The Developing Person
Through the Life Span

Maurice Prendergast, *Yacht Race*, 1900

The Developing Person Through the Life Span

Third Edition

KATHLEEN STASSEN BERGER

Bronx Community College
City University of New York

With the assistance of

Ross A. Thompson
University of Nebraska-Lincoln

WORTH PUBLISHERS

The Developing Person Through the Life Span, THIRD EDITION

Copyright © 1994, 1988, 1983 by Worth Publishers, Inc.

All rights reserved

Printed in the United States of America

Library of Congress Catalog Card Number: 93-60514

ISBN: 0–87901–594–2

Printing: 1 2 3 4 5 - 98 97 96 95 94

Developmental editor: Peter Deane

Design: Malcolm Grear Designers

Art director: George Touloumes

Production editor: Toni Ann Scaramuzzo

Production supervisor: Sarah Segal

Layout: Patricia Lawson

Photo editor: Elyse Rieder

Photo research assistant: Hope Brennan

Line art: Demetrios Zangos

Composition and separations: TSI Graphics, Inc.

Printing and binding: Von Hoffmann Press, Inc.

Cover: Maurice Prendergast, *Yacht Race* (detail), 1900, watercolor, 33.3 × 52.1 cm,

   Watson F. Blair Purchase Prize, 1932. 175. © 1988 The Art Institute of Chicago

Acknowledgments begin on page PA–1, and constitute an extension of the copyright

   page.

Worth Publishers

33 Irving Place

New York, New York 10003

Contents in Brief

Contents

Contents by Topic

This brief index provides a ready reference to the major themes and topics of development through the life span and is intended to be useful for quick reference and review and for researching essays and topical term papers. This index does *not* include all the topics in this text, nor are all minor discussions listed. A complete index appears at the back of the book.

Preface

I began the first edition of this book twelve years ago with a single goal in mind: to reveal the study of life-span development as the intriguing, exciting, and critically important discipline I myself find it to be. Years of teaching and studying had convinced me that a text should respect students' interests and experiences and at the same time reflect the complexity of human development—without being condescending or, alternatively, becoming so overburdened with theoretical and academic details as to be dull and difficult. I sought to present theory, research, practical examples, and controversial issues in such a way as to inspire critical thinking, insight, and pleasure as well. The response of instructors and students to *The Developing Person Through the Life Span* has been enormously gratifying, encouraging me to believe that the book is fulfilling its goal, and at the same time making me eager to improve as well as update each new edition.

The overriding improvement I have worked toward in this edition has been a deepening and strengthening of the contextual perspective. Between the first edition and this one a sea change has occurred in the study of human development, as the old debate between nature and nurture has been dramatically recast. Just as scientists have recently come to realize that genetic influences play a far more extensive role in total human development than had previously been thought, so too are they increasingly recognizing the crucial importance of the specific environmental contexts in which human development occurs. Scientists now view the interaction between heredity and environmental contexts as intensely dynamic and incredibly diverse, an ever changing combination of influences that affect each person differently. For example, certain inherited influences on personality—especially those underlying such basic traits, as extroversion, conscientiousness, openness, and neuroticism—are pervasive, no less so in old age than in youth. But the specific expression of these genetic influences, the actual behaviors they promote, depends not only on the individual's specific genetic makeup but on all the surrounding contexts as well—the intricate and often tangled interplay among cultural and ethnic values and expectations, socioeconomic status, cohort experiences, varying family dynamics, and the myriad other contextual elements that impinge on individual development. Developmentalists now realize that every aspect of human activity, every piece of human behavior, every biological imperative, can be understood only within the framework of the many contexts in which it is imbedded.

Throughout this edition you will see the deeper insights gained from this heightened contextual perspective, insights evident in areas as wide-ranging as attachment between caregivers and infants; the social awareness that begins to emerge as early as 2 years of age; the impact of discipline and affection on the growing child; the specific ingredients that lead to effective schooling; the links between family structure and developmental outcome; the adolescent's search for identity in a multicultural world; the diverse expressions of sexual love; the effects of divorce on ex-spouses and children; the emotional spillover between work and family; the sexism, racism, and ageism that influence health and sickness; and the vast variation in individual responses to the entire process of development, from the moment of conception to the last heartbeat. Analyses of these and many other topics benefit markedly from the field's greater appreciation of the significance of social contexts. This greater appreciation has also added a new challenge to the present edition: to highlight the universals of the human experience even as we portray the many individual paths that development can take.

The new emphasis on social contexts—with a more dynamic cross-group, cross-cultural, and cross-historical perspective—has led me to devote more attention in this edition to some of the controversial social issues of our time. Topics such as prenatal drug abuse, child maltreatment, variations of family structure, homelessness, adolescent pregnancy, AIDS, violent death, health care delivery systems, generational equity, and care for the dying are all discussed in depth. Often an international and multicultural perspective makes it clear that many of the problems commonly associated with such issues are not necessarily inevitable. In every case, when problems are examined, not to bemoan it is our contemporary scene but to understand causes and to point to possible solutions. That is, in fact, the underlying assumption of the entire discipline of human development—that a more informed and scientific understanding of human life will help lead to more fulfilled and less troubled lives for all.

In addition to its intensified contextual approach, this edition contains many new topics and emphases. Topping the list are discussions of

risk analysis and the difficulty of precisely predicting teratogenic harm;

new research on infants' development of perceptual categories, including gender perception;

the importance of "goodness of fit" between the child's temperament and parenting style;

Vygotsky's view of learning as a social interaction and of the role of language as the chief medium of interaction within the "zone of proximal development";

children's fast-mapping of vocabulary;

the cultural, school, and family factors underlying the "academic achievement gap" that exists between the United States and many other nations;

the development of social cognition and social-problem solving;

adolescent reasoning and the threat of AIDS;

person-environment fit in the high schools;

new views of adolescent drug use;

gender and violent death in young adulthood, worldwide;

new reproductive technologies and their implications;

friendship patterns in adulthood and the same-sex differences among them;

the effects of gender bias in health research and treatment;

the latest research and thinking on adult cognitive development, including the most recent views from information-processing and contextual theorists;

the stability of the "Big Five" personality trait clusters;

the significance of "aging in place" for older adults and the emergence of NORCs (naturally occurring retirement communities);

the importance of selective family involvement in old age;

ways to prevent fragility from becoming frailty in the elderly.

In addition to these and many other changes, new photographs, charts, and tables have been chosen, and for the first time the book is full-color throughout.

To help orient students to the contents and direction of individual chapters, each chapter is introduced with a brief, informal overview paragraph and a short list of questions intended to stimulate interest and curiosity.

In a number of important ways, the book remains unchanged, including its basic organization. The first part consists of four chapters that deal with, respectively, the definitions and methodologies of development study, the major theories of the field, the interplay of heredity and environment, and prenatal development and birth. The remainder of the book is divided into seven parts that correspond to the seven major periods of life-span development—infancy, early childhood, middle childhood, adolescence, early adulthood, middle adulthood, and late adulthood. Each of these parts consists of a trio of chapters dealing with, respectively, biosocial development, cognitive development, and psychosocial development. This topical organization within a chronological framework fosters students' appreciation of how the various aspects of development are interrelated—of how body, intellect, and personality develop through interaction rather than separately.

The pedagogical aids have also been retained. Thus, at the end of each chapter there is a chapter summary, a list of key terms (with page numbers indicating where the term was introduced), and a series of key questions for reviewing important concepts. At the end of each part there is a full-page chart that provides an overview of the significant biosocial, cognitive, and psychological events covered in that part. A comprehensive glossary at the back of the book lists all the key terms that appear in the text, along with the page number for each term's initial use.

Supplementary Materials

As one who has taught many courses in college and graduate school for twenty years, I know that some instructor's aids are not very helpful, and that many of my colleagues ignore them. If this describes you, I urge you to examine the resources available with this book. I think you will be pleasantly surprised by the exceptional quality and usefulness of these supplements.

The new *Study Guide* by Richard Straub (University of Michigan, Dearborn) and Joan Winer Brown uses the SQ3R format to help students learn more and retain their learning longer. Each chapter includes a review of the key concepts, guided study questions, and section reviews that make students active participants in the learning process. Two practice tests and a challenge test of multiple-choice, true/false, and matching questions help students to determine their degree of mastery of the material. The correct answers to test questions are explained, to ensure understanding.

Each chapter of the *Instructor's Resource Manual* by Richard Straub features a chapter preview and lecture guide, learning objectives, lecture/discussion/debate topics, handouts for group and individual student projects, and supplementary readings from journal articles with introductions and questions. The general resources include course planning suggestions, ideas for term projects, including observational activities, and a guide to commercially available audio-visual and software materials.

A set of acetate *transparencies* of key illustrations, charts, tables, and summary information from the textbook is available to adopters.

An extensive *Test Bank*, revised by Carolyn Meyer (Lake Sumter Community College) includes approximately 80 multiple-choice questions and 50 fill-in, true/false, and essay questions for each chapter. Each question is keyed to the textbook topic and page numbers, and its level of difficulty is noted. The *Test Bank* questions are also available with test-generation systems for IBM PC, Macintosh, and Apple II.

Finally, *The Developing Person Through the Life Span* is the textbook that accompanies "Seasons of Life," a telecourse produced by The Annenberg/CPB Project that first aired on public television in September 1989. The telecourse study guide is available from Worth Publishers. Information about the telecourse and its other supplements can be obtained by calling The Annenberg/CPB Project at 1-800-LEARNER.

The Author

My theoretical roots are diverse. My graduate-school mentors included gifted teachers who studied directly with Erik Erikson, B. F. Skinner, Carl Rogers, and Jean Piaget, and I continue to have great respect for each of these theorists. However, like most developmentalists today, my overall approach is eclectic, influenced by all the theories rather than adhering to any one. The abiding influence of my academic study and training is in my respect for knowledge attained through the scientific method: I believe that the more we know about development, the better we can help all people fulfill their potential.

As great an influence on my thinking as those who have taught me have been those whom I have taught, for my students have had a powerful effect on how I interpret and envision the material I study and write about. I have taught at a variety of institutions, ranging from the United Nations High School to Fordham University Graduate School to Sing Sing Prison, and I have been a member of the psychology department at Bronx Community College of the City University of New York for the past twenty years. My students have come from a great diversity of ethnic, economic, and educational backgrounds, and my work with them and my ongoing appreciation for their interests and concerns have greatly broadened my own understanding of human development.

Thanks

This book has benefited from the work of the entire community of scholars involved in human development. I have learned much from conferences, journals, and conversations with fellow developmentalists. Of course, I am particularly indebted to the many academic reviewers who have read various drafts of this book in each edition, providing suggestions, criticism, references, and encouragement. Each of them has made the book a better one, and I thank them all. I especially wish to thank those who reviewed this new edition or offered suggestions for its improvement:

Barbara L. Biales, College of St. Catherine

Steven W. Cornelius, Cornell University

Daniel F. Detzner, University of Minnesota

Mary Gauvain, University of California, Riverside

Deborah T. Gold, Duke University Medical Center

Susan Goldberg, The Hospital for Sick Children

Fred W. Grote, Western Washington University

Sharon Karr, Emporia State University

Thomas E. Ludwig, Hope College

Thomas Moeschl, Broward Community College

Robert Plomin, The Pennsylvania State University

Clara C. Pratt, Oregon State University

Scott D. Wright, University of Utah

The editorial, production, and marketing people at Worth Publishers are dedicated to meeting the highest standards of excellence. Their devotion of time, effort, and talent to every aspect of publishing is a model for the industry. When I decided to publish with them, I was told I would have to work twice as hard as I would for any other publisher, and that the result would be many times better. It is true, and I am grateful.

I particularly would like to thank Peter Deane, my editor, who has helped me through every edition of this book, maintaining his perseverance, brilliance, creativity, and humor despite sometimes compelling reasons not to. Without him, the book would lose much of its elegance and good sense. I also deeply appreciate the efforts of the production staff, and of Toni Ann Scaramuzzo, the production editor, who are responsible for the high quality of the book's appearance.

With this edition I have a new person to thank—Ross Thompson, a renowned child-development scholar and professor of psychology at the University of Nebraska, Lincoln. Increasingly, instructors who use my books have been requesting that *The Developing Person Through Childhood and Adolescence* and *The Developing Person Through the Life Span* be put on three-year revision cycles. Given the various demands on my time, this seemed impossible unless the work of the revision could be shared. I therefore invited Ross to help me in the revision of several chapters of the third edition of *The Developing Person Through Childhood and Adolescence,* and our collaboration was such a pleasure that I have asked him to join me as coauthor in the next edition. Ross was also gracious enough to help in preparing several chapters of the present revision, and assuming that his many academic and family responsibilities permit it, he will be joining me as coauthor in future editions of this book as well.

New York City
July, 1993

The Developing Person
Through the Life Span

PART I

Beginnings

The study of human development has many beginnings, as you will see in the following four chapters. First, you will learn about research methods and designs, the building blocks, as it were, of the scientific study of development. But building blocks are useless without a master plan for their use. Chapter 2 presents several such plans, in this case the psychoanalytic, learning, cognitive, and humanist theories of development. A good theory is invaluable in helping researchers examine and explain human development, and these are four of the best psychology has to offer.

A different kind of master plan is described in Chapter 3, which traces the interaction of hereditary and environmental influences. Each human being grows and develops in accordance with chemical guidelines carried on the genes and chromosomes. Interacting with the environment, genes influence everything from the shape of your baby toe to the swiftness of your brain waves to basic aspects of your personality. Thus, understanding the fundamentals of gene-environment interaction is essential to an understanding of human development.

Finally, Chapter 4 details the true beginnings of human life, from the fusing of sperm and ovum to make one new cell to the birth of a new human being, a totally dependent individual who can nevertheless see, hear, and cry, and is ready to engage in social interaction.

CHAPTER 1 | # Introduction

You are about to begin a fascinating journey through the study of human development. To help prepare you for this journey—which explores development from the moment of conception to the final moments of old age—Chapter 1 will serve as a kind of roadmap, outlining your route and familiarizing you with the general terrain. More specifically, it will introduce you to the goals, values, and methods that are involved in the scientific study of human development and suggest some of the practical applications that such study can produce. Among the questions this chapter addresses are the following:

What are the primary concerns and goals of developmental scientists?

What is the relationship between development in the early stages of life and development throughout the rest of the life span?

What innate and environmental factors help shape an individual's ongoing development?

How do variations in cultural context, socioeconomic status, and historical setting affect the course of development?

What ethical values guide the study of human development?

David, my brother's son, is in his junior year of college. Like every young adult, he faces a future that will be strongly influenced by his past. In many ways, David's childhood and adolescence were typical: he had a family that cared for him from the moment he was born; schools that brought out his best, and sometimes his worst; and a social world that gave him both joy and pain. Some of the specifics of his current life will strike a familiar chord in most readers: like many of you, David has become a dedicated student, devoting several hours a day to studying German, his major, as well as Russian, a recently acquired interest. He is also deeply intrigued by politics, and will argue current issues at the drop of a hat. Somewhat of a late-bloomer socially, David is self-conscious about his appearance (he is slight of build and must wear thick glasses) and, though he has yet to develop a serious romantic relationship, he wishes the case were otherwise.

In one very basic way, however, David's development is far from typical. He began life severely handicapped, with little hope for survival, let alone for a life approaching normality. His childhood and adolescence were filled with harsh, often heartbreaking obstacles to normal development, and he still struggles against unusual odds as his life unfolds.

Most of this book is, of course, about "normal" development—that is, the usual patterns of growth and change that everyone follows to some degree and that no one follows exactly. But this chapter will examine David's unusual story for two reasons.

First, David's struggles and triumphs offer a poignant illustration of the underlying goal of developmental study: to help each person develop throughout life as fully as possible.

Second, David's example illuminates, with unusual vividness, the basic definitions and central questions that frame the study of human development. Just as suddenly being thrust into an unfamiliar culture can help us see more clearly our own daily routines, habits, and assumptions, which we tend to overlook precisely because they are so familiar, so, too, can David's story highlight the major factors that influence more typical human development. Let us begin, then, with a brief look at those definitions and questions that underlie the study of human development, and then return to David's story.

The Study of Human Development

Briefly, *the study of human development is the study of how and why people change over time, as well as how and why they remain the same.*

Developmental scientists study development at every stage, from conception to death, in every community and context. They examine all kinds of physical, intellectual, and emotional change—simple growth, radical transformation, improvement and decline—and all sources of continuity from one day, year, or generation to the next. Underlying this study is the goal of identifying the factors that foster healthy development, as well as those that impair it. Thus developmentalists consider everything from the genetic codes that lay down the foundations of growth to the countless environmental factors that shape development across the life span. They look at the impact of prenatal life; of family, school, and peer group; of health and economic well-being; of career aspirations and opportunities; of marriage, parenthood, and grandparenthood; of friendship and religious affiliation. And they examine all these factors—and untold others—in light of the social and cultural contexts that give them meaning and force.

Accordingly, the study of human development involves many academic disciplines, especially biology, education, and psychology, but also history, sociology, anthropology, medicine, economics, and subspecialities such as developmental genetics, public health, and demography.

The Three Domains

To make it easier to undertake this vast interdisciplinary study of myriad developmental changes, human development is often separated into three domains: the **biosocial domain**, including brain and body changes and the social influences that guide them; the **cognitive domain**, including thought processes, perceptual abilities, and language mastery, as well as the educational institutions that encourage them; and the **psychosocial domain**, including emotions, personality, and interpersonal relationships, and the complex social contexts in which they occur.

Figure 1.1 *The division of development into three domains makes it easier to study, but we must remember that very few factors belong exclusively to one domain or another. Development is not piecemeal but holistic: each aspect of development is related to all three domains.*

DOMAINS OF HUMAN DEVELOPMENT		
Biosocial Development	**Cognitive Development**	**Psychosocial Development**
Includes all the growth and change that occur in a person's body—and the genetic, nutritional, and health factors that affect those developments — as well as motor skills—everything from grasping a rattle to driving a car. Social and cultural factors that affect these areas, such as duration of breastfeeding, encouragement of risk-taking, and attitudes toward aging are also part of biosocial development.	Includes all the mental processes that are used to obtain knowledge or to become aware of the environment. It can include perception, imagination, judgment, memory, and language—the processes people use to think, decide, and learn. Education, including formal curriculum within schools, informal tutoring by family and friends, and the accumulated wisdom from life experience, is also part of this domain.	Includes emotional, personality, and social development. The influences of the family, the community, the culture, and the larger society, although relevant to all three domains, are particularly central to the psychosocial domain. Thus, public-policy questions, such as how to prevent child abuse, what the impact of divorce laws might be, and whether retirement should be voluntary, are primarily part of this domain.

All three domains are important at every age. For instance, understanding an infant involves studying his or her health, curiosity, and temperament, as well as dozens of other aspects of biosocial, cognitive, and psychosocial development. Similarly, to understand an adolescent, we consider physical changes that mark the bodily transition from child to adult; intellectual development that leads to thinking about moral issues and future goals; and the emerging patterns of friendship and courtship that prepare for the intimate relationships of adulthood. Inevitably, each domain is affected by the other two: whether or not an infant is well-nourished, for instance, may well affect the baby's learning ability and social experiences. For many adolescents, their perception of their bodies—the way they *think* their bodies look—affects their eating and exercise habits, and these, in turn, affect their physical health and their emotional and social development. Such overlapping influence among the three domains is continual and powerful throughout the life span.

Figure 1.2 *Every aspect of human behavior reflects all three domains. Obviously biosocial factors—such as hormones and body strength—are at work here, but so are cognitive and psychosocial ones. For instance, each student's mental concentration or lack of it is critical to karate success, as is the culture's message about who should learn the martial arts, a message that seems to have made this a nearly all-male class.*

The Many Contexts of Development

Until recently, the study of human development focused primarily on biological, cognitive, and psychological change *within* each developing individual, almost as if growth occurred in social isolation. Increasingly over the past two decades, however, a considerably broader focus has been adopted, as suggested by the labeling of the bio*social* and psycho*social* domains.

An Ecological Perspective

This broader approach to understanding development is often called the **ecological approach**, for, just as a naturalist studying a flower or a fish needs to examine the organism's supporting ecosystems, so a developmentalist needs to look at the ecosystem in which a human being seeks to thrive. The systems that support human development can be seen as occurring at four levels, each nested within the next (Bronfenbrenner, 1979; 1986):

1. the **microsystem**—the immediate social settings, such as the family, the classroom, the peer group, the workplace, that directly affect each individual's life;

2. the **mesosystem**—the links that connect one microsystem to another (such links can be direct, like the parent-teacher conference, or indirect, like the relationship between required overtime at work and problems at home);

3. the **exosystem**—the neighborhood and community structures (including newspapers, television, and public agencies) that directly affect the functioning of smaller systems;

4. the **macrosystem**—the overarching patterns of culture, politics, the economy, and so forth.

Looking at each of these as a *system* means recognizing that no cog in the system moves in isolation and that actions in any one part of the system affect all the other parts, and vice versa. Consider this approach in the study of the most basic microsystem, the family. Not too long ago, psychologists studying family influences on development focused almost exclusively on how mothers affect their young children (Sigel et al., 1984). Now researchers have broadened their study of family influences to include fathers, siblings, and grandparents. Each of these family members can have a significant impact on a child's development, sometimes becoming the deciding factor in whether that development progresses well or badly. Grandparents, for instance, were rarely included in traditional research on the family, yet we now know that they sometimes provide essential stability, especially when illness, divorce, or unemployment undermines parents' ability to function (Cherlin and Furstenberg, 1986).

Further, a systems perspective makes it apparent that family influences are multidirectional: each child influences every member of the household, and each family relationship (such as that between husband and wife, or between siblings) affects all the other family members. Take the case of a child who is "difficult"—disobedient, hostile, demanding. Traditionally, an explanation for the child's behavior was sought, and usually found, in the mother, who was likely to be judged self-absorbed, or cold, or indulgent. Today we realize that the child's own temperament, the father's competence as a parent, the nature of the marital relationship, the rivalries and tensions of other siblings, and a dozen other factors are also implicated in a child's behavior. In the case of our difficult child, we would also realize that the mother's seeming self-absorption, or coldness, or indulgence might be as much a result of the child's actions as a cause of it. Indeed, it is now recognized that each family member is both a victim and an architect of whatever problems the family members might have (Patterson, 1982).

Using a systems approach also provides a larger perspective on family issues, calling attention to the external forces that affect family functioning. For example, until recently, parental employment was thought to have an impact on child development only as it affected the level of family income and the need for outside child care. However, research has revealed that the stresses and satisfactions of parents' work affects the quality of their parenting, and that conditions on the job affect conditions in the home (Greenberger and Goldberg, 1989; Hoffman, 1989; Zedek, 1992). For instance, changes in employment—getting a promotion, losing a job, or returning to work—can affect the psychological interaction among family members (Flanagan, 1990; Elder et al., 1985; McLoyd, 1989; Hetherington et al., 1989). Perhaps the most obvious, and unfortunate, example of this involves the loss of employment. When economic distress in the macrosystem leads to higher rates of unemployment in the exosystem, there is a corresponding increase in child abuse in the family microsystem. Apparently, the psychological strain caused by job loss tends to manifest itself in alcohol abuse, stricter expectations for other family members, and less patience with normal child behavior.

The larger perspective fostered by the ecological approach makes it imperative that human development be understood in both its *cross-cultural context*—that is, in terms of its similarities and variations across cultures and subcultures—and its *historical context*—that is, in terms of its

Figure 1.3 *This family is forcefully experiencing the impact that changes in the macrosystem can have on the family microsystem: dramatic shifts in the agriculture industry have led to foreclosure on the farm. Research has found that the impact of such negative events on younger children depends almost entirely on the way adults adjust to them. If, for instance, the parents are sustained by a strong faith or a sense of family unity, the psychological strain may be lessened for them and, in turn, for their young children. Adolescents, however, have a more difficult time. Even if the rest of the family accepts economic dislocation, most teenagers react to it with signs of stress, such as depression, anger, or a sense of shame.*

similarities and variations over time. Constantly recognizing these two contexts keeps us mindful of an obvious but important fact: if any given individual had been born in another culture or century, or even in another subculture or decade, that person's growth and development would have been quite different from what it is.

From Systems to Individuals

A major way these cultural-historical influences are transmitted to the individual is through sets of experiences, values, and beliefs that tend to be prevalent in certain social contexts and rare in others. It is as if the immensely varied range of human life experiences and options is first filtered and narrowed by particular contextual influences before any individual begins to chart his or her own life course. Now, at the outset of our study, three particularly potent contextual influences need to be recognized and understood—cohort, ethnicity, and socioeconomic status.

Cohort

A **cohort** is a group of people born roughly at the same historical time, usually within the same five- or ten-year period, which means that, as a group, they tend to share certain sociohistorical influences and perspectives in common. Today's teenagers, for instance, experience their sexual awakening with quite different attitudes and expectations from those their counterparts held before 1960, because changes in male and female roles, different attitudes about virginity, and such factors as the birth-control pill, legal abortion, and AIDS have all altered the sexual landscape markedly from what it was three decades ago.

Ethnic Group

An **ethnic group** is a collection of people who share certain attributes, such as national origin, religion, culture, and language, and, as a result, tend to have similar values and experiences. Racial identity is also sometimes considered as an element of ethnicity. As social scientists emphatically point out, however, biological tendencies (such as lighter or darker coloring or characteristic variations in facial features and body shape) that may distinguish one "race" from another are much less significant to development than the sense of cultural and social identity—and the attitudes and experiences resulting from minority or majority status—that may arise from racial consciousness.

The power of ethnicity to affect development comes from the particular behavioral habits, personality patterns, and personal and social values that it fosters. For example, ethnic groups differ in how much they value education, and this affects how strongly parents from various groups encourage their children to attend school, do homework, or aspire to go on to college. Similarly, some ethnic groups respect the elderly much more than the young, expecting children to defer to patriarchs and matriarchs and ensuring that economic and social resources flow from the newer generations to the older ones. Other groups, in contrast, expect the older generations to sacrifice their needs to benefit the younger ones (Keith, 1990; Goodnow and Collins, 1990).

Ethnic groups also vary a great deal in whether they believe that the unity and welfare of the family should supersede the personal well-being of the individuals in it. This can profoundly affect personal decisions. For instance, a Latin-American wife whose husband is a chronic alcoholic might be encouraged by her relatives and her own conscience to protect and nurture him long after an Anglo-American woman, with the identical problem, would have followed her family's advice and her own convictions to confront the man or throw him out. The Latina in this case would believe that she was saving the family honor, avoiding shame (*verguenza*), and preserving her children's respect for their father, while the opposite behavior would be justified by the Anglo as avoiding codependence, saving her own self-respect, and protecting her children from a destructive role model (Inclan and Hernandez, 1992; Zayas, 1988; Kitchens, 1991).

Socioeconomic Status

A third major contextual influence on development is **socioeconomic status,** sometimes called social class, as in "middle class" or "underclass." Socioeconomic status, abbreviated **SES,** is determined by a combination of several overlapping variables, including wealth, education, residence, and occupation. In official government statistics, SES is often measured simply in terms of annual family income, adjusted for inflation and family size, with family income under a certain amount considered to be below the *poverty line* and the family members being officially designated poor.

As an influence on development, many social scientists believe that SES is more potent than either cohort or ethnicity.* People who are highly educated and employed as professionals, for example, share many common experiences and values, tending to create similar lifestyles for themselves and their families and to make choices quite different from those of the same cohort and ethnicity who are undereducated and unemployed.

---

*The overlap between SES and ethnicity sometimes obscures this distinction, because ethnicity affects the likelihood of being poor. In 1989, in the United States, families with incomes below the poverty line included 8 percent of white families, 11 percent of Asian-American families, 24 percent of Native-American families, 24 percent of Hispanic-American families, and 28 percent of African-American families (U. S. Bureau of the Census, 1991).

Figure 1.4 *As you can see, poor health correlates much more powerfully with socioeconomic status than with ethnic background. Presumably, good medical care, nutritious meals, and regular exercise are more the product of income and education than of ethnicity or genetics.*

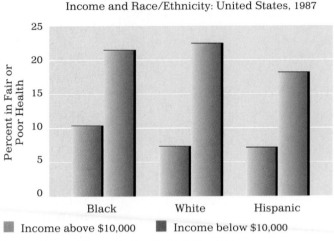

Health Characteristics According to Income and Race/Ethnicity: United States, 1987

Source: National Center for Health Statistics, 1990.

Socioeconomic status becomes a particularly potent contextual factor at the bottom of the SES ladder, where limited opportunities and heightened pressures conspire to make growing up and growing old much more hazardous than it is higher up the ladder. For example, infant mortality, child neglect, adolescent drug abuse, and chronic disease in adulthood are all much more common among the very poor than among the nonpoor. One statistic clearly reveals this effect: poverty is twice as likely as minority status to be associated with poor health (see Figure 1.4).

It is obvious now that the many contexts of development, including cohort, ethnicity, and socioeconomic status, influence each person's life path. However, while these factors affect development, they do not determine it: no one is exactly like the typical person of his or her generation, ethnic group, or SES, and each of us differs in unexpected ways from any stereotypes or generalities that might seem pertinent.

Now let us return to David, a person clearly affected by the social systems that structure his development yet, just as obviously, unique.

David's Story: Domains and Systems at Work

David's story begins in 1967, with an event that seems clearly from the biosocial domain. In the spring of that year, in Appalachia, an epidemic of rubella (German measles) struck two more victims, David's mother, who had a rash and a sore throat for a couple of days, and her 4-week-old embryo, who was damaged for life. David was born in November, with a life-threatening heart defect and thick cataracts covering both eyes. Other damage caused by the virus became apparent as time went on, including minor malformations of the thumbs, feet, jaw, and teeth, as well as brain injury.

From a systems perspective, the larger medical and political systems had already had a major impact, one determined partly by the particular point in historical time at which David entered the world. Had David been conceived a decade later, the development and widespread use of the rubella vaccine would probably have prevented his mother's contracting the disease. On the other hand, had he been born a few years earlier, or in a different part of the world, he would have died, because the medical technology that saved his life would not have been available.

The Early Years: Heartbreaking Handicaps, Slow Progress

As it happened, heart surgery in the first days of life was successful, and it was thought that David would have at least a few years of life. However, surgery to open a channel around one of the cataracts failed, completely blinding the eye.

It soon became apparent that David's physical handicaps were contributing to cognitive and psychosocial liabilities as well. Not only did his blindness make it impossible for him to learn by looking at his world, but his parents overprotected him to the point that he spent almost all his early months in their arms or in his crib. An analysis of the family system would have revealed that David's impact on his family, and their effect on him, were harmful in many ways. Like most parents of seriously impaired infants, David's felt guilt, anger, and despair (Featherstone, 1980); they were initially unable to make constructive plans to foster normal development.

Fortunately, however, David's parents came from a social and educational background that encouraged them to seek outside help, allowing the exosystem to give assistance to their family microsystem. The first step occurred when a teacher from the Kentucky School for the Blind visited David's home and gave his parents some much-needed encouragement and advice. They were told to stop blaming themselves for David's condition and to stop overprotecting him because of it. If their son was going to learn about his world, he was going to have to explore it. To this end, they were told that, rather than confining David to a crib or playpen, they should provide him with a large rug for a play area. Whenever he crawled off the rug, they were to say "No" and place him back in the middle of it, thus enabling him to use his sense of touch to learn where he could explore safely without bumping into walls or furniture. David's mother dedicated herself to this and the many other tasks that various specialists suggested, including exercising his twisted feet and cradling him frequently in her arms as she sang lullabies to provide extra tactile and auditory stimulation.

Figure 1.5 *When the new baby is physically perfect and developmentally "normal," parents take pleasure and pride in recording landmarks in the child's progress—first steps, first words, month-by-month growth, new friends. For parents with a handicapped child, however, milestones are too frequently marked more by relief than by celebration.*

His father helped, too, taking over much of the housework and care of the two older boys, who were 2 and 4 at the time. When he found an opportunity to work in Boston, he took it, partly because the Perkins School for the Blind had just begun an experimental program for blind toddlers and their mothers. At Perkins, David's mother learned specific methods for developing physical and language skills in multihandicapped children, and she, in turn, taught the techniques to David's father and brothers. Every day the family spent hours rolling balls, doing puzzles, and singing with David.

Thus, the mesosystem of communication between home and school worked as it should, expediting the collaboration between the family and educational systems to help young David develop. However, progress was slow. It became painfully apparent that rubella had damaged much more than his eyes and heart. At age 3, David could not talk, nor chew solid food, nor use the toilet, nor coordinate his fingers well, nor even walk normally. An IQ test showed him to be severely mentally retarded. Fortunately, although most children with rubella syndrome have hearing defects, David's hearing was normal. However, the only intelligible sounds he made mimicked the noises of the buses and trucks that passed by the house.

At age 4, David said his first word, "Dada." Open-heart surgery corrected the last of his heart damage, and an operation brought partial vision to his remaining eye. While sight in that eye was far from perfect, David could now recognize his family by sight as well as by sound, and could look at picture books. By age 5, when the family returned to Kentucky, further progress was obvious: he no longer needed diapers or baby food.

David's fifth birthday occurred in 1972, just when the idea that severely handicapped children could be educated in school rather than at home was beginning to be accepted. David's parents found four schools that would accept him and enrolled him in all of them. He attended two schools for victims of cerebral palsy: one had morning classes, and the other—forty miles away— afternoon classes. (David ate lunch in the car with his mother on the daily trip.) On Fridays these schools were closed, so he attended a school for the mentally retarded, and on Sunday he spent two hours in church school, his first experience with "mainstreaming"—the then-new idea that children with special needs should be educated with normal children.

Childhood and Adolescence: Heartening Progress

By age 7, David's intellectual development had progressed to the point considered adequate for the normal educational system. In some skills, he was advanced; he could multiply and divide in his head. He entered first grade in a public school, one of the first severely handicapped children to be mainstreamed. However, he was far from being a normal first-grader, for rubella continued to have an obvious impact on his physical, cognitive, and social development. His motor skills were poor (among other things, he had difficulty controlling a pencil); his efforts to learn to read were greatly hampered by the fact that he was legally blind even in his "good" eye; and his social skills were seriously deficient (he pinched people he didn't like and cried and laughed at inappropriate times).

During the next several years, David's cognitive development proceeded rapidly. By age 10, he had skipped a year and was a fifth-grader. He could read with a magnifying glass—at the eleventh-grade level—and was labeled "intellectually gifted" according to tests of verbal and math skills. At home he began to learn a second language and to play the violin. In both areas, he proved to have extraordinary auditory acuity and memory.

David's greatest problem was in the psychosocial domain. Schools generally ignored the social skills of mainstreamed children (Gottlieb and Leyser, 1981), and David's experience was no exception. For instance, David was required to sit on the sidelines during most physical-education classes, and to stay inside during most recess periods. Without a chance to experience the normal give-and-take of schoolyard play, David remained more childish than his years. His classmates were not helped to understand his problems, and some of them teased him because he still looked and acted "different."

Because of David's problems with outsiders and classmates, his parents decided to send him to a special school when he was ready for junior high. In the Kentucky School for the Blind, his physical, cognitive, and psychosocial development all advanced: David learned to wrestle and swim, mastered algebra with large-print books, and made friends whose vision was as bad as his or even worse. For his high school years, David remained at the Kentucky School, where he mastered not only the regular curriculum but also specialized skills, such as how to travel independently in the city and how to cook and clean for himself.

Figure 1.6 *The enthusiasm expressed by these Special Olympians reflects not only the thrill of competition but also the satisfaction of having one's abilities and interests recognized and accepted. In a highly competitive soceity like the United States, being forced to the sidelines by social attitudes can be far more devastating psychologically than the limitations imposed by a particular disability.*

Looking Back and Looking Forward

Now many of David's worst problems are behind him. In the biosocial domain, he seems certain of a long life, and doctors have helped to improve its quality: an artificial eye has replaced the blind one; a back brace has helped his posture; and surgery has corrected a misaligned jaw, improving his appearance and his speech. In the cognitive domain, the once severely "retarded" preschooler is a bright, articulate college student, who is looking forward to a career as a linguist and translator (an interesting choice for someone who has learned to listen very carefully to what people say because he is unable to read their facial expressions). And in the psychosocial domain, the formerly self-absorbed child is now an outgoing young man, eager for friendship.

This is not to suggest that David's life is all smooth sailing. In fact, every day presents its struggles, and David, like everyone, has his moments of self-doubt and depression. As he once confided:

> I sometimes have extremely pejorative thoughts . . . dreams of vivid symbolism. In one, I am playing on a pinball machine that is all broken—glass besmirched, legs tilted and wobbly, the plunger knob loose. I have to really work at it to get a decent score.

Yet David never loses heart, at least not for long. He continues to "really work" on his life, no matter what, and bit by bit, his "score" improves.

In looking at David's life thus far, we can see how the domains and systems interact to affect development, both positively and negatively. We can also see the importance of research and the application of developmental principles. For example, without research that demonstrated the crucial role of sensory stimulation in infant development, David's parents might not have been taught how to keep his young mind actively learning. Nor would David have been educated in schools had not the previous efforts of hundreds of developmental scientists proved that schools could provide effective teaching even for severely handicapped children. David might instead have led an overly sheltered and restricted life, as many children born with David's problems once did. Indeed, many children with David's initial level of disability formerly spent their lives in institutions that provided only custodial care.

David's immediate future will likewise be influenced by the various systems. The macrosystem, for instance, is becoming increasingly sensitive to the needs of handicapped people: the laws of the land now safeguard the right to a normal life in college, in housing, and in employment. The microsystem of his family will continue to delight in him, and care for him as well. However, as he ventures through adulthood, he will need to find his own social world—a difficult task for most young American adults, especially for those who have an unusual life history and appearance.

At the same time that David's story highlights the influence of domains and systems, it also serves to remind us of a universal truth: none of us is simply a product of these influences. Each person is a unique individual who uniquely reacts to, and acts upon, the constellation of systems that impinges on his or her development. Thus the most important factor in David's past successes may have been David himself, for his determination and stoic courage helped him weather the physical trauma of repeated surgery and the psychological devastation of social rejection. Of all those who should be proud of David's accomplishments—including the scientists, teachers, and family members who directly and indirectly contributed to his growth—the one who should be most proud is David himself. More than anyone else, in the final analysis, David, like each of us, directs his own development.

Three Controversies

As David's case makes abundantly clear, the study of development requires taking into account the interplay of the biosocial, cognitive, and psychosocial domains, within a particular historical time, influenced by familial, cultural, political, and economic forces. Not surprisingly, assessing the relative impact of all these factors is no simple matter. In fact, developmentalists often find themselves on one side or another of three controversies that have been debated since the scientific study of human development began.

Nature and Nurture

The central dispute in the study of human development is the nature-nurture controversy. It is the continuing debate over the relative impact of hereditary and environmental influences in shaping various personal traits and characteristics.

Nature refers to the range of traits, capacities, and limitations that each person inherits genetically from his or her parents at the moment of conception. Body type, eye color, and inherited diseases are obvious examples. Nature also includes those largely inherited traits, such as athletic ability or memory, that appear after a certain amount of maturation has occurred.

Nurture refers to all the environmental influences that come into play after conception, beginning with the mother's health during pregnancy and running through all one's experience with, and learning in, the outside world—in the family, school, community, and the culture at large.

The controversy about nature and nurture has taken on many names, among them *heredity versus environment* and *maturation versus learning*. Under whatever name, however, the basic question remains: How much of any given characteristic, behavior, or pattern of development is determined by genetic influences and how much is the result of the myriad experiences and influences that occur after conception? Note that the question implies that with all characteristics, behaviors, and patterns of development, *both* nature and nurture are influential. All developmentalists agree that, at every point, the *interaction* between nature and nurture is the crucial influence on any particular aspect of development. They note, for example, that intelligence is determined by the interplay of heredity and such aspects of the social and physical environment as schooling and nutrition. Despite their acknowledgment of the interaction between nature and nurture, however, developmentalists can get into heated arguments about the relative importance of each.

One of the reasons the controversy over the relative importance of heredity and environment is very much alive is that it is difficult to prove which is more responsible for a particular developmental outcome. Another is that the practical implications of the controversy are enormous. Consider one example. Although boys and girls in elementary school show similar math aptitude, the mathematical achievement of the typical teenage boy is higher than that of the average teenage girl. Furthermore, high school students who are gifted in math are usually boys, by a 4-to-1 ratio (Benbow and Stanley, 1983). A closer analysis of the male advantage reveals that, beginning at about age 10, boys are better at spatial skills—the kind required for geometry—and this accounts for much of the difference in math achievement (Johnson and Meade, 1987).

Figure 1.7 *It's all in the family, Whitney Houston on the left, her aunt Dionne Warwick on the right, and her mother, Cissy, a gospel singer, in the middle— all descendants of the same woman, a mother and grandmother who sang to her children. But is the musical bond that unites these three women the re- sult of nature or nurture? Perhaps they inherited extraordinary vocal chords and melodic sensitivity, or perhaps long hours in church choirs and family gath- erings encouraged them to sing. The answer, of course, is that both nature and nurture made essential contribu- tions, as is always true for talents and abilities.*

Is nature responsible for this difference? Perhaps some hormonal difference causes early brain differentiation that, at puberty, gives males an advantage (Jacklin et al., 1988). Or is nurture the key factor? Perhaps girls learn that math ability is not considered feminine, and perhaps their parents, teachers, or boyfriends, sharing this view, subtly—or not so subtly— discourage their interest and efforts in math (Eccles and Jacobs, 1986). Whichever the answer, the implications are significant. If the difference between adolescent male and female ability in math is attributable to nature, it is foolish and frustrating to expect males and females to do equally well in math. On the other hand, if the difference is the result of nurture, we are wasting half our mathematical potential by not encouraging girls to develop their full math abilities.

Continuity or Discontinuity?

How would you describe human growth? Would you say we develop gradually and continually, the way a seedling becomes a tree? Or do you think we undergo sudden changes, like a caterpillar becoming a butterfly?

Many developmental researchers emphasize the **continuity** of development. They believe that there is a continual progression from the beginning of life to the end. Accomplishments that may seem abrupt, such as a baby's first step, can actually be viewed as the final event in weeks of growth and practice. In the same way, learning to talk or read, or the physical changes that occur in adolescence, can be seen as gradual processes rather than as abrupt changes.

Other theorists emphasize the **discontinuity** of development. They see growth as occurring in identifiable stages, each with distinct problems and characteristics. Terms such as the "terrible twos" or "teenage rebellion" or "midlife crisis" reflect the popular version of the stage concept. Those who focus on stages of development believe that, at certain times during life, a person moves from one level to another, as though climbing a flight of stairs. Often pivotal events—such as beginning to walk, learning to talk, beginning the sexual changes of puberty, becoming a parent, or entering retirement—signal the beginning of a new stage. Such events are thought to change the individual quite suddenly and in many specific ways, leading to new patterns of thought and behavior.

The stage view of development has been the dominant one in the twentieth century. Indeed, this textbook, like most of its kind, reflects the stage view, at least implicitly, by treating development in terms of distinct periods—infancy, early childhood, middle childhood, adolescence, and then early, middle, and late adulthood. There is, of course, good reason for this organization. To begin with, maturation occurs according to a biologically determined timetable, with the result that people of roughly the same age have in common many physical abilities and limitations, as well as age-related patterns in the way they think about their world and about themselves. Correspondingly, at various ages, many people also experience similar kinds of psychosocial needs and conflicts.

Recently, however, a number of developmentalists have cautioned against overemphasizing distinct stages of development. As Flavell (1982) expresses it, strict stage views "gloss over differences, inconsistencies, irregularities, and other real but complexity-adding features." Although it would be convenient to approach human development as a "neat 'ages and stages' developmental story," Flavell notes, actual development is much more complex, for children grow in varied ways—sometimes in sudden leaps and bounds, sometimes step by step, and sometimes with such continuity that they seem not to change at all. Such variation in stagelike development is even more apparent in adulthood, because the rate of aging varies from person to person and the social expectations related to the aging process vary from one social group to another (O'Rand, 1990). In other words, a given person's **biological clock**—which reflects how rapidly the body matures and ages—and a given culture's **social clock**—which reflects what behaviors and attitudes the culture deems appropriate for a given age—are not synchronized with any universal ages or stages.

For example, a stage such as "midlife," complete with a crisis of soul-searching and dramatic life changes—a stage given much popular attention in the United States—seems an artifact of highly developed, youth-centered cultures. (The idea of a midlife crisis would no doubt be incomprehensible to a Chinese rice farmer or a Masai cattle herder.) Even in the United States, wide variation regarding "midlife" is recognized. Some people might experience it in their thirties, especially if they are out of shape, graying, and/or balding, and live in a subculture where physical prowess and youthful appearance are important for social status. On the other hand, someone in excellent health who appears much younger than his or her chronological age might not feel, or act, or be considered, middle-aged until age 50 or later. This would be especially true in a subculture (such as that of many college professors!) where the accumulation of information and expertise is much more prized than a youthful appearance or physical vigor.

Deficit or Difference?

Is there one pattern of human development that is the usual, normal one? Or are there as many paths of development as there are individuals?

The idea that there is one universal pattern was held by many of the first scientists interested in development. Consequently, a number of early research projects were concerned with determining what constituted "normal" development, particularly in childhood and adolescence. They began with a large group of children of various ages, tested them on one characteristic or another, and averaged the results. This average was used as the **norm,** that is, the typical case. Norms were established for everything from walking without holding onto something to speaking in two-word sentences, from reading simple words to falling in love for the first time (e.g., McCarthy, 1954; Bayley, 1935, 1955; Gesell, 1926; Gesell and Ilg, 1946; Hall, 1904).

One of the most influential of these researchers was Arnold Gesell (1926), who tested over 500 children between the ages of 3 months and 5 years to find the norms for various behaviors and abilities. Among other things, Gesell determined that, by age 3, the average child can be "trusted with breakables . . . such as carrying china, glassware, or grandmother's spectacles from one part of the house to another. A moderate capacity in this direction is, therefore, characteristic of three-year-old maturity." Gesell also found that 3-year-olds use plurals and pronouns correctly, draw circles, put on shoes (lacing them at age 4 and tying them at age 5), and perform dozens of other normative behaviors.

The establishment of norms such as these led, quite logically, to another idea—that children who did not follow the usual path were abnormal and probably deficient or deprived in some way. If a child's development differed from the norm, the assumption was that something must be wrong, either in the child, the family, or the culture.

Recently, however, differences have increasingly come to be seen as alternative paths of development rather than as inferior ones (Rogoff and Morelli, 1989). Consequently, contemporary developmentalists are much more likely to recognize the unique characteristics of each child, each family, each culture, than they are to stress the universal generalities that apply to all of them. The 2-year-old who carries breakables or the 4-year-old who

Figure 1.8 *In a multiethnic society like the United States, preschool is one of the first places where the great diversity among children is apparent. In recognition of this diversity, both developmentalists and educators are increasingly less inclined to measure children's development against a single "norm."*

drops them may both be developing perfectly well, and the 6-year-old who does not know how to tie a pair of shoes may be evidencing the influence of zippers and Velcro rather than slowed development.

One important reason for this shift is that researchers realized that much of the early research on development was done by white, middle-class American researchers, using white, American middle-class children as their sample. For instance, most intelligence tests were standardized using the scores of such children (Anastasi, 1988; Hollander, 1982), as were the norms of physical, cognitive, and social development widely disseminated by Gesell. Some researchers even attempted to describe the normal course of development for both sexes on the basis of studies that involved only males (e.g., Kohlberg, 1966; Levinson, 1986).

Not surprisingly, non-Americans, nonwhites, and females were found to be different in many significant ways from white American males. Interpreting these differences as deficiencies has been vigorously challenged in recent years. For example, if African-American children score below average on standard tests of learning ability, it may well be because these tests emphasize the abstract, analytic thinking valued by the white culture and neglect other, possibly more creative and expressive, modes of thought and self-expression that appear to be more typical of the black culture (Hale, 1982; Heath, 1989). Or if females score lower than males on a particular series of tests of moral reasoning (Kohlberg, 1963), it may be that females, socialized to be nurturing and concerned with others, tend, more than males do, to concentrate on the practical, humane aspects of moral issues rather than on the abstract principles that are more highly rated by the test (Gilligan, 1982). Or if personality tests suggest that Asian-American children are withdrawn, dependent, and passive, it may be because these children are developing the characteristics fostered by families and subcultures that value deference, family loyalties, and self-restraint much more than the outgoing, individualistic, assertiveness encouraged by many families of Western European ancestry (Endo et al., 1980; Super and Harkness, 1982). Similarly, if Navajo children seem unresponsive to a traditional punishment that works well with Hawaiian children—specifically, isolation from the group—it may be that the two cultures have quite different values regarding being alone (Tharp, 1989).

The overall realization that behavior that is desirable and healthy in one culture might be inappropriate and disruptive in another has broadened the scope and the direction of developmental research, and led to an appreciation of cultural and individual differences. This is a trend welcomed by developmentalists, both men and women, of every color and background. Among its many benefits, it has led to more flexible patterns of teaching (as David experienced when he was mainstreamed), to broader perspectives in family counseling, and to a greater appreciation of diversity in people of every group and age.

The Scientific Method

As the above controversies show, developmentalists are no different from other people; they have opinions, too, opinions that are partly the result of their own background and biases. However, as scientists, they are committed to consider insights and evidence from the available research before they draw conclusions and to change their view when new data indicate they should. When doing research, they are expected to follow a general procedural model often referred to as the **scientific method,** which helps them overcome whatever biases they have. Procedures and techniques, not theories and assumptions, are what make the study of development a science (Scarr, 1985).

The scientific method involves four basic steps, and sometimes a fifth:

1. *Formulate a research question.* Build on previous research, or on one of the theories of development, or on personal observation and reflection, and pose a question that has relevance for the study of development.

2. *Develop a hypothesis.* Reformulate the question into a hypothesis, which is a specific prediction that can be tested.

3. *Test the hypothesis.* Design and conduct a scientific research project that will provide evidence about the truth or falsity of the hypothesis. As the Research Report on pages 22–23 indicates, the research design often includes many specific elements that help make the test of the hypothesis a valid one.

4. *Draw conclusions.* Formulate conclusions directly from the results of the test, avoiding general conclusions that are not substantiated by the test data.

5. *Make the findings available.* Publishing the results of the test is often the fifth step in the scientific method. In this step, the scientist must describe the test procedures and the resulting data in sufficient detail so that other scientists can evaluate the conclusions and, perhaps, **replicate** the test of the hypothesis—that is, repeat it and obtain the same results—or extend it, using a different but related set of subjects or procedures. Through replication, the conclusions from each test of every hypothesis accumulate, leading to **more definitive and extensive conclusions and generalizations.**

Figure 1.9 *The scientific method often reveals the unexpected. Popular wisdom usually blames teenage drinking habits on the youth culture and/or state drinking laws. Scientific research has shown that the most influential factor in adolescents' use or nonuse of alcohol or other drugs is the closeness of their relationship with their parents.*

In actual practice, scientific investigation is less straightforward than these five steps would make it appear to be. The link between testing a hypothesis and drawing conclusions is bound to include some speculation and uncertainty (Bauer, 1991). For this reason, scientists use various research methods, sometimes in combination, to test hypotheses, because the accumulated results are likely to provide a clearer picture of the puzzles of human development than any one method alone. Among the most common methods are naturalistic observation, laboratory experiments, and surveys. Each has advantages and disadvantages.

Naturalistic Observation

Scientists can test hypotheses by using **naturalistic observation,** that is, by observing people in their natural environments. This usually means going to a home, a school, an office, or a public place and recording people's behavior and interactions in detail. Typically, the scientist tries to be as unobtrusive as possible, so that the people being observed will act as they normally do. For example, naturalistic observation has been used to study everything from the moment-to-moment interactions of parent and infant to the social patterns of residents in retirement communities.

In one recent study of the former type, researchers wanted to test the hypothesis that "maternal responsiveness is effected by cross-cultural differences" (Richman et al., 1992). Accordingly, they arranged for trained observers, familiar with the local language and culture, to compare mothers and their second- or later-born babies in several communities, among them the Gusii in rural Kenya and middle-class whites in suburban Boston. The observations, which spanned several months, were made in the subjects' homes, with the mothers going about their normal household activities and each observer taking the part of a visiting neighbor, trying to be as casual and quiet as possible while recording mother's and child's behaviors as each responded to the other.

Ways to Make Research More Valid

In scientific investigation, there is always the possibility that the researchers' procedures and/or biases can compromise the validity of their findings. Consequently, scientists often take a number of steps to ensure that their research is as valid as possible. Five of them are explained here.

Sample Size

To begin with, in order to make any valid statement about people in general, the scientist must study a group of individuals that is large enough so that a few extreme cases will not distort the picture of the group as a whole. Suppose, for instance, that researchers wanted to know the age at which the average North American child begins to walk. Since they could not include all 4 million American infants in their study, they would work with a large sample group—a *sample population*—determining the age of walking for each member of the sample and then calculating the average for the group.

The importance of **sample size** can be seen if we assume for the moment that one of the infants in their sample was severely mentally retarded, and did not walk until 24 months. If the sample size were less than ten infants, that one late walker would, relative to the current standard of 12 months, add more than a month to the age when the "average" child was said to walk. However, if the sample were more than 500 children, one abnormally late walker would not change the results by even one day.

Representative Sample

Since the data collected on one group of individuals might not be valid for other people who are different in significant ways, such as gender, ethnic background, and the like, it is important that the sample population be a **repre-**

"I'm walking."

Do babies walk (or talk) when they are ready, no matter how little attention their parents provide? Only careful research can provide the answer.

sentative sample, that is, a group of subjects who are typical of the general population the researchers wish to learn about. In a study of when the average American infant begins to walk, the sample population should reflect—in terms of sex ratio, economic and ethnic background, and so forth—the entire population of North American children. Ideally, other factors might be taken into consideration as well. For instance, if there is some evidence that first-born children walk earlier than later- or last-born children, then the sample should include a representative sample of each birth order.

There were, of course, many cross-cultural similarities in maternal responsiveness that were observed: when the infants cried, for example, mothers in both locations were attentive, rarely ignoring their infant's signs of distress and usually responding to them with some form of social interaction—holding, touching, or talking. (As experienced caregivers, they did not assume that every cry signaled hunger; they offered a breast or bottle to their crying infants less than 10 percent of the time.) In both locations, mothers also took the baby's developmental stage into account: they were more

The importance of representative sampling is revealed by its absence in two studies of age of walking (Gesell, 1926; Shirley, 1933) undertaken in the 1920s. Both studies used a relatively small and unrepresentative sample (all the children were white and most were middle-class), and, consequently, both arrived at a norm that is 3 months later than the current one, which was derived from a much more representative sample.

"Blind" Experimenters

A substantial body of evidence suggests that when experimenters have specific expectations of the outcome of their research, those expectations can affect their perception of the events of the research itself. As much as possible, then, the people who are carrying out the actual testing should be **"blind,"** that is, unaware of the purpose of the research. Suppose one hypothesis is that first-born infants walk sooner than later-borns. Ideally, the examiner who tests the infants' walking ability would not know what the hypothesis is, and would not even know the age or birth order of the toddlers under study.

Experimental Group and Control Group

In order to test a hypothesis adequately, researchers must compare two study groups that are similar in every important way except one: they must compare an **experimental group,** which receives some special experimental treatment, and a **control group,** which does not receive the experimental treatment.

Suppose a researcher hypothesized that children who use "walkers" walk earlier than children who spend several hours a day in a playpen. In order to find out if this is true, the researcher would select two representative groups of children and arrange that one group (the experi-mental group) be placed in walkers for a certain amount of time each day while the other group (the control group) would be put in their playpens for the same length of time. If the infants in the experimental group, in fact, walked *significantly* earlier on average than the infants in the control group, then the hypothesis would be confirmed.

Determining Significance

Whenever researchers find a difference between two groups, they have to consider the possibility that the difference might have occurred purely by chance. For instance, in any group of infants, some would walk relatively early and some relatively late. When the researchers in the "walker versus playpen" study were dividing the sample population into the experimental and control groups, it would have been possible that, by chance, a preponderance of early walkers ended up in one group or the other. To determine whether their results are, in fact, simply the result of chance, researchers use a statistical test, called a test of **significance.** This test takes into account many statistical factors, including the sample size and the average difference between the groups, and yields the *level of significance,* a numerical indication of exactly how unlikely it is that the particular difference occurred by chance. (Note that the word "significance" here means something quite different from its usual sense; that is, it refers to the validity of a study, not to its value.) Generally, in order to be called *significant*, the possibility of the results occurring by chance has to be less than one chance in twenty, which is written in decimals as a significance of .05. Often the likelihood of a particular finding's occurring by chance is even rarer, perhaps one chance in a hundred (the .01 level) or one in a thousand (the .001 level).

likely to cradle their crying 4-month-olds than they were to cradle their older babies.

Confirming the researchers' hypothesis, the observers also noted many cultural differences. One of the more intriguing was that American mothers communicated much more with words and much less with physical contact than Kenyan mothers did. This was apparent not only when the babies cried (see Figure 1.10, p. 24) but also when they made other sounds, played with objects, or merely looked at their mothers.

Figure 1.10 *As apparent from these data and from other research, African mothers are more physical, and North American mothers more verbal, in raising their children. This does not mean that one group is better than the other. For instance, for 10-month-olds, both touching and talking are quite successful methods of hushing an unhappy baby, and mothers from both groups are equally responsive—albeit in different ways. However, the fact that every child is raised within a culture that encourages some aspects of development more than others is one reason adults have the particular values, abilities, and desires that they do.*

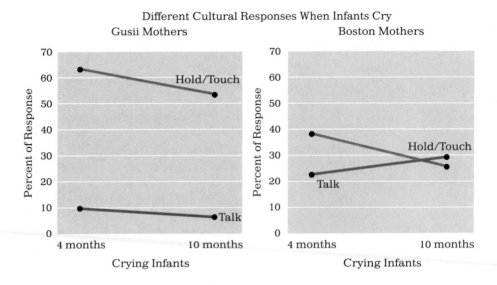

Different Cultural Responses When Infants Cry

The difference is clearly related to cultural views of the mother's role, as the researchers explain:

> Both groups of mothers are responsive to infant signals, but their different behaviors indicate divergent goals and styles. The responsiveness of the Gusii mothers is directed toward soothing and quieting infants rather than arousing them . . . The responsiveness of the Boston mothers, especially as their infants become more communicative later in the 1st year, is designed to engage the infants in emotionally arousing conversational interaction. Gusii mothers see themselves as protecting their infants, not as playing with or educating them. [Richman et al., 1992]

Limitations of Naturalistic Observation

But what more specific factors might underlie these differing cultural views? There are several possible explanations, and they reveal the chief drawback of naturalistic observation—the difficulty of pinpointing the direct cause of the behaviors that are observed. For example, one plausible hypothesis for the above findings relates to infant mortality. In a society in which adequate food and survival are in doubt, as is the case in much of Africa, good parenting may entail soothing and quieting a baby so that he or she can conserve energy, while in an amply fed group such as the suburban Bostonians, a parental priority is likely to be providing the infant with cognitive stimulation (Nugent et al., 1989; Le Vine, 1988).

Another likely hypothesis, posited by the researchers, is that maternal education may influence attitudes about verbal communication: if the mothers are, themselves, well-educated and literate, as the Boston mothers were, they may encourage verbal interactions even before the babies can speak a word. In fact, many Boston mothers were already reading books to their infants before they were a year old, whereas many of the Gusii mothers were illiterate. Some support for this hypothesis comes from a study of Mexican mothers, who were all from the same low-income neighborhood but who had varying levels of education (Richman et al., 1992). This study found that, indeed, the more education the women had, the more likely they were to talk to their babies. In other words, the study found a positive correlation between maternal education and verbalization with infant offspring.

However, we need to be careful in interpreting such findings: **correlation** is a statistic that merely indicates whether two variables are related to each other—specifically, whether changes in one are likely to be accompanied by changes in the other. But in and of itself, *correlation does not indicate causation* (see A Closer Look on p. 26). While it seems logical that something in the educational process might encourage women to be more verbal with their infants, it is possible that some third variable was the underlying cause of the correlation. It could be, for example, that, overall, girls who are higher in verbal skills than other girls tend to spend more years in formal education, and that because of their verbal skills, rather than their education, they tend, as adults, to talk more to everyone—babies included.

Other research does indicate that a mother's education is not the sole explanation for variations in mother-child communication, especially international variations. Other cultural factors, such as the relative emphasis on children's self-reliance, may also play a role. For example, a naturalistic study of international differences in mother-child communication comparing highly educated mothers from Paris, Tokyo, New York, and Buenos Aires found that the Japanese and American mothers talked to their infants at about the same rate (compared to the French who talked less and the Argentineans who talked more), but that the Tokyo mothers were more likely to utter endearments and nonsense syllables, while the New Yorkers were likely to provide information or ask questions (Bornstein et al., 1992). At the very least, this particular difference seems consistent with the tendency of Japanese parents to allow children a much longer period of emotional dependency on adults than do American parents, who tend to push children quickly toward independence.

Obviously, then, naturalistic observation can provide fascinating data and can often generate a number of explanations for the results that it produces. But just as obviously, it cannot definitively link cause and effect, because naturalistic settings contain numerous variables that are, by definition, beyond the researcher's control. To be certain that a particular observation is the result of one variable and not another, and to prove that their speculations are not simply creative hypotheses, scientists must go beyond naturalistic observation to the experiment.

The Experiment

Unlike naturalistic observation, an **experiment** tests a hypothesis in a controlled situation, that is, a situation in which the relevant variables are limited and therefore can be manipulated by the experimenter. Typically the experimenter exposes a group of subjects to the particular variable that is under investigation (for instance, a specific behavior on the part of a caregiver, a new teaching technique, a special diet, a particular social setting, a memory strategy) and then evaluates how they react.

A CLOSER LOOK   Correlation: What It Does, and Does Not, Mean

Correlation is a statistical term that indicates that two variables are somehow related, that is, that one particular variable is likely, or unlikely, to occur when another particular variable occurs. For instance, there is a correlation between height and weight, because, usually, the taller a person is, the more he or she weighs. There is also a correlation between wealth and education, and perhaps even between springtime and falling in love.

Note that the fact that two variables are correlated does not mean that they are related in every instance. Some tall people weigh less than people of average height; some wealthy people never finished high school; some people fall in love in the depths of winter.

Nor does correlation indicate cause. The correlation between education and wealth does not necessarily imply that more education leads to greater wealth. It may be instead that more wealth leads to greater education, since wealthier people are more likely to be able to afford the expense of college. Or there may be a third variable, perhaps intelligence or family background, that accounts for the level of both income and education.

There are two types of correlation, positive and negative. Whenever one variable changes in the same direction as another variable changes (for example, both increase or both decrease), the correlation is said to be *positive*. All the examples given so far are examples of positive correlation. Thus, when education increases, income tends to increase as well; when education is low, so is income likely to be.

When two variables are inversely related (one increasing while the other decreases), the correlation is said to be *negative*. Snow and summertime, maleness and motherhood, and blue eyes and black hair are negatively correlated.

When there is no relationship between the two variables, the correlation is said to be *zero*. It is hard to think of any two variables that have no relationship to each other at all. Probably the correlation between eye color and age is zero (except in infancy, when many babies temporarily have blue eyes), as is the correlation between how much milk you drank yesterday and whether it is raining today (unless seasonal variations in rainfall are related to your thirst).

Correlations can be expressed numerically. They range from plus one (+ 1.0), the highest positive correlation, to minus one (– 1.0), the most negative correlation. Halfway between plus one and minus one is zero, which, as you just learned, indicates no correlation at all.

Correlations are one of the most useful tools in psychology and, at the same time, one of the most often misused. They are useful because knowing how variables are

Like all single parents, this single father is confronted with the research finding that single parenthood correlates with developmental problems for the children involved. However, it must be remembered that correlations nearly always reflect tendencies, not inevitabilities. Nor do they indicate causation. The developmental problems associated with single parenthood may arise from variables other than single parenthood itself—such as reduced family income or ongoing conflict between ex-spouses.

related helps us understand the world we live in. However, as the respected researcher Sandra Scarr (1985) notes, "the psychological world . . . is a cloud of correlated events to which we as human observers give meaning." Unless we are cautious in giving that meaning, we are likely to seize on one or another particular correlation as an explanation, without looking for other possible explanations. For instance, in the 1960s many psychologists noted the correlation between "broken" homes and maladjustment in children and concluded that single parents necessarily put their children at risk. In the 1980s, psychologists looking at the same kinds of homes (now called single-parent families) noted that many children in them do quite well, and that other factors that correlate with such homes (e. g., low income, disrupted education) may be the explanation for children's problems when they occur (see pp. 352–354). The lesson here is clear: we need to be very careful not to jump from the discovery of correlations to conclusions about causes.

Let's take a simple example. Naturalistic observation reveals that children are much more likely to follow their parents' suggestions at certain times than at others. You can probably think of dozens of explanations, but without an experiment, it is impossible to know which are valid. One hypothesis is that children's moods directly affect how they respond to their parents' directives.

To test this hypothesis, twenty-eight 4-year-old children and their mothers were studied in a laboratory playroom (Lay et al., 1989). Half the children were put into a positive mood by being asked to think of some event that had made them feel happy, good, or excited, and the other half were put into a negative mood by being asked to recall some event that had made them upset, scared, or angry. After thinking of the experience, they were asked to relate it to the experimenter, and then to go over it again in their minds, remembering how it made them feel. Such guided memories have, in previous experiments, been proven to affect a person's mood.

Then the experimenter left, and each mother, as directed, asked her child to sort and put away 153 blocks that were scattered on the floor. The mothers were told not to praise or help the child but to simply repeat the instructions if the child stopped sorting. Four minutes later, the experiment was over. The influence of mood on the two groups was striking. All the children in a positive mood began sorting the blocks quickly—averaging only a 15-second delay before beginning. Even the slowest among them started within half a minute after the initial instructions. By contrast, children in a negative mood were much slower to comply, typically waiting 90 seconds to begin and sometimes refusing to begin at all. By the end of the four minutes, the children in a positive mood had sorted and put away an average of 93 blocks each, whereas the children in a negative mood had sorted and put away an average of only 42.

Limitations of the Experiment

As you can see, experiments of this sort, done under very specific conditions that compare two groups of subjects, can make the link between cause and effect quite clear. The question is, To what degree do findings from an artificial experimental situation apply in the real world? In the normal give-and-take at home, for instance, can children be put into a particular mood as easily, and with the same effect, as they were in this experiment? Probably not. In addition, the actual experimental task—sorting the blocks—was an easy and neutral one. All the children could do it, and neither mother nor child had any personal interest in whether or not it got done. In actual life, parents generally ask children to do things that the parents want them to do, and that the children may not want to do, or may not be able to do. The influence of mood may therefore not be as straightforward at home as it was in the experimental setting.

The experiment is subject to an additional limitation when it involves older children and adults, who may alter their behavior in the experimental setting because they know that they are being studied. Subjects sometimes behave in ways that they think will please the experimenter or will make them look good, and, occasionally, some subjects (usually college students) may try to undermine the experiment—all of which adds an additional layer of possible artificiality to this type of research. Nonetheless, experiments can provide invaluable clues regarding cause and effect.

Figure 1.11 *Naturalistic observation reveals that children are sometimes cruel to animals as well as to each other, but it does not reveal why. Laboratory experiments, however, have shown that one factor is the observation of cruelty and aggression in others. Chances are these children have seen someone else try to settle a dispute over possession in a similar fashion.*

Figure 1.12 *"If you want to know what people think, just ask them," is the operating strategy used by survey-takers. Unfortunately, even with interviewers trained to encourage forthright responses, the truth in a survey is sometimes exclusive. For example, will this elderly woman, seemingly proud yet wary, report her age and income accurately, or truthfully relate her own specifics on whatever topic might be of interest to the researcher, such as health habits, sexual activities, religious practices, or relationships with grown children?*

The Survey

In a **survey,** the scientist asks people for information about themselves or for their opinions, either through personal interviews or formal questionnaires. This seems to be an easy, quick, and direct research method. However, it is more difficult to get valid survey data than it seems, because a survey, even more than an experiment, is vulnerable to bias, on the part of the surveyor and the respondents. To begin with, the very phrasing of the survey questions can influence the answers. A survey on the issue of abortion, for instance, might prompt different responses depending on whether it asked about "terminating an unwanted pregnancy" or "taking the life of an unborn child."

In addition, many people who are surveyed give answers that they think the survey expects, or that they think will make them seem "right-thinking" (or, alternatively, unconventional or wicked). Even when people wish to give completely accurate information, their responses may be flawed because their opinion on a particular question varies from day to day, or because their recollection of events is distorted. Interviews can be particularly difficult when they involve young children, who may misunderstand the interviewer's questions, be uneasy with the questioning process, or confuse reality with fantasy.

The Case Study

An additional research tool is the **case study,** an intensive study of one individual. Typically, the case study is based on interviews with the subject regarding his or her background, present thinking, and actions, and often utilizes interviews of others who know the individual. Naturalistic observation and standardized tests may furnish additional case-study material.

Case studies can provide a wealth of detail and therefore are rich in possible insights. However, not only are case studies susceptible to the problems just mentioned in connection with survey interviews, but the interpretation of case-study data depends on the wisdom as well as the biases of the interpreter. Even if the interpretation is valid, it may apply only to the par-

Figure 1.13 *Reconciling the many possible, sometimes conflicting, views about the subject of a case study requires a talented interpreter, whose views and possible biases must also be taken into account.*

"You are fair, compassionate, and intelligent, but you are <u>perceived</u> as biased, callous, and dumb."

Drawing by Mankoff; © 1985 The New Yorker Magazine, Inc.

ticular individual being studied. (The case study of David's encouraging progress over his particular handicaps, for example, applies only to David and might give a misleading picture if used to predict the future outcomes for others with rubella syndrome.) For the most part, then, the case study is not used to do basic research, because no conclusions about people in general can be drawn from a sample size of one.

Designing Developmental Research

Thus, there are many ways to test hypotheses. Researchers can observe people in natural settings, or experiment with them in a laboratory; they can compare one group with another and find correlations and significant differences; they can survey hundreds or even thousands of people about specific aspects of their behavior and attitudes. None of these ways to examine a hypothesis is sufficient in itself, but each one can bring us closer to an understanding of the phenomenon being studied.

However, for research to be truly developmental, scientists must discover how and why people do or do not change *over time*. To learn about the pace and process of change, developmentalists use two basic research designs, cross-sectional and longitudinal, or a combination of the two.

Cross-Sectional Research

The more convenient, and thus more common, way researchers study development is by doing a **cross-sectional** comparison of people of various ages. In this kind of study, groups of people who are different in age but similar in other important ways (such as their level of education, socioeconomic status, ethnic background, and so forth) are compared on the characteristic or tendency that is of interest. Any differences on this dimension that exist among the people of one age and the people of another are, presumably, the result of age-related development.

One recent cross-sectional study compared 1,300 young, middle-aged, and older adults on various emotional dimensions, including the propensity to boredom, to see how they changed with age. With respect to boredom, the findings suggest that, contrary to commonsense expectations, adults are less subject to boredom as they grow older. For example, the youngest, not the oldest adults, were most likely to agree that "It is hard to find things that are new and interesting." The youngest were also most likely to needfully seek out stimulation of various kinds, saying it was "very true" that they craved excitement, liked loud music, enjoyed thriller movies, and were inclined to do "something crazy to spice up the week." Older adults tended to say this was only "somewhat true," with many of the oldest adults saying this was "not at all true" (Lawton et al., 1992).

However, with cross-sectional research it is very difficult to ensure that the various comparison groups are similar in every background variable except age, and that age is therefore the explanation for whatever differences are found among the groups. Of course, good scientists try to make the groups as similar as possible. For example, in this study, ethnicity, SES, and health were comparable in all three groups, and most of the participants were attending college. However, the young adults were full-time undergraduates, while the older ones were part of an adult-education program

Figure 1.14 *The apparent similarity of these two groups in terms of gender and ethnic composition makes them seem potential candidates for cross-sectional research. However, before we could be sure that any differences between the two groups on any given dimension are the result of age, we would have to be sure the groups are alike in other ways, such as socioeconomic background, religious upbringing, and so forth.*

called Elderhostel. There is no way to know if this difference affected the results of the study, but it is theoretically possible that those elderly people who become involved in Elderhostel programs are more intellectually curious, motivated, and absorbed than the typical undergraduate and therefore are less in need of exciting external distractions. It is also probable that the Elderhostel subjects are not typical of older adults as a whole, so the findings of this study could not be applied to the general population of elderly adults.

In addition, every cross-sectional study will, to some degree, reflect cohort differences, and in some cases the findings of cross-sectional research may be more a product of historical time than of chronological age. In the present study, for example, adults who grew up before 1950, prior to the electronic era, had a childhood without television, video games, and computers. Perhaps the reason they are less readily bored is that they learned the joys of reading a good book, engaging in a deep conversation, writing a thoughtful letter, and so forth, while the younger generation, raised in an era of fast-moving, constantly changing, instant-access diversions that require only a short attention span and can be changed at the touch of a button, has developed a greater need for novelty.

Longitudinal Research

To help discover if age, rather than some other background or historical variable, is the reason for an apparent developmental change, researchers use **longitudinal research**, which involves studying the same individuals over a long period of time. This allows information about people at one age to be compared with information about them at another age, thus enabling researchers to find out how these particular people changed over time.

For example, a longitudinal study on the trajectory of boredom and sensation-seeking with age might begin with a group of young adults, perhaps not only asking them survey questions like those in the cross-sectional study just described (such as whether they regularly sought something "crazy to spice up their week") but also interviewing them to find out their interests, hobbies, daily activities, general frustrations, and so on. Then, every decade or so, the same individuals could be surveyed and questioned again, with their responses compared to those of their younger years. If these subjects were less likely to seek external stimulation as they aged, it would be clear that something about the aging process itself decreased boredom, at least within this group. While such a precise study has not been undertaken, longitudinal studies of overall personality patterns suggest that the propensity to boredom and the need for external stimulation do, in fact, decrease with age (Giambra et al., 1992; Haan et al., 1986).

Longitudinal research is particularly useful in studying developmental trends that occur over a long age span. It has produced valuable and sometimes surprising findings on such questions as children's adjustment to divorce (the negative effects linger, especially for school-age and older boys [Hetherington et al., 1989]); the long-term effects of serious birth problems (remarkable resiliency is often apparent [Werner and Smith, 1992]); and the consistency of personality in adulthood (personality patterns do not change much from age 30 to 70, but the expression of a person's particular traits can vary a great deal [McCrae and Costa, 1990]).

However, although longitudinal research is "the lifeblood of developmental science," the actual number of studies that cover more than a few years is "woefully small" (Applebaum and McCall, 1983). The primary reason for this is a very practical one: to follow the development of a group of people over a number of years usually requires great effort, considerable foresight, and substantial funding. Thus, while most developmental researchers consider longitudinal research far more revealing than cross-sectional studies, they are forced to rely heavily on cross-sectional research. (An attempt to combine both types of research—*cross-sequential* research—to maximize their respective advantages is discussed in Chapter 21.)

Ethics and Values

Every scientist must be concerned with ethics, particularly in the conduct and reporting of research. At the most basic level, researchers who study human behavior and development must conduct their studies in an ethical manner, ensuring that the subjects of research are not harmed by the research process, and that their participation is voluntary and confidential. This is particularly crucial when the subjects are children, as reflected in the following precautions urged by the Society for Research in Child Development (1990):

> The investigator should use no research operation that may harm the child either physically or psychologically . . . When in doubt about the possible harmful effects, consultation should be sought from others.
>
> Before seeking consent or assent from the child, the investigator should inform the child of all features of the research that may affect his or her willingness to participate and should answer the child's questions in terms appropriate to the child's comprehension. [The child is free to] discontinue participation at any time. . . . Investigators working with infants should take special effort to explain the research procedures to the parents and be especially sensitive to any indicators of discomfort in the infant.
>
> Informed consent requires that parents or other responsible adults be informed of all the features of the research that may affect their willingness to allow the child to participate.
>
> When, in the course of research, information comes to the investigator's attention that may jeopardize the child's well-being, the investigator has a responsibility to discuss the information with the parents or guardians and with those expert in the field in order that they may arrange the necessary assistance for the child.
>
> The investigators should keep in confidence all information obtained about research participants.

All these goals are ones that developmental researchers endorse. However, in practice, it is not always possible to guarantee that no harm will come of a particular research endeavor, or that subjects understand what their involvement implies. Nor is it a simple matter to make sure that the benefits of the research outweigh any possible costs. For instance, in order to attain the goal of developmental research—all individuals reaching their full potential—developmentalists urgently need more information on children who have learning disabilities or who have been abused, but those children are especially vulnerable to emotional stress in the research process (Thompson, 1990). Indeed, one reason naturalistic observation is used in de-

Figure 1.15 *The long time span of longitudinal research provides a revealing view of how individuals change and how they remain the same. Longitudinal research on this woman would reveal whether her view of a woman's role over the years has changed as readily as her sense of hair style, and whether her outgoing personality has remained as stable as her engaging smile would seem to suggest.*

velopmental research is that inadvertent harm cannot occur if the scientist merely observes children in their normal life.

However, the most difficult ethical question raised by the study of human development is not safeguarding the participants, which is fairly straightforward, but attending to larger implications of the research. As stated in the *Ethical Principles of Psychologists*, the "freedom of inquiry and communication" that is an integral part of science also entails "concern for the best interests of . . . society" (American Psychological Association, 1990). This is essential because controversial issues such as infant day care, parental consent in teenage abortion, custody rights in divorce cases, retirement policies, and "right to die" legislation are often argued using research that is imperfectly interpreted and deliberately overstated in the public press.

Each reader of this book should also try to be mindful of the implications of the various findings, theories, and examples found in the study of human development. As we examine the mechanisms and patterns of development, you will, time and time again, be confronted with both practical and ethical issues—from family-planning and prenatal care to basic education and child discipline, from marriage, divorce, and alternative lifestyles to issues of sexism and racism—many of which may touch on some aspect of your own life. Your growing understanding of the practical and philosophical questions of development is important whether you plan to become a researcher or a practitioner, a teacher or a parent, or simply a more involved and better-informed member of the human family.

SUMMARY

The Study of Human Development

1. The study of human development is the study of how and why people change over time, and how and why they remain the same. Developmentalists include researchers from many academic and practical disciplines, especially biology, education, and psychology, who study people of every age and in every social group.

2. Development is often divided into three domains, the biosocial, the cognitive, and the psychosocial. While this division makes it easier to study the intricacies of development, researchers note that development in each domain is influenced by the other two, as body, mind, and emotion always effect each other and the social context always guides all three.

3. An ecological, or systems, approach stresses the many contexts of development, particularly the influence of family, community, and culture. Each individual is seen as part of many systems, affecting them as well as being affected by them. Three factors that are particularly influential within each system are cohorts, ethnic groups, and socioeconomic status, or SES.

4. The interaction of domains is clearly seen in the example of David, whose handicaps originating in the biosocial domain quickly affected the other two domains. His example also shows how the individual is affected by, and also affects, the surrounding systems of family, society, and culture.

Three Controversies

5. All aspects of development are guided by the interaction of hereditary forces and the particular experiences a person has. The relative importance of these factors is a topic of debate, called the nature-nurture controversy.

6. Another controversy exists between those who think that development is smooth and continuous, and those who think it occurs in stages. Particularly in adulthood, universal age-related stages are difficult to find. The reason is that one adult's developmental timetable is often quite different from another's because of variations in both the individual biological clock that governs the aging process and in the social clock that regulates age-appropriate behavior.

7. Traditionally, many researchers searched for the averages, or "norms," of development, and considered individuals who differed from those norms deficient. Current researchers are much more likely to consider differences as alternative paths of development.

The Scientific Method

8. The scientific method is used, in some form, by most developmental researchers. They observe, pose a question, develop a hypothesis, test the hypothesis, and draw conclusions based on the results of the tests.

9. To check their conclusions and to try to remain as objective as possible, researchers use a variety of methods, among them, selection of a representative sample population, "blind" experimenters, control groups, and tests of statistical significance.

10. One common method of testing hypotheses is naturalistic observation, which provides ecologically valid information but does not pinpoint cause and effect. The laboratory experiment pinpoints causes but is not necessarily applicable to daily life. The interview and case study are also useful.

11. In developmental research, ways are needed to detect change over time. Cross-sectional research compares people of different ages; longitudinal research (which is preferable but more difficult) studies the same individuals over a long time period. Both are valid for the cohorts under examination, but not necessarily for other cohorts.

Ethics and Values

12. Contemporary researchers in the social sciences give considerable thought and attention to safeguarding the rights and well-being of the participants in their research. A more difficult ethical problem is the accurate reporting of research and understanding and dealing with all of its implications.

KEY QUESTIONS

1. What is the main focus of the study of human development?

2. What are the three domains into which the study of human development is usually divided?

3. Give examples of the interaction among the various systems that affect an individual's development.

4. Name and give examples of three contextual factors that developmentalists recognized as powerful influences in every system.

5. What are the steps of the scientific method?

6. What are the advantages of the scientific method?

7. What are the advantages and disadvantages of testing a hypothesis by naturalistic observation?

8. What are the advantages and disadvantages of testing a hypothesis by experiment?

9. Compare the advantages of longitudinal research and cross-sectional research.

10. What ethical precautions should developmental researchers take?

KEY TERMS

biosocial domain (5)
cognitive domain (5)
psychosocial domain (5)
ecological approach (6)
  (also, systems
  approach) (7)
microsystem (6)
mesosystem (6)
exosystem (6)
macrosystem (6)
cohort (8)
ethnic group (8)
socioeconomic status
  (SES) (9)
nature (15)
nurture (15)
continuity (17)
discontinuity (17)

biological clock (17)
social clock (17)
norm (18)
scientific method (20)
replicate (20)
naturalistic observation (21)
sample size (22)
representative sample (22)
blind (23)
experimental group (23)
control group (23)
significance (23)
experiment (25)
correlation (25)
survey (28)
case study (28)
cross-sectional research (29)
longitudinal research (30)

CHAPTER 2

Theories

The patterns of development in everyday life are often complex and not simply explained. Over the past hundred years, social scientists have devised several theoretical perspectives that offer insight into why we develop in the ways that we do and how we learn to act in new ways. In this chapter, we will see how these perspectives suggest answers to such questions as:

How does the mind develop?

Which is more effective in changing behavior—punishments or rewards?

Are humans, including children, motivated by unconscious impulses?

How do children and adults influence their own development?

What psychological needs do all humans have?

Our efforts to understand human development usually begin with questions. How do we develop into the kind of person we ultimately become? How significant and long-lasting are influences from early childhood? To what degree are we the products of our genetic inheritance, or of our environment? How do we learn to think, reason, create, and understand as we do? What are the unique challenges for personality growth at each stage of the life span?

What Theories Do

To begin to answer these questions and many others, we need some way to select significant facts and organize them in a manner that will take us deeper than our first speculations. In short, we need a theory. A **developmental theory** is a systematic statement of principles that explain behavior and development.

Figure 2.1 *No matter what interaction developmentalists study, they can make their observations from various theoretical perspectives—psychoanalytic, which emphasizes unconscious drives and motives; learning, which emphasizes learned responses to particular situations; cognitive, which emphasizes the individual's understanding of self and others; and humanistic, which emphasizes the individual's need for self-fulfillment.*

In developmental research, theories have several purposes. First, they provide a broad and coherent view of the complex influences on human development, and thus they offer guidance for practical issues encountered by parents, teachers, therapists, and others concerned with development. They distinguish certain influences as paramount and others as peripheral, for example, and suggest how to best optimize human growth. Second, theories form the basis for hypotheses—or educated guesses—about behavior and development that can be tested by research studies and either supported or disconfirmed by their results (as you learned in Chapter 1). Third, as theories are constantly modified by research findings, they provide a current summary of our knowledge about development. In this respect, developmental study is never complete, because updated theories give rise to new questions and new hypotheses meriting further investigation. Theories thus help us to ask important and relevant questions as well as leading us to useful answers.

Theories are central to understanding development. Consider why, for example, parents devote such time and energy to caring for offspring. Is it because of the rewards and reinforcement that children provide? Is parenting a basic stage of adult development? Does parental devotion derive from an understanding of, and empathy for, children's needs? Is parenting a fundamental human motive? Does it occur because of cultural expectations? Different theories provide different answers to these questions, and lead us to view parenting in different ways. Furthermore, the answers provided by developmental theories often have important practical applications, such as how best to provide preventive intervention with parents who abuse or neglect their offspring.

Many theories are relevant to the study of development, but in this chapter we will focus on four kinds of theories that have been most influential and useful to developmental psychology—psychoanalytic theories, learning theories, cognitive theories, and humanistic theories. Remember that their purpose is to provide a broad understanding of human development that integrates our knowledge and leads us to ask important questions and make relevant applications of this knowledge.

Psychoanalytic Theories

Psychoanalytic theories interpret human development in terms of intrinsic drives and motives, many of which are unconscious, hidden from our awareness. These basic, underlying forces are viewed as influencing every aspect of a person's thinking and behavior, from the crucial choices of a lifetime to the smallest details of daily life. Psychoanalytic theories also see these drives and motives as providing the foundation for universal stages of development and for specific developmental tasks within those stages, from the formation of human attachments in infancy to the quest for emotional and sexual fulfillment. As a consequence, psychoanalytic theories provide a fascinating window into age-typical developmental processes as well as into the growth of individual differences in personality and behavior.

Origins

The psychoanalytic perspective provided the first comprehensive view of human behavior for the field of psychology. Because of this, the questions it posed and the answers it offered have intrigued psychologists ever since. To understand the tenets of this perspective, it is helpful to know something about the intellectual climate that it challenged. In Europe during the late 1800s, prevailing thought about human behavior included the ideas that people are governed for the most part by reason and mature judgment, and that children are "innocent," devoid of all sexual feelings.

By the 1870s, against the grain of these notions, a number of European intellectuals were developing an explanation of human behavior that emphasized the controlling power of emotional forces and the subordinate role of reason. In particular, Sigmund Freud (1856–1939), the founder of the psychoanalytic approach, began to evolve a theory that pointed specifically to the irrational basis of human behavior. Most notably, it called attention to the hidden emotional content of our everyday actions, to the ways the individual is driven by unconscious but powerful sexual and aggressive impulses, to the inner conflicts surrounding these impulses, and to the ways these conflicts arise in childhood and shape the individual's personality. Freud's depiction of the irrational and destructive forces at work in the normal personality shocked most of his contemporaries, but was soon to become a major influence in the field of psychology.

Freud was a medical doctor who formulated his theory while treating people with various physical disorders. Freud suspected that the origin of their symptoms was in the mind. In an effort to uncover the hidden causes of their problems, Freud would have them recline on his office couch and talk about anything and everything that came into their minds—daily events, dreams, childhood memories, fears, desires—no matter how seemingly trivial or how unpleasant. From these disclosures and such things as the patient's slips of the tongue and unexpected associations between one word and another, Freud discerned clues to the usually unconscious emotional conflicts that paralyzed one person or terrified another. Once the patient, under Freud's guidance, came to understand the nature of these hidden conflicts, the patient's symptoms would frequently diminish or disappear.

Figure 2.2 *Many of Freud's students and patients spoke about his penetrating gaze, which, they said, helped them uncover their hidden thoughts and fantasies. Indeed, some critics contend that much of Freud's success as a psychoanalyst could be credited to his personality and insight, rather than to his methods or theories.*

The medical establishment ridiculed Freud's "talking cure," especially when he reported that many physical and emotional problems were caused by unconscious sexual desires, some of which originated in infancy. This idea was contrary to the prevailing view that children are asexual, and that early life events have little influence on adult personality. But as patients revealed their problems and fantasies, Freud listened, interpreted, and formulated an influential theory of the human personality.

Freud's Ideas

One of Freud's basic ideas is that, long before they reach adolescence, children have sexual—or sensual—pleasures and fantasies, derived from stimulation of various parts of their bodies. According to his theory of **childhood sexuality,** development in the first six years occurs in three **psychosexual stages** (see Table 2.1, p. 40). Each stage is characterized by the focusing of sexual interest and pleasure in a particular part of the body. In infancy, it is the mouth (the **oral stage**); in early childhood, it is the anus (the **anal stage**); in the preschool years, it is the penis (the **phallic stage**). In each stage, the sensual satisfaction associated with these body regions is linked to the major developmental needs and challenges that are typical of various ages in childhood. During the oral stage, for example, physical nurturance is crucial, so the baby experiences pleasure through sucking and (later) biting, and becomes emotionally attached to the person who provides these oral gratifications. During the anal stage, pleasures related to control and self-control—initially in connection with defecation and toilet training—are paramount. During the phallic stage, pleasure is derived from genital stimulation, and the young child's interest in physical differences between the sexes leads to the development of gender identity and to the child's identification with the moral standards of his or her same-sex parent.

It was Freud's contention that each stage also has its own potential conflicts between child and parent, such as those concerning weaning or toilet training. How the child experiences those conflicts influences his or her basic personality and lifelong patterns of behavior. Finally, after a five- or six-year period of sexual **latency,** during which sexual forces are dormant, the individual enters a final psychosexual stage, the **genital stage,** which is characterized by mature sexual interests and lasts throughout adulthood. (These psychosexual stages are discussed in greater detail in chapters 7, 10, 13, and 16.)

Figure 2.3 *This girl's interest in the statue's anatomy may reflect simple curiosty, but Freudian theory would maintain that it is a clear manifestation of the phallic stage of psychosexual development, in which girls are said to feel deprived because they lack a penis.*

Id, Ego, and Superego

To help explain the dynamics of psychological development, Freud identified three components of personality: the id, ego, and superego. The **id,** which is present at birth, is the source of our unconscious impulses toward fulfillment of our needs. It operates according to the *pleasure principle,* that is, the striving for immediate gratification. In other words, the id wants whatever seems satisfying and enjoyable—and wants it *now.* The impatient, greedy infant screaming for food in the middle of the night is all id.

Gradually, as babies learn that other people have demands of their own and that gratification must sometimes wait, the **ego** begins to develop. This rational aspect of personality, which emerges because of frustrating experiences like weaning and toilet training, has the role of mediating between the unbridled demands of the id and the limits imposed by the real world. The ego operates according to the *reality principle:* it attempts to satisfy the id's demands in realistic and appropriate ways that recognize life as it is, not as the id wants it to be.

The ego also strives to keep another irrational force at bay. At about age 4 or 5, the **superego** starts to develop, as children begin to identify with their parents' moral standards during the phallic stage. The superego is like a relentless conscience that distinguishes right from wrong in unrealistically moralistic terms. Its prime objective is to strive for perfection, and to keep the id in check. In this regard, it is the function of the ego to mediate between the primal desires of the id and the superego's unbending effort to inhibit those desires.

The Ego and Development

According to psychoanalytic theory, the ego guides the course of developmental changes that are initiated by physical maturation, pressures and opportunities in the environment, and the child's own internal conflicts. The development of new skills, understanding, and competence is largely an outgrowth of the ego's striving for mastery over intrapsychic and environmental challenges (Loevinger, 1976). Psychologically healthy individuals develop strong egos that can also competently manage the demands of the id and superego. However, in some circumstances, the ego may rely on *defense mechanisms* to cope with internal conflict or with demands from the environment. One of the most commonly referred to of these defense mechanisms is **repression**—that is, the pushing of a disturbing memory, idea, or impulse out of awareness and into the unconscious, where it is no longer actively threatening. Because of repression, for example, a traumatized child may not remember witnessing a terrifying accident, and thus will not be troubled by explicit recollections of the event. At the same time, however, repression prevents the individual from confronting a disturbing experience thoughtfully and rationally. Moreover, memory of that experience remains in the unconscious, where it may continually distort behavior and thinking (for example, the child may have an irrational fear of places and objects associated with the accident). According to Freud, this unconscious legacy can endure throughout life, undermining healthy personality functioning for reasons unknown to the individual.

Psychoanalytic theory thus holds that each adult inherits a legacy of problems from the conflicts of his or her childhood, along with particular ways of coping with them. Depending on our early experiences, some of us are more able to cope with the stresses of daily life than others.

TABLE 2.1   Comparison of Psychosexual and Psychosocial Stages

Approximate Age	Freud (Psychosexual)	Erikson* (Psychosocial)
Birth to 1 year	**Oral Stage** The mouth, tongue, and gums are the focus of pleasurable sensations in the baby's body, and feeding is the most stimulating activity.	**Trust vs. Mistrust** Babies learn either to trust that others will care for their basic needs, including nourishment, warmth, cleanliness, and physical contact, or to lack confidence in the care of others.
1–3 years	**Anal Stage** The anus is the focus of pleasurable sensations in the baby's body, and toilet training is the most important activity.	**Autonomy vs. Shame and Doubt** Children learn either to be self-sufficient in many activities, including toileting, feeding, walking, exploring, and talking, or to doubt their own abilities.
3–6 years	**Phallic Stage** The phallus, or penis, is the most important body part, and pleasure is derived from genital stimulation. Boys are proud of their penis, and girls wonder why they don't have one.	**Initiative vs. Guilt** Children want to undertake many adultlike activities, sometimes overstepping the limits set by parents and feeling guilty.
7–11 years	**Latency** Not a stage but an interlude, when sexual needs are quiet and children put psychic energy into conventional activities like schoolwork and sports.	**Industry vs. Inferiority** Children busily learn to be competent and productive in mastering new skills, or feel inferior and unable to do anything well.
Adolescence	**Genital Stage** The genitals are the focus of pleasurable sensations, and the young person seeks sexual stimulation and sexual satisfaction in heterosexual relationships.	**Identity vs. Role Confusion** Adolescents try to figure out "Who am I?" They establish sexual, political, and career identities or are confused about what roles to play.
Adulthood	Freud believed that the genital stage lasts throughout adulthood. He also said that the goal of a healthy life is "to love and to work well."	**Intimacy vs. Isolation** Young adults seek companionship and love with another person or become isolated from others by fearing rejection or disappointment.
		Generativity vs. Stagnation Middle-aged adults contribute to the next generation by performing meaningful work, creative activities, and/or raising a family, or become stagnant and inactive.
		Integrity vs. Despair Older adults try to make sense out of their lives, either seeing life as a meaningful whole or despairing at goals never reached and questions never answered.

*Although Erikson describes two extreme resolutions to each crisis, he recognizes that there is a wide range of outcomes between these extremes and that most people arrive at some middle course.

Erikson's Ideas

Dozens of Freud's students became famous psychoanalytic theorists in their own right. Although they all acknowledged the importance of the unconscious, of irrational urges, and of early childhood, each in his or her own way expanded and modified Freud's ideas. Many of these neo-Freudians, including Margaret Mahler and Anna Freud, are mentioned at various points in this book. One of them, Erik Erikson (1902–   ), formulated a comprehensive theory of development that will be outlined here and discussed in later chapters.

Psychosocial Development

Erikson spent his childhood in Germany, his adolescence wandering through Europe, his young adulthood in Vienna under the tutelage of Freud and Freud's daughter Anna, and his later life in the United States. In Amer-

Figure 2.4 *Erik Erikson has continued to write and lecture on psychosocial development throughout his long life. His work also emphasizes psychohistory—the relationship between historical factors and personality development.*

ica, he studied students at Harvard, soldiers who suffered emotional breakdowns during World War II, civil rights workers in the South, the play of disturbed and normal children, and Native American tribes. Partly as a result of this diversity of experience, Erikson began to think of Freud's stages as too limited and too few. He proposed, instead, eight developmental stages, spanning the entire life span, each one characterized by a particular challenge, or crisis, that must be resolved.

As you can see from Table 2.1, Erikson's first five stages are closely related to Freud's stages. Freud's last stage occurs at adolescence, however, while Erikson sees adulthood as having three stages. (You will read more about Erikson's theory throughout this book, including chapters on adulthood.) Another significant difference is that all Erikson's stages are centered, not on a body part, but on each person's relationship to the social environment. To highlight this emphasis on social and cultural influences, Erikson calls his theory the **psychosocial theory** of human development.

Cultural Influences

In this theory, the resolution of each developmental conflict depends on the interaction of the individual's characteristics and the support provided by the social environment. In the stage of *initiative versus guilt,* for example, children between ages 3 and 6 often want to undertake activities that exceed their abilities and/or the limits set down by their parents. Their efforts to act independently can thus leave them open to feelings of pride or failure, depending in part on the reactions of parents and on cultural expectations for children's behavior. How a child resolves the challenges of each stage involves both the child's competencies and the response of others to the child's successes and failures. The same is true in adulthood, when, for example, how well the individual negotiates the stage of *intimacy versus isolation* is influenced both by personal needs and by various cultural assumptions, such as those regarding the appropriate age to marry. To be unmarried at age 20 means quite different things in different societies.

Figure 2.5 *It seems quite clear that the toddler here is in the thick of the psychosocial stage Erikson referred to as* autonomy versus shame and doubt. *Whether he emerges from this stage feeling independent or inept depends in part on whether his parents encourage his various efforts at self-control or, instead, regularly criticize him for his failures. It seems equally clear that this young girl is trying to negotiate the stage Erikson called* identity versus role confusion. *In this stage, teenagers try out a number of roles (often focusing on appearance) in an effort to discover who they really are.*

Central to Erikson's theory is the idea that each culture faces particular challenges and, correspondingly, promotes particular paths of development that are likely to meet those challenges. Problems arise when a society's traditional methods of upbringing no longer prepare its children to cope with the demands they face as adults. No culture anticipates the future so well that each member is prepared to live in it without problems. Each society provides better preparation for some crises than for others.

Evaluations of Psychoanalytic Theories

All developmentalists owe a debt of gratitude both to Freud and to the neo-Freudians who extended and refined his concepts. Many of Freud's ideas are so widely accepted today that they are no longer thought of as his—for example, that unconscious motives affect our behavior, that development occurs in a series of stages, and that the early years are a formative period of personality development. While few accept his ideas completely, many have learned from his insights.

Moreover, the psychoanalytic approach continues to shape current thinking about topics as diverse as mother-infant attachment, the effects of parental discipline, gender identity, moral development, adolescent identity, and a variety of other issues that you will study in subsequent chapters. Although the ideas of Freud and his followers have been modified considerably, they remain suggestive and insightful, and many current formulations originate in psychoanalytic ideas.

There are, however, many aspects of the psychoanalytic approach that most contemporary developmentalists find to be inadequate or wrong. For instance, Freud's notion that the child's experiences during the first three psychosexual stages form the basis for character structure and personality problems in adulthood has found little support in studies of normal children. Most researchers agree that, throughout life, personality characteristics and behavior are also affected by genetic traits, current life events, and the overarching sociocultural context, as well as by the experiences of early childhood (Bengston et al., 1985; Ingleby, 1987; Vandenberg et al., 1986; Whitbourne, 1985a). Also lacking support is Freud's depiction of the struggle between the id and the superego—that is, between a torrent of impulses seeking immediate release and a ceaselessly judgmental monitor trying to check those impulses—a notion that seems more an outgrowth of the Victorian morality of nineteenth-century Vienna than a valid depiction of a universal process.

Erikson's interpretation of development has fared better than Freud's, perhaps because Erikson's ideas, though arising from Freudian theory, are more comprehensive, contemporary, and apply to a wider range of behavior. Even so, most of the sources of Erikson's theory are, like Freud's, grounded in his own experiences, the recollections of his patients in therapy, and the insights of classical literature. In general, psychoanalytic theories do not lend themselves easily to laboratory testing under controlled conditions, which leads to the accusation by some that the validity of psychoanalytic ideas is "evaluated by dogma, not data" (Cairns, 1983). Consequently, some psychologists find psychoanalytic theories illuminating and insightful; others find them provocative nonsense; most think they are somewhere in between.

Learning Theories

Early in the twentieth century, John B. Watson (1878–1958) argued that if psychology was to be a true science, psychologists should study only what they could see and measure. In Watson's words: "Why don't we make what we can *observe* the real field of psychology? Let us limit ourselves to things that can be observed, and formulate laws concerned only with those things. . . . We can observe behavior—what the organism does or says" (Watson, 1967; originally published 1930). Many American psychologists agreed with Watson, partly because of the difficulty of trying to study unconscious motives and impulses identified in psychoanalytic theory. Behavior, by contrast, could be studied far more objectively and scientifically. Thus began a major theory of American psychology, **behaviorism**, now more commonly called **learning theory** because of its emphasis on how we learn specific behaviors.

Laws of Behavior

Learning theorists have formulated laws of behavior that can be applied to any individual at any age, from fetus to octogenarian. These laws provide insights into how mature competencies are fashioned from simple skills, and how environmental influences shape individual development, throughout life, in both deliberate and unintentional ways. In this view, development is a process of learning.

The basic laws of learning theory explore the relationship between **stimulus** and **response**, that is, between any experience or event (the stimulus) and the behavioral reaction (the response) with which it is associated. Some responses are automatic, like reflexes. If someone suddenly waves a hand in your face, you will blink; if a hungry dog smells food, it will salivate. But most responses do not occur spontaneously; they are learned. Learning theorists emphasize that life is a continual learning process: new events and experiences evoke new behavior patterns, while old, unproductive responses tend to fade away. One part of this learning process involves **conditioning**, through which a particular response becomes conditional upon a particular stimulus. Conditioning occurs in two basic ways: classical and operant.

Classical Conditioning

More than eighty years ago, a Russian scientist named Ivan Pavlov (1849–1936) began to study the link between stimulus and response. While doing research on salivation in dogs, Pavlov noted that his experimental dogs began to salivate not only at the sight of food but, eventually, at the sound of the approaching attendants who brought the food. This observation led him to perform his famous experiment in which he taught a dog to salivate at the sound of a bell. Pavlov began by ringing the bell just before feeding the dog. After several repetitions of this association, the dog began salivating at the sound of the bell even when there was no food. This simple experiment in learning was one of the first scientific demonstrations of **classical conditioning** (also called *respondent conditioning*), in which an animal or person comes to associate a neutral stimulus with a meaningful one, and then *responds* to the former stimulus as if it were the latter. In this case, the

Figure 2.6 *Pavlov was a physiologist who received the Nobel Prize in 1904 for his research on digestive processes. It was this line of study that led to his discovery of classical conditioning.*

dog associated the bell (the neutral stimulus) with food and responded to the sound as though it were the food itself.

There are many everyday examples that suggest classical conditioning you may have experienced: imagining a succulent pizza might make your mouth water; reading the final-exam schedule might make your palms sweat; seeing an erotic photograph might make your heart beat faster. In each instance, the stimulus is connected, or associated, with another stimulus that regularly produced the physiological response in the past. Classical conditioning can also be observed in a child's crying at being returned to a place where he or she had earlier been frightened by a dog. As Watson (1927) himself noted, emotional responses are especially susceptible to learning through classical conditioning, particularly in childhood.

Operant Conditioning

The most influential contemporary proponent of learning theory was B. F. Skinner (1904–1990). Skinner agreed with Pavlov that classical conditioning explains some types of behavior. However, Skinner believed that another type of conditioning—**operant conditioning**—plays a much greater role, especially in more complex learning. In operant conditioning, the organism learns that a particular behavior produces a particular consequence. If the consequence is useful or pleasurable, the organism subsequently repeats the behavior to achieve that consequence again. If the consequence is unpleasant, the organism will not repeat the behavior.

In operant conditioning, then, a system of pleasurable consequences (such as rewards) might be used to train a dog to perform a specific behavior —fetching newspapers or jumping through hoops—that is not in the dog's usual repertoire. Once the behavior has been learned, the dog will continue to do the work—for example, fetching the newspaper—even when the reinforcement is occasional rather than consistent. Similarly, almost all a person's daily behavior, from socializing with others to earning a paycheck, can be said to be the result of operant conditioning. (Operant conditioning is also called *instrumental conditioning*, bringing attention to the fact that the behavior in question has become an instrument for achieving a particular response.) Children likewise respond to operant conditioning, from the toddler who learns to "stay dry" to obtain parental approval to the adolescent who takes up the latest fad in order to be accepted by peers.

Types of Reinforcement

In operant conditioning, the pleasurable or useful consequence that makes it more likely that the behavior in question will reoccur is called **reinforcement** (Skinner, 1953). A stimulus that increases the likelihood that a behavior will be repeated is therefore called a **reinforcer.** Reinforcers may be either positive or negative. A **positive reinforcer** is something pleasant—a good feeling, say, or the satisfaction of a need, or a reward from another, such as a piece of candy or a word of praise. For a grade-conscious student who has studied hard for an exam, getting an "A" would be a positive rein-

Figure 2.7 *B. F. Skinner is best known for his experiments with rats and pigeons, but he also applied his knowledge to a wide range of human problems. For his daughter, he designed a glass-enclosed crib in which temperature, humidity, and perceptual stimulation could be controlled to make time spent in the crib as enjoyable and educational as possible. He also conceptualized and wrote about an ideal society based on principles of operant conditioning, where, for example, workers at the less desirable jobs earn greater rewards.*

forcer of scholarly effort. A **negative reinforcer** is the removal of an unpleasant stimulus as the result of a particular behavior. When a student's anxiety about test-taking is reduced by extra preparation or, counterproductively, by "getting high," the reduction of anxiety is a negative reinforcer. That is, the anxiety-reduction increases the probability that the next time the student is worried about a test, he or she will again prepare well, or take drugs. Note that a negative reinforcer differs from a **punishment,** because punishment is an unpleasant event that makes behavior *less* likely to be repeated.

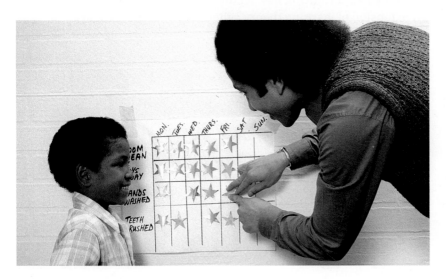 

Figure 2.8 *According to learning theory, the boy on the left is likely to develop good hygiene habits, largely because he is reinforced frequently for his efforts at cleanliness and is aware of the link between behavior and consequence. The girl on the right is obviously thrilled with her accomplishment. Her feelings of satisfaction and self-competence are self-reinforcing.*

Reinforcers may also be either extrinsic or intrinsic. **Extrinsic reinforcers** come from the environment in such varied forms as payment for work, a special privilege for behaving a certain way, good grades, and so forth. **Intrinsic reinforcers** come from within the individual, and typically involve feelings of satisfaction in a job well done and perceptions of self-competence. Thus individuals not only obtain reinforcement from others but are also *self-reinforcing.*

It is important to recognize that not all extrinsic reinforcers have equal significance for those experiencing them. For some people, money is a potent reinforcer; for others, obtaining a special privilege is; and for others, praise and appreciation are most influential. Learning theorists judge the effectiveness of a reinforcer by how strongly it affects behavior.

When behaviorists weigh the methods of creating lasting changes in behavior, they prefer reinforcers to punishments. Harshly criticizing or penalizing someone might immediately change behavior, but research has shown that these are not the best ways to alter behavior permanently. Punishment does not teach a desirable alternative behavior to replace the one that is being punished. Punishment can also have destructive side effects: someone who is punished frequently can become an apathetic, frustrated, or aggressive person (Skinner, 1972).

Social Learning Theory

Learning theorists have sought to explain behavior primarily in terms of the organism's direct experience, for they believe that each individual's current behavior results from the accumulated bits of learning acquired through past conditioning, whether classical or operant. These conditioning processes can explain complex patterns of human interaction, as well as simpler behaviors (Bijou, 1989). However, learning theorists also focus on less direct, though equally potent, forms of learning. They emphasize that people learn new behaviors merely by observing the behavior of others, without directly experiencing any conditioning. These theorists have developed an extension of learning theory called **social learning theory.**

Figure 2.9 *Social learning theory tends to validate the old maxim "Examples speak louder than words." If the moments pictured here are typical for each child, the boy on the left is likely to develop an interest in bicycling that might last a lifetime. On the other hand, the girl on the right may become a cigarette smoker like her mother—even if her mother tells her that smoking is an unhealthy habit to be avoided.*

Modeling

An integral part of social learning is **modeling,** in which we observe other people's behavior and then pattern our own after it. We are more likely to model our behavior after people we consider admirable, or powerful, or similar to us, particularly if we have seen them reinforced for what they do (Bandura, 1977). Often the modeling process is patently obvious, particularly in children. A child who sees another child disobey orders, or share a snack, or play with a toy in an unusual way is likely to imitate the example. Indeed, as one review concludes, "under the right circumstances, children will imitate almost anything, from physical aggression to moral judgment, from taste in candy to patterns of speech" (Hetherington and McIntyre, 1975). Similarly, adults also seem to be surprisingly influenced—by political leaders, media celebrities, coworkers, and friends—in their choices of everything from leisure activities to hairstyles, from slang expressions to personal philosophies.

Cognitive and Motivational Processes

Of course, social learning involves much more than just observing a model and imitating his or her behavior. A person must be motivated to attend to the modeled behavior, to store information about it in memory (perhaps by mentally rehearsing it), and to later retrieve that information when opportunities to use that behavior arise (Bandura, 1977, 1986, 1989). These cognitive and motivational processes help to explain why children's susceptibility to modeling changes as they mature. With increasing age, for example, children become more discriminating observers of other people, and are better able to extract general rules of behavior from the specific examples they observe. This is why young children tend to imitate the most obvious behaviors of a wide range of people, whereas adolescents and adults reproduce more subtle behaviors and styles of conduct (such as a "laid-back air" or a "scholarly manner") from their observations of selected individuals.

Observing others also enables people to develop expectancies for the likely consequences of their actions. With these expectancies, they can mentally test alternative behaviors and choose the one with the most desirable probable outcome. Not surprisingly, children acquire considerable skill in this capacity for "forethought" as they get older (Bandura, 1986, 1989). Whereas preschoolers may react impulsively and regret the consequences, school-age children can, on the basis of memories of past experiences and their observations of others, anticipate the results of their impulses and perhaps act differently. Adults can, in turn, devise sophisticated behavioral strategies based on astute predictions of others' thoughts or reactions and, at times, can use such strategies to manipulate the behavior of others.

Finally, social learning is also affected by perceptions of **self-efficacy,** that is, the person's sense of his or her own aspirations and capabilities (Bandura, 1986, 1989). Because people have different goals, standards, and expectations for themselves, they are naturally drawn to certain social influences, and to certain models, more than to others. Learning is thus affected by self-understanding, because the standards you set for yourself, and your confidence in your ability to meet them, influence your motivation to learn from various sources—whether they be peers, mentors, or media stars. Differences in perceptions of self-efficacy can help explain, for example, why one 10-year-old with good coordination and past athletic successes can be found imitating Michael Jordan's moves on a basketball court, while another 10-year-old whose inclinations are more musical is likelier to be found practicing Eric Clapton's moves on an air guitar. Changing perceptions of self-efficacy may also explain why middle-age men begin to admire and emulate business magnates more than baseball stars. In short, much of our social learning depends on the directions in which our perception of self-efficacy points us.

Reciprocal Determinism

Because of these cognitive and motivational influences on social learning, theorists like Bandura (1986, 1989) regard behavior as an outcome of **reciprocal determinism**—that is, the mutual interaction of the person's internal characteristics, the environment, and behavior itself. One's expectations, self-perceptions, and goals are affected by the social environment, as we have seen, but they also influence that environment. Extroverted individuals, for example, evoke different reactions from others than do withdrawn persons. These reactions, in turn, reinforce their outgoing qualities. Behavior is thus jointly the result of personal and environmental factors, but also influences each. In this concept of reciprocal determinism, social learning theorists seek to encompass the significant personal and environmental determinants of individual development in a comprehensive theory.

Figure 2.10 *Whether children strive to imitate Eric Clapton's moves on an air guitar or Michael Jordan's moves on a basketball court depends, in part, on perceptions of self-efficacy—what people aspire for themselves and believe they can accomplish.*

RESEARCH REPORT   **Children Who Are Out of Control**

One of the most serious problems that developmentalists have been called upon to solve is that of disruptive, antisocial children. Such children not only cause havoc at home and trouble at school but also tend to become juvenile delinquents and even career criminals (Hirschi, 1969).

One social learning researcher, Gerald Patterson, has spent his professional life trying to understand and help "out-of-control" children, that is, children who behave in aggressive and antisocial ways that neither family nor school seems able to control. For the past two decades, Patterson has led a team of scientists at the Oregon Social Learning Center in providing behavioral analysis as well as practical help to families in which one child is disruptively aggressive (Patterson et al., 1967; Patterson, 1980, 1982).

In the tradition of learning theorists, Patterson and his research team have spent thousands of hours observing the moment-by-moment sequences of behavior in hundreds of normal families and in families with an out-of-control child. They have produced a vast amount of data on the frequency of aversive behavior (defined as unpleasant acts such as hitting, yelling, teasing, scolding), as well as on the events leading up to, and the consequences of, such behavior.

It was found that out-of-control children behaved aversively at least three times as often as normal children (the record for frequency was set by a 6-year-old boy who behaved aversively, on average, four times a minute). Patterson determined that the problem is not just in the child but also in the social learning provided by the family.

For one thing, in problem families, the other family members also have higher-than-average rates of aversive behavior, often responding to aggression with aggression in a way that sets up an escalating cycle of retaliation. For example, a problem child and a sibling might begin exchanging increasingly nasty names with each other and

end up exchanging blows. In time, these patterns of attack and counterattack become so well learned that the parties involved become blind to alternative ways of resolving conflict. Siblings also provide each other with potent aggressive models to imitate.

Another factor highlighted by Patterson's research is that mothers of problem children are often unwitting perpetuators of aversive behavior once it occurs. When a child does something aversive, mothers of problem children are twice as likely to end up responding positively—that is, by giving in to the child—or neutrally (allowing the child to continue the aversive behavior) than they are to respond negatively by punishing the behavior. Thus they buy their children candy to stop them from screaming and crying in the supermarket, or they let a child stay up later if he or she vehemently refuses to go to bed. As Patterson analyzes it, the immediate result of such maternal behavior is reinforcing for both the child and the mother. The child gets what he or she wants (positive reinforcement), and the mother avoids further unmanageable behavior that calls attention to her ineffectiveness (negative reinforcement). In essence, the child becomes operantly conditioned to go out of control in order to get his or her way, and the mother becomes operantly conditioned to acquiesce in order to avoid intensifying the child's behavior.

The mother's short-term solution creates a long-term problem, however. Patterson found that mothers are the victims of aversive behavior ten times as often as fathers and three times as often as siblings. As his research clearly shows, the mother's role is typically that of family caretaker and "crisis manager," the one who is almost always at the front lines when problems occur. This is in marked contrast to the role taken by the typical father:

> The role most appropriate for fathers might be that of "guest." They expend much effort on activities which the

Evaluations of Learning Theories

The study of human development has benefited from learning theory in at least two ways. First, the emphasis on the causes and consequences of observed behavior has led researchers to see that many behavior patterns that may seem to be inborn or the result of deeply rooted emotional problems may actually be the result of the immediate environment. As the Research Report on children who are out of control (above) clearly shows, a detailed analysis of environmental influences can sometimes reveal the origins of otherwise perplexing behavioral problems. And even when the immediate environment cannot explain a problem completely, altering that environment may significantly remedy the problem nevertheless.

find reinforcing (e.g., reading the newspaper). They may function as reinforcer, spectator, and participant in games, that is, "the resident good guy." They may even enter into some lightweight child management activities. However, given real crisis or high rate of aversives, they tend to drop out. [Patterson, 1980]

Patterson also notes that mothers who do not generally deal effectively with aversive behavior also tend to respond inappropriately to good behavior, either ignoring it or, about 20 percent of the time, actually punishing it. (One explanation for this involves classical conditioning: the mother becomes so conditioned to interpret her child's behavior as negative that she even interprets positive behavior that way.) Since the child is neither reinforced for good behavior nor punished for bad, the child doesn't learn to do anything differently.

The solution, as Patterson sees it, is for the mothers to become more skilled at conditioning techniques. They must reinforce positive behavior in their children, and, when punishing negative behavior, they must make sure that the punishment is sufficient to stop the outburst, rather than simply escalating and extending it. Here is an observer's account of Patterson's approach to training mothers in appropriate management techniques:

> The child went to bed early only when he felt like it, insisted on sleeping with his mother (she had no husband), rarely obeyed even the most reasonable commands, spread his excrement all over the living room walls, was a terror to other children who tried to play with him, and seemed destined to be a terror to his teachers. The first task was to make the mother realize that he was not minding her in important ways because he was not minding her in small ones. Every day for one hour she was to count the number of times the boy failed to obey an order within fifteen seconds of its being issued and report the results to the therapist. This led the mother to become aware of how many times she was issuing orders and how long she was waiting to get results. . . .

At the third session, the mother was taught how to use "time out" as a means of discipline. She was told that whenever her son did something wrong she should immediately tell him why it was wrong and order him to go to time out—five minutes alone in the bathroom. She resisted doing this, because it forced her to confront all of her son's rule-breaking, and to do so immediately. She preferred to avoid the conflicts and the angry protests. She especially resisted using this means to enforce her son's going to bed at a stated, appropriate time; she was . . . lonely, . . . and it was clear to the therapist that she wanted her son to sleep with her. In time, the woman was persuaded to try this new form of discipline and to back up a failure to go to time out by the withdrawal of some privilege ("no TV tonight"). As the weeks went by, the woman became excited about the improvement in the boy's behavior and came to value having him sleep alone in his own room. [Wilson, 1983]

However, retraining is not easy. In many families, the parents have developed a marriage relationship that works to encourage aggression rather than to limit it (Morton, 1987). For instance, if standard family disputes (over whether a child should have a new bike, or where to go for vacation, or if the television can be on during dinner) are typically resolved by one parent outshouting the other, the children never learn how conflicts can be resolved in an amicable way. It takes a skilled trainer and several weeks or months to undo the habits learned over many years. Ideally, mother, father, and siblings should be brought into the project to change the social network of the family and to become models of appropriate, rather than inappropriate, behavior. They can also practice specific techniques to condition the problem child to behave in a more compliant fashion. If the entire family works to improve their interaction, a family that has been at war with itself can learn to function in a supportive way for every member.

This realization has encouraged many scientists to approach particular problem behaviors, such as temper tantrums, phobic reactions, and drug addiction, by analyzing and attempting to change the stimulus-response patterns they entail. A similar approach has been adopted by programs that help parents to understand how they unintentionally reinforce or model problem behavior in offspring and to learn more successful child-rearing skills. Teachers, too, have benefited from this insight, developing classroom environments that promote learning and cooperation. Even nursing-home policies have been affected, following the discovery that reinforcing and supporting independent decision making on the part of residents can reduce the passive, dependent behavior that typifies many institutionalized older adults (Baltes and Reisenzein, 1986).

Second, learning theory has contributed considerable scientific rigor to developmental study. Learning theorists have challenged researchers to define terms precisely, test hypotheses critically, explore alternative explanations for research findings (especially explanations involving environmental influences), and avoid reliance on theoretical concepts (such as unconscious drives or reasoning structures) that cannot be observed and directly tested. This emphasis has made developmental psychology a more scientific—and less speculative and intuitive—field of study.

At the same time, learning theory is often criticized for being inadequate to the task of explaining complex cognitive, emotional, and perceptual dimensions of human development. Critics point out that these developmental processes are influenced not just by the environment, but also by biological maturation, internal structures of thought, and the developing person's own efforts to comprehend new experiences. From this perspective, behavioral and social learning theories that focus primarily on learning from the environment provide an important but very incomplete picture of the full range of developmental influences at work throughout life.

Cognitive Theories

The prime focus of **cognitive theories** is the structure and development of the individual's thought processes and the way those processes can affect the person's understanding of the world. In turn, cognitive theories consider how this understanding, and the expectations it creates, can affect the individual's behavior.

Piaget's Ideas

Jean Piaget (1896–1980), the most famous of cognitive theorists, first became interested in thought processes while field-testing questions that were being considered for a standard intelligence test for children. Piaget was supposed to find the age at which most children could answer each question correctly, but eventually he became more interested in the children's *wrong* answers. What intrigued him was that children who were the same age made similar types of mistakes, suggesting that there is a developmental sequence to intellectual growth. He began to believe that *how* children think is much more important, and more revealing of their mental ability, than tabulating what they know (Flavell, 1963; Cowan, 1978). Moreover, understanding how children think also reveals how they interpret their experiences and gradually construct their understanding of the world.

Figure 2.11 *All his life Jean Piaget was absorbed with studying the way children think. He called himself a "genetic epistemologist"—one who studies how children gain knowledge about the world as they grow up.*

Stages of Cognitive Development

Piaget held that there are four major stages of cognitive development. Each one is age-related, and each has structural features that permit certain types of thinking (see Table 2.2).

TABLE 2.2 Piaget's Stages of Cognitive Development

Approximate Age	Name	Characteristics	Major Acquisitions
Birth to 2 years	Sensorimotor	Infant uses senses and motor abilities to understand the world. There is no conceptual or reflective thought; an object is "known" in terms of what an infant can *do* to it.	The infant learns that an object still exists when it is out of sight *(object permanence)* and begins to think by using mental as well as physical actions.
2–6 years	Preoperational	The child uses *symbolic thinking*, including language, to understand the world. Sometimes the child's thinking is *egocentric*, causing the child to understand the world from only one perspective, his or her own.	The imagination flourishes, and language becomes a significant means of self-expression and of influence from others. Children gradually begin to *decenter*, that is, become less egocentric, and to understand and coordinate multiple points of view.
7–11 years	Concrete Operational	The child understands and applies logical operations, or principles, to help interpret experiences objectively and rationally rather than intuitively.	By applying logical abilities, children learn to understand the basic ideas of conservation, number, classification, and many other scientific ideas.
From 12 on	Formal Operational	The adolescent or adult is able to think about abstractions and hypothetical concepts and is able to speculate in thought "from the real to the possible."	Ethics, politics, and social and moral issues become more interesting and involving as the adolescent becomes able to take a broader and more theoretical approach to experience.

According to Piaget, infants in the **sensorimotor stage** think exclusively through their senses and motor abilities: their understanding of the objects in their world is limited to the immediate actions they can perform on them and their sensory experiences of them. This is a very practical, experienced-based kind of early intelligence, but infants' thinking is thus limited to the here-and-now. By contrast, preschool children in the **preoperational stage** can begin to think symbolically; that is, they can think about and understand objects using mental processes that are independent of immediate experience. This is reflected in their ability to use language, to think of past and future events, and to pretend. However, they cannot think logically in a consistent way, and thus their reasoning is subjective and intuitive. School-age children in the **concrete operational stage** can begin to think logically in a consistent way, but only with regard to real and concrete features of their world, not abstract situations. In the final, **formal operational stage,** adolescents and adults, in varying degrees, are able to think hypothetically and abstractly: they can think about thinking, solve problems entirely "in the head," and speculate about the possible as well as the real. Each of these ways of thinking is explained in detail later in this book, in chapters 6, 9, 12, and 15.

How Cognitive Development Occurs

Piaget viewed cognitive development as a process that follows universal patterns. This process is guided, according to Piaget, by the need in everyone for **equilibrium,** that is, a state of mental balance (Piaget, 1970b). What he meant is that each person needs to, and continually attempts to, reconcile new experiences with present understanding in order to make sense of them.

Equilibrium is achieved when a person's mental concepts—or, in Piaget's terms, **schemas**—accord well with his or her current experiences. A schema is a general way of thinking about, or interacting with, ideas and objects in the environment. The infant first comes to know the world through schemas involving sensorimotor activities—a sucking schema, a grasping schema, a listening schema, and the like. By adulthood the schemas through which the individual knows the world are innumerable, ranging from something as simple as the schema for doing and undoing a button to the abstract moral schema that a human life is more valuable than any material thing. Equilibrium is experienced when one's present schemas "fit" new experiences, whether this involves a baby's discovery that new objects can be grasped in accustomed ways or an adult's being able to explain current events in terms of his or her political philosophy. When existing schemas do not seem to fit present experiences, the individual falls into a state of **disequilibrium**, a kind of imbalance that initially produces confusion and then leads to growth, as the person modifies old schemas and constructs new ones to fit the new experience. You may experience disequilibrium when a friend's argument reveals inconsistencies in your views, or when your favorite chess strategy fails against a skilled opponent.

Figure 2.12 *To Piaget, a child's stage of cognitive growth influences how the world is experienced and understood. Each of these children is thinking about a plant, but they are thinking in much different ways. To the baby in the sensorimotor stage, the flower is "known" as something that can be looked at and tasted. To the child in the preoperational stage, plants can be named and their needs can be understood through language. To the grade-school child, plants can be analyzed through logical reasoning skills, such as classification.*

Periods of disequilibrium can be disquieting to a child or an adult who suspects that accepted ideas no longer hold true. But they are also exciting periods of mental growth, which is one reason why people of all ages seek new, challenging experiences. By seeking out new experiences, children are constantly putting their current schemas to the test. Babies poke, pull, and taste everything they get their hands on; preschool children ask thousands of questions; school-age children become avid readers and information collectors; adolescents try out a wide variety of roles and experiences; and adults continually increase their knowledge and expertise in areas that interest them—all because people at every age want cognitive challenges. Recognition of this active searching for knowledge is the very essence of Piaget's theory of human cognitive development.

The search for knowledge (provoked, in part, by disequilibrium) is accomplished through two innate, interrelated processes that are, according to Piaget, the core of intelligence. These processes are **organization** and **adaptation.** People organize their thoughts so that they make sense, establishing links between one idea and another and integrating their knowledge in systematic, cohesive ways. In the process of learning about various animals, for example, a child may organize them mentally in clusters according to whether they are birds, mammals, or fishes. At the same time, people adapt their thinking to include new ideas as new experiences provide additional information.

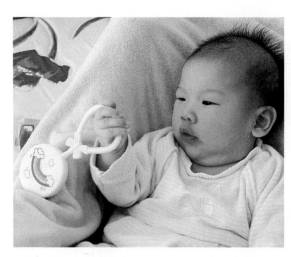

Figure 2.13 *One indication of cognitive growth in infancy is how the baby's inborn grasping schema is used and adapted to different objects. Infants will assimilate just about any object to this schema, whether it is their blanket, a rattle, or Daddy's nose! They also accommodate this schema to the size and shape of the object. In this manner, grasping becomes better adapted to the environment—and the baby grows intellectually.*

This adaptation occurs in two ways, through *assimilation* and *accommodation.* In the process of **assimilation**, new information is incorporated into a current schema; that is, it is simply added to the cognitive organization already in place. In the process of **accommodation**, the intellectual organization has to adjust to the new information. Thus, in watching a nature film on whales, a child may *extend* his or her schema of mammals by learning that whales, like cats and elephants, are members of this class (assimilation). Simultaneously, the child may also *change* the schema through the realization that some mammals, like fish, live in the sea (accommodation). As in this example, assimilation and accommodation work in tandem, because a schema is both expanded and modified when something new is learned.

These basic processes of cognitive change are at work even in the first weeks of life. Consider the grasping reflex, for instance. Newborns curl their fingers tightly around anything that crosses their palm. Soon, however, their grasping reflex becomes organized in specific ways as their particular experiences provide them with new knowledge: they grasp Mother's sweater one way, their bottle another way, a rattle another, and the cat's tail not at all. They have thus adapted their inborn grasping schema to their environment, first by assimilation (grasping everything that comes their way) and then by accommodation (adjusting their grasp to the "graspability" of the object).

The processes of assimilation and accommodation continue throughout life, and help to account for cognitive growth. As a final example, consider one of Piaget's famous experiments, in which a child is first shown two identical glasses, each containing the same amount of liquid (Piaget and Inhelder, 1974). Next, the liquid from one of the glasses is poured into a third glass, which is taller and narrower than the other two, resulting, naturally, in the liquid's reaching a higher level than in the original glass. The experimenter then asks the child which glass contains more. Most children younger than 5 consider the relative levels of liquid and say the taller glass contains more, using the simple schema that "taller is more." They are unshakable in this conviction, even when the experimenter tries to persuade them otherwise.

Figure 2.14 *The author's daughter Sarah, here aged 5¾, demonstrates Piaget's conservation-of-liquids experiment. First she examines both short glasses to be sure they contain the same amount of milk. Then, after the contents of one is poured into the tall glass and she is asked "Which has more?" she points to the tall glass, just as Piaget would have expected.*

By the age of 7 or 8, however, most children have developed the schema that Piaget called **conservation of liquids**—the realization that the amount of liquid does not change even though a different container (in this case, a taller glass) changes the liquid's appearance. They remain steadfast in this conviction, even in the face of contrary arguments.

In both cases, the children's ideas and perceptions are in a state of equilibrium: their mental concepts enable them to make sense of what they see. However, in the transition from the first state of equilibrium to the second, children experience disequilibrium, during which they begin to recognize that some of their ideas conflict with their experiences. They become increasingly aware, for example, of the inconsistency between their perception that the identical glasses originally contained the same amount of liquid and their schema that "taller is more." During this transitional period, the dual processes of assimilation and accommodation yield interim resolutions to this dilemma, such as the idea that the tall glass actually contains *less* liquid because it is narrower.

Taken together, Piaget's portrayal of the child is of a "little scientist" who develops new organizations of thought by exploring the world and modifying his or her understanding accordingly. Piaget's theory also describes the comprehensive changes that occur in thinking and reasoning as children proceed through stages of mental growth that increase their capacity to view the world symbolically, logically, and then abstractly.

Information-Processing Theory

In recent years, another view of cognitive growth has influenced many developmental researchers. Taking its inspiration from modern technology, **information-processing theory** likens many aspects of human thinking and reasoning to the way a computer analyzes and processes complex data. Though obviously not as fast, the human mind is far more sophisticated than the most advanced computer, and no computer can match the mind's capacity for reflection, creativity, and intuition. However, information-processing theorists suggest that by thinking of the mind in terms of the way it processes information, we might derive a more precise understanding of how we develop mentally (Klahr, 1989; Kuhn, 1988; Siegler, 1983a).

Steps of Processing

One example of how researchers portray the information-processing system can be seen in Figure 2.15. Notice that, like the learning theorists, information-processing theorists are interested in the relationship between stimulus and response. But they differ from learning theorists because of their interest in internal mental processes—specifically, in the flow of information between cognitive processes—and in the developmental changes that occur in each of these processes.

The first step in information processing occurs in the **sensory register,** which stores incoming stimulus information for a split second after it is received to allow it to be selectively processed. (You may have noticed that whenever you close your eyes, you retain a fleeting image of what you were last looking at. This is an example of the sensory register at work.) Much of the information that comes into the sensory register is lost or discarded, but what is meaningful or significant is transferred to working memory for further analysis. It is in **working memory** (sometimes called short-term memory) that your current, conscious mental activity occurs. This includes, at this moment, your understanding of this paragraph, any previous knowledge you recall that is related to it, and also, perhaps, distracting thoughts about your weekend plans or the interesting person who sat next to you in class today. Working memory is constantly replenished with new information, so thoughts and memories are usually not retained for very long. Some are discarded, while a few are transferred to your knowledge base. The **knowledge base** (also called long-term memory) stores information for days, months, or years, and has a virtually limitless capacity. Together with influences from the sensory register and working memory, the knowledge base

Figure 2.15 *This is a flow chart of the information-processing system. Solid arrows refer to the transfer of information between system components. Broken arrows refer to influences within the system that affect how information is processed and transferred. (Adapted from Shiffrin and Atkinson, 1969.)*

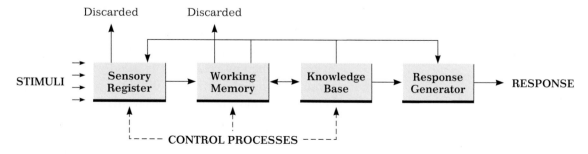

assists in organizing your reactions to environmental stimuli through the **response generator,** a network of mental processes that organize behavior.

Although we do not usually think of our minds as sophisticated computers, this information-processing flow chart helps to explain many features of mental activity. Suppose the radio is playing while you are studying, and a call-in phone number for a contest is announced. If you are distracted or uninterested, this auditory information will get no further than the sensory register, and you will not consciously think about it. If you pay attention to the number, however, it will enter working memory and remain there temporarily—probably long enough for you to call the number. If you get a busy signal, however, you must decide how to retain the number for a longer period of time, perhaps by transferring it to your knowledge base. You might mentally rehearse it, by repeating it a number of times, or divide the digits into groups to make them more memorable, or use some other memory strategy. Thus as you analyze sensory information (in this case, the phone number) further, additional components of the information-processing system are enlisted.

Developmental Changes

These components of the information-processing system function differently as children and adults mature, which explains in part why learning and memory skills change with development. The knowledge base expands throughout childhood and adolescence, for example, as children acquire more information about the world, and this assists new learning because they can more readily relate new information to what they already know. In late adulthood, on the other hand, limitations in the speed and efficiency of working memory may restrict how easily adults can recall complex new information (Hultsch and Dixon, 1990; Salthouse, 1991).

The most significant developmental changes occur in the component called **control processes,** which regulate the analysis and flow of information within the system. When you deliberately use rehearsal or another strategy to remember a phone number, for example, you are using a control process. Control processes are also involved when you try to retrieve someone's name or other specific information from your knowledge base, or listen for a familiar voice in a crowd, or use a rule-of-thumb to solve a problem. In a sense, control processes assume an executive role in the information-processing system, regulating the analysis and transfer of information within the system.

The ways in which control processes become more efficient are most noticeable in young children, as they acquire more sophisticated memory and retrieval strategies, learn to use selective attention, become capable of automatically performing mental activities that formerly required considerable effort (like reading), and develop more effective rules or strategies for problem solving (Kuhn, 1988; Sternberg, 1988). Consider what happens, for example, when a first-grader is faced with a simple problem to solve—like trying to remember what he did after school the day before yesterday. His retrieval of that information from his knowledge base may be limited because he does not yet know how to search his memory thoroughly or deeply. He may remember pieces of events from that time period ("I came home and had a snack"), but may be distracted by other, associated knowledge ("I really like my teacher"). His account is likely to be piecemeal, partly irrelevant, and probably inaccurate. By contrast, a fifth-grader approaches this problem far more effectively, perhaps by bringing to mind her usual after-school routine (or "script") and trying to recall any events that may have modified it on the day in question. The older child will remain focused on this task until she can provide a coherent, complete account of her after-school activities that day. These differences between the first-grader and fifth-grader arise, in part, from the maturation of control processes, which contributes to the more strategic and efficient approaches of the older child.

Similarly, an understanding of control processes can enhance our appreciation of cognitive functioning in adulthood. Young adults think and learn skillfully because they use a broad repertoire of cognitive strategies and can confidently handle complex reasoning tasks with speed and efficiency. Traditional research has pointed to an apparent decline in certain cognitive skills in old age, but many researchers have shown that if older adults are trained to use effective cognitive control processes—such as memory strategies that facilitate their retention of new information—their intellectual skills improve significantly, sometimes equaling those of much younger individuals (Kliegl et al., 1989; Schaie, 1990; Willis and Nesselroade, 1990). These studies underscore the flexibility—or plasticity—of the cognitive changes of later life, and suggest that certain intellectual losses of late adulthood are remediable (Baltes et al., 1984).

As you can see, information-processing theorists view cognitive development differently than Piaget did. Their approach has life-span applications, whereas Piaget's theory ends with adolescence. Moreover, whereas Piaget characterized cognitive development as a series of broad stages of mental growth, information-processing theorists tend to think of development as a more gradual process involving the acquisition of specific strategies, rules, and skills that affect memory, learning, and problem solving. Information-processing theorists believe that by analyzing the development of complex cognitive skills in terms of these component abilities, researchers can better understand how reasoning ability changes with age, and the specific ways individuals' analysis of cognitive challenges matures.

Evaluations of Cognitive Theories

Cognitive theories have revolutionized developmental psychology by focusing attention on active mental processes. The attempt to understand the mental structures and strategies of thought, and to appreciate the internal need for new ones when the old ones become outmoded, has led to a new understanding of certain aspects of human behavior. Thanks to the insights provided by cognitive theories, we now have a greater appreciation of the capacities and limitations of the types of thinking that are possible at various ages—and of the ways in which these capacities and limitations can affect behavior.

Figure 2.16 *Are children more like scientists or computers in their cognitive growth? Elements of each are apparent in this preschooler's enthusiasm for discovering how baby powder looks, feels, and tastes, and in her efforts to relate these discoveries to prior experiences and events (like tasting and touching snow). Unfortunately, her parents are likely to be concerned only with cleaning up this mess!*

Cognitive theories have also profoundly affected education in many countries, allowing teachers and students to become partners in the educational process once the child's own capacities and needs are recognized. Learning through personal discovery, acquiring effective learning strategies, and acting on objects rather than merely being told about them are all contemporary features of educational practice drawn from cognitive theories. For instance, elementary-school math is now taught with objects the child can manipulate, because we now realize that the thinking of school-age children is better suited to working out and understanding solutions through concrete activities, such as measuring blocks or counting pennies, than to using the more abstract learning tasks involved in reading about, and memorizing, mathematical facts. Children can also be helped in developing learning and problem-solving strategies that improve their classroom performance.

Finally, and perhaps most obviously, cognitive theories remind us that "intelligence" involves many factors that are not easily summarized in an IQ score, and reflects the remarkably diverse and complex skills and strategies that people evolve through their interactions with the surrounding world.

At the same time, many people think Piaget was so absorbed by the individual's active search for knowledge that he ignored external motivation or teaching. While it is comforting to think that children can develop their own schemas when they are ready, this implies that teachers should not intervene when a child seems uninterested in learning to add or spell. And even some of those who most admire Piaget believe that he underestimated the role of society and home in fostering cognitive development. Many psychologists believe that culture and education can be crucial in providing the proper mix of equilibrium and disequilibrium.

A number of critics have also found fault with Piaget's depiction of cognitive stages as universal. For example, there are many adults who never develop the capacity for abstract thinking that Piaget described as being typical of adolescence. A number of researchers have also pointed out that Piaget's description of cognitive development tends to make it seem comprehensive, as though once a new stage of cognition has been achieved, it will be reflected in all aspects of the individual's thinking. In fact, the cognitive advance may occur in some areas of thinking and not in others. And particularly with children, the advance in a given area may be evident on one occasion and not on another. Most cognitive theorists now generally believe that "unevenness is the rule in development" (Fischer, 1980; Flavell, 1982). For this reason, some information-processing theorists emphasize that the skills and strategies children acquire may be task-specific, and do not generalize to other situations (Case, 1985; Fischer, 1980).

Of course, information-processing theory has its critics as well. Some take issue with the use of the computer metaphor as a model of human thinking. Computers do not have the capacity for reflection, insight, or self-change that people do, and using this metaphor may mislead researchers into neglecting these essential features of human reasoning. These critics find Piaget's portrayal of the child as a little scientist, actively generating new understanding by acting on the world, to be a far more attractive image of children's thinking.

Humanistic Theories

During the past several decades, an influential group of psychologists has argued that mainstream views of human behavior and development depict people as little more than a collection of drives, prior conditioning, or cognitive processes. By contrast with this "reductionistic" approach, humanistic theorists like Abraham Maslow and Carl Rogers take a **holistic** view of human growth that tries to account for all the diverse aspects of human experience. **Humanistic theory** regards people as unique, self-determined, and worthy of respect, and sees human development as being guided by a variety of basic human needs, among them the need to achieve one's full potential, or **self-actualization.** These needs influence development throughout life, but are most salient during the adult years, when people establish goals for the direction of their lives that are affected, in part, by their awareness of their unique needs.

Maslow's Ideas

Abraham Maslow (1908–1970), who earned his Ph.D. from Columbia University in 1934, began his career by studying the experiences of mentally healthy, creative people. His findings led him to question the assumptions of psychoanalytic and learning theories that dominated psychology at that time. As he explained in *Toward a Psychology of Being* (1968), "Human nature is not nearly as bad as it has been thought to be . . . It is as if Freud supplied us the sick half of psychology and we must now fill it out with the healthy half." And, unlike learning theorists who inferred laws of human behavior from the study of dogs, rats, and pigeons, Maslow believed that humans are not simply another animal species but something greater.

Maslow examined the personalities of people who seemed to have lived life to its fullest, such as Abraham Lincoln and Eleanor Roosevelt, as well as some of his personal friends. He found that such people shared several characteristics: they were realistic, creative, spontaneous, self-accepting, spiritual, independent, purposeful. They had a small number of intimate friends with whom they felt very close and at the same time were deeply concerned for their fellow human beings. Most notably, their lives were marked by what Maslow called *peak experiences*—moments of great happiness and insight in which they transcended ordinary experience and felt whole, integrated, and reconciled to life and to the world.

According to Maslow, each person's behavior is motivated by a variety of universal human needs, ranging from the most basic survival needs for food, sleep, and safety, to the highest needs for self-actualization (see Figure 2.18). If a person's basic, or lower, needs are not satisfied, that person must devote time and energy trying to meet them, thus restricting his or her capacity to seek higher needs for love, esteem, and self-fulfillment. But if a person grows up well-fed, safe, loved, and respected, self-actualization becomes more possible. Indeed, in the last years of his life, Maslow (1971) argued that beyond self-actualization is the experience of *self-transcendence*, in which the person identifies with universal values and has frequent peak experiences, especially of a spiritual or existential quality (Wilber, 1986).

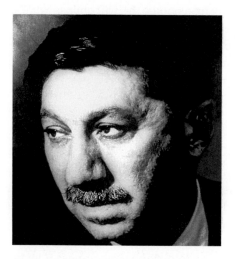

Figure 2.17 *Abraham Maslow had many of the characteristics of a self-actualized person. He was unconventional and intense but not above laughing at himself. He had a deep respect for his fellow human beings and a great love of nature, believing that peak experiences could occur on a solitary walk in the woods as well as through human intimacy.*

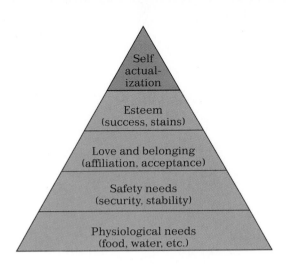

Figure 2.18 *According to Maslow's hierarchy, unless the basic physiological needs are satisfied, people are unable to fulfill their potential. Some of Maslow's followers have taken this literally and become very concerned about the damage to the human spirit, as well as to the body, brought about by poverty, famine, and war.*

In developmental perspective, of course, children are more likely than adults to be primarily concerned with safety, belongingness, or esteem needs. However, Maslow (1968) noted that even children are motivated to fulfill their potential: "Healthy children enjoy growing and moving forward, gaining new skills, capacities and powers. . . . In the normal development of the healthy child. . . . if he is given a really free choice, he will choose what is good for his growth." Nevertheless, the pursuit of self-actualization or self-transcendence is more commonly a concern of later adulthood, when questions about the meaning of life and one's unique purposes in existing are more paramount (as Erikson also noted).

Rogers's Ideas

Figure 2.19 *Thirty years ago, Carl Rogers became one of the leading advocates of group therapy, a logical outcome of his emphasis on the ability of each of us to help one another. Toward the end of his life, Rogers worked to stop the proliferation of nuclear weapons by suggesting constructive ways for nations to resolve conflicts.*

Rogers agreed with Maslow that all people, even in childhood, try to fulfill their potential or, as Rogers would put it, try to become *fully functioning human beings* (Rogers, 1961). Rogers believed that each person has an ideal self—that is, the person that one would like to be—and that healthy people try to become that ideal self as much as possible. This is done in two ways: first, by improving the real self and, second, by modifying the concept of the ideal self in more honest and realistic ways, in order to encompass a wider variety of emotions and behaviors that are part of real life.

Rogers believed that the process of becoming fully functioning is aided throughout life by people who are important to us—the "significant others," such as our parents, a marital partner, and close friends. They are especially helpful when they provide us with **unconditional positive regard**, through which we perceive that we are loved and respected no matter what we do. When a child complains about schoolwork, for example, parents demonstrate unconditional positive regard by acknowledging the child's feelings and helping the child cope with academic demands rather than criticizing the child or arguing that the child should not feel this way. Similarly, one spouse might show unconditional positive regard for the other by respecting the other's anger rather than simply reciprocating with resentment and hostility. Unconditional positive regard is facilitated, according to Rogers, by a **phenomenological** approach to others, that is, an empathic openness to viewing the world from the other person's point of view.

To Rogers, unconditional positive regard derives from respecting each person's human worth and dignity. He believed that experiencing such regard can have powerful therapeutic benefits for disturbed individuals, and this has been shown with young children as well as adults (Axline, 1964).

Evaluations of Humanistic Theories

Although humanistic theorists like Maslow and Rogers contributed mostly to our understanding of adult personality, Crain (1992) has observed that they relied heavily on developmental principles:

> [T]hey have joined the developmentalists in their search for intrinsic growth forces that can lead to healthy development. . . . [T]he humanists' call for a more phenomenological science has been, to an extent, anticipated by developmentalists; for many developmentalists have suggested that we cannot appreciate the growing child's unique ways of thinking and learning unless we approach them with something of a naive openness. Finally, both humanists and developmentalists have been primarily concerned with the universal aspects of human development, with the urges toward growth and health that we all share.

Maslow, Rogers, and other humanistic theorists also advance the optimistic view that it is never too late to develop and become the kind of person one hopes to be. This is true throughout life and, while childhood sets the stage for personality development, adulthood is important also. Indeed, Rogers (1980) wrote convincingly of the significant changes that occurred in his own personality during his 70s. In this regard, humanistic theories are life-span theories of development. Moreover, by portraying human motivation in terms of a succession of basic human needs—ranging from survival-related needs to self-actualization needs—humanistic theorists help to explain why personal goals and interests change in significant ways throughout the life course. Finally, humanistic theory has helped developmental researchers explore and integrate the whole of development—including biosocial, cognitive, psychosocial, and even spiritual growth—in contrast to the tendency to examine developmental processes in isolation from one another.

However, while humanistic theory is optimistic and encouraging, it is, like all theories, not necessarily true. Indeed, critics argue that its adherents are blind to the many ways that growth is stunted and deflected from the optimal route, not just by a deficit of unconditional positive regard, but also by social inequities, governmental policies, and injustices that reflect how complex the achievement of human potential really is. Societies, families, and even individuals themselves do not always encourage or allow human fulfillment. In a sense, humanistic theories provide a better portrayal of our hopes for human well-being than of the present realities of human development.

The Theories Compared

Each of the theories presented in this chapter has contributed a great deal to the study of human development. Psychoanalytic theories have made us aware of the importance of early childhood experiences and of the impact of the "hidden dramas" that influence our daily lives. Learning theories have shown us the effect that the immediate environment can have on behavior. Cognitive theories have brought us to a greater understanding of how our thinking affects our actions. And humanistic theories have given us an encouraging view of the goals of human development.

A CLOSER LOOK   Developmental Theories and Child-Rearing Advice

Theories of human development have had considerable and widespread impact throughout the twentieth century. They have guided researchers in their study of children and adults and have shaped policy in education, pediatrics, and the treatment of troubled children. More noticeably, though sometimes less successfully, they have influenced the advice offered to the public by various child-rearing experts.

Americans have always been drawn to learning theories because they seem to provide straightforward solutions to common child-rearing dilemmas. It is not surprising, therefore, that early in this century John Watson was both a leading theoretician in academic psychology and a popular writer in parents' magazines. In one article, "What to Do When Your Child is Afraid," Watson (1927) applied principles of classical conditioning to the problem of children's fears.

> No child is afraid, at first, to be put to bed alone in the dark, but suppose the wind blows over a screen with a loud bang or causes a shutter to slam, or suppose the wind catches the door and bangs it behind you as you leave the room. You have almost an ideal situation for making the child afraid of the dark. . . .
>
> Suppose this fear of the dark has developed in your child. How will you handle it? You can treat or 'recondition' as we say, the child in a very simple way. When you put him to bed tonight, leave the door partly open and a dim light burning in the hall. The child will go to sleep. Then, gradually, close the door a little and dim the light a little every night. If you work patiently, four or five nights will enable you to recondition the child so that the door can be closed and the light turned out.

Such advice was influential because it offered practical, easy-to-apply solutions and came from a recognized scientific authority. But it also encouraged parents to feel responsible (perhaps too responsible) for their child's development because they controlled many of the environmental influences affecting their offspring. In a sense, Watson gave parents a double message: that they could substantially shape their child's growth through principles of conditioning, but that this also made them responsible for the result.

Following World War II, and the immigration to this country of many of Europe's leading psychoanalysts, popular advice to parents began to reflect Freud's ideas about the emotional, irrational forces within children and the role of parents in understanding and supporting their offspring. Consider this passage from the classic source of parental advice, *The Common Sense Book of Baby and Child Care* (1945), by the leading child-rearing expert of his time, Benjamin Spock.

> New types of fears crop up fairly often around the age of 3 or 4—fears of the dark, of dogs, of fire engines, of death, of cripples. The child's imagination has now developed to the stage where he can put himself in other people's shoes and picture dangers that he hasn't actually experienced. His curiosity is pushing out in all directions. He not only wants to know the cause of everything, but what these things have to do with him. . . .
>
> These fears are commoner in children who have been made tense through battles over such matters as feeding and toilet training, children whose imaginations have been overstimulated by scary stories or too many warnings, children who haven't had enough chance to develop their independence and outgoingness. . . .
>
> Don't make fun of him, or be impatient with him, or try

Each theory has also been criticized. Psychoanalytic theory has been faulted for being too subjective; learning theory, for being too mechanistic; cognitive theory, for undervaluing the power of direct instruction and overemphasizing rational, logical thought; and humanistic theory, for being overly idealistic.

In reviewing these theories, consider how they differ in their portrayals of the child and of human development. As we have seen, each theory has its own unique portrait of what the child is like—a cauldron of unconscious impulses, a little scientist, a computer, a seeker of unconditional love. Similarly, these theories also vary in how they describe the process of human development. Some theories, like those from the psychoanalytic perspective and Piaget's cognitive theory, view development as a succession of stages of growth, with each stage characterized by its own unique challenges and achievements. For other theories, however, development is a much more gradual and continuous process, and the factors that govern human develop-to argue him out of his fear. If he wants to talk about it, as a few children do, let him. Give him the feeling that you want to understand, but that you are sure nothing bad will happen to him. This is the time for extra hugs and comforting reminders that you love him very much and will always protect him.

Notice that Spock analyzed the reasons for children's fears much differently than Watson did: in keeping with the psychoanalytic view, he depicted them as the natural outgrowth of children's irrational imaginative thinking rather than of prior learning experiences. Consequently, his advice to parents was different: they should provide reassurance, security, and emotional support rather than try to recondition the child.

More recent child-rearing advice has drawn from Spock's legacy, but has also been influenced by cognitive and humanistic views. Parents are now encouraged to accept children's needs and desires—however unreasonable they might appear—by respecting the limitations in the young child's intellectual understanding and experience. Consider this excerpt from the highly popular recent volume for parents, *Babyhood,* by Penelope Leach (1989):

> Unfortunately where fears are concerned we tend to treat toddlers as if they were miniature versions of adults. When a child is afraid of something which many adults fear, he is usually sympathetically handled. . . . But when the toddler expresses a fear that seems to the adult to be simply silly, it is often treated with bossiness, irritation, or even shame. We forget that the toddler has an intrinsic fear of the strange; we forget that he does not have our experience or our knowledge to call on. Meeting his first tortoise, an 18-month-old boy reacted immediately with pure horror: "Way, way," he said, scarlet-faced. "It's a tortoise, darling," said his mother, picking it up and moving toward him. "Notty," wailed the toddler, exploding into tears and backing up against the wall. . . . The mother could not see that the child *could* be afraid of a tortoise. He had never met one before; had had no nasty experiences with tortoises; it made no noise. . . . Yet she herself disliked spiders. I wonder how many spiders had bitten or roared at her? . . .
>
> Perhaps we need to rethink our attitudes to two separate issues: fearlessness and bravery. Fearlessness is simply not being afraid. It comes from not feeling fear. Logically, then, the less we frighten children, the more fearless they will be.

The idea that many fears are both natural (including, according to Leach, adults' fears of spiders), and intensified by children's limited understanding, implies that it is probably fruitless to try to talk children out of them. Whereas Watson would seek to recondition the frightened child and Spock would provide reassurance, Leach suggests completely avoiding situations that provoke fear until the child has acquired the cognitive skills necessary for approaching these situations more maturely. In a sense, she argues, a child's fears should be respected by the parents as a natural outgrowth of the child's stage of development.

In these examples, therefore, popular advice to children reflects influential theories of development that guide researchers. As new views of children and their growth continue to emerge within developmental psychology, it is fascinating and provocative to speculate about how these new perspectives will find their way into the next generation of child-rearing manuals.

ment (such as learning processes or structures of information-processing) remain more consistent throughout life. These theories also vary in whether they portray development as a lifelong process, and which periods of the life span (if any) they emphasize as important. Comparing developmental theories in these ways can highlight the unique contributions of each and the ways in which each theory alerts us to important features of the developmental process.

Each theory by itself is, in fact, too restricted to grasp the breadth and diversity of human development (Cairns, 1983; Thomas, 1981). As one researcher explains, we now see people as

> so complex and multifaceted as to defy easy classification . . . [and] multiply influenced by a host of interacting determinants. . . . It is an image that highlights the shortcomings of all simplistic theories that view behavior as the exclusive result of any narrow set of determinants, whether these are habits, traits, drives, reinforcers, constructs, instincts, or genes, and whether they are exclusively inside or outside the person. [Mischel, 1977]

Because no one theory can encompass all of human behavior, most developmentalists would describe themselves as having an **eclectic perspective,** meaning that rather than adopting any of these theories exclusively, they make use of all of them.

In subsequent chapters, as echoes and elaborations of the psychoanalytic, learning, cognitive, and humanistic theories appear, you can form your own opinion of the validity of each theory. The best challenge you can set for yourself—the same one facing developmental researchers—is the integration of theory, research, and applications into an increasingly comprehensive picture of human development.

SUMMARY

What Theories Do

1. A theory provides a framework of general principles that can be used to interpret our observations. Each theory interprets human development from a somewhat different perspective, but all theories attempt to provide a context in which to understand individual experiences and behavior.

Psychoanalytic Theories

2. Psychoanalytic theories emphasize that our actions are largely ruled by the unconscious—the source of powerful impulses and conflicts that usually lie below the level of our conscious awareness.

3. Freud, the founder of psychoanalytic theory, developed the theory of psychosexual stages to explain how unconscious impulses arise and how they affect behavior during the oral, anal, phallic, latency, and genital stages of psychosexual development of the child.

4. Freud interpreted behavior in terms of three components of personality: the id seeks immediate gratification of its desires; the superego acts as a relentless conscience to suppress the id; the ego moderates the demands of the id and superego and copes with the recognition that one must seek satisfaction by realistic and appropriate ways in view of the limitations of the real world.

5. Erikson's theory of psychosocial development describes individuals as being shaped by the interaction of personal characteristics and social forces. Culture plays a large part in each person's ability to deal with the most significant tasks, or crises, of psychosocial development. Erikson described successive stages of psychosocial development through life.

Learning Theories

6. Learning theorists believe that psychologists should study behavior that can be observed and measured. They are especially interested in the relationship between events and the reactions they are associated with, that is, between the stimulus and the response.

7. Learning theory emphasizes the importance of various forms of conditioning, a process by which particular stimuli become linked with particular responses. In classical conditioning, one stimulus becomes associated with another to produce a particular response. In operant, or instrumental, conditioning, reinforcement makes a behavior more likely to occur.

8. Social learning theory recognizes that much of human behavior is modeled after the behavior of others, and that various cognitive and motivational processes influence how we are affected by the behavior of others.

Cognitive Theories

9. Cognitive theorists believe that a person's thought processes—the understanding and analysis of a particular situation—have an important effect on behavior.

10. Piaget, the leading cognitive theorist, proposed that people develop schemas—general ways of thinking about ideas and objects. When a person becomes aware of perceptions or experiences that do not fit an existing schema, the schema changes or a new schema is created, and cognitive growth occurs. Learning is accomplished by a process of organization and adaptation through each of several stages of cognitive development.

11. Information-processing theorists study cognitive development in terms of changes in internal cognitive processes such as working memory and the knowledge

base. Growth and refinement of control processes are especially important to cognitive development.

Humanistic Theories

12. Humanistic psychologists believe that the potential for growth exists throughout life, and is guided by significant human needs. For Maslow, these needs range from survival-related needs to the need for self-actualization. For Rogers, these needs encompass the effort to become a fully functioning person.

The Theories Compared

13. Psychoanalytic, learning, cognitive, and humanistic theories have all contributed to the understanding of human development, yet no one theory is adequate to describe the complexity and diversity of human experience. Most developmentalists incorporate ideas from several developmental perspectives into their thinking.

KEY TERMS

developmental theory (35)
psychoanalytic theory (37)
childhood sexuality (38)
psychosexual stages (38)
oral stage (38)
anal stage (38)
phallic stage (38)
latency (38)
genital stage (38)
id (38)
ego (39)
superego (39)
repression (39)
psychosocial theory (41)
behaviorism (43)
learning theory (43)
stimulus (43)
response (43)
conditioning (43)
classical conditioning (43)
operant conditioning (44)
reinforcement (44)
reinforcer (44)
positive reinforcer (44)
negative reinforcer (45)
punishment (45)
extrinsic reinforcers (45)
intrinsic reinforcers (45)
social learning theory (46)
modeling (46)
self-efficacy (47)

reciprocal determinism (47)
cognitive theory (50)
sensorimotor stage (51)
preoperational stage (51)
concrete operational
    stage (51)
formal operational
    stage (51)
equilibrium (51)
schema (52)
disequilibrium (52)
organization (53)
adaptation (53)
assimilation (53)
accommodation (53)
conservation of liquids (54)
information-processing
    theory (55)
sensory register (55)
working memory (55)
knowledge base (55)
response generator (56)
control processes (56)
holistic (59)
humanistic theory (59)
self-actualization (59)
unconditional positive
    regard (60)
phenomenological (60)
eclectic perspective (64)

KEY QUESTIONS

1. What functions does a good theory perform?

2. What is the major premise of psychoanalytic theories?

3. According to Freud's theory, what is the function of the ego?

4. What is the major difference between Erikson's theory and Freud's theory?

5. What is the major premise of learning theory?

6. What are the differences between classical and operant conditioning?

7. What are some of the cognitive processes in social learning?

8. What is the major premise of cognitive theory?

9. According to Piaget, how do periods of disequilibrium lead to mental growth?

10. What is the difference between assimilation and accommodation?

11. How do information-processing theorists describe cognitive growth?

12. How do humanistic theories view development?

13. What are the main differences between the psychoanalytic, learning, cognitive, and humanistic theories?

14. Why do most developmentalists describe themselves as having an eclectic perspective?

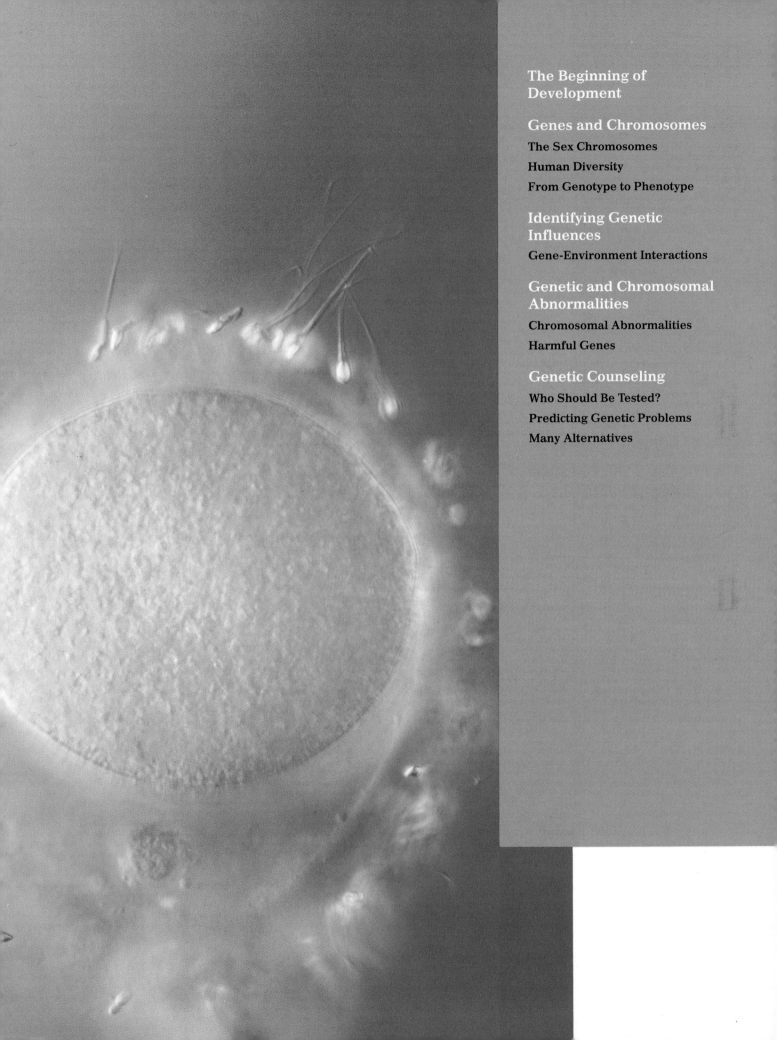

CHAPTER 3

Heredity and Environment

When a sperm and an ovum unite in conception, genetic instructions from both parents combine to direct the growth and development of a unique person. This genetic inheritance influences the course of the individual's entire life, from the moment of conception until the moment of death. However, the ultimate unfolding of that life depends, not on genetic influences alone, but on the interaction that occurs between those influences and an endless array of environmental factors—everything from the mother-to-be's health during the first days of pregnancy to the society's economic policies regarding the elderly, from the cultural routines that regulate everyday life to the unique events that each particular individual encounters.

In this chapter, we will discuss the interactions between genetic inheritance and environment that continually affect every developing person, focusing on questions such as the following:

What does it mean to say that a trait is genetic?

Is personality the result of genes, or upbringing, or culture, or all three?

How much of intelligence is inherited?

Do children in the same family experience the same home environment?

Are some couples more likely than others to have a child with a genetic or chromosomal abnormality?

From the moment of human conception, individual development is driven by the interaction of two prime forces, heredity and environment. At conception, a complex set of genetic instructions takes form to influence every aspect of development, affecting not only obvious characteristics such as sex, coloring, and body shape but also every less visible trait, psychological as well as physical—from blood type to bashfulness, metabolic rate to moodiness, voice tone to verbal fluency.

As we will see throughout this chapter, however, just as no human characteristic is untouched by heredity, no genetic instruction—including those for basic traits such as physical structure and intellectual potential—is unaffected by the environment. Indeed, each person's genetic inheritance and individual experiences are so intertwined that it is virtually impossible to isolate the specific effects of one from the other. The interaction between these two factors is lifelong, shaping the individual from the moment of conception until the moment of death.

The Beginning of Development

Human development is initiated when a male gamete, or sperm, penetrates the membrane of a female gamete, or ovum. Each of these gametes contains more than a billion chemically coded genetic messages, which, taken together, represent one half of a rough blueprint for human development. When the two reproductive cells subsequently fuse, the two blueprint halves combine, interacting to form a complete set of developmental guidelines.

At first, the two gametes maintain their separate identities, side by side, enclosed within the ovum's membrane. Then, after an hour or more, they suddenly merge, their genetic material combines, and a one-celled living organism called a **zygote** is formed.

Within hours after its formation, the zygote initiates a process of duplication and division that starts human development. Just before the zygote divides, all the combined genetic material from both gametes duplicates itself, forming two complete sets of genetic instructions. These two sets move toward opposite sides of the cell; the cell then divides neatly down the middle, and the zygote thus becomes two cells. In identical fashion, these two cells duplicate themselves and divide to become four; these four, in turn, duplicate and divide to become eight; and so on.

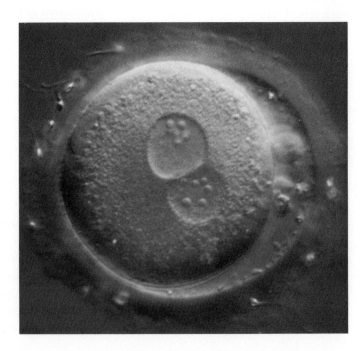

Figure 3.1 *The ovum shown here is about to become a zygote. It has been penetrated by a single sperm, whose nucleus now lies next to the nucleus of the ovum. Shortly, the two nuclei will fuse, bringing together several billion genetic codes that will guide future development.*

Soon, a third process, differentiation, is added to the simple duplication and division. Following a genetic timetable, various cells begin to specialize and reproduce at different rates, according to their programmed function. Following the same timetable, some cells will die early in life and others will continually reproduce for decades; still others will remain dormant until puberty, or adulthood, or old age.

At birth, a baby is made up of about 10 trillion cells. By adulthood, the number has increased to between 300 and 500 trillion. But no matter how many cells a person may have, no matter how much differentiation and specialization has occurred, each body cell carries a copy of the genetic instructions inherited by the one-celled zygote at the moment of conception.

Genes and Chromosomes

The basic units of these genetic instructions are called **genes**, which are segments of **DNA (deoxyribonucleic acid)** molecules, each arranged in particular coded sequences. Overall, genes accomplish an amazing transformation: "they organize nonliving material into living systems" (Scott, 1990). All together, humans have close to 100,000 genes, comprising more than 3 billion codes that direct the form and function of every body cell. Following those genetic directions, certain cells become part of the neurons of the brain; others become part of the lens of the eye; others become part of the heart; and so on.

In addition to directing the differentiation of cells, genes also establish the cells' qualitative functioning—influencing, for example, how rapidly the neurons in each particular part of the brain process information; how efficiently the lens of the eye focuses on various forms; how rapidly the heart beats when exerted.

The genes are able to coordinate this transformation because all 100,000 of them are organized in a precise sequence and position on **chromosomes**, which are threadlike structures of DNA. Every normal human has forty-six chromosomes, arranged in twenty-three distinct pairs, one chromosome in each pair being from the mother and the other being from the father. Each pair member serves as the designated location for a particular portion of genetic material that corresponds to the genetic material on its chromosome mate (see Figure 3.2). For the most part, genes are positioned quite precisely on a particular "leg" or "arm" of a certain chromosome. Thus chromosomes not only carry the genes; they also furnish each gene with a niche opposite a corresponding gene on the matching chromosome, thereby allowing each gene pair to perform its mission in directing development.

The matching of the chromosome pairs occurs at conception. Every human sperm carries twenty-three chromosomes, each one of which corresponds in functioning to one of the twenty-three chromosomes carried in every ovum. Collectively, the twenty-three chromosomes in the sperm and the twenty-three chromosomes in the ovum represent the two halves of the genetic blueprint referred to earlier. When the sperm and ovum unite, their corresponding chromosomes link up, providing complete instructions for the development of a new person. The chromosomal pairing remains lifelong.

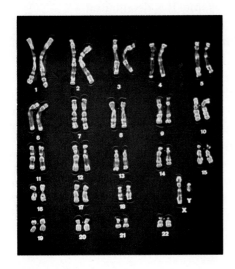

Figure 3.2 *This picture, called a karyotype, shows the forty-six chromosomes from one individual, in this case a normal male. In order to produce a chromosomal portrait such as this one, a cell is removed from the person's body (usually from inside the mouth), processed so that the chromosomes become visible, magnified many times, photographed, and then arranged in pairs according to the length of the upper "arms."*

Figure 3.3 *Whether a fertilized ovum will develop into a male or female depends on whether the ovum, which always has an X chromosome, is fertilized by a sperm carrying an X chromosome (a female will result) or a sperm carrying a Y chromosome (a male will result).*

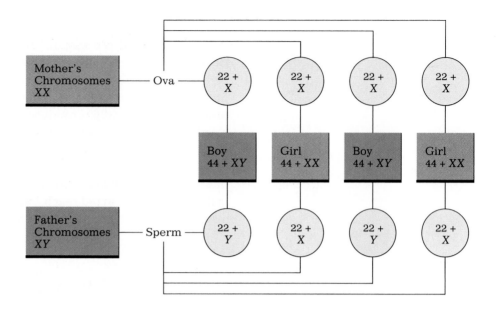

The Sex Chromosomes

Twenty-two of the twenty-three pairs of human chromosomes are closely matched pairs, each half containing similar genes in identical positions and sequence. The **twenty-third pair**, which is the one that determines the individual's sex, is a different case.

In the female, the twenty-third pair of chromosomes is composed of two large, X-shaped chromosomes. Accordingly, it is designated **XX**. In the male, the twenty-third pair is composed of one large X-shaped chromosome and one, much smaller, Y-shaped chromosome. It is designated **XY**.

The reason for this unusual pair is that the duplication-and-division process in the production of gametes differs from that in the production of body cells. When cells make gametes, they do so in such a way that each sperm or ovum receives only one member of each chromosome pair. Thus each sperm or ovum has only twenty-three chromosomes, half as many as the forty-six in every other body cell of that person. This assures that when the chromosomes of the sperm and ovum combine at conception, the total chromosome number for the new organism will still be forty-six.

Obviously, since a female's twenty-third chromosome pair is XX, every gamete she makes will have either one X or the other. And since a male's twenty-third pair is XY, half his sperm will have an X chromosome and half will have a Y. Thus the critical factor in the determination of a zygote's sex will be which sperm reaches the ovum first, a Y sperm, creating a boy (XY), or an X sperm, creating a girl (XX).

Human Diversity

The union of the sperm and ovum accomplishes dual goals, both essential to the survival of the species. First, the vast majority of each person's genes are identical to those of any unrelated person of the same sex (Plomin, 1990a). As a result of the instructions carried by these genes, each new member of the human race shares a common biological heritage, physical structure, and reproductive potential with every other human, allowing each new generation to perpetuate the human species. The remaining genes ensure diversity, such that the person developed from each zygote will be unlike any of the 6 billion or so other people now alive, or any of our billions of ancestors and descendants.

Given that each sperm or ovum from a particular parent contains only twenty-three chromosomes, you may be wondering how it is possible that every conception represents the potential for a genetically unique individual. The answer is that when the chromosome pairs divide up during the formation of gametes, which one of each of the pairs will wind up in a particular gamete is a matter of chance, and many combinations—each totaling twenty-three chromosomes, one from each of the twenty-three pairs—are possible. The laws of probability show that there are 2^{23}—that is, about 8 million—possible outcomes. In other words, approximately 8 million different ova or sperm can be produced by a single individual.

In addition, just before a chromosome pair divides during the formation of gametes, corresponding segments of the pair are sometimes exchanged, altering the genetic composition of both pair members. Through the recombinations it produces, this crossing-over of genes adds greatly to genetic variability. Further, geneticists have recently discovered that certain genes behave differently, depending on whether they are inherited from the mother or the father (Hoffman, 1991). And finally, when the sperm and ovum unite, the interaction of their chemically coded instructions forms combinations not present in either parent. All things considered, any given mother and father can form over 64 trillion genetically different offspring. Thus it is no exaggeration to say that every conception is, potentially, the beginning of a genetically unique individual.

Twins

Although every zygote is genetically unique, not every newborn is. About once in every 200 pregnancies, the growing cluster of cells splits apart during the first two weeks of development, creating two identical, independent clusters. These cell clusters become **monozygotic twins**, so named because they originated from one (mono) zygote. Since they originated from the same zygote, they share identical genetic instructions for physical appearance, psychological traits, vulnerability to certain diseases, and so forth.

Of course, not all twins are monozygotic. In fact, **dizygotic twins**, who begin life as two separate zygotes created by the fertilization of two ova that were ovulated at roughly the same time, are more common, occurring naturally about once in every seventy births, and when fertility drugs are used, about once in every ten births. Dizygotic twins share no more genes than do any other two offspring of the same parents, about 50 percent on average. They may be of different sexes and very different in appearance. Or they may look a great deal alike, just as nontwin brothers and sisters sometimes do. Other multiple births, such as triplets and quadruplets, can likewise be monozygotic, dizygotic, trizygotic, quadrazygotic, and so forth.

From Genotype to Phenotype

As we have seen, conception brings together genetic instructions from both parents for every human characteristic. How do these instructions work to influence the specific characteristics a given offspring will inherit? The an-

Figure 3.4 *Skin color is one of the most variable of human genetic characteristics. A child can be lighter or darker than either parent, or have a skin tone that is somewhere in between, even if in many other features the child seems to take after Mom or Dad.*

swer is usually quite complex, because most traits are both **polygenic**—that is, affected by many genes—and **multifactorial**—that is, influenced by many factors, including factors in the environment.

To grasp the complexity of genetic influences we must first distinguish between a person's genetic inheritance—his or her genetic *potential*—and the actual *expression* of that inheritance. The sum total of all the genes a person inherits for any particular trait is called the **genotype**. The actual expression of traits, observable in the person's physical appearance as well as in his or her behavioral tendencies, is called the **phenotype**. The phenotype of any given characteristic arises from two levels of genetic interaction: (1) the interaction of the specific genes that make up the genotype of the characteristic and (2) the ongoing interaction between the genotype and the environment. Let us look first at the types of interaction that can occur among the genes themselves and then consider some of the ways the phenotype is shaped by environmental factors.

Genetic Interaction

The simplest pattern of genetic interaction occurs when the genes from both parents instruct for the same outcome on a given characteristic. In such cases, the result is usually straightforward: the offspring will display in his or her phenotype the outcome called for by both sets of genes. However, when the genes from the parents carry divergent instructions for a given trait, the genes will interact in one of several alternative patterns.

One common pattern is called **additive**, because each gene in question makes an active contribution to the final outcome. In effect, then, the phenotype in this pattern reflects the sum of all the genes involved. The many genes affecting height, for instance, interact in an additive fashion, as do the various genes underlying most intellectual abilities and temperamental traits.

A less common but more intriguing pattern of genetic interaction is the **dominant-recessive** pattern. In this pattern, some genes are *dominant:* they act in a controlling manner, hiding the influence of the weaker *recessive* genes and directing the outcome of the genetic interaction.

Hundreds of physical characteristics follow the dominant-recessive pattern. Let us consider eye color. Simplifying greatly, let's say that a person inherits two eye-color genes, one from each parent, and that the gene for brown eyes is dominant and that the gene for blue eyes is recessive. (Following traditional practice, we will indicate the dominant gene with an upper-case letter—"B" for dominant brown—and the recessive gene with a lower-case letter—"b" for recessive blue.) If both genes are for brown eyes (BB), the person's eyes will be brown. If one gene is for brown eyes and the other for blue (Bb), the person's eyes will be brown, since the brown-eye gene is dominant. If both genes are for blue eyes (bb), the person will have blue eyes.

Through the dominant-recessive pattern it is also possible for parents to have offspring whose phenotype for a particular characteristic is completely different from theirs, if both parents both have the necessary recessive genes. For example, if each of two brown-eyed parents has a recessive gene for blue eyes (Bb and Bb), there is one chance in four that a particular child of theirs will inherit the recessive blue-eye gene from both of them and will therefore have blue eyes. (The four possible combinations in their offspring would be BB, Bb, Bb—all yielding brown eyes—and bb, yielding blue eyes.)

A person who has a recessive gene as a part of his or her genotype is called a **carrier** of that gene. In fact, we are all carriers of dozens of recessive genes that are in our genotypes but not in our phenotypes. Usually we are unaware of which recessive genes we carry until we have a child with a surprising phenotype (see Figure 3.5).

Figure 3.5 *These two may not look like father and son, but they are. A blue-eyed, blond child could easily be the biological offspring of dark-eyed and black-haired parents, as long as each parent has the requisite recessive genes.*

X-Linked Recessive Genes

Some special recessive genes are called **X-linked** because they are located only on the X chromosome. For example, the genes for most forms of color blindness, certain allergies, several diseases, and some learning disabilities are recessive and are carried by the X chromosome. Since males have only one X chromosome, they are more likely to have these characteristics on their phenotype, because their Y chromosome has no corresponding dominant gene to countermand the instructions of the recessive gene. This explains why some traits often seem to be passed from mother to son but only rarely from mother to daughter or from father to offspring of either sex.

For example, if a male *(XY)* inherits a gene for color blindness on the X chromosome he receives from his mother, he will be color-blind. On the other hand, if a female *(XX)* inherits a gene for color blindness on either one of her X chromosomes, but also inherits a corresponding dominant gene for normal color vision on her other X chromosome, she will be a carrier of color blindness, but she herself will not be color-blind. This pattern holds true for all sex-linked recessive genes: a female can carry them on her genotype, but she will not show their effects on her phenotype unless she has inherited them from both of her parents.

As complex as the preceding descriptions of additive, dominant, and recessive gene interaction may seem, they in fact make gene interaction appear much simpler than it actually is. Some additive genes contribute more substantially than others, either because they are naturally partially dominant, or because their influence is amplified by the presence of certain other genes. When additive genes combine, their final product is not always the simple total of all the contributions.

Nor are recessive genes always completely suppressed by the presence of their dominant gene counterparts. For example, although eye color is listed in many textbooks as either dominant brown or recessive blue, in reality, eyes are many shades of brown, blue, and even green or gray, each revealing the influence of several genes of varied dominance. Many a hazel-eyed child has one parent with blue eyes and the other with brown. In this case, the child's light-brown eyes bear witness to the recessive gene in his or her genotype.

Such polygenic complexity is particularly apparent in psychological characteristics, including everything from personality traits, such as sociability, assertiveness, moodiness, and fearfulness, to cognitive traits, such as memory for numbers, spatial perception, and fluency of expression. Typically, many pairs of genes, some interacting in the dominant-recessive mode, some additive, and some creating new combinations, affect every behavioral tendency (Plomin, 1990; Eaves et al., 1989).

Identifying Genetic Influences

Genetic influence on physical appearance is obvious even to a casual observer—family resemblances in facial features, hair and eye color, and body type are apparent at a glance—but the impact of genes on psychological characteristics is much less easy to identify. Of course, many intellectual abilities, artistic talents, and personality traits seem to run in families, but nurture rather than nature could be the explanation. How, then, do scientists identify genetic influence on various personality characteristics?

Studying children growing up in their birth families is not much help, precisely because of the confounding of genetic inheritance and environmental family influences. For instance, if children of highly intelligent parents excel in school, their school performance could, *theoretically*, be attributed entirely to their genetic inheritance, or entirely to their family environment (which is likely to encourage reading, intellectual questioning, and high academic standards), or to any combination of the two, including a lopsided 99–1 in either the nature or nurture direction, or an even 50–50 split.

One approach to this puzzle has been to study twins. As we have seen, monozygotic twins share all the same genes, while dizygotic twins share only about half the same genes, just like any other two siblings from the same parents. Thus, if monozygotic twins, on the whole, are found to be much more similar on a particular trait than dizygotic twins are, it seems likely that genes play a significant role in the appearance of that trait.

Another way to distinguish the impact of genes from that of upbringing is to study large numbers of adopted children and both their biological and adoptive parents. Traits that show a strong correlation between adopted children and their biological parents suggest a genetic basis for those characteristics; traits that show a strong correlation between adopted children and their adoptive parents suggest environmental influence.

The most telling way to try to separate the effects of genes and environment is to combine both strategies, studying identical twins who have been separated at birth and raised in different families. Although it requires painstaking searching in order to find enough twin pairs to make statistically significant conclusions, several groups of researchers, in the United States, Sweden, England, Denmark, and Australia, have done just that, finding altogether close to a thousand twins raised apart. The results (see A Closer Look, pp. 76–77) provide dramatic confirmation for the general conclusion reached by more conventional research on thousands of single-born adopted children and on twins raised by their biological parents—and that conclusion is that virtually every psychological characteristic and personal trait is genetically influenced (Eaves et al., 1989; Bouchard et al., 1990; Pederson et al., 1988).

At the same time, these very same studies reinforce another, equally important conclusion: that virtually every psychological characteristic and personal trait is affected, throughout the life span, by the environment.

Gene-Environment Interactions

In order to understand the wide-ranging impact of the environment on genetic inheritance, you need to know that when social scientists discuss the effects of the **environment** on the individual, they are referring to a multitude of variables—indeed, everything that can interact with the person's genetic inheritance at every point of life, from the first prenatal days to the last breath, from the impact of the immediate cell environment on the genes themselves to the ways all the elements in the outside world might impinge upon the individual. These external elements include direct effects, such as those of nutrition, climate, medical care, and family interaction; indirect effects, such as the broad economic, political, and cultural context; irreversible effects, such as the impact of severe brain injury on cognitive development; and less permanent effects, such as the impact of the immediate social environment on temper.

Figure 3.6 *Is it heredity or environment that explains the fact that several generations of the Flying Wallendas have pursued the perfection of incredible high-wire feats of balance and coordination? Obviously, body type and a hearty attitude toward danger must play a role, together with family encouragement and practice that begins almost in infancy.*

A CLOSER LOOK   Personal Choices, Private Tastes, Individual Preferences, and . . . Genes?

Your chosen friends, favorite foods, individual idiosyncrasies, and lifestyle preferences all seem a matter of personal choice, part of what makes any given moment of your life uniquely yours to live. To the extent that you think of your personal choices as being subject to influences outside your control, you probably regard environmental circumstances—such as childhood experiences, social pressures, and cultural context—as much more powerful than any particular sequence of DNA in your genetic code. That may be *how it seems*, but is that *how it is*? If, in the early days of prenatal life, the zygote that contained your genes had happened to split, and if you and your twin had happened to be separated at birth and raised by different families, and if you were to one day run into your twin, you might discover that many of your supposedly unique personal choices had also been made by someone else.

Consider the case of Robert Shafran, who, while walking across the campus of the university in which he had recently enrolled, was suddenly greeted by a young woman who kissed him warmly on the mouth and exclaimed, "Where have you been?" That Robert didn't even know this woman was a fact he admitted somewhat reluctantly, since she was just his type. As it turned out, she was also his brother Eddy Galland's type; in fact, it was Eddy, Robert's long-lost twin, whom the woman had taken Robert to be. When Eddy and Robert were reunited, it was soon clear that the resemblance between them was not limited to physical characteristics. Among other striking similarities, the brothers wore the same kinds of clothes; had similar hairstyles; laughed in the same way at the same jokes; drank the same brand of beer; smoked the same brand of cigarettes (which they held in the same way); engaged in the same sports, including team wrestling (in which they had almost identical records); and listened to the same music, at similar volumes.

When the story of Robert and Eddy hit the press, David Kellman looked at their photo and thought he was seeing mirror images of himself—and, in fact, he was, for in this case, monozygotic triplets rather than twins had been separated at birth. When the three brothers were reunited, they (and the psychologists who studied them) were amazed at the number of experiences, tastes, and interests they had in common (*New York Times,* 1980).

Similar amazement was registered, a bit less publicly, by a group of researchers beginning the Minnesota Study of Twins Reared Apart, an extensive study of monozygotic twins who were separated early in life (Bouchard et al., 1990; Holden, 1980). One pair of identical twins, Oskar Stohr and Jack Yufe, were born of a Jewish father and German mother in Trinidad in the 1930s. Soon after their birth,

The sources of triple confusion, from top to bottom: Edward Galland, David Kellman, and Robert Shafran.

Oskar was taken to Nazi Germany by his mother to be raised as a Catholic in a household consisting mostly of women. Jack was raised as a Jew by his father, spending his childhood in the Caribbean and some of his adolescence in Israel.

On the face of it, it would be difficult to imagine more disparate cultural backgrounds. In addition, the twins certainly had their differences. Oskar was married, an employee, and a devoted union member. Jack was divorced and owned a clothing store in southern California. But, when the brothers met for the first time in Minnesota,

similarities started cropping up as soon as Oskar arrived at the airport. Both were wearing wire-rimmed glasses and mustaches, both sported two-pocket shirts with epaulets. They share idiosyncrasies galore: they like spicy foods and sweet liqueurs, are absentminded, have a habit of falling asleep in front of the television, think it's funny to sneeze in a crowd of strangers, flush the toilet before using it, store rubber bands on their wrists, read magazines from back to front, dip buttered toast in their coffee. Oskar is domineering toward women and yells at his wife, which Jack did before he was separated. [Holden, 1980]

Since Oskar Stohr (left) and Jack Yufe (right) are monozygotic twins, it is not surprising that they look very much alike. However, since they have been separated almost from birth, it is more difficult to explain their similarities in many of those characteristics that are usually considered to be acquired, for example, their preference for moustaches and their tastes in food and drink.

Their scores on several psychological tests were very similar, and they struck the investigator as remarkably similar in temperament and tempo. Other pairs of twins in this study likewise startled the observers by their similarities, not only in appearance and on test scores, but also in mannerisms and dress. One pair of female twins, separated since infancy, arrived in Minnesota, each wearing seven rings (on the same fingers) and three bracelets, a coincidence that might be explained by pure chance, but more likely was partly genetic—that is, genes endowed both women with beautiful hands and, possibly, contributed to an interest in self-adornment.

The evidence from monozygotic twins suggests that genes affect a much greater number of characteristics than most psychologists, including the leader of the Minnesota study, Thomas Bouchard, suspected. As Bouchard has noted (Cassill, 1982), he once believed it was "foolish" to think that genes affect almost every trait, but he now finds that the idea is "no longer subject to debate" and that genetic variation is significant for "almost every behavioral trait so far investigated from reaction time to religiosity" (Bouchard et al., 1990).

This does not mean that the seemingly uncanny similarities between monozygotic twins raised in separate homes should automatically be attributed to genetics. For instance, the triplets' taste in cigarettes and beer was also shared by a million or so other young men, who had little in common genetically but a great deal in common culturally, including exposure to advertising messages extolling the manly virtues of particular brands.

Further, most twins reared apart have quite similar home experiences. Typically, they are raised by close relatives in neighboring communities. A review of the research found that, in every case in which separated twins were raised in markedly different homes, such that one twin experienced "extreme deprivation or unusual enrichment," the resemblance between the twins lessened (Scarr and McCartney, 1983).

Only rarely are identical twins separated by language, culture, and religion, as Oskar and Jack were. Even in their case, says Bouchard, beneath the more dramatic differences in background, their upbringing was basically quite similar. Moreover, personality similarities may foster environmental similarities, as much as vice versa. Large-scale research finds that monozygotic twins tend to evoke similar degrees of warmth and encouragement from the adults who interact with them (Plomin, 1990a). Thus a pair of identical twins, making their way in different families, may be similarly influenced by the similar family patterns they themselves may help create.

All these caveats and cautions notwithstanding, most researchers are astonished at the similarities they find in monozygotic twins raised separately (Lykken et al., 1992). Indeed, these twins are sometimes more alike than twins raised together (Juel-Nielsen, 1980). It seems that, when they grow up in the same home, some monozygotic twins deliberately create or emphasize differences between themselves in order to preserve a sense of individuality.

Such findings make one wonder anew about the sources of our own individuality. Are our life choices—large and small—mostly an outgrowth of experience and cultural background, or do the roots go much deeper? Could many of the habits and patterns that distinguish each of us be not so much a matter of personal choice as a matter of genetic push? It is an intriguing question to which we may never have a definitive answer.

By the way, how many rings do you have on your fingers, and why?

Physical Traits

Environment, as broadly defined above, affects every human characteristic—even physical traits that show strong genetic influence. Take height, for example. An individual's potential maximum growth is genetically determined, yet most adults in developed countries are, on average, taller than their grandparents ever were but virtually the same height as their full-grown children. Why? Because to reach the genetically set upper limits of height, a person must have adequate nutrition and good health. In the nineteenth century, these two factors were much less common than they are now, and Americans, for example, were, on average, about 6 inches shorter than they are today (Tanner, 1971). Throughout the twentieth century, however, as nutrition and medical care improved, each generation grew slightly taller than the previous one. Over the past three decades, this trend has stopped, because the prevailing levels of health and nutrition have permitted the vast majority of the population to reach their genetically set height limits, and most children reaching adulthood in the 1990s will, on average, be about as tall as their parents. Of course, in individual cases, environmental factors such as malnutrition, chronic illness, and stress can make a child considerably shorter than his or her heredity calls for.

Psychological Traits

Environmental influences are fairly simple to understand as they affect physical traits. As we have just seen, for example, the effect of nutrition on height is self-evident. More varied, hidden, and intriguing are the effects of the interactions of all the environmental influences on psychological traits.

Take shyness, for instance. No doubt shyness is partly inherited: study after study finds that the levels of a personality trait called extroversion, or sociability, are more similar in monozygotic than dizygotic twins (Bouchard et al., 1990; Eaves et al., 1989; Plomin et al., 1990). However, research on adopted children shows that shyness is affected both by the genetic heritage of the biological parents and the social atmosphere provided by the adoptive parents (Loehlin et al., 1982).

As this research suggests, a genetically shy child whose parents are outgoing would have many contacts with other people, and would observe his or her parents greeting strangers with a friendly hello and socializing freely. Although such a child might cling to his or her parents in the beginning, gradually the child would learn to relax and would become less observably shy. It is not that as life experiences accumulate, genetic impulses disappear: a shy child would always feel twinges of inhibition when entering a new school, or when arriving at a party full of strangers, for instance. But some shy people are able to build on childhood experiences and know how to warm up to others and feel more at ease. Alternatively, of course, if this same shy child's parents are also very shy and socially isolated, the child might grow up much more timid socially than he or she would have with outgoing parents—and considerably more so than most other children.

Thus the expression of shyness will depend on the interactions between parental example, cultural encouragement, school milieu, cognitive awareness, self-understanding, and adult experiences—each of which may exacerbate, diminish, or redirect the impact of the others.

Figure 3.7 *This chart, which reflects more than sixty years of research in several European countries, indicates the lifetime risk of becoming schizophrenic (Gottesman, 1990). As you can see, while any person chosen at random has only about a 1 percent chance of developing the disorder, the more closely one is related to a person with schizophrenia, the more likely one is to develop the problem oneself. The highest risk occurs for monozygotic twins: when one twin is diagnosed as being schizophrenic, the other has almost a 50 percent chance of eventually being so diagnosed. Note, however, that while this chart shows a clear genetic influence on schizophrenia, the odds also show the effects of environment. For instance, over half the monozygotic siblings whose twin is schizophrenic are not schizophrenic themselves.*

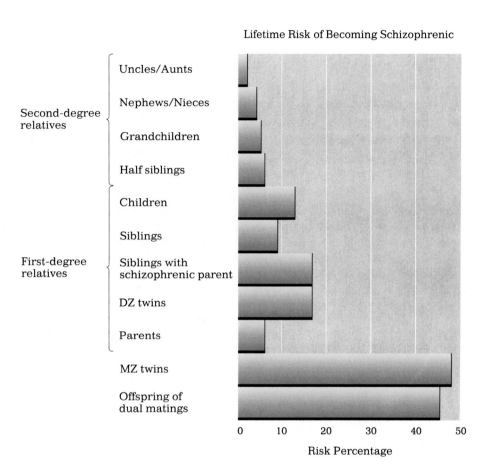

Lifetime Risk of Becoming Schizophrenic

Mental Illness

Overall, research reveals that, as in the case of shyness, genes are never the exclusive determinant of any psychological characteristic, including intellectual abilities and personality traits. This is also true with regard to psychopathologies such as depression, antisocial behavior, and bipolar disorder: here, too, both genes and environment are influential (Gottesman, 1990).

The most extensive research on this question has been done on schizophrenia, and it shows that if one monozygotic twin becomes schizophrenic, the chances are about 50 percent that the other will too, a rate far above the 1 percent incidence in the overall population. Looked at another way, however, the same evidence reveals the importance of the environment: among identical twins, half of those whose twin is schizophrenic are not themselves afflicted. Obviously, schizophrenia is multifactorial, with environmental elements—possibly a slow virus, head injury, or overall stress—playing a pivotal role.

Alcoholism: A Clear Example of Gene-Environment Interaction

One particularly clear example of the way the environment moderates genetic potential in psychological characteristics can be seen in the case of alcoholism. At various times alcoholism was thought to be a moral weakness, a personality flaw, or a sign of psychopathology. We now know that alcoholism is at least partly genetic, although the specific genes involved, the nature of their interaction, and their precise power have yet to be determined (McClearn et al., 1991). We do know that some people's biochemistry makes them highly susceptible to alcoholism; others' biochemistry makes them much less so. Thus, while anyone can abuse alcohol, the addictive pull can be immensely strong or very weak, depending on the person's genetic makeup. In addition to quite specific physiological patterns, certain temperamental traits, themselves partly genetic, also correlate with abusive drinking. Among these are a quick temper, a willingness to take risks, and a high level of anxiety. Thus alcoholism is polygenic, with no two alcoholics inheriting quite the same genetic basis, but with almost every alcoholic inheriting biochemical or temperamental traits that push toward abusive drinking.

Obviously, however, environment plays a critical role in the expression of alcoholism. If a person with a strong genetic affinity to alcoholism spends a lifetime in an environment where alcohol is unavailable, the alcoholic genotype will never become manifest in the phenotype. On the other hand, if the same person is raised in a dysfunctional family within a culture that promotes the use of alcohol, he or she is quite likely to become an active alcoholic. Even in that situation, however, social influences and individual choices can dramatically alter the outcome. Some alcoholics die of the disease before they are 30; others spend a lifetime fluctuating between abuse, controlled drinking, and abstinence; still others recognize the problem by early adulthood, get help, and are sober and productive throughout a long life.

The example of alcoholism also illustrates a final factor influencing the interaction between genes and the environment—the individual's stage of development and the particular expectancies the culture holds for that stage. Alcoholism may be genetically "present" at birth but it is rarely expressed before adolescence. Many other traits become more apparent as children mature and parental restrictions and influence wane (Scarr and Weinberg, 1983; Loehlin et al., 1985). This is especially the case with adopted children, whose genetic predisposition is sometimes at odds with that of their adoptive parents. When they are very young, adoptees reflect many of their adoptive parents' interests, behaviors, and personality traits. However, with maturity, they often choose friends, hobbies, and habits that express their biological, rather than their familial, heritage.

In summary, then, it is quite clear that both genes and environment are powerful influences on development, that their interaction is involved in every aspect of development, and that their interaction is complex, varying from person to person, trait to trait, culture to culture, and stage to stage. On a practical level, this means we should not ignore the fact that there is a genetic component in any given trait—whether it be something wonderful, such as a wacky sense of humor, or something fearful, such as a violent temper, or something quite ordinary, such as the tendency to tire of the same routine. At the same time, we must always recognize that the environment affects every trait in every individual in many ways that change as developmental processes unfold. Genes are always part of the tale, influential on every page, but they never determine the plot or the final story.

Genetic and Chromosomal Abnormalities

In studying human development, we give particular attention to genetic and chromosomal abnormalities, for three reasons. One reason is that, by investigating genetic disruptions of normal development, we can gain a fuller appreciation of the complexities of genetic interaction. A second reason is that an understanding of those who inherit genetic or chromosomal abnormalities is essential to everyone concerned about fostering human development. A lack of such understanding can lead to misinformation and prejudice, which only compound the problems of those affected by such disorders. A third reason is the most practical: the more we know about the origins of genetic and chromosomal abnormalities, the better we understand the risks of their occurring and the better prepared we are to limit their harmful effects when they do occur. First let us look at problems caused directly by the chromosomes. Such genetic abnormalities are, in general, the most serious, but they are also the easiest to detect and prevent.

Chromosomal Abnormalities

Sometimes when gametes are formed, the forty-six chromosomes divide unevenly, producing a sperm or ovum that does not have the normal complement of twenty-three chromosomes. If such a gamete fuses with a normal gamete, the result is a zygote with more or less than forty-six chromosomes. This is not unusual. An estimated half of all zygotes have an odd number of chromosomes. Most of these do not even begin to develop, and most of the rest never come to term, usually because a spontaneous abortion occurs. Once in every 200 births, however, a baby is born with forty-five, forty-seven, or even more chromosomes (Gilbert et al., 1987). In every case, these chromosomal abnormalities lead to a recognizable **syndrome**—a cluster of distinct characteristics that tend to occur together. Individuals who have a particular syndrome do not necessarily have all the distinguishing characteristics, and in any given syndrome, the severity of the symptoms varies from person to person.

In most such cases, the presence of an extra chromosome is lethal within the first days and months after birth. There are two major exceptions in which affected individuals often survive to adulthood—when the extra chromosome is at the twenty-first pair, where the smallest nonsex chromosome pair is located, or at the twenty-third pair.

Down Syndrome

The most common of the extra-chromosome syndromes is **trisomy-21**, or **Down syndrome**, which results from there being three chromosomes at site 21. Some 300 distinct characteristics can result from the presence of that extra chromosome, but as is the case with all syndromes, no Down-syndrome individual is quite like another, either in the specific symptoms he or she has or in their severity (Cicchetti and Beeghly, 1990). Despite this variability, almost all people with trisomy-21 have certain facial characteristics—a thick tongue, round face, slanted eyes—as well as distinctive hands, feet, and fingerprints. Many also have hearing problems, heart abnormalities, muscle weakness, and short stature.

Figure 3.8 *This Down-syndrome child has the round face, almond-shaped eyes, and thick tongue that characterize those who have an extra chromosome at the twenty-first pair. This young girl is fortunate, however, in that her family's affectionate care and support should help to make her comparatively self-sufficient by young adulthood.*

In terms of psychological development, almost all Down-syndrome individuals experience some mental slowness, but their eventual intellectual attainment varies, from severely retarded to average or even above average. Often—but not always—those who are raised at home and given appropriate schooling progress to the point of being able to read and write and care for themselves, while those who are institutionalized tend to be, and to remain, much more retarded. Ability to get along with others does not seem impeded by Down syndrome: in fact, many Down-syndrome children are considered unusually sweet-tempered. By middle adulthood, however, Down-syndrome individuals are more likely to experience a form of dementia similar to Alzheimer's disease, severely impairing their intellectual and social skills. They are also prone to a host of other problems more commonly found in the elderly, including cataracts and certain forms of cancer.

Abnormalities of the Sex Chromosomes

Every zygote that develops long enough to be born has at least one X chromosome. About 1 in every 500 infants, however, has either a missing sex chromosome, so that the X stands alone, or has the X chromosome completed by two or more sex chromosomes. As you can see from Table 3.1, these abnormalities can impair cognitive and psychosocial development, as well as sexual maturation. In many cases, treatment with hormone supplements can alleviate some of the physical problems, and special education may remedy some of the deficits in psychological functioning.

Again, however, remember that the specific features of any syndrome vary considerably from one individual to another. In fact, in many cases, the presence of abnormal sex chromosomes goes undetected until a seemingly normal childhood is followed by an abnormally delayed puberty. Many specialists recommend chromosomal analysis as soon as a problem is suspected, and then carefully individualized counseling and treatment for those with a problem.

Other Chromosomal Problems

Sometimes during the formation of gametes, a piece of a chromosome breaks off and reattaches itself to another chromosome. Depending on the particular gamete that created the zygote, as well as on the specific pattern of early cell division, the result can be a zygote with some genetic material missing or with extra material. Indeed, Down syndrome is sometimes caused by chromosome 21 having an extra arm rather than an entire additional chromosome. Individuals with this pattern often have the facial features of Down syndrome but are less likely to experience serious cognitive deficits. Recently researchers discovered that a small extra piece on chromosome 17 is the cause of an inherited degenerative weakness in the hands and feet, called Charcot-Marie-Tooth syndrome (Patel and Lupski, 1991). Many other genetic diseases, including some forms of Alzheimer's disease and schizophrenia, may also be the result of extra genetic material on a particular chromosome (Angier, 1991).

As you might expect, even more severe problems are caused when genetic material is missing than when additional material is present. Usually the zygote does not grow and develop, and thus is spontaneously aborted.

TABLE 3.1 Common Abnormalities Involving the Sex Chromosomes

Name	Chromosomal Pattern	Physical Appearance*	Psychological Characteristics*	Incidence
Kleinfelter syndrome	XXY	Male. Secondary sex characteristics do not develop. For example, the penis does not grow, the voice does not change. Breasts may develop.	Learning disabled, especially in language skills.	3 in 1,000 males
(No name)	XYY	Male. Prone to acne. Unusually tall.	Tend to be more aggressive than most males. Mildly retarded, especially in language skills.	1 in 1,000 males
Fra-X (Fragile X)	Usually XY	Often, large head, prominent ears. Occasionally, enlarged testicles in males.	Variable. Some individuals apparently normal; others severely retarded.	1 in 1,000 males; 1 in 5,000 females
(No name)	XXX,XXXX	Female. Normal appearance.	Retarded in almost all intellectual skills.	2 in 1,000 females
Turner syndrome	XO (only one sex chromosome)	Female. Short in stature, often "webbed" neck. Secondary sex characteristics (breasts, menstruation) do not develop.	Learning disabled, especially in abilities related to math and science and in recognition of facial expressions of emotion.	1 in 2,000 females

*There is some variation in the physical appearance and considerable variation in the intellectual and temperamental characteristics of these individuals. With regard to psychological characteristics, much depends on the family environment of the child.

Sources: McCauley et al., 1987; Moore, 1989; Vandenberg, 1987; Kaplan et al., 1987; Gardner and Sutherland, 1989.

One exception is *cri du chat* syndrome—so named because the newborn's cry resembles that of a cat—which is caused by a deletion on chromosome 4 or 5. Typically the baby survives, but is severely retarded, requiring lifelong total care.

The Fragile X

One of the most common chromosomal problems is also one of the most variable in its effects. In some individuals, part of the X chromosome is attached by such a thin string of molecules that it seems about to break off. This abnormality, caused by a single gene, is **fragile-X syndrome**.

Of the females who carry it, most are normal (perhaps because they also carry one normal X chromosome), but a third show some mental deficiency. Among the males who inherit a fragile X chromosome, there is considerable variation in effect: about 20 percent are apparently completely normal; about 33 percent are somewhat retarded; and the rest are severely retarded. The last group is sufficiently large that about half the residents in most homes for the retarded have the fragile X (Brown et al., 1987). While the widely variable effects of this disorder are somewhat unusual, some geneticists believe that the more we learn about other abnormal genes and their interactions, the more diversity in the expression of the phenotype we will find (McKusick, 1990).

Causes of Chromosomal Abnormalities

Chromosomal abnormalities are caused by many factors, some genetic and some, such as viruses, environmental. However, among the most common correlates of chromosomal abnormalities, especially Down syndrome and Kleinfelter syndrome, is parental age. According to one detailed estimate,

Figure 3.9 *The fact that older parents have a higher risk of conceiving an embryo with chromosomal abnormalities should not obscure another reality. With modern medical care and prenatal testing, pregnancies that occur when the parents are in their 40s can, and almost always do, result in healthy babies.*

for example, a 20-year-old woman has 1 chance in 500 of having a child with chromosomal abnormalities; a 39-year-old woman has 1 chance in 100; and a 48-year-old woman has 1 chance in 9 (Cefalo and Moos, 1988). One possible explanation for this increasing rate is the aging of the gametes. Since a female is born with all the ova she will ever have, a 48-year-old woman has ova that are 48 years old. Perhaps degeneration of the ova leads to chromosomal abnormalities. However, this cannot be the only reason older parents have more offspring with chromosomal problems, because, no matter how old the mother, the father's age correlates with the birth of a child with an extra chromosome. Perhaps as the male reproductive system ages, it produces a higher percentage of malformed sperm.

Harmful Genes

While relatively few people have abnormal chromosomes, everyone is a carrier of at least twenty genes that could produce serious diseases or handicaps in their offspring (Milunsky, 1989). To date, roughly 5,000 genetic disorders have been identified, many of them exceedingly rare (Mukusick, 1990).

Among the more common genetic disorders are cystic fibrosis, spinal defects, cleft palate, and club feet (see Table 3.2, pp. 86–87 for a detailed listing of genetic disorders). Fortunately, many genetic problems are recessive, so a person will not have a particular condition unless he or she has inherited the genes for it from both parents. In addition, some serious genetic conditions are polygenic, so several specific genes must be present in the genotype before the problem appears in the phenotype. Still others are multifactorial; they do not become apparent unless something in the prenatal or postnatal environment fosters their expression. Thus, most babies have no apparent genetic problems, although all carry some of the destructive genes that their parents have. About one baby in every thirty, however, is not so lucky and is born with a serious genetic problem (Wheale and McNally, 1988).

In most cases, the parents are completely unprepared for the birth of such a child, which compounds the problem. As we will now see, a better understanding of genetics, and a more widespread use of genetic counseling, can make such births less likely and better prepare families and physicians for those births that do occur.

Genetic Counseling

For most of human history, couples at risk for having a child with a chromosomal or genetic problem did not know it. Indeed, if a child was born with a serious defect and died very young, the parents often had a "replacement" child soon after—unaware of the risk they were taking. Today, a combination of testing and counseling before and during pregnancy, as well as immediate medical attention at birth, has transformed the dilemmas faced by prospective parents. Through **genetic counseling,** couples can learn more about their genes, and make informed decisions about their childbearing future.

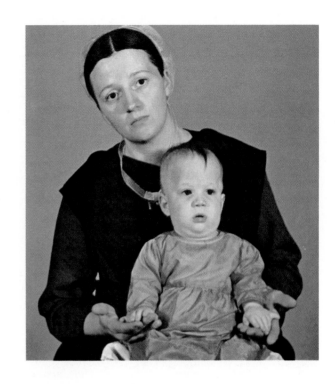

Figure 3.10 *Rare genetic conditions become more common when blood relatives marry, because the chance of a child's inheriting the same recessive genes from both parents increases. This child is a six-fingered dwarf, a condition extremely rare in the general population. However, at least sixty-one cases have occurred among the Old Order Amish, a religious group founded by three couples over 200 years ago. Members of this group are forbidden to marry outsiders, despite the fact that approximately one out of every eight members is a carrier of this gene.*

Who Should Be Tested?

Who should receive genetic counseling? Certainly everyone who plans to become a parent should probably know something about his or her genetic inheritance. Ideally, all couples should have preconceptual counseling, not only exploring their family histories for possible warning signs but also learning about factors in their lifestyle—nutrition, drugs, work, and so forth—that might affect a fetus (Cefalo and Moos, 1989). However, genetic counseling is strongly recommended for couples in five situations:

1. those who already have a child with a genetic disease;

2. those who have relatives with genetic problems;

3. those who have had previous pregnancies that ended in spontaneous abortion;

4. those who have a history of infertility;

5. those in which the woman is over 34 or the man is over 44.

Another group of couples who may be at risk are those whose ancestors came from particular regions of the world where matings almost always occurred between members of the same small ethnic group. Such group inbreeding causes the gene pool to become closed, and the odds of the identical harmful gene being present in both mother and father increase. As indicated in Table 3.2, virtually every ethnic group has an elevated risk for at least one inherited disease. At even greater risk are those couples whose ancestors were from one of the many parts of the world where young people are encouraged to marry cousins or other relatives. Obviously, the more ancestors a particular couple have in common, the more likely they are to carry similar harmful genes, making genetic testing all the more important (Bittles et al., 1991).

TABLE 3.2   Common Genetic Diseases and Conditions

Name	Description	Prognosis	Method of Inheritance	Incidence*	Carrier Detection?[†]	Prenatal Detection?
Alzheimer's disease	Loss of memory and increasing mental impairment.	Eventual death, often after years of dependency.	Some forms are definitely genetic; others are not.	Less than one in 100 middle-aged adults; nearly half of all adults over age 80.	No.	No.
Cleft palate, cleft lip	The two sides of the upper lip or palate are not joined.	Correctable by surgery.	Multifactorial. Drugs taken during pregnancy or stress may be involved.	One baby in every 700. More common in Asian-Americans and Native Americans; rare in African-Americans.	No.	Yes, in some cases.
Club foot	The foot and ankle are twisted, making it impossible to walk normally.	Correctable by surgery.	Multifactorial.	One baby in every 200. More common in boys.	No.	Yes.
Cystic fibrosis	Lack of an enzyme. Mucous obstructions in body, especially in lungs and digestive organs.	Until recently, nearly all CF victims died by adolescence; medical advances now allow some to reach middle age.	Recessive gene.	One white baby in every 2,000. One in 25 white Americans is a carrier.	Yes.	Yes, in some cases.
Diabetes	Abnormal metabolism of sugar because body does not produce enough insulin.	Early onset is total unless controlled by insulin. Diabetes in later adulthood increases the risk of other diseases. Controllable by insulin and diet.	Multifactorial. Exact pattern hard to predict because environment is crucial.	About 10 million Americans. Most develop it in late adulthood. One child in 500 is diabetic. More common in Native Americans.	No.	No.
Hemophilia	Absence of clotting factor in blood. Called "bleeders disease."	Crippling and death from internal bleeding. Blood transfusions can lessen or even prevent damage.	X-linked. Also spontaneous mutations.	One in 1,000 males. Royal families of England, Russia, and Germany had it.	Yes.	Yes.
Hydrocephalus	Obstruction causes excess water in brain.	Can produce brain damage and death. Surgery can sometimes make survival and normal intelligence possible.	Multifactorial.	One baby in every 100.	No.	Yes.
Muscular dystrophy (13 separate diseases)	Weakening of muscles. Some forms begin in childhood, others in adulthood.	Inability to walk, move; wasting away and sometimes death.	Duchenne's is X-linked; other forms are autosomal recessive or multifactorial.	One in every 3,000 males will develop Duchenne's; about 100,000 Americans have some form of MD.	Yes, for some forms.	Yes, for some forms.

*Incidence statistics vary from country to country; those given here are for the United States. All these diseases can occur in any ethnic group of Americans. When certain groups have a higher incidence, it is noted here.

[†]Studying the family tree can help geneticists spot a possible carrier of many genetic diseases or, in some cases, a definite carrier. However, here "Yes" means that a carrier can be detected even without knowledge of family history.

Name	Description	Prognosis	Method of Inheritance	Incidence	Carrier Detection?[†]	Prenatal Detection?
Neural tube defects (open spine)	Two main forms: anencephaly (parts of the brain and skull are missing) and spina bifida (the lower portion of the spine is not closed).	Often, early death. Anencephalic children are severely retarded; children with spina bifida have trouble with walking and with bowel and bladder control.	Multifactorial; defect occurs in first weeks of pregnancy.	Anencephaly: 1 in 1,000 births; spina bifida: 3 in 1,000. More common in those of Welsh and Scotch descent.	No.	Yes.
Phenylketonuria (PKU)	Abnormal digestion of protein.	Mental retardation, hyperactivity. Preventable by diet.	Recessive gene.	One in 80 European-Americans is a carrier; more common among those of Norwegian and Irish ancestry.	No.	Yes.
Pyloric stenosis	Overgrowth of muscle in intestine.	Vomiting, loss of weight, eventual death; correctable by surgery.	Multifactorial.	One male in 200; 1 female in 1,000. Less common in African-Americans.	No.	No.
Sickle-cell anemia	Abnormal blood cells.	Possible painful "crisis"; heart and kidney failure.	Recessive gene.	One in 400 African-American babies is affected. One in 10 African-Americans is a carrier, as is 1 in 20 Latinos.	Yes.	Yes.
Tay-Sachs disease	Enzyme disease.	Apparently healthy infant becomes progressively weaker, usually dying by age 3.	Recessive gene.	One in 30 American Jews is a carrier, as is an estimated 1 in 20 French-Canadians and 1 in 200 non-Jewish Americans.	Yes.	Yes.
Thalassemia	Abnormal blood cells.	Paleness and listlessness, low resistance to infection; treatment by blood transfusion.	Recessive gene.	As many as 1 in 10 Greek-, Italian-, Thai-, and Indian-Americans is a carrier.	Yes.	Yes.
Tourette syndrome	Uncontrollable tics, body jerking, verbal obscenities.	Worsens with age. Often imperceptible in children; becomes crippling in later adulthood. Can be treated with drugs.	Probably dominant gene.	One in 500.	Sometimes.	No.

Source: McKusick, 1990; Moore, 1989; Vandenberg et al., 1986; Milunsky, 1989; Bowman and Murray, 1990; Connor and Ferguson-Smith, 1991.

Figure 3.11 *The first step in genetic counseling is usually the taking of a detailed family history, searching not only for ancestors and descendants with known genetic diseases, but also for relatives with unexplained problems such as infertility, stillborn children, or a seemingly innocuous mental or physical "peculiarity" that might be a marker for a more serious genetic anomaly. The history is typically interpreted as a chart, such as the one here, that helps elucidate inheritance patterns.*

Predicting Genetic Problems

The ease and accuracy of predicting genetic problems varies from condition to condition. In some cases, both the test and the interpretation of it are quite simple. A blood test is all that is needed for carrier detection of the genes for sickle-cell anemia, Tay-Sachs, PKU, hemophilia, and thalassemia; chromosomal analysis can readily reveal fragile X and the inherited form of Down syndrome, as well as many less common abnormalities.

With many other disorders, the specific harmful genes involved have yet to be located, but **markers** for the presence of such genes have been identified. Such markers, usually harmless in themselves, suggest but do not prove that the individual is a carrier. In some cases, the marker is in the carrier's phenotype, such as an oddly shaped earlobe or finger, or a particular pattern of eye movement (Holzman and Matthysse, 1990; Kurnit et al., 1987). Other markers involve specific clusters of genes that are typically linked with a specific disease gene. These markers can be detected only through DNA analysis of several family members (Boehm, 1988).

Rapid progress in locating genes, and markers, is being made as scientists collaborate on the **Human Genome Project**, a worldwide effort to map all 3 billion codes of the 100,000 human genes. Within the past several years, researchers have found more precise markers for cystic fibrosis and for some forms of muscular dystrophy, as well as having located the gene that causes fragile-X syndrome and some forms of cancer (Roberts, 1991; Claibourne et al., 1990).

Knowing the carrier status of a particular set of prospective parents can pin down the odds of their children's inheriting a genetic disease. If the potential problem involves recessive genes, the odds are clear. When two carriers of the same recessive gene procreate, each of their children has one chance in four of having the disease, because each child has one chance in four of inheriting the recessive gene from both parents. (The principle is the same as that in the case [p.73] of two brown-eyed parents who have recessive genes for blue eyes and a one-in-four probability of having blue-eyed offspring.) It is important in this respect to remember that "chance has no memory," which means that *each time* two carriers have another child, the odds of that child's inheriting the disease are one in four. Each child born into the family also stands a one-in-four chance of avoiding the gene altogether and a 50-50 chance of inheriting one recessive gene, making the child a carrier like the parents.

Some genetic diseases are carried by dominant rather than recessive genes. In fact, there are almost twice as many known dominant-gene disorders as recessive ones (McKusick, 1990). Each offspring of a carrier of a dominant-gene disorder has a 50-50 chance of inheriting the disorder.

Once pregnancy has begun, further testing can often reveal definitively if a particular fetus has beaten the odds or not (see Table 3.3). Some of these tests, such as AFP screening and the sonogram, are routine for all pregnancies in certain countries. Others, such as amniocentesis, are suggested whenever the mother is older than 35 or when both parents are carriers of certain genetic diseases. Indeed, in the United States, an obstetrician who fails to advise high-risk patients about prenatal testing can be sued for "wrongful life" (a legal term) if a severely impaired child is born (Blank, 1988).

TABLE 3.3   Detecting Prenatal Problems: Four Special Tests

1. Testing the level of **alphafetoprotein (AFP)** in the mother's blood can indicate the possibility that a fetus has a neural tube defect or Down syndrome. One pregnancy in ten has unusual AFP levels, requiring further tests.

2. A **sonogram** uses high-frequency sound waves to outline the shape of the fetus, allowing the detection of abnormalities in body shape or rate of growth.

3. **Amniocentesis** is done about sixteen weeks after conception, when a small amount of amniotic fluid can be withdrawn and analyzed. Since the fluid contains sloughed-off cells from the fetus, chromosomal abnormalities and many other genetic and prenatal problems can be detected.

4. In **chorionic villi sampling (CVS)**, a tiny piece of the placental membrane is obtained and analyzed, providing much the same information as in amniocentesis, with one advantage: CVS can be done about eight weeks earlier.

All these tests are very low-risk for the mother and quite low-risk for the fetus. However, risk analysis should precede any intervention, assuring that the benefits outweigh the hazards.

Overall, genetic testing is one of the most innovative areas in all of developmental research, raising hopes that within the next decade researchers will be able to detect elevated genetic vulnerability in both fetus and adult for an increasing number of conditions, including not only dominant and recessive diseases but multifactorial ones, among them cancer, heart disease, and diabetes, and many types of mental retardation and psychopathology (Marx, 1991). As scientists home in on particular harmful genes, both prevention and treatment will improve. In some cases, genetic disease will be cured by adding a healthy gene—a practice already in the experimental stage for cystic fibrosis.

Many Alternatives

Fortunately, with proper counseling, those who undergo genetic testing because they are concerned about their potential offspring learn that they have many choices. Often testing reveals that neither partner, or only one, is a carrier of a harmful trait, or reveals that the odds of that couple's having offspring with a serious illness are not much higher than they are for any other couple. If a couple learn that they both are carriers of a recessive disease, or are high-risk in other ways, they have several alternatives—from avoiding pregnancy and, perhaps, planning adoption, to having amniocentesis and, perhaps, considering abortion, to determining how they will care for an affected infant. The specifics will vary, not only by couple, but also by disease.

Preventive measures are usually chosen when the risk is for a devastating disease. For example, no one would willingly have a child with Tay-Sachs, because the disease progressively destroys the infant's mind and body, leading to death by age 5. Between 1970 and 1990, extensive testing and counseling of Jewish engaged couples led to a 95 percent reduction in Tay-Sachs among the Jews of North America (Zeiger, 1990). This dramatic turnaround involved some very painful decisions for the carrier couples involved. Some broke off their engagements; some decided not to bear children; some decided to try pregnancy, with abortion as an option if their fetus was found to have Tay-Sachs. But as a result, almost none had to watch their child suffer a short and ravaged life.

In cases where the consequences of a genetic disease are variable, the decision-making process is even more difficult. For example, some infants born with sickle-cell anemia die in childhood after suffering frequent "crises," in which they experience great pain; others live relatively normal lives into adulthood, with occasional bouts of illness.

Couples at risk of any particular problem should talk with parents who have, or have had, children with the same problem. Almost always, they will gain an important perspective and insight, including a sense of the unanticipated anguish and unexpected fulfillment that having a seriously handicapped child can represent. Most genetic counselors believe very strongly that the final choice should be made by the individuals concerned, whose values must be respected, even if their decision is not what the counselor, or their family members, would make. Indeed, couples with identical genetic risks often make quite different decisions, depending on their personal relationship, values, temperaments, and financial resources.

SUMMARY

The Beginning of Development

1. Conception occurs when a sperm penetrates an ovum, creating a single-celled organism called a zygote. The zygote contains all the genetic material—half from each of the two gametes—needed to create a unique developing person.

Genes and Chromosomes

2. Genes, which provide the information cells need to specialize and perform specific functions in the body, are arranged on chromosomes. Every human cell contains 23 pairs of chromosomes, one member of each pair contributed by each parent. Every cell contains a duplicate of the genetic information in the first cell, the zygote.

3. Twenty-two pairs of chromosomes control the development of most of the body. The twenty-third pair determines the individual's sex: zygotes with an *XY* combination will become males; those with two X chromosomes will become females.

4. Each person has a unique combination of genes, with one important exception. Identical (monozygotic) twins are formed from one zygote that splits in two, creating two zygotes with identical genes.

5. Most inherited characteristics are polygenic and multifactorial, the result of the interaction of many genes and a combination of numerous environmental factors.

From Genotype to Phenotype

6. Genes can interact in many ways. In one of the most intriguing patterns of heredity, a person who inherits a dominant gene and a recessive gene for a particular characteristic develops the phenotype of the dominant gene. If two recessive genes are present, then the phenotype expresses the recessive form of the characteristic.

7. Males inherit just one X chromosome, from their mother, and so, through X-linked inheritance, they have a greater chance than females of inheriting certain harmful recessive genes, including the gene for color blindness.

Determining Genetic Influences

8. Most physical and psychological characteristics are polygenic and multifactorial, the result of the interaction of many genetic and environmental influences.

9. Genes affect almost every human trait, including intellectual abilities, personality patterns, and mental illness. At the same time, the environment—from the moment of conception throughout life—constantly influences genetic tendencies. Gene-environment interaction is thus ongoing and complex, and virtually impossible to separate out.

Genetic and Chromosomal Abnormalities

10. Chromosomal abnormalities occur when the zygote has too few or too many chromosomes. Most of these defects involve the sex chromosomes. The most common autosomal abnormality occurs when an extra chromosome attaches itself to the twenty-first pair, causing Down syndrome. Middle-aged couples are more likely than younger parents to produce a child with a chromosomal abnormality.

11. Every individual carries some genes for genetic handicaps and diseases. However, since many of those genes are recessive, and many of the diseases involved are polygenic, or multifactorial, most babies will not inherit a serious genetic defect.

Genetic Counseling

12. Genetic testing and an evaluation of family background can help predict whether a couple will have a child with a genetic problem. If there is a high probability that they will, they can consider several options, such as adoption, remaining childless, obtaining prenatal diagnosis and, if necessary, abortion. In some cases, appropriate postnatal treatment may remedy or alleviate the problem.

KEY TERMS

zygote (68)
gene (69)
DNA (deoxyribonucleic acid) (69)
chromosome (69)
twenty-third pair (70)
XX (70)
XY (70)
monozygotic twins (71)
dizygotic twins (71)
polygenic inheritance (72)
multifactorial characteristics (72)
genotype (72)
phenotype (72)
additive pattern (72)
dominant-recessive pattern (72)

carrier (73)
X-linked genes (73)
environment (75)
syndrome (81)
Down syndrome (trisomy-21) (81)
fragile-X syndrome (83)
genetic counseling (84)
markers (88)
Human Genome Project (88)
alphafetoprotein (AFP) (89)
sonogram (89)
amniocentesis (89)
chorionic villi sampling (CVS) (89)

KEY QUESTIONS

1. How do chromosomes determine the sex of a zygote?

2. In what ways do monozygotic (identical) twins differ from dizygotic (fraternal) twins?

3. What are the differences among additive, dominant, and recessive genes?

4. What research strategies are used to determine genetic influences on psychological characteristics?

5. How does the interaction between heredity and environment differ for physical traits, such as height, and psychological traits, such as shyness?

6. Why is it that some people who have a genetic predisposition for schizophrenia or alcoholism never develop these conditions?

7. What are some of the causes of chromosomal defects?

8. What are some of the factors that determine if a couple is at risk of bearing a child with genetic abnormalities?

9. How can genetic counseling help those parents who are at risk of bearing a child with genetic problems?

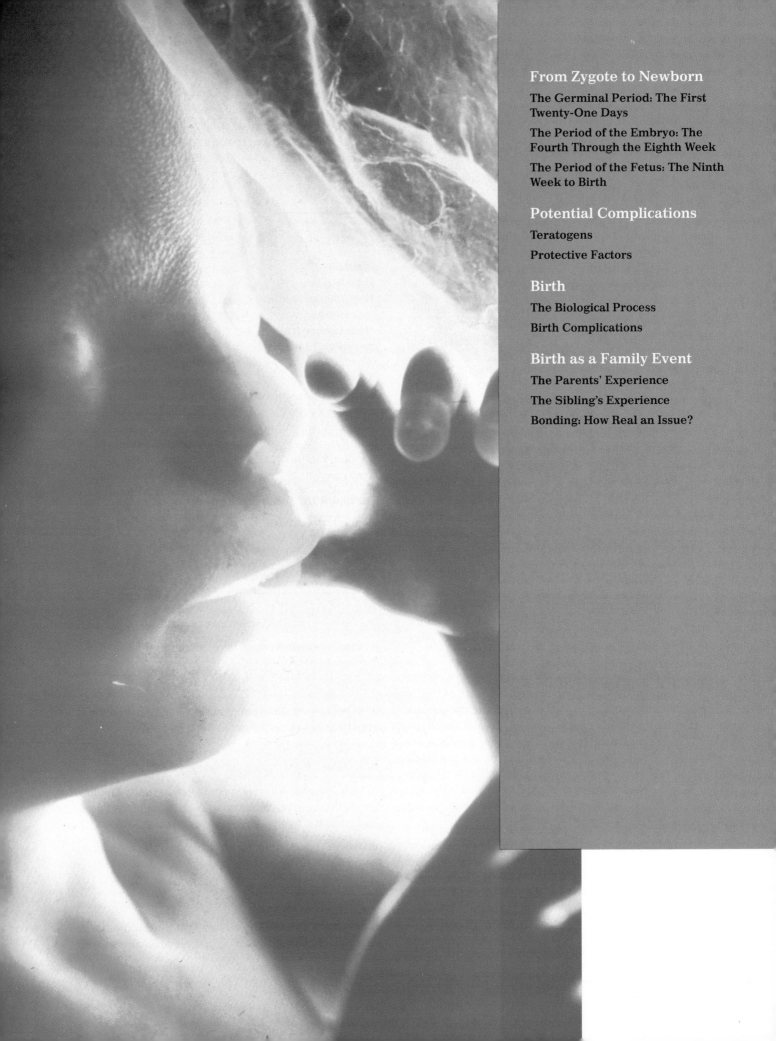

CHAPTER 4

Prenatal Development and Birth

Until the latter half of this century, little serious thought was given to prenatal development: its specifics were known only in a general way, their significance to lifelong development almost completely unsuspected. Thanks to innovations in modern medical research, we now know a great deal about the first nine months of human development, a period that represents the most rapid growth and transformation of the entire life span. Most important, we now recognize that the context and circumstances of prenatal development and birth extend far beyond the immediate biological events, with consequences that affect the child and family for years to come. In this chapter, we will examine in detail the fascinating events of these early days, as we explore a number of crucial questions and issues surrounding them, including the following:

What is the normal process of growth from the one-celled zygote to the newborn infant?

At what point does the developing organism become able to survive outside the mother's body?

What factors in prenatal development can cause birth defects or result in later problems?

What factors can increase the chances that prenatal development will result in a healthy baby?

Why does birth weight vary from less than 2 pounds to more than 10?

How and when does the bond between parents and child form?

As you learned in Chapter 1, to understand any one period of the development of any one individual, we must consider a complex interaction among domains, systems, and contexts. This is no less true for the first 9 months of life than for the remaining 900 or so.

Obviously, one major focus of a chapter on prenatal development and birth will be on the astounding physical growth that transforms a single-celled zygote into a fully formed human baby. However, to understand that physical growth, we must also look at the larger context in which it occurs, including the mother-to-be's health and health habits, the relationship between the parents-to-be, and the various customs and laws that influence prenatal care, particularly those related to such issues as the prevention and treatment of disease, drug use, and the medical management of pregnancy. Because of variations in the overall context, some infants begin life much more capable than others—biologically, cognitively, and psychologically. Understanding prenatal development in all its complexity is therefore essential to helping every developing person enter life better prepared for the years that lie ahead.

From Zygote to Newborn

The process of human growth from a single-celled zygote into a fully developed baby is generally discussed in terms of three main periods. The first three weeks of development are called the **germinal period** (also called the period of the ovum); from the fourth week through the eighth week is the **period of the embryo;** and from the ninth week until birth is the **period of the fetus.***

The Germinal Period: The First Twenty-One Days

Within hours after conception, the one-celled zygote starts to travel down the Fallopian tube and to begin the process of cell division and growth, first dividing into two cells, which soon become four, then eight, then sixteen, and so on (see Figure 4.1). By the end of the first week, the multiplying cells form two distinct masses, a circular mass of outer cells enclosing a mass of inner cells. The outer cells will become the placenta and other membranes that protect and nourish the inner cells, which will become the embryo and then the fetus.

When this body of cells arrives at the uterus, the outer mass begins the process of **implantation,** burrowing into the uterine lining and rupturing its tiny blood vessels to obtain nourishment. This process, in turn, initiates hormonal changes that interrupt the woman's usual menstrual cycle and trigger bodily changes that signify the beginning of pregnancy.

If all goes well, the cell mass will be securely implanted by the tenth day following conception, not to break away until contractions some nine months later begin the birth process. It is important to note, however, that implantation is far from automatic: an estimated 58 percent of all conceptions fail to become properly implanted (Gilbert et al., 1987), thereby terminating the pregnancy (see Table 4.1). Successful implantation marks the end of the most hazardous period of pregnancy.

Figure 4.1 *Within thirty-six hours after fertilization, the one-celled zygote divides into two cells, and then, about one day later, it divides into four cells, as shown here. At the time of implantation, about six days after fertilization, the developing organism consists of more than one hundred cells, each one much smaller than the original cell, but each containing exact copies of the genes and chromosomes in the zygote.*

*Technically speaking, the name of the developing human organism changes several times, depending on the precise stage of development. While there is no need for the student to learn them all, the curious might be interested to know that the organism that begins as a zygote becomes a morula, a blastocyst, a gastrula, a neurula, an embryo, and a fetus before it finally becomes an infant (Moore, 1988).

TABLE 4.1
The Hazards of Prenatal Development

The Germinal Period

From the moment of conception until 21 days later, when the neural tube forms, 58 percent of all developing organisms fail to grow or to implant properly, and thus do not survive the germinal period. Most of these were grossly abnormal.

The Period of the Embryo

From 22 days until 56 days after conception, during which time all the major external and internal body structures begin to form, about 20 percent of all embryos are aborted spontaneously.

The Period of the Fetus

From the eighth week after conception on, about 5 percent of all fetuses are aborted spontaneously before viability at 22 weeks, or are stillborn after 22 weeks.

Birth

Only 31 percent of all conceptions survive prenatal development to become living newborn babies.

Source: Moore, 1988; Gilbert et al., 1987; Volpe, 1987.

While the outer cells are implanting, the inner cells divide into three layers, which will eventually develop into the major body systems. The outer layer becomes the skin and nervous system; the middle layer becomes the circulatory, excretory, and reproductive systems, as well as the muscles and bones; and the inner layer becomes the digestive and respiratory systems. Soon the first perceptible sign of body formation appears, specifically, a fold in the middle of the cell mass that becomes the **neural tube,** the precursor of the **central nervous system,** which will include the brain and the spinal cord. Once the neural tube is fully formed, the mass of cells is ready for a new name, the **embryo.**

The Period of the Embryo: The Fourth Through the Eighth Week

During the embryonic period, growth proceeds in two directions: from the head downward—referred to as **cephalo-caudal development** (literally, "from head to tail")—and from the center, that is, the spine, outward—referred to as **proximo-distal development** (literally, "from near to far"). Thus the most vital organs and body parts form first, before the extremities.

Following this pattern, in the fourth week after conception, the head and blood vessels begin to develop and the heart starts to beat, making the cardiovascular system the first organ system to begin to function (Moore, 1988). At the end of the first month, eyes, ears, nose, and mouth start to form, and buds that will become arms and legs appear, as does a taillike appendage extending from the spine. The embryo is now about ⅕ of an inch long (5 millimeters), about 7,000 times the size of the zygote it was twenty-eight days before.

Even more rapid growth during the early weeks of life occurs in the **placenta** (see Figure 4.3, p. 97), where blood vessels from the mother are interwoven with vessels that lead directly to the umbilical cord, and thus to the circulatory system, of the developing embryo. A network of membranes in the placenta allows substances to be exchanged, through diffusion, from one blood system to another. This makes it possible for the developing organism to have its own independent blood supply, while obtaining oxygen and nourishment from the mother and ridding itself of body wastes by passing them, through the placenta, into the mother's system.

The Second Month

About five weeks after conception, following the proximo-distal sequence, the upper arms, then the forearms, the hands, and the fingers appear. Legs, feet, and toes, in that order, follow a few days later, each having the beginning of a cartilage skeletal structure. By the end of the second month, the fingers and toes, which originally were webbed together, are separate.

Eight weeks after conception, the embryo weighs about ⅓₀ of an ounce (1 gram) and is about 1 inch (2.5 centimeters) long. The head has become more rounded and the features of the face are fully formed. The embryo has all the basic organs (except sex organs) and features of a human being, including elbows and knees, fingers and toes, and even buds for the first baby teeth. The tail is no longer visible, having become incorporated in the lower spine at about 55 days after conception (Moore, 1988). The organism is now

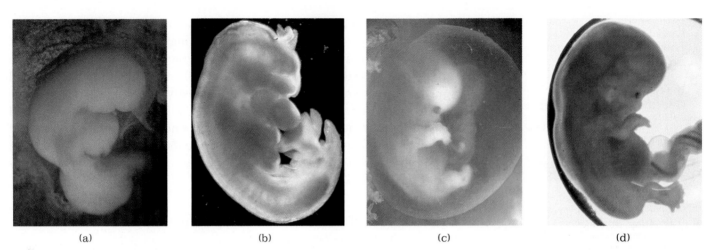

(a)   (b)   (c)   (d)

Figure 4.2 *During the first months of life, growth is rapid and proceeds from the head downward and from the center outward. (a) At about four weeks past conception, the embryo is only about ¹/₅ inch long (5 millimeters), but already the head (top right) has taken shape. (b) At five weeks past conception, the embryo has grown to twice the size it was at four weeks. Its heart, which has been beating for a week now, is visible, as is what appears to be a primitive tail, which will soon be enclosed by skin and protective tissue at the tip of the backbone (the coccyx). (c) By seven weeks, the organism is about an inch long (2 centimeters). Eyes, nose, the digestive system, and even the first stage of toe formation can be seen. (d) At eight weeks, the overall proportions of the developing organism are close enough to those of a full-term baby that we can recognize this 1¹/₂-inch-long (4-centimeter) creature as a human fetus complete with feet, the final step of the proximo-distal development.*

ready for another name, the **fetus,** a term that denotes that the basic body parts have been formed but that the developing organism is dependent on the mother's body.

The Period of the Fetus: The Ninth Week to Birth

During the third month, muscles develop and cartilage begins to be replaced by bone. All the major organs complete their formation, including stomach, heart, lungs, and kidneys.

It is also during this period that the sex organs take discernible shape. The first stage of their development actually occurs in the sixth week, with the appearance of the *indifferent gonad,* a cluster of cells that can develop into male or female sex organs. If the fetus is male *(XY),* one gene on the *Y* chromosome sends a biochemical signal late in the embryonic period that triggers the development of male sex organs, first the testes at about seven weeks and then the other male organs during the early fetal period. If the embryo is female and therefore has no *Y* chromosome, no signal is sent, and the fetus begins to develop female sex organs at about the ninth week (Koopman et al., 1991). Not until the twelfth week after conception are the external male or female genital organs fully formed (Moore, 1988).

By the end of the third month, the fetus can and does move almost every part of its body, kicking its legs, sucking its thumb, and even squinting and frowning. The 3-month-old fetus swallows amniotic fluid, digests it, and urinates, providing its tiny organs with practice for the day when it will take in nourishment on its own. This active little creature is now fully formed—including its fingerprint pattern—and weighs approximately 3 ounces (86 grams) and is about 3 inches (7.5 centimeters) long.*

---

*During early prenatal development, growth is very rapid, and considerable variation occurs between one fetus and another, especially in body weight. The numbers given above—3 months, 3 ounces, 3 inches—have been rounded off for easy recollection. (For those on the metric system, "100 days, 100 millimeters, 100 grams" is similarly useful.) Actually, at twelve weeks after conception, the average fetus weighs about 1½ ounces (45 grams), while at fourteen weeks, the average weight is about 4 ounces (114 grams) (Moore, 1989).

The Second Trimester

As you are no doubt aware, pregnancy is often referred to in terms of three-month-long segments, called **trimesters.** Our discussion so far has involved the events of the first trimester, during which the body structures and organs all form. In terms of basic appearance, only details are added during the second trimester (the fourth, fifth, and sixth months): hair, including eyebrows and eyelashes, begins to grow, and fingernails, toenails, and buds for adult teeth form.

However, in terms of functioning, critical maturation occurs in the second trimester. While the first pulsations of the primitive heart begin early in the first trimester, in the second, the heartbeat becomes much stronger and can be heard with a stethoscope. The digestive and excretory systems develop, as the fetus begins to suck, swallow, and urinate. Weight increases tenfold, a typical fetus increasing from about 3 ounces (86 grams) at the beginning of this trimester to 30 ounces (860 grams) at the end. This increasing body mass means that most women feel first the flutter, and then the thump, of fetal arms and legs during the second trimester.

Most important, during the second trimester the brain undergoes appreciable development. From the beginning to the end of this period, it increases sixfold in size (Moore, 1988), and toward the end of the period exhibits dramatic maturation. Whereas electrical impulses of the brain had previously been virtually absent, as revealed by a flat brain-wave pattern similar to that of brain death, by the twenty-fourth week, occasional bursts of electrical activity similar to that in the newborn reveal that the brain is becoming functional (Parmelee and Sigman, 1983).

This brain development in the second trimester makes possible the regulation of basic body functions and states (breathing, sleep patterns, and so forth) that may be the critical element in attaining the **age of viability** (sometime between the twentieth and twenty-sixth week after conception). Once that age is attained, the fetus has at least some slight chance of survival outside the uterus, if expert care is available (see A Closer Look on very low birth weight, p. 112.)

The Third Trimester

While the first trimester is the time for building basic structures, and the second is the time for the essential organ and brain maturation that makes survival possible, the third trimester is a period of final prenatal maturation that is truly transforming. An infant born at the beginning of this trimester is a tiny creature requiring intensive hospital care, dependent on life-support systems for nourishment and for every breath. The typical newborn born at the end of this period is a lusty, vigorous baby, ready to thrive at home with mother's milk—no expert help, concentrated air, special food, or technical assistance required. As you can imagine, this change is important psychologically as well as biologically, since a full-term birth in which extraordinary care is unnecessary is obviously less stressful for the infant, and more joyful for the parents. (Preterm infants are discussed further on page 109.)

Two important developments underlying this transformation occur in the respiratory and the cardiovascular systems (Moore, 1988). In the last months of prenatal life, the lungs begin to expand and contract, exercising the muscles that will be needed to breathe by using the amniotic fluid that

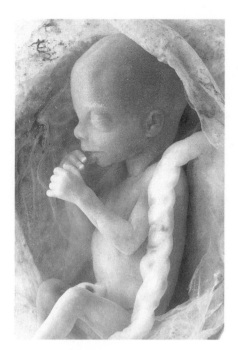

Figure 4.3 *At the end of four months, this fetus, now 6 inches long, looks fully formed, down to the details of eyebrows and fingernails. However, brain development is not yet sufficient to sustain life outside the uterus. For many more weeks, the fetus must depend on the translucent membranes of the placenta and umbilicus (the white cord in the foreground) for survival.*

surrounds the fetus as a substitute for air. At the same time, the valves of the heart go through a final maturation that, at birth, will enable the newborn's circulatory system to function independently.

Brain development is also notable in this period. Beginning about twenty-nine weeks after conception, the brain is rarely completely inactive. By about thirty-four weeks, measurement of the brain's electrical activity reveals distinct sleeping and waking patterns (Parmelee and Sigman, 1983).

In addition, during these final months, the fetus gains substantial weight, increasing, on average, from about 2 pounds (900 grams) at the beginning of the trimester to 7½ pounds (3,400 grams) at the end. An important part of this weight is fat, which will provide a protective layer of insulation when the developing person no longer is surrounded by the mother's body warmth. The added weight also provides nourishment and vitamins that will be used in the early days after birth, when the mother's supply of breast milk is not yet fully established. Thus, until the due date is reached, thirty-eight weeks after conception, every week of prenatal life increases the likelihood, not only of survival, but of healthy infancy.

Potential Complications

As suggested by the fact that less than a third of all conceptions survive to birth, the transformation from the one-celled zygote to viable human being can be highly hazardous. Fortunately, most babies who complete this transformation are born healthy and capable, ready for eighty years or so of life. A minority, about 3 percent, have major malformations that are apparent at birth, and another 3 percent have severe problems, such as deafness or mental retardation, that become apparent within the first year (Moore, 1989). In addition, another group, perhaps as many as 15 percent, are born susceptible to learning problems of various sorts, such as difficulty in developing language or social skills. The cause of such structural, cognitive, and behavioral problems can rarely be traced to any one factor. Even in the case of major abnormalities, the origins are mostly unknown (see Table 4.2).

In the preceding chapter we examined those congenital problems that have definite chromosomal and genetic origins. Here we will turn our attention to those congenital problems that are significantly influenced by environmental factors.

Teratogens

Until recently, little scientific credence was given to the possibility that an unborn child might be affected directly by specific diseases or other environmental agents to which the mother-to-be is exposed. However, thanks to modern **teratology***, the study of birth defects, we now know that hundreds of such agents can, in fact, cause widespread damage to the embryo and

TABLE 4.2
Estimated Causes of Major Congenital Malformations

Cause	Percent
Chromosomal abnormalities	6
Single-gene defects	7
Environmental factors	7
Multifactorial inheritance	25
Unknown sources	54

Source: Moore, 1989.

*"Teratology" stems from the Greek word *tera*, meaning "monster." Coined over a century and a half ago, the term was born out of ignorance of the true nature of birth defects and is no longer read literally. Today, teratology includes the study of all substances that might harm prenatal development, including not only those that lead to visible abnormalities but also those that do invisible damage to the brain, or that threaten the usual course of pregnancy and birth.

Common Teratogens: Risks and Risk Reduction

	Risks	Risk Reduction
Diseases	Many diseases, including common viruses, parasites and sexually transmitted diseases, are teratogenic. One of the most devastating is rubella, also known as German measles. Almost every fetus exposed in the first trimester to rubella is affected, with deafness, blindness, and brain damage the most common results. Another highly teratogenic virus is HIV, which is spreading more rapidly among young women of reproductive age than among any other age or gender group. About one in every four infants born to an HIV-positive woman has already caught the virus in the womb, and will die of AIDS, usually before age 3.	The best way to reduce risk from disease is to avoid the illness in the first place. For many diseases, this entails immunizing all preschool children, and/or all nonimmune adolescent girls, practices that have reduced incidence of rubella syndrome children (like David in Chapter 1) by 99 percent since 1965. Unfortunately, the only way known to reduce the risk of AIDS in children is to stop the spread of the virus to adults, through the use of condoms, clean needles, sexual abstinence, and the like, and through preventing pregnancy in HIV-positive women.
Drugs	Many common medicines, including those containing tetracycline, retinoic acid, lithium, Valium, and hormones, are sometimes teratogenic. However, the most widespread and destructive teratogenic drugs are social drugs—from alcohol and cigarettes to heroin and cocaine (see Research Report on pp. 101–102).	Avoiding certain drugs, and limiting doses of others are the best ways to avoid drug teratogens. Before taking any medicine, pregnant women should check with their doctors, and any pregnant woman who cannot stop or markedly reduce her use of social drugs should seek treatment immediately.
Pollutants	Several pollutants, among them lead, mercury, PCBs, radiation, are teratogenic, if a woman is exposed to an unusually high amount. Exposure *before* pregnancy can be a factor, since these substances can be stored in the body a long time, and sometimes indirect exposure can occur. This is particularly a problem for pesticides, herbicides, and fungicides, which can cause slow growth during prenatal development, higher miscarriage rate, and learning disabilities.	Dosage is critically important for pollutants. For the most part, a small amount is harmless. The possible exceptions are chemicals used to kill bugs or weeds, where even a small bit can do damage. This means pregnant women should garden without pesticides, wash fruits and vegetables, and, if other family members work with such chemicals, they should shower afterward and wash their own workclothes separately.

Source: Ades et al., 1991; Goedert et al., 1989; Klebanoff et al., 1990; MacDonald et al., 1988; Molfese, 1989; Peter, 1992; Savitz et al., 1989.

fetus. The harmful agents, or **teratogens**, that have so far been identified range from many viruses and bacteria to various drugs, chemicals, and types of radiation, and the kinds of damage they can cause range from obvious defects, such as physical malformations, to less visible problems, such as language retardation, poor impulse control, or delayed puberty (see the chart above and the Research Report on pp. 101–102).

The link between cause and effect in teratology is often obscure, however. Even when it is known that a particular fetus has been exposed to a specific teratogen, it can rarely be predicted with certainty that a specific defect will be the result. As the Research Report on pages 101–102 makes clear, this is particularly the case with regard to social drugs.

Overall a complex web of both destructive and protective factors results in one baby's being born problem-free, while another is born with several disabilities. The science of teratology is thus a science of **risk analysis,** which attempts to evaluate what factors make prenatal harm more, or less, likely to occur.

Timing of Exposure

One crucial factor that determines whether a specific teratogen will cause harm, and of what nature, is the timing of the developing organism's expo-

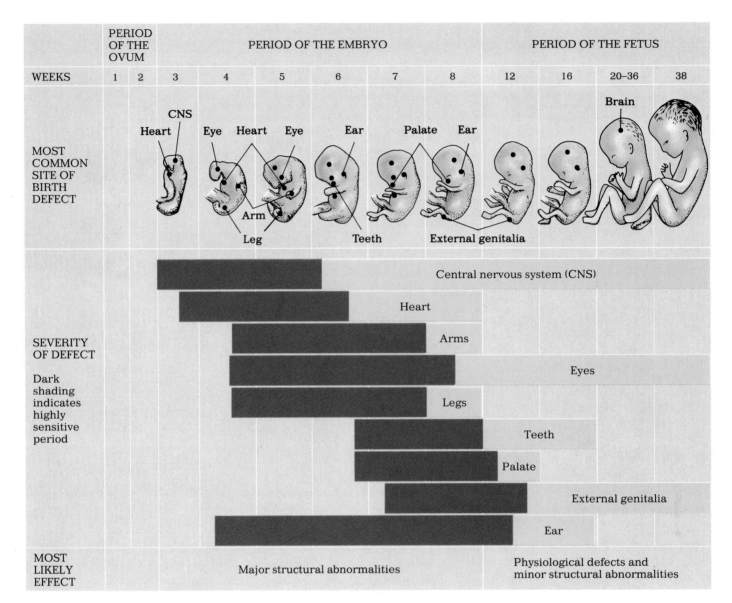

Figure 4.4 *As this chart shows, the most serious damage from teratogens is likely to occur in the first eight weeks after conception. However, damage to many vital parts of the body, including the brain, eyes, and genitals, can occur during the last months of pregnancy as well.*

sure to it. For this reason, the period of the embryo is often called the **critical period,** because teratogenic exposure between the third and ninth week can produce malformations of basic body organs and structure, causing abnormal limbs, or eyes, or spine, for instance. Each body structure has its own most critical time: the eye at about four weeks, the ear and arms at about six weeks, the legs and palate at about seven weeks (see Figure 4.4).

However, with some teratogens, the entire prenatal period is critical. This is particularly true for teratogens that damage the neural networks of the brain, impairing the future child's intellectual and emotional functioning. Such substances are called **behavioral teratogens,** since they chiefly affect the way the child behaves rather than how he or she looks. A 5-year-old who cannot sit quietly and concentrate for more than a minute or an 8-year-old whose handwriting is still illegible may be suffering the effects of a teratogen to which he or she was exposed at any time during prenatal development, from the first hours after conception to the last hours before birth.

RESEARCH REPORT   Social Drugs as Teratogens

The teratogenic damage caused by social drugs usually shows up in behavioral problems, rather than in readily identifiable structural ones, and because such behavioral problems are influenced by many factors not directly related to drug use, teratological research on social drugs is very complex. It is further complicated by the fact that accurate estimates of the total amount of prenatal drug exposure that a particular newborn encountered are hard to come by. Particularly in Western cultures, many pregnant women misrepresent the frequency and quantity of their drug consumption, even to themselves. Keep these complications in mind as you read about the specific teratogenic effects of various drugs. There is no doubt that social drugs are potentially harmful to prenatal development, but much more research is needed before we know all the specifics. Let us begin with the most common drugs, tobacco and alcohol.

Tobacco   Exposure to cigarette smoke is detrimental to the fetus, with the magnitude of harm related to the level of exposure and its duration. Babies born to regular smokers weigh less than they otherwise would, on average 9 ounces (about 250 grams) less, and they are shorter, both at birth and in the years to come. In addition, smoking increases the chances of ectopic (tubal) pregnancy (Coste et al., 1991), stillbirth, premature separation of the placenta from the uterus, and prematurity (Tisi, 1988).

Children whose mothers smoked during pregnancy are also more likely to have a host of problems, including respiratory difficulties (Moessinger, 1989) and learning disabilities, especially in reading, spelling, and verbal expression (Fried and Watkinson, 1990). However, proving that these long-term effects are caused by prenatal exposure to cigarettes is difficult, since pregnant women who smoke are more likely to have additional attributes, including poor health habits and specific personality traits (such as high-strung impatience), that might help account for these physical and cognitive problems (Rush and Callahan, 1989).

Alcohol   Average daily consumption of three or more drinks (a drink being defined as one beer, one glass of wine, or a single shot of liquor), or binge-drinking of five or more drinks on any one occasion, is teratogenic, especially in the first days and weeks after conception. However, most research finds no proven prenatal detriment from moderate drinking, defined as no more than two drinks on any day (Waterson and Murray-Lyon, 1990).

The most obvious effect of prenatal alcohol consumption is **fetal alcohol syndrome (FAS)**, which includes abnor-

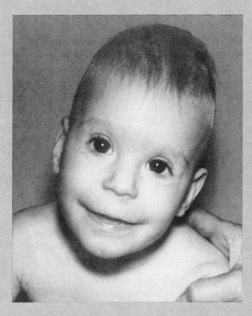

This boy's widely spaced eyes, underdeveloped upper jaw, and flattened nose are three of the typical facial characteristics of children with fetal alcohol syndrome. Many babies born to women who drank alcohol show no signs of FAS; others have more obvious deformities of the eyes and head.

mal facial characteristics (see photo), slowed physical growth, behavior problems (including poor concentration and poor social skills), and mental retardation. FAS does not occur in every fetus exposed to alcohol: likely victims are those who are genetically vulnerable and whose mothers drink more than five drinks on several occasions during the first two months of pregnancy. Incidence varies depending on the culture's encouragement of female alcohol consumption, but a review of studies in Australia, North America, and Europe suggests that overall, about 1 in every 550 babies has FAS, making it a leading cause of mental retardation in the industrialized world (Abel and Sokol, 1987).

Similar but less pronounced symptoms occur in **fetal alcohol effects (FAE)**. Some researchers believe that almost every child whose mother consumes a daily average of three or more drinks in the first month of pregnancy experiences some FAE. According to one estimate, the average intellectual deficit of such a child is 5 IQ points (Streissguth et al., 1989).

(continued on p. 102)

One study found that, compared to babies born to women who drank moderately or not at all, children whose mothers drank beyond the three-drink threshold had almost twice as many minor physical anomalies, such as widely spaced eyes, flat noses, missing earlobes, crooked fingers or toes, and so forth (Ernhart et al., 1989). This study also highlights the complications of research in this area. For one thing, almost everyone has, through natural variations, one or more minor learning or physical problems that resemble the kinds of difficulties caused by prenatal drug exposure. In this particular study, the children of heavy drinkers averaged four or more such anomalies. But at the same time, the children of the abstainers and moderate drinkers averaged two to three.

Obviously, then, distinguishing "natural" problems from drug-related ones is a difficult, sometimes impossible, task. In addition, even for a legal drug such as alcohol, accurate assessment of prenatal drug use remains problematic. In this study, for example, when asked during pregnancy about their drinking patterns, only 4 percent of the women reported that they exceeded three drinks a day; but when asked to recall their prenatal drinking five years later, 12 percent admitted drinking beyond that limit. The later reports were seemingly more accurate, since they correlated more strongly with the rate of birth anomalies than did the initial report. That their children did not seem seriously harmed five years after the fact apparently allowed women to be more truthful about drinking during pregnancy.

Overall, this and other research suggests that efforts to prevent FAS and FAE should focus more on specific programs for those women of childbearing age who have difficulty limiting their consumption to a drink or two per day than on promoting the idea that all pregnant women should totally abstain.

Marijuana   Marijuana is another behavioral teratogen whose damage is dose-related. Heavy marijuana use produces notable effects on the fetus, as shown by a study that followed the pregnancies of rural Jamaican women living in communities where marijuana smoking is generally acceptable and women are sometimes admired if they can smoke "as hard as a man." Half of these women did not use marijuana during pregnancy, heeding warnings from elders that such use would cause "mashed up brains" and "cracked skin." The other half smoked a daily average of four marijuana cigars, estimated to be fifteen to twenty times stronger than the typical American marijuana cigarette (Lester and Dreher, 1989). Infants born to the heavy users of marijuana showed impairment to their central nervous systems—including a kind of abnormal, high-pitched crying that denotes brain damage.

Compared to this Jamaican study, studies conducted elsewhere, particularly in North America, are less clearcut, partly because smoking marijuana in those countries is likely to be underreported and partly because it is difficult to find control groups like those of the Jamaican study, who were very similar in background and lifestyle to the experimental group but dramatically different in marijuana consumption. As best we can tell, however, there may be a threshold for marijuana as a teratogen, with occasional use doing no harm to the fetus. This threshold is not certain, however: some research finds that even moderate use of marijuana correlates with pregnancy problems of many kinds, including miscarriage, prematurity, and stillbirth, and childhood deficits in language and memory (Fried, 1989; Fried and Watkinson, 1990).

Cocaine   Cocaine use affects the fetus throughout pregnancy as well as immediately before and after birth. Early in pregnancy, the use of cocaine increases the risk of structural damage, specifically to the sex organs (Chasnoff et al., 1988). In addition, cocaine use, even more than that of the other social drugs, causes overall growth retardation, affecting head circumference particularly. Another hazard is that the sudden rush and crash of cocaine—especially when smoked—can cause prenatal convulsions, because the fetal brain and heart cannot withstand the stress of such rapid changes. Cocaine consumption in early labor—contrary to the street notion—makes the birth process longer, not shorter, and increases the risk of complications to the fetus (Skolnick, 1990). If newborns have cocaine in their bloodstreams during the hours after birth, when they must adjust to breathing on their own, they are especially vulnerable to seizures that can cause lasting brain damage. They also show evidence of an unstable central nervous system, trembling, startling, or crying at the slightest disturbance or, alternatively, being unusually sleepy and sluggish in their response to stimulation (Lester, 1991).

As you can see, every social drug can affect the fetus, but specifics as to dose and defect are difficult to assay. Consequently, the wisest course for the pregnant individual is to avoid all such drugs completely. However, as long as such drugs are socially accepted and encouraged, such lonely wisdom may be hard for individuals to attain. This raises the thorny issue of apportioning personal and social responsibility for fetal drug exposure, an issue discussed in the Closer Look on pages 105–106.

Amount of Exposure

A second important factor affecting potential teratogenic damage is the amount of exposure. Especially for teratogenic drugs, the more frequent the exposures and the higher the dose on any one occasion, the greater the likelihood and the severity of damage. For some drugs, such as tobacco, the effect is simply cumulative: each cigarette smoked by a pregnant woman reduces birth weight an additional several milligrams. For other drugs, there is a **threshold effect;** that is, the substance is virtually harmless until the mother-to-be's use of it reaches a certain frequency or dosage level.

Compounding the question of the amount of teratogenic exposure is the possible interaction between teratogenic agents. Sometimes, for example, one drug exacerbates the effects of another. Both marijuana and alcohol may be threshold drugs—teratogenic only at a certain level (Waterson and Murray-Lyon, 1990). However, when taken together, their thresholds may drop, making them potentially harmful in combination at a dosage level that, for each drug separately, would be innocuous (Hingson et al., 1982).

Protective Factors

As indicated earlier, the risk that teratogenic exposure can pose for normal development is often moderated by a variety of protective factors. The developmental process itself has several "built-in" defenses. Many spontaneous abortions—especially those that occur in the first months of pregnancy, when widespread structural damage to the fetus is possible—are part of a natural process that tends to ensure normal development. Further, the fact that growth, especially brain growth, is a lengthy process, means that, in most cases, harm at one point of pregnancy can be overcome if the rest of pregnancy and infancy is healthy. Behavioral teratogens, in particular, usually do not do serious damage unless they are one link in a sequence of risk factors, including extensive teratogenic exposure, birth complications, and a neglectful pattern of child-rearing (Kopp and Kaler, 1989).

Three additional protective factors in pregnancy involve adequate nutrition, prenatal care, and social support.

Nutrition

In developed countries, most pregnant women eat a diet high in calcium and protein, take special vitamin supplements, and gain 25 pounds or more. We now know that this is more than adequate: as long as a woman begins pregnancy reasonably well-nourished and gains at least 15 pounds, she is just as likely to have a healthy, full-term baby as a woman who maintains a special prenatal diet and gains twice that weight (Enkin et al., 1989).

In developing countries, of course, many women begin pregnancy poorly fed, and it is particularly important for them to eat well and gain at least 15 pounds. Studies of malnourished women who were given nutritional supplements in the last three months of pregnancy found that the odds of their having healthy births and bright children were significantly improved (Salt et al., 1988). Even here, however, a developmental perspective is important: a 5-pound newborn can gain weight quickly if adequately fed after birth, and will be unlikely to experience cognitive deficits if nourished intellectually as well as physically during the crucial first two years.

At a more specific level, some intriguing research has raised the possibility that particular nutrients may have protective value against certain defects. In this case it was found that folic acid may help to protect against **neural tube defects**. As you may remember from Chapter 3, in about 1 in every 500 embryos, the neural tube does not grow properly: either the lower spine does not close, causing spina bifida, or the upper part of the central nervous system does not develop, causing anencephaly. Genes clearly play a role in neural tube defects. Not only does the rate of the defects vary by population group (fetuses of British descent, for example, are more vulnerable than those of African or Asian descent), but once a given couple has an infant with a neural tube defect, the chance of their next child having the problem rises to 1 in 30.

In addition, however, recent research suggests that the genetic predisposition to neural tube defects may be moderated by the amount of folic acid (an essential vitamin found in many greens) in the mother-to-be's diet. In one study in England, close to 2,000 pregnant women who had already had a child with a neural tube defect were randomly assigned to one of four conditions: vitamins including folic acid; vitamins without folic acid; folic acid but no other special vitamins; and no special dietary supplements at all. Those women who had additional folic acid, with or without the other vitamins, had far fewer children with a neural tube defect: the folic acid reduced their risk from 1 in 30 to 1 in 100 (Ward et al., 1991).

While this study raises the question of whether other vitamins might protect against other defects, it also raises the need for a caution. The protective effect that other specific vitamins might have against specific prenatal damage is not, in fact, known. However, it is known that megadoses of certain vitamins, notably vitamin A, can *cause* defects. Consequently, pregnant women should never undertake an intense regimen of vitamin supplements in a mistaken effort to "play it safe."

Prenatal Care

Medical care that begins in the first three months of pregnancy and includes prenatal counseling as well as basic screening tests is one of the best predictors of a healthy pregnancy, an easy birth, and a normal newborn (Enkin et al., 1989). Of course, one reason for this correlation—at least where health care is privately paid for—is that early prenatal care is usually sought by women of higher socioeconomic status, and higher SES usually entails a number of factors, such as greater education, that may contribute to a lower risk of pregnancy complications. However, prenatal care, in and of itself, helps women avoid some problems and ameliorate others (Kotch et al., 1992). Two examples make the point, First, in China, a network of workers trained in basic medicine—the so-called barefoot doctors—provide prenatal care even in the most remote and impoverished areas. Consequently, China has achieved a lower rate of birth defects and complications than many wealthier nations (United Nations, 1990). Second, in the United States, Mississippi, one of the lowest-ranking states in terms of both education and income, is now ahead of many richer states in prevention of birth complications and infant mortality because almost every pregnant Mississippian is entitled to free prenatal care (DeParle, 1991).

A CLOSER LOOK	Drug Use in Pregnancy: A Woman's Choice?

As made clear in the earlier Research Report, the link between drug use and prenatal damage is uncertain, dependent on a multitude of factors. Despite this uncertainty, or because of it, it is prudent for women who are pregnant, or who might become so, to abstain from all drugs.

The reality is, however, that most sexually active young women use some sort of drug, at least occasionally, and may continue to do so when they become pregnant (Adams et al., 1989). Indeed, a report from thirty-six hospitals across the United States found that in the case of illicit drugs alone, at least 11 percent of all newborns had been exposed to them—a figure that undoubtedly represents an underestimation, since some hospitals tested only those newborns who had apparent complications or abnormalities (Chasnoff, 1989). Given what we do and do not know about the teratogenic effects of drug use, what kinds of social measures are warranted to protect the developing organism?

Education seems to be an obvious measure, yet current education efforts—especially those involving dramatic poster campaigns and TV spots—may not be entirely helpful. As one review explains:

> Any health education intervention, however well intentioned, may have negative side-effects. A large proportion of women worry about having an abnormal baby. It is important to avoid increasing this [anxiety and stress] unnecessarily. . . Scientific knowledge . . . couched in terms of probabilities . . . is not easily simplified into unambiguous health warnings. . . . Exaggeration of risk may result in women disregarding the warnings altogether. [Waterson and Murray-Lyon, 1990]

Perhaps the responsibility of counseling mothers-to-be should be left to medical personnel, who can individualize their advice. Unfortunately, most obstetricians do not inquire about details of their patients' drug use, and even alcohol consumption is more often ignored than discussed (Waterson and Murray-Lyon, 1990). Indeed, according to one leading medical researcher, "substance abuse in pregnancy may be the most frequently missed diagnosis in all of obstetric and pediatric medicine" (Chasnoff, 1989). Doctors seem particularly oblivious to prenatal drug abuse among their private middle-class, white patients, incorrectly assuming that the problem is more likely among minority-group clinic patients (Skolnick, 1990).

One solution that has been suggested is to establish a national standard of health care available for all pregnant women (Kotch et al., 1992). Ideally, this standard of care would not involve urine toxicologies or other laboratory evaluations, but would bring physicians back to the basic practice of medicine; i.e. taking a complete history and performing a thorough physical exam. This approach would establish the necessity of evaluating lifestyle as a part of medical care and of instructing the patient as to the impact that lifestyle may have on her unborn child [Chasnoff, 1989].

Such an approach seems sensible, but even if prenatal care were changed to include such personalized advice, medical personnel would still encounter situations when their advice is not heard or heeded—even when the risks of prenatal damage seem quite high. Consider the following case, reported by a medical team (Mackenzie et al., 1982).

A pregnant woman with a sixteen-year history of alcohol and phenobarbital abuse was hospitalized in a state of stuporous intoxication, with bruises and other signs that she might have been physically abused. In response to the medical staff's concerns, she denied that she was trying to get rid of the fetus, saying she and her husband wanted the baby "very much." Nevertheless, she admitted to two phenobarbital overdoses during the first two months of pregnancy.

Two months later the woman was hospitalized because of premature labor. The pregnancy was successfully prolonged, but the medical staff became more concerned about the fetus, for blood tests revealed that the woman was continuing to abuse phenobarbital, and while she was in the hospital, she covertly took an overdose of diuretics.

With their fears for the well-being of the fetus mounting, the medical team referred the woman to the local Child Protection Service. She attended several counseling sessions, and thereafter no further episodes of drug abuse were reported. The woman subsequently gave birth to a girl who, though low in birth weight, was full-term and seemingly healthy.

As the authors of the report make clear, a case such as this is likely to have aspects that make the decision to intervene prenatally a highly complex one:

> At no time could fetal damage be demonstrated. Further, it could not be established conclusively that [the mother's] behavior, if continued, would have caused significant harm to the fetus. Yet this behavior indisputably increased the risk of neonatal morbidity and mortality and threatened to compromise the child's developmental capacities.

(continued on p. 106)

The medical team concludes that "protective custody" laws should be extended to allow physicians to safeguard the developing fetus in whatever way seems necessary. Although this baby may have escaped harm, and although the woman attended counseling sessions, the authors feel that they should have had the power to intervene earlier and more aggressively.

However, the prospect of prenatal "protective custody" in the form of jailing or hospitalizing the mother-to-be in order to protect her fetus raises a number of problems. Already some states require official reporting of any evidence of drug use during pregnancy. Because of such laws, some women who most need prenatal care avoid it, fearing that they will be arrested or forced to give up their baby after it is born (Skolnick, 1990; Fost, 1989). (This is no idle fear. As of 1991, at least forty-four American women had been prosecuted for using drugs during pregnancy [Mayer et al., 1992].)

There is also, of course, the question of a woman's right to privacy and self-determination—especially given the uncertainties of predicting the consequences of prenatal drug use. Imagine if every pregnant woman could be legally forced to surrender her freedom of choice—over drug use or any other behavior—because some expert concluded that her fetus *might* be harmed. Certainly many women would consider this cruel and needless punishment. Already, many pregnant women who are hospitalized *voluntarily,* because their doctor determines that their fetus needs constant medical attention, become "bad patients," infuriating their doctors and nurses because they refuse to comply with rules, routines, and orders (Snyder, 1985). One such woman complained, "I'm a person too, not just something that happens to be wrapped around a baby" (quoted in Snyder, 1985).

Yet it is an inescapable fact that a woman's right to self-determination can sometimes threaten a child's future. Consider another example, one from a Native American community in which genetics and prejudice conspire to make alcoholism an epidemic. A Native American man adopted Adam, a Sioux from the Pine Ridge reservation in South Dakota. Adam had been neglected, first by his mother who died of alcoholism when he was 2, and then by state institutions and foster parents. His new father recalls diapering 3-year-old Adam for the first time.

I . . . lay him on the floor, and pulled open the snaps of his pants. Then, while he contemplated the ceiling, I wiped and I powdered. It was impossible to see his thin legs, dominated by the thick balls of his knee joints, without making resolutions. He needed nourishment, care, encouragement, stability. I was determined that his development in every area would match his age before another year had passed. [Dorris, 1989]

Despite the adoptive father's determined efforts to ensure Adam's normal development, Adam was slow to talk, to feed himself, to read. Even as a young adult, he could not do math, tell time, plan ahead, make a friend, keep a job, or think for himself. The cause: fetal alcohol syndrome. The consequence:

My son will forever travel through a moonless night with only the roar of the wind for company . . . He doesn't ask who he is, or why. Questions are a luxury . . . A drowning man is not separated from the lust for air by a bridge of thought—he is one with it—and my son, conceived and grown in an ethanol bath, lives each day in the act of drowning. For him there is no shore.

This poignant image leads to the central issue: At what point, in what ways, and with what sanctions can community concern for the well-being of the unborn supersede parents' rights to live as they choose? The urgency of this question is brought home by Adam's adoptive mother:

Because his mother drank, Adam is one of the earth's damaged. Did she have the right to take away Adam's curiosity, the right to take away the joy he could have felt at receiving a high math score, in reading a book, in wondering at the complexity and quirks of nature? Did she have the right to make him an outcast among children, to make him friendless, to make of his sexuality a problem more than a pleasure, to slit his brain, to give him violent seizures?

On some American Indian reservations, the situation has grown so serious that a jail internment during pregnancy has been the only answer possible . . . Some people have . . . called for the forced sterilization of women who, after previously blunting the lives of several children like Adam, refuse to stop drinking while they are pregnant. This will outrage some women, and men, good people who believe that it is the right of individuals to put themselves in harm's way, that drinking is a choice we make, that a person's liberty to court either happiness or despair is sacrosanct. I believed this too, and yet the poignancy and frustration of Adam's life has fed my doubts, has convinced me that some of my principles were smug, untested. After all, where is the measure of responsibility here? Where, exactly, is the demarcation between self-harm and child abuse? . . . Where do we draw the line? [Erdrich, 1989]

Social Support

Another important protective factor in pregnancy is social support (Norbeck and Tilden, 1983; Pagel et al., 1990). The term *social support* refers to the nature and extent of the social networks to which a person has access. Someone who has extensive social support has several people to depend on for encouragement, advice, and practical help. Objective measures of social networks—for example, how many relatives live nearby, whether or not the woman is married, and so forth—are not as accurate in predicting a healthy birth as subjective indices, such as how helpful the woman feels her relatives and friends are (Molfese et al., 1989). Exactly how social support reduces prenatal complications is not clear, but is seems likely that, at the very least, it facilitates the mother-to-be's efforts to maintain good health habits and regular prenatal care.

This highlights a larger question: What role should society, especially the legal system, play in protecting the fetus from a parent's potentially harmful actions? The issues involved in this question are among the most crucial and controversial in all of development (see A Closer Look, pp. 105–106). Definite answers are elusive, but one thing is clear: in preventing birth defects, much emphasis is rightly placed on the mother—on what she does and does not do—but society has an important role as well, promoting adequate nutrition, prenatal care, and social support, as well as preventing teratogenic diseases, controlling environmental teratogens, reducing drug addiction, and the like.

Birth

The moment of birth represents one of the most radical transitions in life. No longer insulated from the harsh conditions of the outside world, no longer guaranteed the nourishment and oxygen that have been provided through the umbilical cord, the fetus is thrust into a new environment where needs and desires will only sometimes be satisfied. The fetus thus becomes a newborn, a separate human being who nonetheless begins worldly existence almost entirely depending on others. Birth is also a transforming experience for parents and other family members.

We will now look more closely at this moment of transition, and at the first days of life for newborns and their families.

The Biological Process

Birth begins, triggered by biochemical signals from the placenta, about 266 days after conception. Strong and regular contractions of the uterus squeeze the fetus downward, usually head first. Gradually, the repeated pressure causes the cervix to dilate to about 10 centimeters in diameter, allowing the head to move past the cervix, through the vagina, and finally to emerge into the outside world. The head is the widest part of the fetus's body, so once it is born, the rest of the body quickly follows. The entire process can be as quick as a few minutes or as long as a few days, but the average length of time is twelve hours for a first birth and seven hours for subsequent births.

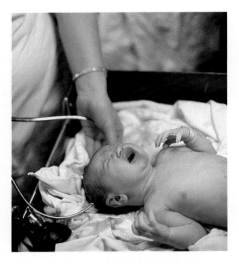

Figure 4.5 *In many hospitals, the first moments after birth are used to make sure the newborn is healthy. Thus the Apgar scale and vital measurements (shown here, the size of the skull) precede cleaning and cradling. This newborn's lusty cry and size indicate that all is well; moments later she should be peacefully snuggled in her mother's arms.*

TABLE 4.3	The Apgar		
Sign	0	1	2
Heart rate	absent	slow (below 100)	rapid (over 100)
Respiratory effort (breathing)	absent	irregular, slow	good, baby is crying
Muscle tone	flaccid, limp	weak, inactive	strong, active
Color	blue, pale	body pink, extremities blue	entirely pink
Reflex irritability	no response	grimace	coughing, sneezing crying

Source: Apgar, 1953.

If the birth is assisted by a trained health worker (as 99 percent of the births in industrial nations and 51 percent of the births worldwide are [United Nations, 1990]), the newborn is immediately checked for problems in body structure and functioning. Usually the doctor, midwife, or nurse rates the infant on the **Apgar** scale (see Table 4.3), assigning a score of 0, 1, or 2 to each of five characteristics—heart rate, breathing, muscle tone, color, and reflex irritability. If the total score is below 4, the newborn is in critical condition and requires immediate expert attention; if the score is between 4 and 6, the baby requires some help establishing normal breathing; if the score is 7 or better, all is well (Harper and Yoon, 1987). The Apgar is taken twice, at one minute after birth and then again four minutes later.

Very few newborns score an immediate perfect 10, but most readily adjust to life outside the womb. Usually, still wet and attached to the umbilical cord, newly born infants cry spontaneously to clear their lungs and then breathe, their chest visibly moving in and out. Soon, as oxygen circulates throughout their system, even their tiny fingers and toes lose their bluish tinge, and they open their eyes wide, staring in seeming awe at the world outside.

Ideally, the newborn is then wiped clean, wrapped for warmth, and given first to the mother to hold and nuzzle at her breast, and then to the father, while the delivery of the placenta is completed. For many new parents, the moments after birth are very special: the baby is usually quiet and alert, and the parents relieved and joyful. In one father's words:

> Christopher was placed in my wife's arms even before the umbilicus was cut; shortly after it was cut, he was wrapped (still dripping and wonderfully new like a chick out of an egg) and given to me to hold while my wife got her strength back. He was very alert, apparently able to focus his attention on me and on other objects in the room; as I held him he blossomed into pink, the various parts of his body turning from deep purple and almost blue, to pink, to rose. I was fascinated by the colors: time stopped. [quoted in Tanzer and Block, 1976]

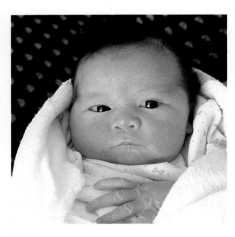

Figure 4.6 *Lily, at 3 days old, has many typical characteristics of the newborn. Her skin is red and splotchy, her chin is recessed, her eyes seem crossed, and there is a red spot on the white of one of them. All of these disappear within a few weeks.*

Birth Complications

As we have seen, birth is usually a short and natural process that results in a healthy newborn. However, this is not always so. When it is not, careful medical monitoring of the birth process and immediate attention to the struggling newborn are saving many lives. Such medical intervention is the main reason that newborn deaths in developed countries in 1990 are less than a third what they were in 1960. While critics contend that many specific intervention practices are overused (e.g., that Cesarean sections account for one out of every four American births), insufficient access to medical technology is a far greater problem, worldwide, than overzealous application (Enkin et al., 1989; Kotch et al., 1992; Bergstrom and Liljestrand, 1988).

However, particularly in developed nations, intensive efforts to save high-risk newborns are not matched by measures to protect against risk in the first place, or, in traumatic cases, to foster development after the emergency is over. Nowhere is this imbalance more evident than in the most common complication of all, birth of an infant weighing less than 2,500 grams.

The Low-Birth-Weight Infant

Most newborns weigh about 3,400 grams (roughly 7½ pounds) and are born full-term, about thirty-eight weeks after conception. As with almost every aspect of development, some variation is completely normal: babies born two weeks early or late, weighing as little as 6 pounds or as much as 9, are just as healthy as those born exactly on time at average weight.

However, worldwide, about one newborn in every seven is **low-birth-weight,** defined internationally as weighing less than 2,500 grams (5½ pounds). Such infants are at risk for many immediate and long-term problems, with the specifics depending partly on the reason for their small size.

Some low-birth-weight infants are simply born too early, before they have reached their full growth, and hence are called **preterm,** defined as being born three or more weeks early. Other low-birth-weight infants weigh substantially less than they should, given how much time has passed since conception. They are called *small-for-dates,* or **small-for-gestational-age (SGA).** A particular baby can be both preterm and small-for-gestational-age, or can be one but not the other. For example, thirty-four weeks after conception, a normal fetus weighs 2,800 grams (almost 6 pounds). If born at that point, a month early, the baby would be preterm but neither small-for-gestational-age nor low-birth-weight. By contrast, a fetus might grow very slowly in the uterus and be born after a full thirty-eight weeks of development weighing only 2,000 grams (about 5 pounds). Such an infant, while not preterm, would be both small-for-gestational-age and low-birth-weight.

The first challenge facing low-birth-weight infants is survival. While they may have many difficulties—maintaining body heat, digesting food, resisting infection—their most critical problem is getting sufficient oxygen. Especially if they are more than a month preterm, their immature reflexes often do not regulate breathing properly. Many experience **respiratory distress syndrome,** the leading cause of preterm death.

Within developed countries, highly technical medical intervention after birth now allows most low-birth-weight infants to live. Indeed, increased survival of very-low-birth-weight infants—those weighing under 1,500 grams (less than 3½ pounds)—is the main reason infant mortality in the United States was down to about 1 in every 110 births in 1990, less than half what it was in 1970, when 1 out of every 50 babies died before age 1. Seventeen other countries, Canada, Japan, and the Scandinavian nations among them, have even lower infant-death rates—not primarily because of intensive postnatal care but because of extensive prenatal care, which results in fewer early, underweight births (see Figure 4.7, p. 111) (Hilts, 1991; Schiff, 1992).

Causes of Low Birth Weight

The most common and direct cause of low birth weight is maternal malnutrition, especially during the last trimester of pregnancy. Another leading cause is the mother's poor overall health, or her poor health habits, including drug abuse. Virtually every social drug impairs fetal nourishment and precipitates labor, causing both preterm and SGA births. In addition, fetal nutrition can be affected by genetic handicaps, prenatal infections, and malfunctioning of the placenta or umbilical cord.

Another common cause of low birth weight, even when the mother and fetus are both healthy, is multiple pregnancies. Twins usually gain weight more slowly than a single fetus does. They also tend to be born early, by three weeks on average. As a result, the typical twin weighs about 5 pounds. Triplets tend to be born even earlier and to weigh even less.

Of particular concern for those interested in child development is that many of these factors are related to poverty. The link between poverty and maternal malnutrition is an obvious example. Poverty is also linked to less education and more stressful living conditions, and these, in turn, are related to poorer health, pregnancies at younger ages, and greater exposure to teratogens of all kinds, from crack cocaine to air pollution. Malfunctions of the placenta and umbilical cord are more likely when pregnancies are closely spaced, and such spacing occurs more often in women of low income. Socioeconomic influences are also a powerful factor in the outcome of multiple pregnancies. Early and adequate medical care can result in newborn twins who weigh 7 pounds each rather than 2, but as noted, especially where most medical care is privately paid for, the likelihood of a pregnant woman obtaining prenatal care in the first half of pregnancy is directly related to her income. Thus sociopolitical factors are an underlying cause of low birth weight, and help explain the wide national and international variations apparent in Figure 4.7 and in the following statistics:

1. Of the 22 million low-birth-weight infants born worldwide each year, 21 million are from developing countries (Bergstrom and Liljestrand, 1988).

2. Developing countries in the same general region, with similar ethnic populations, can have markedly different low-birth-weight rates. Colombia's rate, for example, is 50 percent higher than that of Venezuela, whose per capita income is triple that of Colombia.

3. In many developed countries, including the United States, the rate of low birth weight in the inner cities is more than double that of the nearby suburbs.

4. Ethnic-group variations within nations tend to follow socioeconomic, rather than genetic, patterns (Klineman et al., 1991). The most telling example in the United States is the rate of low birth weight for infants of African-American descent, which is 12.4 percent, more than twice the rates for whites and Asian-Americans, who, as a whole, are considerably higher in socioeconomic standing. The socioeconomic influences behind these differences are underscored by the fact that wealthier African-Americans have lower rates of low birth weight than poor African-Americans do. Similarly, among Latino groups, the rate among Puerto Ricans is 9 percent, whereas the rate for the most affluent group, the Cuban-Americans, is 6 percent. There

Figure 4.7 *Although the incidence of low birth weight varies greatly among developed and underdeveloped countries, socioeconomic factors, such as maternal malnutrition and poverty, have been identified as the underlying cause. In the United States, the rate of low birth weight is higher in the inner cities and poorer rural states.*

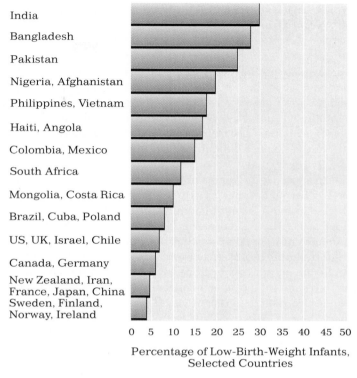

India	
Bangladesh	
Pakistan	
Nigeria, Afghanistan	
Philippines, Vietnam	
Haiti, Angola	
Colombia, Mexico	
South Africa	
Mongolia, Costa Rica	
Brazil, Cuba, Poland	
US, UK, Israel, Chile	
Canada, Germany	
New Zealand, Iran, France, Japan, China Sweden, Finland, Norway, Ireland	

0   5   10   15   20   25   30   35   40   45   50

Percentage of Low-Birth-Weight Infants, Selected Countries

Source: United Nations.

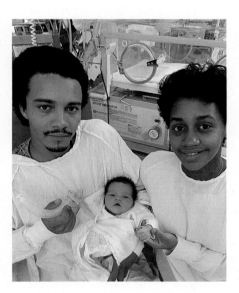

Figure 4.8 *Pictured here is one of the increasingly lucky low-birth-weight infants, who, thanks to medical technologies, have twice the chance of surviving today than they had twenty years ago. The next step is for her parents and community to provide the right mix of attention, patience, and stimulation for her intellectual and social development. She may be fortunate here too: unlike many low-birth-weight infants, she seems to have two parents who are ready and able to give her what she needs.*

is one surprise, however: the Mexican-American rate is only 5.8 percent, perhaps because social support for pregnant women is so extensive that it helps to overcome socioeconomic liabilities.

Consequences of Low Birth Weight

A number of factors in the early days and months of life may put the low-birth-weight infant at risk, especially if the birth was more than six weeks early and if the birth weight was under 1,500 grams. Many such infants experience brain damage as a result of episodes of **anoxia**—a temporary lack of oxygen—or of cerebral hemorrhaging (Beckwith and Rodning, 1991). In addition, the immediate care of such infants is dictated by precaution against disease and infections. Often they are confined to isolettes or are continuously hooked up to medical machinery. Consequently, they are deprived of certain kinds of stimulation, such as the regular handling involved in feeding and bathing a newborn. At the same time, these infants are subject to a number of experiences unknown to the normal infant, such as breathing with a respirator and being fed intravenously.

Parents are also deprived and stressed. They cannot cradle and care for their infant normally, and they must cope with uncertainty, and perhaps with sorrow, guilt, and anger, as well. This can impede the start of normal parent-infant interactions.

As time goes by, difficulties in cognitive development may become apparent as well. Infants who were of low birth weight but had no obvious impairments are more distractible and slower to talk. Such infants sometimes have problems with concentration and language development throughout childhood (Lindahl et al., 1988; Vohr et al., 1989; Robertson et al., 1990).

A CLOSER LOOK   Very-Very-Low-Birth-Weight Infants

A dramatic improvement has occurred over the past twenty years in the survival rate of very tiny infants—those under 1,000 grams. In 1970, virtually all of them died; now about 50 percent survive. Some of the survivors will live essentially normal lives. Unfortunately, some will not. About one-third will be severely handicapped, and another third will have learning difficulties in primary school (Beckwith and Rodning, 1991).

Ironically, the very same medical interventions that save lives sometimes create lifelong handicaps, among them blindness (from the administering of high concentrations of oxygen to aid breathing), cerebral palsy (from brain damage that occurred during the emergency birth), and cognitive deficits (from hemorrhaging during surgery to repair heart and respiratory failure). With very-very-low-birth-weight infants, a choice must sometimes be made between two risks: the risk of visual and intellectual impairment versus the risk of early death (Stevenson and Sunshine, 1987). For all concerned, the choice can be agonizing.

One example makes the point:

Debbie and Bill Lonstein's daughter Joan was born 15 weeks prematurely . . . During her four months in Georgetown's Intensive Care Nursery, she suffered the most serious degree of brain hemorrhaging, and her lungs were badly damaged. Joan is home now, but the uncertainty continues. She may have severe brain damage and cerebral palsy. She may never be able to swallow or suck. "When I hold her in my arms, she's my baby and I want her to live," says Debbie. "We appreciate every day we have with her, but sometimes you can't help but wonder whether this is the best for her. We don't know that she'll ever be able to enjoy her life . . . "

Her husband adds: "There was a time when we were afraid she would die. Now there are times when we're afraid she'll live. Without this technology, she would have died naturally, and we wouldn't have had to ask ourselves these questions. Maybe that would have been better." [Kantrowitz et al., 1988]

This harsh reality has raised a social dilemma. Parents and doctors alike obviously wish every newborn the fullest chance of survival. But some experts question "the practice of providing highly sophisticated and very costly therapies to the extremely small newborns . . . when the probability of intact survival remains very low" (Nordio et al., 1986). It costs about $400,000 to save one 2-pound infant. If the same money were spent on the prevention of very, very low birth weight, there is no doubt that many more lives would be saved and the total hardship and disability would be much less.

Further, the intensive effort to save the life of a tiny baby is seldom matched in the care of the infant once the crisis is over. Few parents are prepared to understand the needs of the very tiny, immature infant, or to cope with the

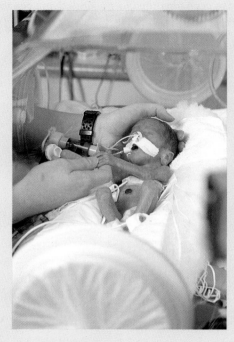

Born weighing only 2 pounds, this infant's heart rate, breathing, temperature, and blood acidity will be monitored continually until he reaches a weight of about 5½ pounds. Although his condition appears to be extremely fragile, current medical technologies give him an excellent chance of survival. However, the medical environment required to meet his most critical physical needs may put him at risk for serious impairment.

demands of the special infant at home. Medical insurance does not usually cover at-home care, and specialized education for children is rarely available until they are preschool age—years after such help is required. Many such children spend months, even years, in custodial care in hospitals because no other alternative is available.

Most developmentalists feel that the choice should not be between ensuring the survival of one tiny infant and providing early prenatal care and nutritional supplements for a dozen high-risk pregnancies. No one would want to suggest that ensuring the survival of any child's life is not worth the cost, but many question our myopia in focusing too narrowly on high-tech heroics: "Our ability to offer expensive, cutting-edge technological support to 1-kilogram infants of homeless mothers contrasts sadly with our inability (or unwillingness) to provide housing for their mothers" (Paneth, 1992). At the same time, it is clear that in the earliest stages of life, as at any point in the life span, the best medicine is preventive medicine that considers family context.

Remedies and Recovery

Recognizing the effects that early hospital experiences can have on low-birth-weight infants, many hospitals now provide special massages to compensate for the infant's lack of normal stimulation, a practice that has been shown to enhance weight gain (Field and Schanberg, 1990). To facilitate early parent-infant interaction, many hospitals also encourage parents to be with their baby as soon as medically possible, perhaps holding and feeding the infant, perhaps simply visiting through the plastic of the isolette.

With time, most parents and preterm infants adjust to each other, just as parents and full-term infants do. For example, parent-infant attachment (explained on pp. 185–190) is often considered a sensitive indication of the overall relationship between a child and parent. A recent longitudinal study of middle-class families found that, even with infants who weighed less than 1,500 grams at birth, secure attachment was just as likely to develop by 18 months as it was with normal-birth-weight infants (Easterbrooks, 1989).

Also with time, most learning problems that low-birth-weight children exhibit in the first years become less problematic, although much depends on the particular family, school, and community. Sadly, but not surprisingly, children born into families of lower socioeconomic status are more likely to continue to have learning problems than are children raised in middle-class families (Beckwith and Rodning, 1991; Butler and Golding, 1986). This is largely because families with little education or income have fewer resources of their own, and the quality of preschool education or of additional medical help available is, apparently, not enough to make up the difference. However, according to one controlled study, special help for such families—in this case, visitors who taught the mothers how to encourage their infants' development, with intensive day care in the second year of life—can result in substantial intellectual growth for the low-birth-weight child.

Overall, low birth weight is a risk factor for slower development, but unless it is actually a symptom of some genetic disorder or teratogenic impairment, or is associated with medical problems soon after birth, the deficits related to it can be overcome. As with so much of development, responsive caregiving can make the difference. Only when the infant is very, very tiny—under 1,000 grams—are early problems unlikely to disappear (see A Closer Look, p. 112).

Birth as a Family Event

Simply describing the sequence and procedures of birth tells little about how the participants are affected by their experience. The psychological and social effects of birth and the days thereafter may have profound and long-lasting influences on all family members.

The Parents' Experience

As we have seen, a number of biological and medical factors can interact to determine whether a birth is fairly simple or complicated. However, psychological factors are also important in determining both the mother's and the father's overall experience of the birth. Psychological factors can make a

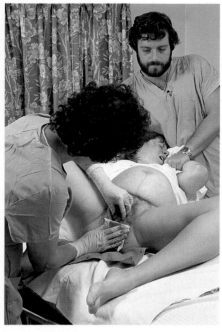

(a)

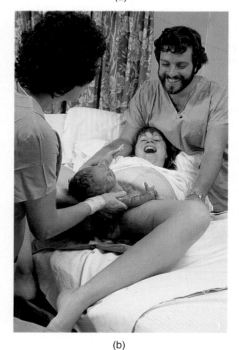

(b)

Figure 4.9 *Many hospitals have tried to make the settings for hospital births more homelike, as in this "birthing room." This birth occurs on a bed, not a steel table, and this woman is aided by a midwife and her husband rather than by unfamiliar doctors and nurses.*

long labor exhilarating, and a short one terrifying. They can make both parents swear "never again" after what physicians would call an easy birth, or they can make even an emergency Cesarean so rewarding that the couple are ready to plan a repeat experience. Two psychological factors that can be especially important are preparation for childbirth and the father's direct involvement in the birth process.

Preparation for Childbirth

Until very recently, first-time parents-to-be often approached childbirth with negative feelings picked up from television dramas or novels. Indeed, one study (Leifer, 1980) of women who were pregnant for the first time found that almost all had negative attitudes about giving birth. Some attributed their apprehension to television programs in which, as one woman put it, "whenever they have a woman bearing a child, it seems like she's screaming horribly or she's fainting, she can't control herself." Others had picked up their attitudes from their mothers and older women whose view generally seemed to be "It's horrible at the time but . . . you soon forget it."

Fortunately, this situation is changing as more and more parents-to-be prepare for birth, not only by learning about the natural processes and medical techniques involved in birth (knowledge that, in itself, reduces fear, tension, and therefore pain [Dick-Read, 1972]), but also by practicing specific breathing and concentration techniques, such as the **Lamaze method** of childbirth. These techniques help the woman focus on the work, rather than on the pain, of giving birth. The Lamaze method, which usually involves the father as a labor "coach," has important psychological as well as physical benefits: both parents are often understandably proud of their active involvement in the safe and speedy arrival of their infant (Bing, 1983). Indeed, when both partners attend childbirth classes and when the husband is an active participant in the labor and birth process, the result for the woman is less pain, less anesthesia, shorter labor, and more positive feelings about birth and about herself. Similar results are found when a "doula"—a woman trained to be supportive throughout labor—provides continuous guidance and reassurance (Kennell, 1990).

Not all parents-to-be prepare for childbirth, however. Middle-income parents are far more likely to attend classes than lower-income parents, especially when the lower-income parents are also relatively young and from minority groups. Partly for this reason, the less education and income women have, the more likely they are to experience pain, loneliness, and confusion during childbirth (Ball,1987; Oakley, 1980).

How much difference is there in women's overall experience of childbirth? According to a study that compared the birth experience of a group of first-time mothers, mostly college-educated and middle class, the difference can be considerable (Leifer, 1980). Those mothers who had general anesthesia and were unconscious during birth felt most negative about the whole event and the baby. Those who went through natural childbirth but had not prepared for it as the Lamaze women had were positive about their babies but negative about the birth process itself—not surprisingly so, since their labors tended to be the most difficult. Those who received conduction anesthesia, which blocks sensation in the lower half of the body while allowing the woman to remain awake, had quite normal labors, and generally positive or neutral attitudes about birth and their babies. They complained, however, that they felt detached from the entire experience. Finally, those who had had Lamaze training had short labors and positive reactions to birth and their babies.

The Father's Participation

Before 1970, fathers everywhere were usually barred from the delivery room. It was thought that, at best, they would merely be in the way and might even disrupt the birth process by becoming faint or ill. Over the past two decades, however, it has become generally recognized that the father can have a highly positive impact during birth, not only as a help to his wife but as an informed participant in the birth process. Accordingly, hospital regulations are changing. Increasingly, fathers are present when their infants are born, even when medical intervention, such as a Cesarean, is needed. This is true, not only in North America, but in many other countries around the world (Lamb, 1987). A review of fatherhood in Britain explains:

> The presence of the father at birth is so clearly expected in Britain that it is probably as hard for a man to stay out of the delivery room as it was for him to get in it only a decade ago. The extent to which this has now become conventional was underlined by the widely reported presence of the Prince of Wales at the birth of both his sons. At the time of the Prince's own birth, as several newspapers remarked, the Duke of Edinburgh was playing squash. [Jackson, 1987]

The results of such participation by the father are generally very positive, for the father as well as for the mother. As the following quotation suggests, for some fathers, being part of the birth process is an indelible, deeply moving experience.

> I administered oxygen to her [his wife] between contractions and coached her on pushing, holding her around the shoulders as support during each push. She was magnificent. Slowly I began to feel a kind of holiness about all of us there, performing an ageless human drama, a grand ritual of life. The trigger was probably the emergence of the baby's head—coughing, twisting, covered with blood, as purple as error, so eager for life—that set me into such intensities of joy and excitement that I cannot possibly adequately describe them. It was all so powerful I felt as though my head might come off, that I might simply explode with joy and a sense of participation in a profound mystery. [quoted by Tanzer and Block, 1976]

Not all husbands are so affected by watching their children born, of course, but overall their reaction to birth is almost always good, just as it usually is for mothers.

The Sibling's Experience

For many children, the birth of a younger brother or sister is a stressful, unhappy event, but several factors can influence whether or not this is the case (Vandell, 1987). One factor is preparation. If the child is told what to expect in the days surrounding the birth, and is reassured that becoming a big brother or sister will have its benefits, adjustment will be easier.

The birth itself can be traumatic for a young sibling. If the mother goes to the hospital, the child at home may feel abandoned and frightened, especially if the child associates hospitals with sickness and death. Showing the child photographs of his or her own early days at the hospital, and making plans for a special outing with the father when Mother is away, may relieve some anxieties. Many hospitals now allow young siblings to visit soon after a birth, and planning trips to see Mom and the new baby can also be reassuring.

If the birth occurs at home, the adults' excitement about the event might make them forget the young child's perspective. As you will see in Chapter 9, most preschool children judge an event by appearances, and thus a joyous, arduous, and naturally bloody birth might be viewed by the child as a frightening trauma. An important part of preparing for home birth, then, might be arranging for the young sibling to be cared for away from the home during labor.

In addition to intellectual and emotional preparation, children benefit from practical preparation as well. If the older child will need to sleep in a new bed, or have a new babysitter, or adjust to a new routine of any sort, it is helpful to initiate the change months before the new baby arrives.

However, even when the child is prepared for the new arrival, and even when the birth itself is not frightening, difficulties often arise. The parents inevitably spend substantial time and effort on the new infant, and less on the older child. They are likely to be more tired, and to have less patience and energy, than usual. Understandably, they hope that the older child will be quiet, self-sufficient, and even helpful. Understandably, the older child may feel slighted and disappoint those hopes. Especially if the big brother or sister had been an only-child, or if the new sibling requires extraordinary attention because of a handicap, many children are considerably disturbed by the newborn's arrival. To try to understand this, one mother imagined how she would feel if her husband brought home a new, younger, and cuter wife, giving this interloper lots of attention, new clothes, and the like while asking her, the "old" wife, to be understanding, helpful, and loving, since he still loved her as much as ever.

Whatever the particular circumstances of a birth in the family, many young siblings feel betrayed, angry, guilty, and jealous. A child who asks "Isn't it time to take it back to the hospital?" or who is inclined to give the baby a bite instead of a kiss is not unusual. Some children revert to babyish behavior, crawling, whining, talking baby talk, or wetting the bed for the first time in months; sometimes they may direct aggression at the baby or at their parents (Field and Reite, 1984). Children who cope with stress in these ways are neither abnormal nor unhealthy, as long as they are able to return to normal behavior when they become accustomed to the presence of the new member of the family.

The birth of a new sister or brother often brings about permanent changes in the family routine, including less parental attention and encouragement for the older children. In many other regards, too, family life never quite returns to what it was before. Indeed, throughout the entire life span, siblings affect each other in countless ways, and at the same time influence the overall pattern of family interaction. (The topic of sibling relations and family dynamics is explored in detail at several points later in the text.)

Bonding: How Real an Issue?

One of the topics in human development that has captured much popular attention is the concept of bonding between parents and newborn children. The term **parent-infant bond** is used to emphasize the tangible, as well as the metaphorical, fastening of parent to child in the early moments of their relationship together. Certainly the quotations and photographs in the past several pages suggest that birth can be an exhilarating and moving experience, and for many parents, the first moments with their newborn provide memories that last a lifetime. And certainly the human touch can convey affection, security, and calm in a way no other form of communication can, especially for infants (Gunzenhauser, 1990). But how important are those first few moments of physical contact to the forming of the parent-infant bond, and to future development?

Animals and Bonding

Questions about the nature of the parent-infant bond in humans actually arose from ethological studies that revealed the formation of a quite specific bond between mother and newborn in virtually every species of mammal. Animal mothers, for instance, nourish and nurture their own young and nearly always ignore, reject, or mistreat the young of others. How, exactly, is this bond formed? Maternal hormones released during and after birth, the smell of the infant, and the timing of the first contact all play a role. In many animals, early contact between mother and infant can be crucial to the establishment of the parent-infant bond. For example, if a baby goat is removed from its mother immediately after birth and returned a few hours later, the mother sometimes rejects it, kicking and butting it away. However, if the baby remains with her for the critical first five minutes and then is separated from her, she welcomes it back. Many other animals react in like fashion (Klaus and Kennell, 1976).

Bonding in Humans

Does a similar critical period exist for humans? While researchers recognize that human behavior is much less biologically determined than animal behavior, nevertheless, they have tried to determine whether the amount of time mothers spend with their newborns in the first few days makes any difference in the mother-child bond. In certain cases—for example, when mothers are young, poor, or otherwise under special stress, or when preterm infants seem too forbiddingly frail, or too dependent on life-support devices, to hold or play with (Leifer et al., 1972; Anisfeld and Lipper, 1983)—early contact does seem to facilitate the initial formation of the mother-child bond.

However, in the vast majority of cases, immediate mother-infant contact does not seem to make any lasting difference in the relationship. Indeed, most developmentalists now believe that the importance of early contact between mother and child has been overly popularized, often resulting in feelings of guilt and blame and sorrow when a woman, for any reason, does not spend much time with her infant in the early days of life (Lamb and Hwang, 1982; Myers, 1984). Even Klaus and Kennell, the original researchers in human bonding, now emphasize that the events right after birth are just

Figure 4.10 *Smell and touch are essential components for mother-infant bonding for many animals, including the nuzzling lions seen here. Fortunately, bonding between humans can occur in varied ways, with early contact not at all essential—though physical intimacy, from breast-feeding at infancy to hugs at adolescence, can obviously foster close attachments between parent and child.*

one episode in a long-term process of bonding between parent and child (Klaus and Kennell, 1982). Research increasingly supports this view with evidence that the strength of the bond between parent and child is determined by the nature of the parent-child interaction throughout infancy, childhood, and beyond (Ball, 1987; Vaughn, 1987). As the next chapters reveal, the relationship between parent and child is critical in the child's development; the specifics of its initial formation are not.

SUMMARY

From Zygote to Newborn

1. The first three weeks of prenatal growth are the germinal period. During this period, the zygote develops into an organism containing more than a hundred cells, travels down the Fallopian tube, and implants itself in the uterine lining, where it continues to grow.

2. The period from four to eight weeks after conception is the period of the embryo. The development of the embryo is cephalo-caudal (from the head downward) and proximo-distal (from the inner organs outward). At eight weeks after conception, the future baby is only about an inch long.

3. From the eighth week after conception until birth is the period of the fetus. The fetus grows rapidly and is fully formed by the end of the third month. The fetus attains viability when the brain is sufficiently mature, sometime between the twentieth and the twenty-sixth week after conception.

Potential Complications

4. It was once believed that the placenta protects the fetus from any harmful substances, but now we know that many teratogens (substances that can cause birth defects) can affect the embryo and fetus. Diseases, drugs, and pollutants can all cause birth defects.

5. As a result of the knowledge derived from teratology, many serious teratogens, including rubella and some prescription drugs, now rarely reach the fetus. However, certain other diseases and social drugs remain hazards that require prevention on the part of the woman. AIDS is the most deadly of these teratogens; alcohol is the most common.

6. In understanding teratology, it is critical to realize that teratogens represent risk factors, not inevitable destroyers. Whether a particular teratogen will harm a particular embryo or fetus depends on many prenatal and postnatal factors. For example, harm is more likely if exposure to the teratogen occurs early in pregnancy and less likely if the mother-to-be is healthy and well nourished.

7. In preventing birth defects, much emphasis is rightly placed on the mother; however, society has an important role also, promoting adequate nutrition, prenatal care, and social support, as well as preventing teratogenic diseases, controlling environmental teratogens, reducing drug addiction, and the like.

Birth

8. Birth typically begins with contractions that push the fetus headfirst, out from the uterus and then through the vagina.

9. The Apgar, which rates the neonates's vital signs at one minute after birth, and again at five minutes after birth, provides a quick evaluation of the infant's health. Although neonates may sometimes look misshapen, most are healthy, as revealed by a combined Apgar score of 7 or more.

10. Preterm or small-for-gestational-age babies are more likely than full-term babies to suffer from stress during the birth process and to experience medical difficulties, especially breathing problems, in the days after birth. Some long-term developmental difficulties may occur as well.

Birth as a Family Event

11. Psychological factors play a large role in the parents' overall experience of birth. Women who are prepared for birth—knowing what to expect and how to make labor easier—and who have the support of their husbands and other sensitive birth attendants are most likely to find the birth experience exhilarating.

12. The father's participation in the birth process generally has several positive effects. Women whose husbands are present throughout delivery feel less pain and use less medication. Fathers, in turn, are often thrilled at being involved in the birth of their child.

13. The arrival of a newborn brother or sister is not necessarily a happy experience. An older sibling's emotional adjustment can be eased somewhat if the birth itself is not frightening and if the child is given extra attention in the days and weeks after the event. Nonetheless, some resentment and jealousy are almost inevitable.

14. Although the idea of early parent-infant bonding has received much popular attention, most developmentalists downplay its importance, stressing that the formation of the parent-infant bond develops continuously over a long period of time.

KEY TERMS

germinal period (94)
period of the embryo (94)
period of the fetus (94)
implantation (94)
neural tube (95)
central nervous system (95)
embryo (95)
cephalo-caudal
   development (95)
proximo-distal
   development (95)
placenta (95)
fetus (96)
trimester (97)
age of viability (97)
teratology (98)
teratogens (99)
risk analysis (99)
critical period (100)

behavioral teratogens (100)
fetal alcohol syndrome
   (FAS) (101)
fetal alcohol effects (FAE)
   (101)
threshold effect (103)
neural tube defects (104)
Apgar scale (108)
low-birth-weight infant
   (109)
preterm (109)
small-for-gestational-age
   (SGA) (109)
respiratory distress
   syndrome (109)
anoxia (111)
Lamaze method (114)
parent-infant bond (117)

KEY QUESTIONS

1. What developmental events occur during the germinal period?

2. What parts of the body develop during the period of the embryo?

3. What parts of the body develop during the period of the fetus?

4. What determines the sex of the fetus?

5. During which trimester of pregnancy is the developing organism most susceptible to damage by teratogens? Why?

6. What are the possible effects of maternal smoking on the fetus?

7. What are the possible effects of drug abuse on the fetus?

8. What factors make a fetus more likely to be harmed by teratogens?

9. What vital body signs does the Apgar measure? What does the Apgar score tell about the health of the newborn?

10. What are the causes of low birth weight?

11. What are the most serious problems of low-birth-weight infants?

12. What are the main advantages of Lamaze-type courses for parents-to-be?

13. What are the advantages of the father's presence during the delivery?

14. How does the arrival of the newborn affect the older children in a family?

15. How is the formation of the parent-infant bond different in animals than it is in humans?

PART **II**

The First Two Years: Infants and Toddlers

Adults usually don't change much in a year or two. Sometimes their hair gets longer or grows thinner, or they gain or lose a few pounds, or they become a little wiser or more mature. But if you were to be reunited with some friends you hadn't seen for several years, you would recognize them immediately.

If, on the other hand, you were to care for a newborn twenty-four hours a day for the first month, and then did not see the baby until a year or two later, the chances of your recognizing that child are similar to those of recognizing a best friend who had quadrupled in weight, grown 14 inches, and sprouted a new head of hair. Nor would you find the toddler's way of thinking, talking, or playing familiar. A hungry newborn just cries; a hungry toddler says "more food" or climbs up on the kitchen counter to reach the cookies.

While two years seem short compared to the more than seventy years of the average life span, children in their first two years reach half their adult height, complete the first of Piaget's four periods of cognitive growth, and have almost finished the second of both Freud's and Erikson's sequence of stages. Two of the most important human abilities, talking and loving, are already apparent. The next three chapters describe these radical and rapid changes.

CHAPTER 5

The First Two Years: Biosocial Development

The biological changes that occur in the child's first two years are swift and dramatic. At birth, infants are totally dependent on others, with only a few reflexive behaviors in their repertoire of abilities. By the end of infancy, changes in size, motor skills, and brain maturation have transformed newborns into resourceful, highly mobile adventurers, able to hold their own on a playground. This chapter traces the impressive physical development of infancy and addresses, among others, the following questions:

How do the proportions of the infant's body change?

What is the relationship between brain maturation and the infant's increasing physical control?

How well can an infant see and hear?

How do a newborn's reflexes indicate brain maturation?

Why might one infant take his or her first steps several months before another?

When is it best for an infant to be breast-fed?

What are the consequences of an infant's being malnourished?

An infant's physical development occurs so rapidly that size, shape, and skills change daily. This is no exaggeration. After an initial weight loss, pediatricians expect normal newborns to gain, on average, an ounce a day for the first few months, and parents who keep a detailed baby diary record new achievements every day, such as taking a first step on Monday, taking two steps on Tuesday, and five steps by the weekend. Let us look at some other specifics of this rapid growth.

Size and Shape

The average North American newborn measures 20 inches (51 centimeters) and weighs a little more than 7 pounds (3.1 kilograms). This means that the average newborn is lighter than a gallon of milk, and about as long as the distance from a man's elbow to the tips of his fingers.

In the first days of life, most newborns lose between 5 to 10 percent of their body weight, mostly in water, before their bodies adjust to sucking, swallowing, and digesting on their own. Once they have made these adjustments, most infants grow rapidly, doubling their birth weight by the fourth month, tripling it by the end of the first year, and growing about an inch longer each month for the first twelve months. By age 1, the typical baby weighs about 22 pounds (10 kilograms) and measures almost 30 inches (75 centimeters) (Lowrey, 1986).

Growth in the second year proceeds at a slower rate. By 24 months, most children weigh almost 30 pounds (13 kilograms) and measure between 32 and 36 inches (81 to 91 centimeters), with boys being slightly taller and heavier than girls. In other words, typical 2-year-olds are almost a fifth of their adult weight and half their adult height (see Figure 5.1).

As infants grow, their body proportions change. Most newborns seem top-heavy because their heads are equivalent to about one-fourth of their total length, compared to one-fifth at a year and one-eighth in adulthood. Their legs, in turn, represent only about a quarter of their total body length, whereas an adult's legs account for about half of it. Proportionally, the smallest part of a newborn's body is that part farthest from the head and most distant from the center—namely, the feet. By adulthood, a person's feet will be about five times as long as they were at birth, while the head will have only doubled in size.

Figure 5.1 *These figures show the range of height and weight of American children during the first two years. The lines labeled "50th" (the fiftieth percentile) show the average; the lines labeled "90th" (the ninetieth percentile) show the size of children taller and heavier than 90 percent of their contemporaries; and the lines labeled "10th" (the tenth percentile) show the size of children who are taller or heavier than only 10 percent of their peers. Note that girls (red lines) are slightly shorter and lighter, on the average, than boys (blue lines).*

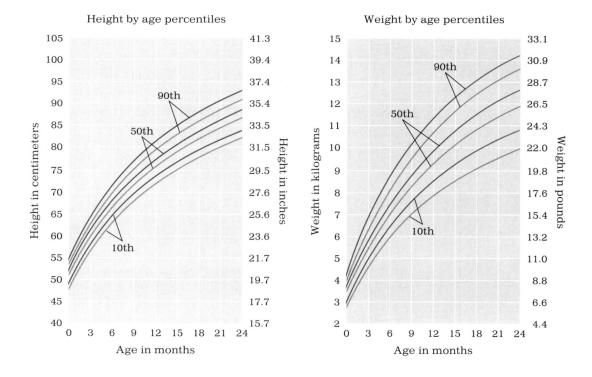

Figure 5.2 *As shown in this figure, the proportions of the human body change dramatically with maturation, especially in the first years of life. For instance, the percentage of total body length below the belly button is 25 percent at two months past conception, about 45 percent at birth, 50 percent by age 2, and 60 percent by adulthood.*

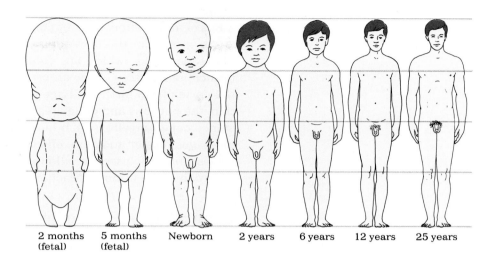

| 2 months (fetal) | 5 months (fetal) | Newborn | 2 years | 6 years | 12 years | 25 years |

Figure 5.3 (a) *Areas of the brain are specialized for the reception and transmission of different types of information. Research has shown that both experience and maturation play important roles in brain development. For example, myelination of the nerve fibers in the visual cortex of the brain will not proceed normally unless the infant has had sufficient visual experience in a lighted environment.*
The role of maturation is apparent in the growth and development of the neurons that make up the nerve fibers. These cells increase in size and in the number of connections among them as the infant matures, enabling impressive increases in the control and refinement of actions. The cross-sectional drawings in (b) and (c) show the development of nerve fibers in the visual cortex between birth and 1 year. Drawings (d), (e), and (f) illustrate changes in the neurons themselves.

Brain Growth and Maturation

One reason the newborn's skull is so disproportionately large is that it must accommodate the brain, which at birth has already attained 25 percent of its adult weight. The neonate's body weight, by comparison, is only about 5 percent of its adult weight. By age 2 the brain is about 75 percent of its adult weight, while the 2-year-old's body weight is only about 20 percent of what it will be in adulthood (Lowrey, 1986).

Weight, of course, provides only a crude index of brain development. More significant are the changes in the maturing nervous system, which consists of the brain, the spinal cord, and the nerves. The nervous system is made up of long, thin, nerve cells called **neurons.** At birth, it contains most of the neurons it will ever have—far more than it will ever need.

During the first months and years, the brain undergoes important changes that greatly enhance its functioning. These changes are particularly notable in the cortex, the outer layer of the brain (about an eighth of an inch of "gray matter") which controls perception and thinking. As you can see in Figure 5.3, specific portions of the cortex are specialized for particular sensory and motor functions, with the remainder of the cortex being "un-

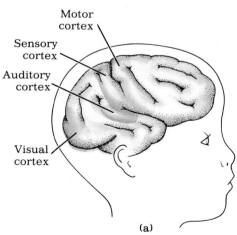

(a)

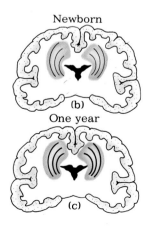

Newborn

(b)

One year

(c)

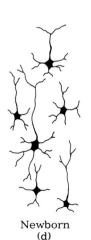

Newborn
(d)

3 months
(e)

15 months
(f)

committed," available for the processing and integration of many different kinds of information. Most important of the changes that occur in the cortex is the growth in the communication networks among its billions of cells. These networks, which are called **dendrites** because they look like the branching of a tree, show an estimated fivefold increase in density within the cortex from birth until age 2 (Diamond, 1988) (see Figure 5.3). In addition, the neurons and dendrites become coated with a fatty, insulating substance called **myelin,** which helps transmit neural impulses, or "electrical messages," faster and more efficiently. This myelination process, which continues until adolescence, allows children to gain increasing neurological control over their motor functions and sensory abilities.

Regulation of Physiological States

An important function of the brain throughout life is the regulation of physiological conditions, or **states.** Just like an older child or adult, a full-term infant normally exhibits several regularly occurring states, the most distinct being *quiet sleep,* in which breathing is regular and slow (about thirty-six breaths per minute) and muscles seem relaxed; *active sleep,* in which the facial muscles move and breathing is less regular and more rapid (forty-six or more breaths per minute); and *alert wakefulness,* in which the eyes are bright and breathing is relatively regular and rapid (Thoman, 1975).

Because each state produces a particular pattern of electrical activity in the brain, referred to as **brain waves,** the patterns can be measured and recorded by an electroencephalogram (EEG), a device which picks up electrical impulses from the nerve cells. Brain waves change rapidly from about three months before term to about three months after, reflecting the maturation that is taking place (see Figure 5.4) (Parmelee and Sigman, 1983).

As the brain develops, physiological states become more cyclical and distinct. With each passing week, for instance, infants are asleep and awake for longer, more regular periods, because their brain maturation allows deeper sleep and more definite wakefulness. Between birth and age 1, the infant's total daily sleep does not change all that much—from about 15 to 13 hours a day—but the length and timing of sleep episodes more closely match the day-night activities of the family. About a third of all 3-month-olds and 80 percent of all 1-year-olds "sleep through the night," defined as sleeping for at least six straight hours during the night. The remainder of each group continue to wake up wanting food and attention (Michelsson et al., 1990; Bamford et al., 1990). As one might expect, preterm newborns sleep more, but less regularly, throughout the first year.

Development of the central nervous system also regulates the degree of the infant's responsiveness to the outside world. For example, a sudden loud noise or a moment of pain (as from a pinprick) makes a normal neonate startle and cry. But soon the baby "self-soothes," that is, becomes more relaxed and quiet on his or her own, as nerve impulses diminish and brain waves display a pattern associated with a calmer state. By comparison, the preterm infant, whose nervous system is less mature, takes longer and requires more intense stimuli, to be aroused; and once crying occurs, the preterm infant takes longer to settle down again. Interestingly, even in normal full-term babies, readiness to become alert, to cry, and to self-soothe correlates with intellectual quickness, as measured by tests of perception later in infancy (Moss et al., 1988).

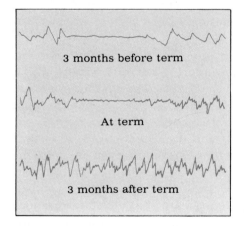

Figure 5.4 *The more mature pattern of brain-wave activity shows many more bursts of electrical activity and greater overall intensity, as can be seen in this electroencephalogram of quiet sleep.*

Sensory Development

Psychologists draw an important distinction between sensation and perception. **Sensation** occurs when a sensory system responds to a particular stimulus. **Perception** occurs when the brain recognizes that response in such a way that the individual becomes aware of it. This distinction may be clear to you if you have ever done your homework while playing the stereo and realized that you had worked through an entire recording but had actually heard only snatches of it. During the gaps in your "listening," your auditory system was sensing the music—your tympanic membranes, hammers, anvils, stirrups, and the like were vibrating in response to the sound waves coming from the speakers—but you were not perceiving the music; that is, you were not consciously aware of it.

At birth, both sensation and perception are apparent. Newborns see, hear, smell, and taste, and they respond to pressure, motion, temperature, and pain. Most of these sensory abilities are immature and very selective. Newborns pay attention to bright lights, loud noises, and objects within a foot of their eyes, and usually screen out almost everything else. Their perceived world is simple—not at all the "great, blooming, buzzing confusion" psychologists once believed it to be (James, 1950).

In this section, we will briefly consider the infant's sensory capacities and basic perceptual abilities. In Chapter 6, we will examine the cognitive dimensions of infant perception.

Research on Infant Perception

Over the past twenty years, there has been an explosion of research on infant perception. Technological breakthroughs—from brain scans to computer measurement of the eyes' ability to focus—have enabled researchers to measure the capacities of infants' senses and to gain a greater understanding of the relationship between perception and physiology (Gottlieb and Krasnegor, 1985).

The basis of this research is the fact that the perception of an unfamiliar stimulus elicits physiological responses, for example, increased heart rate, concentrated gazing, and in the case of infants who have a pacifier in their mouths, intensified sucking. When the new stimulus becomes so familiar that these responses no longer occur, the infant is said to be *habituated* to that stimulus. Employing this phenomenon of **habituation**, researchers have been able to assess infants' ability to perceive by testing their ability to discriminate between very similar stimuli (Bornstein, 1985). Typically, they present the infant with a stimulus—say a plain circle—until habituation occurs. Then they present another stimulus similar to the first but different in some detail—say a circle with a dot in the middle. If the infant reacts in some measurable way to the new stimulus (a change of heart rate, a narrowing of the pupils, a refocusing of gaze), that indicates that the difference in stimulus has been perceived.

Vision

At birth, vision is the least developed of the senses. Newborns focus most readily on objects between 4 and 30 inches (10 and 75 centimeters) away.

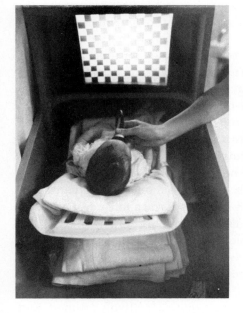

Figure 5.5 *In this experiment in infant perception, the nipple on which the infant is sucking is connected to an element that can focus the image on the screen. Another device records the frequency and strength of the sucking. Typically, infants show their interest by sucking fairly intensely when they see a new image. Then, as they become habituated, their sucking tapers off.*

Their distance vision is about 20/600, which means the baby sees an object 20 feet (6.1 meters) away no better than an adult with 20/20 vision sees the same object 600 feet (183 meters) away. However, distance vision develops rapidly, improving in the first months and reaching 20/20 by 6 months (Aslin, 1987). This improvement results more from changes in the brain than from changes in the eye. Distance focusing is not impossible for the newborn (as it would be for an adult with 20/600 vision), but the immaturity of the brain's neural networks makes such focusing slow and difficult (Braddick and Atkinson, 1988). As neurological maturation and myelination allow better coordination of eye movements and more efficient transmission of information between the eyes and the brain, focusing improves. During the same time period, increasing maturation of the visual cortex accounts for improvements in the other visual abilities. When 1-month-olds look at something, their gaze often wanders, and their ability to scan the object and attend to the critical areas is quite imperfect (Aslin, 1988). However, by 3 months, "striking" improvement has occurred (Braddick and Atkinson, 1988). **Binocular vision,** that is, the ability to use both eyes together to focus on one object, also develops, occurring at about 14 weeks, on average. As a result, depth and motion perception improve dramatically.

Evidence of this comes from infants' ability to "track" a moving object, that is, to visually follow its movement (Nelson and Horowitz, 1987). Although some instances of tracking are apparent in the first days of life, this ability is erratic. Most very young babies "lose sight" of an object that moves slowly right in front of their face. One reason for this is that, even with stationary objects, newborns' eyes do not remain focused for long, and they do not focus on edges (Bronson, 1990). Thus continual, smooth tracking of a moving object is virtually impossible. In the months after birth, tracking improves week by week, with large, fast-moving, high-contrast objects being tracked more readily than small, slow-moving, low-contrast objects.

Interestingly, by 6 months infants can use both eyes to track a moving object quite well and can use both hands to grab a stationary object firmly, but it takes several additional months before they exhibit hand-eye coordination with respect to moving objects. By 8 or 9 months, they can adjust their reach as if to catch, even when an object is thrown fairly fast and from an unusual angle (von Hofsten, 1983). Finally, sometime during the second year, they are able to grab a moving object successfully.

Hearing

Relative to their vision, newborns' hearing is quite sensitively attuned. Sudden noises startle newborns, making them cry; rhythmic sounds, such as a lullabye or a heartbeat, soothe them and put them to sleep. When they are awake, they turn their heads in the direction of a noise (Clarkson et al., 1985), and they are particularly attentive to the sound of conversation. Indeed, even three days after birth, newborns can distinguish their mother's voice from the voice of other mothers (DeCasper and Fifer, 1980).

By the age of 1 month, infants can also perceive differences between very similar sounds. In one experiment, 1-month-old babies activated a recording of the "bah" sound whenever they sucked on a nipple. At first, they sucked diligently; but as they became habituated to the sound, their sucking decreased. At this point, the experimenters changed the sound from "bah" to "pah." Immediately the babies sucked harder, indicating by this sign of interest that they had perceived the difference (Eimas et al., 1971). It may even be that newborns have some ability to discriminate between vowels (Clarkson and Berg, 1983).

Although very young infants can discriminate among a wide variety of sounds, their hearing is not as acute as that of an older child. Even at 6 months, when infants can hear high-frequency sounds as well as older children, their hearing for low-frequency sounds is much less acute (Olsho, 1984; Olsho et al., 1988). Undoubtedly this is one reason most adults use a higher pitch when talking to babies than when talking to other people, as discussed in Chapter 6.

Taste and Smell

Although less developed than their hearing, neonates' sense of taste is clearly functioning. This was vividly shown in a demonstration with a dozen 2-hour-old infants who were each given tastes of sweet, sour, salty, and bitter water (Rosenstein and Oster, 1988). Careful analysis of their video-taped facial expressions revealed distinctive reactions to all the samples except the salty one.

Newborns' sense of smell is even more acute. In a number of experiments, breast-fed infants a few days old have been positioned in a crib between two gauze pads, one worn by their own mother in her bra for several hours, the other similarly worn by another breast-feeding mother. In trial after trial, infants tended to turn their heads toward their own mother's pad, preferring her smell to that of another woman (Schaal, 1986).

Together, taste and smell continue to develop during the early months, and become quite acute by age 1. Indeed, by late infancy, these senses are probably sharper than at any other time in the entire life span. Experts recommend giving infants a wide variety of foods, not because nutrition demands it, but because taste preferences develop so rapidly that introduction of new foods becomes more problematic with each passing year (Birch, 1990).

The Role of Sensory Experience

One of the most intriguing issues in infant development is how important sensory experience is to the development of the infant's sensory abilities, particularly with regard to the establishment of the brain's neural networks. To a great extent, of course, the basic elements of infants' sensory systems are already established at birth. There is no doubt, however, that at least a minimal amount of sensory experience is essential, not only in the development of perceptual abilities, but even in the development of the dendrites and other brain structures that make seeing, hearing, and other sensory abilities possible.

This fact is most clearly shown by research in which animals that were prevented from using their senses or moving their bodies in infancy became permanently handicapped (Parmelee and Sigman, 1983). Kittens who are blindfolded for the first several weeks of life, for example, do not develop the visual pathways in their brains to allow normal vision, even if their blindfolds are removed when they are just a few months old. Indeed, if only one eye is temporarily blinded and the other left normal, kittens can see but will never develop the binocular vision necessary for depth vision (Mitchell,

Figure 5.6 *This 7-week-old's concentrated gaze is a sign that her brain is hard at work processing the visual information provided by her crib toy. Experiences such as this are not only fascinating to infants but are essential for the normal development of the visual pathways of the cortex.*

1988). Significantly, such atrophy of brain pathways occurs only when blindness takes place in the early weeks of life; kittens who have had some normal visual experiences, as well as older cats who are subjected to longer periods of temporary blindness, recover quite well once the sight deprivation is over.

In very simple terms, these abnormalities occur because the deprivation of certain basic sensory experiences prevents the development of the normal neural pathways that transmit sensory information. As researchers explain it metaphorically, the "wiring" of the brain—that is, the basic structures that allow the development of specific capacities—is genetically programmed and present at birth. What is required is the "fine-tuning" that occurs with the development of the connective networks, and it is this fine-tuning process that can be affected by the individual's experience or the lack of it.

As best we know, the brain development that permits seeing and hearing in humans likewise becomes "fine-tuned" through visual and auditory experiences in the first months (Imbert, 1985; Parmelee and Sigman, 1983). This is not to say that an infant would not be able to see colors or understand speech unless he or she had an opportunity to experience them in the first days of life. Nor does it mean that intensive exposure to visual, auditory, and motor stimulation is desirable in the first weeks. (Indeed, many newborns would react to such stimulation by shutting it out with tears or sleep.) However, it does mean that even in the case of a biologically programmed event such as early brain maturation and sensory-system development, experience also plays a role.

Motor Skills

We now come to the most visible and dramatic of the physical changes that occur in infancy, those that ultimately allow the child to "stand tall and walk proud." Thanks largely to the changes in body size and proportion and the increasing brain maturation that we have outlined, infants gain dramatically in their ability to move and control their bodies. Both **gross motor** skills—abilities such as running and climbing that demand large movements—and **fine motor skills**—abilities that require more precise, small movements, such as picking up a coin or using a crayon—develop rapidly during the first two years. Because of the growing independence they afford the child, motor skills become a "catalyst for developmental change" (Thelan, 1987), as they open new possibilities for the child's discovery of the world. For this reason, especially, it is important to understand the development of these skills—including the usual sequence and timing of their emergence—and the various factors that might cause one child to develop certain skills "behind" or "ahead of" schedule.

Reflexes

The infant's first motor skills are not, technically, skills at all but **reflexes,** that is, involuntary responses to particular stimuli. The newborn has dozens of reflexes. Some are essential to life itself; others disappear completely in the months after birth; still others provide the foundation for later motor skills. All are important as signs of neurological health.

Three sets of reflexes are critical for survival and become stronger as the baby matures. One set maintains an adequate supply of oxygen. The most obvious reflex in this group is the **breathing reflex.** Normal newborns take their first breath even before the umbilical cord, with its supply of oxygen, is cut. For the first few days, breathing is somewhat irregular, and reflexive *hiccups, sneezes,* and *spit-ups* are common, as the newborn tries to coordinate breathing, sucking, and swallowing.

Another set of reflexes helps to maintain constant body temperature: when infants are cold, they *cry, shiver,* and *tuck their legs* close to their bodies, thereby helping to keep themselves warm. A third set of reflexes fosters feeding. One of these is the **sucking reflex:** newborns suck anything that touches their lips—fingers, toes, blankets, and rattles, as well as nipples of various shapes. Another is the **rooting reflex,** which helps babies find a nipple by causing them to turn their heads and start to suck when something brushes against their cheek. *Swallowing* is another important reflex that aids feeding, as is *crying* when the stomach is empty.

Other reflexes are not necessary for survival, but they are important signs of normal brain and body function. For example, the following five reflexes are present in normal, full-term newborns. (1) When their feet are stroked, their toes fan upward *(Babinski reflex)*. (2) When they are held upright with their feet touching a flat surface, they move their legs as if to walk *(stepping reflex)*. (3) When they are held horizontally on their stomachs, their arms and legs stretch out *(swimming reflex)*. (4) When something touches their palms, their hands grip tightly *(grasping reflex)*. (5) When someone bangs on the table they are lying on, newborns usually fling their arms outward and then bring them together on their chests, as if to hold on to something, and they may cry and open their eyes wide *(Moro reflex)*.

Tests of these and other reflexes are frequently used to assess the newborn's physical condition and brain development. The most notable of these measures is the **Brazelton Neonatal Behavioral Assessment Scale (NBAS),** which includes twenty reflexes as well as twenty-eight items of infant behavior, such as reaction to cuddling, attentiveness to the examiner's voice and face, trembling, irritability, and so forth (Worobey and Brazelton, 1990). The

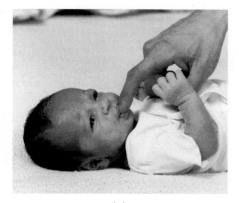

(a)

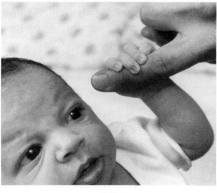

(b)

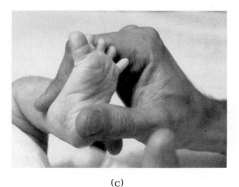

(c)

Figure 5.7 *At 3 weeks, Joanna displays some of the many reflexes of the newborn—sucking, grasping, and fanning her toes.*

underlying premise of the NBAS is that these simple reflexes and responses form the basis of cognitive, social, and motor skills, and thus indicate the infant's overall readiness to respond to the world. As you will now see, some of the infant's early abilities, including the swimming, stepping, and grasping reflexes evolve into gross motor skills that help transform a dependent creature who stays put into an independent explorer who never seems to stay still.

Gross Motor Skills

Even as newborns, infants placed on their stomachs move their arms and legs swim-fashion and attempt to lift their heads to look around. As they gain muscle strength, they start to wiggle, attempting to move forward by pushing their arms, shoulders, and upper body against the surface they are on. Although these initial efforts usually get them nowhere, or even move them backward, infants persist, and over the next two months or so, they become able to use their arms, and then legs, to inch forward. By 6 months, most infants succeed at this type of locomotion (Chandler, 1990). A few months later, usually between eight and ten months after birth, most infants are crawling on "all fours" (sometimes called creeping), coordinating the movement of their hands and knees in a smooth, balanced manner. Within weeks, most infants also learn to climb up onto couches and chairs—as well as ledges, window sills, and the like.

As with every new skill, crawling opens new opportunities and challenges. Once infants can locomote on their own, they can propel themselves toward intriguing objects, whether nearby or across the room. They can even leave the room, exploring new areas and gaining a sense of their own independent actions. New hazards are also within reach, from the stairs they might tumble down to the floor polish they might taste. (The prudent parent seals off all dangerous places and substances by 6 months, if not sooner.) Fortunately, with most infants, the advent of crawling coincides with an emerging sense of wariness about the unfamiliar (see Chapter 7), producing a new measure of caution that tempers their curiosity: infants investigate a novel situation tentatively, frequently interrupting their explorations to glance at a parent for signs of encouragement or disapproval. Thus, a combination of motor skills, cognitive awareness, social interaction, and access to new surroundings makes the crawling 9-month-old a quite different baby from the precrawler (Bertenthal and Campos, 1990).

Walking shows a similar progression, from reflexive, hesitant newborn stepping to a smooth, speedy, coordinated gait (Thelan and Ulrich, 1991). On average, a child can walk while holding a hand at 9 months, can stand alone momentarily at 10 months, and can walk well unassisted at 12 months. In recognition of their accomplishment of walking, babies at this stage are given the name **toddler,** for the characteristic way they move their bodies, toddling from side to side. Interestingly, once an infant can take steps, walking becomes the preferred mode of movement—except when speed is an issue, and then many new walkers quickly drop to their hands and knees to crawl. Within a short time, mastery of walking leads to mastery of running; 2-year-olds almost never crawl except when, with a mocking grin on their face, they pretend to be babies.

4 months

8 months

9 months

10 months

18 months

Figure 5.8 *At 4 months, identical twins Adam and Ryan have enough strength and coordination to lift their heads and their shoulders; by 8 months, they can pull their bodies forward in a crawl. With each new motor skill come new opportunities for exploration and pleasure, as Adam and Ryan demonstrate at 9, 10, and 18 months. (Monozygotic twins usually sit up, stand, and walk within a few days of each other. Dizygotic twins often vary by weeks or even months.)*

In addition to allowing infants freedom of movement, crawling and walking aid their development in other ways. It is no coincidence that with infants' increased mobility and independence comes a forward leap in their cognitive awareness (detailed in Chapter 6) and the opening of new dimensions in parent-infant interaction (described in Chapter 7). In addition, in purely practical terms, upright mobility not only raises the child's vistas figuratively but literally gives the child a new perspective on his or her world. It also frees up the child's hands, fostering the development of fine motor skills.

Fine Motor Skills

As we have seen, infants are born with a reflexive grasp, but they seem to have no control of it. During their first two months, babies will stare and wave their arms at an object dangling within reach, and by 3 months, they can usually touch it. But they cannot yet grab and hold on unless the object is placed in their hands.

By 6 months, most babies can reach for, grab, and hold onto almost any object that is the right size, whether it is a bottle, a rattle, or a sister's braids.

Figure 5.9 *Motor skills develop rapidly during the first two years partly because infants take advantage of every opportunity to use whatever abilities they have. Climbing, perching, and grasping are just some of the motor skills this young muralist is currently refining.*

Once grabbing is possible, infants explore everything within reach, mastering fine motor skills while they learn about the physical properties of their immediate world. As Eleanor Gibson, a leading researcher in infant perception, describes it, the infant at 6 months has "a wonderful eye-hand-mouth exploratory system," which before age 1 is sufficiently developed that the infant can "hold an object in one hand and finger it with the other, and turn it around while examining it. This is an ideal way to learn about the distinctive features of an object" and, bit by bit, about the tangible world (Gibson, 1988).

At the same time, the skill of picking up and manipulating small objects develops. At first, infants use their whole hand, especially the palm and the fourth and fifth fingers to grasp. Later they use the middle fingers and center of the palm or the index finger and the side of the palm. Finally, they use thumb and forefinger together, a skill mastered sometime between 9 and 14 months (Frankenburg et al., 1981). At this point, infants delight in picking up every tiny object within sight, including bits of fuzz from the carpet and bugs from the lawn.

Variations in Timing

Although all healthy infants develop the same motor skills in the same sequence, the age at which these skills are acquired can vary greatly from infant to infant and still be considered normal. Table 5.1 shows the age at which half of all infants in the United States master each major motor skill, and the age at which 90 percent master each skill.

These averages, or **norms,** are based on a large representative sample of infants from a wide range of ethnic groups. Such representativeness is important because norms vary from group to group, as well as from place to place. For example, throughout infancy, African-Americans are more advanced in motor skills than Americans of European ancestry (Rosser and Rudolph, 1989). Internationally, the earliest walkers in the world seem to be

TABLE 5.1   Age Norms (in Months) for Motor Skills

Skill	When 50% of All Babies Master the Skill	When 90% of All Babies Master the Skill
Lifts head 90° when lying on stomach	2.2	3.2
Rolls over	2.8	4.7
Sits propped up (head steady)	2.9	4.2
Sits without support	5.5	7.8
Stands holding on	5.8	10.0
Walks holding on	9.2	12.7
Stands momentarily	9.8	13.0
Stands alone well	11.5	13.9
Walks well	12.1	14.3
Walks backward	14.3	21.5
Walks up steps (with help)	17.0	22.0
Kicks ball forward	20.0	24.0

Source: The Denver Developmental Screening Test (Frankenburg et al., 1981).

Figure 5.10 *At 14 months, this infant taking her first steps is somewhat of a "late walker." The reasons for this slowness to walk could be many, involving both nature and nurture, but none of them is likely to be something her parents should be concerned about.*

in Uganda, in Central Africa, where, if well nourished and healthy, the typical baby walks at 10 months; some of the latest walkers are in France, where taking one's first unaided steps at 15 months is not unusual.

What factors account for this variation in the acquisition of motor skills? Of primary importance are inherited factors, such as activity level, rate of physical maturation, and body type. The power of this genetic component is suggested by the fact that identical twins are far more likely to sit up, and to walk, on the same day than fraternal twins are (Wilson, 1979). Particular patterns of infant care may also be influential. Indeed, in many parts of Africa, infants are held next to an adult's body virtually all day long, cradled and rocked as the adult works. With respect to the development of motor skills, especially walking, this kind of stimulation, which allows the infant to practice movement while in an upright position and to continually feel the rhythm of an adult's gait, may well give African babies an advantage over the typical Western infant who spends much of each day in a crib (Bril, 1986).

Given the evidence, most developmentalists would say that the age at which a *particular* baby first displays a *particular* skill depends on the interaction between inherited and environmental factors. Each infant has a genetic timetable for maturation, which can be faster or slower than that of other infants from the same ethnic group and even from the same family; and each infant also has a family and culture that provide varying amounts of encouragement, nutrition, and opportunity to practice.

Although many parents may take pride in an early walker or fret over a late one, in the long term, it is unimportant if an infant is a little early, or a little late, in walking, or in any other motor skill. However, in cases of significant lateness—as when an 8-month-old does not sit up, grab objects, or attempt to crawl—the parents should have the child medically examined.

Nutrition

As we have seen, under normal circumstances, infants double their birth weight in the first months, a growth rate that often requires feeding every three or four hours, day and night. The actual feeding "schedule," which can vary considerably from one child to another, is not the crucial factor, however. What matters is the overall quality and quantity of the infant's nutritional intake. Adequate nutrition is essential not only to the physical growth described in this chapter but to brain development and skill mastery as well.

The Early Months

At first, infants are unable to eat or digest solid food, but their rooting, sucking, swallowing, and breathing reflexes make them well adapted for consuming the quantities of liquid nourishment that they need.

In these early months, breast milk is the ideal infant food (Eiger, 1987; Jelliffe and Jelliffe, 1977). It is always sterile and at body temperature; it contains more iron, vitamin C, and vitamin A than cow's milk; and it also contains antibodies that provide the infant some protection against disease. In addition, breast milk is more digestible than cow's milk or formula, which

Figure 5.11 *Feeding an infant "solid" foods usually begins in earnest at about 6 months, as the baby's digestive system matures and his or her nutritional needs become more complex. The father of this 7-month-old is obviously an experienced feeder, having mastered the "open wide" expression to signal the arrival of the spoon.*

means that breast-fed babies have fewer allergies and stomach upsets than bottle-fed babies, even when both groups of babies have similar family backgrounds and excellent medical care.

Despite the advantages of breast milk, breast-feeding is no longer the most common method of feeding infants. The advent of the rubber nipple, the plastic bottle, canned milk, powdered milk, and premixed infant formulas available in handy six-packs has meant that many infants now survive and thrive without ever tasting breast milk (see A Closer Look, p. 137). Less than a fifth of all babies born in the United States are breast-fed for six months or more, despite evidence that breast milk is particularly beneficial from the third month to the six month (Rush and Ryan, 1991).

Nutrition After Weaning

Although breast milk can be the exclusive food in the first six months, by 6 months or so, "solid" foods should gradually be added to the diet. Cereals are needed for iron and B vitamins, fruits for vitamins A and C, and when these first solids are well-tolerated, vegetables, meat, fish, and eggs can be introduced to provide additional nutrition (Purvis and Bartholmey, 1988). By the time the infant is a year old, the diet should include all the nutritious foods that the rest of the family consumes.

In most developed countries, an ample and varied diet is fairly easy to obtain. Unfortunately, this is not true in many other areas of the world, and the consequences for the individual's development can be serious (Grant, 1986).

Nutritional Deficiencies

"Nutritional deficiency" covers a wide range of problems and consequences, from anemia and fatigue to outright starvation. In some cases, these conditions are the result of catastrophic circumstances, such as prolonged drought or civil war. In many cases, however, the underlying causes are ignorance or indifference in the family, culture, and community.

Severe Malnutrition

It is estimated that, overall, roughly 7 percent of children in developing nations are severely malnourished during their early years, with rates running above 60 percent in countries like Ethiopia, Pakistan, and Niger (United Nations, 1990). In the first year of life, severe protein-calorie deficiency can cause **marasmus,** a disease that occurs when infants are severely undernourished. Growth stops, body tissues waste away, and the infant dies. During toddlerhood, protein-calorie deficiency is more likely to cause **kwashiorkor,** a condition in which the child's face, legs, and abdomen swell with water, sometimes making the child appear well-fed to anyone who doesn't know the real cause of the bloating. Because in this condition the essential organs claim whatever nutrients are available, other parts of the body are degraded, including, characteristically, the child's hair, which usually becomes thin, brittle, and colorless.

A CLOSER LOOK   Breast versus Bottle

If breast milk is best, why do many women choose to give their infants formula? The reasons have little to do with nutrition directly, but are greatly influenced by the cultural attitudes and social pressures of our modern world and by the mother's socioeconomic circumstances. Ironically, since the practice of breast-feeding in developed countries decreases as the level of maternal education and maternal income decreases, breast-feeding occurs less often among women who would benefit from it most in terms of both health protection for their infant and financial savings for themselves (While, 1989).

Many women find that, even if they want to breast-feed, it may not be easy. Problems may begin in the hospital if procedures make it impossible for the mother to have her newborn near her day and night, so that she can nurse whenever the infant is hungry. Outside the hospital, cultural attitudes may make breast-feeding inconvenient, if not impossible, except in the privacy of one's own home. Even in some cultures that have traditionally regarded breast-feeding in public as completely normal, there has been, as a result of Westernizing influences, a growing trend toward "modern modesty."

Increasing time pressures in many cultures have added to the problem. In order for breast-feeding to succeed, especially in the early weeks, nursing should occur every two or three hours or even more often if the baby demands it (Riordan, 1983), with each feeding lasting twenty minutes or more. Such a schedule is important because the supply of breast milk is closely linked to demand, and frequent sucking helps establish ample quantity in the mother's production of milk. For many women who work outside the home or whose daily activities require them to be out in public much of the time, meeting this kind of schedule is difficult.

In addition, most women today are aware that traces of whatever drugs a breast-feeding mother ingests—cigarettes, alcohol, birth-control pills, and so forth—will show up in her milk. Furthermore, the quantity and quality of the milk are affected by what the woman eats, so weight-loss diets are inadvisable for nursing mothers. Consequently, many women decide that, rather than feeling guilty about compromising the quality of their milk or being as careful about their diet after pregnancy as they had to be before, they would rather feed their baby formula.

Fathers are influential, too. Some men are jealous of the close relationship that exists between a nursing mother and her infant, a relationship that seems to exclude them. Some contemporary fathers want to be involved in all aspects of infant care right from the start, and, especially if they are unaware of the advantages of breast-

feeding, prefer that their child be bottle-fed so they can sometimes do the feeding. Practical advice can also be pivotal. When infant formulas and rubber nipples first became widely available in the 1930s, many hospitals encouraged bottle-feeding as the more "reliable" and convenient method, a trend that accelerated as hospitals and pediatricians endorsed the idea that newborns should be fed every four hours (Apple, 1988). Consequently, breast-feeding became less common, and by 1960 in the United States, three-fourths of all infants were exclusively formula-fed. Then, as the nutritional and health benefits of mother's milk became better understood, expert advice and hospital practices shifted, and by 1980, almost two-thirds of all American newborns were breast-fed. Now there are signs that the trend has reversed again. By the end of the 1980s in the United States, breast-feeding of newborns had fallen to 52 percent, and in the five-year period from 1984 and 1989, breast-feeding after 6 months fell from 24 to 18 percent (Rush and Ryan, 1991).

One reason for this latest reversal is the reduced availability of early help and encouragement. As one physician explains:

> Mothers are now discharged so fast from the hospital they leave even before their milk comes in. They are just handed a package of formula on the way out the door. At home, if their mother didn't breast feed, they have no support. [Lawrence, quoted in Hilts, 1991]

Without practical guidance, many women do not know how to handle all the specifics of breast-feeding—such as positioning the infant, getting the full nipple into the mouth, increasing milk supply, coping with a fussy feeder, relieving sore nipples, protecting against teething—and they quit when the first problem arises. This latest trend is unfortunate, since experts now recommend that breast-feeding continue throughout the first year, not only for optimal nutrition and protection against disease but also for the mutual pleasure and intimacy that helps build a close mother-child relationship.

Breast-feeding, of course, does not guarantee infant health or a good mother-child relationship—any more than bottle-feeding precludes it. And while the consensus among developmentalists is that breast-feeding generally fosters good maternal care, as well as good health and nutrition, it must be remembered that the choice between breast- and bottle-feeding is a personal and sometimes complicated one. Breast-feeding for at least one year may well be ideal, but the practical needs of the mother, father, and other children may mean that the best overall pattern for the entire household entails bottle-feeding for the newest family member.

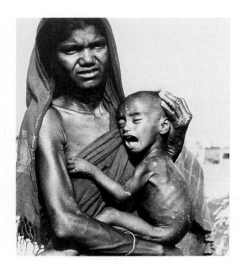

Figure 5.12 *There have been many contributing causes to the recent famine in the countries of Africa, among them weather conditions, farming practices, civil war, and government policies. In each area struck by this disaster, the toll in the health of children has been the same: increases in marasmus and kwashiorkor, and many more deaths from diseases like measles and chicken pox, illnesses that are not often fatal to children who are otherwise in good health.*

The primary cause of malnutrition in developing countries is early cessation of breast-feeding. In many of these countries, breast-feeding was usually continued for at least two years, but now is often stopped much earlier in favor of bottle-feeding, usually with powdered formulas. Under normal circumstances, such formulas are adequate and safe. However,

> for many people in the developing world . . . the hygienic conditions for the proper use of infant formula just do not exist. Their water is unclean, the bottles are dirty, the formula is diluted to make a tin of powdered milk last longer than it should. What happens? The baby is fed a contaminated mixture and soon becomes ill, with diarrhea, which leads to dehydration, malnutrition, and, very often, death. [Relucio-Clavano, quoted in Grant, 1986]

A comparison of the survival rates of breast-fed and bottle-fed babies from the same impoverished background reveals that bottle-fed babies have fared much less well: in Chile, for instance, they are four times more likely to die; in Egypt, five times more likely (Grant, 1982). While death and disease rates are obvious evidence of harm, many malnourished infants who survive carry more subtle handicaps that will remain throughout the life span. Specifically, those who are chronically malnourished early in life are physically shorter and intellectually less able than their peers born in the same community (Bogin and MacVean, 1983). Other deficits are particularly likely to involve visual and auditory skills, probably because the early months of life are the ones when the brain areas for these skills develop rapidly.

Many countries have tried to combat severe infant malnutrition by encouraging breast-feeding. Their efforts are proving successful in some cases. In Brazil, for example, infant mortality was cut in half between 1973 and 1983, even though overall nutrition and living standards did not improve. Longer duration of breast-feeding was one critical factor (Monteiro et al., 1989). In other countries, extensive efforts to promote breast-feeding seem to have had little or no impact. One reason may be that in-hospital campaigns to educate new mothers about breast-feeding through lectures and pamphlets are often cancelled out by such simultaneous in-hospital practices as separating mother and newborn for lengthy periods and providing new mothers with free samples of infant formula (Cunningham and Segree, 1990; Hull et al., 1990).

In developed countries, severe malnutrition in infancy is not widespread, even among families with very low income. This is because social programs, though often inadequate in many ways, tend to meet the essential nourishment needs of infants. Even when a particular impoverished family cannot obtain welfare, food stamps, or other governmental assistance, enough help is usually available from neighbors, relatives, and religious groups to prevent the extremes of marasmus or kwashiorkor. However, isolated cases of severe malnutrition during infancy do occur, when emotional and physical stresses on the caregivers are so overwhelming that they ignore the infant's feeding needs, and when the malnutrition of such an infant is not noticed by the larger community.

Undernutrition

Undernutrition is far more prevalent than severe malnutrition, both in developing and developed countries. Worldwide, according to United Nations

Figure 5.13 *This chart shows the percentage of children in selected countries whose weight is 20 percent below the standard for a well-nourished child, but who do not yet show medical evidence of severe malnutrition. Such undernutrition, if it continues throughout childhood, not only makes a child smaller and shorter than his or her genetic potential would allow, but also undermines intellectual development, resistance to disease, and, eventually, reproductive fitness. For example, even if they are well-fed in adulthood, women who were undernourished as children tend to have more difficult pregnancies and to have a higher rate of low-birth-weight infants than women who were well nourished as children. Given the consequences and pervasiveness of undernutrition, public health officials contend that relief efforts should center as readily on these children as on the emaciated, listless, severely malnourished children who easily capture public sympathy.*

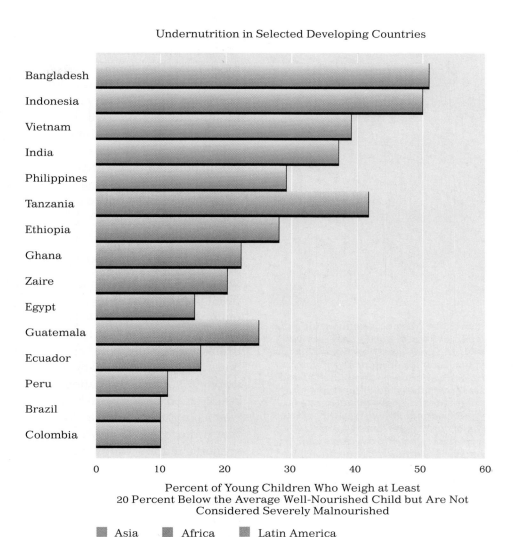

Undernutrition in Selected Developing Countries

Percent of Young Children Who Weigh at Least
20 Percent Below the Average Well-Nourished Child but Are Not
Considered Severely Malnourished

◼ Asia   ◼ Africa   ◼ Latin America

statistics (1990), roughly one-fifth of young children in developing countries are undernourished, and in some developed nations, up to 6 percent are undernourished (see Figure 5.13).

Most commonly, undernutrition is caused by a complex interaction of factors, with social and/or family problems being prime underlying factors. This is most obvious in regions of the world where everyone is undernourished: typically the society's socioeconomic policies do not reflect the importance of infant nutrition, and parents may not even realize that a somewhat thin offspring is undernourished. In developed countries, problems contributing to undernourishment are generally centered in the home. Mothers who are depressed, for example, tend to feed their children erratically and to be highly arbitrary in deciding when an infant has had enough to eat (Drotan et al., 1990). In infancy, as well as later in childhood, emotional stress brought about by conflict at home, or changes in a child's life, can also cause undernutrition (Sinclair, 1978). A previously well-nourished toddler who suddenly fails to gain weight probably has experienced a disruption in his or her life—such as an upsetting entry into day care, or the arrival of a new baby, or the departure of the father—that is expressed in mealtimes that are less frequent, or less healthy, or less pleasant.

Figure 5.14 *Normal genetic variation is apparent here, in appearance, activity level, and body size. However, if this is a typical sample of American infants, at least one infant is undernourished and one is overnourished. Infants who are undernourished have insufficient energy for normal growth and the expression of curiosity; infants who are overfed are slower to develop motor skills and are more likely to have a variety of health problems—ranging from asthma to heart disease—later in life.*

Another cause of undernutrition in developed countries is ignorance of the infant's nutritional needs. For example, one common form of undernutrition in the United States is "milk anemia," so named because it arises from parents' giving their toddler a bottle of milk (which has no iron) before every nap and with every meal, inadvertently destroying the child's appetite for other foods that are iron-rich.

Because of these complexities, programs that see undernutrition as a problem of poor families exclusively, and seek to solve the problem by providing poor families with free food, are too narrowly focused (Ricciuti, 1991). To be successful in staving off the harm of inadequate nutrition, social policy must consider the entire context, including the need to raise parents' "nutritional consciousness."

Consequences of Undernutrition

While severe malnutrition in infancy brings obvious physical and cognitive problems, the toll of less serious undernutrition is not so apparent and is quite variable (Lozoff, 1989). Moreover, research suggests that even when undernourishment occurs during the brain's most rapid growth period, children's intellectual abilities can recover. Such recovery is not automatic, however. It is influenced by the duration of the undernutrition and the quality of intellectual stimulation experienced after infancy. Recent longitudinal research on undernourished children in Mexico, Kenya, and Barbados, as well as in Europe and North America (Galler, 1989; Dobbing, 1987), reveals that if they receive only minimal stimulation from family members or the school, children who were malnourished as infants show impaired learning—especially in ability to concentrate and in language skills—throughout childhood and adolescence. Not surprisingly, these effects are more apparent when the early nutritional deprivation continues into childhood. Thus marginal nutrition in infancy is a risk factor, not necessarily causing deficits, but making problems more likely to occur if other stresses are present (Ricciuti, 1991).

SUMMARY

Size and Shape

1. In their first two years, most babies gain about 20 pounds (9 kilograms) and grow about 15 inches (38 centimeters). The proportions of the body change. The newborn is top-heavy, for the head takes up one-fourth of the body length, partly because the brain, at birth, has attained a high proportion of its adult size in comparison to other parts of the body. In adulthood, the head is about one-eighth of the body length.

Brain Growth and Maturation

2. Although at birth the nervous system has virtually all the nerve cells it will ever have, these neurons grow and form branching networks during infancy and childhood, resulting in increasing efficiency of communication between the brain and the rest of the body.

3. Fetal brain maturation is responsible for the infant's increasingly regular patterns of sleep and wakefulness, and also for changes in the infant's ability to respond to, and to control responses to, the environment.

Sensory Development

4. Both sensation and perception are apparent at birth, and both become more developed with time. Some senses—notably hearing—seem very acute within the first months of life; others—notably vision—develop more slowly throughout the first year.

5. The development of perceptual abilities involves the interaction between brain maturation and the infant's experience.

Motor Skills

6. The development of motor abilities during the first two years allows the infant new possibilities in discovering the world. Gross motor skills involve large movements such as running and jumping; fine motor skills involve small precise movements, such as picking up a penny.

7. At first, the newborn's motor abilities consist of reflexes. Some reflexes are essential for survival; some provide the foundation for later motor skill; others simply disappear in the first months. However, all reflexes are indices of brain development.

8. Although the sequence of motor-skill development is the same for all healthy infants, babies—for both hereditary and environmental reasons—vary in the ages at which they master specific skills.

Nutrition

9. Breast milk is the ideal food for most babies. However, commercial formulas, properly prepared, are an acceptable substitute. A mother's choice to breast-feed or bottle-feed typically depends on many factors, including education, lifestyle, and cultural pressures.

10. In developing countries, severe malnutrition can often be attributed to the early cessation of breast-feeding and improper preparation of commercial formulas. Marasmus and kwashiorkor, two major diseases caused by long-term protein-calorie deficiencies, can result in early death. When not fatal, chronic malnourishment may result in intellectual deficits and in shorter physical stature.

11. Undernutrition is quite common in developing countries and is often apparent in developed countries as well. The consequences vary, depending in part on the child's intellectual stimulation at home and in school.

KEY TERMS

neurons (125)
dendrites (126)
myelin (126)
physiological states (126)
brain waves (126)
sensation (127)
perception (127)
habituation (127)
binocular vision (128)
gross motor skills (130)
fine motor skills (131)

reflexes (131)
breathing reflex (131)
sucking reflex (131)
rooting reflex (131)
Brazelton Neonatal Behavioral Assessment Scale (131)
toddler (132)
norms (134)
marasmus (136)
kwashiorkor (136)

KEY QUESTIONS

1. How do the proportions of the infant's body change during the first two years?

2. What are the primary maturational processes that take place in the infant's brain and how do they affect the infant's physical functioning?

3. How do researchers determine whether an infant perceives a difference between two stimuli?

4. Which reflexes are critical to an infant's survival?

5. What is the general sequence of the development of motor skills?

6. What are the advantages and disadvantages of breast-feeding?

7. What are some of the consequences of serious, long-term malnutrition?

CHAPTER 6

The First Two Years: Cognitive Development

The pace of cognitive development in infancy is dramatic: an infant begins life capable of satisfying his or her curiosity about the world only through such basic activities as sucking, grabbing, staring, and listening, and yet within two years, he or she will be capable of anticipating future events, remembering past ones, imitating the actions of others, and pretending. The development of language is similarly remarkable: for a young infant, crying and smiling are the major modes of expression, yet by age 2, the average toddler will be able to converse simply but effectively with others.

In this chapter, we will discuss how these significant accomplishments occur and look for answers to a number of intriguing questions, including the following:

In what ways can babies think?

Why do babies sometimes grab at objects they are too immature to actually grasp?

When do infants begin to use gestures, such as pointing, to communicate?

When can infants perceive differences between males and females?

Are children born with some of the abilities required for using language, or are all language abilities learned?

Adults throughout the world change their speech patterns in special ways when they talk to children. What are the common features of "baby talk" and how do they promote language learning?

Newborns know nothing about the world around them, but armed with their reflexes, senses, and curiosity, they are ready and eager to begin making sense of the myriad sensations and events that surround them. By age 2 they have already learned a great deal about objects (that some make noise, that others move, that some are fun to play with, that some are not to be touched), about people (that some are familiar and trustworthy, that others are strange and unpredictable), and about experiences (that playing in sandboxes is enjoyable, that visiting the doctor can hurt). Even more impressive, they have learned to communicate, initially with gestures, body movements, and sounds, and then with words—a few by age 1 and a hundred or more by age 2.

All these achievements are part of **cognition,** that is, the interaction of all the perceptual, intellectual, and linguistic abilities that are involved in thinking and learning. If cognitive development is "how we acquire and use knowledge in adapting to the vicissitudes of the world" (Caron and Caron, 1982), then the infant's cognitive development during the first two years is impressive indeed.

We will begin our study of this development by considering the work of Jean Piaget, the foremost theorist of infant cognition.

Sensorimotor Intelligence

As you remember from Chapter 2, Piaget believed that children actively seek to comprehend their world, constructing understandings of it that reflect specific, age-related cognitive stages. This process, he demonstrated, begins at birth and accelerates rapidly in the early months of life. Indeed, Piaget's first, and most basic, contribution to the study of infant cognition was the recognition that infants do, in fact, think. Prior to his work, psychologists grossly underestimated infant intelligence, chiefly because of babies' lack of language. "No talk, no thought; no words, no ideas" was a prevalent and mistaken assumption. However, Piaget, perhaps because of his training as a zoologist, brought to the study of children an unprecedented quality of observation. His very close scrutiny of infant behavior—beginning with that of his own three children—soon convinced him that infants possess a highly active intelligence, one that, in the absence of language, functions exclusively through their *senses* and *motor skills* (Gratch and Schatz, 1987). Accordingly, Piaget called the first period of cognitive development **sensorimotor intelligence.**

Figure 6.1 *This boy's presentation strikes us as funny because we recognize Piaget's basic idea: children's thinking differs from adults' not only in its content but in its structure as well.*

"*But is showing you this toy and telling about it the whole story? Let's take a look at its sales record, as illustrated by this chart, which compares it with other toys in its price class.*"

What does it mean to say that infants think exclusively with their senses and motor skills? Consider this comparison. If a typical adult is presented with a plastic rattle, that person might refer to it by name, classify it according to function, and evaluate it aesthetically, while at the same time having thoughts ranging from the fascinations of infancy to the fluctuating costs of petrochemicals. Give a rattle to a baby and he or she will stare at it, shake it, suck it, bang it on the floor. As Flavell (1985) expresses it, the infant "exhibits a wholly practical, perceiving-and-doing, action-bound kind of intellectual functioning: he does not exhibit the more contemplative, reflective, symbol-manipulating kind we usually think of in connection with cognition."

The Six Stages of Sensorimotor Intelligence

According to Piaget, sensorimotor intelligence develops through six stages, each characterized by a somewhat different way of understanding the world (see Table 6.1).

Stage One: Reflexes (Birth to 1 Month)

Figure 6.2 *At the sensorimotor stage of cognitive development, even Father's face is a site for active exploration by all the infant's senses and motor skills.*

Sensorimotor intelligence begins with newborns' reflexes, such as sucking, grasping, looking, and listening. In Piaget's terms, these reflexes represent the only *schemas* that neonates have. (As you learned in Chapter 2, a schema is a general way of thinking about, and interacting with, the environment.) Take sucking as an example. One of the most powerful inborn abilities of the newborn is the *sucking reflex:* newborns suck everything that touches their lips, using the schema that all objects are to be sucked. Similarly, infants grasp at everything that touches the center of their palm, stare at everything that comes within focus, and so forth. Through the repeated exercise of these reflexes, newborns gain information about the world, information that will be used to develop the next stage of learning.

TABLE 6.1   The Six Stages of Sensorimotor Intelligence

To get an overview of the stages of sensorimotor thought, it helps to group the six stages in pairs. The first two involve the infant's own body.

Stage One (birth to 1 month)	*Reflexes*—sucking, grabbing, staring, listening.
Stage Two (1–4 months)	*The first acquired adaptations*—accommodation and coordination of reflexes—sucking a pacifier differently from a nipple; grabbing a bottle to suck it.

The next two involve objects and people.

Stage Three (4–8 months)	*Procedures for making interesting sights last*—responding to people and objects.
Stage Four (8–12 months)	*New adaptation and anticipation*—becoming more deliberate and purposeful in responding to people and objects.

The last two are the most creative, first with action and then with ideas.

Stage Five (12–18 months)	*New means through active experimentation*—experimentation and creativity in the actions of "the little scientist."
Stage Six (18–24 months)	*New means through mental combinations*—thinking before doing provides the child with new ways of achieving a goal without resorting to trial-and-error experiments.

Stage Two: The First Acquired Adaptations (1 Month to 4 Months)

The second stage of sensorimotor intelligence begins when infants adapt their reflexes to the environment. Again let us take the sucking reflex as an example. Infants first show signs of adapting their sucking to specific objects at about 1 month, according to Piaget, and by 3 months they have organized their world into objects to be sucked for nourishment (breasts or bottles), objects to be sucked for pleasure (fingers or pacifiers), and objects not to be sucked at all (fuzzy blankets and large balls). They also learn that efficient breast-sucking requires a squeezing sucking, whereas efficient finger- and pacifier-sucking do not. In addition, once infants learn that some objects satisfy hunger and others do not, they will suck contentedly on a pacifier when their stomach is full but will usually spit one out when they are hungry.

Stage Three: Procedures for Making Interesting Sights Last (4 Months to 8 Months)

In the third stage, infants become more aware of objects and other people, and they begin to recognize some of the specific characteristics of the things in their environment, particularly how objects respond to their actions on them. One way infants show this new awareness is by repeating a specific action that has just elicited a pleasing response from some person or thing. For example, a baby might accidentally squeeze a rubber duck, hear a quack, and squeeze the duck again. If the quack is repeated, the infant will probably laugh and give another squeeze, delighted to be able to control the toy's actions.

Piaget called stage three "procedures for making interesting sights last," because babies interact diligently with people and objects to produce exciting experiences. Realizing that rattles make noise, for example, babies at this stage shake their arms and laugh when someone puts a rattle in their hands. In fact, even the sight of something that normally delights the infant—a favorite toy, a favorite food, a smiling parent—can trigger an active attempt at interaction. Vocalization of all sorts increases a great deal, for now that babies realize that other people can respond, they love to make a noise, listen for a response, and answer back.

Figure 6.3 *What makes tickling tickle is the realization that someone else is doing it. This realization comes with stage three of sensorimotor development, as infants become more aware of other people and objects as separate from themselves.*

Stage Four: New Adaptation and Anticipation (8 Months to 12 Months)

In stage four, babies adapt in new, more deliberate ways. They can anticipate events that will fulfill their needs and wishes and can set about initiating them. A 10-month-old girl who enjoys playing in the tub might see a bar of soap and bring it to her mother as a signal to start her bath, squealing with delight when she hears her bath water turned on. Similarly, if a 10-month-old boy sees his mother putting on her coat to go out without him, he might begin tugging at it to stop her, or he might signal that he wants her to get his coat too.

Both of these examples reveal anticipation and, even more noteworthy, **goal-directed behavior**—that is, purposeful actions. Thus, stage-four babies might see something clear across the room and crawl toward it, ignoring many interesting distractions along the way. Or they might grab a forbidden object—a box of matches, a thumbtack, a cigarette—and cry with rage when it is taken away, even if they are offered a substitute that they normally find fascinating.

One important element underlying this reaction is **object permanence,** the realization that objects exist even when they cannot be seen. According to Piaget, for babies under 8 months, "out of sight" is literally "out of mind." If a 5-month-old drops a rattle out of the crib, the baby will not look down to search for it. It is as though the rattle has completely passed from the infant's awareness.

To determine if an infant has developed object permanence, Piaget developed a simple test: show a baby an interesting toy and then cover it up with a cloth or a blanket. If the baby tries to uncover it, he or she must suspect that the toy still exists. Here is how Piaget tried this test on his 7-month-old daughter Jacqueline with one of her favorite toys:

> I take the duck . . . and place it near her hand three times. All three times she tries to grasp it, but when she is about to touch it I place it very obviously under the sheet. Jacqueline immediately withdraws her hand and gives up.

Toward the end of stage three, babies might show tentative signs of realizing that when objects disappear, they have not vanished forever. When a toy falls from the crib, the 7-month-old sometimes looks for it for a moment rather than immediately losing interest. At the beginning of stage four, however, object permanence is readily apparent when the momentary impulse to look for an object that has disappeared from sight becomes an active effort to search for it.

Full realization of object permanence—in which the child knows that a toy that has vanished must still be *somewhere*—takes months to emerge. For instance, many stage-four infants make a fascinating mistake, called the **AB error.** Having found an object that was hidden in one place, A, and then observing it being hidden in a second place, B, the infant will subsequently search for the object in the first place, A, and then give up looking. Piaget (1954) described the AB error as displayed by Jacqueline:

> I take her [toy] parrot from her hands and hide it twice in succession under the mattress on her left, in A. Then I take it from her hands and move it very slowly before her eyes to the corresponding place on her right, under the mattress, in B. . . . At the moment when the parrot disappears in B, she turns to her left and looks where it was before, in A.

Figure 6.4 *What do you see in this photo? Instead of a mess that needs to be cleaned up, you might discern a demonstration of intellectual ability. This infant has a goal firmly in mind, and is wielding the tools to attain it—an achievement beyond most younger babies.*

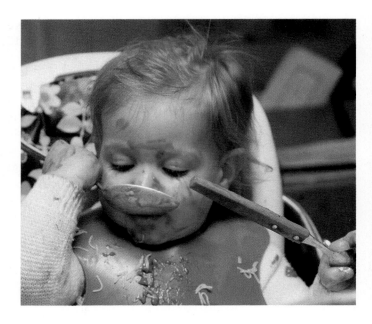

Even though object permanence is only partially established at stage four, its initial emergence, along with that of anticipation and goal-directed behavior, means that caregivers find they have a much different infant to deal with. For example, once infants realize that objects that are out of sight must be somewhere, they become more insistent, demanding specific people and certain toys to which they are attached. One infant cries for several minutes after Mother leaves; another refuses to go to sleep without a particular blanket; a third retrieves a rubber ball that rolled out of sight behind a bookcase; a fourth opens the cupboard to get some cookies. In short, as they gain an understanding of object permanence and act on it, infants become less malleable, more assertive, and, consequently, much more characteristically human.

Stage Five: New Means Through Active Experimentation (12 Months to 18 Months)

Stage five builds directly on the accomplishments of stage four, as the infant's goal-directed and purposeful activities become more expansive and creative. It is a time of active exploration and experimentation, a time when infants "get into everything," as though trying to discover all the possibilities their world has to offer.

The Little Scientist

Because of the explorations that characterize this stage, Piaget referred to the stage-five toddler as a little scientist who "experiments in order to see." Having discovered some action or set of actions that is possible with a given object, stage-five infants seem to ask, "What else can I do with this? What happens if I take the nipple off the bottle, or turn over the trash basket, or pour water on the cat?" Their "scientific method" is trial and error.

Partly because of this experimentation, babies in stage five no longer make the AB error, having learned from their explorations that an object hidden in a given place is likely to remain there. As long as they see an object disappear, they know where to look for it.

Their penchant for experimentation also leads toddlers to find new ways to achieve their goals. Through their trial-and-error explorations they learn, for instance, that they can bring a toy closer by pulling on the string tied to the end of it, or that they can "reach" the plate of cookies in the middle of the dinner table by pulling on the tablecloth (Piaget, 1952a). As parents of toddlers can readily attest, a little scientist's experiments can often wreak havoc. Remembering that these explorations are signs of developing intelligence may help a parent maintain a sense of humor, or at least a sense of perspective, when an infant combines baby powder and vaseline and uses the mixture to "paint" the wall, or takes out all the eggs in the refrigerator and throws them one by one on the floor, or, in a single flush, tries to send toothbrushes, hairbrushes, and a roll of paper down the toilet.

An important element that is missing from stage five is the ability to imagine something that is not tied directly to immediate perceptual experience. Object permanence, again, illustrates the point. According to Piaget, while the 15-month-old knows perfectly well that objects exist when you cannot see them, and that the best place to look is where they last disappeared, the child does not understand "invisible displacements." That is, the child cannot recognize a hiding place as such unless he or she has actually seen the object disappear there. Thus, at stage five Jacqueline Piaget watched her father hide a coin in his hand, and then put his closed hand under a blanket for a moment. When he withdrew his hand, Jacqueline looked in it for the coin, but when she didn't find it, she was perplexed. She didn't think of looking under the blanket for it.

Figure 6.5 *At stage five, as Duncan demonstrates here, the toddler's mission is to discover to what new uses familiar objects can be put.*

Stage Six: New Means Through Mental Combinations (18 Months to 24 Months)

At this stage, toddlers begin to anticipate and solve simple problems by using **mental combinations** before they act. That is, they are able to try out various actions mentally without having to actually perform them. Thus the child can invent new ways to achieve a goal without resorting to physical trial-and-error experiments. Consider how Jacqueline solved the following problem at 20 months:

> Jacqueline arrives at a closed door with a blade of grass in each hand. She stretches out her right hand toward the knob but sees that she cannot turn it without letting go of the grass. She puts the grass on the floor, opens the door, picks up the grass again and enters. But when she wants to leave the room, things become complicated. She puts the grass on the floor and grasps the doorknob. But then she perceives that in pulling the door toward her she will simultaneously chase away the grass which she placed between the door and the threshold. She therefore picks it up in order to put it outside the door's zone of movement. [Piaget, 1952a]

What makes mental combinations possible at this point is what Piaget called **mental representation,** the ability to create mental images of things and actions that are not actually in view. With the emergence of mental representation comes full object permanence. For example, in yet another search for a coin that had undergone an invisible displacement, Jacqueline Piaget this time looked first in her father's hand and then, without hesitation, under the blanket, without having ever seen the coin placed there.

Representation also allows the child to reproduce behavior observed in the past. For example, one day Jacqueline saw a neighbor's child have a temper tantrum: he screamed, shook his playpen, and stamped his feet. She had never seen anything like it. The next day, Jacqueline had a tantrum of her own, complete with stamping. Piaget called this kind of acting-out of a detailed mental image **deferred imitation,** because the reproduction of the image is delayed, or deferred, to another time.

Figure 6.6 *According to Piaget, pretending becomes possible when toddlers reach the stage of mental combinations, at about 18 months. At this point, imagination is expressed primarily through simple actions, such as those performed with a doll or toy animal; but soon it evolves into the elaborate dramas of the preschool and school-age child.*

Pretending

Perhaps the strongest, and most endearing, sign that children have reached stage six is their ability to pretend. Pretending can entail not only deferred imitation (as when a child sings a lullaby to a doll before tucking it into bed) but also mental combinations, as an action from one context (riding in a car) is mentally combined with another (pushing a toy car around a table). In stage six, the teddy whose fur became matted with saliva when every object was to be sucked (stage one), and whose arm got pulled off when every object needed to be experimented with (stage five), now becomes a playmate, to be cradled, cared for, and invited to tea.

The Significance of Stage-Six Behavior

Stage-six behaviors all share an important characteristic. They are a step beyond the simple motor responses of sensorimotor thought and a step toward "the more contemplative, reflective, symbol-manipulating activity" (Flavell, 1985) that we usually associate with cognition. As you will see in Chapter 9, mental representation, deferred imitation, and pretending all blossom into the symbolic thought typical of the next period of cognitive development.

Piaget Reconsidered

Piaget's analysis of infant cognition, published more than half a century ago, is still widely accepted. Many studies on thousands of babies have replicated the results Piaget initially discovered with his own three children. His description of the infant's increasing ability to learn about the world by *acting* on it—sucking, grasping, and experimenting—remains a vivid and useful account.

However, later research has also revealed several problems with Piaget's theories and descriptions. These problems have to do with (1) the seeming strictness of Piaget's timetable for the child's progression through the sensorimotor stages and (2) the implication that the child enters each stage "all at once," in all abilities. Both of these problems have been highlighted by recent research on object permanence, one of the more familiar mileposts of sensorimotor intelligence.

A Second Look at Object Permanence

Literally hundreds of studies of object permanence have been undertaken, most supporting the essence of Piaget's findings. It certainly seems true that, in the first half of the first year, infants do not search for hidden objects and then, sometime in the second half of the first year, they do. It also is true that object permanence is a concept that develops with age, so that the older baby no longer makes the AB error, and even masters invisible displacements.

However, many researchers have added important qualifiers to Piaget's formulations. The central qualifier is that the various phases of object permanence do not appear, suddenly and reliably, in strict accordance with Piaget's schedule. Rather, the schema of object permanence emerges very gradually, and the age at which each new advance is attained can vary somewhat from child to child.

The age at which object permanence is demonstrated can also vary according to how it is being tested. According to Piaget, for example, what proves that the infant understands object permanence is active searching: failure to search means the concept is not yet understood. However, active searching requires a certain amount of motivation, memory, and motor ability, as well as understanding. When simpler criteria are taken as proof of object permanence—perhaps a surprised look when an object suddenly reappears in a place other than where it disappeared, or a sign of anticipation when an adult's search is about to succeed—infants as young as 4 months old have been found to demonstrate at least rudimentary object permanence (Baillergeon et al., 1990).

Even using standard Piagetian tests, the age at which object permanence seems to emerge can vary due to a number of factors that are not directly related to the infant's cognitive maturity (Ruff, 1982; Harris, 1987). For example, the infant's prior experience in searching, and his or her motivation to search, can affect whether object permanence is demonstrated or not. The particular hiding place can make a difference as well: infants who do not pull away a blanket to search for an object might look behind a screen or knock over a cup for one; infants who uncover a toy hidden right in front of them might not uncover a toy hidden a foot or two away.

Memory and Object Permanence

Memory ability may also be critical. An infant may actually realize that a just-hidden object still exists somewhere, but may have swiftly forgotten where it is. This explanation particularly fits the AB error. As we saw earlier, in stage four, infants who see an object hidden in place B, after having earlier seen it hidden in place A, look for it in place A. This error, according to Piaget, disappears at stage five. In fact, however, extensive research has shown that, depending on certain factors, infants younger than 12 months often correctly look in B and infants over 12 months often mistakenly look in A (Harris, 1987).

One factor is the relative "memorability" of the hiding places. It is easier for an infant to remember something dropped into a small, shallow container, covered by a cloth of contrasting color, than to remember something slipped somewhere into a large area filled with possible hiding places. Thus,

Figure 6.7 *In infancy, no less than in the rest of life, passing a test of cognitive ability depends on the specific circumstances surrounding the testing as well as on the age and intelligence of the child. If this infant had had no interest in the hidden object, he would have had little motivation to search for it, even though he might have realized it still existed under the blanket.*

10-month-old Jacqueline Piaget, after having found her parrot in location A, under the mattress, might have then found it in the new hiding place if location B had been on top of the bed beneath a bright scarf rather than merely under another part of the mattress.

Another critical factor is the time interval between the hiding and the searching. If allowed to look immediately for the object, many infants in stage four correctly look in place B. But even a short delay after the object is hidden can cause an infant to lose track and revert to searching in A.

A longitudinal study conducted by Adele Diamond set out to find exactly how time delays affected infants' searching at different ages (Diamond, 1985). In this research, the object-finding abilities of twenty-five infants were measured every two weeks for half a year, beginning at 6 months. At first, none of the infants showed any evidence of understanding the most basic object permanence; they did not search for an intriguing toy that was hidden right in front of them under a highly visible blue cloth. By 7½ months, at their third testing, eighteen of the twenty-five infants demonstrated a basic object permanence by uncovering the hidden toy. These eighteen were then tested on the AB problem. Only four were successful, uncovering the toy in location B after they had previously found it in location A.

In this experiment, once the babies had mastered the basic AB problem, their search was subjected to systematic time delays. For example, the four precocious 7½-month-olds who had already mastered the AB problem were retested immediately. This time they were distracted and prevented from searching for 2 seconds. The result: two of them looked correctly in location B and the other two erroneously searched in location A.

From then on, every month brought improvement for all twenty-five infants. At 8½ months, those who previously hadn't even searched for the hidden toy did so; those who had made the basic AB error no longer did; and the precocious four avoided the AB error after a delay of several seconds. Once each of the infants had overcome the basic AB problem, his or her performance on delayed searches improved at an average rate of 2 seconds per month. By 11 months, eighteen of the twenty-five could wait 8 seconds or longer between the hiding and the search and still find the toy.

This one experiment illustrates two of the central problems with Piaget's delineation of infant cognition. For one thing, it clearly shows variability in age of accomplishment, a variability that occurred even though, in this case, background differences among the subjects were minimal. (All the babies were full-term, healthy, and from two-parent, mostly upper-middle-class families in Boston, and so, presumably, they all experienced the same general patterns of child-rearing and environmental stimulation.) The experiment also clearly shows that the attainment of object permanence, like many other aspects of sensorimotor intelligence, is far from being an all-or-nothing phenomenon. Piaget's cognitive milestones are reached gradually, bit by bit, and their demonstration may depend, in part, on the testing conditions. One reason that Diamond's experiment found object permanence attained at earlier ages than Piaget predicted may have been that it involved repeated practice under highly motivating conditions designed to elicit a search. For example, the infants' every success was greeted with praise, applause, and a chance to play with the toy they had just found. The fact that testing conditions can make a substantial difference in performance is telling, revealing that much more than a natural unfolding of conceptual ability is involved in the acquisition of object permanence. These same general findings apply to many other aspects of Piaget's account of sensorimotor intelligence.

Sensorimotor Intelligence Reevaluated

As you read in Chapter 2, Piaget's theory is a general statement about the developmental path of the human species as a whole. His goal was to understand the grand and universal process of human cognition (Gratch and Schatz, 1987). Consequently, his depiction of the major cognitive stages as well as of the sensorimotor stages is made to seem applicable to every child in the same way, with each child moving uniformly and sequentially through each stage on schedule. Indeed, one of Piaget's major contributions to developmental psychology is his clear delineation of how children at any particular age can be expected to think.

Unevenness and Diversity

However, if too rigidly applied, Piaget's depiction of how children think can also be a liability in two ways. First, it implies that children progress from one stage to another quite suddenly and globally, like climbing from one step of a flight of stairs to the next. As we have just seen with object permanence, (1) cognitive development seems to occur much less evenly than Piaget's descriptions suggest, with the individual demonstrating a new cognitive level bit by bit, ability by ability, and situation by situation; and (2) the specific context—especially the conditions of the testing situation—is far more important than Piaget realized in determining whether or not an infant would appear to have reached a particular sensorimotor stage.

Second, the assumed universality of Piagetian stages may blind us to the diversity and variability of cognitive development. Many factors contribute to this diversity. Of particular importance are individual differences in inherited characteristics and early experiences, which can have a powerful influence on the timing of specific aspects of cognitive growth (McCall, 1981).

Cultural differences in the specific customs and goals of child care also produce notable differences in the nature and pace of cognitive development (Le Vine, 1989), a truism in infancy as well as in childhood and adulthood. For example, babies from the Ivory Coast of Africa reach the stages of sensorimotor development somewhat earlier than French babies, perhaps because their culture generally places greater value on motor skills and provides more opportunities for sensorimotor stimulation (Dasen et al., 1978).

The more we study exceptional babies, non-Western cultures, and specific aspects of cognition, the more we find that Piaget's masterful overview of cognition ignores many of the variations and dimensions of early learning. For the most part, it is not that Piaget was wrong so much as that he was incomplete. One broad area of cognition that was largely ignored because of Piaget's emphasis on practical, skill-related cognition is perception. This is described on pages 154–155. Another area is memory, which we will examine in the Research Report on the next page.

Figure 6.8 *The cultural differences suggested by this photo go beyond costume and setting. Holding an infant upright and engaging in face-to-face dialogue is much more common in some cultures than others. As a result, some infants gain sensorimotor skills, as well as social skills, more quickly than others.*

RESEARCH REPORT   Infant Memory in Context

As you just read, under the right conditions, infants' memory for hidden objects or for actions performed by someone else is much better than predicted by Piaget. Piaget was not alone in his underestimation of what and when babies remember. Until recently, developmentalists agreed that infant memory was fleeting and fragile. Naturalistic observations of babies under 6 months were replete with instances of forgetting. For instance, a trip to the pediatrician for an inoculation at 2 months would be forgotten a month later, when the same doctor in the same setting would be greeted with a smile. Psychoanalytic theory even held that experiences of the first two years were lost to memory in a kind of "infantile amnesia."

Experimental research confirmed that young infants' memories fade very quickly. In a typical experiment, 3-month-old infants might habituate to a series of photographs of the same face and then look at a photo of a new face with interest—a sign not only that the infants could detect the difference but also that they remembered the old face. But then, a few seconds later, if the experimenter showed the photo of the original face, most infants would stare at it as if it were new. Overall, experimental evidence found that, at best, babies under 8 months might remember a stimulus for a minute or so (Werner and Perlmutter, 1979). At about 8 months, according to the research, memory improves, with infants for the first time being able to recall something they have experienced an hour or more before (Schacter and Moscovitch, 1984). Toward the end of the second year of life, when language begins to provide assistance, memory becomes more permanent.

On the whole, this account of infant memory remains fairly accurate. At the same time, however, it now appears that earlier memory research may not have elicited the best of infant performance, particularly in infants under a year (Rovee-Collier, 1987; Siegler, 1986). One of the problems is that much of the research was designed to be free of "contamination" by real-life experiences, and thus was conducted in a laboratory setting with material the infant had never before experienced. Further, the stimulus to be remembered was typically presented in one repetitive installment—such as showing an infant a series of photos of the same stranger, and then showing a photo of another stranger. The result, as Rovee-Collier (1987) points out, was a good deal of information about the infant's short-term memory of unfamiliar stimuli in simple, unfamiliar settings, yet

little understanding of the infant's behavior in a complex environment that contains a variety of sources of *predictive information*. Humans have evolved in a variable environment, yet our typical experimental environments have been relatively barren. [Rovee-Collier, 1987]

By contrast, recent research has shown that when (1) the experiment is carefully tailored to the infant's capacity as it might be demonstrated in real life, and (2) the infant's motivation to remember is high, and (3) special measures are taken to aid retrieval, infant memory is much more capable than was once thought. Notable among this new research has been a series of experiments with 3-month-olds, in which the infants were taught to make a mobile move. This is a highly reinforcing event for young babies, who delight in looking at colorful, moving objects within easy focusing distance. The infants were tested at home, in their own cribs. A brightly colored mobile was placed overhead, and the infants were connected to the mobile by means of a ribbon tied to one of their feet. In this situation, virtually every infant quickly was conditioned to kick to make the mobile move.

Two weeks later, these same infants were again placed in their cribs and the mobile tied to their feet, but they showed no evidence of having remembered how to activate the mobile (Sullivan, 1982). Presumably they were too young to have retained in long-term memory what they had learned about mobile-moving.

However, surprising results occurred when this experiment was repeated with another group of infants who were allowed a "reminder" session two weeks after the initial learning session. In this reminder session, the infants were not tied to the ribbon, and were positioned so they could not kick. They merely watched the mobile move (a hidden experimenter pulled another ribbon). The next day, when they were tethered to the mobile and positioned so that they could move their legs, the infants remembered to kick as they had learned to do two weeks before. Similar experiments have been done with younger infants (as young as 8 weeks) after a longer interval (up to eighteen days) with the same result (Davis and Rovee-Collier, 1983; Linde et al., 1985). Thus infant memory does not necessarily disappear forever within moments after the event, as most experts had previously believed.

Now that we know that young infants can learn a behavior pattern and remember it for longer than a few minutes, the question is, What exactly is it that young infants remember? In the case of the mobile experiment, is the infant's kicking merely akin to a reflexive response, triggered by the sight of the mobile? Or is the infant somehow processing the mobile experience cognitively, perhaps beginning to make a judgment about when to kick and when not to. Continuing research using the mobile has revealed that at least some thought is part of the process. If infants are trained three days in a row with one kind of mobile, say, of zoo animals, and then tested the next day with another kind, say, of circus figures, they show no sign of remembering to kick. Apparently, the specifics of their training caused their memory to focus on a particular visual display.

However, if they are trained on three separate days on three different mobiles—zoo, circus, farm—and then tested on another day with still another mobile—for instance, storybook characters—they do kick to make the unfamiliar mobile move. In this case, their training apparently caused them to form a more generalized memory.

Indeed, the infant's ability to differentiate and generalize is remarkable. In one set of experiments, 3-month-olds were once again conditioned to kick their feet to make a mobile move. The mobile was a series of blocks embossed with either the letter A or the number 2. Two weeks after the original training, infants who had been trained and reminded with an A mobile were more likely to activate an A mobile by kicking than they were a 2 mobile, and vice versa. Infants who had been trained on one mobile, and reminded with another, were not likely to remember what they had learned (Hayne et al., 1987).

Further evidence for the remarkable durability of specific memories comes from a recent longitudinal experiment (Perris et al., 1990). It began with 6-month-olds being trained in a university laboratory to reach for a dangling Big Bird toy when it made a noise, first in the light and then in the dark. Two years later, the children were brought back to the lab and retested on this reaching task, along with a control group of age-mates who had received no training. Prior to the retesting, the trained children were interviewed to see if they had any overt memory of the laboratory setting or the training experience: they did not. Then, thirty minutes before testing, half of all the children who were to participate were randomly selected and given a 3-second exposure to the toy in the dark—intended as a possible "reminder" for those from the trained group.

In the actual experiment, the conditions of the original test were repeated: each child sat in his or her mother's lap and was told the lights would go out. Then, in the dark, the experimenter dangled the noise-making toy in front of the child. Compared with the untrained children, those who had been trained at 6 months were more likely to reach and grab the toy. In fact, among those who experienced the 3-second "reminder" exposure, the previously trained children reached almost four times as often. Moreover, their reaction to suddenly being in the dark was "an

almost global emotional acceptance," a marked contrast to the discomfort and fussiness exhibited by many from the control group. Thus, not only the sensorimotor pattern of a single experience at 6 months, but also its emotional tone, can remain in the memory, dormant, for two full years.

Many developmentalists are now reexploring infant memory, trying to discover exactly when and how it functions (e.g., Moscovitch, 1984; Lipsitt, 1990). Some conclusions are evident.

1. Even under the best of conditions, memory is fragile in the beginning of life, elicited only by particular reminder events.

2. The specific learning situation and the infant's motivation to remember are extremely important, and the best performance is likely to occur when the task and situation have some ecological relevance for the infant.

3. Very young infants can and do remember, not words but sensorimotor experiences—images, smells, movements, and sounds—that are unlikely to be measured by traditional tests of memory.

4. Improvement in memory ability seems tied to brain maturation and language development, with notable increases in memory capacity and duration occurring at about 8 months, and again at about 18 months.

Much more needs to be understood, including answers to the following questions:

1. Are there several forms of memory, perhaps a type for sensorimotor processes (as in kicking) and another for more cerebral processes including language?

2. Is the problem with infant memory primarily one of encoding—that is, getting the event into memory—or of retrieval—that is, getting it back out once it is in?

3. Is the reason that older children and adults seem unable to remember any of the emotions and events of their infancy because these memories are processed through sensorimotor activities exclusively, rather than through language?

4. What is the relationship between infant memory and infant cognition? In what ways does memory relate to perception, to sensorimotor schemas, to language, and vice versa? More research in this area is now underway. As you will see in the next section of this chapter, one of the most promising avenues of inquiry is in perception.

Perception

Infant cognitive development is demonstrated on three different but related fronts. The first to be recognized—by parents and researchers alike—was language, which once was considered the only manifestation of infant intelligence. Piaget, of course, called attention to a second form of infant thinking when he noted that, through sensorimotor intelligence, babies learn by doing long before they learn by listening and talking.

In recent years, a number of researchers have focused on a third way that infant intelligence is revealed—through the infant's perceptual organizations. Using new experimental techniques to study infant perception, these researchers have shown that, beginning in the first days and months of life, infants learn by perceiving, that is, by cognitively selecting, sorting, and organizing the sensory information that bombards them. This work on infant perception has reaffirmed and deepened what Piaget's initial work on sensorimotor intelligence began to reveal fifty years ago—that infants are much more knowledgeable than most people ever imagined.

The Gibsons' Ecological View of Perception

Much of the current research in perception and cognition has been inspired by the work of Eleanor and James Gibson (1969, 1979, 1982). These researchers stress that perception is far from being an automatic phenomenon, which everyone, everywhere, experiences in the same way. Rather, perception is, essentially, an active cognitive process, in which each individual selectively interacts with a dense and richly varied field of perceptual possibilities.

Affordances

In the Gibsons' view, all objects have many **affordances;** that is, they "afford," or offer, diverse opportunities for interaction. What affordances a person actually perceives with regard to any given object depends partly on the individual's past experiences, partly on his or her present needs, and partly on his or her cognitive awareness of what the object might afford. To take a simple example, a lemon, among many other possibilities, affords smelling, tasting, touching, viewing, throwing, and squeezing. Which of these affordances a person perceives depends on the individual and the situation: a lemon might elicit a quite different perceptual response from an artist about to paint a still-life, a thirsty adult in need of a cool, refreshing drink, and a teething baby wanting something to gnaw on.

The idea of affordances thus emphasizes that there is an ecological fit between individual perceptions and the environment, such that affordances do not reside solely in the object itself but arise in large measure from how the individual perceives the object (Ruff, 1984). As one psychologist explains:

> With affordances, a function is defined not by an essence but by its functional use to an organism. For example, if I want to sit down in a sparsely furnished bus station, a floor or a stack of books or a not-too-hot radiator might afford sitting. None of these are chairs, and thus their affordance of "sit-ability" is in relationship to my perception. [Gauvain, 1990]

How does the idea of affordances relate to infants? First of all, it alerts us to consider what the infant needs to perceive from the environment. One such affordance is graspability, that is, whether an object is the right size, shape, and texture for grasping, and whether it is within reach. This is vital information for infants, since they learn a great deal about their world by handling various objects (Rochat, 1989; Palmer, 1989). Extensive research has shown that infants perceive graspability long before their manual dexterity enables them to actually grasp successfully. For instance, when 3-month-olds view objects, some graspable and some not, they reach for those that are the right size and distance for grasping and merely follow the others with their eyes (Bower, 1989).

The fact that babies perceive graspability so early helps explain how they explore a face. Once they have some control over their arm and hand movements, and a face comes within their reach, they immediately grab at it. But their grabbing is not haphazard: they do not grab at the eyes or mouth (although they might poke at them), for they already perceive that these objects are imbedded, and thus do not afford grasping. A pull at the nose or ears is more likely, because these features do afford grasping. Even better, however, are glasses, or earrings, or a long mustache—all of which are quickly yanked by most babies, who perceive at a glance the graspability these objects afford. Similarly, from a very early age, infants understand which objects afford suckability, which afford noise-making, which afford movability, and so forth. An impressive feature of this perceptual capacity is the infant's ability to distinguish affordance similarities in dissimilar objects (rattles, glasses, and pacifiers are all graspable) and affordance differences in similar objects (among objects the same color, size, and shape, furry ones are more likely to be squeezed and plastic ones more likely to be sucked) (Palmer, 1989).

Coordination Between Sensory Systems

Once researchers were alerted to the early development of perceptual skills, they began to look closely at the infant's ability to integrate perceptual information from different sensory systems.

One aspect of this is **intermodal perception,** the ability to associate information from one sensory modality with information from another. For example, when we sit near a lighted fireplace, it is through intermodal perception that we realize that the heat, the crackling, the smokey odor, and the flickering light all come from the same source.

Even newborns exhibit some intermodal perception, as when they look for the source of a sound—though not always in the right direction. By 3 months, they not only look quite accurately for the source of what they hear but also have a notion of which sounds are likely to accompany what events. This has been demonstrated in various experiments that test whether infants can "match up" a film they are watching with an appropriate soundtrack. In one such experiment (Spelke, 1979), infants were shown two films simultaneously, each one displaying a stuffed animal puppet jumping up and down. At the same time, the infants heard a percussion soundtrack, keyed to the dancing movements of one of the puppets. By carefully monitoring the direction of the infants' gaze, the experimenter discovered that the infants looked more often at the film that matched the soundtrack.

Figure 6.9 *This infant is coordinating an intermodal perception by linking the sight of the sponge with its texture and affordance of squeezability. From the looks of it, the next mode of perception to be coordinated may be taste.*

What do these results mean? Were the infants simply responding in a visceral way to the beat of the drum and the accompanying visual rhythm of the puppet's jumping, or were they actually making a mental link between a particular sound and a particular sight? To answer this question, variations of this experiment have been repeated many times, usually with infants less than 6 months old. Even when there is no obvious visual or auditory rhythm, infants typically focus most on the film that matches the soundtrack, whether the sound is music, a voice, or simply noises—such as squishing sounds (matched with a film of a sponge being squeezed) or clacking sounds (matched with a film of wooden blocks hitting one another) (Bahrick, 1983). In one variation, infants about 6 months old simultaneously viewed two films of people talking, one happy and one sad. At the same time, they heard the soundtrack of one of the films (the voice was deliberately not synchronized with the film, so that lip movements would not be a cue). Although the infants at first looked equally at both films, they soon began looking more intently at the one that matched the mood of the soundtrack (Walker, 1982).

The fact that infants 6 months and younger are able to match pictures with sounds in so many different examples suggests that the babies are not simply making a primitive match between visual and auditory rhythms. Rather, they seem to be doing something more complex and more cerebral, turning information from one sensory modality into an expectancy and then matching that expectancy with information from another sensory modality.

Evidence for such cognitive integration of perceptual information also comes from research on a related ability known as **cross-modal perception,** the ability to use information from one sensory modality to imagine something in another—as when you hear the voice of a stranger on the phone and picture the person who is talking, or see a food and imagine how it tastes. In infants, of course, cross-modal perception is extremely rudimentary, but it has nevertheless been demonstrated many times (Rose and Ruff, 1987; Spelke, 1987). The most convincing evidence comes from experiments in which infants create a visual expectancy through their sense of touch. Essentially, experimenters allow infants to manipulate an object that is hidden from view and then show them two objects, one of which is the object they have just touched. By analyzing the infants' gaze, researchers can tell whether the infants distinguish the object they manipulated from the one they have not. In one experiment, for example, 2½-month-olds touched either a plastic ring or a flat disk and then were shown both objects. The duration of their gazing revealed that most of the infants "recognized" the object they had just manipulated (Streri, 1985).

Startlingly, even 1-month-olds have some cross-modal perceptual abilities. Again, visual expectancy derived from touch is involved, but the touch is by mouth, not by hand. In one experiment, infants sucked for a minute on an object, either a rigid one (a lucite cylinder) or a flexible one (a piece of wet sponge). They then observed both objects being manipulated by a pair of black-gloved hands. Analysis of their gazing suggested that they could distinguish the familiar object from the novel one: in other words, just by sucking an object they had gained some understanding of how it might look and move (Gibson and Walker, 1984).

What is the significance of this research? To some investigators, it suggests that, from a very early age, infants are coordinating and organizing their perceptions into categories, such as soft, hard, flat, round, rigid, flexi-

Figure 6.10 *The earliest verifiable instances of cross-modal perception occur when 1-month-olds put something in their mouths and form a concept of how it might look. With experience, infants can reverse the process, imagining how something will taste from the way it looks.*

ble, and so forth. For the preverbal infant, of course, these categories do not have labels, but they are nonetheless useful. Once an object is mentally placed in a category, the infant has a ready set of expectations about it.

Developing Categories

The perceptions infants form may, in some ways, be part of the neurological potential of the human being, the result of the interaction of a prewired intellect and the sensory world (Lockman, 1990). In other words, very young infants, perhaps even newborns, may be predisposed to perceive the world in certain ways, "programmed" as it were, to search for examples of general categories such as suckability, graspability, and squeezability as they encounter various objects.

Indeed, research on perceptual abilities indicates that infants may be neurologically primed to perceive certain characteristics of objects, putting them into categories just as older children do. Some sort of innate categorization process seems the likely explanation for the results of a study of 3-month-olds (Cook and Birch, 1984) who saw a series of pictures, first a sequence of squares and then a parallelogram the same size as the square (see Figure 6.11). When the parallelogram appeared, the infants looked much longer at it than at the squares (7 seconds versus 2 seconds), suggesting that they had some notion of "squareness" in mind and that this notion was "violated" by the appearance of the parallelogram.

An alternative explanation, of course, is that the infants were simply reacting to a change in the stimulus. The experimenters explored this possibility by rotating both the square and the parallelogram 90 degrees. Now both shapes, standing on a corner rather than on a side, looked like diamonds (see Figure 6.11). A group of 3-month-olds were habituated to the first diamond, and then shown the second. In this case, they didn't stare any longer at the second stimulus than at the first. On some level, at least, they seemed to recognize that a parallelogram is not a square, but that a diamond—though shaped somewhat differently from another diamond—is still a diamond.

Similar results—and further evidence for innate categorization—come from the perception of color. Twenty years ago, psychologists wondered if infants could distinguish colors at all. Certainly many preschoolers have difficulty learning the names for various colors, confusing such opposite hues as purple and yellow. However, we now know that babies 4 months and older

Figure 6.11 *Infants as young as 3 months old seem to demonstrate some awareness of the category "squareness" by recognizing the discrepancy between the squares and the parallelogram in the first row of this figure.*

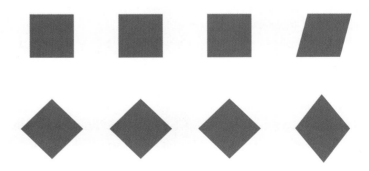

RESEARCH REPORT   Is It a Boy or a Girl?

Very early in life infants have some beginning understanding that people are subdivided into male and female. By 3 months of age, babies seem to realize that male voices and faces are different from female voices and faces. For instance, an infant who is shown a series of photographs of male faces is likely to habituate to the series, even if each face is obviously different. Then, if a female face appears, the infant suddenly pays more attention.

Studies of intermodal perception demonstrate that infants are soon able to coordinate their knowledge of gender-specific voices and faces. One study showed 6-month-olds two photographs, one of a woman and one of a man, and simultaneously played a tape of a person talking. At first the infants scanned both faces equally. Then, gradually, gender expectancies appeared to emerge: the babies looked longer at the male face when the speaker was male, and longer at the female face when the speaker was female (Francis and McCroy, 1983).

By 1 year of age, infants seem to have a firm ability to distinguish male from female, even among young children. In fact, whereas adults frequently have trouble distinguishing the sex of 1-year-olds, especially when the infants are dressed in unisex clothes, 1-year-olds themselves do not share this difficulty (Bower, 1989). When playing with unfamiliar peers, dressed in unisex clothes, boys are much more likely to play with boys, and girls, with girls. Even in looking at video tapes of toddlers, boys pay more attention to the boys, and girls, to the girls.

In one experiment, reported by Bower (1989), researchers made several brief films with a very simple basic script: a toddler walks over to a toy and sits down. The only variations were the sex of the toddler, how he or she was dressed (either in boyish pants and shirt or a frilly dress), and the toy (a drum or a doll). When 1-year-olds were shown two of these films, different only in the actor's biological sex, they looked more intently at the film that showed someone of their own sex, no matter what the other variables. Thus, a girl would tend to look more intently at a girl in pants and shirt playing with a drum than at a boy in a dress playing with a doll. The most interesting specific finding was that boys "spent proportionally far more time" looking at cross-dressed boys than at traditionally dressed boys or cross-dressed girls.

> Their typical pattern of looks at the cross-dressed boy was a long stare, a glance off at nothing, followed by short looks, interspersed with looking off. It was almost as if the boys found the sight of a boy dressed in girls' clothing extremely puzzling, almost shocking. No such pattern was found in girls. [Bower, 1989]

How do these infants detect biological sex when the external clues are deceptive? Bower hypothesized that

Is this a boy or a girl? And what about the infant being tickled on p. 146 or the baby about to taste the sponge on p. 157? Check your guesses by looking on page 162 and realize that your eye for infant gender probably would have been keener if you were a year old.

movement patterns seemed the likely answer. To test his idea, he dressed boy and girl models in black jumpsuits and placed a band of reflective tape on each shoulder, elbow, wrist, hip, knee, and ankle. He then filmed the infants in special lighting that revealed nothing but the movement of the reflective bands. According to Bower, when toddlers are shown these films, "the familiar pattern emerges, with boy babies looking more at boy babies and girl babies looking more at girl babies." On analyzing the films, Bower found that girls take shorter steps, swing their hips more, and seem more fluid in their movements. In addition, boys almost always bend from the waist to pick up a toy, whereas girls bend from the knees.

The fact that 1-year-olds are sensitive to all these subtle differences that escape most adults suggests that they have formed their own version of gender categories, based more on perception of body movement than on culturally determined differences in clothing or playthings. At the same time, the fact that the boys were highly alert to boys in frilly dresses, whereas the girls took no special notice of girls in boyish garb, suggests that by age 1 children have already begun to absorb cultural norms regarding "sex-appropriate" attire among their peers.

not only can perceive the difference between red, blue, green, and so forth but also find it easier to remember a color if it is a basic hue—the reddest red, the bluest blue—just as adults do (Teller and Bornstein, 1987).

Young infants also seem to have some innate notion of similarities and differences with regard to other perceptual distinctions. In one study, a group of 4-month-olds were shown several pairs of geometric forms, identical in shape but different in size. In each case, the smaller shape was pictured above the larger. After seeing several instances of this arrangement, the infants glanced for a shorter and shorter time at each new presentation. Suddenly, the larger shape appeared above the smaller one. Immediately, the infants' length of gazing increased, as if they were trying to figure out what had happened. This suggests that, in a very elemental way, infants may be able to extrapolate a general concept of relative size from a series of instances (Caron and Caron, 1981). The same general research format reveals that infants younger than 8 months can also distinguish sets that differ in density, angularity, shape, and number (up to three items).

Taken as a whole, the evidence suggests that young infants are not merely "seeing the difference" between blue and red, square and parallelogram, larger and smaller; they are also applying some underlying organizing principles that enable them to develop a concept of what is, or is not, relevant for inclusion in a particular category. While this kind of rudimentary understanding of certain categories may be innate—"prewired" as it were—it is through experience that such categories are developed and refined so that they become usable in specific contexts. One clear example involves the ability to distinguish male and female. Although the underlying differences between these categories are biological, and perhaps are biologically recognized, the particular cues attached to them, such as dress and behavior, are largely cultural. As the Research Report on page 160 demonstrates, even young infants show some ability to distinguish male and female, and by age 1, can, in some limited instances, apply cultural cues to these categories.

In truth, the implications of all this perception research are open to question. Some researchers are convinced that it reflects the development of perceptual categories and expectancies that are akin to thinking processes used at later ages, processes of reflection, evaluation, and conceptualization. Other researchers believe that it merely reflects the maturation of the basic senses and the refinement of simple perceptual abilities, rather than the formation of categories and concepts. Certainly infant perceptions do not lead to concepts in the abstract and verbal sense, such as "truth," "beauty," or "justice." However, as one major researcher points out, the linking together of one perception and another within the brain is "where perceiving ends and thinking begins" (Spelke, 1987). The ability to perceive what an object affords, to coordinate one sense and another, to detect the similarities and differences between various shapes and colors and faces, suggests that something cognitive allows infants to organize and interpret reality in a way much more advanced than researchers previously realized. If this is so, it is no wonder that babies become such active explorers once they finally can walk and grab. It is also no wonder that speech development proceeds so rapidly once toddlers learn and are able to use the particular words that express concepts they may have understood for some time. Let us now turn to that third area of cognition, language.

Language Development

Everywhere in the world, in every language, children are talking by age 2, with a grasp of basic grammar and a vocabulary that is frequently surprising in scope. Consider these sentences uttered consecutively by 24-month-old Sarah:

> Uh, oh. Kitty jumping down.
> What drawing? Numbers? [said as her words were being transcribed]
> Want it, paper.
> Wipe it, pencil.
> What time it is? [said upon seeing a watch]

These sentences show that Sarah has a varied vocabulary and a basic understanding of word order. For example, Sarah said "Kitty jumping down," rather than "Down jumping kitty," or "Jumping kitty down," or "Kitty down jumping." They also show that she has much to learn, for she incorrectly uses the pronoun "it" and its referent together, omits personal pronouns, and uses reverse word order in asking the time. Sarah's impressive but imperfect language is quite similar to that of 2-year-olds in many families and cultures. On the basis of detailed studies of thousands of babies, we know quite a bit about the sequence of verbal skills in the first two years of life, and Sarah, both in her early days and here at age 2, is typical.

Steps in Language Development

Children the world over follow the same sequence and approximately the same timetable for early language development (Bates et al., 1987; see Table 6.2). The first area in which they become competent is *language function*—that is, the communication of ideas and emotions. Indeed, considering language solely in terms of its function, it can be said that infants are born using language, a language of noises and gestures. As you will see, within the first

The answers for the figure in the Research Report are girl, girl, boy!

TABLE 6.2	Language Development: The First Two Years
Newborn	Reflexive communication—cries, movements, facial expressions.
2 months	A range of meaningful noises—cooing, fussing, crying, laughing.
3–6 months	New sounds, including squeals, growls, croons, trills, vowel sounds.
6–10 months	Babbling, including both consonant and vowel sounds repeated in syllables.
10 months	Comprehension of simple words; intonation of language; specific vocalizations that have meaning to those who know the infant well. Deaf babies express their first sign; hearing babies use specific gestures (e.g., pointing) to communicate.
12 months	First spoken words that are recognizably part of the native language.
12–18 months	Slow growth of vocabulary, up to 50 words.
16–20 months	More rapid increase of vocabulary, first two-word sentences.
24 months	Vocabulary of more than 200 words. Grammar apparent in word order, suffixes, prefixes, pronouns (specifics depend partly on the particular native language).

two years of life, this rudimentary ability to communicate evolves into an impressive command of *language structure*, that is, the particular words and rules of the infant's native tongue.

Cries, Coos, and Babbling

Infants are noisy creatures, crying, cooing, and making a variety of other sounds even in the first weeks of life. These noises gradually become more varied over the first months, so that by 5 months, squeals, growls, grunts, croons, and yells, as well as some speechlike sounds, are part of most babies' verbal repertoire. Then, rather suddenly, at 6 or 7 months, babies' utterances begin to include the repetition of certain syllables ("ma-ma-ma," "da-da-da," "ba-ba-ba"), a phenomenon referred to as **babbling** because of the way it sounds. In some respects babbling is universal—all babies do it, and all make the same sounds, no matter what language their parents speak. Worldwide, every culture assigns important meanings to some of these sounds, with "ma-ma-ma," "da-da-da," and the like usually being applied to significant people in the infant's life (see Table 6.3).

Babbling in Deaf Infants

Deaf babies begin to make babbling sounds several months later than other infants do (Oller and Eilers, 1988). However, recent research suggests that deaf infants may actually begin a type of babbling—manually—at about the same time hearing infants begin babbling orally (Pettito, 1991). Analysis of video tapes of deaf children whose parents communicate in sign language reveals that before the tenth month, the infants use about a dozen distinct hand gestures—most of which resemble basic elements of the American Sign Language used by their parents—in a rhythmic, repetitive manner analogous to normal babbling. The similar timing of babbling among hearing babies exposed to spoken language and deaf babies exposed to signed language suggests that maturation of the brain, rather than more specific maturation of the vocal apparatus, underlies the universal human ability to develop language.

Gestures

During the same months that babbling appears, gestures become part of the baby's deliberate efforts to communicate (Bates et al., 1987; Oller and Eilers, 1988). Often the first gesture to be used is pointing. When desired objects are out of reach, even very young infants may extend an arm and fuss. But by 9 months they begin to point, vocalize, and look away from the object toward an adult, leaving no doubt about their message. By 12 months, other gestures appear, usually modeled after those used by caregivers. Interestingly, during this period (6 to 12 months), deaf babies tend to show superiority over hearing babies in communicating through gestures and facial expressions.

Comprehension

At every stage of development, including the preverbal stage, children understand much more than they express (Kuczaj, 1986). When asked

TABLE 6.3 First Sounds and First Words: Cross-Linguistic Similarities

	Mother	Father
English	mama, mommy	dada, daddy
Spanish	mama	papa
French	maman, mama	papa
Italian	mamma	babbo, papa
Latvian	mama	tēte
Syrian Arabic	mama	baba
Bantu	ba-mama	taata
Swahili	mama	baba
Sanskrit	nana	tata
Hebrew	ema	abba
Korean	oma	apa

Figure 6.12 *Infants' verbal understanding advances well ahead of their abilities at verbal production. "Fishee" is probably one of dozens of words that this child readily recognizes even though he has yet to say them himself.*

"Where's Mommy?" for instance, many 10-month-olds will look in her direction; or when asked "Do you want Daddy to pick you up?" will reach out their arms. In addition, as the infant learns to anticipate events (stage four of sensorimotor development), words such as "hot!" "no!" or "bye-bye" take on meaning. Of course, context and tone help significantly to supply that meaning. For example, when parents see their crawling infant about to touch the electrical outlet, they say "No" sufficiently sharply to startle and thus halt the infant in his or her tracks. Typically, they then move the child away, pointing to the danger and repeating "No. No." Given the frequency with which the mobile infant's behavior produces similar situations, it is no wonder that many infants understand "No" months before they can talk.

First Spoken Words

At about 1 year, the average baby speaks one or two words, not pronounced very clearly or used very precisely. Usually caregivers hear, and understand, the first word before strangers do, which makes it hard to pinpoint, scientifically, exactly what a 12-month-old can say.

Vocabulary increases gradually, perhaps a few words a month. By 18 months, the average baby speaks about fifty words and comprehends many more. Most of these early words are names of specific people and objects in the child's daily world, although some "action" words are included as well (Barrett, 1986; Kuczaj, 1986). At about the fifty-word milestone, vocabulary suddenly begins to build rapidly, a hundred or more words a month (Huttenlocher et al., 1991).

At first, infants apply the few words they know to a variety of contexts. This characteristic, known as **overextension,** or overgeneralization, might lead one child to call anything round "ball," and another to call every four-legged creature "doggie." But once vocabulary begins to expand, toddlers seem to "experiment in order to see" with words just as they do with objects. The "little scientist" becomes the "little linguist," exploring hypotheses and reaching conclusions. It is not unusual for 18-month-olds to walk down the street pointing to every animal, asking "doggie?" or "horsie?" or "kitty?"—perhaps to confirm their hypotheses about which words go with which specific animals.

As children learn their first words, they usually become adept at expressing intention. Even a single word, amplified by intonation and gestures, can express a whole thought. When a toddler pushes at a closed door and says "bye-bye" in a demanding tone, it is clear that the toddler wishes to go out. When a toddler holds on to Mother's legs and plaintively says "bye-bye" as soon as the babysitter arrives, it is equally clear that the child is asking Mommy not to leave. A single word that expresses a complete thought in this manner is called a **holophrase.** In the early stages of language development, almost every single-word utterance is a holophrase, making toddlers much more proficient linguists than their limited vocabulary would suggest.

Indeed, it is important to note that vocabulary size is not the only, nor the best, measure of early language learning. Rather, the crux of early language is communication, not vocabulary. If parents are concerned about their nonverbal 1-year-old son, they should look at his ability and willingness to make his needs known and to understand what others say. If those skills seem to be normal, and if the child hears enough simple language addressed to him every day (through someone's reading to him, singing to him, talking about the food he is eating and the sights he sees), he will probably be speaking in sentences before age 2 (Eisenson, 1986). On the other hand, infants who show signs of language delay (for example, not babbling back when parents babble to them, or not responding to any specific words by age 1) should have their hearing examined as soon as possible. Even a moderate early hearing loss can delay speech acquisition (Butler and Golding, 1986).

Combining Words

Within about six months of speaking his or her first words, a child begins to put words together. As a general rule, the first two-word sentence appears between ages 16 and 21 months. Combining words demands considerable linguistic understanding because, in most languages, word order affects the meaning of the sentence. However, even in their first sentences, toddlers demonstrate that they have figured out the basics of subject-predicate order, declaring "Baby cry" or asking "Rain stop?" rather than the reverse.

Teamwork: Adults and Babies Teach Each Other to Talk

How do babies learn to talk? Early research on language development tended to take one of two directions, focusing either on the ways parents teach language to their infants or on the emergence of the infant's innate language abilities.

The focus on teaching arose from B. F. Skinner's learning theory, which held that conditioning processes could explain verbal behavior just as well as other types of behavior (Skinner, 1957). For example, if babies are reinforced, with food and attention, when they utter their first babbling sounds, soon they will call "mama," "dada," and "baba" whenever they want their mother, father, or bottle. Similarly, Skinner believed that the quantity and quality of parents' talking to their child will affect the rate of the child's language development, from the first words through complex sentences.

The focus on innate language ability came from the theories of Noam Chomsky, who stressed the universality of early language development (Chomsky, 1968, 1980). According to Chomsky, the fact that all children learn to communicate so rapidly, beginning at the same age, implies that there is something akin to a "language acquisition device" (abbreviated LAD) in the human brain. Thus, just as children are prewired to begin to stand up and walk at a certain point in their maturation, children are similarly prewired to begin to babble and talk, finding words to express concepts that are innate, such as that people and objects have names and that certain intonations indicate a question. This awareness of the basic use and structure of language—which is grasped by infants of every language group—is what makes it possible for communication to develop rapidly. The infant's early vocalizations need only to be fine-tuned by the specifics of a particular language's vocabulary and grammar (e.g., English, Spanish, Urdu) so that the baby's LAD can latch onto the communicative structures within a particular culture.

Research in recent years has suggested that both Skinner and Chomsky's theories have some validity, yet both miss the mark, because the actual language learning process occurs in a social context, framed by the adult's

Figure 6.13 *If his infancy is like that of most babies raised in the Otavado culture in Ecuador, this 2-month-old will hear significantly less conversation than infants from most other regions of the world, including other localities in South America. According to Skinner, such a lack of reinforcement will result in a child who is much less verbal than most children from other cultures. However, since each culture tends to encourage the qualities most needed in the cultures, it may well be that verbal fluency among children is not required in this community.*

teaching sensitivity and the child's learning ability. Infants are genetically primed to pick up language, and, on their part, many caregivers are surprisingly skilled at facilitating the infant's language learning.

The language-learning process begins in the first days of life, as infants turn their heads and open their eyes wide when they hear voices, express excitement when someone talks to them, and show preferences for certain voices. As we saw in Chapter 5, babies under a month old have demonstrated in laboratory experiments that they can hear the difference between very similar speech sounds, suggesting that this ability is inborn (Clarkson and Berg, 1983). As time goes on, infants become attuned to the specific intonations, timing, and phonetic distinctions of the language they hear daily. Japanese infants, for example, become less attentive to the difference between "l" and "r" because there is no "l" sound in the Japanese language. Babies raised hearing English, on the other hand, become highly attuned to the distinction between the two letters, noticing the difference long before they can articulate it themselves.

For their part, adults talk to infants even in the first days of life, using a special form of language called **baby talk,** nicknamed *Motherese*. As used by researchers, the term "baby talk," or "Motherese," does not refer to the way people think babies talk—the "goo-goo-ga-ga" that few infants actually say. Rather, it refers to the particular way people talk to infants. Motherese differs from adult talk in a number of features that are consistent throughout all language communities (Ferguson, 1977): it is distinct in its pitch (higher), intonation (more low-to-high fluctuations), vocabulary (simpler and more concrete), and sentence length (shorter). It also employs more questions, commands, and repetitions, and fewer past tenses, pronouns, and complex sentences, than adult talk does. People of all ages, parents and nonparents alike, speak baby talk with infants (Jacobson et al., 1983), and preverbal infants prefer listening to Motherese over normal speech (Fernald, 1985). Part of the appeal, and the impact, of baby talk may lie in its energy and exaggerated expressiveness. Research has shown that the baby talk of depressed mothers is too flat in intonation and too slow in its conversational responses to hold the baby's interest (Bettes, 1988).

The function of baby talk is clearly to facilitate early language learning, for the sounds and words of baby talk are those that infants attend to, and speak, most readily. In addition, difficult sounds are avoided: consonants like "l" and "r" are regularly missing, and hard-to-say words are given simple forms, often with a "-y" ending. Thus, father becomes "daddy," stomach becomes "tummy," and rabbit becomes "bunny," because if they didn't, infants and parents wouldn't be able to talk about them.

In the earliest stages of baby talk, the conversation is, of course, rather one-sided. However, as the child grows more responsive and communicative, the general interaction between parent and child becomes more like a conversation in its give and take, with turn-taking games such as peek-a-boo becoming more common.

The "conversational" aspect of the parent-child interaction is strengthened between 5 and 7 months, as parents begin to treat burps, smiles, yawns, gestures, and babbling as part of a dialogue. Even when the baby seems to do nothing, the parent is likely to carry on the conversation as though it were actively two-way (Bremner, 1988). A mother might say, "Don't

Figure 6.14 *Peek-a-boo brings great delight to infants as long as the intervals between hiding and revealing are short. Timing is an essential element in many of the interactive games of infancy, as it soon will be when genuine conversations occur.*

you want to take a nap now?" pause a second or two as though allowing the baby to answer, and then say, "Of course you do."

In fact, the response is not all in the mind of the mother. Babies show with facial expressions that they listen to maternal speech, and they indicate when they are ready to hear more. By 9 months, many babies have developed the conversational skill of taking turns, just as adults do, both in vocalization and in gaze (looking intently at the mother when listening, averting the eyes somewhat while "talking"). This skill becomes more efficient and rapid as infants mature, with the number of turns taken per minute increasing from seven at 9 months to sixteen at 24 months (Rutter and Durkin, 1987).

Once the child begins to talk, many conversations between parent and child show the parent interpreting the child's imperfect speech and then responding with short, clear sentences the child can understand, often with special emphasis on important words. Particularly with firstborns, the child's vocabulary expands in the process (Jones and Adamson, 1987). Naturalistic observation is the best way to study this interaction, for facial expression and intonation are as much a part of baby talk as the words spoken. However, recorded dialogues like the following one between a mother and son at bedtime help give the flavor (Halliday, 1979):

> Mother: And when you get up in the morning, you'll go for a walk.
> Nigel: *Tik.*
> And you'll see some sticks, yes.
> *Hoo.*
> And some holes, yes.
> *Da.*
> Yes, now it's getting dark.
> *I wa [repeated thirteen times].*
> What?
> *I wa [seven times]. Peaz.*
> What do you want in bed? Jamie? [his doll]
> *No!*
> You want your eiderdown? [quilt]
> *(grins) Yeah!*
> Why didn't you say so? Your eiderdown.
> *Ella [three times].*

In most episodes of baby talk, the child is an active participant, responding to the speaker and making his or her needs known. In this one, Nigel asked for his quilt a total of twenty times, persisting until his mother got the point.

A Social Interaction

As we have seen repeatedly, infants are motivated to understand the world: the same motivation that makes toddlers resemble little scientists makes infants seek to understand the noises, gestures, words, and grammatical systems that describe the world in which they live. Central to the achievement of understanding language is verbal interaction. As one researcher writes:

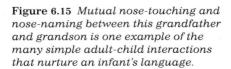

Figure 6.15 *Mutual nose-touching and nose-naming between this grandfather and grandson is one example of the many simple adult-child interactions that nurture an infant's language.*

language . . . could not emerge in any species, and would not develop in any individual, without a special kind of fit between adult behavior and infant behavior. That fit is pre-adapted: It comes to each child as a birthright, both as a result of biological propensities and as a result of social processes learned and transmitted by each new generation. [Kaye, 1982]

The idea that language develops as the outcome of "biological propensities" and "a special kind of fit" confirms that both innate processes and the social context are prerequisites for language development. Humans are biologically destined to communicate, and their brains are primed to develop language. At the same time, verbal interaction between adult and infant is essential, for without a sensitive and responsive conversational partner, a child's language learning will be impeded. Thus parent and baby together accomplish what neither could do alone: teach a person to talk. As we will see in the next chapter, the same parent-infant relationship is at the core of the psychosocial development of the child.

SUMMARY

1. Impressive changes in the infant's capacity to understand and communicate with the world are the result of developments in cognition, the interaction of the perceptual, intellectual, and linguistic abilities that result in thinking and learning.

Sensorimotor Intelligence

2. From birth to age 2, the period of sensorimotor intelligence, infants use their senses and motor skills to understand their environment. They begin by adapting their reflexes, coordinating their actions, and interacting with people and things. By the end of the first year, they know what they want and have the knowledge and ability to achieve their simple goals.

3. According to Piaget, for infants younger than 8 months, when an object disappears from their sight, it no longer exists. But by the age of 1½, when the concept of object permanence is fully developed, toddlers can imagine where to search for an object hidden in their presence, even though the object itself may have been covered from their sight as it was being hidden.

4. In the second year, toddlers find new ways to achieve their goals, first by actively experimenting with physical objects, and then, toward the end of the second year, by manipulating mental images of objects and actions that are not in view.

5. Although Piaget's general description of the six stages of sensorimotor intelligence is still widely accepted, recent research has found several problems with it. Specifically, the experimental demonstration of both object permanence and deferred imitation depends much more on the particular test conditions than Piaget realized.

6. Overall, differences in infants' motivation, experience, and culture affected which particular sensorimotor skills they display and when they display them. Consequently, development of sensorimotor intelligence is much more varied than a strict interpretation of Piaget would suggest.

Perception

7. Infants' perceptual skills reveal early cognitive abilities. For example, within the first six months, infants perceive many of the affordances of their perceptual world—knowing which objects can be grasped, sucked, and so forth.

8. Infants' ability to coordinate their senses indicates some intellectual processing of perceptual information. Both intermodal perception (such as listening to a sound and knowing which object is likely to be the source) and cross-modal perception (as in touching an object and imagining how it might look) are evident in the first months of life.

9. Infants use their perceptual skills to form categories, such as those related to different shapes and colors. One of the most intriguing categories they form involves gender. By age 1, infants distinguish male and female toddlers, a distinction based primarily on patterns of body movement. Whether or not these early perceptual achievements indicate an innate ability to sort and organize perceptions into categories is still an open question.

Language Development

10. Language skills begin to develop as babies communicate with noises and gestures and then practice babbling. Infants say a few words by the end of the first year, and they understand more words than they speak. By age 2, most toddlers can combine two words to make a simple sentence.

11. Children vary in how rapidly they learn vocabulary, as well as in the way they use words. In the first two years, the child's comprehension of simple words and gestures, and willingness and ability to communicate, are more significant than the size of the child's vocabulary.

12. According to Skinner, children learn language through reinforcement and association. Chomsky believes children have an inborn ability to understand and use the basic structure of language and that each culture teaches its children the particular structures, such as vocabulary and grammar, of its own language.

13. Language learning is the result of the interaction between parent and child. The child is primed to learn language, and adults all over the world communicate with children using a simplified form of language called baby talk, which suits the child's abilities to understand and repeat.

KEY TERMS

cognition (144)
sensorimotor intelligence (144)
goal-directed behavior (147)
object permanence (147)
AB error (147)
mental combinations (149)
mental representation (149)
deferred imitation (150)
affordances (156)
intermodal perception (157)
cross-modal perception (158)
babbling (163)
overextension (164)
holophrase (164)
baby talk (166)

KEY QUESTIONS

1. According to Piaget, what is the basic characteristic of infant thought between birth and age 2?

2. What are the first signs of adaptation according to Piaget?

3. Between the ages of 6 and 18 months, what changes occur in the infant's understanding of objects that are out of sight?

4. Why did Piaget call 1-year-olds "little scientists"?

5. What cognitive developments make it possible for the toddler to pretend?

6. What are the major criticisms of Piaget's description of sensorimotor intelligence?

7. How does an understanding of affordances indicate active perceptual ability?

8. What evidence is there that infants form categories to organize their perceptions?

9. In what way do children's first words reflect their stage of cognitive development?

10. What are some of the ways of determining whether the language development of an infant or toddler is normal?

11. What are the differences between Skinner's and Chomsky's theories of language development?

12. How do the special features of baby talk make it easy for parents and children to communicate with each other?

CHAPTER 7

The First Two Years: Psychosocial Development

The social life of the developing person begins very early, earlier even than many researchers have believed. In the first month, in fact, infants can express a number of emotions and can, in turn, respond to the moods, emotions, and attentions of others. One reason these communications are so readily exchanged is that we seem to be born with a capacity for a universal language of emotional expression—a basic understanding of the meaning of each other's smiles, tears, and quizzical glances. Which other aspects of our personalities are we born with, and which develop as we mature and interact with others? This question and the ones that follow reflect some of the topics that will be examined in Chapter 7.

How does the infant's increasing sense of self-awareness affect his or her emotions and relationships with others?

What factors are important in helping a child to develop a sense of trust?

What are the implications of an infant's attachment, or lack of attachment, to his or her mother?

What are the differences in ways mothers and fathers play with their infants and what is the effect of these differences?

What are the characteristics of the child, the parents, and society that lead to an increased risk of child abuse?

As you remember from Chapter 1, psychosocial development includes not only factors that are usually considered characteristic of the individual's psyche, such as emotional expression, self-awareness, and temperament, but also factors that are clearly social, such as the parents' relationship to their offspring or the culture's impact on the child. In addition, these factors are mutually influential, with the individual's personal characteristics shaping, as well as being shaped by, the surrounding social context. As we will see, this mutuality of influence is strongly evident even in early infancy.

Emotional Development

We begin this chapter by examining emotional development, because the child's emerging emotional responsiveness provides a valuable window into early psychological growth. Emotions are also important contributors to parent-infant interaction, for a baby's cry, smile, and other expressions are very significant social signals.

Recently, researchers have taken a new look at infant emotions, partly in response to the surprising discoveries that have been made concerning infant perception and cognition (see Chapters 5 and 6). Using sophisticated systems for deciphering the emotional content of facial expressions, they analyzed videotapes of hundreds of infants, frame-by-frame, and found that even very young infants express many emotions—including joy, surprise, anger, fear, disgust, interest, and sadness (Izard, 1980; Campos et al., 1983). Indeed, it seems as if there is a developmental "schedule" by which infants acquire the capacity for specific emotions. This capacity appears to be related to brain maturation (Fox and Davidson, 1984) and to infants' growing abilities to understand the events around them.

The First Days and Months

The first emotion that can be reliably discerned in infants is distress, most commonly registered in the crying of the infant who is hungry or otherwise uncomfortable. In addition, when infants a few days or even a few hours old hear a loud noise, or feel a sudden loss of support, or see an object looming toward them, they often cry and look upset (Izard and Malatesta, 1987; Sroufe, 1979). Slightly older babies have more pronounced distress reactions, and also seem angry at times, as when, for instance, they are prevented from moving (Stenberg and Campos, 1983).

Sadness, or at least a sensitivity to it, is also apparent early in infancy. In an experiment in which mothers of infants between 1 month and 3 months old were told to look sad and act depressed, their infants responded by looking away and fussing (Cohn and Tronick, 1983; Tronick et al., 1978). More explicit findings were provided by an experiment in which the facial expressions of a 3-month-old girl who had been severely abused were filmed and later shown to "blind" judges for assessment: without knowing anything about her condition, the judges rated her as undeniably sad (Gaensbauer, 1980).

On the positive side, newborns show the wide-eyed look of interest and surprise when something catches their attention (Field, 1982). Smiles also begin early: a half-smile at a pleasant noise or a full stomach appears in the first days of life; a **social smile**—a smile in response to someone else—begins to appear at about 6 weeks (Emde and Harmon, 1972). By 3 or 4 months, smiles become broader, and babies laugh rather than grin if something is particularly pleasing. These patterns are universal, as evident among the hunter-gatherers of the Kalahari as among the upper class of Boston and Paris (Bakeman et al., 1990).

Figure 7.1 *This infant's "pleasure smile" is probably an inborn response to the satisfactions of a full stomach and a smoothly functioning digestive system, just as most of the early cries are automatic responses to hunger or indigestion.*

(a)

(b)

Figure 7.2 *This mother may, at first, be puzzled, or even embarrassed by her child's response to the kind stranger. However, at this stage, this infant's behavior is simply a sign that she understands the difference between the familiar and the unusual.*

The "Older Infant"

At about 8 months, infants' emotions become much stronger, more differentiated and distinct, especially fear, anger, and joy.

One common fear, **fear of strangers** (also called stranger anxiety), is first noticeable at about 6 months and becomes full-blown by 12 months. Perhaps you have observed this fear yourself when offering a 1-year-old a friendly greeting in a supermarket—only to have the child erupt in loud wailing! Contrary to popular belief, however, not all infants experience fear of strangers, and those who do vary considerably in the intensity of their reactions. How a baby responds to a stranger depends on aspects of the infant (such as temperament and the security of the mother-infant relationship), the stranger (including the stranger's gender and behavior toward the baby), and the situation (such as the mother's proximity or the infant's current mood) (Thompson and Limber, 1990). A baby may be friendly toward a stranger who keeps at a distance in the mother's presence, but react fearfully if the same stranger looms suddenly when the mother is away.

A related emotion is **separation anxiety,** the fear of being left by the mother or other caregiver. Like many other fears, separation anxiety emerges at about 8 or 9 months, peaks at about 14 months, and then gradually subsides. Whether or not infants will be distressed by separation depends on such factors as the baby's prior experiences with separation and the manner in which the parent departs—leaving abruptly, for example, or in a relaxed fashion, with goodbyes and reassurance (Thompson and Limber, 1990).

As every parent knows, anger also intensifies in toddlerhood. When videotapes of infants being inoculated between 2 and 19 months were categorized by "blind" raters who could see only the children's faces, ratings of anger increased dramatically between 7 and 19 months. In addition, the duration of anger increased, from a fleeting expression in early infancy to a lengthy demonstration at 19 months (Izard et al., 1987).

Finally, as infants become older, they smile and laugh more selectively, as well as more quickly (Lewis and Michalson, 1983). For instance, the sight of almost any human face produces a stare and then a smile in the typical 3-month-old, but the typical 9-month-old may grin immediately at the sight of certain faces—and might remain impassive or burst into tears at the sight of certain others.

Emotion and Cognition

What might explain this intensification of emotional development that causes the toddler at 12 months or more to be quite a different creature from the infant under 6 months? Since several emotional shifts occur between the ages of 8 months and 12 months, which is the same time that new cognitive and memory abilities appear (see Chapter 6), the emotional changes may be the result of a "cognitive metamorphosis" (Zelazo, 1979). In other words, being able to think and remember in a much more efficient and mature way, the infant can recognize more reasons to be happy or afraid, and be quicker to anger or sorrow (Sroufe, 1979). For example, the emergence of anticipation and goal-directed behavior in stage four of sensorimotor intelligence means that the infant can respond emotionally to *expectations*, such as crying when seeing Mommy putting on her coat to leave the house or laughing excitedly when she brings out the baby's ice-cream bowl.

Moreover, by 10 months infants engage in obvious **social referencing;** that is, they look to trusted adults for emotional cues in uncertain situations. This capacity is built upon the ability to meaningfully interpret the emotional signals of others, and the cues infants receive through social referencing affect how they feel and react (Feinman, 1985; Klinnert et al., 1983). In an experimental situation, for example, infants are more likely to approach a strange-looking toy (such as a green stuffed dinosaur moving around the room buzzing softly) when their mother is smiling, and to withdraw when she looks fearful (Klinnert, 1984). In everyday situations, infants often look to their mother for emotional cues when they encounter a stranger, and the mother's expressions influence whether the baby is friendly or fearful. This occurs partly because infants often spontaneously share the emotion their mother communicates, and thus when mothers look wary or fearful of an unusual person or event, their offspring probably experience similar feelings (Haviland and Lelwica, 1987; Termine and Izard, 1988).

Emotions and Self-Awareness

One of the most important cognitive features of later infancy is the development of a certain measure of **self-awareness.** The emerging sense of "me and mine" makes possible many new self-conscious emotions, including shame, guilt, jealousy, and pride. At the same time, a sense of self allows a new awareness of others, and hence allows such emotions as defiance and true affection.

In the first several months, infants have no sense of self: in fact, they do not even have an awareness of their bodies as theirs. To them, for example, their hands are interesting objects that appear and disappear: 2-month-olds, in effect, "discover" their hands each time they catch sight of them, become fascinated with their movements, then "lose" them as they slip out of view. Even 8-month-olds often don't seem to know where their bodies end

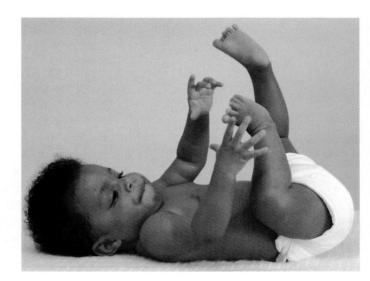

Figure 7.3 *Although young infants have great fun playing with their fingers, toes, and the rest of their bodies, they lack the self-awareness to realize that these things are part of them.*

and someone else's body begins, as can be seen when a child grabs a toy in another child's hand and reacts with surprise when the toy "resists." By age 1, however, most infants would be quite aware that the other child is a distinct person, whom they might hit if the coveted toy is not immediately forthcoming.

Evidence of the emerging sense of self was shown in a classic experiment in which babies looked in a mirror after a dot of rouge had been surreptitiously put on their nose (Lewis and Brooks, 1978). If the babies reacted to the mirror image by touching their nose, it was clear that they knew they were seeing their own face. After trying this experiment with ninety-six babies between the ages of 9 and 24 months, the experimenters found a distinct developmental shift. None of the babies under a year reacted to the mark, whereas most of those between 12 and 24 months did. Before their second birthday, most infants can point to themselves when asked "Where's [child's name]?" and they can use their own name appropriately when asked "Who's that?" (Pipp et al., 1987).

The link between the advent of self-awareness and the emergence of certain self-conscious emotions was shown in a recent extension of the rouge-and-mirror experiment (Lewis et al., 1989). In this study, 15- to 24-month-olds who showed self-recognition in the rouge task described above also looked embarrassed when they were praised by an adult; that is, they smiled and looked away, covered their face with their hands, and so forth. Infants who did not show self-recognition were not embarrassed (Lewis et al., 1989). These changes seem universal, occurring at about the same time among toddlers from varied backgrounds (Schneider-Rosen and Cicchetti, 1991). The shift is apparent at home as well as in laboratory experiments: mothers report that the toddler's sense of shame and guilt appears for the first time after self-awareness begins (Stipek et al., 1990).

Self-awareness also changes the intensity and conditions of the toddler's reactions to others, including affection and jealousy. Indeed, the famous toddler temper develops partly because, when children become more aware of themselves, they take frustration and hurt much more personally, and realize, in turn, that they are more able to respond in kind (Dunn and Munn, 1985).

Figure 7.4 *Mirror images make young infants smile and try to touch "the baby." It is not until after they are a year old that children realize that they are looking at themselves.*

The Origins of Personality

Now that we have seen how emotional capacities develop during infancy, the next questions are: How do the infant's emotional and behavioral responses begin to take on the various patterns that form personality? What happens to evoke or create personality traits and social skills during infancy, leading to the emergence of a distinct individual?

Psychological Theory: The Importance of Nurture

In the first half of the twentieth century, the prevailing view among psychologists in North America, Western Europe, and Australia was that the individual's personality is permanently molded by the actions of his or her parents—most especially the mother's—in the early years of childhood. There were two major theoretical versions of how this came about.

Behaviorist Theory

Those who favored the behaviorist perspective (see Chapter 2) maintained that personality is molded as parents reinforce or punish the child's various spontaneous behaviors, and that how the child turns out is entirely the parents' doing. The strongest statement regarding this came from John Watson, the leading behaviorist of the time, who cautioned:

> Failure to bring up a happy child, a well-adjusted child—assuming bodily health—falls squarely upon the parents' shoulders. [By the time the child is 3] parents have already determined . . . whether . . . [the child] is to grow into a happy person, wholesome and good-natured, whether he is to be a whining, complaining, neurotic, an anger-driven, vindictive, over-bearing slave driver, or one whose every move in life is definitely controlled by fear. [Watson, 1928]

Although later behaviorists saw a more complex link between parental behavior and the child's response, the direct impact of the parents' actions on the child was not doubted.

Psychoanalytic Theory

Beginning with a different set of assumptions about human nature, psychoanalytic theorists (see Chapter 2) reached very similar conclusions about the early, and permanent, formation of the individual's personality. Sigmund Freud, who established the framework for their view, felt that the experiences of the first four years of life "play a decisive part in determining whether and at what point the individual shall fail to master the real problems of life" (Freud, 1963). He also thought that the child's relationship with the mother was "unique, without parallel, established unalterably for a whole lifetime as the first and strongest love-object and as the prototype of all later love relations" (Freud, 1940, 1964).

Freud: Oral and Anal Stages

As we noted in Chapter 2, Freud viewed human development in terms of psychosexual stages that occur at specific ages. According to Freud (1935), psychological development begins with the **oral stage,** so named because in the first year of life the mouth is the infant's prime source of gratification. Not only is the mouth the instrument for attaining nourishment; it is also the main source of pleasure: sucking, especially at the mother's breast, is a joyous, sensual activity for babies. In the second year, Freud maintained, the infant's prime focus of gratification shifts to the anus, particularly the sensual pleasure taken in stimulation of the bowels, and eventually, the psychological pleasure in controlling them. Accordingly, Freud referred to this period as the **anal stage.** This change is more than a simple shift of locus; it is a shift in the mode of interaction, from the passive, dependent mode of orality to the more active, controlling mode of anality.

According to Freud, both these stages are fraught with potential conflict for the infant, conflict that can have long-term consequences. If a mother frustrates her infant's urge to suck—by making nursing a hurried, tense event, or by weaning the infant from the nipple too early, or by continually preventing the child from sucking on fingers, toes, and other objects—the child may be made distressed and anxious. Moreover, the child may become an adult who is "fixated," or stuck, at the oral stage, excessively eating, drinking, chewing, biting, smoking, or talking in quest of the oral sat-

Figure 7.5 *To psychoanalytic theorists, breast-feeding is important not just because it is a source of nourishment but also because the pleasurable, intimate contact it affords strengthens the infant's attachment to the mother and fosters a feeling of "basic trust" in the world.*

isfaction denied in infancy. Similarly, if toilet training is overly strict or premature (occurring before the age of 1½ or 2, when children are physiologically, as well as psychologically, mature enough to participate in the toilet-training process), parent-child interaction may become locked into conflict over the toddler's resistance or inability to comply. Furthermore, it may produce an adult who has an "anal" personality. The person will be either anally retentive—overemphasizing neatness, cleanliness, precision, and punctuality—or anally expulsive—exhibiting messiness and disorganization in nearly all matters.

Although Freud's ideas concerning orality and anality have been extremely influential, research has failed to support the linking of specific conflicts during these stages to later personality traits. Rather, it has shown that the parents' overall pattern of warmth and management is much more important to the child's emotional development than the particulars of either feeding and weaning or toilet-training (Maccoby and Martin, 1983). This broader perspective is reflected in the theories of Erik Erikson and Margaret Mahler, two contemporary psychoanalytic theorists who have studied infancy.

Erikson: Trust and Autonomy

As you will remember from Chapter 2, Erik Erikson believes that development occurs through a series of basic crises, or issues, throughout the life span (see p. 41). The crisis of infancy centers not on experiences related only to oral gratification per se but on the larger pattern of parent-child interaction of which oral experiences are a part (Erikson, 1963). In Erikson's terms, the crisis of infancy is one of **trust versus mistrust** in which the infant learns whether the world is essentially a secure place in which basic needs will be met. Erikson contends that babies begin to develop a sense of security when their mothers provide food and comfort with "consistency, continuity, and sameness of experience." He explains that "the amount of trust derived from earliest infantile experience does not seem to depend on absolute quantities of food or demonstrations of love, but rather on the quality of the maternal relationship" (Erikson, 1963). When this relationship inspires trust and security, the child experiences confidence in engaging and exploring the world.

Similarly, Erikson's view of toddlerhood places the idea of anality in the broad context of the crisis of **autonomy versus shame and doubt.** Toddlers want to rule their own actions and bodies. If they fail in their efforts to do so, either because they are incapable or because their caregivers are too restrictive and forbidding, they come to feel shame and to doubt their abilities. For many toddlers, the struggle for autonomy does, in fact, center on toilet-training, but as Erikson notes, as toddlers' increasing mobility allows them to move from safe, boring experiences toward more exciting and potentially dangerous ones, they encounter many other kinds of conflict that lead to the development of self-confidence or doubt. In Erikson's view, the key to the child's successfully meeting this crisis and gaining a sense of autonomy is parental firmness:

> Firmness must protect him [the toddler] against the potential anarchy of his as yet untrained sense of discrimination, his inability to hold on and let go with discretion. As his environment encourages him to "stand on his own feet," it must protect him against meaningless and arbitrary experiences of shame and of early doubt. [Erikson, 1963]

Figure 7.6 *How will this young child's parents react to his explorations? According to Erikson, parent strictness or permissiveness can shape how young children resolve the psychosocial crisis of autonomy versus shame and doubt.*

Figure 7.7 *According to Erikson, a healthy sense of autonomy encourages young children to master age-appropriate skills (like learning to brush their teeth), and provides self-confidence when encountering new challenges.*

If parents accomplish this, the child is likely to become increasingly self-confident when encountering new challenges as an independent being.

Like Freud, Erikson believed that problems arising in early infancy can last a lifetime. The adult who is suspicious and pessimistic, or who always seems burdened by self-doubt, may have been an infant who did not develop sufficient trust, or a toddler who did not achieve sufficient autonomy. However, Erikson also emphasizes that experiences later in life can alter or transform the effects of early experiences, and that earlier crises can be taken up again and resolved later in life.

Mahler: Separation-Individuation

The need for a proper balance between protection and freedom is also central to Margaret Mahler's theory of infancy. In the first months of life, according to Mahler, the mother-child relationship is symbiotic. The nursing infant feels literally a part of the mother's body, and the mother, ideally, welcomes this temporary intrusion and dependency. At about 5 months, a new period begins that lasts until about age 3. This is **separation-individuation,** when the infant gradually develops a sense of self, apart from the mother. Mahler refers to this as the time of "psychological birth," when babies break out of the "protective membrane" that had symbiotically enclosed them and "hatch" by crawling and walking away from the mother (Mahler et al., 1975).

As toddlers, children attempt greater psychological separation from their mothers, but then become frightened by the independence they have gained, perhaps regressing to a period of babyish clinging. Because they are caught between two opposite needs, toddlers can be moody, showing sorrow and dependence, or anger and aggression. Even well-adjusted 1-year-olds show their ambivalence by darting away, hoping to be chased, or following their mother around, hoping to be noticed. Ideally, the mother will recognize the child's need for both independence and dependence, allowing a measure of freedom as well as providing comforting reassurance.

Like Freud and Erikson, Mahler (1968) believes that each stage of development is important for later psychological health. Indeed, Mahler thinks severe mental illness results directly from maladaptive mothering in the first six months of life. She also maintains that the resolution of the separation-individuation stage likewise has lasting implications: adults

Figure 7.8 *From the parent's perspective, the most difficult aspect of separation-individuation is deciding whether or not to intervene when offspring try to master new skills that may be beyond their capabilities. For the child, acquiring new skills is also an exciting and scary experience—which is why, for this toddler, the company of a grandparent (and a comforting bottle) can be reassuring.*

who avoid intimacy, or fear independence, may still be trying to resolve the tension of separation-individuation and achieve a proper sense of self.

Overall, then, traditional psychological theory maintains that personality is primarily shaped by early nurture, particularly the mother's caregiving. This view has been seriously challenged by those who see basic elements of the infant's personality emerge so early that parental influences cannot be credited or blamed.

Temperament: The Importance of Nature

As you read in Chapter 3, researchers, using a variety of measures and definitions, have determined that each individual has his or her own distinct, genetically based temperament, which permeates virtually every aspect of the person's developing personality. **Temperament** is defined as "relatively consistent, basic dispositions inherent in the person that underlie and modulate the expression of activity, reactivity, emotionality, and sociability" (McCall, in Goldsmith et al., 1987).

Temperament begins in the multitude of genetic codes that guide the development of the brain, and is affected by many prenatal experiences, especially those relating to the nutrition and health of the mother. Elements of temperament are evident from birth, and within the first months, temperament is clearly established. However, although temperament is apparent in the first months of life, as the person develops, the social context and the individual's experiences increasingly influence the nature and expression of temperament.

The most famous and extensive study of temperament is called the New York Longitudinal Study (NYLS), conducted by Alexander Thomas, Stella Chess, and Herbert Birch. According to their initial findings (1963), babies in the first days and months of life differ in nine personality characteristics:

1. *Activity level.* Some babies are active. They kick a lot in the uterus before they are born, they move around a great deal in their basinettes, and as toddlers, they are nearly always running. Other babies are much less active.

Figure 7.9 *At any age, temperamental differences can make a given experience a treat for one person but a trauma for another.*

2. *Rhythmicity.* Some babies have regular cycles of activity. They eat, sleep, and defecate on schedule almost from birth. Other babies are much less predictable.

3. *Approach-withdrawal.* Some babies delight in everything new; others withdraw from every new situation. The first bath makes some babies laugh and others cry; the first spoonful of cereal is gobbled up by one baby and spit out by the next.

4. *Adaptability.* Some babies adjust quickly to change; others are unhappy at every disruption of their normal routine.

5. *Intensity of reaction.* Some babies chortle when they laugh and howl when they cry. Others are much calmer, responding with a smile or a whimper.

6. *Threshold of responsiveness.* Some babies seem to sense every sight, sound, and touch. For instance, they waken at a slight noise, or turn away from a distant light. Others seem unaware even of bright lights, loud street noises, or wet diapers.

7. *Quality of mood.* Some babies seem constantly happy, smiling at almost everything. Others seem chronically unhappy: they are ready to complain at any moment.

8. *Distractibility.* All babies fuss when they are hungry, but some will stop if someone gives them a pacifier or sings them a song, while others keep fussing until they are fed. Similarly, some babies can easily be distracted from their interest in an attractive but dangerous object and diverted to a safer plaything, while others are more single-minded.

9. *Attention span.* Some babies play happily with one toy for a long time. Others quickly drop one activity for another.

Thomas and Chess (1977) believe that "temperamental individuality is well established by the time the infant is two to three months old," before the parents could affect personality much. In terms of various combinations of personality traits, most young infants can be described as one of three types: *easy* (about 40 percent), *slow-to-warm-up* (about 15 percent), and *difficult* (about 10 percent). Note, however, that about 35 percent of normal infants do not fit into these well-defined groups.

In a series of follow-up studies carried into adolescence and adulthood (Thomas et al., 1968; Carey and McDevitt, 1978; Chess and Thomas, 1990), temperamental characteristics showed some stability: the easy baby remains a relatively easy child, while the difficult one is more likely to give his or her parents problems. Similarly, the slow-to-warm-up infant who cried on seeing strangers at 8 months may well hide behind Mother's skirt on arriving at nursery school and avoid the crowd in the halls of junior high.

This does not mean that temperament remains exactly the same throughout life. Indeed, some of the NYLS characteristics are not particularly stable. Rhythmicity and quality of mood, for instance, are quite variable, meaning that the infant who has been taking naps on schedule might not do so a few months later, and the baby who has seemed consistently happy might become a malcontent if life circumstances change for the worse. The age of the child is also important. In the first few years, stability is more evident from month to month than from year to year (Bronson, 1985;

Peters-Martin and Wachs, 1984). Change itself may follow genetic timetables, and inborn traits may be more apparent during particular developmental periods and under certain conditions (Chess and Thomas, 1990).

In addition, there are several ways the caregiving environment can affect a child's temperamental characteristics. One way is through the "goodness of fit," or "match," between the child's temperamental pattern and the demands of the home environment (Lerner and Lerner, 1983; Thomas and Chess, 1977; Buss and Plomin, 1984). When parents accommodate their child-rearing expectations to their offspring's temperamental style, the result is a more harmonious "fit" between them, with good outcomes for both child and family. Consider the effects of "goodness of fit" on one of the original subjects from the NYLS:

> Carl was one of our most extreme cases of difficult temperament from the first months of life through 5 years of age. However, he did not develop a behavior disorder, primarily due to optimal handling by his parents and stability of his environment. His father, who himself had an easy temperament, took delight in his son's "lusty" characteristics, recognized on his own Carl's tendencies to have intense negative reactions to the new, and had the patience to wait for eventual adaptability to occur. He was clear, without any orientation by us, that these characteristics were in no way due to his or his wife's influences. His wife tended to be anxious and self-accusatory over Carl's tempestuous course. However, her husband was supportive and reassuring and this enabled her to take an appropriately objective and patient approach to her son's development.
>
> By middle childhood and early adolescent years, few new situations arose which evoked the difficult temperament responses. The family, school, and social environment was stable and Carl flourished and appeared to be temperamentally easy rather than difficult. . . .
>
> When Carl went off to college, however, he was faced simultaneously with a host of new situations and demands—an unfamiliar locale, a different living arrangement, new academic subjects and expectations, and a totally new peer group. Within a few weeks his temperamentally difficult traits reappeared in full force. He felt negative about the school, his courses, the other students, couldn't motivate himself to study, and was constantly irritable. Carl knew something was wrong, and discussed the situation with his family and us and developed an appropriate strategy to cope with his problem. He limited the new demands by dropping several extracurricular activities, limited his social contacts, and policed his studying. Gradually he adapted, his distress disappeared, and he was able to expand his activities and social contacts. [I]n the most recent follow-up at age 29 . . . his intensity remains but is now an asset rather than a liability [Chess and Thomas, 1990].

By contrast, when the child's temperamental pattern and caregiving expectations are significantly out of sync, parents and offspring are likely to experience greater conflict, and the child's temperamental style may become more difficult. In these ways, both nature and nurture contribute to temperamental individuality.

Parents also soon learn that how their parenting style affects their child depends on the child's temperamental style. A parenting style that provides lots of opportunities for learning and stimulation at home may help a child with a low activity level to explore, but that same approach may overwhelm a highly active child (Gandour, 1989). As a consequence, the effects of parenting style and other early experiences depend on the individual's characteristics, including temperament (Wachs and Gruen, 1982). In essence, everyone approaches the world differently—and is affected by it differently—depending on his or her temperamental style.

RESEARCH REPORT   Early Signs of Shyness

One dimension of infant temperament, extroversion (or sociability) and its opposite, shyness, has been the focus of extensive research, partly because extroversion/shyness has proven to be one of the most durable and significant traits of the human personality. This trait, which relates to such personality dimensions as friendliness, fearfulness, self-confidence, and introspection, has been linked with a variety of life-course events. For example, shy men tend to date, marry, and become fathers later than other men, and shy women are more likely to become full-time homemakers rather than pursue a career. In general, extroverts are more likely to attain higher-paid, stable management positions (Caspi et al., 1990; Caspi et al., 1988).

Although every ethnic and racial group has a portion of individuals who are very outgoing and another portion who are unusually shy, the most detailed research concerning extroversion/shyness has been carried out with white American children. Among this group, about 25 percent are "consistently sociable, affectively spontaneous, and minimally fearful," while about 10 percent are "consistently shy, cautious, and emotionally reserved" (Kagan and Snidman, 1991). Among whites, shyness seems to be genetically linked with certain physical characteristics, among them blue eyes, tall and thin bodies, and allergies, especially eczema and hayfever (Rosenberg and Kagan, 1987).

Although social shyness is difficult to ascertain in young infants, the personality trait of extroversion/shyness is readily observable by age 1, and continues to be apparent in childhood. For example, while all toddlers are somewhat cautious when a stranger appears, some hide their faces or even cry and run away. By the time children join a preschool, differences are even more evident: some children immediately make friends, while others stand quietly on the periphery of a group of children, watching and waiting. In addition, shy children are often unusually fearful in certain nonsocial situations, such as seeing the ocean for the first time or watching a scary movie (Honig, 1987).

Such tendencies have led researchers to theorize that the extroversion/shyness trait might manifest itself even in the first months of life as a general inhibition to unfamiliar objects and experiences. To test this hypothesis, ninety-four healthy middle-class infants were tested longitudinally (Kagan and Snidman, 1991). At 4 months they were videotaped for 10 minutes as they reacted to several new toys, mobiles, and sounds. Blind observers, watching the tapes, rated the infants as high or low on two behaviors: motor activity (for instance, how much they kicked or waved their arms) and crying (including how quickly they could be soothed if they began to fret). Twenty-three percent of the infants were high in both activities, 37 percent were low in both, and the remaining 40 percent were high in one but not the other.

Then, at 9 months and 14 months, the infants were tested again with several possibly unsettling situations, such as a stranger inviting the child to play with a metal robot. All the children showed wariness, but some of them were notably more fearful than others—crying and refusing to play with the novel toy, for instance. Again blind observers rated the number of times each infant showed apparent fear. Given the normal variability of infants, and the difficulties in testing them, the results were amazingly clearcut: those high or low in both crying and motor activity at 4 months were, respectively, high or low in fear at 9 and 14 months. When individual patterns were examined, results were most marked for those who were unusually fearful or fearless. Of the fourteen toddlers who had the lowest fear scores, none had been in the high/high category as infants. Similarly, of the five toddlers who were most fearful, none had been in the low/low category.

Results such as these extend the general finding that extroversion/shyness is an inherited trait and provide two further details. First, they suggest that social shyness is only one manifestation of a more general, physiological pattern of inhibition to new stimuli, apparent in infancy. Second, the fact that the behavior of a specific group of infants was, over time, distinctly more shy or more sociable than the average infant suggests that extroversion/shyness is not inherited in an additive fashion, producing a simple continuum from very social to very shy, with every gradation in between. Rather, the presence or absence of a certain gene, or genes, may produce unusual neurological reactions to novelty. Thus the trait may be inherited discretely, as blood type is, for instance (Kagan, 1989).

Of course, as with all inherited tendencies, the reaction of others can modify or exacerbate a person's tendency toward extroversion or shyness. For instance, children who are genetically predisposed to be timid are more likely to become extremely shy if they have a dominating older brother or sister. Parents also make a difference: even if a child becomes an extremely shy toddler, he or she has about a 50/50 chance of no longer behaving with unusual timidness at age 7, with family encouragement of social play with other children being one deciding factor. Even with parental guidance and preschool experience, however, very few shy toddlers become such spontaneous and social 7-year-olds that they would be mistaken for extroverts (Kagan, 1989; Galvin, 1992).

This research has a very practical application. In cultures in which shyness is considered a fault, the realization that some children may be genetically inhibited should make everyone more accepting and reassuring when a child seems unusually fearful, timid, or quiet.

Parent-Infant Interaction

As we have now seen, neither the parents' method of handling the child nor the infant's innate characteristics are sole determinants of infant psychosocial development: rather, it is the interaction between the parent and the child that is crucial. This interaction is affected by the personality of the parent and the temperament of the child, as well as by the child's stage of development. In infancy, these stages, and the nature of the parent-child interaction, can be described by two words: synchrony and attachment.

Synchrony

As you read in Chapters 5 and 6 and in the beginning of this chapter, even very young infants communicate emotionally, through sounds, movements, and facial expressions. In the beginning, such communications seem to be reflexive responses—the cry when hungry, the smile when a face appears, the waving of arms and legs when excited. But even in the first days of life, the beginnings of more interactive responsiveness appear, as newborns sometimes seem to copy the expression they see on someone else's face and watch intently for a reaction (Field et al., 1982). On their part, of course, many caregivers gaze intently at their baby, trying to decipher what the infant needs and respond accordingly.

By the second month, this tendency toward mutual responsiveness has begun to emerge in episodes of **synchrony**, or coordinated interaction between infant and caregiver. Synchrony has been described by researchers as the meshing of a finely tuned machine (Snow, 1984), or a patterned "dialogue" of exquisite precision (Schaffer, 1984), or an emotional "attunement" of an improvised musical duet (Stern, 1985). It is partly through synchrony that infants learn to express and read emotions (Bremner, 1988).

To be sure, the specific behaviors of caregivers engaged in synchrony are not remarkable in themselves, except that they are used exclusively with babies: mothers and fathers open their eyes and mouths wide in exaggerated expressions of mock delight or surprise, make rapid clucking noises or repeated one-syllable sounds ("ba-ba-ba-ba-ba," "di-di-di-di," "bo-bo-bo-bo," etc.), raise and lower the pitch of their voice, change the pace of their movements (gradually speeding up or slowing down), lean forward and back, tickle, pat, lift, and rock the baby, and do many other simple things. Nor are the infant's behaviors very complex: babies stare at their parent partner or look away, vocalize, widen their eyes, smile and laugh, move forward or back, or turn aside (Stern, 1985).

Typically, the caregiver notices the infant's expression or vocalization and mirrors it with his or her own (such as smiling when the baby smiles), or interprets it as a call for action (such as soothing when the baby looks distressed). While moments of synchrony are usually brief, they sometimes last several minutes, as when caregiver and infant engage in mutual play (see Figure 7.10).

Even in the early months, synchrony is a partnership. Infants modify their social and emotional expressiveness (smiling, looking, cooing) to match or complement the caregiver's overtures, while the adult modifies the timing and pace of his or her initiatives to accord with the baby's readi-

Figure 7.10 *A moment of perfect synchrony!*

ness to respond (Cohn and Tronick, 1987). As a result, the two are "in sync" with each other. Such coordination, of course, is not constant. In fact, episodes of synchrony occur less than 30 percent of the time in normal mother-infant play. Much of the time, the pair is jointly reestablishing coordinated play following periods of dyssynchrony, caused by the baby's becoming fussy or hiccoughing, or by the mother's becoming distracted, or by any number of other factors (Tronick, 1989; Tronick and Cohn, 1989). Thus infants are learning not only how to socialize during periods of parent-infant interaction but also how to remedy or "repair" social encounters that are not going well (Gianino and Tronick, 1988).

Generally, repair is not difficult: the signs of dyssynchrony are obvious—averted eyes, stiffening or abrupt shifting of the body, an unhappy noise—and the alert caregiver can quickly make adjustments, allowing the infant to "recover." Depending on various aspects of their temperament and maturity, of course, some infants take longer than others to recover and to resume synchronous interaction. Since development of the central nervous system improves awareness and timing, 5-month-olds lead the "dance" notably better than 3-month-olds (Lester et al., 1985).

When initiation and repair of synchrony are difficult, it is usually because the caregiver regularly overstimulates the baby who wants to pause, or ignores the infant's invitations to interact (Isabella and Belsky, 1991). If the infant is repeatedly ignored, he or she will quit trying to respond: offspring of depressed mothers, for example, are less likely to smile and vocalize, not only when interacting with their mothers but also when responding to a nondepressed adult (Field, 1987). Infants with an intrusive, overstimulating caregiver defend themselves more obviously, by turning away or even "shutting down" completely—crying inconsolably or simply falling asleep. Unfortunately, some caregivers still do not notice the cues, as in this example:

> Whenever a moment of mutual gaze occurred, the mother went immediately into high-gear stimulating behaviors, producing a profusion of fully displayed, high-intensity, facial and vocal . . . social behavior. Jenny invariably broke gaze rapidly. Her mother never interpreted this temporary face and gaze aversion as a cue to lower her level of behavior, nor would she let Jenny self-control the level by gaining distance. Instead she would swing her head around following Jenny's to reestablish the full-face position. Jenny again turned away, pushing her face further into the pillow to try to break all visual contact. Again, instead of holding back, the mother continued to chase Jenny. . . . She also escalated the level of her stimulation more by adding touching and tickling to the unabated flow of vocal and facial behavior . . . Jenny closed her eyes to avoid any mutual visual contact and only reopened them after [she had moved her head to the other side]. All of these behaviors on Jenny's part were performed with a sober face or at times a grimace. [Stern, 1977]

While this example clearly shows the effects of the caregiver's personality, it should be noted that the infant's personality and predispositions also affect the ease of synchrony. For example, some infants are constitutionally more sensitive to stimulation than others, and these would have particular problems with an intrusive caregiver like Jenny's mother. Fortunately, even with such a mismatch, repair is possible. Sometimes a helpful outsider can teach the mother how to read her baby's signals, and sometimes the baby and caregiver begin to adjust to each other spontaneously (Stern, 1985). In this case, Jenny eventually became more able to adjust to the mother's sudden overstimulation, and the mother, finding her infant more responsive, no

(a)

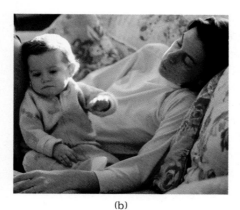

(b)

Figure 7.11 *Adults typically use special social behaviors (a) with their young infants—leaning in close, opening their eyes and mouths wide in exaggerated expressions of surprise or delight, maintaining constant eye contact—because they elicit the baby's attention and pleasure. But these behaviors are subdued or absent when the adult is depressed or stressed (b), and this makes social interaction much less enjoyable for each partner.*

longer felt the need to bombard her with stimulation as she had earlier. With time, Jenny and her mother established a mutually rewarding relationship.

Attachment

Just as the moment-by-moment harmony between parents and young infants has captured scientific attention, so has the **attachment** between parents and slightly older infants been the subject of extensive research. "Attachment," according to Mary Ainsworth (1973), "may be defined as an affectional tie that one person or animal forms between himself and another specific one—a tie that binds them together in space and endures over time." Not surprisingly, when people are attached to each other, they try to be near one another, and they interact with each other often. Thus infants show attachment through "proximity-seeking" behaviors—such as approaching, following, and climbing into the lap—and "contact-maintaining" behaviors—such as clinging and resisting being put down (Ainsworth and Bell, 1970). Parents show their attachment by keeping a watchful eye on their infant, even when safety does not require it, and by responding affectionately and sensitively to the infant's vocalizations, expressions, and gestures.

Measuring Attachment

In studying attachment in England, Uganda, and the United States, Ainsworth discovered that virtually all normal infants develop special attachments to the people who care for them, with some infants much more secure in those attachments than others.

A **secure attachment** is one in which the infant derives comfort and confidence, as evidenced by attempts to be close to the caregiver and by readiness to explore the environment. The caregiver acts as a "secure base," enabling the toddler to venture forth, perhaps scrambling down from mother's lap to manipulate a toy while periodically looking back, vocalizing, or returning for a hug.

By contrast, **insecure attachment** is characterized by the infant's fear, anger, or seeming indifference to the caregiver. The infant has much less confidence, perhaps being unwilling to let go of the mother's arms, or perhaps playing aimlessly with no signs of trying to maintain contact.

While there are many ways to measure attachment, Ainsworth developed a classic laboratory procedure, called the **Strange Situation,** which is designed to evoke the infant's reactions to the caregiver under somewhat stressful conditions. Infants are closely observed in a well-equipped playroom, in several successive episodes of about three minutes, with their mother and/or a stranger, or alone.

About two-thirds of all American infants tested in the Strange Situation demonstrate secure attachment. Their mother's presence in the playroom is enough to give them courage to explore the room and investigate the toys; her departure may cause some distress (usually expressed through verbal protest and a pause in playing); and her return is a signal to reestablish positive social contact (with a smile or by climbing into the mother's arms) and then resume playing.

Other infants, however, show one of three types of insecure attachment. Some are *anxious* and resistant: they cling nervously to their mother even before her initial departure and thus are unwilling to explore the play-room; they cry loudly each time she leaves; they refuse to be comforted when she returns, perhaps continuing to sob angrily even when back in her arms. Others are *avoidant*: they engage in little interaction with their mother; they often show no apparent stress when she leaves; and on her return, they tend to avoid reestablishing contact, sometimes even turning their backs. Others are *disoriented,* or disorganized: they show an inconsistent mixture of behavior toward the mother, such as avoiding her just after seeking to be close to her (Main and Solomon, 1986).

Attachment and Context

Ainsworth's procedure for measuring attachment has been used in thousands of studies. From these we have learned that attachment is one indication of the quality of care in early infancy (Bretherton and Waters, 1985; Lamb et al., 1985; Thompson, 1991). Among the caregiving features that affect the quality of attachment are (1) general sensitivity to the infant's needs, (2) responsiveness to the infant's specific signals, and (3) talking and playing with the infant in ways that actively encourage the child's growth and development. Thus sensitive and responsive caregiving in the early months leads naturally to secure attachment in the later months.

Attachment may also be influenced by the broader context in which infant and mother live. It may be affected, for example, by the extent and quality of the father's involvement in the care of the child, and by the nature of the marital relationship (Easterbrooks and Goldberg, 1984; Goldberg and Easterbrooks, 1984). Furthermore, significant changes in family circumstances—such as a parent's changing jobs—alter the attachment relationship between infant and mother by altering familiar patterns of interaction. This can result in a new relationship that may be more or less secure than before (Thompson et al., 1982). Such influences can affect attachment in diverse ways, so it is not surprising that when researchers have tried to explain why infants become securely or insecurely attached, measures of maternal care taken alone provide only a partial explanation. Measures of infant temperament likewise tell a part of the story (Belsky and Rovine, 1987; Izard et al., 1991). In essence, attachment relationships take shape from the *interaction* of mother and infant within a complex social ecology.

As part of that ecology, cultural context can also affect the development of attachment (Sagi and Lewkowicz, 1987; van Ijzendoorn and Kroonenberg, 1988). In cross-cultural comparisons of the Strange Situation, for example, Japanese and Israeli children show a higher rate of anxiety and resistance than American infants do, while infants from some Western European countries show higher rates of avoidance. Why do these differences exist? Some researchers believe that particular cultural backgrounds may make the Strange Situation too demanding for certain infants, causing them to exhibit insecure behavior. Japanese mothers, for instance, rarely leave their infants with babysitters, and their offspring are thus less prepared to cope with being with a stranger or alone in the Strange Situation than American infants are (Chen and Miyake, 1986). However, an extensive analysis of cross-cultural data on attachment reveals that, in the Strange Situation, infants of various nationalities, overall, exhibit more similarities than differences in their behavior. Most infants worldwide consider their mother's presence a reassuring sign that it is safe to explore the environment, and most infants come back to her for comfort under stress (Sagi et al., 1991). Most infants also show signs of secure attachments to other caregivers—fathers, siblings, day-care workers—although this obviously varies from culture to culture.

The importance of the specific context in assessing attachment was highlighted by a recent controversy involving day care. On the basis of studies showing that infants who experienced early and extended day care (in or out of the home) were more likely to ignore or avoid their mother in the Strange Situation, some researchers concluded that more than twenty hours of day care a week in the infant's first year posed a risk for secure attachment (Belsky, 1986). However, other reviewers have noted that the majority of infants with early and extended day care are, in fact, securely attached (Thompson, 1991). As they point out, when attachment behavior is measured in the Strange Situation, day-care infants may behave differently—that is, seeming blasé about their mother's comings and goings—because of their prior experience of separation and reunion, not because of insecure attachment. As Clarke-Stewart (1989) noted, in the Strange Situation

> the infant plays with someone else's toys in a room that is not his or her own; the infant is left by his or her mother with a woman who is a stranger; the infant plays with and is comforted by that woman in the mother's absence; the mother returns to pick the infant up. Although at least some infants of nonworking mothers undoubtedly have had experiences like these before their assessment in the Strange Situation, infants of working mothers are more likely to have had them regularly and routinely and, therefore, to be more accustomed to them.

The researcher who initiated this controversy, Jay Belsky, now acknowledges that when day care in the first year is of "high quality," there should be "little reason to anticipate negative developmental outcomes (Belsky, 1990).

The Importance of Attachment

Why is attachment considered so important? Part of the reason lies in longitudinal research that documents the results of secure and insecure attachment. It clearly shows that secure attachment at age 1 provides a preview to the child's social and personality development in the years to come. For example, observations in nursery school show that 3-year-olds who are rated securely attached at age 1 are significantly more competent in certain social and cognitive skills: they are more curious, outgoing, and self-directed than those who were insecurely attached. The 3-year-olds who are securely attached are also more likely to be sought out as friends and chosen as leaders. Furthermore, securely attached infants tend to become children who interact with teachers in friendly and appropriate ways, seeking their help when needed. By contrast, infants who show anxious insecure attachment tend to become preschoolers who are overly dependent on teachers, demanding their attention unnecessarily and clinging to them instead of playing with other children or exploring the environment (Sroufe et al., 1983). At age 4, boys who are insecurely attached tend to be aggressive, while girls who are insecurely attached tend to be overly dependent (Turner, 1991). Even at ages 5 and 6, differences are apparent between children who were securely and insecurely attached as infants (Arend et al., 1979; Main and George, 1985).

RESEARCH REPORT   **Father and Infants**

Traditional views of infant development focused almost exclusively on mothers, partly because the received wisdom in most cultures was that fathers are naturally "remote and authoritarian," above any intimate relationship with their young children. And historically fathers were, in fact, removed from most caregiving activities, in response to the cultural expectations as well as to the practical necessities of working long hours away from home while the mothers tended house, children, and garden.

Recently, however, as family size has shrunk and mothers have increasingly become employed outside the home, many fathers have taken on a "significant share of the nurturing responsibilities" for their offspring (Poussaint, 1990). This shift is apparent worldwide, including countries such as Ireland and Mexico where the stereotype is that fathers are above changing diapers or spooning pablum (Nugent, 1991; Bronstein, 1984; Lamb, 1987). Virtually all developmentalists applaud this trend, for fathers who share in child-care responsibilities probably enhance development of their children more than the remote fathers of old did.

As this change occurred, it raised some interesting questions about the relationship between fathers and their infants. The first and most urgent was: Could fathers provide adequate care for newborns and young infants? The answer, quick in coming, was a resounding yes: research found that babies drank just as much formula, emerged from the bath just as clean, and seemed just as content with the caregiving of fathers as with the caregiving of mothers. It was further determined that fathers can provide the necessary emotional and cognitive nurturing as well, coordinating their facial expressions in synchrony, speaking Motherese like a native, and forming secure attachments (Parke, 1981). Overall, researchers found "no evidence that women are biologically predisposed to be better parents than men are" (Lamb, 1981). As one psychiatrist emphatically expressed it:

> There is perhaps no mystique of motherhood that a man cannot master except for the physical realities of pregnancy, delivery, and breast feeding. [Poussaint, 1990]

Given that fathers *can* master caregiving, the next question was: Why don't more fathers develop this skill? Worldwide, women spend far more time in child care than men do, especially in the early months and particularly if the child is a girl (Lamb, 1987). Even in contemporary marriages, even when both parents work outside the home on weekdays, and even when both agree that child care is a shared responsibility, the reality is that, although fathers do some basic caregiving in the evenings and on weekends, mothers do a great deal more (Belsky et al., 1984; Thompson and Walker, 1989; Pleck, 1985).

Surprisingly, although the media, and many mothers, tend to blame the fathers, mothers may actually be more responsible for this unequal distribution of labor than fathers. Indeed, many mothers assume the status of the family child-care authority: they serve as a kind of gatekeeper and judge of the father's performance, forbidding or criticizing certain behaviors, permitting and praising others (Pollack and Grossman, 1985; Kranichfeld, 1987).

In addition, the general social context often works against fathers' being intensely involved in caregiving with infants. The traditional view of child-rearing roles, for example, is reinforced by many cultural pressures—from that of older relatives, who may encourage the mother to provide most of the nitty-gritty child care, to that of the father's friends and colleagues, who may deride the idea of Daddy's doing diapers. Employers too, are more likely to recognize, and make allowances for, the woman's role as caregiver than they are the man's. Finally, the marriage relationship can affect the father-child relationship: when the couple are happy with their relationship, they are more likely to share child-care duties (Belsky et al., 1991).

As researchers looked more closely at the amount of time mothers and fathers spend with their infants, they discovered another curious difference between the caregiving of mothers and fathers: although fathers provide less basic care, they play more—devoting an average of 3 hours a day to such activity, according to one study of first-time fathers and their toddlers (Easterbrooks and Goldberg, 1984). Moreover, compared to mother's play, father's play is noisier, more boisterous, and idiosyncratic, as fathers make up active and exciting games on the spur of the moment (MacDonald and Parke, 1986).

Even in the first months of the baby's life, fathers are more likely to play by moving baby's legs and arms in imitation of walking, kicking, or climbing, or by zooming the baby through the air ("airplane"), or by tapping and tickling the baby's stomach; mothers, on the other hand, are more likely to talk or sing soothingly, or to combine play with caretaking routines such as diapering and bathing (Parke and Tinsley, 1981).

These differences between mothers' and fathers' play

Fathers are significant people to infants because they have a unique style of caregiving and play that typically gets babies excited and delighted. Fathers are important also because their involvement in infant care can make the mother's role either easier or more demanding.

are not lost on infants. Even young infants typically react with more visible excitement when approached by their fathers than when approached by their mothers. In the first months of life infants are more likely to laugh—and more likely to cry—in episodes of play with Daddy.

As infants grow older, fathers generally increase the time they spend with them, and their tendency to engage in physical play becomes more pronounced. Fathers are likely to swing their toddlers around, or "wrestle" with them on the floor, or crawl after them in a "chase."

Mothers, on the other hand, when "playing," are more likely to read to their toddlers, help them play with toys, or play conventional games such as patty-cake or peek-a-boo (MacDonald and Parke, 1986). These differences continue to be reflected in infants' reactions. According to one study (Clarke-Stewart, 1978), 20-month-olds are more responsive during play with their fathers than with their mothers. By 30 months, differences are even more apparent: 2-year-olds are generally more cooperative, involved, and interested in their fathers' games than in their mothers' play, and judging by their smiles and laughter, they have more fun.

What do infants gain from playing with their fathers, in addition to having fun? They may be learning something about social interaction: if they enjoy being with their fathers, they probably will enjoy being with other people as well. For instance, one study looked specifically at the attachment of 12-month-olds to their mothers and their fathers, and then at the infant's reaction to the stranger in the Strange Situation. There was no correlation between attachment to the mother and response to the stranger, but there was a correlation between attachment to the father and response to the stranger: those infants who were securely attached to their fathers were more likely to initiate contact with the stranger, and those who were insecurely attached were more likely to cry (Bridges et al., 1988).

In another study, 18-month-olds who were securely attached to both parents met a stranger while either their father or their mother sat passively nearby. The father's presence made the toddlers much more likely to smile and play with the new person than the mother's presence did, a result especially apparent for the boys. The authors of this study speculated that the child's experiences of boisterous, idiosyncratic play with Dad may make the father's presence a cue for playfulness and embolden the child to engage the stranger. It may also be that the father's style of play encourages risk-taking, especially with sons, with whom they more frequently engage in roughhousing. As the authors of the study note, while

> elements of mothers' play also involve risk (e.g. the mock "scare" at the end of the "peek-a-boo" pattern) . . . being thrown up in the air is probably more highly arousing to the central nervous system, [and] the expectation and relief of being caught may serve to enhance the attraction of risk-taking. [Kromelow et al., 1990]

Findings such as this raise anew the question of whether or not gender-specific caregiving with infants may be best. At the moment, researchers have no definitive answers, but some are beginning to shift the emphasis of the question, suggesting that the division of child-rearing labor that may be best for infants is whatever division is best for the parents. Indeed, when their relationship is good, each parent complements, encourages, and enhances the other in "a balanced system of interactive effects between husbands and wives" (Grossman et al., 1988). Even in today's changing world, mothers and fathers together are more likely to meet all their infant's needs—biological, cognitive, and social—than either one alone is.

Attachment as revealed in the Strange Situation has been used, successfully, to indicate the overall relationship between caregiver and child. If a child is insecurely attached, that signals a poor relationship, one that may become child maltreatment (Crittenden and Ainsworth, 1989). Beyond this specific application, researchers disagree about the significance of attachment status. Some believe that insecure attachment itself can be transitory, evident in the laboratory at age 1 but gone a few months later, especially if the caregiver becomes more attentive.

Lending support to this optimistic view is a study done with the infants of Spanish-speaking immigrants. The study compared three groups of 1-year-olds: a securely attached group, an insecurely attached control group, and an insecurely attached experimental group, who were visited weekly by an empathic bilingual and bicultural adviser. Within a year, the experimental group of mothers and infants were relating to each other almost as well as the group who originally were secure—and far better than the control group on measures of infant anger, maternal responsiveness, and the like (Lieberman et al., 1991).

However, many psychologists believe insecure attachment indicates a flawed caregiver-child relationship that is difficult to alter: perhaps immigrant Latinas in this study were particularly receptive to supportive visitors, while other mothers of insecurely attached infants may be less tractable. In fact, some believe that early attachment is a formative influence on the developing personality, making the insecurely attached infant become fearful or destructive of all intimate relationships, even in adulthood (Ainsworth, 1985; Richman and Flaherty, 1987). Longitudinal research with many groups of infants is needed to establish how long-lasting and powerful early attachment relationships are.

A more immediate consequence of insecure attachment is that the toddler is not free to explore. Experiences such as manipulating toys to understand the characteristics of the object world, or interacting with strangers to expand one's social realm, or toddling into another room to discover what lies out of sight, are all part of healthy child development. The toddler who is filled with enthusiasm and curiosity, and whose parent has the patience, affection, and foresight that encourages "the little scientist" to experiment, becomes the brighter, happier child (Bradley and Caldwell, 1984; Carew, 1980).

Child Maltreatment

Several times in this chapter, you have read that parents are not always sensitive to their infants: they may misread emotions, or foster insecure attachment, or frustrate the child's need for autonomy. Such problems are common, understandable, and relatively easy to remedy. Now, however, we turn to child maltreatment, an interaction that, while common, is at first difficult to understand. Ironically, our difficulty is compounded by the type of attention this topic receives in the media. The stories are familiar to everyone:

> 8-month-old Yessana "began crying and would not stop." The mother . . . had been drinking and could stand the crying no more. She said in a videotaped statement that she shook and struck the baby and twice dropped her on the

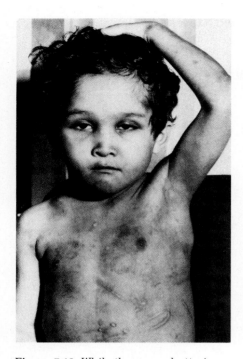

Figure 7.12 *While the severe battering of a child may be the most disturbing kind of abuse to witness, long-term and repeated physical and psychological abuse is much more common and more damaging. When asked about his injuries, which included cigarette burns, welts, and bite marks, this 5-year-old explained, "My stepfather sometimes says 'I'm a lion. You're a piece of meat.' I guess he doesn't like me."*

floor . . . less than 12 hours later, the infant died, apparently of multiple fractures of the skull. [McFadden, 1990]

7-month-old Daniel died of starvation and dehydration after five days without food or water. After his father beat his mother, she . . . "went on a six day crack binge." The next day his father "left the baby alone in the unlocked apartment . . . " According to the police, neither parent intended for the child to die, they were "both remorseful." The mother was known to authorities, because she had several other children, all in foster care. [Duggar, 1991]

Our emotions are caught by the brutality and senselessness of cases like these, and we are filled with outrage at what we perceive to be pathological perpetrators, as well as at the indifferent neighbors and overworked child-welfare workers who often seem to share the blame. According to some critics, however, the media focus on such stories inadvertently does a disservice to the well-being of many children, distracting attention from the more typical case and from the community's collective responsibility to ensure children's well-being (Scheper-Hughes and Stein, 1987).

In fact, even among those children who are seriously maltreated, less than one in a thousand die. Much more common is a persistent pattern of abuse or neglect that, accumulating over the years, affects the child's self-concept and personality, sometimes permanently. And instead of the incomprehensible behavior of the parents cited above, more frequent are the harmful actions of parents who do not understand how to love and guide a child, reasoning, for example, like this mother of a 6-month-old:

If he spits his food at me I slap his leg. No time to learn like the present—if he is old enough to do it, he is old enough to learn not to do it. [Gelles, 1987]

In their efforts to understand and stop maltreatment, social scientists have attempted to get beyond sensationalism and easy blame and apply their knowledge about human development. As you will now see, their recognition of the scope, causes, and consequences of child mistreatment is quite recent, and their approaches to the treatment and prevention of this problem are still emerging.

A LIFE-SPAN PERSPECTIVE

Abuse and Neglect in Context

Child abuse and neglect occur from conception through adolescence and, like other forms of domestic violence, harm every family member—victim, perpetrator, and observer. We will therefore take up our major discussion of maltreatment in this Life-Span Perspective, placing it in the infancy because the early years of the parent-child relationship are the time when maltreatment is most likely to begin and the most likely to result in severe harm, as well as the time it is most easily averted.

Changing Definitions of Maltreatment

Only forty years ago, the concept of child maltreatment was, for the most part, limited to gross physical abuse, which was generally thought to be the rare, violent outburst of a mentally disturbed person (Zigler and Hall, 1989). We now recognize that child maltreatment is neither rare nor sudden, that its perpetrators usually are not deranged, and

RESEARCH REPORT   **Child Maltreatment: How Common in the United States?**

Nobody knows the true prevalence of child maltreatment, since it usually occurs behind closed doors, with the caregiver unwilling, and the child unable, to acknowledge it. However, there are four methods commonly used to estimate prevalence: official reports, professional surveys, general surveys, and retrospective accounts.

The simplest method is to count the number of complaints received by official agencies. Currently about 2.5 million reports are logged annually in the United States—which represents a reporting rate of one in every twenty-five children, double that of ten years ago.

However, tallying complaints is probably the least accurate method of estimating the incidence of maltreatment: while many instances are not reported, others are reported more than once, and of those that are reported, only about half are substantiated—sometimes because the report was completely false, but more often because the seriousness of the offense was insufficient to warrant an official recognition (NCCAN, 1988; Finkelhor, 1992).

A better method of estimating maltreatment is to ask all the trained professionals—judges, probation officers, police, doctors, nurses, teachers, day-care-center staff, child-welfare workers—in representative communities to name every child they are quite sure has been mistreated, and then extrapolate the results to the nation as a whole. This approach, taken by the National Center for Child Abuse and Neglect, produced the results shown in the first table here, indicating that about 1 child in 40 (about 1.5 million) was known to suffer maltreatment of some kind in 1986, with physical abuse affecting 1 child in about 175 (NCCAN, 1988).

Incidence of Child Maltreatment Known to Professionals, per 100 Children: United States, 1986

Rate of Abuse	1.07
Physical	0.57
Sexual	0.25
Emotional	0.34
Rate of Neglect	1.59
Physical	0.91
Educational	0.46
Emotional	0.35
Overall Rate	2.52

Totals of subcategories exceed the overall rate because about 10 percent of the children were known to have experienced more than one type of maltreatment.
Source: National Center for Child Abuse and Neglect, 1988.

A third method is to ask caregivers, confidentially, about their behavior with their children. One study that used this approach conducted a telephone survey of more than 3,000 representative American families from all fifty states (Straus and Gelles, 1986). (If a surveyed family had two parents or several children, only one parent was asked about his or her behavior with one child, to get an accurate incidence per caretaker and child, rather than per family.) The results, shown in the table on the next page, suggest that about one child in forty was abused very violently (kicked, bitten, beaten, burned, hit with a fist, cut with a knife, and/or shot at)—a much higher figure than the estimates derived from cases of physical abuse known to pro-

that serious physical injury is only one of several signs of mistreatment (Ammerman and Hersen, 1990; McGee and Wolfe, 1991; Cicchetti and Carlson, 1989).

As our understanding of child maltreatment has increased, its definition has broadened. Currently the term **child maltreatment** includes all intentional harm to, or avoidable endangerment of, someone under age 18. Specific acts of maltreatment fall into one of two broad categories—**abuse**, which includes all actions that are deliberately harmful to a child's well-being, and **neglect**, which involves failures to act appropriately to meet a child's basic needs.

Most professionals further divide both abuse and neglect into three subcategories of maltreatment:

1. *Physical abuse*—deliberate, harsh injury to the body. Signs of physical abuse include broken limbs and battered bodies, as well

Parents' Reporting of Their Own Violence With Offspring

Type of Violence	Percent Reporting
Cursed or insulted child	63
Slapped or spanked child	55
Pushed, grabbed, shoved child	31
Hit child with something (e.g., belt, stick)	11
Kicked, bit, hit with fist, beat up, burned	3
Used gun or knife	0.2

Source: Gelles, 1987, 1989.

fessionals. Even so, this figure is undoubtedly an underestimate. Not only would some caregivers report less violence than they actually committed, but, as indicated, they were not asked about their abuse of other children in the household or of abuse by other family members. In addition, parents who refused to answer questions or who were without telephones were, obviously, not part of the study. Since being without a telephone is a sign of both poverty and social isolation, the latter group, especially, represents an important missing segment of the population most at risk. Moreover, while this method may be fairly accurate for most forms of physical punishment, it cannot validly assess sexual abuse, about which most perpetrators are ashamed and secretive, or neglect, since many caregivers do not know when they seriously neglect their children.

Finally, a fourth method—asking adults if they have ever been abused or neglected—leads to the highest incidence statistics of all. For example, in one study of families, 30 percent of the fathers and 17 percent of the mothers reported having been regularly hit with a belt, paddle, or other object by their parents when they were about age 12 (Simons et al., 1991). This rate well exceeds the 11 percent rate of hitting acknowledged by parents in the second table. The discrepancy between self-reports of the maltreated and any other source is particularly apparent with regard to sexual abuse, where even the *lowest* rates of childhood abuse recalled by adults are more than twenty times the rates reported or known to professionals (Peters et al., 1986).

Among the reasons that this last method produces notably higher abuse rates is, obviously, that it accounts for victims whose cases never came to official attention and helps compensate for the unwillingness of some parents to be candid about their maltreatment of their children. Another important reason is that the retrospective survey usually asks about a person's entire childhood, while the other techniques focus on a single year. At the same time, however, the higher retrospective rates could reflect a higher actual rate of abuse in previous generations, as suggested by many studies that find maltreatment decreasing (Gelles, 1987; Simons et al., 1991; Besharov, 1992). In addition, some adults may have distorted or exaggerated memories of their mistreatment in childhood.

Thus each method of estimating maltreatment has its drawbacks. Each reflects a part of the picture, and therefore each has some validity and purpose, but none is completely accurate. Nevertheless, taken together, they make it starkly clear that child maltreatment is the most common of the serious developmental problems American children encounter.

as less obvious symptoms, such as similar abrasions on both sides of the face or body, X-rays that reveal old, poorly knit fractures, CAT-scans that show bleeding in the brain, and burn marks that are small and round (from lit cigarettes), lattice-like (from hot radiators), or that stop part-way up the body (from scalding bathwater).

2. *Emotional abuse* (also called psychological abuse)—deliberate destruction of self-esteem and equanimity. The most common type is repeated verbal abuse, ranging from angry threats to incessant criticism. Another type is social isolation, such as shutting a small child in a dark closet or keeping an adolescent housebound and friendless. Overall, any terrorizing, isolating, degrading, or belittling of the child can become emotional abuse.

3. *Sexual abuse*—deliberate involvement in, or exposure to, sexual activities without informed consent. Since children are naive and

| A CLOSER LOOK | Child Maltreatment in Context |

As you remember from Chapter 1, every behavior needs to be considered in perspective. This is especially true when assessing parental nurturance, a topic that involves our deepest and most personal emotions. Developmentalists increasingly believe that "behaviors per se can seldom be defined as harmful or beneficial—the immediate, relational, familial, and cultural contexts in which they occur all play a crucial role in determining what effects the behavior may have" (Sternberg and Lamb, 1991).

Understanding child maltreatment in context begins by considering *community standards*. Each community has somewhat different customs and goals regarding child-rearing, which means that sometimes what is maltreatment in one place is not maltreatment in another. For example, while more than 90 percent of American parents sometimes spank, slap, or push their 3-year-olds, and think such behavior is justified, in Sweden any physical punishment of children at any age is considered abusive and is against the law (Daro, 1988). In some Asian, African, and Caribbean countries, by contrast, to never hit a child is tantamount to neglect (Rohner et al., 1991; Rohner, 1984; Arnold, 1982).

Thus in many cases, before concluding that a particular behavior or practice represents maltreatment, we need to take community standards into account. This is especially important in light of the fact that children everywhere feel loved when their parents raise them not too differently from other children in the same family, neighborhood, and culture, and that parents judge their own child-rearing partly on the basis of the collective wisdom and practice of their peers. Given the diversity of the world's communities, it is "imperative to disentangle the natural from the cultural," distinguishing those practices which hurt any child anywhere from those that are harmful only in a particular place (Woodhead, 1991). Beating a child is one example: for children in the West Indies, being hit for misbehaving is commonplace, and is taken as a sign of the parent's love and concern. But for these children, as for children everywhere, frequent and severe physical beatings result in feelings of rejection and low self-esteem (Rohner et al., 1991).

Understanding maltreatment in context also requires taking into account the impact of a behavior on the particular child. Since each child is unique, and every child changes over time, a practice that harms one child may not negatively affect another, or may not hurt either of them a few years later. For example, some children need much more supervision than others; some wither more quickly under criticism; some are more likely to be injured, physically or emotionally, by corporal punishment. Thus the seriousness of any specific act of maltreatment depends partly on the age, temperament, and abilities of the child (McGee and Wolfe, 1991).

Finally, assessing the effects of any particular behavior requires a developmental view, assessing long-term effects. Often the critical question is whether or not a particular act of commission or omission is part of a repeated pattern. Regular maltreatment—such as frequent beatings or ongoing indifference—is much more devastating in the long run to children than an isolated loss of temper or an occasional neglectful act.

Of course, predicting the effects of potential maltreatment is difficult, for researchers still have much to learn about why one child is hurt by a particular act or pattern of behavior and another is not. However, we already know that immediate and visible damage is not the best predictor of eventual impact. Sometimes there are no visible effects at all, yet an infant whose caregiver is rejecting or indifferent may become a child who cannot make friends; a toddler who is shaken hard in anger may incur lifelong brain damage; a young adolescent who has an erotic relationship with a parent may become an adult who dreads sexual intimacy. For this reason, **endangerment**—putting a child at risk for serious harm—is now accepted as one criterion for child abuse (NCCAN, 1988).

At what point, then, does imperfect parenting become maltreatment? There is no clear line of demarcation. Every case should be judged in terms of its context and developmental history (Zigler and Hall, 1989; Cicchetti, 1991). Beyond that, the question becomes, Who is judging the behavior, and for what purpose? When the issue is whether a particular case should be legally labeled as maltreatment, only those cases in which maltreatment seems clearly dangerous and ongoing, as well as completely unacceptable to the community, merit official intervention (Thompson and Jacobs, 1991). On the other hand, when caregivers wonder if they are crossing the line, they need to remember that every parent's caregiving, is, indeed, sometimes potentially harmful, no matter what the context, and that whenever doubts about the severity of disciplining arise, it is far better to trust those doubts and err on the side of leniency.

vulnerable to the power of adults, they are by definition incapable of informed consent, and thus any erotic activity that arouses an adult and excites, shames, or confuses the child—whether or not the child protests and whether or not genital contact is involved—can be sexual abuse. (This topic is discussed in Chapter 17.)

4. *Physical neglect*—failure to meet basic needs for biological survival. This type of neglect includes the failure to provide adequate food, warmth, or medical care, as well as reasonable supervision and protection from harm or injury.

5. *Emotional neglect* (also called psychological neglect)—failure to meet basic needs for emotional sustenance. Distant, cold, indifferent, and unaffectionate caregivers are emotionally neglectful. So are those who capriciously withdraw love or comfort, who allow the child's self-abuse with drugs or other means, or who do not shield a child from witnessing violence between adults.

6. *Educational neglect*—failure to fulfill the basic need for learning and information. The most common form is not sending a child to school on a regular basis. More broadly, educational neglect can include schools or teachers who do not teach the children entrusted to them.

For reasons cited in the Research Report on page 192 and the Closer Look, specific estimates of the prevalence and destructiveness of maltreatment vary considerably. Even if a conservative approach is taken, however, and only cases known to professionals (doctors, police, social workers, teachers, and so forth) are counted, then about one of every forty American children under age 18—a total of about 1.5 million children—experienced some form of severe maltreatment *within the past year*. Understanding the causes, the consequences, and the ways to prevent such suffering is, obviously, critically important.

Causes of Child Maltreatment

At first it is hard to imagine why anyone would hurt a child entrusted to his or her care. However, research has shown that virtually everything—from the community values to the caregiver's history, from the family culture to the child's temperament—can play a role.

The Community Context

According to the United Nations, concern and protection for the well-being of children varies markedly worldwide. Even countries in the same region of the world, with similar per capita income, differ markedly in measures of child health, education, and overall well-being (United Nations, 1990).

More subjective views of child abuse and neglect find day-to-day caregiving influenced by broad cultural values (Korbin, 1981; Sigler, 1989). What seem to be the values that protect children from abuse? Four seem to be especially important:

1. Children are highly valued, as a psychological joy and fulfillment, as well as an economic asset.

2. Child care is considered the responsibility of the community. If a mother is unwilling or unable to care for her child, other relatives are ready to take over.

3. Young children are not expected to be responsible for their actions. In some cultures, almost any punishment of children younger than age 3, or even age 7, is considered abusive and unnecessary.

4. Violence in any context—between adults, between children, and between caregiver and child—is disapproved.

The role of social values and conditioning in child maltreatment is dramatically highlighted by the different rates of child abuse among the Polynesian people who live in their traditional home, the Pacific Islands, and those who have emigrated to New Zealand. Among the former, abuse is virtually nonexistent (Ritchie and Ritchie, 1981), for their society meets the four criteria listed above: children are highly respected, are cared for by many adults, are considered unteachable until they are at least 2 years old, and adults rarely express their anger through physical aggression (Ritchie and Ritchie, 1981; Reid, 1989).

However, when Polynesians move to New Zealand, the rate of child abuse skyrockets, surpassing the rate of the European New Zealanders many times over. The demands of the new lifestyle, designed for nuclear rather than extended families, make it impossible for the parents to continue their relaxed permissiveness, communal authority, and informal, shared child care. Like every immigrant group entering a radically different culture, these Polynesian parents experience considerable stress until they develop viable new coping strategies, such as learning how to guide children's behavior without resorting to physical punishment, how to replace the freely available caregivers of the past, and how to limit family size so that children are not an overwhelming financial burden. These contextual stresses often lead to a loss of perspective, and abuse results.

Cultural Factors Affecting Maltreatment in the United States

Comparing the four characteristics of nonabusive cultures with the patterns common in the United States explains, to a great extent, why child maltreatment is so prevalent there. First, children are considered to be both a financial and personal burden. Not surprisingly, no matter how maltreatment is defined or counted, it becomes more frequent as family income falls. For example, according to one study, children in families with an annual income under $15,000 were almost five times as likely to be abused, and nine times as likely to be neglected, as those from slightly wealthier families (NCCAN, 1988).

Second, in the United States, social support for parents and young children is scarce. For a variety of reasons, ranging from geographic separation of family members to the cultural emphasis on "looking out for number 1," few relatives, neighbors, and friends are willing and able to help with child care. Grandmothers, for instance, once the mainstay of practical help, are now much more likely to live a distance away and to have their lives taken up with careers and friends outside the family.

Figure 7.13 *Child maltreatment, spouse abuse, and elder neglect—three serious social problems in industrialized nations—are rare in Micronesia. One reason, reflected in this photo of a community on Pulap Island, is that family life occurs largely in the open rather than behind closed doors. Neighbors and relatives immediately notice any lapse of care or outbursts of temper, and remedy the problem before it becomes neglect or abuse.*

Figure 7.14 *Arnold Schwarzenegger's role as The Terminator seems the epitome of Hollywood's tradition of depicting violence as a quick and righteous solution to problems of every sort, a tradition that dates as far back as the silent movies. According to many critics, the high death rate on the silver screen, as well as on television, helps explain why the United States has the highest homicide rate, and perhaps the most widespread domestic abuse, of any developed nation.*

Lacking a supportive network, overburdened parents often take out their problems on their children, with the problems escalating, undetected, until considerable harm has been done. Especially when lack of support results in social isolation, the likelihood of abuse is high, with those who are most isolated being among the most abusive (Kempe and Kempe, 1984; Schilling, 1987).

Third, the American attitude about young children may add to the problem. The emphasis on the infant's and preschooler's ability to learn may cause some parents to forget that young children are also immature, self-absorbed, and dependent on others. For example, many abusing parents consider irritating but normal infant behavior to be deliberate and therefore amenable to correction: they punish their infants for "crying too much" or punish toddlers for being unable to control urination or defecation or punish older children for "immature" behavior, expecting them to get themselves up, dressed, fed and to school, as well as to avoid "trouble" of all kinds long before they are sufficiently mature to do so.

Finally, as many have observed, "violence is as American as apple pie." Indeed, by almost any measure, from the prevalence and prominence of aggression on television to the rate of spouse abuse, from the rates of violent crime to the rate of homicide, the United States is one of the most violent nations of the world (Sigler, 1989; Gelles and Straus, 1988; Benedek, 1989).

The Family Context

Each family has its own culture, including traditions, habits, and values that affect every family member. Many experts believe that the way these are structured in the individual family system can be pivotal in allowing maltreatment to occur. For example, the daily routine of most families is somewhat flexible, with adults and older children being able to make minor adjustments in their schedules and established roles as the occasion requires. However, the routines of maltreating families are typically at one of two extremes: they are either so rigid in their schedules and role demands that no one can measure up, or they are so chaotic and disorganized that no one can be certain of what is expected, or under what circumstances one can count on receiving appreciation, encouragement, protection—or even food and a clean bed. In such families, hostility and neglect are inevitable.

Similarly, while almost every family experiences crises that disrupt their harmony, most also have ways of coping and readjusting so that the family once again functions well. One crucial element in this restabilization is the family's ability and willingness to avail themselves of social support when needed. As already noted, maltreating families tend to lack social support, but problems are especially likely to worsen if a particular family's code includes isolation and distrust of all outsiders, from the neighbor next door to members of the local clergy. If those problems lead to abuse, children are stuck within

> a family system in which exploitation, loyalty, secrecy and self-sacrifice form the core of the family's value system. In a sense, the victim's survival is dependent on adjusting to a psychotic world where abusive behavior is acceptable but telling the truth about it is sinful. [Carmen, 1989]

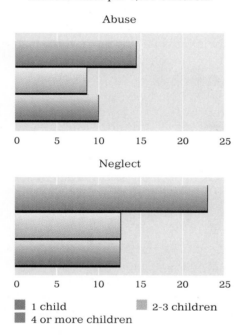

Maltreatment and Family Size
(Annual Rates per 1,000 Children)

Abuse

Neglect

■ 1 child   ▨ 2-3 children
■ 4 or more children

Source: NCCAN, 1988

Figure 7.15 *As suggested by the nursery rhyme about the "old woman who lived in a shoe, she had so many children she didn't know what to do," large families increase the risk of neglecting the children's basic needs.*

Another element within the family system that exacerbates maltreatment is dysfunctional relationships between members other than the perpetrator-victim pair. Child maltreatment is most inevitable within a home where the relationship between the resident adults—especially that between mother and father or between grandparents and children—is either extremely hostile or emotionally neglectful or both.

Another factor that clearly affects the intensity of dysfunctional family relationships is family size and the adult-to-child ratio: when there are more than three young children, mistreatment is more common (see Figure 7.15), partly because each new baby means less money, less space, and less attention for the older ones, which, in turn, means more jealousy and resentment. These effects are more pronounced in single-parent families, since it is even harder for one adult to meet all the needs of several children.

Not surprisingly, low-income single mothers are more abusive than their married counterparts, presumably because the former are often isolated and overwhelmed by being the only adult among a group of children. However, once income rises, single mothers are no more abusive than married mothers, perhaps because the additional income makes social networks more likely, as well as allowing the mother to pay for care by babysitters, day-care centers, and so forth. Unfortunately, no matter what their income, single fathers are more likely to mistreat their children than married fathers (Gelles, 1989). A possible explanation comes from research that found single fathers to be less likely than other parents to ask for, pay for, or accept help in family matters (George and Wilding, 1972).

An additional risk in poorly functioning families is **sibling abuse**, when serious and intentional harm is done to one child by a brother or sister. Typically it begins by parents abusing a child, and then that child, in turn, abusing the younger child. When one sibling is notably stronger than the other, and when parents are themselves abusive and neglectful, serious physical or sexual abuse is common (Goodwin and Roscoe, 1990; Johnson, 1989). Sibling abuse is particularly likely to occur when the aggressor has stresses of his or her own, as happens when a teenage boy must contend with neighborhood toughs, or a pubescent girl has herself been sexually abused.

Problems in the Parents

Contrary to popular misconceptions, most maltreating parents are not markedly different from average parents. Like other parents, they love their children and want the best for them. Only about 10 percent or fewer of them are pathological—so deluded or emotionally and cognitively dysfunctional that they never recognize the basic needs and vulnerabilities of their children.

Overall, however, maltreating parents do tend to have personality traits, thinking patterns, and/or habits that, in combination with stressful situations in a hostile environment, form a volatile constellation likely to lead to an injured child. Personality tests, for example, find that maltreating parents tend to be less trusting, less self-assured, and less adaptable than other parents. They also are less mature, which makes them more concerned with their own needs and less patient with the demands of others (Belsky and Vondra, 1989). Maltreating parents also tend to view the world in negative ways that affect not so much their general attitudes about child-rearing as their attributions for a child's specific behaviors (Newberger and White, 1989). They tend to see the world as hostile and difficult, which leads them to interpret any signs of their infant's discomfort or distress as a personal attack. This negative attribution, especially when combined with immaturity, makes normal coping with the demands and needs of children very difficult (Heap, 1991). Thus two parents may have similar child-rearing attitudes; they may, for instance, both agree that a deliberately disobedient child should be spanked. However, when a particular 2-year-old knocks over the milk, one considers it an accident, while the other "knows" that the "fresh kid" did it out of spite.

Compounding the problem is the fact that some abusive parents completely misread their child's communications. For instance, they are likely to misinterpret the facial expressions and cries of an infant in distress as displays of anger (Kropp and Haynes, 1987), or to mistake the fearful clinging of a genuinely frightened child as a manipulative demand for attention. The effects of this misattribution and miscommunication can be disastrous:

> An average mother will regard a crying or fussy baby as hungry or wet or full of gas. She will proceed to feed, change, burp him, and then put him down in the crib and say, "Baby, you're tired," close the door, then turn on the radio or talk to a friend. The abusive parent is unable to leave the crying child, and tries harder and harder to pacify him until in a moment of utter frustration she is overwhelmed by the thought that the baby, even at two weeks of age, is saying, "If you were a good mother I wouldn't be crying like this." It is precisely because the parent tries to be extra good, to be loved and earn the love of the child, that intractable crying is seen as total rejection and leads to sudden rage. The abuse is clearly not a rational act. It is not premeditated, and it is often followed by deep grief and great guilt. Such parents are seen by doctors and nurses as being very solicitous. Third parties find it hard to believe that so loving a parent could have inflicted such serious injury. [Kempe and Kempe, 1978]

An additional factor that increases the likelihood of maltreatment is drug dependency. One study of addicted parents found that virtually all were neglectful to some degree. In addition, 27 percent of the alcoholics and 13 percent of the heroin addicts physically or sexually abused their children (Black and Mayer, 1980). Another study that focused on Native Americans from the Southwest—who are traditionally very nurturant of their children—found even more striking evidence. Interviews with clinic and hospital staff, community health workers, and tribal leaders revealed that intoxication was a contributing factor in 63 percent of abuse and 85 percent of neglect cases. When both abuse and neglect were present, almost inevitably, alcohol was too (Lujan et al., 1989).

Problems in the Child

Finally, children themselves sometimes inadvertently contribute to their abuse. Babies who are unwanted, who are born too early, who were the product of an unhappy love affair or a difficult pregnancy, who are the "wrong" sex, or who have physical problems can become victims of their parents' disappointment. Even the baby's appearance, as in the case, say, of the little boy who looks just like the father who left the mother early in pregnancy, or the little girl who reminds her father of his abusive mother, can trigger rejection instead of love. Parents may also be unhappy and frustrated over their baby's temperament, wanting a quieter child, or a less active one, or a less difficult one (Steele, 1980). All these disappointments may lead to unresponsive and rejecting parenting, which, as we have seen, is likely to make a child much more difficult than he or she would otherwise have been.

Because the child's nature or behavior can sometimes be a precipitating factor in cases of maltreatment, it is important to stress the obvious: maltreated children are not to be blamed for their fate. While most high-risk babies—especially demanding, irritable, irregular ones—cause stress in their parents, most parents cope well enough without mistreating the infant. Problems arise when the difficult or disappointing child enters a family that is already under strain and unable to function well (Belsky and Vondra, 1989). In addition, although many abused and neglected children are difficult—immature, hyperactive, or deceitful—their difficulties are almost always a result of mistreatment more than a cause of it. Most important, even when a child's actions provoke justifiable anger and merit punishment, abuse is never acceptable, for as you will now see, the consequences of abuse can be devastating.

Consequences of Abuse

The more we learn about child maltreatment, the clearer it becomes that its consequences extend far beyond any immediate injuries. For the victim, it almost always results in impaired development. Compared to well-cared-for children, chronically abused and neglected children tend to be slower to talk, underweight, less able to concentrate, and behind in school (Vondra et al., 1990; Hanson et al., 1989). Deficits are particularly apparent in social skills: maltreated children tend to regard other children and adults as hostile and exploitative, and hence they are less friendly, more aggressive, and more isolated than other children (Haskett and Kistner, 1991; Hart and Brassard, 1989; Mueller and Silverman, 1989). As adolescents and adults, those who were severely mistreated in childhood, either physically or emotionally, often engage in self-destructive and/or other-destructive behavior of every sort, from drug abuse to delinquency, suicide to homicide, isolation to racism.

The human and financial costs, both to the victim and to society, are virtually impossible to measure. In the United States in the 1980s, the annual cost of immediate care (investigation, medical treatment, court costs, emergency shelter) for all reported cases of serious maltreatment was around $500 million, with another $700 million for therapeutic services and long-term foster care (Daro, 1988). Additional costs result when victims of maltreatment later require special education for learning disabilities, therapy or institutionalization for emotional problems, and, in some cases, imprisonment for acts of misdirected anger.

In assessing the outcomes of maltreatment, we must neither minimize nor exaggerate. On the one hand, virtually every child who experiences ongoing maltreatment of any kind will bear some lifelong scars,

Figure 7.16 *No matter how much a harried mother tries to ignore a squalling infant, it is virtually impossible not to feel resentment, anger, or self-blame. If this moment is repeated several times a day, the result is likely to be destructive to both partners.*

with a psychic toll of depression, anger, and fear of intimacy (Rutter, 1989). On the other hand, many adults who were victims of childhood abuse or neglect live relatively normal lives, marrying, working, and raising a family.

One potential consequence that must be considered with particular care is **intergenerational transmission**, that is, mistreated children growing up to become abusive or neglectful parents themselves. Many people erroneously believe that the transmission of maltreatment from one generation to the next is automatic and unalterable. This belief is not only false but destructive. As one review explains:

> Uncritical acceptance of the intergenerational hypothesis has caused undue anxiety in many victims of abuse, led to biased response by mental health workers, and influenced the outcome of court decisions, even in routine divorce child custody cases. In one such case . . . a judge refused a mother custody rights because it was discovered during the trial that the mother had been abused as a child. Despite the fact that much of the evidence supported the children's placement with their mother, the judge concluded that the mother was an unfit guardian, since everyone "knows" abused children become abusive parents. [Kaufman and Zigler, 1989]

In determining the actual rate of intergenerational transmission, it is critical to study the problem longitudinally rather than retrospectively. Retrospective analyses invariably show high rates of transmission because almost every adult who seriously mistreats his or her child does, in fact, remember a very difficult, if not actually neglectful or abusive, childhood. But these analyses, by definition, omit the victims of abuse who do not themselves become abusers.

On the basis of longitudinal studies that begin before the abused individual becomes a parent, experts believe that only about 30 percent of the children who were abused actually become child abusers themselves, a rate about six times that of the general population but much less than that generally assumed to be the case (Kaufman and Zigler, 1989). Those parents least likely to perpetuate the abuse they endured as children are those who subsequently had someone who loved and cared for them, such as the other parent or a foster caregiver in childhood or their spouse in adulthood. In addition, those who are able to remember their mistreatment and understand its effects are much better able to avoid abusing their own children.

Prevention and Treatment

As the scope and consequences of child maltreatment have become better recognized, efforts at prevention and treatment have greatly expanded, particularly in the area of public awareness. In most countries worldwide, as well as throughout the United States, laws have been passed over the past thirty years requiring the reporting of child maltreatment; several public and private national organizations tally reports of abuse and neglect, monitor treatment, and fund research; attention by the popular press has increased dramatically; and a professional journal, *Child Abuse and Neglect*, has been in publication for more than a decade. As a result, professionals and the general public have become much more aware of the problem, and are more likely to report it.

There are a number of signs that such efforts are paying off. One of the most encouraging is that the rate of violent punishment (hitting with a fist or an object, kicking, and the like) reported by American parents fell by 20 percent between 1975 and 1985 (Gelles, 1987), and that the rate of serious injury or death from abuse has also fallen (Besharov, 1992). Further evidence of some progress is that, increasingly, Americans agree that teachers should not use corporal punishment (eleven states forbid it), and that infants should not be hit, while, internationally, a majority in some European nations believe that no child should be physically punished (Daro, 1988). An important reason for this change is growing public awareness of the problem.

Specific Treatment

Reporting, investigating, and substantiating maltreatment, and even punishing the perpetrator, do not necessarily stop abuse, however (Finkelhor,1992). Even with documented cases, between a third and a half of all victims experience another episode of maltreatment (Daro, 1989). While great strides have been made in recognizing and defining maltreatment, and in understanding the causes and consequences, researchers and practitioners are still struggling with the application of these findings to specific cases.

One of the major challenges is how to tailor treatment to fit the particular family context. According to one useful analysis, families involved in maltreatment can be subdivided into four categories: vulnerable to crisis; restorable; supportable; and inadequate (Crittenden, 1992).

Those families that are **vulnerable to crisis** are experiencing unusual problems and need temporary help to resolve them. For example, a divorce, the loss of a job, the death of a family member, or the birth of a handicapped infant can severely strain some adults' ability to cope with the normal demands and frustrations of child-rearing. Especially if other relatives or friends are unable to relieve the pressure, the relationship between parents and children may deteriorate to the point of abuse or neglect.

About a fourth of all mistreating families fall into this vulnerable-to-crisis category. They are relatively easy to help, with services such as crisis counseling and parent training that are already available in most parts of the country. In the majority of cases, once the parents learn to cope with the specific difficulty more effectively, a process that usually takes less than a year, they are once again able to provide adequate child-rearing.

Less easily reached are the **restorable families**, who make up about half of all maltreating families. The caregivers in these families seem to have the potential to provide adequate care, and perhaps have done so in the past, but they have many problems, caused by their immediate situation, by their past history, and by their temperament, that seriously impair their parenting abilities. A given single mother, for example, might have untreated medical problems, inadequate housing, and poor job skills, all fraying against a quick temper, which tends to explode when her toddler is difficult or disobeys her. Or a binge-drinking husband might periodically beat his children, perhaps with the tacit permission of his overly dependent and isolated wife, who herself may

Figure 7.17 *Oprah Winfrey—TV talk-show star, independent producer, and self-made millionaire—is also a victim of childhood sexual abuse. Shown here testifying before a senate committee investigating child abuse, she is open about her experience because she believes secrecy is the abuser's most potent weapon. Researchers all agree that the more we know about child maltreatment, the better we will be able to stop it before it occurs.*

have come from an abusive home. Or a teenage couple might be both emotionally immature and addicted to one or more drugs, causing them to sometimes disregard their infant's basic needs or to seriously overestimate the baby's abilities.

Treatment with restorable families requires a case worker who has the time and commitment to become a family advocate, mediating and coordinating various services, finding help for every family member who needs it, and providing essential emotional support. In actuality, few case workers are trained as, or have the time to be, such advocates. Indeed, one study of child-protection workers found that they spent only 11 percent of their time working directly with families—usually in their offices rather than in the family's home—and that half of the approved treatment plans were not implemented, usually because the case worker or referral agencies were too busy (Crittenden, 1992).

Supportable families, who make up about a fifth of all maltreating families, will probably never be able to function adequately and independently until the children are grown. However, with ongoing support, ranging from periodic home visits by a nurse or housekeeper to special residences that include a variety of services, such as free clinics, day-care centers, recreation programs, social workers, and therapists, these families could meet their children's basic needs for physical, educational, and emotional care.

Foster Care

Because of the lack of services, both restorable and supportable families too often experience a series of inadequate interventions, and then, when maltreatment continues and escalates, the most seriously injured child is placed into foster care. Approximately 350,000 American children—1 out of every 175—are currently cared for by a paid surrogate parent.

As many critics have recognized, foster care should be the treatment of last resort. In general, the relationship between parents and children is such that, even if far less than ideal, both the adults and the children fare better when they are together. Too often, official decisions about placing a child in foster care are affected by implicit socioeconomic and cultural biases—as when, for instance, a middle-class social worker from the majority culture fails to recognize the potential of an illiterate grandmother to care for an abused child, if she is given adequate support (Lindsey, 1991; Pinderhughes, 1991). An additional problem is that foster care is usually hastily begun as a temporary solution, meant to last until the parents correct whatever problems led to the child's removal; but usually once a child is removed, fewer services—material or psychological—are provided to the family than would have been offered if the child were still at home (Lindsey, 1991). The result is that temporary foster care stretches into an uncertain future, and if the child is returned, the family is neither restored nor supported, and thus is still unable to provide good care.

Finally, nearly 10 percent of families are so **inadequate**, so impaired by deep emotional problems or serious cognitive deficiencies, that they may never be able to meet the needs of their children. For children born into these families, long-term foster care is the best solution.

Research over the past decade has shown that, while it is not good for children to be moved frequently from family to family, consistent long-term placement is preferable to allowing a child to remain in a continually abusive or neglectful home (Widom, 1991; Fein, 1991; Wald et al., 1988). Indeed, some foster children do very well, catching up on missed education, learning how to respect themselves and others, and eventually becoming good, nonmaltreating, parents. The children who fare worst in foster care tend to be those who have already endured such extensive maltreatment in their own homes—and hence have developed such low self-esteem, such impaired social skills, and so much anger—that they would encounter difficulty no matter where they were raised.

Specific Prevention

Overall, then, if treatment is geared to the particular needs of the family, and if this treatment is deftly begun early in the maltreatment cycle, then most maltreated children can be helped. Better still, of course, would be to prevent the problem before it begins. There are, in fact, a broad variety of programs that have been designed to this end, including early parent-newborn bonding programs, high school classes in parent education, crisis hotlines, respite care and drop-in centers, home health visitors, and programs to educate children about potential abuse (Olds and Henderson, 1989). Such programs are often targeted for "high risk" individuals, such as teenage or single parents, or parents with a history of domestic violence or drug abuse. While all these efforts make sense, we are just beginning to learn which are most effective.

The best strategy seems to be to focus on first-time mothers who are young and alone, and whose child is newborn. Intervention in infancy is crucial, for four reasons. First, being very needy and demanding, an infant puts great strain on a young, inexperienced parent. Second, abuse and neglect during the early years are likely to be most damaging, causing not only the most serious immediate injuries (child abuse deaths are highest under age 2), but the most troubling long-term consequences. Third, intervention is much easier before either the parent or the child has learned a destructive pattern of interaction. And finally, if the mother and child manage to establish a good caregiving relationship from infancy to age 2, prospects are good for the future (Pianta et al., 1989).

Several recent research projects in North America have assessed the impact of providing emotional support early on, particularly by assigning someone—social worker, nurse, paraprofessional, or trained volunteer—to visit new mothers at home throughout pregnancy and the first year (Olds and Henderson, 1989; Lyons-Ruth et al., 1990; Jacobson and Frye, 1991). The results have been good, especially for women at high-risk. Mothers who are depressed, isolated, unmarried, with unwanted pregnancies are particularly likely to feel more confident and have better attachment relationships with their children when they have experienced a supportive relationship with a trained visitor.

One extensive research project included four groups of high-risk women, ranging from a comparison group who were given only free developmental evaluation at 12 and 24 months to an extensive treatment group, who received free transportation to the clinic for pediatric care and home visits throughout pregnancy and infancy. The visitor was a specially trained nurse, who, among other things, encouraged informal support networks—friends, neighbors, grandmothers, and the like—and taught inexperienced mothers how to interpret and respond to their infant's needs and moods. Once mothers became able to read the infant's emotions, they were able to establish a smoother, happier relationship, as measured by the mother's positive mood and the infant's less frequent crying. On many measures, positive results were especially apparent for those women who were poor, unmarried, and young: not only did the visited teenagers enjoy motherhood more than their unvisited counterparts, but they were much less likely to scold or hit their babies. This difference was reflected in an independent source: according to official reports when the babies were 2, only 4 percent of the extensive-treatment teenagers had abused or neglected their infants as compared with 19 percent of the comparison group (Olds and Henderson, 1989).

As we have seen, the ecological view reminds us that effective prevention and treatment of child abuse requires intervention into social conditions fostering abuse. A look at the broader context of abuse suggests that since poverty, youth, and ignorance correlate with poor parenting, measures that raise the lowest incomes, discourage teenage parenthood, and increase the level of education will probably be needed to reduce the rate of abuse. And since social isolation and unrealistic expectations regarding children make it harder to provide good care for the young, any program that fosters friendly contact with others and an accurate understanding of the needs and abilities of children should be encouraged. Indeed, as this chapter shows, a rewarding parent-infant relationship is within the capacity of virtually all parents, no matter what their age, education, or background. With a little experienced guidance, most parents can become better at appreciating their children and learning how to relate to them with greater respect and with mutual delight.

SUMMARY

Emotional Development

1. In the first weeks and months of life, infants are capable of expressing many emotions, including fear, anger, sadness, happiness, and surprise. Toward the end of the first year, the typical infant expresses emotions more readily, more frequently, and more distinctly.

2. In the second year, cognitive advances cause infants to become more conscious of the distinction between themselves and others and thus new emotions emerge, such as guilt, pride, and embarrassment.

The Origins of Personality

3. In the first half of the twentieth century, the prevailing view among psychologists was that the individual's personality is permanently molded by the actions of his or her parents in the early years of childhood.

4. Freud argued that the child-rearing practices encountered in the oral and the anal psychosexual stages had a lasting impact on the person's personality and mental health.

5. Erikson and Mahler built on Freud's ideas, broadening his concept of the first two stages. According to Erikson, the infant experiences the crises of trust versus mistrust, discovering whether the immediate world is secure or

insecure, and then autonomy versus shame and doubt, as the infant tries to achieve some measure of independence. Mahler describes a period of separation-individuation, in which the infant, with much ambivalence, develops a sense of self apart from the mother. Like Freud, both of these psychoanalytic thinkers stress the lifelong impact of the caregiver's actions during the first two years.

6. Contemporary developmentalists generally do not accept Freud's stages of infant development. Erikson and Mahler have more influence on current thought. All of these theorists, however, neglect the importance of the father, social conditions, and the infant's own contributions to personality development.

7. Temperament, a group of personality characteristics, some largely influenced by genetics, others more susceptible to environmental influences, is another factor in psychosocial development.

Parent-Infant Interaction

8. In addition to the parents' actions and the infant's temperament, developmentalists now stress the interaction between parent and child.

9. The early parent-child interaction is characterized by synchrony, a harmony of gesture, expression, and timing that can make early nonverbal play a fascinating interchange. Attachment between parent and child becomes apparent toward the end of the first year. Secure attachment tends to predict curiosity, social competence, and self-assurance later in childhood; insecure attachment tends to correlate with less successful adaptation in these areas.

Child Maltreatment

10. Child maltreatment can take many forms—from physical, emotional, or sexual abuse to physical, emotional, or educational neglect. Child abuse and neglect occur from conception through adolescence and harm every family member.

11. The causes of abuse are many, including problems in the society (such as exploitive cultural attitudes about children), in the family (such as isolation), in the parent (such as drug addiction), and in the child (such as being sickly or difficult).

12. The consequences of child maltreatment can be far-reaching, impairing the child's learning and social understanding. However, it is not inevitable that abused children will become abusive adults.

13. Once maltreatment occurs, careful intervention must support and restore these families that can be helped and provide stable foster care for the minority of families in which the pattern of maltreatment cannot be halted.

14. The most effective strategies emphasize prevention and treatment rather than blame. In addition, measures that reduce the stresses and increase the social support for families with young children make child maltreatment less likely.

KEY TERMS

social smile (172)
fear of strangers (173)
separation anxiety (173)
social referencing (174)
self-awareness (174)
oral stage (176)
anal stage (176)
trust versus mistrust (177)
autonomy versus shame
   and doubt (177)
separation-individuation
   (178)
temperament (179)
synchrony (183)
attachment (185)

secure attachment (185)
insecure attachment (185)
Strange Situation (185)
child maltreatment (192)
abuse (192)
neglect (192)
endangerment (194)
sibling abuse (198)
intergenerational trans-
   mission (201)
vulnerable to crisis (202)
restorable families (202)
supportable families (203)
inadequate families (203)

KEY QUESTIONS

1. Which emotions develop in the first year?

2. Which factors influence whether a baby will be afraid of a stranger?

3. What are some consequences of the toddler's growing sense of self?

4. What are the similarities among the theories of Freud, Erikson, and Mahler?

5. What are the three most common temperamental patterns in infancy, and how does nurture affect them?

6. What are the similarities and differences between mother-infant and father-infant interactions?

7. What do infants learn from parent-infant interaction?

8. What contributes to a secure attachment?

9. What are some of the reasons parent-infant interaction does not always go well?

10. How common is child abuse and neglect?

11. What are some of the factors in the parent and in the child that may lead to child abuse?

12. What can be done to help abused children and their parents?

Biosocial Development

Body, Brain, and Nervous System

Over the first two years, the body quadruples in weight and the brain triples in weight. Neurons branch and grow into increasingly dense connective networks between the brain and the rest of the body. As neurons become coated with an insulating layer of myelin, they send messages faster and more efficiently. The infant's experiences help to "fine-tune" the brain's responses to stimulation.

Motor Abilities

Brain maturation allows the development of motor skills from reflexes to coordinated motor abilities, including grasping and walking. At birth, the infant's senses of smell and hearing are quite acute, and although vision at first is sharp only for objects that are about 10 inches away, by 6 months, acuity approaches 20/20.

Cognitive Development

Cognitive Skills

The infant progresses from knowing his or her world only through immediate sensorimotor experiences to being able to "experiment" on that world mentally, through the use of mental combinations and an understanding of object permanence. Infants appear to develop perceptual categories very early and by age 2 have developed numerous definite concepts.

Language

Babies' cries are their first communication; they then progress through cooing and babbling. Interaction with adults through "baby talk" teaches them the surface structure of language. By age 1, an infant can usually speak a word or two, and by age 2 is talking in short sentences.

Psychosocial Development

Emotions and Personality Development

Emotions change from quite basic reactions to complex, self-conscious responses. Infants become increasingly dependent, a transition explained by Freud in terms of the oral and anal stages, by Erikson in terms of the crises of trust versus mistrust and autonomy versus shame and doubt, and by Mahler in terms of separation-individuation. Much of basic temperament and mood is inborn, and apparent lifelong.

Parent-Infant Interaction

Parents and infants respond to each other first by synchronizing their behavior. Toward the end of the first year, secure attachment between child and parent sets the stage for the child's increasingly independent exploration of the world. Some cultures emphasize an exclusive mother-infant bond; others encourage wider social interaction with the father and other caregivers.

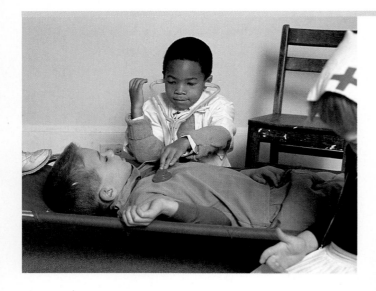

PART III

The Play Years

The period from age 2 to 6 is usually called early childhood, or the preschool period. Here, however, these years are called the play years to underscore the importance of play. Play occurs at every age, of course. But the years of early childhood are the most playful of all, for children spend most of their waking hours at play, acquiring the skills, ideas, and values that are crucial for growing up. They chase each other and dare themselves to attempt new tasks, developing their bodies; they play with words and ideas, developing their minds; they play games and dramatize fantasies, learning social skills and moral rules.

The playfulness of young children can cause them to be delightful or exasperating. To them, growing up is a game, and their enthusiasm for it seems unlimited, whether they are quietly tracking a beetle through the grass or riotously turning their play area into a shambles. Their minds seem playful, too, for the immaturity of their thinking enables them to explain that "a bald man has a barefoot head," or that "the sun shines so children can go outside to play."

If you expect them to sit quietly, think logically, or act realistically, you are bound to be disappointed. But if you enjoy playfulness, you might enjoy caring for, listening to, and even reading about children between 2 and 6 years old.

CHAPTER 8

The Play Years: Biosocial Development

Between the ages of 2 and 6, increases in children's strength and motor skills, along with their more adultlike body proportions, allow the exploration and mastery of their world to proceed by leaps and bounds, both literally and figuratively. In this chapter we will examine not only the biosocial changes that occur in the play years but also the implications these changes have for behavior and learning, including topics such as the following:

What are some of the reasons one child grows markedly taller and heavier than another?

Compared to children of other ages, how likely are preschoolers to be malnourished?

What motor skills can children develop before age 6?

How does children's play affect their physical skills?

How do boys' and girls' bodies differ during early childhood?

Why do children usually play with peers of the same sex?

Between ages 2 and 6, significant biosocial development occurs on several fronts. The most obvious aspect of this development during early childhood, of course, is the striking changes that occur in size and shape, changes that cause many 6-year-olds to find photos of themselves as chubby toddlers unrecognizable. Less obvious but more crucial changes involve the maturation of the brain and central nervous system. This maturation allows the mastery of motor skills that clearly sets the 6-year-old apart from the clumsy toddler and also makes possible the cognitive development that we will discuss in the next chapter. Let us begin our examination of biosocial development in the preschool years by looking at the way children's body proportions change.

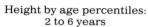

Height by age percentiles:
2 to 6 years

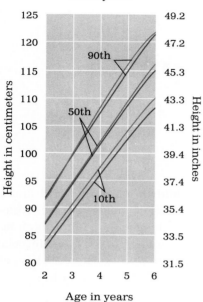

Weight by age percentiles:
2 to 6 years

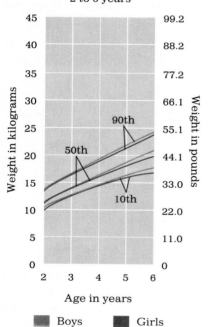

Figure 8.1 *As these charts show, preschool boys (blue line) and girls (red line) grow more slowly and steadily than they did in the first two years of life. Most children actually lose body fat during these years. The weight that is gained is usually bone and muscle.*

Size and Shape

During the preschool years, the child becomes slimmer as the lower body lengthens and some of the fat accumulated during infancy is burned off (Rallison, 1986). The kindergarten child no longer has the protruding stomach, round face, and disproportionately short limbs and large head that are characteristic of the toddler. By age 6, the proportions of the child's body are not very different from those of the adult (Sinclair, 1978).

Steady increases in height and weight accompany the changes in body proportions. From age 2 through 6, healthy, well-fed children add almost 3 inches (7 centimeters) and gain about 4½ pounds (2 kilograms) per year. By age 6, the average child in a developed nation weighs about 46 pounds (21 kilograms) and measures 46 inches (117 centimeters).

The range of normal development is quite broad, with many children being notably taller or shorter than these averages (see Figure 8.1). Weight is especially variable: about 10 percent of American 5-year-olds weigh less than 35 pounds and another 10 percent weigh almost 50 pounds (Lowrey, 1986). Of the many factors that influence height (see Table 8.1) and weight, the most influential are the child's genetic background, health care, and nutrition (Meredith, 1978). It is the last of these factors that is largely responsible for dramatic differences that exist between children in developed and developing countries: the average 4-year-old in Sweden, for example, is as tall as the average 6-year-old in Bangladesh, where roughly 60 percent of the children experience stunted growth due to poor nutrition (Eveleth and Tanner, 1976; United Nations, 1991).

Generally, boys are more muscular, less fat, and slightly taller and heavier than girls throughout childhood, although this varies depending on the culture and the child's age. For example, even in the early years, boys in India are markedly taller and heavier than girls, because boys are more highly valued by the society and therefore are more likely to have their nutritional needs taken care of first when food is scarce (Poffenberger, 1981). In North America, by contrast, children who are in the heaviest 10th percentile are more likely to be girls than boys, primarily for two reasons. First, girls in general have a higher proportion of body fat when they have access to ample food; and second, girls are generally less active than boys and are therefore less likely to burn off excess calories (Lowrey, 1986).

Eating Habits

Whether a child is short or tall, his or her annual height and weight gain is much less from age 2 to 6 than during the first two years of life. In fact, between ages 2 and 3, an average child adds fewer pounds than during any other twelve-month period until age 17 (Rallison, 1986). Since growth is slower during the preschool years, children need fewer calories per pound during this period than they did from birth through toddlerhood, especially if they are among the modern sedentary children who spend much of their time indoors. Consequently, their appetites seem smaller, a fact that causes many parents to worry. In most cases, however, this relative decline in appetite does not represent a medical problem unless the child is unusually

TABLE 8.1   Factors Affecting the Height of Preschoolers

Taller Than Average If	Shorter Than Average If
well nourished	malnourished
rarely sick	frequently or chronically sick
African or northern European ancestors	Asian ancestors
mother is nonsmoker	mother smoked during pregnancy
upper class	lower class
lives in urban area	lives in rural area
lives at sea level	lives high above sea level
first-born in small family	third- or later-born, large family
male	female

Source: Eveleth and Tanner, 1976; Meredith, 1978; Lowrey, 1986.

Figure 8.2 *If this were your son, staring at his dinner, how would you react? Instead of insisting he eat because this food is good for him, or lecturing him about starving children in other parts of the world, you might first consider the situation. Did he just recently consume a candy bar? Is he getting sick? Is the portion too big, or the food strange-seeming? Or is he simply a typical preschooler, who sometimes rejects the meal his parents put before him? In any case, quarreling at mealtime is not likely to improve his appetite.*

thin or is not gaining weight at all. Most parents report a noticeable increase in the child's appetite by age 8—a normal developmental improvement (Achenbach and Edelbrock, 1981). On the whole, then, serious malnutrition is much more likely to occur in infancy (see pp. 136–140) or in adolescence than in early childhood.

Of course, as at any age, the diet during the preschool years should be a healthy one. The most prevalent nutritional problem in developed countries during the preschool years is iron deficiency anemia, the chief symptom of which is chronic fatigue. This problem, which stems from an insufficiency of quality meats, whole grains, and dark-green vegetables, is three times more common among poor families than among nonpoor ones. Although low income makes it harder to purchase the foods highest in iron, it should also be noted that families of every social class are likely to contribute to the problem by giving their children candy, soda, sweetened cereals, and the like. These items can spoil a small appetite faster than they can a large one, and therefore may keep a child from consuming enough of the foods that contain essential vitamins, minerals, and protein.

Brain Maturation

The most important physiological development during early childhood is the continued maturation of the central nervous system. This maturation underlies children's rapidly expanding cognitive abilities as well as their increasing control and coordination of their bodies.

As explained in Chapter 5, during childhood the brain develops faster than any other part of the body. One simple indication of this is weight: by age 5, the brain has attained about 90 percent of its adult weight, even though the average 5-year-old's total body weight is only about 30 percent that of the average adult (Lowrey, 1986). Part of this increase in brain size is due to the continued proliferation of dendrite networks, enhancing communication among the brain's various specialized areas, and to the ongoing process of myelination, which provides the nerves with an insulating sheathing that speeds up the transmission of neural impulses. Myelination bears significantly on the child's developing abilities: the areas of the brain associated with hand-eye coordination, for example, do not become fully myelinated until around age 4; those associated with the ability to maintain focused attention, not until the end of childhood; those associated with language and intelligence, not until the age of 15 or so (Tanner, 1978).

Also of major importance is the myelination process—complete at around age 8—that occurs in the **corpus callosum**, a band of nerve fibers that connects the two halves of the brain.

The Two Halves of the Brain

The brain is divided into two similar halves, the left brain and the right brain. Each controls the functioning of the opposite side of the body as well as being responsible for certain specialized tasks. In 95 percent of right-handed adults and about 70 percent of left-handed adults, the left brain is the location of several key areas associated with logical analysis and language development, including speech; the right brain, meanwhile, is the location of areas associated with various visual and artistic skills, among them recognizing faces, responding to music, and perceiving various types of spatial relations. Obviously, for a person to be fully functioning, both halves of the brain, as well as both sides of the body, need to work together, which is why the maturation of the corpus callosum is a critical factor for advanced motor skills and higher-order cognition (Springer and Deutsch, 1989). Indeed, when the corpus callosum is surgically severed, as it sometimes must be to halt chronic brain seizures, people show dramatic deficits in particular tasks involving left-brain–right-brain coordination (Gazzaniga, 1983). For example, they can see a familiar object with the right eye but are unable to name it, or, given the title of a popular song, they can readily recite the words but have great difficulty recognizing the right melody.

In the early years, considerable flexibility in the functioning of the two halves of the brain and body is apparent. For example, in infancy and early childhood, many fewer areas of the brain are dedicated to specific functions than in adulthood. Consequently, when damage occurs to an area that has begun to specialize, the functions of that area can usually be taken over by some other area. By contrast, functioning that is lost in a given area in adulthood is much harder to remedy, and often remains deficient. This is notable when damage occurs in the language areas of the brain. In children, such damage is more likely to lower overall cognition than to impair specific language abilities (O'Leary, 1990), while in adults, the identical damage might cause the loss of a specific set of verbal abilities. In some cases, an adult might be unable to retrieve whole categories of vocabulary (such as prepositions, or the names of fruits) but otherwise show no language impairment. Similarly, some brain-damaged adults lack other particular skills—such as the ability to move one part of the body or to respond appropriately to social nuances—while young children are less precisely affected.

This early flexibility of brain functioning and specialization is evident in handedness: even by age 5, when more than 90 percent of all children are clearly right- or left-handed, a child can be taught to use his or her nonpreferred hand for certain skills. In fact, in times past, most lefties, under pressure from misguided teachers and parents, learned to write with their right

Figure 8.3 *Sometimes preschoolers use their left hand to paint or to write simply because their right hand is busy doing something else. (One of the author's former undergraduate students had learned to write with his left hand because he usually kept his right thumb in his mouth. As an adult, he is right-handed for everything except writing, the opposite pattern of many left-handed persons.)*

hand. Once any pattern of brain functioning and specialization is firmly set by the end of childhood, it is more difficult to switch sides or to learn new patterns. Adults find it much harder to learn to ice-skate, or knit, or write with their nonpreferred hand than young children do, because bodily-coordination patterns in the brain have become localized and habitual.

Precisely how the two halves and the various sections of the brain function as a whole, and how this relationship changes with time, are a matter of great interest and practical import but little firm knowledge. It does seem clear that, even at birth, the two halves of the brain are already specialized to some degree, and that smooth coordination of the many parts of the brain underlies many intellectual skills (Molfese and Segalowitz, 1988). For example, analysis of the brain's electrical activity reveals that several areas in both sides of the brain are involved in reading, and that some children who are poor readers use one side of the brain considerably more than the other, preventing them from properly connecting visual symbols, phonetic sounds, and verbal meanings (Bakker and Veinke, 1985). However, such specific explanations for cognitive deficits apply only for a minority of children with particular problems. The neurological causes and consequences of most cognitive deficits are yet to be determined. While various researchers disagree about the particulars of specialization and coordination within the brain, all agree that much more research is needed before we understand how the two halves of the brain interact (Molfese and Segalowitz, 1988; Springer and Deutsch, 1989).

Activity Level

Developmental studies of **activity level**, that is, of how much and how often a person moves his or her body, show definite age-related patterns that are assumed to be linked to brain maturation. Although the precise mechanisms are not well understood, they are thought to be related to neurological development, the brain's production of certain hormones, and to the mind's need for a certain level of outside stimulation, a need that changes as the person grows older.

We do know that, in the first two or three years of life, activity level increases in all children, and then decreases throughout childhood (Eaton and Yu, 1989). Thus a 2½-year-old is more likely than a 1-year-old, but less likely than a 5-year-old, to display signs of high activity level, such as fidgeting while being read to, moving about while being dressed and groomed, and being continually on the run, indoors and out (Fullard et al., 1984).

This developmental trend in activity level is universal, but a number of factors contribute to wide variation among individuals. One such factor is that males tend to be more active than females (Eaton and Yu, 1989). (We will discuss this difference at the end of the chapter.) Another very important factor is heredity: variations in activity level are one of the abiding innate distinctions between one person and another (Goldsmith et al., 1987). The genetic component of activity level has been highlighted by comparisons of monozygotic and dizygotic infant twins. In one study, measurements taken by motion meters attached to the infants' arms and legs for two days revealed that activity level for monozygotic twins was almost identical, whereas for dizygotic twins it was no more similar than for regular siblings (Saudino and Eaton, 1989).

Although the normal variation in the activity level of children is substantial, a child who is *much* more active than others the same age and gender may be exhibiting signs of a problem called attention-deficit hyperactivity disorder, or ADHD. There are several potential causes of ADHD that are discussed in Chapter 11, but one cause, *lead poisoning*, merits description here, because the presence of lead toxins should be spotted and treated during early childhood in order to avoid further damage.

Most commonly, children are exposed to lead by breathing or ingesting lead residues, such as those in chips or dust from flaking lead-based paint or those in industrial pollutants. Since lead accumulates in the body, small amounts taken in over a period of time can produce toxicity.

Lead poisoning is diagnosed through blood analysis. If the lead level is above 70 milligrams per deciliter of blood, the toxic damage may include paralysis, permanent brain damage, and even death. If the level is between 25 and 70 milligrams per deciliter, many less obvious problems may result, including abnormally high activity level, poor concentration, and slow language development.

Whether lower levels, between 10 and 25 milligrams, are toxic is controversial. Some research finds an association between such levels of lead and developmental problems, and other research does not (Cooney et al., 1989; Silva et al., 1988). The controversy arises from confounding factors that make it difficult to draw firm conclusions. Looking at the same data, for example, two teams of American scientists both found a correlation between moderate lead levels and behavioral problems, but one team attributed this correlation directly to the effects of the lead (Bellinger and Needleman, 1985; Needleman et al., 1990), while the other team thought the deficits could be better explained by other factors (Ernhart et al., 1985).

As the second team points out, for instance, elevated levels of lead are likely to be found in children who live in old houses with peeling paint or who play near factories that pollute the air—in other words, in children who live in low-income neighborhoods. The proven hazards of poverty (such as troubled families, crowded schools, inadequate nutrition) may be the real culprit, not the hypothetical hazard of low lead levels. Analyzing the data without taking such factors into account, according to noted developmental psychologist Sandra Scarr, is "outrageous," partly because it shifts public attention away from reducing psychosocial risks to attending to purely biological ones (Palca, 1991).

Nevertheless, to be on the safe side, in 1991 the federal government lowered the level at which lead is considered toxic to 10 milligrams per deciliter. The Centers for Disease Control now recommends that all children under age 6 be tested for lead, and that when levels higher than 10 are found, precautions be taken. Obvious first steps include removal of any deteriorating lead-paint dust in window casements, eliminating lead contaminants from the yard, and keeping the child from licking or eating anything that might contain lead (Hilts, 1991).

Although not all developmentalists are convinced that the estimated 4 million young American children (about one out of every five) whose lead level is higher than 10 are at risk, most agree that lead testing of all young children and decreasing the pollutants in their environment—not just in their homes but also in the air and water—are wise public health precautions. When certain 3-year-olds would consistently rather run than walk and jump up and down and fidget rather than ever being still, it would be reassuring to know that this high activity is age-related normal behavior that will improve in a few years, rather than a toxic reaction that might worsen.

Activity level can also be affected by environmental factors. For example, family and cultural differences regarding "acceptable" levels of activity in various contexts can intensify or dampen the child's rate of activity. (Some children, for instance, seem much more fidgety when their movement is forbidden, as in a quiet church service.)

In practical terms, what is the relevance of this developmental trend? First, it suggests that it is a mistake to expect young children to sit quietly for very long, whether at home or in nursery school. Nor should anyone expect every child to be as quiet as his or her peers. Some children are naturally much more active than others, as well as more active than the typical younger child (though they are, fortunately, likely to be less active than they themselves were a few years before). Since activity level is sometimes associated with the ability to concentrate and to think before acting, expectations, especially for preschoolers, should be tempered in these respects as well. As with many developmental patterns, a combination of patience and an appreciation for individual differences is likely to be more productive than merely ordering a child to stay still or pay attention.

Mastering Motor Skills

As their bodies grow slimmer, stronger, and less top-heavy, and as their brain maturation permits greater control and coordination of the body, children between ages 2 and 6 are able to move with greater speed and grace, and become more capable of focusing and refining their activity. The result is a notable improvement in their various motor skills.

Gross Motor Skills

Figure 8.4 *No matter where they live and play, preschoolers find ways to develop their gross motor skills, using their entire bodies in running, kicking, jumping, and climbing activities. In this respect the variable that matters most across environmental contexts is safety.*

Gross motor skills, that is, large body movements such as running, climbing, jumping, and throwing, improve dramatically during the preschool years (Clark and Phillips, 1985; Du Randt, 1985; Kerr, 1985). The improvement is apparent to anyone who watches a group of children at play. Two-year-olds are quite clumsy, falling down frequently and sometimes bumping into stationary objects. But by age 5, many children are both skilled and graceful. Most North American 5-year-olds can ride a tricycle, climb a ladder, pump a swing, and throw, catch, and kick a ball. Some of them can even skate, ski, and ride a bicycle, activities that demand balance as well as coordination. These specialized abilities obviously require practice, as every parent who has run beside a child on a wobbling bicycle knows. However, a certain level of brain maturation is also necessary. This is readily apparent in hopping on one foot, a skill that requires fluid coordination between the two halves of the brain. It is a skill very few 3-year-olds can master, no matter how often they try, and one almost all 5-year-olds can perform (Sutherland et al., 1988).

Most young children practice their gross motor skills wherever they are, whether in a well-equipped nursery school with climbing ladders, balance boards, and sandboxes, or on their own, with furniture for climbing, fences for balancing, and gardens or empty lots for digging up. On the whole, preschool children learn basic motor skills by teaching themselves and learning from other children, rather than by specific adult instruction. So as long as a child has the opportunity to play with other children in an adequate space and with suitable play structures (none of which is to be taken for granted in today's neighborhoods, especially in large cities [Garbarino, 1989]), gross motor skills will develop as rapidly as maturation, body size, and innate ability allow.

Figure 8.5 *Two of the oldest childhood games are follow-the-leader and show-and-tell, both usually played informally, without adult input. One result is that children teach each other gross and fine motor skills by example—often a better route toward mastery than explicit adult instruction.*

Fine Motor Skills

Fine motor skills, the skills that involve small body movements, are much harder for preschoolers to master than gross motor skills. Such things as pouring juice from a pitcher into a glass without spilling, cutting food with a knife and fork, and achieving anything more artful than a scribble with a pencil are difficult even with great concentration and effort. Preschoolers can spend hours trying to tie a bow with their shoelaces, often producing knot upon knot instead.

The chief reason many children experience these difficulties is simply that they have not developed the muscular control, patience, and judgment needed for the exercise of fine motor skills, in part because the myelination of the central nervous system is not complete. For many preschoolers, this liability is compounded by their still having short, fat fingers. Unless these limitations are kept in mind when selecting utensils, toys, and clothes for the preschool child, frustration and destruction can result: preschool children may burst into tears when they cannot button their sweaters, or mash a puzzle piece into place when they are unable to position it correctly.

The Value of Fine Motor Skills

Many educators consider the development of fine motor skills to be an important goal of the preschool curriculum. One of the first and most influential of these was Maria Montessori, who nearly a century ago designed a series of puzzles, pegboards, and fine motor tasks that encourage coordination among the eye, the hand, and the brain. Her approach gave rise to Montessori schools, which continue to emphasize development of fine motor skills and respect for the child's accomplishments. Comparison studies suggest that such schools prepare children well for formal learning (Miller and Bizzell, 1983; Miller and Dyer, 1975). Happily, the fine motor skill that seems most directly linked to later development is one that is easy for parents and teachers to encourage—the skill of making marks on paper.

Children's Art

Developmentalists agree that arts and crafts are an important form of play. On the simplest level "the child who first wields a marker is learning in many areas of his young life about tool use" (Gardner, 1980). In addition, in thinking about what to draw, manipulating the pencil, crayon, or brush to execute the thought, and then viewing, and perhaps explaining, the end product, the child is experiencing a sequence of events that not only provides practice with fine motor skills but also enhances the child's sense of accomplishment. Children's artwork also provides a testing ground for another important skill, self-correction. A developmental study of children's paintings found that whereas 3-year-olds often just plunked their brushes into the paint, pulled them out dripping wet, then pushed them across the paper without much forethought or skill, by age 5 most children took care to get just enough paint on their brushes, planned just where to put each stroke, and stood back from their work to examine the final result (Allison, 1985). Older children also show an eagerness to practice their skills, drawing essentially the same picture again and again.

Physical Play

As should now be apparent, developmentalists view children's play as work, a major means through which physical, cognitive, and social skills are strengthened and honed. Indeed, most developmentalists believe that a healthy child is a playing child, using toys, daily play routines, imagination, and friendships to learn about life (Cohen, 1987). The varied social interaction that occurs in play is discussed in Chapter 10. Here, let us look at three types of play that are especially well suited to developing motor skills.

Sensorimotor Play

Play that captures the pleasures of using the senses and motor abilities is called **sensorimotor play**. We have already seen that infants regularly engage in this kind of play, delighting in such things as watching a turning mobile or kicking the side of the bassinet. This pleasure in sensory experiences and motor skills continues throughout childhood. For example, given the chance, preschool children will happily explore the many sensory experiences that can be extracted from their food, feeling various textures as they mix noodles, meat, and gravy together with their hands, watching peas float after they put them in their milk, listening to the slurping sound they make as they suck in spaghetti, tasting unusual combinations such as cocoa sprinkled on lemonade. Children find similar opportunities for sensorimotor play in almost any context, in the sandbox, the bathtub, or a mud hole.

Mastery Play

Much of the physical play of childhood is **mastery play**, a term used to describe the play that helps children to master new skills. Children waste no opportunity to develop and practice their physical skills. A simple walk down the block can become episode after episode of mastery play, as the child walks on top of a wall, then jumps over every crack in the sidewalk (so as not to "step on a crack and break your mother's back"), then skips, or walks backward, or races ahead. Along the way, there may be ice patches to slide across, or wind to run against, or puddles to jump over, or into. Similarly, making a snack, getting dressed, or singing along with music all are occasions for mastery play. Hand skills are also developed in mastery play, as when children intentionally tie knots in their shoelaces, put pegs in pegboards, or use a pair of scissors to make snippets of paper out of a single sheet.

Mastery play is most obvious when physical skills are involved, but it includes almost any skill the child feels motivated to learn. For instance, as children grow older, mastery play increasingly includes activities that are clearly intellectual, such as play with words or ideas. While the impulse to engage in mastery play comes naturally to preschool children, their parents' example and encouragement influence which skills a child will master. Parents who enjoy throwing balls will find their children are much better catchers than the children of those who prefer spending their spare time watching TV (East and Hensley, 1985).

The other critical role of parents is providing a safe setting for mastery of skills, for in their curiosity and eagerness to challenge themselves, children are often oblivious to the hazards that surround them (see the Closer Look that follows).

Figure 8.6 *"Finger painting" frequently seems an understatement for sensorimotor work in this artistic medium, which often requires involvement of the whole arm right up to the elbow, and sometimes even the nose.*

Injury Control Is No Accident

As children gain control of their motor skills, they practice them continually—wherever and however they can. They climb trees and fences; they run along open fields and busy streets; they find ways to play with almost anything they can get their hands on. All this activity and exploration is healthy in many ways, but it also poses dangers, exposing the child to far greater risks than those parents usually worry about, such as abduction or cancer (MacDonald, 1990).

In fact, in all but the most disease-ridden or war-torn countries of the world, accidents are, by far, the number one cause of childhood death, killing more young people than all other causes combined (National Safety Council, 1989). An American child, for example, has twice the chance (about 1 in 500) of dying an accidental death before age 10 as dying from disease. Injuries, of course, are even more common. In the United States, a child has about 1 chance in 3 *each year* of having an injury that needs medical attention. Virtually every child will need stitches or a cast sometime before adolescence and 44 percent of all serious injuries requiring hospitalization occur among children under age 15.

The accident risk for any particular child depends on several factors, some within the child and some within the surrounding systems. Naturally, the child's own judgment, motor skills, and activity level are crucial, as are the caregivers' forethought and supervision. Also of major importance are community standards and cultural norms that either foster or impede safety practices. Because of variations in all these factors, some groups of children suffer many more serious injuries than others. For instance, no matter where they live, boys, being more active than girls, as well as more willing to take risks, have more injuries and accidental deaths than girls—about one-third more between ages 1 and 5 and twice as many between ages 5 and 10. Asian-Americans, the most closely supervised among American ethnic groups, have the lowest accident rate of any American children (Heckler, 1985). Children in poor urban neighborhoods, which are often hazard-filled, have twice the accidental death rate of children in wealthy suburbs.

For all children, however, the risk of accidents could be much lower than it is. Accidents are certainly the most preventable cause of childhood death, and both the individual and the community can do much to reduce the risk of accidents generally (Margolis and Runyan, 1983; Butler et al., 1984; Garbarino, 1988). The first step, many believe, is to approach the problem in terms of **injury control** instead of "accident prevention." The word "accident," they point out, implies that no one was at fault, whereas most serious accidents involve someone's inadequate forethought.

In addition, since the complete prevention of childhood injuries is impossible, the focus should be on controlling their damage. For instance, bicycle accidents, a seemingly inevitable part of childhood, are a major source of serious injuries. In fact, each year hospitals in the United States report roughly a quarter of a million bicycle-related injuries involving children. Yet the public seems largely unaware of the magnitude of the danger or of the steps that would reduce the risk. Such steps—including intensified safety education, stricter traffic enforcement, the wearing of protective gear (especially helmets), and the use of reflectors on bikes—could avert thousands of serious injuries as well as a large portion of the 1,200 bicycle-related deaths that occur each year (Siegfried, 1990).

Once a risk has been identified, and injury control is accepted as a possible goal, many educational and legal measures may be taken to reach that goal. The question is, Which measures work best? Overall, broad-based safety education, such as television announcements and poster campaigns, rarely have a direct impact on risk-taking habits, although they may foster a general climate that makes more specific measures likely to work. Similarly, educational programs in schools and preschools may be successful to the extent that they enable children to verbalize safety rules, but they appear to have little effect on children's actual behavior. The best approaches to safety education are those that reach both parents and children, individually or in small groups, in situations where motivation is high (as when a child known to those involved has been injured) (Garbarino, 1988).

Interestingly, new and expectant parents are much more likely than experienced parents to heed safety suggestions, such as using an infant car seat, turning down the household water heater to avoid accidental scalding, or placing all poisons in locked cabinets (Christophersen, 1989). Apparently, experienced parents whose children have not yet had serious injuries become complacent, reasoning "We've never had a car accident . . . no one we know has ever been scalded . . . our kids don't play with detergents, medicines or matches—so why worry?"

More effective than educational measures, apparently, in reducing the overall injury rate are safety laws that include penalties for noncompliance. Among such measures that have led to significant reductions in accidental death rates in the United States are

1. a federal law requiring child-proof safety caps on medicine bottles—credited with an 80 percent reduction in poisoning deaths of 1- to 4-year-olds;
2. state laws requiring car safety seats for infants and children—credited with the significant declines over the past decade in child motor-vehicle deaths;

(a)

(b)

(c)

3. city laws requiring window guards on every apartment where children live—credited with a 50 percent drop in fall-related deaths in New York, for instance.

Largely as a result of laws like these, the accidental death rate for American children between the ages of 1 and 5 has been cut in half in the past two decades, from over 40 per 100,000 in the late 1960s to roughly 20 per 100,000 in the late 1980s. Nevertheless, this means that nearly 4,000 children in this age group are still being killed by accidents each year, so much remains to be done. Although child safety restraints in cars can reduce deaths by 90 percent, only about a third of all parents use them, possibly because the laws requiring their use are underenforced (Garbarino, 1988). Similarly, about half of all children who are killed by cars are pedestrians, yet in most heavily trafficked areas, safe outdoor play spaces for young children are probably even more scarce now than they have ever been.

In many cases, child experts and public officials do not know what the precise impact of various injury-control measures might be, yet money for research on injury control is hard to find, partly because of the prevailing notion that childhood accidents cannot be prevented. For every year of productive life lost through accidents, only $3 is spent on accident research, compared to more than $500 per lost year on cancer research (Foege, 1985).

The issue of injury control is now capturing the attention of many experts—pediatricians, developmental psychologists, and teachers alike. It is increasingly apparent that the child who escapes serious injury in childhood is not *just lucky*, and that accidents are not *just an accident*.

In order for parents to safeguard their children from injury, they first need to be aware of safety hazards, and then need to take whatever action is necessary. In two of these photos, the parents are to be commended: the parents in (b) not only put a helmet on their child but demonstrate by example the importance of this measure; and as suggested by the smiles in (c), the mother probably has been securing her child in a safety seat from early infancy. However, the children in (a) are swinging perilously close to a table that might injure them if they fall. In all likelihood, their parents are unaware that home playground equipment is a common source of childhood injury.

If the general public, and the political leaders, become more aware of the relationship between policy, practice, and child safety, more children will survive the hazardous years of childhood intact.

Rough-and-Tumble Play

The third type of physical play we will describe here is called **rough-and-tumble play**. The aptness of its name is made clear by the following example:

> Jimmy, a preschooler, stands observing three of his male classmates building a sand castle. After a few moments he climbs on a tricycle and, smiling, makes a beeline for the same area, ravaging the structure in a single sweep. The builders immediately take off in hot pursuit of the hit-and-run phantom, yelling menacing threats of "come back here, you." Soon the tricycle halts and they pounce on him. The four of them tumble about in the grass amid shouts of glee, wrestling and punching until a teacher intervenes. The four wander off together toward the swings. [cited in Maccoby, 1980]

One distinguishing characteristic of rough-and-tumble play is its mimicry of aggression, a fact first noted in observations of young monkeys' wrestling, chasing, and pummeling of each other (Jones, 1976). The observers discovered that the key to the true nature of this seemingly hostile behavior was the monkeys' **play face**, that is, a facial expression that seemed to suggest that the monkeys were having fun. The play face was an accurate clue, for only rarely, and apparently accidentally, did the monkeys actually hurt each other. (The same behaviors accompanied by a frown usually meant a serious conflict was taking place.)

In human children, too, rough-and-tumble play is quite different from aggression, even though at first glance it may look the same. This distinction is important, for rough-and-tumble play is a significant part of the daily activities of many children in preschool, especially after they have had to sit quietly for a period of time. In general, rough-and-tumble play, unlike aggression, is not only fun for children; it is also constructive, developing interactive skills as well as gross motor skills (Pellegrini, 1987). Adults who are unsure whether they are observing a fight that should be broken up or a social activity that should be allowed to continue may be helped by knowing that facial expression is as telltale in children as it is in monkeys: children almost always smile, and often laugh, in rough-and-tumble play, whereas they frown and scowl in real fighting.

Figure 8.7 *Time to intervene to protect the victim from the attacker? Not as long as the "victim" is smiling. This is rough-and-tumble play.*

Rough-and-tumble play is universal, occurring everywhere children play, including Japan, Kenya, and Mexico, as well as in every income and ethnic group in North America, Europe, and Australia (Boulton and Smith, 1989). There are some cultural and situational differences, however. One of the most important is space and supervision: children are much more likely to instigate rough-and-tumble play when they have room to run and chase, and when adults are not directly nearby. In addition, rough-and-tumble play usually occurs among children who have had considerable social experience, often with each other. Not surprisingly, then, among children in nursery schools, newcomers, younger children, and only-children take longer to join in rough-and-tumble play than to participate in any other form of play (Garvey, 1976; Shea, 1981). Gender differences are also evident in rough-and-tumble play and these, too, vary from culture to culture. In some cultures, such as traditional Moslem ones, girls almost never engage in rough-and-tumble play. Among North Americans, girls sometimes engage in such play, but not as often as boys do: one carefully controlled study found that boys spent three times as much time in rough-and-tumble play as girls did (DiPietro, 1981).

A LIFE-SPAN PERSPECTIVE

Gender Distinctions in Play Patterns

Some differences between males and females, not only in body size and shape but also in motor skills and activity level, are apparent throughout childhood, as well as throughout the rest of the life span. Such differences have fascinating, but controversial, implications for other male-female differences that emerge in childhood, such as in accident rates, academic achievement, and, one we will examine here, play patterns. The basic question for social scientists is whether such differences are **sex differences**—arising from the differences between male and female chromosomes and hormones—or **gender differences**—arising from the special customs, values, and expectations that a particular culture attaches to one sex or the other. As we will see, the implications of this question with regard to children's play patterns may well extend into adulthood.

In the preschool years, and indeed, throughout childhood, boys, compared with girls, typically spend more playtime outside, engaging in gross motor activities like running, climbing, and playing ball. Many, if not most, of boys' activities involve playful aggression and competition, as in rough-and-tumble play. Girls, by contrast, spend more time indoors, typically engaging in activities that demand fine motor coordination and a relatively lower activity level, such as arts and crafts, sewing, or dressing and undressing their dolls. When they do play outside, girls are more likely to engage in cooperative, turn-taking games (Crum and Eckert, 1985; Harper and Sanders, 1975). Take jump rope, for example, a girls' outdoor activity much more than a boys'. Two rope turners must synchronize their efforts, with each other and with the jumpers, who, in turn, are not so much competing as displaying their skills—to the audience of other jumpers, who contribute by chanting rhythmic rhymes as they wait their turn. In the preschool and early school years, at least, there are no winners or losers in girls' jump-roping, no aggressors or victims, just some who can jump faster, or longer, or with fancier footwork.

Another distinction in children's play involves choice of playmates: boys tend to play with boys, and girls, with girls. This preference for same-sex play partners, as well as the tendency for masculine play to be more aggressive and active than feminine play, is evident even in infancy (Maccoby, 1980) and becomes more apparent as children grow older (La Freniere et al., 1984). The same general trends are found in every culture (Whiting and Edward, 1988), every historical period (Herron and Sutton-Smith, 1971), and—as you can confirm by observing the recess activities at your local school—persist in the 1990s.

Figure 8.8 *Obviously, girls can wield a sword and boys can play "tea party," but it is hard to imagine either of these photos with the sex of the subjects reversed. Sex differences in play patterns during childhood are universal. However, the reasons for this, and the implications of it, are the subject of vigorous disputes among researchers, teachers, and parents—especially parents whose child prefers playing with the other sex.*

Are these sex differences or gender differences? Certainly there are some biological differences between the sexes that might help to explain their play differences. As noted, for example, boys, on average, are slightly taller and more muscular, with less body fat than girls, and their forearm strength is notably greater. In addition, boys' higher activity level, which is evident even in infancy, increases steadily, so that by age 8, only about one girl in five is as active as the average boy (Eaton and Yu, 1989). Girls, on the other hand, mature more quickly than boys in a number of ways, including bone maturation, which gives them more dexterity and control in fine motor skills.

Thus if some children's innate activity level is high, and they are physically suited to activities involving arm strength, it seems quite natural that they (mostly boys) will want to engage in play that involves running, climbing, and throwing, as well as rough-and-tumble play. On the other hand, if some children have a relatively low activity level, and if they are physically suited to activities involving fine motor skills more than strength, it seems equally natural that they (mostly girls) will enjoy sitting and working with their hands.

The fact is, however, that such physical differences as do exist between the sexes during the preschool years are slight. Until puberty, both sexes follow very similar paths of biological development, being about the same size, and able to do the same things, at the same age (Tanner, 1978). In those abilities in which one sex is more advanced or skilled than another, the advantage is small compared to the advantages of individual genetic endowment and/or repeated practice. This means that in every ability in which boys, in general, excel, most boys know several girls their age who are better than they are. The reverse is equally true.

This fact suggests that, if children played at whatever activities seemed within their capacity, many girls would be regularly engaged in "boys" games, and vice versa. In fact, this often occurs at home if a particular child has no playmates other than a sibling or neighbor of the other sex (Bloch, 1989). However, mixed-sex play is generally not the case, especially in public places such as school playgrounds. This suggests, in turn, that social pressures add to, and foster, the biological differences that exist. Parents and other adults typically encourage children, directly and indirectly, to play with peers of their own sex. They also tend to give them "gender-appropriate" toys, thereby strengthening whatever physical differences there may actually be (Sutton-Smith, 1986). Dolls and play dishes obviously elicit quite different motor skills and activities than footballs and toy guns do.

In recent years, of course, some adults have made a deliberate effort to diminish gender stereotypes among children. Within the preschool classroom particularly, many teachers have tried to accomplish this goal by encouraging children of both sexes to engage in all forms of play, and by deliberately seating the children in mixed-sex groups (Swadener and Johnson, 1989). However, the children's socialization into traditional notions of gender generally proves unshakable. The children increasingly take on "gender-specific" roles and sort themselves into same-sex friendships. The pattern becomes more distinct as preschoolers grow older. As one teacher notes:

> Kindergarten is a triumph of sexual self-stereotyping. No amount of adult subterfuge or propaganda deflects the five-year-old's passion for segregation by sex. Children of this age think they have invented the differences between boys and girls and, as with any new invention, must prove that it works. [Paley, 1984]

As this observation suggests, an important source of social pressure for gender stereotyping is children themselves. Because of this, if a child wanted to spend a great deal of time in a particular activity favored by the other sex, he or she would probably hesitate, since his or her favorite playmates would be doing something else—not to mention the fact that girls rarely welcome the lone boy who wants to play hopscotch, and boys usually turn away the girl who wants to play cops and robbers. By elementary school, when there are sufficient children of the same sex and age to play with, gender roles are firmly entrenched: the "tomboy" is regarded as unusual, and the "sissie" is not only considered odd but is teased for his preferences.

Figure 8.9 *Boys and girls sometimes play together in games usually reserved for one or the other sex—but only in special circumstances. Would these two be playing hopscotch if they were at recess in school, with dozens of same-sex playmates available? Or if this were a busy sidewalk instead of an isolated field, would awareness of what strangers might think make them hesitate?*

What, then, are the implications of sex differences in children's play patterns? Cross-cultural research finds that, in all societies, children are encouraged to engage in activities that teach them their culture's traditional adult roles. Indeed, in those societies where adults have quite distinct gender roles, girls and boys virtually never play together (Whiting and Edward, 1988). In modern, technological societies, where adult roles are not so rigid, boys and girls do sometimes spontaneously play together, but usually in games where one sex teams up against the other. More significant, in modern societies, the gender-specific play of boys may serve to ready them for the largely male-dominated business world, where self-assertion and competitiveness lead to success. The activities of girls, by contrast, teach them cooperation, patience, and relative passivity, qualities that might help them in family life, but would handicap them in many careers.

This raises an important question for the future. Given that women are increasingly working outside the home, and that men are becoming more involved in family life, should preschool girls be urged to play rougher, more competitive games, and boys, to spend more time in gentler cooperative play? Should both sexes be encouraged, or even pushed, to play together? Or should parents and teachers remain on the sidelines, and neutral, allowing play patterns to emerge as they will?

Obviously, there is no easy answer. Not only is this a question on which it seems impossible to sort out the influences of nature and nurture; it is a question framed by a wide array of individual and cultural values. Some regard the two sexes as "opposites" and believe that gender differentiation should be encouraged; others believe that the sexes are much more similar than dissimilar, and that, as much as possible, gender distinctions should be obliterated. In Chapter 10, where gender-role development is examined in greater detail, these questions will be raised again, not to find definitive answers but to explore the implications of our diverse value judgments.

SUMMARY

Size and Shape

1. During early childhood, children grow about 3 inches (7 centimeters) a year. Normal variation in growth is caused primarily by genes, nutrition, and health care.

Brain Maturation

2. Brain maturation, including increased myelination and improved coordination between the two halves of the brain, brings important gains in children's physical abilities and higher-order cognition. In the early years, considerable flexibility in the functioning of the two halves of the brain and body is apparent. Once any pattern of brain functioning and specialization is firmly set by the end of childhood, it is more difficult to switch sides or to learn new patterns.

3. Activity level is assumed to be associated with brain maturation in several ways. It is highest at around age 2 or 3, and then declines throughout the rest of childhood.

Mastering Motor Skills

4. Gross motor skills improve dramatically during this period, making it possible for the average 5-year-old to do many things with grace and skill.

5. Fine motor skills, such as holding a pencil or tying a shoelace, also improve, but more gradually. Many tasks, including writing, remain difficult and frustrating.

6. Play is the work of early childhood. Through sensorimotor play, mastery play, and rough-and-tumble play, children develop their bodies and skills.

7. Children's play is marked by distinct gender differences, which may reflect some differences in physical development. The average boy is taller and more muscular than the average girl. He is usually better at gross motor skills, such as throwing a ball, than she is, but she is usually better at fine motor skills, such as drawing a person. These differences may be part of the reason that boys tend to play more actively and aggressively than girls and that both sexes prefer playmates of the same sex.

8. However, during these years the physical similarities between the sexes are much more apparent than the differences. Although the extent to which differences in play patterns are influenced by either biological or social factors is not known, it is clear that social and cultural pressures play a role in their expression.

KEY TERMS

corpus callosum (214)
activity level (215)
gross motor skills (217)
fine motor skills (218)
sensorimotor play (219)
mastery play (219)

injury control (220)
rough-and-tumble play
  (222)
play face (222)
sex differences (223)
gender differences (223)

KEY QUESTIONS

1. How does the shape of the child's body change during early childhood?

2. What causes variations among children in height and weight during early childhood?

3. What are some of the important brain developments during early childhood?

4. How do gross motor skills develop?

5. What difficulties do children experience in mastering fine motor skills?

6. What measures seem most effective in reducing the rate of accidents in childhood?

7. Why is play called "the work of childhood"?

8. What are some of the gender distinctions that are typical of children's play patterns, and how might they be explained?

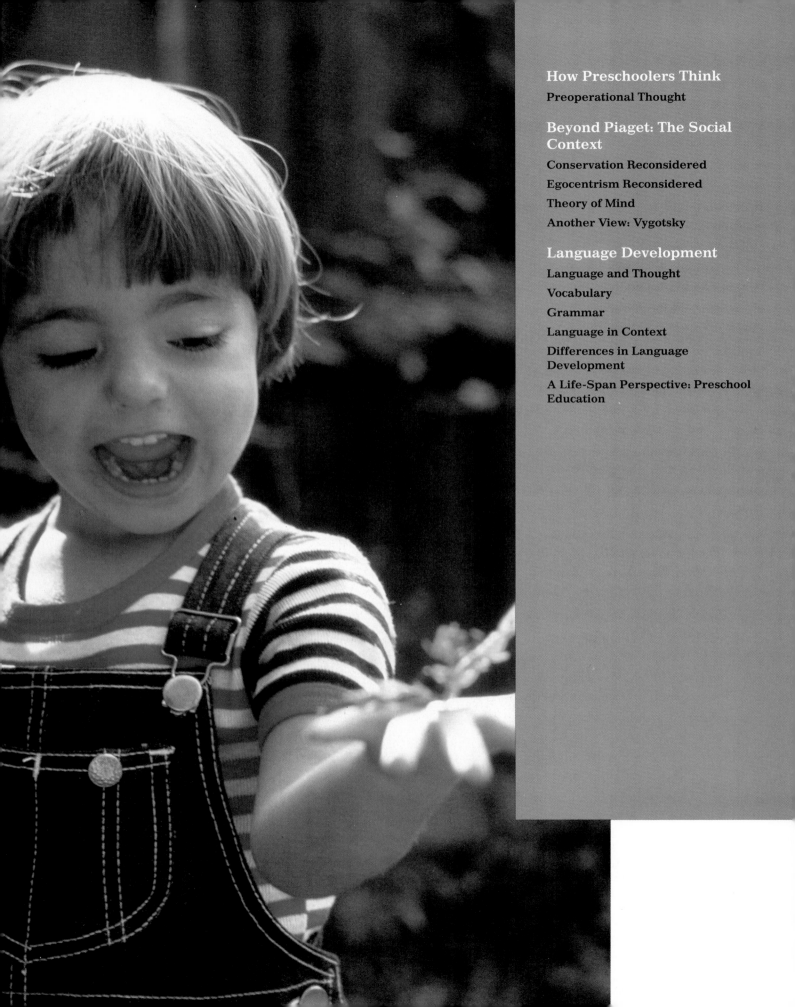

CHAPTER 9

The Play Years: Cognitive Development

An adult who asks a preschool child "What is it?" or "How does it work?" is likely to hear some surprising answers. Although children at this age are never at a loss for an explanation, they seem to formulate their ideas according to entirely different rules of logic than those used by adults. What are the characteristics of children's thinking at this stage and how do mature patterns of logical thinking develop? These and the following questions will be among the topics discussed in this chapter:

How do children progress from understanding the world through actions and perceptions to using symbols such as words?

Why do preschoolers often seem to understand everything from their own point of view?

How do children use language to help their thinking?

What factors are conducive to language learning?

Does preschool education really teach children?

Jeremy (aged 3): Mommy, go out of the kitchen.
Mother: *Why, Jeremy?*
Jeremy: Because I want to take a cookie.
[quoted in Peskin, 1992]

The thoughts and verbal expressions of children between the ages of 2 and 6 have always amused, delighted, and surprised adults. A child who wonders where the sun sleeps, or who comforts a sad parent by offering a lollipop, or who announces to his mother that he plans to sneak a cookie is bound to make us smile. Recently, however, researchers studying the intellectual underpinnings of preschool thought have found that they involve much more than charming nonsense. As you will soon learn, early childhood is an impressive period for the development of imagination and language, and even of the basic structures of logic.

How Preschoolers Think

The mind of the young child has been the topic of thousands of research studies over the past ten years. One reason for this wealth of research is that, on the face of it, thinking during early childhood seems a jumble of surprising competencies and incompetencies. Logic and illogic, honesty and deception, imaginative flights of fantasy and rigid literal-mindedness combine in puzzling ways.

Given such variability in intellectual display, scientists find it difficult to conclude exactly what preschoolers understand or do not understand: again and again the general findings of one study are modified by the next. In this chapter we will begin with Piaget's analysis of preschoolers' cognitive development, not because his views are the final word—in fact, much of the recent research activity in this area centers on qualifying Piaget's views—but because his theories and experiments provide a solid foundation on which to build our understanding of the young child's mind.

Preoperational Thought

As you remember, at the end of the period of sensorimotor thought, Piaget found that children's thinking is no longer tied to their immediate actions and perceptions. They become able to think symbolically; that is, they can think by forming mental representations of things and events that they are not immediately experiencing. Symbolic thought develops rapidly throughout the preschool years.

The growth in the use of symbolic thinking occurs as the child develops, and becomes able to mentally coordinate, an increasing number of schemas for the objects in his or her world. This progression is particularly clear when children play with something that could represent a person, such as a doll or stuffed animal. When children first play with such toys, at about age 1½, the doll or animal is used to represent one fairly simple action at a time. For example, a doll might be put to bed and left there, ending that particular episode of pretend play. With time, the child will put the doll through a sequence of related behaviors—making her wash her hands, cook the dinner, and eat it. Finally, at age 3 or 4, the child has the doll taking on more complex roles, talking and interacting with other dolls and toys, forming a family, or a school group, or a group of friends and foes. As children become older, they share their symbols in play with others: by age 4 or 5, many children are quite delighted to develop pretend dramas—such as "hospital," "store," or "family"—with their friends.

Typically, each of these levels of symbolic play is accompanied by more elaborate use of spoken language, itself an indication of symbolic thought, since words are the most common symbols we have. Thus the sequence of

Figure 9.1 *In pretend play, preoperational thinking tends to blur the distinction between the real and the imaginary, so this doctor might believe he hears a heartbeat, and his patient might feel better after doing what the doctor orders.*

symbolic play, with objects, words, and other children, is evidence of increasing cognitive development, distinguishing the preschooler from the infant (Piaget, 1951; Case, 1985; Garvey, 1989; Lyytinen, 1991).

Limits of Logic

Although children's capacity to coordinate symbols in a meaningful way increases dramatically during the preschool years, children are not necessarily able to coordinate symbols in a meaningful way that is consistently logical. According to Piaget, their thinking from about age 2 until 7 is characterized by **preoperational thought;** that is, they cannot yet perform logical "operations," using ideas and symbols to develop logical principles about their experiences. At the simplest level, they cannot regularly apply a general rule, such as "If this, then that . . . " or "If not this, then not that."

One example of this operational inability is the preschooler's failure to grasp the idea of **reversibility**—that is, the logical idea that reversing a process will bring about the original conditions from which the process began. This sounds much more complicated than it actually is, for what it means in practical terms is that the child may know that $3 + 2 = 5$ but not necessarily realize that the reverse is true, that $5 - 2 = 3$. It also means that a preschooler who walks to school every day but gets a ride home would, if asked to walk home one afternoon, probably reply, "But I've never walked home before. I don't know the way."

The most notable characteristic of preoperational thought, as described by Piaget, is **centration,** the tendency to think about one idea at a time—that is, to "center" on it—to the exclusion of other ideas.

Preoperational children are particularly likely to center on their perceptions, especially on the more obvious aspects of their visual perceptions, rather than consider a broader view of a situation or experience. Thus, in the preschooler's mind, the tallest child or adult is probably the oldest and the best as well (Kuczaj and Lederberg, 1977). Similarly, in the preschooler's view, a cut "hurts" because it bleeds, so covering it with a bandage will make it feel better. Likewise, if the morning sun is streaming through the bedroom window, that means it is time to get up and have breakfast—never mind that it is 5 A.M. on a June morning and Mommy and Daddy are sound asleep.

Because children are so inclined to center on one idea, their understanding is static rather than dynamic (Flavell, 1985). According to Piaget, they understand the world in terms of an either/or framework rather than as a flux of possibilities. For example, they think of themselves as a "good" child or a "bad" one, not as a child who is sometimes good in some ways and sometimes bad in others (Harter, 1983). Because they think in terms of absolutes, they also have trouble understanding transitions and transformations. A 3-year-old who is asked to put a series of pictures of a growing flower in order is likely to organize the pictures into simple categories, little and big, rather than into a continuous series (Voyat, 1982).

A related problem is preschoolers' difficulty in understanding cause and effect, partly because they center on one aspect of an event rather than on the relationship between events. This difficulty is particularly apparent when some mishap occurs. Children who fall down might blame the sidewalk or another child several feet away. Or a 3-year-old might say, and believe, that a vase fell and broke because it wanted to, or even that it fell *because* it now lies in dozens of pieces on the floor.

The characteristics of preoperational thought are demonstrated most clearly in Piaget's experiments. Let us look closely at his experiments in conservation, the most famous of the concepts that Piaget considered impossible for preoperational children to grasp.

The Problem of Conservation

As you read in Chapter 2, **conservation** (the idea that amount is unaffected by changes in shape or placement) is not at all obvious to young children. Rather, when comparing the amount of liquid in two glasses, they are impressed solely by the relative height of the fluids. If they are shown two identical glasses containing equal amounts of lemonade, and then watch while the lemonade from one glass is poured into a taller, narrower glass, they will insist that the taller, narrower glass has more lemonade than the remaining original.

Preschool children usually have the same problem with regard to conservation of many other sorts (see chart below). Consider **conservation of matter.** Make two balls of clay of equal amount, and then ask a 4-year-old child to roll one of them into a long skinny rope. When this is done, ask the child whether both pieces still have the same amount of clay. Almost always, 4-year-olds will say that the long piece has more.

Tests of Various Types of Conservation

	Start with:	Then:	Ask the child:	Preoperational children usually answer:
Conservation of Liquids	Two equal glasses of liquid. 	Pour one into a taller, narrower glass. 	Which glass contains more?	The taller one. 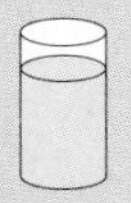
Conservation of Number	Two equal lines of checkers. 	Increase spacing of checkers in one line. 	Which line has more checkers?	The longer one. 
Conservation of Matter	Two equal balls of clay. 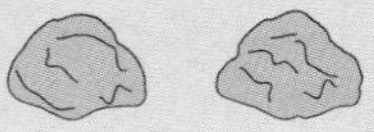	Squeeze one ball into a long, thin shape. 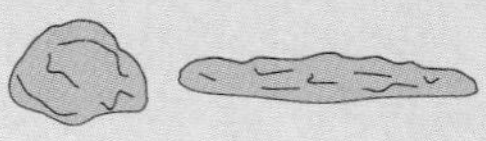	Which piece has more clay?	The long one. 
Conservation of Length	Two sticks of equal length. 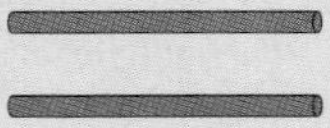	Move one stick. 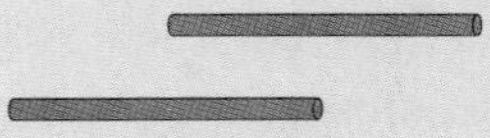	Which stick is longer?	The one that is farther to the right. 

Figure 9.2 *When tested on conservation of number, Sarah was not positive that the top row had as many checkers as the bottom row, no matter how they were arranged. Her response to this uncertainty was to count the rows—a sign that she is beginning to use the logical operations of the school-age child rather than the magical, preoperational thinking of the preschooler.*

Similarly, **conservation of number** is beyond preschoolers, according to Piaget. In one Piagetian test (Piaget, 1952), an experimenter lines up pairs of checkers into two rows and asks the child if both rows have the same number of checkers. The child will almost always say yes. With the child watching, the experimenter next elongates one of the rows by spacing the checkers farther apart, and then asks the child if the rows now have the same number or if one has more. The preoperational child almost always says that the longer row has more.

In such tests of conservation, the problem is that the preschooler centers on appearances and thus ignores or discounts the transformation that has occurred. Because of their tendency toward centration, and their resulting immature reasoning, Piaget contends that it is impossible for preoperational children to grasp the concept of conservation, no matter how carefully it is explained.

Egocentrism

One of the things preschoolers center on most is themselves, producing a type of thinking referred to as egocentrism. **Egocentrism** means that thinking centers on the ego, or self. Thus the egocentric child's ideas about the world are limited by the child's own narrow point of view: the child does not take into account that other people may have thoughts and feelings different from the ones he or she is having at the moment.

To say that preoperational children are egocentric means only that because of their cognitive immaturity, they are naturally self-centered, not that they are selfish (Piaget, 1959). A 3-year-old boy hearing his father crying, for instance, might try to comfort his daddy by bringing him a teddy bear. Obviously, this child is not being selfish: he is willing to give up something of his own. But he is egocentric: he assumes that his father will be consoled by the same things he himself finds consoling.

Egocentrism is also apparent in **animism,** the idea held by many young children that everything in the world is alive, just as they are. When thinking animistically, children whose play is interrupted by nightfall might get angry at the sun for "going to bed" too early, or they might begin to cry when they drop a stuffed animal because they think they have hurt it. Animism, as well as egocentrism, is what allows children to accept as literal truth many of the mythical explanations that adults offer them—that the Sand Man visits each night with "sleepy seeds" to make the child fall asleep; that Jack Frost brings winter's snows so that the child can make snowmen; that Mother Nature brings spring so that the child can smell the flowers. Children create their own animistic, egocentric explanations as well: they say the moon follows them when they walk outside at night or that the thunder comes because they have been bad.

Piaget's Three Mountains

According to Piaget, children are, because of their egocentrism, unable to take another's point of view until at least age 7. The basis for this assertion is Piaget's classic experiment (Piaget and Inhelder, 1963) in which children between the ages of 4 and 11 were shown a large three-dimensional exhibit of three mountains of different shapes, sizes, and colors (see Figure 9.3). First, the children would walk around the exhibit and view it from all sides, and then they would be seated on one side of the table that held the exhibit, with a doll seated on another side. Each child was then asked to choose which one of a series of photos showed the scene that the doll was viewing.

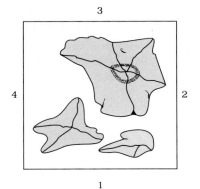
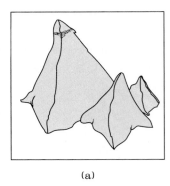
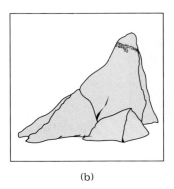
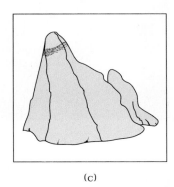

3

4   2

1   (a)   (b)   (c)

Figure 9.3 *Replications of Piaget's three-mountains experiment are used to measure the ability to imagine a different point of view. The child is first shown a display model of three mountains, and then is shown ten drawings of various views of the mountains. The child is asked to select the drawing that most accurately portrays the point of view of a doll seated at various positions around the table. For instance, if a child were sitting in position 1 looking at the three-mountain display (here shown in an overhead view) and asked how the display would look from sitting-position 4, which picture—(a), (b), or (c)—should the child select? Preoperational children often wrongly select their own view (b) rather than correctly choosing (a).*

No matter where the doll was seated, children younger than 6 mistakenly chose the photo that showed the mountains as they themselves were viewing them. By age 6 or 7, most children realized that the doll's view would be somewhat different from their own, but they often failed to pick the correct photo. Between 7 and 9, children generally chose correctly, with occasional errors, and finally at ages 9, 10, and 11, most of the children performed this task perfectly. From these results, Piaget concluded that children under 7 were too egocentric to take the perspective of another.

Beyond Piaget: The Social Context

The standard Piagetian experiments have been replicated hundreds of times with children from various cultures, and the results have nearly always been the same: preoperational children make many mistakes with the three-mountains experiment, just as they do with the conservation experiments using glasses of lemonade, or lumps of clay, or rows of checkers (Dasen, 1977; Donaldson et al., 1983).

However, many developmentalists now offer a new explanation for some of these mistakes. They suggest that the failure of preschoolers to demonstrate any sign of conservation or perspective-taking on Piaget's standard tests has more to do with context than content. In other words, children's failures on these tests may in part be related to the wording of test questions and to the specific test conditions rather than to a complete inability to grasp the concepts that are being tested. Accordingly, many researchers have attempted to change the context of Piaget's tests in order to determine if preschoolers are capable of more advanced thinking than Piaget believed them to be.

Conservation Reconsidered

One aspect of Piaget's theory that has been reexamined extensively is the concept of conservation (Gelman and Baillargeon, 1983). It is now clear that this concept does not appear, full-blown, at age 7 or 8, in accordance with Piaget's schedule, but instead develops slowly and unevenly. Piaget acknowledged this to some degree himself, noting, for instance, that most 7-year-olds understand conservation of liquids but that many 10-year-olds still have trouble with conservation of volume.

However, Piaget did not recognize what many other researchers have now shown: that children as young as 4 can succeed at some tests of conservation—if they are given special training and if the tests are simple and gamelike (Field, 1987). The best results occur when training includes not only careful verbal instructions and demonstrations but also an opportunity for the children themselves to perform the experiments while the instructor provides feedback on their performance. Under such conditions children sometimes show evidence of much more understanding than Piaget's more formal testing procedures ever brought forth.

Conservation of Number

Even in the absence of explicit instruction from an experimenter, preschoolers show some evidence of conservation of number, when the conditions are playful rather than serious. Several researchers have followed the standard conservation-of-number experiment with one telling exception. Rather than having an adult experimenter deliberately elongate one row of checkers, they made the change seem accidental by having it occur as a result of the actions of a "naughty" teddy bear (Dockrell et al., 1980; McGarrigle and Donaldson, 1974). In this case, when the teddy bear rather than an adult caused the elongation, preschool children were much more likely to recognize that both rows still contained the same number. One explanation is that, in the gamelike condition, children are not distracted from the realization that the teddy's "messing up" the display would not change the number of checkers, whereas in the standard Piagetian conditions, they are misled by the deliberateness of the experimenter's actions, assuming that if an adult took the time and trouble to reposition a row of checkers, something—such as the total number of checkers—must have changed.

Another group of experiments was designed to discover if children between 3 and 5 years old could recognize when a row of several identical toys was surreptitiously rearranged to make a longer or shorter line, or when one or two toys were taken away from a group of five (these transformations were done "magically," while the display was hidden under a cup). Virtually every child tested showed that he or she noticed the changes. Moreover, many of the children gave evidence that they were counting the display—often with idiosyncratic number sequences (instead of "1-2-3," counting, say, "1-2-6" or "A-B-C"). Despite their use of these irregular designations, however, the children knew what they were doing: when one toy was missing, they would say something like "Look, it used to be 1-2-6 but now it's only 1-2."

Thus, it is clear that some concept of number is present among young children (Gelman and Gallistel, 1978). However, it is also clear that even though preschoolers have some understanding of number, their understanding of the number system is fragile—apparent at some moments and not at others (Siegler, 1986; Frye et al., 1989; Becker, 1989). For example, 4-year-olds can typically count to 20, and have some recognition that one set of objects is comparable to another set of an equal number. They could understand, for instance, why a birthday party with five guests would require five party favors—or six, if the birthday child is to get one. However, the same child might not know how many favors are needed if one guest cannot come or might not realize that purchasing a pack of eight favors would be more than enough for the entire group. Thus, while they can say their numbers very well, they frequently misunderstand the implications of what they are saying (Fuson, 1988).

Egocentrism Reconsidered

Is Piaget's three-mountains experiment a valid test of the ability to take someone else's perspective? Considering that a child must choose a photo depicting a doll's view of a particular three-dimensional configuration of three abstract shapes seen for the first time moments earlier, this experiment would seem to test memory, spatial perception, and comprehension of an unusual experimental task, in addition to perspective-taking. What would happen if the task were simplified? Could children younger than 7 succeed?

Literally dozens of experiments have answered this question. In one group of studies, children between the ages of 3 and 6 are seated in pairs, and the contents of a box are shown to one member of each pair but not the other. Each child is then asked if he or she knows what is in the box, and if the other child knows. When answering from their own perspective, almost all answer correctly. However, virtually none of the 3-year-olds seem to realize what their partner's view would be, and many of the 4-year-olds also become confused. By ages 5 and 6, however, almost every child is equal to this task (Wimmer et al., 1988; Ruffman and Olson, 1989).

Even earlier perspective-taking was found in an experiment that involved playing a game rather than answering questions (Hughes and Donaldson, 1979). Children between the ages of 3½ and 5 were asked to hide a little boy behind a series of "walls," so that police who were looking for him could not find him. In one version, the walls made four quadrants (Figure 9.4), and the police were placed so that they could see into three of them. Almost always, the children, regardless of age, correctly placed the boy in the only quadrant where he would be safe from view. Perfect scores were attained by 73 percent of the children and another 17 percent made only one error in their four chances.

Perspective-taking was similarly impressive in a more complicated version of this game (Figure 9.4). Eight out of ten 4-year-olds scored perfectly, and seven out of ten 3-year-olds made no errors, or only one error. In fact, two of the 3-year-olds who were technically counted as failures in the experimental task actually did very well at protecting the boy—one by hiding the boy under the table, and one by hiding him in her hand. (Despite the experimenter's best efforts to explain that this was not the way to play the game, both refused to risk police detection by releasing the boy.) Thus it seems

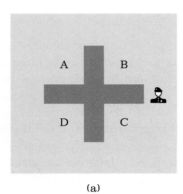

(a)

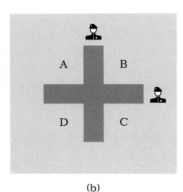

(b)

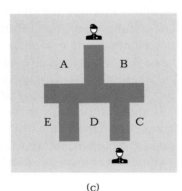

(c)

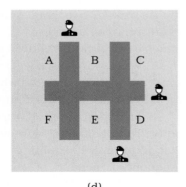

(d)

Figure 9.4 *Although the problem of hiding the little boy behind "walls" where the policemen will not be able to see him becomes increasingly complex in the sequence from (a) to (d), even very young children performed surprisingly well.*

that the conditions of this experiment elicit perspective-taking, even in 3-year-olds.

Why is it that young children succeed at these tasks but fail at the three-mountains task? The researchers who devised the policemen games believe it is because

> the policemen tasks make human sense in a way that the mountain task does not. The motive and intentions of the characters (hiding and seeking) are entirely comprehensible, even to a child of three, and he is being asked to identify with—and indeed do something about—the plight of a boy in an entirely comprehensible situation. This ability to understand and identify with another's feelings and intentions is in many ways the exact opposite of egocentrism, and yet it now appears to be well developed in three-year-olds. [Hughes and Donaldson, 1979]

Several additional factors also seem to be involved, including the child's direct participation in the task and the playful and nonverbal nature of the task itself. Certainly these factors make the policeman task quite different from answering an adult's questions about precisely what someone else's perspective might be. In general, as perspective-taking tasks become more verbal and more formal, they become more difficult for young children, while those that are designed to be gamelike and do not involve answering questions make perspective-taking easier to demonstrate (Cox, 1986).

Theory of Mind

The suggestion that children's mastery of the policeman task reveals an "ability to understand and identify with another's feelings," which is the "exact opposite of egocentrism," raises an intriguing possibility which Piaget and, until recently, most other developmentalists never considered: that preschoolers might have a "theory of mind."

All adults have what psychologists call a **theory of mind.** That is, we each have our own personal understanding of mental processes, of the complex interaction among emotions, perceptions, thoughts, and actions—in ourselves, as well as others. This allows us to analyze and interpret (with varying degrees of accuracy) human behavior. When two people give different interpretations of someone's actions (whether, say, the person broke a dish carelessly, clumsily, nervously, or deliberately), they are, essentially, utilizing alternative theories of mind.

Some thinking about the mental processes in oneself and others is certainly evident by the end of the preschool years. In fact, a theory of mind for 6-year-olds can include not only a knowledge of one's own emotions, which might be different from those of another, but also some understanding of the possible implications of those differences. This is illustrated by the following interchange between a mother and her 6-year-old son:

> Mother: "It's hard to hear the baby crying like that."
>   Son: *"Yes it is. But it's not as hard for me as it is for you."*
>   "Why is that?"
>   *"Well, you like Johnny better than I do. I like him a little, and you like him a lot, so I think it's harder for you to hear him cry."* [quoted in Bretherton et al., 1986]

Figure 9.5 *The best evidence for early development of a theory of mind comes from siblings, who often show impressive understanding of each other's emotions. This is obvious in older children. Some mental understanding is also apparent in younger children; many preschoolers seem to know just what will make their baby sibling smile or cry.*

If Piaget is correct in describing the thinking of younger preschoolers as basically egocentric, action-oriented, and appearance-bound, then a theory of mind would be logically impossible for them. They would center so much on what they see and do that they would not be able to think about another person's mental processes. Yet once researchers began to look for them, they found signs that a theory of mind may begin developing as early as age 2 (Astington et al., 1988; Miller and Aloise, 1989). Two-year-olds, for example, were noted to say things such as "Don't be mad, Mommy," "Mama having a good time?" and even "Maybe Craig would laugh when he saw Beth do that" (Bretherton and Beeghly, 1982). In addition, many young siblings seem to have a remarkable ability to know what soothes, amuses, or angers each other (Dunn, 1988). Consider the apparent nonegocentric awareness in the following episode of aggression and revenge between a 3-year-old girl and her 16-month-old brother:

> Anne is playing with her teddy bear, her favorite comfort object. She is making a tent for him in the kitchen with a chair and a cloth. Eric, her younger brother, watches. Five minutes later both children are in the front room, and they have a fight over the possession of a toy car. Anne wins the fight. Eric is angry. He runs back to the kitchen, pulls Anne's tent to pieces, and hurls the teddy bear across the room. Anne bursts into tears. [Dunn, 1985]

Spontaneous remarks and actions such as these seem to reveal an impressive understanding of the emotions of others. However, we should not jump to conclusions. Note that this research involves naturalistic observation, which can be interpreted in many ways. A 2-year-old who says "Don't be mad, Mommy" may have just heard an older child use the same phrase, and may not really understand what might make Mommy mad or what might placate her. And the interaction with the teddy bear involved siblings, who, after all, have compelling reason to anticipate each other's emotions and have lots of practice at it. Nevertheless, the possibility that a theory of mind may begin to emerge early in childhood has led researchers to try to pinpoint, experimentally, whether and when preschoolers have, and can act upon, an understanding that someone else's thoughts and perceptions might be quite different from their own.

Deception

One of the best ways to elicit evidence of a theory of mind is through games that ask the child to try to mislead another person. To understand that someone else might hold false beliefs, and, more significant, to know how to create such beliefs in another, is, obviously, to realize that someone else can have thoughts different from one's own. A substantial body of research has shown such understanding in 4-year-olds but has not found it consistently in children younger than 4 (Perner et al., 1987).

However, under the right set of experimental conditions, even 2½-year-olds showed that they had some understanding of deception (Chandler et al., 1989). While a child watched, an experimenter made a doll named Tony carry a treasure of gold coins across a white, washable surface and hide it in one of four boxes. Tony was designed to leave inky purple footprints that could be sponged off after each episode of "hide and seek." Once the child understood how the doll worked, he or she was urged to make Tony hide the treasure so another adult, waiting in a different room, couldn't find it.

Figure 9.6 *Given motivation, encouragement, and method, preschoolers are surprisingly capable of developing strategies to fool an adult. Most impressive in this experiment was the fact that 40 percent of the children between 2½ and 4 years old used not one strategy but two—erasing the telltale purple footprints and creating a new set of prints leading to a box that did not contain the treasure.*

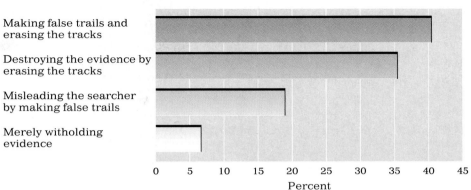

Deceptive Strategies Used by All Children

All fifty children, aged 2½ to 5 years, who participated in this experiment played their part. At the least, they were secretive, not telling where the treasure was or lying about its location. Most were even more misleading, putting down false trails, or erasing the telltale tracks, or both. Significantly, the 2½-year-olds were as likely as the 4-year-olds to demonstrate the most sophisticated level of deception (see Figure 9.6). The authors of the study explain:

> . . . the obvious conclusion demanded by these data is that even the youngest subjects of this study already have at their disposal an early theory-like understanding of the mind. It is equally clear that these results are at serious odds with those reported by others . . . who commonly find nothing to suggest that children younger than 4 years of age are aware that others will act on beliefs that are false . . . . [Chandler et al., 1989]

Interestingly, in this experiment, when the youngest children were asked why they chose the deceptive strategies that they did, many of them had no explanation. This may be an important key to understanding young children's performance on standard Piagetian tests of cognitive development, including those for perspective-taking and conservation: children can demonstrate understanding before they can verbalize it. Thus in a given situation, a preschooler may have a hypothesis about another person's thoughts and possible reactions, and may also be able to test it out through actions. Yet the same child may be unable to describe even his or her own feelings and mental processes, much less his or her reasoning about someone else's.

Given all the evidence, it seems that preschoolers do, in fact, have a "theory-like understanding of the mind," and that in perspective-taking, as well as in conservation, Piaget underestimated the preoperational child's ability.

Remember, however, that the experiments we have been considering were *designed* to challenge Piaget by evoking whatever conservation or perspective-taking abilities the young child might possess. While quite young children may have a rudimentary grasp of these concepts, that grasp is weak and fluctuating, apparent in certain (sometimes carefully designed) circumstances and not in others. As Rochel Gelman, a leading researcher on children's cognitive development, cautions:

> Despite the many competencies of the young, they nevertheless fail or err on a wide range of tasks that do not seem to be that difficult . . . The young child, to be sure, has many pieces of competence. However, they are exceedingly fragile. The older child can show that competence across a wide range of tasks. Hence, the idea is that development involves going from the fragile (and probably rigid) application of capacity to a widely based use of these. [Gelman et al., 1982]

Thus, no 3-year-old and few 6-year-olds have the solid, logical, understanding that the typical concrete operational child possesses (Becker, 1989). Such "widely based" understanding does not become firmly established until sometime during the school years.

Another View: Vygotsky

Much of the new research on, and appreciation of, the young child's emerging cognition is inspired by the writings of Lev Vygotsky, a Russian psychologist. Although Vygotsky was born in 1896, the same year as Piaget, his ideas have only recently reached the mainstream of Western thought, in part because he died young, at age 38, and in part because of national and international political barriers (Belmont, 1989).

Like Piaget, Vygotsky was intrigued by the ways in which differences in people's basic assumptions and perceptions created structural differences in their thinking. However, Vygotsky's approach to understanding such differences was unlike Piaget's in a very fundamental way. Piaget focused on age-related factors that he believed were at the root of cognitive development, and he described cognitive growth in terms of the child's innate curiosity, working within certain maturational constraints. Vygotsky, by contrast, believed that the structural differences in people's thinking arose primarily from cultural variations in the goals, experiences, and linguistic tools that foster mental growth. Those cultural variations are transmitted, according to Vygotsky, by parents and other teachers, as they motivate, guide, and channel a child's learning.

In short, Vygotsky saw learning as a social activity more than as a matter of individual discovery, propelled by cultural goals more than by maturational disequilibrium. The distinction between these two theorists has been forcefully delineated by Carol Rogoff (1990), a leading American researcher:

> According to Piaget, the young child is largely impervious to social influences because egocentricity blocks the establishment of reciprocity and cooperation in considering differing points of view. . . . Young children would generally find it so difficult to consider the logic of another's point of view that they would either continue to see things from their own perspective or switch to the other person's perspective without understanding the rationale and hence without actually advancing developmentally.
>
> In contrast with Piaget, Vygotsky assumes that social guidance aids children in learning . . . from the first years of life. This guidance provides children with the opportunity to participate beyond their own abilities and to internalize activities practiced socially, thus advancing their capabilities for independently managing problem solving.

To see how Vygotsky's approach works in practical terms, let's look at an example that can be taken both literally and metaphorically. Say that a child quits after trying unsuccessfully to assemble a puzzle. Does that mean the task is beyond the child's ability? Not necessarily—that is, if the child is given guidance that provides motivation, focuses attention, and restructures the task to make its solution more attainable. In this case, an adult or older child might begin by encouraging the child to look for a likely piece ("Does it need a big piece or a little piece?" "Do you see any blue pieces with a line of red?") Suppose the child finds some pieces the right size, and then some blue pieces with a red line, but again seems stymied. The tutor might then be more directive, selecting out a piece to be tried next, or rotating a piece so that its proper location is more obvious, or actually putting a piece in place with a smile of satisfaction.

The critical element in guided assistance is that the adult and child interact to accomplish the task. Eventually, such guided assistance enables the child to independently accomplish the task. Once the child puts the puzzle together with adult help, chances are he or she will try it again soon, needing less help, or perhaps none at all. Such interactions are commonplace: in every culture of the world, adults direct children's attention and provide assistance to teach various skills, and, soon, children who are given such guided practice learn to perform the skills on their own (Tharp and Gallimore, 1988; Rogoff, 1990).

To further elaborate his conception of the social nature of learning, Vygotsky suggested that each individual is surrounded by a **zone of proximal development (ZPD)**, which represents the cognitive distance between the child's "actual level of development as determined by independent problem solving and the level of potential development as determined through problem solving under adult guidance or in collaboration with more capable peers" (Vygotsky, 1978). It is as if, at any given moment, everyone is surrounded by an area of potentiality, a zone of possibilities, including all the ideas, knowledge, and skills that are almost, but not quite, within one's intellectual grasp.

How and when a person moves through that zone, and whether the new, socially induced understanding becomes incorporated into independent thinking, depends a great deal on the social context. The instructor's tone and choice of words in giving instructions, the learner's attention and motivation, and the familiarity of the particular materials (it is easier to teach math with everyday objects than with abstractions) are all crucial contextual elements. Since every culture values some cognitive skills more than others, the social context is also crucial in determining which particular parts of potential understanding become actually understood and incorporated into independent thought. It is not surprising, for example, that children in the Micronesian islands are much better at interpreting weather and navigation signs than American children, or that American children are more likely to be computer-literate than their Micronesian peers.

Family context also helps explain why some young children demonstrate much less egocentric, and more insightful, theories of mind than others: as noted, for example, preschoolers in competition with several siblings

Figure 9.7 *While this child is quite capable of looking at photographs by himself, without his mother's verbal guidance he could not realize that these pictures depict himself at younger ages. Such interactions within the zone of proximal development foster cognitive growth.*

have considerable motivation for, and practice in, figuring out what their "rivals" think and feel, as well as reason to use that information to be defensive or devious if necessary. In addition, how much attention and guidance the parents give to understanding emotions, as measured by how much of their conversation with the children focuses on what someone is feeling and why, directly affects how adept preschoolers become at understanding and expressing emotional states, as well as how advanced they are at perspective-taking tasks that are more obviously cognitive (Dunn et al., 1991).

Overall, then, researchers draw quite different conclusions about children's cognitive accomplishments if they examine what children can do alone or with social guidance. Many developmentalists now think the Vygotskiian way, engaging the child within the zone of proximal development, provides the more rewarding and productive way to understand cognition. Taking this perspective, a child's language development becomes critically important as a cognitive tool.

Language Development

As noted in Chapter 6, babies normally begin talking at about a year, with language development occurring slowly at first. Toddlers typically add only a few new words to their vocabulary each month, speak in one-word sentences, and sometimes have trouble communicating, frustrating themselves as well as even the most patient caregiver who tries to understand what the 1-year-old wants to say.

During the preschool years, however, as cognitive powers increase, the pace and scope of language learning increases dramatically. Indeed, an "explosion" of language occurs, with vocabulary, grammar, and the practical uses of language showing marked and rapid improvement.

Language and Thought

What is the relationship between language and thought in the child's cognitive growth? Does the child first get an idea and then try to find the words to express it, or does the child's language ability enable the child to think new thoughts?

Piaget (1976) believed that cognitive development precedes language: children must first have an experience or understand a concept before they are capable of using the words that describe it. This explains, for instance, why the first words that children learn are ones that refer to objects that can be manipulated and explored with the senses. The noun "watch" is usually used before "crib," for example, because, although infants hear the word "crib" more often, they cannot play with it in the same sensorimotor way they can play with a watch. Similarly, words for the appearance and disappearance of things and people ("bye-bye," "allgone," "no more," "where . . . ?") emerge only after full object permanence has been attained.

Most developmentalists agree with Piaget that infants form concepts long before the first signs of language appear. But most American developmentalists also believe that, beginning in early childhood, language helps children form ideas (Bruner, 1983; Rice, 1989).

Talking to Learn: Vygotsky's Theory

This idea was expressed over fifty years ago by Vygotsky, who believed that language is essential to the advancement of thinking in two crucial ways. The first is through **private speech,** the internal dialogue in which a person talks to himself or herself (Ziven, 1979; Vygotsky, 1987). In adults, private speech is usually silent, but in children, especially preschoolers, it is much more likely to be uttered out loud. With time, this self-talk becomes a whisper, and then becomes inner, private speech.

Researchers studying private speech have found that preschoolers use it to help them think, reviewing what they know, deciding what to do, and explaining events to themselves. Interestingly, many researchers have found that children who have learning difficulties tend to be slower to develop private speech, or to use it to guide their behavior (Diaz, 1987). Training in private speech sometimes helps them learn, another sign that language, in this form, aids the learning process.

The second way language advances thinking, according to Vygotsky, is as the *mediator* of the social interaction that is a vital part of learning. Whether it involves explicit instruction or casual conversation, verbal interaction with others helps to refine and extend one's present level of understanding. This function of language is essential to traversing Vygotsky's zone of proximal development, because verbal interaction provides the bridge from the child's current understanding to the almost understood.

In any case, during the preschool years, both private and social language erupt in a verbal explosion, as children spend hour upon hour asking question after question, telling stories that seem endless, or just talking and singing to themselves. This explosion is most evident in the growth of preschoolers' vocabulary.

Vocabulary

The rapid growth of vocabulary during early childhood is astonishing, especially when we remember that it takes most infants a year to utter one intelligible word, and several months more before they master a dozen words. As one summary describes it:

> Children typically produce their first 30 words at a rate of three to five new words per month. The same children learn their next 30,000 words at a rate of 10 to 20 new words per day. [Jones et al., 1991]

Indeed, words are often learned after only one hearing, through a process called **fast mapping,** in which the child immediately assimilates new words by connecting them through their assumed meaning to categories of words the child has already mastered (see A Closer Look, p. 244).

The learning of new words follows a predictable sequence according to parts of speech. Nouns are generally learned more readily than verbs, which are learned more readily than adjectives, adverbs, conjunctions, or interrogatives. Within parts of speech, the order is predictable as well. For instance, the first interrogatives children learn are "where?" and "what?" then "who?" followed by "how?" and "why?" (Bloom et al., 1982). Basic general nouns, such as "dog," are learned before specific nouns, such as "collie," or more general categories, such as "animal" (Anglin, 1977; Blewitt, 1982).

A CLOSER LOOK   Fast Mapping: Advantages and Disadvantages

Considerable research has attempted to determine how children master vocabulary so quickly. This inquiry begins with the realization that after the first year or so of language acquisition, learning vocabulary is no longer simply an additive process, with each word, in isolation, being added to the child's current stock of words. After age 2, there is an acceleration of vocabulary growth that soon seems like an explosion, with words being added daily in chunks. How does this happen?

One explanation is that the child's mind seems to develop an interconnected set of categories for vocabulary, a kind of mental map that charts the meanings of various words (Golinkoff et al., 1992). Hearing a new word, the child uses the context in which it is being used to create a quick, partial understanding and then to categorize it, placing it in his or her existing lexicon. Thus children learn new animal names so quickly, for instance, because new animals can be mapped close to the old ones—"zebra" is easy to learn if you know "horse"; "fox" is easy if you know "dog"; and so forth. This process is called "fast mapping," as if, rather than stopping to figure out an exact definition, and waiting until a word has been understood in several contexts, the child simply hears it once or twice and adds it to his or her mental language map (Heibeck and Markman, 1987).

The quickness of fast mapping is phenomenal: a word can be learned after a single exposure (Dickinson, 1984). Moreover, several new words can be learned over a short time period. In one experiment, 3- and 5-year-olds were first given a multiple-choice vocabulary test on twenty words they were unlikely to know, such as "gramophone," "nurturant," "artisan," "malicious," and "contentment." Their scores were just about what they would be by chance, between five and six correct of the twenty. Then, in two 15-minute sessions, they viewed cartoons with the twenty words used about ten times each in context. On retesting, 3-year-olds averaged eight correct answers and the 5-year-

olds averaged eleven right. Object words (e.g., "gramophone," which 93 percent got right) were easiest to learn, and emotional-state words (e.g., "contentment," which only 20 percent got right) were hardest. This is not at all surprising, since the language map for objects is well formed during preschool years, but the map for emotions is not (Rice and Woodsmall, 1988).

Fast mapping has obvious advantages, in that it fosters quick vocabulary acquisition. However, it also means that a child might seem to understand a word because he or she uses it in an appropriate context, when, in fact, the child has no real understanding of the word's meaning or understands it only in a limited way. One very simple, common example is the word "big," a word even 2-year-olds use and seem to understand. In fact, however, young preschoolers often use "big" when they mean "tall," or "old," or "great" ("My love is so big!"), and only gradually use "big" correctly (Sena and Smith, 1990).

If adults realize the difficulty children often have in comprehending exactly what the words they use mean, it becomes easier to understand, and sometimes forgive, the mistakes that children make. I can still vividly recall an example of fast mapping that arose when one of my daughters, then 4, was furious at me. She had apparently fast-mapped several insulting words into her vocabulary. However, her fast map did not contain precise definitions, or reflect the nuances. She first called me a "mean witch," and then a "brat." I smiled at her innocent imprecision. Then she let loose with an X-rated epithet that sent me reeling. Struggling to contain my anger, I tried to convince myself that fast mapping had probably left her with no real idea of what she had just said. "Language like that is never to be used in this house!" I sputtered. My appreciation of the quickness of fast mapping was deepened by her response: "Then how come my big sister called me that this morning?"

The speed with which a child acquires words and relates them to categories and concepts depends partly on the particular conversations the child has with adults, who may or may not stress the linkage between one noun and another (Markman, 1989). When adults do describe categories—not in a formal lesson but simply in the course of normal speech—children are able to map new words more quickly, just as Vygotsky's stress on the pivotal role of social interaction would suggest. For example, when a child meets a dog named Lassie, and repeats "Lassie," a parent might say "Yes, Lassie is a dog, a collie dog," helping the child make the connection between the specific name, the breed, and the kind of animal.

The vocabulary-building process happens so quickly that, by age 5, some children seem to understand and use almost any specific term they hear. In fact, 5-year-olds can learn almost any word or phrase, as long as it is explained to them with specific examples and used in context. One 5-year-old surprised his kindergarten teacher by explaining that he was ambidextrous. When queried, he said, "That means I can use my left or my right hand just the same." In fact, preschoolers are able to soak up language like a sponge, an ability that causes most researchers to regard early childhood as a crucial period for language learning.

The spongelike fast mapping of vocabulary during these years is so impressive that we need to remind ourselves that young children cannot readily grasp every word they hear. Abstract nouns, such as "justice" or "government," are difficult to understand because there is no referent in the child's experience to link them to. Metaphors are also difficult, because the fast-mapping process is often quite literal, allowing only one meaning per word. When a mother, exasperated by her son's frequent inability to find his belongings, told him that someday he would lose his head, he calmly replied, "I'll never lose my head. If I feel it coming off, I'll find it and pick it up."

Further, because preschool children tend to think in absolute terms, the idea of relativity is beyond them, and they consequently have difficulty with words expressing comparisons, such as "tall" and "short," "near" and "far," "high" and "low," "deep" and "shallow" (Reich, 1986). Once they know which end of the swimming pool is the deep one, for instance, they might obey instructions to stay out of deep puddles by splashing through every puddle they see, insisting that none of them are deep. Words expressing relativities of place and time are difficult as well, such as "here" and "there," "yesterday" and "tomorrow." More than one pajama-clad child has awakened on Christmas morning and asked "Is it tomorrow yet?"

Grammar

Grammar includes the structures, techniques, and rules that languages use to communicate meaning. Word order and word form, prefixes and suffixes, intonation and pronunciation, all are part of grammar. Grammar is apparent even in toddlers' two-word sentences, since they almost always put the subject before the verb.

By age 3, children typically demonstrate extensive grammatical knowledge. They not only put the subject before the verb but also put the verb before the object, explaining "I eat apple" rather than using any of the other possible combinations of those three words. They can form the plural of nouns, the past, present, and future tenses of verbs, the subjective, objective, and possessive forms of pronouns. They are well on their way to mastering the negative, progressing past the simple "no" of the 2-year-old ("No sleepy," "I no want it," "I drink juice no") to more complex negatives such as "not," "nobody," "nothing," and even "never."

Children's understanding of grammar is revealed when they create words that they have never heard, like those in the chart on page 246. Each of the words in the chart shows not only the child's mastery of grammatical rules but the presence of egocentrism as well, in that the children all expected others to understand their linguistic creations.

Difficulties with Grammar

Children tend to apply the rules of grammar even when they should not. This tendency, called **overregularization,** can create trouble when their language is one that has many exceptions to the rules, as English does. For example, one of the first rules of grammar that children use is adding "s" to form the plural. Thus many preschoolers, applying this rule, talk about foots, snows, sheeps, and mouses. They may even put the "s" on adjectives, when the adjectives are acting as nouns, as in this dinner-table exchange between a 3-year-old and her father:

> Sara: I want somes.
> *Father: You want some what?*
> I want some mores.
> *Some more what?*
> I want some more chickens.

Once preschool children learn a rule, they can be surprisingly stubborn in applying it. Jean Berko Gleason reports the following conversation between herself and a 4-year-old:

> She said: "My teacher *holded* the baby rabbits and we *patted* them." I asked: "Did you say your teacher *held* the baby rabbits?" She answered: "Yes." I then asked: "What did you say she did?" She answered again: "She *holded* the baby rabbits and we *patted* them." "Did you say she *held* them tightly?" I asked. "No," she answered, "she *holded* them loosely." [Gleason, 1967]

Although technically wrong, such overregularization is actually a sign of verbal sophistication, since children are, clearly, applying rules of grammar. Indeed, as preschoolers become more conscious of grammatical usages, they may exhibit increasingly sophisticated misapplications of them (de Villiers and de Villiers, 1986). A child who at age 2 says she "broke" a glass may at age 4 say she "braked" one and then at age 5 say that she "did

Children's Knowledge of Grammar in Creating Words

Rule Followed	Word	Context
Add "un" to show reversal.	"unhate"	Child tells mother: "I hate you. And I'll never unhate you."
Use a limiting characteristic as an adjective before a noun to distinguish a particular example.	"plate-egg," "cup-egg" "sliverest seat"	Fried eggs, boiled eggs. A wooden bench.
Add "er" to form comparative.	"salter"	Food needs to be more salty.
Create noun by saying what it does.	"tell-wind"	Child pointing to a weather vane.
Add "er" to mean something or someone who does something.	"lessoner" "shorthander"	A teacher who gives lessons. Someone who writes shorthand.
Add "ed" to make a past verb out of a noun (as in punched, dressed).	"nippled"	"Mommy nippled Anna," reporting that Mother nursed the baby.
	"needled"	"Is it all needled yet?" Asking if Mother has finished mending the pants.
Add "s" to make a noun out of an adjective.	"plumps"	Buttocks.
Add "ing" to make a participle out of a noun.	"crackering"	Child is putting crumbled crackers into soup, thereby crackering it.

Source: Examples come from Bowerman, 1982; Clark, 1982; Reich, 1986; and the Berger children.

No, Timmy, not "I sawed the chair."
It's "I saw the chair" or "I have seen
the chair."

Figure 9.8 *This mother has obviously*
become accustomed to her son's use of
overregularization.

Drawing by Glenn Bernhardt

broked" another. After children hear the correct form often enough, they spontaneously correct their own speech, so parents can probably best help development of grammar by example rather than explanation or criticism—in the present case, for example, by simply responding "You mean you broke it?" While few children will immediately correct their grammar, the cumulative effect of correct demonstration will lead to more rapid language mastery (Farrar, 1992).

During the preschool years children are able to comprehend more complex grammar, and more difficult vocabulary, than they can produce. Thus, while it is a mistake to expect preschoolers to use proper grammar and precise vocabulary, it is also an error to simply mirror the child's speech, "talking down" to his or her level. And while an adultlike understanding of some grammatical forms is beyond many preschoolers, that does not mean that their language-learning abilities are severely limited. Vygotsky's concept of the zone of proximal development is useful here: between the grammar forms that are understood, and those that are, as yet, ununderstandable, lies a zone of potential, a zone that, with adult guidance and the child's natural intellectual curiosity, can be used to expand the child's grammatical comprehension. While adults from various cultures differ in their readiness to teach language to their children, all children, as we will now see, are extraordinarily receptive to whatever communication patterns they experience.

Language in Context

In addition to studying the growth of children's grasp of the meanings and forms of language, developmentalists have recently undertaken the study of **pragmatics**, the practical communication between one person and another in terms of the overall context in which language is used (Rice, 1982). The major emphasis of this study is that a person's communicative competence depends on that person's knowing how to adjust vocabulary and grammar to the social situation.

Children learn these practical aspects of language very early. Evidence of such pragmatic understanding of language can be seen, for example, in 2- or 3-year-olds' use of high-pitched "baby talk" when talking with younger children or with dolls and in their using a deeper, "adult" voice when giving commands to dogs and cats. Similarly, preschoolers use more formal language when playing the role of doctor or teacher or train conductor, and they use "please" more often when addressing someone of higher status (Rice, 1984). Children also gradually master proper listening behavior, such as nodding the head and saying things like "Uh huh" and "Really?" to continue a conversation by indicating that the speaker is heard and understood, even when this is not the case (Garvey, 1984). As every adult knows, this practical skill facilitates social interaction as well as further understanding, and thus smoothes the way for learning.

Another pragmatic development is shown in children's developing ability to relate an event sequentially, as they become more aware of the usual "scripts" for various everyday events. By age 3 or 4, children can follow the script in telling what happened at, say, a restaurant (order food, eat it, and pay for it), or a birthday party (give presents, play games, have cake and ice cream). Here is one 5-year-old's description of how to buy groceries:

Figure 9.9 *It is obvious from their body language that these two children have different points of view. Their ability to communicate their opinions and come to an agreement is an indication of their pragmatic skills.*

Um, we get a cart, uh, and we look for some onions and plums and cookies and tomato sauce, onions, and all that kind of stuff, and when we're finished we go to the paying booth, and um, then we, um, then the lady puts all our food in a bag, then we put it in the cart, walk out to our car, put the bags in our trunk, then leave. [quoted in Nelson, 1986]

Not only is the sequence correct, enabling listeners to understand exactly what happens, but the child also has the ability to find adequate substitutes for words that are not yet in his vocabulary, in this case, identifying the checkout counter as "the paying booth."

Children can also relate specific details of those experiences that are different from the usual sequence. Thus, in the middle of a description of birthday parties in general, a child sadly mentions, "It was just at my birthday party. Someone cried there and she ruined the whole party" (Hudson, 1986). From a practical language perspective, the ability to make meaningful conversation about events that happened some time before is even more important than the breadth of one's vocabulary or the correctness of one's grammar.

Differences in Language Development

Families and cultures differ in how much they stress language development. Consequently, by the time children enter kindergarten, differences in language skill are great. While one child seems to know the name of almost every object and action within that child's experience, and can converse in complex sentences, another child has only a basic vocabulary and uses only a few words at a time.

To some extent, one can predict which groups of children are likely to be more advanced in language (Bates et al., 1987). On most measures of language production, girls are more proficient than boys; middle-class children, more proficient than lower-income children; first-borns, more proficient than later-borns; single-born children, more proficient than twins, who, in turn, tend to be ahead of triplets.

Researchers who try to explain these differences usually look first at the familial and cultural variations in the language children hear. In general, they have found that mothers talk more to daughters than to sons; that middle-class parents provide their children with more elaborate explanations, more responsive comments, and fewer commands than lower-income parents do; and that parents talk more to first-borns and single-borns than to later-borns or twins. Particularly important are the attitudes about children's language: in cultures where it is thought that children should be seen and not heard, where "idle talk" is frowned on, and where "talking fresh" is punished, children's language production is not encouraged, and, not surprisingly, most children from such cultures do quite poorly on tests of language development (Schieffelin and Eisenburg, 1984; Ward, 1982). Note, however, that these group variations are small compared with the differences among individual children from the same group. Thus some lower-income twin boys know far more words than other lower-income twin boys. Similarly, a linguistically advanced lower-income twin boy may have a far better grasp of language than the average middle-class, single-born girl.

If we look more closely, research finds that measures of the overall relationship between parent and child, such as strength of attachment and the amount of time spent together, are *not* especially good predictors of a child's language competence. However, the particulars of conversation between adults and children are relevant. Children become more linguistically competent if the significant adults in their lives encourage them to talk, and reply to their comments with specific and contingent responses (Snow, 1984). (If, for instance, a child says, "I saw a fire engine," a response like "Was it a long red fire engine?" is much more helpful than something like "That's nice.")

Adults can also provide experiences that act as a "scaffold" on which to build language skills (Genishi and Dyson, 1984; Schiefelbusch, 1984). Such experiences might include looking at picture books together, going on excursions that provide opportunities for new vocabulary and topics of discussion, and pretending together (pragmatic skills can be evoked by almost any imaginary venture, from a tea party to a trip to the moon). Measures like these work as well for learning a second language as they do for learning a first (McLaughlin, 1984).

In thinking about these differences, it is useful to keep Vygotsky's idea about the zone of proximal development in mind. During preschool years, the lower boundary of the zone—what the child is capable of expressing at the moment—includes basic vocabulary and rudimentary grammar, the simple telegraphic, egocentric sentences of the toddler. The upper boundary—what is within the child's present learning abilities—includes thousands of words, hundreds of grammar rules and exceptions, and dozens of pragmatic skills. By nature, the preschool child is a language learner, ready to follow a fast map into new territory. How far a child actually travels within that zone depends on the extent to which others are ready and willing to nourish the child's eagerness for new words and ideas. Accordingly, Vygotsky (1986) stresses the importance of adults' sensitivity to the child's abilities at the moment.

> The only good kind of instruction is that which marches ahead of development and leads it. It must be aimed not so much at the ripe as at the ripening functions. It remains necessary to determine the lowest threshold at which instruction may begin, since a certain ripeness of functions is required. But we must consider the upper threshold as well: instruction must be oriented toward the future, not the past.

As we will now see, the obvious importance of language encouragement, and of regular opportunities to communicate with adults and other children, is one reason quality preschool education can be a vital enhancement to early cognitive development.

A LIFE-SPAN PERSPECTIVE   ## Preschool Education

The cognitive experiences of preschool-age children are quite different now than they were thirty years ago. Whereas children formerly almost always stayed at home until about age 6, now—in almost every developed nation and in many of the developing ones—most children enter some form of school during the time still referred to as the "preschool" years.

There are two primary factors behind this change. The first is a dramatic shift in maternal work patterns. Whereas once few mothers of young children were employed away from the home, now most are. This shift has occurred in industrialized nations worldwide, but it is particularly noticeable in the United States: since the beginning of the 1960s, the percentage of employed mothers of preschool-age children has risen from below 20 percent to over 65 percent. Coinciding with this shift, there has been an increase in the number of single parents, a rise in the number of grandmothers employed, and a decrease in average family size—all of which has meant that there are fewer family members available to care for young children while their mothers are at work.

The second factor is related to research on child development. Over the past thirty years, scientists have shown not only that the years before age 6 are a time of rapid learning but also that young children can learn at least as well outside the home as within it—an idea that directly contradicted both popular and professional wisdom. According to several thorough reviews of the research, good preschool education advances cognitive development as well as social development sufficiently so that when preschool students are compared with other children from the same backgrounds who stay at home, the preschool children generally fare better (Clarke-Stewart, 1984; Scarr, 1984; Haskins, 1989).

The clearest and most extensive evidence for the benefits of preschool education comes from high-quality schools characterized by (1) a low teacher-child ratio, (2) a staff with training and credentials in early-childhood education, (3) a curriculum geared toward cognitive development rather than behavioral control, and (4) an organization of space that facilitates creative and constructive play. Research has found that preschools and day-care centers that include cognitive development among their goals but do not have all these costly resources can also foster children's learning, though not as much (Lee et al., 1988; Burchinal et al., 1989).

Most of the research on early childhood education comes from the United States and Canada, but similar results have also been found in research conducted in other countries. For example, a large comparison done in Bermuda (McCartney, 1984), where 84 percent of the children between 2 and 4 years old spend their days in some sort of care outside their homes, found that quality of care in the day-care centers, particularly the amount of adult-child conversation, had noticeable effects on the children's verbal skills and on their overall intellectual development. The best centers were the ones where teachers spent more time teaching children (usually with small groups of children) and less time controlling them (usually done one child at a time), and where the children engaged in a variety of activities designed to foster motor, social, and language skills.

As a result, then, of both the increased need for child care and the proven benefits of preschool education, more and more young children are in some sort of educational milieu. In 1970, only 20 percent of all 3- and 4-year-olds in the United States were in some sort of preschool; in 1990, close to half were. In many other countries, especially in Western Europe, the numbers are even higher, because the government sponsors education in early childhood.

While we know that preschool education provides short-term benefits for children, until recently it was not known what the long-term benefits might be. Fortunately, we now have longitudinal data which show intriguing results.

Headstart: A Longitudinal Look

In the early 1960s, social scientists and social reformers advocated giving low-income children who might be disadvantaged by their home environment or "culturally deprived" by their community some form of compensatory education during the preschool years, since these years were increasingly being regarded as critical for later cognitive development. Such children were thought to need remediation for the deficiencies of their early experiences and a head start on the skills required in elementary school (Zigler and Berman, 1983).

This idea caught on, and as part of the federal government's "war on poverty," **Project Headstart** was inaugurated in 1965. In its first year some 20,000 children, from many racial and ethnic backgrounds, from virtually every pocket of rural or urban poverty in the nation, attended a variety of Headstart programs—some full-time, some part-time, some concentrating on classroom activity, some teaching parents how to educate their children in the home. Despite these somewhat improvised and hasty beginnings, the initial results from Project Headstart were encouraging. Children learned a variety of intellectual and social skills between September and June of their Headstart year, averaging a gain of 5 points on intelligence tests.

Although longitudinal research found that the early IQ advantage of Headstart graduates often faded by the third grade, it also revealed important **sleeper effects,** or results that become apparent sometime after the precipitating event (Consortium for Longitudinal Studies, 1983; Haskins, 1989). As they made their way through elementary school, for example, the Headstart graduates scored higher on achievement tests and had more positive school report cards than non-Headstart children from the same backgrounds and neighborhoods. By junior high, they were significantly less likely to be placed in special classes or made to repeat a year.

In adolescence, Headstart graduates had higher aspirations and a greater sense of achievement than their non-Headstart peers, and as they entered adulthood, Headstart graduates were more likely to be in college and less likely to have a criminal record or a dependent child. Similar findings appear in longitudinal research, begun in the 1960s, on participants in the Perry Preschool Program, a well-financed project in Ypsilanti, Michigan, that was much like Headstart in design. The latest survey of the Perry subjects, now in their late 20s, indicates that, compared to the study's control group, they have greater earning power, greater family stability, and have required fewer social services over the past decade (Schweinhart and Weikart, 1993).

Conclusion

While no developmentalist believes that a year or two of preschool education will necessarily transform an impoverished child's life, almost all

Figure 9.10 *One of the original goals of Project Headstart was to expand the children's understanding of their aspirations of what they might become, through trips such as this one, taken in 1981, to the local fire company. If these children are typical of most who experienced Headstart, they are now more outgoing, confident, and accomplished than their peers who had no preschool education. It would not be surprising if at least one of them—of any color or either sex—planned to be a firefighter.*

agree that, on the evidence from Headstart, most disadvantaged children will benefit from early education beginning at age 3 or even sooner. This education can be in the form of a Headstart program (the program is the only antipoverty measure that survived government spending cuts in the 1980s) or in another setting, as long as trained teachers implement a child-centered curriculum.

The program's sleeper effects include economic benefits as well. Various studies comparing the cost of publicly financed preschool in the United States to the later savings from lower rates of special education, crime, and welfare dependency all find that early education is a sound public investment. Indeed, the more intensive, and expensive, the programs, the greater the dividend (Barnett and Escobar, 1987). Not surprisingly, those preschool programs that involve parents and community most intensely are also those that show the strongest long-term benefits for children and families. Too often, unfortunately, those children who most need quality care are least likely to get it, because their parents cannot find or afford it (Hayes et al., 1990).

Do the same generalities hold for children who are not poor? Yes, to a degree. Longitudinal research on more advantaged children in the United States and elsewhere finds that they also benefit from a quality preschool setting, although the better the home environment, the less pronounced the influence of the preschool is likely to be (Anderson, 1989; Larsen and Robinson, 1989). Such benefits are cumulative: the more months and years a child spends in preschool, the more the cognitive and emotional benefits accrue (Field, 1991).

Considering all we now know about cognitive development between ages 2 and 6, we should not be surprised at the benefits of a well-run nursery school. Children develop cognitive skills as a result of many interactive experiences with adults and children, in settings with many activities and much opportunity to play. That is precisely what a good preschool provides. In the next chapter, you will see that many aspects of emotional and social development occur in the same kinds of settings, and for the same reasons, as cognitive growth.

SUMMARY

How Preschoolers Think

1. When children become capable of symbolic thought—that is, of using words, objects, and actions as symbols—their ability to understand, imagine, and communicate increases rapidly. According to Piaget, they are no longer bound by the immediate experiences that characterize sensorimotor thinking, but are now in a period of preoperational thought.

2. Piaget describes preoperational thought as, essentially, prelogical. Children center on one feature of an experience rather than looking at the relationship among several features. What something appears to be, or what imagina-

tion says it might be, is more salient than what logic would dictate it actually is.

3. The preoperational child, according to Piaget, believes that other people and even objects think and act the same way he or she does. This general characteristic, called egocentrism, is quite different from selfishness. One consequence of egocentrism is that preoperational children have difficulty understanding a point of view other than their own.

Beyond Piaget: The Social Context

4. In playful situations—both in naturalistic observation and in experimental conditions—preschool children often demonstrate an understanding of logical ideas that Piaget did not expect them to show until an older age. Among

these are some of the underlying concepts of mathematics, conservation, and perspective-taking.

5. Preschoolers are not always appearance-bound and egocentric. They have some understanding of emotions and mental processes, in other people as well as in themselves. This understanding, called a theory of mind, is sometimes reflected in preschoolers' efforts to comfort, irritate, or deceive other people. The theory of mind develops throughout the preschool years, with some evidence of such a theory apparent by age 2.

6. While experimental evidence reveals that preoperational children can sometimes demonstrate more logical thinking than Piaget believed them capable of—especially in contexts specifically designed to elicit such thinking—it nonetheless remains true that the young child's ability to demonstrate an understanding of conservation, number, or perspective is fragile. Not until the concrete operational period of cognitive development are these basic ideas firmly established.

7. Vygotsky saw learning as a social activity more than as a matter of individual discovery. He believed that structural differences in people's thinking arises from cultural variations in the goals, experiences, and linguistic tools that foster mental growth. These cultural variations are conveyed by parents and other teachers as they guide and stimulate a child's learning.

Language Development

8. Most developmentalists agree that infants form concepts first and then learn the words to express them. At some point in early childhood, language becomes a tool for forming ideas and regulating action.

9. According to Vygotsky, the ability to use and understand language is one powerful way that children learn. This occurs in private speech, when children use language to review what they know and to regulate their actions, and in social speech, when children communicate with others.

10. Language accomplishments during early childhood include learning 10,000 words or more, and understanding grammatical forms. Children at this age, however, have difficulty with abstract words and often misunderstand grammatical rules.

11. Children's language can be evaluated from the perspective of pragmatics—the use of practical communication in a variety of contexts. The ability to make meaningful conversation often develops before the acquisition of a complete vocabulary and perfect grammar. As impressive as they are, however, children's communication skills are sometimes hampered by their egocentrism.

Preschool Education

12. Due to the increasing number of working mothers and evidence that young children learn outside the home as well as within it, more and more children today attend preschools and day-care centers.

13. Children who have attended preschool programs designed to improve their intellectual abilities tend to show improvements in social and cognitive skills through adolescence and young adulthood.

KEY TERMS

preoperational
  thought (231)
reversibility (231)
centration (231)
conservation (232)
conservation of matter (232)
conservation of number (233)
egocentrism (233)
animism (233)

theory of mind (237)
zone of proximal
  development (241)
private speech (243)
fast mapping (243)
overregularization (246)
pragmatics (247)
Project Headstart (251)
sleeper effects (251)

KEY QUESTIONS

1. How does symbolic thinking expand the cognitive potential of the young child?

2. What are the characteristics of preoperational thought?

3. What are several examples of the concept of conservation?

4. Under what conditions do preschool children seem to understand conservation and perspective-taking?

5. How well can preschoolers understand the number system?

6. What evidence is there that young children have a theory of mind?

7. How does the increasing capacity to use language affect thought in early childhood?

8. What are the impressive language accomplishments of the young child?

9. What are the limitations of the language ability of the young child?

10. Why do young children have difficulty understanding grammatical rules? How is this difficulty shown in their language?

11. How do preschool programs, such as Headstart, affect children?

CHAPTER 10

The Play Years: Psychosocial Development

In the preschool years, children become increasingly aware of themselves and of others. Their growing capacity for communication, imagination, and social understanding allows them to participate in ever-more-elaborate play scenarios with other children and to explore various social roles. In this chapter we will consider the ways preschoolers develop their ideas about themselves and their relationships to the social world, including topics such as the following:

How does the development of a child's self-understanding influence his or her ability to form relationships with others?

What do children learn from playing with other children?

What are the various types of caregiving patterns that parents adopt, and how do these patterns affect children's behavior?

Is it normal for a child to hit another child?

How do children learn sex roles?

Picture a typical 2-year-old and a typical 6-year-old, and consider the psychosocial differences between them. Chances are the 2-year-old still has many moments of clinging, of tantrums, and of stubbornness, vacillating between dependence and self-determination. Further, many 2-year-olds cannot be trusted alone, even for a few moments, in any place where their relentless curiosity might lead them into destructive or dangerous behavior.

Six-year-olds, by contrast, have the confidence and competence to be relatively independent. They can be trusted to do many things by themselves, perhaps getting their own breakfast before school and even going to the store to buy some more cereal. They also can show affection with parents and friends without the obvious clinging or exaggerated self-assertion of the younger child. Six-year-olds are able to say goodbye to their parents at the door of the first-grade classroom, where they go about their business, befriending and playing cooperatively with certain classmates and ignoring others, and respecting and learning from their teachers.

It is apparent that in terms of self-confidence, social skills, and social roles, much develops during early childhood. Cognitive growth permits children a greater appreciation of psychological roles, motives, and feelings, deepening their understanding of others and of themselves. At the same time, their social world also becomes more diverse, with the introduction of new social partners (in preschool or in the neighborhood) and richer roles for familiar partners (such as parents, siblings, and peers). Catalysts for psychosocial development thus come from within and around the child, and this chapter examines that development.

The Self and the Social World

Self-concept, self-confidence, and self-understanding, as well as social attitudes, social skills, and social roles, are familiar topics for psychologists who study adults. Increasingly, these same topics are central to researchers studying children, especially those looking at early child development. Between ages 1 and 6, children progress from a dawning awareness that they are independent individuals to a firm understanding of who they are and how their selfhood relates to others. In the course of this progression, children move from the first fleeting recognition of themselves in a mirror, to knowing their name, gender, and what is theirs, to knowing what they need and want from their family and friends and how to get it.

Theories of Early Childhood

As you will shortly see, each of the major theories has a somewhat different explanation for the emergence of children's self-understanding, particularly with regard to how children develop sex roles, a topic explained at the end of the chapter. At the same time, the major theories share a common theme, each portraying early childhood as a time of emerging competency and self-awareness, when children seem to come into their own.

Psychoanalytic Theory

The most encompassing psychoanalytic view is that of Erik Erikson (1963), who notes that the child comes into "free possession of a surplus of energy which permits him to forget failures quickly and to approach what seems desirable . . . the child appears 'more himself,' more loving, relaxed, and brighter in his judgment, more activated and activating." The child initiates new activities with boldness and exuberance.

Indeed, the crisis of this stage, according to Erikson, is **initiative versus guilt.** In this crisis, which is closely tied to the child's developing sense of self and the awareness of the larger society, preschoolers eagerly take on new tasks and play activities and feel guilty when their efforts result in failure or criticism. Their readiness to take the initiative reflects preschoolers' desire to accomplish things, not simply to assert their autonomy as they did when toddlers. Thus, in a nursery-school classroom the older preschoolers take

Figure 10.1 *According to Erikson, how parents react to the excesses of exuberant initiative—when, say, a child's efforts to prepare a meal or repair a toy result in chaos—can influence whether children experience guilt concerning their desire to accomplish and learn new things.*

the initiative to build impressive block towers, whereas younger children in the autonomy stage are more likely to be interested in knocking them down. The enthusiasm of older children to learn and master many things derives, in part, from their growing sense of membership in the larger culture and a desire to acquire the skills of citizen and worker as well as of family member.

When initiative fails, according to Erikson—when eager exploration leads to a broken toy, a crying playmate, or a criticizing adult—the result is guilt, an emotion that is beyond the scope of the infant because it depends on an internalized conscience and a sense of self (Campos et al., 1983).

Cognitive Theory

As we saw in Chapter 9, cognitive theory reveals that preschool children acquire a dawning awareness of psychological processes within themselves and others. As they develop a "theory of mind," preschoolers can better identify and distinguish their own perceptions, emotions, thoughts, and intentions from those of others, and can coordinate them intellectually (Bretherton and Beeghly, 1982; Miller and Aloise, 1989). For example, most 4-year-olds realize that parents are more likely to be upset when a misdeed is deliberate rather than unintentional. Consequently, when some bad behavior of theirs is discovered, they often plead accidental misfortune ("I didn't *mean* to!") in an effort to conceal their culpability.

Even so, preschoolers' psychological understanding remains fairly simplistic. They do not grasp the complexity of personality or the variability of a person's competencies: they cannot appreciate, for example, that a person can be mean to people but kind to animals, or can be good at math but poor in reading. Preschoolers also do not clearly distinguish between different psychological causes of their actions or skills as well as older children and adults do. For example, they believe that ability—like effort—is self-controlled and can be changed (Nicholls, 1978). Thus their understanding of themselves and others is global and general (Miller and Aloise, 1989).

Learning Theory

Learning theory notes that toward the end of early childhood, praise and blame, as reinforcements and punishments, become powerful, as they could not be earlier, because now children are aware of themselves and of how others perceive them (White, 1965). Furthermore, preschoolers can be self-reinforcing (acting in ways that provoke pride in oneself) and self-controlling (flexibly regulating their behavior in light of adults' expectations) (Kopp, 1982). Increasingly, then, preschool children can take pride in their ability to spontaneously comply with the standards of being a "good boy" or a "good girl," and this is an important cornerstone of self-image.

Humanism

Similar themes are sounded in humanist theory, which points to the child's drive for competency and achievement (Kagan, 1984). As we saw in Chapter 2, the core idea of humanism is that every human being has innate drives to fulfill his or her potential. This is first apparent in **mastery motivation,** as young children spontaneously seek to develop all their skills and competencies, whether or not adults provide incentives for them to do so (Messer et al., 1987).

Of course, the fact that children are naturally inclined to strive for mastery does not diminish the parents' role in this endeavor. As you will recall, humanists maintain that it is the parents' overall acceptance of the child—their "unconditional positive regard" for the child—that provides the emotional ambience in which the child can fully thrive. Further, according to humanist theory, anyone, of any age, who does not have this feeling of acceptance will be handicapped in his or her striving for self-actualization. Research on children confirms this basic concept: if parents are too punishing or restrictive, preschoolers are less likely to show evidence of self-esteem or to exhibit the drive to master their environment (Vondra et al., 1990); and if parents are too controlling—for instance, by commenting on every action with praise or criticism—the child's natural drive to mastery will diminish (Lutkenhaus, 1984).

Overall, then, humanists emphasize that preschoolers on their own want to be more efficacious. The persistent efforts of 2-year-olds to button their sweaters or of 5-year-olds to write their own names, even when parents could do it much more quickly and better, are simple but telling examples. In many ways, humanism stresses that the parents' role is to provide general encouragement and some of the specific wherewithall—big-enough buttonholes, sharp-enough pencils, or whatever—and then stay out of the way.

Self-Concept and Social Awareness

As you can see, every theory describes the child's developing sense of self. Indeed, early childhood is filled with examples of an emerging self-concept, as preschoolers assiduously note which possessions are theirs, claiming everything from "my teacher" to "my mudpie"; repeatedly explain who they are and who they are not ("I am a big girl," "I am not a baby"); and relish many forms of mastery play that allow them to show that "I can do it."

Almost as soon as their sense of self is established, they use this awareness to facilitate their interaction with others. One aspect of the relationship between self-awareness and social interaction was shown in a study that tested seventy-eight 2-year-old boys for their self-understanding (Levine, 1983). Their comprehension of possessive pronouns was assessed by seeing if they could correctly follow commands such as "Tickle your stomach," "Touch my nose," and "Touch your toes." The accuracy of their use of "I" and "me" was also tested. In addition, their self-recognition was measured by means of the mirror-and-a-dot-of-rouge experiment described in Chapter 7. Then they were paired off and put in a playroom together. Typically, the first step of interaction was asserting selfhood, usually in terms of ownership, as shown in the following dialogue between two boys who are relatively advanced in development of self-concept. (Each boy is sitting on a toy car, and holding his own Nerf ball.)

> John: My ball.
> *Jim: Mine ball.*
> My ball. [I] have this. No. [The warning came in spite of the fact that Jim has made no move toward the toy.]

My ball.
No.
No ball.
No ball ball. Two ball ball.
Mine.
No.
My ball. Boon ball. [Smiles]
Bump!
Yup!
Car's going bump.

This particular play session began with ten statements of self-assertion before a joke ("boon ball") was used to initiate actual play. Finding this pattern repeated again and again in her study, the author concludes: "A child's increased interest in claiming toys may not be a negative sign of selfishness but a positive sign of increased self-awareness . . ." With development, a toddler's interactions take on a different character, marked by possessiveness and an attempt to make sense of the other child as a separate social being (Levine, 1983).

In this study, those children who had the more firmly established self-understanding as measured by the pretests were also those who engaged in more interactive play. Similar results have been found in a number of contexts: the children who are most social are those who have a better-developed sense of self, as well as a more secure feeling of self-assurance in a given setting (Hartup, 1983). Further, children who are skilled at social interaction tend to be those who are quite confident of their own ability. For example, they are less dependent on teachers in a nursery school or parents at a playground than children who are more awkward at the skills of friendship (Rubin, 1980).

Figure 10.2 *Self-concept and social awareness are allied achievements during the play years: children become more sensitive and understanding of their friends as they become aware of the feelings and interests that make them unique and different from others.*

Self-Evaluation

For children of all ages, psychologists emphasize the importance of developing a positive self-concept. Preschoolers usually have no problem in this regard. Typically they form quite general, and quite positive, impressions of themselves. Indeed, much research, as well as anecdotal evidence, shows that preschool children regularly overestimate their own abilities. One reason is that they do not spontaneously compare their skills and abilities with those of others (Ruble, 1983). As every parent knows, the typical 3-year-old believes that he or she can win any race, do perfect cartwheels, count accurately, and make up beautiful songs. In a laboratory test, even when preschoolers had just scored rather low on a game, they confidently predicted that they would do very well the next time (Stipek and Hoffman, 1980).

In addition, most preschoolers think of themselves as able in all areas—competent at physical skills as well as at intellectual ones (Harter and Pike, 1984). This is greatly different from children older than age 8, who make clear distinctions between domains of competence, asserting, for example, that they are rather good in intellectual skills but poor in athletic ones (Harter, 1983).

Figure 10.3 *Social play—in this case, rough-and-tumble wrestling—helps young animals learn skills related to conflict and conflict-resolution, whether it involves young gorillas or preschool boys.*

Social Play

As we saw in Chapter 8, and in the preceding discussion, play is the work of preschoolers: through it they develop physical skills and expand their cognitive grasp of their world. Play is also important to preschoolers' psychosocial development because of the opportunities it provides for children to develop social skills and roles. As their play activity becomes more complex with increasing age—encompassing not only sensorimotor and mastery play (Chapter 8) but also rough-and-tumble play, pretend (or dramatic) play, and games with rules—it becomes more social. In social play, children acquire skills of initiating and maintaining friendly interaction with peers, and the themes of their play activity enable children to explore and rehearse the social roles they observe around them. Healthy animals of all species, and both sexes, play when they are young, developing practical and social skills that may be critically important for survival. For example, most kinds of monkeys live in fairly large groups: in order to live together peacefully, all the adults must know how to assert their rights without antagonizing other adults to the point of a serious fight. By pretending to fight with each other, young monkeys learn complicated behaviors of dominance and submission, using facial expressions, body language, and mock chase and retreat to regulate their interaction.

Nurturant behaviors are learned through play as well. Primates in early adolescence seem particularly interested in infants, playing with them and caring for them whenever the infants' mothers allow it. Such play is evident in juveniles of both sexes, although male monkeys tend to play more actively, and less gently, with younger monkeys than female juveniles do (Mitchell and Shively, 1984).

There is evidence that, for humans, social play in early childhood similarly affords crucial experiences that would be hard for adults to provide and that would be difficult to acquire at a later stage of life (Howes, 1987). For example, learning to play with friends teaches reciprocity, nurturance, and cooperation much more readily than interaction with adults does (Eisenberg et al., 1985; Youniss, 1980). This is because with peers, children are on a much more equal footing and must assume greater responsibility for initiating and maintaining harmonious social interaction. In play with peers—whether they are learning how to share crayons or the sandbox, or how to include everybody in the construction of a spaceship, or how to respond to a friend's accusation that "it's not fair!"—children cannot rely on their partners to make all the effort, as they can in encounters with adults. Similarly, dramatic play enables children to explore and rehearse various social roles, and to examine personal concerns in ways that would not be possible with adults.

The nature and significance of dramatic play have been vividly documented in classic research by Catherine Garvey (1977), who found many examples of dramatic play when she studied forty-eight preschool children ranging in age from 2 years and 10 months to 5 years and 7 months. Each child was paired with a playmate the same age; then both children were placed in a well-equipped playroom to do whatever they wanted.

Many of these pairs, even some of the youngest, chose to engage in dramatic play. The 2- and 3-year-olds often played a simple mother-and-

Figure 10.4 *In dramatic play, children cooperate in creating an imaginary story that may involve the assignment of roles, sudden shared plot changes, and corrective instructions. Can you guess what roles these young dramatic actors are assuming?*

baby game; older children sometimes played a parent-child game or, if they were of different sexes, a husband-wife game (which tended to be a somewhat more complicated interaction, since it usually involved making some compromises about who did what). Older children created many other roles, including Hansel and Gretel, Dr. Jekyll and Dr. Hines (sic), and their own version of the latest TV shows.

Although Garvey found that most dramatic play involves standard plots such as these, she also noted other types of scenarios, such as one player announcing that a child or pet is sick or dead and the other player automatically becoming the healer, administering food or medicine, or performing surgery, to restore life and health. In a third standard type of drama, one child announces a "sudden threat" (the appearance of a monster, for instance), then both children take the role of victim or defender, attacking or fleeing. The episode can end happily ("I got him!") or unhappily ("He ate me. I'm dead."), unfolding naturally yet without prearrangement.

As suggested by the last example, dramatic play is, for the most part, creative and fluid, with children making up and embellishing the drama as they go along. Yet underlying the seemingly improvisatory nature of this play are surprisingly complex rules and structures enabling children to smoothly coordinate their pretend activity (Garvey, 1977). Preceding the onset of play, for example, children negotiate the themes they will enact, the roles they will assume, and the imaginary setting. These joint decisions are provisional, however, and can be changed at a moment's notice by any actor ("Let's say this is a secret cave. OK?" "OK!"). Children use vocal inflections and other cues to signal when they are acting in-role or are instead providing out-of-role instructions or questions ("I'm feeling sick." "Really?" "No, pretend."). And preschoolers are quick to correct play partners who assume roles deemed inappropriate (such as an older boy wanting to play "mommy") or who play their roles inadequately (failing to "fall dead" when shot in a game of cops-and-robbers, for instance, or talking too much when playing the role of "baby").

Dramatic play such as this not only is fun but it also helps children try out and rehearse social roles, express their fears and fantasies, and learn to cooperate.

Siblings in Early Childhood

For many children, the first and foremost lesson in social interaction comes from their brothers and sisters. To a child, sibling relationships are unique, different from relationships with parents and peers. As they do with parents, siblings share lifelong relationships and common backgrounds and experiences. Like peers, however, siblings are closer (although usually not equal) in age, abilities, and outlook, and their interests are often different from those of parents. Perhaps for these reasons, siblings assume significant roles in a child's life. For a younger child, an older sibling is an enticing model, a source of learning, and occasionally a reservoir of comfort and security. For an older child, a younger sibling is an important benchmark of social comparison ("Mark can't jump rope, but *I* can!"), and permits the

Figure 10.5 *The ambivalent emotions of sibling relationships are apparent during playful conflict like pillow fights, which can evolve from friendly pummeling to angry hitting back to delighted shoving in a remarkably short period of time!*

growth of new social skills related to nurturance and authority (Abramovich et al., 1979, 1982; Dunn, 1983, 1988).

Not surprisingly, the emotional quality of sibling relationships varies dramatically. Much attention, of course, has been given to sibling rivalry, and it is true that siblings are more likely to quarrel with each other than they are with nonrelated children. However, researchers have found that the flip side of sibling rivalry has been understressed: siblings are also more likely to have positive interactions with each other, showing more nurturance and cooperation than with an unrelated child (see Lamb and Sutton-Smith, 1982). Consequently, *ambivalence* might be the best single word to describe the emotional quality of most sibling relationships.

In most families, parents greatly influence the nature of sibling interactions, setting the stage for cooperation, or for rivalry—by comparing one sibling unfavorably with another, for example, or by regularly forcing an older child to include a younger sibling "tag along" in his or her activities. Parental influences actually begin with the birth of the second child: one research group discovered that preschool-age siblings whose mothers frequently discussed the newborn sibling as a person with feelings and desires had considerably greater interest and nurturance toward the younger child (Dunn, 1988).

In fact, because each sibling has a particular position within the family, the home experiences of each child in a given family are quite different from those of the other children. This helps explain a phenomenon that had, at first, puzzled researchers in behavioral genetics. Earlier researchers had assumed that, if two children from the same family were markedly different in personality, intelligence, and so forth, the differences must be genetic, since the environment was the same. However, careful analysis finds that environmental variations within families are substantial (Plomin, 1990). Home is a quite different place for the first-born big brother than for the last-born baby sister (Dunn and Plomin, 1990).

While there are many reasons for marked experiential differences between siblings, one of the most important is that parents' differential treatment of their children, even when well-intentioned and justifiable, fuels feelings of jealousy, anger, dominance, or inferiority (Daniels et al., 1985; McHale and Pawletko, 1992). Preschoolers, particularly, are very sensitive to social interactions between their parents and their siblings: they interrupt conversations, claim moral superiority when a sibling has transgressed, and make invidious comparisons, often to their own detriment (Dunn and Plomin, 1990).

One example comes from a 2½-year-old, Andy, and his 14-month-old sister:

> Andy was a rather timid and sensitive child, cautious, unconfident, and compliant. His younger sister, Susie, was a striking contrast—assertive, determined, and a handful for her mother, who was nevertheless delighted by her boisterous daughter. In the course of an observation of Andy and his sister, Susie persistently attempted to grab a forbidden object on a high kitchen counter, despite her mother's prohibitions. Finally, she succeeded, and Andy overheard his mother make a warm affectionate comment on Susie's action: "Susie, you *are* a determined little devil!" Andy, sadly, commented to his mother, "*I'm* not a determined little devil!" His mother replied, laughing, "No! What are you? A poor old boy!" [Dunn, 1992]

Multiplied hundreds of times over during Andy's growing up, such feelings of inadequacy might spur him toward success or failure, bravery or timidity, but they certainly would not be neutral. Not all siblings are rivals, but almost all are reciprocally involved in ways that affect the personality and social understanding of both (Dunn and Plomin, 1990).

In terms of the specific topic here, the development of social skills, it is easy to see that, given the attentiveness they bring to their relationship, siblings might provide better instruction than any other person, since they are likely to guide, challenge, and encourage a child's social interactions more frequently and intimately than most adults do. Very practical lessons in self-defense, sharing, and negotiation are part of every younger sib's childhood.

This raises, of course, the question of the only-child, who is becoming increasingly common in many Western homes. In the United States, for example, 13 percent of all wives in the 1980s expected to have only one child, compared with just 6 percent in the 1960s (U. S. Bureau of the Census, 1991), and many women who plan to have more than one child actually stop childbearing after their first. Do only-children suffer from the lack of siblings? Generally not. In fact, in most ways, only-children fare as well or better than children with siblings (Mellor, 1990; Falbo, 1984). They are particularly likely to benefit intellectually, becoming more verbal, more creative, and more likely to graduate from college, even when compared to their peers from the same social class and of the same intellectual ability (Blake, 1989). The one problem specific to their being an only-child might be in social skills, if they miss out on some of the benefits of social play. However, parents can compensate for that by making sure that, in the preschool years, they have regular contact with other children.

Parenting

Thus far we have not discussed the most crucial influence on preschool children—their parents. Not only do most children—even those in full daycare—typically spend more time with their parents than with anyone else, but parents also make the crucial decisions that establish the various contexts of the child's everyday life.

Some of these parental choices—what neighborhood the family lives in, whether or not the child attends preschool, whether or not the child has siblings, and so forth—have obvious impact. Others—the myriad little choices a parent makes each day—may seem inconsequential at first glance, but over time, they add up. It matters, for instance, whether, when the child asks a typical question like "Can I have some juice?" the typical answer is "Yes," "No," "Not now," "I'll get it," "Get it yourself," "Say please," or "Shut up." While the parent's response to the daily flood of child-related demands obviously depends on the particulars of each specific situation, it also depends on the parent's overall approach to child-rearing. As the Life-Span Perspective on parenting styles makes clear, the approaches to child-rearing usually follow one of several general patterns, each one of which, over the years of parenting, can have a distinct impact on the child's confidence and competence.

Styles of Parenting

Figure 10.6 *The modern supermarket is rife with temptations for small children and corresponding provocations for parents. Children climb on or off the shopping carts, nibble food that has not been purchased, grab for candy placed enticingly beside the check-out, and, as shown here, demand boxes of sugary junk. How parents respond in such situations often reflects their overall style of parenting. Some would let this boy have his way; others might negotiate for a healthier treat; others would simply say "no." Then if the boy started to cry, some parents might ignore him; others might resort to yelling or spanking; others might try to distract or comfort him. Over the years, such differences in parenting style may influence whether a child becomes confident and self-controlled or anxious and immature.*

What kinds of parenting help children to develop a positive sense of themselves, as well as to interact positively with others, and to be competent at school? This question has no simple, universal answer because there is no guaranteed relationship between how a parent rears a child and how a child turns out. (As we saw in Chapter 7, even abusive and severely neglectful parenting can vary in the damage it does.) Indeed, parents adopt many acceptable styles, from quite strict to very permissive, from intensely involved to rather laid back, and a child reared in one type of family may not be markedly different from a child reared in another type.

However, twenty-five years of careful research have led to an important insight about the impact of certain parental styles—not that one style is always best, but that some styles are more likely to produce confident and competent children than others. The seminal study in this research was begun in the early 1960s, when Diana Baumrind set out to study 110 middle-class preschool children in California (Baumrind, 1967, 1971). She used many measures of behavior, stressing naturalistic observation. First, she observed the children in their nursery-school activities and, on the basis of their actions, rated their self-control, independence, self-confidence, and the like. She then interviewed both parents of each child, and observed parent-child interaction in two settings, at home and in the laboratory, in order to see if there was any relationship between the parents' behavior with the child and the child's behavior at school.

There were four features of parenting that stood out in Baumrind's observations and interviews. First, parents differed in their warmth or *nurturance* toward offspring. Second, they varied also in their efforts to *control* the child's actions through rules and punishment. Third, parents also differed in how well they *communicated* with offspring. Fourth, and finally, they varied in their *maturity demands*—that is, in their expectations for age-appropriate conduct. On the basis of these features, Baumrind delineated three basic patterns of parenting:

1. **Authoritarian** The parents' word is law, not to be questioned, and misconduct is punished. Authoritarian parents seem aloof from their children, showing little affection or nurturance. Maturity demands are high, and parent-child communication is rather low.

2. **Permissive** The parents make few demands on their children, hiding any impatience they feel. Discipline is lax. Parents are nurturant, accepting, and communicate well with offspring. They make few maturity demands because they view themselves as available to help their children but not as responsible for shaping how offspring turn out.

3. **Authoritative** The parents in this category are similar in some ways to authoritarian parents, in that they set limits and enforce rules, but they are also willing to listen receptively to the child's requests and questions. Family rule is more democratic than dictato-

Figure 10.7 *Parental maturity demands are an important aspect of parenting style, and they concern the expectations parents have for age-appropriate conduct in offspring. Chances are that these siblings not only learned to help with the dishes but are also expected to perform a number of chores around the house, like making their beds and getting themselves dressed in the morning.*

rial. Parents make high maturity demands on offspring, communicate well with them, and are nurturant.

Baumrind and others have continued and extended this research, following the original children as they grew into adulthood and studying hundreds of other children of various backgrounds and ages (Clark, 1983; Baumrind, 1989; Baumrind, 1991; Steinberg et al., 1989; Lamborn et al., 1991). The basic conclusions of the original studies have been confirmed: children whose parents are strict and aloof are likely to be obedient but unhappy; those whose parents are quite lenient are likely to lack self-control; those whose parents provide both love and limits are more likely to be successful, happy with themselves, and generous with others. In addition, the follow-up research found that the initial advantages of the authoritative approach are likely to be even stronger over time, in that authoritative parents "are remarkably successful in protecting their adolescents from problem drug use and in generating competence" (Baumrind, 1991).

Other Styles

The later research has also found that the original description of only three types of parenting was too limited. While various studies have proposed several new types—more than can be described here—three additional styles merit attention.

The permissive pattern, in particular, can take two distinct forms. While both forms are quite undemanding and uncoercive—that is, the parents rarely control, restrict, or punish the children unless health or safety are obviously jeopardized—some permissive parents are quite warm and responsive. They might best be called **democratic-indulgent.** Other permissive parents are quite cold and unengaged, and are called **rejecting-neglecting.** Although they fall far short of the extreme neglect that characterizes official maltreatment, rejecting-neglecting parents permit the child to do almost anything, and seem relatively uninvolved in, and even ignorant about, what the child actually does (Maccoby and Martin, 1983; Baumrind, 1991; Lamborn et al., 1991).

An example of the difference between the two types of permissive parenting might be that, while both would allow a 5-year-old to play unsupervised in the kitchen making a "cake" by mixing flour, sugar, water, baking soda, and cinnamon, the democratic-indulgent parent might taste the dough, pronounce it delicious, and bake it in the oven for the family dinner, whereas the rejecting-neglecting parent might simply pour the unappetizing mess into the garbage. Both of these, of course, differ from nonpermissive parents: the authoritarian parent might not allow such a young child to be involved in any kind of food preparation, while the authoritative parent would be right there with guidance and a cookbook.

As Baumrind collected more information on parenting styles, she found another distinct type of parenting which she called **traditional** (Baumrind, 1989). Parents in this category take somewhat old-fashioned male and female roles, the mother being quite nurturant and permissive, while the father is more authoritarian. In the cake-baking example, for instance, the mother might allow and even encourage the child's "creative cooking" (especially if the child is a daughter), but might warn that the mess must be cleaned up before Father gets home.

Although psychologists often stress that, ideally, both parents should be consistent and should agree on the specifics of child-rearing, in fact, traditional parents often agree to disagree in their approaches, each one hewing to the expectations of his or her respective gender role. The result for the children appears to be much better than the advocates of consistency might expect: longitudinal research suggests that traditional and democratic-indulgent parenting are midway on the scale of successful parenting—less successful than authoritative parenting but more successful than authoritarian or rejecting-neglecting parenting (Baumrind, 1989).

Further Complexities

Any generalizations about the outcome of particular parenting styles—including the idea that authoritative parents produce the most competent children—must be interpreted with caution. In truth, parenting styles and children's responses to them are among the most complex and diversified aspects of family life. Thus, direct effects are hard to measure, and simple conclusions are usually misleading. While research confirms a longitudinal correlation between specific parental styles and a child's personality, values, and achievement, the impact of parenting style is actually quite modest when other elements that also have an impact on the child's development are taken into account. In addition, parenting style itself is affected by many factors. As we will now see, one of the most important of these factors is the child's own temperament. Others include the nature of the parents' relationship and the influence of the culture and the community.

Direction of Effects

Through their temperament, children may affect parenting styles as much as they are affected by them (Bell and Harper, 1977). It may be, for example, that children who have some measure of self-reliance and self-control sometimes "produce" relaxed, flexible parents. Similarly, it may be that temperamentally angry and unfriendly children may tend to produce overcontrolling, cold parents, even as such parents tend to foster hostile, antisocial children. Indeed, initially, the parents' strictness or laxness is less important than their warmth toward the child in the early years and their establishment of a secure and strong attachment relationship. A good early relationship is like "money in the bank," ready for use in later childhood and adolescence (Maccoby and Martin, 1983). As one reviewer explains, "If parents can do what is necessary early in the child's life to bring about a cooperative, trusting attitude in the child, that parent has earned the opportunity to become a nonauthoritarian parent" (Maccoby, 1984).

Also complicating the predictive power of parenting typologies is the fact that the impact of specific styles varies with family size and with the child's age and gender. Parents with many children tend to be more controlling, partly because allowing too much freedom with too many children is an invitation to anarchy. The relevance of the child's age is particularly obvious with democratic-indulgent parents: during early and middle childhood, their children tend to be mediocre in school achievement, perhaps because they are somewhat lost without the structure and daily push provided by stricter parents, but teenagers of democratic-indulgent parents often do quite well, probably because they have developed their own sense of structure and motivation to achieve. The girls, particularly, tend to have high math and verbal scores (Baumrind, 1989; Baumrind, 1991). Authoritarian parenting, on the other hand, is likely to work quite effectively in middle childhood but become increasingly debilitating as children grow older. This tendency is particularly obvious for boys, since they are caught between the culture's expectations for males to stand up for themselves and their authoritarian parents' insistence on obedience with no back talk. Teenage boys of authoritarian parents tend to be alienated from school, to dislike themselves, and to blame their problems on other people (Lamborn et al., 1991; Baumrind, 1991).

The Marital Relationship

One of the truths to emerge from a life-span perspective on development is that the interaction between any two family members may have an impact on the rest of the family. Certainly the relationship between husband and wife affects the style of parenting both use, and thus affects the children. When the marriage is satisfying and mutually supportive, both parents tend to be authoritative, setting high standards and responding with pleasure to their children's actions (Goldberg, 1990). On the other hand, when they are unhappy with each other, parents are more likely to be authoritarian, using threats and punishments and showing little patience for their children's explanations. Parents are particularly likely to be rejecting and neglecting when the marriage is falling apart, or already broken (Baumrind, 1991).

Marital stress can also indirectly affect parenting practices because of its effects on children. In one experimental study, young children were observed playing while two adults simulated either a loud, angry argument, or a warm, friendly conversation, elsewhere in the

Figure 10.8 *Marital stress can affect children in various ways— by heightening the likelihood that frustrated parents will act punitively with offspring, by increasing children's distress and anger when they hear parents arguing, and by providing a salient model of conflict within the home. As a consequence, it is not surprising that when parents begin fighting, the rest of the family often erupts in conflict and anger as well.*

room. Children who played with anger in the background were significantly more distressed and aggressive toward other children (Cummings et al., 1985).

Similar reactions have been observed in children at home, suggesting that loud marital conflict increases the distress and misbehavior of the offspring, which in turn, makes authoritative parenting more difficult, since it is hard to be firm yet flexible, responsible yet responsive, when the children are crying, fighting, and out of control. If the children from such a marriage turn out to be adolescents who are depressed or rebellious, this outcome could be caused as much or more by the parents' treatment of each other as by their treatment of the children.

Cultural and Community Context

The cultural and community context also plays a role in parenting patterns, affecting not only parental goals and values but also the appropriateness and efficacy of various parenting styles (Goodnow and Collins, 1990). For example, while the extreme forms of both authoritarian control and permissive freedom tend to be destructive no matter what the community situation, the best balance between those extremes depends, in part, on the stability and safety of the larger society, and also of the particular family (Bronfenbrenner, 1985). In chaotic and dangerous environments, such as the urban ghettos of contemporary America, or in the disequilibrium of an event like divorce, responsible parenthood in a particular family might well require a high level of parental control, whereas the same family in more secure and stable circumstances might find a democratic-indulgent style to be preferable and more effective.

Overall, then, research reveals that child-rearing patterns, and their effects, are moderated by a host of complex and wide-ranging factors: parental actions are imbedded in community and family settings, influenced by children's temperament, age, and gender, shaped by prior parent-child and father-mother interactions, and subject to change when historical and social conditions change. While the authoritative style may represent the ideal for effective parenting, in actual day-to-day child-rearing the ideal balance between freedom and control is not so clear.

Possible Problems

No matter how careful and judicious parents are, preschool children sometimes do and say things that cause worry. They seem too ready to strike out at others, or they retreat into their own imaginary world, or they refuse to play. At what point does normal social immaturity become abnormal psychological development? Of course, there is no simple answer to such a question, because there is no clear dividing line between normal and abnormal behavior. However, developmentalists have learned a great deal about usual and unusual behavior during early childhood, and about how to help those children who have special problems.

Figure 10.9 *These preschoolers show instrumental aggression at its simplest, in which the goal is to obtain possession of the toy. This is different from hostile aggression, in which the goal is to hurt someone rather than just acquiring an object or privilege.*

Aggression

When children first start playing with other children in toddlerhood, they are rarely deliberately aggressive. They might pull a toy away from another child or even push someone over, but they do so to get an object, or remove an obstacle, rather than to hurt. As they become more aware of themselves as separate individuals, however, they become increasingly aware that other people have things they want, or are thwarting their wishes, and they often assert themselves through physical aggression, grabbing, hitting, biting, and so forth. As children grow older, the frequency of deliberate physical aggression increases, normally peaking during the preschool years, and then declining (Parke and Slaby, 1983; Achenbach et al., 1991).

The decline in the frequency of aggression over childhood is particularly apparent for **instrumental aggression,** which involves quarreling over an object, territory, or privilege. **Hostile aggression,** which is an attack against someone rather than a fight about some thing, also becomes less frequent over this period but does not decline as rapidly (Hartup, 1974; Parke and Slaby, 1983). One reason aggression declines is that it is one of the least successful strategies for resolving conflict with a peer, and as children gain increased experience playing with others, they develop alternative, more workable strategies, like negotiation (Shantz, 1987).

These developmental trends are equally apparent in both sexes, although boys are more frequently involved in aggressive encounters than girls at every age—a sex difference that has been found in many cultures (Whiting and Whiting, 1975). Friendship status also affects the probability that conflict will result in aggression. In an observational study of preschoolers, conflict between friends and nonfriends occurred with equal frequency and duration—but conflict between friends was less intense and more often resulted in compromise solutions (Hartup et al., 1988). Another factor related to the frequency of aggressive behavior in preschoolers is the frequency of their exposure to television violence (see A Closer Look, p. 270).

Thus a certain amount of aggression in preschoolers is normal. If two 3-year-olds are playing with a toy and a sudden argument about whose toy it is results in a hit on the head or a slap on the face, that is not unusual. Indeed, a certain amount of aggression is not only normal; it is a healthy sign of self-assertion as well as an occasion for social learning, for the reaction of other children and adults may help children learn about the dynamics of social relations (Hay and Ross, 1982).

Fantasy and Fear

Another characteristic of preschool children is that they sometimes have vivid nightmares, elaborate daydreams, and imaginary friends and enemies. These flights of fancy can worry their parents, but in fact this active fantasy life is normal and healthy. Young children sometimes have difficulty distinguishing reality from fantasy; for them, dreams are believable. A child waking up from a nightmare might insist that there is a rhinoceros under the bed and refuse to be comforted by assurances that rhinoceroses are confined to zoos and, in any case, cannot fit under beds. Instead of trying logic, parents should use actions—perhaps turning on the light, looking under the bed, and announcing that there is nothing there except, of course, dirty socks, broken crayons, and cookie crumbs.

| A CLOSER LOOK | **Television and Aggression** |

According to Nielsen Media Research, in 1990 children between the ages of 2 and 5 watched an average of 29 hours and 19 minutes of television each week, over 2 hours more than the 1984 average (and the highest of any age-group). Such high rates of TV-viewing have raised concern on a number of fronts, from the possible role of television-watching in childhood obesity (see pp. 288–290) to the possible effects of preschoolers' exposure to grossly manipulative advertising. The question of most concern, however, involves the effect that observing violence on television has on children.

Most psychologists now agree that TV violence promotes physical aggression in children, primarily through example. The effect is reciprocal and cumulative: children who watch a lot of television are likely to be more aggressive than children who do not, and children who already tend to be aggressive are likely to watch a lot of TV violence (Friedrich-Cofer and Huston, 1986; Huston et al., 1989).

Preschool children are even more likely to be influenced by violence on television than older children are, because they have an especially hard time differentiating reality from fantasy, and they are uncritical television viewers. In television cartoons, which are designed primarily for young children, physical violence occurs an average of seventeen times per hour. The good guys (Popeye, Dinoriders, Teenage Mutant Ninja Turtles) do as much hitting, shooting, and kicking as the bad guys, yet the consequences of their violence are made comic or sanitized, never being portrayed as bloody or evil. In cartoonland, demolition, whether of people or things, is just plain fun.

A related concern over the cumulative effects of watching repeated violence on television is that children will become desensitized to the fact and consequences of violence, a hypothesis with experimental support (Parke and Slaby, 1983). Children who see a lot of violence on television may thus become more passive when viewing actual violence in real life and may be more likely to regard violence as a "normal" part of everyday life. Ironically, although the negative impact of TV violence is now accepted by social scientists as fact, not hypothesis, violence actually increased in American children's television programs during the 1980s (Pearl, 1987), at the same time that many current TV heros are more hostile, critical, and aggressive than those of past years (Pena et al., 1990).

A related criticism is that even the best television does more harm than good, because it robs children of play time and tends to cut off social communication, which, as we have seen, is essential for enhancing the social skills that children must develop. In contrast to social play, television watching is an essentially passive, noninteractive process, even when others are present.

What can parents do? Some professionals, in fact, recommend no television at all for preschoolers. Others suggest that parents watch with their children, so that they can monitor or criticize the content of television shows. Many parents have found it easier to impose a simple rule—TV only an hour a day, or only before dinner, or only on Saturday—than to try to prohibit television completely or censor each program (Sarlo et al., 1988). Others try to sensitize their children to the actual consequences of violence portrayed on television. Although there is no clear consensus on how parents should control their children's TV-viewing, one thing is certain: no psychologist who has studied the effects of children's television thinks preschoolers should watch whatever and whenever they want.

In addition, because young children focus on physical appearance, many of them are genuinely frightened at the sight of a friend wearing a Halloween costume or of a parent pretending to be a lion. They also worry about bodily wholeness and can be quite troubled when they see a person who has an obvious physical abnormality. In addition, everyday objects that make things disappear—the toilet bowl, vacuum cleaner, or bathtub drain—may also seem ominous to many small children, because they wonder if these devices might make them disappear, too.

Because their thinking is so centered on subjective experience, young children can imagine something and then act as though what they have imagined is real. For instance, many children create imaginary playmates, who serve as companions for games, reassurance in scary situations, and sometimes as scapegoats for mischief or accidents. Preschool children with such creative imaginations are neither liars nor disturbed; they are simply showing a normal characteristic of preoperational thought.

Figure 10.10 *Preschoolers' inability to disentangle the real from the imaginary means that they can become genuinely frightened by movie scenes, sometimes with unexpected results. For example, after seeing the Wicked Stepmother poison Snow White, a 3-year-old might refuse to eat apples or have nightmares about a harmless old lady who lives nearby.*

Distinguishing Fact and Fantasy

While preschool children typically have vivid imaginations, and while their grasp of logic is not solid, it is important not to exaggerate their irrationality. For example, careful questioning of a group of British 4- and 6-year-olds found that most of them could clearly distinguish between real people and monsters, ghosts, or witches. At the same time, many of them were not positive that such imagined characters might not become real under certain circumstances (Harris et al., 1991). Given this kind of mind set, it is important that adults not try to scare the preschooler into good behavior with fantasy untruths: many children, when warned by an adult that a witch might snatch them or a dog might eat them up, have nightmares about the possibility.

The ability of young children to distinguish between fantasy and truth has become of considerable legal interest when children are called as witnesses in court cases. To counteract the idea that children are unreliable witnesses, some child advocates have attempted to promote the idea that "children don't lie," at least not in court. In most circumstances the essence of that idea is accurate; young children generally have a firm enough grasp of reality to report accurately what they have experienced or observed, and it is a rare child that can make up elaborate and plausible fantasies and report them as fact. They are particularly unlikely to report details of sexual molestation, for instance, if nothing of the kind occurred.

At the same time, however, it must be acknowledged that preschool children are highly suggestible: if a questioner, like an abuse investigator, intentionally or inadvertently puts ideas and phrases into the child's mind, and reinforces a particular version of events in subsequent interviews, over time the child may come to believe and report the "suggested" events as the actual events (Doris, 1991).

Serious Psychological Problems

At every part of the life span, certain behaviors that are normal can also be signs of serious psychological difficulty. This is true for the aggression, fantasies, and fears that every normal preschooler expresses to some degree.

Antisocial Behavior

As we have seen, some aggression is a normal part of self-assertion, especially if the attack follows a threat or obvious provocation. However, if a preschool child is unusually aggressive, this may reflect emotional problems, perhaps deriving from difficulties at home. Patterson (1982), for example, found that parents of very aggressive preschoolers either overuse physical aggression themselves or have given up trying to control the child's aggression. The most frightening evidence of this comes from children known to be physically abused. Even at age 2, such children typically are not only more aggressive than other children, but they are also aggressive in contexts in which other children would not be. In addition, aggressive children tend to have deficient social problem-solving skills, misinterpreting neutral or even positive social cues as threatening and creating a hostile environment for themselves that heightens their tendency to act aggressively (Mueller and Silverman, 1989; Dodge et al., 1990).

Thus, while a show of force is a normal response to provocation in a 3-year-old, this does not mean that adults should simply ignore preschool aggression entirely. During early childhood, children need to learn how and when to modify their aggressive impulses, partly because, by school age, aggressive children are often decidedly unpopular with peers as well as with teachers (Patterson, 1982). In addition, if a pattern of aggression continues into the later years of school, it may be a precursor of delinquency and adult criminality (Rutter and Garmezy, 1983).

For many reasons, the unusually aggressive child needs help to learn the social skills that will temper his or her outbursts. Obviously, if the cause is hostile parents, the family needs help as well.

Phobias

A **phobia** is an irrational fear that becomes so powerful and overwhelming that it interferes with the person's normal life. Many preschoolers have occasional phobias, in part because their active imaginations and imperfect grasp of reality make them vulnerable, especially after watching a television program about, for instance, monsters from the deep, or seeing an adult who is frightened of some particular nonthreatening experience, such as a trip to the dentist or a visit to the zoo (Rutter and Garmezy, 1983). While some common childish phobias—of bumblebees or tidal waves, for instance—are not crippling, others are much more pervasive, preventing such healthy and needed experiences as playing outside, separating from mother to attend preschool, or even going to sleep without being terrified.

As with older children and adults, bringing the phobic child to a gradual, step-by-step familiarity with the feared object or event in a reassuring context is usually the best answer. Ridicule and forced exposure only increase the power of the fear. A child who is terrified of dogs should never be told that only babies are afraid of dogs, nor should a child who is afraid of the water be thrown into it so that he or she will "get over" the fear. In most cases, phobias such as these tend to diminish over time, with or without specific treatment.

Gender Roles and Stereotypes

An important feature of self-understanding during the play years is the child's developing understanding of gender roles and personal gender identity. As we saw in Chapters 6 and 8, gender preferences and play patterns emerge early in childhood. Not surprisingly, preschoolers have quite remarkable ideas about gender. Consider this account by Sandra Bem (1989), a leading researcher of gender identity, concerning a day when her young son Jeremy

> naively decided to wear barrettes to nursery school. Several times that day, another little boy insisted that Jeremy must be a girl because "only girls wear barrettes." After repeatedly asserting that "wearing barrettes doesn't matter; being a boy means having a penis and testicles," Jeremy finally pulled down his pants as a way of making his point more convincingly. The boy was not impressed. He simply said, "Everybody has a penis; only girls wear barrettes."

Children learn about gender very early (Huston, 1985). Most 2-year-olds know whether they are boys or girls, and identify strangers as mommies or daddies. By age 3, children have a rudimentary understanding of the permanence of their own sex and can consistently apply gender labels (Kuhn et al., 1978). Further, children's behavior acknowledges traditional distinctions between boys and girls at a very early age. By age 2, children prefer to play with gender-typed toys (dolls versus trucks) (Weinraub et al., 1984) and at age 3, they enact gender-typed roles (nurses versus soldiers) (Eisenberg-Berg et al., 1979; Huston, 1983, 1985; O'Brien et al., 1983). At these young ages, children also have definite ideas of typical male and female behavior and misbehavior, believing that girls are more likely than boys to clean the house and to "talk a lot" and that boys are more likely than girls to mow the lawn and to hit others (Kuhn et al., 1978; Weinraub et al., 1984).

By age 6, these notions become full-blown prejudices, when most children (even those from feminist homes) express stereotypic ideas of what each sex should do, wear, or feel (Huston, 1983). Indeed, by age 4, preschool girls and boys are quite judgmental about their peers' choice of gender-appropriate toys and play patterns (Roopnarine, 1984). The boy who wants to help the girls dress the dolls or the girl who wants to be one of the space warriors is likely to be soundly criticized by his or her friends.

Three Theories of Gender-Role Development

We have already discussed the nature-nurture issue several times, and you are well aware that developmentalists disagree about what proportion of observed sex differences is biological—perhaps a matter of hormones, of brain structures, or of body size and muscular distribution—and what proportion is environmental. However, even for differences that seem most closely related to nurture, theorists hypothesize various reasons for their existence; specifically, they ask: What is the origin of gender-role preferences and stereotypes that children develop during the preschool years? Three of the major psychological theories have somewhat different answers.

Psychoanalytic Theories

Freud (1938) called the period from about age 3 to 7 the **phallic stage,** because he believed its center of focus is the penis. At about age 3 or 4, said Freud, a boy becomes aware of his penis, begins to masturbate, and develops sexual feelings about his mother, who has always been an important love object for him. These feelings make him jealous of his father—so jealous, in fact, that, according to Freud, every son secretly wants to replace his father. Freud called this phenomenon the **Oedipus complex,** after Oedipus, son of a king in Greek mythology. Abandoned as an infant and raised in a distant kingdom, Oedipus later returned to his birthplace, and, not realizing who they were, killed his father and married his mother. When he discovered what he had done, he blinded himself in a spasm of guilt.

According to Freud, little boys feel horribly guilty for having the feelings and thoughts that characterize the Oedipus complex and imagine that their father will inflict terrible punishments on them if he ever finds out about these thoughts. They cope with this guilt and fear by means of **identification,** a defense mechanism through which people imagine themselves to be like a person more powerful than themselves. In a sense, if they cannot replace the father, young boys strive to be *like* the father. As part of their identification with their father, boys copy their father's masculine behavior and adopt his moral standards. Through this process, they develop their superego, to control the forbidden impulses of the id (see page 39).

Freud offered two overlapping descriptions of the phallic stage as it occurs in little girls. One form, the **Electra complex,** follows the reverse pattern of the Oedipus complex: the little girl wants to get rid of her mother and become intimate with her father. In the other version, the little girl becomes jealous of boys because they have a penis, an emotion called **penis envy.** Somehow the girl decides that her mother is to blame for this state of affairs, so she becomes angry at her and decides the next best thing to having a penis of her own is to become sexually attractive so that someone with a penis, preferably her father, will love her (Freud, 1965; originally published in 1933). (See A Closer Look, p. 275.)

In both versions, the consequences of this stage are the same for girls as for boys: guilt and fear, which are resolved by adoption of gender-appropriate behavior and the parent's moral code.

Learning Theories

Learning theorists take another view about gender-role development during early childhood. They believe that virtually all role patterns are learned, rather than inborn, and that parents, teachers, and society are responsible for whatever gender-role ideas and behaviors the child demonstrates.

Preschool children, according to learning theory, are reinforced for behaving in the ways deemed appropriate for their sex and punished for behaving inappropriately. In some ways, research bears this out. Parents, peers, and teachers are all more likely to reward "gender-appropriate" behavior than "gender-inappropriate behavior" (Huston, 1983; Langlois and Downs, 1980). This kind of learning may be strongest within sex-segregated peer groups, where, beginning in the early preschool years, children acquire gender-typical play styles and social skills, including strategies for influencing others (Maccoby, 1988, 1989).

A CLOSER LOOK   Berger and Freud

As a woman, and as a mother of four daughters, I have always regarded Freud's theory of female sexual development as ridiculous, not to mention antifemale. I am not alone in this opinion. Psychologists generally agree that Freud's explanation of female sexual and moral development is one of the weaker parts of his theory, reflecting the values of middle-class Victorian society at the turn of the century more than any universal pattern. Many female psychoanalysts (e.g., Horney, 1967; Klein, 1957; Lerner, 1978) are particularly critical of Freud's idea of penis envy. They believe that girls envy, not the male's sexual organ, but the higher status the male is generally accorded. They also suggest that boys may experience a corresponding emotion in the form of womb and breast envy, wishing that they could have babies and suckle them.

However, my own view of Freud's theory as complete nonsense has been modified somewhat by the following experiences with my four daughters when each was in the age range of Freud's phallic stage. The first "Electra episode" occurred in a conversation with my oldest daughter, Bethany, when she was 4 or so.

Bethany: When I grow up, I'm going to marry Daddy.
I: *But Daddy's married to me.*
Bethany: That's all right. When I grow up, you'll probably be dead.
I: *(Determined to stick up for myself) Daddy's older than me, so when I'm dead, he'll probably be dead, too.*
Bethany: That's O.K. I'll marry him when he gets born again. [Our family's religious beliefs, incidentally, do not include reincarnation.]

At this point, I couldn't think of a good reply. Bethany must have seen my face fall and taken pity on me.

Bethany: Don't worry Mommy. After you get born again, you can be our baby.

The second episode was also in a conversation, this time with my daughter Rachel, when she was about 5.

Rachel: When I get married, I'm going to marry Daddy.
I: *Daddy's already married to me.*
Rachel: (With the joy of having discovered a wonderful solution) Then we can have a double wedding!

The third episode was considerably more graphic. It took the form of a "valentine" left on my husband's pillow by my daughter Elissa, who was about 8 at the time. It is reproduced in the next column.

Finally, by the time my youngest daughter, Sarah, turned 5, she also expressed the desire to marry my husband. Her responses to my statement that she couldn't marry him because he is already married to me reveals one of the disadvantages of not being able to ban TV in our household: "Oh yes, a man can have two wives. I saw it on television."

I am not the only feminist developmentalist to find Freud's theories on this matter surprisingly perceptive. Nancy Datan (1986) writes about the Oedipal conflict: "I have a son who was once five years old. From that day to this, I have never thought Freud mistaken."

Obviously, these bits of "evidence" do not prove that Freud was correct. But Freud's description of the phallic stage seems not to be as bizarre as it first appears to be.

Theodore Lidz (1976), a respected developmental psychiatrist, offers a plausible explanation of the process evident in my daughters and in many other children. Lidz believes that all children must go through an Oedipal "transition," overcoming "the intense bonds to their mothers that were essential to their satisfactory pre-Oedipal development." As part of this process, children imagine becoming an adult and, quite logically, taking the place of the adult of their own sex whom they know best, their father or mother. This idea must be dispelled before the sexual awakening of early adolescence, otherwise an "incestuous bond" will threaten the nuclear family, prevent the child's extrafamilial socialization, and block his or her emergence as an adult. According to Lidz, the details of the Oedipal transition vary from family to family, but successful desexualization of parent-child love is essential for healthy maturity.

Figure 10.11 *Most parents derive considerable pleasure from children's efforts to imitate them in gender-appropriate ways, whether it is shaving for boys or using make-up for girls. Parental modeling— and the approval parents provide for children's imitative efforts—are important influences on sex-role socialization, especially for preschoolers who are learning the traits and characteristics associated with their sex.*

Interestingly, boys are criticized more than girls for wanting to play with "gender-inappropriate" toys. Even between ages 1 and 5, boys are discouraged from wanting to play with dolls (Fagot, 1978; Robinson and Morris, 1986). Furthermore, fathers are more likely to expect their girls to be "feminine" and their boys to be "masculine" than mothers are. As we saw in Chapter 7, fathers are more gentle with their daughters and are more likely to engage in rough-and-tumble play with their sons. Thus, in American society at least, gender-role conformity seems to be especially important for males.

Modeling

Social-learning theorists (Bandura, 1977; Mischel, 1970, 1979; Sears et al., 1965) say that children learn much of their gender and moral behavior by observing other people, especially people whom they perceive as nurturing, powerful, and similar to themselves. For all these reasons, parents are important models during childhood, although models in the neighborhood, at school or day care, and in the popular media are also very influential.

Social-learning theorists are not surprised when preschool children seem precociously and dogmatically conscious of gender roles, even when the parents espouse less traditional views. In this case, actions speak louder than words, and most adults are more gender-stereotyped, in their behaviors as well as self-concept, during the years when their children are young than at any other time in the life span (Feldman et al., 1981; Gutmann, 1975). Imagine a typical modern child-free couple who try to avoid traditional gender roles, both of them being employed and both sharing the housework. Then the wife becomes pregnant. The most likely sequel is that she will take a maternity leave, quit her job, or work part-time. This traditional pattern is reinforced by the biological fact that only the woman can breast-feed, the sociological fact that relatives and friends generally expect the woman to provide most infant care, and the economic fact that the man's salary is usually higher than the woman's. If the wife stays home, it is likely that she will do more than half the housework. If she does go back to work full-time, typically she will find another woman to care for her child, either at home or in a day-care center. In addition, influences from the macrosystem, including everything from who runs for president, to who does what in television commercials, to which characters take the initiative in children's books, teach children those behaviors that are considered gender-appropriate (Barnett, 1986; Huston, 1983).

Cognitive Theories

In explaining gender identity and gender-role development, cognitive theorists focus on children's understanding of gender and male-female differences, and on how children's changing perceptions of gender motivate their efforts to behave consistently with their gender-role. Two theories of gender identity have been proposed by cognitive theorists.

According to *cognitive-developmental theory* (Kohlberg, 1966, 1969), young preschoolers' understanding of gender is limited by their belief that sex differences depend on differences in appearance or behavior rather than on biology. Thus boys believe that they could become mommies; girls think they could be daddies; and children of both sexes think boys would be girls if they wore dresses and girls would be boys if they cut their hair very short. It is not until after age 4 or 5 that children realize that they are permanently male or female on the basis of their unchanging biology. This realization, called **gender constancy,** motivates, in turn, their efforts to learn about gender roles and to adopt appropriate gender-role behavior.

There is strong evidence for the first part of this view. Kohlberg and Ullian (1974), for example, interviewed boys and girls between the ages of 3 and 18 and found that, by age 6, children understood that sex is a permanent characteristic and were pleased to be whatever sex they were. However, researchers have failed to confirm that an awareness of gender constancy underlies children's knowledge of gender-role behavior or their motivation to adopt appropriate behavior. Instead, children have a surprisingly sophisticated understanding of gender roles and behave in many sex-typed ways long before they have acquired an awareness of gender constancy (Fagot, 1985; Huston, 1985).

Because of this, *gender-schema theory* (Bem, 1981, 1984; Martin and Halverson, 1981) argues that young children's motivation to behave in gender-appropriate ways derives instead from their **gender schemas,** that is, the ways they organize their knowledge about people in terms of gender-based categories and evaluations. A gender schema might dictate that women care for young children, for example, or that men do heavy labor. Children acquire gender schemas quite early in life because our society makes many gender-related distinctions between people that young children can easily comprehend. Thus as soon as children start to become aware of gender schemas and can accurately label themselves as male or female, they try to conform to these schemas and use them to evaluate others' behavior. In support of this view, Levy and Carter (1989) found that children's accuracy in attributing gender stereotypes to others was related to development in their knowledge of gender schemas.

In a sense, each of the theories we have discussed points to different, but important, ingredients in gender-role development in early childhood. To psychoanalytic theorists, the emotional attachments to parents and identification with the same-sex parent within the family are most significant. Learning theorists, by contrast, emphasize reinforcement and modeling processes that occur not just at home but in all the child's social environments. To cognitive theorists, in turn, the child's developing understanding of gender schemas are paramount, together with the characteristics that constitute these schemas in society at large. As we have seen, these theories vary also in the extent to which parents—who may or may not emphasize traditional gender roles at home—are viewed as the most significant influences on the gender-role development of their offspring. In this respect, learning and cognitive theorists point out what most parents themselves acknowledge: that there is an overabundance of sources outside the family through which children learn about expected gender-role behavior.

Figure 10.12 *As social-learning theorists point out, not all gender-role learning occurs at home, and sometimes children acquire, from peers or the media, gender stereotypes that parents oppose. This boy is adding to his gender schemas concepts of masculinity that may conflict with his parents' efforts to encourage nontraditional portrayals of masculine roles.*

A Different Goal: Androgyny

In recent years, many developmentalists, and many parents as well, have encouraged the concept of androgyny. As a biological term, of course, "androgyny" refers to an organism's having both male and female sexual characteristics. As developmentalists use the term, **androgyny** refers to a per-

Figure 10.13 *This daughter's evident delight in "driving" her daddy's fire truck mirrors her father's pleasure in her. It is worth noting, however, that our culture generally allows greater sex-role latitude to girls than to boys. Would this father be equally pleased if his son showed a strong interest in ballet?*

son's having a balance of what are commonly regarded as "male" and "female" psychological characteristics. The idea behind the emphasis on androgyny is to break through the restrictiveness of traditional gender roles and to encourage the individual to define himself or herself primarily as a human being, rather than as a male or female. An additional goal has been to counter the misconception that masculinity and femininity are opposites.

Several measures of androgyny have been developed in which a person chooses which adjectives are closest to describing his or her own personality (Bem, 1974; Spence and Helmreich, 1978). For instance, someone who scores high in instrumental characteristics such as aggression, dominance, competitiveness, and activity, and low in expressive characteristics like gentleness, kindness, emotionality, and warmth, would be rated as typically masculine; someone with opposite scores would be rated typically feminine. A person who scored high in both sets of characteristics would be considered androgynous.

Thus androgynous men and women share many of the same personality characteristics, instead of following the traditional gender-role patterns. For instance, traditional males rate significantly higher than traditional females on a personality trait labeled "dominant-ambitious," but androgynous males and females score about the same, because the men see themselves as less dominant than the traditional male does while the women see themselves as more dominant than the traditional female does (Wiggins and Holzmuller, 1978). Androgynous people are nurturing as well as independent and try to be neither unemotional nor passive. They are more flexible in their sex roles, able to display the best qualities of both of the traditional stereotypes.

Certainly in contemporary society, androgyny seems an admirable and highly functional goal. Yet comprehensive longitudinal research on the development and effects of an androgynous persona is lacking, and the research that is available shows mixed results—or at least different effects at different points in the life span. Some of the first studies on androgyny showed that androgynous individuals are generally more competent and have a higher sense of self-esteem than people who follow traditional gender-role behavior (Spence and Helmreich, 1978). And while more recent research has generally found that androgynous college students, particularly, have higher self-esteem than more traditional young adults, at certain other stages of life, this does not seem to be the case. At age 16, for instance, those who consider themselves relatively traditional for their sex also tend to be high in self-esteem. This is particularly true for boys of average intellectual achievement, who take pride in having masculine qualities and in not having feminine ones (Allgood et al., 1991).

Another time when traditional values may foster self-esteem is when parents are raising young children. In her research on parenting styles, Diana Baumrind found that traditional parents—relatively nurturant and emotional mothers and relatively strict and less emotional fathers—often did a better job of child-rearing than more androgynous parents, and were more pleased with themselves. The reason suggested by Baumrind is that they tend to be more child-centered: in such families all the needs of the children are met because both parents value raising the next generation and know what is expected of them to accomplish the task (Baumrind, 1982).

Overall, the fact that gender awareness and gender-role distinctions develop so early in a young child's life suggests that on some level young children welcome the simplistic clarity of a male-female dichotomy and resist the androgynous ideal. In fact, Sandra Bem (1985), one of the designers of an androgyny scale, recognizes that ideas about gender differences are useful to help young children organize their perceptions of the adult world. The problem comes, if at all, when children and their parents remain rigid in applying these schemas, causing the fixed stereotyping to stifle the full development of the child or the adult. Thus the child's gender-role concepts, like the child's definition of selfhood, mode of play, use of aggression, and all the other themes of this chapter, should change with exposure and maturity. These changes help the preschool child gradually become ready for the next stage of life, the school years, which are presented in the next trio of chapters.

SUMMARY

The Self and the Social World

1. As children develop a more clearly defined idea of self, they become more confident and eager to take on new activities. According to Erikson, the accomplishments of this age help to resolve the crisis of initiative versus guilt.

2. An increasing sense of self-understanding helps children to increase their social understanding and to become more skilled in their relationships with others.

3. Playing with other children prepares preschoolers for the demands of school and the social relationships they will later develop. In particular, it requires them to take responsibility for maintaining harmonious social interaction through sharing and reciprocation. Dramatic play teaches social skills and permits children to explore social roles, examine personal concerns, and learn to cooperate.

4. Children's relationships with their brothers and sisters are unique and different from relationships with parents and peers. Although siblings may quarrel, they are also more likely to show each other more nurturance and cooperation. One of the most important factors in shaping the relationship between siblings is the differential treatment they may receive from their parents.

Parenting

5. Parent-child interaction is complex, with no simple answers about the best way to raise a child. However, in general, authoritative parents, who are warm and loving but willing to set and enforce reasonable limits, have children who are happy, self-confident, and successful. Authoritarian families tend to produce aggressive children. Children from permissive families often lack self-control.

6. Although parenting style is an important element in shaping a child's development, it is only one of many, and its importance should not be overestimated. Often children shape the parents as much as they are shaped by them. Other factors, such as children's changing needs, the nature of the parents' relationship to each other, and the cultural and community context affect the parenting style of any given family.

Possible Problems

7. Normal preschool children sometimes use physical force to get what they want. They may also have vivid fantasies that they think are real. These behaviors are to be expected in a child who is trying to cope with the many ideas and problems of social interaction but whose thinking remains immature.

8. Some children show signs of more serious psychological problems, such as antisocial behavior and phobias. Children who are prone to antisocial behavior need help developing the social skills to control their outbursts. Children who suffer phobias generally can overcome their fear through gradual, unforced exposure to whatever is causing them.

Gender Roles and Stereotypes

9. While all psychologists agree that children begin to learn gender roles and gender identity during early childhood, they disagree about how this occurs.

10. Freud believed that during the phallic stage, the fears and fantasies produced by the Oedipus and Electra complexes lead to adoption of gender-appropriate behavior and development of the superego, both through identification with the same-sex parent.

11. Learning theorists think children learn expected gender-role behavior from the reinforcement they receive for acting appropriately, and from the punishment they get for behaving inappropriately. The example set by their parents, as well as cultural role models, is also important.

12. Cognitive theorists remind us that young children are slowly constructing an understanding of gender. As their comprehension of sex differences increases, they are motivated to behave in gender-appropriate ways.

13. According to the goal of androgyny, individuals who are less rigid in their gender roles and seem to have a balance of both male and female characteristics tend to be more confident and have a higher sense of self-esteem than those who follow more traditional gender-role behavior. In many ways, children seem to resist this goal, preferring the simplicity of a fairly strict male-female dichotomy.

KEY TERMS

initiative versus guilt (256)
mastery motivation (257)
authoritarian parenting (264)
permissive parenting (264)
authoritative parenting (264)
democratic-indulgent
    parenting (265)
rejecting-neglecting
    parenting (265)
traditional parenting (265)
instrumental aggression (269)

hostile aggression (269)
phobia (272)
phallic stage (274)
Oedipus complex (274)
identification (274)
Electra complex (274)
penis envy (274)
gender constancy (277)
gender schemas (277)
androgyny (277)

KEY QUESTIONS

1. How does children's increasing self-knowledge affect their relationship with others?

2. Why is social play important?

3. As children grow older, how does their dramatic play change?

4. What are the three basic patterns of parenting?

5. What influences contribute to the complexity of parenting?

6. What word best describes sibling relationships, and why?

7. What pattern does aggressive behavior in preschoolers typically follow?

8. How does the preschooler's stage of cognitive development affect the fantasies and fears that may occur at this stage of development?

9. What are the essential disagreements among psychoanalytic, cognitive, and learning theorists about the origin of gender roles during early childhood?

10. How would androgynous individuals describe their personality traits?

Biosocial Development

Brain and Nervous System

The brain continues to develop faster than any other part of the body, attaining 90 percent of its adult weight by the time the child is 5 years old. Myelination proceeds at different rates in various areas of the brain. This differential neurological development has some bearing on the child's readiness for certain types of activity.

Motor Abilities

The child becomes stronger, and body proportions become more adultlike. Large body movements, such as running and jumping, improve dramatically. Fine motor skills, such as writing and drawing, develop more slowly. Gender differences in motor skills become apparent.

Cognitive Development

Cognitive Skills

The child becomes increasingly able to use mental representation and symbols, such as words, to "figure things out." However, the child's ideas about the world are sometimes illogical. Throughout this period, children begin to develop a theory of mind, as they take into account the ideas and emotions of others. Social interaction is both a cause and a consequence of this cognitive advancement.

Language

Language abilities develop rapidly; by the age of 6, the average child knows 14,000 words and demonstrates extensive grammatical knowledge. Children also learn to adjust their communication to their audience, and use language to help themselves learn. Specific contexts affect the particulars of what, and how much, children say and understand.

Psychosocial Development

Emotions and Personality Development

According to Erikson, increased levels of energy at this stage enable the child to boldly and exuberantly initiate new activities, especially if the child is praised for his or her endeavors. The child's ability to interact with others depends on a well-developed sense of self. As children's social and cognitive skills develop, they engage in increasingly complex and imaginative types of play, sometimes by themselves and, increasingly, with others.

Parent-Child Interaction

As children become more independent and try to exercise more control over their environment, the parents' role in supervising the child's activities becomes more difficult. Some parenting styles and some forms of discipline are more effective than others in encouraging the child to develop both autonomy and self-control. At the same time, parenting styles are influenced by cultural and community standards, various environmental pressures, and the characteristics of the individual child.

The School Years

PART IV

If someone asked you to pick the best years of the entire life span, you might choose the years from 7 to 11 and defend your choice persuasively. To begin with, biosocial development is usually smooth and unremarkable, making it easy to master dozens of new skills.

With regard to cognitive development, most children are able to learn quickly and think logically, providing that the topic is not too abstract. Moral reasoning has reached that state where right seems clearly distinguished from wrong, with none of the ambiguities that complicate moral issues for adolescents and adults.

Finally, the social world of middle childhood seems perfect, for most school-age children think their parents are helpful, their teachers fair, and their friends loyal. The future seems filled with promise—at least most of the time it does.

However, school and friendships are so important at this age that two common events can seem crushing: failure in school and rejection by peers. Some lucky children escape these problems; others have sufficient self-confidence or family support to weather them when they arise; and some leave middle childhood with painful memories, feeling inadequate, incompetent, and inferior for the rest of their lives.

The next three chapters celebrate the joys, and commemorate the occasional tragedies, of middle childhood.

CHAPTER 11

The School Years: Biosocial Development

For most children, the school years are a time of stable growth and notable improvement in physical skills. For some, unfortunately, it is a time when certain types of disabilities become more pronounced in their consequences. In this chapter, we will examine the physical changes and variations that are characteristic of middle childhood, as well as certain difficulties that sometimes occur in biosocial development during this period. The following questions reflect some of the topics we will consider in this chapter:

How is a child's biosocial development affected by genetic and cultural patterns?

What are the effects of being overweight on a school-age child?

Which games and sports are best suited to the skills of children in middle childhood?

What kinds of learning disabilities appear in middle childhood, and how do they affect school achievement?

What are the true symptoms of attention-deficit hyperactivity disorder, and what are some of the methods used to treat this disorder?

Compared to that of other periods of the life span, biosocial development in middle childhood seems, on the whole, to be relatively smooth and uneventful in a number of ways. For one, disease and death are rarer during these years than during any other period. For another, most children master new physical skills (everything from tree-climbing to roller-blading) easily and without much adult instruction, provided their bodies are sufficiently mature and they have an opportunity to practice these skills. In addition, sex differences in physical development and ability are minimal, and sexual urges seem to be submerged. Certainly when physical development during these years is compared with the rapid and dramatic changes that occur during infancy and adolescence, middle childhood seems a period of relative tranquility. Now let us look at some of the specifics, as well as at some of the special needs, that may emerge during this period.

Size and Shape

Children grow more slowly during middle childhood than they did earlier or than they will in adolescence. Worldwide, the typical well-nourished child gains about 5 pounds (2¼ kilograms) and 2½ inches (6 centimeters) per year, and by age 10 weighs about 70 pounds (32 kilograms) and measures 54 inches (137 centimeters) (Lowrey, 1986).

During these years children become slimmer than in earlier years, as they grow taller and their body proportions change. In addition, muscles become stronger, enabling the average 10-year-old, for instance, to throw a ball twice as far as the average 6-year-old. The capacity of the lungs also increases, so with each passing year children are able to run faster and exercise longer than before.

Variations in Physique

In some regions of the world, most of the variation in children's height and weight is caused by malnutrition, with wealthier children being several inches taller than their contemporaries from the other side of town—whether the town is Hong Kong, Rio de Janeiro, or New Delhi. But most children in developed countries get enough food during middle childhood to grow as tall as their genes allow.

Genetic factors and nutrition affect not only size but rate of maturation as well. This is particularly noticeable at the end of middle childhood, as some 10- and 11-year-olds begin to undergo the changes of puberty, and may find that they are ahead of their peers not only in height but in strength and endurance as well. Among Americans, those of African descent tend to mature somewhat more quickly (as measured by bone growth and loss of baby teeth) and to have longer legs than those of European descent, who, in turn, tend to be maturationally ahead of those with Asian ancestors.

While it may be comforting for parents and teachers to know that healthy children come in all shapes and sizes, it is not always comforting to the children themselves. In elementary school, children compare themselves with one another, and those who are "behind" their classmates in areas related to physical maturation may feel deficient. Physical development during this period even affects friendships, which are based partly on physical appearance and competence (Hartup, 1983). Consequently, children who look "different," or who are noticeably lacking in physical skills, often become lonely and unhappy.

Childhood Obesity

One difference in size that, from middle childhood on, can seriously affect emotional as well as physical well-being is **obesity.** Although the point at which an overweight child qualifies as "obese" depends partly on the child's body type, partly on the proportion of fat to muscle, and partly on the culture's standards on this question, most experts define obesity as body weight that is more than 20 percent greater than average for one's age, sex, and body size (Epstein, 1985) (see Table 11.1). By this criterion, at least 10 percent of American children are sufficiently overweight to need slimming down (Grinker, 1981; Lamb, 1984).

Figure 11.1 *Chronological age accounts for differences in the physical size of school-age children, but so also do hereditary differences. Each of these fifth-graders is close to his or her 10th birthday, but their variability in height and weight means that, at this age, some are more likely to excel at athletic competition than others.*

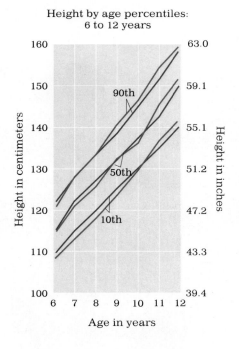

Height by age percentiles:
6 to 12 years

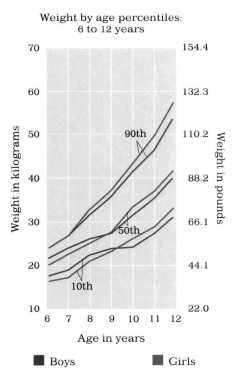

Weight by age percentiles:
6 to 12 years

■ Boys   ■ Girls

Figure 11.2 *As you can see, growth is quite steady throughout middle childhood, except for those girls in the 90th percentile (the heaviest 10 percent). Typically, they begin puberty at about age 10, which accounts for their increasing rate of weight gain at ages 11 and 12.*

Obesity is a physical and medical problem at any stage of life, for the obese person runs a greater risk of serious illness (Lamb, 1984). In children, orthopedic and respiratory problems are especially associated with obesity (Neumann, 1983). It is often a psychological problem as well. Children begin developing negative beliefs about fat people even as preschoolers (Fritz and Wetherbee, 1982), but it is not known if being fat themselves affects their self-concept. In middle childhood, however, fat children are teased, picked on, and rejected. They know they are overweight, and they are more likely to experience diminished self-esteem, depression, and behavior problems as a result (Israel and Shapiro, 1985; Strauss et al., 1985). Obese children have fewer friends than other children (Strauss et al., 1985), and when they are accepted in a peer group, it is often at a high price, such as answering to nicknames like "Tubby" or "Blubber," and having to constantly suffer jokes about their shape. A vicious cycle of rejection, isolation, and low self-esteem leading to inactivity, compensatory overeating, and, in turn, to further rejection by peers, may cause obesity to persist in children (Neumann, 1983).

Help for Overweight Children

Clearly, an overweight child needs emotional support for a bruised self-concept, as well as help in losing weight. But reducing is difficult, and psychological encouragement is often scarce, partly because obesity is usually fostered by entrenched family attitudes and habits that promote a fattening diet and, most likely, a sedentary lifestyle (see A Life-Span Perspective, p. 288). Thus changes in family patterns, as well as in the child's food intake, are an essential to effective treatment.

Obese children sometimes try crash diets, which make them irritable, listless, and even sick—adding to their psychological problems without accomplishing much long-term weight loss. To make matters worse, strenuous dieting during childhood can be physically harmful, since cutting down on protein or calcium could hinder important brain and bone growth (Winick, 1975). Unless a child is seriously obese, in which case careful weight reduction is in order, nutritionists generally recommend stabilizing the weight of overweight children to allow them to "grow out" of their fat. In some cases, a family-based treatment program involving nutrition education and exercise may be recommended (Epstein, 1985). In the case of extremely obese children, a family-intervention process similar to that for severely malnourished children may be necessary, for excessive overfeeding of a child is often a sign of family depression and disorganization (Christoffel et al., 1989).

The best way to get children to lose weight is to increase their physical activity. However, exercise is hard for overweight children, for they are not often chosen to play on teams, and they are likely to be teased and rebuffed when they try to join in group activities.

Parents and teachers can help overweight children to do the kinds of exercise in which their size is not a disadvantage, such as walking to school rather than taking the bus, or doing sit-ups at home. Parents can also exercise with their children, not only making activity easier and providing a good model, but bolstering the child's self-confidence as well. Children can share responsibility by monitoring their eating, recreation, and other activities related to their weight. The importance of changing the child's eating

Figure 11.3 *Even if they join in physical activities and are accepted by their peers, overweight children often feel painfully self-conscious, especially when the activity requires donning a costume that calls more attention to one's appearance.*

and exercising patterns is apparent when one realizes that if the childhood weight problem reaches the point that the child is obese, and continues at that level throughout the childhood years, it is likely to last a lifetime (Grinker, 1981; Lamb, 1984). Treatment of obesity may be more successful early in life before the habits and attitudes contributing to weight gain have become well established. Thus, parents of the obese child who do nothing about the child's weight problem are jeopardizing the health as well as the happiness of their child in later years.

A LIFE-SPAN PERSPECTIVE

Causes of Obesity

Typically, no one explanation suffices for a particular instance of obesity; rather, the problem is generally created through the interaction of a number of influences (Grinker, 1981; Lowrey, 1986). These influences begin in infancy, continue through childhood, and remain influential in adulthood.

1. *Heredity.* Body type, including the amount and distribution of fat, as well as height and bone structure, is inherited. So are individual differences in metabolic rate and activity level. Therefore, not everyone can be "average" in the ratio of height to weight.

2. *Activity level.* Inactive people burn fewer calories and are more likely to be overweight than active people. This is even more true in infancy and childhood than in the rest of life. Activity level is in-

fluenced not only by the child's willingness to become involved in strenuous play but also by the availability of safe places to play.

3. *Quantity of food eaten.* In some families, parents take satisfaction in watching their children eat, always urging them to have another helping. The implication is that a father's love is measured by how much food he can provide; a mother's love, by how well she can cook; and a child's love, by how much he or she can eat. This is especially true when the parents or grandparents grew up in places where starvation was a real possibility. Not surprisingly, in the United States, immigrants from developing countries and their children and grandchildren have the highest risk of being overweight.

4. *Types of food eaten.* Choice of food is important as well. Diets that emphasize fruits, vegetables, and grains do not lead to excess weight gain, whereas diets that are high in fat and sugar obviously do. Besides the unquestionable culprits, many common foods, from breakfast cereals to ketchup, have sugar as a major ingredient. In addition, many snack foods contain saturated fats, which the body metabolizes slowly. Unfortunately, but understandably, the diet of North American families who are below the poverty line tends to be high in fat, containing more pork than other meats and more fried foods than those that are broiled or steamed (Eichorn, 1979). There are also ethnic and subcultural food preferences that affect fat intake. Traditional Chinese and Japanese foods, for example, include much more fiber and less fat than traditional northern and eastern European foods do. Research also shows that people develop tastes for certain types of foods, depending on what they have become accustomed to eating, especially in childhood (Rozin, 1990). Thus the "treats" and "junk food" that some parents regularly give their children may be creating dietary cravings that will lead directly to lifelong weight problems.

5. *Attitude toward food.* Some people consider food a symbol of love and comfort, and eat whenever they are upset. This pattern may be initiated in infancy, if parents feed their babies whenever they cry, rather than first figuring out if the baby is lonely or uncomfortable rather than hungry. The pattern may be reinforced through childhood, if parents use sweets as a reward or consolation, or as a substitute for emotional warmth (Lowrey, 1986).

6. *Overfeeding in infancy and late childhood.* For most of life, the number of fat cells in a person's body remains relatively constant, no matter what that person eats. Adults become fatter because each fat cell becomes fuller, or thinner because each cell loses fat. However, in the prenatal period and the first two years of life, and again during early adolescence, when total body fat increases in anticipation of the rapid growth that follows, the number of fat cells is likely to increase. Malnutrition slows down the rate of cell multiplication, and overfeeding speeds it up (Grinker, 1981). This is one more reason why fat babies and adolescents become adults who want more food and gain weight more easily than people who were not overfed as children. Even when these adults diet and lose

weight, their bodies still contain those extra cells, just waiting to fill up with fat again, like sponges ready to soak up water.

7. *Television-watching*. In cultures where it is a regular pastime, television-watching is another factor in obesity, one that exacerbates several of the influences already cited. According to a large longitudinal study (Dietz and Gortmaker, 1985), children's excessive television-watching is directly correlated with their being overweight. In addition, those children who watch several hours of TV a day during middle childhood are more likely to become obese adolescents. The researchers suggested three factors that make TV fattening: while watching television, children (1) are bombarded with, and swayed by, commercials for junk food, (2) consume many snacks, and of course (3) burn fewer calories than they would if they were actively playing. In fact, they appear to burn fewer calories when watching TV than when doing *nothing*. A recent study found that when glued to the tube, children fall into a deeply relaxed state, akin to semiconsciousness, that lowers their metabolism below its normal at-rest rate—on average, 12 percent below normal in children of normal weight and 16 percent below normal in obese children (Klesges, 1993). In all probability, many of these factors apply to obese adults as well.

8. *Repeated dieting*. People who fast or severely cut back their calorie intake over a period of days or weeks find that they gain weight even more quickly when they return to their normal eating habits. The reason is that the body reacts to protect itself during periods of severe dieting as it would during periods of famine. The rate of metabolism becomes slower, enabling the body to maintain its weight with fewer calories. One consequence is that after a certain amount of weight loss, additional pounds become much more difficult to lose. Another problem is that dieting helps the body become more efficient at storing fat. Thus each new round of dieting is harder than the last one, and each temporary weight loss is followed by an even greater and more permanent gain when the dieter returns to normal eating habits (Striegel-Moore et al., 1986).

9. *Precipitating event*. For many children, the onset of obesity is associated with a critical event or traumatic experience—a hospitalization, a move to a new neighborhood, a parental divorce or death—that creates a sense of loss or diminished self-image and a corresponding need for an alternative source of gratification, in this case, food (Neumann, 1983).

10. *Physiological problems*. One more cause of obesity should be mentioned, even though it is rare. In a few instances, an abnormality in the growth process or in metabolism is to blame (Lowrey, 1986). In these cases, obesity is only one sign of a complex physiological problem that usually involves retardation of normal physical and mental growth. It must be stressed, however, that disorders of this type account for less than 1 percent of all cases of childhood obesity. Therefore, parents of the fat school-age child should, in all likelihood, be much more concerned about the child's diet and exercise than about the possibility of physiological disturbances.

Motor Skills

The fact that children grow more slowly during middle childhood may be part of the reason they become so much more skilled at controlling their bodies during these years. (Compare their self-control, for instance, with the clumsiness that typically accompanies sudden changes in body shape and size during puberty.) School-age children can perform almost any motor skill, as long as it doesn't require very much power or judgment of speed and distance.

Of course, which particular skills a child masters depends, in part, on opportunity and encouragement. The skills of typical North American 8- and 9-year-olds may include swinging a hammer well, sawing, using garden tools, sewing, knitting, drawing in good proportion, writing or printing accurately and neatly, cutting fingernails, riding bicycles, scaling fences, swimming, diving, roller-skating, ice-skating, jumping rope, and playing baseball, football, and jacks (Gesell et al., 1977). Halfway around the world, in Indonesia, children master many of these same skills—though for environmental reasons they do not learn to ice skate, for cultural reasons they do not learn to play baseball or football, and, in Bali, for religious reasons, they do not learn to swim (water is considered to harbor evil) (Lansing, 1983). At the same time, Indonesian children learn skills not common among North American children, like the use of sharp knives and the weaving of intricate baskets.

Differences in Motor Skills

Boys and girls are just about equal in physical abilities during these years, except that boys have greater forearm strength (Tanner, 1970) and girls have greater overall flexibility. Consequently, boys have an advantage in sports like baseball, whereas girls have the edge in sports like gymnastics. But for most physical activities during middle childhood, sex is not as important as age and experience: boys can do cartwheels, and girls can hit home runs, if given an opportunity to learn these skills.

However, the maxim "Practice makes perfect" does not always hold true. Every motor skill is related to several other abilities, some depending on practice, but others relying on body size, brain maturation, or genetically based talent. For example, brain maturation is a key factor in **reaction time,** which is the length of time it takes a person to respond to a particular stimulus. One study of reaction time in people between the ages of 7 and 75 found that the 7-year-olds took about twice as long as the typical adult to press a button in response to a flash of light (.75 seconds as opposed to .37 seconds). The 9-year-olds were notably better than the 7-year-olds, and the 11-year-olds were better still, but none of these three age groups did as well as any adult group (Stern et al., 1980). Another study of reaction time in children aged 5 through 14 found that the older children were almost twice as fast as the younger ones (Southard, 1985). Thus in any sport in which reaction time is crucial, the average older child has a decided advantage over a younger one, and the average adult is quicker than the average child.

Other individual and age differences also come into play. Some are obvious, such as the advantage of height in basketball and of upper-body strength and size for tackle football. Other differences may not be so obvi-

Figure 11.4 *Sex differences in motor skills make boys slightly better at pulling themselves up with their arms— as illustrated by this smiling treeclimber—while girls, like these rollerskaters, are slightly better at twisting and bending.*

ous to the teacher or parent. For example, children vary in the ability to co-ordinate their body movements, so some children are not able to aim a kick in soccer, or execute a leap in gymnastics, nearly as well as others. Individual differences in these characteristics derive from experience and training, and from one's heredity.

Looking closely at the sports that adults value reveals that few are well-suited for children, because they demand precisely those skills that are hardest for them to master. Even softball is much harder than one might think. Throwing with accuracy and catching both involve more distance judgment and eye-hand coordination than many elementary-school children possess. In addition, catching and batting depend on reaction time. Younger children are therefore apt to drop a ball even if it lands in their mitt, because they are slow to enclose it, and they are similarly likely to strike out by swinging the bat too late. Thus a large measure of judgment, physical maturity, and experience is required for good ball-playing. As always, of course, underlying differences between individuals are key. Some children will never be able to throw or kick a ball with as much strength and accuracy as others, a fact that parents, teachers, and teammates sometimes tend to forget.

Figure 11.5 *The games that are well-suited for school-age children focus on the skills they can perform well, such as running and kicking. Not surprisingly, these are the activities that children themselves often choose, rather than the sports involving complex coordination and one-on-one competition commonly favored by adults.*

Learning Disabilities

The obvious fact that children are not all equally adept at motor skills is also obviously true for the skills required in school. For example, after a year or two of formal education, most 8-year-olds can sit attentively in class while they listen to the teacher's instructions, and can read simple books, add a short column of numbers, or write several sentences, as required. However, some children have difficulty with one or another of these tasks. In some children, these difficulties are consistent with their lower level of overall intelligence. In others, however, such difficulties are in surprising contrast with their overall intelligence level. These children are said to have a **learning disability,** a failing that is not attributable to an overall intellectual slowness, to a specific physical handicap such as hearing loss, or to a lack of basic education.

While almost everyone has some unexpected incompetencies (perhaps in his or her sense of direction or ability to remember names), children who are learning-disabled are markedly below other children in their achievement in a particular academic domain, such as reading or math. Generally, part of the diagnosis involves a series of tests, with the learning-disabled child scoring two or more grades below what his or her intellectual potential, as determined by measures of aptitude, would predict (see A Closer Look, p. 294). Currently, about 5 percent of all American schoolchildren are so designated, and are receiving special instruction because of it (U.S. Department of Education, 1991). In all probability, at least another 5 percent are learning-disabled but have not been officially labeled as such.

Problems in a Particular Academic Area

By definition, a learning-disabled child is average or above average in some intellectual areas and below average in others, experiencing great difficulty in learning certain material (Rourke, 1989). For example, a child might have **dyslexia,** which is a disability in reading. Dyslexic children may seem bright and happy in the early years of school, volunteering answers to some difficult questions, diligently completing their worksheets, sitting quietly and looking at their books. However, as times goes on, it becomes clear that they are not really reading: rather, they are guessing at simple words (occasionally making surprising mistakes) and explaining what they have just "read" by telling about the pictures.

Another common disability is **dyscalcula,** that is, great difficulty in math. This problem usually becomes apparent somewhat later in childhood, at about age 8, when even simple numbers facts, such as 3 + 3 = 6, are memorized one day and forgotten the next. Soon it becomes clear that the child is guessing at whether two numbers should be added or subtracted, and that everything the child knows about math is a matter of rote memory rather than understanding.

Other specific academic subjects that may show learning disability are spelling and handwriting: a child might read at the fifth-grade level but repeatedly make simple spelling mistakes ("kum accros the rode") or take three times as long as any other child to copy something from the chalkboard and still produce an illegible scrawl. In addition, although they are not usually so labeled and given special help, some children are learning-disabled in an underlying skill—such as spatial relations, sequential processing, memory, or attention span—that affects all intellectual areas (Rourke, 1989).

Causes

None of these learning problems is caused by a lack of effort on the child's part, although, unfortunately, parents and teachers sometimes treat children who are learning-disabled as though they are not trying hard enough. In fact, the precise causes of learning disabilities are hard to pinpoint (Chalfant, 1989). Many professionals believe that the origin is often organic. It seems as if some parts of the learning-disabled child's brain do not function as well as they do in most people.

(a)

(b)

(c)

Figure 11.6 *The classroom behavior of children with learning disabilities is most apparent when they are faced with academic demands beyond their capabilities. This boy* (a) *listens to the teacher's question,* (b) *thinks hard and gets part of the answer correct, and then* (c) *temporarily despairs when he learns that part of his answer is wrong. Whether this stressful moment becomes a productive pause, the prelude to an angry outburst, or the beginning of a despondent day depends, in part, on how this child's teacher and classmates respond to his faltering.*

A CLOSER LOOK   Aptitude and Achievement Testing

One of the most important steps in approaching learning disabilities is obtaining an accurate and early diagnosis. This is essential to helping learning-disabled children before they fall so far behind their classmates that their self-esteem is damaged and valuable learning years are lost. It is also essential to preventing normal children who are somewhat delayed in their development from being misdiagnosed as learning-disabled.

Teachers and psychologists who suspect that a particular child may have a learning disability look primarily for two elements: discrepant performance and exclusion of other explanations. Discrepant performance refers to the child's performing notably lower than what would be expected on the basis of the child's age and ability. Exclusion of other explanations means that, when a child does not seem to be learning as well as expected, other factors—such as hearing loss, language difficulties, mental retardation—must be ruled out.

While learning disabilities are quite obvious by the end of middle childhood—something is clearly wrong when a seemingly bright child who reads well cannot do simple math problems—a combination of achievement and aptitude tests can usually pinpoint discrepancies much sooner than that.

Achievement tests are designed to measure actual learning—for example, how well a child reads, or adds, or understands science concepts. Typically, achievement tests focus on a particular subject and ask the child questions that are variously easy, average, and difficult. The child's score is then either compared with that of the typical child with the same amount of schooling or the same background or it is measured against some objective standard. For instance, the reading achievement of a Latino fourth-grade boy might be compared to other fourth-graders nationwide, or to other male Latino fourth-graders, or to a standard such as being able to read and understand a basic reading vocabulary of 5,000 words. The results of several such achievement tests might be that this particular fourth-grader reads at the third-grade level, spells at the fourth-grade level, and does math at the fifth-grade level. Such minor differences are common; most of us achieve better in some areas than in others because of specific instruction, particular interest, or general motivation. However, sometimes a fourth-grader might read at the first-grade level. In this case, further examinations are clearly in order.

Among the next steps would be to check the child's school records for factors, such as poor attendance or possible vision problems, that might explain a deficit and to corroborate the test results by seeing if the deficit emerges in an informal setting, as when the child is reading one-on-one with the teacher. Before a child is officially designated as learning-disabled in the absence of such factors, an aptitude test is usually administered.

Aptitude tests are designed to measure potential, such as how well and how quickly a person could learn a new subject if given the chance. When the potential to learn academic knowledge is under examination, the aptitude tests that are usually administered are intelligence tests, which are made up of hundreds of questions that involve various abilities thought to be among the basic intellectual skills, such as memory, vocabulary, knowledge, and spatial perception.

In the original versions of these tests, a person's score was translated into a mental age and that was divided by the person's chronological age to find the intelligence quo-

As detailed in Chapters 3 and 4, many prenatal factors can have a detrimental effect on brain functioning. Genetic inheritance is one of them, since learning disabilities tend to run in families (Oliver et al., 1991; Silver and Hagan, 1990). Teratogens, of course, are another factor, with maternal drug use, particularly of crack cocaine, being the latest teratogenic influence that may be associated with brain damage and later learning disabilities. Prenatal exposure to other toxins, notably mercury and PCBs, is likewise linked to learning disabilities (Jacobson et al., 1992), as is postnatal damage, such as that from convulsions caused by high fever, or from eating or inhaling leaded contaminants (Needleman et al., 1990). The children most affected are those who are both genetically vulnerable and prenatally or postnatally exposed to insult.

tient (IQ). For instance, of three 8-year-olds, one child's score might be equal to that of a typical 6-year-old; another's might be the same as that of most other 8-year-olds; and the third's might be as high as a typical 10-year-old's. To find the intelligence quotient, the child's intellectual age was divided by his or her chronological age, and the resulting number was multiplied by 100. Thus, for the three 8-year-olds above, the first's IQ would be 75 (6/8 x 100), the second's would be 100 (8/8 x 100), and the third's would be 125 (10/8 x 100).

While current tests do not literally apply that formula, their scoring concept is comparable, with two-thirds of all children scoring within a year or two of their age-mates, an IQ somewhere between 85 and 115. Typically, the scores on the various subtests are comparable: thus a child who is above average in reasoning would usually be average or above average in vocabulary. Specific labels are sometimes used to designate children who score above or below the expected scores for their age:

Above 130	Gifted
115–130	Superior
85–115	Average
70–85	Slow learner
Below 70	Mentally retarded

As you undoubtedly know, both aptitude and achievement tests are controversial, since an individual child's test performance can be affected by many factors other than the child's intellectual potential or academic achievement. Emotional stress, visual or hearing problems, language difficulties, educational background, and the like all play a role. Especially when the child's scores are compared to those of children from a different culture or socioeconomic status, interpretation must be very carefully done.

However, the basic idea is sound: serious learning problems are best spotted early so that remediation can prevent educational loss, and IQ tests are a useful tool in the early identification of such problems (Rispens et al., 1991; Snider and Tarver, 1989; Taylor, 1988). For example, if a child does poorly on all the subtests of the IQ test, then a slower pace of teaching may eventually lead to more learning. Without such an adjustment in the teaching pace, the child might fall further and further behind, pretending to understand and hiding his or her shame until dropping out of school. Similarly, the gifted child, scoring high in every part of the IQ test, may need accelerated instruction or additional work to prevent boredom, frustration, and wasted potential. Finally, the learning-disabled child, whose IQ scores scatter high and low from subtest to subtest, or whose tested aptitude is much higher than tested achievement, can benefit from quite specific instruction targeted to the specific disability.

An important caution should be noted in using test scores, however. While virtually every educator is convinced that children benefit from early, individualized instruction to meet their special needs, many educators also believe it is destructive to label young children "retarded," "gifted," or "disabled," or to isolate them from their peers on the basis of ability or achievement tests (Wang et al., 1988; Oakes, 1986). **Homogeneous grouping**—all the slow learners in one class, the gifted in another, and learning-disabled in a third—is not necessarily best for the children or for the community.

However, every specialist cautions that the connection between organic damage and learning problems is not straightforward. Some children are learning-disabled even when nothing untoward occurred in their prenatal or early postnatal environment (Vandenberg et al., 1986), and some who experienced quite obvious insults, including prenatal exposure to crack and other illegal drugs, sometimes suffer no measurable deficits, especially if they are raised in a loving and stable family (Johnson et al., 1990; van Baar, 1990).

Most important, even if a particular learning problem is of proven organic origin, that does not mean that it is impossible to ameliorate. In fact, no matter what the cause of learning disabilities, the way teachers and parents respond to a child who displays difficulties in learning can make an enormous difference to the child's chances of overcoming the problem. If teachers and parents recognize that a child with a learning disability is neither lazy nor stupid, they can help the child become a competent adult with patient, individual tutoring. With such assistance, many children with learning disabilities develop into adults who are virtually indistinguishable from other adults in their educational and occupational achievements (Goodman, 1987). In general, the earlier a learning-disabled child gets special help, and the more that help is tied to the particular problem (giving the child with dyscalcula specific help with number concepts or math strategies, or giving the dyslexic child direct assistance with letter recognition or phonics, as the case requires), the better the child's future prospects are (Wilson and Sindelar, 1991; Achenbach, 1982). In addition, attention should be given to social interaction, because social skills are often directly or indirectly affected by the underlying neurological problem.

While the underlying problem is likely to remain lifelong (Spreen, 1988), training the child how to leapfrog, sidestep, or undercut the difficulty can minimize its effects, not only aiding the child in making and keeping friends but also helping with academic learning (McIntosh et al., 1991).

Attention-Deficit Disorder

As you have read, some learning disabilities do not manifest themselves in a particular academic skill but instead appear in specific psychological processes that affect learning and understanding generally. One of the most puzzling and exasperating of such problems in childhood is **attention-deficit disorder,** or **ADD,** in which the child has great difficulty concentrating for more than a few moments at a time. Sitting down to do homework, for instance, an ADD child might repeatedly look up, ask irrelevant questions, think about playing outside, get up to get a drink of water, and then get up again to get a snack. Often this need for distraction and diversion is accompanied by excitability, impulsivity, and a need to be active, in which case, the child actually suffers from **ADHD,** that is, **attention-deficit hyperactivity disorder**. Such children often are easily frustrated and quick-tempered.

Figure 11.7 *Many children have periods when they seem out of control—too active, too aggressive, and too inattentive for adults (or the children themselves) to manage. While these behaviors are symptoms of attention-deficit hyperactivity disorder, a child is not considered to have this condition unless these characteristics are apparent over a long period of time and in several different settings.*

The crucial, underlying problem seems to be a neurological difficulty in screening out irrelevant and distracting stimuli. This deficit makes "paying attention" difficult, and therefore makes it hard for the child to focus on any one thought or experience long enough to process it. Thus a child might impulsively blurt out the wrong answer to a teacher's question, or might not have the patience to read and remember a passage in a school textbook. In addition to these handicaps, ADHD is often accompanied by other learning disabilities (Dykman and Ackerman, 1991; Cantwell and Baker, 1991).

Estimates of the prevalence of this problem vary, from about 1 percent to 5 percent, depending partly on diagnostic criteria, which vary by nation. British doctors, for example, are less likely to diagnose children as having ADHD than American doctors are, and are more likely to diagnose such children as having conduct disorders (Rutter and Garmezy, 1983; Epstein et al., 1991). Generally, however, the sex-ratio of diagnosed ADD and ADHD children is four boys for every one girl (Bhatia et al., 1991).

Causes of Attention-Deficit Hyperactivity Disorder

When confronted with a school-age child who is considerably more active than other children and cannot concentrate very well, it is not easy to explain that child's behavior. However, we do know at least six reasons why such a child is different from the normal child, and attention-deficit hyperactivity disorder may arise from one or more of these factors.

1. *Genetic differences*. Twin studies have shown that the concordance rate for attention-deficit hyperactivity disorder is significantly higher for identical twins than for fraternal twins: if one member of the monozygotic twin pair has this disorder, the other member is also likely to have it (Shaywitz and Shaywitz, 1983). In addition, a comparison of biological and adoptive parents of hyperactive children found that only the biological parents had attentional difficulties similar to those of their offspring (Alberts-Corush et al., 1986). Taken together, these studies indicate that hereditary factors contribute to attention-deficit hyperactivity disorder. This genetic element may manifest itself in abnormal brain metabolism. A brain-scan study (Zametkin et al., 1990) of twenty-five adults who had had the disorder in childhood and who have at least one child with the disorder revealed that, on average, their overall rate of brain metabolism was 8 percent lower than that of a control group. More significant, the areas of lowest metabolism were in two areas of the brain that are associated with the control of attention and motor activity.

2. *Prenatal damage*. One precursor of this disorder is prenatal damage of some sort (Hartsough and Lambert, 1985). Thus, a person who was prenatally exposed to a teratogen may have escaped major harm but show minor problems in physical development and learning ability. Maternal drug use during pregnancy and pregnancy complications have both been implicated (Varley, 1984).

3. *Lead poisoning*. Lead poisoning in its early stages leads to impaired concentration and hyperactivity, as discussed on page 218.

4. *Diet*. Severe vitamin deficiencies, especially of the B vitamins, impair concentration. In addition, certain foods, such as milk, chocolate,

and some chemical additives, may make some children restless (Conners, 1980). However, in view of the amount of popular concern about diet and dietary remedies (such as the Feingold Diet), it is important to recognize that individual children are affected in different ways by these substances, so diet will not have predictable consequences for all children (Kaplan et al., 1989).

5. *Family influences.* Compared with other children, children diagnosed with attention-deficit hyperactivity disorder come from families who move often, are stressed, have fewer children, and are less concerned about the child's academic performance than about controlling the child's behavior. Obviously, each of these factors may be the result, rather than the cause, of the child's difficulties, or they might contribute to maintaining these difficulties once they have begun for other reasons. However, after elaborate study, some researchers are convinced that these family differences contribute as much to a child's attention problems as genetic or temperamental variables (Lambert and Hartsough, 1984).

6. *Environment.* The ecological niche in which some children find themselves may exacerbate attention-deficit hyperactivity disorder. The child is especially likely to "misbehave" in an exciting but unstructured situation (such as the typical birthday party) or in a situation with many behavioral demands (such as a long church service, or dinner in a fancy restaurant). Children with no place to play, or who watch television hour after hour, may become restless, irritable, and aggressive. In one study of Puerto Rican children living in overcrowded apartments in New York City (Thomas et al., 1974), the parents' concern for their children's safety led them to keep their children in school or at home virtually all the time. Not surprisingly, 53 percent of these children were considered hyperactive by their parents. In one case, a family with a son described as a "whirling dervish" moved to a new house, which had a small yard. To his parents' delight, the boy quickly "outgrew" his hyperactivity.

Figure 11.8 *Anticipation, excitement, and lots of stimulation are all elements that make self-control difficult for many children. Especially for those children with attention-deficit hyperactivity disorder, these elements in an unstructured setting may lead to behavior that is hard even for adults to control.*

Help for Children with Attention-Deficit Hyperactivity Disorder

Not surprisingly, children with attention-deficit hyperactivity disorder are annoying to parents and teachers and are rejected by peers (Henker and Whalen, 1989). Many children with the disorder continue to have problems in adolescence, not only with hyperactivity but with academic demands and social skills as well (Nussbaum et al., 1990; Barkley et al., 1991). Many become disruptive and angry. In fact, more than half of all children with attention-deficit hyperactivity disorder have continuing problems as adults in pacing their work, controlling their temper, and developing patience. However, as they grow older, many people learn to cope with these problems, for example, by choosing occupations that suit their skills but that do not emphasize patience and control (Gittelman et al., 1985; Weiss and Hechtman, 1986). In childhood, the most effective forms of help are medication and cognitive and psychological therapy.

Drugs

The most frequent therapy for children with attention-deficit hyperactivity disorder is medication (Copeland et al., 1987). For reasons not yet determined, certain drugs that stimulate adults, such as amphetamines and methylphenidate (Ritalin), have a reverse effect on hyperactive children. For many children, the results are remarkable, allowing them to sit still and concentrate for the first time in their lives (Sprague and Ullman, 1981). Indeed, some physicians think that an overactive child who does not respond to such drugs does not really have this disorder, although others disagree with this claim.

Drug therapy is not a panacea, however. Unfortunately, drugs are sometimes prescribed for children without proper diagnosis or without follow-up examinations—an abuse that can harm the child. For instance, children are sometimes prescribed an excessively large dosage and become lethargic. Further, by the time a child has become a candidate for psychoactive drugs, the child's behavior has usually created school, home, and personal problems that no drugs alone can reverse. Psychoactive drugs should never be given as a one-step solution; instead, they should be part of an ongoing treatment program that involves the child's cognitive and psychosocial worlds (Wender, 1987).

Psychological Therapy

Usually, the child with attention-deficit hyperactivity disorder needs help overcoming a confused perception of the social world and a bruised ego, while the family needs help with their own management techniques and interaction. As noted in Chapter 2 (see Research Report, pp. 48–49), many families with difficult children unwittingly get caught in a vicious cycle of aggression and anger, in which the parents' and siblings' responses to the problem child perpetuate that child's problem behavior (Patterson, 1982). Although some forms of therapy may work better with certain children than with others, the most effective types of therapy have generally been those developed from learning theory, such as teaching the parents how to use behavior-modification techniques with their child, guiding their efforts to organize and structure the child's environment in subdued and nondistracting ways, and helping the child see the effect of his or her own behavior (Henker and Whalen, 1989; Ross and Ross, 1982).

Teacher Response

Teachers are often the first professionals to suggest that a particular child might have attention-deficit hyperactivity disorder, for they are able to compare these children with their peers in a relatively structured setting. However, teachers, like parents, are often not aware that they themselves may be contributing to the child's difficulties. One study showed that some classroom environments, labeled **provocation ecologies,** made the problem worse, while others, called **rarefaction ecologies,** ameliorated the problem. In the former, structure was either unusually rigid or completely absent, and noise was either completely forbidden or tolerated to a distracting degree. In rarefaction ecologies, teachers who managed to diminish hyperactivity were flexible in their reactions to minor disruptions (for example, allowing children to ask questions of their neighbors as long as they did so quietly), but also provided sufficient structure so that the children knew what they should be doing and when (Whalen et al., 1979). Short periods of concentrated schoolwork in a quiet room alternating with opportunities for physical activity can also be helpful (Zadig and Meltzer, 1983). Often hyperactive children have other learning disabilities. Once these are recognized and attended to, the child's hyperactivity tends to diminish.

This is not to say that, with proper teaching, children with attention-deficit hyperactivity disorder suddenly quiet down and concentrate on their work. On the contrary, as with all physical handicaps and learning disabilities, no school, family, or neighborhood, no matter how structured or flexible, can make the problem disappear. However, like all children, children who have attention-deficit hyperactivity disorder can be greatly helped or harmed by the particular ecosystem of which they are a part.

Conclusion

It should be clear from our discussion of learning disabilities and attention-deficit disorder that physiological, educational, and social influences can interact to produce problems, and that all such influences must be understood before the impact of these problems can be reduced. However, our focus on such problems must not blind us to the reality that the same interactional approach should characterize attempts to understand and meet the needs of all school-age children. Further, we must remember that each child has some of the strengths and liabilities typical of children in middle childhood, as well as capabilities and problems that few others share. This is, of course, true whether we are looking at biosocial development, as in this chapter, or at cognitive development, which we shall investigate in the next chapter.

SUMMARY

Size and Shape

1. Children grow more slowly during middle childhood than at any other time until the end of adolescence. There is much variation in the size and rate of maturation of healthy North American children, primarily as a result of genetic, rather than nutritional, differences.

2. Overweight children suffer from peer rejection and low self-esteem. More exercise, rather than severe dieting, is the best solution, along with new attitudes toward food and recreation.

3. Many influences throughout the life span interact to cause obesity. Hereditary factors, overfeeding in infancy and late childhood, repeated dieting, lack of exercise, and other factors contribute to the incidence of obesity.

Motor Skills

4. School–age children can perform almost any motor skill, as long as it doesn't require much strength or refined judgment of distance or speed. The activities that are best for children are ones that demand only those skills that most children of this age can master.

Learning Disabilities

5. Children with problems such as dyslexia (severe reading problems) or with attention-deficit hyperactivity disorder (high activity levels with low concentration ability) need special attention and help to learn to cope with their problems.

6. Some learning disabilities may originate in genetic or physical problems of some sort, but whether or not the cause is organic, many educational and psychological programs can help children with these disabilities. Psychoactive drugs also help some children, but these should be used carefully and cautiously.

KEY TERMS

obesity (286)
reaction time (291)
learning disability (292)
dyslexia (293)
dyscalcula (293)
achievement tests (294)
aptitude tests (294)
homogeneous grouping (295)
attention-deficit disorder (ADD) (296)
attention-deficit hyperactivity disorder (ADHD) (296)
provocation ecologies (300)
rarefaction ecologies (300)

KEY QUESTIONS

1. What are some of the causes of variation in physical growth in middle childhood?

2. How does obesity affect a child's development?

3. What are the causes of obesity?

4. What are some of the reasons for the notable improvement in children's motor skills during the school years?

5. What kinds of considerations come into play when determining the appropriateness of physical activities for children?

6. What are the symptoms of learning disability?

7. What are the possible causes of attention-deficit hyperactivity disorder?

8. What are the arguments for and against the use of psychoactive drugs to control attention-deficit hyperactivity disorder?

9. What other types of treatment are helpful in controlling attention-deficit hyperactivity disorder?

CHAPTER 12

The School Years: Cognitive Development

During the school years, children's cognitive development enables them to focus their thinking less intuitively and more accurately on the facts and relationships that they perceive in the world. They become astute observers who can organize objects according to their particular characteristics and understand ideas of time and distance. These new abilities to investigate the world more objectively will be among the topics of this chapter, as will the questions that follow:

How does the ability to recognize that people and objects can simultaneously belong to a number of different categories affect the child's understanding of subjects as diverse as mathematics and family relationships?

What cognitive developments account for the child's new grasp of concepts such as conservation, seriation, and reciprocity?

What are some of the factors that affect how children remember and how well they learn new information?

What factors may influence a child's success in learning a second language?

The thinking and reasoning of the typical 11-year-old is radically different from that of the typical 6-year-old. For example, most sixth-graders can figure out which brand and size of popcorn is the best buy, can be taught to multiply proper and improper fractions, can memorize a list of fifty new spelling words, and can use irony appropriately—accomplishments beyond virtually every first-grader.

Their approach to learning is different as well. Take the first day of school, for example. Six-year-olds enter school filled with excitement and fear, wondering if the teacher will be mean or nice and clinging tightly to their mother's or father's hand. By age 11, children arrive at school with new notebooks and sharpened pencils, ready for the serious business of learning. They appear casual and confident, even when they aren't, and they would angrily resist if their parents offered to walk them to the classroom. While first-graders worry about making friends or getting lost, sixth-graders worry about finishing homework, memorizing new concepts, or failing a test.

Not surprisingly, there is a vast difference as well in what teachers expect of students over this five-year period. If first-graders can learn to stay quiet when they are supposed to, read simple words, and add simple numbers, that's considered accomplishment enough. Sixth-graders are expected to know their multiplication tables and spelling rules; and they are supposed to understand the themes of the stories they read and the general principles underlying the science experiments they perform. They are urged to plan ahead and to hand in work that is neat and correct.

These changes in behavior, attitudes, and expectations reflect, in part, the growth of children's cognitive abilities as their thinking becomes more systematic and logical. This chapter describes the cognitive processes that produce new skills and reasoning strategies and the language development that expresses them.

Concrete Operational Thought

What underlies the differences we have just described is, according to Piaget, the attainment of **concrete operational thought,** through which children can reason logically about the things and events they perceive. Between ages 7 and 11, children begin to understand logical principles, as long as the principles can be applied to concrete, or specific, cases.

One reason for this advance is that children become increasingly able to **decenter,** that is, to move away from an intuitive, perceptual focusing on one aspect of a problem. Thus they are able to think more objectively: they are less likely to be misled by mere appearances or to peg their judgments on a single feature of an object or situation. They can watch water being poured from a narrow glass into a wide one, for example, and explain why the quantity of liquid remains the same (see Chapters 2 and 9). They are quick to debunk a younger child's fallacious reasoning, asserting "Maybe it *seems* that way to you, but *really* it's . . . " They can also reverse their thinking, moving forward or backward in their problem-solving to reexamine earlier assumptions or return to the beginning. Moreover, according to Piaget, their reasoning can be generalized across tasks and situations: thus, if they can apply a logical principle in one context, they can often apply it in other analogous contexts. However, they can reason only about the concrete, tangible things in their world: they are not yet able to reason about abstractions, as can the adolescent or adult who has reached formal operational thought.

According to Piaget, "experimentation has shown decisively that until the age of seven, the child remains prelogical." True concrete operational thinking is preceded by a transitional period between the ages of 5 and 7— sometimes called the **5-to-7 shift**—in which the child has not quite outgrown preoperational thought nor firmly reached concrete operational thought. Piaget noted that although children of this age sometimes intuitively grasp the right answer on tests of concrete operational logic, they frequently cannot explain the underlying principles that led them to their conclusion.

Logical Operations

At about age 7 or 8, maturation and experience allow the child to become a true concrete operational thinker. The hallmark of concrete operational thought is the ability to understand certain logical operations, or principles—such as *identity* and *reversibility*—when these principles are applied to specific, or concrete, cases. Behind this understanding of concrete operations is the newly acquired ability to simultaneously remember and compare various characteristics of objects, or persons, or situations (Biggs and Collins, 1982; Case, 1985).

Consider three logical operations: identity, reversibility, and reciprocity. **Identity** is the idea that an object's content remains the same despite changes in its appearance. In a typical experimental example, a grasp of identity enables the child to realize that rolling a ball of clay into a long, thin rope of clay does not alter the amount of clay. **Reversibility** is the idea that a transformation process can be reversed to restore the original form. With a grasp of this concept, the child in the preceding example would realize that the clay rope could be rerolled into a ball again. **Reciprocity** is the idea that a transformation in one dimension is compensated for by a transformation in another. In this case, the child would be able to explain that the rope of clay is longer but skinnier, and thus contains the same amount as in the beginning.

According to Piaget, once these principles, or operations, are mastered, they can be applied in many contexts. Once children have a firm grasp of identity, for instance, they know that the number 24 is always 24, whether it is arrived at by adding 14 and 10 or 23 and 1; they also understand that their mother was once a child, and unlike preoperational children, can accept that a baby picture of their mother is, in fact, a picture of their mother. The same logical ideas can be applied to the social world. For example, while two arguing 4-year-olds might yell "Is," "Is not," back and forth until one gives up, or hits, or calls a parent, two 8-year-olds can argue by appealing to logic, reasoning, for example, that "Even though it fell on the floor it is still my pencil" (identity), "If you take back all the mean things you said to me, I can be your friend again" (reversibility), or "You can play with my dolls if I can ride your bike" (reciprocity).

This application of logical principles can also be seen in two additional concepts, classification and seriation.

Classification is the concept that objects can be organized in terms of categories, or classes. For example, a child's parents and siblings belong to the class called *family. Toys, animals, people,* and *food* are other everyday classes. A related but more complicated concept is **class inclusion,** the idea that a particular object or person may belong to more than one class. Most preschool children have some understanding of how to apply classification labels, but they do not have a good grasp of the complex relationships between general and specific categories (Flavell, 1985).

Younger children have particular trouble with the hierarchical relations between categories and subcategories. Consider the following experiment, modeled on a series of experiments conducted by Piaget. An examiner shows children seven toy dogs. Four of them are collies, and the others are a poodle, an Irish setter, and a German shepherd. First, the examiner

Figure 12.1 *As experienced concrete operational thinkers, this group of fifth-graders can classify rocks and minerals into categories and subcategories as easily as they can classify more familiar animals and people. For preschoolers, however, this kind of hierarchical classification would have been unmanageable.*

questions the children to make sure that they know that all the toys are dogs and that they can name each breed. Then comes the crucial question: "Are there more collies or more dogs?" Until the concept of classification is firmly established, most children say "More collies." They cannot simultaneously keep in mind the general category *dog* and the subcategory *collie*, mentally shifting from one to the other. When they can eventually do so, it strengthens their understanding of the world around them. They realize that people, objects, and events can belong to more than one category, and that these categories can be hierarchically organized (a child is simultaneously a "human being," "mammal," and "animal"), overlapping (in many families a child is an "offspring" and a "sibling") and, at times, diverse (a child is a "family member" and a "peer-group member").

Seriation refers to the arrangement of items in a series, as in the laying out of sticks from shortest to longest, or of crayons from lightest to darkest. Like other logical operations, seriation begins to be understood toward the end of the preoperational period, but the concept is usually not firmly established until age 7 or 8. Thus, during the 5-to-7 shift, if a typical 6-year-old is asked to arrange a series of ten sticks according to length, the child might first put together three sticks—short, medium, and long—and then insert the others, rearranging several of the sticks before getting the correct order. A typical 8-year-old, in contrast, would look at the whole jumble of sticks, pick out the shortest, then the next shortest, and so on, quickly arranging the series. This is because, rather than using trial-and-error, the older child can systematically arrange the sticks according to an underlying concept of seriation.

Many of the logical operations of concrete operational thought underlie the basic ideas of elementary-school math and science. For instance, the principle of seriation is necessary for a firm understanding of the number system. Similarly, classification is essential to grasping the taxonomic relations between different kinds of insects, plants, or birds, and identity is helpful in appreciating how these life forms change (or metamorphosis) in the course of their development. Indeed, one reason for Piaget's interest in the development of these logical operations is that they are crucial to the kind of scientific reasoning that is necessary to understand the world accurately

Figure 12.2 *To prepare their contribution to this science fair, these students had to draw on their familiarity with logical operations—such as reciprocity and reversibility—as well as on the creative ingenuity that often accompanies the growth of logical reasoning during the school years.*

and objectively. The growth of these reasoning abilities during middle childhood also helps explain how children can quickly learn and remember information that they want to know. This is true for nonacademic as well as academic pursuits, whether it concerns the characteristics of dinosaurs or the batting averages of baseball stars.

Modifying Piaget

As noted in earlier chapters, a number of cognitive researchers have modified certain of Piaget's ideas by emphasizing the individual differences in, and the unevenness of, children's progress through cognitive stages. Whereas Piaget tended to describe the child's movement from one stage to the next as occurring fairly quickly once begun, and also as occurring across the board in all domains, these researchers maintain that the child enters a new stage gradually, and more readily in some domains than in others. A certain type of reasoning might be apparent in, say, math or science but not social understanding.

Particularly in the case of concrete operational thought, many studies find that cognitive development is considerably more heterogeneous, or inconsistent, than Piaget's descriptions would suggest. According to Flavell (1982), two of the factors that account for this heterogeneity are the hereditary differences among individuals in their abilities and aptitudes and the environmental differences in "cultural, educational, and other task-related experiential background." The sum of these differences, says Flavell, might well produce a great deal of cognitive heterogeneity:

> Imagine, for example, a child or adolescent who is particularly well-endowed with the abilities needed to do computer science, has an all-consuming interest in it, has ample time and opportunity to learn about it, and has an encouraging parent who is a computer scientist (whence much of the aptitude, interest, and opportunity, perhaps). The quality and sophistication of the child's thinking in this area might well be higher than that of most adults in any area. It would also likely be much higher in this area than in most other areas of the child's cognitive life. His level of moral reasoning or skill in making inferences about other people might be considerably less developed, for instance. The heterogeneity could be a matter of time constraints as well as a matter of differential aptitudes and interests: that is, time spent at the computer terminal is time not spent interacting with and learning about people.

As we saw in Chapter 9, most researchers also believe that children demonstrate partial entrance into concrete operational thought earlier than Piaget predicted. This contention is bolstered by studies (de Ribaupierre et al., 1985; Blevins-Knabe, 1987; Smith, 1989) showing that on simplified versions of Piagetian tests for classification and seriation, preschoolers often reveal the same kind of grasp of these concepts that we saw them reveal for conservation and perspective-taking in Chapter 9. Many aspects of concrete operational thought appear, therefore, to have much earlier origins than Piaget believed.

The Legacy of Piaget

Despite these revisions and criticisms, Piaget's comprehensive view of children's cognitive development is considered correct in most aspects. With

Figure 12.3 *Piaget's influence on American education has helped to change many classrooms from the kind in the first photo—in which teachers use "talk and chalk" to direct student learning from the front of the classrooms—to the kind in the second photo, in which teachers work with individual children who are pursuing activities that are well-suited to their particular needs and interests.*

regard to school-age children, three of Piaget's ideas in particular have provided valuable insights into the cognitive skills of children of this age.

1. Compared with that of the preschool child, the thinking of the school-age child is characterized by a more comprehensive logic and markedly broader grasp of the underlying principles of rational thought. The overall thinking of an 8-year-old on almost any issue is less intuitive and more logical than it was a few years earlier.

2. Children are active learners. They learn best by questioning, exploring, and doing. In fact, Piaget's theories provided the theoretical framework for making most classrooms today quite different places from those in the 1950s (Ravitch, 1983). The reason was interest in what is called *open education*, which encourages individualized learning by discovery, discussion, and deduction. This approach to learning, in various forms, has tended to replace much of the passive, teacher-centered, lock-step education of a few decades ago.

3. How children think is as important as what they know. Piaget's interest in the underlying structures of thought has led to a realization that what distinguishes the thinking of school-age children from that of preschoolers is not new information alone but new cognitive organizations. What children acquire, then, is not only new facts but also new ways to assemble facts (Flavell, 1985).

The Information-Processing Perspective

Many of the current developmental researchers who share Piaget's interest in the growth of reasoning and learning in middle childhood begin their analysis with a different image of intellectual development. Rather than conceptualizing cognitive growth as being like that, say, of a flower, which, provided it has sufficient sunlight and nutrients, unfolds according to an organic timetable, they think of the mind as being like a computer, whose capacity can be upgraded with development. Accordingly, these researchers apply an **information-processing** approach to their studies. As we saw in Chapter 2 (pp. 55–58), information-processing theorists are interested in the processes through which the mind analyzes, stores, and retrieves information, and in the cognitive changes that make these processes more reliable and efficient as the child matures.

Information-processing theorists begin with the same question that fascinated Piaget: What accounts for the remarkable changes in thinking, learning, and problem-solving that occur between the preschool years and middle childhood? To answer this question, they explore the age-related changes that take place in the child's selective attention, memory skills, processing capacity, knowledge base, and cognitive and problem-solving strategies (Kuhn, 1988; Sternberg, 1988; Bjorklund, 1990). Researchers have discovered that as children mature, they employ their cognitive skills more strategically and resourcefully in challenging tasks—and they do so because they have learned *what they must do* to succeed at such tasks. Whereas most preschoolers do not have a clue about how to learn and reason well, most school-age children have several strategies and tactics. To understand why, we will consider some of the cognitive advances of the school years that have most interested information-processing theorists.

Selective Attention

We all know that it is easier to understand new ideas when we can focus our attention on them without distractions. Most students can study more easily in the quiet of the library, for example, than in the dorm with roommates and rap music in the background. Most students also know how to focus their attention, concentrating on the task at hand when taking an exam, for instance, rather than letting their mind wander to plans for the coming weekend.

This ability to use **selective attention**—to screen out distractions and concentrate on relevant information—improves steadily during middle childhood. In one classic investigation, children between the ages of 6 and 13 were asked to remember the distinctive background colors of pictures of an elephant, a scooter, and other objects (Maccoby and Hagen, 1965). They were not asked to remember the particular objects in each picture. As expected, memory for background colors improved steadily with age: 13-year-olds remembered them almost twice as accurately as 6-year-olds. But then the children were unexpectedly asked to remember the objects in the pictures. The ability to remember this distracting (or incidental) information improved up to age 11, but then decreased sharply. In other words, the older children had learned to focus their attention and to ignore unnecessary information—so well that the 13-year-olds were actually worse than the 6-year-olds at remembering the objects in the pictures. Their developing skills at selective attention probably contributed both to their improved memory for the relevant information (i.e., the background colors) and their diminished recall of the irrelevant information.

Selective attention is important for reasoning and problem solving. To complete a challenging problem, a person must first focus on the information that is likely to lead to a solution, and then proceed straightforwardly until a successful outcome is achieved. Many preschoolers fail at simple problem solving, not because they are ignorant or lazy, but because their selective attention is inconsistent, and they become distracted on the way to the solution. Sometimes they even forget the problem itself! By contrast, older children are more planful and strategic: they know when selective attention is called for and know how and where to focus their attention (Flavell, 1985).

Memory Skills

If you wanted to remember some new information—a list of names, say—you could simply look at the list for a while and hope it sinks into your memory. This ineffective approach (you might call it the "osmosis strategy") is precisely the one that most preschool children use. During middle childhood, however, children's repertoire of procedures for retaining new information—their memory **storage strategies**—broadens significantly (Kail, 1990). They begin to use **rehearsal,** repeating the information to be remembered. Somewhat later, they also use **organization,** regrouping the information to make it more memorable. For example, to memorize the fifty states, one could learn them by region, or in alphabetical order. By early adolescence, children are capable of more complex storage strategies, such as associating information with personal experiences or hypothetical examples, and they have thus become quite skilled at knowing *how* to remember.

Figure 12.4 *How best to remember the names and locations of countries around the world? These boys know that any of a variety of memory strategies would be helpful—including simple rehearsal, grouping countries by region or in alphabetical order, or color-coding them on maps according to their location or other features.*

In addition to storage strategies, of course, learning also requires **retrieval strategies,** that is, procedures to access previously learned information. As an adult, you use a variety of devices for recalling information from memory: you think of associated information (hoping it will jog your memory), or you try to create a mental image of the event or object you are trying to recall. You can also use clues from others to assist your recollection. The last time you encountered someone whose name you could not remember, for instance, you probably tried to recall the context in which you knew the person or called to mind other people this person was associated with. In general, whereas preschoolers do not search their memories very thoroughly or deeply, the ability to use retrieval strategies emerges in middle childhood and improves steadily thereafter (Kail, 1990). By the sixth grade, many students would not be panicked in a geography test if they did not immediately remember the exact location of Bolivia or Bulgaria: they know that mentally visualizing a map of the world, or reconstructing the context of the last study session, will likely bring it to mind.

Taken together, storage strategies and retrieval strategies are called **mnemonics,** or memory aids. One reason older children are such better students than younger children is that they have a broader repertoire of mnemonics, can use them spontaneously and skillfully, and are aware of the situations in which they are most useful.

Processing Capacity

Another reason that children in the school years are better learners and problem-solvers is that they have a larger **processing capacity**—that is, they can hold more information in working memory, where reasoning and thinking occur. Enhanced processing capacity enables children to consider different aspects of a situation simultaneously, or to apply more information to a problem. A larger processing capacity means, for example, that children can mentally coordinate the height of the liquid and the volume of the container in the conservation-of-liquids test, or can image different visual viewpoints to an event. It also means that children can better predict whether an adult will think a joke is funny by considering that person's preferences and values—as well as the joke itself!

Most theorists think that processing capacity expands, not because of changes in the actual size of working memory, but because individuals learn to use their working memory more efficiently (Flavell, 1985). Improvement in their cognitive skills (including selective attention, mnemonics, and some other strategies we will discuss) enhances schoolchildren's ability to eliminate distracting or irrelevant information, thereby making more space available in working memory for other things, such as additional information about the task, or thinking carefully about a solution. In a sense, schoolchildren's thinking is less "cluttered" than that of preschoolers.

Processing capacity also becomes more efficient through automatization, as familiar and well-rehearsed mental activities become routine and automatic. Recall how much concentrated effort you needed to read words or add numbers when you were young, or to use a foreign vocabulary before you were fluent, or to hit the ball correctly when you first tried to play tennis. As these activities became more familiar and routine, less mental work was required to carry them out successfully, making more of working memory available to devote to other things. As a result, you can now (most likely)

Figure 12.5 *During this instant of focused concentration on connecting racket with ball, you can see how difficult it would be for this young tennis novice to consider, at the same time, where to direct his shot, where to move after hitting the ball, or the finer points of tennis strategy. However, after the ability to hit the ball accurately has become more routine and automatized, this boy will have greater processing capacity available to simultaneously think about these other aspects of his game.*

comment to yourself mentally on what you are reading at a given moment—even in the foreign language—or plot strategy while hitting the tennis ball. In this manner, as children get older, more mental activities become automatized, and this frees up processing capacity for other things.

Some theorists believe that the enhanced capacity of working memory during middle childhood accounts for many significant changes in children's thinking and reasoning (Case, 1985). For example, the preschooler's tendency to center on only one aspect of a problem, noted by Piaget (Chapter 9, pp. 230–234), may derive from limitations in the capacity of working memory. With enhanced processing capacity in middle childhood, centration and egocentrism diminish because the child can keep in mind multiple perspectives or viewpoints at one time.

Knowledge

As we have seen, having a body of knowledge or skills in a particular area makes it easier to understand and learn new information in that area because it can be integrated with what is already known. The more expanded one's knowledge base becomes, the easier it is to add to it. Thus, one reason children become better learners in middle childhood is that they have an expanded knowledge base.

If this is so, are children who have a greater knowledge base on a particular topic than adults actually able to remember and reason better on that topic than the adults? Are their memory and reasoning skills stronger? This question was explored by Michelene Chi (1978) in a study of young chess experts recruited from a local chess tournament. These children, who were from the third through the eighth grade, were compared on their recall of complex chess positions against a group of adults who were acquainted with the game but were not experts. The children were strikingly more accurate in their recall than were the adults, and their mental organization of the chess pieces into logical, interrelated memory "chunks" was also more efficient. By contrast, when the same children and adults were compared in another test of memory recall for digits—in which the children did not have expertise—the adults were more proficient (see Figure 12.6). The better memory skills of the children were apparent, therefore, only when they had greater knowledge and experience.

Chi's findings are not a surprise to any parent who has been rebuked by his or her 6-year-old for mistaking a diplodocus for a brontosaurus. But the implications of this study may be surprising, since they suggest that adults are not always more cognitively competent than children. Many differences between schoolchildren's and adults' memory and reasoning may be due, in fact, to the children's more limited knowledge and experience (Keil, 1984). As the child's storehouse of knowledge increases with age, concepts become more elaborated and interconnected with each other, the mental framework for organizing knowledge becomes more sophisticated, and the young learner can ask better questions to gain new understanding. Many theorists believe that knowledge, not maturation, is the basis for Piaget's concrete operational thought. As Robert Sternberg (1990), a scholar of cognition, has expressed it:

> Piaget's theory seems severely to underestimate the role of knowledge in intellectual development. In many instances, children cannot solve a problem not because of a lack of logical operations, but because they do not know enough.

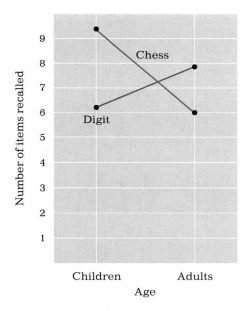

Figure 12.6 *The number of items recalled by children and adults in tests measuring memory for chess pieces, and memory for digits, in the study by Michelene Chi (1978).*

Figure 12.7 *Collections of all sorts—from stamps to baseball cards to Barbie dolls—take on new dimensions with the metacognition of middle childhood, as many schoolchildren spend happy afternoons counting, categorizing, and calculating the worth of their particular treasures.*

Metacognition

A final reason school-age children advance in learning and reasoning is their developing awareness of cognitive strategies. In essence, during the school years, children acquire a "sense of the game" of what thinking is about (Flavell, 1985): they become aware that learning and problem-solving require that they *do* something, and they increasingly understand *what* they must do to perform well. The ability to evaluate a cognitive task to determine how to best accomplish it—and to monitor one's performance—is called **metacognition.** In a sense, this term means "thinking about one's thoughts," and its development is related to the "theory of mind" children begin to acquire in the preschool years (see Chapter 9, pp. 237–242). School-age children's better use of selective attention, mnemonics, and other cognitive strategies all derive from metacognitive growth.

There are other indicators of this developmental change as well (Flavell, 1985; Kail, 1990). Preschoolers have difficulty judging whether a problem is easy or difficult and thus they devote equal effort to each kind. By contrast, children in the school years know how to identify challenging tasks and they devote greater effort to these challenges, with greater success. School-age children also spontaneously monitor and evaluate their progress in a manner that is rare in preschoolers, so they are usually able to judge when they have adequately learned a set of spelling words or science principles. Older children are also more likely to use external aids—such as writing things down, or making lists—to enhance their memorization and problem-solving efforts. In short, older children approach cognitive tasks in a more strategic and planful manner. Their efforts are thus more comprehensive and exhaustive, because they have a heightened metacognitive awareness.

Not surprisingly, research on metacognition is relevant to education: children's learning can be improved if teachers can teach them more effective cognitive strategies (Kail, 1990; Weissberg and Paris, 1986). Children can be encouraged to analyze whether a problem is likely to be easy or difficult, select an appropriate learning or memory strategy, and monitor their progress throughout. One information-processing theorist, Robert Siegler (1983a, 1983b), has studied the intuitive strategies that children commonly employ in problem-solving situations, and he has noted that children learn most when they are shown the specific shortcomings in the strategies they use and are led to more advanced strategies. In general, children benefit from educational practices that not only impart knowledge but also foster cognitive strategies.

As you can see, information-processing theorists have identified a variety of mental processes that develop during middle childhood in ways that enhance the child's learning, thinking, and problem-solving capabilities. It is no surprise, therefore, that formal education usually begins at the age that these capabilities start to unfold. Children become far more educable when they can deliberately use selective attention and mnemonics to assist their learning, when they become aware of cognitive strategies and other aspects of metacognition, and when they can benefit from expanded knowledge and enhanced processing capacity in their efforts to think and reason. In each of these ways, the older child can benefit from formal instruction in ways the preschooler cannot.

However, while the information-processing perspective has helped researchers identify and study these components of cognition, its proponents have failed to reassemble these mental processes to show how the child develops as a coherent, integrated thinker. As Sternberg notes on this point:

> Because they tend to deal with information processing at a nitty-gritty level, it is easy . . . to get wrapped-up in the details of information processing and at times to lose sight of . . . where performance on a task fits into the grander scheme. [Sternberg, 1990]

This shortcoming—which, ironically, highlights the comprehensiveness of Piaget's theory—suggests that there may be limitations to depicting children's minds as computerlike information-processors. Because children are so much more than data analysts—approaching their worlds inventively, creatively, and insightfully—there remains considerably more to cognitive growth than the development of information-processing skills.

Language

As you saw in Chapter 9, the preschool years are the time of a language explosion, in which children's vocabulary, grammar, and pragmatic language skills develop with marked rapidity. Language development during the years from age 6 to 11 is also remarkable, though much more subtle, as children consciously come to understand more about the many ways language can be used. This understanding gives them greater control in their comprehension and use of language, and, in turn, enlarges the range of their cognitive powers generally. Their understanding of language is a powerful key to new understanding of themselves and their world.

Vocabulary

During middle childhood, children begin to really enjoy words, as they continue to fast-map new ones into their vocabularies. Their delight in verbal play—clearly demonstrated in the poems they write, the secret languages they create, and the jokes they tell—makes middle childhood a good time to explicitly help children expand their vocabularies, thus providing a foundation for more elaborate self-expression.

One of the most important language developments during middle childhood is a shift in the way children think about words. Gradually they become more analytic and logical in their processing of vocabulary, and less restricted to the actions and perceptual features directly associated with particular words (Holzman, 1983). When a child is asked to say the first word that comes to mind on hearing, say, "apple," the preschooler is likely to be bound to the immediate context of an apple, responding with a word that refers to its appearance ("red," "round") or to an action associated with it ("eat," "cook"). The older child or adult, on the other hand, is likely to respond to "apple" by referring to an appropriate category ("fruit," "snack") or to other objects that logically extend the context ("banana," "pie," "tree").

Similarly, when they define words, preschoolers tend to use examples, especially examples that are action-bound. For instance, while preschoolers understand that "under," "below," and "above" refer to relative position, they define these words with examples such as "Rover sleeps under the bed," or

"Below is to go down under something." Older children tend to define words by analyzing their relationships to other words: they would be more likely to say, for instance, that "under" is the same as "below," or the opposite of "above" (Holzman, 1983).

Drawing by Charles Schulz © 1980 United Feature, Syndicate, Inc.

Figure 12.8 *With a language as irregular as English, it should be no surprise that many children (as well as adults) sometimes generate grammatical errors by applying logic to their language constructions.*

Older children's more analytic understanding of words is particularly useful as children are increasingly exposed to words that may have no direct referent in their own personal experience. This understanding makes it possible for them to add to their conceptual framework abstract terms such as "mammal" (extracting the commonalities of, say, whales and mice) or foreign terms such as *yen* (relating this unit of currency to the dollar), and to differentiate among similar words such as "big," "huge," and "gigantic," or "running," "jogging," and "sprinting." Thus, the cognitive maturation of middle childhood, coupled with the school experiences that children have, encourages children to link words with other words. The combination of maturation and experience leads to more rapid intellectual processing, as well as continued vocabulary development.

Grammar

Similar progress occurs in grammar. Although most grammatical constructions of the child's native language are mastered before age 6, knowledge of syntax continues to develop throughout elementary school (Chomsky, 1969; Romaine, 1984). Children are increasingly able to use grammar to understand the implied connections between words, even if the usual clues, such as word order, are misleading.

For instance, children younger than age 6 often have trouble understanding the passive voice, because they know that the agent of an action in a sentence usually precedes the object that is being acted upon. By middle childhood, however, most children realize that the sentence "The truck was bumped by the car" does not state that the truck did the bumping (de Villiers and de Villiers, 1978). The increasing understanding of the passive voice is reflected in children's spontaneous speech as well as in research studies: compared with 6-year-olds, 8-year-olds use the passive voice two-and-a-half times as frequently, and 10-year-olds, three-and-a-half times as often (Romaine, 1984).

The school-age child's gradual understanding of logical relations helps in the understanding of other constructions, such as the correct use of comparatives ("longer," "deeper," "wider"), of the subjunctive ("If you were a millionaire . . . "), and of metaphors (that is, of how a person could be a dirty dog or a rotten egg) (Waggoner and Palermo, 1989). The ability to use these constructions depends on a certain level of cognitive development that typically occurs during elementary school. This is true even with languages in which the particular construction is relatively simple. For instance, the subjunctive form is much less complicated in Russian than in English, but Russian-speaking children master the subjunctive only slightly earlier than English-speaking children, because the concept *if-things-were-other-than-they-are* must be understood before it can be expressed (de Villiers and de Villiers, 1978).

School-age children have another decided advantage over younger children when it comes to mastering the more difficult forms of grammar. Whereas preschool children are quite stubborn in clinging to their grammatical mistakes (remember the child in Chapter 9 who "holded" the baby bunnies?), school-age children are more teachable. They no longer judge correctness solely on the basis of their egocentric version of the rules, or on their own speech patterns. Assuming that they have had ample opportunity to learn the correct grammar, by the end of middle childhood, children are able to apply the rules of proper grammar when asked to, even if they don't use them in their own everyday speech. Thus, even if they themselves say "Me and Suzy quarreled," they are able to understand that "Suzy and I quarreled" is considered correct.

Pragmatics

You have already seen that preschoolers have a grasp of some of the pragmatic aspects of language: they change the tone of their voice when talking to a doll, for instance, or when pretending to be a doctor. However, preschoolers are not very skilled at modifying vocabulary, sentence length, semantic content, and nonverbal cues to fit particular situations. The many skills of communicating improve markedly throughout middle childhood.

Communicating effectively requires, for instance, considering the needs and capacities of the listener. Although preschoolers show an early sensitivity to listener needs—by using simpler speech with a younger child (Shatz and Gelman, 1973), for example—these communications seldom take into account the specific listener's background or characteristics. In one study, Sonnenschein (1986) asked first-grade and fourth-grade children to pretend that they were instructing a playmate on how to find a particular toy in their room at home. The playmate was either a best friend who was familiar with the toys in that room, or a child who was visiting for the first time. Sonnenschein found that although children at each age gave more instructions to the first-time visitor, only the fourth-graders' instructions were consistently well-suited to finding the toy: those of the first-graders included both helpful and irrelevant additional information.

One of the clearest demonstrations of schoolchildren's improved pragmatic skills is found in their joke-telling, which demands several skills not usually apparent in younger children—the ability to listen carefully; the ability to know what someone else will think is funny; and, hardest of all, the ability to remember the right way to tell a joke. Telling a joke is beyond most preschool children. If asked to do so, they usually just say a word (such as "pooh-pooh") or describe an action ("shooting someone with a water gun") that they think is funny. Even if they actually use a joke form, they usually miss the point. One preschooler attempted a joke after listening to her

Figure 12.9 *Chances are that if the words this girl is whispering to her friend were written here, few of us would find them funny. Humor depends on its context, and also on the ability of the joke-teller to use the pragmatic skills of intonation and gestures.*

older sisters tell jokes on a long car trip. "What happens when a car goes into a tunnel?" she asked. "What?" her sisters chorused. "It gets dark" came the punch line. By contrast, almost every 7-year-old can successfully tell a favorite joke upon request (Yalisove, 1978).

The process of asking a riddle shows another pragmatic skill that develops during middle childhood—verbally teasing or tricking someone, especially an adult. Whereas a 7-year-old is likely to deliver the punch line as soon as the listener says "I don't know," or even before, a 10-year-old is more likely to demand several guesses before giving the correct answer with a self-satisfied grin.

Further evidence of increased pragmatic skill is shown in children's learning the various forms of polite speech. School-age children realize that a teacher's saying "I would like you to put away your books now" is not a simple statement of preference but a command in polite form (Holzman, 1983). Similarly, compared with 5-year-olds, 7- and 9-year-olds are quicker to realize that when making requests of persons of higher status—particularly persons who seem somewhat unwilling to grant the request—they should use more polite phrases ("Could I please . . . ?") and more indirect requests ("It would be nice if . . . ") than when they are negotiating with their peers (Axia and Baroni, 1985).

Code-Switching

Changing from one form of speech to another is called **code-switching.** As we will see, children in middle childhood can engage in many forms of code-switching, from the relatively simple process of censoring profanity when they talk to their parents to switching back and forth from one language to another.

A very obvious example of code-switching is children's use of one manner of communicating when they are in the classroom and another when they are with friends after school. In general, the former code, called *elaborated,* is associated with middle-class norms for correct language, while the latter, called *restricted,* is closer to the norms for pronunciation, vocabulary, and grammar associated with lower socioeconomic levels (Bernstein, 1971, 1973). The **elaborated code** is characterized by extensive vocabulary, complex syntax, and lengthy sentences: the **restricted code,** by comparison, has a much more limited use of vocabulary and syntax and relies more on gestures and intonation to convey meaning. The elaborated code is relatively context-free; the meaning of its statements is explicit. The restricted code tends to be context-bound, relying on the shared understandings and experience of speaker and listener to provide some of the meaning. Switching from one code to another, a dispirited student might tell a teacher, "I am depressed today and I don't feel like doing anything," and later confide to a friend, "I'm down, ya know, really wiped." Research has shown that children of all social strata engage in this type of code-switching, and that their pronunciation, grammar, and slang all change in the process (Holzman, 1983; Rogers, 1976; Romaine, 1984).

It seems clear that both elaborated and restricted codes have their place. It is important to be able to explain one's ideas in elaborate and formal terms when appropriate. In fact, two of the basic skills taught during these years, reading and writing, depend on the comprehension of language in a situation devoid of gestures and intonations. At the same time, it is useful to be able to express oneself informally with one's peers, using more emotive, colloquial, and inventive modes of communication than those of the standard, accepted code. While many adults rightly stress the importance of children's mastery of the elaborated code ("Say precisely what you mean in complete sentences, and no slang"), the code that is used with peers is also evidence of the child's pragmatic skill (Goodwin, 1990).

Nonstandard English

Another, more difficult type of code-switching is required of those whose ethnic or regional heritage includes vocabulary, grammar, and pronunciation quite distinct from the "standard" form of their native language. This is clearly the case with regard to "standard English," which in English-speaking countries is the form of the language written in most books and magazines, spoken by national newscasters, and understood by the educated public.

To some degree, nonstandard English is pervasive: idiosyncrasies in speech patterns between one Canadian province and another, or one U.S. state and another, or even one side of town and another, are often strong enough to identify an individual's cultural and geographic origins (Wells, 1982). The Boston "r" (as in "Pahk the cah"), the Ontario "o" (as in "Talk a'boot a lucky break"), the Mississippi "a" (as in "Cayan ya dayance?"), or the preferred regionalisms used for ordering for a "hero"/ "hoagy"/ "submarine"/ "grinder"/ "dagwood" and a "soft drink"/ "cola"/ "pop"/ "soda"/ "fizzy water"/ "tonic" to wash it down are among the most obvious examples.

For some groups, however, language differences form a distinct code.

This is especially true for groups that are cohesive, geographically isolated, and culturally distinct, as reflected in the English spoken in Jamaica, Ireland, Liverpool, and Pakistan. Within the United States, the distinctive pattern most frequently studied is called **Black English.** This form of English has linguistic roots from Africa and the antebellum South, yet is also very contemporary, repeatedly influencing standard American English and continuously revised by many young African-Americans (Labov, 1972; Baugh, 1983).

Many users of standard English consider such variations simply wrong, a collection of mispronunciations, malapropisms and grammatical mistakes that call for disdain or derision. Actually, however, each dialect has particular rules, rhythms, and phrases that survive because they hold communicative power beyond that of the standard language. Within the United States, the work of African-American novelists, filmmakers, and songwriters using Black English is testimony to this power.

Both academic and social problems can arise, however, if a child's primary language is a nonstandard form, spoken by everyone at home and in the neighborhood. Success in school requires learning to read and write standard English—a task that is made much more difficult if standard speech is unfamiliar. This task is further complicated if classmates tease the child for his or her unusual speech and if the teacher takes the stance that nonstandard English is incorrect, incomprehensible, and "illegitimate"— both responses representing an attack on the child's primary identity (Hemmings and Metz, 1990). Faced with such treatment, many children either become silent in the classroom or rebel, defiantly refusing to learn standard English, and often rejecting behavior codes and achievement expectations from the school as well. In addition, the school's reaction undercuts the merits of the child's own culture, causing a double blow to self-esteem. Thus the school's "denial, punishment, and truncation of family and community language socialization patterns minimize the chances that students will manage to transfer these profitably to either the classroom or workplace" (Heath, 1989).

Other teachers, taking the opposite tack, treat nonstandard English as legitimate, accepting it in classwork and speaking it with the students (Hemmings and Metz, 1990). This reaction may unintentionally handicap the child's chances for advancement, not only in school and college, but also in the job market and the larger society, by impeding his or her ability to communicate clearly and comfortably with those in the mainstream culture.

The best path is for the child to learn standard English as a distinct code, a task well-suited to middle childhood because of the concrete operational thinking and metacognition that characterize these years. Children are young enough to hear and notice the nuances of various codes and old enough to comprehend language rules and apply them logically. At the earlier stages of language learning, during toddlerhood and the preschool years, children seem to learn well by simply listening and talking, without specific correction, but during middle childhood, explicit language instruction that delineates the differences between the two codes is useful. For example, pointing out that whereas double negatives in Black English are used for emphasis (as in the spiritual "I Couldn't Hear Nobody Pray"), double negatives in standard English cancel each other, is much more effective than merely criticizing and correcting the child's poor grammar. As long as they feel respected when using their usual speech forms, children are generally open to learning the pragmatics of code-switching and rule-changing, becoming competent in a standard code without being cut off from their original code. As we will see, the same general strategy applies to teaching children an entirely new language.

Learning a Second Language

Few nations are without a minority who speak a different language, and a majority of the citizens of the world are bilingual. Linguistically and culturally, and probably cognitively as well, it is an advantage for children to learn more than one language (Diaz, 1985). Although some critics of bilingualism have correctly noted that one language sometimes seems to interfere with verbal fluency in another, such interference seems to be either the result of poor teaching or else a temporary condition that ends when both languages are eventually separated in the child's mind (McLaughlin, 1984; Cummins, 1991). Moreover, bilingualism may actually enhance children's grasp of linguistic rules and concepts (Bialystok, 1988), as well as further their cognitive development in other ways (Diaz and Klinger, 1991). Thus in the United States the question is how to teach English to the approximately 4.5 million schoolchildren who have another native language, as well as how to help the English-speaking children learn at least one other language before adulthood (Hakuta, 1986; Rotberg, 1982). In Canada, the question is even more complex, since bilingualism is part of a cultural and political struggle that, for many, goes to the heart of Canadian identity.

Unfortunately, although this question has been one of intense concern and emotion, no simple answer is apparent. Almost every educational approach has been tried—from total **immersion,** in which the child's instruction occurs entirely in the second language, to "reverse immersion," in which the child is taught in his or her native language until most of childhood is over and the second language can be taught as a "foreign" language. Variations on these approaches present some topics of instruction in one language and other topics in the other language. However, few carefully controlled, longitudinal studies have been done to evaluate the effectiveness of the various approaches.

Of the research that is available, some of the most thorough comes from Canada, where both English and French are official languages that all children are expected to learn. Immersion programs seem to work best when children are young (Harley et al., 1987). In Canada, immersion has proven successful not only with immigrant children who speak neither English nor French, but also with English-speaking children who are taught exclusively in French in their first years of school and then gradually given more instruction in English. These children eventually match their English-speaking English-taught peers in academic subjects, and surpass them in French (Genesse, 1983).

However, in most such instances of successful immersion, parents voluntarily placed their children in a special program designed to teach the second language. As the Research Report on pages 320–321 points out, variations in attitudes within the family and within the culture are often transmitted to the classroom, in some cases causing the child to cling steadfastly to his or her first language, in others, helping the child to readily learn a second language, perhaps even to become truly bilingual and bicultural.

Figure 12.10 *Bilingual education works best when it is bicultural as well, that is, when teachers and students understand that language is not simply a collection of words to be translated but a set of values, perceptions, and experiences to be appreciated. This occurs best in a classroom that encourages student participation, as seems to be the case here.*

RESEARCH REPORT   Bilingual Education

At some stages of development, learning a second language can happen as naturally as learning a first language. Most kindergartners arrive at school knowing such basics of communication as expressive gestures and turn-taking, as well as relevant social and cognitive strategies for "getting along" in whatever language the other children speak (Saville-Troike et al., 1984). To be more specific, in a study of Spanish-speaking children aged 5 to 7 in a largely English-speaking setting, Lily Wong Fillmore (1976) found that children relied on eight strategies for learning English.

Social Strategies

1. Join a group and act as if you know what is going on, even if you don't.

2. Give the impression, with a few well-chosen words, that you speak the language.

3. Count on your friends to help.

Cognitive Strategies

1. Assume that what people are saying is directly relevant to the situation at hand. GUESS.

2. Use some expression you understand and start talking.

3. Look for recurring parts in the formulas you know.

4. Make the most of what you've got.

5. Work on the big things first: save the details for later.

Obviously, the children need to feel fairly self-confident, and their peers need to be relatively receptive, before these strategies can be used effectively. Unfortunately, such is not always the case for many minority-language children, especially older children. In order for language learning to occur between one child and another in elementary school, the teacher must encourage communication between the children, even if the form is not precisely what he or she would hope for. Indeed, in one study many of the first phrases the children used would not be in any textbook: "Lookit," "All right you guys," "I wanna," "I don't wanna," "How do you do these (little tortillas/flowers/etc.) in English?" and "Shaddup your mouth."

The success of formal bilingual education, of course, varies greatly from child to child, teacher to teacher, and program to program (Wong Fillmore, 1987). As you might expect, one critical difference between success and failure is whether or not the children have ample opportunity to converse, either with other children or with the teacher, in the new language. As Piaget, Vygotsky, and information-processing theorists would have predicted, large-group instruction and rote learning do not lead to language fluency. One-on-one communication between the language learner and the language teacher is crucial (Van Lier, 1988; Wong Fillmore, 1991).

Overall, the context of language learning seems as important as the curriculum. In general, children can successfully take on a second language in the early grades if the following conditions obtain (Rotberg, 1982; McLaughlin, 1985):

1. The program is specifically designed for language learning, with bilingual teachers who are trained and skilled in language teaching.

2. The child already has a mastery of the native language, and wants to learn the new language.

3. The language to be learned, and the native language, are both of relatively high status in the culture.

4. The parents and the community are supportive of the program.

When these conditions do not exist, children have great difficulty learning a new language to which they are suddenly exposed, especially if that language is the primary language of the culture and the school and therefore is simultaneously used for instruction in reading, writing, and math. For such children, bilingual-bicultural education may be best. This type of instruction first reinforces the children's native language and culture, so that they are able to master reading and writing in their first language, as well as to feel proud of themselves and their heritage. At the same time, the children can learn to speak the second language. By age 9 or so, these children are better able to use their logical skills to learn the formal grammar and spelling of a second language.

Bilingual education of any kind is expensive; since classes should be small and teachers specially trained. Moreover, even if money is available, teachers may not be: typically, the minority-language group has relatively few adults who are proficient in both languages and trained to teach. Not surprisingly, then, in the United States and in many other countries, most non-English-speaking children are simply placed in standard English classes, with no special language-learning arrangements whatsoever (O'Malley, 1982). How do they do? For the most part, not very well. Not only do they have difficulty mastering the majority language and maintaining their native tongue; they also fall behind in other academic subjects. Far too often, they drop

Figure 12.12 *International differences in educational achievement are widespread, particularly in subjects that are heavily dependent on classroom instruction. As this graph shows, for example, almost twice as many Korean as Irish 13-year-olds score at the 500 level (able to solve two-step verbal problems) in math, and children in the United States are at the bottom of the heap in science.*

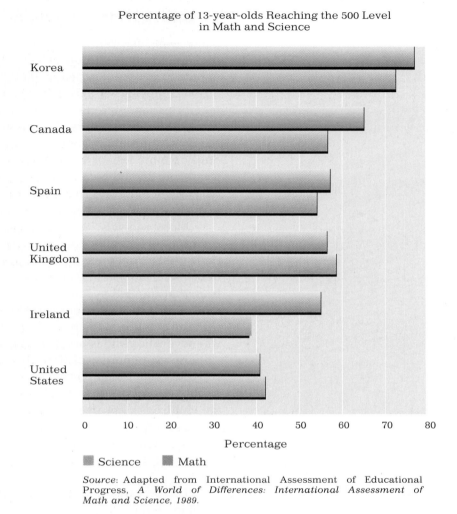

Percentage of 13-year-olds Reaching the 500 Level
in Math and Science

Source: Adapted from International Assessment of Educational Progress, *A World of Differences: International Assessment of Math and Science, 1989.*

concern about certain educational processes that now seem to be inadequate. This is particularly apparent in the United States, because achievement scores show American children behind their counterparts in most other industrialized countries, especially in math and science (Stevenson and Stigler, 1992; International Assessment of Educational Progress, 1989). The differences are most marked when children of the United States are compared with those from the Pacific-rim countries (Japan, Hong Kong, Korea, the Republic of China) but they are also apparent in comparisons with children from European nations and Canada (see Figure 12.12).

Consequently, almost every aspect of the schooling process, from teacher selection to public financing, from racial integration to religious instruction, from parental involvement to curriculum balance, has been the target of criticism. While most of the issues in these controversies are more appropriately discussed in a textbook on political processes than here, research in cognitive development provides valuable insights into the basic question of how children learn best.

Cognitive Development and Classroom Learning

School-age children are active learners, seeking to master logical principles and learning strategies, as well as to develop academic skills and accumulate knowledge—which means that passive learning, such as sitting quietly and copying work from the blackboard, and piecemeal learning, such as memorization, by repetition and rote, of the sounds of the alphabet, of the sums of simple numbers, of the names of the continents, and so forth, is not the most appropriate means of instruction overall. Educators influenced by developmental theory, particularly Piaget's, have rightly concluded that the classroom should be a busy place, in which children's curiosity is met with an array of materials to explore and discuss, such as coins to count, objects to measure, books to read, stories to dramatize.

More recently, the information-processing perspective has led to a reemphasis on explicit instruction, which was sometimes shunted aside in the initial excitement about Piagetian discovery methods. However, the information-processing emphasis on skills and knowledge is quite different from that implicit in the workbooks and rote memorization of old. Student motivation, attention, and mastery of strategies and principles are the key, with the teacher at the ready to provide the necessary knowledge and skills whenever the child is prepared to open a new cognitive door.

An even more recent insight from developmental research has been a recognition of the importance, as highlighted by Vygotsky, of social interaction in the classroom, not only between teacher and student but also among the children themselves. Numerous studies have shown that if their task is structured to encourage cooperation, classmates can draw each other into the zone of proximal development (see pp. 240–242), expanding each other's knowledge as well as, and more often than, any one teacher can (Rogoff, 1990).

This fact was clearly demonstrated in an extensive experiment on the development of reading skills, in which teachers of 3,345 children in Hawaii followed a Vygotskiian model that emphasized social interaction within the zone of proximal development. Instead of the usual practice of having students read silently to themselves, with the teacher asking the entire class some simple comprehension questions, the teachers in this experiment used such strategies as having groups of children read a paragraph aloud together, and then collectively respond to a series of questions designed to elicit discussion as well as confirm understanding. Compared to a control group who received more conventional teaching within the same schools, the experimental children scored significantly higher on standard tests of reading achievement. Indeed, by the end of first grade, the experimental group's scores were 41 percent higher than the control group's (Klein, 1988).

A similar approach is being taken in many math classes, as workbooks, rote learning, and pure memorization are being replaced by instruction that involves "hands-on" materials and active discussion, both designed to elicit conceptual understanding, problem solving, and the ability to verbalize math concepts.

Such new approaches are sorely needed. According to a nationwide exam, for example, almost all American high school students educated in

Figure 12.13 *In this New Zealand classroom, children learn to read and write using the highly successful "whole language" approach, figuring out how to write their own stories and then reading them to each other. As you can see, proper spelling is not essential to getting a foothold on basic literacy.*

the traditional way knew that a square has four equal sides, and that the formula for finding the area of a rectangle is L × W = A—yet less than half could find the area of a square given the length of one side (Sizer, 1985). This particular difficulty points to the central problem of the traditional approach to math—rote memorization of method with little attention to the underlying concepts. As a result, in this case, many students relied on knowing specific formulas for specific problems, rather than on a conceptual understanding of what "area" entails. With the new approach, the schoolchild's introduction to "finding the area" would center on the concept itself. A teacher might ask, for example, how many desks could fit into the classroom—and allow the children in groups to use such strategies as moving furniture, using measuring sticks, drawing diagrams, and so forth to come to the answer. With such a tactic, children are more likely to understand and remember what area is and how to find it, and years later they will be able to apply that knowledge whether they remember the formula or not.

That goal has not yet been broadly realized, however. Published results of national and international testing still show American students far behind what might be expected, as well as behind many of their foreign peers. Consequently, politicians, scholars, and the general public are curious about what other nations are doing to foster learning. In fact, both the reading and math innovations beginning to emerge in American schools are influenced by successful programs abroad. Other practices, such as extending the school day or year to equal that of European or Asian countries, have also been proposed. Before adopting any one reform, however, we need to compare educational systems more closely.

Education in the United States, Japan, and the Republic of China: A Cross-Cultural Comparison

The same tests that find American children's achievement close to the bottom, internationally, find Japan, Korea, and China at the top. One early explanation of this difference was genetic: since Japanese children scored higher than American children on standard IQ tests, perhaps, it was suggested, they are innately smarter (Lynn, 1982).

However, a group of researchers studying this issue has found a quite different explanation (Stevenson et al., 1990; Stevenson and Stigler, 1992). Comparing first- and fifth-grade children from the cities of Minneapolis (USA), Taipei (the Republic of China), and Sendai (Japan) on a variety of tests of reading, math, and other cognitive abilities, they found that although Chinese and Japanese schoolchildren frequently outperformed American children, these differences were due not to higher intellectual aptitude but to educational experiences in the school and in the home.

In Japan and the Republic of China, for example, children go to school five and a half days a week, compared to five in the United States; the average school year is one-third longer than in the United States; and the children are in school more hours each day than American children are. Further, Japanese children in particular are likely to attend supplemental classes at private cram schools called *juku*.

But according to these researchers, even more important than how much time children spend in the classroom is how that time is spent. American schoolchildren devoted far less classroom time to academic activities than Japanese and Chinese students, more frequently engaging in inappropriate activities (getting out of their seats, chatting with friends, etc.). By fifth grade, American students were spending 64 percent of the schoolday in academic work, whereas Japanese students were academically engaged 87 percent of the time. One notable result of this difference in the use of classroom time is that American children spent an average of only three hours a week on math, whereas Japanese children spent an average of seven. American children were also more inclined to work alone than in groups, compared with Japanese and Chinese children. American teachers, in turn, worked more frequently with individual children or in small groups than with the class as a whole, while teachers in Japan and China strongly emphasized group instruction with every child actively participating. As a consequence, children from these Asian nations had greater overall opportunity to learn from their teachers in class.

Education also involves the home, of course, and the most recent report from these researchers reveals important differences in parental support and attitudes toward the child's educational progress. According to Stevenson and Stigler (1992), academic achievement was a much more central concern to Japanese and Chinese parents, who had higher expectations for their offspring and were more involved in fostering their children's success. The Minneapolis mothers, according to these researchers, believed instead that "it is better for children to be bright than to be good students." Perhaps as a consequence, parents in Japan and the Republic of China were much more involved in the child's education, encouraging and supervising homework, (91 percent of Japanese children had their own desk at home), obtaining tutoring if their child encountered problems, maintaining high standards for academic work, and emphasizing the value and importance of hard work over innate capabilities. By contrast, American parents were far more likely to be satisfied with their child's current progress and achievement, and their offspring likewise gave themselves the highest ratings on their ability in reading and math, brightness, and academic performance. This is sadly ironic, of course, in view of their actual achievement in relation to that of children from other developed countries.

Values in the macrosystem are highly influential as well. In keeping with the culture's regard for education, Japanese teachers are highly trained, greatly esteemed, and well paid (their salary is 2.4 times the average Japanese salary, in contrast with that of American teachers, which is 1.7 times the national average). Similarly, Japanese schools are clean and very well equipped, with almost all having libraries, music rooms, and science laboratories, and 75 percent of them having swimming pools.

Figure 12.14 *The enthusiasm for learning and academic achievement of these Japanese schoolchildren has many catalysts: how teachers organize their activities in the classroom, how parents encourage intellectual accomplishment at home, and how the culture emphasizes hard work and every person's capacity to contribute. An added element is that Japanese schoolchildren tend to be interactive and cooperative. In elementary school, for instance, it is typical for desks to be pushed together and for children to discuss their work with each other. Japanese classrooms are organized heterogeneously, with children of varying ability learning cooperatively.*

As this research indicates, educational achievement entails a complex interaction of a child's aptitude and motivation, the school environment, and support from the home. While American parents tend to be very concerned about their child's progress during the preschool years,

> they abdicate some of these responsibilities to the teacher once the child enters school. This trend is opposite from that which occurs in Chinese and Japanese families . . . From the time that child enters school, life for the Chinese and Japanese child becomes purposeful; the child, the parents, and the teachers begin the serious task of education. [Stevenson and Lee, 1990]

An awareness of the importance of cultural context reminds us that no one national educational system can be transmitted, wholesale, to another. It is tempting to focus on one or two distinctive traits of successful education in another country, and consider them the solution to domestic educational problems. Unfortunately, the easiest solutions, such as extending the school day, tend to be the most superficial. The researchers in the comparison study warn that:

> increasing the amount of time spent in academic activities without modifying the content of the curriculum and the manner of instruction might further depress American children's interest in school and increase their dislike of home-

work. Greater time on task is not the primary basis for the high achievement of Chinese and Japanese children. The answer lies instead in the high quality of experiences that fill this time. . . . Chinese and Japanese elementary school classrooms, contrary to common stereotypes, are characterized by frequent interchange between teacher and students, enthusiastic participation by the students, and the frequent use of problems and innovative solutions. [Stevenson and Lee, 1990]

As you have just read, this is precisely the direction suggested by developmental theory, a direction more and more educators in the United States, Canada, and elsewhere are pursuing. Perhaps combining more time on task and better instructional methods will soon boost American children's achievement.

The contextual view reminds us, however, that school is not isolated from society and that cognitive development does not occur in isolation from the biosocial development described in Chapter 11 or the psychosocial development discussed in the next chapter. In some ways, American values may undermine school reform; in some cases, specific children may, because of the effects of poverty, racism, divorce, abuse, rejection, or self-doubt, be unable to learn in class. Chapter 13 explores some of these cultural, familial, and personality factors that impede or enhance development during middle childhood.

SUMMARY

Concrete Operational Thought

1. According to some developmental psychologists, the years from ages 5 to 7 are a time of transition, when new memory skills, reasoning abilities, and capacity to learn appear. During this period, children sometimes intuit the right answers to logical questions without knowing how they got them.

2. According to Piaget, beginning at about age 7 or 8, children are able to think using the logical operations of concrete operational thought. They can apply their logic to problems involving classification and seriation and can use reversibility and reciprocity. Mathematics and scientific principles are also better understood, as are others' points of view.

3. While Piaget's ideas about the sequence of cognitive development have been generally acknowledged to be correct, many researchers believe that cognitive changes occur more gradually and more heterogeneously than Piaget's theory suggests.

The Information-Processing Perspective

4. Information-processing theorists seek to explain development in learning, thinking, and problem-solving in middle childhood in terms of the growth of selective attention, the acquisition of memory skills, an increase in the child's

processing capacity, a growing foundation of knowledge, and a developing awareness of cognitive strategies.

5. The study of developmental changes in specific mental components has helped researchers delineate aspects of cognitive growth with important educational implications. However, it has not yet provided a picture of how these components are integrated in the child's development.

Language

6. Language abilities continue to improve during middle childhood, partly because schools and families encourage this learning, and partly because increased cognitive development makes it easier to understand difficult grammatical and pragmatic distinctions.

7. The ability to understand that language is a tool for communication makes the school-age child more able to use different forms of language in different contexts. For example, a child can use Black English on the playground and standard English in the classroom.

8. Teaching children a second language can be accomplished by a number of different methods—from total immersion in the new language to gradually increasing exposure. However, the most important factors seem to be the commitment of home and school.

Thinking, Learning, and Schooling

9. The school-age child is someone who is thoughtful, eager to learn, able to focus attention, to master logical operations, to remember interrelated facts, and to speak in several linguistic codes.

10. Although basic literacy is universally sought, who receives instruction, the curriculum offered, and pedagogical techniques vary widely.

11. School-age children are active learners, which means that passive learning is not the most appropriate means of instruction. Recent developmental research has shown the pedagogical benefits of greater classroom interaction, both between teachers and students and among the students themselves.

12. Cross-cultural studies show that effective education depends not only on how time is spent in the classroom but also on how education is valued in the home and the larger culture.

KEY TERMS

concrete operational
  thought (304)
decenter (304)
5-to-7 shift (304)
identity (305)
reversibility (305)
reciprocity (305)
classification (305)
class inclusion (305)
seriation (306)
information-processing
  (308)
selective attention (309)

storage strategies (309)
rehearsal (309)
organization (309)
retrieval strategies (310)
mnemonics (310)
processing capacity (310)
metacognition (312)
code-switching (316)
elaborated code (317)
restricted code (317)
Black English (318)
immersion (319)

KEY QUESTIONS

1. What are some of the cognitive characteristics of the 5-to-7 shift?

2. What are some of the cognitive changes that enable children at 7 or 8 to reason logically and objectively?

3. What are some of the concepts that children must be able to apply to understand mathematical and scientific principles?

4. What are some of the factors responsible for the improvement in learning and problem-solving during middle childhood, according to information-processing theory?

5. Why do preschoolers tend to be more optimistic about their cognitive skills than school-age children?

6. What are some of the language skills that develop in middle childhood?

7. How does code-switching enable children to speak both standard English and Black English?

8. What are some of the factors that encourage learning of a second language?

9. How do the educational experiences of an American child differ from those of either a Chinese or a Japanese student?

CHAPTER 13

The School Years: Psychosocial Development

During the school years, emotional and social development occurs in a much more elaborate context than the closely supervised and circumscribed arenas of the typical younger child. As school-age children explore the wider world of neighborhood, community, and school, independent of parental control, they experience new vulnerability, increasing competence, ongoing friendships, challenging, and sometimes troubling, rivalries, deeper social understanding, and conflicting moral values. Personality attributes, coping mechanisms, and future aspirations are all formed by their developing social cognition. This chapter describes their reaction to their expanding horizons, answering questions such as the following:

How does self-understanding evolve during the school years?

What familial factors foster healthy development?

Is it destructive for children to live in a single-parent household?

Does divorce harm every child, or only children of a certain age, sex, and family background?

How does it affect a child to be poor or homeless?

What types of social support are most helpful to children who are experiencing serious stress?

As children between the ages of 6 and 11 become physically stronger and more capable (Chapter 11), and cognitively wiser and more logical (Chapter 12), their growing abilities serve as the foundation for remarkable psychological and social accomplishments. For example, as they become more independent, children also begin to make their own decisions and govern their own behavior, including everything from the mundane selection of which socks to wear, to the social choice of whom to befriend, to the moral decision about whether to lie or steal. In so doing, children increasingly experience the influence of other children, as well as of the community as a whole.

This interplay between increasing competence and an expanding social world is the theme of psychosocial development in middle childhood, and thus the theme of this chapter. First let us look specifically at the psychic growth that characterizes these years, and then at some of the contexts, particularly those associated with family structure, that shape and propel that growth. Finally, we look at the stresses that many children this age confront, and at their ways of coping with those stresses.

An Expanding Social World

Throughout the world, school-age children are recognized as markedly more independent and more capable than younger children. As a result, children go to school, or outside to play, or off to work, out of their parents' view, meeting friends and strangers unknown to their families, and experiencing adventures and challenges that adults often know little about.

A Common Theoretical Thread

This new competence has been recognized by every developmental theorist who has attended to this period. Freud describes middle childhood as the period of **latency,** when children's emotional drives are quieter, their psychosexual needs are repressed, and their unconscious conflicts are submerged, features that make latency "a time for acquiring cognitive skills and assimilating cultural values as the child expands his world to include teacher, neighbors, peers" (Miller, 1983).

Erikson (1963) likewise agrees that middle childhood is a quiet period emotionally and that it is productive as well, as the child "becomes ready to apply himself to given skills and tasks." The specific crisis that Erikson sees for this developmental period is **industry versus inferiority.** According to Erikson, as children busily try to master whatever skills are valued in their culture, they develop views of themselves as either competent or incompe-

Figure 13.1 *The Brazilian boy fashioning arrows in the Amazon jungle and the American boy in a woodworking class are both engaged in essentially the same task—attaining competence in their respective societies.*

(a)   (b)

tent, or, in Erikson's words, as either industrious and productive or inferior and inadequate.

Operating from quite different theoretical bases, developmentalists influenced by behaviorism or social learning theory, or by the cognitive or humanist perspectives, are less interested in the school-age child's convoluted emotional life and more concerned with the step-by-step acquisition of new cognitive abilities, and the steady unfolding of self-understanding, that characterize middle childhood. However, their overview of this period is quite similar to the psychoanalytic depiction: children during middle childhood meet the challenges of the outside world with an openness, insight, and confidence that few younger children possess. Middle childhood is seen as a time when many distinct competencies coalesce. The abilities to learn and to analyze, to express emotions, and to make friends have been in evidence from infancy, but now they come together in a much more focused and consistent manner, forming a much stronger, unified, and self-assured personality (Collins, 1984; Bryant, 1985; Bandura, 1981, 1989).

Now let us look at some of the specific manifestations of this developmental period.

Social Cognition

An integral key to the psychosocial development of school-age children is an advance in **social cognition,** that is, in the understanding of other people and groups. As we saw in Chapter 9, preschoolers first evidence social cognition in a simple, one-step theory of mind, when they begin to realize that other people's actions can be motivated by thoughts and emotions that are different from their own. But such "theorizing" as young children do in this respect is ephemeral and episodic—a break in the egocentric thinking that is more typical of preschoolers. During the school years, children's theory of mind evolves into a complex, multistep view of others. Children begin to understand human behavior not just as responses to specific contiguous antecedents but as actions that are influenced, simultaneously, by immediate needs and emotions and by long-term human relationships and motives (McKeough, 1992; Bruner, 1986).

This developmental progression was shown explicitly in a very simple experiment in which children between the ages of 4 and 10 were shown pictures of various domestic situations and asked how the mother might respond and why (Goldberg-Reitman, 1992). In one scene, for example, a child curses when playing with blocks. In assessing what the mother might do, the 4-year-olds attended only to the immediate behavior, whereas older children recognized the implications and possible consequences of the behavior, as reflected in the following typical responses:

Age 4: "The mother spanks her because she said a naughty word."

Age 6: "The mother says 'Don't say that again' because it's not nice to say a bad word."

Age 10: "The mother maybe hits her or something because she's trying to teach her . . . because if she grew up like that she'd get into a lot a trouble . . . she might get a bad reputation."

In a variety of similar research studies, as well as in everyday spontaneous examples, younger children are much more likely to focus solely on observable behavior, not on underlying motives, feelings, or social consequences: they know when an adult might protect, nurture, scold, or teach a child but not necessarily why. Older children tend not only to understand the affective origins of various behaviors but also to analyze the future impact of whatever action they might take.

This more complex social cognition is also shown in children's advancing realization that individuals differ in personality traits. Compare the following two descriptions from an extensive study (Livesley and Bromley, 1973) in which children aged 7 and older described other children:

> 7-year-old: Max sits next to me, his eyes are hazel and he is tall. He hasn't got a very big head, he's got a big pointed nose.

> 10-year-old: He smells very much and is very nasty. He has no sense of humor and is very dull. He is always fighting and he is cruel. He does silly things and is very stupid. He has brown hair and cruel eyes. He is sulky and 11 years old and has lots of sisters. I think he is the most horrible boy in the class. He has a croaky voice and always chews his pencil and picks his teeth and I think he is disgusting.

As you see, the 7-year-old's description focuses exclusively on physical characteristics. Children of this age are, in fact, aware of personality traits and can infer them from others' behavior (Berndt and Heller, 1985; Miller and Aloise, 1989), but they usually do not spontaneously think of others in terms of personality dispositions. Instead, they focus either on outward appearance or behavior that can be more easily observed and interpreted (Feldman and Ruble, 1988). Older children, by contrast, are aware of the importance of personality traits. They organize their perceptions of a person around the traits they observe in the individual and frequently use those traits as a basis for predicting the person's future behavior and emotional reactions (Gnepp and Chilamkurti, 1988).

During the school years, children's emotional understanding deepens in a number of other ways as well. They begin to appreciate, for example, that emotions have internal causes that can sometimes be personally redirected (such as thinking happy thoughts in a sad situation); that someone can feel several emotions simultaneously (and can thus have conflicting or ambivalent feelings); and that people sometimes disguise or mask their emotions to comply with social rules (such as looking delighted after opening a disappointing gift) (Harris et al., 1981; Harter and Whitesell, 1989; Saarni, 1989).

This expansion of emotional understanding has several important consequences for social interaction. It means that children are likely to become more sensitive to, and empathize with, the emotional experiences of others. This heightened sensitivity influences children's willingness to be kind and helpful to others. Another advance, for which adults may be grateful, is that older children are better able to recognize and rephrase or avoid potentially offensive statements (Johnson et al., 1984). Thus the 11-year-old is much less likely than the 6-year-old to tell you that your stomach is too fat.

Children's enhanced emotional understanding also increases their sensitivity to the social purposes of emotional expressions, and to the possibility that their own expressions—and those of other people—may not reflect what they truly feel. As a consequence, they are harder to fool: it is the school-age child who shrugs off a parent's sympathy by saying "You're just

Figure 13.2 *Will this gift be a treat or a turkey? Whichever it is, this girl knows that she should look pleased with the gift in the presence of the person who gave it to her. Contrary to most preschoolers, in other words, she knows that people often mask their true emotions for social purposes—in this case, to protect the feelings of the gift-giver.*

trying to make me feel better," or dismisses a parent's praise with "You have to say that because I'm your kid!"

The child's increasing ability to recognize others' personality and emotional characteristics, and to anticipate how these characteristics might affect their behavior, helps the child to get along better with other people. In one detailed study (Gottman, 1983) in which children between the ages of 2 and 11 were told to play with an unfamiliar peer, the younger children (up to about age 5) tended to just start playing at whatever came to mind. The older children were more likely to introduce themselves and search for some common ground between them to provide a basis for their play. In addition, the older children had a better sense of proper pacing of personal communication: they first discussed the similarities between them before discussing the differences. Unlike the younger children, they also knew whether and when to reveal private information. For example, one 5-year-old told her new playmate that her mother didn't love her anymore—because, she said, her mother wanted to be left alone with Jimmy (her new boyfriend) instead. Older children never shared such personal information on first meeting. Finally, the older children were better at resolving conflict, using humor, for example, rather than confrontation when disagreements occurred. For all these reasons, the older children were more likely than the younger children to be on friendly terms when the play session was concluded. Their social understanding contributed to more successful social interaction.

Understanding Oneself

As we saw in Chapters 9 and 10, preschoolers have begun to develop a theory of mind, although they have little, if any, stability in their specific ideas of self, at least in the sense of having a theory about themselves that they can verbalize and use to guide their actions (Harter, 1982). However, children's thoughts about themselves develop rapidly during middle childhood, as their cognitive abilities mature and their social experience widens. In the beginning of the school years, for example, children often explain their actions by referring to the events of the immediate situation; a few years later they more readily relate their actions to their personality traits and feelings (Higgins, 1981). Thus, whereas the 6-year-old might say that she hit him because he hit her, the 11-year-old might also explain that she was already upset because she had lost her bookbag and that, besides, he is always hitting people and getting away with it. Further, children's self-understanding becomes integrated even as it becomes more differentiated (Harter, 1983), enabling schoolchildren to view themselves in terms of several competencies at once. They might, for example, recognize themselves as weak at playing sports, good at playing a musical instrument, and a whiz at playing Nintendo. Similarly, they might feel that they are basically good at making friends, and are considerate of others, but that they have a quick temper that sometimes makes them do things that jeopardize their friendships.

Along with their developing self-understanding comes greater self-regulation, as children learn to control their reactions for strategic purposes. With respect to emotion, for example, children in the school years acquire skills at monitoring and modifying their emotional experiences (Band and Weisz, 1988; Merum Terwogt and Olthof, 1989; Thompson, 1990).

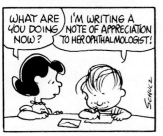

Drawing by Charles Schulz; © 1967, 1968 United Feature Syndicate, Inc.

Figure 13.3 *As children grow older, they become increasingly adept at understanding that situations look different to people with different viewpoints, and that friendship and interpersonal understanding are complex processes. Linus's social cognitive skills are revealed in his awareness that Miss Othmar's difficulties in visual perspective accounted for his misunderstanding of her social perspective toward him.*

This might involve reinterpreting an emotionally arousing situation (such as deciding that a teacher's crankiness isn't to be taken personally), intentionally distracting oneself (such as reading a book while parents are arguing), and other deliberate strategies. Being able to understand various aspects of their emotions and personality *sometimes* helps children to modify their behavior. For example, they might apologize for an outburst of anger by referring to their hot temper, or they might even take steps to protect a friend from such an outburst by, say, going for a walk to "cool off."

The Rising Tide of Self-Doubt

As their self-understanding sharpens, children gradually become more self-critical, and their self-esteem dips. One reason is that they are more capable of comparing their skills and achievements with those of others (Ruble et al., 1980), and thus they can critically evaluate their strengths and weaknesses. Further, as they mature, children are more likely to feel personally to blame for their shortcomings, and less likely to believe, as younger children often do, that it is bad luck that makes them do poorly (Powers and Wagner, 1984). Girls are especially likely to blame themselves for their difficulties (Stipek, 1984), a tendency apparent throughout childhood. Thus, while children are better able to recognize the diverse areas in which they succeed and fail as they grow older, they are more likely to take failures seriously, and thus their overall self-esteem, which is usually quite high in early childhood, decreases throughout middle childhood, reaching a low at about age 12 before it gradually rises again (Harter, 1983; Savin-Williams and Demo, 1984; Simmons et al., 1973; Wallace et al., 1984).

Several studies have shown that children's perceptions of their intellectual competence also decline steadily through the elementary-school years (Marsh et al., 1984; Pintrich and Blumenfeld, 1985). This is in striking contrast to the self-evaluations of preschoolers, who usually remain buoyantly optimistic and confident of their own abilities, even in the face of negative evaluations by others (Stipek, 1984).

One reason for preschoolers' persistently sunny view of their cognitive skills is that they think of intellectual ability as a changing attribute that can be improved through practice and effort. When preschoolers confidently predict success on a task they have consistently failed at, it means that they intend to try harder next time. In contrast, by the middle school years, children can better distinguish between ability and effort, and they regard intellectual abilities as relatively enduring traits that can promote or limit success (Benenson and Dweck, 1986; Nicholls, 1978). Just as they see themselves as weak in some social skills and strong in others, they may believe that they are "good at," say, math or reading, but just "can't do" science or social studies.

These developmental changes in intellectual self-evaluation are illustrated in an observational study of children in kindergarten, first-, second-, and fourth-grade classrooms by Frey and Ruble (1987). Observers made detailed ratings of the spontaneous comments of these children during independent work, devoting particular attention to self-congratulatory comments ("Know how I did it? BRAINS!") and self-critical comments ("I missed a lot"). They found that self-congratulatory comments peaked at first grade and then declined markedly by fourth grade, while self-critical comments increased steadily throughout this period. According to the researchers, these changes were largely due to increasing self-criticism in the older children, together with increased social sensitivity to classmates (which meant not bragging about academic success).

Learned Helplessness

Altogether, these developmental changes in self-esteem can affect children's willingness to try to master new skills and learn new material. As one review explains, "developmental change can be a risky business. Greater cognitive capacity for self-reflection can provide the tools for new levels of mastery but can also result in greater inhibition of mastery attempts" (Dweck and Elliott, 1983).

Put another way, compared with younger children, older children are more vulnerable to **learned helplessness:** that is, their past failures in a particular area have taught them to believe that they are unable to do anything to improve their performance. Many children who experience learned helplessness attribute their failures—but not their success—to their ability. Consequently they tend to lack self-confidence in challenging situations, and their performance deteriorates as a result: they use poor problem-solving strategies, their attention wanders, they feel that they are struggling for nothing. Thus learned helplessness leads to a self-fulfilling prophecy. Whereas children who believe in their ability will continue to work at a task they have not yet mastered—confident that their efforts will pay off—children experiencing learned helplessness "know" that they are bound to fail, and so give up trying.

This is especially true if parents or teachers indicate that the child's failure was due to limited competence rather than to not trying hard enough—a message, by the way, that girls tend to receive more often than boys (Dweck et al., 1978). As Erikson predicted when he described industry versus inferiority, a child with few successes may develop a sense of inferiority that leads to anticipation of continued failure and a lower self-esteem. Thus the child who experiences learned helplessness in middle childhood is likely to experience continuing social and/or academic problems unless parents and teachers can change how the child attributes successes and failures (Fincham et al., 1989).

However, as we will now see, in many respects, adults may be less crucial in fostering self-esteem and in other aspects of psychosocial development than peers are.

Figure 13.4 *The best antidote to learned helplessness is a competent and encouraging teacher. Given this girl's expression, her father has probably already begun to teach her some fundamentals of the game—rather than assuming that girls can't hit hard, throw straight, or catch—and to make her feel relaxed about messing up. In general, children learn much more from adults who believe that every child can become competent than from adults who think innate ability is the determining factor.*

The Peer Group

Perhaps the most influential system in which the school-age child develops his or her self-esteem is the **peer group,** a group of individuals of roughly the same age and social status who play, work, and learn together. Acceptance in one's peer group can go a long way toward building a sense of competence, particularly in middle childhood, when frequency of contact with nonfamily peers increases as contact with family members declines (Feiring and Lewis, 1989). Not surprisingly, children become increasingly dependent on their peers, not only for companionship but also for self-validation and advice (Nelson-Le Gall and Gumerman, 1984). Indeed, the peer group becomes a kind of separate society from that of adults.

The Society of Children

When groups of children play together, they develop particular patterns of interaction that regulate their play, distinguishing it from the activities of adult-organized society. Some social scientists call the peer group's subculture the **society of children,** highlighting the distinctions between children's groups and the general culture (Knapp and Knapp, 1976; Opie and Opie, 1959; Davies, 1982).

The society of children typically has a special vocabulary, dress codes, and rules of behavior that flourish without the approval, or even the knowledge, of adults. Its slang words and nicknames, for instance, are often ones adults would frown on (if they could understand them), and its dress codes become known to adults only when they try to get a child to wear something that violates those codes—as when a perfectly fine pair of hand-me-down jeans is rejected because, by the standards of the dress code, they are an unfashionable color, or have the wrong label, or have legs that are too loose, or too tight, or too short, or too long. If parents find a certain brand and style of children's shoes on sale, they can bet that they are the very ones that their children would not be caught dead wearing. Sex differences in clothes, behavior, and play patterns and partners become increasingly salient as children move from kindergarten to the sixth grade (Furman, 1987; Hayden-Thompson et al., 1987).

The distinction between those who are "in" and those who are "out" is perhaps most obvious in children's spontaneous organization of clubs, in which much attention is given to details concerned with rules, officers, dress, and establishing a clubhouse, often deliberately distant from adult activity. Sometimes the club has no announced purpose, its only apparent function being the exclusion of adults and children of the other sex. From a developmental perspective, however, such clubs serve many functions, including building self-esteem, sharpening social skills, and teaching social cooperation. As one researcher describes his club:

> I was a charter member of a second-grade club called the Penguins, whose two major activities were acquiring extensive information about penguins and standing outside in the freezing weather without a coat for as long as we could. Like most other groups of this sort, the Penguins did not last very long, but in the making and unmaking of such groups, children are conducting what may be informative experiments in social organization. [Rubin, 1980]

Unfortunately, for some children, youth gangs serve similar functions, with acceptance into them being dependent upon the child's willingness to engage in certain forms of tough talk and bravado, risk-taking, and flaunting of conventions. All too often, it also requires a willingness to engage in criminal activities.

Even when it does not involve a specific club, gang, or group, the society of children entails general codes of behavior, many of which demand independence from adults. By age 10, if not before, children (especially boys) whose parents walk them to school or kiss them in public are pitied; "cry babies" and "teachers' pets" are criticized; children who tattle or "rat" to adults are despised. As they did at younger ages, school-age children (again, especially boys) engage in rough-and-tumble play, but, observing the codes of their group, they become increasingly selective in when, where, and with whom they do it (Humphreys and Smith, 1987).

Figure 13.5 *A snowball fight is an example of a complex peer-group event—choosing teammates and targets, building forts and planning strategy, and agreeing on rules (such as no iceballs or aiming at the face)—that requires lots of cooperation and trust.*

Norms for Aggression

Closely related to their increasing selectivity in friendly roughhousing is children's growing sensitivity to the norms for nonplayful aggression—the teasing, insulting, and physical threatening that are at the edge of many episodes of children's social interaction. Indeed, a certain amount of aggression, counteraggression, and reconciliation is expected in every children's society, and children often risk social isolation if they do not readily defend themselves against sarcastic comments, implied insults, or direct verbal or physical attacks.

The specifics regarding when aggression is appropriate, in what forms, and to what degree depend, of course, on the specifics of the social context. A study in England, for example, found that children who were most socially accepted were those who "gave as much as they got," sometimes teasing and mocking each other and—girls as well as boys—coming to blows. In fact, reciprocity of aggression was such a part of peer-group acceptance that those who suffered attack without retaliating were rejected as "piss weak" (Davies, 1982). At the same time, arrogance beyond a certain limit was considered out of bounds, for children were quite critical of "getting the snobs, getting the cranks, . . . lying, showing off, getting too full of yourself, posing, . . . wanting everything your way, being spoilt . . ." (Davies, 1982).

A somewhat different distinction between proper and improper aggression was found in a study of first-grade African-American boys: instrumental aggression (e.g., fighting to get one's own way) did not enhance a boy's status, but relatively quick retaliation against an implied threat or insult or a show of force to establish dominance was likely to inspire admiration. As the boys grew older, aggression was less positively viewed, but it still did not undermine acceptance. Even with maturity, a certain amount of preemptive self-defense was expected (Coie et al., 1991).

As these examples suggest, variation in the norms for aggression can occur by ethnic and economic group, by neighborhood, and by the specific social situation, with different rules about hitting someone smaller, or boys attacking girls, or girls using physical force, or the appropriate role of friends and bystanders, or the specifics of which contacts (e.g., a slap in the face, a kick in the shins, a step on the shoes) or insults (directed at one's relatives, one's sexual preferences, or one's intellect) should be ignored, reciprocated, or avenged.

Customs and Principles

While they are developing the social codes for their own societies, children also become more aware of the customs and principles of the larger society. This is shown in a series of studies by Elliot Turiel (Turiel, 1983; Turiel et al., 1991), who found that school-age children not only understand social conventions and ethical principles but can also distinguish between them.

For example, Turiel asked one typical 8-year-old what rules he knew. The boy cited a rule that the children in his house must clean up the mess that their guests make, and he explained that this rule could be easily changed if his parents decided to do so. He also knew another rule, that children should not hurt each other, and he explained that this rule could *not* be changed because hurting is always wrong whenever and wherever it occurs. Similarly, he felt that the rule against stealing could not be changed because "people would go crazy." He added, with an impressive sense of social justice, "People that don't have anything should be able to have something, but they shouldn't get it by stealing."

Older children also understand that people sometimes obey customs more readily than they follow principles. For example, Turiel (1983) found that 10-year-olds, but not 6-year-olds, were convinced that it is a more serious transgression for a child to steal an eraser than to wear pajamas to school, because stealing is wrong while the question of appropriate clothing is simply a custom. At the same time, however, the 10-year-olds admitted that they personally would be more likely to commit a minor theft than to dress inappropriately.

Prosocial Behavior

Figure 13.6 *School-age children have the social cognitive skills to visualize—and feel for—the circumstances of people who are completely unfamiliar to them, such as victims of tornados and floods. This can motivate prosocial behavior, such as the clean-up efforts of these preteens following a tornado in Texas.*

While they are following the social conventions for their own microsociety, children also become more aware of the laws and values of their city and nation, and of the ethical principles that benefit humanity as a whole. They appreciate and respect **prosocial behavior,** acts of sharing and caring that benefit others more than the individual who performs them. As we have already seen, school-age children learn to curb and redirect their antisocial or destructive behavior. Now we will see that, given the appropriate context, children become more sensitive and selective in their prosocial actions as well.

For example, as they grow older, children are better able to explain why a particular action is just or unjust, and why people should help each other, even when no personal gain is involved (Eisenberg et al., 1987). This larger understanding enables many older children to be quite adamant and emotional about the evils of war, racism, sexism, or poverty. One 8-year-old, for instance, was playing with her Barbie dolls. Suddenly she began crying. When asked the reason, she explained that she was pretending that her Barbies were homeless and it made her very sad. Similar sensitivities are apparent in many children, who raise money to help the less fortunate, or refuse to eat tuna that is not caught in dolphin-safe nets, or who write letters to impoverished children in distant countries.

However, although grade-school children are more likely than preschoolers to want to assist those who are completely unfamiliar (such as the victims of famine or earthquake), they are more restrictive when it comes to aiding those they know, and are more likely to assist and share only with someone they like or admire, or with someone who they know needs their help, or with younger children (Burelson, 1982; French, 1984). Perhaps most important, prosocial behavior is increasingly seen as a sign and obligation of friendship, and, as we will see below, friendship becomes more selective and exclusive as middle childhood progresses. Thus the expanding social understanding that is sometimes a catalyst for prosocial behavior during the school years may also restrict its range of recipients within the peer group.

A similar tension between concerns about larger principles and the demands of the immediate situation is shown when children are asked whether they would break a law to help their siblings or peers. In general, school-age children consider loyalty to siblings or peers, especially to a close friend, compelling reason to bend one's allegiance to impersonal standards of right action: most children say they would cheat, lie, or steal to help a needy friend (Turiel et al., 1991).

Friendship

Throughout childhood, friendships become increasingly important, and children's understanding of friendship becomes increasingly complex, as children learn to balance honesty with protectiveness, mutual dependence with a respect for independence, and competition with cooperation, shared conversation, and shared actions (Berndt, 1989b; Rawlins, 1992).

These changes are reflected in a study of hundreds of Canadian and Scottish children, from first grade through the eighth, who were asked what made their best friends different from other acquaintances. Children of all ages tended to say that friends did things together and could be counted on for help, but the older children were more likely to cite mutual help, whereas younger children simply said that their friends helped *them*. Further, the older children considered mutual loyalty, intimacy, and interests, as well as activities, to be part of friendship (Bigelow, 1977; Bigelow and La Gaipa, 1975). Similarly, in a United States study (Berndt, 1981), children were asked "How do you know your best friend?" A typical kindergartner answered:

> I sleep over at his house sometimes. When he's playing ball with his friends he'll let me play. When I sleep over, he lets me get in front of him in 4-squares (a playground game). He likes me.

By contrast, a typical sixth-grader said:

> If you can tell each other things that you don't like about each other. If you get in a fight with someone else, they'd stick up for you. If you can tell them your phone number and they don't give you crank calls. If they don't act mean to you when other kids are around.

As suggested by the sixth-grader's account, older children increasingly regard friendship as a forum for self-disclosure, and expect that their intimacy will be reciprocated (Rotenberg and Mann, 1986; Rotenberg and Sliz, 1988). Partly because friendships become more intense and more intimate as children grow older, older children demand more of their friends, change friends less often, find it harder to make new friends, and are more upset when a friendship breaks up. They also are more picky: throughout childhood, children increasingly tend to choose best friends who are of the same sex, race, and economic background as they themselves are (Hartup, 1983).

As children become more choosy about their friends, their friendship groups become smaller. Whereas most 4-year-olds say that they have many friends (perhaps everyone in their nursery-school class, with one or two notable exceptions), most 8-year-olds have a small circle of friends, and by age 10, children often have one "best" friend to whom they are quite loyal. Although this trend toward an increasingly smaller friendship network is followed by both sexes, it tends to be more apparent among girls. By the end of middle childhood, many girls have one and only one best friend on whom they depend (Gilligan et al., 1990).

Thus, as children grow older, friendship patterns become more rigidly set, so that by age 9 or so everyone knows who hangs out with whom, and

Figure 13.7 *What distinguishes these grade-school friends from preschool pals is that they understand their relationship as a forum for mutual assistance, self-disclosure, and psychological compatibility. This makes friendships more intimate and intense, but also makes the emotional consequences greater when friendships break up.*

few dare to try to break into an established group or pair of friends. With the changes of early puberty (at about age 10), some children come to be more advanced than others, disrupting former social patterns and wrecking many friendships. As one girl named Rachel put it:

> Oh, I feel so horrible about friends. Everybody is deserting their best friend and everybody hates someone else and Paula Davis has been stranded with nobody—except me and Sarah. Cristine has run off with Liz and Joan has moved up from being an eleven-year-old . . . and, oh well, I suppose it happens every year.

Social Problem-Solving

Children's deepening social understanding during the school years enhances their social problem-solving skills, which, in turn, makes their peer relations become more intimate and sophisticated (Dodge, 1986; Rubin and Krasnor, 1986). Among preschoolers, peer conflict frequently results in retaliation, an appeal to an adult authority, or distress. In the school years, however, children master a variety of alternative strategies for resolving conflict. They can cajole the adversary, use bargaining, suggest compromise or cooperation (like turn-taking), and redirect conflict through humor. Children also acquire different strategies for accomplishing different social goals, such as gaining entry to a group, organizing cooperative activity, or getting to know an unfamiliar peer (Putallaz and Wasserman, 1990). These problem-solving strategies enable children to become more sensitive and successful social partners.

Social problem-solving requires several steps (see Figure 13.8). Consider the following exchange between two third-graders who are building with blocks (Rubin and Krasnor, 1986):

> Sarah: "Hey (reaches over). We can make it wider. Here, wanna do it?"
> Lisa: (no response)
> Sarah: "Don't you think it should be a bit wider?"
> Lisa: (no response)
> Sarah: "Yeah, let's make it wider."
> Lisa: (makes construction wider)

Sarah's goal is to involve Lisa in her modified construction plan. She suggests to Lisa that they "make it wider" together because Lisa's previous social cues caused Sarah to interpret their relationship as cooperative. When this initial strategy fails, Sarah reinterprets the situation, and then devises two alternative strategies (a direct inquiry and a restatement of her goal) that eventually accomplish her goal.

As you can see, the social problem-solving flow chart shown in Figure 13.8 resembles an information-processing approach to social understanding (see Chapter 2). Using the information-processing perspective, researchers have begun to examine how specific skills at each step of social problem-solving change during childhood. The ability to generate alternative strategies to resolve conflict and to evaluate their potential outcomes increases during the school years, for example, and leads to improved social competence with peers (Dodge, 1986; Dodge et al., 1986). Children who can predict which strategies will best resolve disagreements tend to be more popular and well-liked among friends. Not surprisingly, this approach has also been useful in improving the social skills of children who are rejected, aggressive, or otherwise deficient in their social skills (see A Closer Look, p. 343).

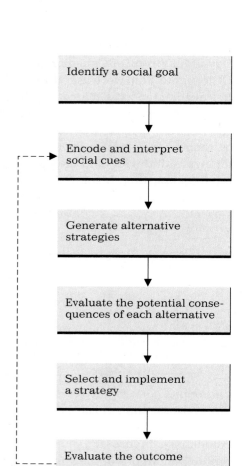

Figure 13.8 *Steps of social problem-solving (adapted from Rubin and Krasnor, 1986, and Dodge, 1986).*

A CLOSER LOOK   **The Rejected, Neglected, or Controversial Child**

All children sometimes feel left out or unwelcome among their peers. As a children's ditty puts it, "Nobody likes me, everybody hates me, think I'll eat some worms."

However, an estimated 5 to 10 percent of all schoolchildren are unpopular and friendless most of the time (Asher and Renshaw, 1981). During the school years, these children develop increasingly negative reputations (Rogosch and Newcomb,1989), which may help explain why they tend to remain shunned (Coie and Dodge, 1983). Using ratings in which children are asked to nominate peers they especially like or dislike, researchers have identified several groups meriting special concern (Coie et al., 1982). *Rejected* children are actively disliked by others, often because of their aggressive, disruptive behavior. *Neglected* children, by contrast, are seldom nominated at all (either positively or negatively), and are ignored by peers because they tend to be shy and withdrawn. *Controversial* children, on the other hand, receive a high number of both positive and negative peer nominations, reflecting ambivalence in how others regard them.

Many of these children have problems: not only are they lonely and unhappy but they have low self-esteem, which affects their learning in school and happiness at home. As they and their classmates grow older, their problems may get worse, because children become more critical of themselves and their peers as adolescence approaches. These concerns are especially great for rejected children, who are most likely to have adjustment problems in adolescence and adulthood (Parker and Asher, 1987).

Several studies have shown that children who are rejected by their peers are immature in their social cognition. Compared with popular or average children, for instance, they tend to misinterpret social situations, considering a friendly act to be hostile (Dodge et al., 1984) or, especially when they feel anxious, interpreting accidental harm as intentional (Dodge and Somberg, 1987). Typically, they might interpret a compliment as sarcastic, or regard a request for a bite of candy as a demand. They also have difficulty sharing and cooperating (Markell and Asher, 1984) and in understanding what other children's needs might be (Goetz and Dweck, 1980).

Unfortunately, since the way most children develop their social understanding and skill is from normal give-and-take with their peers, rejected children are excluded from the very learning situation they need most (Rubin, 1980; Youniss, 1980).

Unpopularity among peers is also affected by social influences outside the peer network. To some extent, a particular ecological milieu encourages or discourages constructive interaction among children. For example, the offspring of authoritarian mothers (see pp. 264–268) use power-assertive strategies themselves to get their way with peers. Not surprisingly, these children are very unpopular (Hart et al., 1990). Another influential factor is the school. On the whole, an informal, open-classroom setting fosters more mutual respect and friendship among the children (Minuchin and Shapiro, 1983). Further, children have more difficulty getting along with peers with whom they share few similarities, so it is probably unwise to place a child with poor social skills into a class where peers have little in common with the new child.

Unfortunately, many parents change neighborhoods (perhaps moving to a "nicer" house) and many principals reassign students (perhaps to create a class that is easier for a teacher to handle) without considering the friendships that might be disrupted or the rejected children who might become even more hostile.

Why is this child sitting by herself apart from the others? She may be a neglected or a rejected child who experiences difficulties with peers, or she may be merely taking a rest from vigorous play. Researchers have discovered that these three alternative interpretations have significantly different long-term implications for the child.

(continued p. 344)

Can anything be done directly to teach children better social skills? Such attempts have been tried, with some success, when the strategies taught were quite specific, such as how to make a positive comment on what someone else says, or how to devise alternative strategies for conflict resolution (Asher and Renshaw, 1981; Bierman and Furman, 1984).

However, a less direct route may also succeed. One surprising study divided socially rejected, low-achieving boys into four groups. One group learned social skills, one academic skills, one both social and academic skills, and one was a control group. Those who concentrated on academic skills improved across the board, in reading and math as well as social acceptance. The boys who learned just social skills improved in only one area, reading comprehension. The authors of this study suggest that children who improve their academic skills are likely to improve in self-esteem as well. This helps them concentrate better in class and feel at ease with their classmates, changes that may be more crucial to improved social status than simply learning how to engage in social interaction (Coie and Krehbiel, 1984; Rabiner and Coie, 1989).

One caution is in order, however: too much emphasis may be placed on the need for children to "fit in." As Robert White (1979) warns:

> Historically we have clamored too loud for social adjustment. We have not been sensitive to the dangers of throwing children together regardless of their anxieties and their own social needs. We have been enchanted with peer groups, as if the highest form of social behavior were getting along with age equals . . .

One indication of the necessity for sensitivity to individual needs, researchers have discovered to their surprise, is that neglected children—that is, those who are ignored because they are withdrawn—do not necessarily lack social skills, but often merely prefer to play alone and do not have long-term adjustment problems (Asher, 1983; Coie and Kupersmidt, 1983; Parker and Asher, 1987). While it is apparent that unpopular children need to be helped with social skills and social acceptance, all children also need to develop their own interests, talents, and self-confidence apart from the social scene.

Family Structure and Child Development

Figure 13.9 *For much of human history, the typical family contained three generations and at least five children, a pattern still followed in many cultures and by some families in the United States. An increasingly common alternative family arrangement today is one parent with one child, a family structure that can function well if the social milieu is supportive.*

Historically and cross-culturally, children have thrived robustly in many kinds of **family structures**, that is, in households composed of people connected to each other in various legal and biosocial ways. At mid-twentieth century, for example, a family of two biological parents living with their own two or three dependent children was both the cultural ideal and the reality for the great majority in most industrialized nations, including the United States. At the same time, the preferred family structure in most developing countries in Asia and Latin America was the large extended family, with grandparents and great-grandparents, and often cousins, aunts, and uncles, living within the same large household, while in many African and Arab nations, a variety of family structures flourished, including the polygamous household, with each child growing up in the company of a dozen or more siblings and half-siblings. In historical America, both the extended family and the polygamous family have existed, but were relatively rare. Much more common were other alternative family forms, usually necessitated by the death of young parents, especially of women in childbirth. These included single-parent and stepparent family structures, as well as households in which children were informally raised by relatives or neighbors (Uhlenberg, 1980).

As we approach the twenty-first century, of course, the "traditional" family form that predominated during most of America's history is becoming increasingly less common. If current trends continue, only a minority—about 40 percent—of American children born in the 1990s will live with both biological parents from birth to age 18. Another 30 percent will begin life with married parents who will later divorce, while the remaining 30 percent will be born to an unmarried woman (Furstenberg and Cherlin, 1991). In addition, many children in the latter two groups will experience several changes in household composition—spending part of childhood living with a grandparent, or with a stepparent, or with a parent's live-in lover—and several marital transitions, from divorce to remarriage to divorce again.

Not all of American culture seems to have caught up to this reality. Common pejorative phrases such as "broken home," "wicked stepmother," "fatherless household," and "illegitimate child" imply that every family structure except that headed by married biological parents (often termed the "natural" parents) is deviant and destructive of the child's well-being. However, current longitudinal research in the United States confirms the historical and international evidence: children can thrive in almost any family format. Specifics of family function or dysfunction, such as excessive conflict, overly authoritarian parenting, and coldness among family members, are much more crucial than specifics of family structure, such as whether the family is headed by one adult or two, and what the genetic or legal relationship among the household members might be (Rutter, 1982; Werner and Smith, 1982; Hetherington, 1989; Demo, 1992). That said, however, we will now see that each structure can have particular advantages and liabilities.

Living with Both Biological Parents

According to large-scale surveys that compare various family structures, children living with both biological parents tend to fare best, having fewer physical, emotional, or learning difficulties from infancy throughout childhood than do children in other family structures. Further, at adolescence, they are less likely to abuse drugs or be arrested and more likely to graduate from high school; and, in adulthood, they are more likely to graduate from college and to continue to develop with self-confidence, social acceptance, and career success (Amato and Keith, 1991; Dawson, 1991; Zill, 1988; Emery, 1988).

Reasons for the Benefits

Two reasons for this seem clear. The most apparent is that two adults, both of whom have known and loved the child since birth, generally provide more complete caregiving than one. Not only can a mother and father together give an extra measure of the warmth, discipline, and attention that all children need (see Chapter 10), but they can also try to compensate for each other's parental shortcomings and enhance each other's parental strengths (Pedersen, 1981; Zaslow et al., 1985).

Second, two-parent homes usually have a financial advantage over other forms—especially the single-parent home—enabling better health care, housing, nutrition, and education for their children. This advantage occurs, in part, because (1) most contemporary two-parent households have two wage-earners; (2) two parents are less likely than single parents to have to pay for various household and child-care services; and (3) couples who decide to marry and stay married tend to be those who already have an adequate and stable income. Thus there is a monetary advantage for matrimony, at least as far as the children involved are concerned. One indicator of this is that for two-parent homes in the United States in 1989, the median income was almost three times that for one-parent homes—$34,000 compared to $13,000 (U.S. Bureau of the Census, 1991). Two-parent families containing a stepparent also tend to be somewhat disadvantaged financially when compared with families containing both biological parents.

Caveats

However, it is important not to conclude from such a broad overview that original two-parent homes are inevitably best, or that development is sure to falter in other family types. The advantage of traditional families, and the disadvantages of alternative family structures, are often "vastly overstated" (Demo, 1992).

Contributing to this overstatement is the fact that many studies indicating an apparent advantage of original two-parent homes do not take sufficient account of other factors that affect child development. The most obvious one, which we have already touched on, is income: since a disproportionate number of one-parent families, for example, are also low-income families, difficulties that are more common in them than in two-parent homes, and that therefore correlate with single parenthood may, in fact, be caused by poverty.

Look, for instance, at the data correlating grade repetition and family structure (Figure 13.10). They seem to show a clear advantage for children in original two-parent families, who are only half as likely to be left back as children in other types of families. However, when the data on the same children are organized according to family income, it is apparent that economic factors interact with, and outweigh, the influence of family structure per se. If family income is below the poverty line (about $13,000 for a family of four), almost three times as many children repeat a grade as when family income is well above poverty (more than $36,000 for a family of four). Even in two-parent households, 23 percent of all poor children repeat a grade, as do about 31 percent of those in other family types.

Figure 13.10 *As you can see, a child's likelihood of repeating a grade, whatever his or her ethnic background, is influenced by the family structure in which the child lives. However, as the chart on the facing page reveals, income is a more potent influence than either family structure or ethnicity, probably because income is more pervasive, affecting the quality of the neighborhood and the school as well as the home.*

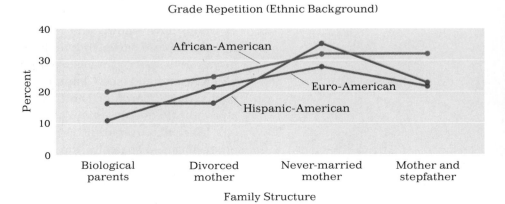

Grade Repetition (Ethnic Background)

African-American

Euro-American

Hispanic-American

Percent

40

30

20

10

0

Biological parents

Divorced mother

Never-married mother

Mother and stepfather

Family Structure

Other powerful factors including race, ethnic background, and religion, also correlate with family structure as well as family functioning, and may underlie what at first looks like a link between family type and child outcome. For example, children of Mormons, or Mennonites, or Orthodox Jews are almost always raised in two-parent households *and* are almost never drug abusers, at least while still living at home. It would be an obvious mistake to ascribe their resistance to drugs primarily to their parents' marital status, ignoring the powerful influence of religious upbringing on abstinence (Jesser et al., 1992). Yet national surveys that suggest a link between family structure and developmental outcome rarely take into account the influence of religion and other factors not directly related to family make-up.

More important, in acknowledging that two parent-homes are generally best we should always bear in mind two important qualifications: (1) not every biological father or mother is a fit parent; and (2) not every marriage creates a nurturant household. As described in Chapter 7, some parents are so disturbed, addicted, or self-absorbed that they mistreat their children or undercut their partner's child-rearing efforts, causing harm that overwhelms any benefits usually associated with the presence of two parents in the home. Many others are adequate parents, individually, but are caught in a marital relationship characterized by such frequent and open conflict that their children are at far greater risk of psychological harm than they would be in a tranquil, one-parent home.

A review of cross-sectional and longitudinal research finds that, while all children are "harmed by intense conflict, whether or not their parents live together . . . children who live in intact families with persistently high levels of conflict are the most distressed of all" (Furstenberg and Cherlin, 1991). Such families are not the norm, but they are surprisingly common. Especially when the partners are under age 35, many couples disagree frequently, and in about one marriage in four that disagreement erupts in destructive ways. For example, when researchers asked a cross-section of Americans about their own behavior toward their mate, among the couples under age 35, more than one spouse in four admitted to engaging in nonphysical aggression—cursing, insulting, slamming doors—at least once a month, and in physical aggression—pushing, slapping, hitting—at least once a year (Gelles and Straus, 1988; Strauss and Sweet, 1992).

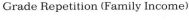

Grade Repetition (Family Income)

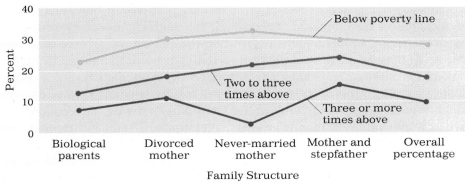

Figure 13.11 *For this young girl, the divorce of her parents might provide a needed respite from recurring, bitter marital arguments like the one shown here. However, it is also possible that she will continue to be drawn into her parents' conflict even after the divorce—in which case she is likely to experience significant amounts of emotional turmoil of her own.*

Most such couples spend years fighting before separating or getting help. In fact, most simply acclimate themselves to the tension, perhaps trying to avoid blow-ups but ultimately falling back into a pattern of mutual attack and counterattack, blaming each other and justifying themselves to the children. From the child's point of view, of course, the justification matters much less than the result—a home where blame and anger destroy the emotional safety that enables healthy growth. Although adults may become impervious to conflict, young children do not: unless both parents find a better way to disagree, instead of staying together "for the sake of the kids," divorcing for the children's benefit may be best.

When the Two-Parent Family Breaks Down

Even though divorce does, in fact, eventually benefit many children, the disruption and discord surrounding divorce almost always adversely affects the children for at least a year or two. They show signs of emotional pain, such as depression or rebellion, and symptoms of stress, such as having lower school achievement, poorer health, and fewer friends (Emery, 1988). Whether this distress is relatively mild and short-lived, or serious and long-lasting, depends primarily on three postdivorce factors: the harmony of the parents' ongoing relationship, the stability of the child's life, and the adequacy of the caregiving arrangement.

Harmony at Home

As already noted, the aspect of the parents' relationship that seems most critical for the development of children is the degree of harmony or discord between them. Unfortunately, even when the reason for divorce is to end long-standing hostility, the years immediately preceding and following the marital break-up are usually characterized by an escalation, not a cessation, of conflict. Most divorcing parents yell insults, exchange blows, destroy each other's property, or undermine each other's dignity and equanimity with greater intensity than ever before (Furstenberg and Cherlin, 1991; Peterson and Zill, 1986; Vaughn, 1987).

The more bitter and open the conflict, the more likely the children are to become depressed and angry, losing interest in schoolwork and in play, or becoming hostile with friends and teachers, as well as with both parents. Of course, this worsens the situation for everyone. Many parents find that, just when they need sympathy and cooperation, their children become more "aggressive, noncompliant, whining, nagging, dependent, and unaffectionate" than ever before. As one mother described it, she felt as though she were being bitten to death by ducks (Hetherington and Camara, 1984).

Relationships between siblings are likely to deteriorate as well, adding to the stress on parent-child relationships and removing a possible source of comfort for each child. Those exceptional children who do manage to maintain a close relationship with at least one brother or sister while their parents are at war are much more likely to escape serious emotional problems (Jenkins, 1992; MacKinnon, 1989).

Stability of Daily Life

The second critical factor determining the ease or difficulty of divorce for children is the stability of the child's life. One major source of instability is the child's being separated completely from a caregiver to whom he or she is highly attached, whether it be a parent, grandparent, or other relative. Another major source of instability is a reduction in household income, especially if it leads to a dramatic decline in the family's standard of living and/or unwelcome transitions such as a move to a less expensive neighborhood and entry into a different school. The need for more money may also dramatically reduce the time and energy the custodial parent has available for the children, because he or she must spend more time working—entering the job market for the first time, or taking full-time instead of part-time work, or seeking overtime or a second job.

Instability also commonly arises from the disorientation parents experience as they undergo the "eradication of the marital subworld," the habits and interactions that formed the structure of married life (Vaughn, 1987). Typically, a custodial mother is initially overwhelmed with the burden of having to run the household and care for the children while worrying about financial problems and coping with her own emotions and changes in self-esteem. Many women become depressed and withdrawn or, alternatively, try to find jobs, develop new skills, and expand their social lives, just when their children need and demand even more attention than before. Correspondingly, mothers frequently become more strict, less playful, and more inconsistent in their disciplining (Hetherington, 1989; Spanier and Thompson, 1984; Wallerstein and Blakeslee, 1989).

Fathers also change, especially in the first year. Typically, if they are the noncustodial parent, they become more indulgent with their children. Many fathers also adopt a more "youthful" lifestyle, including dating a variety of women, often younger. Many change their appearance, adopting a new hairstyle or growing a beard, or taking on a new look in their wardrobe. All such changes, especially in combination, can greatly increase the child's sense of instability in his or her life.

Even more stressful for children is that fathers, as noncustodial parents, tend to visit their offspring less frequently and more inconsistently over time, and their children miss them. A nationwide survey in 1989 found that only 25 percent saw their fathers at least once a week, while 33 percent saw their fathers no more than once a year (Seltzer, 1991). As low as this visitation rate is, it represents an improvement over the rate of a decade ago, when only 16 percent of children of divorce visited their fathers once a week, and almost half had not seen their fathers at all the previous year (Furstenberg and Nord, 1985). (As we will see shortly, however, frequent visitation can present problems of its own.)

Stability for Younger and Older Children

While the instability of divorce affects children at every age, the immediate disruptions of family life are generally harder on younger children, whose world is almost completely confined to the family attachments that they see disappearing in front of their eyes, and who have little understanding of why that world is changing so dramatically. Children who themselves are in transition, such as when they are beginning kindergarten, also find divorce particularly hard (Hetherington, 1989; Wallerstein and Blakeslee, 1989; Allison and Furstenberg, 1989).

As children grow older, they are better able to absorb the immediate impact of divorce, because usually they have some understanding of what is happening and why. They also have areas of interest and emotional investment that lie outside the family, and they often have friends who can offer support because their own parents have divorced. Nevertheless, they too can be hard hit, especially when divorce coincides with, or requires, changes in the mainstays of middle childhood—neighborhood and school. In such circumstances, not only must children adjust to new family routines, patterns, and demands, but they must also leave old friends and enter a new society of children, something which is problematic even for children whose family is stable. In addition, as they enter their teens, children often view events with what is referred to as adolescent egocentrism (see Chapter 15), a kind of self-centered thinking that causes them to see these events as revolving primarily around themselves. As a result, they tend to overpersonalize their parents' divorce, viewing themselves as the rejected party, wondering how their parents could be so selfish as to ignore their interests, and becoming mired in self-pity. This kind of reaction, in combination with the various transitional stresses that often accompany the onset of puberty, make early adolescence, overall, the worst time for children to experience divorce (Hetherington and Clingempeel, 1992). For older adolescents, the chief disruption of divorce is likely to be economic, as everything from clothing purchases and leisure expenditures to college plans and career aspirations are put on hold.

Custody and Caregiving

One aspect of divorce that has received a great deal of attention is how to best adjudicate custody to maintain adequate caregiving when a marriage ends. Until fairly recently, custody of children in a divorce was based almost exclusively on gender. In the nineteenth century, for example, custody nearly always went to the father, and for most of this century, it nearly always went to the mother. The current view of the judicial system, and of the general public, is that whoever was the most competent, involved parent before the divorce should continue to be the primary caregiver (Price and

Drawing by Schwadron

"Must I pick one of my parents? I'd rather live with Bill Cosby."

Figure 13.12 *For many children, the problems of their own family life are a sharp contrast to the humor, affluence, and closeness they witness in typical "family fare" on television. Such a gap between reality and expectation may actually make coping with the difficulties brought on by their parents' divorce even harder.*

McHenry, 1988; Felner and Terre, 1987), a view that is strongly supported by extensive research.

However, another common assumption is not supported by the research—that the more often the children see the nonresident parent, the better off they are. Following from this assumption is the idea that frequent visitation of the noncustodial parent is to be encouraged, and that joint custody, with both parents involved in child-rearing decisions and with children spending substantial time in both parental homes, is the best arrangement of all. Somewhat surprisingly, data comparing children in various custody arrangements show that, in fact, children who are in joint custody, or who see their noncustodial parents very frequently, generally develop no better than those who rarely or never see their noncustodial parent (Luepnitz, 1986; Maccoby et al., 1990).

There are several reasons behind this unexpected finding, beginning with the fact that frequent visitation and joint custody are generally much more problematic than most people—including psychologists and judges, as well as parents and the general public—imagine. Among the most common problems are the logistics of coordinating the schedules and routines of everyone involved; the disorientation of the child who shuttles back and forth between homes with distinctly different rules, expectations, and emotional settings; and the disagreements that arise between former spouses as a result of their frequent interaction (Johnston et al., 1989; Kline et al., 1989; Folberg, 1991).

In addition, many ex-spouses find that, for their own reasons, they must abandon hopes of shared parenting because their most immediate and compelling psychic need is to extricate themselves from the emotional entanglements and dependencies of their former life. As these ex-spouses work "to establish a separate identity and an independent perspective . . . the social and psychological tasks of divorce directly collide with the normal expectations of parenthood," (Furstenberg and Cherlin, 1991).

Many ex-spouses also find shared parenthood very difficult when one of them is out of the flow not only of the child's daily life but also of the other parent's insights and observations about it. Given the realities of scheduled visitation—however liberal—it is almost impossible for a noncustodial parent to maintain the level of intimacy that is necessary to provide love and discipline with sensitivity and finesse. Indeed, cut off from sustained close contact and restricted to the artificiality of a visitation schedule, many noncustodial parents err by being too authoritarian or too permissive, as well as by being critical of their former spouse. None of this helps the children, who, more than ever, need authoritative child-rearing and harmonious family life (Hetherington and Clingempeel, 1992).

In general, if the custodial parent provides both warmth and a stable structure for the child's daily life, the noncustodial parent can help the child most by providing ongoing support—financial as well as psychological—to that parent. Unfortunately, tensions between the ex-spouses, often exacerbated by the legal system, tend to work against this ideal, evoking adversarial attitudes and begrudging child-support payments. Indeed, about half of all noncustodial parents provide no child support at all, while many of the remainder provide less than the court mandates, which itself is usually less than the family needs (Weitzman, 1985).

Single-Parent Households

The number of single-parent households has increased markedly over the past two decades in virtually every major industrialized nation except Japan (see Figure 13.13). Although the specific reasons and consequences of this trend vary somewhat from nation to nation, worldwide this family structure tends to be blamed for all manner of developmental problems, from rioting in the streets to adolescent suicide, from health problems to academic failure (e.g., U.S. Department of Education, 1991; National Center for Health Statistics, 1991; Roll, 1989; Burns, 1992). Such blanket condemnation often is linked to an unfortunate stereotype—that of a single mother with little education, many neglected children, few conventional morals, and no ambition, spending her time collecting government checks and watching TV.

However, once we look at the data on single parenthood, we find that the reality is much more complex, both nationally and internationally (Burns, 1992; Roll, 1989). Even within the United States, it is not easy to generalize about single parenthood, partly because the reasons for it vary: divorce accounts for about 60 percent of single parents, death for about 8 percent, and out-of-wedlock birth for about 32 percent, with each of these patterns having different problems and strengths. Further, even within these categories, the functioning of families differs depending on ethnic, economic, and community patterns. For example, among Puerto Ricans living on the mainland, most "single" mothers are actually living with the father of their children, and have much more in common with married mothers than with truly single parents (Landale and Fennelly, 1992).

However, while it is not easy to generalize about single parenthood, it is easy to show that the stereotype of it is usually false: in the United States in 1990, compared to married parents, single parents were *more* likely to be employed (e.g., 80 percent of divorced mothers compared to 68 percent of married mothers were in the labor force); their households had *fewer* children (half had only one child); and only a minority received government assistance of any kind, including welfare, unemployment, or Medicaid (U.S. Bureau of the Census, 1991; Johnson et al., 1991). No matter what nationality,

Figure 13.13 *Beyond the obvious—that single-parent households are increasing worldwide—this chart also reflects a combination of two trends, liberalized divorce laws and increasing acceptance of never-married mothers. The country with the lowest rate of single parenthood, Japan, has experienced neither of these factors. The country that had the highest rate in the 1970s, Sweden, had already experienced both, and still has many adults who prefer to raise a family together without marriage rather than to formalize their union and then risk divorce.*

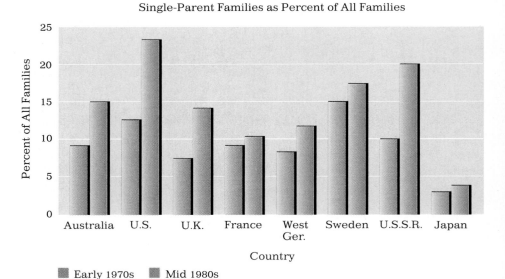

Single-Parent Families as Percent of All Families

■ Early 1970s   ■ Mid 1980s

Figure 13.14 *This young, single mother is likely to experience significant "role overload" as she tries to make ends meet financially, care for two young preschoolers, and maintain some time for her own needs. Her capacity to successfully juggle these multiple responsibilities depends, in part, on the support she receives from extended family members, friends, and in some cases, the children's father.*

ethnicity, or education a lone parent has, he or she is most likely to work hard to fill both the role of major income-producer and that of major caregiver, surrendering personal recreation, social life, and sleep to do so.

How do children actually develop in such households? Surprisingly, when compared to others of the same ethnicity and socioeconomic status, in many ways children develop just as well living with one biological parent as with two (Adams et al., 1984). With the exception of children whose parents are recently divorced, children from single-parent families are usually on a par with other children, especially in three crucial areas: school achievement, emotional stability, and protection from serious injury. This generality holds for preschoolers, school-age children, and adolescents (Hawkins and Eggebeen, 1991; Milne et al., 1986; Smith, 1990; Dawson, 1991).

If all factors are equal, then, the structure of single-parent households does not necessarily impair the functioning of such homes, and thus has few disadvantages. However, other factors are almost never equal, because single parents are vulnerable to many kinds of stress that can and do affect children. To begin with, most single parents suffer from "role overload," as they try to provide nurturance, discipline, and financial support all at the same time (Zill, 1983). Having a full-time job and a young family is not easy, no matter what one's marital status, but the single parent is particularly likely to be squeezed when a child is sick, when the job demands overtime, or when school holidays conflict with work obligations. These problems of the single parent increase markedly as family size increases: one child does not put nearly as much strain on the parent as two or more children do (Polit, 1984).

Another major problem is that the income of single-parent households is substantially lower than that of two-parent households, even when only one of those two parents is employed. Indeed, about a third of all American single parents are forced to rely on public assistance, at least temporarily, a solution that does not provide adequate income or self-respect. With or without government assistance, half of all American children living in single-parent households are living in households below the poverty line, the level officially determined as adequate to pay for basic family expenses (e.g., in 1990, the poverty line for a family of four was $13,500).

Given these problems, how do single parents manage to cope as well as they do? Social support is often critical, as friends and relatives can relieve some of the single parent's stress by helping with child care, with overdue bills, and with low self-esteem. This may explain an intriguing finding: regardless of ethnic group or income, children of widows and widowers generally develop as successfully as their peers who have both parents alive, perhaps because social support is generally much more freely given to widows than to divorcées or unwed mothers (Rutter, 1982; Adams, 1984).

Single Fathers

Most public discussion about single parents proceeds as though they are all mothers, but in the United States in 1990 almost one single parent in five was a man, compared with one in nine in 1980. Generally, children develop quite similarly in father-only homes as in mother-only homes (Thompson et al., 1992). In fact, if anything, children in father-headed homes fare better, especially if those children are boys, as they tend to be, since fathers are more likely to have custody of their sons than daughters.

Among the possible reasons for the father-advantage is that growing boys, particularly, sometimes respond better to a man's authority than to a woman's, and are thus likely to be less disruptive and destructive in father-headed households (Santrock et al., 1982; Peterson and Zill, 1986; Hetherington, 1989; Wallerstein and Blakeslee, 1989). In addition, since the father's having custody is still somewhat unusual, those fathers who seek and gain such arrangements are, on the whole, those who are likely to be suited for it, whereas mothers typically have custody whether they prefer it or not.

Beyond the possible psychological benefits of a father-headed household, such families also have some practical advantages over mother-headed families. They are, on average, more secure financially (even though fathers are less likely to receive substantial child support from their former mates than mothers are). Fathers also get more child-care assistance from other people, particularly from women: former wives, childless women, and their own mothers tend to be more helpful to single fathers than former husbands, childless men, and their own grandfathers are to single mothers (Seltzer and Bianchi, 1988; Weitzman, 1985; Risman, 1987).

Blended Families

Most divorced parents remarry within a few years, and many unmarried parents eventually marry as well. When remarriage means less loneliness for the custodial parent, improved finances, less conflict between former spouses, and more stable household organization, it eventually benefits all concerned. However, while the new partners are initially likely to be happy with the remarriage, such is almost never the case for the children, who must suddenly negotiate a new set of family relationships, not only with a stepparent but often also with stepsiblings, stepgrandparents, and so forth, most of whom they would not have chosen on their own.

The same factors affecting children in marriage and divorce—parental cooperation, stability, and adequacy of caregiving—affect children in stepfamilies (Keshet, 1988; Kurdek, 1989). Even in the best of circumstances, however, harmony takes time to achieve, as the blended family must develop a new style and culture that all members can live with, each member

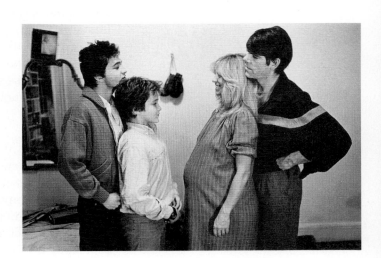

Figure 13.15 *On the left, adolescent boys from the mother's first marriage; on the right: their mother and stepfather; in the future, a half brother or sister who may either draw this blended family together or cause it greater stress—or do both.*

making certain accommodations to the others. In the process, some members are more likely to benefit, especially younger boys from mother-headed families. Others are more likely to suffer, among them adolescent girls who are particularly likely to resent their new stepfathers, only-children who suddenly lose privacy to new siblings, and children who become indirect targets of the nonremarried parent's jealousy (Furstenberg and Cherlin, 1991; Allison and Furstenberg, 1989; Giles-Sims and Crosbie-Burnett, 1989; Hetherington and Clingempeel, 1992).

While most remarriages eventually work out for the children as well as for the adults, many do not: the divorce rate is higher for second marriages than first marriages, and this is particularly true if there are young adolescent children involved. Overall, the stress of a second divorce adds disruption to the child's life as well as to the adult's, a fact that itself should caution any single parent hoping to marry primarily in order to give the children a two-parent home.

Grandparent Households

As we will discuss in greater detail in Chapter 22, grandparents often play an important role in children's adjustment to stresses of every kind—providing extra income, emotional support, continuity, and child care, all of which are especially needed during divorce and in single-parent homes. However, when the child and a single parent move into a grandparent's household, notable stresses are likely to occur, as reflected in children's behavior. For example, one study comparing young children in various family structures found that those living with both grandparents had poorer language skills and more behavior problems, among them disobedience, dependence, and aggression, than children in any other kind of home, including homes headed by both biological parents, by single mothers, or by a mother and stepfather (Hawkins and Eggebeen, 1991).

Interestingly, this effect was not seen for African-American children, who, in this study and others, appear to benefit by living with grandparents (Pearson et al., 1990; Wilson, 1989). One suggested reason is that, among whites, the grandparent-headed household is traditionally unusual, even aberrant, and thus is a sign of trouble, a source of shame, and a cause of stress (Clemens and Axelson, 1985). Among nonwhites, however, extended family structures have always been more common, and more accepted, with established patterns of interaction to ease tensions when three generations share one roof. For example, traditional respect for the older generation among nonwhites may cause both the child and the parent to more readily defer to a grandparent in matters of child discipline than would their white counterparts, who may view grandparents' attempts to discipline a child as intrusive.

Social context is thus a critical variable in the actual functioning of a family: if the community accepts and supports a particular family type, the chances are good that the adults will be able to nurture the children entrusted to them. Indeed, over the past thirty years, as social acceptance of nontraditional families in America has been increasing, the negative effects of "alternative" families on children have been decreasing (Amato and Klein, 1990; Demo, 1992).

Poverty in Middle Childhood

As you remember from Chapter 1, socioeconomic status affects developing persons throughout life, with low SES, particularly, affecting development for the worse. The precise impact of poverty depends, of course, on many factors, among them the person's age, the specific domain under consideration, and the public policies that soften or sharpen the blow. Each of these factors is relevant to understanding the effects of poverty during middle childhood.

The Biosocial Domain

For children of every age in every nation, poverty takes a toll on biosocial development: as SES decreases, the risk of health hazards—including malnutrition, disease, accidents, abuse, and neglect—increases. However, for two reasons, the specific toll of poverty on growth and health in middle childhood is blunted. First, their natural immunities, physical strengths, and growth patterns make school-age children relatively unlikely to suffer the most devastating consequences of malnutrition and disease. Second, their developing independence and reasoning ability make them better able to protect themselves against dangers of every kind, from household fires to abusive parents. As a result, worldwide, poverty in middle childhood is less damaging biosocially than in infancy or early childhood.

The Cognitive Domain

As Chapter 12 detailed, school-age children depend on the particular lessons of formal education to fully develop their minds, with the number of days and years a person attends school being directly reflected in the individual's tested intelligence and thinking ability, as well as in his or her proficiency at the specific tools of learning—including reading, writing, and math—that make further cognitive development possible (Fiati, 1991; Ceci, 1991). In addition, of course, the quality of education is also crucial to the child's cognitive development. Since both the extent and the quality of education are in many ways tied to socioeconomic factors, poverty during the middle years can be particularly detrimental to intellectual growth.

In some nations, for example, an elementary school education must be paid for directly by the child's parents, including fees for tuition, uniforms, and books. As a result, poverty means little or no schooling for many children. By contrast, in other countries, a substantial portion of the national income is dedicated to providing free, quality education for all. Those nations devoting the highest proportion (about 7 percent) of their GNP to education are Canada, Sweden, Denmark, Norway, Israel, and Saudi Arabia (United Nations, 1990).

Still other countries are somewhere between these extremes, the United States, the United Kingdom, Australia, and New Zealand among them, spending about 5 percent of their GNP on education. In the United States, public schools are free, open to everyone, and are attended by 90 percent of the children between ages 6 and 16 (the other 10 percent attend private schools, mostly church-affiliated). However, the United States' method of supporting education makes poverty a particular liability. Be-

Figure 13.16 *A child's ability to learn depends partly on receiving encouragement from teachers, as shown here. Unfortunately, many poor children do not have this benefit: their teachers are often overworked and discouraged, unable to show even one terrific thing to do with a book.*

cause public school funding depends primarily on local property taxes, wide disparities in neighborhood wealth translate into per-pupil expenditures more than twice as high in rich districts as in poor ones, even within the same region of the same state (Kozol, 1991). While, in general, per-pupil expenditure is not *the* determining factor in quality of education, there comes a point at which the cumulative effects of substantially larger class size, lower salaries, less maintenance, and fewer new materials undercuts teacher morale and seriously compromises student learning.

A case in point is one Chicago school, where many teachers are chronically late or absent, the building is crumbling,

> there are no hoops on the basketball court and no swings in the playground. For 21 years . . . the school has been without a library. Library books, which have been piled and abandoned in the lunch room of the school have "sprouted mold". . . Some years ago the school received the standard reading textbooks out of sequence: The second workbook in the reading program came to the school before the first. The principal, uncertain what to do with the wrong workbooks, was told by the school officials it was "all right to work backwards." [Kozol, 1991]

The attitudes and atmosphere in such an institution are antithetical to the ingredients for good learning, as reviewed in Chapter 12: dedicated teachers, age-appropriate curriculum, and structured materials that excite the children's intellectual curiosity. Not surprisingly, achievement scores in this school showed that, with each year of education, the children fell further behind their peers in better schools.

The Psychosocial Domain

In middle childhood, the toll of poverty on psychosocial development, while harder to measure than biosocial or cognitive growth, may be the most devastating of all. Many children from low-income homes—especially those in dangerous neighborhoods—come to think of themselves as worthless and their futures as hopeless, and this makes them unmotivated, depressed, and angry (Garbarino et al., 1991).

One reason that poverty has such a debilitating effect during these years is that, being in the stage of concrete operational thinking, children focus on the tangible and thus are highly susceptible to assessing individual and family worthiness in terms of material possessions. Unlike younger children, who do not recognize the difference between cheap and chic, or adults, who may esteem inner dignity and worth, school-age children are preoccupied with the status conveyed by consumer items, by advertised brands and "in" styles. Thus the child with tattered, ill-fitting clothes and a rusty second-hand bike becomes self-conscious, teased, and ashamed, as movingly illustrated by Shawn, a 10-year-old boy:

> Me and my brother are a little hard on shoes. This summer the only shoes we had were thongs and when church time came, the only shoes we had to wear were a pair of church shoes. The one that got them first got to wear them. The one that didn't had to wear a pair of my mom's tennis shoes or my sister's.
>
> Sometimes I pray that I won't be poor no more and sometimes I sit up at night and cry. But it didn't change anything. Crying just helps the hurt and the pain. It doesn't change anything.
>
> One day I asked my mom why the kids always tease me and she said because they don't understand but I do understand about being on welfare and being poor, and it can hurt. [Johnson et al., 1991]

One crucial factor in how psychologically debilitating poverty can be is in **social comparison,** a practice school-age children seem compelled to engage in, as they check each other out on everything from who got the highest grade and who has the hippiest fad item to who gets the highest allowance and whose family has the hottest car. Realizing that one is at the bottom of the heap with respect to one's peers, or remembering better days—for instance, before the family income plummeted when Dad or Mom was laid off or left the family—can be emotionally destructive (Weitzman, 1985; Newman, 1988).

As children grow older, social comparison broadens to include not only one's immediate experience, but the somewhat larger community, depicted on television, or viewed as the child begins to travel outside the neighborhood. In the Chicago school described above, for instance, the first-graders seemed happy and quite eager to learn in their ill-equipped classrooms with unmotivated teachers; older children, however, were discouraged and bitter at the contrast between their schools and the local suburban schools they had seen, with landscaped lawns, computer laboratories, and well-prepared teachers (Kozol, 1991).

The personality attributes and coping methods nurtured by such discouraging comparisons are not constructive for later success. For example, the conviction that society does not care about them can lead some children to a general attitude of resignation and indifference and excite in others a penchant for dangerous, self-destructive actions. Overall, children who feel overlooked or cast aside by society are less likely to feel responsible for their own destiny, and to believe that their fate lies in the hands of luck or other people.

Neighborhood and Residence

Because school-age children are voyaging beyond the confines of their immediate home for the first time, developing an independent social life and devising their own adventures, the surrounding neighborhood has a powerful impact on them (Bryant, 1985). For many poor children, however, their surroundings make mastery of the normal skills of middle childhood very difficult. As Kenneth Keniston describes it, it is a

> dangerous world—an urban world of broken stair railings, of busy streets serving as playgrounds, of lead paint, rats and rat poisons, or a rural world where families do not enjoy the minimal levels of public health . . . It is a world where even a small child learns to be ashamed of the way he or she lives. And it is frequently a world of intense social dangers, where many adults, driven by poverty and desperation, seem untrustworthy and unpredictable. Children who learn the skills for survival in that world, suppressing curiosity and cultivating a defensive guardedness toward novelty or a constant readiness to attack, may not be able to acquire the basic skills and values that are needed, for better or worse, to thrive in mainstream society. [Keniston, 1977]

The world of poverty has gotten even more dangerous since Keniston's analysis, as hard drugs and hand guns have flooded the inner cities of America. Newspapers, television, and especially the movies have given the public a sense of the dramatic danger of living in an urban environment

Figure 13.17 *Does this scene look familiar? For most of us, it probably doesn't—because these young boys are growing up in a lower-SES setting where, compared to that of most youths who go on to college, the risks to their health and safety are greater, and the chances for completing their education and experiencing future employment and financial success are diminished.*

where brutality, random violence, and drive-by killings punctuate daily life, but much less attention has been devoted to the ongoing emotional price paid by those struggling to maintain a normal life in the midst of such surroundings. Young children tend to internalize constant fear, sensing death around every corner. For older children, this premonition of mortality sometimes turns into malaise and indifference (Kotlowitz, 1991).

Homelessness

Between 100,000 and 500,000 American children are homeless each night, about half of them school-age. Those literally without a roof over their heads are most often adolescent runaways or throwaways, whose parents have abused them or disowned them. Homeless children under age 12 usually live with their families in shelters. Although these children have, for the moment, the assurance of a bed and meals, they are troubled in many ways. As one report explains:

> By the time they arrive in a shelter, children may have experienced many chronic adversities and traumatic events. More immediately, children may have gone hungry and lost friends, possessions, and the security of familiar places and people at home, at school, or in the neighborhood . . . Locations [of shelters] are usually undesirable, particularly with respect to children playing outside. Moreover, necessary shelter rules may strain a child and family life. For example, it is typical for no visitors to be allowed, and for children to be . . . accompanied at all times by a parent. [Masten, 1992]

Comparing homeless children in middle childhood with their peers of equal SES finds that the homeless children have fewer friends, more fears, more fights, more chronic illnesses, more changes of school, and lower school attendance. They are also about fourteen months behind academically (Masten, 1992; Rafferty and Shinn, 1991). In terms of long-term development, the most chilling result is a loss of faith in life's possibilities: compared even to other impoverished children, they have lower aspirations and less hope for the future or for their fellow humans, expressing doubt that anyone will ever help them. Clinical depression is common, striking almost one homeless child in every three (Bassuk and Rosenberg, 1990). When such attitudes develop in a child, they may take a lifetime to reverse.

At this point in human history, poverty affects more children than adults, and because they are still developing, they are affected in more devastating ways. The percentage of children affected varies a great deal from nation to nation, from nearly 100 percent in the Indian subcontinent to less than 10 percent in northern Europe. Between those extremes is the United States, where in 1990 one child in five lived in a family with income below the poverty line, up 60 percent from a decade before (Johnson et al., 1991).

The growing numbers of poor children are especially troubling, since many of today's impoverished children must also cope with other problems, including learning difficulties, crowded households, and troubled parents. Fortunately, as we will now see, even children growing up in such families sometimes find ways to survive, managing to develop normally despite their problems.

Coping with Life

As we have seen throughout these three chapters on middle childhood, the expansion of the child's social world sometimes brings with it new and disturbing problems. For example, the beginning of formal education forces any learning disabilities to the surface, making them an obvious handicap; playing with friends beyond the home may result in peer problems, such as rejection and attack that can take a serious toll; leaving the protection of the family can expose the child to social prejudices such as sexism, racism, and classism, in some cases causing shame, self-doubt, and loneliness. Such troublesome problems of middle childhood often piggyback on those chronic stresses that are detrimental at every age, such as living in an impoverished, overcrowded, or violent home, or having a parent who is emotionally disturbed, drug-addicted, or imprisoned. Because of problems such as these, many children fail at school, fight with their friends, fear the future, cry themselves to sleep. Indeed, the entire range of academic and psychiatric difficulties that school-age children sometimes display can be traced, in part, to psychosocial stresses (Luthar and Zigler, 1991; Anthony, 1987; Rutter, 1987).

Fortunately, although the potential stresses and hassles are many during middle childhood, so are the coping measures that children develop. As a result, between ages 6 and 11, the overall frequency of various psychological problems decreases while the number of evident competencies—at school, at home, and on the playground—increases (Achenbach et al., 1991). Two factors described in this chapter—the development of social cognition and an expanding social world—seem to combine to buffer school-age children against the many stresses they may encounter. According to some observers, many children seem "stress-resistant," even "invulnerable" and "invincible" (Murphy and Moriarty, 1976; Werner and Smith, 1982; Werner, 1992; Garmezy, 1985). Let us look more closely at how some children rise above problems that might seem potentially devastating.

Assessing Stress

The first important point to recognize in studying the effects of various stresses on children is that there is no simple correspondence between a given stress and a given result. Detailed longitudinal studies find that the likelihood that a given stress will produce psychological fallout depends on the number of stresses the child is experiencing concurrently and on their pervasiveness, that is, on the degree to which they affect the overall patterns of the child's daily life (Seifer and Sameroff, 1987; Luthar and Zigler, 1991).

Typical of this research is a study which found that children coping with one, and only one, serious, ongoing stress (e.g., poverty, large family size, criminal father, emotionally disturbed mother, frequent fighting between the parents) were no more likely to develop serious psychiatric problems than children with none of these liabilities. However, when there was more than one risk factor present, "the stresses potentiated each other so that the combination of chronic stresses provided very much more than a summation of the effects of the separate stresses considered singly" (Rutter, 1979). Indeed, the finding of a number of other studies is that, in general, a

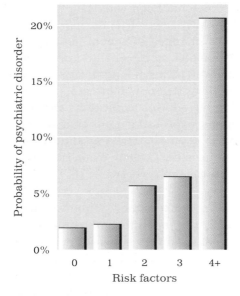

Figure 13.18 *Rutter found that children who had to cope with one serious problem ran virtually as low a risk of suffering a psychiatric disorder as did children who faced no serious problems. However, when the child had two problems, the chances more than doubled. Four or more problems produced about ten times the likelihood of psychiatric disorders as one. About one child in five who experienced four or more serious stresses actually became emotionally disturbed.*

single chronic problem creates vulnerability in a child without causing obvious harm, but if that vulnerability is subjected to additional stresses—even mild ones that are more often termed "daily hassles" rather than "stressful events"—the child can suffer evident damage (Luthar and Zigler, 1991).

The underlying reason is that the impact of stresses depends on how they affect the moment-by-moment tranquillity of daily life. For example, living with an emotionally dysfunctional parent may mean that a child has to prematurely assume many of the responsibilities for his or her own daily care and school attendance, often in the midst of a chaotic household; and/or has to listen to an adult's confused, depressed, or irrational thinking; and/or has to supervise and discipline younger siblings. The net result is a child who never has a moment to play, to relax, to develop his or her own personality. On the other hand, the impact of having a disturbed parent can be minimized if the child's daily life remains stable and peaceful, if, say, another adult protects the child from disruptions caused by the dysfunctional parent, or if the parent's illness is controlled in such a way that the child never feels its full force. This was suggested by a study of the effects of the stresses associated with maternal mental illness on children. The specific diagnosis of the mothers' mental disorder, such as schizophrenia, manic depression, and so forth, did not correlate with the children's reactions, nor did the seriousness of a single episode. However other factors that affect daily life did have an effect, among them how anxious the mother became, and how long-standing and severe her manifest symptoms were (Seifer and Sameroff, 1987).

Focus on Strengths

Particularly important to a child's ability to cope with problems is that child's competencies, especially well-developed social, academic, or creative skills. Each of these skills can help the child deflect or avoid many of the problems he or she may encounter at home or in the community.

There are several reasons why competence can more than compensate for disabling factors. One is self-esteem: if children feel confident in any area of their lives, they are better able to put the rest of their life in perspective. They believe, for example, that despite how others might reject or belittle them, they are not a worthless failure, and that despite the voices of despair within them, life is not hopeless.

More directly, children with better-developed cognitive and social skills are better able to employ various practical strategies, such as changing the conditions that brought about a problem in the first place, or restructuring their own reactions to the problem. This explains why older children tend to be less vulnerable to the stresses of life than are children who are just beginning middle childhood. For example, when a peer is antagonistic, a 6-year-old is likely to dissolve into tears or to launch a clumsy counterattack, which merely brings further rejection. Older children, on the other hand, are more adept at finding ways to disguise their hurt, or at keeping a bully at bay, or at repairing a broken friendship, or at making new friends to replace the old ones (Compas et al., 1991).

Schools and teachers can obviously play a significant role in the development of competence. Even for children from seriously deprived backgrounds, school achievement can make it possible for them to aspire beyond the limited and constricting horizons that they may encounter in their daily lives.

Of course, much depends on the nature of the particular school the child attends. Even more important than the academic quality of the curriculum or the size of the classes is the overall emotional tone of the school. This was found in a study of twelve London schools that served low-SES children, many of whom came from crowded families that were headed by single parents or who had parents with serious psychological problems (Rutter, 1979). Some of these schools had markedly more students who passed higher-level exams, fewer students who dropped out, and lower rates of juvenile delinquency than would be expected on the basis of the students' backgrounds. One crucial factor that distinguished the more successful schools was that they cared about the children, as evidenced by such simple things as the student's work being displayed on the walls and the frequency of praise from the teachers. Another factor was that the administration of these schools had high expectations of their teachers, who, in turn, had high expectations of their students. Apparently, in environments that expect and encourage competence, children tend to meet the challenge, overcoming home and community handicaps to do so.

Social Support

Another important element that helps children deal with problems is the social support they receive. The companionship and comfort provided by a grandparent, a sibling, or even the family dog can relieve some tension in a child's life. In addition, one of the benefits of the expanding social world of middle childhood is that the child can venture forth to seek out many more potential sources of social support. For example, a child whose parents are fighting bitterly on their way to divorce may spend hours on the phone with a friend whose parents have successfully separated, or may frequently drop in for dinner at a neighbor's house where family harmony still prevails, or may devote himself or herself to helping a teacher, a coach, or a church group (Hetherington and Clingempeel, 1992; Bryant, 1985; Rutter, 1987).

An additional source of support for many children is religious faith and practice. Especially for children in difficult circumstances—such as the impoverished child in a single-parent family in a dangerous neighborhood—religious faith itself can be protective. School-age children, almost universally, develop their own theology—influenced by whatever formal religious education they might receive but by no means identical to it—that helps them structure life and deal with worldly problems (Hyde, 1990; Coles, 1990). Their view of a god figure is generally very personal, enabling troubled children to believe that they are being watched over and protected. One example is an 8-year-old African-American girl who, in the 1960s, was one of the first to enter a previously all-white school. She remembers walking past a gauntlet of adults yelling insults:

> I was all alone, and those people were screaming, and suddenly I saw God smiling, and I smiled. A woman was standing there, and she shouted at me "Hey you little nigger, what are you smiling at? I looked right up at her face, and I said 'At God.' " Then she looked up at the sky, and then she looked at me, and she didn't call me any more names. [quoted in Coles, 1990]

Figure 13.19 *Parents are the most important social supports available to a child. For this reason, one way of assisting children under stress is to enable their parents to function more successfully as supportive figures in the child's life, perhaps through financial supports, counseling, or assistance from friends or relatives.*

In a way, this example illustrates many aspects of children's coping abilities, for not only faith but a measure of self-confidence, social understanding, and skill at deflecting one's own emotional reactions enabled this child to overcome a very real threat.

While adults may wish that all children could have an idyllic childhood, such is almost never the case. Nor is it necessary for healthy development: research on coping in middle childhood clearly suggests that, as they grow older, most children develop ways to deal with all sorts of stress, from the major traumatic events to minor hassles.

However, some children are at risk of developing serious psychological problems if they are faced with multiple problems that affect their daily routines. To help these children the best strategy may be, not simply to reduce stress, but to increase competencies within the child or the social supports surrounding them. If the home situation is problematic, for instance, having access to anyone from a caring teacher to a best friend to a loving grandparent can make a difference (Rutter, 1987). Or if a child has a severe reading difficulty, developing the child's talents in other areas, such as math and music, may be as important for the child's overall well-being as specific tutoring to overcome the dyslexia.

As you will see in the next three chapters, in many ways adolescence is as much a continuation of middle childhood as a radical departure from it. Stresses and strains continue to accumulate during adolescence, and destructive coping mechanisms, such as drug use and dangerous risk-taking, become more available. Fortunately, constructive coping methods also increase: personal competencies, family supports, and close friends get most young people through adolescence unharmed.

SUMMARY

An Expanding Social World

1. All the major perspectives recognize the importance of children's growing independence and competence during the school years. Freud believed that, during middle childhood, most of the child's emotions are quiet or latent, especially their sexual and aggressive urges.

2. Erikson calls middle childhood the stage of industry versus inferiority, because children are busy learning new skills. As they attempt to develop the competencies their society values, they gain self-esteem, or else come to see themselves as inferior and inadequate.

3. In various ways, learning, cognitive, and humanist theorists stress school-age children's increasing ability to master new skills and develop new abilities, particularly in understanding others and themselves.

Social Cognition

4. School-age children develop a multistep theory of mind, becoming increasingly aware that other people have complex personalities, motives, and emotions that are different from their own. At the same time, they become better able to adjust their own behavior to interact appropriately with others.

5. Children also develop theories about themselves and their own behavior. As they become more knowledgeable about their abilities and shortcomings, both personal and academic, they become more self-critical, and their self-esteem often dips.

6. School-age children also create their own subculture, with language, values, and codes of behavior. The child who is not included in this society often feels deeply hurt, for social dependence on peers is strong at this age, even as independence from adults is valued.

7. As children develop their own social codes, they become increasingly aware of the principles of the larger society. They do not necessarily follow these principles, however, especially if acceptance within their group or loyalty to their friends is at stake.

8. Friendships become more selective and exclusive as children grow older. Social problem-solving skills also develop during this period, as children acquire more sophisticated strategies for resolving differences and gaining social goals.

Family Structure and Child Development

9. Family functioning is far more crucial to children's well-being than family structure is. Whether a child lives in a two-parent, one-parent, or blended family is less important than whether the child's home situation is relatively stable, conflict-free, and supportive.

10. While functioning is key, nonetheless certain structures—especially one-parent, low-income homes and family arrangements that change dramatically from year to year—tend to be stressful on development. Since more than half of all American children will spend some of their childhood in a single-parent home, and since many children must undergo several family transitions, community attitudes and practical support from family and friends can play a crucial role to ensure children's well-being.

11. During middle childhood, poverty can be especially detrimental to cognitive and social development. One reason is that school-age children increasingly compare themselves with others, particularly on visible signs of status. This often leads children in poverty to feel ashamed and hopeless.

12. Another problem is that many very poor children live in violent neighborhoods, which restricts their independence and limits their willingness to plan ahead. Homeless children are especially vulnerable, because they experience not only poverty but often a dangerous, unstable life.

Coping with Life

13. Almost every child has some difficulties at home, school, or in the community during middle childhood. Most children cope quite well, as long as the problems are limited in duration and degree.

14. How well particular children cope with the problems in their lives depends on the number and nature of the stresses they experience, the strengths of their various competencies, and the social support they receive. Those children who seem "invulnerable" are usually those who have some special skills—intellectual, social, or artistic—and some person—parent, teacher, friend—to help them overcome whatever difficulties life presents.

KEY TERMS

latency (332)

industry versus inferiority (332)

social cognition (333)

learned helplessness (337)

peer group (337)

society of children (338)

prosocial behavior (340)

family structure (344)

social comparison (358)

KEY QUESTIONS

1. What features of development during middle childhood do all the major theoretical perspectives recognize?

2. How does the child's understanding of other people change during the school years?

3. How does a child's self-understanding change from the preschool years through middle childhood?

4. What factors typically cause children's self-esteem to drop during middle childhood?

5. What is the role of the peer group during the school years?

6. What are some of the factors that may cause a child to be rejected by the peer group?

7. What are the steps of social problem-solving?

8. What are the advantages and possible disadvantages of the two-parent home?

9. What are some of the factors that influence how parental divorce will affect a child?

10. What are some of the problems that are experienced by single-parent households?

11. What factors tend to make blended and dual-earner families beneficial or harmful to a child's development?

12. How does socioeconomic status affect development in middle childhood?

13. What are some of the stresses associated with a high risk of serious problems in a child's life?

14. What factors can help a child cope with stress?

Biosocial Development

Growth

During middle childhood, children grow more slowly than they did during infancy and toddlerhood or than they will during adolescence. Increased strength and heart and lung capacity give children the endurance to improve their performance in skills such as swimming and running.

Motor Skills

Slower growth contributes to children's increasing bodily control, and children enjoy exercising their developing skills of coordination and balance. Which specific skills they master depends largely on culture, gender, and inherited ability.

Cognitive Development

Thinking

Beginning at about age 7 or 8, children develop the ability to understand logical principles, including the concepts of reciprocity, classification, class inclusion, seriation, and number. They also become better able to understand and learn, in part because of their growing memory capacity and an increasing ability to use mnemonics. At the same time, metacognition techniques enable children to organize their learning.

Language

Children's increasing ability to understand the structures and possibilities of language enables them to extend the range of their cognitive powers and to become more analytical in their use of vocabulary. Most children develop proficiency in several language codes, and some become bilingual.

Education

Formal schooling begins worldwide, with the specifics of the curriculum depending on economic and societal factors.

Psychosocial Development

Emotions and Personality Development

Erikson sees the crisis of this stage as one of industry versus inferiority, while learning theorists suggest that children's greater awareness of the actions and attitudes of others makes them more susceptible to reinforcement and modeling techniques. The peer group becomes increasingly important to children as they become less dependent on their parents and more dependent on friends for help, loyalty, and sharing of mutual interests. A child's specific personality traits can make peer acceptance or rejection an important aspect of life. Children are also increasingly aware of, and involved in, family life, as well as in the world outside the home, and therefore are more likely to feel the effects of family, economic, and political conditions. Whether or not particular situations will be stressful for a child will depend, in part, on the child's temperament, competence, and the social support provided by home and school.

PART V

Adolescence

Adolescence is probably the most challenging and complicated period of life to describe, study, or experience. The biological changes of puberty are universal, but in their particular expression, timing, and extent, the variety shown is enormous and depends, of course, on sex, genes, and nutrition. There is great diversity in cognitive development as well: many adolescents are as egocentric in some respects as preschool children, while others reach the stage of abstract thinking that characterizes advanced cognition. Psychosocial changes during the second decade of life show even greater diversity, as adolescents develop their own identity, choosing from a vast number of sexual, moral, political, and educational paths. Most of this diversity simply reveals the productive variation that typifies the human life course, but for about one adolescent in four, fateful choices are made that handicap, and sometimes destroy, the future.

Yet such differences should not mask the commonality of the adolescent experience, for all adolescents are confronted with the same developmental tasks: they must adjust to their changing body size and shape, to their awakening sexuality, to new ways of thinking, and they must begin to strive for the emotional maturity and economic independence that characterize adulthood. As we will see in the next three chapters, the adolescent's efforts to come to grips with these tasks is often touched with confusion and poignancy.

CHAPTER 14

Adolescence:
Biosocial Development

In the teenage years, adolescents are caught up in a torrent of biosocial, cognitive, and emotional changes. Not only do they grow taller, heavier, and stronger at a rate more rapid than at any time since early childhood; they also experience changes associated with sexual growth that contribute a new dimension to the way their bodies function and to the ways they think about themselves and others. In this chapter we will focus on the nature and consequences of the biosocial changes that occur in adolescence, focusing on such questions as the following:

Is adolescence always a time of stress for teenagers, and consequently for their parents?

In which ways are the patterns of physical and sexual growth similar for both sexes?

What are some of the factors that affect the timing of puberty for a particular individual?

Why do early-maturing girls and late-maturing boys tend to have more problems than peers who experience puberty "on time"?

Between the ages of 10 and 20, humans everywhere cross a great divide between childhood and adulthood, biosocially, cognitively, and emotionally. No one would call this process of becoming an adult simple or easy. In modern society, at least, adjusting to the many changes that adolescence entails can be difficult and stressful, turbulent and unpredictable.

Before beginning our discussion of adolescence, however, we should acknowledge that no period of life is problem-free, and none—including adolescence—is defined only by its problems. There are moments, it is true, of moodiness, confusion, and anger in almost every teenager's life, and many adolescents make serious missteps on the path toward maturity. This chapter and the two that follow will examine some of these problems, putting them in perspective and focusing on causes and prevention. However, the major theme of these chapters is that the same developmental changes that may be a source of difficulty are also the source of new excitement, challenge, and growth of many kinds. Seriously troubled adolescents are in the minority. Moreover, many of the so-called problems of adolescence are actually problems more for parents and society than for teenagers themselves: the same music that makes adults shake their heads in disbelief makes young people jump with joy; the telephone time that exasperates parents is a social lifeline for teenagers; the sexual awakening that society fears is, for many individuals, the beginning of thrilling intimacy. Thus, any generalization about the "nature" of adolescence, especially about its turbulence, must be made cautiously and applied with care.

Puberty

The period of rapid physical growth and sexual maturation that ends childhood and brings the young person to adult size, shape, and sexual potential is called **puberty.** For girls, the visible physical changes of puberty include, in order, the emergence of breast buds, the initial appearance of pubic hair, widening of the hips, peak growth spurt, first menstrual period, final breast development, and completion of pubic-hair growth. For boys, the visible physical changes include, in order, growth of the testes, growth of the penis, initial appearance of pubic hair, first ejaculation, peak growth spurt, voice changes, and then beard development and completion of pubic-hair growth (Rutter, 1980; Malina, 1990).

Figure 14.1 *Increases in height, weight, musculature, and body fat are characteristics of all adolescents, but the range of these changes varies considerably, not only between the sexes but also between individuals of the same sex. While all the teenagers in this photo are developing normally, not all of them may feel that way at the moment.*

The age at which puberty starts is variable: normal children begin to notice body changes anywhere between ages 8 and 14. (The reasons for this variation, and the impact of it, are discussed at the end of this chapter.) Once puberty begins, the changes almost always occur in the sequence just outlined, and barring unusual events such as extreme malnutrition, con-

TABLE 14.1 Sequence of Puberty

Girls	Approximate Average Age*		Boys
Ovaries increase production of estrogen and progesterone	9	10	Testes increase production of testosterone
Internal sex organs begin to grow larger	9½	11	Testes and scrotum grow larger
Breast "bud" stage	10	12	Pubic hair begins to appear
Pubic hair begins to appear	11	12½	Penis growth begins
Weight spurt begins	11½	13	First ejaculation
Peak height spurt	12	13	Weight spurt begins
Peak muscle and organ growth (also, hips become noticeably wider)	12½	14	Peak height spurt
Menarche (first menstrual period)	12½	14½	Peak muscle and organ growth (also, shoulders become noticeably broader)
First ovulation	13½	15	Voice lowers
Final pubic-hair pattern	15	16	Facial hair appears
Full breast growth	16	18	Final pubic-hair pattern

*Average ages are a rough approximation, with many perfectly normal, healthy adolescents as much as three years ahead or behind these ages. In addition, sequence is somewhat variable. For instance, many girls have some pubic hair before their breasts start to grow, and some boys have visible mustaches before their voices have completely changed.

tinue steadily (see Table 14.1). About three or four years after the first visible signs of puberty, the major events are over, although individuals may gain an inch or two of height and add some additional fat and muscle in early adulthood.

The entire process begins with hormone production in the brain. Hormones from the hypothalamus trigger hormone production in the pituitary gland (located at the base of the skull), which, in turn, triggers increased hormone production by the adrenal glands (two small glands at either side of the mid-section) and by the gonads, or sex glands (the testes in the male and the ovaries in the female).

While about a dozen distinct hormones are involved in puberty, the most important are **GH,** the growth hormone (which rises steadily in both sexes), **testosterone** (which increases dramatically in boys and slightly in girls), and the **estrogens** (which increase markedly in girls and slightly in boys). These hormones begin their increase at least a year before the first perceptible signs of puberty. Rapidly increasing hormones, especially testosterone, can effect various personality traits and, particularly, sexual interest (Udry, 1990), but the emotional impact of puberty depends more on other factors—including the reaction of others to the visible signs of puberty—than on the concentration of hormones in the bloodstream (Nottelman et al., 1990).

The many observable changes of puberty outlined above are often grouped into two categories: rapid increase in body size, called the growth spurt, and the emergence of sexual characteristics. We will describe both sets of changes in turn.

The Growth Spurt

The first sign of the **growth spurt** is increased bone length and density, a process that begins in the ends of the extremities and works toward the center. Thus adolescents' fingers and feet lengthen before their arms and legs do. The torso is the last part of the body to grow, making many adolescents temporarily big-footed, long-legged, and short-waisted.

At the same time that the bones begin to lengthen, the child begins to gain weight much more rapidly than before, because fat begins to accumulate more readily. In fact, parents typically notice that their children are emptying their plates, cleaning out the refrigerator, and straining the seams of their clothes even before they notice that their children are growing taller. Toward the end of middle childhood, usually between the ages of 10 and 12, both boys and girls become noticeably heavier, primarily through the accumulation of fat. The specific parts of the body that take on fat, and the total amount of fat increase at each site, vary a great deal, depending partly on gender (girls accumulate more fat generally, especially on their legs and hips, than boys), partly on heredity, and partly on diet and exercise.

Soon after the onset of the weight increase, a height increase becomes notable, burning up some of the recently accumulated fat and redistributing some of the rest. On the whole, a greater percentage of fat is retained by females, who naturally have a higher proportion of body fat in womanhood than in girlhood. About a year after these weight and height increases take place, a period of muscle increase occurs: consequently, the pudginess and clumsiness exhibited by the typical child in early puberty generally have disappeared by late pubescence, a few years later. The muscle increase is particularly notable in boys' upper bodies: between ages 13 and 18, arm strength more than doubles (Beunen, 1988).

Overall, the typical girl gains about 38 pounds (17 kilograms) and 9⅝ inches (24 centimeters) between the ages of 10 and 14, while the typical boy gains the same number of inches and about 42 pounds (19 kilograms) between the ages of 12 and 16 (Lowrey, 1986). Note, however, that the cross-sectional data, which average out the individual growth spurts, are somewhat deceptive, because the chronological age for the growth spurt varies considerably from child to child. In any given year between ages 10 and 16,

Figure 14.2 *At the beginning of puberty, adjustment to the growth of fat, bone, and finally muscle entails a certain amount of awkwardness, both physical and psychological. Most of the youths pictured here seem to reflect the physical ungainliness and self-consciousness that are typical of early puberty.*

Figure 14.3 *Because of the sequence of physical growth in puberty, buying a new pair of jeans can be a major project for young teenagers. Almost all pants ready-made for adults are too short in the legs, or too low in the waist, or too tight in the buttocks. And if these girls do succeed in finding a pair that fits just right, in six months they will probably have outgrown them.*

some individuals will not grow much at all because their growth spurt has not begun or is already over, while others will grow very rapidly. Records of individual growth during this period make it obvious why the word "spurt" is used to describe these increases (Tanner, 1978). During the twelve-month period of their greatest growth, many girls gain as much as 20 pounds (9 kilograms) and 3½ inches (9 centimeters), and many boys gain up to 26 pounds (12 kilograms) and 4 inches (10 centimeters).

One of the last parts of the body to grow into final form is the head. To the embarrassment of many teenagers, the facial features—especially the markedly larger ears, lips, and nose that differentiate adults from children—increase in size before the head itself takes on the large, more oval shape typical of adults. At least as disturbing to some young people can be the fact that the two halves of the body do not always grow at the same rate: one foot, breast, testicle, or ear can be temporarily larger than the other. None of these anomalies persist very long. Once the growth process starts, every part of the body reaches close to adult size, shape, and proportion in three or four years. Of course, for the adolescent, these few years of waiting for one's body to take on "normal" proportions can seem like an eternity.

Organ Growth

While the torso grows, internal organs also grow (Lowrey, 1986). The lungs increase in size and capacity, actually tripling in weight, allowing the adolescent to breathe more deeply and slowly. The heart doubles in size, and heart rate decreases, slowing from an average of ninety-two beats per minute at age 10 to eighty-two at age 18. In addition, the total volume of blood increases.

These changes increase physical endurance in exercise, making it possible for many teenagers to run for miles or dance for hours without stopping for rest. However, the fact that the more visible spurts of weight and height precede the less visible ones of the muscles and organs means that athletic training and weight-lifting should match a young person's size of a year or so earlier. Exhaustion and injury might result if the physical demands on a young person's body do not take this lag into account (Thornburg and Aras, 1986).

Figure 14.4 *It is not until several years after the growth spurt begins that outward appearance and organ maturation reach adult form. However, because of the social pressures they feel to be "grown up," many young girls turn to cosmetics and other aids to make themselves look womanly.*

One organ system, the lymphoid system, including the tonsils and adenoids, actually decreases in size at adolescence, making teenagers less susceptible to respiratory ailments. About half the victims of childhood asthma, for example, improve markedly in adolescence (Markowitz, 1983).

The eyes also undergo a change, as the eyeballs elongate, making many adolescents sufficiently nearsighted to require glasses.

Finally, the hormones of puberty cause many relatively minor physical changes that, despite their insignificance in the grand scheme of development, can have substantial psychic impact. For instance, oil, sweat, and odor glands of the skin become much more active during puberty. One result is acne, which occurs to some degree in about 85 percent of all adolescents (Lowrey, 1986). Another result is oilier hair and smellier bodies, which make adolescents spend more money on shampoo and deodorants than any other age group.

Nutrition

The rapid body changes of puberty obviously require additional calories, as well as additional vitamins and minerals (Taitz and Wardley, 1989). In fact, the recommended daily intake of calories, as well as of calcium and iron, is higher for an active adolescent than for a person at any other time during the entire life span. The typical adolescent needs about 50 percent more calcium, iron, zinc, and vitamin D during the growth spurt than two years earlier (Sinclair, 1978).

In developed nations, where quality food is sufficiently available, most adolescents, most of the time, meet their basic nutritional needs, consuming four or more meals a day in spite of often skipping breakfast (Leon et al., 1989; Thornburg and Aras, 1986). If a seemingly well-nourished adolescent is nutritionally deficient at all, it is likely to be in iron (most commonly found in meat, egg yolks, and dark-green vegetables), since fewer than half of all adolescents daily consume the recommended 15 milligrams. Because each menstrual period deletes some iron from the body, adolescent females are more likely to suffer iron-deficiency anemia than any other subgroup of the population. This means, for one thing, that if a teenage girl seems apathetic and lazy, she should have her iron level checked before it is assumed that she suffers from a poor attitude or other psychosocial difficulties. It also means that if a teenager becomes pregnant, she will most likely be in need of iron supplements.

While it is true that most adolescents in developed countries are well nourished most of the time, it is also true that most experience periods of overeating, undereating, or nutritional imbalance. For many reasons, the typical adolescent is especially vulnerable to food fads and strange diets. These can be harmful at every age, but they are particularly so during the rapid growth of early adolescence, when the body must have sufficient nourishment to reach full growth potential. Teenagers who systematically deprive themselves of basic nourishment throughout the growth spurt will become shorter and less well formed adults (Tanner, 1978).

Indeed, a sizable minority of adolescents have problems that interfere with normal, healthy eating. Childhood obesity often worsens in adolescence if the young person experiences increased social rejection and a further lowering of self-esteem. Addictive drug use also affects eating patterns,

Figure 14.5 *In their efforts to see that their teenage children are well-nourished, many parents feel they are engaged in a lost cause: they urge fruits, vegetables, and lean meat, while their offspring stoke up on sugary, greasy, salty, fast foods. However, given the high calorie needs of the growing young person, fast foods are not unequivocally bad. For instance, milk shakes are rich in calcium, French fries, in vitamin C, and pizza, in iron, and all provide ample calories necessary to sustain rapid growth.*

altering the appetite and digestive processes and depriving the young person of growth and energy.

Another problem, particularly for girls, is the preoccupation with being thin, which can lead to serious undernourishment, halting growth and sexual maturation. Most adolescent girls wish they were thinner. Indeed, a large longitudinal study of younger adolescents found that even at sixth grade many girls were unhappy with their weight. By ninth grade, not only were most girls dissatisfied with their weight but they also "cared very much" about it. No other problem with appearance was of such concern (Simmons and Blyth, 1987).

Another study found that older girls (aged 14 to 18) typically wanted to be about 12 pounds lighter (Brooks-Gunn et al., 1989). Amazingly, this held true across the board—regardless of the girls' maturation status or their exercise levels. For example, girls who matured late, and thus had relatively thin, girlish, bodies, wanted to lose almost as many pounds as those more womanly shaped girls who had matured on time. Similarly, competitive swimmers, whose bodies were quite muscular and who needed some fat to help them with buoyancy and endurance, wanted to lose weight just as much as the nonathletes, who had somewhat more fat on their bodies and less reason to need it. Even the thinnest group, late-maturing girls who practiced daily in professional dance training schools, wished they weighed 10 pounds less.

Because of this pervasive desire among adolescent girls to be ever thinner, many of them seem to be either continually dieting or continually worried that they should be dieting. This is often unfortunate, because chronic unrealistic concern about one's weight and repeated dieting can be destructive, not only for peace of mind and self-confidence, but also for physical health. (The cultural and psychological causes of destructive eating habits and their potentially serious consequences, are discussed in Chapter 16, pp 455–457.)

Sexual Maturation

While the growth spurt is taking place, another set of changes occurs that transforms boys and girls into young men and women. As we have seen, before puberty, the physical differences between boys and girls are relatively minor. At puberty, however, sexual maturation results in many significant body differences. These include changes in both the primary and secondary sex characteristics.

Changes in Primary Sex Characteristics

Changes in **primary sex characteristics** involve those sex organs that are directly involved in reproduction. During puberty, all the sex organs become much larger. In girls, the uterus begins to grow and the vaginal lining thickens, even before there are visible signs of puberty. In boys, the testes begin to grow, and about a year later, the penis lengthens and the scrotal sac enlarges and becomes pendulous.

By the end of puberty, the young person's sex organs have become sufficiently mature to make reproduction possible. For girls, the specific event that is taken to indicate fertility is the first menstrual period, which is re-

Figure 14.6 *In recent years, adolescent girls have been much more likely to engage in strenuous sports. This has revealed two interesting facts about the adolescent menstrual cycle. First, it is more often irregular or absent altogether if the girl is very physically active, and very lean as a result . Second, menstrual cramps are real—not just an excuse for laziness or a factor of poor health. Even star athletes can be handicapped by physical changes on or about the first day of their period.*

ferred to as **menarche.** For boys, the comparable indicator of reproductive potential is **spermarche,** that is, the first ejaculation of seminal fluid containing sperm. Ejaculation can occur during sleep in a nocturnal emission (a wet dream), through masturbation, or through sexual intercourse, with masturbation being the most common cause for the first ejaculation.

Actually, both menarche and spermarche are simply one more step toward full reproductive maturity, which occurs several years later (Thornburg and Aras, 1986). In fact, a girl's first menstrual cycles are usually *anovulatory*; that is, they occur without ovulation. Even a year after menarche, most young women are still relatively infertile: ovulation is irregular, and if fertilization does occur, the probability of spontaneous abortion is much higher than it will be later, because the uterus is still relatively small. In the case of boys, the concentration of sperm usually necessary to fertilize an ovum is not reached until months or even years after the first ejaculation of seminal fluid (Chilman, 1983). (As many teenagers discover too late, unfortunately, this relative infertility does not mean that pregnancy is impossible at puberty; it is simply less likely than it will be a few years later. When pregnancy does occur before a girl's body is fully developed, the combined nutritional demands of her own growth and her fetus's increase the risk of her having a low-birth-weight infant and lessen her chances of ever reaching her maximum potential height.)

Attitudes toward menarche, menstruation, and spermarche have changed over the past two decades, and, for the most part, young people no longer face these events with anxiety, embarrassment, or guilt. Indeed, these events are looked on positively today, and adolescents are more worried if they experience them after, rather than before, most of their friends do. Most feel quite well informed about these first signs of sexual maturity. In particular, masturbation, once a source of overwhelming fear and shame, is now commonly accepted by adolescents of both sexes (Chilman, 1983).

Nevertheless, a strong sense of sexual privacy remains. Virtually no young adolescent discusses these private events with friends or parents of the other sex. Indeed, although most boys are proud to reach spermarche, few of them tell other boys the details of their experiences with masturbation or ejaculation. They are also unlikely to discuss instances of unexpected or unwanted arousal, such as to a photo, to another boy, to a relative, even though such arousal is fairly common (Gaddis and Brooks-Gunn, 1985). For their part, girls, who typically promise to tell their close friends when menarche arrives, are usually more reticent than they had anticipated (Brooks-Gunn et al., 1986).

One negative still associated with menstruation is occasional cramping, which in about half of all adolescent girls is sufficiently painful that it may preclude normal activities (Widholm, 1985). Further, in this age group, moodiness in the days before menstruation is quite common. Teachers and parents need to know that although psychological tension may exacerbate these problems, the primary cause is in the body, not the psyche, and medical diagnosis and treatment may help (Dawood, 1985).

Secondary Sex Characteristics

While maturation of the reproductive organs is the most directly sexual development of puberty, changes in many other parts of the young person's body also indicate that sexual maturation is occurring. These changes are called **secondary sex characteristics,** for while they are not directly related to the primary sexual function of reproduction, they are clearly signs of sexual development. Most obviously, the body shape of males and females, which was almost identical in childhood, becomes quite distinct in adolescence (Malina, 1990). Males grow taller than females and become wider at the shoulders than at the hips. Females become wider at the hips, an adaptation for childbearing that is apparent even in puberty and becomes increasingly so over the teenage years.

Another obvious difference in the shape of the female body, and the one that receives the most attention in Western cultures, is the development of breasts. For most girls, the first sign that puberty is beginning is the "bud" stage of breast development, when a small accumulation of fat causes a slight rise around the nipples. From then on, breasts develop gradually for about four years, with full breast growth not being attained until almost all the other changes of puberty are over (Malina, 1990). Since our culture misguidedly takes breast development to be symbolic of womanhood, girls whose breasts are very small or very large often feel worry and embarrassment; small-breasted girls often feel "cheated," even disfigured; large-breasted girls may become extremely self-conscious as they find themselves the frequent object of unwanted stares and remarks.

In boys, the diameter of the areola (the dark area around the nipple) increases during puberty. Much to their consternation, many boys develop breast tissue as well. However, their worry is usually short-lived: about 65 percent of all adolescent boys experience some breast enlargement, typically at about age 14 (Smith, 1983), but this enlargement normally disappears by age 16.

Another secondary sex characteristic that changes markedly is the voice, which becomes lower as the larynx grows. This change, of course, is most noticeable in boys. (Even more noticeable, much to the chagrin of the young male, is an occasional loss of voice control that throws his newly acquired baritone into a high squeak.) Girls also develop somewhat lower voices, a fact reflected in the recognition of a low, throaty female voice as more womanly.

During puberty, both sexes also experience changes in head and body hair, which usually becomes coarser and darker. In addition, new hair growth occurs under the arms, on the face, and in the pubic area. Indeed, for many young people, the appearance of a few light-colored straight strands of pubic hair is the first apparent sign of puberty. As puberty continues, pubic hair becomes darker, thicker, and curlier, and covers a wider area. Girls reach the adult pubic-hair pattern in about three years; for boys, the process takes somewhat longer.

Facial and body hair are generally considered distinct signs of manliness in American society, a notion that is mistaken for three reasons. First, the tendency to grow facial and body hair is inherited; how often a man needs to shave, or how hairy his chest is, is determined by his genes rather than his virility. In addition, facial hair is usually the last secondary sex characteristic to appear, sometimes long after a young male has become sexually active. Finally, girls typically develop some facial hair and more noticeable hair on their arms and legs during puberty—a sign not of masculinity but of sexual maturation.

Figure 14.7 *Although sex differences in appearance are biological, emerging in dozens of ways at puberty, much of the gender differences that adolescents display are cultural. The obvious male-female distinctions here are mostly a matter of hair style, body language, and clothes—or lack of them.*

A CLOSER LOOK   Body Image

The physiological changes of puberty necessitate a drastic revision of adolescents' **body image**, that is, their mental conception of, and their attitude toward, their physical appearance. According to many developmentalists, developing a healthy body image is an integral part of becoming an adult (e.g., Erikson, 1968; Simmons and Blythe, 1987). However, few adolescents are satisfied with their physical appearance, most imagining that their bodies appear far less perfect than they actually are.

As a result, many adolescents spend hours examining themselves in front of the mirror—worrying about their complexions, about how their hair style affects the appearance of their face, about whether the fit of their clothes makes them look shapely. Some exercise or diet with obsessive intensity (e.g., lifting weights to build specific muscles, or weighing food to the gram to better calculate calories). Such self-absorption can seem nearly psychopathological to outsiders, or even to other adolescents, who tire of hearing each other fretting endlessly about their appearance.

Indeed, the quest for the ideal body can become physically as well as psychologically unhealthy. At one time or other, almost every American girl undereats for an extended period, sometimes drastically, in order to be thinner, and 6 percent of all American high-school boys take steroids to build up their muscles, risking a variety of serious health problems, especially if they obtain the drugs illegally, and "stack" one drug with another, as many do (Yesalis et al., 1989). Further, although most adolescents believe that smoking cigarettes puts their health "at great risk," about one in four 16-year-olds smokes regularly—partly because cigarettes are thought to reduce the appetite. Given that fact, it is not surprising that, contrary to the pattern for other drugs, teenage girls are more likely than boys to smoke (Johnston et al., 1991).

Before dismissing adolescents' preoccupation with their looks as narcissistic, we should recognize that teenagers' concern for appearance is, in part, a response to the reactions of other people. Parents and siblings, for example, sometimes make memorable and mortifying comments about the growing child's appearance—"You look like a cow," "You're flat as a board," "Your feet look like gunboats"—that they would not dare make with anyone else. Strangers, too, offer commentary (usually unwanted and disconcerting) on adolescents' growing bodies: pubescent girls suddenly hear whistles, catcalls, and lewd suggestions; boys, depending on their level of maturation, often find themselves labeled as studs or wimps. Adolescents may even get subtle messages about their appearance from their teachers: in junior high school, at least, teachers tend to judge new students who are physically attractive as academically more competent than their less attractive classmates (Lerner et al., 1990).

The concern with physical appearance dominates the peer culture as well, with the most obvious impact on self-esteem occurring in early adolescence (Harter, 1990). Teenagers who are unattractive tend to have fewer friends—of either sex—than the average teenager (Rutter, 1980). And, of course, physical attractiveness is an especially important sexual lure during adolescence. One researcher asked teenagers what, among all the possible abilities, traits, or characteristics, they looked for in the other sex. Ranked in order of importance, the traits boys most wanted in girls were good looks, a good body, friendliness, and intelligence. Girls wanted similar traits in boys: intelligence, good looks, a good body, and conversational ability (Hass, 1979).

Adolescents also receive powerful messages from the macrosystem regarding the importance of physical appearance. They are daily bombarded with media images of handsome faces and beautiful bodies selling everything from clothes and cosmetics to luncheon meats and auto parts. These images reinforce the "cultural ideal" that men should be tall and muscular, that women should be thin and shapely, and—at least in the United States, Canada, and Australia—that both should have features suggesting an Anglo-Saxon heritage. Obviously, few people fit this so-called ideal. Indeed, many ethnic groups are genetically endowed with shorter stature, or broader hips, or chunkier bodies, and so forth than those called for by the cultural ideal. Often these genetic differences are not very salient in childhood, before hormones evoke the adult body type the person is destined to have. This means that puberty suddenly requires many young adolescents to come to terms with a body form, inherited from their ancestors, that is a far cry from those of the models and movie stars they idolize.

It is no wonder, then, that many adolescents are dissatisfied with their emerging bodies (Simmons and Blythe, 1987). Overall, compared to boys, girls are more dissatisfied with their appearance and more likely to be concerned about particular parts of their bodies (Clifford,

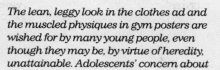

The lean, leggy look in the clothes ad and the muscled physiques in gym posters are wished for by many young people, even though they may be, by virtue of heredity, unattainable. Adolescents' concern about their body image is such that even the two teenagers shown here—whose genes allow them to approach the cultural ideal—are likely to be overly worried about how their bodies look.

1971; Koff et al., 1990; Rauste-von Wright, 1989). For example, in addition to being dissatisfied with their weight, girls are more likely to be unhappy about their hips, legs, knees, and feet. Even girls who appear flawless seem eager to recite their imperfections—a crooked finger, a short neck, thin eyebrows, a slight bump on the nose. Other than wishing they were taller, few boys are so specific in their concerns.

With time, the intense self-preoccupation and concern about body image typical of the pubescent young person lessens, and adolescents gradually become more satisfied with their physical selves (Rauste-von Wright, 1990). By adulthood, most people have learned to accept the discrepancy between the cultural ideal and their own natural appearance, an acceptance that becomes easier once they are assured, over the years, that they and their bodies are loved "just as they are."

Meanwhile, however, teenagers' concern over their body image should not be taken lightly. For most adolescents, thinking that they look "terrible" makes them feel terrible. In adolescence, particularly, feelings of depression among both males and females correlate strongly with a negative body image (Rierdan et al., 1988). Girls are particularly vulnerable: compared to happier girls, depressed girls tend to be more dissatisfied with particular parts of their bodies, and to think of their bodies as ugly, sick, useless, boring, weak, and out of control (Rierdan et al., 1987). Instead of ignoring or belittling the adolescent's self-preoccupation, adults should provide whatever practical help seems warranted—such as clothing suggestions, encouragement to exercise, or medical treatment for acne. Understanding and compliments, instead of criticism and derision, might have far-reaching benefits, not only for the adolescent's body image but also for his or her self-esteem and social acceptance.

The Timing of Puberty

While the sequence of pubertal events is very similar for all young people, there is great variation in the age of onset. Healthy children begin puberty any time between ages 8 and 14, with ages 10, 11, and 12 being the most typical. The child's sex, genes, body type, nourishment, metabolism, and both emotional and physical health all affect this variation (Cameroon, 1990; Hopwood et al., 1990).

Factors Affecting When Puberty Occurs

Male-female differences are one factor affecting when a particular person will experience puberty, although the average time differential between female and male development depends on which particular event in puberty is being compared. The first signs of reproductive capability appear only a few months later in boys than in girls: the average American girl reaches menarche at about age 12½, while the average boy first ejaculates at age 13 (Schoof-Tams et al., 1976; Thornburg and Aras, 1986). However, since the growth spurt appears later in the sequence of pubertal changes in boys, the average boy is two years behind the average girl in this respect. Consequently, between ages 12 and 14, most girls are taller than their male classmates.

Genes are a second important factor in the age at which puberty begins. This is most clearly seen in the case of menarche. Although most girls reach this milestone between 11 and 14, the age of onset varies from 9 to 18. However, sisters reach menarche, on the average, only 13 months apart, and monozygotic twins differ by a mere 2.8 months. Recognition of this genetic influence is particularly important in the case of early or late maturation. For the one girl in fifty who shows breast "bud" development before age 8 or after age 13, or the one boy in fifty whose testes begin to enlarge before age 9 or after age 14, the most likely explanation is normal genetic variability.

Perhaps for genetic reasons, the average age of onset of puberty varies somewhat from nation to nation, and from ethnic group to ethnic group. Within Europe, for example, onset tends to be relatively late for Belgians and relatively early for Poles (Malina et al., 1988). Within the United States, African-Americans often begin puberty earlier, and Asian-Americans later, than Americans of European ancestry.

Some of these genetic differences may be related to body type. In general, stocky individuals tend to experience puberty earlier than those with taller, thinner builds. Menarche, in particular, seems related to the accumulation of a certain amount of body fat, and thus does not usually occur until a girl weighs about 100 pounds. Females who have little body fat, such as dancers, runners, and other athletes, menstruate later than and more irregularly than the average girl, while those who are generally inactive menstruate earlier (Frisch, 1983). (This is one explanation for the fact that blind girls, who are usually less active than sighted girls, normally have their first period earlier than sighted girls. It may also explain why menarche is more likely to occur in winter than in spring or summer.)

One intriguing final factor may influence the onset of puberty: the relative degree of warmth or emotional distance in the relationship of the child to his or her parents. Many studies have found a correlation between early

Figure 14.8 *The growth spurt occurs later in male than in female maturation, so it is not unusual for a group of junior high school students to include boys who appear quite childlike. However, sexual development occurs almost at the same age in both sexes, so to the extent that sexual interest is hormonal, the boy playing the mandolin is probably experiencing the same feelings as the girl playing the guitar.*

puberty and parent-adolescent strife. The traditional explanation always was that the combination of the young person's "raging hormones" and emotional immaturity was at the root of such conflict. Surprisingly, longitudinal research suggests that the effects sometimes flow in the other direction: family distance and stress may accelerate onset of puberty (Steinberg, 1988; Moffit et al., 1990; Surbey, 1990), although the particulars vary a great deal depending on the overall situation (Ellis, 1991; Belsky et al., 1991).

<table>
<tr><td>A LIFE-SPAN PERSPECTIVE</td></tr>
</table>

Early and Late Maturation

Young people who experience puberty at the same time as their friends tend to view the experience more positively than those who experience it earlier or later (Dubas et al., 1991). As Table 14.1 (p. 371) reveals, timing is particularly important for girls. Compared to boys, girls who are "on-time" are more happy and those who are "off-time" are less happy.

Early-Maturing Girls

Girls who are taller and more developed than their classmates discover that they have no peers who share their interests or problems. Prepubescent girls call them "boy crazy," and boys tease them about their big feet or developing breasts. Almost every sixth-grade class has an 11-year-old pubescent girl who slouches so she won't look so tall, wears loose shirts so no one will notice her breasts, and buys her shoes a size too small. There are additional hazards for the early maturer. If she begins dating, it will probably be with boys who are older, and her self-esteem is likely to fall for a number of reasons (Simmons et al., 1983): she may feel constantly scrutinized by her parents, criticized by her girlfriends for not spending time with them, and pressured by her dates to be sexual. In fact, age at menarche is a stronger predictor of age of first sexual intercourse than almost any other factor, including religion, race, and socioeconomic standing (Bingham et al., 1990).

In general, those who date early (by age 14) are likely to have sexual intercourse before high school is over (Miller et al., 1986). And those who have sexual intercourse early are less likely to use contraception (see Chapter 15), more likely to become pregnant, and, if they keep the baby, more likely to find their educational and career accomplishments deflected downward for at least a decade (Furstenberg, et al., 1987).

Of course, this path is not inevitable. Social pressures and constraints are at least as important as biological ones in determining the age of dating (Wyatt, 1990). Many early-maturing girls, for example, are prevented from dating by their parents or by their own shyness; and others may not begin dating unless they associate with older peers (Magnussen et al., 1985). Furthermore, dating does not always lead to sexual activity, and sexual activity does not necessarily lead to motherhood. Nevertheless, the link is there, and some young women find their

Figure 14.9 *Both 14-year-olds pictured here experienced puberty "off-time." Probably the early-maturer suffered considerable stress at around age 11, when her feet, hips, and breasts provoked unwanted attention. By this point, however, she may already have learned to cope with her body image, and the late-maturing girl may be wishing her body would "hurry up."*

adult lives and the lives of their children restricted by a chain of events that began when they reached menarche at age 10 or 11 rather than later.

Most early-maturing girls weather their first years of adolescence without premature sexual experiences, however, and most soon find that they benefit more than they suffer from the difference between themselves and their peers. By seventh or eighth grade, early maturation bestows increased status, respect, and popularity (Faust, 1983). Initial problems often lead to more mature thought as well as appearance (Livson and Peskin, 1980). After a few years of awkwardness and embarrassment, the early-maturing girl is able to advise her less mature girlfriends about topics that they find increasingly important, such as bra sizes, dating behavior, menstrual cramps, and variations in kissing. In general, the early-maturing girl has more close friends than those who have not yet begun to mature (Brooks-Gunn et al., 1986). She also becomes more comfortable with her body, and with whether and how she expresses her sexual feelings.

Further research suggests that, in the long run, girls who are late to mature may have more problems than girls who are early. As one review explains:

> The stress-ridden early-maturing girl in adulthood has become clearly a more coping, self-possessed and self-directed person than the later-maturing female in the cognitive and social as well as in emotional sectors . . . . By contrast, it is the late-maturing female, carefree and unchallenged in adolescence, who faces adversity maladaptively in adulthood. [Livson and Peskin, 1980]

Late-Maturing Boys

In contrast to temporarily troubled early-maturing girls or to the temporarily carefree late-maturing girls, late-maturing boys may have problems that last into adulthood. They must watch themselves be outdistanced, first by the girls in their class and then by most of the boys, and they are forced to endure the patronizing scorn of those who only recently were themselves immature. Extensive longitudinal data from the Berkeley Growth Study (Jones, 1957, 1965; Jones and Bayley, 1950; Mussen and Jones, 1957) showed that in high school, late-maturing boys tend to be less poised, less relaxed, more restless, and more talkative than early-maturing boys, who were found to be more often chosen as leaders. The late-maturing boys were more playful, more creative, and more flexible, qualities that are not usually admired by other adolescents. One study found that late maturity in boys is associated with more conflicts with parents than early maturity in boys or later maturing in girls (Savin-Williams and Small, 1986).

However, particularly for boys, generalizations based solely on age of puberty are difficult to make. A review of all the research on timing of puberty in boys finds that, while the effects of early puberty are generally positive, the effects of late puberty are mixed, dependent not only on the particular traits and particular population under study but also on other factors (Downs, 1990). For example, no matter what the timing of their development, boys who are unusually short, who are not ath-

Figure 14.10 *Nature often forces different roles on early- and late-maturing boys of the same age. The early-maturing boy generally feels compelled to show his strength, with a cocky self-assurance that is hard to shake. The late-maturer, on the other hand, compensates, perhaps becoming a "brain," a trouble-maker, or the class clown.*

letic, who appear physically weak or unattractive, and/or who are slow to become sexually involved, tend to have lower self-esteem and create more problems for themselves and others during adolescence. This occurs no matter what the timing of the boy's development, but the later puberty begins, the more likely each of these liabilities is to occur. Obviously the extent to which a particular boy experiences them will vary—some late developers are quite handsome and athletic—and, further, some peer groups value each of these attributes more than others. Thus, the impact of later maturation varies a great deal, from person to person and culture to culture.

Follow-up studies of the Berkeley late-maturing boys when they were 33 years old, and again when they were 38, found that most of them had reached average or above-average height but that some of the personality patterns of their adolescence had persisted. Compared with early- or average-maturing boys, those who had matured late tended to be less controlled, less responsible, and less dominant, and they were less likely to hold positions of leadership in their jobs or in their social organizations. Some still had feelings of inferiority and rejection. However, in several positive characteristics they scored well. They were likely to have a better sense of humor and to be more egalitarian and more perceptive than their early-maturing peers. Especially in an era of greater liberation from traditional sex roles, later-maturing boys became more adaptive men (Livson and Peskin, 1980).

Of course, not all late-maturing boys feel inferior during adolescence. And, in fact, late maturation today may be less difficult than it was decades ago; for example, because of the greater freedom allowed young girls, the late-maturing boy can now gain experience with the other sex by dating girls several years younger than he is. If he attends a school where most students are placed in classes according to interests and abilities, rather than age, he will be less likely to feel inferior and more likely to develop his skills.

School, Family, and Cultural Factors

Adolescents are affected not only by how their development meshes with that of others in their class but also by how it compares with that of others in their school. For example, one study shows that tall, early-maturing sixth-grade girls score higher in measures of social competence when they are enrolled in a middle school where they are among similarly mature seventh- and eighth-graders than when they are the tallest, most mature girls in an elementary school that ends at sixth grade (Nottelmann and Welsh, 1986).

Another important factor may be the timing between puberty and various forms of social transition—entry to junior high, moving to a new neighborhood, beginning to date, and so forth. In general, the more social changes adolescents go through, the more likely they are to experience such typical problems as a drop in school grades, a decrease (especially among girls) of self-esteem, and an increase (especially among boys) of difficulties with teachers (Simmons et al., 1988).

The family context is important as well. No matter what their timing, the physical events of puberty and the budding drives for sexual expression and freedom of action typically increase the distance between parents and their adolescent children, particularly between mothers and daughters. When the family already has a pattern of dysfunction, or when stressful family events such as divorce coincide with puberty, then the adolescent is likely to have difficulty adjusting to the normal changes of adolescence. (The relationship between family patterns and adolescent problems is discussed in Chapter 16.)

In many ways, cultural values can intensify, or lessen, the problems of early or late maturation. The effects of early or late maturation are more apparent, for example, among adolescents of lower socioeconomic status because physique and physical prowess tend to be more highly valued among teenagers of low SES than among middle- or upper-class teenagers. Correspondingly, alternative sources of status for the early or late maturer, such as academic achievement or vocational aspiration, are less available and valued among lower-SES adolescents (Rutter, 1980).

The impact of school and culture was further revealed in a longitudinal study showing that, unlike their American counterparts, early-maturing girls in Germany do not experience lower self-esteem. The authors of the study speculate that the reason may be that sex education is more extensive in German schools than in American schools, leading to less confusion and embarrassment about sexual maturation, as well as to a reduced likelihood of pregnancy (Silbereisen et al., 1989).

As always in development, the interaction among the three domains is more potent than changes in any one area. In the next chapter, we will look at the adolescent's ability to understand, and thus cope with, these changes.

SUMMARY

Puberty

1. While the sequence of pubertal events is similar for most young people of both sexes and in every culture, the timing of puberty shows considerable variation. Normal young people experience their first body changes any time between the ages of 8 and 14. The process begins with hormone production in the brain. Three of the most important hormones are the growth hormone, testosterone, and the estrogens.

2. The growth spurt—first in weight, then in height—provides the first obvious evidence of puberty, although some hormonal changes precede it. During the year of fastest growth, an average girl grows about 3½ inches (9 centimeters) and an average boy about 4 inches (10 centimeters).

3. Growth usually begins with the extremities and proceeds toward the torso. By the end of puberty, the head, muscles, lungs, heart, and digestive system also change in size and shape.

4. To fuel such growth, adolescents experience increasing nutritional demands, for vitamins and minerals as well as for calories—more than at any other period of life. Several specific problems can interfere with normal nutrition.

5. During puberty, all the sex organs grow larger as the young person becomes sexually mature. Menarche in girls and ejaculation in boys are the events usually taken to indicate reproductive potential, although full fertility is reached years after these initial signs of maturation.

6. Many adolescents are intensely concerned over, and somewhat dissatisfied with, their appearance. For some, this leads to health problems and psychological depression. Girls are particularly vulnerable, as dissatisfaction with weight can trigger dangerous dieting and anxiety.

7. Most secondary sex characteristics—including changes in the breasts and voice, and the development of pubic, facial, and body hair—appear in both sexes, although there are obvious differences in the typical development of males and females.

8. As the body changes, so must the individual's body image—the person's conception of what he or she looks like. For many adolescents, this is problematic, because their actual new shape and appearance are not what they expected, or what the cultural ideal promotes.

The Timing of Puberty

9. The individual's sex, genes, body type, and nutrition all affect the age at which puberty begins and ends. Girls typically begin puberty ahead of boys, and children with more body fat begin earlier than those who are lean. Consequently, some young women are, essentially, full-grown by age 13, while some young men still are growing at age 18.

10. While not all teenagers have a difficult adolescence, early-maturing girls and late-maturing boys are more likely to experience stress because of their off-time physical development. This problem has no long-lasting impact for girls, as long as they do not become sexually active and pregnant, but the lack of confidence of late-maturing boys may continue into adulthood. For both sexes, the ecological context—specifically, other changes such as the transition from elementary school to junior high—can ameliorate or exacerbate the problem.

KEY TERMS

puberty (370)
GH (growth hormone) (371)
testosterone (371)
estrogens (371)
growth spurt (372)
primary sex
   characteristics (375)

menarche (376)
spermarche (376)
secondary sex
   characteristics (377)
body image (378)

KEY QUESTIONS

1. What is the usual sequence of biological changes during puberty?

2. What are the main changes that characterize the growth spurt?

3. What are the nutritional needs and possible eating problems of adolescence?

4. How is the sexual maturation of males and females similar, and how is it different?

5. How do adolescents react to the changes in their body shape and size?

6. What factors make puberty occur early, late, or on time?

7. How does the age at which puberty occurs interact with psychosocial development?

CHAPTER 15

Adolescence:
Cognitive Development

Having a conversation with a 15-year-old about international politics, or the latest rage in music, or the meaning of life, is obviously quite different from trying to have the same conversation with an 8-year-old. Because of advances in their cognitive abilities, adolescents are increasingly aware of both world concerns and personal needs—others' as well as their own—and they can reason about them logically, at least some of the time. This chapter examines the cognitive developments of adolescence, exploring such topics as the following:

What are the characteristics of scientific reasoning?

In which ways does adolescent egocentrism limit teenagers' ability to think rationally?

What characteristics tend to make some schools highly effective in advancing adolescents' cognitive development?

How does moral thinking develop?

What aspects of adolescents' thinking can interfere with their ability to make responsible decisions about such matters as sexual activity?

The biological changes of puberty that we have just reviewed are universal and visible, transforming children by giving them adult size, shape, and sexuality. However, another set of changes, more variable and less apparent, is equally pivotal in turning a child into an adult. Cognitive maturation that occurs during adolescence makes teenagers much more adultlike in their use of analysis, logic, and reason.

As we will see, however, acquiring such intellectual perspectives opens young persons up to new vulnerabilities because their thoughts can now take a more comprehensive, less practical, sweep. Many adolescents appear tough-minded; at least their displays of sarcasm, cynicism, and seeming selfish indifference to public opinion give this impression. But the opposite is more likely to be true: adolescents tend to be self-absorbed, often troubled by their own introspections, and hypersensitive to criticism, real and imagined.

Recognizing this peculiar mixture of intellectual bravado and fragile self-centeredness is especially important for parents and teachers as they try to guide and advance adolescents' thinking abilities and social problem-solving skills.

Adolescent Thought

Piaget was the first theorist to recognize what many psychologists now consider the distinguishing feature of adolescent thought—the capacity to think in terms of possibility rather than merely concrete reality (Inhelder and Piaget, 1958). As John Flavell (1985) explains, before adolescence, the child has "an earthbound, concrete, practical-minded sort of problem solving approach . . . and speculations about other possibilities . . . occur only with difficulty and as a last resort." The adolescent and the adult, by contrast, are more likely to approach problems "quite the other way around . . . reality is subordinated to possibility."

This means that, on the whole, adolescents are able to fantasize, speculate, and hypothesize much more readily and on a much grander scale than children, who are still tied to concrete operational thinking. By the end of adolescence, many young people can understand and create general principles or formal rules to explain many aspects of human experience in the abstract. For this reason, Piaget calls the last stage of cognitive development, attained at about age 15, **formal operational thought.** At this point the adolescent "begins to build systems or theories in the largest sense of the term" about literature, philosophy, morality, love, and the world at large (Inhelder and Piaget, 1958).

Formal Operations and Scientific Reasoning

One specific example of formal operational thought is the development of **scientific reasoning.** Inhelder and Piaget (1958) undertook a classic series of experiments that revealed how children between the ages of 5 and 15 reason about certain laws of physics, chemistry, and so forth. Children were asked to put objects in a pail of water and explain why some sank and others floated; they were given different weights to hang on a string pendulum and asked to figure out which factors might affect the speed of the pendulum's swing (length of string, size of weight, height of release, force of release); they were asked to roll marbles down an incline onto a flat surface and estimate how far they would go. In all these experiments, Piaget and Inhelder found that reasoning abilities developed gradually in the years before adolescence, culminating at about age 14 with an understanding of the general principles involved.

For instance, the children in one experiment were asked to balance a balance scale with weights that could be hooked onto the scale's arms (see Figure 15.1). This task was completely beyond the ability of most preoperational children (typically, a 4-year-old might put two weights on the same side of the scale and none on the other).

By age 7 (the usual age for the beginning of concrete operational thought), children realized that the scale could be balanced by putting the same amount of weight on both arms, but they didn't realize that the distance of the weights from the center of the scale is also an important factor.

By age 10 (near the end of the concrete operational stage), they were often able, through trial and error, to see that the farther from the fulcrum a given weight is, the more force it exerts (in one child's words, "At the end it makes more weight"), and to find several correct combinations that would balance the scale. Note, however, that, although they had discovered the importance of the weights' distance from the fulcrum in their trial-and-error experimenting, they still had to try out different weights at different distances to get the scales to balance. They could not hypothesize a general principle to guide their placement of the weights.

Finally, at about age 13 or 14, some children hypothesized the general law that there is an inverse relationship between a weight's proximity to the fulcrum and the force it exerts. Thus, they correctly concluded that if the weight on one arm of the balance is three times as heavy as the weight on the other, it has to be a third as far from the center as the other weight in order for equilibrium to be achieved, and they were able to correctly predict which other combinations of weights and distances would achieve balance.

True, False, or Impossible to Judge?

Another way to measure formal operational thinking is to look at children's ability to assess the inherent logic of various statements. In one classic series of experiments designed to do this, an investigator spread many solid-colored poker chips out on a table and asked adolescents and preadolescents to judge whether various statements about the chips were "true," "false," or "impossible to judge" (Osherson and Markman, 1974–1975).

For instance, the investigator hid a poker chip in his hand without letting the child see what color it was and then asked the child to judge the veracity of the statement "Either the chip is green or is it not green." Almost every preadolescent replied that the statement was "impossible to judge" rather than saying it was true. They also thought that the statement "The chip in my hand is green and it is not green" was impossible to judge rather than false.

When the investigator held a red chip so that it could be seen and said "Either the chip in my hand is green or it is not yellow," only 15 percent of the preadolescent children correctly answered "true." Beginning at age 11, however, the number of children answering correctly increased. By age 15, about half were able to accurately evaluate the logic of this kind of either/or statement, realizing that such a statement is true if only one of the clauses is true, and thereby demonstrating what Flavell (1985) calls the **game of thinking.** That is, they were able to suspend their knowledge of reality (such as knowing that the chip is red) and think playfully about the possibilities suggested by the statement itself.

Flavell (1985) gives another example of the adolescent's ability to ignore the real and think about the possible. If an impoverished college student is offered $10 to argue in favor of the position that government should *never* give or lend money to impoverished college students, chances are, he or she can earn the money. By contrast, concrete operational children have great difficulty arguing against their personal beliefs and self-interest. The

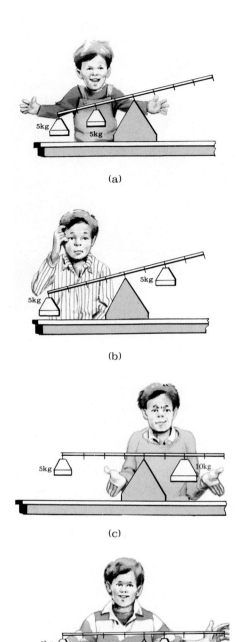

Figure 15.1 *These drawings illustrate Piaget's balance-scale test of formal reasoning, as it is described in the text and is attempted by a 4-year-old (a), a 7-year-old (b), a 10-year-old (c), and a 14-year-old (d).*

Figure 15.2 *In an attempt to score a point for his debating team, this young man may be constructing an eloquent and logical argument for a point of view he truly opposes. He also may be using humor to disarm criticism of his stand. If so, he is engaged in the game of thinking, a favorite pursuit of many adolescents but an incomprehensible puzzle for younger children.*

ability to divorce oneself from what one believes to be the case and argue from other premises makes adolescents much more interesting and adept as participants in intellectual "bull sessions" or as partners in debate.

The formal operational adolescent sometimes enjoys the game of thinking so much that logic seems to outweigh common sense. An adolescent who is adept at "thinking about thinking" and making "statements about statements" (Piaget, 1980) may find logical flaws in virtually every utterance a friend, teacher, or parent makes. Knowing when to stop looking for possibilities and begin dealing with the practical realities of life is difficult when "reality has become simply one of many possibilities" (Muuss, 1988).

Piaget Reevaluated

Piaget's measures of formal operational thought have been replicated many times, with similar results. Not only Piaget's defenders but also his critics agree that "children with age become increasingly systematic in their exploration of scientific-type problems," with the adolescents notably more logical and systematic than preadolescents or younger children (Braine and Rumain, 1983).

However, many adolescents arrive at formal operational thinking later than Piaget predicted, if at all. In fact, many older adolescents, including college students, do poorly on standard tests of formal operational thought. Many adults likewise have difficulty. Thus formal operational thinking—as measured by standard tests—is not inevitable with puberty.

Piaget (1972) himself acknowledged that society and education are crucial factors in enabling an individual to attain formal operational thought. He believed that the maturation of brain and body that occurs at puberty makes these intellectual achievements possible, but certainly not inevitable. Without experiences such as formal education, or social interactions that stress science, math, or logic, adults still think like concrete operational children.

Furthermore, formal operational thinking is more likely to be demonstrated in certain domains than in others, depending upon an individual's intellectual endowments, experiences, talents, and interests. Even on Piaget's classic tests of formal operations, which measure scientific logic in problems of physics and chemistry, the correlations between performance on various tests are, in general, quite low (between .30 and .40), which means that an adolescent who is quite logical in figuring out the balance-beam problem may not be nearly as logical in figuring out the pendulum problem (Muuss, 1988). Such variability is even more obvious when looking at adolescents' logic in nonscientific areas. The ability to analyze the themes of *Hamlet*, or to assess the multiple causes and consequences of the famine in Ethiopia, or to anticipate and counter the possible calls of the opposing quarterback are all formal operational abilities, yet the adolescent who can do one of these tasks very well may be quite inept at the other two.

In general, however, as at earlier stages of cognitive development, there are many differences between potential and performance, as well as variations from domain to domain. These discrepancies are much more apparent during adolescence than Piaget's description of formal operational thinking would seem to suggest.

Adolescent Egocentrism

While many adolescents and adults have the cognitive competence to think logically, they do not always do so, especially when thinking about themselves. Adolescents, in particular, often have difficulty thinking rationally about their immediate experiences. Their thought patterns tend to be flawed by a characteristic called **adolescent egocentrism** (Elkind, 1985). While they are long past the global egocentrism of the preschool child, adolescents tend to see themselves as much more central and significant on the social stage than they actually are. For example, the limits of adolescent judgment and logical reasoning often lead teenagers to believe that no one else has ever had the particular emotional experiences they themselves are having—that no one else, for example, has ever felt so angry, or so elated, or so misunderstood.

As David Elkind (1978) explains, this form of egocentrism occurs because adolescents fail

> to differentiate between the unique and the universal. A young woman who falls in love for the first time is enraptured with the experience, which is entirely new and thrilling. But she fails to differentiate between what is new and thrilling to herself and what is new and thrilling to humankind. It is not surprising, therefore, that this young lady says to her mother, "But Mother, you don't know how it feels to be in love."

Fantasies and Fables

Adolescent egocentrism can lead to several kinds of distorted, unrealistic thinking (Elkind, 1974). One example is what might be called an **invincibility fable.** Many young people feel that they are somehow immune to the laws of mortality and probability; they take all kinds of risks, falsely secure in the notion that they will never get sick, or killed, or caught. One clear example of this involves cigarette smoking. Although today's adolescents are fully aware of the proven health risks of smoking, two-thirds of all high school seniors have tried cigarettes and almost half of these are frequent smokers. Virtually none of the regular smokers thought they would ever become addicted, yet more than half have tried to stop and failed (Johnston et al., 1989). The invincibility fable also plays a role in adolescents' sexual behavior, as we will see later in this chapter, and in their use of drugs as well (Chapter 16).

Another example of far-fetched egocentrism is what Elkind (1974) calls the **personal fable,** through which adolescents imagine their own lives as heroic or even mythical. They see themselves destined for great fame and fortune, discovering the cure for cancer, authoring a masterpiece, or becoming a rock or movie star, a sports hero, a brain surgeon, a business tycoon, or whatever else will make millions—sometimes having already decided that a high school education is a waste of time.

Theater of the Mind

One of the most telling features of adolescents' thinking is the concern teenagers have for others' opinion of them. As part of their egocentrism, adolescents often create for themselves an **imaginary audience,** as they fantasize how others will react to their appearance and behavior. For instance, adolescents are so preoccupied with their physical appearance, sometimes spending hours in front of a mirror, that they assume that everyone else judges the final result. Anticipation of a favorable judgment can cause teenagers to enter a crowded room with the air of regarding themselves as the most attractive and admired human beings alive. On the other hand, something as trivial as a slight facial blemish can make them wish that they could enter the room invisibly. Similarly, school phobia (a fear of school that often keeps the student from attending) is particularly likely in adolescence—and often centers more on worries about physical appearance (particularly on being viewed in the locker room) than about academic achievement (Rutter, 1980).

In general, a preoccupation with the imaginary audience can be taken as an indication that the young person is not at ease with the larger social world. This helps to explain some interesting variations in the intensity of adolescent egocentrism and the power of the imaginary audience. According to a self-report questionnaire designed to measure these concepts, girls are generally more concerned with the imagined opinions of onlookers than boys are (Elkind and Bowen, 1979; Gray and Hudson, 1984), and, among middle-class teenagers, younger teens are more self-conscious than older ones. However, delinquent boys think more about the imaginary audience than do nondelinquents of either sex (Anolik, 1981). Further, concern about the imaginary audience, rather than decreasing, *increases* from early to late adolescence in at least two groups: rural, low-SES whites (Adams and Jones, 1981) and Native Americans (Markstrom and Mullis, 1986).

Thus, adolescent thought processes are usually a mixture of the abilities to imagine many logical possibilities and to deny reality when it interferes with hope and fantasies.

Drawing by W. Miller; © 1986
The New Yorker Magazine, Inc.

Figure 15.3 *Fantasies are certainly not the exclusive domain of adolescents. They occur at every age, and are usually more helpful than harmful. They can help in getting a necessary task done with pleasure or in venting negative emotions harmlessly.*

Figure 15.4 *Nearly all teenagers suffer from chronic anxiety about their complexions, even if they don't actually suffer acne itself. At times their thinking is so egocentric that a single blemish is enough to make them want to go into hiding, as though the whole world were waiting to condemn them for a pimple.*

Finally, a high degree of egocentrism is usually an indication that an adolescent has not yet mastered formal operational thought (Pesce and Harding, 1986), although, as you have learned, it is possible to think formally in one domain and not in another. By late adolescence, however, as young people become better able to reason logically, they gradually become more secure, more realistic, and more positive in their understanding of themselves (Denny and Thomas, 1986).

Schools, Learning, and the Adolescent Mind

Given the cognitive changes that adolescents typically experience, what kind of school best fosters their intellectual growth? That straightforward question has no single answer, because, with regard to education, the optimum **person-environment fit**—that is, the best setting for personal growth—depends not only on the individual's developmental stage, cognitive strengths and weaknesses, and learning style but also on the society's traditions, educational objectives, and future needs, which vary substantially from place to place and time to time.

This cultural variation in the goals, and therefore in the content, of education was cogently expressed by Native Americans in colonial America in the year 1744, when members of the Council of Five Nations politely declined scholarships to William and Mary College with these words:

> You who are wise must know, that different nations have different conceptions of things; and you will therefore not take it amiss if our ideas of this kind of education happen not to be the same with yours. We have had some experience of it; several of our young people were formerly brought up at the college of the northern provinces; they were instructed in all your sciences; but when they came back to us . . . [they were] ignorant of every means of living in the woods . . . neither fit for hunters, warriors, or counsellors; they were totally good for nothing. We are, however, not the less obliged by your kind offer . . . and to show our grateful sense of it, if the gentlemen of Virginia will send us a dozen of their sons, we will take great care of their education, instruct them in all we know, and make *men* of them. [Drake, cited in Rogoff, 1990]

The goals of the American education system have, themselves, changed dramatically over the generations. In the beginning of the twentieth century, young people needed preparation for work on the assembly line, on the farms, or in the home; as the century draws to a close, American students require computer literacy, scientific understanding, and critical thinking (Graff, 1987). But even within these broad needs, diversity in learning environments is widespread and deep, as some communities and groups have quite different educational goals than others. However, what we know about adolescent cognition and about the intellectual demands on young adults does enable us to describe aspects of education which are likely to foster the learning needed for the future.

Adolescent Vulnerability

As we have seen, as the capacity for formal operational thought starts to emerge, adolescents begin to abandon simplistic, concrete thinking and to construct more comprehensive and complex worldviews. Consequently, they become increasingly interested in the opinions and judgments of others—adults as well as peers from a variety of backgrounds. At the same time, their adolescent egocentrism makes them highly sensitive to actual or anticipated criticism. This combination of openness and egocentrism puts them in a cognitive bind, eager for lively intellectual interaction yet highly vulnerable to self-doubt.

As a result, their increasing ability to imagine and theorize often takes a self-defeating tone, creating a "great potential for distortion," as youngsters fear that making one mistake will trigger a chorus of criticism (Harter, 1990). One outcome of this tendency is a widespread dip in academic self-confidence just when young people enter secondary school, with many students feeling less able, less conscientious, and less motivated than they did in elementary school (Eccles and Midgley, 1989).

Given these tendencies, one might expect that educational settings would be designed to encourage supportive interactions, both among students and between teachers and students, as well as to find ways to buttress students' self-confidence. Too often, the opposite is the case, as "a volatile mismatch" is formed between many adolescents and their schools (Carnegie Council, 1989). Compared to elementary schools, most secondary schools have more rigid behavioral demands, intensified competition, and more punitive grading practices, as well as less individualized attention and procedures. Particularly antithetical to the facilitation of a smooth person-environment fit may be the bureaucratic structure of the educational setting: many secondary schools attempt to educate more than a thousand students, each of whom travels from room to room to learn in 40-minute segments from numerous teachers—some of whom do not even know the names, much less the personality traits, intellectual interests, and personal aspirations of their students (Sizer, 1984; Lightfoot, 1983; Carnegie Council, 1989).

Teacher Expectations

Because of this mismatch between student needs and the school environment, learning suffers. To make matters worse, many teachers accept "the pervasive stereotype regarding the near impossibility of teaching young adolescents" (Carnegie Council, 1989). For example, one longitudinal study compared 171 math teachers, half teaching sixth-graders in elementary schools and half teaching seventh-graders in junior high (Midgley et al., 1988). The junior high faculty were more likely to regard their students as unmotivated, inclined to cheat, and needing to be kept in their place. Further, compared with elementary school teachers, junior high teachers tended to expect less of themselves, believing that they could not raise student achievement very much.

These lower expectations had a direct impact on the students, for, as they moved from the sixth to the seventh grade, most experienced a drop in motivation, and their achievement fell. That this decline was directly related to teacher expectations—rather than simply to the overall school setting, the sudden onset of puberty, or some other variable—was shown by a minority of students whose seventh-grade teachers actually held higher expectations for their students, and for their own ability to influence them, than the children's sixth-grade teachers had. Unlike their peers, these students showed an increase in motivation and achievement over the two-year period.

Classroom Interaction

Research such as this has clear implications for the social interaction between students and teachers and among students themselves. Since safeguarding of self-esteem, reduction of egocentrism, and exposure to new perspectives all facilitate the emergence of formal thinking—precisely those critical, imaginative, and logical processes the student will need in adulthood—developmentalists generally agree that cooperation, rather than competition, should predominate in the classroom, and that the motivation for learning should be mastery of an intellectual challenge rather than advancement of one's own ego in a grading contest.

This emphasis has led to a distinction between ego-involvement learning and task-involvement learning (Nicholls, 1989). In **ego-involvement learning**, academic grades are based solely on individual test performance, and students are ranked against each other. In this setting, students who try to succeed and fail experience embarrassment as well as a low grade, while exceptionally good students risk being ostracized as "a brain," "a geek," "a nerd." In such competitive conditions, many students—especially girls and students from minority backgrounds—find it easier, and psychologically safer, not to try, thereby avoiding the potential pains of both success and failure.

Given this reaction, it is noteworthy that the areas of the curriculum in which standardized, competitive achievement scores have predominated—specifically, math and science—are exactly those areas in which girls suddenly score lower in high school than in elementary school and subsequently shun advanced courses, protecting their self-esteem in the process (Roberts and Petersen, 1992). As you know, there are many plausible explanations for this pattern, but the most likely one is that individualistic, competitive standards discourage girls from achieving, because, in general, girls are socialized to be nurturant and noncompetitive (Huston and Alvarez, 1990). The same pattern of avoiding advanced math and science is also followed by many minority students, especially from cultures, such as Latino and Native American ones, that stress cooperation and collaboration. Part of the reason may be that they experience similar social pressures against competition (Tharp, 1989). An additional result of ego-involvement learning is that those who are labeled inferior consider themselves doomed to failure, and often drop out (see A Closer Look).

By contrast, in **task-involvement learning**, grades are based on acquiring certain competencies and knowledge that everyone, with enough time and effort, is expected to attain. Unlike ego-involvement learning, task-involvement learning, which typically utilizes such practices as team research projects, in-class discussion groups, and after-school study groups, allows all students to improve if they cooperate, and one person's success can foster another's. In this situation, when the task is assisting, rather than surpassing, one's peers, the social interaction that teenagers cherish is actually constructive for education.

A CLOSER LOOK   Tracking

One outgrowth of competition that has been widely used as an attempt to boost achievement and widely criticized for destroying motivation is **tracking**, the separation of students into distinct groups based on standardized tests of ability and achievement. Ironically, in many nations, this practice is typically instituted for the first time at about age 12, the age at which it is particularly deleterious. As one report explains:

> In theory, this between-class "tracking" reduces the heterogeneity of the class and enables teachers to adjust instruction to students' knowledge and skills. Greater achievement is then possible for both "low-" and "high-ability" students.
>
> In practice, this kind of tracking has proven to be one of the most divisive and damaging school practices in existence. Time and time again, young people placed in lower academic tracks or classes, often during the middle grades, are locked into dull, repetitive instructional programs leading at best to minimum competencies. The psychic numbing these youth experience from a "dumbed-down" curriculum contrast sharply with the exciting opportunities for learning and critical thinking that students in the higher tracks or classes may experience. [Carnegie Council, 1989].

The evidence supporting the efficacy of tracking high-achievers is mixed, but the evidence regarding the effect on those at the bottom is clear, both in Japan (Rohlen, 1983) and in the United States (Oakes, 1985; Slavin, 1987).

Part of the problem is that many teachers and administrators are unaware that cognitive development, especially during adolescence, is almost always uneven. A student could test very poorly at, for instance, solving quadratic equations or interpretation of textbook paragraphs, but nonetheless be highly motivated, capable, and logical in intellectual discussions of hypothetical ideas. Without realizing this, a teacher of lower-track students is likely to provide repetitive, uninteresting classwork, leading to more boredom, distraction, and disturbances and,

consequently, to disciplinarian instruction rather than to creative attempts to foster intellectual growth. It should be no surprise that the lower-track students' pace of learning slows markedly, as the curriculum generally repeats basic skills that should have been mastered years before.

A description of the regular and lower-track classes within a large high school in the Midwest makes the impact very clear:

> Teachers expect the socially-advantaged, high-achieving, regular track students to contribute valuable, diverse opinions in lessons that foster debate and discussion. Several emphasize the teaching of "critical thinking skills" [and] . . . welcome disagreement as events that "liven up the lesson," signal student involvement, and confirm the teacher's professional expertise and skill . . . . students may confront a teacher with the question "How do you know that?" and the query will not be regarded as impertinent . . . .

Within lower-track classes in the same school, however, the same teachers discourage talk of any kind as distracting and an invitation to "trouble" from students "lacking the critical thinking skills to participate in a discussion." With lower-track students, teachers see their task as being limited to providing "the basics" and "structure."

> Individualized work on noncontroversial topics—worksheets, films, and silent reading—is . . . much more common in lower-track classes than in regular classes. Silent seatwork constituted a major portion of all lower-track classes which [were] observed and a near-invariant routine in some. [Page, 1990]

Not infrequently, and not surprisingly, the lowest track in the middle grades becomes the truant track and then the drop-out track in high school. Studies find that, most often, the precipitating reason for dropping out is not lack of ability, irrelevance of curriculum, or even lack of achievement, but rather the overall lack of encouragement, acceptance, and intellectual excitement from teachers and classmates (Pittman, 1991; Fine, 1989).

Cooperative learning provides an added benefit for students whose secondary school is their first extended exposure to people of differing backgrounds—economic, ethnic, religious, and racial—and thus to ideas, assumptions, and perspectives that are quite different from their own. In a competitive setting, racial or other types of integration can lead to rivalry, social distance, and open hostility, as insecure adolescents protect their own self-concept by exaggerating group differences and rejecting anyone who represents a challenge to their sense of identity. In a cooperative setting, however, these differences can expand learning opportunities, bringing to the classroom a variety of perspectives that is exciting and enriching rather than threatening. When we look at the demographics of the future, with more and more migration from one nation to another, it certainly benefits young people to deepen their understanding of other groups.

School-Wide Goals

How can schools, overall, be organized so that each student's cognitive needs are likely to be met? First, it is important to realize that schools can make a decided difference—in academic achievement, in self-image, in delinquency, and in future success. Too often, poor student achievement has been blamed on everything but the schools—on the student's native intelligence, on low SES, on minority background, or on family disorganization. All these factors can be relevant, of course, but many studies over the past fifteen years have shown that, when these factors are controlled, some schools simply educate much more effectively than others (Wilson and Corcoran, 1988; Kach et al., 1986; Carnegie Council, 1989; Rutter, 1979; Page and Valli, 1990). And virtually every study finds that those schools which are more effective share a central characteristic—educational goals that are high, clear, and attainable, and that are supported by the entire staff, from the principal on down.

Initially, it may sound contradictory for goals to be both high *and* within reach of everyone. However, study after study finds that this combination is not only possible; it is pivotal, particularly for students from whom teachers have traditionally demanded little, such as those from minority ethnic groups or from impoverished families (Wilson and Corcoran, 1988; Carnegie Council, 1989; Rutter, 1979; Page and Valli, 1990; Pink, 1986). A variety of practices—including serious attendance and homework demands, teacher involvement in curriculum decisions, manageable class size, after-school tutoring, and activities such as sports and clubs that foster student involvement—make it more likely that teachers will be able to expect and get high achievement from all their students (Liston and Zeichner, 1991; Oakes and Lipton, 1990; Wilson and Corcoran, 1988).

The goals of the school must not only be high and attainable; they must also be clear to everyone. Precisely because of their egocentrism and emerging formal thinking, many adolescents are lost in a "vertigo of relativity" with "disabling uncertainties" (Chandler, 1987), making it hard for them to recognize implicit standards and set their course for long-term gain. For instance, the purpose of such simple practices as coming to class on time and doing the work is not always obvious to many adolescents: they feel genuinely offended if points are taken off for lapses in these areas. Teachers may be dumbfounded to have a chronic truant tell them "You didn't seem to care about attendance" or to hear from a failing pupil, "You never said the homework affected our grade," but such students often believe they are being unjustly penalized. On a broader level, the goals and relevancy of the curriculum must be made explicit. Many young people do not realize the connection between specific course work and later accomplishment: advanced math, foreign language, and laboratory science too often fall by the wayside as irrelevant, especially when they compete with the more compelling needs of adolescents to look good and feel accepted.

Good schools and good teachers cut through this confusion by making expectations explicit. A study of 571 effective schools found not only that their standards of attendance, punctuality, homework, class performance, and graduation requirements were higher than the national norms, but also that their students were well aware of each demand and proudly "praised their teachers for making them work harder than they might have if left to their devices" (Wilson and Corcoran, 1988). Even more telling, among these particular effective schools, the average drop-out rate was about 7 percent, while the college enrollment rate was about 51 percent—compared with national averages of about 27 percent and 30 percent, respectively. The contrasts were most dramatic in those effective schools in which poor and minority students predominated: in their "ineffective" counterparts it was typically the case that less than half the students graduated and virtually none went on to college (Wilson and Corcoran, 1988).

We should close this section with a cautionary reminder: the best particular teaching practices will be determined partly by the specific social context. Indeed, even practices that are usually destructive, such as individual competition and tracking, sometimes facilitate learning if goals are high, if every student feels the process is fair, and if the school is relatively small (Page and Valli, 1990). However, given what we know about cognitive development, any measure that uses cooperative social interaction to reach greater intellectual understanding is likely to produce academic as well as emotional growth.

Moral Development

The development of moral actions, attitudes, and arguments is lifelong, from the toddler's grabbing a toy and insisting "Mine!" (a primitive statement about individual property rights) to the elderly adult revising provisions of a living will (an intricate balancing of individual desires, community values, and religious or philosophical faith). However, adolescence appears to be the time of greatest upheaval in moral behavior as well as the period of most rapid development of moral reasoning (Colby et al., 1983; Eisenberg, 1990). Moral habits taught by parents and religious institutions in childhood often weaken when the impulse to experiment becomes strong, and old codes crumble under the barrage of intellectual questioning and criticism that besets most adolescents.

Indeed, during adolescence every aspect of growth accelerates the progress of moral reasoning: biosocial development awakens drives and permits actions that were impossible before; cognitive development allows adolescents to think more deeply and abstractly as well as to question the moral strictures of home and church; social development exposes them to a variety of conflicting values; and personal experiences compel them to face ethical dilemmas. As a result, between ages 10 and 20, many people come to see moral issues more broadly, going beyond their own narrow personal interests to consider community, cultural, and universal values (Langford and Claydon, 1989; Damon, 1984). This changing perspective has been charted and studied extensively over the past two decades, particularly with regard to thoughts about morality. While many scholars have contributed to this research, the basic framework has been most clearly described by Lawrence Kohlberg.

A LIFE-SPAN PERSPECTIVE

Kohlberg's Stages of Moral Development

Building on Piaget's theories and research, Lawrence Kohlberg (1963, 1981) studied the development of moral reasoning by presenting children, adolescents, and adults with a set of hypothetical stories that pose ethical dilemmas. The most famous of these is the story of Heinz:

> A woman was near death from cancer. One drug might save her, a form of radium that a druggist in the same town had recently discovered. The druggist was charging $2,000, ten times what the drug cost him to make. The sick woman's husband, Heinz, went to everyone he knew to borrow the money, but he could only get together about half of what it cost. He told the druggist that his wife was dying and asked him to sell it cheaper or let him pay later. But the druggist said "no." The husband got desperate and broke into the man's store to steal the drug for his wife. Should the husband have done that? Why?

Kohlberg examined the responses to such dilemmas and found three levels of moral reasoning: preconventional, conventional, and postconventional—with two stages at each level.

I. **Preconventional** *Emphasis on avoiding punishments and getting rewards.*

Stage 1: Might makes right (punishments and obedience orientation). At this stage the most important value is obedience to authority in order to avoid punishment.

Stage 2: Look out for number one (instrumental and relativist orientation). Each person tries to take care of his or her own needs. The reason to be nice to other people is so they will be nice to you. In other words, you scratch my back and I'll scratch yours.

II. **Conventional** *Emphasis on social rules.*

Stage 3: "Good girl" and "nice boy." Good behavior is considered behavior that pleases other people and wins their praise. Approval is more important than any specific reward.

Stage 4: "Law and order." Right behavior means being a dutiful citizen and obeying the laws set down by those in power.

III. **Postconventional** *Emphasis on moral principles.*

Stage 5: Social contract. The rules of society exist for the benefit of all, and are established by mutual agreement. If the rules become destructive, or if one party doesn't live up to the agreement, the contract is no longer binding.

Stage 6: Universal ethical principles. General universal principles determine right and wrong. These values (such as "Do unto others as you would have others do unto you," or "Life is sacred") are established by individual reflection and meditation, and may contradict the egocentric or legal principles of earlier reasoning.

Figure 15.5 *The teen years are often characterized by intense ethical debates and religious study, as adolescents move up the hierarchy of moral thinking. The fact that this girl is wearing a Coptic cross and holding a crystal in her right hand suggests that she may be exploring values that are different from those she grew up with.*

According to Kohlberg's longitudinal research, people advance up this moral hierarchy as they become more mature. At every age, *how* people reason morally, rather than what specific moral conclusions they reach, determines their stage of moral development. For example, moral reasoning at stage 3 might produce opposite conclusions—either that the husband should steal the drug (because people will blame him for not saving his wife) or that he should not steal it (because he has already done everything he could legally and people would call him a thief if he stole). Kohlberg thinks that a person must be at least at the cognitive level of early formal operations before he or she can reach stage 3, and that a certain amount of life experience and responsibility is a prerequisite for reaching stage 5. For these reasons, Kohlberg generally sees relatively little progress in moral development during middle childhood, and believes few adolescents can go beyond stage 4.

Kohlberg and His Critics

Originally, Kohlberg's ideas were the product of three sets of observations: Piaget's theory of cognitive development; various philosophers' delineations of ethical behavior; and Kohlberg's own research on a group of eighty-four boys, ages 10, 13, and 16, who provided Kohlberg with his original empirical data on the development of moral thinking. From these three elements, Kohlberg created and validated his moral dilemmas, his stages of moral thinking, and his theory of moral development.

His theory attracted a great deal of attention, because many people had apparently been searching for a way to clarify and focus their concern about moral education and growth. However, with this attention came criticism on a number of counts:

1. Kohlberg's "universal" stages seemed, generally, to reflect liberal, Western values (Reid, 1984; Miller, 1991). (In some cultures, serving the needs of kin may have a higher moral priority than observing principles that presumably apply to all of humankind.)

2. The structure of moral thinking is much less stagelike than Kohlberg implies, especially when practical rather than theoretical dilemmas are analyzed (Eisenberg, 1986).

3. Kohlberg's moral stages overemphasized rational thought and underrated religious faith (Lee, 1980; Wallwork, 1980). (Some people believe that divine revelation, rather than intellectual reasoning, provides the best standards for moral judgment.)

4. Kohlberg's original moral-dilemma scheme was validated only on males but was applied to females as well (Gilligan, 1982). (It may be that females and males are socialized to approach moral questions in different ways.)

Each of these criticisms has some validity, but, on balance, Kohlberg's scheme has withstood major attack. For example, cultural differences have been found, but not as many as critics predicted (Snarey et al., 1985; Nisan, 1987). Also, while individuals are much less rigid in their moral reasoning than a strict interpretation of Kohlberg implies, they show a clear consistency in reasoning across various types of moral dilemmas (Walker, 1988; Denten et al., 1991). And instead of underrating religious faith, Kohlberg's ideas have been incorporated in some religious education and have prompted one psychologist (Fowler, 1981) to delineate stages of faith (see pp. 472–473).

Gender Differences

Now let us consider one criticism in detail—that Kohlberg's stages of development are biased against females. The most compelling and best-

Figure 15.6 *Imagine that these two teenagers are having a difference of opinion about the morality of a friend's behavior. According to Gilligan's understanding of male and female moral reasoning, the girl's basic position is likely to be "If you knew what he's been going through, you wouldn't condemn him." The boy's, on the other hand, is more likely to be "If you stuck to your principles, you wouldn't justify his actions."*

known expression of this position has come from Carol Gilligan (1982).

According to Gilligan, girls and women tend to see moral dilemmas differently than boys and men do. In general, the characteristic male approach seems to be "Do not interfere with the rights of others"; the female approach, on the other hand, seems to be "Be concerned with the needs of others." Females give greater consideration to the context of moral choices, focusing on the human relationships involved, Gilligan contends that women are reluctant to judge right and wrong in absolute terms because they are socialized to be nurturant, caring, and nonjudgmental.

As evidence, Gilligan cities the responses of two bright 11-year-olds, Jake and Amy, to the dilemma of Heinz, who must decide whether to steal drugs for his dying wife. Jake considered the dilemma "sort of like a math problem with humans," and he set up an equation that showed that life is more important than property. Amy, on the other hand, seemed to sidestep the issue, arguing that Heinz "really shouldn't steal the drug—but his wife shouldn't die either." She tried to find an alternative solution (a bank loan, perhaps) and then explained that stealing wouldn't be right because Heinz "might have to go to jail, and then his wife might get sicker again, and he couldn't get more of the drug."

While Amy's response may seem equally ethical, it would be scored lower than Jake's on Kohlberg's system. Gilligan argues that this is unfair, because what appears to be women's moral weakness—their hesitancy to take a definitive position based on abstract moral premises—is, in fact,

> inseparable from women's moral strength, an overriding concern with relationships and responsibilities. The reluctance to judge may itself be indicative of the care and concern that infuse the psychology of women's development. [Gilligan, 1982]

Of course, the difference between male and female moral thinking is not absolute. Gilligan is aware that some women think about moral dilemmas the way men do, and vice versa. Nor does she think that either way of reasoning is better than the other, or even in itself sufficient. If people stress human relationships too much, they may overlook the principles involved and may be unable to arrive at just decisions; if they stress abstract principles too much, they may blind themselves to the feelings and needs of the individuals affected by their decisions. The best moral thinking synthesizes both approaches (Gilligan, 1982; Murphy and Gilligan, 1980).

Gilligan maintains that Kohlberg's scoring system tends to devalue the female perspective. However, an exhaustive review of sex differences in moral reasoning (Walker, 1984) finds that there is no evidence that these differences systematically affect the scores on Kohlberg's dilemmas. Many studies in which males and females are compared find no sex differences at all. Those studies that do find differences confirm Gilligan's hypothesis to some degree: females do focus on interpersonal issues more than on moral absolutes—but the differences are not large (Walker et al., 1987; Gulotti et al., 1991). Taking a life-span perspective, it may be that females begin with an ethic of personal relations and males begin with an ethic of principles, but that these different orientations converge with experience (Gilligan and Attanucci, 1988).

Moral Behavior

The various findings of the research on moral development raise a crucial and very practical question. What is the relationship between moral thinking and moral behavior? A classic series of studies found that although most children can explain why honesty is right and cheating is wrong, most children cheat under certain circumstances, such as when their friends put pressure on them to do so, and when the chance of being caught is slim (Hartshorne et al., 1929). The same can be said of adolescents and adults, most of whom "bend" the rules when their own self-interest is at stake (Lickona, 1978). Obviously, then, the translation of the intellectual understanding of rules into moral behavior is far from automatic.

On the other hand, most studies have shown that moral thought can have a decided influence on action and vice versa (Rest, 1983; Eisenberg, 1986). Beginning in middle childhood, children try to apply their moral standards to their own behavior. Increasingly, as they grow older, children try to figure out what the "right" thing to do is, and feel guilty when they do "wrong." Significantly, juvenile delinquents generally score lower on tests of moral reasoning than do other adolescents their age (Nelson et al., 1990), suggesting that one reason they violate the norms of society is that they are less likely to consider those norms morally relevant. At the same time, of course—especially with the egocentrism of adolescence—it is easier to recognize and condemn immorality and hypocrisy in others than in oneself. Many teenagers, for example, justify marijuana or cocaine use by noting society's acceptance of tobacco and alcohol, or forgive their own petty lawbreaking by expounding on white-collar crime.

Before being too critical of adolescent moral thinking and behavior, however, we need to acknowledge the complexity of moral decision making. As young people become more aware of their social world, and better able to analyze it, they are increasingly confronted with problematic moral dilemmas, requiring some balance between their own self-interest, the codes of the peer group, the morality of their parents and teachers, the tenets of their religion, and the values of their culture. It takes substantial maturity and analytic ability—more than many adolescents possess—to coordinate all these values.

Sexual Decision Making: A Study in Adolescent Cognition

Sexual interest during adolescence is a normal, even essential, part of development, with the particular expression of that interest affected by a host of factors, including biology and culture, family and friends, and, our focus here, cognition. Study after study confirms that beliefs, values, and reasoning processes affect what kind of sexual activity adolescents engage in, when, and with whom. Unfortunately for many adolescents, especially younger ones, their minds are not as ready for sex as their bodies are, and their decision making on sexual matters often leads to two serious problems that can hinder, or even halt, development.

Figure 15.7 *This girl is not alone in her condition: nearly one million American teenagers become pregnant each year. For most of these girls, the decision to have unprotected sex was probably based more on immediate concerns, such as what their boyfriend would say if they didn't, than on long-term concerns, such as how prepared they are to raise a child.*

Unanticipated Outcomes: Pregnancy and Disease

The first potential problem resulting from adolescent sexuality is teenage pregnancy, which is a problem worldwide. Adolescent pregnancy is particularly problematic in the United States, which has the highest teenage pregnancy rate in the industrialized world (Jones et al., 1986). Each year about a million American teenagers—80 percent of them unmarried—become pregnant. Currently, an American girl has about one chance in six of becoming pregnant before her 17th birthday, and more than one chance in three of becoming pregnant at least once before she is 20 (Trussell, 1988). Very few of these pregnancies are wanted by both parents, and many are aborted. For girls under age 15, two-thirds of all pregnancies result in abortion. For 15- to 19-year-olds, the ratio is about one in two. Nevertheless, close to half a million American teenage girls have babies each year.

The likely consequences of American adolescents' giving birth are well documented: for the mother, immediate interference with her education and long-term slowing of her social and vocational growth; for the child, greater risk of prenatal and birth complications, of lower academic achievement, and at adolescence, of drug abuse, arrest, and—against the advice of the mother—parenthood (Furstenberg et al., 1987; Dubow and Luster, 1990; Hayes, 1987; McKay, 1984).

The second possible problem that adolescents are likely to face is **sexually transmitted disease (STD)** (formerly called venereal disease, or VD). Indeed, the highest rates of all the most prevalent STDs—gonorrhea, herpes, syphilis, and chlamydia—occur in sexually active people between the ages of 10 and 19 (Bell and Hein, 1984; Children's Defense Fund, 1990). Most cases of STDs are not serious, if promptly treated, but adolescents are less likely to obtain prompt medical care. Untreated, STDs are likely to cause sterility, and some, like gonorrhea and syphilis, can eventually result in life-threatening complications.

Ominously, the high rate of sexual disease among adolescents suggests that many teenagers are engaging in unprotected, nonmonogamous sex, putting them at risk of exposure to another, always fatal disease, AIDS. Although the human immunodeficiency virus, or HIV, that causes AIDS can be spread through direct blood contact (typically through shared hypodermic needles in intravenous drug abuse), the most common transmission is through sexual contact. Once a person contracts the virus, AIDS will eventually develop, typically ten years or so after initial exposure.

Primarily because of this long latency period, less than 1 percent of reported AIDS cases involve teenagers. However, about 20 percent of all current AIDS deaths involve people in their late 20s. Given the slowness of the virus to develop, many of these individuals must have become infected during their teens (Hein, 1993; Centers for Disease Control, 1992; Kirp, 1989). Indeed, AIDS and HIV infection are now rising fastest among high school and college-age youth, and experts are now concerned that thousands of teenagers who are sexually active in the early 1990s will become AIDS statistics in the twenty-first century (DiClemente, 1990). It is presently estimated that one in every five teenagers is at "high risk" for AIDS because of such unsafe practices as having several sexual partners and failing to use condoms (Centers for Disease Control, 1992).

Why are the rates of unwanted pregnancy and STD so much higher among adolescents than adults, even though adults are more active sexually? A logical explanation would be that adolescents are uninformed about sex, or that contraception is unavailable to them. But this explanation does not fit the reality of the 1990s. Although as recently as 1980 only three American states (Kentucky, Maryland, and New Jersey) required sex education in public schools, by 1988 seventeen states required it, and all the others except Utah strongly encouraged it (Kenney et al., 1989). In addition, the media are quite open about sexuality—particularly the problems it can cause—and condoms are available in drug stores, supermarkets, and even in some schools.

Clearly, then, information about, and protection from, pregnancy and STD are within reach of today's teenager. However, various studies have found that merely understanding the facts of sexuality, and knowing how to obtain contraception, do not correlate with more responsible and cautious sexual behavior (Hanson et al., 1987; Howard and McCabe, 1990). For example, a survey of ten exemplary sex-education programs found that students who scored well on tests measuring sexual knowledge were neither more nor less sexually active, or careful, than students without formal sex education (Kirby, 1984). Similarly, programs to help adolescent mothers usually succeed in improving their parenting skills and furthering their education, but are less successful in reducing repeat pregnancies (Polit, 1989). The same patterns are found worldwide. For example, a study of 17-year-olds to 20-year-olds in Australia found that most were well informed about AIDS, but that only 22 percent of those who were sexually active always used a condom (Moore and Rosenthal, 1991).

Reasoning About Sex

To understand why knowing sexual facts has so little effect on adolescent sexual behavior we need to consider the limitations that typify adolescents' thinking, particularly that of younger adolescents (Gordon, 1990). Young adolescents, who may have only a fragile ability at formal reasoning, have difficulty envisioning alternatives, and then evaluating each one, choosing the best option among many (Case, 1985). They also tend to focus on immediate considerations rather than on future ones. Consequently, they may fail to measure the difficulty and inconvenience of using contraception against the difficulty and inconvenience of pregnancy. Similarly, when imagining possible parenthood, they may fail to measure the status and love that they think a baby might bring against the consuming responsibility that caring for an infant entails. This failure to think through possible consequences helps explain an interesting finding. Although few teenage girls actually want a baby, most who do not practice contraception think that having a child would not necessarily be so bad (Hanson et al., 1987). In other words, not having carefully considered the future implications of an unwanted pregnancy, they do not regard the possibility of one as something to be assiduously avoided. Focusing on immediate consequences might also lead a pregnant teenager to rule out abortion because it is painful, risky, and expensive, ignoring the much greater pain, risk, and expense of birth. Or it

Figure 15.8 *In the normal course of events, certain milestones happen on schedule: high school graduation, then marriage after a few years, then parenthood. This young graduate has reversed the order, making each transition more difficult.*

could just as well lead her to have an abortion primarily because of fears about giving birth.

A related problem is egocentric thinking, which leads adolescents to reason in terms of their own immediate needs, rather than considering the consequences of their behavior for their sexual partner or for a possible child. Boys, for example, often insist upon sexual intercourse as their "due" or as proof of devotion, and girls often consent for fear of losing the boy's interest. Boys may also decline to use contraception because they find it inconvenient, or regard it as unmanly; girls may decline to use it—especially in a casual or new relationship—because they think that being "prepared" is a sign of being "easy." Typical of this egocentrism is the view of one 15-year-old who maintained that, although he and his friends would not ordinarily use a condom because "it is not really a good sensation," they might use one with a girl who was poorly dressed or didn't look clean. He indicated that he wouldn't use one with his steady girlfriend, however, even if it might mean getting her pregnant. "If it happens, it happens. There's nothing I can do about it" (Berger, 1990).

Similar egocentrism is likely to be exhibited by teenagers when they are confronted with a pregnancy. Gilligan and Belensky (1980) found that adolescent girls were more concerned about themselves (for example, seeing their dilemma as how to avoid embarrassment and criticism from boyfriends, parents, and friends) rather than being concerned about whether they could love and care for a child. Boys, too, are likely to respond to pregnancy with egocentric thinking, initially reacting with pride at the idea that they have demonstrated their manhood—usually with no thought about the responsibilities involved, or the fact that, in most cases, they will be unable to fill the traditional provider role (Hardy et al., 1989).

Egocentrism also leads adolescents to be embarrassed to get treatment for STDs, and ashamed to tell their sexual partners about it. Thus STD spreads much more quickly among adolescents than among older adults (Karp, 1989; DiClemente, 1990).

Another problem with adolescents' thinking about sex is that their sense of personal invincibility is compounded by difficulty in grasping the logical laws of probability. This combination makes clear thinking about risks almost impossible. Many, for instance, seriously underestimate the chances of pregnancy, or of contracting a disease, reasoning that either is unlikely to occur from just one episode of unprotected intercourse. Then, if no misfortune occurs, the adolescent does the same thing again, reinforced by the belief that past experience has already shown that he or she is lucky. As one family-planning counselor put it, "The biggest thing is that they just don't think it's going to happen to them. As my mother would say 'They don't believe fat meat is greasy.' They feel they are invincible, and they are risk takers" (Shipp, 1985). Similarly, adolescents generally believe that other teenagers are more likely to contract the AIDS virus than they themselves are, with females being especially likely to underestimate their own risk (Moore and Rosenthal, 1991).

Because of their faulty risk assessment, many teenagers are incredulous when a pregnancy occurs. Consequently, they take longer than adults to confirm the pregnancy, to seek advice, to obtain prenatal care, or to have an abortion. Each of the delays increases the actual risk of problems.

The New Wave of Sex Education

How can adolescents be helped to make more rational decisions about their sexuality? A first step, according to many experts, is for adults to be more rational in *their* thinking, and to understand that almost every adolescent will have some sort of sexual experience. Some parents seem to believe, or hope, that if they ignore the question of sex in their teenagers' lives, their children will ignore it too. The reality is usually quite different. Often it is a question, not of whether their children will become sexually active, but of when, how, and with whom they become active.

In the United States, even before puberty, most children have already "liked" a member of the other sex. Most 14-year-olds have experienced mutual kissing, hugging, and body touching, and by age 16, 35 percent of girls and 50 percent of boys have had sexual intercourse, as have about 80 percent of 19-year-old girls and almost 90 percent of 19-year-old boys (Chilman, 1983; Koch, 1988; Weddle et al., 1988; Sonenstein et al., 1989).

Despite these rates, many parents do not talk to their children about sexuality until years after the child has been informed, or misinformed, by friends and personal experience. Of course, no one denies that parents have an influence on children's sexual behavior: their overall relationship with the child, their values, beliefs, or religious convictions about sex, and their attitudes about higher education can all have an effect (Hanson et al., 1987). However, when it comes to specific sex education in the home, parents often deny the realities and try to lay down the law rather than help the child think about the options. Indeed, one study found that parents' conversations about sex with their daughters tended to have the opposite effect from the desired one, making the daughters more permissive in their attitudes. With sons, however, parental discussion correlated with less precipitous sexuality and increased use of contraception. The explanation suggested by the authors is that sons listen more to their parents on the topic of sex because the underlying message is somewhat accepting of sexuality, while the message to daughters is "Don't, and if you do, we don't want to know about it" (Treboux and Busch-Rossagel, 1990).

Figure 15.9 *Sexual intercourse during adolescence can have many risks, and abstinence, correspondingly, can have many advantages, but fewer and fewer American teenagers agree with this view. Consequently, some sex educators are now focusing on trying to help adolescents postpone becoming sexually active, at least until they are able to understand, and take responsibility for, the possible consequences of their sexual behavior. The most worrisome data reflected in this chart may not be that the vast majority of 19-year-olds have had sex but that almost a third of 15-year-olds have—triple the rate of earlier generations.*

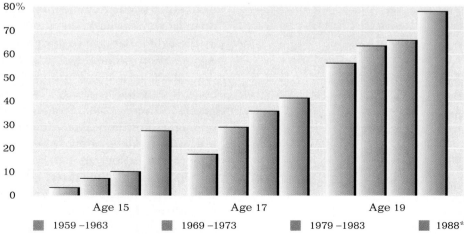

*Participants in the 1988 survey were 1/2 year older than earlier surveys.
Source: National Center for Health Statistics

Figure 15.10 *Some embarrassed laughter is almost inevitable in sex-education classes. The test of effective sex-education here is whether the instructor can successfully get past the tittering about anatomy and focus on serious discussion of interpersonal relationships and responsibility.*

Traditional sex education may be similarly irrelevant, especially when the teacher tries to fit a lot of factual information, mostly about biology, into a ten-hour course (the usual time allotted). Adolescents are often put-off by sex-education courses that are merely "organ recitals," or that seem to have little bearing on their actual sexual dilemmas and pressures. As one 17-year-old mother regretfully recalled: "I found the course boring and I tried to cut as often as possible. I didn't know how it applied to my life. I wish I had listened" (Williams and Kornblum, 1985).

In recognition of these realities, a new form of sex education is emerging that attempts to take into account adolescent thinking patterns, particularly the difficulty many adolescents have in reasoning logically and abstractly and in accepting prohibitions imposed by adults, no matter how well intentioned.

Some of the specific methods are quite ingenious. For instance, to help adolescents imagine the constant care and attention that a baby needs, some classes require students to keep an uncooked egg with them, twenty-four hours a day, without breaking it. To make the possible consequences of sexual activity more immediate, first-hand accounts are used in place of textbook examples. Typically, someone with AIDS talks about safe sex; a teenage parent discusses the responsibilities of parenthood; older teenagers explain the kind of pressures that often push one into becoming sexually active. While concrete examples are stressed, formal thinking is also fostered, through discussions and specific exercises, helping adolescents weigh alternatives, think of others' needs, and analyze risks. Role-playing is used extensively, so that students can test and develop responses to various "real-life" situations.

One sex-education program for eighth-graders made significant gains by using several of these techniques to help adolescents resist peer pressure to become sexually active (Howard and McCabe, 1990). This approach was initiated after a survey of 1,000 adolescent girls revealed that the topic most girls (84 percent) were interested in was "How to say 'no' without hurting the other person's feelings." The heart of the program involved a **social inoculation** procedure in which the adolescents, through role-playing and discussions, were gradually exposed to the various kinds of sexual pressures and problems they might face in the future. In this way, it was hoped they might build up a kind of cognitive immunity to these pressures by developing the reasoning skills to analyze and deal with them. A special feature of this program was that each class was led by an older teenage girl and boy, who had received special training in the role. As the researchers who followed this program explain:

> Teenage leaders have been shown to produce greater and more lasting effects than adults. Young people want to be and act older than they are. Besides imparting attitudes and skills, slightly older teenagers illustrate that those who "say no" to the pressured behavior can be admired and liked by others. They also clearly demonstrate to the younger teenagers that the behavior—for example, having sex—is not the way to attain such status.

Overall, this inoculation program showed striking, though mixed, results. For those participants (about one-fourth of the students) who already had had intercourse prior to entering the program, it appeared to have little effect, since they were no more likely to abstain from sex or use contraception than the nonparticipant control group. However, for those who were not already sexually active at the start of the program, the results were

Longitudinal Impact of Sex
Education on 8th Grade Virgins
(18 months)

	Sex Education	No Sex Education
Percent Remaining Abstinent	71	62
Percent of Nonabstainers Using Protection	76	66
Percent of Nonabstainers Not Using Protection	24	34

Source: Kirby et al., 1991

Figure 15.11 *Given the many forces propelling teens toward sexual activity, it is not surprising that most programs of sex education have little impact. However, when carefully designed, sex education can have notable positive results, as shown here.*

quite positive (see Figure 15.11). Further, of those who did become sexually active after taking the class, the number of partners was lower and the use of contraception higher than in the control group.

A similar program for older adolescents was successful in promoting parent-adolescent discussions about sex and in postponing sexual intercourse for those who were virgins when they began the program. For those who had already engaged in sexual intercourse, however, the program was less successful. Eighteen months after the program's completion, 44 percent of these adolescents reported not having used birth control during their most recent act of intercourse, a figure comparable to the results associated with more conventional sex-education efforts (48 percent) (Kirby et al., 1991).

Collectively, these findings clearly point to the need for sex-education curricula to begin early and to be geared to the cognitive abilities of the participants, fostering attitudes and social skills that can help them refrain from sexual activity until they are mature enough to recognize, and take responsibility for, the possible consequences of their actions.

Indeed, this case study can be seen as applicable to all forms of adolescent education, outside the schools as well as inside them. Given the nature of adolescent thinking, open discussion of logical possibilities and the use of hypothetical scenarios seem critical to developing the cognitive maturity required for effective decision making. Of course, cognition is not the whole story for adolescents' sexual decisions or for any of the choices teenagers must make about their present and their future. The next chapter explores the psychosocial influences that shape teenagers' lives, including the impact of family, friends, and society.

SUMMARY

Adolescent Thought

1. During adolescence, young people become better able to speculate, hypothesize, and fantasize, emphasizing possibility more than reality. Unlike the younger child, whose thought is tied to concrete operations, adolescents can build formal systems and general theories that transcend, and sometimes ignore, practical experience. Their reasoning can be formal and abstract, rather than empirical and concrete.

2. The ability to think logically is the hallmark of formal operational thought. Between the ages of 12 and 15, many young people become able to articulate scientific principles when given Piagetian tests of formal operational thought. They are also much more able to follow logical arguments and reason about social problems.

3. Many adolescents and adults never attain formal operational thinking, as measured by Piaget's tests. In addition, those who do attain it may exhibit it strongly in some areas and weakly or not at all in others.

Adolescent Egocentrism

4. Another characteristic of adolescent thought is a particular form of egocentrism that leads young people to overestimate their significance to others. This characteristic is sometimes expressed in a personal fable about the grand and glorious deeds they will perform in adulthood. It also leads many young people to imagine themselves as continually being at center stage, the focus of everyone's attention.

Schools, Learning, and the Adolescent Mind

5. During this time of mixed openness and egocentrism, adolescents find themselves eager for intellectual interaction yet highly vulnerable to self-doubt. Many students enter secondary school feeling less able, less conscientious, and less motivated than they did in elementary school.

6. Compared to elementary schools, most secondary schools have more rigid behavioral demands, intensified competition, more punitive grading practices, and less individualized attention and procedures.

7. Schools can be organized to make a decided difference in academic achievement, self-image, delinquency, and future success by setting educational goals that are high, clear, and attainable, and that are supported by the entire staff.

Moral Development

8. Moral reasoning also becomes more complex during adolescence, for the young person who can grasp general laws of physics or principles of logic is more likely to articulate moral laws and ethical principles.

9. Kohlberg proposes that the development of moral reasoning occurs through six stages of increasing complexity, from the elemental "might makes right" to the recognition of universal ethical principles. Entry into the postconventional stages of moral reasoning require a certain amount of life experience and responsibility, according to Kohlberg, so few adolescents progress beyond stage 4.

10. Kohlberg's critics suggest that his theory reflects particular cultural values and gender socialization rather than universal stages. However, Kohlberg's theory seems to be generally valid, and, although males and females may analyze problems differently, neither sex is deemed to be better at solving moral dilemmas.

Sexual Decision Making: A Study in Adolescent Cognition

11. Cognitive immaturity makes it difficult for adolescents to arrive at rational decisions about sexuality. Adolescents who believe that they are above many of the normal problems that humans experience may also believe that they will never be confronted with pregnancy or sexually transmitted diseases, even when they don't take precautions against them.

12. The best way to help adolescents avoid problems with sexual behavior may be to encourage them to postpone sexual exploration until they are able to reason more maturely. Role models provided by peers seem especially influential, as does education that encourages thinking and discussion.

KEY TERMS

formal operational thought (388)
scientific reasoning (388)
game of thinking (389)
adolescent egocentrism (391)
invincibility fable (391)
personal fable (392)
imaginary audience (392)
person-environment fit (393)
ego involvement learning (395)

task involvement learning (395)
tracking (396)
preconventional moral reasoning (399)
conventional moral reasoning (399)
postconventional moral reasoning (399)
sexually transmitted disease (STD) (403)
social inoculation (407)

KEY QUESTIONS

1. What are some of the tests that determine whether or not a person has attained formal operational thought?

2. What improvements in the ability to think logically occur during adolescence?

3. How is research on adolescent thinking relevant to education?

4. What are some of the characteristics of adolescent egocentrism?

5. What are some of the reasons for a decline in academic achievement in high school?

6. How should schools be organized to achieve better academic success and strong social interaction among teens?

7. What stages of moral development are reached during adolescence?

8. What are some of the criticisms of Kohlberg's theory?

9. What are some of the explanations for the high rates of sexually transmitted disease and pregnancy in adolescence?

10. What are some of the ways of helping adolescents to avoid early sexual experience?

CHAPTER 16

Adolescence: Psychosocial Development

One of the challenges of adolescence is to establish a sense of individual identity, to find a way to be one of the group and yet stand out from the crowd. In meeting this challenge, teenagers must make some important decisions about a wide, and sometimes bewildering, array of personal questions. These tasks of the teenage years, the problems they may involve, and the role of family and friends in helping adolescents confront them are among the topics discussed in this chapter.

How do changes in economic and political circumstances affect the development of identity for different cohorts?

In what ways might it be more difficult for minority-group teenagers to achieve identity than for members of the majority culture?

How does the peer group ease the transition from dependence on parents to true intimacy with a member of the other sex?

When is there a "generation gap"?

What are the differences between teenage drug use today and a decade ago?

What are some of the social and personal characteristics that are associated with such problems as teenage suicide and sexual abuse?

The physical changes of puberty begin the process of adolescence by transforming the child's body into an adult's, and the cognitive developments described in the preceding chapter enable the young person to begin to think logically. However, it is psychosocial development—such things as relating to parents with new independence, to friends with new intimacy, to society with new commitment, and to oneself with new understanding—that helps the young person eventually attain adult status and maturity. Taken as a whole, these aspects of psychosocial development can best be understood in terms of the adolescent's quest for identity, that is, for answers to a question that never arose in younger years: "Who am I?"

Identity

In the 1940s, Erik Erikson became absorbed with the question of **identity,** the individual's attempt to define himself or herself as a unique person. For Erikson, the search for identity represents a basic human need that begins to be felt in adolescence. Indeed, according to Erikson, the search for identity is the primary task and crisis of adolescence, a crisis in which the young person struggles to reconcile a quest for "a conscious sense of individual uniqueness" with "an unconscious striving for a continuity of experience . . . and a solidarity with a group's ideals" (Erikson, 1968). In other words, the young person seeks to establish himself or herself as a separate individual while at the same time maintaining some connection with the meaningful elements of the past and accepting the values of a group. In the process of "finding themselves," adolescents attempt to develop a sexual, moral, political, and religious identity that is relatively stable, consistent, and mature. This identity ushers in adulthood, as it bridges the gap between the experiences of childhood and the personal goals, values, and decisions that permit each young person to take his or her place in society (Erikson, 1975).

Identity Statuses

The ultimate goal, called **identity achievement,** occurs when adolescents attain their new identity through "selective repudiation and mutual assimilation of childhood identifications" (Erikson, 1968). That is, the adolescent, ideally, establishes his or her own goals and values by abandoning some of those set by parents and society and accepting others.

For many young people, however, identity achievement is quite difficult, and even the process of accepting some parental values while rejecting others is problematic. The result often is **foreclosure,** or premature identity formation. In this case, the adolescent accepts earlier roles and parental values wholesale, never exploring alternatives or truly forging a unique personal identity. A typical example might be the young man who from childhood has wanted to, or perhaps was pressured into wanting to, follow in his father's footsteps, as, say, a doctor. He might diligently study chemistry and biology in high school, take premed courses in college, and then perhaps discover in his third year of medical school (or at age 40, when his success as a surgeon seems hollow) that what he really wanted to be was a poet.

Other adolescents may find that the roles their parents and society expect them to fill are unattainable or unappealing, yet they may be unable to find alternative roles that are truly their own. Adolescents in this position often take on a **negative identity,** that is, an identity that is the opposite of the one they are expected to adopt. The child of a teacher, for instance, might drop out of high school, despite having the capacity to do college-level work. The child of devoutly religious parents might defy his or her upbringing, stealing, taking drugs, and the like.

Figure 16.1 *Staring into the mirror, thinking "Who are you?" exemplifies the search for identity in adolescence. The answer a schoolchild might give—for instance, "I am an Asian-American girl"—is no longer sufficient, as the teenager now realizes there are many ways to be Asian, American, and a girl. How traditional, how liberated, and how "feminine" to be, for example, is a matter of complex self-definition, and only a part of identity formation.*

Figure 16.2 *Scottish punkers and rookie Marines may actually have a great deal in common. Many of them may be avoiding identity achievement by opting for a negative identity, a foreclosure, or a moratorium. In any of these cases, where they are, who they are with, and how they wear their hair and clothes suggests "I'm not ready to decide my unique, personal identity quite yet."*

Other young people experience **identity diffusion:** they typically have few commitments to goals or values—whether those of parents, peers, or the larger society—and are often apathetic about trying to find an identity. These young people have difficulty meeting the usual demands of adolescence, such as completing school assignments, making friends, and thinking about the future.

Finally, in the process of finding a mature identity, many young people seem to declare a **moratorium,** a kind of time-out during which they experiment with alternative identities without trying to settle on any one. In some cases, a society may provide formal moratoriums through various of its institutions. In the United States, the most obvious example of an institutional moratorium is college, which usually requires young people to sample a variety of academic areas before concentrating in any one and forestalls pressure from parents and peers to choose a career and mate. Other institutions that permit a moratorium are the military, the Peace Corps, and various service internships, many of which enable older adolescents to travel, acquire valuable skills, and test themselves while delaying lifetime commitments.

Research on Identity Status

Following Erikson's lead, many other developmentalists have found the concept of identity a useful one in understanding adolescence. Foremost among these is James Marcia, who has defined the four major identity statuses (achievement, foreclosure, diffusion, and moratorium) in sufficiently precise terms that he and other investigators can interview an adolescent and determine his or her overall identity status (Marcia, 1966, 1980).

TABLE 16.1   **Characteristics of the Various Identity Statuses**

	Foreclosure	Diffusion	Moratorium	Achievement
Anxiety	repression of anxiety	moderate	high	moderate
Attitude toward parents	loving and respectful	withdrawn	trying to distance self	loving and caring
Self-esteem	low (easily affected by others)	low	high	high
Ethnic identity	strong	medium	medium	strong
Prejudice	high	medium	medium	low
Moral stage	preconventional or conventional	preconventional or conventional	postconventional	postconventional
Dependence	very dependent	dependent	self-directed	self-directed
Cognitive processes	simplifies complex issues; refers to others and to social norms for opinions and decisions	complicates simple issues; refers to others in both personal and ideological choices	thoughtful; procrastinates, especially in decisions; avoids referring to others' opinions or to social norms	thoughtful; makes decisions by both seeking new information and considering others' opinions
College	very satisfied	variable	most dissatisfied (likely to change major)	high grades
Relations with others	stereotyped	stereotyped or isolated	intimate	intimate

Adapted from research reviewed by Berzonsky, 1989; Marcia, 1980; Streitmatter, 1989.

Dozens of studies have compared adolescents' identity statuses with various measures of their cognitive or psychological development and have found that each identity status is typified by a number of distinct characteristics (see Table 16.1). For example, each of the four identity statuses correlates with a somewhat different attitude toward parents: the diffused adolescent is withdrawn, perhaps deliberately avoiding parental contact by sleeping or listening to music on headphones when the rest of the family is together; the moratorium adolescent is not withdrawn as much as independent, busy with his or her own interests; both the foreclosure and the achiever are loving, but the foreclosure evidences more respect and deference, while the achiever treats parents with more concern, behaving toward them as an equal or even as a caregiver rather than as a care-receiver.

Table 16.1 shows some revealing combinations of statuses and traits. Note, for instance, that both adolescents who have achieved identity and those who have prematurely foreclosed their search for self-definition have a strong sense of ethnic identification, seeing themselves as proud to be Irish, Italian, Latino, or whatever. However, those who have foreclosed are relatively high in prejudice, while the identity achievers are relatively low, presumably because they are sufficiently secure in their ethnic background that they do not need to denigrate that of others.

Extensive research, much of it longitudinal, confirms that many adolescents go through a period of foreclosure or diffusion, and then a moratorium, before they finally commit themselves to a mature identity. The process can take ten years or more, with many college students still not clear about who they are or what they want to do (Marcia, 1980; Waterman, 1985). Within the four categories of identity formation, subcategories are evident. For example, some individuals in diffusion are apathetic, seeming not to care about anything, while others are alienated, rebelling against everything. Similarly, in foreclosure, some prematurely take on the identities their parents urge on them, while others choose totalitarian groups—such as a religious cult or a doctrinaire political organization—that take over all independent decision making (Archer and Waterman, 1990). No matter what the age or identity status of the individual, however, it is obvious that answering the question "Who am I?" is an important psychosocial task.

There is also no doubt that the ease or difficulty of finding an identity is very much affected by forces outside the individual. One of the most influential of these is the surrounding society, which can aid identity formation primarily in two ways: by providing values that have stood the test of time and that continue to serve their function, and by providing social structures and customs that ease the transition from childhood to adulthood. Whether these factors are present and actually do make the search for identity easy depends primarily on the degree to which the members of the society are agreed on basic values, and the degree to which the individual is exposed to social change. In a culture where virtually everyone holds the same moral, political, religious, and sexual values, and social change is slow, identity is easy to achieve. The young person simply accepts the only social roles and values that he or she has ever known. In modern industrial and postindustrial societies, by contrast, rapid social change, a broad diversity of values and goals, and an ever expanding array of identity choices can make identity formation a formidable task. As the Closer Look on pages 416–417 points out, some aspects of identity formation can be particularly difficult for minority-group members, who may feel pulled in opposite directions by their group and by the majority culture.

Now let us look at two other forces—the immediate family and the peer group—that are instrumental not only in the young person's quest for identity but in all other aspects of navigating the passage to adulthood.

Family and Friends

Sailing the changing seas of development is never done alone; at every turn, each voyager's family, friends, and community provide provisions and directions, ballast for stability, and an anchor when it is time to rest, or, through example and pressure, reasons to move full speed ahead. In adolescence, when the winds of change blow particularly strong, parents and peers become especially powerful, for good or ill.

Parents

Often adolescence is characterized as a time of waning adult influence, when the values and habits of young people are said to become increasingly distant from those of their parents and other adults. According to all reports, however, the **generation gap,** as the differences between the younger generation and the older one have been called, is not very wide. Younger and older generations have very similar values and aspirations. This is

Identity for Minority Adolescents

In most contemporary societies, finding an identity is extremely complex: many alternative paths are open and a multitude of choices must be made. For members of minority ethnic groups, identity achievement may be particularly complicated, and often painful (Spencer and Markstrom-Adams, 1989; Phinney et al., 1990). On the one hand, democratic ideology espouses a color-blind, multiethnic society, in which background is irrelevant to achievement and all citizens develop their potential according to their individual merits, particular characteristics, and personal goals. This ideal is sought by parents and adolescents from every ethnic group: more than one teenager, filling out a form that asks "Race?" writes "human."

On the other hand, most minority ethnic groups place major emphasis on ethnicity and expect their teenagers to honor their roots and take pride in their heritage. Thus, identity formation requires finding the right balance between transcending one's background and immersing oneself in it. In Erikson's words, during adolescence "each new generation links the actuality of a living past with that of a promising future" (Erikson, 1968).

Making this link is difficult for many North American children from minority groups, since their group's past is likely to be either ignored or implicitly slighted by educational institutions. School curricula, especially when most teachers and administrators come from a majority group, rarely include more than a superficial historical look at famous figures from minority groups (O'Connor, 1989). School staff are often ignorant of very real differences among members of minority groups, assuming, for example, that all Chicanos speak Spanish, or referring to Vietnamese or Hmong students as "Chinese" (Goldstein, 1990).

Parents and other relatives, meanwhile, are unsure how much to encourage their children to adapt to the majority culture for the sake of future success and how much to preserve past tradition. For example, some non-English-speaking parents push their children to learn English to the point of sacrificing fluency in their native tongue, while other parents downplay the importance of mastering the dominant language. As a result, many young people never feel at home with the language or literature of either traditions.

Compounding this problem is the social reality that in the world outside their own neighborhoods and extended families, minority children experience discrimination, prejudice, and stereotyping. Playful or deliberately hurtful comments about the size of one's nose, the shape of one's eyes, the texture of one's hair, the cadence of one's speech, or the style of one's clothes are particularly painful and common during the self-conscious years of early adolescence. Even worse, as minority teens start to plan for adulthood, are the various forms of hidden discrimination that may impede their higher education and career development.

In coping with such problems, adolescents might find it too difficult to forge their own solutions to the complicated issues of self-determination. Instead they may embrace a negative identity—rejecting wholesale the traditional values of both their ethnic group and the majority culture—or foreclose on identity prematurely—choosing the values of one culture exclusively (Phinney et al., 1990). More often the latter is the case. According to one study, African-American, Native American, Mexican-American, and Asian-American adolescents were all more likely to have foreclosed on identity questions than were European-Americans (Streitmatter, 1988). Thus, they had stopped searching for their own values and selfhood, perhaps because the process was too painful or confusing.

The primary effect of such foreclosure is to prevent mature reconciliation of both wellsprings of identity, the minority and the majority culture. For example, in a study of black adolescents (Miller, 1989) bused into high schools that were 95 percent white, one student remarked:

> I don't consider myself to be a minority because my [White] friends, they don't even consider or even look at it as me being a different color, just being regular, being just like them. They [other bused students] prefer to be Black, they want to just hang around with the Blacks, they don't want nothing to do with the Whites . . . I'm not like that . . . I attended the ski club and I asked if anyone else wanted to get into it, and you should have seen their faces, it was hysterical. What is this kid talking about, the ski club? It's a bunch of "honkies" gonna be there.

By contrast, another of the bused students, who socialized almost entirely with other black students and thought both the school rules and the principal were unfair, said:

> I think this school is prejudiced. I didn't want to come out here . . . And this school does not do things that Black people can get into. Like at our prom, we wanted to have a D.J. that could play White music and Black music. But they [White students] didn't want that. They wanted a band, which we can't comprehend.

Relationships with parents and other relatives are often particularly stressful for minority adolescents in the United States. Many minority groups revere family closeness—respecting elders and accepting self-sacrifice for the sake of the family—more than most members of the majority culture do (Harrison et al., 1990). Yet this ideal clashes with the majority culture's glorification of adolescent freedom and self-determination, exacerbating the normal conflict that arises when the adolescent's need for independence and friendship is incompatible with parental demands and cultural expectations. Some minority adolescents (mostly girls) give in to parental control (perhaps docilely living at home until marriage), while others (mostly boys) rebel completely (perhaps leaving home in a mad fury). In both cases, the normal search for identity is sacrificed. Finding a balance between these two extremes has its own price. As one girl lamented:

> I don't know who I am. Am I the good Chinese daughter? Am I an American teenager? I always feel I am letting my parents down when I am with my friends because I act so American, but I also feel that I will never really be an American. I never really feel comfortable with myself anymore. [quoted in Olson, 1988]

While adolescents from every minority group encounter additional complications in finding their own identity, the particulars vary depending on the subculture. Asians feel the stress of becoming an "achieving Asian," with academic pressure that precludes much of a social life and may, in fact, undermine school success (Natagata, 1989). African-Americans and Latin-Americans who are academically talented may feel the opposite pressure, hiding their ability in order not to be perceived as a "brainiac" by their peers (Fordham and Ogbu, 1986; Matute-Bianchi, 1986). In addition, members of minority groups often experience intense criticism from peers if they make an effort to join the majority culture: typically they are branded as an "oreo," a "banana," an "apple"—of color on the outside but white inside.

Of course, these generalities themselves are stereotypic, overlooking both individual and group differences. Depending on the particular national origin, socioeconomic status, and acculturation of the family, pressures differ. The Cuban-American is quite distinct from the Mexican-American; the impoverished inner-city African-American differs from the middle-class, suburban one; the newly arrived Cambodian is very different from the third-generation Japanese, just as the Aleut from Northern Canada is different from the Navaho in New Mexico.

Even within each subgroup, further distinctions arise. As one ninth-grade Mexican immigrant complained:

> There is so much discrimination and hate. Even from other kids from Mexico who have been here longer. They don't treat us like brothers. They hate even more. It makes them feel like natives. They want to be American. They don't want to speak Spanish to us, they already know English and how to act. If they're with us, other people will treat them more like wetbacks, so they try to avoid us. [quoted in Olson, 1988]

In addition, historical changes can present each generation with a somewhat different array of possibilities and problems. The past forty years in America, for example, have seen swings from legal and de facto segregation and discrimination to enforced integration and affirmative action to, more recently, signs of movement in the opposite direction; from the traditional social separation of racial groups to the ideal of the racial and ethnic "melting pot" to, more recently, a new emphasis on racial and ethnic heritage. Given these differences, even if schools taught a more diverse history and parents provided more cultural education, each individual must wage his or her own fight to achieve an ethnic identity, perhaps with the aid of slightly older adolescents from the same subculture. Ethnic identity, like identity of all sorts, takes time to find, with individuals usually going to extremes of assimilation and separation before reaching a mature self-affirmation (Cross, 1991). Eventually, every young person should find his or her own historical roots, gender roles, vocational aspirations, religious beliefs, and political values, all influenced by his or her own community and culture, but each nonetheless unique.

Most high schools today are made up of adolescents of different ethnic backgrounds, and almost every student willingly talks, argues, and jokes with those from other groups. Many, indeed, cherish close interethnic friendships, partly because one's understanding of life is deepened by such relationships. Nonetheless, this photo depicts a typical scene: most students socialize primarily with others from their own group in the lunchroom, between classes, and after school. Ethnic roots become a bond that cannot be denied, and associations with others of the same race, religion, or national origin often make finding an identity seem easier.

Figure 16.3 *Most parents and adolescents have quite similar values and enjoy the same activities. When differences do occur, they are likely to be relatively minor—such as how to wear one's hair, what and when to eat, and who is responsible for cleaning up what.*

especially true when adolescents are compared, not with adults in general, but with their own parents (McClelland, 1982).

Numerous studies have shown substantial agreement between parents and adolescents on political, religious, educational, and vocational opinions and values (Feather, 1980; Youniss, 1989). Most young people, for instance, favor the same candidate for president or prime minister and follow the same religion as their parents do. Interestingly, daughters are even more similar to their parents on numerous value questions, ranging from religion to drug use, than sons are (Feather, 1980)—with one notable exception, attitudes about sex (Treboux and Busch-Rossnagel, 1990).

Other similarities between parents and adolescents are apparent as well. For example, regardless of academic potential, adolescents who do relatively well in high school and college tend to be the offspring of parents who value education and did well in high school and college themselves. By contrast, most high school dropouts report that their parents do not understand, accept, or care about them or their education (Dunham and Alpert, 1987). Similarly, whether or not an adolescent experiments with drugs is highly correlated with his or her parents' attitudes and behavior regarding drugs (Jurich et al., 1985). Indeed, virtually every aspect of adolescent behavior is directly affected by the family.

How small or big the generation gap is also depends on who assesses it. Generally, parents and adolescents tend to believe that they understand each other as well as, or better than, most other families do (Noller and Callan, 1988). Further, parents estimate the size of the gap as smaller than adolescents do. The reason for this is that each generation in the parent-adolescent relationship has a psychic need to view that relationship somewhat differently. In effect, each group has its own **generational stake** in the family (Bengston, 1975): because of their different developmental stages, each generation has a natural tendency to see the family in a certain way.

Parents are concerned about continuity of their own values, so they tend to minimize the import of whatever differences occur, blaming them on hormones or peer influences rather than anything long-lasting. Adolescents, on the other hand, are concerned with shedding many parental restraints and forging their own independent identity, so they are likely to exaggerate problems. Thus a conflict about a curfew may be seen by the teenager as evidence of the parents' outmoded values, or lack of trust, whereas the parents may see it merely as a problem of management, the latest version of trying to get the child to bed on time.

Conflict and Harmony

A certain amount of conflict between parents and adolescents is apparent in virtually every culture and every historical period, as the young person's innate drive for independence clashes with the parents' traditional control (Schlegal and Barry, 1991). In fact, an absence of conflict may indicate a disturbed parent-child relationship—one in which the young person is so cowed, or the parent so permissive, or the parent-child bond so tenuous that disagreements rarely emerge (Grotevant and Cooper, 1985). As at other periods of life, authoritative parenting—which usually includes some heated discussions—is better for the adolescent's achievement and self-esteem than either authoritarian or permissive parenting (see pp. 264–268). Especially harmful are parents who are permissive because they do not seem to care what their child does: their teenagers are likely to lack confidence and to be depressed, low-achieving, and delinquent (Baumrind, 1991; Lamborn et al., 1991).

Conflicts need not be monumental, knock-down fights about critical philosophical issues. Instead, in contemporary Western cultures, parents and adolescents typically do battle over mundane matters, such as "hair, garbage, dishes, and galoshes," (Hill and Holmbeck, 1987). According to one study in which parents and children were asked to cite specific conflicts, most families could describe about three or four such recurring disputes, each arising about once a week (Smetana et al., 1991). The reason is that, while the specifics seem petty, the underlying issue—adolescents' freedom to make their own decisions—is not. In general, adolescents believe that they should be granted this freedom much earlier, and more extensively, than parents do. Disagreement is particularly likely to occur over questions the adolescent thinks are simply matters of personal choice, such as what clothes to wear, how neat to keep one's room, when to eat or sleep, or whom to have as a friend. For example, in one study, only 10 percent of a group of 10- to 16-year-olds thought parents had a legitimate authority over whether an adolescent could sleep late on weekends or talk on the phone to friends when no one else had to make a call. By contrast, half of all the parents thought they could and should intercede in such matters (Smetana, 1988).

The frequency and nature of parent-adolescent conflict are affected by a number of factors, beginning with the child's age and maturity level: parent-child spats are most common in early adolescence, and are much more likely to involve mothers and their early-maturing offspring than fathers and late-maturing children (Montemeyer, 1986; Steinberg, 1990; Hetherington, 1989). Family structure makes a difference as well. Conflicts are less frequent in stable, single-parent homes than in families where the parents are married, newly divorced, cohabiting, or remarried—perhaps because most single parents have already worked out a system in which children have more independence and authority than in other homes. For these families, personal autonomy is not such an urgent and controversial issue (Smetana et al., 1991; Stinson, 1991).

Birth order is a factor as well, with first-borns having more conflicts with parents than later-borns do (Small et al., 1988). As one older adolescent explained to a younger sibling, "You should be grateful to me. I had to break them in, so you have it easy."

Finally, factors in the macrosystem also affect the frequency and severity of conflict. Parents' expectations for their children are influenced by income, education, culture, and traditions, and these vary widely from place to place (Goodnow and Collins, 1990; Steinberg et al., 1991). For example, while parents of every socioeconomic status want their children to be honest, happy, and considerate, lower-income families are likely to also value politeness, neatness, and obedience—qualities for which many adolescents do not have equal enthusiasm (Kohn, 1979). Further, one of the key components of SES is education, and families with less education are particularly likely to lose patience with the kinds of endless discussion, debate, and disagreement that puberty seems to evoke.

As a result, adolescents who lack confidence or who rebel by leaving home, taking drugs, or becoming sexually active before age 16 are more likely to come from very strict, or very permissive, lower-income homes than from homes that are more moderate in discipline and average in SES. Note, however, that one large study of American adolescents of every background (including European, African, Latino, and Asian) found that parenting style is associated with such problems even more than income level is. Those adolescents from authoritative low-income families were better adjusted and more confident than those from nonauthoritative, middle-income families (Steinberg et al.,1991).

There is another more immediate reason that lower-SES homes may tend to be more strict than middle-income homes. Many poor families live in neighborhoods where drugs, violence, and crime are all too prevalent. One critical factor that can keep a particular young person from being caught up in the social destruction of such communities is **parental monitoring,** that is, parental watchfulness about where one's child is and what he or she is doing and with whom (Snyder et al., 1986). The worse the social milieu, the more likely monitoring is to result in curfews, restrictions on friends, and other seemingly authoritarian measures. The higher the family's SES, the less the need for such stringent measures, and the more emphasis there tends to be on self-direction and curiosity—values many adolescents do share with their parents.

While parent-child conflicts are normal in adolescence, and parents often have good reason to be concerned about their youngsters' habits and whereabouts, with time such conflicts and concerns gradually subside. Parents' first reaction to the emergence of assertiveness in their adolescent is to be more assertive themselves, reiterating general rules and principles the child seems to have forgotten, exaggerating the dangers of independence, and insisting on the obedience and respect that the young person suddenly seems disinclined to give. As the months go by, parents tend to

Figure 16.4 *If parents try to lay down the law about obedience, hard work, and responsibility every moment of the adolescent's life, the adolescent—especially if a boy—is likely to rebel, either with open defiance or passive resistance. Many a parent has ended yet another lecture wondering "I don't understand what his problem is. I've told him again and again."*

yield more often, in part because they recognize that their child is growing up, in part because some of the adolescent's arguments start to make sense, and in part because the young person begins to act in more mature ways. Usually by late adolescence, parent-child relations are more harmonious, a trend found among children of both sexes, adopted as well as nonadopted children, in all family types, and in many nations (Montemayor, 1986; Hurrelmann and Engel, 1989; Maughan and Pickles, 1990).

All told, then, if there is a "generation gap," it is more likely to occur in early adolescence, and to tend to center on issues of self-discipline and self-control. During these years, teenagers and their parents are more likely to have disagreements about the adolescent's musical tastes, domestic neatness, and sleeping habits than about world politics or deep moral concerns. Fortunately, the bickering and alienation that occur in many families in early adolescence diminish with time. Those who do not follow this generally benign pattern—the roughly 20 percent of all families who find that conflict appears and reappears throughout adolescence (Montemeyer, 1986; Offer and Offer, 1975)—are those who are the most vulnerable to the special problems discussed later in this chapter (Dryfoos, 1990).

Peers

The socializing role of peers, which begins to emerge during the latter part of middle childhood, becomes even more prominent during adolescence (Berndt, 1989). From "hanging out" with a large group to whispered phone conversations with a trusted confidant, relations with peers are a vital part of the transition from childhood to adulthood.

Adolescents help each other in many ways, with identity formation, value clarification, independence, and social skills. As John Coleman (1980) explains, although "the peer group has a continuous part to play in the socialization process during the whole span of school and college years . . . there are undoubtedly special factors operating during adolescence that elevate the peer group to a position of unusual prominence." Coleman finds three of these factors noteworthy:

1. The physical and social changes typical of adolescence cause the young person to confront new experiences and challenges to self-esteem. At such times, the peer group can function as a self-help group, a sounding board of contemporaries who may be going through the same sorts of struggles.

2. A crucial task in adolescence is questioning the validity of adult standards and authority. As a consequence, "at a time when uncertainty and self-doubt are greatest and support is most needed, many adolescents find themselves in an emotional position where it is difficult, if not impossible, to turn to their parents. Under such circumstances, it is hardly surprising that peers play an unusually important role."

3. Adolescents need to experiment, discovering which of their personality characteristics and possible behaviors will be accepted and admired. "This process of discovery, sometimes rewarding, sometimes painful and embarrassing, is dependent on the involvement of the peer group" (Coleman, 1980).

Figure 16.5 *In the search for identity, peers provide a temporary haven—often with very obvious clothing rules that indicate "you are one of us." Taste in music, food, and slang are also identifying marks. One group's "real cool" might be another group's "total def."*

Another way that peers aid in the quest for identity is to help adolescents define who they are by helping them define who they are not. In American culture, every adolescent is exposed to not just one peer group but to many, each with distinct preferences in activities, dress, and music, and differing values about school and society (McClelland, 1982). As adolescents associate themselves with this or that subgroup (the jocks, the brains, or the druggies, for instance), they are rejecting others—and the particular self-definitions that would go with them.

Boys and Girls Together

One of the most important means by which adolescents help each other is by easing the way into relationships with the other sex. As you remember, voluntary sex segregation is the common practice among children during most of early and middle childhood. Neither sex pays much attention to the other. Then, as puberty begins, boys and girls begin to notice one another in a new way.

Usually, the first sign of heterosexual attraction is not an overt positive interest but a seeming dislike. A study of adolescents in New Zealand (Kroger, 1989), for example, found that a typical feeling among girls at age 11 was that "boys are a sort of disease"; at age 13, that "boys are stupid although important to us"; at age 15, that "boys are strange—they hate you if you're ugly and brainy but love you if you are pretty but dumb"; and at age 16, that "boys are a pleasant change from the girls." Similarly, a typical feeling among boys at age 11 was that "girls are a pin prick in the side"; at age 13, that "girls are great enemies"; at age 15, that "girls are the main objective"; and at age 16, that "girls have their good and bad points—fortunately, the good outnumber the bad." Similar patterns of "warming up" to the other sex have been found in many nations, although the pace of change depends on various factors. The hormonal changes of puberty obviously affect when sexual interest occurs, although they are probably not as powerful in this regard as the influence of the culture and personal experience (Coe et al., 1988).

Typically, the peer group plays an important part in the "warming-up" process, as friendships within the group become a launching pad for romantic involvements, providing peers with security and role models as well as people to talk to while sparing them the embarrassment of being alone for any period of time with a member of the other sex without knowing what to do or say. It also provides witnesses and companions of the same sex who will help the young person evaluate whether so-and-so (male) is really nice or a nerd, whether so-and-so (female) is cute or stuck up, and, equally important, whether a particular attraction is mutual or not. Not surprisingly, then, the typical adolescent friendship circle is quite large and fluid. For example, one study found that the average tenth-grader had ten friends of the same sex and seven friends of the other sex, and that between the beginning and end of the school year, more than half of the old friends had been replaced by new ones (Fischer et al., 1986).

Similar trends were documented in a study of students in a large, multiethnic public school outside Chicago (Csikszentmihalyi and Larson, 1984).

Figure 16.6 *Adolescent couples often double date, observing each other for cues to appropriate couple behavior. Double-dating also provides a bridge over awkward silences and, often, an opportunity to "debrief" with a close friend about how the date went.*

Not only did these adolescents gradually spend more time with the other sex, but they enjoyed it more: freshmen were happiest when they were with companions of their own sex or in mixed-sex groups; and juniors and seniors were happiest when with members of the "opposite" sex.

As romantic relationships develop, a social support network of friends continues to be important. For many adolescents, the first experiences with intimacy are fraught with problems, especially the likelihood of rejection. Indeed, the fear of rejection keeps many adolescents from trying to form intimate relationships, and when rejection does occur, adolescents are likely to experience it as devastating (Mitchell, 1986). Having friends to cushion this pain by offering reassurance and solace and by validating one's feelings and sense of self-worth is essential. For those adolescents who are homosexual, the added complications of finding both romantic partners and friends as confidants usually slow down the entire process. Generally, feeling at ease with one's sexual identity takes longer if one's orientation is toward one's own sex, in part because finding an accepting peer network is more difficult (Bell et al., 1981).

Finally, in late adolescence, true intimacy usually occurs. At this point adolescents no longer need the company of their peers, or their friends' specific reactions to their dates, in order to validate their own feelings. Of course, the pace and character of this transition to adult male-female relationships depends a great deal on the social context. An anthropological survey of adolescence in several eras and on every continent found wide variations. Some cultures rush the process; others delay it many ways, for many different reasons. Some cultures allow both sexes similar freedom; others are much more restrictive with girls than with boys. Some cultures tolerate homosexual expression; others rigidly prohibit it. Almost universally, however, peers play an important role in easing and guiding the process (Schlegal and Barry, 1991).

Overall, then, research suggests that peers are a positive aid in every major task of adolescence, from adjusting to the physical changes of puberty, to searching for identity, to forming romantic attachments. These findings help put the much overemphasized problems of "peer pressure" in perspective. Many parents worry that their children might be transformed during adolescence by the pressure of their friends, becoming, perhaps, sexually promiscuous, or drug-addicted, or delinquent. In some cases, of course, parents are right to worry, and may even have to intervene. However, while certainly some young people do things with their friends that they would not do alone or with a different peer group (the first drag on a cigarette or the first swig of beer is almost always related to the urging of friends), in general, peers are more likely to complement the influence of parents during adolescence than to pull in the opposite direction (Fasick, 1984; Hartup, 1983).

Parents and Peers

Despite the complementary nature of their influences, there are distinct differences between parents and peers as sources of social support. For one thing, the mutuality of peer friendships helps distinguish them from parent-child relationships (Youniss, 1980).

Consider a study in which groups of adolescents rated how often they discussed various topics with their parents and with their peers, as well as the character of the conversations. As one might expect, most of the conversations about family relationships occurred with their parents, and most of their discussions about their peer relationships were with their friends. On academic, vocational, religious, ethical, and political topics, the young adolescents talked more with their parents, whereas older adolescents talked more about these topics with their peers. More significant, no matter what the adolescent's age or what the issue, parents were reportedly more likely to offer and justify their own thoughts than to try to understand the adolescent's ideas. Peers, on the other hand, listened as much as, or more than, they presented their own views (Hunter, 1985).

Another study found that adolescents give high praise to those who are good listeners and are highly critical of anyone who "just won't listen" (Gilligan et al., 1990). Thus, while having a parent's opinion may often be appropriate, and clarifying, at least about what the parent thinks, having a peer who listens sympathetically while a teenager gives a blow-by-blow account of a social interaction, or thinks out loud about a complex issue, helps the teen gain insight into his or her own ideas, values, and actions. In the process, self-definition, and hence identity, become strengthened. Not surprisingly, then, while school-age children are typically even closer to their parents than to friends of the same sex, as young people leave childhood and enter adolescence, they are much more likely to share personal information and find companionship with peers—of both sexes—than with parents or teachers (Buhrmester and Furman, 1987).

Perhaps for this reason, and increasingly as they grow older, adolescents typically spend much more time with peers than with parents, and the time they spend with peers is more enjoyable. This was revealed in detail in an extensive study (Csikszentmihalyi and Larson, 1984) in which high school students reported that they spent six times as much time exclusively with friends as exclusively with parents and, overall, had much more positive emotions when with their friends than when with their parents (see Figure 16.7). However, those adolescents whose parents maintained a relatively high level of involvement with them while at the same time allowing them considerable autonomy reported higher than average levels of happiness when interacting with their family (Rathunde and Csikszentmihalyi, 1991).

Thus, parents and peers represent influences that are usually compatible and supplemental, not antithetical. Those adolescents who have good relationships with friends also, generally, have good relationships with parents—and most adolescents need both for a healthy transition to adulthood. Problems emerge when either of these influences is overpowering (as when parents insist on unquestioning obedience in the name of respect or closeness, or when peers insist on group conformity and risk-taking in the name of loyalty and independence) or when either is, in effect, missing (as when adolescents feel that their parents don't care or that their peers don't notice). While most adolescents do not experience these extremes in their parent or peer relationships, those who do are vulnerable to a variety of special problems.

Figure 16.7 *When a group of high school students wearing beepers were asked to record who they were with when paged randomly during the day, it was revealed that they were strongly tied to their own generation. All told, time spent exclusively with adults took up only 7 percent of their day.*

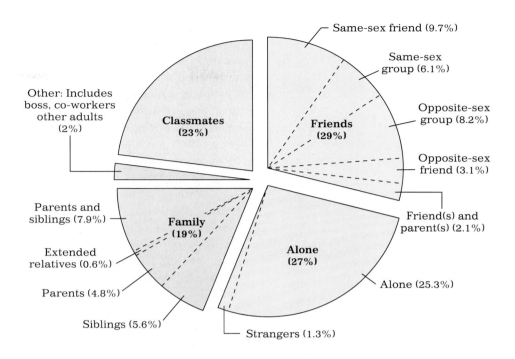

Special Problems

As we have seen, for the majority of adolescents the voyage to young adulthood is fairly smooth sailing, and they are able to ride out whatever rough seas may arise. For a minority of teenagers, however, the rough seas can become a boiling tempest that threatens development, or even life itself. When serious problems do occur, they usually are a consequence of a wide range of factors—including long-standing problems in the home and persistent vulnerabilities in temperament, as well as the special strains of adolescence and the particular peer and neighborhood context (Robins and Rutter, 1990).

Let us begin with the most common problem of all, drug use.

Drug Use

For many adolescents, a certain amount of rebellion against adult authority in general, and parental authority in particular, seems part of making one's own decisions and living one's own life. In addition, during identity formation, experimentation with new attitudes and roles is commonplace.

In recent decades especially, this combination of rebellion and experimentation has made the use of alcohol and other drugs a part of many young people's lives in every industrialized nation in the world. This trend has been chronicled in many studies, one of the most notable of which has been an annual, detailed, confidential survey of more than 15,000 American high school seniors from a cross-section of over 100 high schools. Since its inception in 1975, this survey has consistently shown that at least nine out of ten seniors have tried alcohol, that two out of three have tried tobacco, and that half have tried at least one illegal drug, most commonly marijuana (Johnston et al., 1992).

The survey has also found interesting variations among various subgroups: students from the east and west coasts use more drugs than students from the Midwest and South; and Native Americans are more likely to use alcohol and various illegal drugs than other ethnic groups, with European-Americans close behind. The lowest rates of alcohol and illegal-drug use are among Asian-Americans, followed in ascending order by those of African-Americans, Latinos, and then Chicanos. Generally males use more drugs than females, although among all groups, the sexes are becoming more equal. Indeed, among whites, women actually exceed white men in some categories, such as the use of alcohol and stimulants.

While drug use is prevalent among every group of adolescents, longitudinal data from this survey, confirmed by other research, shows encouraging signs. Compared to the late 1970s, drug use gradually decreased among every group of high school students throughout the 1980s, with 1991 data showing a continued decline. Not only have fewer high school seniors in the past decade ever tasted alcohol, puffed a cigarette or tried an illegal drug, but regular drug use, defined as use within the past 30 days, is down (see Figure 16.8). For instance, regular marijuana use peaked in 1978 at 37 percent, and has declined every year since then, reaching an all-time low in 1991 at 13.8 percent. Cocaine use peaked later, in 1985, when 7 percent of all seniors reported regular use; this compares to only 1.4 percent in 1991.

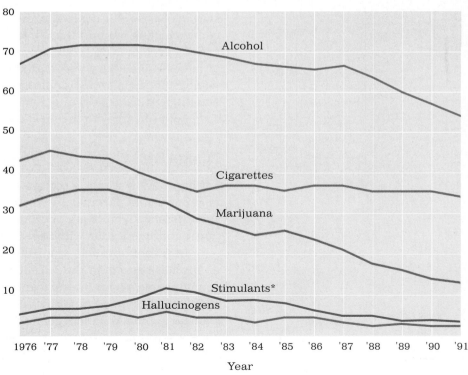

Percentage of High School Seniors
Using Drugs in Past 30 Days

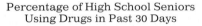

Figure 16.8 *This graph can be seen optimistically: since 1980, regular drug use among American high school students has been steadily declining. On the other hand, since every one of these drugs impairs physical health and judgment, many would argue that the rates are still alarmingly high.*

* Data on stimulants is adjusted to exclude drugs taken under doctor's orders.

Another example is the rise and fall of crack-cocaine use. By 1987, the first year crack cocaine was included in the nationwide survey, almost 6 percent of all high school seniors had already tried it, with 1 in every 77 (22 percent of those who had tried it) smoking it within the past month. One year later, slightly fewer had tried it, but the number of regular users was up to 1 senior in 62, about 30 percent of those who had ever tried it (Johnston et al., 1989). Since then, however, both one-time experimentation and regular use have decreased: in the 1991 survey, only 1 senior in 150 had used crack in the past month (Johnston et al., 1992).

Of course, the trend toward less drug use among adolescents is good news, but serious problems persist, particularly with regard to the traditional social drugs. The number of seniors who smoked a cigarette within the past month has been steady at about 30 percent throughout the 1980s, despite the overwhelming evidence of tobacco-related health risks. Although regular alcohol use has declined, it is still high: 90 percent have tried alcohol, 57 percent have used it recently, and, most troubling of all, 32 percent have consumed five or more drinks on one occasion within the past two weeks. Those 32 percent, as well as those abusing any other psychoactive drugs, are more vulnerable to virtually every other serious problem that plagues adolescents, including a rate of violent death (through accidents, homicide, and suicide) that is by far the leading cause of adolescent mortality. Furthermore, every psychoactive drug clouds the individual's thinking, and adds an element of artificiality to one's social relationships. Consequently, frequent drug use impairs normal learning and social growth. Many adults who were addicted to drugs as adolescents find that they missed important lessons in how to relate to other people (Newcomb and Bentler, 1988).

Moreover, many students begin their drug use before the twelfth grade, with those who began tobacco and alcohol before ninth grade being likely to use illegal drugs in high school (Dryfoos, 1990). While early drug experimentation does not inevitably lead to multidrug abuse, those individuals who use more drugs, more often, at younger ages, than their classmates are also more likely to have multiple drug- and alcohol-abuse problems later on (Newcomb and Butler, 1990).

Finally, the fifteen-year trends in drug use, while encouraging overall, contain a serious warning. The rise and fall in adolescents' use of LSD, PCP, (Angel Dust), cocaine, and crack suggests that this age group is continually vulnerable to new, and potentially more devastating, drugs: experimentation with XTC, "ice," or not-yet-known drugs may, in some cases, lead to patterns of escalating use.

Diverse Dimensions to the Problem

In their efforts to gain a comprehensive understanding of adolescent drug use, psychologists have learned an important lesson: too simplistic a view of adolescents' drug use makes the problem more difficult to deal with. Many adults act as if drug addiction occurs the moment a teenager takes one drag, swallow, or snort. The assumption seems to be that, if a teenager begins to use a drug, all is lost, but that if the teenager can somehow be dis-

Figure 16.9 *One characteristic of drug abuse is denial of the seriousness of the problem. Many adults inadvertently encourage this denial in adolescents by simplistically exaggerating the consequences of occasional experimentation. While it is true that alcohol and marijuana are "gateway" drugs, making it more likely for other drugs to enter into one's life, and that experimentation with cocaine often does lead to abusive use of the drug, it is also true that most users of alcohol and marijuana do not go on to hard drugs, and that most young people who try cocaine do not become addicts.*

suaded from ever trying drugs, all will be well. The reality is usually more complex, as was suggested by the findings of a fifteen-year longitudinal study that followed children from the age of 3. By age 18, most had tried marijuana as well as alcohol and tobacco. This led the researchers to wonder if such experimentation was normative in "psychologically healthy, sociable, and reasonably inquisitive individuals" (Shedler and Block, 1990).

To explore this question, they divided their sample into three groups: *abstainers*—those who had never tried any illegal drug; *experimenters*—those whose marijuana use was no more frequent than once a month, and who had tried no more than one other illegal drug; and *frequent users*—those who used marijuana once a week or more, and who had used at least one other illegal drug. (Those who did not fit into any of the groups were omitted from the analysis.)

To no one's surprise, the researchers found the typical frequent user to be a "troubled adolescent, an adolescent who is interpersonally alienated, emotionally withdrawn, and manifestly unhappy, and who expresses his or her maladjustment through undercontrolled, overtly antisocial behavior." Somewhat surprisingly, however, the typical abstainer was found to be not much better off—a "relatively tense, overcontrolled, emotionally constricted individual who is somewhat socially isolated and lacking in interpersonal skills." The experimenters, by contrast, were the most outgoing, straightforward, cheerful, charming, and poised of the three groups. Compared to the other two, they were least likely to distrust others or to keep them at a distance.

The longitudinal data in this study reveal that these patterns were not caused by the drug use but reflected preexisting personality characteristics. Even as young children, the frequent drug users and the abstainers tended to be more tense, distressed, and insecure, while the experimenters were more curious, open, happy, warm, and responsive. Further, the parents of the future frequent users and the future abstainers had much in common: they tended to be cold and unresponsive, pressuring their children to achieve but not encouraging them for what they did.

This study by no means suggests that drug use during adolescence should be looked on benignly. The authors emphasize that drug use, especially in early adolescence, is not only a sign of preexisting problems but most likely makes them worse: those who were already using marijuana by age 14 tended to be maladjusted, unhappy, and rebellious. The authors also stress that, for adolescents who are emotionally vulnerable, abstinence is the best choice, because in their case especially, drug experimentation may lead to drug addiction.

However, the authors do take strong exception to the present thrust of drug prevention in the schools and media. They suggest that telling teenagers that one taste will lead to addiction and that they should "just say no" to their friends is likely to foster, not abstinence, but the notion that adults are hopelessly misguided. Moreover, this approach, they contend, focuses on the symptom rather than the problem:

> Current efforts at drug "education" seem flawed on two counts. First, they are alarmist, pathologizing normative adolescent experimentation and limit-testing, and perhaps frightening parents and educators unnecessarily. Second, and of far greater concern, they trivialize the factors underlying drug abuse, implicitly denying their depth and pervasiveness. [Shedler and Block, 1990]

It seems, then, that the problem of drug abuse during adolescence is really two problems (Brown and Mills, 1987; Dryfoos, 1990). One applies to all adolescents, whose poor judgment about when and how to experiment with drugs, and whose behavior when "under the influence," might lead to fatal accidents or other serious consequences. The second applies to those adolescents who use drugs as an attempt to solve or forget long-standing problems. For them, drugs may bring temporary relief but, as time goes on, only add to their difficulties with growing up. Many of them have other problems as well—with school, with sexual relationships, with the law—problems that are made worse by drug abuse. They need much more help than a lecture on the evils of addiction.

Now let us look at juvenile delinquency, to discover to what extent it too is a time-limited phenomenon or a symptom of serious trouble.

Juvenile Delinquency

Accurate information on the extent of juvenile delinquency is difficult to come by. It is true, worldwide, that arrests are far more likely to occur during the decade of adolescence than in any other decade of life. In the United States, for example, a third of all arrests are of people between the ages of 11 and 21 (U.S. Department of Justice, 1990). However, simply looking at arrest statistics is not sufficient to reveal the prevalence or seriousness of delinquency. The actual prevalence might be overestimated, if, as some contend, a small minority of repeat offenders is responsible for a highly disproportionate share of juvenile offenses. Or the statistics may underestimate the problem, because, as others point out, most offenses never come to police attention, and of those that do, few lead to an arrest. Even data on gender, class, and ethnic differences in arrests is open to question. Boys are four times as likely to be arrested as girls, lower-SES adolescents are almost twice as likely to be arrested as middle-class adolescents, and African-American and Latino youth are close to twice as likely to be arrested as European-Americans, who, themselves, are more than twice as likely to be arrested as Asian-Americans (Farrington, 1987). But it has been consistently shown that, at least in some jurisdictions, the police are more inclined to arrest lower-SES or dark-skinned teenagers than middle-class or light-skinned ones, and they may be similarly more inclined to arrest boys than girls. Moreover, arrest statistics are subject to marked variations from place to place and time to time—probably more because of the changing politics and policies of law enforcement than because of any changes in adolescent behavior.

Thus, we need to study individuals longitudinally, obtaining confidential information from the adolescents themselves. When such research is done, it reveals that law-breaking that could lead to arrest seems to be part of normal adolescence. If all illegal acts—including such minor infractions as under-age drinking, disorderly conduct, breaking a curfew, playing hooky, driving over the speed limit—are included, virtually every adolescent is a repeat offender. In addition, at least in North America, Great Britain, and Australia, most studies reveal that somewhat more serious crimes—vandalism, theft, causing bodily harm—are also common, being committed at least once by about 80 percent of all adolescents (Rutter and Giller, 1984; Binder et al., 1988).

Figure 16.10 *Whether this boy gets arrested may depend on a number of factors besides his alleged offense and the evidence against him. Research has shown that arrest rates follow racial and social-class lines. In cases of minor offenses, an arrest may also hinge on whether the young person exhibits defiance or contrition.*

Developmental Trends in Delinquency

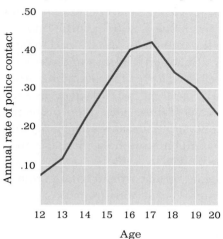

Figure 16.11 *While these data come only from one group—boys in a Wisconsin town—two characteristics are equally true, no matter where the information is collected. First, the rate of police contact rises and then falls during the years from age 10 to 20. Second, almost every American boy has some brush with the law. According to this graph, the average boy has almost three police interactions by age 20. Of course, not every transgression is caught: the actual average number of delinquent acts is much higher.*

This is not a new phenomenon. Shannon (1988) found similar patterns in a study of three cohorts of young people born in 1942, 1949, and 1955 in one Wisconsin town. Using longitudinal research that included self-reports, interviews, and police statistics, he determined that well over 90 percent of the boys and 65 to 70 percent of the girls had engaged in illegal acts.

The period of greatest increase in illegal activity appears to be age 15 or 16, with a rate about three times that of age 12 (Shannon, 1988). Thereafter it levels off and then drops, so that by age 20 it is about half the rate at age 17 (see Figure 16.11). Interestingly, being caught and being punished do not seem to affect the frequency of law-breaking, or the time span it includes: those whose law-breaking ends as adulthood approaches usually cite maturity, rather than any contact with the criminal justice system, as their reason for stopping their criminal behavior (Shannon, 1988; Rutherford, 1986; Quay, 1987).

Obviously, however, this does not mean that adolescent law-breaking should be allowed to run its course. For one thing, some adolescent crime is very serious. In the United States, of all those arrested in 1989 for serious crimes—including murder, rape, assault, and robbery—11 percent were under age 15 and another 17 percent were between the ages of 15 and 18 (Department of Commerce, 1990). Similar rates are found in other nations: arrests for sudden, impulsive, destructive crimes tend to occur most often at adolescence. Further, although many who engage in repeated delinquency at age 15 cease their criminal activity before adulthood, a significant minority do not, going on to become career criminals.

Unfortunately, attempts to discover the best approach to juvenile delinquency are fraught with problems. Some headway has been made toward identifying a child at risk for serious delinquency. According to a number of studies, those children who by age 10 have learning difficulties in school, especially in reading, *and* significant stresses at home (such as a single parent, a large family, or low income) are more likely to become delinquent. This is especially true if, as early as age 6, they have signs of attention-deficit disorder and antisocial behavior (Moffitt, 1990; Wilson and Herrnstein, 1985). However, trying to differentiate those children and adolescents who are likely to become serious adult criminals from those who are not is, in most cases, virtually impossible (Arbuthnot et al., 1987; Trasler, 1987). One reason is that so many factors bear on the outcome—from prenatal brain damage to the availability of guns, on the negative side, and from being a first-born child to attending a well-structured junior high school, on the positive side—that it is very difficult to identify and weigh all the factors that might be relevant. Thus, if an adolescent is statistically at risk of committing a serious crime someday, he or she may never actually do so, for reasons that never enter the calculation, and an adolescent who has already broken the law and been caught may not necessarily be one of the ones who most need special treatment. Finally, the array of intervention options is very broad—ranging from vocational help to incarceration in adult prisons, from reading lessons to family therapy—yet none of them has been shown to be consistently effective.

However, from a developmental and scientific point of view, we have learned some things. Most experts agree that those adolescents whose crimes include antisocial acts—the lone mugger as opposed to the adolescent who joins friends for a joy ride in a stolen car—need intensive intervention. With this subgroup, carefully structured rehabilitation—which may involve removal from the community to a place where the adolescent can learn academic and interpersonal skills he or she has thus far failed to acquire—can help (Garrett, 1985; Morris and Braukmann, 1987).

For most delinquents, however, such drastic programs are not needed, and may even prove harmful, segregating them with a peer group that prizes possessions more than people, and that survives with deceit and self-centeredness rather than trust. Further, the adolescent may adopt a negative self-image, while learning how to elude further arrest.

While no response to adolescent crime is always successful, the best outcomes result when the teenager is encouraged to understand the social consequences of his or her offense—as when the punishment is restitution or the performance of unpaid community service (Schneider, 1990). Most effective in the long run would be an ecological approach that simultaneously aids families, schools, and the community, as well as the adolescent. Helping parents discipline their children in an authoritative manner, strengthening schools so that fewer young people have learning problems, and shoring up neighborhood networks so that community institutions provide constructive challenges for the youth would be a far better way to prevent delinquency than attempting to retrain every offender—or to answer the frequent outcry for a cop on every block and a cell for every law-breaker (Gold, 1987; Lorion et al., 1987; Snyder and Patterson, 1987; Rutherford, 1986). True prevention begins early, from birth throughout childhood.

Abuse and Neglect

In some troubled families the stresses of normal adolescence become the final straw, breaking the family structure. One result is reflected in the divorce rate, which rises when the oldest child reaches about 12. A more direct consequence is child maltreatment, which remains relatively constant from about age 6 to 10, and increases again at about age 11. This includes psychological abuse, such as the constant nagging, belittling, and humiliation that some parents heap on their maturing children; physical abuse, often with objects such as bats and belts and threats with knives and guns not used when children were smaller; and neglect, as some children become "throwaways," tossed out of the house to the streets.

The seriousness of adolescent maltreatment is often underestimated, with the mistaken idea that harsh measures are justified because adolescents are naturally and inevitably out of control, or that their size enables them to defend themselves. The truth is that, with apparent maturity comes greater danger, because adolescents react to maltreatment in ways that younger children rarely do, with self-destruction, such as suicide, drug abuse, or running away, or with counterattack, such as the vandalism and violence aimed at society or at the perpetrator—including patricide (Ewing, 1990).

Adolescent problems that do not seem directly tied to maltreatment often, on closer analysis, are. For example, researchers studying a representative group of pregnant teenagers from every ethnic and economic group in Washington state were astonished at the number who had been abused: 36 percent had been sexually molested by a family member, including

7 percent who had been raped; 64 percent had been physically abused by a caretaker; and 36 percent had been emotionally abused by one or both parents (Boyer and Fine, 1992).

Now let us focus on sexual abuse, which is the type of maltreatment that most often affects adolescents. (A detailed discussion of child maltreatment in general can be found on pp. 191–205.)

Sexual Abuse

As you remember from Chapter 7, our understanding of child maltreatment is evolving, as ongoing research provides new insights into its dimensions, causes, consequences, treatment, and possible prevention. This is particularly true for child sexual abuse, which only recently has come to public attention as a widespread and damaging form of maltreatment. Many people still have a distorted view of this form of abuse.

Typically, sexual abuse is not a single event but series of episodes over the years, beginning with seemingly harmless fondling in childhood and then a marked increase in obvious sexual activity at puberty. While young children are sometimes sexually abused, it is a mistake to think that this form of abuse is particularly prevalent during early childhood: the rates of sexual abuse rise dramatically at about age 11, and then continue to climb throughout adolescence, until whatever age victims are considered adults (NCCAN, 1988).*

Even more than with other forms of maltreatment, precise data on sexual abuse are hard to come by, because abuse is variously defined and its occurrence is, clearly, underreported. For example, some reporting agencies include only cases in which the child has been physically penetrated; most developmentalists, on the other hand, believe that "sexual abuse" is the appropriate label for any act in which an adult uses a child or adolescent for his or her own sexual needs, whether it be through some form of intercourse, or through a less serious act, such as intentional touching of clothed breasts or genitals. Depending partly on the definition of sexual abuse, various surveys report that between 6 and 62 percent of women and between 3 and 31 percent of men have been sexually abused (Peters et al., 1986). Virtually every expert believes that the actual rates may be even higher than that, for many adults are reluctant to admit, even to themselves, that they were sexually abused as children. Memories of parents manually examining the child's genitals with great concern, or kissing the child's body in a prolonged, erotic manner, or intruding on the adolescent during bathing or dressing are likely to stir feelings of confusion and guilt, and thus not be recognized as indications of abuse—particularly by abused males who have been taught by the culture that men cannot be sexual victims (Hunter, 1990).

Typical Sexual Abuse

Given the difficulties of definition and reporting, it is difficult to describe typical abuse. However, as with other forms of maltreatment, the particular act is only one measure of the seriousness of the abuse. More important, in

---

* The age at which a victim of sex abuse is no longer considered a child ranges from 13 to 18 in the various states of the United States and 14 to 16 in Canada.

terms of developmental consequences, is whether the abuse is ongoing, and whether it interferes with normal development.

Unfortunately, sexual abuse typically meets both criteria: it usually evolves over a period of years, beginning with sexual fondling, explicit nudity, and teasing comments in childhood, and escalating during early adolescence with intercourse; and it distorts the young person's emerging sexuality. Overt force is seldom involved, because the perpetrator is usually someone who can easily dominate the child, typically a father, relative, or trusted family friend. The powerlessness of the child is particularly apparent when the victim is a pubescent girl and the perpetrator her own father.

While girls are the most common victims, increasingly it is recognized that boys are also often sexually abused. Compared to that of girls, sexual molestation of boys occurs more often outside the home and is committed by someone, most often a male, who is not a family member. In this regard, it is less devastating than the girl's incestual experiences. However, for sexually abused boys, added to the stigma of unwelcome sexual activity is shame at the idea of being weak, unable to defend oneself, and engaged in homosexual activities, all contrary to the macho image that many boys, especially young adolescents, strive to attain (Bolton et al., 1989). When the sexual abuse of a boy does occur at home, typically by the father or stepfather, the problems of vulnerability and self-esteem are multiplied.

Although mothers and other female relatives seem to be less often perpetrators of obvious sexual abuse, they are sometimes guilty of sexual teasing and fondling, especially of sons when the father is absent, that can evoke feelings of confusion, shame, and victimization (Hunter, 1990). However, with daughters as well as sons, mothers are often part of the problem in a different way, in that they fail to notice or to believe that sexual abuse is occurring, or fail to support and protect the child when the child reports it.

As with other manifestations of maltreatment, parents who are immature, socially isolated, alcoholic, or drug-abusing are much more likely to be sexually abusive, or so neglectful that their children are vulnerable to abuse from others. However, unlike other forms of maltreatment, parents of every income and level of education are well-represented among sexual abusers.

Consequences of Sexual Abuse

The psychological effects of sexual abuse depend largely on the extent and duration of the abuse, and on the reaction of other people—family as well as authorities—once the abuse is known. If the abuse is a single nonviolent incident, and a trusted caregiver believes and reassures the victim, taking steps to make certain the incident does not happen again, the psychological damage may last only a few days (Schlesinger, 1982). Even with abuse that is more serious, children and adolescents can be quite resilient if they are cared for with sensitivity, confidentiality, and respect.

If an adolescent is abused by a family member, if the problem is ongoing, and if psychological manipulation and humiliation are part of the pattern, much damage may occur before the abuse is uncovered. As Kempe and Kempe (1984) report, under these circumstances

> victims have a much higher than normal incidence of poor sexual adjustment and difficulties in sexual identity and preference. As teens they are likely to run away from an intolerable situation, become pregnant, get involved in delin-

quency such as theft and substance abuse (both alcohol and other drugs), engage in teenage prostitution and, as has been the experience for some of our clients, make a significant number of attempts at suicide. Some have, indeed, killed themselves . . .

From a developmental point of view, one of the most troubling long-term sexual abuse consequences of incest is that the young person may never learn what a normal adult-child or man-woman relationship should be. Studies have shown that female victims of sexual abuse may have a distorted view of sexuality, and thus are more likely to marry men who are abusive. If these men begin to abuse their daughters, the mother is less alert to the problem or feels trapped again, unable to help (Kempe and Kempe, 1984). In addition, adolescent victims of abuse, whether they are male or female, tend to become involved again in violent relationships, either as the abuser or the abused (Billingham and Sack, 1986; Bolton et al., 1989). Thus, in several ways, the effects of sexual abuse may be transmitted from generation to generation.

Prevention

Obviously, prevention of sexual abuse requires recognizing factors that foster sexual abuse and putting a stop to, or at least guarding against, them. As the table below reveals, these factors begin in the macrosystem—with cultural values and practices that encourage sexual feelings toward children—and continue at each level down to the microsystem of the family.

Not all these factors can be changed or controlled. One that can be changed, however, is the culture's values about sex and about children. Already, rising awareness of the problem of sexual abuse has increased public pressure against the eroticization of children and pubescent young people in pornography and advertising. In addition, certain preventive measures

---

Preconditions for Sexual Abuse of Children

1. *Adults must have sexual feelings about children.* Such feelings are encouraged by:

childhood sexual experiences;
exposure to child pornography;
exposure to advertising that sexualizes children;
male sex-role socialization that devalues nurturance and encourages sexual aggression;
"successful" adult sexual experiences with children.

2. *Adults must overcome internal inhibitions against abuse.* These inhibitions are weakened by:

cultural values that accept sexual interest in children;
low impulse control;
alcohol;
stress;
low self-esteem;
fear of, or frustration with, sexual relationships with adults;
values that emphasize father's unquestioned authority.

3. *Adults must overcome external inhibitions to committing*

sexual abuse. These obstacles to contact with a child are minimized by:

an absent, sick, or powerless mother;
a mother who is neglectful, unaware of her children's need for protection;
crowded living conditions or sleeping together;
opportunities to be alone with the child;
social isolation—family members have few friends;
geographical isolation—family has few nearby neighbors.

4. *Adults must overcome the child's resistance.* Overcoming this barrier is easier if the child is:

emotionally deprived;
socially isolated;
acquainted with the adult;
fond of the adult;
vulnerable to incentives offered by the adult;
ignorant of what is happening;
sexually repressed and sexually curious;
weak and frightened of physical force.

Source: Finkelhor, 1984.

can be established in the social institutions of the community. Since vulnerability is fostered by ignorance, sex education in the schools should begin at younger ages, and should include not just the specifics of biology but also discussion of appropriate relationships between adults and children, and between men and women. This may not only prevent young people from being victims; it may also help them become adults who would not permit abuse to occur. A related step would be to make teachers aware of the preconditions for, and the symptoms of, sex abuse, so they could be alert to help victims early on.*

Adolescent Suicide

One of the most perplexing problems that may occur in adolescence is suicide. From an adult's perspective, the teenager is just at the start of the many wondrous and exciting experiences that life offers. It seems inexplicable that a young person would end his or her life just as it is about to really begin. Yet about 1 adolescent in every 10,000 does that each year—triple the rate of twenty-five years ago.

As can be seen in Figure 16.12, the suicide rate between ages 15 and 19 is lower than half that for any subsequent age group. As an index of despair, however, this differential may be misleading, because it probably results from the higher failure rate of teenagers' suicide attempts. Further, many people who commit suicide as young adults were unsuccessful attempters as adolescents.†

Contributing Factors

What factors cause a young person to take his or her own life? Do adolescents who commit suicide differ in personality from normal adolescents or from disturbed nonsuicidal teenagers? And what circumstances drive a young person to the point of self-destruction? Answers to these questions are hard to arrive at. For one thing, obviously, information about suicide victims cannot be gotten directly: it must come from those acquainted with the victims, or be inferred from studies of adolescents who have failed in their attempts on their lives. The information from the former source, usually parents, may be tainted for several reasons, including grief, guilt, or a denial of, or blindness to, serious problems that may have existed. The data from the second source may also be faulty, for it simply may not be valid to generalize from studies of failed suicides to successful ones.

Allowing for these limitations in the study of teenage suicides, we can see certain rough patterns emerge from the research. Suicidal adolescents tend to be more solitary than normal adolescents and, compared with disturbed nonsuicidal adolescents, they show a greater tendency to be depressed, self-punishing, and emotional. Research has also shown that there

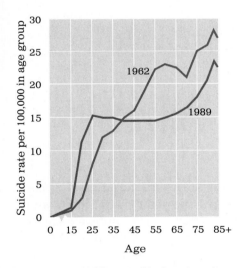

Figure 16.12 *A historical look at American suicide statistics reveals two trends. First, although their rate is still below that of adults, teenagers are three times as likely to take their own lives as they once were. Second, this increase in teen suicide is part of a lifespan trend. Whereas once suicide rates used to rise in middle age, recently young adults are more suicidal and older adults less so. Among the possible reasons are the facts that drug abuse and divorce rates have made early adulthood more problematic, and that better health care and pension plans have made the later years easier.*

---

* A national hotline, 1–800-422-4453, or 1-800-"4" A CHILD, is open day and night for questions and problems related to child abuse of any kind.

† Accurate statistics on attempted suicide in adolescence are hard to come by, because many attempts are hidden by embarrassed parents, and many apparent accidents may actually have been suicides. However, it is generally believed that adolescents attempt suicide at least as often as adults do.

A CLOSER LOOK   Warning Signs of Suicide

A number of warning signs should alert family and friends that a young person may be becoming dangerously overwhelmed with emotional difficulties and may be at increased risk of suicide (Curran, 1987):

1. *A sudden decline in school attendance and achievement, especially in students of better-than-average ability.* While about a third of the young people who attempted suicide had recently failed or dropped out of school, only 11 percent were in serious academic difficulty before their precipitous decline.

2. *A break in a love relationship.* This is the precipitating event for many adolescent suicides. The fact that such events are relatively common in adolescence sometimes blinds parents and teachers to the pain and depression they cause, especially in the egocentric young person who believes that the lost love is the only love he or she could ever have.

3. *Withdrawal from social relationships, especially if the adolescent seems no longer to care about social interaction.* The adolescent who decides that suicide is the solution sometimes seems less depressed than previously and may cheerfully say something to the effect of "It's been nice knowing you." A joking or serious "goodbye" accompanied by a sudden desire to be alone is a serious sign.

4. *An attempted suicide.* An attempted suicide, however weak it might seem, is an effort to communicate serious distress, and therefore must be taken seriously. If nothing changes in the adolescent's social world, an attempted suicide may turn out to have been a trial run for the real thing. Almost all adolescent suicides follow failed attempts.

5. *Cluster suicides.* Adolescents, given their egocentrism, are particularly likely to be influenced by knowing, or even reading about, another adolescent who committed suicide. Thus, whenever a suicide is publicized, concerned adults and adolescents need to be particularly sensitive to the more vulnerable young people in their midst (Davidson, 1986).

When such warning signs have been detected, they must be quickly acted upon. As Edwin Shneidman (1978) has written:

the act of suicide is an individual's effort to stop unbearable anguish or intolerable pain by doing "something." Therefore, the way to save a person's life is also to do "something," to put your knowledge of the person's plan to commit suicide into a social network—to let others know about it, to break the secret, to talk to the person, to talk to others, to offer help, to put action around the person, to show response and concern, and, if possible, to offer love.

Figure 16.13 *Suicidal adolescents may spend a lot of time alone with their own thoughts—especially despairing thoughts about life. This boy may merely be having a momentary reaction to an argument with his parents or a downturn in his love life. However, if he spends much of his time this way and has lost interest in his usual activities, these signs should be taken seriously.*

is usually no single event that triggers a suicide attempt; rather, it "occurs within the context of long-standing problems," one of the most prominent of which is chronic family conflict, characterized by "anger, ambivalence, rejection, and/or communication difficulties." However, while the problems are long-standing, the actual suicide attempt may be impulsive and thus unpredictable—another reason the long-standing problems need attention (Curran, 1987).

Professional help for suicidal adolescents and their families can often open up channels of communication that had been blocked by the self-absorption of the adolescent, and perhaps by the parents' insensitivity as well. One important goal of therapy is to keep expectations in line with reality. Parents often demand too much. As one pediatrician explains, "A lot of families expect that the minute the youngsters become thirteen or fourteen, they should be capable of making it on their own. In reality, teenagers probably need as much support at that point in their lives as toddlers need, although of a different sort" (Langone, 1981).

Conclusion

As this trio of chapters draws to a close, let us look again at the years from age 10 to 20. Except perhaps for the very first months of life, no other period is characterized by changes so multifaceted and inexorable. Nor is the developing person likely to experience a sequence of changes more fascinating, or more potentially confusing, than those that adolescents typically undergo. Their developmental tasks—to grow to adult size and sexuality, to adjust to different educational expectations and intellectual patterns, to develop autonomy from parents and intimacy with friends, to achieve a sense of identity and purpose—are too complex to be accomplished without some unanticipated surprises. No wonder every young person, in every family and culture, experiences some disruption (Barry and Schlegal, 1991).

As we have seen, most adolescents, most families, and most cultures survive this transition fairly well. Parents and children bicker and fight, but they still respect and love each other. In America, many teenagers skip school, eat unwisely, drink too much, experiment with drugs, break laws, feel depressed, rush sexual expression, conform to peer pressure, disregard their parents' wishes—but all these behaviors stay within limits. They do not occur too often or last too long; they do not lead to lifelong or life-threatening harm. For most young people, the teenage years overall are happy ones, as they escape serious problems and discover the rewards of maturity.

Unfortunately, while all adolescents have some difficulties, those with one serious problem seem to have several others as well (Dryfoos, 1990). For instance, girls who become teenage mothers also tend to be those from troubled families, likely to leave school and experiment with hard drugs before age 16. Boys who become repeat delinquents also tend to be alienated from their families, failing in school, drug-abusing, and lacking in close friends. Suicidal adolescents typically are heartbreakingly lonely, with inadequate social support, from family, friends, and school.

In almost every case, these clusters of problems stem from earlier developmental events, beginning with genetic vulnerability and prenatal insults and continuing with family disruptions and discord in early childhood and with learning disabilities and aggressive behavior in elementary school—all within a community that does not provide adequate intervention. With the inevitable stresses of puberty, such early handicaps become worse and more obvious, as well as more resistant to change. If these chronic patterns are not somehow altered, they are not "grown out of"; they persist into adulthood and begin to disrupt the development of the next generation, when those who should become responsible workers and nurturing parents are unable to do so.

Fortunately, an encouraging theme is apparent in all three adolescent chapters. No developmental trajectory is set in stone by previous events, and adolescents are, by nature, innovators, idealists, risk-takers, open to new patterns, goals, and lifestyles. Research on effective schools, on teenage drug programs, on the positive role of friendship, and on identity achievement shows that some individuals take a path distinct from the limitations and burdens of their past. For some of those who find adolescence sorrowful, humiliating, and problem-filled, the next stage of life—early adulthood—can be a time for growth, achievement, and fulfillment.

SUMMARY

Identity

1. According to Erikson, the psychosocial crisis of adolescence is identity versus role confusion. Ideally, adolescents resolve this crisis by developing a sense of both their own uniqueness and their relationship to the larger society, establishing a sexual, political, moral, and vocational identity in the process.

2. Sometimes the pressure to resolve the identity crisis is too great, and instead of exploring alternative roles, young people foreclose their options, establishing a premature identity. Other young people simply choose values and roles opposite to those expected by parents and society, thus forming a negative identity.

3. The process of identity formation depends partly on the society: if its basic values are consistent and widely accepted, and if social change is slow, the adolescent's task is fairly easy.

4. By contrast, in industrial and postindustrial societies, social change is rapid, and identity possibilities are endless. Consequently, identity achievement typically takes a decade or more and can be very difficult, especially for those—such as members of minority groups—who are caught between diverse cultural patterns.

Family and Friends

5. Parents are an important influence on adolescents: the generation gap within families is usually not very large, especially with regard to basic values. Children, especially daughters, tend not to stray too far from parental ideals, and parents have a personal stake in minimizing whatever conflicts there are.

6. The peer group is an important source of information and encouragement for adolescents. The adolescent subculture provides a buffer between the world of children and that of adults, allowing, for example, a social context for the beginning of heterosexual relationships.

7. Thus parents and peers are both important social influences on the adolescent, filling complementary rather then conflicting roles. However, especially as they grow older, adolescents spend much more time with peers (who usually listen to them) than with parents (who often tell them what to do). While most close friendships in early adolescence are from the same sex, by late adolescence friendships typically include members of the other sex.

Special Problems

8. While drug use is prevalent among every group of adolescents, hard drug use has gradually decreased among high school students throughout the 1980s and into the 1990s. Serious problems, however, persist with regard to the traditional social drugs—tobacco and alcohol. Frequent drug use impairs normal learning and social growth.

9. Information on the prevalence or seriousness of juvenile delinquency is difficult to come by. Law-breaking that could lead to arrest seems to be part of normal adolescence. Boys are four times more likely to be arrested as girls. Progress has been made toward identifying a child at risk for serious delinquency—those children who by age 10 have learning difficulties in school and significant stresses at home are more likely to become delinquents.

10. Adolescents react to maltreatment, such as psychological abuse, physical abuse, and neglect, with self-destruction or with counterattack. Sexual abuse is the type of maltreatment that most often affects adolescents. The most common types of sexual abuse occur between children and relatives and family friends. Patterns of family interaction may allow such abuse to continue over long periods of time. Abused children tend to develop distorted views of parent-child relationships and adult sexuality.

11. Most adolescent suicides are preceded by a long sequence of negative events, including family problems and breakdowns in family communication. Suicide prevention requires heeding the preliminary warning signs.

KEY TERMS

identity (412)	moratorium (413)
identity achievement (412)	generation gap (415)
foreclosure (412)	generational stake (418)
negative identity (412)	parental monitoring (420)
identity diffusion (413)	

KEY QUESTIONS

1. What are some of the difficulties adolescents might experience on the way toward identity formation?

2. Which parenting styles seem least helpful to adolescents?

3. What is the function of the peer group during adolescence?

4. What social and cultural characteristics tend to be associated with delinquency?

5. What family and social patterns are preconditions for sexual abuse of children?

6. What are some of the psychosocial and cognitive patterns that tend to be associated with adolescent suicide?

Biosocial Development

Physical Growth

Between the ages of 8 and 14, puberty begins with increases in male and female hormone levels. Within a year, the first perceptible physical changes appear—enlargement of the girl's breasts and the boy's testes. About a year later, the growth spurt begins. During adolescence, boys and girls gain in height, weight, and musculature. The growth that occurs during these years usually proceeds from the extremities to the torso and may be uneven.

Changes in Sex Organs and Secondary Sex Characteristics

Toward the end of puberty, menarche in girls and ejaculation in boys signals reproductive potential. On the whole, males become taller than females and develop deeper voices and characteristic patterns of facial and body hair. Females become wider at the hips; breast development continues for several years. Puberty that is early or late can be stressful.

Cognitive Development

Adolescent Thinking

Adolescent egocentrism, along with feelings of uniqueness and invincibility, often clouds teenagers' judgment. At the same time, many adolescents gradually become capable of formal operational thought, enabling them to understand and articulate general principles and hypotheses.

Education

The specific intellectual advancement of each teenager depends greatly on education. Each culture and each school emphasizes different subjects, values, and modes of thinking, a variation which makes some adolescents much more sophisticated in their thoughts and behavior than others. The interplay between education and egocentrism helps explain why some teenagers are at greater risk for STDs, AIDS, and pregnancy than others.

Psychosocial Development

Identity

One of the major goals of adolescence is identity achievement, which can be affected by personal factors—including relationships with family and peers—the nature of the society, and the economic and political circumstances of the times. Identity achievement can be especially problematic for members of a minority group in a multiethnic society.

Peers and Parents

The peer group becomes increasingly important in fostering independence and interaction with members of the other sex. Parents and young adolescents are often at odds over issues centering on the child's increased assertiveness or lack of self-discipline. These difficulties usually diminish as teenagers become more mature and parents allow more autonomy. While most adolescents try drugs, break the law, and sometimes get depressed, the small minority who have serious problems in these areas often come from a troubled family and a debilitating social context.

PART VI

Early Adulthood

As young children, we look forward to the day when we will be "all grown up," imagining that when we attain adult size, we will automatically master the roles, privileges, and responsibilities of adulthood. As young teenagers, we likewise impatiently await our high school graduation or 18th or 21st birthday, anticipating that independence, and the competence to cope with it, will be bestowed when we arrive at these "official" milestones.

But young adults, who must make their own decisions about career goals, intimate relationships, social commitments, and moral conduct, usually find these aspects of independence, though exciting, far from easy to deal with. This is especially true today because the array of lifestyle choices seems so vast and varied. No matter which of the roles of adulthood they choose to take on, or how thoughtfully and eagerly they strive to play them, they are bound to be confronted with stresses, set-backs, and second thoughts. Yet for most young adults, it is problems faced and usually solved, and limitations accepted or overcome, that make the decades from ages 20 to 40 an exhilarating period when people often feel they are living to the fullest. The next three chapters describe how many young adults cope with the engrossing, multidimensional realities of early adulthood.

CHAPTER 17

Early Adulthood: Biosocial Development

Young adults are in their prime biologically. They are full-grown, at full-strength, and are as able as they will ever be to physically do whatever they feel they want to do—from driving themselves full-tilt at work, to playing fiercely competitive sports, to having baby after baby. Illness is rare, and death from disease is even rarer. As you will learn, however, problems of their own making—with nutrition, with aggression, and with sexual activity—can impair normal biosocial development, sometimes curtailing and even cutting short the physical health and sexual-reproduction potential that should be a privilege attained by every young adult.

When and how does the aging process affect overall health?

How do muscles, skin, and body fat change during adulthood?

Do men and women experience similar changes in sexual responsiveness?

What is the best age to have a baby?

Why do many young adult women diet too much?

Why do many young adult men seem prone to violent death?

As we have seen again and again, cognitive and psychosocial development from birth through adolescence are closely tied to physical growth and maturation. Just as the exploration and autonomy of the toddler must await the development of walking, and the formal education of the schoolchild must await certain levels of brain maturation, so must many of the cognitive and psychosocial aspects of adolescence be preceded by the body growth and hormonal changes of puberty.

With the attainment of full maturity, human development is released from the constraints inherent in genetically programmed maturation. At the same time, however, a new aspect of development comes into play—**senescence,** or age-related decline, which in some cases begins even before maturation is complete. Each of the three chapters on adult biosocial development will, therefore, be centered on the declines that occur with age, but they will also emphasize a crucial fact: how people perceive changes that occur in their bodies over time, and what decisions they make regarding health habits and lifestyle, can have nearly as great an impact on the course of their overall development as the changes themselves.

In terms of physiological development, early adulthood can be considered the prime of life. Our bodies are stronger, taller, and healthier than during any other period. The first years of young adulthood (the early 20s) are the best ones for hard physical work, for problem-free reproduction, and for peak athletic performance. As we will see, although the advancing years of early adulthood are accompanied by some senescence throughout the body, whatever difficulties young adults experience in biosocial development are usually related to factors other than aging per se.

Growth, Strength, and Health

For most people, noticeable increases in height have stopped by the beginning of early adulthood, at about age 18 in females and 21 in males, although late-maturers can grow an inch or so during their 20s (Sinclair, 1989). Growth in muscle and increases in fat continue into the 20s, as the body fills out, women attaining their full breast and hip size, and men reaching their full shoulder and upper-arm size. Partially because of these increases, weight typically increases as well, especially during the early 20s. Before middle age, the average man adds 15 pounds, and the average woman, 14 pounds, to their weight at age 20 (U.S. Bureau of the Census, 1986). Women typically have a higher percentage of body fat and a lower metabolism than men do, a sex difference that increases throughout life (Striegel-Moore et al., 1986).

Since more of their body mass is comprised of muscle, men are typically stronger than women. For both sexes, however, physical strength, as evidenced in the ability, say, to run up a flight of stairs, lift a heavy load, or grip an object with maximum force, generally increases during the 20s, reaches a peak at about age 30, and then decreases (Sinclair, 1989). In terms of overall health, all the body systems, including the digestive, respiratory, circulatory, and sexual-reproductive systems, function at an optimum level during early adulthood. Visits to the doctor and days in the hospital are significantly lower for this age group than for later ages, and medical attention in early adulthood is more often necessitated by injuries (often drug- or sports-related) or by normal pregnancy than by disease. Even the common cold is less frequent in early adulthood than in any other part of the life span. Self-reports reflect this healthy state. Seventy-three percent of those in early adulthood rate their health as very good or excellent, and only 5 percent rate it as fair or poor (Public Health Service, 1990).

Correspondingly, death from disease is rare in early adulthood. Of the fatal diseases, cancer is the leading killer of young adults, yet the annual cancer death rate between ages 20 and 35 is less than 1 person in 10,000, compared with 16 per 10,000 between the ages of 45 and 54, and 108 per 10,000 over the age of 65. The data in Table 17.1 make especially clear the relatively low mortality rate that young adults have for disease overall (U.S. Bureau of the Census, 1992).

All told, then, most adults from age 20 to 40 are strong and healthy, with disability arising from personal actions rather than from the universal processes of aging. Nevertheless, many signs of aging are already apparent before middle age.

TABLE 17.1 Annual U.S. Death Rates from Disease and Chronic Conditions

Age	Deaths per 100,000 Americans
1–14	16
15–24	22
25–34	70
35–44	164
45–54	422
55–64	1,149
65–74	2,576
75–85	6,007
85+	14,747

Source: U.S. Bureau of the Census, 1992.

Age-Related Changes

By the late 20s, most people notice the first signs of aging in their physical appearance. Slight losses of elasticity in facial skin produce the first wrinkles, usually in those areas most involved in their characteristic facial expressions. As the skin continues to lose elasticity and fat deposits build up, the face sags a bit with age. Indeed, some people have drooping eyelids, sagging cheeks, and the hint of a double chin by age 40 (Whitbourne, 1985). Other parts of the body sag a bit as well, so as the years pass, adults need to exercise regularly if they want to maintain their muscle tone and body shape. Another harbinger of aging, the first gray hairs, is usually noticed in the 20s and can be explained by a reduction in the number of pigment-producing cells. Hair may become a bit less plentiful, too, because of hormonal changes and reduced blood supply to the skin.

Changes that are not so visible or obvious occur in every body system (Brooks and Fahey, 1984). As you can see in Figure 17.1, the efficiency of most body functions begins to decline in the 20s. The decline in efficiency proceeds at a somewhat different rate for each organ system, and is affected, too, by the individual's genetic makeup; however, in general, the body systems of the typical 40-year-old are already 20 percent less efficient than they were at age 20. Of course, lifestyle, especially exercise, can affect the rate of decline in every individual, making some 40-year-olds more physically fit than some 20-year-olds. (Health habits are discussed in Chapter 20.)

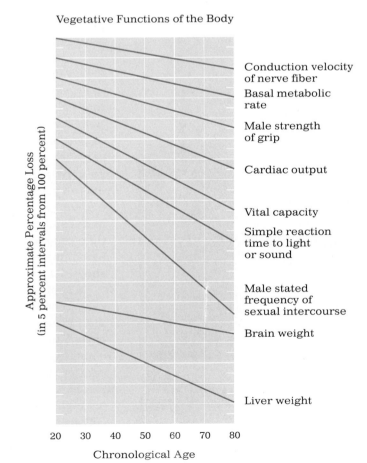

Vegetative Functions of the Body

Conduction velocity of nerve fiber

Basal metabolic rate

Male strength of grip

Cardiac output

Vital capacity

Simple reaction time to light or sound

Male stated frequency of sexual intercourse

Brain weight

Liver weight

Approximate Percentage Loss (in 5 percent intervals from 100 percent)

20   30   40   50   60   70   80

Chronological Age

Figure 17.1 *As this graph clearly shows, all body functions steadily decline after age 20. Fortunately, for reasons made clear in the next section, the effects of age-related physical declines are much less dramatic than one might imagine from a glance at these plot lines. In addition, this chart shows averages; individuals actually can do a great deal to change the rate, if not the direction, of physiological change.*

Figure 17.2 *As firefighters age, they are increasingly likely to die in the line of duty, but not because they are less able to cope with dangerous situations. Rather, sudden exertion and stress can put an overwhelming strain on an aging body, so the older they are, the more likely professional firefighters are to die of heart attacks than of burns or smoke-poisoning.*

Figure 17.3 *Declining physical strength is irrelevant in modern-day occupations, even in the steel industry, where brute strength and unflagging endurance were once essential. Today's hard-hatted steel workers can perform most of their jobs with their fingertips.*

Homeostasis

Many of our body functions serve to maintain **homeostasis;** that is, they adjust automatically to keep our physiological functioning in a state of balance, or equilibrium. For instance, when we are very active, our breathing and heart rate increase to bring us more oxygen. When we are hot, we sweat to give off body heat.

The older a person is, the longer it takes for these homeostatic adjustments to occur, making it harder for older bodies to adapt to, and recover from, physical stress (Brooks and Fahey, 1984). For example, even if a younger and an older player are otherwise equally matched in a sport that doesn't demand stamina, the older adult would need a longer warm-up period before the game, and more rest afterward, to allow heart rate, breathing, blood pH (acidity), and blood glucose (sugar) to return to normal. Similarly, older adults might have a harder time adjusting to work that is physiologically stressful. These changes become sufficiently apparent during early adulthood that the average 35-year-old might notice that he or she can no longer skip a night's sleep and still function adequately or can no longer bounce back the next day after a full day of unusually heavy exertion.

Organ Reserve

In bare outline, the declines of adult aging might seem steep. However, the actual experience of aging is usually much less perceptible than it might seem from looking at the graph in Figure 17.1. In day-to-day life, most adults of all ages feel that their bodies are quite strong and capable, not much different than they were ten years earlier.

In fact, for most of us, our bodies, if adequately maintained, are capable of functioning quite well until we are at least age 70. The reason is that the declines of aging primarily affect our **organ reserve,** the extra capacity that each organ has for responding to unusually stressful events or conditions that demand intense or prolonged effort (Fries and Crapo, 1981). In the course of normal daily life, however, we seldom have to call upon this extra capacity, and except for when we do, the deficits in organ reserve generally go unnoticed. Thus, while 50-year-olds are somewhat slower than 20-year-olds at, say, running up several flights of stairs, because the reserve capacity of their hearts and lungs is not as great as it once was, they move with ease in normal activity. In the same fashion, a woman in her late 30s might find that pregnancy puts measurable strain on her kidneys, or elevates her blood pressure, more than a pregnancy at an earlier age did, but that when she is not pregnant, these organs function very well.

There is a kind of muscle reserve as well, for few adults develop, or ever need to use, all the muscle capacity that they could develop during their years of peak strength. Whatever one's level of muscle development in early adulthood, maximum strength potential typically begins to decline at about age 30, but so gradually that 50-year-olds can expect to retain 90 percent of the strength they had at age 20, and the 10 percent that is lost is rarely missed (Hodgson and Buskirk, 1981). Consequently, among adults living in developed countries where hard manual work is not a daily necessity, a healthy 50-year-old can perform virtually all the tasks of everyday living as well as a 20-year-old and still have strength to spare.

The most important muscle of all, the heart, shows a similar pattern.

Figure 17.4 *Professional athletes are one of the few groups for whom the bodily declines of early adulthood may have significant consequences. Even here, however, the benefits of experience overcome many of the liabilities of advancing age. While Michael Jordan may have been a quicker basketball player in his late teens, at age 29 he and most other members of the Olympic "Dream Team" (average age 29) were at the peak of their careers.*

TABLE 17.2 Heart Functioning

	Decade of Life				
Average Maximum Heart Rate	20s	30s	40s	50s	60s
Men	195	190	182	175	162
Women	188	185	178	172	152
Average Resting Heart Rate					
Men	75	75	75	75	72
Women	72	72	72	72	70

The average maximum heart rate—the number of times the heart can beat a minute under extreme stress—declines steadily, as organ reserve is reduced with age. But the resting heart rate remains very stable, as Table 17.2 shows (Brooks and Fahey, 1984). Once again, while peak performance shows declines, this aspect of heart functioning for most of daily life is unaffected by aging until late adulthood.

Thus, most of the age-related biological changes that occur during the first decades of adulthood are of little consequence to the individual in the normal course of events, especially if the person develops a lifestyle that safeguards health. There are two notable exceptions. The first is athletic performance. Minor differences in strength, reaction time, and lung efficiency can have a notable impact on the ability of professional athletes, as well as on that of serious weekend players. However, for athletes, as for the rest of us, much depends on lifestyle and the willingness to adapt to changing abilities. Maintaining good health habits and a rigorous training schedule will enable many athletes to extend the years of their star performance (Lamb, 1984). Indeed, conditioned older athletes can perform so much better than most unconditioned younger persons that they should serve more as an inspiration than as an example of inevitable physical decline. Practiced marathoners in their 60s have run 26 miles at less than 8 minutes a mile, yet many sedentary 20- and 30-year-olds can't even run around the block.

The second exception involves changes in the sexual-reproductive system, changes that we will now discuss.

The Sexual-Reproductive System

The decades from 20 to 40 are the most likely time for adults to begin a long-term sexual relationship and to reproduce. The changes that occur in the sexual-reproductive system during this period have very little effect on sexual activity, but they can have a major impact with regard to the timing of parenthood.

Sexual Responsiveness

In both sexes, sexual responsiveness, sexual preferences, and sexual orientation vary for many reasons—innate predispositions, childhood experiences, and cultural norms and taboos among them. Age is also a factor, one that affects men and women somewhat differently.

During the early years of manhood, sexual excitement, which includes a faster heart beat and penile erection, can occur very quickly and frequently, in response to many things—even an idea, a photograph, or a passing remark. Typically, orgasm also occurs fairly quickly. For both young and older men, orgasm usually is followed by a refractory period during which sexual arousal is not possible, but for some young men, a second sexual cycle can regularly follow the first almost immediately.

As men grow older, they often need more direct or explicit stimulation to initiate the excitement phase. In addition, as men age, a longer time elapses between the beginning of excitement and full erection, between erection and ejaculation, and between orgasm and the end of the refractory period (Whitbourne, 1985). Nevertheless, age-related declines in sexual responsiveness are, for the most part, not a concern until middle or late adulthood. Indeed, for most men, frequency of sexual intercourse increases from adolescence until about age 30, because, although their sexual responses are somewhat diminished from when they were teenagers, they are more likely to have a steady sexual partner (Harman, 1978).

Age-related trends in sexual responsiveness are not as clear-cut for women as for men. In general, however, it seems that as they mature from early adolescence toward middle adulthood, women become more likely to experience orgasm during love-making rather than less likely (Sloane, 1985). Part of the reason for this may be that the slowing of the man's responses makes the sex act likely to last longer, providing the more prolonged stimulation that many women need to reach orgasm. Another possible explanation for women's increased sexual responsiveness during early adulthood may be that, with experience, both partners may be more likely to recognize and focus on those aspects of love-making that intensify the woman's sexual responses.

A third explanation is that the current generation of women between young and middle adulthood came of age in an era of increasing sexual awareness and openness. Learning about other people's sexual experiences on television talk shows, in mass-market magazines, and through conversations with friends leads many people to explore more of their own sexuality as they grow older. Consequently, research finding that women's sexual responses are heightened by maturity may actually be reflecting cohort differences rather than increasing sexual sensitivity with age.

Further complicating the developmental picture are notable differences between one couple and another (Turner and Adams, 1988). This variety overshadows any solid biological trends, so that, in terms of intensity and frequency, the sexual relationship of some young adult couples may resemble that of a typical couple three times their age, and vice versa. (The topic of age-related trends in sexual arousal is further detailed in Chapter 20.) However, one conclusion is clear: in terms of biological capacity for sexual expression, healthy young adults need not fear imminent decline.

Fertility

While young adults need not worry about the effects of aging on their capacity for sexual pleasure, the same does not hold true for the effects of aging on their reproductive potential. Nevertheless, most young couples, confident that they have ample time for starting a family, worry more about having children before they are ready than about not having children when they choose to do so. Theoretically, they are right: most women can still bear a first child as late as age 40, and most men can father a child throughout late adulthood. However, about 15 percent of all married couples discover that they are **infertile**—usually defined as being unable to conceive a child after a year or more of trying—and since many couples today are waiting until their 30s before trying to start their families, age is often a contributing factor to the problem. One specific statistic makes the point: about one couple in twenty is infertile when the woman is in her early 20s, whereas about one couple in seven has this problem when the woman is in her early 30s (Menken et al., 1986). It should be noted that, although fertility statistics are often based on the age of the woman, until middle age both sexes are equal contributors to fertility problems: in about 40 percent of the cases, the woman is the primary source; in another 40 percent, the man is the primary source; and in the remaining 20 percent, both partners are equally implicated or the source is unknown (Van Davajan and Israel, 1991).

Male Infertility

The most common fertility problem in men lies in the low number of their sperm or in the sperm's poor **motility**, or ability to swim quickly and far enough to reach an ovum. In order for a single, normal sperm to reach and fertilize an ovum, the mathematical probabilities of conception require that a man produce at least 20 million sperm per milliliter of ejaculate and that at least half of them be normal in shape and have normal motility (Van Davajan and Israel, 1991). For a number of reasons, including genital abnormalities, about 5 percent of young American adult males do not meet these requirements and therefore are infertile (Lipshultz and Howards, 1983). Most young men, however, have more than twice the required number of normal, motile sperm. As these men grow older, the number, shape, and motility of their sperm are adversely affected, but the declines are very gradual. Changes in sperm caused by normal aging usually do not result in sterility, but a man in middle age will probably require more attempts to impregnate a woman than he would have required in early adulthood.

Age is not the only factor that can affect sperm production in normally fertile men, however. Sperm grow in the testes, in tiny long tubes, over a period of seventy-four days. Thus, at any given moment, billions of sperm are in the process of development, and the lengthiness of this process increases the sperm's vulnerability. Anything that impairs normal body functioning, such as an illness with a high fever, or medical therapy involving radiation or a high dosage of prescription drugs, or exposure to environmental toxins, or unusual stress, or an episode of drug abuse, can affect the number, shape, and motility of the sperm for several months (Bardin, 1986; Newton, 1984). Although this type of impairment is not necessarily age-related, age might be a factor: since the incidence of illness rises with age, the chances of a man's fertility being periodically reduced also increase with age.

Female Infertility

One common fertility problem in women is difficulty with ovulation. A small percentage of women, perhaps 2 percent, do not ovulate naturally, no matter what their age. Most other women ovulate regularly once their menstrual period is well established by late adolescence, but find that ovulation becomes less regular as middle age approaches. There may be cycles with no ovulation, and other cycles when several eggs are released. Thus older women take longer to conceive, and they are more likely to have twins when they do. In addition, as we saw in Chapter 4, a woman is born with all the ova she will ever have, and with every passing year her ova become not only older but less fertile.

The other common fertility problem for women is blocked Fallopian tubes, often caused by pelvic infections—called **pelvic inflammatory disease, or PID**—that were not treated promptly. If a woman experiences one or more episodes of PID, she has about one chance in five of becoming sterile (Menken et al., 1986). Although blocked Fallopian tubes are not caused directly by age, if a woman is sexually active with a number of partners over a number of years, she obviously is more likely to get sexually transmitted diseases, such as gonorrhea or chlamydia, which can cause PID (Stanton and Dankel-Schetter, 1991).

Finally, if a woman has difficulty conceiving, it may be that she has **endometriosis,** a condition in which fragments of the uterine lining become implanted and grow on the surface of the ovaries or the Fallopian tubes, blocking the reproductive tract. Endometriosis is most common between the ages of 25 and 35, and about a third of those who have it are infertile (Van Davajan and Israel, 1991).

Age and Fertility

Because successful conception and pregnancy gradually become more difficult with each passing year, most physicians recommend that women begin their childbearing before age 35, and that men realize that fatherhood is less likely to occur once early adulthood is over. Nevertheless, it is important not to exaggerate the relationship between age and infertility. While age is one factor, it rarely is the primary cause until middle age. Many adults who postpone parenthood until their 30s and then find conception difficult to achieve might have had the same problem if they had tried to have a baby ten years earlier (Menken et al., 1986).

Further, many fertility problems can be solved by modern medical techniques. Minor genital abnormalities that cause infertility in the male are often correctable through surgery. Alternatively, a man with a low sperm count can store his sperm over a period of days, and then his partner can be artificially inseminated with sufficient sperm for conception to occur. In women, an inability to ovulate can usually be treated with drugs to stimulate ovulation. Blocked Fallopian tubes can often be opened surgically.

Many of these problems can also be overcome by recent technological innovations. In **in vitro fertilization (IVF),** for example, ova are surgically removed from the ovaries and fertilized by sperm in the laboratory. The resulting embryos are then inserted into the uterus to await implantation (or are sometimes frozen for later use). This technique, experimental in 1978 when the first "test tube" baby was born, is now widely available, with a success rate of about one baby in seven attempts. Two recent variations of IVF, GIFT (gamete intra-Fallopian transfer) and ZIFT (zygote intra-Fallopian transfer), which involve inserting either sperm and unfertilized ova (gametes) or fertilized ova (zygotes) into a Fallopian tube, and have success rates of about one in five attempts.

Figure 17.5 *Although they obviously differ in age, brothers David and Nicholas might be called "twins," since they were conceived at the same time. Because their mother had a blocked Fallopian tube that prevented normal conception, the boys' parents turned to IVF. One of the embryos that resulted from the procedure (David) was used immediately; another embryo (Nicholas) was kept frozen and then used about a year later.*

In addition, all these innovations make possible, when needed, a variety of "third-party" contributions—donor sperm, donor ova, even donor wombs. It is now even possible, among other revolutionary possibilities, for a postmenopausal woman to carry a pregnancy conceived through the artificial insemination of a donor ova by her husband's sperm.

Obviously, these alternative paths to reproduction raise profound legal and ethical questions, not the least of which is why couples should go to great lengths to have their own (or partially their own) biological offspring in a world where millions of unwanted newborns seem destined to suffer neglect and abuse. Socioeconomic inequalities make the question even more complicated, for a birth achieved through one of these fertilization technologies typically costs between $10,000 and $50,000 and is rarely covered by insurance. Consequently, a couple's ability to have a child by these methods is based as much on their income as on their desire for pregnancy.

These questions are made all the more pointed by the fact that infertility treatment is not always necessary or helpful. About a third of all infertile couples who remain untreated eventually have a baby, and about half the couples who are treated never do. Further, treatment itself has psychological as well as financial costs, making it more difficult and painful for the individual to accept his or her barrenness. People who spend years of their lives and thousands of dollars on medical measures without success often find their marital relationship sorely strained and their self-concept badly damaged (Dunkel-Schetter and Lobel, 1991).

As with every developmental problem, the best strategy is to try to prevent its occurrence in the first place. Since a major contributor to infertility is STDs, this means practicing safe sex and seeking prompt treatment of sexually transmitted diseases from the moment a young person becomes sexually active. Further, individuals who feel strongly that parenthood is important to their life should probably try to begin childbearing before age 30, when fertility is more likely. If a couple has unprotected intercourse during every ovulation for six months or more without conception, early consultation with a fertility clinic, and perhaps a genetic counselor, will improve the chances of their success. Beginning this entire process relatively soon in adulthood also speeds acceptance of failure, allowing a couple to adopt several children before middle age, if that is what they choose.

Three Troubling Problems

Although the picture of physical development and health in early adulthood has been fairly sanguine so far, it, of course, is not trouble-free for all young adults. A number of diseases that commonly appear in middle or late adulthood—such as cancer, cirrhosis of the liver, coronary heart disease—may have already gotten a toehold in early adulthood, although the symptoms are not yet apparent. The course of these diseases, and of physical development generally, is substantially affected by the individual's lifestyle, and in Chapter 20 we will examine the overall systemic impact of such lifestyle factors as cigarette smoking, years of heavy alcohol consumption, nutrition, exercise, and stress. In this section we will address three problems that are more prevalent in early adulthood than at any other stage—drug abuse, destructive dieting, and violent death.

A LIFE-SPAN PERSPECTIVE

Drug Abuse

Drug abuse—defined as any drug use that impairs one's physical, cognitive, or social well-being—is a topic that touches every point in the life span. To begin with, many of the factors influencing drug abuse start early in life. Indeed, at the moment of conception, genetic interactions begin to shape one's propensity for, and response to, any given drug, from a physician's prescription to a pusher's latest product.

As we saw in Chapter 3, the role of heredity in drug abuse has been most clearly demonstrated in connection with alcohol, the drug most often abused. Part of the genetic vulnerability to alcohol abuse is directly biochemical, in the physiological tolerance of, and response to, alcohol. Other aspects of alcoholism are related to heritable personality traits, among them a powerful attraction to excitement, a low tolerance for frustration, and a vulnerability to depression. These same traits make a person susceptible to almost any mood-altering drug, especially cocaine, which is one reason that many drug abusers become multidrug users before they realize they are vulnerable to psychoactive drugs in general, not just to one specific substance (Winger et al., 1992; Miller and Gold, 1991; Cadoret, 1992; Bardo and Mueller, 1991).

Of course, the likelihood of a person's abusing alcohol or other drugs in adulthood is affected not just by genetics but also by gender, family upbringing, and cultural context. For example, a person who was an easy-going, confident child raised in a warm and stable family, and who lives in a culture that promotes moderation or abstinence regarding drug use, is unlikely to become a drug abuser, especially if that person is female. On the other hand, a person who was a hostile child with low self-esteem raised in a discordant, drug-abusing family, and who lives in a culture that implicitly encourages and glamorizes drug use, is a prime candidate for becoming a substance abuser, especially if that person is male (Kaplan and Johnson, 1991).

The effects of drug abuse are likewise apparent at every stage of the life span. As we have already seen at various points in this text, the fetus may suffer brain and body damage if the mother is an alcoholic or drug abuser; children of any age are at higher risk of maltreatment if their parents are drug users; and adolescents may put themselves at risk by using mind-altering substances. Throughout adulthood, too, drug abuse impairs cognitive processes and distorts motivation, resulting in any number of interpersonal problems, from spouse abuse and broken families to job loss and criminal behavior. And, as we will see in Chapter 24, drug misuse can have particular consequences for many of the aged, who may be dismissed as being senile when, in fact, they are suffering from a drug reaction, sometimes involving a combination of prescription drugs but more often involving abuse of a social drug. Indeed, adults never lose the potential for addiction, as shown by one 68-year-old man who, with no history of alcoholism or drug abuse, tried crack cocaine one night after his wife had berated him for playing cards. At first he used the drug occasionally and moderately, but then blew $200 on it in a single evening, felt "out of control," and sought treatment (Woody et al., 1992).

Of all the stages of life, however, the beginning of young adulthood is the time when problem drinking and illicit drug use are not only most common but also most likely to result in serious harm to many people. The widespread substance abuse during this stage, shown by many longitudinal as well as cross-sectional studies, generally increases steadily each year from early adolescence through early adulthood, peaking at about age 23 and then gradually declining throughout the rest of adulthood (Clayton, 1992). For example, a nationwide cross-sectional study found that, for both sexes and every ethnic group, those between the ages of 18 and 25 were most likely to use both alcohol and illicit drugs than were people of the same gender and ethnicity who were older or younger (see Table 17.3). Interactions between gender and age are especially noteworthy: females are less likely to be polydrug users, and their drug use is particularly likely to peak at about age 20 and then dip dramatically by the late 20s.

Why the high rate of drug use and abuse in the first years of adulthood? There seem to be at least four reasons:

1. Many young adults are in transition between families, becoming increasingly independent of their family of origin but not yet established in a family of their own. In fact, for some young adults, drug abuse is a way of striving for independence from parents, even to the point of forcing the parents to push them away (Stanton, 1985). Being single, as most young adults are, correlates with drug and alcohol abuse.

2. A number of life stresses—completing an education, finding a mate, establishing a career—cluster during the 20s. Many people abuse alcohol and other drugs in an effort to escape these stresses, if only for the moment (Yost and Mines, 1985).

TABLE 17.3 Percent Using Alcohol and Illicit Drugs Simultaneously

	Age Range			
	12–17	18–25	26–34	35 and older
Males				
White	9	24	18	3
Black	7	20	17	8
Hispanic	7	18	17	3
Females				
White	9	21	11	1
Black	5	14	8	4
Hispanic	4	10	4	1

Source: National Institute of Drug Abuse, 1988.

3. The need to feel sexually attractive and fulfilled is often very intense during these years, as is the fear of social rejection and sexual unresponsiveness. Many young adults believe that alcohol and other drugs enhance sexual responses, and take them for that reason. In fact, moderate use of most psychoactive drugs does lift inhibitions, and for certain people, certain drugs have the momentary effect of intensifying almost any feeling, including lust. But, for the most part, the connection between drugs and heightened sexuality is more myth than reality, more in the distorted perceptions and wishful thinking of the drug user than in the functioning of the sexual organs. Indeed, heavy drug use diminishes, and sometimes even eliminates, sexual responsiveness and potency (Kolodny, 1985).

4. Young adults are the group least likely to be regularly exposed to one of the most powerful factors halting drug and alcohol abuse —religious faith and practice (Brunswick et al., 1992; Jessor et al., 1991). Only about half of all adults in their 20s attend religious services, a significantly smaller representation than that of older adults.

5. The social surroundings of many young adults encourage alcohol and drug use. For example, compared to older adults, those in their 20s are more likely to frequent bars, clubs, large parties, sports events, and huge concerts, are more likely to be away from home at college or in the military, and are more likely to live in large urban areas. In these contexts, drugs are more accessible than in society as a whole, and their use is more accepted and even expected, increasing pressure on the individual to "go with the flow." Especially influential is the immediate friendship circle: a careful longitudinal study found that the single most important factor encouraging drug abuse among young adults—even more important than life stress, temperament, and personal attitudes— was having friends who used drugs (Jessor et al., 1991). Such friends are more plentiful at the beginning of adulthood than earlier or later, particularly for women, who typically find that motherhood narrows their social circle considerably before age 30.

Does drug abuse in early adulthood signal a lifetime of addiction? Not usually (Woody et al., 1992). Although some individuals, with some drugs, can become "hooked" very quickly, compulsive drug dependency more often occurs after years of abuse. The lengthiness of the addiction process allows most abusers to get control of their drug excesses before addiction sets in. Most young adults who drink to drunkenness or who abuse illicit drugs gradually realize that such behavior is destructive and curtail or eliminate it.

In the meantime, however, many young drug abusers do themselves or others serious harm. Sometimes the drug itself proves lethal. Rapid ingestion of large amounts of alcohol (as a young adult might attempt on a dare) can produce unconsciousness, coma, and death, and even one-time use of cocaine can cause a massive heart attack (Winder et al., 1992). Drug-overdose deaths have increased over the past two decades, particularly for young adults. While such deaths are still quite

Figure 17.6 *For some young adults, social camaraderie demands abuse of alcohol and other drugs. These fraternity brothers are playing a card game—one of many that require the losers to consume so much beer that some will throw up or pass out, perhaps later to brag about becoming "smashed," "plastered," or "blasted." In such circumstances, alcohol becomes not only a social facilitator but a dangerous drug.*

rare, drug-related accidental injuries are not. In fact, drug use is implicated in most single-car crashes, homicides, and suicides involving young adults, as well as in many accidents that involve innocent victims. For example, only 14 percent of the licensed drivers in the United States are between the ages of 18 and 24, but this age group is responsible for 30 percent of the nation's fatal drunk-driving accidents, causing an estimated 6,500 deaths in 1990 (U.S. Bureau of the Census, 1992; Centers for Disease Control, 1992).

Even if drug abuse in young adulthood does not lead to addiction or serious injury, it nonetheless can take a serious toll on development. The ability to master the developmental tasks of young adulthood—getting an education, finding a suitable career, establishing lifelong friendships and love relationships—is impaired by the irrationality, social misjudgment, and eventual isolation that heavy drug use entails. Even occasional drug abuse often leads to missing some school or work, decline in productivity and learning ability, and mistreatment of sexual partners, close friends, or family members. The conclusion for all young adults is that their age puts them at risk, and that the sooner they recognize an alcohol or other drug problem in themselves or their friends, the sooner they will be able to treat the problem and get on with their lives.

Dieting as a Disease

The processes of homeostasis work to maintain body weight just as they do to maintain sufficient oxygen in the blood or normal body temperature. Obvious mechanisms such as pangs of hunger and the feeling of fullness, and less obvious ones such as fluctuations in hormonal levels and neurotransmitter activity, regulate the urge to eat. Healthy and active adults and children tend to "automatically" consume sufficient calories to maintain their required energy level. In addition, many scientists now believe that each person has a certain "set point" for his or her weight, that is, a general weight that the body strives to maintain (Schlundt and Johnson, 1990). Each person's particular set point is determined by factors such as heredity, age, gender, childhood eating habits, and exercise levels.

Cultural pressures and personality patterns can undermine this tendency toward biological balance, however. A prime example is the present trend in the United States and other Western nations toward an ideal of feminine beauty that is virtually "fat-free"—a trend that has promoted the quest for an elusive and unreasonable thinness and turned that quest into a "cultural obsession" and a "current epidemic" (Gordon, 1990). A national survey of 15,000 American women, for example, found that 44 percent of those between the ages of 17 and 60 were dieting at that moment, as were 29 percent of those aged 60 and older. On average, they hoped to lose 30 pounds—a goal that, if attained, would make most of them underweight (Williamson et al., 1992).

As a result of this cultural obsession, millions of women share a self-defeating set of circumstances—feeling fat, reading diet books, dieting, doing spot exercises, losing weight, and then repeating this cycle again and again, because the vast majority who lose weight by dieting eventually regain all the weight they lost and more. Most often, this is because repeated or extensive weight loss alters the metabolism in such a way that the body, as though protecting itself from starvation, begins to maintain its weight on fewer calories, so that "even normal eating after dieting may promote weight gain" (Stregel-Moore et al., 1986).

Indeed, most women, dieting or not, normally gain weight over the years of adulthood, and although "lean and mean" has become touted as the sure way to good health, gradual weight gain over the decades of adulthood is not unhealthy for most women. Indeed, while even 10 pounds of extra body fat may be unhealthy for men, "there is no evidence that being a little fat is any kind of health hazard" for women (Sloane, 1985). In fact, for women, thinness is more disruptive of normal development: insufficient fat halts the natural hormonal rhythms that are the hallmark of healthy womanhood, making menstruation irregular and reproduction difficult or impossible (Hsu, 1990).

Not only is strict leanness uncalled for in terms of good health, but repeated dieting can be very unhealthy as well as counterproductive. This is especially true when it involves crash diets, which nearly all result in nutritional imbalance and sometimes can lead to death. In addition, if the long-term pattern of weight-watching becomes a yo-yo pattern of dieting losses followed by substantial gains, this can put significant strain on the heart—much more than maintaining a steady elevated weight does.

For many dieters, the health consequences are even more deleterious when, frustrated, guilty, or depressed at having their best efforts "sabotaged" by their body's natural chemistry, they become dependent on diet drugs. Women are particularly likely to abuse illegal or prescribed stimulants that work for a few weeks until tolerance builds, requiring the person to quit or become hooked, or to rely on over-the-counter appetite suppressants which can produce such side effects as insomnia, tenseness, anxiety, and, in megadoses, psychosis. Young women are also more likely than

Figure 17.7 *The image in this trick mirror may be closer to the young woman's own sense of her body than what she sees when she views herself in a true mirror. At some point, almost every young woman in today's developed nations considers herself too fat, even though far more young women are dangerously thin than are unhealthily overweight.*

young men to smoke in order to suppress appetite and relieve depression, running such well-known long-term risks as cancer, heart disease, and emphysema (Hsu, 1990; Johnson and Conners, 1987).

For some dieters, the problem becomes even worse, as dieting triggers physiological changes that lock them into an eating disorder, creating an addiction no less powerful or shameful to the addict than alcoholism or heroin (Gordon, 1990). One such problem is **anorexia nervosa**, an affliction characterized by self-starvation, sometimes to the point of death. Typically, a high-achieving girl who is in early puberty or early adulthood restricts her eating so severely that she weighs a bony 80 pounds or less, still exercising and complaining about being fat. To an observer, the anorexic's obsessive, irrational, and dangerous thinking is even more horrifying than his or her emaciated body. Much more common, especially among young adults, is the other major eating disorder of our time, **bulimia nervosa,** which involves compulsive binge eating followed by purging through vomiting or taking massive doses of laxatives. While people who suffer from bulimia are usually close to normal in weight and therefore unlikely to starve to death, they can experience a wide range of serious health problems, including severe damage to the gastrointestinal system and cardiac arrest from the strain of electrolyte imbalance (Hsu, 1990). College women are at particular risk for eating disorders (depending on the college, between 12 and 22 percent of women students are sometimes bulimic), and college athletes—who, in theory at least, should be most concerned about health and fitness—are even more vulnerable to eating disorders than women in general (Guthrie, 1991; Cohn and Adler, 1992; Pertschuk et al., 1986; Pope et al., 1984).

Intertwined with the physical consequences of excessive dieting are the psychological ones, including low self-esteem and depression, which can act as a stimulus for an eating disorder and then as a reason to continue this destructive pattern. Fasting, binging, and purging "have powerful effects as immediate reinforcers—that is, in relieving states of emotional distress and tension" (Gordon, 1990). The result is that the person becomes enmeshed in an increasingly destructive and addictive cycle, usually requiring outside intervention—individual psychotherapy or group therapy (such as Overeaters Anonymous)—to break the chains of depression and dieting, binging and purging. Without help, the problem can get very serious, not only causing the physical damage outlined above but also creating a despair so severe that it can lead to suicide (Johnson and Conners, 1987).

Why do women torture themselves so with eating habits that are contrary to health and happiness? The most obvious explanation is, as outlined above, the cultural pressure to meet the current, and arbitrary, "slim and trim" female ideal, a pressure exerted particularly on unmarried young women seeking autonomy from their parents' nurturance. Other possible explanations range from the psychoanalytic theory that women with eating disorders have a conflict with their parents, who provided their first nourishment, to the more sociological explanation that, as women enter the workplace, they try to project a strong, self-controlled, masculine image.

No matter what the explanation, it seems clear that for many of today's young women, "dieting is a disease" (Herman and Poliby, 1987), and that during the young adult years when women are supposed to be at their peak, many jeopardize their health with distorted ideas of how their bodies should appear.

Although young men worldwide are more likely to engage in unnecessary bravado and irrational risk-taking than young women or older adults are, the chances of a particular young man dying a violent death, and the specific type of death he risks, depend on many factors within him and within his family, neighborhood, and culture. Maleness is much more hazardous to some men in some social settings than in others.

This variability is apparent in international comparisons of homicide rates (see figure). One reason for these differences is the variation in cultural ideals of what constitutes a "real man," variations that can, for example, encourage young men to master the art of gentlemanly compromise or propel them to exhibit an uncompromising macho facade. Family discipline techniques, school curricula, television heroes, religious values, and alcohol availability also vary markedly from nation to nation and from subculture to subculture, and these differences have obvious effects on how predisposed young men are to various expressions of violence.

An additional contextual factor frequently cited for the variation in homicide rates, and especially for the extremely high rates of homicide among American young men, is the availability of firearms. There are an estimated 60 million guns distributed throughout the United States (an average of one per family), with almost 3 million more being purchased every year (Centers for Disease Control, 1992). While some argue that "guns don't kill people, people kill people," public-health and law-enforcement experts emphasize that the presence of a gun often transforms nonlethal aggressive impulses into deadly ones (Centers for Disease Control, 1992).

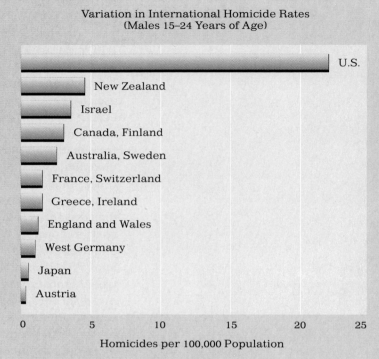

Variation in International Homicide Rates
(Males 15–24 Years of Age)

U.S.
New Zealand
Israel
Canada, Finland
Australia, Sweden
France, Switzerland
Greece, Ireland
England and Wales
West Germany
Japan
Austria

0   5   10   15   20   25
Homicides per 100,000 Population

Source: National Center for Health Statistics, World Health Organization, and country reports for 1986–1987.

Research tends to verify this. Consider the violent-death statistics in the mid-1980s from two demographically, economically, and geographically similar cities in the Pacific Northwest—Seattle, Washington, and Vancouver,

Violent Death

Just as contemporary notions about "feminine" appearance may promote the excessive dieting and eating disorders that afflict many young women, stereotypes about "manly" behavior may lead to a problem that afflicts mostly young men—**violent death,** that is, death from accident, homicide, or suicide.

Indeed, relative to all other age groups, young adult males are at increased risk for virtually every kind of violent death, from car crashes to gang shoot-outs, from jumping off roofs to overdosing on drugs. More specifically, between his 15th and 35th birthday, one American male in every forty-four dies violently. Such deaths are most likely to involve young men in their early 20s, who are four times more likely to die violently than women the same age.

British Columbia. The data reveal that the residents of Vancouver were no less aggressive than those of Seattle: both cities had similar rates of violent assault and similar rates of arrest, conviction, and punishment. However, murder in Seattle was almost twice as common as in Vancouver (Sloane et al., 1988). The most likely explanation for this disparity lies in the relative prevalence and legality of guns: Seattle had no restrictions on gun ownership or use—except the need for a permit to carry a loaded, concealed weapon on public property—while in Vancouver, gun possession was severely curtailed.

Gun availability also seemed to affect suicide rates. Overall suicide rates were similar in the two cities, but fewer young men killed themselves in Vancouver than in Seattle. The researchers suggest that, for the youthful Canadians, not having a gun at hand allowed time for self-destructive impulses to subside before it was too late, while their armed, suicide-prone peers sixty miles southward had no such buffer (Sloane et al., 1990).

Within nations, violent death varies by subgroup, largely because of cohort, ethnic, and socioeconomic forces. For example, overall, African-Americans are less likely to kill themselves than European-Americans are, a racial disparity that increases with age to the point that, among 80-year-olds, the white rate is five times that of blacks. In general, the suicide rate of young Native Americans is well above the national rate, and that of Hispanic-Americans is well below it, although marked differences occur within specific tribes and Latino subgroups (Centers for Disease Control, 1992). Among the reasons for these differences are that, compared to European-Americans, African-Americans tend to have more extensive family and friendship networks, which helps protect against the sense of isolation that is typically a precondition to suicide. Further, the suicide rates for Hispanic-Americans and Native Americans are partly explained by religious influences: the Catholic tradition of most Hispanic-Americans holds suicide to be a mortal sin, whereas in some Native American traditions, suicide can be an honorable act.

Another notable ethnic variation in violent death is that homicide is the leading cause of death for young African-American men, while among European-American men, accidents are the number-one cause. The reason is primarily economic: white young men are more likely to be middle-class and living in the suburbs, and hence are more likely to own and drive cars—a potentially dangerous tool in the hands of a young man. By contrast, the conditions of daily life for many young black men include survival in the inner city—overcrowded, crime-torn, drug-infested, and job-poor—where violent impulses often intensify to the breaking point, turning even minor disagreements between friends into deadly confrontations (Centers for Disease Control, 1992; Wilson, 1987). Indeed, a black 10-year-old male has one chance in twenty-one of being murdered before reaching old age.

Whatever the economic, cultural, or other explanations for national and ethnic differences in violent death, one thing is clear: it is not maleness per se that puts a young man at risk. Instead, it is a lethal combination of biological maleness and cultural values, encouraging young men to act, or not act, in ways that carry the risk of death.

Values and Violence

According to James Harrison, who titled his critique "Warning: The Male Sex Role May Be Dangerous to Your Health," the explanation for this propensity toward an untimely violent end lies in prevailing cultural concepts of masculinity, including that men need to "give 'em hell" with "no sissy stuff," a notion that leads many young adult males to put themselves and others at deadly risk in a wide variety of contexts (Harrison, 1984).

Miriam Miedzian, another social scientist, goes deeper into the fundamental causes of masculine violence, suggesting that the tendency of young men to perpetrate and to suffer harm is due to a cascade of biosocial factors (Miedzian, 1991). Among these are factors that influence every young man, such as higher testosterone levels, and less common ones that nevertheless affect males disproportionately, such as dyslexia, attention-deficit disorder with hyperactivity, and certain genetic abnormalities. In addition, cultural and familial factors, including child maltreatment, divorce, movie and television violence, the glorification of war, and the lure of drug abuse all seem to promote destructive behavior in males more than females.

In the final analysis, however, both Miedzian and Harrison agree that social values are at the root of the problem. A society that turns positive masculine tendencies such as courage, independence, and competitiveness (all of which might have an evolutionary biological base) into such negative male traits as recklessness, callousness, and "an egocentric and often obsessive need to be dominant and to win" is bound to suffer violent consequences. Young men taught to avoid being a wimp or a sissy at all costs will eventually pay a price (Miedzian, 1991).

Living up to a tough-guy image, for example, makes it hard for a young man to back down from a confrontation, to back away from a dangerous challenge, or to admit that he needs help—especially emotional help—even if so doing would remove him from a life-threatening situation. Of course, cultural and familial influences make it much harder for one man to seek help than another (see Research Report, pp. 458–459).

It should be noted that gender is not necessarily protective for any of these three troubling problems: many young women die of violence, many young men develop abnormal eating habits, and many young adults of both sexes abuse drugs. However, it certainly seems true that all three hazards spring partly from cultural pressures to fit a particular gender stereotype, and that these pressures affect men and women in divergent ways.

Given the grimness of the three troubling problems we have been considering, we should end this chapter with a reminder that all the self-destructive behaviors just discussed are evident in only an unfortunate minority of young adults. Most young people, no matter what their ethnic group, economic status, or gender, manage the transition from adolescence to adulthood well and pass through their early adulthood healthy and robust. As we will see in the next two chapters, although early adulthood is not easy, most young people become increasingly capable of understanding and coping with their lives during their prime years.

Figure 17.8 *Running with the bulls in Pamplona, Spane, is one of thousands of public events worldwide that idealize and ritualize the urge of young males to confront danger. In some situations, the risk is largely symbolic, but too often it becomes shockingly real: in every nation, far more men between ages 18 and 30 are killed by accident than by any other cause, often in some conscious or unconscious test of manhood.*

SUMMARY

Growth, Strength, and Health

1. While young adults do not grow significantly taller in their 20s, they typically grow stronger and fuller as their bodies reach adult size. In terms of overall health, as well as peak physical condition, early adulthood is the prime of life.

Age-Related Changes

2. With each year from 20 to 40, all the body systems gradually become less efficient—losing about 20 percent of their efficiency over that time span—and homeostasis takes increasingly longer to reach.

3. However, because of organ reserve, none of these changes is particularly troublesome or even noticeable for most people most of the time. Even athletic performance, while slowed somewhat, can remain at a high level.

The Sexual-Reproductive System

4. As middle age approaches, the speed of sexual responses slows down in men, but not in women. These modest declines usually have no negative effect on the man's sexual experiences, and, in some cases, they may enhance the woman's experience.

5. When they reach their early 30s, about 15 percent of all couples have fertility problems. One common reason is that the man's sperm are insufficient in quantity or motility. Another common problem is that the woman's ova do not reach the uterus because the Fallopian tubes are blocked, or because ovulation itself does not occur.

6. The normal aging process is rarely the primary cause of infertility in the two decades of early adulthood, but age can be a contributing factor. While most couples can conceive a child even in their early 40s, those who have fertility difficulties should get medical assistance early so that the age-related declines in the reproductive system do not make existing problems worse.

Three Troubling Problems

7. Young adults are more likely to use alcohol and illicit drugs than are people of any other age, often doing themselves or others serious harm.

8. Eating disorders are also more common during young adulthood than at other ages, as some young women feel a compulsion to be thinner than their bodies naturally tend to be.

9. Suicide, homicide, and fatal accidents are a serious problem for young adults, especially for young men in American society. The reasons are at least as much cultural as biological, as revealed by ethnic differences in the rates of these three causes of violent death.

KEY QUESTIONS

1. In what specific ways is early adulthood the prime of life?

2. How is the physical performance of a 20-year-old athlete likely to be different from that of a 40-year-old?

3. As a person ages, what are the changes that occur in organ reserve? How do these changes affect a person's activities?

4. What are some of the factors that tend to diminish fertility toward the end of early adulthood?

5. What can be done to prevent and remedy the main causes of infertility?

6. Why are young adults particularly susceptible to drug use and abuse?

7. How can concern about being fat become a health hazard?

8. What are the sex differences in the rate of violent deaths, and how do you explain them?

KEY TERMS

senescence (443)
homeostasis (446)
organ reserve (446)
infertile (449)
motility (449)
pelvic inflammatory
   disease (PID) (450)

endometriosis (450)
in vitro fertilization (IVF)
   (450)
drug abuse (452)
anorexia nervosa (457)
bulimia nervosa (457)
violent death (458)

CHAPTER 18

Early Adulthood: Cognitive Development

In early adulthood there are many catalysts to cognitive growth: the challenges of higher education, the responsibilities of work and parenthood, and (perhaps most important) the personal dilemmas and inconsistencies of everyday life. As a result, cognitive development during the adult years becomes more practical, integrative, and resourceful—by contrast with the abstract and absolute reasoning that typifies formal operational thinking. Cognitive growth opens the young adult to new ways of thinking and reasoning about life experiences, but also may introduce greater relativism and doubt about one's beliefs. In exploring this developmental process, we will pose the following questions:

Is there a stage of cognitive development beyond Piaget's formal operational stage and, if so, what are its characteristics?

How is moral reasoning in the early adult years influenced by the practical dilemmas of adult responsibilities at home and work?

Does the experience of higher education yield new ways of thinking and reasoning?

How do life events like parenthood or personal hardship affect cognitive development during the early adult years?

Over the course of adulthood, many changes occur in our thinking processes. There are changes in our store of knowledge and experience, in how fast we think, in what we think about, in how efficiently we process new information, in how deeply or reflectively we relate new experiences to previous ones, and in how we use our intellectual skills. Unlike the relatively "straightforward" cognitive growth of childhood and adolescence, these changes are *multidirectional*: some abilities increase, others wane, and some remain stable throughout this period (Uttal and Perlmutter, 1989). Understanding adult cognitive development thus involves appreciating how thinking and reasoning reflect an interplay of growth and decline in intellectual abilities.

Developmental theorists have used three different approaches to explain the cognitive changes that occur in adulthood. Picking up where Piaget himself left off, the Piagetian approach emphasizes the possible emergence of new stages of thinking and reasoning in adulthood that build on the skills of formal operational thinking. The psychometric approach, which analyzes components of intelligence such as those measured by IQ tests, examines whether these components improve or decline during adulthood. The information-processing approach, which studies the encoding, storage, and retrieval of information throughout life, considers whether the efficiency of these processes changes as the individual grows older. In a sense, the three approaches can be viewed as studying changes in *thinking, knowing,* and *processing* during adulthood (cf. Rybash et al., 1986).

All three approaches provide valuable insights into cognitive development across adulthood, but to bring each one to bear in each of the cognitive chapters in early adulthood, middle adulthood, and late adulthood would be repetitive and, potentially, confusing. Therefore, we will concentrate on each approach separately. In this chapter, our primary focus will be on the Piagetian approach, since it identifies stages of cognitive development that follow up on the achievements of formal operational reasoning in adolescence. The psychometric approach will be emphasized in our discussion of middle adulthood cognition in Chapter 21, and the information-processing approach to cognition in late adulthood will be considered in Chapter 24. To begin the present chapter, however, we will consider in broader terms the nature of the adult cognitive changes that each approach seeks to explain.

Adult Thinking

Adult thinking seems different from adolescent thinking in many ways. While adolescents often try to distill universal truths from their personal experiences and tend to think about resolving the world's problems in terms of rational absolutes, adult thinking is more personal, practical, and integrative. Similarly, adults are less inclined toward the "game of thinking" (see Chapter 15), as their intellectual skills become enlisted in the occupational and interpersonal demands that shape adult life, and thus become more specialized and experiential. Broader experience also leads most adults to accept, and adapt to, the contradictions and inconsistencies of everyday experience, rather than decrying them or trying to resolve them definitively. Indeed, one hallmark of mature adult thinking is the realization that most of life's answers are provisional rather than necessarily enduring. As Gisela Labouvie-Vief (1992) explains, adult thinking

> is less and less considered a purely objective, impersonal, and rational activity. Instead, it embraces dimensions that are subjective, interpersonal, and nonrational. By establishing a dialogue with those dimensions, thinking becomes rebalanced . . .

One important catalyst for these cognitive changes is commitment to the responsibilities of career and family that most adolescents can only anticipate (Labouvie-Vief, 1985). As a result, the development of cognitive abilities and interests becomes oriented and focused in specific ways. Commitment also deepens the person's ties to others in the surrounding world, requiring an awareness of people's differing needs and viewpoints, and the ability to cope with incompatible roles and expectations.

Schaie's Stages

The idea that personal commitment guides the development of adult thought is stressed particularly by K. Warner Schaie (1977–1978), who has proposed four stages of adult cognition that correspond to the patterns of commitment and social emphases in adult life (see Table 18.1). Schaie believes that childhood and adolescence constitute a **period of acquisition,** during which information is absorbed and problem-solving techniques are learned with little regard for their actual importance or usefulness in the young person's life. Thus a bright high school senior could, with equal enthusiasm, devote time and energy to learning political theory, analyzing poetry, and taking quilt-making lessons, all in the same day. The acquisitive thinker learns a subject because it is interesting, in much the same way that the famous mountaineer Lord Mallory climbed Mount Everest "because it is there." These unspecialized skills provide considerable flexibility to intellectual growth, however, because they can be applied to a broad variety of tasks and problems.

Figure 18.1 *According to Schaie, thinking during early adulthood is largely achievement-oriented. Being focused on the attainment of specific goals, it tends to be narrower and more intense in its concerns than the "responsible" mode of thinking that may emerge as the individual approaches middle adulthood.*

TABLE 18.1 **Schaie's Stages of Adult Thought**

Childhood and Adolescence	Early Adulthood	Middle Adulthood	Late Adulthood
Acquisition (unspecialized knowledge and skills)	Achieving (goal-directed learning)	Responsible (integrating personal and familial goals) Executive (concern for social systems)	Reintegrative (wisdom)

Beginning in the late teens or early 20s, a shift occurs as young people move away from an indiscriminate acquisition of knowledge and enter the **achieving stage,** in which they *use* knowledge to establish themselves in the world. According to Schaie, the thinking of young adults is "much more goal-directed," displaying "more efficient and effective cognitive function with respect to tasks which have role-related achievement potential." In contrast to the indiscriminate high school learner, a young adult might well strive to excel at politics or poetry or quilt-making, but unless a very unusual career goal is in sight, he or she is unlikely to specialize in all three.

As middle adulthood approaches, many people enter a third stage, called the **responsible stage,** in which "the goal-directed entrepreneurial style of the achieving stage will be replaced by a pattern which facilitates integrating long-range goals as well as consequences for one's family unit in the solution of real-life problems" (Schaie, 1977–1978). In other words, while the young businessperson might have a clear goal of professional achievement—perhaps to be a corporation president by age 35—in ten years or so he or she tries to adjust professional goals to fit with other personal and family goals. Being rich and powerful may no longer seem as important as

Figure 18.2 *A sense of responsibility for others, and for the broader social institutions that affect others, can motivate participation in school boards, civic committees, or community programs during the middle adult years.*

having well-nurtured, happy children, and the personal risk-taking or 80-hour work weeks that seemed an acceptable part of striving for professional achievement may be tempered by a greater concern for the needs of the people one loves, or an interest in developing personal pursuits.

For some adults, according to Schaie, the middle years also bring an unusually broad and deep sense of responsibility, which leads to a particular new stage of cognition called the **executive stage.** People at this stage are concerned about larger social systems: they may well be in charge of a company, a school, a town government, and so forth. Their concerns and obligations are more complex and stretch further than those of the usual person in the responsible stage, for they must coordinate the needs of various social groups, some of whom may have conflicting interests, and the needs of various individuals under their direction.

Finally, in late adulthood a **reintegrative stage** appears, when thoughts turn to making sense of life as a whole. At this point, people may turn inward to focus on their own lives or turn outward to the cosmos, seeking the purpose of life in general. They are also likely to more selectively devote their intellectual skills to problems that are personally meaningful. According to Schaie, this final stage completes a three-step transition in adult thinking—from "What should I know?" to "How should I use what I know?" to "Why should I know?"

Schaie's description of adult thinking is, of course, very general, and obviously does not apply to everyone in every culture. Taken as a whole, however, the direction of adult thinking described by Schaie points to the emergence of a type of thought that can be distinguished from the concrete or formal operational thinking of the younger person. These are one of many adaptations of intellectual skills that occur because of the unique requirements of adulthood. Several other researchers have described adult thought in ways that fit in with Schaie's overview, and we will now turn to their ideas.

Beyond Formal Operations: Postformal Thought

As we saw in Chapter 15, Piaget's theory of cognitive development culminates in formal operational thought, the stage in which the individual can engage in truly scientific reasoning which involves systematic hypothesis-testing and consideration of multiple theoretical possibilities. The formal operational thinker can solve logical problems entirely through the use of mental constructs and can coordinate logical relationships (such as negation, correlation, and incompatibility) when doing so. This is a significant advance over the reality-bound concrete operational thinker whose use of logical reasoning is tied to tangible events. (As pointed out in Chapter 15, however, not all adolescents—or adults, for that matter—achieve formal operational thinking, and Piaget himself [1972] realized that whether an individual does so depends on the challenges and opportunities provided by culture and education, especially in the fields of science and mathematics.)

Piaget regarded the development of formal operational thought as the pinnacle of cognitive development and envisioned no new cognitive stages in adulthood. Other researchers have questioned this conclusion, arguing that the cognitive challenges of adulthood described by Schaie and others result in a new, *postformal,* stage of cognitive development that builds on the accomplishments of formal operational thought. In general, **postformal thought** is less abstract, and less absolute, than formal thought, and therefore it can better adapt to life's inconsistencies. Although developmental theorists portray postformal thought in somewhat different ways, Deidre Kramer (1983) has identified three basic characteristics of postformal thought that most formulations share in common:

1. *relativism*—an understanding that one's own perspective is only one of many potentially valid views of reality, and that knowledge is not necessarily absolute or fixed (Sinnott, 1989);

2. *acceptance of contradiction*—an appreciation that reality embraces inconsistencies, such as the awareness that light travels both as waves and as particles, or that seemingly incompatible emotions like love and anger might coexist in our feelings toward another (Kramer, 1989);

3. *integration*—a capacity to synthesize apparently conflicting ideas or views into a more coherent whole, rather than feeling compelled to choose between them (Benack and Basseches, 1989).

These features of postformal thought are evident in two important ways: the ability to apply adaptive logic and problem finding to the challenges of everyday life and the capacity for dialectical thinking. We will look at each of these characteristics of postformal thought in detail.

Adaptive Thought

The central features of postformal thought permit reasoning that is adapted to the subjective, real-life contexts to which it is applied. Labouvie-Vief (1985, 1986) points out that the traditional models of mature thought stress objective, logical thinking and devalue the importance of subjective feelings and personal experience. This kind of thinking, she maintains, is adaptive for the schoolchild, the adolescent, and the "novice adult," because it permits them to "categorize experience in a stable and reliable way." However, it may be maladaptive in trying to understand, and deal with, the complexities and commitments of the adult world. For the adult, subjective feelings and personal experiences must be taken into account, or the result will be reasoning that is "limited, closed, rigidified in relation to the complex human dimensions of everyday experience." In this view, truly mature, **adaptive thought** involves the interaction between abstract, objective forms of processing and expressive, subjective forms that arise from sensitivity to context.

To demonstrate the development of this form of thought, Labouvie-Vief and her colleagues presented subjects between the ages of 10 and 40 with brief narratives that tested problem-solving logic. Because the researchers were more interested in their subjects' problem-solving approach than in their specific solutions, the tests were designed to be superficially simple and logical but to allow for deeper interpretations outside the straightforward propositions of the text. One such story went as follows:

John is known to be a heavy drinker, especially when he goes to parties. Mary, John's wife, warns him that if he comes home drunk one more time, she will leave him and take the children. Tonight John is out late at an office party. John comes home drunk.—Does Mary leave John?

In arriving at their answers, all the young adolescents and many of the older ones reasoned strictly according to the basic premise of the story: in the case of the drunken husband, it was evident to them that Mary would leave John because that is what she said she would do. Older respondents, of course, recognized the explicit logic of the story, but they resisted the limitedness of the narrative's logical premise and explored the real-life possibilities and extenuating circumstances that might apply—whether, for example, Mary's warning was a plea rather than a final ultimatum, whether John was apologetic or abusive upon his return home, whether Mary had somewhere to go, what the history of the marriage relationship might be, and so forth. At the most advanced level, adults tried to "engage in an active dialogue" with the text, forming multiple perspectives as a result (Adams and Labouvie-Vief, 1986). This appreciation and reconciliation of both objective and subjective approaches to real-life problems are the hallmarks of adult adaptive thought.

Problem Finding

By contrast with the systematic problem-*solving* abilities of the formal operational thinker, sometimes the most distinctive feature of adult thought is **problem finding** (Arlin, 1984, 1989). In essence, this refers to the capacity to formulate new questions from ambiguous or ill-defined problems or situations—to "go beyond the information given" to raise more searching issues. This capacity to ask deeper questions is, according to Patricia Arlin (1984), based on "relativistic logic"—the recognition that problems can look different depending on one's viewpoint, and that adopting different perspectives can result in new and interesting problems.

Problem finding typically involves assessing whether "tried and true" approaches are still the most effective and whether a given goal is as important as it was once thought to be. In a sense, problem finding involves standing a particular set of circumstances on its head to see what might result if things were other than they are. Problem finding may lead to difficult questions regarding the meaningfulness of one's work, the satisfaction of one's marriage or parenthood, or the value of one's legacy for the future. Problem finding may also involve devising a new and creative solution to a technical problem, making a novel artistic statement, or approaching the balance of career, family, and personal needs in an unconventional way. Not surprisingly, therefore, problem finding is a central ingredient to artistic and scientific creativity (Getzels and Csikszentmihalyi, 1976). But as a catalyst for personal inquiry, problem finding can also generate the kinds of probing, searching, self-examination that contribute to personal growth—and, at times, personal crises—in adulthood.

Figure 18.3 *Sometimes problem finding rather than problem solving is the key to scientific insight, especially when conventional ways of thinking about an issue seem too limiting. Scientists may propose radically different models of organic growth or light energy, for example, not just to explain their research findings but also to raise interesting new questions for further study.*

Dialectical Thought

Some theorists consider **dialectical thought** the most advanced form of cognition (Basseches, 1984, 1989; Leadbeater, 1986; Riegel, 1975). The word "dialectical" refers to the philosophical concept that every idea, every truth, bears within itself the suggestion of the opposite idea or truth. In terms used by philosophers, each new idea, or *thesis,* implies an opposing idea, or *antithesis.* Dialectical thinking involves considering both of these poles of an idea simultaneously and then forging them into a *synthesis,* that is, a new idea that integrates both the original idea and its opposite. The idea of the dialectical process also emphasizes that, because ideas are always initiating new syntheses, constant change is inevitable, and the dialectical process is continual. Moreover, because each new synthesis is a deepening and refinement of the idea that initiated it, dialectical change results in developmental growth.

For our purposes here, we may say that in daily life, dialectical thinking involves the constant integration of one's beliefs and experiences with all the contradictions and inconsistencies they encounter. The result of dialectical thinking is a continuously evolving view of oneself and the world, a view that recognizes that few, if any, of life's most important questions have single, unchangeable, correct answers.

This does not mean that dialectical thinkers adopt the idea that "everything is relative" and stop there, unable to commit themselves to broader values. On the contrary, a dialectic view explicitly recognizes the limitations of extreme relativistic positions such as "If you think it is true, then it's true for you" (Leadbeater, 1986). Truly dialectical thinkers, in fact, acknowledge both the subjective nature of reality *and* the need to make firm commitments to values that they realize are likely to change over time. They recognize that while many viewpoints may be potentially valid, some can be better justified or defended than others and thus provide a better basis for thoughtful decisions.

Let us see how the dialectical process might work in a simple example. Take the aphorism "Honesty is the best policy," which many people accept uncritically. A dialectical thinker, too, might begin by agreeing with this thesis, but would then consider the opposite idea: that honesty can cause hurt feelings, or foolish behavior, or destructive emotions, and so it is sometimes *not* the best policy. From these conflicting conclusions, a dialectical thinker might synthesize a new idea: that honesty is a desirable goal in human relationships because it fosters trust and intimacy, but honesty should not conflict with respect for the other person. The dialectical process does not stop here, however, for this new synthesis is itself constantly refined by new real-life situations. Does "respect for the other person" mean complimenting someone for a poor achievement in which he or she feels pride and has worked hard, for example? The answer to this question might vary depending on such factors as whether the person in question is a child or an adult, has achieved the maximum he or she is capable of or can improve, is spurred on by constructive criticism or is discouraged by it, and so on. In each new case, the dialectical thinker attempts to ascertain how, why, and in what form of expression honesty is best, recognizing all the while that whatever choices he or she makes may have to be subsequently reconsidered in light of new information or changing circumstances. This is different from an extreme relativism, which asserts that honesty may be best for some people and not for others. You can see that dialectical thought is a complicated process, seeking answers that are integrative rather than simple or fixed.

Now let us look at another example of dialectical thought as it applies to an experience familiar to many: the fading of a love affair (Basseches,

Figure 18.4 *A capacity to integrate one's beliefs with all the contradictions and inconsistencies they encounter may be essential to the growth of close relationships, whether in marriage or in parenting, because they help us realize how people and relationships are constantly changing.*

1984). A nondialectical thinker is likely to see each of the partners in a relationship as having stable, independent traits and to define their relationship in terms of the enduring interaction of these traits in compatible ways. Faced with a troubled romance, then, the nondialectical thinker is likely to conclude that one partner or the other is at fault; or that the relationship was a mistake from the beginning because the two partners are basically incompatible. By contrast, the dialectical thinker sees relationships as constantly changing rather than as stable, and understands that the partners are changed by their relationship as much as they create it. Thus the dialectical thinker realizes that the personalities, needs, and circumstances of any relationship change over time, making alterations in the relationship necessary and inevitable. A troubled romance may occur, therefore, not because the partners are fundamentally incompatible but because both have changed without adapting their relationship accordingly. Rather than concluding that one partner is at fault, therefore, the dialectical thinker can pose a new alternative: both partners can accommodate their relationship to the changes that have already occurred in it and in themselves, creating in effect, a new relationship between them.

A recognition of the continually evolving quality of human relationships gives the dialectical thinker a broader and more flexible perspective on many aspects of personal and social interaction, making that person better able to adapt to the flux of life and to perceive the disequilibrium of new demands, roles, and responsibilities as new opportunities for growth and synthesis rather than as sources of stress and dysfunction.

A Fifth Stage?

These characteristics of postformal thought provide a rich portrayal of new forms of thinking that emerge in early adulthood. They suggest—optimistically—that new cognitive capacities emerge in young adults that enable them to confront life experiences more adaptively, realistically, and competently than they could as adolescents.

But this formulation of adult cognition also has its critics. Although there is research evidence that dialectical and relativistic thought increase during the adult years (e.g., Kramer and Melchior, 1990; Kramer and Woodruff, 1986), in general, research on postformal thought has not kept pace with theories about it. Critics note that we have especially little knowledge about the maintenance of postformal thought into late adulthood, when the narrowing of certain cognitive competencies may alter styles of reasoning and thought (see Chapter 24).

On the question of whether postformal thought represents a distinct fifth stage of cognitive development, theorists are also divided. On the one hand, some claim that the unique features of postformal reasoning justify claims that a Piagetian stage beyond formal operational thought has been discovered (Commons and Richards, 1984). On the other hand, critics contend that the characteristics of postformal thought are not universal and do not necessarily build on the prior accomplishments of formal operations, and thus do not resemble the characteristics of Piaget's earlier stages (Kramer, 1983; Rybash et al., 1986). On balance, it is probably wisest to regard postformal thinking as a constellation of several styles of thought that are based on life experience, education, and other factors associated with adult maturity. Indeed, the picture of adaptive, dialectical thinking presented by postformal theory should probably also be viewed as ideal rather than normative. In describing the best accomplishments of young adult cognitive development, theorists have provided a conception of postformal reasoning that some adults use regularly, that others never use, and that many use irregularly or in specific areas.

Adult Moral Reasoning

According to many researchers, the responsibilities and concerns of adulthood can also affect moral reasoning, propelling a person from a lower moral stage to a higher one (Kohlberg, 1973; Rest, 1983; Rest and Thoma, 1985). In fact, Kohlberg states that in order to be capable of "truly ethical" reasoning, a person must have "the experience of sustained responsibility for the welfare of others and the experiences of irreversible moral choice which are the marks of adult personal experience." The development of faith follows a similar path, for the same reasons (see A Closer Look on pp. 472–473).

However, the challenges and dilemmas of adult responsibilities, in tandem with the emerging relativistic and dialectical features of adult thought, can lead to new and different qualities of moral reasoning. Carol Gilligan has looked particularly at the relationship between adult life experiences and a broader understanding of moral issues. As we saw in Chapter 15, Gilligan believes that in matters of moral reasoning, males tend to be more concerned with the question of rights and justice, whereas females are more concerned with personal relationships, tending to put human needs above justice principles. According to Gilligan, however, as all people's experience of life expands, and especially as they become committed to, and responsible for, the needs of others, they begin to realize that moral reasoning based chiefly on justice principles or on individual human needs is inadequate to resolve real-life moral dilemmas (Gilligan, 1981, 1982). Consequently, they begin to construct principles that are relative and changeable, seeking a synthesis of ethical principles with life experience (Gilligan and Murphy, 1979; Murphy and Gilligan, 1980).

Figure 18.5 *Regardless of whether one is prolife or prochoice, the American debate over abortion reveals that complex moral issues are not easily resolved through logic or moral principles alone, but must include the confrontation of ethics with life experience.*

| A CLOSER LOOK | The Development of Faith |

Thinking about religious matters is another aspect of adult cognitive development that has interested some researchers. Like morality, faith obviously is not only a cognitive process: it involves practice as well as preaching, and it arises from religious experience as well as religious education. Nonetheless, one view of faith is as a developmental process; as a person has more experience trying to reconcile religion with daily life, his or her faith may reach higher levels.

The most detailed description of the development of faith comes from James Fowler (1981, 1986), who delineates six stages of faith. It should be noted that when Fowler describes "faith," he does not necessarily mean religious faith. He agrees with Paul Tillich (1958) that all humans need to have faith in something, whether that something is a god figure, philosophical principles, country, or simply oneself. Faith gives humans a reason for living their daily lives, a way of understanding the past, a hope for the future. It is whatever each person really cares about, his or her "ultimate concern" in Tillich's words.

Stage One: Intuitive-Projective Faith

Stage-one faith is magical, illogical, imaginative, and filled with fantasy, especially about the power of God and the mysteries of birth and death. It is typical of children, ages 3 to 7.

Stage Two: Mythic-Literal Faith

At this stage, the individual takes the myths and stories of religion literally and believes simplistically in the power of symbols. In a religious context, this stage usually involves reciprocity: God sees to it that those who follow his laws are rewarded, and that those who do not are punished. Stage two is typical of middle childhood, but it also occurs in adulthood. For example, Fowler cites the case of a woman who says extra prayers at every chance, in order to put them "in the bank." Whenever she needs divine help, she thinks she can withdraw some of her accumulated credit.

Stage Three: Synthetic-Conventional Faith

A nonintellectual, tacit acceptance of cultural or religious values in the context of interpersonal relationships is typical of stage three. Unlike stage-two faith, stage-three faith serves to coordinate the individual's involvements in a complex social world, providing a sense of identity and adding significance to the rituals and symbols of daily life. For example, Fowler describes one man who puts his faith in his relationship with his family, a man whose personal rules include "being truthful with my family. Not trying to cheat them out of anything . . . I'm not saying that God or anybody else set my rules. I really don't know. It's what I

feel is right." Because of his commitment to his family, he has learned to accept the "rat race" of his daily work. These responses are typical of the conformist stage of faith, which is conventional, concerned about other people, and values "what feels right" more than what makes intellectual sense.

Stage Four: Individual-Reflective Faith

By contrast, stage-four faith is characterized by intellectual detachment from the values of the culture and from the approval of significant other people. The experience of college can be a springboard to stage four, as the young person learns to question the authority of parents, teachers, and other powerful figures and to rely, instead, on his or her own understanding of the world. An unexpected experience in adulthood, such as a divorce, the loss of a job, the death of a child, can also lead to stage four. The adult's understanding of faith ceases to be a matter of acceptance of the usual order of things and becomes, instead, an active commitment to a life goal and lifestyle that differs from that of many other people.

Fowler's example of someone at the fourth stage of faith is Jack, whose time in the army provided him with a chance to think and to talk with people from other backgrounds, and gradually to develop a personal philosophy. Jack explains:

> I began to see that the prejudice against blacks that I had been taught, and that everybody in the projects where I grew up believed in, was wrong. I began to see that us poor whites being pitted against poor blacks worked only to the advantage of the wealthy and powerful. For the first time I began to think politically. I began to have a kind of philosophy.

Jack's ability to articulate his own values, distinct from those of family, friends, and culture, makes his faith an individual-reflective faith.

Stage Five: Conjunctive Faith

This type of faith incorporates both powerful unconscious ideas (such as the power of prayer and the love of God) and rational, conscious values (such as the worth of life compared with that of property), and is characterized by a willingness to accept contradictions. It involves a synthesis of the magical understanding of symbols and myths that characterized stage two and the conceptual clarity of stage four. Fowler cites one woman at this stage who believes strongly in God, but adds, "I don't think it matters a bit what you call it. I think some people are so fed up with the word God that you can't talk to them about God." Her recognition that the word "God" may be distracting and misleading is typical of the ability of the stage-five thinker to articulate paradoxes and contradictions in faith. Also typical of this stage is an openness to new truths; this

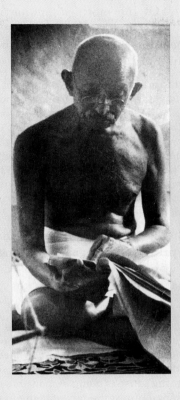

Neither Gandhi (who helped lead India to independence from Great Britain through his campaign of nonviolent resistance) nor Mother Hale (who cared for hundreds of infants born addicted to drugs) planned to take on the heroic roles they eventually did. As Fowler and Kohlberg explain, people often develop a deeper and more universal faith or moral vision, and sometimes transform their lives, as events and experiences lead them to feel a greater connectedness to their fellow beings.

woman explains her beliefs by referring to Jesus, George Fox, Krishna-Murti, and Carl Jung. Fowler says this cosmic perspective rarely comes before middle age.

Stage Six: Universalizing Faith

People at stage six have a powerful vision of universal compassion, justice, and love that compels them to live their lives in a way that, to most people, seems either saintly or foolish. They put their own personal welfare aside, and sometimes even sacrifice their lives, in an effort to enunciate universal values. Often, a transforming experience converts an adult to stage six, as happened to Moses when he saw the burning bush, and to Mohammed, Buddha, and Paul. Fowler mentions some twentieth-century people who have reached this level, among them Gandhi, Martin Luther King, Jr., and Mother Theresa, each of whom radically redefined their lives after a particular experience produced a new understanding of human brotherhood. Clearly, a person reaching stage six of faith is an exceedingly rare individual.

Indeed, the scarcity of people at the upper stages of Fowler's hierarchy might make one wonder how useful it is. Moreover, it may be galling to read that there are "higher" stages of faith than most adults are likely to reach—especially when some of the "lower" levels of thinking can be seen as no less valid than the "higher" levels. Describing levels of faith seems to imply values about the nature and object of belief. It is easy to imagine, for instance, Fowler's students coming to class, as Kohlberg's once did, wearing buttons proclaiming "Stage Two and proud of it" and insisting that what Fowler characterizes as "childish" stage-two faith is actually the purest kind.

In Fowler's defense it should be noted that he never explicitly says that the higher stages are better. In fact, Fowler explains:

> Each stage has its proper time of ascendancy. For persons in a given stage at the right time *for their lives,* the task is the full realization and integration of the strengths and graces of that stage rather than rushing on to the next stage. Each stage has the potential for wholeness, grace and integrity, and for strengths sufficient for either life's blows or blessings.

If Fowler is correct, faith, like other aspects of cognition, may progress from a quite simple, self-centered one-sided perspective to a more complex, altruistic, and multi-sided view.

One young man whom Gilligan studied illustrates this shift very well. In late adolescence he was able to reason abstractly, and at an advanced level, about the moral dilemma involving Heinz and his dying wife (see p. 399), citing valued the principle that life is more than money. But seven years later, in early adulthood, he had become much more aware of the personal implications of his answer:

> This is a very crisp little dilemma and you can latch onto that principle pretty fast and say that life is more important than money. But then, when you reflect back on how you really act in your own life, you don't use that principle, or I haven't yet used that principle to operate on. And none of the people who answer that dilemma that way use that principle to operate on because they were blowing $7,000 a year for their education at Harvard instead of giving it to the Children's Fund to give porridge to the kids in Botswana and to that extent answering the dilemma with that principle is not hypocritical, it's just that you don't recognize it. I hadn't recognized it at the time, and I am sure they didn't recognize it either. [Gilligan and Murphy, 1979]

Similarly, a woman stated that she once thought there were no absolute principles of right and wrong: "I went through a time when I thought things were pretty relative, that I can't tell you what to do and you can't tell me what to do, because you've got your conscience and I've got mine." But at age 25, she held these views:

> Just seeing more of life [led me to recognize] that there are an awful lot of things that are common among people. There are certain things that . . . promote a better life and better relationships and more personal fulfillment than other things, and . . . you would call [those things] morally right . . . I have a very strong sense of being responsible to the world, that I can't just live for my enjoyment, but just the fact of being in the world gives me an obligation to do what I can to make the world a better place to live in, no matter how small a scale that may be on.

According to Gilligan, one reason that adulthood involves new forms of moral thought is that life experience poses more complex moral dilemmas than such straightforward problems as that of human welfare versus property rights framed by Kohlberg's story about Heinz. In one case, for example, a young district attorney interviewed by Gilligan had to decide whether to prosecute a gang member who was probably innocent of the present charges against him but was undoubtedly guilty of other crimes he had gotten away with (Gilligan et al., 1990). Should the gang member be prosecuted on the basis of flimsy, perhaps perjured evidence? Suppose he was unlikely to afford a good attorney who could effectively defend him? Would justice be served if he were convicted in this manner, or would the system be corrupted? Experiences like this, together with the capacity for asking deeper questions about such dilemmas ("problem finding"), cause many young adults to retreat from the certainty they had formerly placed in the purely logical analysis of moral questions and to realize that determining the "right thing to do" is often highly ambiguous and uncertain, and possibly unknowable.

Out of the uncertainties caused by questioning, probing, and reworking ethical principles in light of the complexities of life experience, however, many adults forge new principles that guide their decisions, but which also may be revised in time. In true dialectical fashion, this process of continuous change in moral thinking results in less moral absolutism, according to Gilligan, but fosters true moral growth.

Cognitive Growth and Higher Education

Figure 18.6 *Many parents today wonder whether a college education is worth the cost. Purely in terms of enhancing an offspring's earning potential, it usually is. But a full answer to the question involves intangibles that are impossible to measure. The value of the cognitive growth that can result from the college experience cannot be expressed in dollars and cents.*

Of particular interest to many developmental researchers, and to readers of this text, is the relationship between college education and adult thinking processes. Although most people today attend college to secure a better job and to learn specific information (such as how to program a computer or how to prepare and interpret balance sheets), the avowed goal of most colleges and universities is the intellectual development of the students who attend them. How successful are they in this objective? Do people think deeper and better because they have been to college? To be more specific, is there any sign that they are more likely to reach postformal thinking, combining the practical and the theoretical in a flexible, dialectical way?

There is no doubt that, in general, education powerfully influences cognitive development. Years of education are strongly correlated with virtually every measure of adult cognition, even more so than other powerful variables such as age and socioeconomic status (Kitchener and King, 1990; Labouvie-Vief, 1985; Reese and Rodeheaver, 1985). College education not only improves students' verbal and quantitative skills and their knowledge of specific subject areas but also enhances the flexibility and resourcefulness of their reasoning abilities. In the words of one review,

> compared to freshmen, seniors have better oral and written communication skills, are better abstract reasoners or critical thinkers, are more skilled at using reason and evidence to address ill-structured problems for which there are no verifiably correct answers, have greater intellectual flexibility in that they are better able to understand more than one side of a complex issue, and can develop more sophisticated abstract frameworks to deal with complexity. [Pascarella and Terenzini, 1991]

The same findings appear even when studies control for age differences among the students and for any preexisting factors that might influence the cognitive growth of those young adults who go on to college. These accomplishments represent significant cognitive advancement over a four- to five-year period of young adulthood!

In addition, research has shown that college education leads people to become more tolerant of political, social, and religious views that differ from their own and to be more flexible and realistic in their attitudes (Chickering, 1981; Pascarella and Terenzini, 1991; Webster et al., 1979). Indeed, some research even finds a year-by-year progression in this process. It begins with the first year of college, when students believe that there are clear and perfect truths to be found, and are disturbed if they do not discover them or if their professors do not provide them. This phase is followed by a wholesale questioning of personal and social values and of the idea of truth itself. Finally, after carefully considering many opposing ideas, students become committed to certain values, at the same time realizing the need to remain open-minded and prepared for change (Clinchy and Zimmerman, 1982; Perry, 1981; Sanford, 1979).

This progression has been described in detail by William Perry, primarily on the basis of an intensive study of Harvard students. As you can see from the chart on page 476, Perry found that, over the course of their college careers, the thinking of his subjects progressed through nine levels of complexity, going from a simplistic either/or dualism (one is either right or wrong, a success or a failure) to a relativism that recognized a multiplicity of perspectives. Position 5, which recognizes that knowledge and values (including those of authorities) are relative but not equally valid, is pivotal in this developmental scheme.

According to Perry, this progression was a product of the college environment; when students reached a new level, their peers, professors, reading, or classwork stimulated new questions that opened the way to the next level. However, Perry (1981) acknowledged that this developmental process does not end with college but, rather, continues throughout adulthood.

These findings do not mean that students necessarily switch from conservative to liberal values during their college years. In fact, the difference is not so much a change in attitudes as a change in the way one's attitudes are held—with greater confidence and tolerance. College experience seems

Scheme of Cognitive and Ethical Development

	Position 1	Authorities know, and if we work hard, read every word, and learn Right Answers, all will be well.
Dualism Modified	Transition	But what about those Others I hear about? And different opinions? And Uncertainties? Some of our own Authorities disagree with each other or don't seem to know, and some give us problems instead of Answers.
	Position 2	True Authorities must be Right, the others are frauds. We remain Right. Others must be different and Wrong. Good Authorities give us problems so we can learn to find the Right Answer by our own independent thought.
	Transition	But even Good Authorities admit they don't know all the answers *yet!*
	Position 3	Then some uncertainties and different opinions are real and legitimate *temporarily,* even for Authorities. They're working on them to get to the Truth.
	Transition	But there are *so many* things they don't know the Answers to! And they won't for a long time.
	Position 4a	Where Authorities don't know the Right Answers, everyone has a right to his own opinion; no one is wrong!
	Transition *(and/or)*	But some of my friends ask me to support my opinions with facts and reasons.
Relativism Discovered	Transition	Then what right have They to grade us? About what?
	Position 4b	In certain courses Authorities are not asking for the Right Answer. They want us to *think* about things in a certain way, *supporting* opinion with data. That's what they grade us on.
	Transition	But this "way" seems to *work* in most courses, and even outside them.
	Position 5	Then *all* thinking must be like this, even for Them. Everything is relative but not equally valid. You have to understand how each context works. Theories are not Truth but metaphors to interpret data with. You have to think about your thinking.
	Transition	But if everything is relative, am I relative too? How can I know I'm making the Right Choice?
Commitments in Relativism Developed	Position 6	I see I'm going to have to make my own decisions in an uncertain world with no one to tell me I'm Right.
	Transition	I'm lost if I don't. When I decide on my career (or marriage or values), everything will straighten out.
	Position 7	Well, I've made my first Commitment!
	Transition	Why didn't that settle everything?
	Position 8	I've made several commitments. I've got to balance them—how many, how deep? How certain, how tentative?
	Transition	Things are getting contradictory. I can't make logical sense out of life's dilemmas.
	Position 9	This is how life will be. I must be wholehearted while tentative, fight for my values yet respect others, believe my deepest values right yet be ready to learn. I see that I shall be retracing this whole journey over and over—but, I hope, more wisely.

Source: Perry, 1981.

to make people more accepting of other people's attitudes and ideas because it makes people less threatened by them (Katz and Stanford, 1979). Research that focuses specifically on dialectical reasoning suggests that the more years of higher education a person has, the deeper and more dialectical that person's reasoning is likely to become. This was shown in a detailed study of students at Swarthmore (Basseches, 1984), as well as in more general research elsewhere (King et al., 1983; Kitchener and King, 1990; Rest and Thoma, 1985).

The College Student of Today

Adding complexity to these conclusions is the fact that the collegiate population, and the institutions they attend, have become more diverse and heterogeneous in recent years, as the number of students in higher education has multiplied significantly, in the United States and in virtually every country worldwide (Geiger, 1986). Correspondingly, the demographic characteristics of the student body have changed both in the United States and elsewhere. There are more women students, more low-income students, more ethnic-minority students, more older students, more students who choose quite specific career-based curricula (computer programming, health services, engineering, accounting, business) rather than a broad liberal arts education, and more part-time students.

As both a cause and a consequence of this shift, attendance at four-year residential colleges has held steady, while nonresidential, public, and/or two-year colleges have expanded their enrollment dramatically. At such colleges, faculty tend to have fewer advanced degrees, to teach more classes, and to spend more time developing basic skills than discussing abstract formulations.

Does it make a difference for cognitive growth, then, whether one attends a four-year residential school or a nonresidential community college, or attends a large university or a small, liberal arts college? Although one's collegiate experience is affected in many ways by the differences among these schools, they have only a minor impact on cognitive growth (Pascarella and Terenzini, 1991). Compared to non-college-bound young adults, those who attend college will grow in various intellectual skills ranging from verbal competence to abstract reasoning, regardless of which college they attend.

This does not mean that the *kind* of education students receive has no important impact. Pascarella and Terenzini (1991) found that factors such as the amount of contact between students and faculty, the degree of emphasis on individualized forms of instruction and hands-on learning (as opposed to lecture and recitation), the educational background of the faculty, and the student's personal involvement in the intellectual and cultural life of the university can have a significant impact on the extent of cognitive growth during the collegiate years. The choice of a major also influences the growth of formal reasoning and critical thinking, but primarily on issues and problems associated with that subject area. Finally, there is also research evidence that a collegiate education succeeds in accomplishing perhaps its most important goal: preparing students to become lifelong learners.

Figure 18.7 *For many young adults, college today provides a unique opportunity to learn about the life experience of people who are different from themselves—not only in ethnic, religious, socioeconomic, and cultural background but often in age as well.*

Figure 18.8 *Life events—both the commonplace and the catastrophic—can lead to new patterns of thinking. In some cases, for example, entering into marriage can begin a series of cognitive shifts that intensify the individual's sense of commitment to others. In other cases, being a victim or observer of a tragedy like the bombing of the World Trade Center can radically alter one's perspective on the meaning of one's own life, or of life itself.*

Thus, as you may already have personally concluded, the collegiate years are a potentially significant period of cognitive growth, and college is a catalyst for mature thought at whatever age one attends. From orientation day to graduation, you are learning not only the information and issues pertaining to your major and other curricular topics but also how to think and reason more deeply, reflectively, and searchingly.

Cognitive Growth and Life Events

Research on one final topic is spotty, but the tentative conclusions are intriguing, especially from a developmental perspective. It has been suggested that many life events, or specific notable occurrences, can trigger new patterns of thinking and thus cognitive development.

Parenthood is a prime example. From the birth of a first child, which tends to make both parents feel more "adult"—thinking about themselves and their responsibilities differently—through the unexpected issues raised by adolescent children, parenthood is undoubtedly an impetus for cognitive growth (Feldman et al., 1981; Flavell, 1970; Galinsky, 1981). One reason is that parenthood offers "insights into the interdependence of the larger social system" (Veroff and Veroff, 1980), which is, as we have learned, an important aspect of mature thought.

Similarly, other life events also might make people think more deeply about the nature and meaning of their lives and their relationship with others. A new intimate relationship or the end of an old one, a job promotion or dismissal, being the victim of a violent attack or, unexpectedly, someone's savior, exposure to a radically different lifestyle, an intense religious experience or in-depth psychotherapy, experiencing the serious illness or death of a loved one—all these can occasion cognitive disequilibrium and reflection, which, in turn, can result in a new view of oneself and the meaning of one's life.

Evidence for this abounds in biographical and autobiographical literature and in personal experience. Probably every reader of this book knows someone who seemed to have a narrow and shallow outlook on the world in early adulthood, but who later developed a deeper and broader perspective as experiences and insight accumulated.

A Case of Cognitive Maturity

One particularly poignant example, reported in a study of adult psychosocial development (Kotre, 1984), is the life of a woman called Dorothy Woodson. She was the last of seven children, born to a poor rural family who, she thought, never loved her. She grew up feeling "horribly ugly," stupid, and neglected, and her perspective on life as she approached adulthood was constricted and bleak. She had no confidence in herself nor any plans for the future. As she later said of herself, "Inside I was very fearful and uncertain. I always wanted somebody just to hold my hand through something. I didn't want to do anything by myself." Dorothy's early adult life reinforced her narrow life view. At 18 she had married a man on whom she felt desperately dependent but who rarely seemed to care about her. Within a year her first baby was born, weighing only 3 pounds. Neither her family nor her husband seemed very interested in him and gave Dorothy no help or encouragement in the difficult task of caring for a premature child. The infant developed slowly and died before his first birthday. Her second child, born soon after that, was "an extremely beautiful and precious" girl named Diana. Shortly after Diana's birth, Dorothy's husband moved to a city 200 miles away, leaving Dorothy alone with their daughter and afraid to protest his absence or to follow him. At one point when Diana was 2, Dorothy was desperate to see her husband and went to visit him, leaving Diana with a 13-year-old babysitter. The sitter's inexperience led to a tragic accident that killed Diana.

Not surprisingly, Dorothy's childhood experiences, her empty marriage, and the deaths of her first two children numbed Dorothy in many ways. Her view of life was shallow and pessimistic. She just barely managed to get through each day and was not at all ready to make commitments or to try to build any kind of future for herself. When she had her third child, she thought, "You're just going to die anyway, I'm not going to love you."

But then, gradually, Dorothy began to develop a new perspective on herself and her life. With the help of a friend, she became involved with a religious community, where she found not only emotional support but also encouragement to read and study. The real turning point for Dorothy came when she found a mentor who spurred and nurtured her intellectual and spiritual growth:

> I began to discuss my thoughts with him. He made me aware of studying critically. He started me wondering about a lot of things. He planted a lot of seeds in my mind, things I never even considered or aspired to. He would question me about everything and make me think about how I really felt, my gut reaction to things rather than parroting what I thought somebody wanted to hear. That opened up a whole new world for me.

As a result of this cognitive awakening, Dorothy began to see herself as worthwhile and her life as meaningful. More particularly, she began to be able to clarify her values and to see the issues in her life in a much fuller dimension.

This is not to suggest that her whole life suddenly changed for the better. To the contrary, she was faced with continual struggle—with the self-doubt and pain that she carried from the past; with the difficulties of raising a child alone; with the tedium of the jobs she was restricted to because of her lack of formal education; with disillusionment in personal relationships; with various medical crises. What did change, increasingly over time, were the depth and complexity of the thinking she brought to these struggles. Listening to her speak of her life, and especially of her son, one is struck by the sense of balance she eventually achieved:

> I feel life is a process and that your experiences bad or good, specifically bad experiences, can either build character or destroy character. And if individuals are seeking a higher good or a higher reason for life, then the experiences will add to their character and add to their life. . . . One of my thoughts is that I've got to make every day count with my son. I mean every day. Not a day should pass that he's not loved and that his ideas and he as a person are not acknowledged and guided in some way. . . . I see family traits that I have, that I've seen in my sisters and my mother and my son. It's like ancestral influences I'm trying to overcome and replace with stronger, more transcendental values. I guess that's what I'm trying to do with him, to let him see that I've passed things on to him—and his dad has too. He's got some pretty good stuff from both of us, but he's got

some weaknesses too. If he doesn't focus on them and just concentrates on those strong areas and replaces the weak areas with the creative things he likes to do, then he's going to be that much more valuable to society. . . . He's turning out to be such a fine, fine individual that I want to be a part of that and his posterity. . . . I guess what I'm saying is that there is a reason to fight for life.

Thus certain key life experiences enabled Dorothy to break through her self-defeating, helpless view of herself, and to experience considerable cognitive growth. Her view of life, of parenthood, of her role in the larger society had become more complex, and at the same time more adaptive and more responsive to the contradictions inherent in personal experience.

Case studies, of course, do not prove general trends: they simply indicate what can sometimes happen. However, longitudinal studies that include many cases point in the same general direction. While there are always exceptions, the general movement of thinking about one's own life in adulthood is toward a more responsible and committed view of the world (Haan, 1985a; Vaillant, 1977).

While much more longitudinal research needs to be done before firm conclusions can be drawn, the general theme of this chapter seems plausible. As people move from late adolescence toward middle adulthood, the interplay between thought and experience, between the logic of formal operational intelligence and the sometimes erratic, sometimes confusing challenges of daily life, may propel adults to new, postformal styles of thought. At that point, they may be able to recognize and adjust to the contradictions and conflicts of adulthood, conflicts that become more apparent in the next chapter.

SUMMARY

Adult Thinking

1. Adult cognition can be studied in several ways, from a Piagetian stage perspective; from a psychometric perspective, focusing on measurement of specific cognitive abilities; or from an information-processing perspective. This chapter focuses on the stage perspective.

2. A number of researchers believe that adult thinking is rooted in, and shaped by, the specific commitments the individual takes on. According to Schaie, as a person makes the commitments of adulthood and sets goals, he or she may pass through several cognitive stages: achieving, responsible, executive, and reintegrative.

Beyond Formal Operations: Postformal Thought

3. Piaget's last stage of cognitive development, formal operational thought, is characterized by the ability to solve problems logically and systematically. Many researchers believe that, in adulthood, the complex and often ambigu-

ous or conflicting demands of daily life produce a new type of thinking, called postformal thought, which is better suited than formal thinking to coping with problems that may have no correct solutions. Postformal thought is adaptive, integrating thinking processes and experience.

4. Postformal thinking is also characterized by relativism, acceptance of contradiction, and problem finding. At its most advanced, postformal thinking may also be characterized as dialectical, capable of recognizing and synthesizing complexities and contradictions. Instead of seeking absolute, immutable truth, dialectical thought leads to a flexible, ever changing approach.

5. Although postformal thinking is sometimes described as a stage, it is not the same kind of universal, age-related stage that Piaget described for earlier cognitive growth. Its appearance is more gradual, dependent on particular experiences and education rather than on a universal, chronologically determined restructuring of mental processes.

6. Thinking about questions of morality, faith, and ethics may also progress in adulthood, along the lines of postformal thought. For example, Gilligan suggests that men and women come to recognize the limitations of basing moral reasoning solely on abstract principles or personal concerns and try to integrate the two with life experience to forge a more reflective, less absolute, moral awareness.

Cognitive Growth and Higher Education

7. College education tends to make people more flexible, thoughtful, and tolerant because they are less threatened by conflicting views. They decreasingly seek absolute truths from authorities and increasingly acknowledge that knowledge and values are relative (but not equally valid).

8. Collegiate education heightens cognitive skills regardless of where one goes to school, but factors like teacher-student interaction and student involvement in learning affect the extent of cognitive growth.

Cognitive Growth and Life Events

9. Life events also promote cognitive growth. Parenthood is one example, unexpected life events another. However, while life events certainly affect the cognition of some people, they have not been shown to have this effect universally.

KEY TERMS

period of acquisition (465)
achieving stage (465)
responsible stage (466)
executive stage (466)
reintegrative stage (465)

postformal thought (467)
adaptive thought (467)
problem finding (468)
dialectical thought (468)

KEY QUESTIONS

1. What are three approaches to the study of adult cognition?

2. How do Schaie's stages reflect the effects of adult commitments on cognitive growth?

3. What are the limitations of formal operational thought?

4. What are the main characteristics of postformal thinking?

5. Can you describe an instance of dialectical reasoning in addition to the two cited in the text?

6. What are "adaptive thought" and "problem finding"?

7. In what ways is postformal thinking not a stage in the Piagetian sense of the term?

8. How might the moral thinking of adults be different from that of children and adolescents? Why?

9. According to research, how does college education affect the way people think?

10. According to your own observation, how does college education affect the way people think?

11. How might life events affect cognitive development?

CHAPTER 19

Early Adulthood: Psychosocial Development

Psychosocial development is the domain where personal emotions and values most directly confront social forces, a private-public interplay that can be quite intense during early adulthood, as young people attempt to master (or modify or reject) the many tasks of adulthood. The emotions and passions of sexual love, for example, often come to fruition in marriage, an institution laden with socially prescribed expectations and obligations that frequently make unanticipated demands on the individual's personal resources. Similarly, entry onto the career path puts personal ambitions and ideals face to face with the realities and priorities of the workplace. Although such juxtapositions are sometimes unsettling and painful, you will see in this chapter why most adults find such struggles worthwhile. Among the questions the chapter will address are the following:

Why do people have different expectations of themselves at different ages?

How do close friendships between men compare with those between women?

How does love change from one stage of a relationship to another?

What factors make marriage likely to succeed or divorce likely to occur?

What factors are instrumental in feelings of job satisfaction?

How is adoptive parenting or stepparenting similar to, or different from, biological parenting?

In terms of psychosocial development, the hallmark of adulthood in the modern world is diversity. No longer limited by the pace of biological maturation or bound by parental restrictions, adults are much freer to choose their own developmental path—and in the final decade of the twentieth century, the array of choices that adults in contemporary society face regarding career, marriage, parenthood, lifestyle patterns, and friendship is wide and varied. Let us examine several themes that underlie and help to organize the complexity and diversity of adulthood.

The Two Tasks of Adulthood

No matter what specific pattern a particular adult life may form, two basic psychosocial needs drive its development. Various theorists describe these needs in somewhat different terms. For example, in the third tier of his hierarchy of human needs (p. 60), Maslow (1968) cites the need for *love and belonging,* which, if met, is followed by the need for *success* and *esteem.* Other psychologists have described these two needs in terms of *affiliation* and *achievement,* or *affection* and *instrumentality,* or social *acceptance* and *competence.* Freud (1935) put the same duality more simply, explaining that a healthy adult was one who could *love* and *work.*

Building on Freudian theory, Erik Erikson suggested that there are two basic crises, or tasks, in adulthood. One is **intimacy versus isolation,** which involves the need to share one's personal life with someone else or risk profound aloneness. As Erikson (1963) explains:

> . . . the young adult, emerging from the search for and the insistence on identity, is eager and willing to fuse his identity with others. He is ready for intimacy, that is, the capacity to commit himself to concrete affiliations and partnerships and to develop the ethical strength to abide by such commitments, even though they call for significant sacrifices and compromises.

In Eriksonian theory, the crisis of intimacy is followed by the crisis of **generativity versus stagnation,** which involves the need to be productive in some meaningful way, usually through work or parenthood. Without a sense of generativity, says Erikson, life seems empty and purposeless; adults have "a pervading sense of stagnation and personal impoverishment."

No matter what terminology is used to describe them, these two themes of adult life are recognized by almost all developmentalists, although researchers find considerable diversity in the particular ways, as well as in the sequence, that people meet these basic needs. While Erikson placed intimacy as a need met primarily during the very beginning of adulthood, and generativity as a need met between ages 25 and 65, most contemporary theorists and researchers see both needs evident throughout adulthood (Wrightsman, 1988).

Ages and Stages

Within the broad themes of love and work, several researchers have suggested that adults typically shift back and forth between periods of openness and change and periods of commitment and constancy. They explore alternatives in their lives, particularly those involving love and work, make choices among them, and follow through on those choices; later they reexamine their earlier choices and either recommit themselves to them or make changes in their lives. As depicted by these researchers (Levinson 1978, 1986; Gould, 1978; Reinke et al., 1985; Harris et al., 1986; Jessor et al., 1991), the most common patterns of early adulthood are as follows.

The 20s

The early 20s are considered the time to finish breaking away from one's parents (a task begun in adolescence, but now given new form through eco-

Figure 19.1 *One of the most frustrating challenges of early adulthood is illustrated here, as this young woman answers help-wanted ads, often to find that the job is unsuitable, nonexistent, or already filled. One contextual factor that mitigates the stress of the early job hunt is that its difficulties are shared by so many of today's cohort of young people that not being able to land a job right away is less likely to create an immediate sense of having failed.*

nomic and residential independence) and to begin making choices concerning affiliation and achievement—choices regarding marriage, parenthood, further education, employment specialization, political allegiance, community involvement, religious participation, and so forth. These choices are not necessarily considered lifetime ones; indeed, they are often explicitly provisional in nature, particularly those involving employment and social-group association.

By their mid-20s, most adults have made some important commitments and decisions, and have a sense of who they are. They have completed the move from the period of late adolescent exploration to adult stabilization, refining the patterns of their lives by accepting and accommodating to social norms. In choices regarding both the superficial aspects of life—such as, say, clothing style and leisure activities—and the more abiding aspects—such as holding down a steady job and getting married—people in their 20s become recognizably adult. Often this is in marked contrast to the experimental and sometimes rebellious adolescents they once were (Haan, 1981; Jessor et al., 1991). Both affiliation and achievement needs now begin to be met.

The 30s

As age 30 approaches, many young adults reexamine and question whatever commitments they have taken on. As Daniel Levinson (1986) expresses it:

> At about age 28 the provisional quality of the 20s is ending and life is becoming more serious, more "for real." A voice within the self says: If I am to change my life—if there are things in it I want to modify or exclude, or things missing I want to add—I must now make a start, for soon it will be too late.

Age 30 has particular salience for many women (Reinke et al., 1985). Those who have no children must confront the fact that their childbearing years will soon be running out. For many, this necessitates a reexamination of career goals, of self-image, and of their relationship to their husbands or potential husbands and to their parents. This rethinking might lead to new directions in their lives (Notman, 1980; Wilk, 1986).

Similarly, at about age 30, many women who are mothers realize firsthand how quickly their children become more independent. Once these young mothers can again envision having time to themselves, they may renew or begin educational or career plans. Closely related to this is the economic reality that, as children grow older, they become more costly to raise, giving many mothers added reasons to increase their own wage-earning ability. Another major decision that many women in their 30s make is to avoid future childbearing forever: for American women, age 30 is, in fact, the peak age for having a last child (Koo et al., 1987), and by age 35, more than a third of married American women are surgically sterilized, with the early 30s being the most common age for this operation (Bachrach, 1984).

Men also undergo a period of questioning at age 30, although often they focus more on vocation than on parenthood. Typically, they seek greater independence from the supervisors and advisers who helped them in their 20s (Bray and Howard, 1983), entering a stage Levinson calls BOOM (Becoming One's Own Man). They also reassess their position at work, asking for more responsibility, money, and power.

After resolving whatever questions age 30 brings, adults typically spend the rest of their 30s following through on work begun: men and women continue up the career ladder, bear their last child, and in many ways come as close to the stereotype of the dedicated, hard-working, career and family men and women as they will ever be. However, according to a number of stage theories, the relatively conservative stage of career and family consolidation in the 30s might evolve into a new questioning phase as age 40 approaches, sometimes referred to as the midlife crisis, a topic discussed in Chapter 22.

The Social Clock

Although these rough chronological stages seem broadly applicable, they need to be put into perspective. With the exception of women's fertility, which decreases gradually and then ends at about age 50, development is no longer propelled by the biological clock of maturation. Consequently, whatever stages of adulthood there might be are determined in large measure by a kind of **social clock,** a culturally set timetable that establishes when various events and behaviors in life are appropriate and called for. Each culture, each subculture, and every historical period has a somewhat different social clock, with variations in the "best" age to become independent of one's parents, to choose a vocation, to marry, to have children, and so on (Keith, 1990).

A prime influence on this cultural clock-setting—worldwide—is socioeconomic status: the lower a person's SES, the younger the age at which he or she is expected to leave school, begin work, marry, have children, quit working, and become "old." The influence of socioeconomic background is particularly apparent with regard to the age at which women become wives and mothers. In the United States and other Western countries, women from low SES backgrounds may feel pressure to marry at 18, and most stop childbearing by age 25, while wealthy women may not feel pressure to marry until age 30 or to stop childbearing until age 40. Although such pressures are not always heeded, they nonetheless have a clear effect on actual childbearing behavior: in the United States, most low-SES women have had at least one child before age 25, whereas nearly a third of high-SES women wait until they are in their 30s to begin motherhood. Consequently, among high-SES women, the rate of first births after age 30 is more than four times that of women at the bottom of the SES ladder. Internationally, the social clock varies even more: in Venezuela, for instance, marriage is legal at age 12 for females and 14 for males, and more than half of all women are married before they are 19. By contrast, men and women in Sweden cannot legally marry until they are at least 18. Most Swedes wait much longer, with the median age of first marriage being 26 for women and 30 for men (UNESCO, 1985).

The social clock's regulation of marriage varies historically as well. To pick one specific example, in the United States, the median age for becoming a new bride was 22 in 1910, 20 in 1956, and then 23.6 in 1987, the oldest since Americans have been recording this statistic (U.S. Bureau of the Census, 1976, 1991).

Similarly, the social clock affects, and varies on, the question of when men should be settled in a career. For example, the idea that men should be fixed on a definite career by their mid-20s was endorsed by almost three out

Figure 19.2 *According to her culture's social clock, this young Moroccan adolescent has become a mother "right on time."*

Figure 19.3 *The social clock once "dictated" that college graduation should occur between ages 21 and 23—and certainly not after age 40. Fortunately for this proud graduate, standard time is no longer the only setting.*

of every four American adults in the late 1950s but by only one out of every four two decades later (Rosenfeld and Stark, 1987).

In contemporary American culture, social time allows more diversity than it once did. However, prescribed ages for many adult roles still tend to cluster in the early and mid-20s. Young adults experience considerable social and personal pressure to take on new responsibilities and get on with adult life. Many people think that, by age 30, they should be educated, employed, married, and raising children, or be prepared to explain why they're not. This can make early adulthood a highly stressful period for psychosocial development, not only for those who, for various reasons, do not take on expected roles, but also for those who do and try to juggle several simultaneously (Pearlin, 1982; Jessor et al., 1991).

Let us look now at some of the ways young adults attempt to satisfy their needs for intimacy and generativity.

Intimacy

To meet the need for intimacy, or affiliation, an adult may take on many roles—friend, lover, and spouse among them. Each role demands some personal sacrifice, a giving of oneself to others. In the process of becoming more open and more vulnerable to others, the individual gains deeper self-understanding and avoids the isolation caused by too much self-protection. As Erikson explains, the young adult must

> face the fear of ego loss in situations which call for self-abandon: in the solidarity of close affiliations . . . sexual unions, in close friendship and in physical combat, in experiences of inspiration by teachers and of intuition from the recesses of the self. The avoidance of such experiences . . . may lead to a deep sense of isolation and consequent self-absorption. [Erikson, 1963]

The two main sources of intimacy in early adulthood are close friendship and sexual partnership. (A third source, ongoing family ties across the generations, is discussed in Chapter 22.) We will begin our study of intimacy here with an examination of friendship, a bond that is almost universal in early adulthood, and then discuss the more variable bond of sexual-emotional intimacy.

Friendship

Friends are very important at every stage of development, a reality increasingly recognized and studied by researchers (Rawlins, 1992). Even more than family members, friends are a buffer against stress and a source of positive feelings (Antonucci, 1990; Vega et al., 1986). One probable reason for this is that friends *choose* each other, often for the very qualities (understanding, tolerance, loyalty, affection, humor) that make them good companions, trustworthy confidants, and reliable sources of emotional support. In addition, the mutuality and voluntary nature of the choosing process, in contrast to obligatory basis of family ties, makes close friendship a testimony to one's personal worthiness, and thus an invaluable source of self-esteem (Allan, 1989).

Because at the start of adulthood most individuals are quite mobile and relatively free of overriding commitments (such as marriage, dependent children, or filial obligation to aging parents), they find it relatively easy to form extensive and varied social networks, as they explore a broad range of goals and interests in many settings—at college, work, or social gatherings, and among political, cultural, athletic, or religious groups. Within this wide array of social contexts, they are usually able to find many peers who can provide much-needed advice, information, companionship, and sympathy to ease the numerous challenges that early adulthood entails.

Indeed, almost never do young adults feel bereft of friendship. One research study found, for example, that less than 2 percent of young adults said they were without close friends (Jessor et al., 1991). Those young adults who live alone are particularly likely to develop an elaborate friendship circle, and to spend as much leisure time with their friends as they do by themselves (Alwin et al., 1985). Not surprisingly, during early adulthood, both men and women tend to be more satisfied with the size and functioning of their friendship networks than with almost any other part of their lives.

Gender Differences in Friendship

As might be expected, in friendships with members of their own sex, men and women tend to differ in many ways—in what they do together, in what they say to each other, and in how they feel about each other. In general, men's friendships are based on shared activities and interests. In contrast, friendships between women tend to be more intimate and emotional, based on shared confidences and practical assistance in times of crisis.

One sign of this gender difference is in what same-sex friends talk about. For women, both the "substance" and "the central feature" of friendship are self-disclosing conversations (Ariès, 1983). As one scholar explains, even when they are "addressing the same basic list of topics as men, women talk more often about their intimate concerns as well as routine matters and mutual endeavors, delving deeper than men into personal and family issues" (Rawlins, 1992).

Among men friends, talk typically centers on practical matters, or on opinions about politics, sports, or people in general, and conversation tends to be peripheral to the social interaction:

> Men's adult friendships . . . are often geared toward accomplishing things and having something to show for their time spent together—practical problems solved, the house painted or the deck completed, wildlife netted, cars washed or tuned, tennis, basketball, poker, or music played, and so on. Shared talk may occur during these pursuits, but it is not the principal focus. [Rawlins, 1992]

As a result of these basic gender differences, women tend to discuss problems with their friends, expecting an attentive and sympathetic ear, and if necessary, a shoulder to cry on. Men, on the other hand, are less likely to talk about their problems, and, when they do, they expect practical solutions rather than sympathy (Tannen, 1990).

One comparison study of men's and women's friendships found that women were much more likely to reveal their weaknesses to their friends, whereas men were more likely to reveal their strengths (Hacker, 1981). In fact, about 25 percent of the women (but none of the men) revealed *only* their weaknesses, fearing that sharing strengths might be considered bragging. By contrast, 20 percent of the men (but none of the women) revealed *only* their strengths, fearing that admitting weaknesses might be consid-

Figure 19.4 *Friendship patterns vary from person to person, of course, and gender stereotypes regarding these patterns are often wide of the mark. Nonetheless, on the whole, friendships between men tend to take a different direction than those between women. Men typically do things together—with outdoor activities frequently preferred, especially if they lend themselves to showing off and friendly bragging. Women, on the other hand, tend to spend more time in intimate conversation, perhaps commiserating about their problems rather than calling attention to their accomplishments.*

ered unmanly. (Interestingly, for many men, the only person they revealed their vulnerabilities to was a woman, usually a romantic partner.)

Closely related to this gender difference in self-revelation is the fact that men's friendships are more clearly tinged with open competition, as reflected in the "bantering, kidding, and needling" that often characterize them (Wright, 1982). Close men friends learn to handle this rivalry with some care. In the words of one man: "I'm sure each of us wants to gain greater status in the eyes of the other . . . but I can't think of any competition where one comes out a winner and the other a loser" (Rawlins, 1992). Thus, whereas friendship for women may be important as a way of coping with problems via shared fears, sorrows, and disappointments, for men, friendship serves primarily as a way of maintaining a favorable self-concept.

Many social scientists have asked why men's friendships seem so much less intimate than women's (e.g., Rawlins, 1992; Fox et al., 1985; Allan, 1989). One reason is that intimacy is grounded in mutual vulnerability, a characteristic that is discouraged by the cultural pressure on men to be strong and hide their fears. Another reason is that, from childhood, boys seem inclined to be more active and girls more verbal, and this early difference may lay the groundwork for interaction patterns in adulthood (Tannen, 1990). A third reason is homophobia: many men avoid any expression of affection toward other men because they fear its association with homosexuality. Ironically, the most open expressions of affection between men tend to occur in situations where they are banded together in the name of aggression, such as intensely competitive team sports or in military combat, perhaps because in such situations, few people would think to question a man's masculinity.

Male-Female Friendship

Overall, the basic differences in male and female same-sex friendships pose important opportunities and problems for cross-sex friendships. For one thing, in the face of society's tendency to overemphasize the differences between the sexes, cross-sex friendships offer men and women an opportunity to learn more about their commonalities, as well as to gain practical skills that may have traditionally been "reserved" for the other sex—from mending to car repair, from money management to child care. Further, to the extent that men and women do indeed have separate experiences and perceptions, cross-sex friendships can help expand each partner's perspective on key social and ethical issues.

At the time, cross-sex friendships also have special problems, as each sex tends to have its own expectations for the friendship process. For example, a woman can be genuinely upset at what her male friend considers good-natured teasing (the kind he applies to his male friends), while a man is likely to wonder why his woman friend continues to talk about her problems rather than taking *his* advice on how to solve them (Tannen, 1990). An additional hazard is that men are often inclined to try to sexualize a platonic friendship, while women may be offended when a man does not understand that they are "just good friends" (Rawlins, 1992).

All told, then, the typical female friendship pattern seems, at first blush, to be better in terms of meeting intimacy needs. Even though men are sometimes critical of women for gossiping, sharing secrets, or simply spending too much time on the phone with their friends (Allan, 1989), these patterns help prevent the loneliness and self-absorption that Erikson describes as a danger of the stage of intimacy versus isolation. As one study of college students summarized:

> for both males and females, more interaction with females was related to less loneliness . . . for both males and females and for both male and female partners, disclosure, intimacy, pleasantness and satisfaction were related to less loneliness. The implication is that both sexes need the same qualities in their interaction to avoid loneliness but that females are more adept at providing them. [Wheeler et al., 1983]

It must be noted, however, that, on the job, the male pattern of keeping one's distance while sharing useful information, productive activities, and reciprocal assistance may be more effective and efficient. In fact, in the work setting, where "the shifting sands of promotion and demotion render some friends expendable," a woman's tendency to seek mutual loyalty among confidantes who know each other's secrets can undermine her ability to do the job (Rawlins, 1992). Women may be handicapped vocationally if they cannot treat their work colleagues with some distance and dispatch, just as men may be handicapped psychologically if they cannot share their problems with their personal friends.

Friendship and Marriage

For most young adults, the friendship circle remains robust until they marry, and then it typically shrinks. The main reason is a practical one: in the busy years of simultaneously building a marriage, establishing a home, pursuing a career, and raising children, there is only limited time and energy for friendship (Rawlins, 1992; Jessor et al., 1991).

Marriage brings other complications to the friendship network. In some cases, friends are seen as a potential threat to the marriage, particularly in the case of cross-sex friendships. A man's major concern in this regard is that his mate's relationship with a close male friend may involve sexual attraction, while women become more upset if their partner seems emotionally involved with another woman (Rawlins, 1992; Buss et al., 1992).

Even close friends of the same sex are sometimes considered rivals by newly married spouses, partly because neither sex necessarily understands the typical friendship patterns of the other. Many husbands feel excluded and even subverted by their wife's eagerness to discuss personal information, including marital matters, with her friends, while many wives feel neglected because of their husband's desire to be off with his buddies (Allan, 1989). Typically, as a marriage lasts over a period of years, both partners become less jealous of outsiders, as well as better able to develop "couple friends," sharing activities and confidences with another married pair.

The Development of Love and Marriage

Although, for almost everyone, having close friends is one important way to satisfy one's need for affiliation, for most adults, having a close relationship with a mate is an even more important goal, a goal that often culminates in marriage.

In much of the world, of course, marriage is not what it once was—a legal, and usually religious, arrangement, sought at the onset of adulthood and socially sanctioned as the sole avenue for sexual expression, as the only legitimate context for childbearing, and as a lifelong source of intimacy and support. Among the statistics that make this point are the following: in the United States today, the proportion of adults who are unmarried is higher than at any other time in this century; only 10 percent of brides are virgins; 30 percent of all births are to unmarried mothers, with at least another 10 percent of first births conceived before marriage; the divorce rate is 48 percent of the marriage rate; and the rate for first marriages in young adulthood is the lowest in fifty years (U.S. Bureau of the Census, 1991; Kahn and London, 1991).

Indeed, between ages 20 and 30, the unmarried are in the majority, with 60 percent of the men and 45 percent of the women never having been married and an additional 3 percent of men and 5 percent of women being already divorced and not yet remarried. Most American adults now spend about half of their twenty years between ages 20 and 40 single (U.S. Bureau of the Census, 1991). Similar trends are apparent in virtually every industrialized nation (Burns, 1992).

At the same time that values and practices regarding the institution of marriage have shifted in many ways, the basic needs underlying it have not: adults still seek romance, sexual fulfillment, and commitment to one partner (White, 1990; Robinson et al., 1991), and generally feel happier with life when they are in such a relationship (Lee et al., 1991; Blumstein and Schwartz, 1990). The result of this seeming paradox has been the emergence of **serial monogamy,** a *series* of intimate, committed, relationships, with only one person at a time, inside or outside of the marriage contract. While many people still seek and maintain a single lifelong monogamous relationship, more and more experience serial monogamy over the sixty or so years of their adulthood.

These relationship patterns, it should be noted, are not exclusive to heterosexual couples: long-term homosexual relationships, once rare, or at least hidden, are now more common and open. An estimated 5 to 10 percent of all American adults spend some part of their lives in gay or lesbian partnerships, choosing such commitments either exclusively or in a sequence that includes heterosexual relationships (Peplau and Cochran, 1990; Gonsiorek and Weinrich, 1991).

Whatever one's sexual orientation, establishing a committed relationship of sexual bonding and intimacy is, of course, a complex personal, pragmatic, moral, and sometimes religious matter. Let us now look at what developmental study has revealed about some of this complexity, including some of the expected and unexpected research findings regarding the relationship between personal happiness and cohabitation, marriage, and divorce. We will begin with one of the most complex matters of all—love.

Figure 19.5 *Traditionally, both friendship and love flourished within boundaries set by neighborhood and religion. Today, however, affiliation needs are more often met informally across traditional boundaries, as common interests outweigh origins in bringing people into contact with one another. An event like this Colorado bluegrass festival, drawing together people of varied backgrounds, is a likely site for the beginning of new relationships.*

The Dimensions of Love

People sometimes talk and act as though love were a simple, universally understood experience—as though the lyric "All you need is love" says it all. In fact, over the life span, love takes many forms, affected not only by personal preferences and the mutual interactions between the two participants in an ongoing relationship but also by developmental stages, gender differences, socioeconomic forces, and historical and cultural context—all of which makes love complex and often confusing (Sternberg and Barnes, 1988).

To begin with, love styles are quite individualistic, affected by the person's temperament and the history of his or her childhood attachments. Thus some people seem susceptible to passionate and irrational love at first sight; others prefer a loving affection that develops slowly over time; others seek a playful, uncommitted love (Lee, 1988). Still others seek some combination of these, or change from one form to another as they mature.

In addition, partners in a love relationship almost never have precisely the same needs, and thus both almost always experience differing, and varying, degrees of lust and loyalty, jealousy and trust, hot romance and placid companionship—a complex shifting mix that often leads to misunderstanding and the accusation that the other partner does "not know the meaning of love" (Hatfield, 1988; Dion and Dion, 1988).

One theory that might decrease such misunderstandings comes from Robert Sternberg, who says that we should recognize that love does not have one simple form but instead has three distinct components: (1) passion, (2) intimacy, and (3) commitment. Sternberg believes that the relative presence or absence of these three components typifies seven different forms of love (see chart). Further, he finds that the emergence and prominence of each of these components tends to follow a usual developmental pattern as a relationship matures.

Seven Forms of Love

	Passion	Intimacy	Commitment
Liking		●	
Infatuation	●		
Empty love			●
Romantic love	●	●	
Fatuous love	●		●
Companionate love		●	●
Consummate love	●	●	●

Passion

As many researchers have found, passion generally is highest early in a relationship. This is the period of "falling in love," an intense physical, cognitive, and emotional onslaught characterized by excitement, ecstasy, and euphoria. Such moonstruck joy is often a bittersweet business, however, beset with uncertainties about intimacy and commitment and "fueled by a sprinkling of hope and a large dollop of loneliness, mourning, jealousy and terror" (Hatfield, 1988).

The truth is that, early in a relationship, while physical intimacy and feelings of closeness may be strong, true emotional intimacy is not high, because the partners have not shared enough experiences and emotions to be able to understand each other very well. Nor have they gained the firm sense of commitment that comes when various obstacles have been overcome together.

Intimacy

If the relationship is to grow, personal intimacy must intensify: a good, lasting partnership depends on a high level of trust, openness, and acceptance that enables "honest, graceful, complete, and patient communication" without anger or guilt (Hatfield, 1988). Attaining such a high level of intimacy is no simple matter. Every time one partner allows the other to share in a secret, to witness a vulnerability, or understand a hidden shame, he or she takes the risk of misunderstanding, rejection, and pain.

Commitment

As intimacy continues through time, the third aspect of love, commitment, is gradually established, expressed, and strengthened. Commitment grows through a series of day-to-day decisions to spend time together, care for each other, share possessions, and overcome problems even when it involves some personal sacrifice. Signs of commitment range from formal acknowledgments such as engagement rings, weddings, and childbearing to less dramatic but equally important aspects of mundane life—from shared morning meals to joint checking accounts, from compromises about leisure activities to dividing up the household work.

The Developmental Pattern of Love

As you can see from Sternberg's chart, in the Western ideal, when commitment is added to passion and intimacy, the result is consummate love. For developmental reasons, however, this ideal is difficult to achieve, partly because both passion and intimacy are stimulated by unfamiliarity, unexpectedness, uncertainty, and risk. In the beginning of passion, a reciprocated touch of the hand, a certain smile, or a mere glance at the lover's body will produce sexual excitement. As lovers get used to their physical relationship with each other, more stimulation is required for the same arousal. Similarly, early in a relationship, the simplest shared confidence will promote trust, but once a certain level of intimacy is taken for granted, deeper sharing is required to trigger the rush of relief and togetherness that intimacy brings. In other words, with time, passion tends to fade and intimacy tends to stabilize, even as commitment develops (Sternberg, 1988). This developmental pattern is true over the years for all types of couples, married, unmarried, and remarried, heterosexual and homosexual, young and old (Kurdek and Schmitt, 1986; Coleman and Ganong, 1990).

Figure 19.6 *"How do I love thee? Let me count the ways." If these couples are typical, the older one makes up for fading passion by enjoying a strong and steady commitment to each other.*

Added to this uneven synchrony in types of love is a gender complication. Men are more likely to be "romantics": for example, they are more inclined to believe in love at first sight, to feel that each person has one true love they are destined to find, and to regard true love as magical, impossible to explain or understand. Women, by contrast, are more likely to be "pragmatists," who stop to think before giving themselves over to love. Women tend to believe that financial security is as important as passion in nourishing a close relationship, to feel that there are many possible individuals that a person could learn to love, and to doubt that "love conquers all"—especially barriers such as economic and ethnic differences (Peplau and Gordon, 1989).

Partly because of these divergent approaches toward the idea of love, men are more likely to consider a woman's willingness to engage in erotic physical contact as an expression of her love, while women see a man's willingness to discuss problems and to compromise about domestic disputes as evidence of his love. A prime example of this difference is the way men and women approach makingup after a fight: women feel that the best way a man can apologize is to engage in a long, heartfelt conversation; men feel that the best way for a woman to say she's sorry is with passionate sex (Peplau and Gordon, 1985).

In keeping with these gender biases, women tend to be more cautious than men before engaging in sexual intimacy or marriage. Once they commit themselves to a relationship, however, women tend to be less willing than men to give it up: typically men are the first to fall in love and the first to fall out of it; the first to insist on exclusive sexual commitment, but the first to become unfaithful; the first to suggest marriage, but the first to move toward divorce. A man's dissatisfaction with a romantic relationship is a better predictor that the relationship will end than a woman's dissatisfaction, partly because in their pragmatic approach to love, women tend to consider working on the relationship as a more preferable course of action than leaving one partnership to find another (Gottman and Krokoff, 1989; Cowan and Cowan, 1992).

Cohabitation

Whereas traditional signs of commitment involved engagement announcements and wedding bells, in contemporary times, many couples take their first steps toward commitment with an informal sharing of domestic life. They might first deepen their intimacy by spending occasional nights and weekends together—learning what it is like to be in each other's company in a domestic setting around the clock. If the partners enjoy the experience but are not prepared—financially, legally, or emotionally—to marry, this intimacy often leads to their living together, or **cohabitation.**

Cohabitation has become increasingly common, not only in the United States (see Figure 19.7) but also in, most notably, Canada, Australia, France, and Sweden, as well as in many other countries (Evans, 1992; Rao, 1990; Leridon and Villeneuve-Gokalp, 1989). Indeed, published statistics undoubtedly underestimate the numbers of young unmarried adults who live together, partly because survey respondents do not always give honest answers on this question, and partly because many couples cohabit for a relatively short time, either breaking up or getting married within two years. Overall, probably about half of all young adult North Americans cohabit for at least a few months.

One major reason for the sharp increase in cohabitation over the past twenty years is financial, particularly among young adults, who were the hardest hit by the economic recession of the late 1980s. However, for most

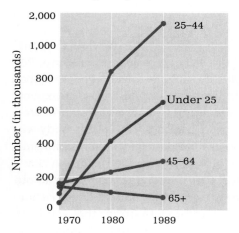

U.S. Cohabiting Couples, in Thousands

Number (in thousands)

2,000 — 25–44
1,000
800 — Under 25
600
400 — 45–64
200
0 — 65+
1970   1980   1989

Source: U.S. Bureau of the Census, 1991.

Figure 19.7 *One reason unmarried couples live together is that cohabitation has many financial advantages over living alone, especially for young adults today, who find their resources stretched thin by the current cost of living. Unfortunately, while cohabitation does save money, it does not protect against broken hearts or broken homes.*

cohabiting young adults, living together is seen less as an economic arrangement than as a tryout for marriage: half have definite plans to marry their current partner, a third are thinking about it, and only one out of five plans not to marry their current roommate, mostly because they plan never to marry anyone (Bumpass et al., 1991). Not only do many couples consider cohabitation a first step toward marriage; they also believe that cohabitation improves the chances of marital success. In a large survey in which cohabiting adults were asked to check the most important reasons to live together, half cited "ensuring compatibility before marriage" (Bumpass et al., 1991).

Despite such youthful hopes, cohabitation does not appear to strengthen marriage. In fact, the opposite seems true. In many studies in North America as well as in Western Europe, marriages that are preceded by cohabitation typically are less happy and less durable (Booth and Johnson, 1988). Of course, correlation does not prove causation, and many factors confound any clear link between cohabitation and marital outcome. For instance, couples who decide to cohabit are already at higher risk of divorce than couples who do not, since they tend to be less conventional, less religious, and lower in SES (DeMaris and Rao, 1992). However, even when such factors are taken into account, studies still find cohabiters overrepresented in the ranks of the divorced. One possible explanation is that cohabitation may decrease the sense of commitment the act of marriage traditionally entails, because, for a couple who have been living together, uniting formally is a much less dramatic turning point in the relationship than it is for couples who share a household for the first time after the wedding (Thompson and Colella, 1992).

Marriage

Although subject to many problems, with its success dependent on dozens of personal and social variations and alternatives, marriage remains the most enduring evidence of couple commitment, celebrated in every culture of the world by the wedding—complete with special words, attire, blessings, food, and, usually, many guests and ostentatious expense. The hoped-for outcome, of course, is a love that deepens over the years, cemented by events such as bearing and raising children, weathering economic and emotional ups and downs, surviving serious illnesses or other setbacks, and sharing a social life and financial commitments. Ideally, over the long run, the marriage is mutually beneficial, with each spouse taking distinct and complementary roles, both strengthened by their relationship.

Given the high rate at which these expectations are dashed, however, many experts and lay people have tried to figure out what makes a marriage work. One important developmental factor is clear: the age and maturity of the partners. In general, the younger marriage partners are when they first wed, the less likely their marriage is to succeed (Martin and Bumpass, 1989). For example, in the United States, marriages involving brides under age 20 end in divorce three times as often as marriages involving brides in their 20s, and about six times as often as marriages begun when either spouse is 30 or older (U.S. Bureau of the Census, 1991). One reason for the high failure rate of marriages begins at a young age is that, as

Erikson explains, intimacy is hard to establish until identity is reached. Many older adolescents and young adults are still figuring out their values and roles, so a young couple might initially see themselves as compatible only to find their values and roles diverging as they become more mature. Further, the compromise and interdependence that are part of establishing intimacy are hard to achieve until one has a clear notion of self and has experienced independence. This correlation between age at marriage and risk of divorce does not indicate straightforward causation, however. For instance, those couples who marry young are often burdened with other factors that make success less probable, such as a pregnant bride, an unemployed groom, and unhappy in-laws.

Another factor influencing marital success is the degree to which a couple is homogamous or heterogamous. When studying various cultures around the world, anthropologists draw a distinction between the custom of **homogamy,** that is, marriage within the same tribe or ethnic group, and **heterogamy,** or marriage outside the group. In industrialized nations, homogamy and heterogamy are more a matter of the degree to which the partners are similar in interests, attitudes, and goals, as well as in background variables such as cohort, religion, SES, ethnicity, and local origin. In general, the more heterogamous a marriage is, the less likely it is to succeed, perhaps partly because every difference creates the potential for tension and disagreement.

A third factor affecting the fate of a marriage is **marital equity,** the extent to which the two partners perceive a rough equality in the partnership. According to one theory, called **exchange theory,** marriage is an arrangement in which each person contributes something useful to the other, something the other would find difficult to attain alone (Edwards, 1969). The marriage becomes a stable and happy one when both partners consider the exchange a fair one. Historically, the two sexes traded quite gender-specific commodities: men provided social status and financial security, while women provided beauty, sex, homemaking skills, and childbearing potential.

In many modern marriages, however, the equity that is sought involves shared contributions of a similar kind: instead of husbands earning all the money and wives doing all the domestic work, both are now expected to do both. Similarly, both partners expect sensitivity to their needs and equity regarding dependence, sexual desire, shared confidences, and so on. Equity is not easy to achieve or maintain, as many factors—including the arrival of children and the aging process itself—can shift the balance between the spouses. In some marriages, the balance changes as one or the other spouse becomes much better educated or attains increased job status, making the marriage less equal, and usually less happy (Tzeng, 1992). Even if the balance does not change in such obvious ways, feelings of inequality arise in almost every modern marriage because the ideology of the changing roles of husbands and wives is not synchronized with actual practice, making both spouses feel somewhat resentful. One widespread instance occurs during early parenthood, when the pressures of infant and child care make women, particularly, feel household labor is not equitably divided (Suitor, 1991). Most marriages weather such temporary inequities, finding ways to redress the balance if time alone does not solve the problem. Other marriages, of course, founder on this very issue.

Figure 19.8 *Whether or not this family is as "traditional" as its size and setting suggest, the longevity and harmony of the parents' relationship to each other depends, according to exchange theory, on each partner's perception of how balanced their mutual contributions to the marital relationship and the family unit are.*

Divorce

Throughout this book, adopting a life-span view of development has enabled us to recognize that many events that seem isolated, personal, and transitory are actually interconnected, socially mediated, and have enduring implications. Divorce is a prime example. The ending of a marriage does not occur in a social vacuum but, rather, is influenced by factors in the social macrosystem as well as in the family microsystem, affecting the lives of many people for years to come (White, 1990).

One indication of the impact that social systems have on divorce is the wide variation in divorce rates from nation to nation. The United States has the highest rate of any major country: almost one out of every two marriages ends in divorce. Many other industrialized countries (including Canada, Sweden, Great Britain, and Australia) have a divorce rate close to one in three, while others (including Japan, Italy, Israel, and Spain) have a markedly lower rate—only about one marriage in ten (Tremblay, 1988; U.S. Bureau of the Census, 1991).

Historical variations are as marked as national ones. Worldwide, divorce increased over most of the past fifty years but stabilized in more recent years. This trend is particularly apparent in the United States (see Figure 19.9).

Certainly some of those cultural and historical variations occur because of differences and fluctuations in laws and social norms (White, 1990). For example, in the United States, laws that had "preserved" a vast number of troubled marriages by permitting divorce only on proof of serious spousal misconduct gave way in the 1970s to "no fault" laws that granted divorce simply on the assertion of incompatibility. One result was a sudden increase in the number of divorces, as many marriages that had limped along for years were finally dissolved. Similar booms occurred later in other countries when their divorce laws also eased.

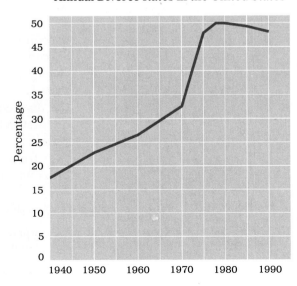

Annual Divorce Rates in the United States

Figure 19.9 *That the divorce rate has leveled off in recent years in the United States can be seen as an encouraging sign—except for the fact that the leveling-off has occurred at about one divorce for every two marriages, a rate that is higher than that of any other nation in the world.*

This boom is now over, but the divorce rate remains high and will probably continue to, as suggested by another historical trend: married couples today are less likely than their counterparts in earlier cohorts to consider their marriages very happy (Glenn, 1991).

Why are there fewer long-lasting, happy marriages than there once were? The reasons suggested range from cultural values that now extol individualism and denigrate family unity to changing gender roles and greater economic opportunity for women (White, 1990; Trent and South, 1989). No doubt, marital outcome is affected by all manner of social, economic, and demographic factors. However, from a life-span developmental perspective, cognitive factors may outweigh sociological ones: crucial to the endurance of a particular marriage are the expectations for the marriage, and of each other, that each partner holds.

The Role of Expectations

Many developmentalists believe that a substantial part of the increasing divorce rate is the result of a cognitive shift that has led most spouses today to expect a great deal more from each other than spouses in the past did. As we have just seen, in earlier decades marital equity was judged on the basis of firm gender roles. As long as both partners did their jobs, the marriage usually survived. As one woman, married in 1909, advised newlyweds on her seventy-first wedding anniversary:

> Don't stop on the little things. Be satisfied whatever happens. Ben didn't commit adultery, he's not a gambler, not a liar . . . So what's there to complain about? [Elevenstar, 1980]

In addition, husbands and wives in the past usually did not expect to really understand each other: they generally assumed that masculinity and femininity are opposites, and that the sexes therefore are naturally a mystery to each other. Today, marriage partners have a much more flexible view of marriage roles and responsibilities and are likely to expect each other to be a friend, lover, and confidant as well as a wage-earner and caregiver.

Evidence for this shift in what is expected from marriage partners is seen in the changing reasons given for divorce. In 1948, recently divorced women were asked what had caused the break-up of their marriage. Cruelty, excessive drinking, and nonsupport were among the most common reasons cited (Goode, 1956). A comparable survey during the divorce boom of the 1970s found lack of communication and poor understanding to be the most common reasons (Kitson and Sussman, 1982).

Ironically, while couples expect more from a relationship than couples once did, they may at the same time devote less of themselves to a marriage because they are alert to the possibility of divorce. As one review of declining happiness in marriage notes, it would seem that

> when the probability of marital success is as low as it is in the United States today, to make a strong, unqualified commitment to a marriage—and to

make the investment of time, energy, and foregone opportunities that entails—is so hazardous that no totally rational person would do it. . . . If this reasoning is sound, the current low probability of marital success in the United States will tend to be self-perpetuating, and disseminating information on the low probability may have a negative effect on marital success. Indeed, the institution of marriage may be as healthy as it is only because of the unrealistic optimism of many persons who marry. [Glenn, 1991]

Assessing Alternatives

Expectations play a role in another sense, too, in that the likelihood of a marital breakup depends more on how the partners assess the alternatives to the marriage than on how they assess the relationship itself (Udry, 1981; Drigotas and Rusbult, 1992). Thus, people who are relatively happy in marriage might nevertheless divorce if they think that they would be even happier single or with another partner (Felmlee et al., 1990). Correspondingly, unhappy spouses might stay married if they see no better options, which is more often the perspective of people who have children, or low income, or who are over age 30 (Heaton and Albrecht, 1991). This helps explain why marriages that fail usually do so within the first five years: men and women who are still relatively young have an easier time coping with the adjustment to divorce, and the chances of finding a new lasting relationship are higher for them than for older divorced persons.

As more and more people have become divorced, the stigma once attached to that status has largely disappeared, and, for some, divorce seems a "normal" stage of family life (Kitson and Morgan, 1990). As one father, himself married three times, said of his 28-year-old son who was about to wed, "Twenty-eight is about the right age for a first marriage." As divorce becomes more acceptable, fewer individuals in unhappy marriages feel compelled to avoid divorce at almost any cost. At the same time, however, most people undertake their first divorce underestimating the psychic costs of severing a marriage bond.

The Impact of Divorce

What is the actual impact of divorce on the separating couple? Initially it is usually quite negative in almost every dimension—health, happiness, self-esteem, financial stability, social interaction, and child-rearing (Kitson and Morgan, 1990). Overall, adjustment to divorce is much more difficult than the ex-spouses had anticipated, for several reasons. One is that, prior to quitting a marriage, spouses are often so focused on what is missing in their relationship that they are "hardly aware of needs currently being well served" (Glenn, 1991). Thus many newly divorced adults suffer from the loss of benefits they did not realize they had. Correspondingly, because they underestimated their emotional dependence on each other, feuding ex-spouses find that the unrestrained rejection they are experiencing is unexpectedly painful, while friendly ex-spouses find that their positive relationship impedes their postdivorce adjustment (Tschann et al., 1989).

In addition, in the first year of divorce, many ex-spouses become even angrier and more bitter with each other than they were in the last months of the marriage. Often this is not entirely their fault: the legal system fosters contention over alimony, the division of property, and/or child custody. Then, too, the need to preserve a sense of self-esteem in the face of a failed marriage almost requires that each spouse direct some fury and blame at the other.

Another adjustment problem is that the ex-spouses' social circle almost always shrinks in the first year after divorce: former friends and in-laws find it difficult to remain on good terms with both halves of a severed couple; neighborhood friends are lost when one or both spouses move away; and casual friends and work colleagues tend to distance themselves when the emotional demands of the newly divorced person suddenly escalate. The cumulative result is the loss not only of friendships but of vital support at a time of high need.

Given all this, it is not surprising that newly divorced people are more prone to loneliness, disequilibrium, irrational sexual behavior, and erratic patterns of eating, sleeping, working, and drug and alcohol use. Fortunately, in most cases, such effects generally dissipate with time (Price and McHenry, 1988; Vaughn, 1987).

For many people, however, certain effects linger over the years (Kitson and Morgan, 1990). National surveys find that single divorced adults of every age are least likely to be "very happy" with their lives, not only when they are compared to married people but also when they are compared to never-married or widowed adults (Glenn and Weaver, 1988; Lee et al., 1991). Ten years after the divorce, many still have ongoing episodes of intense anger, loneliness, and disappointment, with enduring feelings of betrayal and abandonment (Wallerstein and Blakeslee, 1990). One reason for this long-term effect is that divorced individuals who do not remarry generally have less income (especially true for women with children) and a smaller social circle (especially true for men) than their never-divorced peers. Even taking finances and friendship into account, however, those who are divorced, especially if they have been divorced more than once, have higher rates of depression and poor health (Menaghan and Lieberman, 1986; Kurdek, 1991).

Extensive research confirms that the presence of children is a key factor that makes adjustment to divorce more difficult. Especially in the first year or two after the divorce, children often create additional direct stresses as they become more demanding, disrespectful, or depressed. The presence of children also adds financial pressures, forces the ex-spouses to maintain contact with each other, visibly reminds them of what might have been (or of what actually was), and makes remarriage less likely (Masheter, 1991; Maccoby et al., 1990). The financial burden of child-rearing usually falls heaviest on custodial mothers, who typically lose about 30 percent of their total available income because whatever child support payments they receive and salary they earn do not offset their increased child-care expenses and the loss of the father's direct

Figure 19.10 *Ensuring good child care is one of the hardest problems facing divorced parents. Fortunately, as the sheer number of divorced families increases, so do the creative alternatives to traditional homes. Many divorced parents with children share a household with another adult who also has children—a solution that seems to work out well for these two fathers and their children.*

contribution to total household expenses (Kitson and Morgan, 1990). (It can be even worse than that: one careful study of California divorces found that, on average, divorced women with dependent children experienced a 73 percent decline in their standard of living in the year after a divorce, while their ex-husbands experienced a 42 percent rise [Weitzman, 1985].) Some of this disparity is caused by fathers who provide no child support at all—about 40 percent of the total nationwide. But even paying fathers typically contribute far less than when they were married, often because neither they nor the courts appreciate the full cost of raising a child (fathers often think solely in terms of food and clothing) or the practical impact of the gender gap in average salary.

Although noncustodial fathers may benefit financially, they suffer in another way. Many of today's fathers want to be active in their children's lives, but few divorced fathers are, often for reasons they neither understand nor control. One is that, as children develop, their interests and emotional needs change, and parental anticipation of, and adjustments to, these changes are difficult without frequent, ongoing interaction with the child. In addition, in many traditional couples, fathers are the source of most of the demands and discipline and mothers are the source of most of the warmth and indulgence, a balance that fosters healthy child development when both parents support each other (see Chapter 10). But after divorce, mothers typically assume much more authority, and children are less likely to accept their father's attempts at discipline and direction.

Finally, many custodial mothers express their anger at their reduced financial circumstances by limiting the father's physical and emotional access to the child—either directly by forbidding contact without support payments, or indirectly by creating practical obstacles to visitation or otherwise trying to undermine the father's role.

The net result for divorced fathers is that most of them become peripheral to their children's lives, as shown in one national study (Seltzer, 1991) that found fathers less involved with their children with every passing year (see Figure 19.11). As time goes on, these trends continue, with many aging divorced fathers having virtually no contact with their grown children, paying a steep developmental price in old age for their marital problems decades earlier.

Remarriage

For many divorced individuals, the perceived solution to the problems arising from a failed marriage seems to be another marriage. Almost 80 percent of divorced people remarry—on average, within three years of being divorced (Glick and Lin, 1986). In fact, in the United States, almost half of all marriages (47 percent) are remarriages for at least one of the spouses (U.S. Bureau of the Census, 1991). Remarriage is more likely if the divorced person is relatively young, in part because there are more potential partners still available. For the same reason, especially at older ages, men are more

Father's Role After Separation and Divorce

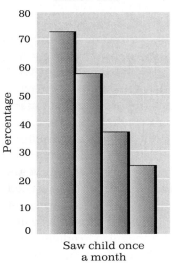

Saw child once a month

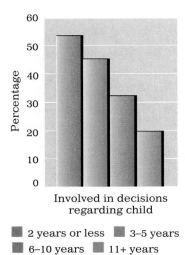

Involved in decisions regarding child

■ 2 years or less ■ 3–5 years
■ 6–10 years ■ 11+ years

Source: Seltzer, 1991.

Figure 19.11 *As graphically shown here, time tends to weaken the bonds between divorced fathers and their growing children, even when both generations wish it were otherwise.*

Figure 19.12 *This football star is surrounded by his family—father, stepmother and baby half-brother. This and other types of "nontraditional" family structures, which are becoming as all-American as football itself, can function very well, even though they inevitably encounter additional stresses as their family interactions require forging new paths of authority and affection.*

likely to remarry than women, because men tend to marry younger women, whereas women tend to marry older men, which means that there is a substantial sex difference in the number of available partners. For every divorced man between the ages of 30 and 34, there are three unmarried women in his age group, and twelve between ages 20 and 29; for every divorced woman between the ages of 30 and 34, there are only two unmarried men in her age group, and 2.5 between ages 35 and 44.

Remarriage often brings initial happiness and other benefits: divorced women typically become financially more secure, and divorced men typically become healthier and more social once they have a new partner. For men, in particular, remarriage often restores the fulfillment of parenthood in one of three ways: improved relationships with their original children, new bonds with custodial stepchildren, or the birth of a baby—an event that typically strengthens the second marriage while loosening the holdover emotional bonds of the first.

Popular wisdom to the contrary, however, there is no guarantee for either sex that love is better the second time around: remarried people generally report lower rates of happiness than people in first marriages, and their divorce rate is about 25 percent higher (Glenn, 1991; Martin and Bumpass, 1989). One reason is that some lonely divorced people marry too quickly, "on the rebound" (sometimes to the first person who seems interested). In many instances, however, an important factor is the disruptive effects of stepchildren. Within three years after marriage, the divorce rate of remarriages involving stepchildren is 17 percent, compared with 10 percent for childless remarriages and 6 percent for first-time marriages (White and Booth, 1985).

Another reason is that remarried individuals may have learned from their first marital experience, being quicker to recognize problems and thus to either resolve the conflict or sever the tie. Some indication of this is that, compared with people in first marriages, remarried people are more likely to describe their marriages as either very happy or quite unhappy, with less middle ground (Coleman and Ganong, 1990).

It may also be that remarriages break up more often than first marriages because of the temperament of the people who find themselves remarried. That is, some individuals may be temperamentally prone to divorce (perhaps by virtue of being unusually impatient, dissatisfied, or adventurous), as suggested by another statistic: the more often a person has been married, the more likely their current marriage is to end in divorce.

One final comment. Most of the comparative research reported above was designed to spot the problems in each form of intimacy, and to highlight the differences between one marital status and another. Consequently, it is easy to exaggerate the developmental impact that a stable marriage, or no marriage, or a string of divorces has on the individual. In truth, marital status is only one of dozens of factors affecting adult psychosocial development, and the similarities between first and second marriages, or between parenthood alone or with a mate, or between being single, divorced, or widowed, are more apparent than the differences. Certainly many happy and fulfilled individuals, as well as many miserable and lonely ones, can be found in every status category. As we will now see, diversity also is apparent in the ways individuals approach the other task of adulthood, generativity.

Generativity

The motivation to achieve is one of the strongest, and most frequently studied, of human motives. The observable expression of achievement motivation, of course, varies a great deal from person to person and culture to culture. For example, some people and some cultures are much more competitive or cooperative than others; some seek tangible signs of success, while others strive for less materialistic attainments; some emphasize college degrees or official titles, while others strive for neighborhood respect or family attainments. But in one way or another, for our self-esteem as adults, we all need to feel successful at something that makes our lives seem productive and meaningful. Adults meet their need for achievement, confronting what Erikson describes as the crisis of generativity versus stagnation, primarily through their work and through child-rearing. Let us look first at career development, then at family development, to see what the possibilities and problems with both are.

The Importance of Work

For many people, their job is central to their life for reasons additional to economic ones. This fact is highlighted by studies in which workers have been asked what they would do if they were to become sudden millionaires. In study after study, in many countries, more than 80 percent of the workers replied that they would keep on working (Harpaz, 1985). The centrality of work is also revealed in research on unemployment, which finds that many laid-off workers feel lost, depressed, and empty without a job (Kelvin and Jarrett, 1985). In addition to putting bread on the table, work clearly serves other functions. As Marie Jahoda (1981) explains, employment

> imposes a time structure on the waking day . . . implies regularly shared experiences and contacts with people outside the nuclear family . . . links individuals to goals and purposes that transcend their own . . . defines aspects of personal status and identity, and . . . enforces activity.

Other activities could perform a similar function, of course. Attending school or volunteering to help others also meets similar needs. But, in most Western cultures, paid employment is the most common source of generativity, and happiness or unhappiness at work is likely to spill over to the rest of life (Ferber and O'Farrell, 1991; Zedeck, 1992).

Young Adults and Work

Finding satisfying work, however, is not easy for the young adult. Typically, a person's first job is taken without much forethought, and sometimes without regard for the person's own abilities and inclinations or for the changing demands of the job market. Most often the first job is chosen because it is readily available and because friends or family members suggested it. New workers usually have fairly high expectations of what their job will be like, and experience "reality shock" when the job turns out to be less exciting and purposeful than anticipated (Reilly et al., 1981). Since almost every job involves more dull moments, and more bureaucratic hassles, than the naive worker imagined, it is not surprising that young workers tend to be less satisfied with their jobs than older workers are, and are more likely to switch

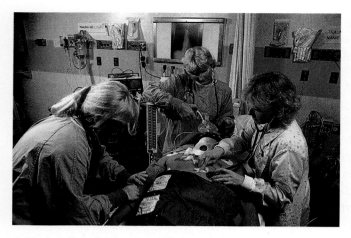 

Figure 19.13 *Which would you rather be, a nurse working in the trauma room of a hospital or an engineer figuring out a design problem? Your answer is likely to depend to some degree on your sex, because in addition to talent, personality, and working conditions, gender expectations affect the probability of a particular young adult's choosing a particular career. In America in 1991, 95 percent of all nurses were women and 92 percent of all engineers were men.*

jobs and careers. In fact, the average American working adult has had three distinct occupations by age 30 (Goldstein, 1984). Naturally, some of these shifts occur in response to changes in the employment market, but, in early adulthood, most shifts occur as the young worker gains a better understanding of his or her own abilities, aspirations, and personality, with or without the help of career counseling (Loman, 1991).

Interestingly, satisfaction with work is less related to variations in wages and benefits than to workers' feelings that their work is meaningful and that their supervisors and coworkers recognize their efforts (Dawis, 1984; Roth, 1989). Also important are the chance to learn new skills and the opportunity to realize one's potential.

At the same time, for many workers, the degree to which their job allows them to mesh work with the rest of their life is a major determinant of job satisfaction. For example, the opportunity to choose one's own work hours, called **flextime,** generally increases worker satisfaction and thereby reduces absenteeism (Ralston and Flanagan, 1985). Other variations in the work schedule, such as job-sharing, home-based work, a compressed work week, or paid leave to care for family needs, all increase job satisfaction (Vanderkolk and Young, 1991). These innovations were originally designed for working mothers, but they are equally beneficial to men in dual-earner families. In fact, one study of 149 such men found that those who worked longer hours on a flexible schedule were less stressed than those who worked a shorter, rigid shift. As the researchers state: "Having a schedule flexible enough to take care of family needs was associated with lower role strain, less marital, parental, and professional stress, and, ultimately, with lower physical distress" (Guelzow et al., 1991).

Another related factor in overall work satisfaction is the social culture within a particular organization, which may foster either cooperative interactions that continue to provide stimulation and encouragement or critical evaluations that undercut the individual's motivation (Schein, 1990; Katzall and Thompson, 1990).

Mentoring

One particular aspect of the organizational culture that is crucial to the success of new workers is the availability of a **mentor,** a more experienced worker who helps guide a younger one. While some firms assign supervisors to teach newcomers, the most effective mentoring relationship often arises spontaneously within a work setting that provides time and a social climate to nurture such relationships. Ideally, the mentor fills many roles—teacher, sponsor, coach, protector, role model, confidant, counselor, and friend (Krim, 1985). In these various capacities, the mentor passes on not only "formal" know-how about the technical aspects of the job but also "informal" tips, such as how to deal with a difficult superior, what office rivalries to beware of, where to find shortcuts through the bureaucratic maze, and the like. Given the closeness of the mentor-mentee relationship, most workers feel more comfortable with mentors of the same sex, because cross-sex mentoring raises the possibility or suspicion of a sexual relationship. Difficulties in finding a suitable mentor may be one important reason many women have a hard time advancing in male-dominated occupations (Keele, 1986), bumping up against a **glass ceiling,** an invisible barrier that halts promotion and undercuts their power at a certain managerial level.

Similar difficulties are encountered by members of minority groups, especially when they are entering a work setting in which their supervisors are from another group. Without some mutual adjustment, ideally mediated by a mentor or manager who understands the subtleties of corporate norms, ethnic values, linguistic etiquette, and gender differences, many workers feel underutilized, misunderstood, and disrespected (Keele, 1986; Thiederman, 1991). Indeed, this is not just a perception; it is a reality: African-, Hispanic-, and Asian-Americans often bump against a glass ceiling of their own, preventing all but a token few from rising in the work hierarchy (Morrison and Glinow, 1990). Not only does this reduce productivity and thwart generativity; it often results in the pain of racial discrimination, sexual harassment, and ethnic bias—all avoidable hazards of the modern workplace. (Other work-related psychosocial problems that are more common as workers grow older, including burn-out, alienation, and early retirement, will be discussed in Chapter 22.)

While employment is often a major source of fulfillment *and* frustration for many adults, the other major source of generativity—parenting—generally produces more of both, as we will now see.

Figure 19.14 *The lasting impact of the Clarence Thomas confirmation hearings in 1991 will lie not in who was telling the greater portion of the truth but in the effect the hearing process itself had in galvanizing women across the country to speak out openly about the many forms of sexual harassment and discrimination they face on the job. Not the least of the factors that stirred women so strongly were the "old boy" attitudes that seemed entrenched among certain members of the Senate Judiciary Committee.*

Parenthood

When one stranger asks another "What do you do?" the answer is rarely "Raise children." Yet adults are as likely to be parents as to be employed, and many of them consider the successful rearing of their children to be their most important achievement. As Erikson points out, while generativity can take many forms, its chief form is "establishing and guiding the next generation," usually through parenthood. Caring for children fulfills an important adult need, according to Erikson (1963), for "the fashionable insistence of dramatizing the dependence of children on adults often blinds us to the dependence of the older generation on the younger one. Mature man [and woman] needs to be needed." The interdependence of parents and children is a lifelong process, which begins at conception and continues throughout late adulthood.

A LIFE-SPAN PERSPECTIVE

Stages of the Family Life Cycle

The family life cycle can be seen as developing through several fairly distinct stages, which are based primarily on the age of the oldest child in the family (see Table 19.1).

Each stage of the family life cycle has its own characteristics and requirements. How parents respond to them varies greatly because of the diversity of both children's and parents' personality structures and psychological needs. Some parents, for instance, like the dependence of infants, enjoying the feeling of being totally needed; others feel much more comfortable in the later stages, when children are more independent. Some parents feel lost, sometimes even purposeless, when their last child leaves home; others feel as though they have been given a new lease on life.

TABLE 19.1   Stages in the Family Life Cycle

Honeymoon Period	Lasts from the wedding until the birth of the first child.
Nurturing Period	Lasts until the first child is 2.
Authority Period	Spans the years between 2 and 5.
Interpretive Period	Spans the years between 5 and 12.
Interdependent Period	Occurs when children are adolescents.
Launching Period	Lasts from the home-leaving of the first child to the home-leaving of the last.
Empty-Nest Period	Begins when the last child leaves home.

It is also true that many families do not follow the stages straightforwardly. The many parents who are separated, divorced, single, or remarried experience any number of variations in the family life cycle, from going through all or parts of the cycle without a partner to going through different stages of the cycle simultaneously with children from different marriages. Despite all the diversity in family life cycles, however, some general trends are apparent.

The Honeymoon Period

As noted earlier, many couples today begin sexual intimacy and domestic life before the formal wedding: when this is the case, the "honeymoon" begins at that point. In terms of the family life cycle, the honeymoon period, which is the time of most passion and intimacy, as well as of the least commitment, provides the happiest and, ironically, the most volatile and conflict-filled years. In troubled marriages, this is the time when physical and verbal abuse is most common and separation and divorce are most likely.

During the honeymoon period, most couples must eventually make one crucial decision that will affect the rest of their life together—whether or not to have children. For those couples who make a mutual decision not to have children, or who agree on when to become parents, and are able to postpone childbearing until they are ready, honeymoon happiness tends to remain fairly steady as the years go on. In many cases, however, the initial happiness dips because childbearing does not go according to plan. For one thing, planned children do not always arrive on schedule: as we saw in Chapter 17, about a fifth of all couples are unable to conceive after a year or more of trying, a stress that diminishes intimacy and happiness while increasing conflict (Abbey et al., 1992). The opposite problem also is stressful: about half of all married couples become pregnant unintentionally. While American couples who are committed to each other usually continue the pregnancy (the abortion rate for married women is only about one pregnancy in twelve), many couples are ambivalent and frightened, and often in conflict, about suddenly becoming parents-to-be, and they may remain so even as the pregnancy develops. As described in Chapter 4, every pregnancy is stressful; for those who face parenthood with mixed feelings, it is especially so. Most stressful of all is when the woman wants the baby and the man does not: such couples usually separate before the child is 2 years old (Cowan and Cowan, 1992).

The Nurturing Period: Birth to Age 2

The joy of this period is getting to know a new human being who is just beginning to take shape as an individual. The drawback is that, from virtually the moment of birth, most parents are overwhelmed by the necessity of meeting the infant's need for twenty-four-hour care (Galinsky, 1981; Cowan and Cowan, 1992). In a longitudinal study that followed women from early pregnancy through the first year of motherhood, Myra Leifer (1980) reports that many of the mothers-to-be looked forward to quitting their jobs to be full-time mothers and wives, imagining that they would then have time to prepare gourmet candlelit dinners for their husbands, fashion clever decorations for their homes, and sit in rocking chairs, crooning lullabies to their sleeping infants. The reality was quite different. Their babies needed to be fed, changed, burped, bathed, carried, and cuddled so often that there was little time for anything else in the mother's life, day or night. As one woman said, "For the first time in my life, I'm doing everything in a mediocre way. I don't have enough time, energy, or ability to do things I want to do."

Parenthood and Employment

Until the Industrial Revolution, most married couples worked together all their lives. Wives would help husbands on the farm or in the shop, and husbands helped their wives oversee the children, especially once the children had begun to participate in the family work (at about age 6.). However, with industrialization, workplaces became distant from living places, and women more often stayed home tending to house and children while men earned their living outside the family setting.

In recent decades, smaller families, greater financial pressures, more employment opportunities, and higher education have put many women in the labor market. Virtually all contemporary women are employed at some point in their lives, and most young women today hope to finish their education and find a job before they begin marriage and parenthood. Unlike women of earlier generations who tended to leave work when their children were small, the typical pattern for today's young women is to continue working throughout motherhood, except for a short break in the months immediately following birth. In fact, young women with dependent children are *more* likely to be in the labor market than older women whose children have grown. One reason is that the expenses of child-rearing, coupled with the comparatively low income of young fathers, make the mother's income particularly useful. Another reason is that, as noted, the younger cohorts of women were raised and educated to have careers (Moen, 1991).

When the Mother Leaves Her Job

If a new mother quits her job, she is usually giving up an important external source of self-esteem, social support, and status. Nevertheless, most mothers who have left the work force completely believe that the disruption of their career is worth it (O'Donnell, 1985), partly because they feel that their relationship with their children is warmer and more secure than it would be if they were still employed (Glass, 1992).

In some cases, however, the mother's departure from the work force may boomerang, especially if the mother was happier with her work outside the home than in it—as most women are. Research clearly shows that unsatisfied workers, whether they work outside the home or solely in-

side it, are more likely to be rejecting and punitive toward their families and therefore tend to have the least happy, most troubled children (Spitze, 1988; MacEwen and Barling, 1991). And the truth is that, contrary to the television commercials depicting women happily sniffing the odor of fresh laundry or admiring the shine on their waxed floors, women are less likely to enjoy housework than paid employment (Shaw, 1986), and women who are exclusively homemakers are more likely to be depressed than women who combine parenthood and work.

A mother's departure from the work force is also likely to put stress on the father by making him the sole breadwinner for a growing family. In fact, virtually every American father who is the sole financial support of his family works more than a regular work week to fulfill his provider role. As a result, fathers are overtired and see less of their family, usually to the distress of all concerned (Hochschild, 1989; Piotrkowski, 1979). Further, hard-working fathers are likely to think that their full-time-mother wives are less appreciative than they ought to be, while the most common complaint of full-time mothers is that their husbands do not help enough around the house (Rhyne, 1981; Suitor, 1991).

As financial pressures accumulate, comments and "helpful" advice from friends and relatives often make the psychic problem worse (Robertson et al., 1991). As one father said:

> Most of my responsibility for the family is providing the bread. You know, Daddy is at work, Mommy is at home. Daddy makes the money, Mommy makes the house and takes care of Faith. I get really pissed off at Celia's friends. They're always asking her "How come Ray doesn't look after Faith more?" Man, I'm looking after Faith six days a week, ten hours a day, busting my ass at the plant. [Cowan and Cowan, 1992]

When the Mother Is an Employee

Given the considerable financial pressures of raising children today, it is not at all surprising that most married mothers are working outside the home. Even mothers of infants are likely to stay employed if they possibly can: according to 1990 statistics, 57 percent of married women with a baby under age 1 were in the labor force (U.S. Bureau of the Census, 1992).

Obviously the mother's employment helps with the financial squeeze, but not as much as one might imagine. Because of the generally lower wages of women, employed women, after expenses and taxes, typically boost household income only 16 percent if the husband earns more than $25,000, 24 percent if he earns between $13,500 and $25,000, and 43 percent if he earns less than $13,500 (Hanson and Ooms, 1991).

This financial boost frequently comes at an emotional cost, more often to the adults than to the children. Almost every couple is stressed by the "second shift" of domestic work that awaits their return home (Hochschild, 1989). Almost always, even when they work as many or more hours outside the home, employed wives do much more housework and child care than employed husbands (Brayfield, 1992). In addition, their tasks are those repetitive ones that must be redone daily—meal preparation, cleaning, child care—while the husband's tasks tend to be more flexible in timing, such as taking care of the car or of household repairs. Typically, both partners say they believe in gender equity more than they actually practice it, with wives resenting that husbands do much less than an equal share, while husbands feel that the fact that they do so much more domestic work than their own fathers or their unmarried friends goes unappreciated. For example, in one two-career marriage, the husband thought he was doing his fair share because he took care of all the tasks related to the first floor of the house—the floor that had the car, his workshop, and their dog—while the wife seethed that "her floor" had the kitchen, all the living and sleeping areas, and, not incidentally, their 3-year-old son (Hochschild, 1989).

The more children a couple has, the less likely they are to share equally in household tasks, even if both work the same number of hours outside the home. Not surprisingly, then, division of household labor is more likely to add stress to families that have several young children than to marriages with only one child (Suitor, 1991; Guelzow et al., 1991).

Another potential problem involves the husband's pride. While most men welcome their wife's contribution to the family income, and prefer to marry a woman who can hold a job (South, 1991), many men were raised believing firmly that husbands should be the major breadwinners. Thus, especially if his wife's income surpasses his own—a circumstance most common among younger, low-income men who already feel disrespected by the work world—a man may lose an important measure of self-esteem (Staines et al., 1986).

To make matters worse, stresses of employment and parenthood exacerbate each other and impinge on the marriage (Eckenrod and Gore, 1990; Hughes et al., 1992; MacEwen and Barling, 1991). The worst situation occurs when both spouses are under pressure at work that directly, or indirectly takes away time from their family. (a condition that is typical in the first stages of career development). Not surprisingly, in a national survey, 38 percent of employed fathers and 53 percent of employed mothers said that they would prefer to work fewer hours in order to "spend more time with their spouse and children, even if it meant having less money" (Moen and Dempster-McClain, 1987).

Fortunately, most dual-career families find ways of meeting the demands of family and work, as both government and business are becoming increasingly aware of, and responsive to, family-work interactions (Vanderkolk and Young, 1991; Ferber and O'Farrell, 1991). For example, laws allowing workers to take time off to care for a new baby or a sick family member have now been passed in almost every developed country, most recently the United States, in 1993. Certainly, there are particular times (especially when the children are small), and personalities (such as the ambitious perfectionist), and social contexts (such as employers that expect single-minded dedication, or national policies that idealize traditional gender roles) that make combining career and child-rearing very stressful. Overall, however, at least for most contemporary Americans, those who combine all three roles—spouse, parent, and employee—are healthier and happier than those who do not (Barnett and Baruch, 1987; Howard, 1992; Broman, 1991; Verbugge, 1983).

Many new fathers find that their wives are making more demands on them and giving them less love and care than they did before the baby's arrival. In addition, couples often quarrel over who should do what. One father described a shouting match in which both he and his wife insisted that they were contributing more than their fair share to maintaining the family:

> The answer was that we were both giving a lot, and it was a drain . . . We never did the simplest things to give ourselves time together. We never got a baby-sitter, never went out together. Our lives together just ceased to exist. [Galinsky, 1981]

The Authority Period: Ages 2 to 5

When children become preschoolers, the issue of authority, over the child and within the marriage, becomes crucial. This is often the period of greatest direct confrontation between husband and wife, and between parent and child, due to mounting pressure from increased financial burdens, multiplying household tasks, and shifting roles, as well as to the child's growing need to assert his or her independence, sometimes in strident, destructive ways (Crnic and Booth, 1991). Fathers usually become more involved parents during this period, providing help that mothers welcome but also expressing much more pointed and detailed comments about matters of discipline, education, and the like, a shift that often sets the stage for potential disagreement. An added complication is that many couples have a second child while the first child is under age 6. This doubles the challenges relating to child care, increasing the need for both parents to be directly involved, and adds a new challenge—teaching an egocentric young child to be nurturant and sharing (Stewart, 1990).

The Interpretive Period: Ages 5 to 12

In many ways, parenting grows easier as children become increasingly self-sufficient and as parents' experience at child-rearing accrues. In general, from the time the first child enters school until adolescence, parents need only set realistic goals for their children and provide encouragement and guidance, allowing their children to develop all their latent competencies. During this period, parents' main task is to interpret, adjudicate, and modify the broadening experiences that come from the outside world, as well as from the child's own expanding cognitive awareness. This period is the best time for parents to establish open communication with their child in preparation for the potentially difficult period of adolescence.

The Interdependent Period: Adolescence

Adolescence brings new challenges, as the young person who is developing the body of an adult demands the privileges of adulthood before knowing how to handle the responsibilities that go with them. New alliances are formed in the family: parents feel the need to stand together,

Figure 19.15 *Parenthood changes an adult's life in many ways. Home becomes a place of work, and vacations are less vacations than relocations of that work site, particularly when children are preschoolers. For example, a vacation at the beach usually involves all the standard child-care chores plus extra efforts to keep young children entertained in unfamiliar surroundings, and especially at a place like the beach, constant vigilance toward the children's safety. A day at the beach for this couple is definitely not the carefree respite it might have been a few years before.*

even though a teenager's strivings for independence might provoke quite different responses from mother and father. Meanwhile, siblings, who once took opposite sides on every issue, may unite to defend their own common interest. Each generation has a different stake in the outcome of the various conflicts between adult and teenager, as parents seek to ensure continuity from generation to generation, and adolescents seek their own independent identity (see pp. 412–417).

The Launching Period and the Empty-Nest Period

The remaining stages of the family life cycle are the launching stage, in which one's grown children begin to set out on their own, and the empty-nest stage, in which the last of the "fledglings" have flown. For many middle-aged parents, the successful launching of an adult child, and eventually all of the children, is a time of rejoicing. According to several surveys, the "empty-nest" period of marriage is generally more satisfying than any of the previous stages since the honeymoon, with love between the partners remaining steady, and the problems with the marriage declining, as explained in more detail in Chapter 22.

Alternative Forms of Parenthood

Thus far, we have focused mainly on parents with their own biological children. However, about a third of all North American adults will become stepparents, adoptive parents, or foster parents at some point in their lives. As you learned in Chapter 13, whatever the particular family structure they are in, the outcome for the children depends more on the quality of their care than on the legal or biological ties to their caregiver.

But how do adults fare when they become parents to children who are not their biological offspring? In many ways, they find that these alternative forms of parenthood can be just as "real" or "natural" as any other, entailing the same satisfactions and frustrations as traditional parenthood. At the same time, however, these alternative forms are open to special problems.

The core problem facing many nonbiological parents involves the strength of the parent-child bond. Strong bonds between parent and child are particularly hard to create when a child is old enough—a year or more—to have formed definite attachments to other caregivers who are still available to the child, as is usually the case with stepchildren—the average age of a new dependent stepchild being about 9 years. Stepmothers often enter the marriage with visions of healing a broken family through love and understanding, while stepfathers typically believe that their new children will welcome a benevolent disciplinarian who can bring some order to their lives. Neither of these expectations usually develops. If all goes well, the stepparent usually becomes a close friend, an "intimate outsider," who nonetheless remains much more distant from the stepchild's personal life than he or she initially imagined (Papernow, 1988; Hetherington and Clingempeel, 1992).

Indeed, many stepchildren are fiercely loyal to the absent parent, sabotaging any newcomer's effort to fill the traditional parent-role perhaps directly challenging his or her authority ("You're not my *real* father, so don't tell me what to do"), or continually intruding on the couple's privacy, or evoking guilt by getting hurt, sick, lost, drunk, arrested, and so on (Pasley and Ilhinger-Tallman, 1987). Such childish reactions, often unconscious, may cause the stepparent, or both parents, to overreact in ways that further alienate the child. Even if the stepparent is patient and understanding, it often takes years before children adjust to the changes in the family dynamics that any new spouse creates. It might take forever before the children express the appreciation and affection that a caring stepparent deserves. The dilemmas of stepparenting are reflected in one stepfather's advice for taking on stepchildren:

> Don't ever expect to replace the natural father in their eyes; win their respect; treat them as your own; love them and discipline them as your own; let nothing come between you and your woman—especially the kids. [quoted in Giles-Sims and Crosbie-Burnett, 1989]

This father's final caution is particularly poignant because disobedient and difficult stepchildren, especially those aged 10 and older, are often a precipitating factor in a second divorce (White and Booth, 1985).

Some foster and older adopted children are likewise attached to their birthparents, an attachment that can be especially volatile because of the destructive treatment many of them have experienced. Other foster children present the opposite problem: they never were attached to anyone, and thus rebuff the foster and adoptive parents' attempts to win them over. The attachment between foster parents and children is further handicapped by the fact that the bond can be suddenly severed for reasons that have nothing to do with the quality of foster care, ranging from the biological mother's completing a drug-treatment program and thus qualifying for another attempt at motherhood to a policy shift at the child welfare agency that requires placing the child somewhere else.

Stepparents face different but equally significant threats to their relationship with their children. One potential problem is divorce, which occurs in about half of all marriages involving stepchildren. Usually such divorces halt the children's relationship with their ex-stepparents, who have no legal visitation rights regarding their ex-stepchildren, no matter how strong or long-lasting their emotional bond with them. Even if the marriage continues, at some point the child's other biological parent may take over custody, formally or informally, legally or not. These various realities make both stepparents and foster parents less likely to invest themselves completely in the parent-child relationship.

Adoptive families have an advantage here: they are legally connected for life. Nevertheless, during adolescence, their emotional bonds may abruptly stretch and loosen, for many adoptive children become intensely rebellious and rejecting of family control, even as they insist on information about, or reunification with, their birth parents. The reasons—whether to test their parents' devotion, or to follow the lead of their native temperament, or to discover their roots, or to establish an identity independent from their adoptive family—are understandable, but the result is often a painful demonstration that the parent-child relationship is more fragile than the law pretends (Rosenberg, 1992).

One sign of the difficulties with parent-child attachments in all three situations is that stepchildren, foster children, and adoptive children tend to leave home—running away, marrying, joining the military, being sent away to school, or moving out on their own—earlier than adolescents living with one or both biological parents (Aquilino, 1991). Early home-leaving is particularly likely for adopted children, as they seek their own identity distinct from parental expectations.

All these potential complications certainly make nonbiological parenthood riskier than it is generally pictured to be. However, we must not exaggerate the difficulties here. Most adoptive and foster parents cherish their parenting experiences so much that they try for more of the same, typically seeking a second child within a few years after the arrival of the first. Similarly, once stepparents realize that they cannot fill the shoes of the absent biological parent, they usually find satisfaction in the role they do play. On their part, the children usually reciprocate, if not immediately, then later on when they have a clearer understanding of the voluntary sacrifices their nonbiological parents have made (Rosenberg, 1992; Keshet, 1988).

Indeed, for some stepparents, foster parents, and adoptive parents, the rewards of their work go beyond the immediate household. This is exemplified in the reflections of one American mother of an adopted Korean child, who writes of her deepened understanding of the "global family," and of the bonds that connect one human being with another:

> We [adoptive parents], like these children whom we claim so adamantly as our kids, have deeper roots than we knew, an enlarged sense of family, another place in the heart, and a rich and varied history of facing life issues we would never have encountered without them . . . I hear news about the mudslide [in Brazil, that buried the shacks of 50 families], or the orphans or the starving children, with a refrain at the end: These could be my kids. [Register, 1991]

Perhaps even more than biological parenthood, alternative routes to parenthood tend to make adults more humble, less self-absorbed, and more aware of the problems facing children everywhere. When this occurs, adults become true exemplars of generativity as Erikson and others (1986) described it, characterized by the virtue that is, perhaps, the most important of all—caring for others.

SUMMARY

The Two Tasks of Adulthood

1. Adult development is remarkably diverse, yet it appears to be characterized by two basic needs. First is the need for affiliation, also called the need for love, belonging, and/or intimacy. Second is the need for achievement, as the need for success, esteem, generativity, and work can be called.

2. A number of researchers describe adulthood as occurring in stages, with periods of notable reevaluation and change occurring every decade, and more stable periods occurring between these transitions.

3. Once young adults break away from dependence on their parents, usually by their early 20s, they begin to make commitments to career, marriage, and parenthood.

4. Age 30 can be a turning point, as many men and women reevaluate their earlier decisions and begin what tasks of adulthood, in work, family life, or education, they have not yet started.

5. Adult stages are propelled more by social standards than by biological processes. The social clock varies from time to time and place to place, and this is one reason for the many variations in adult developmental paths.

Intimacy

6. During early adulthood, a primary source of intimacy is the friendship circle, with notably different needs being served by men's and women's same-sex friendships.

7. For most people, the deepest source of intimacy is found through sexual bonding with a mate, a bonding that frequently involves cohabitation, marriage, and/or serial monogamy.

8. Of the many factors that can affect the success or failure of a marriage, three are particularly notable: the age of the partners at marriage, the similarity of their background and values, and the couple's perception of the balance of equity in the marriage.

9. The divorce rate has risen dramatically over the past fifty years, internationally and especially in the United States. The primary factors contributing to this increase include changing divorce laws and changing expectations regarding both the partners' respective marital roles and the permanence of marriage.

10. Divorce is emotionally draining on both partners and is particularly difficult for those who have children. While some divorced parents manage to maintain good relationships with each other and with their children, more typically the mothers have more work and less money than before, and fathers become estranged from their children.

11. Most divorced people remarry, usually attaining more happiness than in their former marriages or than in their divorced state. Especially if there are children from former marriages, however, a new marriage also creates additional stresses.

Generativity

12. For most adults, work is an important source of satisfaction and esteem, as it helps meet the need to be generative.

13. Finding appropriate work is not easy. Most young adults go through a period of career exploration, during which their jobs and vocational goals change. Ideally, the young worker finds not only a fulfilling job but also a mentor, who will guide him or her through the first steps of the career ladder.

14. Parenthood is the other common expression of generativity. Families go through various stages, depending on the ages of the children, with the hardest adjustment to parenthood usually occurring when the children are very young.

KEY TERMS

intimacy versus
   isolation (484)
generativity versus
   stagnation (484)
social clock (486)
serial monogamy (491)
cohabitation (494)

homogamy (496)
heterogamy (496)
marital equity (496)
exchange theory (496)
flextime (504)
mentor (504)
glass ceiling (505)

KEY QUESTIONS

1. How does the social clock affect life choices?

2. What are some typical gender differences in friendship patterns?

3. What are some of the major factors that are likely to affect marital outcome?

4. Why has the divorce rate risen dramatically over the past fifty years?

5. What factors tend to make some divorced people more unhappy than others?

6. Why is work important beyond supplying income?

7. What factors in the workplace tend to enhance job satisfaction?

8. How does the arrival of children affect the honeymoon period?

9. What are some of the rewards and costs of parenthood?

Biosocial Development

Growth, Strength, and Health

Noticeable increases in height have stopped by about age 18 in females and age 20 in males. Physical strength increases through the 20s and peaks at about age 30. Although all body systems function at optimum levels as the individual enters early adulthood, declines in body functions begin to diminish the efficiency of most organ systems at the rate of about 1 percent a year.

Gender Differences and The Sexual-Reproductive System

Both men and women have particular risks during the beginning of adulthood—the men, for violent death, and the women, at least in Western cultures, for dangerous dieting. For both sexes, sexual responsiveness remains high in early adulthood; the only notable changes are that men tend to experience some slowing of their responses with age, and women tend to become more likely to experience orgasm. Problems with fertility, however, become increasingly frequent.

Cognitive Development

Adult Thinking

As an individual takes on the responsibilities and commitments of adult life, thinking may become more adaptive, practical, and dialectical to take into account the inconsistencies and complexities encountered in daily experiences. Years of education is the variable that has been shown to have one of the most powerful effects on the depth and complexity of adult thinking. Significant life events can also occasion cognitive development.

Psychosocial Development

Intimacy

The need for affiliation is fulfilled by friends and, often, by a marriage partner. Friendships are important throughout adulthood but are particularly so for individuals who are single. Men's friendships and women's tend to follow different patterns. The developmental course of marriage depends on several factors, including the presence and age of children and whether the interests and needs of the partners converge or diverge over time. Divorce, if it is to occur, is most likely three or four years after the wedding.

Generativity

The need for achievement can be met both by finding satisfying work and establishing a career and by parenthood, including several types of nonbiological parenthood.

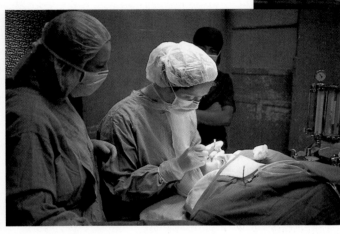

PART VII

Middle Adulthood

Popular conceptions of middle adulthood are riddled with clichés like "midlife crisis," "middle-aged spread," and "autumn years" that conjure up a sense of dullness, resignation, and perhaps a touch of despair. Yet the tone of these clichés is far from reflecting the truth of the development that can and often does occur between the ages of 40 and 60. Many adults feel healthier, smarter, more pleased with themselves and their lives during these two decades than they ever did.

Of course, such a rosy picture does not apply to everyone. Some middle-aged adults are burdened by health problems, or a decline in intellectual powers, or unexpected responsibilities for aged parents or adult children. Some feel trapped by choices made in early adulthood. But the underlying theme of the next three chapters is that in middle age, much of the quality of one's life is directly related to how one views it and to decisions, sometimes new ones, about how to live it. There are still many turning points ahead where new directions can be set, new doors opened, and a healthier and happier life story written.

CHAPTER 20

Middle Adulthood:
Biosocial Development

Middle age is a period when every part of the body gives clear evidence of the accumulating years. From wrinkling of the skin to the decreased frequency of sexual activity, from the lowering of endurance to increased evidence of heart diseases, everything seems, at first glance, to be getting worse, However, this chapter provides a more detailed look at the biosocial changes of middle adulthood, revealing that most middle-aged people feel as healthy as ever, and that they have it in their power to stay vital throughout the middle years. Among the questions that this chapter will examine are the following:

Which signs of aging are superficial and which are significant?

Why are mortality statistics not the best indicator of health?

Do people usually improve or decline in health habits as they grow older?

How are women's illnesses typically different from men's?

Which people are most likely to experience vitality in their sex life during middle age?

What can be done to protect against stress?

In Chapter 17 we saw that the first two decades of adulthood can be considered the prime of life as far as biosocial development is concerned, with the effects of aging being, for many people, barely perceptible. Between the ages of 40 and 60, aging continues at the same steady rate, but the levels of change that are now reached are more difficult to ignore. As we will see, however, adults in middle age can do a great deal to safeguard their vitality and to remedy, or compensate for, many of the physiological declines they experience, discovering in the process that though aging is inevitable, it is not inevitably bad.

Normal Changes in Middle Adulthood

As people advance in age past 40, their hair usually turns noticeably gray and thins appreciably; their skin becomes drier and more wrinkled; and their body shape changes, as "middle-age spread" develops and pockets of fat settle on various other parts of the body—the upper arms, the buttocks, even the eyelids.

For some people, the size as well as the shape of their body changes. As back muscles, connecting tissues, and the bones lose strength, the vertebrae collapse somewhat, causing some individuals to lose nearly an inch in height by age 60 (Whitbourne, 1985). In addition, overeating and underexercising result in more people being noticeably overweight during middle age than during any earlier period.

For the most part these changes in appearance have no significant health consequences. The consequences for self-image, however, can be substantial, particularly for women, because the cultural link between youthful beauty, sexual attractiveness, and social status is much stronger for them than for men (Katchadourian, 1987). The French writer Simone de Beauvoir (1964) probably spoke for many middle-aged women when she confessed in her 50s:

> I loathe my appearance now: the eyebrows slipped down toward the eyes, the bags underneath, and the air of sadness around the mouth that wrinkles always bring. Perhaps the people I pass in the street see merely a woman . . . who simply looks her age, no more, no less. But when I look I see my face as it was, attacked by the pox of time for which there is no cure.

Most developmentalists would find these feelings both understandable and unfortunate. As we will see throughout the rest of this book, the overall impact that aging has on the individual in middle age, and in late adulthood, depends in large measure on the individual's attitude toward growing old.

Figure 20.1 *Advertising images like this one daily reinforce our culture's emphasis on youthful appearance. As the baby-boomers approach middle age, the market for skin-care products to mask the signs of aging is booming. Some people go even further: according to the American Society of Plastic and Reconstructive Surgeons, in 1990 its members alone performed 644,000 cosmetic procedures, one of the more common procedures being a face-lift.*

For those who develop a constructive, adaptive attitude, the difficulties of the aging process can be greatly diminished, and the pleasures, significantly enhanced. Regarding the "pox of time" and the superficial physical changes of middle age, many developmentalists might wish for both men and women a view closer to the one expressed by another writer in her middle years, Germaine Greer (1986):

> Now, at last, we can escape from the consciousness of glamour; we can really listen to what people are saying, without worrying whether we look pretty doing it. . . . We ought to be turning ourselves loose, freeing ourselves from inauthentic ideas of beauty, from discomfort borne in order to be beautiful.

This is not to suggest that developmentalists are in favor of people just "letting themselves go" in middle age. On the contrary, they emphasize that throughout adulthood, the benefits of staying in shape are far more than cosmetic. What they urge is a more balanced view of the changes of aging, one that is, literally and figuratively, more than skin deep.

Now let us take a look at some of the less obvious but more crucial physical changes that occur during middle adulthood.

The Sense Organs

Sometimes before age 60, virtually all adults notice that the functioning of their sense organs is not as acute as it once was. Although all the sensory systems decline at about the same rate, age-related deficits are most obvious in the two most crucial systems, hearing and vision.

Hearing

Most of the hearing losses that adults experience involve three factors: sex (men are more likely than women to develop difficulties), genetic tendencies, and age. In addition, some decline is environmentally caused. Performing very noisy work for long periods without protective headphones, for example, or habitually listening to music at ear-splitting levels, increases hearing loss, both in the short and the long term.

Although some hearing loss is inevitable in middle age, most middle-aged adults can still hear quite well, as the statistics on the ability to hear speech at age 50 suggest (see Table 20.1). It should be noted, however, that these data may underestimate overall hearing losses, because ability to distinguish pure tones declines faster than ability to understand conversation: often the first sign of a hearing loss is difficulty hearing a doorbell or telephone ring in the distance, or a tendency to turn up the stereo. Hearing

TABLE 20.1 Hearing Loss at Age 50

	Men	Women
Can understand a whisper	65%	75%
Cannot understand a whisper, but can understand soft conversation	28%	22%
Cannot understand soft conversation, but can understand loud conversation	5%	2%
Cannot understand even loud conversation	2%	1%

losses are also more evident in the case of high-frequency noises, especially for men.

Fortunately, most hearing losses in middle adulthood are easy to remedy. Usually only a minor accommodation is needed, such as asking others to speak up, adjusting the ring of the telephone, and the like. In the case of more serious loss, today's tiny wireless hearing aids can usually correct the problem much more efficiently than the hearing aids of even a few years ago could.

Vision

The standard measure of visual acuity, which is the ability to focus on objects at various distances, shows great variation from person to person across adulthood, largely because, after puberty, heredity affects focusing much more than age does.

Nevertheless, older adults are more likely to need corrective lenses, and age-related changes in the shape of the cornea affect the kind of lenses they need (Whitbourne, 1985). Young people tend simply to be nearsighted, whereas older adults tend also to be farsighted and astigmatic, necessitating bifocals or two pairs of glasses.

Several other aspects of vision, among them depth perception, eye-muscle resilience, and adaptation to darkness, decline steadily with age (Kosnik et al., 1988). Each of these changes can affect daily life. Decreasing depth perception makes people more likely to trip going down stairs; muscle weakness makes it harder for them to focus on small print for several hours; slower adaptation to darkness increases the time it takes them to begin to find their way in a dark room after coming in from the bright light, or, more ominously, to see the road at night after experiencing the momentary blindness caused by oncoming headlights. These changes are particularly likely to become apparent after age 50. It is noteworthy, however, that middle-aged adults seem to adjust to these changes without major difficulty. Serious accidents, either in a fall or while driving a car, are much more common in late adolescence or late adulthood than in middle adulthood.

Although most age-related vision problems are minor, and relatively easy to correct or compensate for, one can be very serious. **Glaucoma,** an eye disease characterized by an increase of fluid within the eyeball, becomes increasingly common after age 40, and in the United States, Canada, and Great Britain, is the leading cause of blindness by age 70. The incidence of glaucoma is especially high among African-Americans, who are also more likely to suffer serious impairment when it does occur (Wilson, 1989). Luckily, the serious consequences of glaucoma can usually be prevented by early treatment; unfortunately, the disease has no obvious early warning signs. There is, however, a simple optometric test (a puff of air to detect increasing pressure within the eyeball) that spots glaucoma in the early stages, and it should be part of routine health care for every middle-aged person.

Changes in Vital Body Systems

Systemic declines, as outlined in our discussion of early adulthood, continue in the efficiency and the underlying organ reserve of the lungs, the heart,

TABLE 20.2 The Increments of Chronic Disease

Age	Stage	Atherosclerosis (Hardening of Arteries)	Cancer	Arthritis	Diabetes	Emphysema	Cirrhosis
20	Start	Elevated cholesterol	Carcinogen exposure	Abnormal cartilage staining	Obesity, genetic susceptibility	Smoker	Drinker
30	Discernible	Small lesions on arteriogram	Cellular metaplasia*	Slight joint space narrowing	Abnormal glucose tolerance	Mild airway obstruction	Fatty liver on biopsy
40	Subclinical	Larger lesions on arteriogram	Increasing metaplasia	Bone Spurs	Elevated blood glucose	Decrease in surface area and elasticity of lung tissue	Enlarged liver
50	Threshold	Leg pain on exercise	Carcinoma *in situ*	Mild articular pain	Sugar in urine	Shortness of breath	Upper GI hemorrhage
60	Severe	Angina pectoris	Clinical cancer	Moderate articular pain	Drugs required to lower blood glucose	Recurrent hospitalization	Fluid in the abdomen
70	End	Stroke, heart attack	Cancer spreads from site of origin	Disabled	Blindness; nerve and kidney damage	Intractable oxygen debt	Jaundice; hepatic coma
Prevention or Postponement		No cigarettes; no obesity; exercise	No cigarettes; limit pollution; diet; early detection	No obesity; exercise; minimize stress on any one joint	No obesity; exercise; diet	No cigarettes; exercise; limit pollution	No heavy drinking; diet

*Abnormal replacement of one type of cell by another.
Source: Adapted from Fries and Crapo, 1980.

"*Structurally, you're sound. It's your facade that's crumbling.*"

Figure 20.2 *In addition to maintaining better health habits, such as cutting down on fatty foods and not smoking, many middle-aged people are coming to realize the benefits of active conditioning. A moderate diet and a program of regular exercise can produce wonders of restoration, even for a facade like this.*

Drawing by Ross; © 1986 The New Yorker Magazine, Inc.

the digestive system, and so forth, making people more vulnerable to disease (see Table 20.2). However, for most middle-aged people, none of these changes is critical. Indeed, in a nationwide survey of people between the ages of 45 and 64, more than half rated their health as excellent or very good, and only one-fifth rated their health as merely fair or poor (National Center for Health Statistics, 1985).

Reflecting this self-reporting of good health is the fact that, thanks to better health habits and disease prevention, death rates among the middle-aged have declined dramatically over the past fifty years, especially those relating to the two leading killers of this age group, heart disease and cancer. Overall, the death rate of people between ages 40 and 60 in 1990 was only half what it was in 1940. Current estimates are that only 3 out of every 100 40-year-olds will die before age 50, and only 8 out of every 100 50-year-olds will die before age 60 (U.S. Bureau of the Census, 1991).

Variations in Health

Overall statistics about health in midlife are generalities that veil many variations. For example, worldwide, individuals who are relatively well-educated, financially secure, and living in or near cities tend to live longer, with fewer chronic illnesses or disabilities, and to feel healthier than those who are less well educated, with less money, and living in rural areas.

Further, within every nation, certain regions seem healthier than others: in the United States, middle-aged people living in the West and Midwest are healthier than those in the South and Middle Atlantic; in Canada, those in Ontario are healthiest; in Great Britain, health among the middle-aged tends to improve as one moves from north to south (Cruickshank and Beevers, 1989).

The reasons for such differences range from variations in the quality of the environment and of health care to more personal factors relating to the population of a given region. For example, genetic, dietary, religious, and cultural patterns of their respective populations may explain why fatal heart attacks are twice as common in Mississippi as in Utah (Smith, 1987; U.S. Bureau of the Census, 1992). (See Table 20.2 and the Research Report on pp. 527–528 for an assessment of the impact of health habits on disease.)

Four Measures of Health

Before discussing these variations, it is important to recognize that there are at least four distinct measures of health: mortality, morbidity, disability, and vitality.

In one sense, the most solid indicator of the health of given age groups is its irrevocable absence, specifically, the **mortality,** or death rate, as measured by the number of deaths each year per thousand individuals. Mortality statistics are based on legally required death certificates, which indicate age and sex of the deceased as well as the immediate cause of death. This measure allows international and historical comparisons of the health of any age or gender group.

However, while such mortality statistics are obviously useful for developmental comparisons, a much more comprehensive measure of health is **morbidity,** defined as disease of all kinds, "the numerous acute and chronic problems that course through an individual's life, that remit or repeat, worsen or stand still, simply accumulate in number or interact synergistically" (Verbrugge, 1989). Morbidity can be *acute,* that is sudden and severe, ending in either death or recovery, or it can be *chronic,* extending over a long time period.

To truly portray a person's overall health, the picture must be broadened to include two additional measures, disability and vitality. **Disability** refers to a person's inability to perform activities that most others can. A victim of heart disease, for example, might be unable to walk more than a block without stopping to rest. Morbidity does not always result in disability, however: by taking appropriate measures, some people with heart disease not only walk but run longer and faster than they did before becoming ill.

The final measure of health, **vitality,** refers to how healthy and energetic, physically, intellectually, and socially, an individual actually feels. Vitality is, of course, a subjective measure—some people say their health is very good even when they have several chronic diseases and obvious disabilities—but for that very reason, vitality is probably more important to quality of life than any other measure (Havlik, 1989). Although there is no consensus about how to define quality of life, most experts, as well as the general public, now agree that the goal of medicine should be extending and improving vitality rather than simply postponing mortality (Homer and Holstein, 1990).

Health Impact of Ethnicity and SES

At first glance, ethnicity, with its attendant genetic and cultural factors, seems to be a powerful influence on all four measures of health in middle age (Jones, 1989; James et al., 1992). American mortality data make the point clearly: between the ages of 40 and 60, the chance of dying is twice as high for African-Americans, and only half as high for Asian-Americans, as it is for Americans of European descent, whose mortality rate is about one in seven in these two decades. Native Americans and Hispanic-Americans are in between these three groups, with the chance of dying being 10 percent higher for Native Americans than for whites and about 10 percent lower for Hispanic-Americans (Fingerhut and Makuc, 1992). Ethnic groups within each of these five broad groupings differ as well. For example, among middle-aged Hispanic-Americans, the death rate of Cuban-Americans is quite low, while that of Puerto Ricans is relatively high; among Asian-Americans, Japanese-Americans tend to live longer than Indian-Americans.

In general, self-reported health status, morbidity, and disability follow the same ethnic patterns as mortality in middle age. For example, close to 60 percent of all middle-aged Americans of European or Hispanic backgrounds say their health is good or excellent, compared with only 45 percent of African-Americans (U.S. Department of Health and Human Services, 1990). African-Americans are particularly likely to suffer illnesses and disabilities related to high blood pressure and poor health habits, including poor diet and cigarette smoking, and their health problems are less likely to be diagnosed in the early stages. This combination of factors makes heart disease, stroke, and cancer morbidity and mortality especially high for this group (Wilson, 1989; Johnson et al., 1990; U.S. Bureau of the Census, 1992).

However, while genetic and cultural factors undoubtedly play a role, especially in the occurrence of particular diseases, the major reason for ethnic variations in health and illness during middle age is socioeconomic status. The evidence is particularly clear for black-white differences in the United States. Indeed, when middle-aged and older people of the same income and education are compared, European-Americans actually have higher death rates than African-Americans (Wilkinson, 1992).

Sex Differences in Health

In middle age, mortality rates continue to favor females, as is the case from conception on, with men twice as likely to die of any cause and three times as likely to die of heart disease. Not until age 85 are the rates equivalent. However, beginning in middle age and beyond, women have higher morbidity rates than men, a difference particularly apparent after menopause.

This sex difference is exacerbated by an unfortunate gender difference in health research and care. Traditionally, the focus in the medical community has been on acute illnesses rather than chronic conditions, on preventing death rather than avoiding disability—which has meant that a disproportionate share of medical research focuses on the problems of men rather than the problems of women. For example, relatively little research money is dedicated to arthritis, osteoporosis, lupus, or migraine headaches—all of which affect more women than men but none of which typically leads to sudden death.

Even with diseases that can be fatal, there is often a gender bias in research and treatment. For example, heart disease, which is the leading cause of mortality in both sexes, eventually kills women at the same rate (one death in every three) as men (U.S. Bureau of the Census, 1992). However, for women, heart disease is more often chronic, and death rates do not rise until after menopause, while men are more vulnerable at younger ages to acute heart disease. Especially in middle age, men die from heart disease three times as often as women. As a result of this disparity, heart failure has sometimes been seen as a man's problem, and key longitudinal and large-scale studies of heart disease have excluded women.

Consequently, diagnosis and treatment of heart disease in women has been based on a male model, and the medical community has only recently begun to recognize that diagnostic procedures, heart surgery, and protective factors may produce different effects in women than in men (Altman, 1991). Because women's responses to exercise are not identical to men's, for example, standard treadmill tests often give false results for women. More telling, the mortality and morbidity rates for both by-pass surgery and angioplasty are notably higher for women than for men. In part, this may be because women have smaller arteries, but it also may be that women's heart problems are often not correctly diagnosed until they have resulted in a medical emergency.

Fortunately, this pattern of gender bias in health research and care is changing across the board, as research increasingly focuses on gender and genetic variations in mortality, morbidity, and disability. In 1993, the National Institutes of Health launched a fifteen-year, $625 million longitudinal study of 160,000 women between the ages of 50 and 79, specifically designed to overcome the neglect that women's health issues have suffered. As the director of the institutes noted, "For far too long . . . men were the normative standard for medical research and treatment. The corollary for this, of course, is that men's hormones set the standard for us all" (*New York Times*, March 31, 1993).

Changes in Health Habits

As signs from their bodies, advice from their doctors, and the celebration of a 40th or 50th birthday drive home the reality of aging, middle-aged adults become more likely to improve their health habits (Katchadourian, 1987; Tough, 1982). For example, almost half of all middle-aged nonsmokers are former smokers (U.S. Bureau of the Census, 1991). Alcohol and drug abuse, especially binge drinking, also become less common as adulthood progresses (Robins et al., 1984).

While some of these improvements may be developmental, reflecting a greater wisdom, or moderation, attendant to aging, they also reflect a cultural shift that places greater emphasis on disease prevention. For example, overall since 1970, the rate of adult smoking has declined from about 50 percent to about 30 percent; the average quantity of hard liquor (excluding beer and wine) consumed has decreased about 20 percent; consumption of animal fat has declined while that of fiber has increased; and seat-belt use has increased dramatically (Cahalan, 1991; U.S. Bureau of the Census, 1991; Chung et al., 1992).

Five Lifestyle Factors and Their Impact on Disease

Over the past twenty years, several large longitudinal studies have followed the lives of thousands of healthy adults, noting the relationship between their lifestyles—particularly health habits—and the later incidence of disease. As you will see, the links between certain lifestyle factors and health are many more than previously thought. Choices made daily in adulthood affect a person's health, not only in the short term but also in the years ahead.

Cigarette-Smoking

About 32 percent of all middle-aged men, and 29 percent of all middle-aged women, smoke cigarettes, at significant peril to their health. Smoking is a known risk factor for most serious diseases that beset adults, including cancer of the lung, bladder, kidney, mouth, and stomach (Engstrom, 1986), as well as heart disease, stroke, and emphysema. Marijuana and low-nicotine cigarettes increase the risk of the same diseases, although researchers are uncertain whether they are equally, more, or less harmful. Second-hand smoke is also deleterious—so much so that it is now considered "the third leading preventable cause of death after active smoking and alcohol" (Cahalan, 1991). One clear example of this is the fact that nonsmokers have a 30 percent higher risk of lung cancer if they are married to smokers than if they are married to nonsmokers (Brownson et al., 1992).

Alcohol

Some studies find that adults who drink wine or other alcohol in moderation may live longer than those who "never touch the stuff." One possible reason is that alcohol increases the blood's supply of HDL (high-density lipoprotein), a protein that aids in reducing cholesterol, thereby helping to prevent clogged arteries and reducing the chance of blood clots. Another possible explanation is that moderate drinking is not itself a health benefit but rather reflects the link between good health and economic well-being, moderate drinking being more common among people of high SES than among people of low SES, who, by comparison, tend to be either abstinent or heavy drinkers (Cahalan, 1991).

Whatever the explanation for the possible beneficial effects of alcohol in moderation, the clear fact is that many people do not drink in moderation, and that while binge drinking is more common in early adulthood, alcohol dependence and abuse are most common at about age 40 (Cahalan, 1991). Alcohol abuse is considered the most expensive health problem in the United States, one that costs the economy well over $100 billion annually, primarily in the loss of productive labor due to workers' being too ill to work (Holden, 1987). Heavy drinking, which is the main cause of cirrhosis of the liver, also puts a stress on the heart and stomach and destroys brain cells. Further, it has-

tens the calcium loss that causes the bone-weakening known as osteoporosis, and it is a risk factor in many forms of cancer, including breast cancer, the most common cancer for women (Edwards, 1987). Finally, alcohol is implicated in about half of all accidents, suicides, and homicides. All told, alcohol is responsible for about 105,000 deaths in the United States each year (Lewis, 1990). Thus the fact that moderate, occasional drinking may have some health benefits should not delude anyone: for many adults, alcohol is a major health risk.

Nutrition

As we have seen, nutrition plays a central role in development throughout the life span. During middle adulthood, it may play an important part with regard to the onset and progress of the two major killers of the middle-aged, heart disease and cancer. Adults in industrialized countries typically consume 40 percent of their calories as fat. Much of it is animal fat (in whole milk, cheese, butter, beef, pork, and eggs), and therefore is high in cholesterol, a contributor to coronary heart disease, particularly in middle age. High-fat, low-fiber diets also make several types of cancer, including stomach, colon, and breast cancer, more likely. Consequently, the National Cancer Institute recommends that adults reduce the fat content of their daily diet to below 30 percent and increase their consumption of fiber from the current average of 20 grams per day to 30.

Weight

A third of all middle-age people are obese, that is, 20 percent or more above the average weight for their particular height (National Center for Health Statistics, 1985). Obesity is a definite risk factor for heart disease, diabetes, and stroke, and is a contributing factor for arthritis, the most common disability for older adults. For obese persons in middle age, then, weight reduction is essential.

As long as a person is not obese, however, physicians disagree about how thin he or she should be. Some believe that it is better to be overweight than underweight, a conclusion suggested by longitudinal research that found that death was no more likely to occur among those who were 30 percent overweight than among those who were a mere 10 percent underweight (Kaplan, 1992). On the basis of data from twenty-five insurance companies, the National Institute of Aging recently raised the weight standards that are considered safe for middle-aged and older people (see table on next page).

However, other experts hypothesize that every excess pound increases the risk of disease and death, a view that finds substantial support from research on lower animals such as mice and rats, whose life span has been doubled by reducing their normal calorie intake by roughly a third

(continued)

Desirable Weight Tables

Height	Metropolitan* Ages 25–59		Gerontology Research Center Men and Women				
	Men	Women	20–29	30–39	40–49	50–59	60–69
4'10"		100–131	84–111	92–119	99–127	107–135	115–142
4'11"		101–134	87–115	95–123	103–131	111–139	119–147
5'0"		103–137	90–119	98–127	106–135	114–143	123–152
5'1"	123–145	105–140	93–123	101–131	110–140	118–148	127–157
5'2"	125–148	108–144	96–127	105–136	113–144	122–153	131–163
5'3"	127–151	111–148	99–131	108–140	117–149	126–158	135–168
5'4"	129–155	114–152	102–135	112–145	121–154	130–163	140–173
5'5"	131–159	117–156	106–140	115–149	125–159	134–168	144–179
5'6"	133–163	120–160	109–144	119–154	129–164	138–174	148–184
5'7"	135–167	123–164	112–148	122–159	133–169	143–179	153–190
5'8"	137–171	126–167	116–153	126–163	137–174	147–184	158–196
5'9"	139–175	129–170	119–157	130–168	141–179	151–190	162–201
5'10"	141–179	132–173	122–162	134–173	145–184	156–195	167–207
5'11"	144–183	135–176	126–167	137–178	149–190	160–201	172–213
6'0"	147–187		129–171	141–183	153–195	165–207	177–219
6'1"	150–192		133–176	145–188	157–200	169–213	182–225
6'2"	153–197		137–181	149–194	162–206	174–219	187–232
6'3"	157–202		141–186	153–199	166–212	179–225	192–238
6'4"			144–191	157–205	171–218	184–231	197–244

All heights without shoes, weights in pounds without clothes
*Combining Metropolitan's ranges for small, medium, and large body frames

Regular aerobic exercise, complete with stretches, is likely to be even more beneficial to the health of these middle-aged men than to the health of the young women who usually frequent such classes.

Snyder, 1989). These experts suggest that the correlation between underweight and disease cited above occurs because those who are underweight at the time of death are so because of illness. Thus, they contend, illness causes low weight, but low weight does not cause illness—quite the opposite.

If it is true that even a little extra fat is hazardous to health, then every middle-aged person who does not drastically reduce his or her calorie intake below that of the younger years is at risk. The reason is that between age 20 and 50 a person's metabolism normally slows down by about a third, which means that simply eating at the same level as at younger ages would cause ballooning weight gain (Ausman and Russell, 1990).

Exercise

There is no dispute about the relationship between exercise and health: active people have much lower rates of serious illness and death than inactive people (Kaplan, 1992). Just being in an active job is beneficial. For example, British bus conductors, who are constantly moving through the bus and up and down the stairs of double-deckers to collect tickets, are generally in better health than their coworkers who drive the buses. Similar findings come from a comparison of San Francisco longshoremen who had active jobs with those who did not (Oberman, 1980).

Even better than having an active job is engaging in exercise that is sufficiently strenuous to raise the pulse to about 75 percent of its maximum capacity—three or more times a week for at least 30 minutes per workout. Such exercise increases heart and lung capacity, lowers blood pressure, increases HDL in the blood, and even if weight remains the same, reduces the ratio of body fat to body weight. Each of these results helps prolong life.

Regular exercise has a number of other benefits as well. Especially in middle-aged and older people, it enhances cognitive functioning, probably because it improves blood circulation in the brain (Stones and Kozina, 1989). Exercise is also the best method of weight reduction: it not only burns calories but decreases the appetite and increases metabolism, so the person continues to benefit for several hours after a workout is over (Sloane, 1985). In addition, for many people, exercise is the pathway to establishing control over other poor health habits, including smoking and drinking (Brownell et al., 1986).

Finally, exercise sometimes helps reduce depression and hostility, making a person psychologically healthier as well as physically more fit (Holroyd and Boyne, 1984; Folkins and Sime, 1981). Indeed, since exercise makes people look good, feel good, and stay healthy, the puzzle is why most adults—especially as they grow older and presumably wiser—would rather park themselves in front of the TV than go for an hour's swim, run, or aerobic workout.

The historical and developmental data are not as encouraging with regard to exercise. Not only is there suggestive evidence that the overall rates of exercise, which rose during the early 1980s, are now decreasing, but there is solid evidence that most individuals exercise much less as they grow older, a trend apparent by about age 30 in men and by about age 40 in women (Kaplan, 1992; Chung et al., 1992; U.S. Bureau of the Census, 1986, 1988).

These data obscure some important individual differences, however. One survey of 10,000 households found that while young adults were most likely to exercise, a sizable minority of adults aged 35 to 54 claimed to exercise regularly—by walking (31 percent), swimming (28 percent), bicycling (17 percent), doing aerobics (10 percent), and jogging (8 percent) (U.S. Bureau of the Census, 1988). Certainly some individuals exercise more than they did when they were younger. At age 45, Jane Fonda, movie star and aerobic guru, maintained that she could "run farther, stretch deeper, climb steeper, lift heavier, stand taller, and dance longer" than when she was 20 (Fonda, 1984). Fonda represents a small minority of highly committed middle-aged fitness buffs, but the very existence of that minority reminds us that many developmental paths are open as people age: sloth and sickness are not inevitable; health and vitality are quite possible instead.

The healthy path is not always the easy one, of course. Many more middle-aged adults attempt to change poor health habits than actually succeed. Most unhealthy lifestyle habits are hard to alter, and each individual has a different set of reasons for trying to improve, and a different likelihood of succeeding with any given strategy. Some find that a small improvement (such as switching to low-fat milk or low-tar cigarettes) is the best they can do; others find that a sudden dramatic shift (such as going on the wagon or working out regularly in the gym) succeeds for a while, and then the old habits creep back. Research on addictions—food, tobacco, alcohol, and other drugs—teaches four lessons relevant to trying to improve any destructive health habit (Brownell et al., 1986; Schachter, 1982; Cahalan, 1991): (1) acknowledging the problem is the first step toward solving it; (2) several attempts might be needed before success is achieved; (3) every step in the right direction and every healthy day are better than no improvement at all; (4) lapses do not have to be relapses: they can be temporary obstacles that need to be overcome.

Overall attitude is crucial to improving health habits: those who succeed are those who believe that change is possible and who recognize that they may have to try various approaches until they find the one best suited to their individual needs. As we will now see, a basic faith in one's ability to control, cope, or overcome is also the key to managing one of the most unavoidable health problems of contemporary life—stress.

Figure 20.3 *To quit smoking, people have resorted to dozens of different techniques, from hypnosis to acupuncture. Shown here is aversive conditioning. Would-be quitters sit together in a small room and smoke continually, puffing hard, until they literally get sick of it. Later, if they are tempted to light up, feelings of revulsion and even nausea usually stop them. When this method works, the new nonsmokers often become the most dedicated opponents of second-hand smoke.*

Stress

Stress is a critical but extremely complex factor in the overall determination of health (Eisdorfer, 1985). Even the definition is somewhat complicated. **Stress** is the adverse physical and emotional reaction to demands put on the individual by unsettling conditions or experiences, which are called **stressors** (Selye, 1982). Central in this definition is the recognition of the importance of context; that is, what is a stressor for one individual on any given occasion may not be one for someone else, or even for the same person on some other occasion. In other words, what makes a potential stressor in fact stressful is the individual's reaction to it.

For example, attending a noisy, crowded party is, obviously, fun for many people, a chance, perhaps, to make new acquaintances, to show off, to flirt, or to just relax and let go of the day's tensions. For other people, the same type of party may, to varying degrees, represent a stressor, because they hate crowding and noise, or worry that they are dressed inappropriately, or feel awkward among strangers, or have difficulty making "party conversation," or regard such gatherings as a waste of time, or fear that the arrival of a former love is going to stir old feelings—the list of possible reasons is virtually endless. And so is the list of possible stress reactions that one person or another might experience: a vague sense of unease; restlessness and an inability to concentrate; headache; indigestion; a feeling of deep fatigue; streams of self-conscious, troubling thoughts; elevated blood pressure; excessive talkativeness; an outbreak of hives; sudden fits of stammering or slips of the tongue; a case of hiccups; a chronic urge to urinate; an onset of nervous laughing; blushing or the appearance of a rash; a pounding heart and sweaty palms; fainting. Any of these reactions, and a host of others, are typical stress responses.

Also endless are the ways various people might try to cope with their feelings of stress. One person might develop a migraine and never get to the party; another might make up an excuse for an early departure; another might stay glued to a close friend for the entire evening; another might sulk in a corner all night; another might retreat to the kitchen to "help out"; another might get drunk; another might decide to look at the party as a challenge and figure out ways of making the best of it. As you can infer from this lengthy but rather simple example, the variables of stress are usually hard to pin down. What, in fact, causes stress in any given individual, and how that person responds to a particular stressor physiologically and behaviorally, depend on the individual's temperament, past experiences, physical vulnerabilities, resources and strategies for coping, the overall context, and, perhaps most important, how all these factors influence the way the individual interprets a potential stressor.

Despite this variation, however, study after study finds that psychological stressors ranging from the devastation of war to the hassles of everyday life correlate with a wide range of health problems. Indeed, virtually every physical disease and psychological disability, from arthritis to alcoholism, heart attacks to headaches, strokes to suicides, is more likely to occur in people who experience significant stress.

How exactly might disease and stress be linked? In addition to the numerous physiological stress reactions like the increased heart rate and elevated blood pressure mentioned in our party example, the experience of stress produces changes in the concentration of many of the hormones and other chemicals in the body (Zales, 1985). Any of these physiological changes could certainly take a toll on the various organs over an extended period of time, and many could harm the body in the short term as well.

Stress may also be less directly involved in causing disease, in that stress over time reduces the effectiveness of the immune system (Stein and Schleifer, 1985). Thus people who are under constant or severe stress are

Figure 20.4 *Stress can occur during many of the happy occasions of life, as well as during troubling ones. These guests at a reception seem to be enjoying themselves, but, chances are, some of them had "butterflies" in their stomachs or sweat on their palms or other signs of stress as they got ready to present themselves to total strangers.*

more vulnerable to a variety of illnesses, ranging from the common cold to cancer (Levy, 1991).

Also likely to turn potential stressors into stress are those individuals who refuse to seek help from others: in general, those who feel supported by the social community are better able to cope, physiologically as well as psychologically, with stress (Uchino et al., 1992; Krause et al., 1990).

Finally, the people who tend to be most troubled by stress are those who are unable to see life in a positive light. Of course, it is often not hard to justify a dark view: almost everyone's life includes some serious illness, career disappointment, or loss of an important friendship or love relationship, and certainly everyone recognizes that sorrow, hate, and disaster are daily risks. However, those who can manage an optimistic view, believing that the world is generally a benevolent place, that improvements are possible, and that they themselves are likely to forestall illness, cope with problems, and better their lives, actually do live longer, healthier, and happier lives than pessimists do (Taylor, 1989).

Developmental Changes in Coping with Stress

As we have seen, there are many ways to cope with stress, from altering the stressor, to denying it, to escaping from it, to reevaluating it. Each coping strategy is well suited to some stresses and poorly suited to others. Ideally we all should have several strategies available so that we can approach some problems directly and avoid or ignore others, and ideally we should assess each stressor in its full context so that the strategy we choose is the one most likely to succeed. Unfortunately, many people tend to be locked into one coping pattern or another, without considering all the alternatives (Roth and Cohen, 1986).

Are middle-aged people any better than younger people at reducing or coping with stressors? Overall, research finds such great individual variations that it would be a mistake to say that aging per se results in better adaptation to stress. Indeed, because the body's organ reserve gradually declines with age, physiological adjustments to stress take longer as people grow older.

Psychologically, however, many people do seem to experience stress less, or to be better at handling stressors, as they grow older (Lazarus and DeLongis, 1983). A longitudinal study that followed men from college days through middle age found that they gradually became more likely to use adaptive defense mechanisms, such as humor, rather than maladaptive ones, such as anger, when they were in potentially stressful situations with other people (Vaillant, 1977). Another longitudinal study that followed college women found that in middle adulthood they too used better coping methods and thus experienced less stress (Helson and Moane, 1987). In both studies, one of the most effective coping strategies was to try to fully understand others' points of view and to depersonalize conflict, concentrating on the issues involved rather than on the emotions surrounding them.

Since stress is a major contributor to most forms of mental illness, additional evidence for improved stress responses over time comes from a large, carefully constructed study of the prevalence of fifteen mental disor-

TABLE 20.3   Incidence of Psychological Problems

Age	Men	Women
18–24	23%	23%
25–44	21%	22%
45–64	13%	14%
65+	12%	13%

ders among a cross-section of adults living in three major U.S. cities (Robins et al., 1984). As you can see from Table 20.3, "the total rates of disorders drop sharply after age 45." Virtually every specific disorder became less common with age, not only ones that you might expect, such as drug abuse (ten times less likely in middle adulthood than in early adulthood) but ones that might not seem age-related, such as schizophrenia (less than half as common over age 45 as under). Similarly, depression among the middle-aged was almost half that of adults between the ages of 25 and 44 (4.6 percent compared with 9 percent). Other studies also find that having problems with sleeping and eating, feeling tired and sad, as well as thinking that other people are unfriendly, are less common during middle age than in early or late adulthood (Kessler et al., 1992).

There are several possible explanations for the apparent developmental changes that may occur in the way stress is experienced and dealt with:

1. As you read in Chapter 19, compared with young adults, middle-aged people on the whole experience fewer psychosocial demands, since they generally have already chosen a career, a spouse, and so forth.

2. Because they tend to be more settled with family, friends, and work, middle-aged people may be better buffered by their social networks against whatever stresses they encounter.

3. Middle-aged people may be more likely to seek, and more able to afford, professional help for their problems, and therefore may have fewer long-standing difficulties.

4. As Chapters 18 and 21 make clear, over time, many people evidence a more flexible cognitive approach, and this flexibility no doubt enhances one's ability to both appraise and deal with potential stressors.

Certainly it would seem that the combination of these psychosocial and cognitive factors could result in a general pattern of reduced stress during middle adulthood.

The Sexual-Reproductive System

As the sexual-reproductive system continues to age during middle adulthood, sexual responses gradually become slower and less distinct. We will soon discuss the consequences of these ongoing changes, but first let us look at one change that is definitive: the cessation of reproductive potential in women.

Menopause

After about age 35, many women find that the time between their menstrual periods becomes shorter, from about every twenty-eight days at age 35 to twenty-five days at age 40, to twenty-three days by the mid-40s (Whitbourne, 1985). Then toward the end of the 40s, periods become erratic, with some coming fairly close together, and others being missed entirely.

Sometimes between her late 40s and early 50s (the average age is 51), a woman reaches **menopause,** as ovulation and menstruation stop and the production of the hormone estrogen drops considerably. Strictly speaking, menopause is dated one year after a woman's last menstrual cycle.

The Climacteric

The term "menopause," and the misnomer "change of life," are also sometimes used to refer to the time, lasting about three years, during which the woman's body adjusts to much lower levels of estrogen, a drop that causes a variety of physical changes. A more inclusive term for these years is the **climacteric,** which refers to all the various biological and psychological changes that accompany menopause.

The most obvious symptoms of the climacteric are hot flashes (suddenly feeling hot), hot flushes (suddenly looking hot), and cold sweats (feeling cold and clammy). These symptoms are all caused by **vasomotor instability,** that is, a temporary disruption in the body mechanisms that constrict or dilate the blood vessels to maintain body temperature. Lower estrogen levels produce many other changes in the female body, including drier skin, less vaginal lubrication during sexual arousal, loss of some breast tissue, more brittle bones, and an increased risk of heart attack. Many women also find that, during the climacteric, their moods change inexplicably from day to day. Despite these changes, however, the prevalent conception of menopause as a time of difficulty and depression is largely myth. For most women, the anticipation of menopause is usually worse than the actual experiencing of it.

While almost all women experience some menopausal symptoms, those most likely to need **hormone replacement therapy,** or **HRT,** are those who have an abrupt drop in hormonal level because their ovaries are surgically removed. This is very common as part of a hysterectomy (surgical removal of the uterus), an operation undergone by an estimated one-third of all women in the United States before age 60 (Sheehy, 1992; Crowe, 1992). Such women are particularly likely to feel physically and emotionally troubled by menopause (McKinlay, 1992).

HRT is not generally needed for the symptoms of a natural menopause. However, low doses of estrogen are strongly recommended for women who are at risk for **osteoporosis,** the condition of thin and brittle bones that leads to increased fractures and frailty in old age (Prince et al., 1991). High risk is suggested by a woman's being thin, Caucasian, and postmenopausal, and is confirmed by X-rays of bone density. For most women, a childhood diet high in calcium, regular weight-bearing exercise (such as walking or running), and avoiding cigarettes and alcohol significantly lessen the likelihood of their developing osteoporosis, particularly if their daily diet in adulthood includes 1,000 milligrams of calcium. It should be noted that the best sources of calcium are food products such as milk, cheese, and yogurt—and that calcium supplements may be of little help unless combined with HRT, despite advertising to the contrary (Culliton, 1987).

HRT also reduces the risk of fatal heart attacks in postmenopausal women—by as much as 50 percent according to some research (Stampfer et al., 1991). However, whether it is wise for women to use HRT for the thirty or

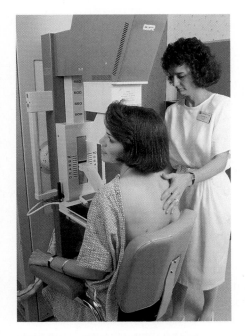

Figure 20.5 *While menopause brings relief from possible complications of birth control, pregnancy, and menstruation, it also brings increased risk for heart disease, osteoporosis, and breast cancer. Fortunately, preventive medicine can halt most problems before they do serious damage. Unfortunately, many women do not get the care they need until symptoms emerge. Less than half of all American women over age 50 get their annual mammograms, even though doing so would save thousands of lives.*

so years that follow menopause is controversial, in part because HRT is associated with a higher incidence of cancer and in part because the results of long-term use of HRT are not yet known. Decisions regarding the prolonged use of HRT therefore need to be made on the basis of a specific risk analysis for each individual.

Reproductive Changes in Context

How strong is the psychological impact of the sudden loss of reproductive potential in women? In this day and age, not very. Traditionally, childbearing was particularly important for women, since most women attained social status directly from their role as mother: indeed the more children a couple had, the more fortunate they were considered to be. In these circumstances, the psychological impact of declining fertility and menopause may have been substantial. Especially if a couple had only one or two children, menopause may have been greeted with considerable sorrow as the final "closing of the gates" of reproduction, as psychoanalyst Helene Deutsch (1945) once described it.

However, historical changes have meant that the end of childbearing is now determined less by age than by personal factors, such as the number of children a couple already has or the couple's financial situation. In fact, for the most part, the end of childbearing occurs through a conscious decision that is usually made when a woman is in her 30s, long before reproduction becomes biologically impossible. Menopause, then, as the time when sexual activity is no longer accompanied by fear of pregnancy, and the inconveniences and risks of contraception are a thing of the past, is more often welcomed than regretted (Luria and Mead, 1984).

Male Menopause?

For men in middle age, there is no sudden downward shift in reproductive ability or hormonal levels, as there is with women. Thus, physiologically, men experience nothing like the female climacteric. Most men continue to produce sperm indefinitely, and although there are important age-related declines in the number and motility of sperm (see Chapter 17), men are theoretically (and in some cases, actually) able to father a child in late adulthood. Similarly, the average levels of testosterone decline gradually, if at all, with age (Whitbourne, 1985).

Although strictly speaking there is no "male menopause," this phrase may have been coined to refer to another phenomenon: testosterone can dip markedly if a man suddenly becomes sexually inactive or unusually worried, as might happen if he were faced with unemployment, marital problems, serious illness, or unwanted retirement. Levels of testosterone correlate with levels of sexual desire and speed of sexual responses, so a man with low testosterone might find himself unable to have an erection when he wanted to. Thus, the effects of this dip, especially when added to whatever age-related declines have already occurred, may make a man highly anxious about his sexual virility, which, in turn, may reduce his testosterone level even more (Katchadourian, 1987).

Age-Related Changes in Sexual Expression

One usual way to measure sexual activity is in terms of the frequency of intercourse and orgasm. By this measure, sexual activity usually declines during middle age, though with wide individual differences, including some people who stop having intercourse altogether and others who continue to have intercourse on a regular basis (Comfort, 1980; Adams and Turner, 1985).

Even for the sexually active, however, the specifics of their activity change with age, especially for men. Sexual stimulation takes longer, and needs to be more direct than earlier. Further, as Herant Katchadourian (1987), a physician who studies sexuality, writes about men, "orgasmic reactions become less intense with age . . . contractions are fewer, ejaculation is less vigorous, and the volume of the ejaculate is smaller." Changes in the woman's orgasmic ability are harder to measure, but many researchers think a woman's eroticism is at least as strong in middle age as in early adulthood (Masters and Johnson, 1966; Van Keep and Gregory, 1977). After menopause, signs of arousal, including sexual lubrication, may be less apparent, but none of these changes need impair a sexual relationship. As Katchadourian explains it, "while the intensity of the physiological responses clearly diminish over time, the subjective experience of orgasm continues to be highly satisfying, though not as explosive as in previous years."

One final fact seems to be suggested by the research: couples do not move from active happy sex lives to passive troubled ones unless their relationship is plagued by other problems that are reflected, but not caused, in the bedroom. Quite simply, people who have active sex lives in young adulthood are most likely to have active sex lives in middle and late adulthood, and couples who were never comfortable with their sexual relations are likely to end them in later years. For middle-aged and older adults, both overall enjoyment of sex and preference for particular sexual activities are

Figure 20.6 *Throughout adulthood, continued, pleasurable sexual relations depend much less on the partners' age than their attitudes toward each other and toward sex itself. As many experts have noted, the most important human sexual organ is the brain.*

more closely related to past sexual interests and desires than to more global variables such as current income, education, or life satisfaction (Pfeiffer and Davis, 1972; Turner and Adams, 1988).

Throughout life, it seems that sexual activity itself helps promote sexual interest and excitement; correspondingly, absence of sexual activity results in lower levels of sex hormones and a loss of sexual interest (Katchadourian, 1987; Masters and Johnson, 1981). Putting it into a broader context, Pfeiffer (1977) concludes:

> Examination of all the available data makes it clear that successfully aging persons are those who have made a decision to stay in training in the major areas of their lives. In particular, they have decided to stay in training physically, socially, emotionally, and intellectually. We have every reason to believe that staying in training sexually will also help improve the quality of life in later years.

Again, it seems that, as adults grow older and biosocial development is much less tied to chronological age, personal choices become increasingly important in affecting the course of development. In the next chapter, we will see that choice can influence our intellectual skills as well. At least in some abilities, to some extent, we can choose to be smarter, wiser, or more expert by staying in training cognitively.

SUMMARY

Normal Changes in Middle Adulthood

1. A person's appearance undergoes gradual but notable changes as middle age progresses, including more wrinkles, less hair, and new fat, particularly on the abdomen.

2. Hearing gradually becomes less acute, with noticeable losses being more likely for high-frequency sounds, particularly in men. Vision also becomes less sharp with age. Two particular difficulties for many middle-aged people are reading small print and adjusting to glare at night.

3. Overall, health is generally quite good during middle age, with a death rate significantly lower today than for earlier cohorts.

Variations in Health

4. Variations in health—which can be measured in terms of mortality, morbidity, disability, and vitality—arise from a combination of many factors, chief among them, race, ethnicity, socioeconomic status, and gender.

5. The most important reason for individual variations in health during middle age, however, is personal lifestyle. Cigarette-smoking, heavy alcohol consumption, high-fat diets, obesity, and lack of exercise are all risk factors for heart disease and cancer, as well as for other ailments.

6. Stress also correlates with virtually every physical and psychological impairment that middle-aged people can have. Great individual variation exists, however, in what constitutes a stressor, in how the person copes with it, and in the particular impact that a stressor will have on the body or the psyche. In general, middle-aged people may experience less stress, or cope with it better, than younger adults.

The Sexual-Reproductive System

7. At menopause, as a woman's menstrual cycle stops, ovulation ceases and levels of estrogen are markedly reduced. This hormonal change produces various symptoms and possible problems, although most women find the experience of menopause much less troubling than they had expected it to be.

8. Men do not have sudden age-related drops in hormone levels or in fertility. In this sense, there is no "male menopause."

9. As a man's sexual responses slow down with age, many couples find that they engage in intercourse less often. However, active sexual relationships can, and often do, continue throughout adulthood, to the satisfaction of both sexes.

KEY TERMS

glaucoma (522)

mortality (524)

morbidity (524)

disability (524)

vitality (524)

stress (529)

stressor (529)

menopause (533)

climacteric (533)

vasomotor instability (533)

hormone replacement
    therapy (HRT) (533)

osteoporosis (533)

KEY QUESTIONS

1. What changes in appearance typically occur during middle age, and what is their impact?

2. What are the reasons one person might have a greater hearing loss than another in middle adulthood?

3. What are the likely changes in a person's vision during middle adulthood?

4. What characteristics and health habits would you expect a middle-aged person in excellent health to have?

5. If an overweight, underexercising, cigarette-smoking, alcohol-drinking adult could change just one bad habit, which one would you recommend changing and why?

6. Do you think you will be less stressed ten years from now? Why or why not?

7. What are the differences between the changes men and women experience in their sexual-reproductive systems in middle adulthood?

CHAPTER 21

Middle Adulthood: Cognitive Development

During middle adulthood, the straightforward cognitive growth of earlier years begins to wane, and intellectual development becomes more multidirectional, multifaceted, and individualized. Rather than mastering skills that are suited to a wide variety of situations, the adult acquires more specialized knowledge and expertise that reflect professional, personal, and relational needs. Life circumstances related to health, marriage, occupation, and other events also influence the course of cognitive development. As a result, intellectual growth moves in more idiosyncratic directions during the middle adult years. To understand this, we will consider the following questions:

Which aspects of intelligence decline with increasing age, and which features become enhanced or remain stable over time?

In what ways does cognitive competence become more individualized during adulthood, with strengths and weaknesses becoming tailored to a person's interests, needs, and motivation?

What are the factors that predict whether an adult will experience intellectual growth or decline during the middle adult years?

How does "practical intelligence" compare with the intellectual skills commonly studied by researchers?

What distinguishes experts from novices in terms of their cognitive skills and competencies?

Overall, would you say that adults become more intelligent, or less, as they grow older? On one hand, the growth of new, postformal styles of thought (such as those described in Chapter 18) and broader experience might yield intellectual progress. On the other hand, intellectual decline might derive from the biological and perceptual changes that accompany aging. No matter which way you answer, you are in good scientific company. Investigators who have spent their professional lives gathering and reviewing research on this question have reached opposite conclusions.

On one side, researchers such as John Horn assert that intellectual decline during adulthood is inevitable (Horn, 1985; Horn and Hofer, 1992; Horn and Donaldson, 1976, 1977). These investigators maintain that although increases in knowledge also occur, there is an undeniable decrease in the flexibility of thinking and problem solving with age. On the other side, researchers such as K. Warner Schaie contend that, throughout life, intelligence is quite plastic, molded by health, education, life experiences, and many other factors (Schaie 1989a, 1990a, 1990b). Depending on the impact of these factors, various aspects of intelligence can either increase or decrease. The idea that intelligence necessarily declines with age is, Schaie argues, a dangerous simplification (Baltes and Schaie, 1974, 1976; Schaie, 1983; Schaie and Baltes, 1977).

How could researchers looking at the same issue, and at much of the same evidence, come to such different conclusions? Which view is more accurate? Is there any synthesis that combines these opposing points of view? This chapter attempts to answer these questions.

Decline in Adult Intelligence?

For most of the twentieth century, psychologists were convinced that intelligence reaches a peak in adolescence, and then gradually declines during adulthood. This belief was based on what seemed to be solid evidence. For instance, all literate American draftees in World War I were given an intelligence test, called Alpha, that tested a variety of cognitive skills. When the scores of men of various ages were compared, one conclusion seemed obvious: the average American male reached an intellectual peak at about age 18, stayed at that level until his mid-20s, and then began to show a decline (Yerkes, 1923).

Similar results came from a classic study of 1,191 subjects between the ages of 10 and 60, chosen from nineteen carefully selected, insular, New England villages. (The purpose of the sampling procedure was to achieve an ethnically homogeneous group of adults who had had fairly similar life experiences. Thus age would be the only significant difference among the test-takers.) IQ tests from this group showed intellectual ability peaking between ages 18 and 21, and then slowly and steadily declining to the point that the average 55-year-old scored the same as the average 14-year-old (Jones and Conrad, 1933). The case for age-related decline in intelligence was considered proven beyond a reasonable doubt.

Contrary Evidence

The first evidence to contradict the assumption that intelligence declines with age was uncovered by Nancy Bayley and Melita Oden (1955). They were analyzing the adult development of the children originally selected by Lewis Terman in 1921 for his study of child geniuses, a group that has been studied by a succession of researchers over the past sixty years. As Bayley later explained, she fully expected to find a decline in these subjects' cognitive de-

Figure 21.1 *The problem of whether intelligence grows or declines in adulthood raises further questions about how intellectual activity changes with increasing age, and whether it should be assessed in different ways as the person matures.*

velopment because in previous cross-sectional studies "the invariable findings had indicated that most intellectual functions decrease after about 21 years of age" (Bayley, 1966). But on several tests of concept mastery, including questions that involved use of synonyms, antonyms, and analogies, the scores of these gifted individuals increased between ages 20 and 50.

Bayley decided to follow this clue by retesting a more representative group of adults who had also been tested as children. (These subjects, as members of the Berkeley Growth Study, had been selected in infancy to be representative of the infant population of Berkeley, California.) Bayley's results again showed a general increase in intellectual functioning from childhood through young adulthood. Instead of reaching a plateau at age 21, the typical person at age 36 was still improving on the most important subtests of the Wechsler Adult Intelligence Scale, specifically, Vocabulary, Comprehension, and Information. On only two of the ten subtests—Arithmetic, which measures speed and accuracy of mathematical ability, and Picture Completion, which requires the person to spot an element that is missing from a picture of a common object (such as an ankle from a foot, or a pair of legs from a bee)—did scores decline. Bayley (1966) concluded that "intellectual potential for continued learning is unimpaired through 36 years."

Cross-Sectional and Longitudinal Studies

Why did Bayley find such a different pattern of intellectual aging? Recall that her study used a longitudinal design (studying the same people repeatedly as they grew older), whereas earlier studies were cross-sectional (studying groups of people that differed only in age).

As we saw in Chapter 1, developmentalists now recognize that cross-sectional research can sometimes yield a misleading picture of adult development, not only because it is impossible to select adults who are similar to each other in every important aspect except age, but also because of the cohort effects created by each group's own unique history of life experiences. Cohort effects, in particular, complicate the interpretation of adult differences in intellectual performance. Adults who grew up during the Great Depression, for example, or during World War II, might have acquired different cognitive skills than younger cohorts who grew up during the 1950s or 1960s. Among other influences, the quality of public education, the variety of cultural opportunities, and the dissemination of information in the popular media have provided advantages to later-born cohorts. Even more significant, elderly adults who grew up before every 16-year-old was expected to be in high school rather than in the work force are likely to differ intellectually from those who grew up later, when a high school education was more normative.

Schaie was one of the earliest researchers to recognize the potentially distorting cohort effects on cross-sectional research. In 1956 he tested a cross-sectional sample of 500 adults aged 20 to 70 on five "primary mental abilities," essentially verbal comprehension, spatial visualization, reasoning, mathematical ability, and word fluency. His initial results showed some gradual decline in ability with age, but Schaie wondered whether cohort effects accounted for these cross-sectional findings. Therefore, he retested his original subjects at seven-year intervals in 1963, 1970, 1977, and 1984 (Schaie, 1989a, 1990a, 1990b). The results of Schaie's Seattle Longitudinal Study confirmed what Bayley had found many years earlier: most people improve in primary mental abilities during most of adulthood. Cross-sectional research had, apparently, given misleading testimony regarding adult intelligence.

But longitudinal findings might be misleading also (Cunningham and Tomer, 1990; Horn and Hofer, 1992). People who are retested several times on similar tests might improve their performance as they become practiced at taking the tests. Moreover, it is hard to retain adults in a longitudinal sample over long periods of time: often 50 percent or more of Schaie's adults could not be found for the next testing period. Adults move away, become ill or die, or may refuse to return for another round of testing. Like those who show up at class reunions, the subjects who return for long-term longitudinal studies may be the most stable, healthy, well-functioning adults who are happy to be retested; those who are ill or who are troubled by their declining abilities are more likely to drop out. Thus, while cross-sectional studies may *overestimate* adult intellectual decline, longitudinal designs may *underestimate* it.

To correct for some of these problems, Schaie went one step further, developing a new research design called *sequential research,* which is a combination of cross-sectional and longitudinal approaches. Each time he retested his original subjects he also tested a new group of adults at each age interval, and then he followed this new group longitudinally as well. The cross-age comparisons that Schaie was able to make with this accumulation of longitudinal and cross-sectional data over many years allowed him to analyze the possible effects of retesting, cohort differences, and other influences on adult changes in intelligence.

Schaie's findings are both important and encouraging:

> On average, there is gain until the late 30s or early 40s are reached, and then there is stability until the mid-50s or early 60s are reached. Average decrements from age 53 to 60 are quite small and are statistically significant only for number and word fluency. Beyond age 60, 7-year decrements are statistically significant throughout. These data suggest that average decline in psychological competence may begin for some as early as the mid-50s, but that it is typically of small magnitude until the 70s are reached. [Schaie, 1990a]

Schaie also found notable cohort differences. In general, more recently born cohorts outperformed earlier cohorts when they were the same age. There were also cohort differences in specific abilities. For instance, recent cohorts of young and middle-aged adults were much better at reasoning ability, but worse at number skills, than those who were young and middle-aged in previous decades (Schaie, 1990b). This trend was especially apparent in comparisons between adults born at mid-century—when progressive education was on the rise—and adults born at the beginning of the century—when rote learning was stressed. However, Schaie has observed fewer recent cohort effects for many abilities, suggesting greater commonalities in the developing experiences of adults in American culture.

We should remember that these patterns of intellectual change represent averages across large numbers of adults. Individual changes in intelligence are likely to be highly variable, and related to a person's life experiences. As Schaie (1990a) notes,

> very few individuals show global decline. It is particularly noteworthy that by age 60, 75% of the study participants maintained their level of functioning over 7 years on at least four out of the five abilities monitored and that this level of

Figure 21.2 *One reason that young adults outperform their elders in mathematical reasoning is that their educational instruction in mathematics is advanced over what most adults received years ago, which illustrates an* important *cohort effect* on adult differences in number skills.

maintenance was true even at age 81 for slightly more than half of the sample. Virtually no individuals contained in our data set showed universal decline on all abilities monitored even by the 80s.

In other words, changes in intelligence are individualized: some abilities are maintained or even strengthened over time, while others decline with increasing age.

An Assessment

Overall, the results of this and other research have led to three general conclusions about intellectual changes during adulthood (Cunningham, 1987; Cunningham and Tomer, 1990; Horn and Hofer, 1992; Schaie, 1989a, 1990a, 1990b):

1. In general, most intellectual abilities increase or remain stable throughout early and middle adulthood until the 60s, at which time selective decrements in certain skills can be noted. However, there is little evidence for comprehensive declines in intelligence, even in very old adults.

2. Cohort differences have a powerful influence on intellectual differences in adulthood, but the effects vary with different intellectual abilities and the age of the sample.

3. Intellectual functioning is also affected by educational background, current health status, and mental well-being. Adults who experience major illnesses or depression, for example, also show concurrent declines in intellectual performance. Conversely, intellectual functioning is enhanced by good health, involvement with others, and intellectual stimulation in adulthood. In these respects, intelligence becomes more individualized and specialized with increasing age.

These conclusions provide a fairly optimistic view of adult intellectual changes. However, before accepting this happy portrayal, let us see why John Horn, an expert psychometrician, calls this view "wishful thinking" and insists that crucial aspects of intellectual functioning decline steadily as adulthood progresses.

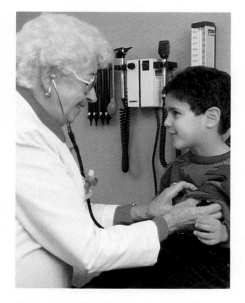

Figure 21.3 *Adult changes in intellectual functioning are affected by the cognitive stimulation the individual receives from peers, a hobby, further education, or a stimulating occupation.*

Fluid and Crystallized Intelligence

Horn began his work on intellectual development with an idea, originally suggested by Raymond Cattell (1963), that the various types of intellectual ability can be divided into a number of global competencies. The more important of these are fluid intelligence and crystallized intelligence. As its name implies, **fluid intelligence** is flexible reasoning used to draw inferences and understand relations between concepts. It is made up of those basic mental abilities—inductive reasoning, abstract thinking, speed of processing, and the like—required for understanding any subject matter, particularly material that is unfamiliar. Someone high in fluid intelligence is quick and creative with words, numbers, and intellectual puzzles. Among

Figure 21.4 *Fluid intelligence consists of flexible reasoning that can be enlisted for solving mental puzzles, abstract dilemmas, or professional challenges.*

the questions that might be used to test fluid intelligence are the following (Horn, 1985):

What comes next in these series?*
4 5 6 3 4 5 6 2 3 4 5 6
B D A C Z B Y A

Another standard type of item that is used to measure fluid intelligence is the timed assembly of puzzles, with credit given for completion within 2 minutes, bonus points for completion within 1 minute, and no credit after 2 minutes.

Crystallized intelligence is the accumulation of facts, information, and knowledge that comes with education and experience within a particular culture. The size of vocabulary, the knowledge of chemical formulas, and long-term memory for dates in history are all indications of crystallized intelligence (Horn, 1982). Test items designed to measure crystallized intelligence might include questions such as these:

What is the meaning of the word "temerity"?†
What do you do with a mango?
What word is associated with bathtubs, prizefighting, and weddings?
In what year was the Magna Carta enacted?

Originally, Cattell and Horn thought fluid intelligence was primarily genetic, and crystallized intelligence, primarily learned. Now Horn (1985) thinks this nature-nurture distinction is invalid, in part because the acquisition of crystallized intelligence is affected by the quality of fluid intelligence. For instance, the strength of your present vocabulary is partly the result of your reading speed and of your ability to make logical associations among words—both of which are related to fluid intelligence.

In adulthood, fluid intelligence declines markedly according to Horn's research. So also do related abilities like processing speed and short-term memory (Horn and Hofer, 1992). This decline is temporarily disguised by an increase in crystallized intelligence, which continues to expand throughout most of adulthood. Take verbal ability as an example. Once you have acquired, via fluid intelligence, a working knowledge of your native language, you are likely to remember it all your life, as long as you continue to use it. This crystallized ability to speak, read, and write your native language makes it easier to enlarge your understanding of it, because you can relate new words to, or define them with words already familiar to you. However, if you had to learn to write and speak a new phrase in a language quite different from any you knew, it would take you longer the older you were. The reason is that your crystallized knowledge of language would be of little use to you, so you could not compensate for the decline in your fluid ability to learn new material.

Horn believes that fluid intelligence declines during adulthood because of the gradual accumulation of irreversible damage to brain structures that results from disease, injury, and biological changes associated with age (Horn and Hofer, 1992). Because these structures guide the attentional and processing capabilities that are necessary for quick, flexible reasoning, the speed and efficiency of thinking progressively declines with age. Crystallized intelligence, too, is affected by these changes, but the knowl-

---

*The correct answers to these two test items are "l" and "x."

†The correct answers to these test items are "Boldness," "Eat It," "Ring," and "1215."

edge structures underlying crystallized intelligence are overlapping and interconnected, such that losses can be more easily compensated. If an adult happens to forget a name or date, that information can be easily retrieved in other ways (such as by looking it up, asking someone, or using mnemonic devices to aid remembering). However, because the maintenance of crystallized intelligence depends partly on how it is used, Horn and Hofer (1992) have also found that individual differences in crystallized intelligence increase with age, whereas individual differences in fluid intelligence remain fairly consistent over time. In other words, the consequences of remaining involved with stimulating people and events—or of being socially isolated and withdrawn—become increasingly important to crystallized intelligence in adulthood, but individual differences in fluid intelligence are neither so variable nor so changeable.

Is Faster Thinking Better Thinking?

It is significant that speed of thinking is a critical element of fluid intelligence. In fact, many standard intelligence tests include speed of response as one component, limiting how much time can be spent on any one problem, and giving bonus points for quick answers. The same is true of many other assessments of adult intelligence. This is one aspect of intelligence testing that some specialists in adult development consider inappropriate.

The reason they think it inappropriate is that older adults are slower than younger adults at almost everything. In fact, James Birren and his colleagues consider slowing of behavior and thought to be one of the most important "markers" of aging (Birren and Fischer, 1992). Between ages 20 and 60, for example, the average adult slows down about 20 percent in basic reaction time on tasks that involve such simple behaviors as pushing a button in response to the sound of a buzzer (Birren et al., 1980). With more complicated activities, reaction time is even slower. Handwriting, for instance, takes twice as long at age 60 than at age 30 (Salthouse, 1985b). In general, decreased speed of thinking and behavior is one of the most significant influences on adult intelligence (Cunningham, 1987; Schaie, 1989b).

How is age-related slowing related to the quality of intelligence? Obviously, it results in poorer performance in timed tests or assessments requiring quick reactions. More broadly, however, Timothy Salthouse (1985b, 1986, 1991) argues that slower thinking is also less efficient thinking: if one cannot process information or ideas quickly enough, then one cannot remember or think about many facts or ideas at once, cannot sequentially relate incoming information, and cannot encompass new information as quickly as it arrives. The result, he contends, is that thinking becomes not only slower but also simpler and shallower, as important information is lost. Speed of thinking may also influence attentional processes and aspects of fluid intelligence (Birren and Fisher, 1992; Cunningham, 1987).

But not *all* features of intelligence are linked to speed of thought. In fact, slower thinking may be deeper, more reflective, and better thinking. As Botwinick (1977) has noted, "if the young are to be compared to the hare, the old may be compared to the tortoise—slow and steady, sometimes to win the race." Moreover, there are many ways that older adults can compensate for age-related slowing in thinking and reasoning, allowing them to perform comparably with younger adults. (The Research Report on p. 546 offers an illustration of how this can happen.)

Figure 21.5 *According to some researchers, slower reaction time is one of the biological "markers" of aging, which may impair performance on tasks (like pitching or hitting a baseball) that cannot be effectively performed at a slower pace. Slower reaction times also diminishes the speed and efficiency of thinking—but not necessarily its quality.*

RESEARCH REPORT   Adaptive Competence in Adulthood

Evidence for a slowing down of behavior and thinking in later adult years does not tell the whole story of cognitive change, because adults often find ways to compensate for their loss of speed and efficiency. Indeed, many researchers believe that a hallmark of "successful aging" is the ability to strategically use one's intellectual strengths to compensate for declining capacities associated with age (Charness, 1989; Dixon, 1992; Salthouse, 1987). Paul Baltes and his colleagues call this "selective optimization with compensation," and they believe that it accounts for the ability of many older adults to maintain the levels of performance of their younger years (Baltes, 1987; Baltes and Baltes, 1990; Baltes et al., 1984). This kind of adaptive competence can be found not just in research laboratories but in everyday workplaces and recreational settings as well.

Take waiting on tables in a restaurant for example, a job that demands a wide range of cognitive skills, including knowledge of menu items, memory for ordering and delivery procedures, simultaneous management of several tables (each at a different stage of the meal), the ability to combine, order, and prioritize different tasks, and monitoring social relations with customers and coworkers—as well as physical stamina! Adolescents and young adults in these roles have an advantage over much older adults in their physical dexterity and endurance and in their cognitive speed and flexibility, and this may account for why restaurant managers sometimes prefer younger employees. But are older employees less efficient, or do they have ways of compensating for the declines they experience?

Marion Perlmutter and her colleagues sought an answer to this question by analyzing the skills required for successful performance in restaurant work and then assessing these skills in a sample of sixty-four restaurant and cafeteria employees who varied in age and prior work experience (Perlmutter et al., 1990). These workers were assessed on tests of memory ability, physical strength and dexterity, knowledge of the technical and organizational requirements of the job, and social capacities. They were also observed during different periods of the work day, such as during "rush" and "nonrush" hours, to determine their effectiveness. Perlmutter and her colleagues wanted to know if younger and older employees would differ in their overall job performance—and if so, whether this difference was due to differences in their physical and cognitive skills, their work experience, or both.

They were surprised to discover that, independent of age, the amount of prior work experience had little impact on the employees' work performance or on their physical or cognitive skills. Apparently, after one has learned the basic requirements of the job, additional experience does not necessarily yield better performance (Ceci and Cornelius, 1990). However, the employee's age (independent of prior experience) made a significant difference. Younger employees, as expected, had better physical skills, better memory abilities, and greater efficiency in computation (such as when calculating the check). Nevertheless, when the two groups were compared on their work performance, older employees outperformed their younger counterparts in the number of customers served during rush and nonrush periods of the day.

Perlmutter found that this was consistent with the reports of some of the restaurant managers she interviewed. For example,

> it was consistently reported that older workers chunk tasks to save steps by combining orders for several customers at several tables and/or by employing time management strategies such as preparing checks while waiting for food delivery. . . . Although younger experienced food servers may have the knowledge and skills necessary for such organization and chunking, they do not seem to use the skills as often, perhaps because they do not believe they need to.

Thus older employees devised cognitive strategies to compensate for the narrowing of some of their other job-related skills. These researchers concluded "that this evidence of adaptive competence in adulthood represents functional improvements that probably are common, particularly in the workplace." And indeed, this appears to be so. Salthouse (1984) found, for example, that older skilled typists could perform at speeds comparable to younger typists by using cognitive strategies (such as reading ahead) to compensate for age-related declines in their perceptual motor skills. Through such "selective optimization with compensation," older adults like these learned to maintain their performance levels, but through strategies that were well-suited to the changing complexion of their cognitive capacities.

Growth, Decline . . . or What?

Horn and his colleagues clearly offer a portrayal of adult intellectual change that is different from that of Schaie and other researchers. Although both groups agree that some decline in intellectual capability is inevitable, they differ in their descriptions of its onset—with Horn arguing that fluid intelligence begins to decline from the mid-20s onward—and in the kinds of intellectual abilities that are vulnerable to decrements. Not surprisingly, many students of adult intellectual development find Schaie's conclusions a more attractive, and optimistic, portrayal of age-related changes. But we should ponder Horn's rejoinder:

> There are powerful reasons for wanting to believe that intellectual decrement does not occur. . . . Humans have a well-developed ability for wishful thinking, and most humans who derive their livelihood and status from exercise of their intellectual abilities have a strong wish that these abilities will not wane . . . The audience for abilities research is thus set to hear what it wants to hear, and what it wants to hear is that intelligence does not decline with age. [Horn, 1976]

On the other hand, each researcher notes that we do not reach an intellectual peak in adolescence and then decline, and that some forms of intelligence continue to grow during the adult years. Moreover, each agrees that intelligence becomes more individualized with increasing age, reflecting the unique background and current experiences that exercise intellectual capabilities. And many researchers—including both Schaie and Horn—are beginning to develop more complex views of intelligence, leading to new answers to classic questions about intellectual development in adulthood. We now turn to these emerging new views.

Intelligence Reconsidered

In the social sciences, breakthroughs are likely to occur, not because someone discovers an astonishing new answer to an old problem, but because someone asks an important new question that transforms the problem. This may be happening in the study of adult intelligence. The question, according to a number of researchers on both sides of the controversy, should not be "What happens to intelligence in adulthood" but "What happens to intelligences in adulthood" (Denney and Thisson, 1983–1984; Dixon et al., 1985; Horn, 1985; Schaie, 1990a, 1990b; Willis and Baltes, 1980).

Historically, psychologists as well as laymen have thought of intelligence as a single entity, a single ability that people possess in greater or lesser amounts. A leading theoretician, Charles Spearman (1927), argued that there is such a thing as general intelligence, which he called "g." Although it cannot be measured directly, he contended, it can be inferred from various abilities that can be tested, such as vocabulary, memory, and reasoning. Just the fact that psychologists give IQ tests with various subtests, and then calculate an overall IQ for the person tested, implies that intelligence can be thought of as an integrated whole. To be sure, a number of psychologists have seriously questioned whether anything like "g" exists. Nevertheless, the idea that there is such a thing as "intelligence" continues to influence research.

Recently, however, several researchers have proposed that there are many quite distinct cognitive abilities. They also maintain that these abilities, or intelligences, follow different developmental paths depending not only on the age of the person but also on the individual's life experiences, interests, and education. Paul Baltes and his colleagues (Baltes, 1987; Dixon and Baltes, 1986; Dixon et al., 1985), leading proponents of this new view, describe adult intellectual competence as being multidimensional and multidirectional, characterized by interindividual variation and plasticity. Let us look at each of these four characteristics in some detail.

Multidimensionality

The closer researchers look at adult intellectual abilities, the clearer it becomes that they are **multidimensional,** that is, that they involve several distinct dimensions. As we saw, Cattell and Horn proposed that intelligence is made up of two sets of abilities, fluid intelligence, which declines during adulthood, and crystallized intelligence, which increases. Horn (1985; Horn and Hofer, 1992) has further suggested that intelligence may consist of as many as ten distinct elements, including visual processing, auditory processing, short-term memory, and long-term memory retrieval. Schaie, too, asserts that intelligence involves distinct abilities, each of which should be conceptualized and measured differently (Schaie, 1990a). In each case, their view of the multidimensional quality of adult intellectual functioning has enabled Horn and Schaie to portray growth and decline more carefully and accurately.

Other theorists have proposed different lists of distinct factors. For example, Howard Gardner (1983) believes that there are seven autonomous intelligences: linguistic, musical, logical-mathematical, spatial, bodily-kinesthetic, self-understanding, and social understanding, each with its own neurological network in the brain. (One reason for this view is that brain-damaged people sometimes lose one or more of these abilities while the others remain intact.) The specific value placed on each of these seven intelligences depends on the cultural values of the evaluator. For instance, in contemporary Western cultures, linguistic and logical-mathematical skills are highly valued. Therefore reading and math are the core of their school curricula, and any hint of lessened reasoning ability with age is viewed with alarm. By contrast, some other cultures gives primary emphasis to social relationships. Therefore they train their children to be good listeners and careful observers of human behavior, and they take it for granted that their elders have greater social wisdom.

Robert Sternberg (1985; Berg and Sternberg, 1985) has proposed that intelligence is composed of three distinct parts. The *componential* part consists of mental processes fostering efficient learning, remembering, and thinking. These include planning, strategy selection, attention, performance monitoring, and other aspects of effective information-processing. The *contextual* part enables the person to accommodate successfully to changes in the environment and to adapt his or her abilities to environmental demands. This involves the problem-solving skills needed, for example, to adjust to retirement or to a new grandparenting role or to new demands on the job. Finally, the *experiential* part concerns the extent to which intel-

Figure 21.6 *Each adult gradually discovers and develops his or her individual capacities and benefits from the specialized abilities of others, whether it be their skill with clay or with circuitry.*

lectual functions are applied to situations that are familiar or novel in one's personal history. Most adults must put forth greater intellectual effort when they have to absorb and use new information than when they can rely on skills that are well-rehearsed and automatized.

Like Gardner, Sternberg, Schaie, Horn, and other theorists (such as Foder [1983]) believe that these multiple dimensions of intelligence are deeply rooted in how mental processes are innately organized. However, these dimensions of intelligence may also be affected by one's personal history. As we will see shortly, some theorists argue that one's interests, experiences, and work-related skills lead an adult to develop intellectual competencies in specific types of thinking and not in others (developing acute musical sensitivity, for example, but not advanced mathematical skills). But whether multidimensionality is regarded as biological or experiential, this new view of intelligence means that appreciating an adult's cognitive skills requires sensitive assessments of more than one feature of their intellectual abilities.

Multidirectionality

No matter which particular list of intelligences one considers, it is clear that the abilities involved are **multidirectional** in that they can follow different trajectories with age. Thus short-term memory generally falls quite steadily, while vocabulary generally rises. Other abilities—such as mathematical reasoning—might rise, fall, and rise again, depending on how much they are used in daily life. Still others might hold steady until a sudden drop occurs because of such factors as illness and depression. Since virtually every pattern is possible, it is misleading to ask whether intelligence, in general, either increases or decreases. An either/or answer is too simplistic.

Interindividual Variation

One reason many patterns exist, of course, is that each individual is genetically unique and has unique experiences, and both of these factors affect the pattern of a particular person's intellectual development (see A Closer Look, p. 551). The result of this **interindividual variation,** as shown by longitudinal research, is that some individuals decline in some or all mental abilities by age 40, while others are just as capable at age 70 as they were at earlier ages. Often such variations are related to changes in family and career responsibilities (Eichorn et al., 1981; Schaie, 1983). The housewife who finds that an "empty nest" brings empty days, and who suffers from, say, hypertension, might begin to show noticeable declines in certain kinds of intellectual functioning. On the other hand, someone who replaces a stimulating career as a parent or a worker with some equally stimulating form of retirement is likely, given continued good health, to maintain fairly steady levels of cognitive functioning well into late adulthood. Educational level, income, and marital status are additional contributors to individual differences in intellectual aging: to be well-educated, financially secure, and happily married to a stimulating spouse has intellectual as well as emotional gains (Schaie, 1990a).

As just suggested, physical and mental health status also strongly influences the course of a person's intellectual functioning (Field et al., 1988). Depression is common in later adulthood, for example, which can contribute to the general slowing of behavior and thinking we noted earlier (Cunningham and Tomer, 1990). Cardiovascular disease and other physical ailments are also associated with declining intellectual abilities, as are degenerative conditions like alcoholism (Cunningham, 1987; Cunningham and Tomer, 1990; Schaie, 1990a, 1990b).

Adding to these individual differences are cohort differences, which may be quite strong, as we have seen, when generations differ not only in the average number of years of education they received but also in the emphasis of that education (Kaufman et al., 1989). Probably for this reason, current cohorts of young adults score higher on conventional IQ tests, even while their arithmetic skills are lower (Bower, 1987b).

Plasticity

Instead of being innate and immutable, the actual pattern of the various intelligences is shaped by experience, education, interests, and motivation. Thus differences in intelligence are not inflexible, but can be altered through experience. This characteristic is called **plasticity,** to suggest that intelligences can be molded in many ways. Abilities can become enhanced or diminished, depending on how, when, and why a person uses them. Intellectual abilities can also be deliberately altered through training. Numerous studies of middle-aged and older adults find that training in a specific area—such as techniques of memory improvement or mathematical problem solving—can result in greatly improved proficiency levels (Baltes and Willis, 1982). This is especially true when the area of training is relevant to the older person's actual life. To be sure, intellectual plasticity declines to some extent with increasing age (Baltes and Lindenberger, 1988). But a capacity for change and improvement is always there. (Some of the specifics of this research are reviewed in Chapter 24.)

It should be clear at this point that the recognition of adult cognition as multidimensional, multidirectional, variable, and plastic greatly defuses the debate about the course of intelligence throughout adulthood. The dispute now can take a much clearer form: Who develops which intelligences for what reasons? It also moderates the common argument about who is more intelligent, the "absent-minded" professor or the "street-smart" illiterate.

| A CLOSER LOOK | Individual Profiles of Adult Intellectual Change |

The portrayal of adult intelligence as multidimensional, multidirectional, and individually variable can seem terribly abstract when it is based on group averages. But one of the advantages of longitudinal studies is that individual profiles of intellectual change can be separated out from group trends, allowing the reasons for growth, decline, and stable functioning to be examined on a case-by-case basis. Case studies like these reveal that the reasons for intellectual growth or decline are complex and multifaceted, based on the unique experiences of adult life.

Using data from his Seattle Longitudinal Study, K. Warner Schaie (1989c) has provided the following portrayals of changes in word recognition (a measure of crystallized intelligence) in two pairs of adults of comparable age. More important, information about each person's occupation, health, marital status, and significant life events was used to assess why patterns of growth, decline, or stability emerged.

The first two profiles [figure (a)] represent two young-old women who throughout life functioned at very different levels. Subject 155510 is a high school graduate who has been a homemaker all of her adult life and whose husband is still alive and well-functioning. She started our testing program at a rather low level, but her performance has had a clear upward trend. The comparison participant subject (154503) had been professionally active as a teacher. Her performance remained fairly level and above the population average until her early sixties. Since that time she has been divorced and retired from her teaching job; her performance in 1984 dropped to an extremely low level, which may reflect her experiential

losses but could also be a function of increasing health problems.

The second pair of profiles [figure (b)] shows the 28-year performance of two old-old men now in their eighties. Subject 153003, who started out somewhat below the population average, completed only grade school and worked as a purchasing agent prior to his retirement. He showed virtually stable performance until the late sixties; his performance actually increased after he retired, but he is beginning to experience health problems and has recently become a widower, and his latest assessment was below the earlier stable level. By contrast, subject 153013, a high school graduate who held mostly clerical types of jobs, showed gain until the early sixties and stability over the next assessment interval. By age 76, however, he showed substantial decrement that continued through the last assessment, which occurred less than a year prior to his death.

Looking at the relative scores of each pair of subjects at their first testing, it is clear that no one could have predicted their later-life intellectual performance solely on the basis of the changes in group averages that occur with increasing age. For each pair, the influences of education, occupation, and idiosyncratic events like a divorce, problems with physical health, and death of a spouse contributed to unique profiles of intellectual growth. For one, in fact, intellectual *growth* rather than decline was the rule in later life. The lesson: intellectual changes are complexly interwoven into the variety of changing life circumstances that a given individual experiences during the adult years, resulting in variations in intellectual development that defy precise prediction.

These figures index changes in word recognition scores (which are used as a measure of crystallized intelligence) for two pairs of comparable adults over time. Notice how distinctly different the profiles of individual change for each person are—even though each is the same age and part of the same birth cohort. These differences underscore how much intellectual change in adulthood is affected by occupational, marital, health, and other experiences that vary from one person to another.

Source: K. Warmer Schaie (1989).

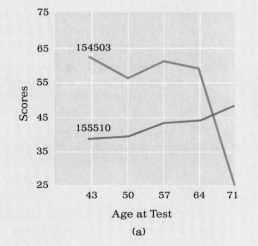

(a)

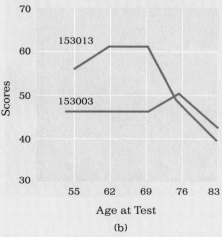

(b)

They are both intelligent in different ways, because each has fostered a different type of intelligence. And as we shall see, this conclusion is confirmed by the study of "practical intelligence" in adults.

Practical Intelligence

In thinking about the course of adult intellectual development, we have assumed that measures of fluid and crystallized intelligence, or of the five primary mental abilities, capture the quality of thinking and reasoning that most adults experience. But is this really true? Is intelligence truly "what intelligence tests measure" (Boring, 1950), or are there other intellectual qualities we use that are not included in these tests?

Many developmentalists who study adult intelligence believe that traditional measures assess little-used knowledge and skills, and that decline in these abilities with age reflects their waning due to lack of use (Denney, 1982, 1989; Labouvie-Vief, 1985). Certainly most adults do not occupy their time trying to define obscure words or deduce the next element in a number sequence, but instead try to solve the real-world challenges of managing a home, advancing a career, balancing family finances, analyzing information from the newspaper or television, and understanding the needs of family members, neighbors, and colleagues. According to contextual theorists of adult development like Roger Dixon (1992; Dixon and Baltes, 1986) and Stephen Ceci (1990), assessments of adult intelligence should encompass the skills and knowledge that are relevant to practical functioning. This has led to a new approach to adult intelligence—the study of **practical intelligence,** or the intellectual skills used in everyday problem solving (Poon et al., 1989; Sinnott, 1989; Sternberg and Wagner, 1986).

In contrast to the examples of measures of fluid and crystallized intelligence on page 544, consider, for example, these items from a measure of practical intelligence that focuses on real-life "domestic" problem solving (Denney, 1989, 1990):

> Let's say that one evening you go to the refrigerator to get something cold to drink. When you open the refrigerator, you notice that it is not cold inside, but rather, is warm. What would you do?

> Let's say that a young man who is living in an apartment building finds that the heater in his apartment is not working. He asks his landlord to send someone out to fix it and the landlord agrees. But, after a week of cold weather and several calls to the landlord, the heater is still not fixed. What should the young man do?

> Let's say that a 60-year-old man who lives alone in a large city needs to go across town for a doctor's appointment. He cannot drive because he doesn't have a car and he doesn't have any relatives who live nearby who could drive him. What should he do?

Other measures of practical intelligence concern career decisions, consumer behavior, conflict resolution, finding one's way in complex physical spaces, and managing an office. Problems in areas like these not only concern real-life situations but also involve the kinds of intellectual abilities and knowledge that most adults consider to be increasingly important as one matures (Cornelius, 1990; Sternberg and Berg, 1987).

Figure 21.7 *Intellectual decline in adulthood is not inevitable: to be well-educated, financially secure, happily married to a stimulating partner, and engaged in cognitively stimulating activities has intellectual—as well as emotional—gains for adults at all ages.*

Such practical problems differ from traditional adult intelligence measures in several ways (Wagner and Sternberg, 1986). First, because these challenges entail everyday, real-world reasoning, adults are often more intrinsically motivated to master them than they are with abstract intelligence measures. Second, because they draw more heavily upon an adult's personal experiences and background, they are more likely than traditional intelligence tests to involve skills that have been strengthened and improved through regular use. Third, unlike conventional intelligence measures, which allow for a single correct answer, solutions to these practical problems can be evaluated in a number of different ways. For example, with respect to the problems listed above, an adult's response could be evaluated in terms of overall problem-solving style (e.g., problem-focused action; help-seeking; avoidance or denial; etc.); or in terms of the number of different solutions proposed; or in terms of the effectiveness of the solutions (Camp et al., 1989; Cornelius, 1990).

When responses are evaluated in terms of the effectiveness of solutions, researchers have found that practical intelligence increases throughout most of the adult years, with some decline in late adulthood (Denney, 1989, 1990). Because real-world intelligence depends partly on experience, it is not surprising that middle-aged adults perform better on these measures than do young adults. But there are limits to the benefits of additional experience, and by the late adult years the skills of practical intelligence may become more narrowed to those capabilities that are especially pertinent to one's personal life.

Figure 21.8 *The skills of* practical intelligence—*which involve reasoning applied to real-world rather than abstract dilemmas, and draw on an adult's wealth of experience and knowledge— are exemplified by counselors and therapists, but are used in a variety of everyday situations by many adults.*

In closing, it should be noted that measures of practical intelligence are not unrelated to traditional adult intelligence measures. Practical intelligence draws upon the skills of both fluid and crystallized intelligence (depending on which kind of measure is used), because real-world dilemmas require not only flexible problem solving but also cultural knowledge and experience (Camp et al., 1989; Cornelius, 1990; Willis and Schaie, 1986). In other words, knowing what to do when the refrigerator doesn't work requires a capacity for insightful inferences and some knowledge of how refrigerators operate. Moreover, it may be due to their reliance on fluid intelligence that some forms of practical intelligence show later-life declines (just as conventional measures of fluid intelligence do), while other kinds of practical intelligence that rely more on crystallized intelligence continue to grow.

Current interest in practical intelligence underscores that adult intelligence is truly multidimensional and multidirectional in quality, and that interindividual variability is related to differences in the life experiences of individuals. As we turn to another form of specialized knowledge—expertise—we see that individual patterns of adult intelligence can assume even more unique, personalized forms.

Expertise

Recognizing the plasticity of intelligence, some developmentalists believe that as we age, we each develop **expertise** at whatever is important to us, in our work, in our leisure activities, in our relationships with others. That is, we tend to become selective "experts," developing specialized competencies in activities that are personally meaningful, whether fixing a car, preparing gourmet meals, diagnosing an illness, or mastering fly fishing (Dixon et al., 1985). This helps to explain the multidimensional and individualized patterns of adult intellectual skills, as adults acquire expertise in some areas while remaining novices in others.

What Makes an Expert?

When developmentalists use the term "expert," they do not mean someone who is extraordinarily gifted at a particular task. They simply mean someone who is significantly better at a task than people who have not put time and effort into doing that task. The difference between experts and novices cannot be reduced to merely differences in the amount of experience and knowledge, however. Research suggests that there are several distinctions to be made between those who are experts and those who are less skilled (Charness, 1986, 1989; Rybash et al., 1986; Salthouse, 1985, 1987).

Expert vs. Novice

First of all, novices tend to rely on formal procedures and rules to guide them. Experts, on the other hand, rely more on their accumulated experience and on the circumstances of the immediate context, and they are therefore more intuitive and less stereotyped in their performance. For example, experienced physicians interview patients with more varied questions, following up on verbal and nonverbal cues that seem to pass unrecognized by less experienced physicians (Elstein et al., 1978; Leaper et al., 1973). Similarly, when they look at X-rays, expert physicians interpret them more accurately, though often they cannot verbalize exactly how they arrived at their diagnosis. As one pair of researchers explain:

> The expert physician, with many years of experience, has so "compiled" his knowledge that a long chain of inference is likely to be reduced to a single association. This feature can make it difficult for an expert to verbalize information that he actually uses in solving a problem. Faced with a difficult problem, the apprentice fails to solve it at all, the journeyman solves it after long effort, and the master sees the answer immediately. [Rybash et al., 1986]

In much the same way, the expert artist, or musician, or scientist is not simply a practiced technician but is an intuitive creator as well (Charness, 1986; John-Steiner, 1986).

Figure 21.9 *Expertise—which is often, but not always, associated with increasing age—entails efficient information-processing and diverse problem-solving strategies, as well as cognitive flexibility and creativity drawn from experience. In this picture, however, either the younger or the older chess player may be an expert, depending on each one's knowledge of the game.*

Second, many elements of expert performance are automatic: that is, the complex action and thought they involve have become routine, making it appear that most aspects of the work in question are performed "instinctively." Instead, experts are processing incoming information more quickly and analyzing it more efficiently than nonexperts, and in well-rehearsed ways that make their efforts appear almost nonconscious.

Third, the expert has better strategies, and more of them, for accomplishing a particular task. In fact, this may be the crucial difference between a skilled and an unskilled person (Welford, 1980). The superior strategies of the expert also permit the "selective optimization with compensation" that we examined in the Research Report on p. 546. As noted there, many developmentalists regard the capacity to accommodate to changes in ability over time as an essential element in "successful aging" (Charness, 1989; Charness and Bosman, 1990).

Finally, perhaps because of all these differences, experts are more flexible. The expert artist, musician, or scientist, for example, is more creative and curious in his or her work, deliberately experimenting and enjoying the surprise when things do not go according to plan (Arlin, 1984; John-Steiner, 1986). Another example of the flexibility arising from expertise

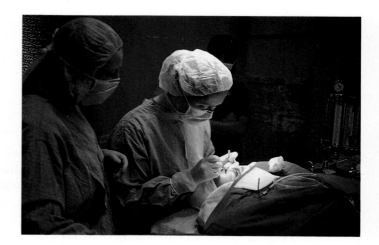

Figure 21.10 *The importance of experience is obvious for a surgeon. Almost any one would agree that if a child needs to have a cleft palate fixed (as shown here), the more practice the surgeon has had with this particular operation, the better. Less obvious, but equally valuable, is expertise in other areas. For example, for the auto mechanic, the airplane pilot, the cook, and the parent, years of pratice produce a combination of intuition, creativity, and wisdom that makes the job easier and the results better.*

comes from surgeons (Salthouse, 1985). Obviously, since no two patients are exactly alike, every type of operation has the potential for sudden, unexpected complications. Not only will the expert surgeon be more likely than the novice to notice little telltale signs (an unexpected lesion, an oddly shaped organ, a rise or drop in a vital sign) that may signal a possible problem, but the expert will be better able to deviate from standard textbook procedure to devise strategies to overcome the problem. Similarly, experts in all walks of life seem better able to adapt to individual cases and exceptions to the rule—somewhat like an expert chef who adjusts ingredients, temperature, technique, and timing as things develop, and virtually never follows a recipe exactly.

How, then, can we best answer the question with which we began this chapter? Perhaps with cautious optimism. The longitudinal evidence reviewed in the first half of the chapter is encouraging: certainly on some basic abilities, many adults improve over most of adulthood, and show no decline by age 60. Indeed, as you will see in Chapter 24, some people show no evidence of decline at all, and continue to master new areas of knowledge even in late adulthood. The suggestion that we are most likely to improve and perhaps develop expertise in those areas that capture our attention and intelligences is also heartening.

Still, the evidence for cognitive growth is not definitive, and there is strong evidence for cognitive declines in some people. On the whole, however, it does seem clear that in middle adulthood individual differences are much more critical in determining the course of cognitive development than chronological age alone is. In other words, you would be better able to predict an adult's intellectual competencies by sampling his or her background, interests, and motivation than by knowing his or her age. And, as we will see in Chapter 24, even in old age, many cognitive declines seem more closely related to particular personal circumstances, such as health and social context, than to age alone.

SUMMARY

Decline in Adult Intelligence?

1. On the basis of many large cross-sectional studies, psychologists once believed that intelligence inevitably declined in adulthood. Within the past twenty-five years, longitudinal research has led to the opposite conclusion, that intelligence may improve during adulthood.

2. Sequential research, which attempts to distinguish the general aging process from the specific experiences of each generation, finds that cohort effects have considerable impact on measurements of intelligence during middle adulthood as well as chronological age.

Fluid and Crystallized Intelligence

3. Despite evidence for cognitive growth during middle adulthood, the impact of age on intelligence is still controversial. Some psychologists believe that while crystallized intelligence, which is based on accumulated knowledge, increases with time, one's fluid, flexible reasoning skills inevitably decline with age.

4. All researchers agree that speed of thinking, as well as speed of behavior, slows down with age. Tests that measure rapidness of thought therefore show an age-related drop. Theorists disagree, however, about whether a slowing of mental processes necessarily affects quality of thought.

Intelligence Reconsidered

5. Most researchers now think that, rather than there being one entity called intelligence, there are several distinct intelligences.

6. Each intellectual ability may increase, decrease, or remain stable with age, depending on such factors as education and experience. Adult intellectual competence is multidimensional and multidirectional, characterized by interindividual variation and plasticity.

Practical Intelligence

7. The study of practical intelligence is based on the view that typical measures of adult intelligence do not include the knowledge and skills employed in everyday problem solving. Measures of practical intelligence involve real-world situations that draw upon an adult's personal experiences.

8. Practical intelligence seems to increase throughout most of adulthood, with some later-life decline. It is related to both fluid and crystallized intelligence.

Expertise

9. As people grow older, they may become more expert in whatever types of intelligence or skills they choose to develop. Meanwhile, abilities that are not exercised may fall into decline.

10. In addition to being more experienced, experts are better thinkers than novices in many ways. Experts are more intuitive and flexible, and use better strategies to perform whatever task is required. Their cognitive processes are more specialized, as well as automatic, often seeming to require little conscious thought.

KEY TERMS

fluid intelligence (543)
crystallized
    intelligence (544)
multidimensional (548)
multidirectional (549)

interindividual
    variation (549)
plasticity (550)
practical intelligence (552)
expertise (554)

KEY QUESTIONS

1. What evidence suggests that intelligence declines during adulthood?

2. What evidence suggests that intelligence increases during adulthood?

3. What are the advantages of longitudinal research on adult intelligence?

4. What are the advantages of sequential research on adult intelligence?

5. What differences would you expect to find in your own intelligence ten years from now? Why would they occur?

6. How is fluid intelligence different from crystallized intelligence? How does each change in adulthood?

7. What are the four recently recognized dimensions of intelligence and how do they broaden the picture of "intelligence" and of cognitive development in adulthood?

8. What is practical intelligence? Why is it important to a complete picture of adult intelligence?

9. What are the differences between an expert and a novice?

CHAPTER 22

Middle Adulthood: Psychosocial Development

Middle age is often said to represent a time of personal crisis, or, at the least, to be a troubling transition between the prime of life and the decline of old age, as the individual measures his or her goals, accomplishments, and commitments in terms of "time left" in life. The popular image of midlife upheaval depicts last-ditch efforts to recapture youth and last-chance efforts to start a new life. However, as you will see, in midlife, continuities of love, relationships, family commitments, work involvements, and personality patterns often seem more salient than any changes that occur. This chapter will explain why this is so, as well as answer the following questions:

How common is the midlife crisis, and what circumstances are likely to bring it on?

Why are the sorrows of the "empty nest" more myth than present-day reality?

What happens when the career ladder leads to a plateau?

What factors cause a job to "burn out" the worker's dedication?

Do men become more feminine and women more masculine as they grow older?

The social clock—the cultural timetable that suggests when various stages and landmark events of adulthood should occur—continues ticking in middle adulthood as it did in early adulthood. Although no dramatic biological shifts occur to signal it, our society recognizes a point called **midlife** at about age 40, when the average adult has about as many years of life ahead as have already past. Midlife ushers in **middle age**, which lasts until about age 60.

As you will soon see, however, while it may be easy to designate an age for midlife, it is not simple to describe what occurs during these years. Much depends on the cultural context and the particular ecological niche in which individuals find themselves at age 40.

Midlife: Crisis, Shift, or Transition?

Midlife is popularly thought of as a period of crisis and dramatic change (Brandes, 1985). Indeed, one of the first best-selling books to broach this idea, *Passages,* describes the "age 40 crucible," when various psychological pressures supposedly compel people to take apart their lives and then put them together into "a whole new puzzle" (Sheehy, 1976).

That middle age might be a time of crisis is certainly a plausible idea, for a number of potentially troubling personal changes often do cluster in the 40s. The most obvious is simply the awareness that one is beginning to grow old. Birthdays tend to be seen in a new perspective—a measure less of time lived than of time remaining. This perceptual shift is often highlighted by the death or serious illness either of a close relative from the next older generation—perhaps a parent or a favorite aunt or uncle—or of a friend or colleague, perhaps someone only a few years older than oneself. Such events bring not only feelings of personal loss but also thoughts about one's own mortality (Katchadourian, 1987).

For many middle-aged parents, an additional source of upheaval is the need to make important, and not always easy, adjustments in their parental roles. Typically, at just about the time that parents enter midlife, children become adolescents, demanding greater independence and putting their parents' authority, and sometimes their values, to the test. No sooner have parents adjusted to these changes than their children set out on their own as adults, perhaps distancing themselves from their parents initially and then calling forth a different form of nurturance and closeness when they make their parents become parents-in-law and grandparents.

Achievement-related shifts may also hold the possibility for difficulty. At about age 40, many individuals reach the limits of their vocational potential and enter a career plateau. With no more opportunity for advancement, the next work-related step seems to be retirement, a prospect that is unsettling to almost everyone, although the specific emotional reactions vary somewhat between pure joy and near terror.

Further, whatever choices adults may have made about generativity, midlife is an occasion to question those decisions. Many who thought that time was on their side in the quest for certain life goals suddenly see the door to the future closing. Many reassess the balance between work and family: those who have been single-mindedly climbing the career ladder often become concerned about the loved ones they have neglected; those who have concentrated on child-rearing often worry about what they will do when their children are gone.

All of these midlife shifts are recognized by most developmentalists who study adulthood (Katchadourian, 1987; Wrightsman, 1988). However, there is substantial debate about whether such changes more commonly produce a **midlife crisis**, provoking radical reexamination and sudden transformation in people's public or personal lives, or simply provide an occasion to reaffirm the overall rightness of one's present course and to look for ways to make minor adjustments to it.

Research on Midlife

How should we decide if midlife represents a crisis, a shift, or a transition? The first step is to look at longitudinal research, which finds somewhat different answers for middle-age adults generally, and especially for men and women.

Levinson's Findings

The researcher offering the strongest evidence for the idea of a midlife crisis is Daniel Levinson (1978, 1986), who originally studied forty men intensely over several years and then did follow-up research on additional adults of both sexes. According to Levinson's findings, sometime between ages 38 and 43, virtually everyone is faced with a basic question:

> "What have I done with my life? . . . What is it I truly want for myself and others? What are my central values and how are they reflected in my life? What are my greatest talents and how am I using (or wasting) them? . . . Can I live in a way that combines my current desires, values, and talents?" [Levinson, 1978]

In addressing this question, the majority of the men in Levinson's study concluded that much of their life had been based on illusions, that they had mistakenly placed too much importance on money, or public achievement, or a particular personal relationship. Although some men maintained psychic equilibrium during this period, making only minor adjustments in the structure of their lives, 80 percent of Levinson's original group experienced

> tumultuous struggles within the self and with the external world. . . . Every aspect of their lives comes into question, and they are horrified by much that is revealed. They are full of recriminations against themselves and others.

As a result, many of these men made major shifts in their lives, ranging from external changes—such as divorce, or remarriage, or a shift in occupation, or an alteration in lifestyle—to internal changes, such as a modification in social outlook or a reordering of personal values. Levinson maintains that while the specifics vary from individual to individual, few can avoid this midlife reappraisal.

Other Research

Other studies also have found that many people, especially men, experience some form of midlife distress (Bergler, 1985; Gould, 1978; Vaillant, 1977). For instance, a study of a representative group of 300 middle-aged men (Farrell and Rosenberg, 1981) found that a higher proportion of them had psychological problems of one sort or another than a comparison group of younger men. As you can see in Figure 22.1 (p. 562), only 12 percent had an obvious, classic midlife crisis, openly wrestling with feelings that their life was goalless and empty, analyzing what they really wanted in life and wishing they could start over afresh. However, another 30 percent expressed even greater dissatisfaction, but rather than questioning their own life

Figure 22.1 *About two-thirds of all the middle-aged men in Farrell and Rosenberg's study experienced significant levels of distress, anger, or depression regarding their lives, but most of them did not acknowledge themselves as being in a crisis: in one way or another, they managed to mask their lack of self-satisfaction. The same study also investigated younger men and found that some, but not as many, had similar feelings.*

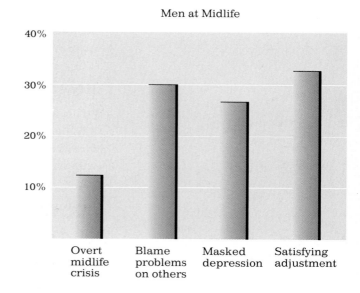

choices and trying to make changes, "they attributed their unhappiness to external circumstances and other people," blaming their jobs, their children, their marriages, and people from other races and ethnic groups.

A third group, 26 percent of the total, tended to deny that anything was generally wrong with their lives, but they had many specific complaints that could well have been caused by their inability to cope with psychological difficulties. For example, they were likely to feel that their intellect was fading, that their children needed authoritarian control, that their enjoyment of food had diminished, and that their sex lives were unsatisfying. The researchers concluded that for this group, "the effort to avoid experiencing their own feelings and changing selves" took its toll "in immobilization, loss of appetites, and depression."

Finally, only 32 percent seemed completely crisis-free, satisfied with their work, their marriages, their children, and their health. This group, rather than experiencing midlife as a disorienting crisis, were able to deal actively and constructively with whatever problems they encountered.

As you see, this study found that men's responses to midlife depended largely on their personal style of coping with problems. Interestingly, education and socioeconomic status seemed to affect coping style. Those who were relatively affluent and well educated were more likely either to have a crisis or to cope effectively; those with less education and lower SES were likely either to blame others or to "punish" themselves psychosomatically.

Gender Differences in the Midlife Crisis

Whereas the idea of a male midlife crisis has been around only twenty years or so, it has long been assumed that, for biological reasons, women inevitably experience a crisis in middle age. If a woman in her 40s or 50s seemed sad or angry, or behaved in unexpected ways, it would automatically be ascribed to the "change of life." (In fact, the assumption that women had a crisis at midlife was so strong that it led to the misnaming of a midlife crisis in men as the "male menopause.")

Figure 22.2 *One of the most striking and well-noted midlife transitions in recent years was that of film actress Audrey Hepburn, who in her 50s became a roving ambassador for UNICEF, traveling to underdeveloped nations on behalf of their starving children.*

Surprisingly, when researchers began to study the lives of adult women, they found relatively little age-related stress in middle age, with tension and depression more likely to occur at age 30 than at 40 or 50 (Baruch and Burnett, 1987; House et al., 1990; Reinke et al., 1985). Instead of being a time of depression brought on by the fear of growing old, an empty nest, or menopause (see Chapter 20), midlife for women may be, as one review concludes, "a time of great growth, expansion, and satisfaction" (Brooks-Gunn and Kirsh, 1984). During the same years that Levinson found men's dreams shattered and their illusions exposed, other research (Baruch and Barnett, 1987; Shaw, 1986; Moch, 1991) found many women (especially those who focused their early adulthood years on motherhood) discovering new opportunities. They went back to school, began careers, became more involved with their community. Even Levinson, while insisting that women as well as men restructure and reappraise their lives every decade, agrees that the full-blown midlife crisis seems more often to be a masculine affair.

Cohort, Context, and Crisis

More detailed analysis of the incidence of midlife crisis and middle-age difficulties for both sexes reveals the importance of contextual factors. For example, a woman might be considered either "finished at 40" or "stronger with age," depending partly on her socioeconomic status and partly on her culture's expectations regarding women in midlife (Gergen, 1990; Todd et al., 1990; Brown and Kerns, 1985). Obviously, a woman's emotions at reaching midlife will be affected by her perception of which characterization more closely applies to her.

Cohort differences are apparent as well. A nationwide American survey in the 1950s found that, as women grew older, their self-esteem fell (Gurin et al., 1960). Twenty years later, women responding to the same questions no longer felt lower self-esteem with age (Veroff et al., 1981). Similarly, the rate of psychological problems among middle-aged women was substantially higher during the 1950s than the 1970s, according to two similar surveys done twenty years apart (Srole et al., 1962; Srole and Fischer, 1980).

The reason for these differences clearly seems to lie in changes in social conditions. Most women who reached middle age several decades ago had been homemakers exclusively, and for most, their chief sources of self-esteem were their roles as mother and wife and their physical attractiveness. When their children left home, these women had no jobs and no marketable skills. Nor were they encouraged to get them. Unless their husbands, for some reason, could not provide for them, they were supposed to stay at home, keeping house and waiting to become needed again as grandmothers. No wonder middle-aged and older women, their children grown, their beauty fading, experienced a fall in self-esteem, and a rise in depression, with age.

However, beginning about 1970, American women started to enter or reenter colleges and the labor market in far greater numbers than before (Shaw, 1986; Moen, 1991). Today, women in middle age are likely to have trained for a career, to have been employed for much of their adult lives, to have work opportunities available to them at midlife, and therefore to have a source of self-esteem that women in earlier cohorts did not have. Of course, this does not mean that motherhood and wifehood have necessarily diminished in importance. Most middle-aged women who have both career and family believe that their family roles are the more important ones (Lopata and Barnewoolt, 1984). However, when women have both work and family roles, each role provides an important buffer to protect against whatever midlife strains may arise in the other (Baruch et al., 1982). If midlife difficulties occur at all in this cohort, unmarried women without children (Mellinger and Erdwins, 1986) or married women without jobs (Baruch, 1984) are more likely to experience them than women who have combined both roles.

Men reaching midlife in recent years may also have been affected by the particular experiences of their cohort, but, in their case, historical change may have worked to make their lives more difficult. As you know, psychologists' interest in adult development is fairly recent. Their collection of data on men in midlife began in earnest primarily during the 1960s and 1970s, so the generation of American men that provided most of the data for the midlife crisis were born in the 1920s. For the men in this cohort, early adulthood went particularly well, especially if they were veterans of World War II (receiving such benefits as free college education and low-cost mortgages), or if they were starting up the career ladder in the prosperous 1950s. Most of them were happy and successful both at work and at home: they married full-time housewives who took care of them, their homes, and their children.

However, when these men reached midlife during the 1960s, many of the nation's youth were seriously questioning authority—not only the authority of parents and teachers but also the authority of church (on sex) and country (on civil rights, civil liberties, and Vietnam). Thus, many fathers found their fundamental values and assumptions being challenged by their own children.

Further, society as a whole was shifting in a way these men had never anticipated: women of all ages began questioning traditional gender roles, often fiercely, and middle-aged men found their wives, daughters, and female employees changing in disconcerting ways. Wives insisted on taking jobs, and on having equal marital rights; daughters wanted to live on their own, or worse, with a boyfriend; secretaries refused to make coffee, and began to protest sexism in the office. Many women who were dissatisfied with the progress of their lives blamed the "male chauvinist pigs," a term applied most freely to the very type of middle-aged, middle-income males that researchers were studying.

Obviously these were not comfortable times for such middle-aged men, and because things had previously been going so well for them, this cohort was particularly unprepared for the issues they were suddenly facing. It is hardly surprising, then, that researchers at this time found that many midlife males to be in crisis.

Now, however, the full limitations of this finding are becoming more apparent. Not only was the notion of a universal "midlife crisis" derived from research on a particular cohort of mostly white, middle-class males, but it was greatly overblown by the media, feeding into the 1970s pop-psych *zeitgeist* that "psychological problems could be attributed to universal developmental changes" and that "predictable crises added both security and spice to adult life" (Costa and McCrae, 1989). Embracing this view uncritically, many people were all too ready to interpret any kind of upheaval in the middle years as a bona fide midlife crisis, often using the label as an excuse for problems they were experiencing themselves or creating for others.

So is there a midlife crisis or not? The answer, now based on several decades of research on people of both genders and several cultures, is yes—for some people, some of the time, in certain contexts. In traditional societies, where aging brings increased power and respect, the midlife crisis is very rare. In more fluid societies, a midlife crisis is likely to be found in those people who reach middle age just when a sociocultural shift and the particulars of their own lives undercut the values and goals they have pursued throughout early adulthood. If such anchors as career, marriage, financial goals, or parental roles no longer seem worthwhile when the fourth or fifth decade begins, the combination of personal aging and sociocultural shift may trigger a crisis. Even in this case, however, the result of the difficult circumstances may be a gradual transition or an abrupt change, accompanied by feelings of either depression or liberation.

Given this diversity, let us examine more closely the two significant arenas of adulthood, family and work, searching for particular patterns and events that are likely to bring stress or satisfaction.

Family Dynamics in Middle Adulthood

Family ties across the generations are particularly important for those in the middle-aged generation, precisely because they are the "generation in the middle," between aging parents and adult children. Often they have grandchildren and sometimes grandparents as well.

It is easy to underestimate the role of the middle generation because, in contrast to the traditional extended family found in many other cultures, with several generations living under the same roof and intensely involved in each other's lives, the various generations of the American family are popularly perceived as being geographically and emotionally remote. Certainly it is true that, by age 50, most middle-aged Americans today live only with a spouse or a friend from the same generation, or alone. However, this does not mean that family links are weak. Researchers have found that relatives typically have frequent contact with each other, exchanging a great deal of support (Barresi and Menon, 1990; Hagestad, 1988; Crimmins and Ingegneri, 1990). They stay in touch by telephone and travel (much easier and less expensive than in earlier times) and provide each other substantial help, both emotional and material (ranging from gifts and loans to babysitting, home repair, and health care). Indeed, while it is tempting to romanticize the idea of households in which relatives of various ages live together, the truth is that many contemporary family members provide better assistance to each other, with less tension and trouble, when they live apart (Umberson, 1992; Coward et al., 1992).

Overall, in these times of societal and economic change, the family bond is often more precious and more extensive (spanning four or even five generations) than ever. Typically, as we will now see, middle-aged adults are the pivotal link in this family chain.

Middle-Aged Adults and Their Aging Parents

The relationship between most middle-aged adults and their parents improves with time. One reason is that, as adult children mature, they develop a more balanced view of the relationship as a whole, especially with regard to their years of growing up. This change is particularly apparent in men who had a tendency as adolescents and young adults to blame their fathers for not having been sufficiently helpful and understanding. In middle age they are likely to reevaluate the "old man" and become more appreciative

Figure 22.3 *Like the middle-aged woman on the right, many adults find their understanding and love of their parents increasing as they themselves become older. Father-son and mother-daughter relationships are particularly likely to become closer than they were when the child was an adolescent.*

of his good qualities and more accepting of his limitations (Farrell and Rosenberg, 1981). Women, too, become more appreciative of the older generation, as they better understand their role in safeguarding traditions and linking the generations (Helson and Moane, 1987).

The improvement in relationships between middle-age children and their parents is particularly likely to occur in the current social setting because most of today's elderly are healthy, active, and independent. They typically prefer not to live with their adult children, and, thanks to a changed economic picture in the past several decades, most of them can afford to live on their own, giving both themselves and their grown children a measure of freedom and privacy that enhances the relationship between them. Indeed, the current financial picture is such that many of the older generation continue to provide financial assistance for their children and grandchildren, just as they did in middle age.

Middle-Aged Adults and Their Adult Children

Likewise, the relationship between middle-aged parents and their children improves throughout middle age, especially if the children have emerged from adolescence successfully. Of course, it seems as though there is almost always some aspect of a young adult's life that parents find fault with, particularly in the case of fathers and their young adult sons (Nydegger, 1986). About a third of all fathers, for example, complain about their son's lack of achievement. Interestingly, when parents complain about their daughters, it more often relates to the daughter's love life than to the daughter herself. Parents are less likely to approve of their daughter's live-in lover than of their son's, and about a third of all fathers feel that their sons-in-law are not worthy husbands (Nydeggar, 1986). When the relationship between young adults and their parents becomes uncomfortably tense, the usual strategy is for the younger generation to limit contact with the parents, a step that may make the relationship less close but often, in fact, makes it more affectionate (Green and Boxer, 1986).

Despite the possible conflicts, being the parent of a young adult child who is beginning college or a career, and perhaps marriage and parenthood, is usually a source of pride. In addition, the younger generation serves as a "cohort bridge," a source of information and advice about new developments in the culture (Green and Boxer, 1986). Many a middle-aged woman has gone to college because her adult children urged her to; many a middle-aged man has begun to take better care of himself because his children provided specific health information. For their part, most young adults benefit not only from the material aid and advice their parents provide, but also from the self-confidence that results from realizing their parents treat them as adults.

Finally, for many middle-aged adults, a new intergenerational tie is formed when their adult children have children themselves. Most grandparents are pleased with their new status, happy to give presents and provide occasional babysitting, and hesitant to give too much advice. In today's society, grandparenthood brings pride and companionship to many middle-aged adults, without the day-to-day responsibility and worries that they had with their own children (Cherlin and Furstenberg, 1986). (Grandparenthood and great-grandparenthood are discussed in Chapter 25.)

In terms of midlife fulfillment and midlife distress, it should be noted that women, as they do throughout adulthood, tend to focus more on family than men do. Women tend to be **kinkeepers,** the people who celebrate family achievements, gather the family together, and keep in touch with family members who no longer live at home. For this reason, family accomplishments are particularly likely to be rewarding to the middle-aged woman who sees her parents happy in retirement, her grown children become responsible adults, and her grandchildren reaffirm the significance of human growth and family continuity.

The Sandwich Generation

Thus far we have outlined the many ways family ties provide stability and gradual improvement in the lives of adults. However, under some circumstances, family ties can become quite burdensome. Because of their position in the generational hierarchy, the middle-aged feel obligated to help both the older and younger generations. Especially if a family member becomes divorced, as many of the younger generation do, or widowed, as many of the older generation do, the middle generation is often called on to provide crucial emotional support, and often financial support as well (Cherlin and Furstenberg, 1986; Troll, 1986). In recent years, such demands have so increased on the middle-aged that they are commonly referred to as the **sandwich generation,** a generation that is often caught between, and squeezed by, the needs of two adjacent generations.

Caring for Adult Children

The number of young adults living with their parents has risen sharply over the past two decades. At any given moment, almost half of all middle-aged adults who have grown children have at least one of their children living with them (Acquilino, 1990). This arrangement is much more likely to exist to help out younger generation than to assist the older one, as suggested by two statistics. First, middle-aged adults in good health are twice as likely to have their adult children with them as those in poor health. Second, parents continue to do most of the household work, with the adult children taking over only 12 percent of the household chores (Ward et al., 1992).

Neither generation is particularly happy with this state of affairs. Parents as well as adult children regard independent living as the natural order of things and neither appreciates the loss of privacy that sharing a household entails. But the circumstances of this cohort of young adults, including longer education, lower salaries, higher unemployment, fewer marriages, and more single parenthood, often make it difficult for them to leave the nest or necessitate their return (sometimes several times) after venturing forth (Ward et al., 1992).

Even when young adults have households of their own, the gap between their income and their expenses often compels the middle-aged generation to provide a great deal of support, particularly in material aid and child care. For example, almost a fourth of all the employed mothers who have infant children use grandparents as their chief alternative caregivers (Klein, 1985).

 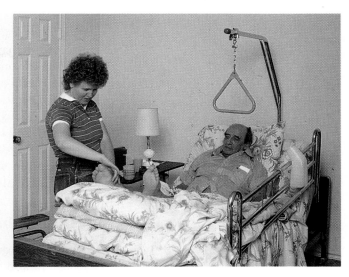

Figure 22.4 *The male bond can be a strong one across the generations. The elderly man at the left enjoys the company and the respect of both his son and grandson, who are visiting him in a nursing home. However, when an elderly man needs daily nursing care, the relative most likely to provide it is a female. For example, when the man at the right lost the use of his legs, the family decided that the best place for him was in his son's home, at least in part because the best caregiver was his son's wife, shown here.*

Caring for Aged Parents

Another, usually more stressful form of caregiving is often required of middle-aged adults. Almost everyone, sometimes before age 60, is called on to provide care for a frail, elderly relative. Such caregiving is required much more often of the current generation of middle-aged adults than of the previous generation, primarily because the numbers of frail elderly, and the number of years that they live, have increased (Coward et al., 1992). Indeed, the latest statistics indicate that nearly a third of the elderly spend some portion of their last years unable to care for themselves, and that they are four times as likely to be cared for by family members at home than in nursing homes or hospitals. If the frail elderly person has a spouse who is capable of providing normal daily care, the middle-aged generation may be called on only for occasional assistance. Often, however, a spouse is frail, too, or the elderly person is widowed, divorced, or has never married. In such cases, it is most often the middle-aged generation that assumes the burden of daily care.

Partly because of their role as kinkeeper, women are much more likely to be cast in the caregiver role than men, and the unexpected divorce of a child or illness of a parent can well become a source of crisis and depression in a middle-aged woman. Daughters and daughters-in-law, for example, are about twice as likely to be caregivers for elderly parents as sons and sons-in-law are (Coward et al., 1992). In some cases, just when a woman has began to appreciate the freedom of an "empty nest" or the satisfaction of her own career, she finds that she is called on to babysit for grandchildren and care not only for her own parents but for her husband's as well (Stueve and O'Donnell, 1984). While middle-aged men are less often caregivers, they do, however, feel financially obligated to help the older and younger generations if necessary. This is one of the factors that contribute to the "financial squeeze" of middle age.

Because intergenerational family caregiving is sometimes idealized by those not directly involved in it (Dwyer and Coward, 1992), we should not minimize these burdens: they have a high potential for precipitating a family crisis of some sort, or for casting a shadow over a time of life that most people find freer of burdens and restriction than earlier years (Gutmann, 1987). (Specific causes of, and solutions to, stressful caregiving relationships with the elderly are discussed in Chapter 25.) However, for the most part, both men and women welcome their continuing family responsibilities during middle age, especially when those responsibilities are shared by several relatives and are part of a lifelong family pattern of mutual affection and obligation (Walker et al., 1990; Blieszner and Hamon, 1992).

Marriage in Middle Adulthood

Throughout adulthood, marriage is the family relationship that seems most closely linked to personal happiness and companionship. This does not mean that single people are necessarily unhappy, or that married people are necessarily happy. Indeed, in recent decades, the "happiness gap" between married and single adults has narrowed: while about 35 percent of the married adults over age 40 claim they are very happy, so do 20 percent of their never-married peers, double that of twenty years ago (Lee et al., 1991).

For those who are married, however, the marital relationship is potent, with a person's overall happiness strongly correlated with his or her marital happiness (Benin and Nienstadt, 1985). The effect of marriage on general happiness is most apparent when the relationship is not going well. Serious trouble in a long-term marriage can be more devastating, leading to greater loneliness, low self-esteem, and depression, than equivalent trouble in a young marriage (Helson, 1992; Chiriboga, 1982; Keith and Schafer, 1991).

Fortunately, most of the research indicates that, after the first ten years or so, the longer a couple has been married, the happier they are (Glenn, 1991). There are several possible reasons for this improvement. One is that, particularly for women, financial security is an important correlate of marital satisfaction, and disagreement over finances is one of the chief sources of marital tension (Berry and Williams, 1987). Overall, families at the empty-nest stage typically have more income—because employed wives can devote more time and energy to their work, thus increasing their pay—and fewer expenses, because the children are, at least partly, self-supporting.

Another reason is that, for many married couples, one of the major goals of the relationship was to raise a family, again a goal that women, particularly, make sacrifices to attain. Once the children are successfully raised and launched, the parents are relieved of many anxieties concerning their children's development and are able to share with each other important feelings of achievement.

In addition, in typical marriages, doing things together—everything from fixing up the house to taking a vacation—contributes to marital satisfaction. Once children leave home and a career plateau has been reached, there is more time for such activities. As a result, married couples often recapture some of the close companionship and marital intimacy that were not possible in the hectic child-rearing , career-building years.

Figure 22.5 *During the empty-nest period, many middle-aged parents regain the freedom to frolic, invigorating their marriage with renewed closeness and the sharing of activities that the emotional and financial demands of earlier years may have compromised.*

Another reason there may be some improvement involves marital equity. In general, the longer couples are married, the more likely both spouses are to consider their mutual contributions to the relationship and the household as equal and just, with "reduced concern for repayment of favors in a marriage as the relationship matures" (Keith and Schafer, 1991).

A final factor, related to all the others, is that the growing accumulation of experiences that a married couple shares over the years, simply by virtue of living in the same community, raising children together, and dealing with the same financial and spiritual circumstances, brings them closer together in personality and values (Caspi et al., 1992).

This does not mean that all marriages improve in middle age. Obviously illness and unemployment of either spouse, or of parents or adult children, increase strain while reducing the time and money for doing things together. Further, some relationships survived to middle age not because the couple did things together but because they learned to do them apart, in effect, becoming "emotionally divorced" (Fitzpatrick, 1984). If middle age means that such a couple must now spend more time together, their marriage may be sorely tested.

Career Dynamics in Middle Adulthood

The need to achieve through work continues in middle adulthood as earlier. In general, workers gain more autonomy over their own work life as they grow older, and, largely for this reason, job satisfaction generally rises with age, especially if status and salary continue to rise (Warr, 1992).

Further, compared to younger adults who are sometimes overwhelmed by the demands of new marriages and young children, and by the pressure they add to career-building, many middle-aged and older adults find that both family and career roles tend to be less burdensome, and that satisfaction with family life tends to mitigate stress at work and vice versa (Baruch et al., 1992; Barnett et al., 1992). As a result, they are less likely to experience role overload and are more likely to find that their various roles act as a buffer against any psychic disruptions caused by the aging process (Keith and Schafer, 1991).

Work-Related Problems in Middle Age

However, this stage of one's work life contains several hazards. Many of those who have been working for several decades enter the "maintenance phase" of their work lives, as they achieve a career plateau. This can mean coming to grips with less success than anticipated. As one expert explains, "the prospect of no further advancement to someone who has counted on it as a measure of success is quite devastating, and those who have been standing still all along have even more to worry about" (Katchadourian, 1987).

When they reach this phase, many workers feel pressure to redefine their work goals and their relationship to work. Often this redefinition makes them see their career in a more balanced perspective, no longer wanting to achieve for achievement's sake. When this happens, workers generally invest less of their ego and energy in the work world; they can afford to be more relaxed in their approach to their job, more satisfied with the work itself, more helpful to others (Karp, 1985–1986). This is a likely time for them to become mentors to their younger fellow workers.

One particular aspect of this redefinition is reassessment of the balance between commitment to, and satisfaction from, work and family. A twenty-year longitudinal study of managers at AT&T (see Figure 22.6) found that work became even more important as a source of satisfaction to those middle-aged managers who were rapidly gaining authority, remained somewhat important to those who were promoted at a more gradual pace, and became less important to those who did not advance very much. In middle age, this last group, particularly, reported that they valued family, recreation, and community service more than they did when they were younger. These men also became more nurturant and helpful, in a word, more communal, while those at the highest levels were more likely to be dominating and less likely to be sympathetic and helpful to their fellow workers (Howard, 1992).

Figure 22.6 *At American Telephone and Telegraph (AT&T), young managers at the beginning of their careers ranked the importance of work about equally. By midlife, however, those who were at the top of the heap, or were still rising to it, thought work was very important, while those who had less success valued other aspects of their life more than their work. One likely explanation is that once people no longer feel the pressure to be intensely competitive and to continually prove themselves in the workplace, they are able to develop other dimensions of their personality more fully.*

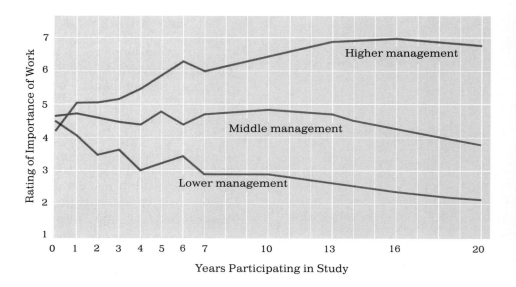

Because of the worldwide economic recession beginning in the late 1980s, the current cohort of workers have several additional adjustment problems not experienced by the workers in the AT&T study. For one thing, they are working longer hours and earning less than they had expected. Specifically, the average American worker spends 163 more hours per year on the job than twenty years ago (Schor, 1991), but his or her salary buys less than before. Even more troubling is that many middle-aged workers fear that they will be laid off or retired before they are ready. This is a realistic fear, especially for men: in 1990, about one in every ten American men between age 45 and 55, and one in every three between 55 and 65, were not employed (U.S. Bureau of the Census, 1992).

Figure 22.7 *Community service is an important source of generativity, and may be particularly so for adults who find that their paid employment does not provide the personal satisfaction they seek. These volunteers from Habitat for Humanity are raising the walls of a house for the homeless—a task that fills essential personal needs as well as community goals.*

One reaction to this situation is that many employees, particularly those in middle age who have some security and health benefits, tend to stay in whatever job they have, unwilling to take the risk of moving to a more desirable but less certain one. They pay a price, however: in general, all other factors being equal, the longer one has a particular job, the less one tends to like it (Warr, 1992). Two particular problems that may occur when a worker has been in the same job for years are **burn-out**—in which a professional feels disillusioned and exhausted by the demands of trying to help others—and **alienation**—in which a factory or service worker feels distant from the actual product being produced or service being offered (see A Closer Look on pp. 574–575).

The various job-related stresses of middle age are most often experienced by those who have invested a great deal of themselves into their work life, a pattern typical of middle-aged men, and of those middle-aged women who have neither children nor spouse. In this respect, the current cohort of married mothers seem to have somewhat of an advantage—in a sense, the flip side of their earlier disadvantage when they had to balance child care, housework, and career, adapting their lives to those of their husbands and children and, consequently, limiting their commitment to their job (Moen, 1991). Born of the necessity, their experience of managing a daily "mosaic of activities and . . . conflicting demands on their time and attention" now gives these women an advantage—"the ability to shift from one preoccupation to another, to divide one's attention, to improvise in new circumstances" (Bateson, 1990)—an ability that is increasingly prized in a work world characterized by continual and rapid change.

Consequently, in today's economic and vocational climate, just at the time many men are hitting a work plateau, perhaps with burn-out and alienation, many women, now free from consuming family responsibilities, increase their personal involvement at their jobs, or renew an abandoned career goal, with commensurate increase in status, authority, and self-esteem (Shaw, 1986; Bateson, 1990).

A CLOSER LOOK   **Burn-out and Alienation**

Every job has its down side, its unpleasant or unrewarding tasks that must be done. But in some cases, the down side is so deep and so pervasive that workers become completely overwhelmed, with all sense of purpose buried by depressing and demeaning demands. Social scientists have identified two common forms of this deep-seated unhappiness with one's work, burn-out and alienation.

Burn-out—so named after a fire-fighting technique in which a forest fire is isolated from further fuel and then allowed to burn full force until it dies—is a state in which the pace and conditions of work totally deplete the worker of energy and enthusiasm. Although burn-out can occur in almost any occupation, it seems particularly prevalent in the helping professions (Souter et al., 1990).

Typically, dedicated workers such as teachers, nurses, doctors, and social workers enter their field determined to change the lives of those they serve, solving such social problems as ignorance, disease, family violence, and poverty. However, such problems are not susceptible to easy solution, and often the helped do not readily appreciate the helper. Moreover, administrative procedures—such as paperwork in triplicate—and institutional needs—such as protecting the school, or the hospital, or the agency from public criticism—deplete energy, time, and hope from those most dedicated to providing service. A typical example is the one cited in Chapter 7, in which factors in the institutional and political macrosystems meant that child-protection workers in Florida spent only 11 percent of their work time actually interacting with troubled families, with most of that interaction taking place in the agency rather than the home (Crittenden, 1992). After years in such a job, frustration turns high ideals, great expectations, and dedicated action into bitter disillusionment and emotional exhaustion.

A clear case of burn-out can be seen in Jessica Siegel, a dedicated high school English teacher in her ninth year of teaching (Freedman, 1990). Jessica's work days are spent instructing five classes, publishing the school paper, conferring with students, and trying to scavenge books and supplies within an urban school district where such things were always scarce. Her evenings and weekends are given over to planning lessons and marking papers, with the goal of "empowering kids with content and ideas." For example, her annual opening assignment for seniors is to write an autobiographical essay, hoping that the very act of writing about themselves would "help a few kids discover the validity in their lives." These assignments benefit Jessica as well:

> Every year she finishes the autobiographies feeling the same way. Her students are heroes. Her heroes, even some who fail the coursework. Could anyone else under-

stand that? How they fill her with awe. How they, yes, inspire her. How their struggles and survivals distract her from the lonely alleys in her own life. And sometimes that is a blessing. When she reads their words, when she hears their voices . . . she knows her life has a reason.

However, in the process of doing her job, striving to teach sentence structure and grammar to teenagers whose papers are error-filled, she also loses something of herself.

> . . . She covers the pages with red ink, a kind of blood. She spills serum drop by drop, transfusing enthusiasm and knowledge and ability. But the donor of time, unlike the donor of blood, cannot regenerate what is given.

And over time, Jessica has become exhausted. She has coached and cajoled a few students into college, but she has also watched many more drop out and disappear, seen young men wounded in gang violence and young women pregnant with babies they do not want. She blames herself for taking too long to mark her papers or for teaching a lesson that does not succeed. She feels isolated from her colleagues and unappreciated by her supervisors. And she sees herself going through all this "for a pittance in salary and respect." Like many who are approaching burn-out, Jessica is like a marathon runner:

> She possesses a tolerance for pain, isolation, and deferred gratification that a spectator may confuse for masochism. If she drops out of the race, then, it is not because a boulder landed on her head, but because she has been plodding for twenty miles with the same pebble in her shoe. [Freedman, 1990]

How can burn-out be prevented? At the individual level, two remedies are to reduce one's expectations of what can be accomplished and to share responsibilities. For instance, instead of hoping to ignite an intellectual fire in each and every student, a teacher in Jessica's situation might settle for helping some students become a little more skilled, and might attempt, with the help of other teachers and parents, to find a private company to donate new textbooks or a working copying machine to the English department. Even sharing frustrations can help: unfortunately, Jessica did not tell any of her colleagues how "soul-deep" her unhappiness was until she announced that she was quitting.

A more encompassing, but less accessible, remedy for burn-out is to change the overall structure and communication patterns in the institutions in which service workers function (Pines and Aronson, 1981). Let us consider another setting in which burn-out often occurs, the hospital system in the United States. In many cases, every patient is seen by a dozen or so personnel, each with a particular task but isolated from the others. Shift schedules and status hierarchies mean that doctors, interns, nurses, and aides have little opportunity to confer about, or even to tend and befriend, the same patient from one day to the next. Economic concerns add to the difficulty: insurance paperwork and defensive medicine (to avoid lawsuits) deflect time and attention from treatment. As a result, many hospital staff feel burned-out by bureaucratic, institutional, impersonal demands, and far removed from the goals they had when they first entered their profession.

What might the solutions be in this case? A first step would be to enhance communication among staff members, arranging regular case reviews that involve all concerned and allow nurses and doctors to puzzle out together why a particular patient is not getting well and to feel a shared sense of achievement when treatment leads to renewed health. One team might be assigned to a small group of patients and their families, with responsibility for everything from admission to discharge. In addition, while many nonprofit or public institutions try to save money on amenities, the specifics of the work environment—a clean and quiet staff room, a coffeemaker, duty-schedules that allow some personal life—can mitigate against some of the conflagrations that contribute to burn-out.

Another problem occurs when workers feel that their work is uninteresting and unimportant. Alienation, as this feeling is called, is theoretically likely to occur when workers do not see the relationship between their work and the final product. Such a feeling is particularly likely to occur in large factories or corporations in which the individual worker is not recognized as a person but is simply regarded as a means of performing some task—usually the same task for hours and years on end.

The feeling, and consequences, of alienation are reflected in the following interview conducted some years ago on an assembly line, long regarded as the archetypal setting for alienation. The interviewee is an auto worker whose job was painting cars, a job, incidentally, that today is performed mostly by robots:

"There's a lot of variety in the paint shop. You clip on the color hose, bleed out the old color, and squirt. Clip, bleed, squirt, think; clip, bleed, squirt, yawn; clip, bleed, squirt, scratch your nose."

I asked about diversions: "What do you do to keep from going crazy?"

There's always water fights, paint fights, or laugh, talk, tell jokes. Anything so you don't feel like a machine."

But everyone had the same hope: "You're always waiting for the line to break down. . . ." [Carson, 1979]

Alienation is particularly likely when the relationship between management and worker is structured as a hostile one. Workers demand pay increases and threaten to

This handshake between management and labor does more than seal a new contract. It symbolizes the need for cooperation among all the workers in a given setting in order to halt the spread of alienation and dissatisfaction endemic to many large corporations.

strike; bosses watch suspiciously for worker laziness, cheating, and sabotage. Eventually, many younger workers respond to alienation by quitting their job or by getting themselves fired. Middle-aged workers, however, are generally more concerned with job security and are reluctant to risk long-term unemployment, which in fact, can be particularly devastating to the 40-to-60 age group in terms of health, self-esteem, and income.

Alienation can be mitigated by policies that make workers more involved in the total decision-making and production process, or that allow workers more say in their own work activities, through flexible job schedules and retraining that allow workers to move to different types of tasks as their interests, needs, and abilities change (Roth, 1991; Lendler, 1990; Hackman, 1986). Indeed, many companies around the world are already employing such policies as they see that avoiding alienation and encouraging participation and pride in the final product not only improves morale but saves money in fewer sick days and higher-quality work (Offermann and Gowing, 1990).

Personality Throughout Adulthood

So far we have discussed some of the many circumstances and patterns that might lead to continuity or crisis, stability or change, in middle adulthood. However, we have yet to consider the most crucial variable of all, individual personality. Personality traits lead us to interpret and react to life events in ways that are distinctly our own. If personality traits remain stable throughout life, the impact of the age-related events and changes we encounter will be powerfully affected by the continuity of who we are.

Although the degree of stability of personality traits is still controversial (Mischel and Peake, 1983; Pervin, 1990), longitudinal research over the decades of adulthood has, for the most part, found notable continuity in many personality characteristics. As two leading researchers explain:

> Personality forms part of the enduring core of the individual, a basis on which adaptation is made to an ever-changing life . . . Lives surely change, perhaps in stages; personality, we maintain, does not. [McCrae and Costa, 1984]

This may come as a surprise to many middle-aged adults, partly because people tend to overestimate whatever personality changes they think they have undergone (Costa and McCrae, 1988). A study that clearly showed this (Woodruff, 1983) began with a group of college students who rated themselves on various personality traits—such as whether they saw themselves as aggressive, tender, cheerful, and so on. Twenty-five years later, the same people rated themselves again twice, first as they currently saw themselves, and then as they thought they had been twenty-five years earlier. There was a clear similarity between the original college rating and the current one, but little similarity between either of those ratings and the way people remembered themselves as having been.

Stable Traits: The Big Five

This is not to deny that people behave differently as their experiences and responsibilities change. However, extensive longitudinal and cross-sectional research, among adults of many nations and linguistic groups, finds five basic clusters of personality traits that remain quite stable throughout adulthood (Loehlin, 1992; Digman, 1990; Eaves et al., 1989; McCrae and Costa, 1990; Paunonen et al., 1992). Although various experts use somewhat different terms to refer to each of these clusters, all would agree that, in essence, they follow along the lines of what is called the **Big Five** (John, 1990):

1. **extroversion**—the tendency to be outgoing, assertive, and active;

2. **agreeableness**—the tendency to be kind and helpful;

3. **conscientiousness**—the tendency to be organized, deliberate, and conforming;

4. **neuroticism**—the tendency to be anxious, moody, and self-punishing;

5. **openness**—the tendency to be imaginative, curious, and artistic, willing to welcome new experiences when they arise.

These trait clusters are determined by many factors, including genes, culture, early child-rearing, and the experiences and choices made during

Figure 22.8 *Laid-back, outgoing, and willing to go with the flow—all characteristics of the nonneurotic, open, extrovert. Someone who exhibits these characteristics as an older adult most likely possessed them as a young person, too.*

Figure 22.9 *Continuity of basic personality traits is apparent throughout the life span and even from generation to generation within families. Nelson Mandela, shown on the right, continues to display the same courage and charisma in late adulthood that he did as a young man, despite the intervening decades of imprisonment. The young congressman presenting an award to Mr. Mandela is Joseph Kennedy, who already seems to reflect many of the renowned Kennedy traits.*

late adolescence and early adulthood. Up through the first years of early adulthood, there is likely to be some fluctuation in these five trait clusters, but by about age 30, their manifestation is usually quite stable, and is likely to remain so throughout the rest of adulthood. One reason for this stability is that, by age 30, most people have settled into an ecological niche—including vocations, mates, and lifestyles—that evokes and reinforces their particular personality needs and interests. The fact that people choose their surroundings to suit their temperament leads two personality researchers to quip: "Ask not how life's experiences change personality; ask instead how personality shapes lives" (McCrae and Costa, 1990).

Using some highly simplified examples, let us see how this niche selection might work with particular traits. For instance, by age 30, those high in extroversion would likely have found a mate who shares, or at least appreciates, their outgoingness and also would have established a busy social life with a wide circle of friends and acquaintances. Their jobs would allow them to interact with many people, perhaps working as a salesperson, a politician, a teacher, a counselor, a personnel director. Similarly, their lifestyle details would foster social contact: their phone would ring often (with an answering machine always on when they were out); they might join amateur sports leagues or engage in volunteer work at their school or community center; and they would most likely prefer to live in a relatively active and crowded neighborhood.

Similarly, those fairly high in neuroticism, with their anxiety and moodiness, might have chosen a job that draws on their general apprehensiveness and vigilance against things going wrong—perhaps as a lawyer, a safety inspector, a cost accountant, a proofreader. Unfortunately, whatever their career, those who are very high in neuroticism would tend to expect the worst of their jobs, their mates, their children, and themselves, and this very expectation would make things go less well than they otherwise might. A substantial body of research indicates that "people with negative self-views consistently enact behaviors that alienate the people around them" (Swann et al., 1992). Further, their fearfulness would make them afraid to take a new job, or to travel to a new place, to join a new group of people. Thus they are likely to be stuck in a cycle of self-pity, a life pattern that would, in itself, perpetuate their unhappiness.

Paradoxically, the continuity of personality helps explain the lifestyle of those adults who lives are in constant flux—with a frequent turnover of jobs, or residences, or spouses. While such seeming discontinuity appears to indicate an unstable personality, it may, in fact, be the hallmark of someone who is quite stable in one underlying trait—openness to new experiences (McCrae and Costa, 1984).

As we will see in Chapter 25, such continuity of temperament continues throughout late adulthood, with agreeable persons, for example, being quite happy with life and willing to help others, and neurotic persons still worrying about the future, however brief the future might appear to be.

In one way at least, this research is reassuring: we are who we are, even when buffeted by events and burnished by time. As Costa and McCrae (1989) explain:

> The impressive degree of stability seen in longitudinal studies over several decades suggests that human beings are . . . not passive victims of life events, historical movements, or changing social roles. They maintain their distinctive characteristics in the face of all these forces.

Developmental Changes

Does the stability of the Big Five mean that there are no changes in personality as people age? Not quite. A series of studies finds several age-related trends. One is a general trend toward improvement in personality, with the particular improvements dependent partly on those valued within the particular culture. In middle-class American culture, for example, many people become less defensively neurotic, more confident, and more open (Haan et al., 1986; McCrae and Costa, 1990; Vaillant, 1977; Whitbourne et al., 1992).

Another change in personality during middle age seems to occur in many cultures—the loosening of rigid gender-role demands, allowing both men and women to move toward androgyny. Middle-aged women find it easier to assert themselves with confidence, while middle-aged men find it easier to express emotions such as tenderness or sadness, a trend apparent even in cultures that endorse quite rigid gender roles for young adults (Gutmann, 1987; Helson and Wink, 1992; Bengston et al. 1985).

One explanation for this shift is biosocial: to the extent that the male tendancy toward aggressiveness and dominance and the female tendancy toward passiveness and nurturance are influenced hormonally, reduced levels of their respective sex hormones may free both men and women from the restriction of traditional gender roles, allowing them to express previously suppressed traits (Rossi, 1980).

A more complex explanation comes from Carl Jung, a psychoanalyst, who believed that everyone has both a masculine and a feminine side, but that in the first half of life, society pressures everyone to develop only those traits that it has reserved for his or her own gender. Thus women strive to be more tender and diffident than they might naturally be, while men try to be brave and assertive even when they would rather not. According to Jung, the demands of achievement mean that young people have no time for self-doubts, fantasy, and introspection (Crain, 1992), and, consequently, they continue to unquestioningly adhere to their prescribed gender roles. However, as Jung explains, middle-aged adults begin to realize that

> the achievements which society rewards are won as the cost of a diminution of personality. Many—far too many—aspects of life which should have been experienced lie in the lumber-room among dusty memories. [Jung, 1933]

Thus, in middle age, adults of both sexes explore the "shadow side" of their personality—women, their repressed "masculine" traits, and men, their repressed "feminine" traits.

Still another explanation comes from David Gutmann (1987), who believes that the changing demands of daily life as people grow older are the main reason for whatever blurring of the gender roles and traits may occur. In childhood, of course, boys and girls are quite similar until puberty, when adolescents of both sexes exaggerate their masculine and feminine traits in order to establish their own sexual identity and to attract the opposite sex. Then, during the early years of family and career development, men and women are pressured by the demands of daily life into quite traditional male and female roles. Particularly critical is the "parental imperative," the pressing demands of raising young children, demands that make many mothers more nurturant and self-effacing, and many fathers more competitive and ambitious, than they might otherwise have been.

Figure 22.10 *A combination of historical events, cultural shifts, and personal traits resulted in the 1992 election of both Barbara Boxer and Diane Feinstein to the U.S. Senate—the first time California has had even one woman senator. Given what is now recognized regarding the potential of both men and women in middle adulthood, it is not surprising that many women are moving into roles once exclusive to the other sex. What is surprising is that so many people once believed it couldn't and shouldn't be done.*

However, with time, the urgency of child-rearing lessens, and more latitude is possible, allowing some middle-aged adults to develop broader gender roles, especially if events push them in this direction. For example, as their children become more independent and they are able to devote more time to their careers, women tend to become more self-confident and assertive. Men, on the other hand, may become more considerate and tender as career goals become less pressing and their need to be competitive diminishes. Later on, the birth of a grandchild, especially if it coincides with retirement, may make a man become more nurturant. Similarly, the illness or death of her husband may cause a woman to become more assertive, especially if she must earn a living for the first time.

Reflecting on this chapter, it is possible to see the overall events of midlife as having been set in motion by choices made in early adulthood, played out on a stage that also arose from those choices. As Gutmann intimates, however, as the decades pass, the stage setting begins to include more circumstances that are less a matter of choice than of the passage of time—retirement, widowhood, diminished strength, approaching death. The surprise of the next stage of life, as you will soon see, is not the diversity of life events but the diversity of the ways people react to them.

SUMMARY

Midlife: Crisis, Shift, or Transition?

1. Midlife is often thought of as a period of crisis, a time when self-doubt and unhappiness lead to radical change. Reasons for such a crisis include shifts in family and work responsibilities, as well as a growing awareness of the limited time left to live.

2. Evidence that a midlife crisis is normative comes from Levinson's longitudinal research. He finds that, at about age 40, most men begin a serious reexamination of their lives, and many make radical changes in connection with their career or family. Other research also suggests that distress is not unusual in midlife men, although in most cases it does not constitute a full-blown crisis that is directly attributable to factors relating to middle age.

3. While women may once have been likely to become depressed during middle age, contemporary women seem more likely to experience middle age as liberating. One explanation for this is that women may now be buffered against a crisis by having careers of their own. Men in recent cohorts, on the other hand, may have suffered from changed expectations of the male role, and thereby may have been made more susceptible to whatever stresses occur in midlife.

Family Dynamics in Middle Adulthood

4. Middle-aged adults generally find their relationships with their own parents, and with their young adult children, improving, particularly if each generation lives under separate roofs. Middle adulthood is also the time people are likely to become grandparents for the first time, usually a welcome event.

5. However, under some circumstances, family ties can be particularly burdensome in middle age, making adults feel like the sandwich generation, squeezed by the financial and emotional needs of both their parents and their adult children.

6. Young adults today often cannot afford to leave the family home, and, if they have children, often need their parents' help with child care.

7. Even more draining on the middle generation can be the care of an elderly relative, a task many adults—usually women—eventually perform.

8. Marriage often improves in middle age, as parents become free of children and have more time and money for themselves. Another factor contributing to marital satisfaction is a rise in marital equity.

Career Dynamics in Middle Adulthood

9. For most adults in midlife, work continues to be a source of satisfaction. At some point, adults typically reach a career plateau, a point at which further advancement no longer seems desirable and/or possible. At this juncture, many adults redefine their relationship to their work. Some strike a new balance between work and family commitments, and may also become more willing to help younger adults find their way.

10. However, for some adults, work itself becomes a reason for dissatisfaction. Burn-out or alienation makes them feel that their efforts are unproductive and meaningless.

Personality Throughout Adulthood

11. After about age 30, several personality traits, referred to as the Big Five, tend to remain quite stable, and these influence the course of development.

12. This stability of personality is partly genetic, partly the result of early life experiences, and partly the result of choices made in early adulthood. However, personality changes occur as well. Two changes are notable. People generally improve in personality traits, and both sexes typically become more androgynous.

KEY TERMS

midlife (559)

middle age (559)

midlife crisis (560)

kinkeepers (568)

sandwich generation (568)

burn-out (573)

alienation (573)

the Big Five (576)

extroversion (576)

agreeableness (576)

conscientiousness (576)

neuroticism (576)

openness (576)

KEY QUESTIONS

1. What factors can be seen as contributing to a crisis at midlife?

2. How has the study of different middle-aged cohorts affected views about midlife crisis?

3. What are some of the stresses involved in being a member of the "sandwich generation"?

4. What are some of the career developments that are more likely to occur in middle age?

5. What are the five trait clusters in personality that tend to be quite stable after about age 30?

6. What factors contribute to stability of these clusters?

7. How do male and female gender roles tend to change in middle age?

Biosocial Development

Normal Changes in Appearance and the Senses

Changes in the appearance of the skin, hair, and body shape are benign, but can be disconcerting. Losses of acuity in hearing and vision are usually gradual, and individuals usually learn to compensate quite easily. In many ways, health in middle age and attitudes about it depend on social context.

Health

Overall health is influenced by variables such as sex, race, SES, and long-term health habits. Susceptibility to stress may also play a role.

The Sexual-Reproductive System

In their late 40s and early 50s, women experience the climacteric during which the body must adjust to changing hormonal levels. Menopause, the cessation of menstruation, signals the end of a woman's reproductive capacity. Men experience no comparably dramatic decline in reproductive ability.

Cognitive Development

Types of Intelligence

Fluid intelligence tends to decline over time, while crystallized intelligence tends to remain steady or increase. Reaction time and speed of thinking slow. Some abilities improve with age, while others decline. Adult intelligence tends to flourish in areas of the individual's particular interests, leading to the development of expertise, characterized by cognitive processes and responses that are intuitive, automatic, and flexible.

Psychosocial Development

Crisis, Shift, or Transition

Whether or not one experiences a midlife crisis depends, in part, on one's sex and cohort. Men are more likely to experience some form of midlife distress than women are, but most men are likely to feel greater satisfaction in middle adulthood than before.

Affiliation and Work

Friendship and marriage continue to be the prime sources of affiliation. The relationship between middle-aged adults and both their parents and their adult children generally improves with time, although many middle-aged adults may feel "sandwiched" between the needs of both, especially when young adults live at home. With the extra time and money available during the "empty-nest" period, satisfaction with marriage usually rises. Most adults reach a "maintenance phase" in their career. Individuals may sometimes experience negative feelings of "burn-out" and alienation, but, generally, middle-aged workers are more likely to feel satisfaction with their work accomplishments than younger or older workers are.

PART VIII

Late Adulthood

What emotions do you anticipate experiencing as you read about development in late adulthood? Given the myths that abound regarding old age, you may well expect to feel discomfort, depression, resignation, and sorrow. Certainly there are instances in the next ninety pages when such emotions would be appropriate. However, your most frequent emotion in learning about late adulthood is likely to be surprise. For example, you will learn in Chapter 23 that most centenarians are active, alert, and happy; in Chapter 24, that marked intellectual decline is the fate of only a minority of the elderly, who are sometimes victims of conditions that can be prevented; in Chapter 25, that relationships between the older and younger generations are neither as close as some sentimentalists idealize them to be nor as distant as some critics claim. Overall, late adulthood is much more a continuation of earlier patterns than a break from them, and, instead of falling into a period of lonely isolation, most older adults become more social and independent than ever.

If surprise does indeed dominate your reactions in learning about late adulthood, you are not alone. Few people, young or old, know much about the actual experiences of most of the elderly, and most people, of every age, fill the gaps in their knowledge with dated clichés and misleading prejudices.

Why does this period of life, more than any other, seem to be a magnet for misinformation and mistaken assumptions? Think about this question when the facts, theories, and research of the next three chapters are not what you expected them to be.

CHAPTER 23

Late Adulthood: Biosocial Development

The hallmark of good scientists is as much in the questions they ask as in the answers they know. This chapter is filled with crucial and intriguing questions, including one of the most profound developmental issue of all—why do all living creatures age and die? While the answer to this question is not precisely known, scientists appear to be closing in on it. Other questions that they are pursuing regarding old age include the following:

What factors lead to ageism, and how is ageism like racism and sexism in its effects?

Does brain shrinkage result in cognitive loss?

What accounts for the notable changes in older adults' sleep patterns and how can they best be adapted to?

Is disease an inevitable part of the aging process in late adulthood?

Does senescence switch on at a certain time, just like puberty?

What factors might contribute to some people living into their 100s?

Imagine that you are a scientist about to study the usual course of life from age 60 on. For practical reasons, you decide to begin your research in the United States and to exclude people currently in hospitals and nursing homes. With those two limitations, you ask a representative cross-section of 1,600 older adults—some employed full-time and some bedridden, from every region, race, religion, and SES—to answer dozens of questions relating to their well-being and happiness.

Like every honest scientist, you recognize that you are beginning your research with certain expectations. Do you think that most of your sample are isolated, depressed, handicapped by disabilities and illness? Or do you believe that most are happy and healthy, able and active? What percentages do you predict on the question asking, "Overall, how satisfied are you with your life?"

Your Predictions

Completely satisfied	_____ percent
Very satisfied	_____ percent
Somewhat satisfied	_____ percent
Not very satisfied	_____ percent
Not at all satisfied	_____ percent

Now compare your expectations and predictions with the data from an actual study that was recently undertaken (Herzog, 1991). Overall, the findings were quite upbeat. Even though 62 percent of the sample had two or more chronic conditions (such as arthritis and high blood pressure), most said that their health does not limit their activities at all, and only 15 percent said their health limits them a great deal. Few were lonely: most visited with friends at least once a week and talked on the phone every day. And you probably will be surprised at the results on the question of life satisfaction, which were more positive than those of some samples of college students. Specifically, twelve times as many older adults said they are completely or very satisfied with their lives as said they are not very or not at all satisfied (the actual percentages were 32 and 41 versus 5 and 1, respectively, with 21 percent saying they are somewhat satisfied).

If your guesses were far from the mark, you might think that this study is a fluke or that you are unusually pessimistic. Neither is the case: other research finds very similar results (Havik, 1991; Costa et al., 1987), and many younger adults mistakenly believe that the elderly are often unhappy and lonely, spending "a lot of time" doing very little (Schick, 1986).

Do you wonder how much the exclusion of nursing-home residents skews the results? Very little. Although the general public estimates that about one older adult in three is institutionalized, the actual number is only about one in twenty. The proportion is higher in some other developed countries, such as Canada and Australia, and lower in others, such as Japan and Hong Kong, but no nation in the world has more than 8 percent of its older population in nursing homes.

Ageism

Why are people's perceptions of the elderly so much worse than the reality? The reason is that most of us tend to be prejudiced about older people. **Ageism,** as this prejudice is called, is similar in many respects to racism and sexism, and is equally harmful. It fosters a stereotype of the elderly that makes it difficult to see them as they actually are, and, by permitting policies and attitudes that discourage the elderly from participation in work and leisure activities, it prevents many older people from living their lives as happily as they might. Ageism also isolates the older generation socially, reducing their ability to contribute to the larger community and perpetuating the fear of aging in all of us.

Why Is Ageism So Strong?

Perhaps the main reason for the strength of ageism in the United States is the culture's emphasis on growth, strength, and progress. The veneration of youthfulness is so great that, as Butler and Lewis (1982) point out, any sign of a person's "beginning to fail" is feared and exaggerated. Furthermore, for many people, interaction with the very old is a reminder of their own mortality. They develop self-protective prejudices against the old as a way of "avoiding and denying the thought of one's own decline and death."

Another factor that reinforces ageism is the increasing age segregation of society, which limits contact between the generations. Fewer and fewer Americans live in multigeneration families; and more and more neighborhoods, voluntary organizations, and workplaces tend to involve one age group of adults more than others. This makes contact between the oldest generation and younger ones increasingly limited, giving young people little chance to compare the myths of old age against its realities.

Also contributing to ageism is the human tendency to generalize about any group on the basis of its most noticeable members, often those who draw attention because they belong to a problem-prone minority. Here we can make a useful distinction between the **young-old,** and the **old-old,** a distinction based not on age but on characteristics related to health and social

Figure 23.1 *A cross-section of the population, like these people at a festival in San Antonio, always includes some old, some young, and some in between. In the future, however, when the baby-boomers reach old age, a representative sample of festival-watchers will include a great many more of the elderly than are present here. It seems safe to predict that as the elderly come to represent an ever increasing proportion of the general population, the culture's extreme emphasis on youth, and its attendant ageist biases, will fade considerably.*

well-being. The young-old, who make up the large majority of the elderly, are, for the most part, "healthy and vigorous, relatively well-off financially, well integrated into the lives of their families and communities, and politically active" (Neugarten and Neugarten, 1986). The old-old are those who suffer "major physical, mental, or social losses" and who are likely to require supportive services or to be spending their days in nursing homes or hospitals. It is the latter group on whom the ageist stereotype is based. Although the young-old are much more numerous than the old-old, we tend not to notice them, precisely because they do not fit the stereotype.

Professionals and Ageism

Ironically, many professionals who work with the elderly have inadvertently strengthened ageist prejudices (Quinn, 1987). The majority of these professionals are in the field of medicine and social work. They spend most of their time working with the minority of the elderly who are sick and infirm, and seldom see those who are well and active. This quite naturally leads them to develop, and to report, a rather dismal view of old age. Even gerontologists—professionals specializing in **gerontology,** the study of old age—have contributed to the stereotype. Until recently, they focused, almost exclusively, on the difficulties and "declines" of old age, ignoring strengths and stability. In addition, they usually studied the aged who were in nursing homes or retirement communities, ignoring the majority who lived in their own homes in the general community and who often maintained the activities, friends, and interests they had at younger ages (Butler and Lewis, 1982).

Fortunately, this picture is rapidly changing. Contemporary gerontologists are among the leading foes of ageism. The cultural bias that associates youth with health and vigor, and age with disease and fragility, is weakening. As A Closer Look (next page) reveals, the number of older adults in the population has been increasing dramatically, and this fact has been instrumental in getting professionals, politicians, and the general public to reconsider their ageist assumptions. Now let us look at what the aging process actually entails.

The Aging Process

In old age, as in earlier periods of adulthood, **senescence,** or the weakening and decline of the body, continues at a gradual but steady pace. Appearance continues to change, senses continue to lose acuity, major body systems continue to slow down as organ reserve continues to shrink. As in earlier periods, too, diet, exercise, and other aspects of lifestyle can do much to soften the impact of senescence. Barring the effects of serious illness, no sudden downturn in health or activity occurs simply because a person is now 60 or 70 or 80.

Nonetheless, for many people, sometime after age 60, the cumulative effects of the aging process reach a point at which body image may be altered and adaptive measures in daily activities may be required. Let us now reexamine the major changes of aging in terms of their physical and psychological consequences.

| A CLOSER LOOK | **Squaring the Pyramid** |

One reason that ageism used to go relatively unchallenged was that the number of elderly was small. Consequently, there was little incentive for professionals, politicians, and others to try to look beyond the stereotypes of old age. Their lack of numbers left the old politically powerless and easy to ignore. In recent years, this "numerical weakness" has been fading fast, worldwide, as **demography**—the study of population—reveals.

In the past, when populations were sorted according to age, the resulting picture was a **demographic pyramid**, with the youngest and largest group at the bottom and the oldest and smallest at the top. There were two reasons for this picture. First, each generation of young adults gave birth to more than enough children to replace themselves, thus ensuring larger cohorts at the bottom of the pyramid. Second, a sizable number of each cohort died before advancing to the next higher section of the pyramid.

Today, however, because of falling birth rates and increased longevity, the shape of the population is becoming closer to a square. In the United States in 1900, there were 5 million people over age 60, a total of 6 percent of the population. In 1991, there were more than 42 million people over the age of 60, representing 17 percent of the population. Almost a third of them (5.3 percent of the total population) were 75 and older. This group of the oldest-old is the fastest-growing segment of the population (U.S. Bureau of the Census, 1992). (See chart.)

The increase in the numbers, as well as in the proportion, of aged citizens will continue well into the future, although it is impossible to predict exactly at what rate. However, if (1) the birth rate remains level, and (2) improvements in health habits and medical care continue to add to life expectancy at the rate they have in recent decades, and (3) the ages of new immigrants are not appreciably lower than the current population, then by the year 2025, when the baby-boom generation are elderly, the American population will be divided roughly into thirds—one-third below age 30, one-third aged 30 to 59, and one-third aged 60 and older.

What will be the result of this "squaring of the pyramid"? Some experts warn about new social problems, such as increased expense for medical care and decreased concern for the quality of education for children. Others envision social benefits, such as lower crime rates and more civic involvement (Pifer and Bronte, 1986b). This much is clear: in order to successfully meet the changes and challenges brought about by a growing older population, we must all understand what the effects of aging actually are, so we can separate the ageist myths from reality.

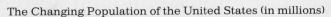

The Changing Population of the United States (in millions)

As the demographic pyramid becomes more square, people of every age are affected. For example, as more people reach late adulthood, the political power of this age group increases, ensuring that their needs will be included in the national public agenda. However, as the number of people who are parents of dependent children declines, the needs of the youngest, nonvoting age group may be neglected, unless those not directly responsible for their care become concerned.

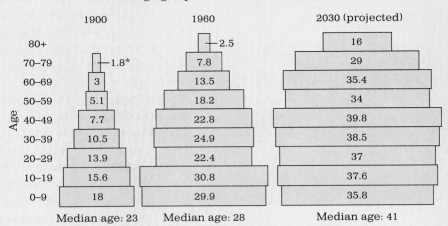

*Those older than 79 are included in the figure for those aged 70–79.

Appearance

Looking "old" is something most adults dread and try to avoid, by many means, no matter what age they are. However, there comes a time for everyone when the superficial changes of aging are beyond concealment. One of the most obvious of these changes occurs in the skin, which becomes dryer, thinner, and less elastic, producing marked wrinkling and making blood vessels and pockets of fat much more visible (Kligman et al., 1985). In addition, the dark patches of skin known as "age spots" are visible in about 25 percent of adults by age 60, about 70 percent by age 80, and in almost everyone by age 100. Hair also undergoes very apparent changes, continuing to become thinner and grayer, and, in many people, eventually becoming white.

Changes in overall body height, shape, and weight also occur in late adulthood (Whitbourne, 1985). Most older people are more than an inch shorter than they were in early adulthood, because their vertebrae (the small bones that make up the spine) have settled closer together. Further, the muscles that hold the vertebrae have become less flexible, making it harder to stand as straight as in earlier years. Body shape is affected by redistribution of fat, which collects less in the arms, legs, and upper face, and more in the torso (especially the abdomen) and the lower face (especially the jowls and chin).

Body weight is often lower in late adulthood, partly because muscle tissue becomes reduced, a difference particularly notable in men, who have relatively more muscle and less body fat than women. For both sexes, the reduction in muscle strength is especially apparent in the legs, necessitating slower walking and sometimes use of a cane or walker. Another reason for lower body weight is osteoporosis, the loss of bone calcium that causes bones to become more porous and fragile. Bone loss usually occurs at a rate of 1 to 2 percent a year after menopause in women and after age 55 in men (Nordin and Need, 1990). Osteoporosis is the main reason some older people walk with a marked stoop, and also the reason the elderly are much more likely to break a bone, particularly the hip bone, when they fall.

All these changes in appearance have serious social and psychological implications: in an ageist society, those who look old are treated as old, in a stereotypic way. This fact is poignantly underscored by the reactions of the elderly themselves. Most older people consider their personality, values, and attitudes quite stable, and except for acknowledging that they may have slowed down a bit, do not feel that they have changed all that much from their younger days (Kaufman, 1986). Therefore, when older people see a recent photograph of themselves, or catch an unguarded glimpse of themselves in the mirror, or merely notice how others treat them, they are often taken with surprise and regret, even in late-late adulthood. As one 92-year-old woman described this experience:

> There's this feeling of being out of one's skin. The feeling that you are not in your own body . . . Whenever I'm walking downtown, and I see my reflection in a store window, I'm shocked at how old it is. I never think of myself that way. [quoted in Kaufman, 1986]

Similar feelings were expressed by a man, also 92, who needed a cane to get around:

> I look like a cripple. I'm not a cripple mentally, I don't feel that way. But I am physically. I hate it. . . . You know, when I hear people, particularly gals and

ladies, their heels hitting the pavement . . . I feel so lacking in assurance—why can't I walk that way? . . . I have the same attitude now, toward life and living, as I did 30 years ago. That's why this idea of not being able to walk along with other people—it hurts my ego. Because inside, that's not really me. [quoted in Kaufman, 1986]

When elderly people associate appearance and identity, or depend on the reactions of others to validate their self-concept (as we all do sometimes), the realization that they look like, or are treated like, an old person may make them act and think like the stereotype of the elderly—with harmful consequences. As you will learn in Chapter 25, activity and feeling young promote psychological as well as physical health in the aged.

Sense Organs

The incidence of impaired vision and hearing increases with each decade. A nationwide survey of Americans over age 65 found that 90 percent had some visual impairment, and that only 10 percent had good vision without glasses (U.S. Bureau of the Census, 1986). Virtually no one hears as well in late adulthood as they did earlier (Olsho et al., 1985), and about a third of all the elderly find that inadequate hearing hampers them in their daily lives (Whitbourne, 1985).

Most of the visual and auditory losses of the aged can be corrected. Approximately 80 percent of the elderly have glasses and can see well when wearing them; only 10 percent still have serious vision problems when using corrective lenses. Even most of the very old can see fairly well. In a study of more than a thousand Americans who had reached age 100, 9 percent could see well without glasses, 62 percent could see well with glasses, and 29 percent (including 4 percent who were blind) had vision deficits that glasses did not correct (Segerberg, 1982).

Unfortunately, far fewer people who need them use hearing aids than use glasses. Although most people using the new types of hearing aids are well satisfied with them, and although nearly a third of the elderly could benefit from them, less than 10 percent use them (Olsho et al., 1985). One important reason is that the hearing aid is regarded as a symbol of agedness, and many people would rather miss some of the sounds of daily life

Figure 23.2 *The man on the left seems eager to hear what these children have to say. However, he is making a mistake common among many of the hard-of-hearing elderly—trying to get by with guesswork and cupped hands rather than using a state-of-the-art hearing aid.*

than risk being considered old. Ironically, this is usually what their poor hearing causes them to be thought of as anyway, often with unanticipated consequences. The person who frequently mishears and misunderstands conversation or who often asks "What did you say?" is likely to be thought of as a bit dottering and to be excluded from much social give-and-take, thereby being deprived of important cognitive stimulation (Whitbourne, 1985). Furthermore, the hard-of-hearing suffer more from their impairment than do those with poor vision: they tend to withdraw socially when others become annoyed at not being heard properly and to become suspicious of inaudible conversation that seems to be about them (Busse, 1985).

Body Systems

At some point in old age, the depletion of organ reserve and the ongoing slowdown of body functioning reaches a level where daily routines need to be adjusted. For the healthy young-old, the changes may be minor, such as eating smaller, more frequent meals and devoting more time to stretching and warm-ups before heavy exercise. For some of the old-old, energy and effort may need to be conserved, requiring that, beyond the basic routines of life, each day be limited to only one or two activities—having lunch with a friend *or* working in the garden *or* visiting a grandchild.

Exercise

Even for the very old, however, some physical activity is beneficial, not only for the cardiovascular system but also for the respiratory, digestive, and virtually every other body system. In late adulthood, of course, the pace of exercise must be carefully adjusted to match the declines that have occurred in heart and lung functioning. For some, this means that jogging replaces running; for others, that brisk walking replaces jogging; for others, that strolling replaces brisk walking. Nonetheless, regular exercise—three or more times a week for half an hour—is even more important in late adulthood than earlier to help maintain the strength of the heart muscle and the lungs. Activities that involve continuous rhythmic movements for an extended period are more beneficial than those that require sudden, strenuous effort (Berg and Cassells, 1990).

If an older person does not exercise regularly (and, unfortunately, the elderly are much less likely to exercise than the young), a sudden, unusual exertion—which would have been absorbed by the organ reserve and homeostatic reactions of a younger person—can result in a heart attack. Not only is regular, measured exercise more likely to strengthen the heart and protect against potentially fatal effects of exertion; it is likely to improve the overall quality of life as well (Harris, 1986).

The Aging Brain

Physiologically, the brain in late adulthood is notably smaller and slower in its functioning than in early adulthood, a fact that once led many people to jump to the conclusion that aged minds are necessarily feeble. The evidence for the physical decrements was fairly clear: the brain loses at least 5 percent of its weight and shrinks in size by about 15 percent by late adulthood.

Figure 23.3 *Regular exercise in old age not only maintains and prolongs one's physical abilities (and even one's cognitive performance, as we will see in the next chapter), but also helps to sustain a vital and active self-image. George Blair, who at age 78 performs six days a week at Cypress Gardens, is an exceptional—but instructive—example.*

One reason for this change is that neurons, which do not reproduce themselves, die throughout life, and die at an increasing rate after about age 60. The amount of cell death varies across different areas of the brain: in the primary visual area of the cerebral cortex, it is about 50 percent; in the motor areas, between 20 and 50 percent; in the areas related to memory and reasoning, 20 percent or less (Whitbourne, 1985).

Changes in the brain are not solely in the size and the number of cells. There are many indications that the neural processes in the brain become markedly slower with age, noticeably so beginning in the late 50s. The most obvious measure of this slowdown is reaction time: in laboratory tests the elderly are much slower to push a button in response to a light flashing on than younger adults are. Slowed neural processes are also reflected in changes in brain-wave patterns, as measured by the EEG (Obrist, 1980). For example, alpha waves, the waves that appear when a person is awake and relaxed, occur at the rate of eleven cycles per second in young adulthood, nine cycles per second by age 65, and eight cycles over age 80.

This slowing of various neural processes may be related to reduced production of **neurotransmitters**—chemicals in the brain that allow a nerve impulse to be communicated from one cell to another. Several neurotransmitters are present in smaller concentrations in the aged brain than in the young one. The slowing may also be related to reduced blood flow to the brain. It is interesting to note that exercise, which increases this blood flow, has been shown to significantly improve several cognitive abilities (Dustman et al., 1984; Shay and Roth, 1992).

However, the practical implications of all this evidence of brain decrement are not obvious. Except in cases of extreme damage and loss, there is no proof that brain activity is directly related to the brain's size or weight or number of cells. When brain cells die, existing cells routinely take over their function. Further, the dendrites reaching out from the remaining neurons continue to develop throughout adulthood (Cotman and Holets, 1985). It is quite possible that, while discrete brain cells are dying, the connections among the remaining cells increase, a compensation that might allow older adults to think as well as they did, although somewhat more slowly.

Even this may be too pessimistic, according to some recent research. First of all, most studies of cognition and aging are cross-sectional, which leads to overestimates of decline (see Chapter 24), and most average their results, which masks some important variations. According to one expert, "it is clear that there's a population of old people [about 20 percent] . . . whose brain function is like that of a younger person" (Plum, in Kolata 1991). Second, virtually all estimates of the aging brain's relative size, weight, and number of cells have been based on autopsy examination, and since most older people die of diseases that affect the entire body—heart disease, diabetes, spreading cancer, and the like—it is impossible to distinguish the effects that aging might have had on the brain from those that might have been caused by pathologies.

To learn more about aging brains, Marion Diamond, a neurobiologist, has spent years studying brain structure and function in lower animals, particularly the rat. Although rats normally lose brain cells with age, especially if underfed, understimulated, and overstressed, Diamond found that with well-fed rats living in enriched environments, such as large cages with many toys, aging does not reduce the number of cortex cells to any appreciable degree. As a result, says Diamond, the old brain is still "plastic," that is, sufficiently flexible that new learning can occur. Diamond concludes:

> The results demonstrating cortical plasticity in the very aged animal contain both caution and promise for our aging human population. They caution us against entering into inactive life styles that reduce the sensory stimuli reaching our brains, and they provide hope, if we continue to stimulate our brains, for healthy mental activity throughout a lifetime. [Diamond, 1988]

Sleep

Brain-wave patterns reveal another interesting difference between young and old adults. Although older adults get about as much light sleep and REM (dreaming) sleep as younger adults, they get significantly less deep sleep, which is the most restorative kind. Either as a cause or a consequence, older adults tend to wake up numerous times each night, an average of twenty-one times according to one study (Hayashi and Endo, 1982). Among the immediate causes of such wakefulness are frequent leg movements, extended pauses in breathing, and an increased sensitivity to noise. As a result of such interruptions to their sleep, many of the elderly have sleep patterns—including being fully awake several times in the middle of the night—that would be considered pathological in a younger person (Dement et al., 1985). These sleep problems can, and often do, create chronic fatigue, as well as psychological difficulties, particularly anxiety and depression (Rodin et al., 1988). Unfortunately, many of the insomniac elderly take over-the-counter or prescription sedatives that can create dependence and eventually make the problem worse.

Figure 23.4 *Sleeping midday or even mid-page is actually an expedient way for older adults to deal with their changing sleep patterns. A solid night's sleep may be hard to come by, but a satisfying nap can become a welcome alternative.*

Instead of treating insomnia as a disorder that should be medicated, a more promising strategy is to help older people understand that changes in their sleep patterns are normal and can be successfully adapted to. For example, in one approach, older adults with sleeping problems are told that midnight waking and getting fewer than eight hours of sleep a night can be perfectly healthy. They are then given explicit instructions on adjusting to their particular patterns, including not going to bed until they are actually tired, not staying in bed after their designated wake-up time, and getting up, even in the middle of the night, if they lie in bed wide awake for more than twenty minutes. This program has been highly successful, in part because once older adults understand that their changing sleep patterns are normal, and not a symptom of disease, they are better able to cope with and control both wakefulness and tiredness (Edinger et al., 1992; Morin and Azrin, 1988). The distinction between the normal effects of aging and those of pathology is an important one in many other respects as well, as we will now see.

Aging and Disease

The relationship between aging and disease is a complex one. On the one hand, aging and disease are not synonymous: it is inevitable that a person's body will gradually weaken overall with age; it is not inevitable that the person will develop any particular disease. Most aged people, most of the time, consider their health good or excellent and, on physical examination, are found to be quite well. Whether a particular elderly person is seriously ill, somewhat ailing, or in fine health depends, not on age, but on genetic factors, past and current lifestyle (including eating and exercise habits), and psychological factors such as social support and a sense of control over one's daily life (Rowe and Kahn, 1987).

On the other hand, it is undeniable that the incidence of chronic diseases—long-standing diseases that are generally irreversible—increases significantly with age. One reason is that the older a person is, the more likely he or she is to have accumulated several risk factors for such diseases. For example, decades of smoking, drinking, and inactivity eventually lead to osteoporosis in many elderly men as well as women.

In addition, many of the biological changes that occur with aging reduce the efficiency of the body's systems, making the older person more susceptible to disease. Because of these changes, aged people are not only more likely to develop a disease; they also take longer to recover from illnesses, and are more likely to die of them (see Figure 23.5). If a younger person contracts pneumonia, for example, he or she almost always is fine again in a few weeks, but if pneumonia comes to a person already seriously weakened by very old age, it is often the immediate cause of death. Even the flu can kill an older person, which is why flu shots are recommended for everyone over age 65 but not for younger people unless they have some chronic condition—such as a heart or kidney disease—that makes them particularly vulnerable.

Figure 23.5 *The death rate from the eight leading causes of death is significantly higher for elderly people than for younger people. This table shows approximate ratios between the death rates for Americans aged 65 and older and those under 65. A finer analysis reveals some interesting age differences. For example, elderly pedestrians are much more likely to be killed in auto accidents than other adult pedestrians are, whereas younger adults are more likely to be killed in auto accidents when they are the drivers or passengers.*

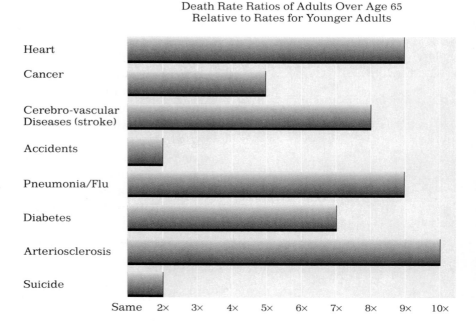

Death Rate Ratios of Adults Over Age 65
Relative to Rates for Younger Adults

Not surprisingly, then, the elderly see doctors more often, and spend more time hospitalized, than younger adults do. Contrary to the ageist stereotype, however, the elderly are not more likely to be hypochondriacs, imagining or exaggerating health complaints (Shock, 1985). In fact, compared with younger adults, the elderly are less likely to seek medical attention for problems that can be treated (Rowe and Minaker, 1985; Siegler and Costa, 1985), largely because they interpret the symptoms as the signs of normal aging, and try to overlook them. Some doctors make the same mistake, because they consider the "aches and pains of old age . . . inevitable, thus warranting less medical attention." As a result, doctors spend less time with elderly patients than they do with younger ones (Stohl and Feller, 1990).

Significant variations in the relationship between aging and disease occur according to gender and national origin, for reasons not completely understood. For example, worldwide, the rates of cancer increase dramatically with age, but the absolute rate of cancer overall, as well as the rate of specific cancers, is amazingly variable. For instance, the breast cancer rate in the United States is more than four times that of Japan, but the stomach cancer rate in Japan is eight times that in the United States; in Australia, men are almost twice as likely to die of cancer as women are, whereas in New Zealand—with a similar population in roughly the same part of the world—the cancer death rate is almost equal for both sexes (Smyth, 1987). In the United States, cancer rates among African-Americans are higher than among European-Americans, but among Hispanic-Americans, Asian-Americans, and Native Americans, they are lower (Jones, 1989).

Sex and gender differences are also omnipresent. As already noted in Chapter 20, in middle and late adulthood, men are more likely to die but women are more likely to be unwell (Ory and Warner, 1990). Of twenty-four common chronic conditions, men are higher in only one—hearing impairments; both sexes are about equal in eleven; and women are higher in the remaining twelve, including arthritis, bronchitis, constipation, eczema, hypertension, hemorrhoids, migraine, sinusitis, urinary diseases, and varicose veins (U.S. Bureau of the Census, 1991). This pattern continues through old age: even in their 80s, men die at a higher rate than women, but women are more likely to be disabled.

There are some plausible psychological or sociological explanations for this difference. One is that women are more likely to notice disease symptoms and go to a doctor, thus getting earlier treatment or preventive care. Another is that men are more likely to tempt death by drug use (including tobacco and alcohol) and by impatient and hostile behavior patterns. However, while such factors play a part, women outlive men even when specific risk factors are equal (Verbrugge, 1990). Indeed, despite the social changes in the lives of both sexes over recent decades, and despite many cultural variations in gender roles, the sex differential in life expectancy from birth is remarkably steady, with females having about a six-year advantage over males. In fact, worldwide, once middle adulthood is reached, life expectancy is several years longer for females than for males (United Nations, 1990).

Let us look more closely at the complex relationship be veen aging and disease with two examples, heart disease and cancer, the leading killers of the aged.

Heart Disease and Cancer

Normal aging reduces the functioning of the heart—especially in times of exercise and stress—partly because it reduces the strength of the heart muscle and lengthens the time the heart needs to relax between contractions. Normal aging also reduces the elasticity of the cardiovascular system. But aging in itself does not cause heart disease. Most aged people have quite healthy, although aging, hearts, capable of sustaining life for many more years (Harris, 1986). However, many older people also show a number of risk factors related to heart disease, including elevated blood pressure, a high cholesterol level, obesity, lack of exercise, a history of smoking. Over time, the interaction of these accumulating risk factors with the general weakening of the heart and relevant genetic weaknesses makes the elderly increasingly vulnerable (Lau, 1991). Thus it is not surprising that heart disease causes about 40 percent of all deaths over age 65, with an increasing proportion of such deaths being the result of gradual heart failure rat ier than sudden massive heart attack.

A similar relationship exists between aging and cancer, the cause of about 20 percent of all deaths in the aged. The predisposing factors that may lead to cancer—genetic vulnerability and environmental insults (such as exposure to asbestos or tobacco smoke) among them—typically predate old age by half a century or more, and the cancer process probably begins years before it is evident. As people age, however, the latent potential for cancer is more likely to become manifest, and cure is more difficult: a person older than 85 is more than a hundred times as likely to die of cancer as a person aged 30. In fact, among those over age 85, the rate of cancer death has increased over the past twenty years by about 20 percent. This is largely because the cohort that currently makes up the old-old was the first group to enthusiastically take up cigarette-smoking as the "modern," sophisticated thing to do. Compared to earlier cohorts, they also ate more animal fat and were exposed to more pollution (Smith, 1987).

Thus far we have discussed two of the reasons that the aged are more vulnerable to disease: their bodies are weaker overall and they have been exposed to environmental stresses for a longer period of time. There is a third factor, however, which may be particularly important in affecting the person's ability to recover from whatever illnesses may strike: diminished immunity.

Immunity

The immune system determines the body's ability to defend itself against invaders from without (such as viruses) and from within (such as cancer cells). The immune system works by recognizing foreign or abnormal substances in the circulatory system, and then isolating and destroying them, mainly with two types of "attack" cells. The first are called **B-cells** because they are manufactured in the bone marrow. B-cells create antibodies that attack specific invading bacteria and viruses. Since these antibodies remain in the system, we do not get measles, mumps, or specific strains of flu more than once. The second type are called **T-cells** because they are manufactured by the thymus gland. T-cells produce specific substances that attack infected cells of the body. T-cells also help the B-cells produce more efficient antibodies and strengthen other aspects of the immune system as well.

The first notable change in the immune system involves the thymus gland, which begins to shrink during adolescence and by age 50 weighs between 5 and 10 percent of what it did at age 15 (Lewis and Cavagnaro, 1991). The production of T-cells declines as well, although not as dramatically. With age there also is a reduction in the power of both T- and B-cells, as well as in the efficiency of the mechanisms that regulate them. These changes help explain why most forms of cancer become much more common with age, and why various other illnesses—from chicken pox to the latest strain of influenza—are much more serious in an adult than in a child. As noted, by late adulthood, the "flu" can be fatal.

In fact, according to one theory, the gradual breakdown of the immune system accounts for the aging process itself, allowing genetic vulnerabilities (such as diabetes) or disease processes (such as the growth of cancer cells) that had been kept in check earlier in life to take over (Hausman and Weksler, 1985). Further, even in the absence of diagnosed illness, older adults with stronger immune systems outlive their contemporaries whose immune systems are less strong (Weksler, 1990).

The immune system is also a candidate to explain the sex differences in morbidity and mortality as people age (see Chapter 20). One reason women outlive men may be that, throughout life, females tend to have stronger immune systems than males: their thymus is larger, and laboratory tests reveal that their immune responses are more efficient. This advantage may be a mixed blessing, however, because women are more vulnerable to autoimmune diseases such as rheumatoid arthritis and lupus, in which an overactive immune system attacks the person's own body (Verbrugge, 1990; Weksler, 1990).

Additional support for the idea that impairments of the immune system are closely involved in aging as well as disease comes from research on AIDS. Some specific cancers and signs of dementia that occur in younger persons with AIDS are also much more common in later life. Changes in the immune system are just one of several explanations for the aging process. We will now look at the others.

Causes of the Aging Process

The attention of many researchers is turning toward making all the years of the life span good ones. The goal is not only a longer life, if possible, but even more important, a **compression of morbidity,** that is, a limiting of the time any person spends ill or infirm. The hope is that improvements in lifestyle and in medical treatment will eliminate more and more diseases once thought to be inevitable with age. As a result, more people will be active, alert, and enthusiastic until age 85 or so, when they will experience an easy and natural death caused by a relatively sudden accumulation of aging effects in all parts of the body (Fries, 1990).

This possibility raises other questions. Might we ever be able to control aging sufficiently that late adulthood never brings frailty, senility, disability, and pain? Can aging be slowed down so that death itself can be postponed, allowing the average person to live 90 or 100 healthy years instead of simply 75 or 85? Underlying these questions is the fundamental one, Why does aging occur? As you will see, there are many intriguing answers to the question, some implicating the environment, some, our genetic makeup, and some, the simple passage of time (Ludwig, 1991; Cooper et al., 1991; Harrison, 1990; Rosenfeld, 1985).

Wear and Tear

The oldest, most general theory of aging, the **wear-and-tear theory,** compares the human body to a machine. It maintains that just as, say, the parts of an automobile begin giving out as mileage adds up, so the parts of the human body deteriorate with each year of use, as well as with accumulated exposure to pollution, radiation, inadequate nutrition, disease, and various other stresses. According to this theory, we wear out our bodies just by living our lives.

Figure 23.6 *Stretching and bending regularly, in any context, at any age, are much more likely to maintain and extend one's physical capabilities than to diminish them.*

Although appealing in its simplicity, the wear-and-tear theory seems to be of limited usefulness. Certainly it is true that an athlete who puts repeated stress on elbows or knees is likely to have damaged joints by middle adulthood; or that an outdoor worker whose skin is continuously exposed to sunlight is likely to have damaged skin; or that an industrial worker who inhales asbestos and smokes cigarettes over many years will eventually have damaged lungs. But, overall, the analogy to a machine's wearing out simply doesn't hold up. In many respects, the human body is its own repair shop, replacing or mending many of its damaged parts. In addition, unlike most machines, many parts of the human body benefit from use. As we have seen, the heart functions better if the person regularly makes it work faster than normal; the respiratory system benefits from routine exertion; the sexual arousal system is more likely to function in old age if the person has been sexually active throughout adulthood; the digestive system benefits from raw fruits and vegetables that require vigorous digestive activity. It seems clear, then, that the notion of wear and tear applies to some diseases and problems in some organs and body parts, but it is not very helpful in explaining the aging process overall.

Cellular Theories

More promising theories of aging begin at the cellular level, suggesting that some occurrence in the cells themselves causes aging. The most prominent of these theories center on the cumulative effects of cellular mishaps.

Cellular Accidents

One cellular theory of aging proposes that senescence is the result of the accumulation of accidents that occur during cell reproduction. With the exception of certain types of cells, notably those of the nerves, the cells of the human body continue to reproduce throughout life. An obvious example is the outer cells of the skin. Under normal conditions, these cells are entirely replaced every few years; the process occurs much more rapidly when a cut or scrape is healing. Thanks to precise functioning of DNA and RNA, each replacement cell is the exact copy of an old cell, or ought to be.

However, "an ever growing number of chemical agents discharged in our environment, [and] . . . an increased possibility for the interaction of different toxicants," as well as radiation from the sun and other sources, all cause mutations in the DNA structure of more and more cells as a person ages (Cooper et al., 1991). Mutations may also occur in the process of DNA repair. As a consequence, the instructions for creating new cells become imperfect, so the new cells are not quite exact copies of the old. Over time, such changes may result in aging of the skin, or benign skin changes, or possibly cancer. Throughout the body, cellular imperfections and the body's declining ability to detect and correct them can result in harmless changes, small declines in function, or sometimes, potentially fatal damage.

Figure 23.7 *The "beauty benefits" of devoted sunbathing are transient; the damage is cumulative. Age spots, wrinkles, and leathery skin texture associated with aging become exaggerated from lengthy exposure to the sun.*

Free Radicals

Another aspect of this theory of aging began with the observation that some of the body's metabolic processes can cause electrons to separate from their atoms, resulting in atoms with unpaired electrons. These atoms, called **free radicals,** are highly unstable and capable of reacting violently with other molecules in the cell, sometimes splitting them or tearing them apart. The most critical damage caused by free radicals occurs in DNA molecules, producing errors in cell maintenance and repair that, over time, may eventually contribute to such diseases as cancer, diabetes, and arteriosclerosis (Harman, 1984). In addition, free radicals formed from oxygen molecules appear to aggravate these diseases, causing many doctors to be selective in giving affected patients pure oxygen (Marx, 1987). The potential for damage from free radicals is also increased by exposure to ultraviolet radiation, which is one of the reasons scientists are concerned about the loss of the ozone layer protecting the earth's atmosphere (McCachran et al., 1991). It seems, then, that since free radicals damage cells, affect organs, and accelerate diseases, the gradual accumulation of damage as the individual ages may be one of the causes of the aging process (Harman, 1984).

Error Catastrophe

When the systems of the body, especially the immune system, are in shape, the effects of cellular damage are minor, held in check by other cells that destroy seriously damaged cells and take over the work that imperfect cells no longer perform (Schneider and Reed, 1985). However, according to some theories, as the immune system declines and the processes of repair become less efficient, the constellation of errors can become so extensive or affect such critically important cells that the body can no longer control or isolate the errors, leading to what has been called an **error catastrophe** (Cohn, 1987). At this point the normal, healthy aging process gives way, disease overtakes the person, and death occurs. This theory of accumulating errors in cell reproduction is one possible explanation for the fact that cancer, a disease in which normal cell reproduction somehow goes awry and cells reproduce so rapidly that malignant tumors are formed, is much more common in humans, and indeed all mammals, as they reach old age. It may also explain why the older a person is, the more likely he or she is to die of a cascade of illnesses, rather than simply one. As noted by the chief mortality statistician of the Centers for Disease Control:

> Death among the oldest old appears to have a somewhat opportunistic character, with many chronic conditions competing to be the precipitating cause. The particular cause of death is less the result of a clearly defined etiological path than the random result of a more generalized deterioration of the capacity for life. [Rosenberg et al., 1991]

Programmed Senescence

Certainly it seems plausible that the changes in cellular processes that occur over time eventually lead to aging and death. However, many scientists suspect that the aging process, while reflecting these changes, is not caused by them. They contend that, just as we are genetically programmed to reach various levels of biological maturation at fixed times, we are genetically programmed to die after a fixed number of years. Thus, even if no particular illness or accident occurs, **programmed senescence** will inevitably bring about death at a certain age.

That "certain age," the maximum number of years that a particular species is genetically programmed to live, is called **maximum life span,** a number that is based on the oldest age to which members of each species have been known to live (Kirkwood, 1985). For the house mouse, the maximum life span is 3 years; for the house cat, 28; for both the horse and the golden eagle, 46; and for the elephant, 70. For humans, the maximum life span is 115 years.

Maximum life span is quite different from **average life expectancy,** which is the number of years the average newborn of a particular population of a given species is likely to live. In humans, life expectancy varies according to historical, cultural, and socioeconomic factors that affect frequency of death in childhood, adolescence, or middle age. In the United States in 1990, average life expectancy at birth was about 72 years for men and 79 years for women. Americans who already are 60 years old, and thus no longer at any risk of an early death, are expected to live to 79 if male and to 83 if female. Current average life expectancy is about four times what it was for people of ancient times, and twenty-eight years more than it was at the turn of the century. The reason for this improvement is not that the maximum life span has increased but that people are less likely to die in infancy or childhood.

A Genetic Clock?

According to one theory, the DNA that directs the activity of every cell in the body also regulates the aging process, not as a mutation over time but as a proper function. Our genetic makeup acts, in effect, as a **genetic clock,** triggering hormonal changes in the brain (similar to the hormonal changes that produce puberty, for instance) and regulating the cellular reproduction and repair process. As the genetic clock gradually "switches off" the genes that promote growth, there is speculation that genes that promote aging are switched on. Aging processes continue to accumulate until one or more body systems can no longer function, and a natural death occurs.

Genetic regulation of aging is suggested by several genetic diseases that include premature signs of aging and early death as part of their symptoms. Down syndrome is the most common: people with Down syndrome who survive childhood almost always die by middle adulthood, with symptoms of heart disease and Alzheimer's disease, a type of dementia that occurs most frequently in old age. Children born with a rare genetic disease called **progeria** have a normal infancy but by age 5 stop growing and begin to look like old people, with wrinkled skin and balding heads. They develop many other signs of premature aging during middle childhood, and die by their teens, seemingly of heart diseases typically found in the elderly (Brown et al., 1990).

The Hayflick Limit

Evidence for a genetic clock that limits the life span also comes from laboratory research, particularly from the work of Leonard Hayflick (Hayflick, 1979; Hayflick and Moorhead, 1961). In this research, cells cultured from human embryos were allowed to "age under glass" by providing them with all the necessary nutrients for cell growth and replication and protecting them from external stress or contamination. In such ideal conditions, it was believed, the cells would multiply forever. Instead, the cells stopped replicating after about fifty divisions. Cells similarly cultured from children showed a smaller number of doublings before they stopped dividing, and cells from adults divided even fewer times. The total number of cell divisions was shown to be roughly related to the age of the donor.

This research has been repeated by hundreds of scientists, using many techniques and various types of cells from people and animals of various ages. The result is always that the cells stop replicating at a certain point, referred to as the **Hayflick limit**. Even in ideal conditions, the replication of cells of living creatures is roughly equal to that occurring in the maximum life span of their particular species. Cells from people with progeria, Down syndrome, and other genetic conditions characterized by accelerated aging show fewer numbers of doublings than would be expected given the age of the donors (Tice and Setlow, 1985).

In all cases, at the point where cell division stops, analysis of the cells shows that they are different from young cells in many ways. This provides new support for the idea that DNA and RNA are responsible for cell death, not only because of random errors but, more important, because of programmed senescence.

The fact that aging and death seem to be genetically programmed helps explain the variability we see in the "normal" life span. Although the maximum life span may be predetermined for each species, how close each particular individual comes to reaching that maximum is genetically influenced. Longevity, for example, runs in families; and compared with dyzygotic twins, monozygotic twins are much closer in rate of aging and age at death (McClearn and Foch, 1985; Tice and Setlow, 1985). Most people, if they escape specific diseases in their younger years, die in their 80s, but some individuals live quite naturally without debilitating chronic diseases until their 100s. Such variation is seen in all animals. In fact, research with fruit flies has shown that they include a small group that survive almost twice as long as the maximum life span of fruit flies was thought to be (Carey et al., 1992).

One major reason many scientists are now focusing on the link between aging and genetics is that the genetic clock itself may be resettable. Genetic engineering is on the brink of allowing children to escape the consequences of genetic diseases they inherit (see pp. 88–90); the same engineering techniques may also be able to reprogram the genes that control the "fixed" limit of human life (Harrison, 1990).

Life Extension

A growing number of gerontologists are becoming convinced that breakthroughs once thought impossible, such as genetic engineering, synthetic boosts to the immune system, dramatic alterations of the usual diet, and eradication of major diseases, might soon increase the average human life span, and, more significantly, the average **healthspan,** that is, the period of vital and vigorous years. Indeed, some believe that the size of such an increase might be a decade or more, a significant jump from the four years or so added since 1950.

Whether or not the dream of extending the life span might be beneficial to the individual or to society is debatable: many people now shudder at the idea of late adulthood lasting fifty years or more, or at the concept of a society in which the elderly outnumber the young by two to one. However, before drawing your own conclusions, remember that ageism clouds our perceptions of late adulthood. A look at some people who have lived to be very old might be instructive.

May You Live So Long

Three remote areas of the world—one in Georgia in the former Soviet Union, one in Pakistan, and one in Peru—have become famous for having large numbers of people who enjoy unusual longevity. In these places, late adulthood is not only long but is also usually quite vigorous.

One researcher describes the Abkhasia people in Georgia as follows:

> Most of the aged [those about age ninety] work regularly. Almost all perform light tasks around the homestead, and quite a few work in the orchards and gardens, and care for domestic animals. Some even continue to chop wood and haul water. Close to 40 percent of the aged men and 30 percent of the aged women report good vision; that is, that they do not need glasses for any sort of work, including reading or threading a needle. Between 40 and 50 percent have reasonably good hearing. Most have their own teeth. Their posture is unusually erect, even into advanced age. Many take walks of more than two miles a day and swim in mountain streams. [Benet, 1974]

Among the people described in this report are a woman said to be over 130 who drinks a little vodka before breakfast and smokes a pack of cigarettes a day; a man who sired a child when he was 100; and another man who was a village storyteller with an excellent memory at a reported age of 148.

A more comprehensive study (Pitskhelauri, 1982) finds that all the regions famous for long-lived people share four characteristics:

1. Diet is moderate, consisting mostly of fresh vegetables and herbs with little consumption of meat and fat. A prevailing belief is that it is better to leave the dining table a little bit hungry than too full.

2. Work continues throughout life. In these rural areas, even very elderly adults help with farm work and household tasks, including child care.

3. Family and community are important. All the long-lived are well integrated into families of several generations, and interact frequently with friends and neighbors.

4. Exercise and relaxation are part of the daily routine. Most of the long-lived take a stroll in the morning and another in the evening (often up and down mountains), most take a midday nap, and most spend several hours socializing in the evening, telling stories and discussing the day's events.

Figure 23.8 *Three remote regions of the world are renown for the longevity of their people. In Vilcabamba, Ecuador, (a) 87-year-old Jose Maria Roa stands on the mud from which he will make adobe for a new house, and (b) 102-year-old Micaela Quezada spins wool. In Abkhasia in the Republic of Georgia, companionship is an important part of late life, as shown by (c) Selakh Butka, 113, posing with his wife Marusya, 101, and (d) Ougula Lodara talking with two "younger" friends. In this remote area of the former U.S.S.R., the elderly continue to work long past the usual American retirement age, so (e) Gumba Tikhed, age 98, still picks tea on a collective farm. (f) Temir Tarba rides his horse daily, as he has for almost all of his 100 years. Finally, Shah Bibi (g), at 98, and Galum Mohammad Shad (h), at 100, from the Hunza area of Pakistan, spin wool and build houses. Alexander Leaf, the physician who studied these people, believes that the high social status and continued sense of usefulness of the very old in these cultures may be just as important in their longevity as the diet and exercise imposed by the geographical conditions in each region.*

(a)

(b)

(c)

(d)

(e)

(f)

(g)

(h)

A CLOSER LOOK   Nutrition and Aging

There is a clear consensus regarding three key aspects of nutrition during late adulthood (Chen, 1986; James, 1989; Maruyama, 1986; Horwitz et al., 1989):

1. Vitamin and mineral needs do not decrease with age. If anything, they increase, as the body's ability to break down food and use the nutrients in it becomes less efficient.

2. Calorie requirements decrease by about 20 percent from those of early and middle adulthood. Although variations in height, weight, and activity are obviously relevant, the average older man should take in about 2,200 calories a day, and the average woman, about 1,700. During the years of late adulthood, calorie needs continue to decline.

3. Because more nutrients need to be packed into fewer calories, a varied and healthy diet, emphasizing fresh fruits and vegetables, lean meats and fish, and complex carbohydrates (cereals and grains), is even more important in late adulthood than earlier.

For many reasons, getting enough nutrients is more problematic for the aged than for younger adults (Chen, 1986; Davies, 1990). The chief age-related factor is the reduced efficiency of the digestive system, which makes absorption of nutrients more difficult. The senses of smell and taste also diminish with age, making food less appealing. A number of external factors may also affect the nutrition of certain segments of the elderly: (1) poverty (high-quality nutrients are more expensive); (2) living alone (those who eat alone tend to eat quick, irregular meals); (3) dental problems (missing teeth and gum disease make people eat softer food and less of it).

Furthermore, many of the elderly take drugs that affect nutritional requirements. For example, aspirin (taken daily by many who have arthritis) increases the need for vitamin C; antibiotics reduce the absorption of iron, calcium, and vitamin K; antacids can reduce absorption of protein; oil-based laxatives deplete vitamins A and D; and so on (Kart and Metress, 1984; Rikaus, 1986). Alcohol, especially in large amounts, is very detrimental to good nutrition, depleting B vitamins, calcium, magnesium, and vitamin C in particular (Ibey, 1990). Alcohol and caffeine, as well as many prescription drugs, reduce the water in the body, making the elderly especially vulnerable to dehydration (Reiff, 1989).

In an effort to maintain health and vigor, about two-thirds of the elderly take vitamin and mineral supplements (Read and Graney, 1982), a practice encouraged by many of the advocates of life extension (Demopoulus, 1982; Rosenfeld, 1985; Walford, 1983), some of whom recommend massive doses of certain vitamins as well as a low-calorie diet.

Some believe that antioxidants, which reduce the number of free radicals of oxygen (pp. 600–601) by forming

A hot balanced meal, a chance to socialize, and a good reason to take a midday walk—all provided by this senior-citizen lunch program, which serves the inner-city elderly who otherwise might eat less nourishing food, alone, at home.

a bond with their unattached oxygen electron, might slow down the disease and aging process. Antioxidants include vitamins C and E, and beta-carotene (most commonly found in carrots), as well as some enzymes and minerals, notably selenium (Mertz, 1989). However, a direct link between these substances in the human bloodstream and a reduction in free radicals is not proven (Canada and Calabrese, 1991; Weber and Miquel, 1986).

Many nutritionists find that most of the elderly are relatively well nourished, and that they are more likely to overspend and overdose on vitamins than to be deficient in them (Bailey, 1986; Chen, 1986; Kart and Metress, 1984). At the moment, there is no clear and compelling evidence one way or the other for the usefulness of vitamin supplements in old age. However, enough is known to advise caution. Some vitamins, such as vitamin A, are toxic in large doses (Lyles, 1991), and large doses of vitamins, in general, may well harm an individual by upsetting the natural nutritional balance in the system, creating vitamin needs and dependencies where there were none before (Cutler, 1984; Hsu and Smith, 1984). The uncertainty in this area is reflected by the strikingly contradictory opinions of experts in various countries regarding what supplements, in what dosages, might be beneficial to what ends (Mertz, 1989; Wahlquist and Flint-Richter, 1989).

Given this state of affairs, it seems reasonable to conclude that the elderly should consume a healthy diet, and beyond that, proceed cautiously. Diagnosis of particular individual vitamin deficiencies should be the only basis for undertaking any expensive or unusual vitamin regimen, and acceptance of any life-extending recommendations should await controlled longitudinal research that uses a sufficient sample size, control groups, and blind experimenters.

Beyond these four aspects of the individual's life, geography and tradition may be influential as well. All three places famous for long-lived people are in rural, mountainous regions that are at least 3,000 feet above sea level. This minimizes pollution and maximizes lung and heart fitness, for even walking in these regions can be considered aerobic exercise. Furthermore, in all three, the aged are respected, and strong traditions ensure the elderly an important social role.

Some researchers suggest that another factor may account for some of these cases of unusual longevity—lying. None of the communities of the long-lived have birth or marriage records from the nineteenth century that are verifiable, at least to the satisfaction of critics. In fact, beginning at about age 70, many people in these areas systematically exaggerate their age, although how greatly is debatable (Leaf, 1982; Mazess and Forman, 1979; Pitskhelauri, 1982). It may be that persons who claim to be 100 years old are only in their 80s, and that those who are supposedly long past 100 are only a little bit past it.

This does not render the earlier reports useless, for no one doubts that an unusual number of very old and healthy people thrive in these isolated areas of the world. While their genetic clocks almost certainly do not allow them to live to age 148, their habits and culture do allow a surprising number of them to reach 100.

Research on those who reach late-late adulthood in countries where records are accurate show lifestyle patterns similar in many ways to those of the long-lived of isolated areas: a lifetime of moderate diet, hard work, optimistic attitude, intellectual curiosity, and social involvement is typical of the oldest old in developed countries as well (Beard, 1991; Poon et al., 1992). For example, between 1955 and 1968 more than a thousand Americans on Social Security reached their 100th birthday and were interviewed by a Social Security representative (Segerberg, 1982). Time after time the interviewer arrived dreading the encounter (and cursing the administrator who had ordered it), and left amazed and heartened that the centenarian still chopped wood, or did the housework, or, in the case of one physician, still saw patients. Very few were in wheelchairs, or had serious illnesses such as cancer or heart disease; only one suffered from senile dementia.

A general impression of these centenarians is conveyed by the following description of one of their members, Francisco Guerra:

> His close cropped hair is black except on the sides, where it is white. His lean body looks hard and sinewy, not an excess ounce of flesh on it. His skin, broiled for years under the Southwest sun, is like leather—but malleable enough for smiling eyes and mouth.
>
> "I have never been sick a day in my life," he says. "I feel good."
>
> Why? How has he been able to do it?
>
> "I have lived so long because there's a Chief up there. Maybe it's punishment, maybe it's glory. I am happy." [quoted in Segerberg, 1982]

Taken together, these and many other studies of the old-old lead to a ready conclusion: If people reach late adulthood in good health, their attitudes and activities may be even more important in determining the length and quality of their remaining years than purely genetic or physiological factors.

SUMMARY

Ageism

1. Prejudices about the elderly are common and destructive, for they result in the old living lives that are more limited and isolated than they need to be. Contrary to the stereotype, most of the aged are happy, healthy, and active. Fortunately, ageism is weakening as gerontologists study more of the elderly who live in the community, and as the sheer number of the aged in the general population increases.

The Aging Process

2. The many apparent changes in the skin, hair, and body shape that began earlier in adulthood continue. In addition, most older people are somewhat shorter and weigh less than they did, and walk more stiffly. Such changes in appearance can affect the self-concept of the older person.

3. Vision and hearing are almost always impaired by late adulthood, to the point that nine out of ten of the elderly need glasses, and one out of three would benefit from a hearing aid. Most who need glasses get them, but, unfortunately, most who need a hearing aid do not get one, fearing that it would make them appear old.

4. The age-related declines of the major body systems and organ reserve eventually reach a point—different for everyone—at which some of the routines of daily life need adjusting. For example, although exercise is just as important during late adulthood as earlier, its pace needs to be slower.

5. By late adulthood, the brain has become smaller and works more slowly, the result of cell death and overall circulatory slowdown. However, the implications of these changes are controversial. Because of research on dendrite development and on learning in old age, many developmentalists think that, barring disease, the brain continues to function well in late adulthood.

6. Sleep patterns in late adulthood are quite different from those in early adulthood, and can lead to chronic fatigue and depression. In most cases, these sleep patterns are normal and can be adapted to healthily if they are regarded as such.

Aging and Disease

7. The aging process is not synonymous with the disease process. We should not assume that illness is an expected, and thus an accepted, companion during the later years. Unfortunately, many of the elderly—and some of their physicians—attempt to overlook problems that need medical attention because they believe their symptoms are just part of growing old.

8. It is true, however, that aging makes people more susceptible to most chronic and critical diseases, and makes recovery slower. At some point, usually in late-late adulthood, multiple problems may occur, and death will result.

9. The decline in the immune system also contributes to the elderly's increasing vulnerability to disease. As the thymus shrinks and production of both B- and T-cells decreases, the body becomes less able to fight against diseases.

Causes of the Aging Process

10. There are many theories that address the environmental and genetic causes of aging. One theory is that as we use our bodies we wear them out, just as a machine wears out with extended use. This wear-and-tear theory does not, however, explain much of what research finds—that activity promotes longer life and healthier aging.

11. Cellular theories of aging seem more plausible. Perhaps the DNA duplication and repair processes are affected by radiation and other factors, leading to an accumulation of errors when new cells are made. These errors may eventually produce an error catastrophe, in which the body suddenly reaches the point that it is much more vulnerable to disease and death.

12. The maximum life span may well be fixed by a kind of genetic clock that switches the aging process on at some point. The theory that genes may be responsible for aging is buttressed by evidence that several conditions that are accompanied by premature aging, such as Down syndrome and progeria, are caused by genetic abnormalities.

13. Further evidence for programmed senescence is found in the Hayflick limit. Even in ideal conditions, cells in the laboratory stop reproducing themselves after a certain number of divisions. This number decreases as the age of the cell donor increases.

Life Extension

14. Theoretically, once the cause of the aging process is understood, it can be altered so that the maximum human life span will increase. Whether or not this is a good idea depends on what quality of life very old people could be expected to have.

15. Wherever they live, those who live to be 100 typically continue to live happy and active lives. In three regions of the world, parts of the former Soviet Union, Pakistan, and Peru, large numbers of people seem to live to be very old. Moderate diet, high altitude, hard work, and traditional respect for the aged characterize all three places.

KEY TERMS

ageism (586)
young-old (587)
old-old (587)
gerontology (588)
senescence (588)
demography (589)
demographic
   pyramid (589)
neurotransmitters (593)
B-cells (598)
T-cells (598)
compression of
   morbidity (599)

wear-and-tear
   theory (599)
free radicals (601)
error catastrophe (601)
programmed
   senescence (601)
maximum life span (602)
average life
   expectancy (602)
genetic clock (602)
progeria (602)
Hayflick limit (603)
healthspan (604)

KEY QUESTIONS

1. To what extent are the elderly inactive, lonely, and frail?

2. What are the advantages of exercise in old age?

3. What changes occur in the brain in old age and how do they affect thinking?

4. What is the relationship between aging and disease?

5. How is the immune system affected by aging?

6. Why is the wear-and-tear theory not very helpful in explaining the aging process?

7. In what ways do the cellular theories of aging seem plausible?

8. What does Leonard Hayflick's research on cells from individuals of various ages tend to show?

9. What are some of the characteristics of people who live to a very old age?

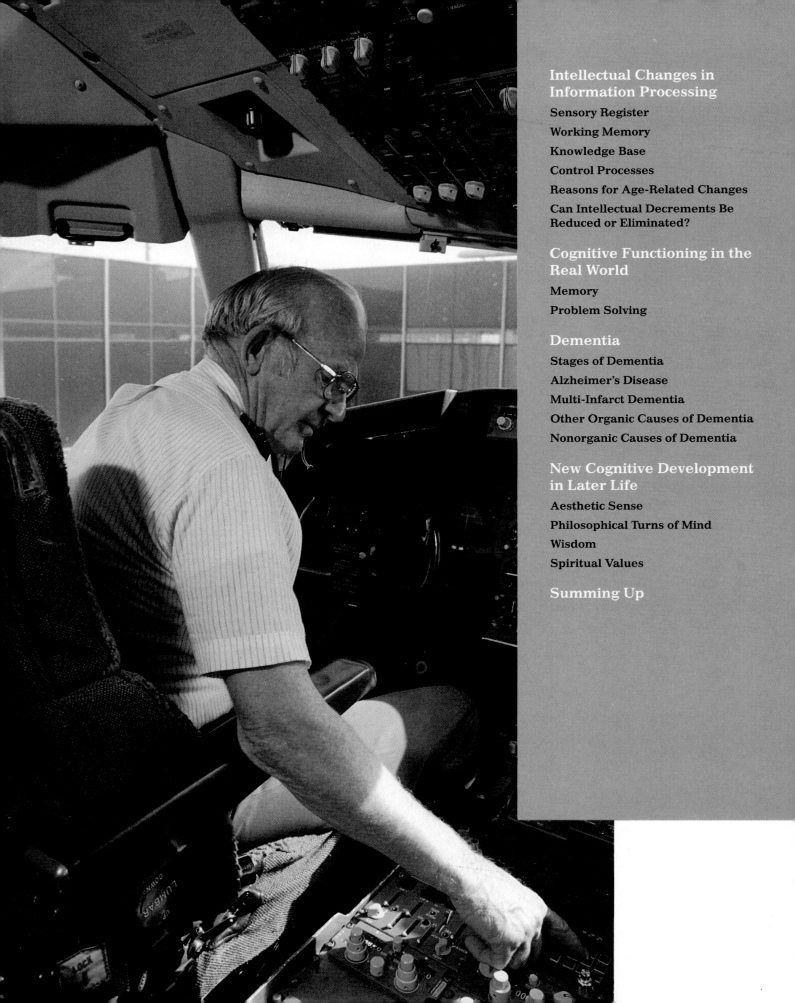

CHAPTER 24

Late Adulthood: Cognitive Development

In late adulthood, the forces of biological decline and accrued experience exert different pulls on intellectual development, accounting for decrements in memory retrieval and abstract thinking on one hand, and the growth of insight and expertise on the other. Indeed, while some older adults experience serious cognitive impairment due to health-related problems—sometimes to the point of dementia—others remain intellectually vital and may even develop an enhanced perspective on life experience. In trying to understand this diversity, researchers have also tried to determine whether the intellectual decrements of later life can be reduced or eliminated. Thus the dynamics of growth and decline in intellectual competencies are the theme of this chapter, which addresses the following questions:

What changes in information processing might account for the intellectual changes of later life?

How modifiable are the intellectual decrements of late adulthood?

What are the characteristics and origins of dementia and related disorders?

What opportunities exist for continued cognitive growth to the end of life?

As we have seen, adult cognitive development is best described as *multidirectional*: over the course of adulthood, some abilities increase, others wane, and some remain stable. In early adulthood, continued cognitive progress is most apparent in the growth of postformal thought and the changes that arise from higher education. In middle adulthood, intellectual changes are more diverse, with some competencies (such as crystallized intelligence) showing sustained growth while others (related to fluid intelligence) begin to decline. Continuing through middle adulthood, adults achieve mastery and expertise in areas of reasoning that are most meaningful and useful to them.

By late adulthood, the cumulative effects of increasing experience and declining biological capacities push cognitive development in opposite directions. On one hand, older adults have a broader history of personal experiences, relationships, and knowledge to draw on when facing the intellectual challenges of later life, and this period often witnesses a deepening in the individual's perspective on life. On the other hand, the effects of health impairments, perceptual declines, and decreases in energy and reaction time exact a greater toll on cognitive competence during the later adult years than in any earlier period. As a consequence, many aspects of intelligence begin to decline during late adulthood. In this chapter, we complete the story of multidirectional cognitive development in adulthood by examining the factors that are most influential in shaping the course of that development during old age.

Intellectual Changes in Information Processing

Although most intellectual abilities increase or remain stable throughout early and middle adulthood, beyond age 60 many individuals begin to experience decrements in certain abilities. In Schaie's Seattle Longitudinal Study (described in Chapter 21), for example, older adults began to show significant declines over seven-year intervals on the five "primary mental abilities" (verbal comprehension, spatial visualization, reasoning, mathematical ability, and word fluency) (Schaie, 1990a, 1990b). Why do these decrements occur? Many researchers believe that an answer to this question can be found by examining age-related changes in the various processes by which the human mind accesses, stores, and retrieves information. More specifically, researchers have sought to understand intellectual changes in late adulthood by studying changes in how the sensory register, working memory, knowledge base, and control processes function in older adults (Salthouse, 1992).

Sensory Register

As we saw in Chapter 2, the **sensory register** stores incoming sensory information for a split second after it is received, allowing it to be selectively processed by other components of the system. (You will recall that the sensory register is revealed in the momentary afterimage, visual or auditory, that remains in the brain after you perceive something. If, for example, you hear someone say something and then realize that the person was speaking to you, you can usually remember what the person said, even though you weren't listening at the time.) Research suggests that the effects of aging may create small decrements in the sensitivity of the sensory register. As a result, it may take longer for information to register via the senses and longer for it to fade once it has registered.

This decrement can be demonstrated experimentally by showing a person two pictures on a screen, one a fraction of a second after the other. If the second picture follows too closely after the first, only one of the two pictures will actually be perceived. On such experiments, older adults need significantly more time between pictures than younger adults do in order to perceive both pictures (Kline and Szafran, 1975). Other laboratory studies similarly suggest that, in late adulthood, the speed with which the brain registers new information declines—so if information is presented too rapidly, some of it may be lost (Fozard, 1990; Poon, 1985). Thus an older adult who is searching for a friend at a busy airport, or who is trying to understand instructions from a fast-talking doctor or lawyer, will be likely to miss some of the information that a younger adult would obtain.

In general, however, the age-related slowdown in sensory registration is rather minimal and can easily be compensated for (such as by asking an informant to slow down, or by writing down and rereading instructions). It is certainly not enough to account for the overall decline in information processing associated with age, which most researchers attribute to memory deficits rather than to sensory difficulties (Craik, 1977; Poon, 1985).

However, it is important to note that because of age-related changes that occur in the sensory systems, the information that reaches the sensory register may differ between older and younger adults (Verrillo and Verrillo, 1985). The older person's sensory receptors, especially the eyes and ears, become less adept at picking up sensory stimuli, especially stimuli that are ambiguous or of low intensity (Fozard, 1990). The vision and hearing losses that often accompany late adulthood mean that in addition to perceptual slowing, older people cannot even begin to register some information—like the details of a dimly lit room or a soft conversation spoken against a noisy background—because the sensory stimuli in question are undetected.

Figure 24.1 *Asking your partner to speak louder, or leaning closer to hear better, are strategies that many older adults use to compensate for the decreased acuity of sensory systems that accompany aging.*

Working Memory

Once information is perceived, it must be placed in working memory. As discussed in Chapter 2, **working memory** is the processing component through which your current, conscious mental activity occurs. Like a PC, working memory has two interrelated functions (Salthouse, 1990). The first is to temporarily store information so it can be consciously used. As in a PC,

Figure 24.2 *Decreases in the capacity of working memory with aging can make it difficult to remember and analyze complex instructions by phone unless the information is written down.*

working memory is constantly replenished with new information (from the sensory register or the knowledge base) that it retains for current use, and it discards old information (or transfers it to the knowledge base) when it is no longer relevant to current tasks. The second function of working memory is to process information: using the information it has stored, working memory enables integrative reasoning, mental calculations, the drawing of inferences, and other mental processes. In a sense, working memory functions both as a temporary information repository and as an analytical processor of information.

In terms of both storage and processing functions, older adults seem to have smaller working-memory capacity than do younger adults (Hultsch and Dixon, 1990; Lovelace, 1990a, 1990b; Salthouse, 1990). Older individuals are particularly likely to experience difficulty holding new information in mind while simultaneously analyzing it in complex ways. Laboratory research indicates, for example, that older adults are not quite as good as younger adults at remembering a short series of numbers they have just heard, and have even greater difficulty if they have to work with the numbers while remembering them—repeating them in reverse order, for instance.

The same trend is true of more meaningful material, such as remembering and analyzing the content of a paragraph or an essay (Rice and Meyer, 1986; Zelinkski et al., 1984). In one study (Light and Capps, 1986), younger and older adults (averaging ages 24 and 71, respectively) were asked to listen to short sentences and designate the probable antecedent for ambiguous pronouns. In each case, the context provided clear clues to the likely answer. For example, in *"Henry spoke at a meeting while John drove to the beach. He brought along a surfboard,"* it is likely that "He" refers to John, whereas in *"Henry spoke at a meeting while John drove to the beach. He lectured on the administration,"* it is likely that "He" refers to Henry. On tasks such as these, older and younger adults performed equally. However, when a sentence or two separated the pronoun and its antecedent—as in *"Henry spoke at a meeting while John drove to the beach. It was a nice day, and there was the the sound of activity in the streets. He brought along a surfboard"*—older adults were significantly less adept at identifying who "He" referred to, because the intervening sentence made it more difficult for them to integrate information from the first and the third sentences while keeping the entire paragraph in mind. As the authors of this study concluded, "under conditions of high memory load . . . , memory problems may masquerade as comprehension problems." If memory load or processing demands are not influential, however, older adults understand and remember the meanings of text passages just as well as younger adults.

One way to compensate for declines in storage and processing functions in older adults is to provide them with additional time to analyze information coming into working memory. In one study (Pezdek and Miceli, 1982), subjects of various ages were tested on their ability to recall forty-eight slides (half of them pictorial, half of them single sentences) presented at the rate of one every 8 seconds. College-age students performed the best on this task, and older adults the worst. However, when the older adults were given 15 seconds per slide, their performance increased markedly. Evidence such as this suggests that if older adults are given additional time to actively process information while trying to remember it, their memory can be quite accurate.

Knowledge Base

The **knowledge base** consists of one's long-term storehouse of information and memories. In adults, the knowledge base involves two subcomponents. The first, called secondary (or long-term) memory, consists of information that is stored for several minutes to several years. The second, called tertiary (or remote) memory, includes information remembered for years or decades.

With increasing age, adults experience greater difficulty accessing information from secondary memory (Lovelace, 1990a; Salthouse, 1991). In laboratory studies that test long-term recall of word associations and other simple concepts, younger adults demonstrate faster and more accurate recall than do older adults. This difference is especially apparent when the memory task requires a deliberate effort to retain and later retrieve the information (such as when memorizing a telephone number, or a list of items to purchase, or directions to a particular location). Many researchers believe that one reason older adults experience difficulty with long-term memory is that they do not use efficient memory strategies for storing incoming information. Their failure to do so may be related to the diminished capacity of their working memory: the most effective memory strategies (such as devising some method of association, or reorganizing the information to be remembered) require considerable processing of information while it is still in working memory—and as we have seen, it is more difficult for older individuals to simultaneously store and complexly process information in working memory.

On the other hand, retrieval of information from remote, or tertiary, memory may be quite good in older adults, perhaps because it was stored at a much earlier age and/or has been frequently retrieved. Of course, definitive research comparing tertiary memory in older and younger adults is difficult because it is almost impossible to verify personal recollections, especially with a large, representative sample of adults (Erber, 1982; Poon, 1985). One approach has been to compare people's memories of public events. But this approach may give an advantage to adults of one age group or another, depending on the particular question. For example, asking for the names of the heads of state at the Yalta Conference might favor people who were politically aware in 1945, whereas asking for the names of the Beatles may favor those who were teenagers in the 1960s. Since the interests and experiences of older and younger cohorts vary a great deal, it is hard to find any item that should be equally accessible from the memory of the average 70-year-old and the average 30-year-old.

Nevertheless, when attempts are made to compare tertiary memory across age groups, the results have been mixed, but often favorable to older persons (Botwinick and Storandt, 1980; Salthouse, 1991). One study compared how well Americans of various ages remembered the Spanish they had studied in high school or college—and had used very little since then. As might be expected, those young adults who had studied Spanish within the past three years remembered it best. Thereafter, however, the amount of forgetting was very gradual, with the older persons who studied Spanish fifty years earlier remembering about 80 percent of what the young adults who had studied it a mere five years earlier remembered. The crucial variable in how much Spanish was remembered was not how long ago the lan-

Figure 24.3 *Retrieving information efficiently from one's knowledge base can be a challenge to older adults when they must, for example, begin conversing in a foreign language learned long ago. Relying on memory aids, such as a bilingual dictionary, is a good way of adapting to this challenge.*

guage had been studied but how well the person had learned it in the first place: those who had received As in Spanish fifty years earlier outscored those who had received Cs a mere twelve months before (Bahrick, 1984).

Control Processes

The final component of the human information-processing system functions in an executive role, regulating the analysis and flow of information within the system (Salthouse, 1992). These **control processes**, as you recall from Chapter 2, include memory strategies used to retain information in the knowledge base, retrieval strategies for reaccessing that information on a later occasion, and rules-of-thumb that aid problem solving. For example, when you are unable to spontaneously retrieve information from memory, you probably do not just "wait around," hoping it will spring to mind. More likely, you begin a systematic search for it, or try to "prime" your recall by remembering related information. Your selection of a retrieval strategy and evaluation of its success reveal your use of control processes in analyzing information.

Older adults use simpler, less efficient control processes to remember new information (Herzog et al., 1990; Lovelace, 1990a, 1990c). For example, in laboratory studies, older adults are less likely to rehearse new information, or to chunk items together, or to try to link a new piece of information with something familiar (Bruce et al., 1982; Rice and Meyer, 1986). Furthermore, when approaching a task involving memory, older adults are more likely to underestimate the difficulty of the task than younger adults, and may consequently use simpler memory strategies. On other control processes, however, older and younger adults show considerable similarity: their knowledge of how their own memory works is comparable and they are equally skilled at monitoring their memory and recall abilities (Lovelace, 1990c; Salthouse, 1991). Thus the deficits in memory-related control processes that older adults experience are specific rather than global, and are especially associated with using complex memory strategies to aid in their storage of new information.

Similarly, the use of less efficient strategies helps account for the fact that older adults are not as good at abstract problem solving as young adults are (Arenberg, 1982; Reese and Rodeheaver, 1985). One standard test of problem-solving ability is the game of Twenty Questions. As you probably know, the object of this game is to guess the person, place, or thing another player has in mind, using no more than twenty questions that can be answered "yes" or "no." The best strategy is to begin with broad, general questions and then ask increasingly specific ones, progressively narrowing the categories to which the object might belong. Asking if the object is animate or inanimate, human or nonhuman, living or dead, male or female, and other general questions is clearly a better problem-solving method than starting off with specific guesses such as "Is it this chair?" "Is it Uncle Glen?" or "Is it Canada?"

Laboratory tests on Twenty Questions reveal distinct age-related differences in the logical structures used to discover the secret object (Denney and Palmer, 1981). Children, for instance, tend to guess impulsively and redundantly; teenagers and young adults are much more systematic in their approach. However, as Denney and Palmer found, in concurrence with many other studies of problem solving, skill level falls as adulthood progresses. Older adults are less adept at logically narrowing the possibilities than are middle-aged adults, who themselves are less skilled than younger adults. This finding is one of many that show that problem-solving strategies decline with age, beginning in early adulthood.

Reasons for Age-Related Changes

We have seen that advanced age brings some decrement to cognitive functioning, but not in every area (Perlmutter et al., 1987). These changes pose a challenge for theorists who seek to explain why these changes occur. Of course, declines in cognitive functioning may be tied to the aging process itself, and result from the neurophysiological and biological changes described in the previous chapter. However, there are other factors affecting cognitive performance that are also associated with age and which provide alternative—or supplementary—explanations for the cognitive changes we have noted. These include changes in the self-perceptions of older adults, diminished resources for information processing, and the effects of health and education.

Self-Perceptions of Cognitive Abilities

To an older adult, one of the most salient and significant changes associated with aging is memory decline (Cavanaugh and Green, 1990; Hertzog et al., 1990; Hultsch and Dixon, 1990; Salthouse, 1991). Because cultural stereotypes of aging emphasize memory impairment and the loss of control over memory ability, even unimportant experiences like forgetting somebody's name or misplacing reading glasses can seem ominous if they are perceived as signs of growing forgetfulness or even dementia. It is one thing to experience memory lapses in one's mid-30s, when they can be attributed to absentmindedness or a hectic schedule; it is quite another to experience these lapses in one's mid-60s, when they seem to confirm cultural expectations of memory declines in old age (Thompson, 1992). Indeed, under the influence of such expectations, older adults may tend to overestimate the memory

Figure 24.4 *Practice, or the lack of it, is one reason cognitive abilities remain strong in some older adults and fade in others. Dr. Eileen Gersh, shown here in her 70s, continued to teach college biology as she had done much of her life, and published her first book,* The Biology of Women, *after her 70th birthday.*

skills they had in young adulthood and so perceive their current memory loss to be greater than it actually is.

The consequence of such misperception may be the loss of **memory self-efficacy**—that is, a loss of confidence in one's memory and related cognitive skills (Cavanaugh and Green, 1990). In turn, this loss of memory self-efficacy can diminish motivation—and the effort—to succeed in situations requiring these skills (Perlmutter et al., 1987). Older adults may be more cautious, and thus slower, in responding to questions requiring recall, and their lack of self-confidence and accompanying anxiety may undermine the accuracy of their recollections. Correspondingly, others may perceive the older person's hesitancy as a sign of impaired memory and react in ways that reinforce the person's uncertainty about his or her memory. Laboratory studies indicate that differences in memory self-efficacy correlate with actual performance in memory and reasoning tasks—adults who have low memory self-efficacy also perform poorly on memory tests—but it is unclear whether these differences in self-perception are a cause or a consequence of memory decline (Lovelace, 1990c; Salthouse, 1991). Quite likely, they are *both*: self-perceptions of memory ability probably decline as actual memory decrements occur, and some older adults may have diminished motivation to adapt to, or compensate for, memory loss because of their diminished sense of self-efficacy.

Reduced Processing Resources

Another way of thinking about the cognitive changes of late adulthood has been proposed by Timothy Salthouse (1990, 1991, 1992). He believes that these changes can be attributed to decrements in one or more of the processing resources that enable, or enhance, certain cognitive abilities. This explanation emphasizes that certain cognitive resources are necessary for one to be an efficient, insightful thinker, and the progressive loss of these resources undermines effective information-processing.

Processing resources include the speed of behavior and thought, a large capacity in working memory, and the efficient deployment of attention. As we have seen, older adults experience decrements in all three of these resources. We have seen, for example, that one significant difference between older and younger adults is that older adults require more time to accomplish certain aspects of cognitive processing—that is, they are slower thinkers (Cerella, 1990). Recall that older adults experience greater difficulty when required to simultaneously store and analyze information in working memory because their capacity is more limited. Finally, especially when older people must pay attention to several things at once, they are more likely than younger people to be distracted by irrelevant stimuli (Hoyer and Plude, 1980; Welford, 1985). That is, their attention processes have become less efficient.

One implication of this view is that when cognitive demands are reduced, the processing resources of older adults are sufficient to enable them to do well. As we have seen, this is generally true. Thus the portrayal of late adult cognitive changes based on diminished processing resources not only provides a broad view of why many features of cognitive processing decline with age, but also offers suggestions for how older adults can compensate for these changes.

Health

Virtually every study has found that good cognitive functioning and good health are positively correlated (Labouvie-Vief, 1985): middle-aged and older adults in good physical health have a clear intellectual advantage over their less healthy contemporaries. Longitudinal research also shows that intellectual quickness and acuity fall when health fades or, more accurately, that they follow the same trajectory.

One category of health problems that seems to be particularly detrimental to cognitive functioning involves the circulatory system. People who have heart disease or untreated hypertension, for example, also tend to show reduced intellectual ability, perhaps because the same circulatory problems that caused those conditions also affect blood flow to the brain (Cunningham, 1987; Eisdorfer, 1977; Schaie, 1990a). Degenerative physical conditions like alcoholism, and mental-health problems like depression, also reduce intellectual capability (Cunningham and Tomer, 1990).

As you can see, there are a variety of possible explanations for the kinds of cognitive declines that can appear in late adulthood, ranging from the motivational (self-perceptions of memory ability) to the decremental (diminished processing resources) to the biological (health problems). Quite likely, a constellation of influences explains these age-related intellectual declines, and also accounts for individual differences in cognitive functioning among older adults. The next question for researchers, then, is, How modifiable are these age-related decrements?

Can Intellectual Decrements Be Reduced or Eliminated?

Researchers have recently designed a variety of training procedures intended to improve the memory and reasoning skills of older adults (Kotler-Cope and Camp, 1990; Willis, 1987, 1990a). Some procedures have provided guided instruction in using mnemonic or problem-solving strategies; others have provided practice in various cognitive tasks to increase familiarity with them; some have focused on heightening self-confidence and reducing anxiety. Such training interventions have lasted from one session to fifty conducted over a period of months, and follow-up studies of the effectiveness of training have occurred several days to several years afterward.

One of the best-known programs is the Adult Development and Aging Project (ADEPT), designed by Sherry Willis and Paul Baltes (Baltes and Willis, 1982; Willis, 1990a; Willis and Nesselroade, 1990). These researchers sought to improve cognitive skills related to fluid intelligence, which, as we saw in Chapter 21, involves flexible reasoning used to draw inferences or understand relations between concepts and which typically begins to decline in late adulthood. Accordingly, they had adults in their 60s participate in five, one-hour, small-group training sessions that involved demonstrations of appropriate problem-solving skills by a trainer, individual practice on these skills, with feedback from the trainer, and, finally, group discussion of what skills seemed to work best. Follow-up assessments one week, one month, and six months after the training sessions demonstrated significant gains for the adults in the training groups compared to a control group that

RESEARCH REPORT   Practical Competence in a Nursing Home

The picture that research presents of cognitive functioning in late adulthood is fairly optimistic: despite age-related declines in memory and abstract reasoning, older adults often acquire strategies for adapting to these changes so they can competently manage the demands of everyday life. But remember that this picture is based largely on studies of healthy, well-educated older adults living independently in the community. These adults are easiest for researchers to enlist in their studies and they are cooperative subjects—but they may also provide an overly rosy view. Consider as an alternative, for example, the elderly residents of a nursing home. Quite clearly, their living conditions often do not foster the kinds of practical competencies that are experienced by older adults living independently. Indeed, many nursing homes reinforce passive, dependent, and predictable behavior, and discourage behavior that is active, independent, or innovative. For example, residents who do not manage their own personal care or hygiene—who, say, just sit staring at their food when it is placed before them—are likely to receive help and attention from the staff; those who manage for themselves are likely to be ignored. Similarly, those who stick to the nursing home's schedules and routines are much more likely to be praised than those who, against the rules, attempt to get a midnight snack, or want to go shopping on a day not designated as a shopping day, or try to keep a pet in their room. When older patients ask for an explanation of some medicine or therapy or, worse, refuse to cooperate with some aspect of their medical treatment, they are likely to be labeled as mentally impaired and disruptive, and to be treated accordingly. (Similar behavior in younger persons is much more likely to be regarded as a sign of mental alertness.) One review sums up, with frightening clarity, the conditions that prevail in many nursing homes:

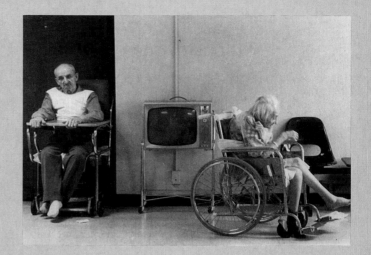

When nursing-home residents are isolated and dependent (note the physical restraints that prevent the people on the left from trying to stand), their cognitive abilities are likely to deteriorate. By contrast, residents can find zest in life when they have the opportunity to socialize and to maintain their interests or develop new ones. In some nursing homes, "visiting

. . . the individual. . . gives up control over the most mundane daily activities, when to sleep, wake, visit, perform toileting activities, bathe, and shop. The patient is exposed to infantilization and numbing bureaucratic and health routines that are of obscure purpose due to the invariably poor communication and misinformation given to placate the patient. Information is withheld or distorted under the assumption that it will not be understood or well-tolerated by the patient. [White and Janson, 1986]

However, research has shown that when the opposite approach is used, and nursing-home patients are encour-

received no training. Furthermore, in a long-term follow-up study of adults in their 70s and early 80s—who had participated in several training sessions in their 60s and 70s—Willis and Nesselroade (1990) reported that these old-old adults were still performing at a level surpassing their initial performance on cognitive tests seven years earlier!

Do findings such as these reflect the remediation of age-related cognitive declines? Without data on the performance of these adults in middle adulthood it is difficult to tell. However, a similar training procedure has been used with subjects in the Seattle Longitudinal Study (SLS) which, as you recall from Chapter 21, was initiated by K. Warner Schaie in 1956 as a sequential research study of adult intellectual development (Schaie and Willis, 1986; Willis and Schaie, 1986). For these subjects, therefore, there

pet" programs provide the elderly with an undemanding companionship that can lighten spirits and improve cognitive and social functioning. These lessons learned from the minority of older adults who are in nursing homes apply also to the majority of older adults in the community at large.

aged to manage on their own as much as possible, many learn to take more control of their activities, developing their own schedules and social lives as well as becoming more responsible for their daily care (Piper and Langer, 1986).

Other research shows that nursing-home residents can learn to improve their perspective-taking skills. One commonly cited characteristic of nursing-home residents is their egocentrism: on Piagetian tasks, they often show themselves to be limited to their own perspective; in daily life, they typically seem greatly absorbed in their own problems and needs, with little awareness of those of their fellow residents. The goal of one research project was to reduce this egocentrism (Zaks and Labouvie-Vief, 1980). The researchers tested the ability of nursing-home residents to understand other points of view and then divided the residents into three groups that were equal in terms of age, health, and performance on the tests. One group was given special training in social understanding. The members participated in discussions and role-playing, centering on problems that might occur in the home (such as what could be done if one roommate liked to watch television late at night and the other liked to sleep). A second group discussed such problems but did not role-play. The third group, the control group, had no special training at all.

On retesting after the training period, the residents in the first group who had had the most active social-learning training were markedly less egocentric than the other two groups, and they improved in their ability to communicate with each other. As the authors of the study concluded, a substantial part of the egocentrism of older institutionalized adults may be caused by their lack of social interaction rather than by their cognitive inability to see other points of view.

Together, these research projects lead to a clear conclusion. Overall, when cognitive deficits appear in older people, trying to find a way to remedy them is a better approach than sympathetically accepting the deficits as inevitable. This is as true for nursing-home residents as for older people who live independently, and the social environment of the nursing home can play an important role in enhancing—or blunting—practical competence in nursing-home residents.

were longitudinal data concerning their cognitive performance for the fourteen year period prior to their training. Like the adults in the ADEPT study, those who participated in the training sessions from the SLS improved significantly in measures of fluid intelligence. Indeed, approximately 40 percent of those who had earlier experienced decline in these measures improved to the levels they had shown fourteen years earlier. Moreover, even adults who had *not* declined during this fourteen-year period showed improvement from training, suggesting that the gains shown by both groups may have been due to the learning of new problem-solving skills as well as to the reacquiring of lost skills. For those who had declined, these new skills compensated for earlier decrements; for those who had remained stable, these new skills improved their abilities.

Sherry Willis (1990b) has summarized these investigations by noting that they highlight

> the considerable plasticity in older adults' cognitive performance. . . . If some of the improvement through training in the elderly represents remediation of previous age-related decline, then training research is useful in examining the question of in which individuals, for what abilities, and under what conditions intellectual decline is reversible or remediable. . . . Finally, cognitive training research has the potential to contribute relevant information to the development of programs and services for the elderly that will enhance their ability to live independently and productively in our society.

This is good news, but some qualifications are necessary. First, this research (and most studies like it) enlists relatively healthy, well-functioning adults who are living independently in the community (Willis, 1990). Consequently, we know much less about how effective cognitive training might be for older adults who are institutionalized, cognitively impaired, or in poor health (see Research Report on pp. 620–621). Second, although plasticity may characterize the intellectual performance of adults of all ages, there is evidence that plasticity declines with increasing age (Denney, 1990; Kliegl et al., 1989, 1990). As a result, the gains that older adults might derive from cognitive training are unlikely to match the gains that younger adults would derive from the same kinds of training. In sum, the results of cognitive-training studies indicate that many of the intellectual decrements that occur with advancing age can be remediated, or compensated for, by new strategies, but that there may be limits to the plasticity of later-life cognition.

But another question can be posed. In practical terms, how important or meaningful are the intellectual decrements that occur with age? Do they significantly impair everyday behavior? And can older adults find ways of compensating for them in their daily lives?

Cognitive Functioning in the Real World

When older people are asked about their memory, most readily acknowledge that it is not as keen as it used to be, corroborating the laboratory research that finds deficits in memory with age. However, most older adults do not consider memory loss a significant handicap in daily life (Sunderland et al., 1986). What's more, when older adults are asked about their problem-solving ability, they say that they are better at solving "everyday problems" than they used to be (Williams et al., 1983). How do we explain this difference between scientists' findings in the laboratory and older adults' "findings" in the real world? Part of the answer lies in the difference between the cognitive skills tested in laboratories and those used in everyday situations.

Memory

In the typical laboratory experiment on memory, adults are given items to remember within a specific time, and then are tested on the accuracy and speed of their retrieval processes. In order to control for the unfair advantage that would result if someone was very familiar with, or unusually interested in, the material to be remembered, memory tests usually consist of items that are fairly meaningless, perhaps a string of unrelated words or numbers. This control, in combination with time limits, also has the effect of making it difficult for subjects to repeat and review the test material. This is particularly deleterious to older adults, since they are more likely than their younger counterparts to benefit from working with familiar materials and being given additional time and repeated practice. For example, practice in various cognitive tasks can bring the performance of older people beyond that of younger, less practiced people (Beres and Baron, 1981; Bruce and Herman, 1986).

The typical memory experiment may also put older persons at a disadvantage with respect to spontaneous priming. Priming refers to the fact that bringing one item forth from memory makes it quicker and easier to bring forth other, related items. We all use priming in daily life: if you misplace your wallet, for instance, you may mentally review the activities of your day, hoping to trigger a memory of the place you put your wallet last; if you forget someone's name, you may try to recall other things about that person, or go through the letters of the alphabet, until the name comes to you. Most memory experiments, however, are constructed to exclude much opportunity for spontaneous priming, thereby depriving older adults of a cognitive tool that is very useful to them in daily life (Howard et al., 1986).

Finally, motivation may be a critical variable in tests of memory. Young college students might have an advantage in a laboratory because they are accustomed to learning material that is not immediately relevant to their lives. As Schaie noted, they are in the "acquiring" stage of cognitive development (see Chapter 18). Older adults, by contrast, may be much more likely to question the purpose of such learning, and therefore may try less hard to commit test items to memory. In daily life, however, older people are more motivated to work at remembering by using memory aids, especially if they are aware of possible memory problems (Perlmutter, 1986).

In many cases, the cumulative effect of practice, priming, and enhanced motivation can offset the memory loss that laboratory research has so often found in older adults. One study designed to mimic the memory demands of daily life illustrates this point well. Older and younger adults (all living busy lives) were asked to call a telephone answering service every day for two weeks, at a designated time they had picked as convenient. One reason this activity was chosen is that remembering appointments is something everyone must do in daily life, and is also something many older people say they have difficulty with. The researchers were surprised to find that only 20 percent of the younger adults remembered to make every call, and that 90 percent of the older adults did.

Why the dramatic difference? Younger adults, it seems, were likely to put excessive trust in their memories ("I have an internal alarm that always goes off at the right time") and therefore were less likely to use mnemonic devices. Older adults, with a heightened awareness of the vagaries of memory, used reminders, such as a note on the telephone or a shoe near the door, and thus almost always called on time.

The experimenters then attempted to increase the rate of forgetting in the older adults by asking for only one call per week, at a time designated by the researcher, and by making the subjects promise to avoid using any visible reminders of the appointment. This time the results were, indeed, much different: about half the elderly and an equal proportion of the young missed calling at the appointed time. And it seems likely that the number of old people who forgot the appointment might have been greater, since some of the older subjects continued to use some memory-priming measures of sorts, carrying the phone number in a visible place in their wallet, for instance, despite instructions to keep it out of sight. One of the researchers concludes:

> With more effort, we are sure we can bring old people's memory to its knees . . . , but that hardly seems to be the point of this research. The main lesson of this venture into the dangerous real world is that old people have learned from experience what we have so consistently shown in the laboratory—that their memory is getting somewhat poorer—and they have structured their environment to compensate. [Moscovitch, 1982]

As we saw in Chapter 21, many researchers believe that a hallmark of "successful aging" is the capacity to strategically compensate for intellectual declines associated with age—what Paul Baltes and his colleagues call "selective optimization with compensation" (Baltes, 1987; Baltes and Baltes, 1990; Baltes et al., 1984). Using mnemonic devices, allowing additional time for problem solving, and practice all reflect this adaptive quality of practical intelligence in later life.

Problem Solving

Research on reasoning ability also shows that problem solving in daily life is far less impaired with age than problem solving in the scientist's laboratory (Cavenaugh et al., 1985; Reese and Rodeheaver, 1985). For example, after giving adults of various ages the test of Twenty Questions, and finding, as expected, that the youngest adults did best, Denney and Palmer (1981) gave these same adults problems of practical intelligence (see Chapter 21)—such as what to do if you are caught in a blizzard, or if your refrigerator feels warm, or if your 8-year-old daughter is not home from school when you expect her. On these problems, the highest scores were attained by adults in their 40s, with only a very gradual decline in the scores after that. Adults in their 60s scored only slightly below the adults in their 20s.

Other studies using real-life contexts have found similar results. For example, in a study comparing young, middle-aged, and older adults (average ages 19, 46, and 68) on answers to complex real-life problems (such as how to solve a hostage dilemma), the oldest were the most dialectical and least mechanistic in their solutions (Kramer and Woodruff, 1986). Another study compared levels of moral thought in two groups of adults, one between the ages of 30 and 49, and the other between the ages of 63 and 85. When years of education were taken into account, the two groups showed no age-related differences in moral thinking overall. However, older adults were better at dilemmas that involved an older person, such as what should be done with an elderly man who lived alone on a fixed income and who occasionally shoplifted items of food (Chap, 1985–1986). This difference suggests, once again, that whether a person finds cognitive tests interesting or personally relevant affects his or her performance on them.

Of course, even these examples are artificial. What about the real-life problems that people actually face? One researcher asked 405 people how they coped with their problems (McCrae, 1982). Contrary to the popular stereotype of the elderly as rigid, stubborn thinkers, the older people were as likely as younger adults to think rationally about their problems, to seek help, and to express their feelings to someone else. At the same time, their thinking differed from that of younger people in several constructive ways:

Figure 24.5 *The idea that reasoning and moral judgment may remain strong even as the body weakens is illustrated in many real-life cases. Popes, heads of state, and supreme Court justices (shown here) often deliver their most memorable and powerful pronouncements when they are over age 70.*

they were less likely to use escapist fantasies, to react with hostility, or to blame themselves. Although older adults must sometimes cope with social environments, such as nursing homes, that undermine rather than enhance their practical competence (see Research Report, pp. 620–621), most older adults are capable of tackling real-life cognitive challenges with skill and determination, if given the opportunity to do so.

When all the evidence is considered, then, it seems that although information processing of all kinds slows down in late adulthood (Hale et al., 1987; Herzog et al., 1986), and that memory and abstract problem-solving ability probably decline in other ways as well, an older adult's ability to cope with the cognitive demands of daily life may not be significantly impaired by these changes. While declines are observable for most people in their 60s, and for virtually everyone by their 80s, these declines are limited in scope and severity, are more apparent in the laboratory than in daily life, and are affected a great deal by factors other than age—health, self-perceptions, and specific learning experiences among them.

In short, the picture of cognitive ability in old age appears to be quite good—with one notable, heartrending exception—dementia.

TABLE 24.1 Estimated Prevalence of Dementia	
Age	Prevalence
65–69	2%
70–74	3%
75–79	6%
80–84	12%
85–89	22%
90 +	41%

Based on studies in Japan, Australia, New Zealand, Britain, Sweden, and Denmark (Preston, 1986).

Dementia

In ordinary conversation, pathological loss of intellectual ability in elderly people is often referred to as "senility." However, this term inaccurately emphasizes the factor of age. A better and more precise term for pathological loss of intellectual functioning is **dementia**—literally, severely impaired thinking, memory, or problem-solving ability (Davies, 1988). Although dementia is more likely to occur among the aged, it can occur before old age. At the same time, it is by no means an inevitable occurrence of old age, even among the very old (see Table 24.1).

Dementia can be caused by a variety of diseases and circumstances, but the general symptoms are similar: severe memory loss, rambling conversation and language lapses, confusion about place and time, inability to function socially or professionally, and changes in personality. Traditionally, when dementia occurred before age 60, it was called *presenile dementia*; when it occurred after age 60, it was referred to as *senile dementia* or *senile psychosis*. This age-based distinction was quite arbitrary, for the symptoms, causes, and treatments are the same no matter what the person's age.

Stages of Dementia

Dementia is usually progressive, with identifiable stages (Reisberg et al., 1985). It begins with a general forgetfulness, particularly of names and places. A common problem is putting something away and then forgetting where it is.

In this early stage, most people recognize that they have a memory problem and try to cope with it, writing down names, addresses, appointments, shopping lists, and other items, much more than they once did. This first stage is often indistinguishable from the "benign forgetfulness" that many older people experience, according to a leading researcher (Reisberg, 1981). Many people reach this first stage and remain somewhat forgetful for the rest of their lives, but never get any worse (Roth et al., 1985).

In the second stage, more general confusion occurs, and there are noticeable deficits in concentration and short-term memory. People at this stage are often aimless and repetitious in conversation, and frequently mix up words, using "tunnel" when they mean "bridge," for instance. They are likely to read a newspaper article and forget it completely the next moment, or to put down their keys or glasses and within seconds have no idea where they could be. Personality changes also occur, with the individual becoming somewhat withdrawn and out of touch—except for occasional overreactions, such as a sudden outburst of temper or tears.

The accumulation of symptoms in the second stage makes it quite clear to others that something is seriously amiss, but most of the people who are in this stage of dementia deny that anything is wrong, to themselves and to others. When asked a question that tests their memory, say, "Who is president now?" they are likely to answer evasively and defensively, with something like "I don't follow politics any more" (Roth et al., 1985). One woman, a lawyer, insisted that it was obvious she had no serious memory loss: "Otherwise I couldn't work as an attorney. I couldn't go to court. I couldn't prepare a case." However, as her husband and law partner explained the actual situation:

> She doesn't really have clients anymore. I let her come to the office, but she hasn't tried a case in years. . . . She keeps misplacing and losing documents. But I'd rather have her at the office. It makes her feel better. She's always worked, she wouldn't know what to do at home. [quoted in Reisberg, 1981]

The third stage begins when memory loss becomes truly dangerous and people are no longer able to take care of their basic needs. They may take to eating a single food, like bread, exclusively, or they may forget to eat at all. Often they fail to dress properly, going out barefoot in winter or walking about the neighborhood half-naked. They are likely to turn away from a lighted stove or a hot iron and completely forget about it for the rest of the day. They might go out on some errand and then lose track not only of the errand but also of the way back home.

Eventually, demented persons need full-time care. They not only cannot take care of themselves; they also do not respond normally to others, sometimes becoming irrationally angry or paranoid. At the end, they no longer can put even a few words together to communicate, and they fail to recognize their closest relatives.

While these general symptoms and stages are the same for all forms of dementia, there actually are several distinct types, each with different risk factors and treatment.

Alzheimer's Disease

Approximately 70 percent of all people who suffer from dementia are afflicted with **Alzheimer's disease**, a disorder characterized by the proliferation of certain abnormalities in the cerebral cortex, called plaques and tangles, that destroy normal brain functioning (Roth et al., 1985). Until recently, the term "Alzheimer's disease" was reserved for symptoms of dementia in people under age 60, while the same symptoms in people over age 60 were termed "senility." However, new techniques for analyzing brain tissue on autopsy show that no matter what the age of the victim, the brain damage takes the same form, and that the amount of plaques and tangles correlates not with the victim's age but with the degree of intellectual impairment before death.

These are some age-related characteristics, however. When Alzheimer's disease appears in middle age, it usually progresses more quickly, reaching the last phase within three to five years, while in late adulthood it can take ten years or more to run its course. Alzheimer's disease in middle age is relatively rare. By late adulthood it affects one in every twenty adults (mostly over age 75), altogether affecting an estimated 3 million people in the United States. This number is expected to rise dramatically in the next decades, when the baby boomers reach late adulthood (Holden, 1987).

Figure 24.6 *"What day is it? Where am I?"—These are two questions that are frequently asked by Alzheimer's victims. In the early stages of this disorder, memory for dates, places, and names fades much more quickly than memory for basic skills, such as reading, so visual aids like the one shown here are likely to help when memory falters.*

While Alzheimer's disease does not usually appear until late adulthood, the disease probably originates decades earlier. In fact, one form is inherited, caused directly by a dominant gene located on chromosome 21 that synthesizes toxins that gradually build up (Hardy and Higgins, 1992; Kosik, 1992; Selkoe, 1990). Many forms of Alzheimer's disease are multifactorial, caused by the combination of a genetic vulnerability and other life circumstances—although no one knows what these circumstances are (Breitner, 1988; St. George-Hyslop et al., 1987). It is believed that one likely causative agent might be a "slow" virus, perhaps one contracted in childhood but kept at bay by the immune system until old age; another might be the cumulative effect of toxins derived from one's diet or the environment. Whatever its origins, Alzheimer's disease undermines the neurons and neurotransmitters of brain systems that are directly relevant to memory, planning, and other kinds of intellectual processes (Katzman, 1987).

There is no way to definitely diagnose Alzheimer's disease apart from examining brain tissue for plaques and tangles, either by biopsy (surgically removing a small piece of brain tissue) or, after death, by autopsy. Most commonly, a diagnosis of Alzheimer's disease is based on a complex medical assessment (involving a patient history, a physical, psychological, and neurological exam, and other tests) to assess symptoms and eliminate alternative explanations (Crystal, 1988).

Early and accurate diagnosis is important chiefly to help the patient and family begin to cope and plan for the future, for despite intense research efforts to control Alzheimer's disease with special diets or drugs, at the moment nothing seems to prevent the disorder or slow its progress. The victim of Alzheimer's disease eventually becomes utterly powerless: inexorably, day by day, month by month, memory fades, until the individual cannot remember how to do something as simple as using a fork; cannot recognize loved ones; cannot even control body functions.

Thus, the victims of Alzheimer's disease include not only the patient but the patient's family, who typically are the main source of care until the last stages of the disease. It is particularly hard for the family members to be understanding and patient with a person who seems in good health but is unable to behave or think normally, and who sometimes becomes angry at efforts to help (Deimling and Bass, 1986; Gatz et al., 1990). Almost always, the time comes when the family must seek help in caregiving, but paying for home-care aides or for nursing-home care is usually problematic: few insurance plans cover the long-term care of those with Alzheimer's disease.

The burden that Alzheimer's disease places on the family makes it difficult not to blame the victim. One man writes movingly about his feelings of helplessness as his father shouted at his mother to "think harder, think harder" when she forgot where she had placed something. She was sufficiently early in the disease to be distressed at his shouting and at her loss of memory and she wandered about the house close to tears searching randomly for whatever she had lost (Sayre, 1979). Understandably, for family members, feelings of sadness and anger are often intermingled with feelings of guilt. In recent years, support groups and respite care services have arisen to help family members cope with the practical and emotional fallout of this disease (Lipkowitz, 1988).

Younger family members suffer in another way as well. Knowing that Alzheimer's disease is sometimes inherited inevitably makes them wonder if they, too, will be victims some day. Although genetic mapping may soon make it possible for some of them to find out for sure if they will develop the disease, probably many of them would rather not know unless a cure can be found.

Multi-Infarct Dementia

The second major type of dementia is **multi-infarct dementia (MID)**, which by itself is responsible for about 15 percent of all dementia, and in combination with Alzheimer's disease, accounts for another 25 percent. MID occurs because an *infarct*, or temporary obstruction of the blood vessels, prevents a sufficient supply of blood from reaching an area of the brain. This causes destruction of brain tissue, in what is commonly called a stroke, or ministroke, often so small the person is unaware that it has occurred.

The underlying cause of such obstructions is general arteriosclerosis (hardening of the arteries). People who have problems with their circulatory systems, including people with heart disease, hypertension, numbness or tingling in their extremities, and people with diabetes are at risk for arteriosclerosis and MID. Therefore, measures to improve circulation such as exercise, or to control hypertension and diabetes, such as diet and drugs, help to prevent MID and to slow or halt the progression of the disease if it occurs.

The progression of MID is quite different from that of Alzheimer's disease (see Figure 24.7). Typically, the person with MID shows a sudden drop in intellectual functioning following an infarct. Then, a., other parts of the brain take over some of the functions of the damaged area, the person becomes better.

However, the prognosis for MID is poor (Crook, 1987). As the name of the disease denotes, multiple infarcts typically occur, making it harder and harder for the remaining parts of the brain to compensate. If heart disease, major stroke, or other illnesses do not kill the MID victim, and ministrokes continue to occur, the person's behavior eventually becomes indistinguishable from that of the person suffering from Alzheimer's disease. On autopsy, however, it is clear that parts of the brain have become destroyed while other parts seem normal; the many plaques and tangles characteristic of Alzheimer's disease are not present.

Other Organic Causes of Dementia

Several other diseases also can cause dementia. The best-known of these is **Parkinson's disease**, which produces dementia—as well as the distinctive rigidity and/or tremor of the muscles—in 30 to 40 percent of its victims (Crook, 1987; Elias et al., 1990). Parkinson's disease is more likely to strike the aged than the young, but it is not exclusively an old person's disease: an estimated 8 percent of the victims are under age 40 when the disease is first diagnosed (Lewin, 1987). Parkinson's disease is related to the degeneration of neurons in an area of the brain that produces dopamine, a neurotransmitter essential to normal brain functioning. The underlying reason for this

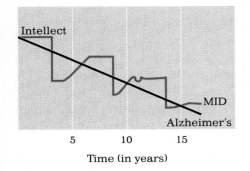

Figure 24.7 *As shown on this chart, cognitive decline is apparent in both Alzheimer's disease and multi-infarct dementia. However, the pattern of decline for each disease is different. Victims of Alzheimer's disease show steady, gradual decline while those who suffer from MID get suddenly much worse, improve somewhat, and then experience another serious loss.*

degeneration is not known. Among the factors implicated as contributors to Parkinson's disease are genetic vulnerability and certain viruses. An interesting finding is that dementia in Parkinson's is not usually evident until the destruction of brain cells has reached a certain threshold. It is likely that forgetfulness and confusion are caused when, and only when, the normal ability of the aging brain to compensate for neuron loss is overloaded (Roth et al., 1985). Other diseases that can result in dementia are Huntington's disease, Pick's disease, and AIDS.

Another cause of dementia is Down syndrome. Individuals with Down syndrome who survive to adulthood often develop the same patterns of memory losses and personality changes that occur in victims of Alzheimer's disease (Kolata, 1985). Since Down syndrome usually involves an extra chromosome at pair 21, the same location where the genetic defect for Alzheimer's disease is located, the same underlying problem probably causes dementia in both cases (Barnes, 1987a).

Brain tumors can also cause dementia, as can head injuries that result in an excess of fluid pressing on the brain. In these cases, surgery can often remedy the problem and restore normal cognitive functioning.

Nonorganic Causes of Dementia

It is not uncommon for the elderly to be assumed to be suffering from one form or another of brain disease when, in fact, their "symptomatic" behaviors are being caused by some other factor such as medication, alcohol, mental illness, or depression.

Medication and Malnutrition

Drug-related changes in intellectual functioning are common in the elderly for several reasons. First, adults over 65 use a disproportionately higher amount of prescription drugs than does any other age group (Perlmutter et al., 1987). Second, the appropriate dose of most prescription drugs is usually determined by tests on younger adults, yet the correct dose for a 30-year-old may be an overdose for the elderly, whose physiological ability to get rid of excess drugs is impaired. Not surprisingly, adverse reactions to various drugs are at least twice as common in adults over age 60 as they are in younger adults (Vestal and Dawson, 1985).

Third, many of the elderly, both at home and in institutions, take several prescription drugs every day, and a number of the drugs commonly taken (such as most of those to reduce high blood pressure, or combat Parkinson's disease, or mitigate pain) can, by themselves, slow down mental processes (La Rue et al., 1985). The intermixing of drugs can also have a deleterious effect. One survey found that 22 percent of the elderly took six or more drugs, often using drugs that interact with each other, exacerbating or negating their effects (Krupka and Vener, 1979).

In addition, malnutrition (see Chapter 23), especially deficiencies of B-vitamins and folic acid, can cause confusion and loss of memory, and can further exaggerate the effects of various drugs. Finally, if an older adult is already forgetful, he or she may take several pills on one day and none the next, compounding any drug-induced mental disorder.

Alcohol

One drug known to have serious effects on memory and other aspects of functioning is taken by an unknown number of the elderly—alcohol. While the rate of alcoholism is lower among elderly men than among younger men, the same cannot necessarily be said for women. It seems that a significant number of women, especially widows who live alone, become alcoholics in their later years (Nathan, 1983). Alcoholism among the elderly is more likely to take the form of steady, measured drinking rather than heavy drinking at a single sitting (La Rue et al., 1985). This type of "maintenance" drinking may be difficult for others to notice, since they might assume that some unsteady movement or slightly slurred speech or lapse of memory is attributable to age rather than to alcohol (Craik and Byrd, 1982).

Unfortunately, at the same blood alcohol levels, older adults show greater impairment of reaction time, memory, and decision making than younger adults. When these functions are already affected by age, the further declines produced by alcohol may reach the point where serious errors of judgment are likely to occur. As at every age, alcohol is a major contributor to accidental and suicidal death in old age. And when alcohol abuse is chronic, disruptions in central nervous system processes impair learning, reasoning, perception, and other mental functions in alcohol dementia (Thompson et al., 1987).

Psychological Illness

In general, psychological illnesses such as schizophrenia and personality disorders are less common in the elderly than in younger adults (La Rue et al., 1985). Nonetheless, about 10 percent of the elderly who are diagnosed as demented are actually experiencing psychological, rather than physiological, illness. In some cases, however, the person is merely unusually anxious, which, as anyone who has taken a final exam under pressure knows, can make even a bright and healthy person forget important information. For many older people, the anxiety that occurs on arrival at a hospital or nursing home is sufficient to cause substantial disorientation and loss of memory. If the anxious new arrival is tested immediately, a misdiagnosis of organic brain damage is possible.

Depression

Most older adults experience symptoms of depression at some time during their later years (Thompson et al., 1987). When depression is sufficiently debilitating to become a clinical disorder, however, its symptoms sometimes resemble those of dementia.

Depressed people are usually slow-moving, often do not seem to care about such basics as eating and dressing, ignore or become distracted during conversation, and, in late adulthood, may talk about losing their mental ability. In fact, talk about fading intellect is one clue that depression, not dementia, is the problem. People who are suffering from organic brain disease usually are ashamed of their loss, and often use denial as a coping mechanism, while those suffering from depression tend to exaggerate any loss of mental functions (Reisberg, 1981). In these cases, the cognitive declines as-

Figure 24.8 *Many older adults who seem to be demented are suffering from curable maladies that have symptoms similar to those of organic dementia. Among these diseases are malnutrition, depression, and alcoholism.*

sociated with depression are sometimes called "pseudodementia" (Kaszniak, 1990; Thompson et al., 1987; Teri and Reifler, 1987). To be sure, older adults with organic dementia (like Alzheimer's disease) may also be depressed. But it is important to distinguish whether intellectual declines are due to depression or to an organic dementia, because although the latter cannot be treated, depression can.

Depression in late adulthood, as at younger ages, is one of the most treatable mental illnesses (La Rue et al., 1985). Psychotherapy and pharmacotherapy usually effect notable improvement in a few weeks. However, even more than at younger ages, most depressed older people are not treated because no one recognizes their depression as a curable disease. Instead, many caregivers consider depression a natural consequence of aging, or they confuse the symptoms with those of brain disease. If the depressed person has recently lost a loved one, the symptoms of depression may mistakenly be attributed to bereavement. It is normal, of course, for the elderly who are in mourning to be sad and to have difficulty eating and sleeping, but the symptoms of bereavement do not normally include strong feelings of guilt and self-deprecation, or last longer than a few months (Breckenridge et al., 1986).

Sadly, one consequence of untreated depression among the elderly is that the suicide rate is higher for those over age 60 than for any other age group, and is one of the ten leading causes of death among older adults (Blazer et al., 1986; Sainsbury, 1986). In the United States, the suicide rate for white males at age 85 is three times that of white males at age 20 (Manton et al., 1986). Comparable statistics in other countries show an even wider disparity: in Japan, the ratio of suicide for those over age 75 is five times that of those between ages 15 and 24; in France, the rate is six times higher (Palmore and Meada, 1985).

In most cases, the precipitating event for the suicide is a social loss, with retirement or widowhood being the most common. A related cause is illness, particularly cancer or illnesses that affect the brain (Whitlock, 1986).

Figure 24.9 *One cause of depression in older adults is social isolation—when too many moments in the day are like this one. Although depression has become one of the easiest psychological disorders to treat, thanks to advances in psychotherapy and pharmacotherapy, many depressed older adults do not get treatment because their symptoms are misattributed or because they themselves are unlikely to believe that help is possible.*

About half of the elderly men, and a third of the elderly women, who commit suicide are physically ill. Even in cases of illness, however, severe depression, generally arising from fears about the possible consequences of the disease rather from the disease itself, is a factor in the suicide. On the whole, old people's fears about their illness are worse than the likely outcome. They do not realize that chronic pain, disability, and depression can usually be treated with drugs and other therapy (Whitlock, 1986). Depression is not an inevitable reaction to either the losses of age or the problems of illness, and thus it should not be accepted as such.

New Cognitive Development in Later Life

So far in this chapter we have mainly considered possible declines in the intellectual functioning of older adults. What about positive changes? Can older adults develop new interests, new patterns of thought, a deeper wisdom? Most of the major theorists on human development believe that they can. For example, Erik Erikson finds that the older generation are more interested in the arts, in children, and in the whole of human experience. They are the "social witnesses" to life, and thus are more aware of the interdependence between one generation and another (Erikson et al., 1986). Abraham Maslow maintains that older adults are much more likely than younger people to reach self-actualization, which, as you remember from Chapter 2, includes heightened aesthetic, creative, philosophical, and spiritual sensitivity (Maslow, 1970). Let us look, then, at these areas of life during late adulthood.

Aesthetic Sense

Many people seem to experience nature and the arts in a deeper, more appreciative way, as they get older. As two leading gerontologists explain, "healthy late life is frequently a time for greater enjoyment of all the senses—colors, sights, sounds, smells, touch—and less involvement in the transient drives of achievement, possession, and power" (Butler and Lewis, 1982).

For many older people, this heightened appreciation leads to active expression. They may begin gardening, bird-watching, pottery, painting, or playing a musical instrument—and not simply because they have nothing better to do. Among those who painted in earnest after age 60 were Winston Churchill, Dwight Eisenhower, and Henry Fonda—all of whom had many other activities (such as heading a nation or making major films) with which to fill up their days. The importance that creativity can have for some in old age is wonderfully expressed by a 79-year-old man, unfamous, little educated, yet joyful at his workbench:

> This is the happiest time of my life. . . . I wish there was twenty-four hours in a day. Wuk hours, awake hours. Yew can keep y' sleep; plenty of time for that later on . . . That's what I want all this here time for now—to make things. I draw and I paint too . . . I don't copy anything. I make what I remember. I tarn wood. I paint the fields. As I say, I've niver bin so happy in my whole life and I only hope I last out. [quoted in Blythe, 1979]

Figure 24.10 *While an enhanced appreciation of aesthetic beauty is typical of the elderly, the particular expression varies depending on the individual's talents, interests, and personality. An extrovert, for example, would be more likely to join some sort of group activity, such as singing in a chorus, while the introvert might choose a solitary activity, such as photography.*

For this man, and for many people, the impulse to create did not suddenly arise in late adulthood; it was present, although infrequently expressed, in earlier years. What does seem to occur in late adulthood is a deepening need to express and develop that impulse, perhaps because, as the years left to live become fewer, those people who were "bearers of a secret dream" decide to defer that dream no longer (McLeish, 1976). This was the case with Laura Ingalls Wilder, who did not begin to write her first book, *Little House in the Big Woods*, until she was 64. By the time she was 75, she had produced seven more novels in the world-famous "Little House" series (Kerber, 1980).

One of the most remarkable examples of late creative development is found in Anna Moses, a farm wife and mother of ten. For most of her life, she expressed her artistic sensitivity by stitching quilts and doing embroidery during the long farm winters, when little outside work could be done. At age 75, arthritis made needlework impossible, so she took to "dabbling in oil" instead. Four years later, three of her oil paintings, displayed in a local drugstore, caught the eye of a New York City art dealer who happened to be passing by. He bought them, drove to her house to buy fifteen more, and began to exhibit them in the city. One year later, at age 80, "Grandma Moses" had her first one-woman show in New York, receiving international recognition for her unique "primitive" style. She continued to paint, "incredibly gaining in assurance and artistic discretion" into her 90s (Yglesias, 1980).

Philosophical Turns of Mind

Many older people become more reflective and philosophical than they once were. In most cases, this reflectivity is personally centered, as the individual attempts to put his or her life in perspective, assessing accomplishments and failures in terms of what the person perceives to be the overall scheme of life. Neugarten (1973) refers to this turn of mind as **interiority**, a heightening of the older person's propensity for introspection. Erikson points to a similar pattern in his depiction of the final stage of psychosocial development, integrity versus despair, in which the individual attempts to see his or her life as a meaningful whole.

Another formulation of this attempt to put one's life into perspective is called the **life review** (Butler, 1963), in which an older person recalls and recounts various aspects of his or her life, remembering the highs and lows, and comparing the past with the present. In general, the life-review process connects one's own life with the future as one tells one's story to younger generations; at the same time, links with past generations are renewed as one remembers what one's parents, grandparents, and even great-grandparents did and thought. One's relationship to humanity, to nature, to the whole of life also becomes a topic for reflection. For some, the life review becomes a psychological survey that leads to resolution of past conflicts and reintegration of the entire life course.

Often the person reflects on the relationship between his or her personal history and the social history of the times, a reflection of great interest to certain historians, who now recognize the life-review process as oral history, an important primary source of historical data (Davis, 1985). The process can take written form as well: many of the famous and not so famous write their autobiographies in their later years.

Sometimes the life review takes the simple form of nostalgia, reminiscence, or story-telling, which may be quite helpful to the older person, although not always easy to listen to. According to Butler and Lewis,

> one of the greatest difficulties for younger persons (including mental health personnel) is to listen thoughtfully to the reminiscences of older people. We have been taught that this nostalgia represents living in the past and a preoccupation with self and that it is generally boring, meaningless, and time-consuming. Yet as a natural healing process it represents one of the underlying human capacities on which all psychotherapy depends. The life review as a necessary and healthy process should be recognized in daily life as well as used in the mental health care of older people. [Butler and Lewis, 1982]

In some cases, the reflectivity of old age may lead to, or intensify, attempts to put broader historical, social, and cultural contexts of life into perspective. It is interesting to note that when Wayne Dennis (1966) studied

Figure 24.11 *Many cultures recognize and appreciate, far more than ours, the contributions of wisdom drawn from years of experience with the "pragmatics of life."*

the production of professionals in sixteen different fields, he found that in two of them—history and philosophy—production peaked in the 60s and 70s. Certainly one of the most famous examples is Will and Ariel Durant's *The Story of Civilization*—a monumental, ten-volume history of civilization written mostly in late adulthood—followed by *The Lessons of History* and *Interpretations of Life,* published when the Durants were in their 80s. The "philosophical bent" of old age is also reflected in the growing number of older adults showing up in the classroom to take courses in ethnic roots, history, and philosophy, sometimes in greater numbers than the young.

Wisdom

Wisdom is one of the most positive attributes commonly associated with older people. This association reflects the view that years of experience confer uniquely valuable insights on important life issues that are complex and often involve uncertainty. Wise perspectives are thought not only to be well-informed but to also accept the contradictions and ambiguities of life experience in offering constructive, and often novel, approaches to practical problems.

Wisdom is difficult to define precisely, and even more difficult to study. Paul Baltes is one of a small number of developmental scientists who have attempted to do both. He defines wisdom as "expert knowledge in the fundamental pragmatics of life permitting exceptional insight and judgment involving complex and uncertain matters of the human condition" (Baltes et al., 1992). Baltes and his colleagues argue that five features distinguish wisdom from other forms of human understanding (Baltes et al., 1992; Dittmann-Kohli and Baltes, 1990; Smith and Baltes, 1990):

1. unspecialized expertise that concerns the broad topic of human experience;

2. knowledge of the "pragmatics of life"—that is, practical and factual knowledge about the conditions of life and its variations;

3. a contextual approach to life problems that defines them in terms of the broader ecological, social, and human contexts in which these issues arise;

4. acceptance of the uncertainty in defining and solving life problems and of the unpredictability of one's future life course;

5. recognition of individual differences in values, goals, and priorities, and the use of relativistic as well as reflective thinking in tackling the contradictions of life experience.

Wisdom thus involves both the elements of dialectical thinking that emerge in early adulthood and the years of personal history through which thinking becomes refined by experience. But is wisdom a typical characteristic of older adults' thinking?

In one effort to study wisdom, Smith and Baltes (1990) asked sixty adults of various ages to assess the lives of four fictitious persons who each faced a difficult decision regarding the future. Here is an example of one story concerning a young adult.

> Elizabeth, 33 years old and a successful professional for 8 years, was recently offered a major promotion. Her new responsibilities would require an increased time commitment. She and her husband would also like to have children before it is too late. Elizabeth is considering the following options: She could plan to accept the promotion, or she could plan to start a family.

The other three stories concerned dilemmas over parental responsibilities at home, accepting early retirement, and intergenerational commitments. After hearing these stories, subjects were asked to formulate a course of action for each fictitious person and to think aloud as they did so, indicating when they thought additional information was needed about certain issues. Their responses were subsequently transcribed and rated by a panel of human-service professionals according to whether they exhibited the characteristics of wisdom described above.

Not unexpectedly, wisdom appeared to be in fairly short supply. Of the 240 responses to their hypothetical stories, Smith and Baltes found that only 5 percent were judged as truly wise. Somewhat more surprisingly, the distribution of responses judged to be wise was fairly even across young, middle-aged, and old adults in the sample. That is, wisdom was not reserved for later life, but could be found at any phase of adulthood, depending, presumably, on one's life experiences and reflective insight about them. As the researchers noted, "adults may be best in those areas of wisdom-related knowledge that are specific to their age and life circumstances." In this regard, it may be possible to identify varieties of "wisdoms," each suited to the challenges and conflicts of different practical dimensions of life.

Spiritual Values

Closely related to the idea that the old are more wise and philosophical than the young is the idea that the old are more spiritual. In many cultures over many centuries, the very old have been the spiritual leaders (Clayton and Birren, 1980). They are the "elders" of the church. More popes, for instance, have been elected in their 80s than in any other decade of life.

Obviously, it is hard to measure spirituality, just as it is hard to measure wisdom. We do have data, however, on the importance of religion in people's lives. As can be seen in the chart here, those 65 and older are likely to value religion more highly than people under age 65 do. These data are cross-sectional, and thus may reflect cohort differences. However, a review of all the research on the importance of religion during old age, including longitudinal studies, confirms a general increase in religious faith, prayer, and spirituality in later years (Achenberg, 1985; Moberg, 1965).

There is some indication that the substance of religion, not just the formal trappings, is of more interest to the elderly (Achenberg, 1985). For example, the numbers agreeing that religion is the most important influence in their lives show a greater age contrast than the numbers attending church. Perhaps by late adulthood, one's own religious beliefs are sufficiently strong that following particular rituals or rules of a particular faith becomes less critical than following the spiritual dictates of that faith.

Measures of the Significance of Religion in Adulthood

	Those Under 65 Answering "Yes"	Those Over 65 Answering "Yes"
Personal Importance of Religon		
Is religious faith the most important influence in your life?	56%	82%
Do you get personal comfort and support from religion?	69%	87%
Do you try to put religious beliefs into practice?	69%	89%
Church Attendance		
Do you attend church weekly	31%	48%

Source: Schick, 1986; The Gallup Organization, 1993.

Summing Up

On balance, then, it seems fair to conclude that the mental processes in late adulthood can be adaptive and creative, not necessarily as efficient as thinking at younger ages, but more appropriate to the final period of life (Labouvie-Vief, 1985). An illustrative and exemplary case in point is the following poem, written by Henry Wadsworth Longfellow at age 80.

> But why, you ask me, should this tale be told
> Of men grown old, or who are growing old?
> Ah, Nothing is too late
> Till the tired heart shall cease to palpitate;
> Cato learned Greek at eighty; Sophocles
> Wrote his grand *Oedipus*, and Simonides
> Bore off the prize of verse from his compeers,
> When each had numbered more than four score years,
> And Theophrastus, at four score and ten,
> Had just begun his *Characters of Men.*
> Chaucer, at Woodstock with the nightingales,
> At sixty wrote the *Canterbury Tales;*
> Goethe at Weimar, toiling to the last,
> Completed *Faust* when eighty years were past.
> These are indeed exceptions, but they show
> How far the gulf-stream of our youth may flow
> Into the arctic regions of our lives
> When little else than life itself survives.
> Shall we then sit us idly down and say
> The night hath come; it is no longer day?
> The night had not yet come; we are not quite
> Cut off from labor by the failing light;
> Some work remains for us to do and dare;
> Even the oldest tree some fruit may bear;
> And as the evening twilight fades away
> The sky is filled with stars, invisible by day.

SUMMARY

Intellectual Changes in Information Processing

1. Thinking processes, as measured by standardized tests, become slower and less sharp once a person reaches late adulthood.

2. The sensory register declines relatively little in late adulthood. However, working memory shows notable declines, especially when one must simultaneously store and process information in complex ways. One reason for this loss is that processing takes longer with age.

3. With increasing age, adults experience greater difficulty accessing information from secondary, or long-term memory. Tertiary, or remote memory, by contrast, appears to decline very little with age. It seems that, once information is securely placed in remote memory, it tends to stay there, no matter how many years elapse.

4. On intelligence tests and laboratory studies of memory, older people use fewer and less efficient strategies to help them reason and remember. In tests of memory, for example, they are less likely to use mnemonic devices. When trying to solve abstract problems, they are likely to be distracted by irrelevant information, or to follow their hunches rather than use logical techniques.

5. One reason older adults, on average, do not perform as well as younger adults on tests of cognitive functioning is that more of the older group have negative self-perceptions of their memory skills that undermine their motivation to succeed. Some theorists believe older adults have reduced internal resources for processing information. Older adults also have health problems, especially undetected cardiovascular difficulties, that slow down thinking.

6. Efforts at cognitive-skills training have shown that the cognitive and memory skills of older adults can be improved, underscoring the plasticity of intellectual decrements in later life.

Cognitive Functioning in the Real World

7. In daily life, most of the elderly are not handicapped by memory difficulties, for several reasons. One is that they can use practice and priming, two memory techniques that are often excluded from the laboratory but are very helpful in daily life. Another is that most of them, once they recognize deficits in memory, develop strategies that aid their memory. The decline in problem-solving ability, evidenced in the laboratory, is also much less apparent in daily life.

8. Older adults are able to learn new learning strategies, as research on the elderly in the community, as well as those in nursing homes, confirms.

Dementia

9. Dementia, whether it occurs in late adulthood or earlier, is characterized by memory loss—at first minor lapses, then more serious forgetfulness, and finally such extreme losses that recognition of closest family members fades.

10. The most common cause of dementia is Alzheimer's disease, an incurable ailment that becomes more prevalent with age. While some cases of Alzheimer's disease are genetic, for the most part the cause is unknown.

11. Multi-infarct dementia is caused by a series of mini-strokes that occur when impairment of blood circulation through stroke destroys portions of brain tissue. Measures to improve circulation and to control hypertension can prevent or slow the course of this form of dementia.

12. In addition to Alzheimer's disease and multi-infarct dementia, other organic causes of dementia are brain tumors, Parkinson's disease, and Down syndrome. Non-organic problems that are frequently misdiagnosed as dementia include drug misuse, alcohol abuse, and psychological illness, especially depression.

New Cognitive Development in Later Life

13. Many people become more responsive to nature, more interested in creative endeavors, and more philosophical as they grow older. The life review is a personal reflection that many older people undertake, remembering earlier experiences and putting their entire lives into perspective. For the individual, this is a valuable psychological experience; others who listen to the life review can gain a new view of a family and social history.

14. Religious concerns and spiritual awareness may also increase in old age. So, too, may wisdom.

KEY TERMS

sensory register (612)
working memory (613)
knowledge base (615)
control processes (616)
memory self-efficacy (618)
dementia (625)

Alzheimer's disease (627)
multi-infarct dementia (MID) (629)
Parkinson's disease (629)
interiority (634)
life review (635)

KEY QUESTIONS

1. In terms of the information-processing approach, how are the sensory register, working memory, the knowledge base, and control processes affected by age?

2. What are some of the reasons for age-related declines in cognition? Can these declines be reversed?

3. What are some of the factors that help older adults show better memory skills in everyday life than on laboratory tests of memory?

4. In what ways do the everyday problem-solving skills of older and younger adults differ?

5. What is the general pattern of cognitive decline in all types of dementia?

6. What are some of the other factors, besides brain disorders, that can cause older individuals to exhibit symptoms of dementia?

7. What are some of the positive cognitive developments that are likely to find expression in older adulthood?

CHAPTER 25

Late Adulthood: Psychosocial Development

Contrary to ageist stereotypes, the social lives of the elderly are full of surprises regarding not only who they are involved with but how often and why. Similarly, the overall outlook and emotional tone expressed by the elderly are much more positive, and less often depressed, than is commonly assumed. The reasons behind these discrepancies between stereotype and reality will be explored in this chapter, as will such questions as the following:

What factors affect whether, and to what degree, older adults might want to withdraw from the social scene?

What determines whether older adults experience retirement as being "turned out to pasture" or as a welcome turn of events?

Does intergenerational assistance generally go from adult children to their parents or the other way around?

Why are some grandparents much more involved with their grandchildren than others?

> Living is not the good, but living well.
> The wise man therefore lives as long as he should, not as long as he can.
> He will observe where he is to live, with whom, how, and what he is to do.
> He will always think of life in terms of quality, not quantity.

This view, expressed by the first-century Roman philosopher, Seneca, reflects the overall perspective of this chapter on psychosocial development in late adulthood and draws attention to one of its central questions: What factors contribute to "living well" in old age? As you know from the previous two chapters, ageism distorts popular perceptions of the later years with negative stereotypes. It recites a litany of old-age circumstances—such as retirement, widowhood, moving away from one's lifelong home, failing strength, increased time on one's hands, decreased income—and despairs over the prospects. Certainly these factors can be a source of disruption and sorrow, but do they necessarily degrade the quality of the individual's life? If not, what elements in the person's personality and circumstances might prevent them from doing so? Our search for an answer begins with an examination of three contradictory theories about development in old age.

Theories of Psychosocial Aging

How do the elderly react to the psychosocial changes of later life? Do they become conservative, withdrawn, and uninvolved, allowing the world to pass them by? Or do they explore new vistas, reinvesting their energies when the daily demands of career-building and child-rearing recede? Or are they essentially unaffected by the shifts of old age, with their basic personality and lifestyle patterns continuing as before? Each of these possibilities has given rise to a theory about development in later life.

Disengagement versus Activity

Disengagement theory (Cumming and Henry, 1961) maintains that, in old age, the individual and society mutually withdraw from each other. This uncoupling occurs in four steps:

1. Beginning in late middle age, a person's social sphere becomes increasingly narrow, as traditional roles, such as worker and parent, become less available or less important and one's social circle shrinks because friends die or move away.

2. People anticipate, adjust to, and participate in this narrowing of the social sphere, relinquishing many of the roles they have played and accepting the gradual closing of their social circle.

3. As people become less role-centered, their style of interaction changes from an active to a passive one.

4. Because of this more passive style of interaction, older people are less likely to be chosen for new roles, and therefore are likely to disengage even more.

In this view, then, the elderly's participation in the disengagement process is voluntary. By old-old age, it is said, people prefer to be quite withdrawn from most social interaction, avoiding the noisy bustle and insistent demands of the younger person's world.

Disengagement theory has provoked a storm of protest and controversy among gerontologists, many of whom object strenuously to the implication that the elderly disengage and withdraw, or that when they do, they do so willingly (Lemon et al., 1972; Rosow, 1985; Sill, 1980). Acknowledging that disengagement does occur for some elderly people in some areas of life, a number of researchers claim that disengagement in one area can lead to reengagement in other areas. Disengagement from work roles, for instance, may promote more involvement in social and community activity (Parnes and Less, 1985); the death of a spouse may reactivate involvement in friendship networks (Adams, 1987).

Figure 25.1 *Although some of the elderly obviously disengage, many others become active in new ways. This woman is telling a Black-history class about her personal experiences as a Black person in America, a way to interweave memories and thoughts about the past with concern for the future.*

The most unfortunate aspect of disengagement theory may be that it seems to justify many of the ageist stereotypes of elders as "useless, withdrawn, inactive, and isolated" and thus perpetuates ageist discrimination—from forced retirement to socially sterile nursing homes—on the grounds that the elderly, after all, want to withdraw (Palmore, 1990).

Nothing could be further from the truth, according to some critics of disengagement theory. Even when an older person seems to be disengaging voluntarily, such withdrawal into a smaller social world may, in fact, be an attempt to cope with the ageism of the surrounding society, an attempt by the old to salvage some self-esteem as society strips them of social roles, powers, and status (Rosow, 1985).

Many critics of disengagement theory endorse an opposing theory, called **activity theory.** Essentially, activity theory holds that older people need to and want to substitute new involvements and new friends for the roles that they lose with retirement, relocation, and so forth. It may well be that the constraints of a fixed income or physical impairment keep an older person quite inactive, but according to activity theory, if social policy and social support networks were available to help the individual overcome such constraints, he or she would once again engage in the maelstrom of modern life. Indeed, according to this theory, the more active the elderly are and the more roles they play, the greater their life satisfaction and the longer their life.

While such suggestions have merit, they have been criticized for creating the potential for a kind of reverse ageism that might force roles and activities onto those elderly who actually would rather quietly withdraw (Callahan, 1990). It also seems that activity theory, like disengagement theory, is not unequivocally supported by research either (Carstensen, 1987). The best sign of satisfaction among the elderly, for example, is not their absolute number of roles or activities but how close their level of activity is to the level they individually desire (Lomranz et al., 1988). And contrary to the assertions of some activity theorists, remaining highly active socially does not necessarily extend longevity: indeed, some of the oldest-old have a very small social circle (Lee and Markides, 1990; Poon et al., 1992). It does seem, however, that social isolation at any age diminishes happiness, impairs health, and shortens life (Keith, 1989; Antonucci, 1990). Thus, while healthy development in late adulthood may be characterized by a very active life or by a rather quiet one, extremes of disengagement are destructive.

Continuity

The underlying premise of both disengagement and activity theory is that old age entails reactions and adjustments to the many disruptions in work roles, family obligations, social circles, and so forth, and that this discontinuity dramatically affects the individual's experience of later life. However, another theory suggests that the discontinuity of the later years is much less influential than it appears.

According to **continuity theory,** each person copes with late adulthood in much the same way that he or she coped with earlier periods of life (Atchley, 1989). Reinforced by the ecological niches that individuals have carved out for themselves, the so-called Big Five personality traits (described in Chapter 20) are maintained throughout old age as they were in younger years. In very broad terms, this means that, for instance, when the elderly confront a health problem such as high blood pressure, how they react will depend a great deal on their individual temperament. Someone who strongly tends toward neuroticism, for example, might spend hours morose and alone, imagining an impending stroke lurking behind every stress. The hypertensive person who is highly extroverted, by contrast, is likely to seek out advice and suggestions, organizing a support group or joining an exercise class.

In recent years, continuity theory has received substantial confirmation from behavioral genetics. Longitudinal studies of monozygotic and dizygotic twins finds that, contrary to the logical idea that genetic influences weaken as life experiences accumulate, some traits seem even more apparent in late adulthood than earlier. Various life events—from how early a person retires to how often a person marries—seem to be at least as much affected by genetics as by life circumstances (Plomin et al., 1990). The explanation for this unexpected result is that, as older adults emerge from the harness of family and work obligations, their temperament receives freer rein.

Diversity

One more point must be made regarding psychosocial development in late adulthood. Elderly individuals are an incredibly diverse group. Consider, for example, the demographic diversity one would find in a cross-section of 65-year-olds within any of the developed nations. Most would be married, but about a fifth of the men and almost half of the women would be single, with the men being divided among the widowed, divorced, and never-married, while the unattached women would be mostly widows. The majority of these elders would have children and grandchildren and some even great-grandchildren, but almost a fourth would have no living offspring. Most would be retired, but some would be still employed, including a disproportionate number performing in their nation's most powerful roles—such as heads of state, religious leaders, and top executives of major corporations.

Even the biological aging process itself would show great diversity. A minority of our cross-section would not only look wrinkled and wizened but would also be feeble, with 2 percent destined to die within a year. By contrast, the typical 65-year-old would appear healthy and attractive, and live many more years—an average of seventeen years longer, with a fourth of all 65-year-olds destined to reach age 90. Obviously, while everyone is affected in some way by his or her own biological clock and by the social clock of their culture's expectations, age as a common denominator becomes increasingly irrelevant as life goes on.

Underlying these and most other areas of diversity in aging processes are the powerful influences of individual temperament and the specifics of culture, profession, gender, health, personal history, ethnic-group membership, and economic circumstances. All told, the diversity in aging adds enormous complexity to our study of late adulthood, because any research finding, or social trend, or gerontological theory that applies to one group may be inappropriate to another.

For example, where and with whom an elderly individual lives, and how he or she feels about it, is determined less by age or by other factors

Figure 25.2 *Of all the many sources of diversity in late adulthood—ethnicity, gender, health, religion, and interests among them—income is probably the most powerful of all.*

that might seem directly relevant (such as marital status and health) than by culture and economics (Kendig, 1990). Most aged Japanese, Koreans, and Filipinos, in keeping with their culture's expectations, live with their adult children and are quite satisfied with this arrangement: indeed, many appreciate the respect they are given and would likely be ashamed and depressed if they lived alone (Andrews et al., 1986; Palmore and Maeda, 1985). By contrast, few elderly North American, British, and Australians live with their children, not because they are disengaging but because they prefer to avoid an anticipated dependency relationship.

Even within a given nation, the living arrangements of older adults are strongly influenced by cohort, income, and ethnicity. For example, in North America forty years ago, most single elderly people lived with their children, in part out of economic necessity. Now most can afford to live alone and do so. If they become very frail and cannot care for themselves, the elderly who are female and European-American are more likely to enter nursing homes and live there for many years than are those who are male, or who are African-, Asian-, or Hispanic-American of either sex (Krause and Wray, 1991).

Varied and changing living arrangements are only one example of an overall pattern of diversity that seems to be increasing, especially in the United States, as growing numbers of individuals from ethnic minorities reach late adulthood (Torres-Gil, 1992). Indeed, as one gerontologist expresses it, "current and future generations of the elderly are part of a quiet revolution—a revolution of older individuals representing the broadest range of ethnic, racial, cultural, regional, religious, political, and socioeconomic diversity ever witnessed in American society" (Burton et al., 1991). As you read about the specific events of psychosocial development in the rest of this chapter, keep in mind the multifaceted diversity of older persons as well as the universal impact of the aging processes.

Generativity in Late Adulthood

In early and middle adulthood, as you remember, almost everyone seeks fulfillment by working—career-building or child-rearing or both. In late adulthood, these sources of generativity typically cease, as retirement and an empty nest replace the work of earlier years. How do these events affect older adults?

Retirement

For most of human history, no one stopped working unless their health failed. Today, however, the vast majority of people in every developed nation are employed for thirty years or more and then quit when late adulthood begins. Even compared to their counterparts a decade ago, more adults now retire while they are still able to work, some as early as age 55, most by age 65, and almost all by age 70 (U.S. Bureau of the Census, 1992; Schor, 1991). In the United States in 1990, for instance, only 11 percent of adults over age 65 (both men and women) were in the labor force (mostly self-employed or part-time), compared to 56 percent of those aged 55 to 65 and 84 percent of those aged 25 to 55.

Figure 25.3 *Employment in late adulthood is an option that is rarely chosen but one that is usually enjoyed when it is taken. Among those who prefer to work are the three shown here: a master book binder, a blacksmith, and a deputy sheriff. The majority of employed elderly work part-time, often at a job related to their previous career or in which independence and conscientious work habits are an asset.*

Reasons to Retire

This trend toward earlier retirement is occurring primarily because of choice, not compulsion or age-related incapacity. In 1986, the practice of mandatory retirement was made illegal in the United States, except in certain professions such as that of airline pilot and police officer. Further, this move was consistent with research that finds that older workers generally perform well and offer employers an additional bonus: they are more loyal and conscientious than younger workers, and consequently are rarely late or absent unless they are truly sick (Davies and Sparrow, 1985).

For various reasons, of course, some older workers still leave the labor market before they would prefer to. About 25 percent of all retirees leave work because failing health makes full-time employment too demanding. Another group, about 10 percent of all current retirees, lost their jobs when their company closed, relocated, or downsized, and then subsequently found that a combination of age discrimination, job scarcity, and their personal reluctance to retrain or relocate made early retirement the only viable option (Walker, 1989).

The majority of retirees, however, leave the work force because they want to and their employers encourage it (Quinn and Burkhauser, 1990). This is in dramatic contrast to the situation in the first half of the twentieth century, when the elderly depended on their jobs for survival and hung on to them for dear life, rightly fearing poverty and depression if they quit. However, poverty in old age is much less common today (see A Closer Look on pp. 648–649), primarily because pensions are almost universal. For example, in 1950, only one out of every three older Americans received any pension income, including Social Security; by 1990, 95 percent had Social Security and 60 percent had private pensions as well. The latter often include bonuses for early retirement, offered by employers eager to reduce their payroll by replacing high-paid senior workers with relatively low-paid younger ones (Clark, 1990). Such inducements are particularly attractive to blue-collar and service workers who never found work particularly satisfying and who thus retire as early as age 55, as soon as they think they can afford it (Hardy, 1985).

Adjustment to Retirement

Research accumulated over the past twenty years finds that, contrary to popular expectations, most retirees not only adjust well to their change in work status but even improve in health and happiness (Betancourt, 1991; Herzog et al., 1991; Quinn and Burkhauser, 1990). The exceptions are primarily among those who retire prematurely and involuntarily, who are abruptly severed not only from productive work but also from their major source of status and social support (Swan et al., 1991). As one policeman expressed it:

> What the hell do I do now? I thought I would feel differently now that I'm retired. I still want to work but they won't let me . . . I always thought that I wanted to rest and fish at this age. I never dreamed I would be in such good physical health. I thought I would be all dilapidated . . . I'm raring to go, but there is no place to go. Rest is O.K. for a couple of months. In fact, I've looked forward to this all my life, lying around, doing what I want to do. But now I know this is crazy. A person's got to be wanted and needed. A person's got to do something with people. This retirement stuff is a myth, a rip-off as the kids say. [quoted in Kornhaber and Woodward, 1981]

For such individuals, a more gradual transition makes psychological sense. Indeed, if employees are given the choice, about three-fourths prefer to retire gradually (Jondrow et al., 1987). Unfortunately, most employers and unions make this difficult, not only by their work schedules and pay scales but also by pension policies that base retirement benefits on the final year's salary—thereby encouraging extensive overtime in the final months rather than a gradual tapering off.

Some of the elderly find their own way to retire gradually: after leaving their career job, they take on another with shorter hours and less pay or they become self-employed (Quinn and Burkhauser, 1990). Many of the new employment practices that originated to help women with small children—such as flextime, family leave, job-sharing, and part-time work—are now helpful to the elderly as well. Whether they continue working or not, however, most retirees remain productive. Their activities may not be financially rewarding but, as we will see, they are worthwhile in many other ways—creating, helping, learning, and loving.

Achievement Patterns in Late Adulthood

Almost every adult in contemporary society has interests, talents, and curiosities that he or she wishes to pursue but cannot because of the pressing obligations of daily life. Further, with their culture's emphasis on individual advancement, many American adults feel unable to give adequate time and concern to meeting the needs of their family, friends, or community while at the same time trying to "get ahead." For many of these people, retirement allows them finally to be able to follow their own inclinations and simultaneously become more involved with others.

Interests and Hobbies

Many of the elderly use the time they once spent earning a living to develop hobbies and interests that had already been part of their life (Kunkel, 1989).

A CLOSER LOOK   Poverty, Age, and Equity

In the second half of this century, the economic circumstances of the elderly have changed dramatically. More than thirty years ago, Michael Harrington's *The Other America* drew a chilling picture of the extent of poverty among adults who were then above age 65.

> Fifty percent of the elderly exist below minimal standards of decency, and this is a figure much higher than that for any other age group . . . We have given them bare survival, but not the means of living honorable and satisfying lives. [Harrington, 1962]

Harrington was not far from wrong. In actuality, one out of every three elderly Americans was then living below the poverty line, and a substantial additional number were "near poor," living at the very edges of poverty.

Since that time, various economic, demographic, and political changes have raised both the personal income and the living standard of many of the elderly throughout the world. In the United States, for instance, the "war on poverty" in the 1960s extended Social Security and provided a range of medical and social benefits to the aged, reducing the proportion of the elderly below the poverty line to about one in eight in 1991. Private firms have followed suit, with subsidies ranging from pensions that afford many older adults a comfortable retirement to symbolic measures such as weekday discounts at movie theaters and fast-food restaurants.

Ironically, during the same years that the American elderly were growing richer, thanks, in part, to increases in their government benefits, other age groups, notably children, were growing poorer, thanks, in part, to cuts in government benefits to young families, including low-cost mortgages, public child care, and income supplements. More than one American child in five now lives below the poverty line (see figure) compared to one in seven in 1970. This economic disparity between young and old has been exacerbated by periods of inflation that have undercut every public benefit except Social Security, which automatically rises with the cost of living.

A backlash against this reversal of financial fortunes has led to calls for **generational equity,** defined as equal contributions from, and fair benefits for, each generation (Hewitt, 1986). Some argue that limits must be put on public money that flows to elders at the expense of the children, a situation that is particularly imbalanced for non-

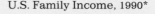

U.S. Family Income, 1990*

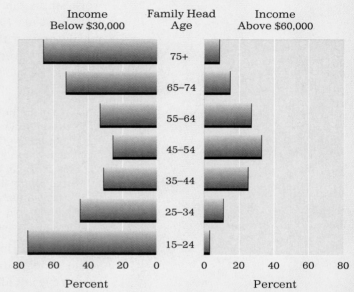

Income Below $30,000	Family Head Age	Income Above $60,000
	75+	
	65–74	
	55–64	
	45–54	
	35–44	
	25–34	
	15–24	

80 60 40 20 0   0 20 40 60 80

Percent   Percent

*Including wages, investment, income, rental income, profits, and pensions.

As you can see, the notion that the wealthy elderly are robbing from the impoverished youth is based more on myth than reality. The richest age groups are actually those in the middle years. Of course, many in these groups might well point out that their seeming affluence is offset by the cost of college for their children and the health expenses of their parents. In truth, every generation today can make a good case that they suffer from an imbalance between available income and necessary expenses.

white minorities, who tend to be overrepresented among the young and underrepresented among the old. One example often cited is health care: costly public outlay for doctors and hospitalization of the aged results in grossly inadequate funding of preventive medicine in childhood and adolescence (Callahan, 1990). At their fiercest, critics argue that "we soak the young to enrich the old" (Taylor, 1986), that "greedy geezers" are living off the regressive Social Security taxes that deplete the wages of younger workers, and that "age wars" will soon ensue (Longman, 1987).

Different Age Groups Living
Below the U.S. Poverty Level

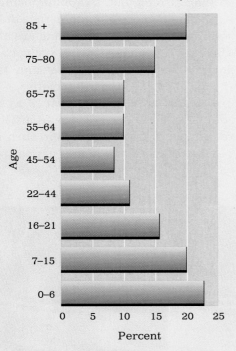

Source: U.S. Bureau of the Census, 1992;
Kleyman, 1992

If any age group is unfairly burdened by poverty, it is the youngest, whose ill health, miseducation, and undernutrition can affect them for years to come.

Gerontologists do not accept this framing of the problem. First of all, these generalities obscure the tremendous diversity of income among the elderly. True, the average older person now has enough income for food, shelter, and other basic expenses, but few are wealthy (see figure). Despite government and private help, those elderly who need costly medications or out-patient care must pay sizable portions of their income and savings or "spend down," that is, get rid of all their assets until they are so poor that they qualify for full government subsidy.

Thus for most of the nonpoor elderly, whatever extra savings they might have are their bulwark against two dreaded circumstances, lingering helplessness and abject poverty. Often this defense fails: many of the most vulnerable older individuals, especially the widowed, the divorced, the nonwhite, and the physically frail, still suffer cruel effects of poverty, living in dangerous and dilapidated housing with insufficient food or heat. This is particularly likely to be the fate of the oldest-old, whose poverty rates are similar to those of the youngest-young. Compared to those just starting their lives, however, the older poor suffer an additional burden: they have little hope of marked financial improvement.

However, even this broader perspective on the distribution of wealth and poverty misses a critical contribution that is implicit in a life-span view of human development—that is, that every age and cohort has its own particular and legitimate economic needs that other generations might fail to appreciate (Deutscher, 1988; Torres-Gil, 1992). For instance, whether one gives greater legitimacy to federally funded day-care programs, or to low-interest government loans for college tuition, or to protecting entitlements for the elderly depends largely on the immediate interests of one's own age group—yet in the long term, each of these subsidies works to the betterment of all.

Taking a developmental view, then, instead of a battle among age groups each generation must try to balance its own needs with those of the others, because *interdependence* is at the heart of intergenerational relationships. It is thus both unfair and counterproductive to pit one generation against another, on the basis of a "flawed and dangerous premise" of exclusionary self-interest, such as "that America's younger generations are suffering *because* of the elderly population" (Minkler, 1991). Instead, the fact that fewer of the elderly are poor today benefits not only the older generations but their descendants and the entire nation. Correspondingly, the fact that more children are poor today imperils not only the children themselves but also the whole community. The crucial needs of every generation need to be seen in full perspective and addressed accordingly: the solution to impoverished youth cannot be found in scapegoating the old.

Some of these pursuits are aesthetic, such as painting or playing a musical instrument. Others are more literary: most of the elderly increase their reading, and many begin writing, with particular interest in the autobiographical account (Parnes and Less, 1985). About a third increase their sports activities, with hiking, golfing, fishing, and swimming being among the favorites that many retirees engage in more often than they did in middle age. Gardening, carpentry, sewing, knitting, and cooking are also common pastimes of the elderly. While the young may look on such activities as mere busywork or puttering, it should be noted that these same tasks are the life work of many people who live in labor-intensive societies.

Sometimes practical interests lead to new careers, such as that of a handyman, gardener, caterer, or quilt maker; and sometimes artistic interests blossom into a publicly recognized talent. More often, such new endeavors simply come in handy at home, and at the homes of nearby friends and family members.

Figure 25.4 *For the elderly who are among the young-old, a wide variety of achievement patterns is available. Shown here are a first-term Texas legislator evaluating a proposed law, gardeners tending their crop, and Elderhostel students searching for tropical fish in the waters around Bermuda.*

Education

For many of the elderly, retirement offers them the opportunity for pursuing educational interests. At any given time about one out of twenty adults aged 60 and older is enrolled in classes of some sort, ranging from courses in the practical arts to those leading to advanced college degrees. Given that career advancement is seldom their motive for renewed schooling, the elderly are more likely to study for the joy of learning, or to master some specific skill, than younger adults are.

The eagerness of the elderly to learn is best exemplified by the rapid growth of **Elderhostel,** a program in which older people live on college campuses and take special classes, usually during college vacation periods. Begun in 1975 with 220 students, Elderhostel now operates at 1,800 sites in the United States and Canada, with an annual enrollment of more than 250,000 (Goggin, 1992).

While older students eagerly enroll in programs designed specifically for them, some hesitate to enter academic classes populated by mostly younger students. This is unfortunate, because many of the elderly who do enter the standard classroom outperform younger students and enjoy the experience once they start, and many younger students and professors benefit from the involvement and example of older students (Shevron and Lumsden, 1985; Watkins, 1990). One man surprised himself by taking drawing, painting, and Spanish classes at a community college, explaining:

> When I first retired, I couldn't wait to pack up and go to a warm climate and just goof off. But now, retirement is an enormous challenge. Once you start learning about yourself, you get the feeling that anything is possible. [Goldman, 1991]

Service in the Community

Many older adults feel a strong commitment to their community and, even more than younger people, believe that older people should be of service. For example, when a cross-section of close to 3,000 Americans were asked whether older adults have an obligation to help others and serve the community, about twice as many older adults as younger adults strongly agreed. Strong disagreement with this idea was expressed by only 6 percent of those over age 60, compared to 12 percent under 60 (Herzog and House, 1991). Perhaps because of their perspective on life, or because of their patience and experience, older adults are particularly likely to do volunteer work with the very young, the very old, or the sick.

Much of this volunteer work is informal. In stable neighborhoods that have a sizable number of elderly, the more capable residents often run errands, fix meals, repair broken appliances, and perform other services that generally make it possible for the disabled elderly to continue to live at home. For example, in one four-block residential area, routine sharing and socializing allowed three widows in their late 80s, one of them blind, one obviously failing cognitively, and one physically disabled, to remain in the community. Their neighbors shopped for them, cooked for them, and simply checked in on them often enough to make them feel part of the neighborhood, while still allowing them some privacy and independence (Rosel, 1986).

While such informal volunteer help to friends and family is the most frequent, performed by two-thirds of all the elderly, over a third are involved with more structured volunteering, often through churches, hospitals, or schools (Herzog and House, 1991). Several volunteer organizations now appeal directly to the retired senior citizen. One such organization is SCORE (Service Corps of Retired Executives), whose volunteers provide advice to owners of small businesses. Another is Foster-Grandparents, which is designed to help an older person "adopt" a child who needs the help a grandparent could provide. Volunteering would probably be more common if other agencies and the elderly themselves realized how useful they could be. The response of one older woman when she and her husband were asked to work with stroke victims is not unusual:

> Of what possible use could we be, a seventyish couple who had none of the seemingly necessary skills, no knowledge of speech or physical therapy, no special social skills either?

Figure 25.5 *While the politically active older citizen is more likely to vote, write letters, and make phone calls than to take to the streets, the Gray Panthers are an important exception. They participate in public demonstrations, organize economic boycotts, and even engage in civil disobedience. Perhaps their biggest success is in public relations: they jostle our ageist stereotypes about the elderly as passive, docile, and conservative.*

Several months after this couple overcame their self-doubt and began the volunteer work, the woman wrote:

> The real question was [not] "What can we do?" [but] "What can we be?" Can we be warm, caring unstroke-damaged human beings, to meet . . . with stroke-damaged ones, exchanging concerns, playing word games, encouraging them to feel at ease, to talk and tease and laugh with us and with each other . . . I wish everyone who feels so useless and lonely could have such a completely satisfying experience as Tom and I are having. [quoted in Vickery, 1978]

The major United States organization affecting the elderly is the **American Association of Retired Persons (AARP)**, "the largest organized interest group in America" (Jacobs, 1990). In 1991, AARP had a membership of more than 33 million (members must be over 50 but need not be retired), employed nearly 50 congressional lobbyists, and involved over 400,000 volunteers in various projects related to advancing the interests of the elderly or to benefiting the overall community. The political influence of this organization is one reason Social Security is usually immune to the budget-cutting that affects almost every other domestic subsidy, from public assistance to highway repair.

The elderly do not necessarily use their political clout exclusively for their own self-interest, however. They are particularly likely to care about future generations, and thus some of the elderly are very concerned with issues related to family values, the federal deficit, nuclear war, pollution, and the preservation of the environment. Nor do they necessarily vote for people of their generation: in the 1992 presidential election, 50 percent of the elderly voted for the youngest candidate, 46-year-old Bill Clinton, giving him a larger plurality than any other age group (Kleyman, 1992).

Children and Grandchildren

Almost all elders who have children and grandchildren devote time and attention to them. The "empty nest" is not always empty, and few older adults stop parenting simply because their children are full-grown, independent, or even married or parents themselves. As one 82-year-old woman succinctly put it: "No matter how old a mother is, she watches her middle-aged children for signs of improvement" (Scott-Maxwell, 1968). On their part, most children feel substantial **filial obligation,** that is, the sense of duty and need to protect and care for their aging parents (Blieszner and Hamon, 1992). Grandparenthood adds another dimension to these intergenerational ties, for most older adults have quite definite concerns about how their children and children-in-law are raising the next generation, while most parents prefer to do it their own way.

Such overlapping family concerns highlight the complexity of the ongoing relationship among the generations of a family. Most families evidence three signs of intergenerational closeness—mutual assistance, frequent contact, and shared affection, each one signifying a somewhat different aspect of the intergenerational bond (Mangen et al., 1988). In general, assistance arises as much from the need for it as from the desire to provide it; contact is more dependent on geographical proximity than on any other factor; and affection is strongly influenced by a family's past history of mutual love and respect. This means that a family can be high on the first two signs of closeness—assistance and contact—without necessarily being high on warmth and affection.

Since most of the elderly are quite capable of caring for themselves, assistance typically flows from the elder generation to their children instead of vice versa. In fact, most elders are pleased to be able to buy things for their children and help out occasionally with the grandchildren, and do not expect large gifts in return, even if someday their financial circumstances change (Hamon and Blieszner, 1990). The older generation also typically enjoys social contact with the younger generations, but on their own turf and terms: most would rather the children visit them at their invitation for a few hours rather than come uninvited, or stay too long, or expect the elders to do the traveling.

As you might expect, the most complex aspect of the relationship among the generations involves the exchange of advice and respect. It is not unusual for there to be a "generation gap" between the elderly and their children and grandchildren (Hagestad, 1985). When the generations differ in their views on such areas as politics, sex, child-rearing, and religion, family members, in the name of "good relations," may confine their conversation to "demilitarized zones," involving topics that are unlikely to provoke anger or hurt feelings. Frequently this results in superficial relations, with the different generations hesitating to offer constructive criticism or advice, even when it might be needed. Thus the price of intergenerational harmony may be intergenerational distance.

This was clearly the case for the following couple, who felt they were viewed as "outmoded and irrelevant" rather than "wise or expert." They explained:

> Our grandson just got married. They both have fancy taste and fancy plans, and they mean to have it all. When we asked about a baby, they said they wouldn't even think about having a child until they could afford a full-time nanny to raise it. Imagine planning to have children so that you won't have to raise them! Whose children are they anyway? Why have them? We love him so much, and we don't want to hurt him, so we didn't say anything. As long as we keep rather quiet, he thinks we're sweet and lovable—and rather silly . . . [Erikson et al., 1986]

Figure 25.6 *The grandfather teaching about how to grow flowers, and the grandmother showing her granddaughter how to quilt are both providing more than information and guidance. As with many abilities, interests, and values, the notion that life is worth living is best learned by example, an example that a loving grandparent can furnish.*

In fairness, however, we should note that most of the elderly keep their children and grandchildren on the periphery of their lives, and are highly selective regarding when, how, and with whom to interact. That pattern is what many of the elderly and their children think they want, but such an arrangement may not actually be best for all concerned (see A Closer Look on p. 655).

Today's pattern of detachment between grandparents and grandchildren is quite different from the one that was typical in the first half of the century when many grandparents were central to the lives of their children's children. What caused this change? Researchers have suggested several reasons (Bengston and Robertson, 1985; Kornhaber and Woodward, 1981; Rodeheaver and Thomas, 1986; Troll, 1980):

1. Increased geographical mobility of offspring has meant that many grandparents live quite far from their children and grandchildren. This makes visiting infrequent and the relationship less intimate.

2. Because grandparents of today are more financially independent than earlier generations of grandparents were, they are more likely to have homes, friends, and interests apart from those of their children and grandchildren.

3. Grandmothers are more often employed than they were earlier, so they have less time, energy, or need to make their grandchildren central to their lives.

4. Because of the rising divorce rate, some grandparents rarely see their grandchildren, who are living with their former daughter- or son-in-law.

5. Finally, the relationship between parents and children has become more egalitarian in recent decades, with the result that the deference once automatically accorded to the older generation has diminished: since their advice regarding child-rearing is likely to go unheeded, the elders take a background role in order to keep family harmony.

Most grandparents are comfortable with their reduced role: they like to play with their grandchildren, give them presents, and baby-sit occasionally—and they are quite happy to leave parenting up to the parents. In fact, those who feel responsible for advising their grandchildren (which grandfathers do more than grandmothers, and young grandparents more than older ones) tend to be less satisfied with the grandparenting role than those who feel their role is simply to enjoy their grandchildren (Thomas, 1986).

These generalities should not obscure the diversity of grandparenting style. As we have seen, some grandparents are so involved with their grandchildren as to be surrogate parents; others are very distant, and rarely heard from; and most are only modestly involved. Styles of grandparenting also vary by sex, age, and ethnic group. In general, grandmothers are more active and more comfortable in the grandparenting role than grandfathers, and grandparents in their 60s are able to be more actively involved in grandparenting than younger or older ones.

In the United States, African-Americans, Asian-Americans, Italian-Americans, and Hispanic-Americans are likely to be more involved in the lives of their children and grandchildren than members of other groups are (Lockery, 1991). Ethnic differences are also apparent in whether a child is

Figure 25.7 *This grandparent appears quite comfortable and content in an active caregiving role. If this is so, the reasons are many, including her particular temperament, age, and health. Cultural background also plays a part, since grandmothers from Asian groups tend to be highly involved, and esteemed, in their grandparenting role.*

A CLOSER LOOK   The Luxury of Selective Family Involvement

In studies of adults' relationships with younger family members over time, one striking feature is how much more selective and enjoyable those relationships become as people age. A fifty-year longitudinal study found that child-rearing overwhelmed many young parents, but that as grandparents, the same individuals could

> love, care for, and be helpful to the grandchildren—all without bearing the responsibility inherent in parental generativity. This freedom from middle age's responsibility for maintaining and perpetuating the world is central to the grand-generativity that characterizes old-age caring. And this very freedom is something many elders relish about being grandparents. [Erikson et al., 1986]

Another study of 300 grandparents and 300 grandchildren of many ethnic and economic backgrounds found that only about 5 percent were closely involved with each other. Another 5 percent had no contact at all. The remaining 90 percent visited occasionally but did not develop intimate relationships (Kornhaber and Woodward, 1981).

While many grandparents have moments of regret that they are not closer to their grandchildren, few would give up their independence and freedom in order to become more involved in their lives. In general, the older a grandparent is, the less likely he or she is to see the grandparent role as central (Cherlin and Furstenberg, 1986). The majority of grandparents seem in accord with the one who confessed of his own grandchildren, "Glad to see them come, and glad to see them go."

Although most older adults today are reasonably satisfied with their less active grandparenting role, whether it be relatively detached or involved, about a third feel a certain amount of discontent. Some are not pleased with the way their grandchildren are being raised, but feel unable to do much about it. Others feel disappointed that their re-

When grandfathers become active with their progeny, they typically do so in the ways traditional to their gender—providing instruction, advice, and, as shown here, play.

lationship with their grandchildren is not more affectionate. This sense of distance is especially likely to occur if their own memories of their grandparents are positive and warm. As one woman said:

> I would have loved for my grandchildren to grow up the way I grew up. A close family, lots of people around all the time. I loved my grandparents. I would go over to their house all the time. It was wonderful. I would so love to have that feeling of closeness to the children. But there's a wall, a barrier. . . . I've lost my grandchildren and they've lost me. [quoted in Kornhaber and Woodward, 1981]

likely to be cared for full-time by a grandparent, or to live with a grandparent instead of a parent, with many older African-Americans being extensively involved in the ongoing care of their grandchildren and great-grandchildren (Barresi and Menon, 1991). Indeed, an estimated 13 percent of African-American children live with their grandparents, compared to about 3 percent of Hispanic-American children and 2 percent of European-American children (Minkler and Roe, 1991). Part of the reason for this racial difference is tradition, since the multigenerational family has been a mainstay of African-American survival, both in the United States and in the Caribbean, for centuries. Another part of the reason is age of parenthood:

African-Americans tend to begin and end their childbearing earlier than other groups, which means that many of the caregiving grandparents are relatively young. Probably more important than either age or history, however, are current economic and social conditions, as indicated by the statistic that grandparent care among African-Americans increases as income falls. Such care is particularly common when the parents live in crowded, dangerous cities and the grandparents live in safer, more rural areas. In such families, having young children live with their grandparents instead of their parents aids economic survival for the family as well as healthier development for the youngest generation (Barresi and Menon, 1991).

Many other ethnic, gender, economic, and cohort factors influence the degree and the nature of grandparent-grandchild contact. For example, Italian-American grandmothers tend to be much more satisfied and involved with grandparenting than Italian-American grandfathers, who tend to be more distant. Among Hispanics, Cuban-Americans are least, and Mexican-Americans most, likely to be involved with the daily lives of their descendants (Bengston, 1986). The timing of grandparenthood can be crucial to satisfaction with the role, and this is particularly true for black grandmothers, who are traditionally very involved in their grandchildren's lives. Black grandmothers who are under age 40 or so often feel pressured to provide care for a new grandchild they were not eager for, while those over age 60 tend to feel that they are fulfilling a cherished role.

It is important to note that specific styles of grandparenting vary greatly. This fact is highlighted by the case of an 18-month-old child who had grandparents from very different ethnic backgrounds, one pair Latin, the other Nordic:

> Her Latin grandparents tickled, frolicked with, and cajoled her. Her Nordic grandparents (who loved her no less) let her "be." Her Latin mother thought her in-laws were "cold and hard" while her Nordic father thought his in-laws were "driving her crazy." The youngster was perfectly content with both sets of grandparents. [Kornhaber, 1986]

Developmentalists are convinced that the particular style of grandparenting is probably not relevant, so long as it is loving, and comfortable for those involved. However, in the opinion of many researchers, the more remote and uninvolved grandparenting that is increasingly common in today's affluent families provides more independence for each generation but at considerable cost. While certainly there are times when neither generation benefits by unwelcome closeness (Thompson et al., 1989), overall both the old and the young suffer when too much distance diminishes the sense of generational continuity and interdependence (Cherlin and Furstenberg, 1986; Troll, 1983). One might hope that more grandchildren and grandparents could share the kinds of feelings expressed in the following quotations from a study of grandparents' practices (Kornhaber and Woodward, 1981):

> Grandma has got a bad leg, so she can't walk around without her cane. I can sit on her lap, though, and she tells me stories about when she was young and I can cuddle up with her . . . She is so cozy. She can't walk too well, but she can talk. And she is the best back rubber in the world.

> I guess my grandchildren are a big part of my life right now. They come over very often, spend the night . . . In some way it is my job to spoil the kids a bit when they are young, listen to them when they are older and do things for them that their parents do not have time to do. It's different from being a parent. Special for me and for the kids . . . Let's get it straight—I need them.

Affiliation: The Social Convoy

The phrase **social convoy** highlights the truism that we travel our life course in the company of others (Antonucci, 1985). At various points, other people join and leave our convoy, but just like members of a wagon train headed West, we could never make the journey successfully by ourselves. Furthermore, the bonds formed as we journey together help us in good times and bad. It is more pleasant to share triumphs with those who know how important the victory is; it may be critical for our survival in times of defeat and sorrow to have familiar confederates whom we have helped in the past. For older adults particularly, the social network's continuity over time is an important affirmation of who they are and what they have been. Friends who "knew them when" are particularly valuable, as are family members (especially a spouse) who share a lifetime of experiences.

Friends

By late adulthood, many members of the social network have been part of a person's convoy for decades. This helps explain a surprising finding: older people's satisfaction with life bears relatively little relationship to the quantity or quality of their contact with the younger members of their own family, but shows substantial correlation with the quantity and quality of their contact with friends (Antonucci, 1985; Essex and Nam, 1987).

Particularly important is the quality of friendship. Having at least one close friend in whom to confide acts as a buffer against the loss of status and roles that comes with such common experiences as retirement and widowhood. Given the importance of friendship, it is comforting to know that most elderly people have at least one close friend. In fact, older adults are less likely than younger ones to want more friends (Antonucci, 1985).

In some ways, older friendships follow the same patterns as friendships earlier in life. As at younger ages, older women tend to have larger social circles than men do, and to have more intimate relationships, especially if intimacy is measured by how often and how revealingly people talk with their closest friends. In late adulthood, this gender difference is particularly apparent for widows, who tend to be more involved in friendship networks than married women, never-married women, or men of any marital status (Hatch and Bulcraft, 1992; Keith, 1989; Wright, 1989).

Figure 25.8 *Sitting in the park on a sunny day, with good friends, watching the world go by—a favorite activity for the young and old. Looking at the posture and expressions of these four, it is not hard to imagine them sixty years earlier, as young teenagers, hanging out on the same bench.*

Also as at every age, the strength of late-life friendship correlates with feelings of well-being and self-esteem (Crohan and Antonucci, 1989). In this respect, however, long-standing friendships in late adulthood have added depth, in that each year that a particular friendship lasts increases the shared memories, intimacies, and gratitude for past support. Not surprisingly, then, while older people sometimes enjoy relationships with much younger people, they particularly cherish their long-term friendships with those they knew in their youth. Unfortunately, this preference can eventually lead to sorrow, as some treasured friends die and others become disabled, making the simple act of getting together much more arduous (Rawlins, 1992). In the latter case, many of the elderly turn to letters, cards, and phone calls to sustain their friendships, making the post office and the telephone as vital to social life in old age as it was in early adolescence.

The importance of long-standing friendships is also reflected in a related phenomenon in late adulthood—the intensification of friendly bonds between siblings (Cicirelli, 1985; Kendig et al., 1988, Moyer, 1992). Of course, greater closeness is not inevitable: sibling rivalries set in childhood often continue lifelong (Greer, 1992). Nevertheless, siblings who respected and liked each other throughout adulthood but who never spent much time together often become close confidants and even share residences once again when a spouse dies.

Neighbors

The social convoy—particularly with regard to the need for friends—is one factor underlying a notable characteristic of most older adults: they like to "age in place" (Mutschler, 1992). Indeed, a recent nationwide survey found that 86 percent of the American elderly want to "stay in their present home and never move" (AARP, 1990). This preference is clearly reflected in United States statistics: the older an adult is, the less likely he or she is to move, with the relocation rate of households headed by young adults being seven times that of households headed by older adults (see Table 25.1). Moreover, when older Americans do move, they more often move nearby, with only one out of six crossing state lines, usually relocating near old friends or family members (Lawton, 1985).

The need to be near familiar people may be particularly important for the current cohort of older Americans, about a fourth of whom are immigrants or first-generation Americans. For them, having neighbors, grocery stores, churches, temples, social clubs, and other cultural sources reflecting their own ethnic and linguistic background often makes the difference between social interaction and lonely isolation. Elders from ethnic minorities are particularly reluctant to move if they anticipate being exposed to racial or religious prejudice from their new neighbors.

Retirement Communities

The fact that the elderly want to stay put has come as something of a surprise to many government bureaucrats, private builders, and gerontologists, who, during the 1970s, championed the construction of tens of thousands of government-subsidized housing units designed for the growing aged population (Dobkin, 1992). **Planned retirement communities,** where all

Table 25.1 Percent of U.S. Population Who Changed Residences Within a Year

Age Group (years)	Moved	Moved to Another State
1–4	26	4.3
5–9	20	2.9
10–14	15	2.0
15–19	17	2.7
20–24	35	5.6
25–29	32	4.8
30–44	18	2.8
45–54	10	1.6
55–64	7	1.2
65–74	5	1.0
75 plus	4	0.4

Source: U.S. Bureau of the Census, 1991

Figure 25.9 *A major advantage of retirement communities is that the older person is surrounded by people with whom he or she is likely to share many things in common—including an appreciation for another year lived.*

the residents must be over a certain age, are now widely available, not only in the temperate climate of the Sunbelt but also in every state of the United States and every province of Canada.

Planned retirement communities usually are a bargain, not only because they are publicly subsidized but also because they do not need expensive amenities such as large private yards, easy access to schools and places of employment, and large kitchens. Other advantages include security, quiet, and nearby medical care. In addition, many retirement communities offer services, from housekeeping to communal dining, for those who want them. Most important of all, age-segregated housing provides a natural setting for making friends, since all the residents are about the same age and often share similar hopes, memories, and problems.

Given the advantages of planned retirement communities, many gerontologists are trying to figure out why relatively few of the elderly—only about 10 percent—move into them. For some, this reluctance may be part of the ageism of our culture, which derides these communities as "geriatric ghettos" or "fogey farms" (Ross, 1977), while ignoring the many benefits they can provide. Others may prefer not to think about their changing needs as they age (Dobkin, 1992). Ironically, those who are most likely to benefit from retirement communities—those who are over 75, or widowed, or relatively poor—are least likely to want to move (AARP, 1990). This is particularly true for the urban-dwelling African-American and Puerto Rican elderly—despite the fact that fear of crime and dangerous traffic make them "vulnerable to a hostile environment . . . not only aging in place [but] stuck in place, prisoners in their own homes" (Skinner, 1992).

While most of the elderly are reluctant to join planned retirement communities, an estimated 27 percent of elderly Americans live in **NORCs, or naturally occurring retirement communities,** defined as neighborhoods or apartment complexes where more than half the residents are elderly. Many NORCs originated in the 1950s, in the new housing developments designed for couples with young children. As their baby-boom offspring grew up and moved out, the parents often stayed put, consulting with their neighbors on the problems of aging just as they had once consulted with them on techniques of toilet-training their toddlers or on curfews for their teenagers (Hunt and Ross, 1990).

Once a NORC develops, it often attracts other older people, who form an active social network, with card parties, carpools to the mall, low-impact aerobic classes, and quilting circles to replace the babysitting coops and PTA meetings of the past. NORC residents tend to be pleased but somewhat surprised at this turn of events. As one man notes:

> We were younger when we moved in but we kept staying, and we all got older. If I were stuck in a retirement home, I'd say 'Heavens get me away from all these old people' but I have had quadruple-bypass surgery, and it's good to be around people who understand that. [Lewin, 1991]

Marriage

Being "around" friends and neighbors who understand is obviously important, but for many older people, a spouse is the best antidote to the problems of old age. Most (about 60 percent) of all Americans currently aged 60 and older are married, and they tend to be healthier, wealthier, and happier than those who never married, or who are divorced or widowed (Haring-Hidore et al., 1985; Bengston et al., 1990).

The Nature of Long-Lasting Marriages

Do marriage relationships change as people grow old, and if so, how? According to longitudinal as well as cross-sectional research, both continuity and discontinuity are apparent. The single best predictor of the nature of a marriage in its later stages is its nature early on: while the absolute levels of conflict, sexual activity, or emotional intensity drop over time, over time couples who were high or low in these dimensions early on tend to remain so relative to each other.

In general, most older married couples believe their marriage has improved over the years (Erikson et al., 1986; Glenn, 1991). Older husbands and wives tend to be happier with each other, and with their marriages, than they have been since they were newlyweds, a continuation of an upward trend that begins about ten years after the wedding (see Figure 25.10).

One reason for this improvement may be that the accumulation of shared life experiences makes husbands and wives become more compatible. That is, all the shared contextual factors—living in the same community, raising the same children, and dealing with the same financial and spiritual circumstances—tend to change both partners in similar ways, bringing long-married couples closer together in personality, perspectives, and values (Caspi et al., 1992).

A cause as well as a consequence of this trend may be a precipitous decline in how often couples fight. Everything from cursing and insulting to pushing and punching one's partner declines, with the result that the frequency of both verbal and physical spouse abuse in late adulthood is less than a fifth that of early adulthood (Stets, 1990; Egley, 1991). Even the rate of disagreement falls; according to one study of communication patterns, older couples who are happily married defer to one another more often than younger couples who are happily married (Zietlow and Van Lear, 1991). Indeed, in many aspects of shared life, from dividing the housework to deciding where to go for vacation, the longer a couple is married, the more likely both are to believe that their relationship is a fair and equitable one (Keith and Schafer, 1991; Suitor, 1992).

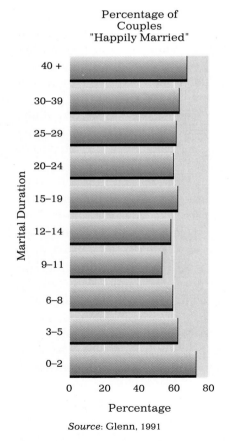

Percentage of Couples "Happily Married"

Marital Duration: 40+, 30–39, 25–29, 20–24, 15–19, 12–14, 9–11, 6–8, 3–5, 0–2

Percentage: 0 20 40 60 80

Source: Glenn, 1991

Figure 25.10 *As you can see, duration of marriage has some effect on likelihood of wedded bliss, with the best years more often being the early and late ones.*

Figure 25.11 *Browning's famous lines "Grow old along with me/The best is yet to be" seem prophetic of many marriages that last forty years or more.*

Poor Health and Marital Support

The perception of fairness among older married couples is particularly striking when one of them becomes seriously disabled, as occurs eventually in about half of all marriages that last fifty years or more. As we will see later in this chapter, the enormous burden of caring for a seriously ill person over a long period of time cannot be minimized. However, if the demands on the healthier spouse are not too great, most older couples adjust fairly well. Indeed, one study of seventy-six older couples in which one spouse or the other was ill found that although sickness did change the marriage relationship somewhat, it did not affect overall marital satisfaction. As the researcher learned from her interviews:

> With the illness of one spouse, when additional demands are placed on the marriage, the interdependence that had developed over the years appears to provide the means to meet these needs, usually without reservations. . . . some conflict was observed in these interviews but . . . disagreements are handled with a good-humored joking, sarcastic remarks, or teasing, rather than overt arguments. [Johnson, 1985]

Generally, older spouses accept their mutual frailties, tending to each other's physical and psychological needs as best they can. This mutual dependency allows most married elders to age in place, in better health, for a longer time than most of their unmarried contemporaries.

This does not necessarily mean that every unmarried elder is destined for loneliness, illness, and misery. For a variety of reasons, some single elders manage to meet their needs quite well, better than some married ones. As we will now see, diversity is readily apparent in this aspect of later life.

The Single Older Adult

About a third of the young-old and two-thirds of the old-old are not presently married. Approximately 80 percent of this group are widows or widowers, while 10 percent have never been married. Another 10 percent are divorced, a number that will probably triple by the year 2010, when the cohort that was caught in the divorce boom of the 1970s reaches old age.

Being old and single is quite different from what it was a generation or two ago, when it was considered a cause for ridicule or pity. The never-married were regarded as immature or selfish, and the widowed and divorced were thought to need supervision, and were often taken in by younger relatives (Keith, 1989). Now, for the most part, as long as health is maintained, being single and elderly means living quite happily and actively—and alone.

Indeed, while attitudes about singleness have gradually improved over the years, the most striking historical shift in the lifestyle of the unmarried elderly is the increasing numbers preferring to live alone, a trend apparent throughout North America and Europe. In the United States, about 12 million people aged 60 and older live by themselves, compared to about 3.5 million in 1960. Of the remaining 5 million single adults, most live with relatives, but about a third live with nonrelatives—friends, acquaintances, or lovers. While some factors, among them gender and marital status (divorced, never-married, or widowed), do affect a single elder's likelihood of happiness or social activity, type of household structure does not seem to do so: those living alone are often as active, healthy, and socially connected as those living with others (Keith, 1989; Kovar, 1991).

The Never-Married

The never-married tend to be particularly content with their independent state of affairs. Since they have spent a lifetime without a spouse, they usually have developed long-standing, alternative social patterns and activity preferences that keep them active and happy in late adulthood as long as their health is reasonably good. Perhaps half of the never-married are gays and lesbians, many of whom have long-time companions as well as extensive social networks (Lee, 1987; Berger, 1982).

Never-married women, in particular, tend to be much involved with their relatives, caring for an aged parent, living with a sibling, or actively helping nieces and nephews (Allen and Pickett, 1987). In fact, one study of loneliness found that never-married women compared favorably with married ones (Essex and Nam, 1987).

Loneliness in Elderly Women

How often lonely	Never	Hardly Ever	Some-times	Often
Married women	38%	33%	23%	6%
Never married	29%	44%	24%	3%
Formerly married	15%	33%	36%	16%

Of course, not every single person is socially inclined. There are some "lifetime loners," usually men who chose long ago to avoid close ties. In urban areas, many live in single-room occupancy (SRO) hotels, where, as one observer explains, "isolation and loneliness is a price they are prepared to pay to maintain their independence" (Stephens, 1976).

The Divorced Older Adult

Divorce *during* late adulthood can be devastating, disrupting long-standing lifestyle patterns, habits, and self-esteem. However, divorce is very rare in late life, except with marriages that have recently been entered into (Uhlenberg and Myers, 1981). Thus most divorced older adults have been single for decades and adjusted to the major disruptions of the break-up long ago.

For divorced older women, in particular, life is likely to improve with age. Especially if they have successfully raised children as single mothers, or succeeded in a career despite all odds, they feel quite proud of past accomplishments. Further, they are less lonely than they were as young divorcees, when married couples tended to exclude them and when the demands of survival and child-rearing cut into their social lives. Now their friendship circle grows as more and more of their contemporaries become widows and their adult children typically keep in contact, often with grandchildren in tow.

As a group, older divorced men do not fare so well, however. Because women are usually the kin-keepers and social secretaries within a couple, and because father-child contact typically diminishes toward nonexistent over time when mothers have custody (see p. 501), many former husbands find themselves isolated from children, grandchildren, and old friends (Keith, 1986). Formerly married men have a higher rate of problems with their physical and psychological health than any other category of seniors (Kurdek, 1991).

Widowhood

Half of all married older adults will, obviously, experience the death of a spouse, one of the most serious stresses a person can undergo. Most surviving spouses will then spend several years, even decades, alone. This is particularly likely for widows: because the average adult woman lives six years longer than the average man, and the average husband is three years older than his wife, a wife is much more likely to be the surviving spouse. In fact, there are five times as many widows as widowers over the age of 65.

For both widows and widowers, the first months alone are generally hardest, for obvious reasons. The death of a mate usually means not only the loss of a close friend and lover but also a lower income, less status, a broken social circle, and disrupted daily routines. It is not surprising, then, that widows and widowers are more likely to be physically ill in the months following the death of their spouse than their married contemporaries are. Widowers particularly are also at a markedly increased risk of death, either by suicide or by natural causes (Stroebe and Stroebe, 1983; Osgood, 1992).

Sex Differences in Adjustment. In general, living without a spouse is somewhat easier for widows than for widowers, especially in the first few months (Stroebe and Stroebe, 1983). One reason is that, most likely, elderly women expect to outlive their husbands and, to some degree, anticipate and make arrangements for some of the adjustments that widowhood will require. In addition, the recently widowed usually have friends and neighbors who themselves are widows and who are ready to provide sympathy and support.

In most communities, widows can also get help from formal widow-support groups.* One longitudinal study found that widows who participated in a widow-to-widow support program were, two years after their husband's death, significantly less anxious, less distressed, and less impelled to hide their true emotions than were the control-group widows who had not been in the program and instead relied solely on friends and family for help (Vachon et al., 1980).

Another gender difference also favors widows. Many of the men who now are elderly grew up with restrictive notions of masculine behavior, and tended to depend on their wives to perform the basic tasks of daily living (such as cooking and cleaning) and to be their main source of emotional support and social interaction. When their wives die, they often find it hard to reveal their feelings of weakness and sorrow to another person, to ask for help, or even to invite someone over to chat.

While women have an easier time coping with the emotions of losing a spouse, they have a harder time with the financial consequences. They tend to have smaller pensions (they are eligible for only half of their husband's Social Security benefits), and less knowledge about savings and investments, than their husbands did. In many cases, widowhood precipitates poverty (Smith and Zick, 1986).

Widows must also come to grips with a hard truth: they are probably never again going to find a man to be their close friend and lover. Men, however, once they have gotten over their initial depression, discover that they are a much-sought-after item—the unmarried, mature male. There are many women who would happily fix their meals, clean their houses, and marry them, if possible. Statistics on remarriage bear this out: widowers are far more likely to remarry (often to women considerably younger than themselves) than widows are.

Remarriage

Not surprisingly, remarriage in late adulthood tends to be happier than remarriage in earlier adulthood (Campbell, 1981). One reason is that both partners are usually widowed rather than divorced. Their former experience of a lasting love relationship helps them build another such relationship. In addition, since any children from former marriages are usually full-grown, neither spouse needs to take on the often troubling aspects of an active stepparent role.

This does not mean, of course, that remarriage in late adulthood is problem-free. Some widows and widowers idealize their first spouse and fault the second by comparison. Sometimes, children, grandchildren, or siblings-in-law also make comparisons that can hurt the "interloper." In some instances, inheritance is a bone of contention if grown children think that money that should have gone to them is being spent on an elderly stepparent.

Yet even when such problems exist, marriage in late adulthood is usually much better for the couple than are the alternatives (Kohn and Kohn,

Figure 25.12 *Remarriage between widow and widower in late adulthood is likely to benefit them both, financially, socially, and sexually. The only likely problem is grown children, who sometimes complain about their parent's choice of partner in words quite similar to those used by parents to complain about their children's mates.*

---

*Addresses for self-help groups of various kinds, including those for widows, can be obtained from the Self-Help Clearinghouse, City University of New York, 33 West 42nd Street, New York, NY, 10036.

1978). In most respects, it is less expensive and less lonely than living alone. For many older people, it also provides sexual affirmation. As one 82-year-old widower, recently remarried, explained: "Everyone tells me about companionship. It gets me mad. Sure, I want companionship, but I also got married for sex. I always had an active sex life and still do" (quoted in Starr and Weiner, 1981).

The Frail Elderly

So far in these chapters we have emphasized the majority of the elderly—those who are alert and active, financially secure, supported by friendship and family ties. They are quite different from the group we focus on now—the physically infirm, the very ill, the cognitively impaired, who are called the **frail elderly.**

No single demarcation differentiates the frail from their hardy contemporaries (Pinholt et al., 1987). However, beyond simple vulnerability and fragility, the crucial sign of frailty is probably an inability to perform, safely and adequately, the various tasks of self-care. Gerontologists often refer to the **activities of daily life,** abbreviated **ADLs,** typically comprising five tasks: eating, bathing, toileting, walking, and dressing. If a person needs assistance with even one of these, he or she may be considered frail, although for some purposes (such as medical insurance compensation or government research on dependency), frailty is not considered to begin until a person is unable to perform three or more.

Equally, if not more, important to independent living are the **instrumental activities of daily life,** or **IADLs,** actions that require some intellectual competence and forethought (Katz, 1983). As one might expect, specific IADLs vary somewhat from culture to culture (Andrews, 1991). For most of the elderly in the United States, they include items such as shopping for groceries, paying bills, making phone calls, taking appropriate medications, and keeping appointments. For some of the elderly in other nations, tending the animals, cultivating the garden, mending clothes, and baking bread might be among the culture's list of IADLs.

Increasing Prevalence of the Frail Elderly

Worldwide, the frail elderly are a minority, even in those nations where universal health care successfully prolongs life for the most vulnerable individuals. Overall, no more than 15 to 25 percent of the world's senior citizens are frail at any given moment, which puts their proportion of the general population at about 4 percent in the most developed nations and about 1 percent in the least developed (United Nations, 1990). However, in every nation their numbers are increasing, for three reasons.

The first reason is demographic. As average life expectancy increases and fewer individuals die young, more people reach old-old age. In the United States, for instance, the number of Americans aged 85 and older quadrupled between 1960 and 1990, making this age group the fastest-growing segment of the population. As more people reach old age, the absolute numbers of frail individuals will increase. This was clearly shown by one extensive study of functional capacity in the year before death (see Fig-

Figure 25.13 *While most elderly people, most of the time, function quite well, the older a person is and the closer to death, the more likely it is that he or she will be unable to perform all the normal activities of daily life. As you can see, after age 85 less than one person in ten is functioning at full capacity in the last year of life.*

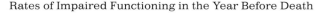

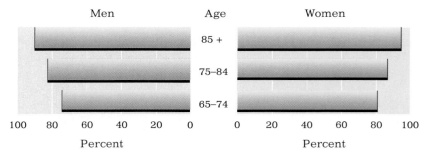

Rates of Impaired Functioning in the Year Before Death

Source: Lentzner et al., 1992.

ure 25.13). Among the oldest-old in that final year, half required assistance with all five ADLs and more than a third exhibited cognitive impairment as well (Lentzner et al., 1992).

The second reason for the rise in frailty is that, as we have seen, the medical establishment is still more geared toward death prevention rather than life enhancement, focusing on dramatic, life-saving intervention for acute illness rather than on the prevention and treatment of chronic illness. Since chronic problems—everything from Alzheimer's disease and arthritis to ulcers and varicose veins—are the ones that most commonly sap the elderly's strength, pride, and independence, the result of these medical priorities is the increasing prevalence of morbidity even as mortality rates fall (Verbrugge, 1989). Just using the knowledge already available, frailty could be decreased substantially if medical efforts were redirected to ameliorating or preventing nonfatal diseases (Fries, 1989). For instance, current therapies, if fully utilized, could cut in half the rate of urinary incontinence, which is a problem for about a fourth of all the elderly. Focusing the attention of general practitioners on the available solutions to this problem would thus improve the quality of life for about 10 million older Americans (Ouslander, 1989; Mitteness, 1987).

The third reason that frailty is increasing among the elderly is that the political process has failed to ensure their ready and timely access to measures that could prevent or reduce their impairment—everything from adequate nutrition to safe housing, from hearing aids to hip replacements. This neglect occurs in spite of the fact that the United States and many other nations spend substantial money on services for the elderly. However, critics find significant gaps in the practical benefits afforded to the needy elderly. While the specifics vary from nation to nation, in general the problem is that adequate services do not reach the most frail in the community. For example, in 1965 the American Congress passed the **Older Americans Act,** providing every older person, regardless of income, a wealth of benefits—from subsidized meals at over 15,000 locations to community services offered by over 20,000 agencies (Quirk, 1991). One result was, as intended, better health, less dependence, and improved morale for many seniors.

However, these benefits are neither comprehensive nor free, with housing and health benefits particularly likely to require copayment. In addition, obtaining these benefits requires some mobility, planning, and initiative. This tends to exclude precisely the poor, uneducated, or isolated who are most likely to become frail (Zopf, 1986). As one gerontologist explains, most housing for the elderly

> is filled with the relatively less needy seniors. Most services . . . [senior centers, meal sites] are captured by the less needy who often actively discriminate against the needy, the culturally different, the eccentric, and the mentally ill. The senior in need is thus faced with a series of "no vacancy" signs and overt and covert discouragement to participate. The tragedy is compounded by the realization that often the places are taken by people who could afford to compete in the real world market for meals, housing, and nursing service. [Knight, 1982]

Finally, social services of every kind—from senior citizen centers to visiting nurses—are relatively scarce in rural areas, where a disproportionate share of the elderly reside. This is particularly the case for "elders of color," such as the African-American elderly in the Deep South and the Native American and Chicano elderly in the Southwest. Because of their age, race, SES, and location, these older people in rural communities are said to live in "quadruple jeopardy" for frailty (Bane, 1991; American Society on Aging, 1992).

Of course, long life does not inevitably include years of frailty: the likelihood of disability depends less on chronological age than on factors such as social support, attitudes, and the physical setting (see A Closer Look on p. 668). However, the best defense against extended frailty—the resources of family members—is increasingly being stretched too thin to prevent frailty as it once did. As one study explains, the combination over the past fifty years of a rapidly increasing population of elderly and a steadily declining birthrate is setting the stage for a "disturbing scenario," that of a "vast army of people whose advanced age and frailty assumes that they will need to depend on others for basic care, and a relatively small cohort of close relatives to provide this care" (Kaye and Applegate, 1990). Obviously, then, caring for the frail elderly will increasingly become a concern for the community as a whole, as well as the family.

Caring for the Frail Elderly

When thinking about the care of the frail elderly, it must be kept in mind that their main goal is not necessarily to keep on living as long as possible but to keep on living as independently as possible. Quality of life is crucial. Because of their wish to be independent, most do not want to enter nursing homes, but they do not want to "burden" their children either. When a sample of older Americans were asked "Would you like to live with one of your children if something happens that you cannot live alone?" 96 percent of the whites, 90 percent of blacks, and 50 percent of Mexican-Americans answered no (Bengston, 1986).

Nevertheless, as in the past, most of the frail elderly are cared for by relatives. Indeed, of every ten frail American elders, six depend exclusively on family and friends. The other four receive a combination of family and professional care, half within a nursing home and half in the community (U.S. Department of Health and Human Services, 1990; DeFriese and Woomert, 1992). Even those who are mentally incompetent as well as physically frail are usually cared for by family in the community: those in nursing homes are disproportionately unmarried and childless.

Between Old, Fragile, and Frail—Protective Buffers

Frailty is not automatically defined by either age or illness. Both advanced years and specific infirmities may make someone more fragile, but neither necessarily makes that person frail, because the health and independence of the elderly depend not only on intrinsic impairment but also on extrinsic resources (Davies, 1991). Many elderly persons never become helpless because four protective factors—their attitude, their social network, their physical setting, and their financial resources—act as a buffer, preventing or postponing the progression from fragility to frailty.

Consider the hypothetical example of two 80-year-old childless widows who have the same failing eyesight and advanced osteoporosis. One widow might live alone in an old, rundown house in an isolated neighborhood. Among the particulars of her residence and daily life are uneven hardwood floors covered with braided scatter rugs, a flight of steep stairs separating the bedroom and the kitchen, dimly lit rooms and hallways, and rumors of a recent robbery two blocks away. After falling and fracturing her wrist on the way to the toilet one night, she is now apprehensive about walking around anywhere without help, and she refuses to go downstairs to prepare meals. She, of course, never ventures outside anymore, and is frightened to answer the door or the phone. Further, she no longer tries to wash or dress herself, or even feed herself as much as she should, citing some lingering pain in her fingers and the fact that "no one cares anyway."

Obviously, this widow is very frail, requiring ongoing care. At present, a home attendant comes every morning to bathe her and prepare the day's food, but the attendant is worried about the woman's depression. This is a valid concern, since suicide is more prevalent among the elderly than among any other age group, and is particularly common among those over 75 who live alone (Osgood, 1992). This widow is on the waiting list for a nursing home, where she will probably become even more frail, since nursing homes tend to discourage independent functioning (Van Nostrand, 1991).

The other widow, by contrast, might have had the financial resources and foresight to have purchased, with two old friends, a large coop apartment near a small shopping center. As all three are aging, they have reduced their vulnerability by outfitting their home with precautionary amenities such as bright lighting, sturdy furniture strategically placed to aid mobility, secure grab rails in the bathroom to ease bathing and toileting, wall-to-wall carpeting nailed to the floor, a telephone programmed to dial numbers at the push of one button, a stove that automatically shuts off after a certain time, a front door that buzzes until it is properly locked with the key, and so forth.

In addition, all three women gladly compensate for each other's impairments: the one who sees best reads the fine print on all the medicine bottles, legal papers, and cooking directions; the one who is the sturdiest sweeps, mops, and vacuums: and our poorly sighted, osteoporotic widow, who has excellent hearing, responds to the phone, the doorbell, the alarm clock, the oven timer. All three regularly eat, converse, and laugh together—a practice that is good for the digestion as well as the spirit.

Unlike the first widow, who will soon be institutionalized, the second widow with the same physical problems is safe and happy in her apartment, caring for herself, socializing with friends, shopping in the community, and so forth. For her, protective buffers will continue to defend against many factors that could otherwise be disabling. For example, she will be motivated, encouraged, and financially able to obtain good medical care and enabling accessories, such as corrective eye-drops and special glasses, or calcium supplements and a hip replacement, or even, if both major disabilities worsen, home delivery of books-for-the-blind and the purchase of a small, motorized wheelchair.

The lesson here is that a certain degree of fragility and vulnerability does not necessarily translate into an equivalent degree of frailty. Just as a fine crystal goblet—admired, lovingly handled, and carefully stored in soft cloth—is unlikely to break despite its fragility, so an older person, surrounded by crucial buffering, is less likely to become frail.

Figure 25.14 *Although the popular press sometimes bemoans the indifference of the younger generations, the facts are otherwise: most of the frail and widowed elderly, like these two, are cared for by their children at home. Only when aged people are very ill, or have no descendants able to help, do they enter a nursing home.*

 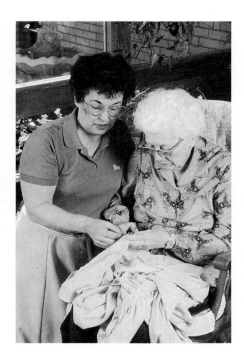

Interestingly, while almost all family members feel an obligation to help their elderly relatives, the specific task of providing care usually falls primarily on one person. If the dependent person is married, their primary caregiver is usually the spouse. If the person is a spouseless parent, the caregiver is usually a daughter or daughter-in-law; otherwise, a sister, niece, or granddaughter is the likely caregiver.

Note that caregivers are usually women, with wives particularly likely to become primary caregivers, partly because they tend to be younger and therefore less frail than their husbands and partly because everyone—from the doctor to the children to the wives themselves—expects them to. However, as a result of low birthrates, high divorce rates, and more women being employed, an increasing number of families have no available female caregivers. Consequently, many husbands, sons, and brothers now provide extensive, nurturant, intimate care (Stoller, 1992; Kaye and Applegate, 1990).

Burdens and Benefits

The demands of providing care for a frail elderly relative should not be underestimated. In many cases, the caregiver must forgo all other activities, because the physical work and psychological stress are overwhelming. One daughter reports on the strain she and her elderly father experienced when her mother developed Alzheimer's disease:

> I worked the entire time through four pregnancies . . . returning to work within six weeks of delivery. It was a piece of cake compared to trying to cope with a combative, frustrated adult who cannot dress, bathe, feed herself; who wanders constantly. A person faced with this situation . . . having to work a full day, raise a family, and take care of an "impaired" relative would be susceptible to suicide, "parent-abuse" . . . possibly murder.

My father tried very hard to take care of her, but a man 84 years old cannot go without sleep, and cannot force her to take care of her personal cleanliness. Up until two years ago, she was taking care of the finances and household. Her signature was beautiful . . . . now it's just a wavy line. An 84-year-old man does not learn to cook and balance the budget very easily, and he becomes bitter. He did not want to put her in the nursing homes he visited in, and so he reluctantly sold his house and moved to a city he didn't like so that his children could help with her care. It has been a nightmare . . . she obviously belonged in a secondary-care facility because no one can give her 24-hr. care and still maintain their sanity and families. But the real victim is Dad . . . his meager income eaten away by the nursing home . . . separated from his wife of 50 years . . . stripped of his house, car, acquaintances . . . dignity. He is the real victim.

Sometimes everyone, from the care-receiver and other family members to neighbors and community professionals, appreciates the caregiver's efforts and attempts to relieve the burden as much as possible, a situation that allows caregivers to feel fulfilled by their experience. As one man caring for both his parents said, "There's so much love in this family; that's what keeps me going" (Kaye and Applegate, 1990).

Often, however, caregivers feel unfairly burdened and resentful, for three reasons. First, if one relative seems to be doing the job, other family members tend to feel relief rather than an obligation to do their share. Second, care-receivers and caregivers often disagree about the nature and extent of care that is needed and of whether the caregiver has the right to set the daily schedule, regulate menus, arrange doctor's visits, and so forth. Such disagreements are bound to cause strain, not only in the caregiver who feels frustrated but also in the carereceiver who wants to be self-determining. Finally, in an effort to contain costs, social agencies rarely offer services unless they are urgently and obviously needed. Most difficult to obtain are those services, such as respite care or support groups, that are designed primarily for the caregiver.

As a result of these circumstances, many caregivers feel that they are "left to care alone," resentfully resigning themselves to years of sacrifice (Cicirelli, 1992; Kaye and Applegate, 1990; Wright, 1986). Indeed, many studies show that the amount of stress, resentment, and ill health experienced by caregivers correlates more with their subjective interpretation of the support they experience than with any other variable—including how impaired the aged person actually is (Zarit et al., 1980; Kaye and Applegate, 1990; Biegel et al., 1991; Uchino et al., 1992). Sadly, as the Closer Look on page 671 explains, when caring for a frail elder creates feelings of resentment and entails social isolation, the consequence sometimes is elder maltreatment.

The Place Where Care Occurs

As explained earlier, most elders want to "age in place," remaining in their own homes as long as possible. For many reasons, this wish should be heeded, even with the frail elderly, and often can be through such strategies as remodeling crucial areas of the home and scheduling daily visits by family members and/or professional aides.

Sometimes, however, independent living becomes truly dangerous or even impossible. The task of finding appropriate housing at this point is critical, because the right setting can reduce frailty in many ways, while the wrong setting can increase dependence and hasten death. In some cases, the best solution is for the older relative to move in with a younger relative.

Elder Maltreatment: A Closer Look

Although professional caregivers, con-artists, mean-spirited strangers, and the like sometimes abuse the elderly, the facts show that **elder maltreatment** is primarily a family affair. Indeed, in many ways, elder abuse and neglect parallel child and spouse maltreatment, both in kind and in cause, ranging from direct physical attack to ongoing emotional neglect, and involving such underlying factors as the social isolation and powerlessness of the victim, mental impairment or drug addiction of the perpetrator, and inadequate education and poverty within the household (Pillemer and Finkelhor, 1988).

The typical case of elder maltreatment begins benignly, as an outgrowth of a mutual caregiving relationship within the family (Steinmetz, 1988). For example, an elder may begin to financially assist someone of the younger generation, who then gradually takes control of and misuses more and more of the elder's assets; or a younger family member may assume care of an increasingly frail relative, only to become so overwhelmed by the task that gross neglect and psychic abuse seem inevitable.

Sometimes however, it is a dependent elder who is the perpetrator of abuse. For example, one Chinese-American woman, age 73, was admitted to the hospital with bruises and a broken wrist. On careful questioning, she admitted that her husband, suffering from Alzheimer's disease, had battered her when she tried to care for him (Elder Abuse Project, 1991).

These examples make it clear that elder abuse within the family must be diagnosed, treated, and prevented case by case. As one noted researcher explains, "elder abuse is not a monolithic problem that can be solved with blanket programs, such as those resulting from mandatory reporting" (Pillemer, 1991). The best solution would be the provision of extensive public and personal safety nets of support for those elderly who are frail or powerless, so that no one—caregiver or receiver—gets to the point of abuse (Johnson, 1991; Steinmetz, 1988).

This solution is sometimes romanticized by the inexperienced and uninformed, but the reality is that sharing a household of two or more generations requires many compromises in independence and well-being (Noelker, 1990). For example, life may become difficult if one of the parties in question feels he or she has the right to comment on the other's choice of friends, especially of the other sex, or to call into question habits of a lifetime—from religious practices to food preferences to sleeping schedules. All this adds to the burdens of caregiving, already described, and of care-receiving, which is not easy for an elder who would much rather be independent in his or her own home than dependent in someone else's.

In many cases, a better solution is some form of **congregate care,** in which a group of older people live together with help from outside personnel. The availability of congregate-care housing (called "sheltered housing" in England, "hostels" in Australia, and "retirement hotels" in the United States) varies considerably from nation to nation. England, for instance, has an extensive network of such housing, with paid "wardens" who typically live nearby and check daily on the well-being of each resident, supervise medical care, organize transportation, and respond to emergencies on a twenty-four-hour basis. As a result, England has one of the highest rates of the elderly in such housing (about 5 percent) and lower rates of nursing-home residents than Canada, Australia, or the United States (Schwenger, 1989).

The main advantage both of living with a relative and of living in congregate housing is that everyone concerned tries to strike a balance between providing social interaction and assistance on the one hand and allowing personal privacy and independent functioning on the other. As we will now see, failure to seek this balance is one of several potential drawbacks to nursing-home care.

Nursing Homes

Many older Americans and their relatives feel that nursing homes should be avoided at all costs, usually because they believe that all nursing homes are horrible. Some nursing homes are indeed horrible. The worst tend to be those profit-making ventures where most patients are subsidized entirely by Medicaid. The only way for these institutions to make a profit is to cut down on expenses. Consequently, they are staffed by overworked, poorly trained aides who provide minimal, often dehumanizing care.

However, some profit-making nursing homes are excellent. Consider the case of Laura Hunter (Hunter and Memhard, 1981), for example. She had reached the age of 80 "bedridden, arthritic, and crotchety . . . relying on drugs, and incapacitated by fears of impending change, illness, and death, [she] clung to the radio for company and turned away even her closest family and friends." A period of hospitalization convinced her children that something had to be done. After much soul-searching, they decided to place her in a nursing home, one of the best in the country. Residents there had their own rooms and were able to carry on private lives, having friends in to visit, for instance, or going to sleep when they wanted to. The staff encouraged the residents to stay active, and the residents had their own council, which helped determine residence policies.

Initially, Laura was despondent and uncommunicative, but gradually she came out of her shell and joined the community life around her. Among other things, she made friends, joined a book-review club and an exercise class, won election to the residence council, worked as a reporter for the residence newspaper, and developed a romance. She also kept a journal of all those activities. Reading it, one gets the impression of a spunky, good-humored lady with a love of life. She needed good nursing-home care, surrounded by people who could become her friends, to help her express that love.

Fortunately, most nursing homes are better than the one in the first example; unfortunately, few are as good as the one in the second. One problem with many homes is that they concentrate almost exclusively on the physical maintenance of their residents and give insufficient attention to the residents' psychological needs, such as social interaction and a feeling

Figure 25.15 *Good nursing homes encourage residents to participate in regular physical exercise, and the best provide physical therapy for those who need it. Good nursing homes also encourage contact with the outside community, sometimes including visits from schoolchildren to allow friendship between the generations. This type of social contact is especially important, since a disproportionate number of nursing-home residents have no living relatives.*

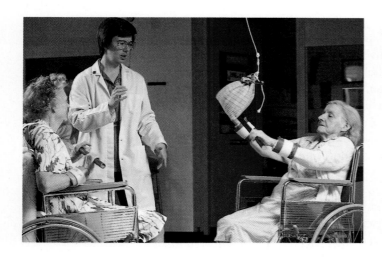

of social control. As we saw in Chapter 24 (pp. 620–621), too often the staff pay more attention to those patients who docilely wait for their needs to be met, thereby reinforcing the dependence of many patients who could learn to fill some of these needs themselves. Correspondingly, the more independent patients suffer from inattention and, even worse, they learn that the best way to cope with life is by becoming passive and relinquishing control. An immediate consequence is that they become less active; in the longer term, they become less healthy, lose self-esteem, and die earlier than they would have (Baltes and Reisenzein, 1986).

One simple research project illustrates this pattern. Forty-seven residents on one floor of a nursing home were asked to help in their own care as much as possible, and were given plants to care for. Forty-five residents on another floor were told that the staff was responsible for their care, and even for the care of their plants. Three weeks later, 93 percent of the first group showed improvement on measures of activity level, alertness, sociability, and self-reliance. In marked contrast, 71 percent of the second group showed declines on the same measures (Langer and Rodin, 1976). The initial experimental treatment apparently set in motion a series of positive reactions that were self-perpetuating. A follow-up study found that even two years later, the group that had been encouraged to be more independent was healthier than the conventional-care group (Rodin and Langer, 1977).

Increasingly, professionals are becoming involved in developing good nursing-home care, where the goal is to help each patient gain as much independence, control, and self-respect as possible (Burger et al., 1986). Thus it is possible to find good care, if one knows what to look for, and can afford it. For those who need nursing-home care, the quality and suitability of that care can make the difference between the final years being full and satisfying or a desolation.

Integrity and Community

Let us conclude this chapter by first reviewing our basic perspective on old age. Aging is neither as distressful and disruptive as ageist stereotypes might depict it to be nor as smooth as phrases such as "the golden years" imply. Instead, three themes that are apparent throughout the life span emerge even more strongly at the end, emphasizing the enormous variety that "growing old" can entail.

One theme is the interplay among the domains: genetic and biosocial foundations affect longevity and vitality; perceptions and cognitive interpretations shape every age-related change; and social supports and public policies determine whether or not a particular elder can find a comfortable niche in which to live and thrive. A second theme is that developmental diversity is to be expected, welcomed, and even celebrated; each person ages in his or her own way, bringing to every aspect of growing old a different set of circumstances and personal history. A third theme is that every life is shaped by its place and time in human history: every cohort in every culture faces new opportunities and new challenges in old age that are peculiar to its historical location. Thus, while relentless, inevitable processes of aging are universal, the particular course of any life within any context is an ongoing process, with the final result not determined until the end.

Figure 25.16 *Eugene Lang (center), a self-made millionaire, was invited to address sixty-one children from the graduating class of the public grade school he had attended in Harlem. During the ceremony, he reflected on the outlook for the graduates, many of whom had grown up in poverty, and suddenly made an astonishing offer: he would pay for their college education if they graduated from high school. In the interim, he arranged tutoring, workshops, and cultural field trips for the children and became their adviser and advocate. In the end, nearly all the students graduated from high school and over half went on to college. In his gesture of extraordinary generosity and integrity, Lang affirmed his personal history and made it meaningful for the next generation.*

For a final view of this process, let us turn again to the most comprehensive of the life-span theorists, Erik Erikson, who is now in his 90s and still writing about the vitality of life.

Erikson calls the final crisis of development the crisis of **integrity versus despair.** His depiction of the diversity of late life is framed in terms of what he sees as the universal attempt of older adults to integrate and unify their unique personal experiences with their vision of the future of their community. Some develop a sense of pride and contentment with their past and present lives, as well as a "shared sense of 'we' within a communal mutuality" (Erikson et al., 1986). Others experience despair, "feeling that the time is now short, too short for the attempt to start another life and to try out alternate roads to recovery" (Erikson, 1963).

As at each of Erikson's eight stages, tension between the two opposing aspects of the developmental crisis helps move the person forward. This is particularly apparent in this eighth stage, when

> life brings many, quite realistic reasons for experiencing despair; aspects of the present that cause unremitting pain; aspects of a future that are uncertain and frightening. And, of course, there remains inescapable death, that one aspect of the future which is both wholly certain and wholly unknowable. Thus, some despair must be acknowledged and integrated as a component of old age. [Erikson et al., 1986]

Ideally, coming to grips with death leads to a new view of survival, through children, grandchildren, and the human community as a whole. This vision of the integrity of the generational life cycle allows a "life-affirming involvement" in the present.

In order to reach integrity, an individual must review his or her life, coming to terms with the personal choices and events that have shaped it. For the most part, even those who earlier in adulthood

> experienced periods of profound unhappiness and restlessness, which they attributed to misguided decisions concerning spouse, career, child-rearing . . . look back now, quite satisfied with how they have chosen to live their lives— with the people they married, with the ways they raised their children, with the kinds of work they did. [Erikson et al., 1986]

Some, however, are mired in bitterness and blame, fearful of death, unable to accept either the past or the future.

What kind of vision enables a person to reach integrity rather than despair? As we have seen throughout this book, there is no one true path, no one lifestyle, no one cultural route toward personal or community wholeness, but each person must believe in the direction his or her own life has taken within the context of the individual's particular culture. As Erikson (1963) explains, people of every background and income can reach integrity, "each aware of the relativity of all the various lifestyles which have given meaning to human striving . . . [yet knowing] that for him all human integrity stands or falls with the one style of integrity of which he partakes."

In other words, instead of comparing themselves with others, those who achieve integrity become self-affirming and self-actualizing, able to judge their life by their culture's standards and to find it good. This is a goal we could all keep in mind at whatever stage of development we are in, seeing our own unique, ongoing existence as an integral thread woven into the multicolored tapestry that depicts the human story.

SUMMARY

Theories of Psychosocial Aging

1. Several theories have been offered to explain how the elderly react to their changing experiences with age. According to disengagement theory, late adulthood is a time when mutual withdrawal occurs between the elderly and society, as work and family roles become less available or less important.

2. Activity theory holds that the less older people disengage, the happier they are. According to this theory, most of the elderly replace one form of activity with another; if an elderly person becomes less active, it is because society or ill health requires it, not because the older person chooses to withdraw.

3. Continuity theory emphasizes the stability of personality traits and behavior patterns across adulthood, including ongoing genetic influences that become even more apparent in the later years. According to this theory, the changes that occur with age are much less disruptive than they appear, because each person's social supports, attitudes, and coping patterns are quite stable.

4. Overall, the elderly are more diverse, in lifestyle, income, and personality than adults at earlier periods of life. Thus each of the major theories is true for some people some of the time, but not for all the people all of the time.

Generativity in Late Adulthood

5. More and more people are retiring, at earlier ages than ever before, partly because the financial incentives to do so have increased, and partly because the jobs available have decreased. After a period of transition, most retirees enjoy retirement.

6. Many retired people do volunteer work, attend classes, pursue hobbies, join organizations, and extend their social activities. Which of these activities a particular person chooses depends largely on lifelong interests that the person always wanted to devote time and energy to.

7. The activities of children and grandchildren also continue to be a source of pride and concern. While each generation is interested in the activities of the other, and is willing to help out if necessary, relationships among the generations are not as intimate as they once were. One important reason is that today's grandparents are more likely to have homes, social lives, and interests of their own.

Affiliation: The Social Convoy

8. Friendship continues to be important in late adulthood, as a source of happiness and as a buffer against trouble. If the elderly have lived in the same neighborhood for many years, their friends are likely to be neighbors. If the elderly move to a senior-citizen community, they are also likely to find social support there.

9. Marriage also provides important social support in old age. Older adults in long-standing marriages tend to be quite satisfied with their relationships, as reflected by a significant drop in conflicts and disagreements. Spouses also safeguard each other's health and provide major care when illness or disability strikes, and for this reason married elders tend to live longer, healthier lives than unmarried elders.

10. The single older adult and the divorced older adult usually have long-standing friendships and interests that keep them active in late adulthood. Health problems, however, might be particularly discouraging.

11. About 80 percent of elderly married women, and 20 percent of elderly married men, must adjust to being widowed at some point in late adulthood, usually before age 75. The ease of this adjustment is affected by the gender of the surviving spouse: men are more likely to experience health problems as widowers, but they are also much more likely to remarry. Women are more likely to have financial difficulties, but they are also more likely to be comforted by friends, who are probably widows themselves.

12. Remarriage in late adulthood is usually a happy event, helping both spouses feel younger, less lonely, happier, and sexier than they did before.

The Frail Elderly

13. Some of the elderly are frail, too feeble or ill to provide basic self-care, either for routine activities such as eating and dressing, or for more intellectual tasks such as shopping and keeping appointments. While this group is a minority at any given moment, most older people will eventually become frail, with those who are female, poor, and over age 85 particularly likely to experience an extended period of frailty.

14. When older persons are unable to care for themselves, they are usually cared for by a close relative—typically their spouse, daughter, or daughter-in-law. Despite the personal sacrifices this entails, most relatives consider such care part of being a close family member.

15. For a minority, however, caring for a dependent and needy older person leads to frustration, anger, or maltreatment. The scope of the problem is not yet known, but we do know that greater community services are needed for the frail elderly living at home.

16. When family members are unable to continue providing care for a frail elderly person, a nursing home is the usual alternative. For the minority of the elderly who must be placed in a nursing home, the quality of their final years of life can vary enormously, depending on the quality of the home.

Integrity and Community

17. In Erikson's final stage of life, the older person attempts to accept and appreciate the essential worth of his or her own particular life, seeing the continuity of that life in relationship to the lives of all humankind.

KEY TERMS

disengagement theory (642)

activity theory (643)

continuity theory (643)

generational equity (648)

Elderhostel (650)

American Association of Retired Persons (AARP) (652)

filial obligation (652)

social convoy (657)

planned retirement communities (658)

naturally occurring retirement communities (NORCs) (659)

frail elderly (665)

activities of daily life (ADLs) (665)

instrumental activities of daily life (IADLs) (665)

Older Americans Act (666)

elder maltreatment (671)

congregate care (671)

integrity versus despair (674)

KEY QUESTIONS

1. Which theory of late adulthood do you think is most accurate and why?

2. Which theory of late adulthood do you think is least accurate and why?

3. What are some of the factors that lead to a satisfying adjustment to retirement?

4. What factors are associated with dissatisfaction with retirement?

5. How and why has the experience of being a grandparent changed in recent times?

6. What specific needs of the elderly do friends fill?

7. What are the changes that occur in marriages of long duration in late adulthood?

8. What accounts for the increasing prevalence of the frail elderly?

9. What are some of the important factors in providing good nursing-home care for the elderly?

Biosocial Development

Senescence

Changes in appearance and decline of the sense organs and major body systems continue at a gradual but steady pace. Because of declines in organ reserve, the immune system, and overall muscle strength, older adults are at greater risk of chronic and acute diseases, heart disease, and cancer. However, risk is also related to long-standing health habits and quality of health care. The brain becomes physically smaller and slower in its functioning. Slowing of brain processes may be due in part to reduced production of neurotransmitters and to reduced blood flow.

Cognitive Development

Decline in Information-Processing Capacity

Experimental testing of older adults reveals deficits in their ability to receive information, store it in memory, and organize and interpret it. These deficits may result from decrements in memory self-efficacy, declines in processing resources, and/or health impairments. However, in the tasks of real life, most older adults develop ways to compensate for memory loss and slower thinking.

Dementia

Dementia, with its progressive impairment of cognitive functioning, is not inevitable in old age but it does become more common, especially in the very old. Symptoms of dementia may be caused by Alzheimer's disease, problems in the circulatory system, other diseases, depression, or drugs.

New Cognitive Development

Many older individuals develop or intensify their aesthetic, philosophical, and spiritual interests and values in later life.

Psychosocial Development

Activities

Retirement is a major economic, social, and psychological event that can be either stressful or benign for both the worker and his or her spouse, depending on an individual's circumstances, including finances, health, outside interests, and new opportunities for achievement.

Affiliation

Older adults' satisfaction with life depends in large part on continuing contact with friends and family. Generally, marital satisfaction continues to improve. Family involvement, especially voluntary interactions with grandchildren, is often a source of pride and joy. The death of a spouse can cause extreme stress for both sexes, but men generally have more difficulty than women in coping with the loss of their partner. Overall, older adults' ability to cope with ageism and frailty depends on many factors, including self-attitude, income, and social support.

Epilogue: Death and Dying

One goal of the study of human development, as outlined in Chapter 1, is to help each person realize his or her full potential. According to many developmental theorists, including Freud, Erikson, and Maslow, achieving an understanding of death and dying is essential to the complete realization of self. The ability to accept death and to work through one's grief over the death of others is crucial if life is to be lived to the fullest.

Death in Context

Death can have many meanings: it can be seen as "a biological event, a rite of passage, an inevitability, a natural occurrence, a punishment, extinction, the enforcement of God's will, the absurd, separation, reunion, . . . a reasonable cause for anger, depression, denial, repression, guilt, frustration, relief . . . " (Kalish, 1985). The specific meanings that actually are attached to death, and the reactions that death prompts, vary, of course, from individual to individual and case to case. They also vary according to their historical and cultural context.

Throughout many cultures, past and present, death has been seen as a quite social moment, witnessed and shared by the community as a whole. In most African traditions, for example, elders take on an important new status through death, joining the ancestors who watch over not only their own descendants but over the entire village as well. Therefore everyone in the village participates in a funeral, preparing the body and providing food and money for the deceased's journey to the ancestral realm. The death of the individual becomes an occasion for the affirmation of the entire community, as members jointly celebrate their connection with each other and with their collective past (Opaku, 1989).

In many Muslim nations, death affirms not so much faith in the group as faith in Allah. In Islam, religious teaching emphasizes that the achievements, problems, and pleasures of this life are transitory and ephemeral, and that everyone should be mindful of, and ready for, death at any time. Therefore, for believers, caring for the dying and the dead is a holy reminder of their own mortality, and specific rituals—including reciting prayers, carrying the coffin, and attending the funeral—are performed by devout strangers as well as by relatives and friends (Muwahidi, 1989; Knappert, 1989).

In Hinduism, helping the dying to relinquish their ties to this world and prepare for the next is a particularly important obligation for the immediate family. A holy death is one that is welcomed by the dying person who lies on the ground chanting holy words at the very last moment, surrounded by family members also reciting sacred texts. Such a holy death is believed to ease entry into the next life (Firth, 1989).

Throughout most of Western history, death was likewise an accepted, familiar event that usually occurred at home (Ariès, 1981). Family members of all ages had intimate contact with death that resulted from childbirth, from disease and infection, from accidents, and from the consequences of old age. In general, they were the ones who tended to the dying person and then to the corpse: in most cases they built the coffin, dug the grave, and buried the body themselves.

In twentieth-century North America and Western Europe, however, death came to be withdrawn from everyday life. More and more, people died alone in hospitals rather than at home among family. The disposition of the deceased passed into the hands of professionals, who sanitized and euphemized death in an effort to disguise its reality. They embalmed and made up the corpse to give it a normal and "healthy" look; they coined terms like "slumber room" (referring to the room in which the corpse was displayed) that gave no hint of death; they supervised the burial and formalized the grieving.

This denial of death likewise came to permeate the medical profession. Doctors and nurses routinely resisted telling terminal patients the truth about their condition, and, in fact, avoided the dying as much as possible. Before the end of biological life, the dying, in effect, experienced a "social death," a kind of institutionalized isolation in which they found themselves shunned by their medical caregivers and constricted in their intimacy with family and friends by hospital procedures and protocol (Kastenbaum, 1992).

Figure 1 *An outdoor funeral procession in Indonesia is a marked contrast to the quiet memorial service that is more typical in the West. No matter what form it takes, community involvement in death and dying seems to benefit the living.*

Research on Death and Dying

Recently there has been a shift away from the denial of death to a more accepting view. A major factor leading to this change in attitude about death was the pioneering work of Elizabeth Kübler-Ross, a physician who was asked in 1965 by four seminary students for help in doing research on people close to death. When Kübler-Ross approached her professional colleagues for permission to interview the dying, they responded with anger and shock, and even denied that any of their patients were terminally ill. "It suddenly seemed that there were no dying patients in this huge hospital" (Kübler-Ross, 1969). Finally, the first interview was obtained, and thereafter Kübler-Ross found many dying people who were eager to talk about their feelings, and many others who were ready to listen to the truth about their condition.

One of the first things Kübler-Ross learned from her interviews was how important informing the dying of their condition can be. She discovered that doctors sometimes told the immediate family of a member's terminal illness and then explicitly instructed them to keep "the facts from the patient in order to avoid an emotional outburst." In many cases the patients eventually guessed their fate but were unable to talk about their feelings because family and staff continued to pretend that all would be well. The result was increased isolation and sorrow for both the patients and their families. In other instances, patient and family were told of the probability of death in such an abrupt and insistent manner that all hope was destroyed. And sometimes the truth was hidden from everyone until the last moment, allowing the dying no time to put their affairs in order or to share their final expressions of love with their family.

Fortunately, Kübler-Ross found some doctors "who quite successfully present the patient with the awareness of a serious illness without taking away all hope" (Kübler-Ross, 1969). To ensure that this approach would be more typical in the future, she instituted seminars designed to help health professionals interact with the terminally ill with sensitivity, honesty, and understanding. Her seminars became increasingly popular, for they apparently met a need that had previously been ignored. Now **thanatology,** as the study of death is called, is a respected field of research. In medical schools, seminaries, colleges, high schools, and even elementary schools, students study death and dying just as they study the other critical moments of human existence.

Reactions to Dying in Context

Kübler-Ross's research on death and dying (1969, 1975) led her to propose that the dying go through five emotional stages in confronting their impending death. The first is *denial,* in which they refuse to believe that their condition is terminal. Typically, they convince themselves that their laboratory tests were inaccurate, or that the disease will have an unexpected remission. The second stage is *anger*—at everyone else, for not caring enough, or for caring too much, or simply for being alive and well. The third stage is *bargaining,* in which a person tries to negotiate away the death, promising God or fate to, say, pray more or to live a better life. When bargaining appears to have failed, *depression* sets in, causing the dying person to mourn his or her own impending death and to be unwilling to make any plans or to take an interest in medical treatment. Finally, *acceptance* can occur. Death is understood as the last stage of this life and, perhaps, the beginning of the next—a transition, not a trauma. Kübler-Ross (1969) writes:

> Acceptance should not be mistaken for a happy stage. It is almost void of feelings. It is as if the pain had gone, the struggle is over, and there comes a time for "the final rest before the long journey" as one patient phrased it. This is also the time during which the family usually needs more help, understanding, and support than the patient . . .

Kübler-Ross's findings have been investigated by many other researchers, few of whom have found the same five stages occurring in sequence. More typically, denial, anger, and depression appear and reappear during the dying process (Kastenbaum, 1992), depending largely on the specific context of the death. For example, denial often occurs when the illness is one of the forms of cancer that has periods of remission. Anger often predominates when the dying feel that others are responsible for their condition, or are not sympathetic to it, as many victims of AIDS feel. Some studies show that depression increases as death nears, but it should be noted that what often appears to be depression related to dying may, in many cases, be a side effect of pain killers or other drugs.

The age of the dying person also affects the way he or she feels. Young children, not understanding the concept of death, are usually upset by the thought of dying because it suggests the idea of being separated from those they love. A dying child therefore needs constant companionship and reassurance. The developing cognitive competencies of the school-age child often lead the very ill young person to become absorbed with learning the facts about his or her illness and treatment and about the "mechanics" of dying. Adolescents tend to think not about the distant future but about the quality of present life. Thus, to the dying or seriously ill adolescent, the effect of their condition on their appearance and social relationships may be of primary importance. For the young adult, coping with dying often produces great rage and depression at the idea that, just as life is about to begin in earnest, it must end. For the middle-aged adult, death is an interruption of important obligations and responsibilities, so most middle-aged people who know they are dying need to make sure that others will take over those obligations. An older adult's feelings about dying depend a great deal on the particular situation. If one's spouse has already died, and if the terminal illness brings pain and infirmity, acceptance of death is comparatively easy.

From all this it is clear that Kübler-Ross's five stages make feelings about death seem much more predictable and universal than they actually are (Kastenbaum, 1992). It is also clear that there is no one approach to death that is universally "best," and that any specific prescription for the proper approach to death is limited, partly by the cultural context and partly by the particular needs and circumstances of the individuals who are directly involved. As one critic of the "stages of death" notion has observed:

Just as no one would listen to music because it is "right" but because it is beautiful, so no one should be urged to accept a specific metaphysical notion because it is "right" . . . but only because it enriches someone's life and makes a positive difference in how he or she . . . endures pain or deprivation. The criterion, it is suggested, for either adopting or rejecting a certain concept of death is not "correctness" but social, spiritual and emotional relevance. [Klatt, 1991]

Dying a Good Death

What constitutes "a good death"? Most people would agree that it is one that occurs after a person has put his or her affairs in order, reached some spiritual understanding of life and an acceptance of death, and said goodbye to loved ones. Once that is complete, a good death involves a swift and peaceful end.

As old age progresses, or as terminal illness takes hold, most individuals do, in fact, prepare in some way for death, drawing up a will, reconciling with friends, ending each family visit with loving goodbyes, and/or establishing spiritual peace. However, while most people can prepare for death in those ways, a swift and easeful death is more difficult to ensure.

The reason is that, increasingly, modern medicine can sustain life beyond its time, holding off death with all manner of technological interventions—able even to maintain organ functioning after brain death has occurred. Obviously, when there is a chance for recovery, extraordinary and "heroic" medical procedures make good sense, and even people of advanced age who have life-threatening illnesses sometimes get well when given appropriate surgery, chemotherapy, resuscitation, or the like. However, when death is inevitable and near, the same procedures rob the patient of a good death and deprive loved ones of their final goodbyes. Indeed,

Figure 2 *For many of those who are nearing death, spiritual counseling, or just talking about one's feelings with someone who is trained to listen and respond sensitively, can be a source of great peace.*

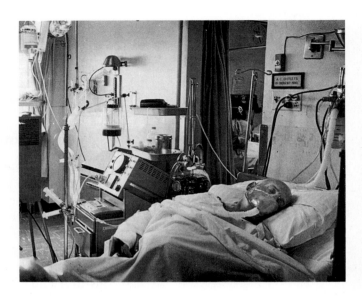

Figure 3 *Life-support equipment, like that pictured here, can often work miracles in sustaining life. However, if this extension of life merely prolongs a person's dying and suffering, it may amount to what one nurse calls "needless torture."*

the majority of people who die in hospitals are likely to depart this life after an extended period of confused semiconsciousness, attached to an assortment of machines, tubes, and intravenous drips. Often they die in discomfort or outright pain, largely because analgesic medications tend to be underprescribed (because of fear of addiction!) (Solomon et al., 1993). And when the dying are maintained on life-support systems, the actual moment of their death is not only unpredictable; it is sometimes unrecognizable.

This situation is often compounded by the attitudes of some doctors who view death as an enemy to be fended off at all costs. Their blind zeal is reflected in this man's bitter account of his mother-in-law's final months:

> She had wasted down to less than half her normal weight. One evening my wife got a call that she was failing and drove to the hospital. "I think I have saved your mother," a young doctor beamed to my wife. He had applied heart and lung resuscitation. My wife loved her mother very much, but her immediate response to the young man was "Why?" [Smyser, 1982]

Fortunately, both the medical profession and the general public are becoming increasingly aware of the undesirability of using extraordinary measures that prolong the suffering of terminal patients and deprive them and their families of a good death. Indeed, "good modern palliation is concerned with relief of all forms of suffering—physical, psychological, social, and spiritual—whereas a few years ago it would have been legitimate (if cruel) to say to a dying agonized patient "Nothing more can be done" (Ahmedzai and Wilkes, 1988). In the **hospice,** an alternative to hospital care for persons who are terminally ill, both patients and their families are given every aid to not only relieve suffering but to make the last days of life filled with love and meaning (see A Closer Look on the next page).

There is also a growing consensus, both in law and in hospital practice, that the ultimate authority regarding what measures are to be used in terminal cases should be made by the person most directly concerned, the patient. To this end, many people, long before death is imminent, make a **living will,** a document that indicates what kind of medical intervention they want should they become terminally ill and incapable of expressing their wishes.

A CLOSER LOOK   The Hospice

One effort to help ensure that more of the terminally ill die a good death began in London during the 1950s, when a dedicated woman named Cecily Saunders opened the first hospice, a place where the terminally ill could come to die in peace. Conceived in response to the dehumanization of the typical hospital death, hospices provide the dying with skilled medical care—which includes pain-killing medication but shuns artificial life-support systems—and a setting where their dignity as human beings, and that of their family members, is respected.

In the hospice, visitors are encouraged day and night. One close friend or family member, called a *lay primary caregiver*, is present much of the time and is responsible for some of the routine care. This arrangement makes the dying person feel less alone and helps the caregiver to be involved rather than excluded as he or she would be in most hospital settings. The hospice staff direct their care to both the patient and the patient's family. When death comes, the staff continue to tend to the family's psychological and other needs.

In some cases, the person's home can become a hospice, allowing the individual the emotional comfort of being in familiar surroundings. In addition, having the home as the hospice can actually prolong life, since it is free of the infections and contagious diseases that the weakened elderly often contract, and die of, in hospitals. When hospice care does occur in the home, doctors and nurses visit regularly, to give comfort as well as medication and therapy and to instruct family members in how to provide daily care.

Obviously, the hospice has much to recommend it. However, the hospice concept is not accepted uncritically. First of all, to be accepted by a hospice, patients must be diagnosed as terminally ill; that is, they must have no reasonable chance of recovery. Such a diagnosis can be made for only a minority of the dying. Second, they and their family must accept this diagnosis, agreeing that longer life and cure are virtually impossible, and that a good death is the only remaining choice. Understandably, even for some who are extremely ill, hope is so crucial that they would rather have one last operation, with all odds against success, than wait for death in a hospice.

Further, hospice care does not always reach its goals of meeting all the needs of the dying and their families. One reason is cost: while the well-functioning hospice uses less high-technology equipment and fewer surgical procedures than a comparable hospital would to treat the same patients, good hospice care is labor-intensive. All the providers of hospice care—doctors, nurses, psychologists,

A dying man has been granted his wish—to spend his last days at home. This is possible because a hospice worker—whose occupation was nonexistent twenty years ago—provides medical and emotional support to him and his family.

social workers, clergy, and volunteers—must be well-trained and must be available to provide continuity of individualized care until the patient dies. Meeting such staffing demands is costly, and most insurance plans are less likely to cover hospice care than hospital care. In addition, even with careful staff development, burn-out is a common problem, and replacements are not easy to find (Lafer, 1991).

All these criticisms have some validity, and the people who are most directly involved in the hospice movement are well aware of them (More, 1987). However, the problem that most concerns them is a more practical one—namely, that a hospice death is available to only a limited number of even those people whose condition qualifies them for acceptance. For example, many hospices admit only patients who have a primary caregiver available on a twenty-four-hour basis. As a result, a disproportionate number of hospice patients are married and relatively young—only 17 percent are over age 75 (More, 1987).

For all these reasons, there is a scarcity of hospice facilities, even in developed nations. One solution to this problem is to change medical training and hospital procedures so that hospicelike care will become more widely available at home and in hospitals. This solution is gradually coming about. At the moment, however, the good death that the hospice can provide is a privilege available only to a relative few.

However, many aspects of this decision remain controversial. Almost everyone—healers, judges, theologians, and the general public—agrees that when vital-organ failure occurs in a terminally ill person who has already experienced severe pain, fearful confusion, and loss of consciousness, medical personnel are not obligated to restore breathing, restart the heart, and so forth. Such **passive euthanasia**—defined as mercifully allowing a person to die by not doing something that might extend his or her life—is permitted when, at the patient's or family's request, the orders *DNR* (do not resuscitate) have been placed on a person's hospital chart. Similarly, it is becoming more common to provide the dying with ample morphine and other medication to reduce pain, even if thus improving the quality of their last days of life might weaken breathing and possibly hasten death.

However, even doctors and nurses disagree regarding the specifics of passive euthanasia. For instance, many medical experts and professional societies make no practical or ethical distinction between ordinary and extraordinary measures to prolong death, or between not starting life support when it seems pointless and stopping it when it is no longer warranted. And the closer doctors and nurses are to the actual care of terminal patients, the more troubling this lack of distinctions becomes. For example, most doctors find it much harder to order a respirator turned off than to not use it at all. Similarly, extraordinary measures—such as a high-voltage shock to a non-beating heart—and more ordinary ones—such as intravenous feeding—may both work to merely prolong dying rather than to enhance living, and are thus identical in their practical outcome. Yet many hospitals routinely administer IV-feeding, antibiotics, and other life-prolonging therapies to patients on whom they would not begin to consider using more drastic measures. Given the ambiguities involved, it is not unusual for medical personnel working together on the same ward to have quite different attitudes on these questions (Solomon et al., 1993).

The controversies intensify over the question of suicide—especially **assisted suicide,** in which someone provides the means for a person to end his or her life—and **active euthanasia,** in which someone intentionally acts to terminate the life of a suffering person. Worldwide, the ethics of such actions are hotly debated in many forums, even by people who believe that passive euthanasia is highly ethical and humane. In the United States, both assisted suicide and active euthanasia are illegal, yet it is rare for someone who commits such acts to be convicted by a jury and then sent to prison. Nonetheless, the threat of prosecution and punishment certainly reduces the incidence, and increases the shame and secrecy, of such acts.

Recent developments in the Netherlands will no doubt add to the intensity of this debate. Although both assisted suicide and active euthanasia are still technically illegal there, in 1993 the Dutch legislature passed a law that guaranteed that doctors would not be prosecuted for such acts, if they follow certain strict guidelines. Among the requirements are that the dying person (1) be certified as terminally ill by an outside physician; (2) be of sound mind; (3) have asked on several occasions for help in dying; and (4) have a present existence so painful and restricted that extending it would bring only suffering. Finally, all the specifics—reasons, witnesses, means of death, and so forth—must be reported in a timely manner to the authorities, a requirement that will undoubtedly help shed light on the true frequency of assisted death.

While such an orderly approach to this issue may seem rational, in actual fact, the decisions involved in both passive and active euthanasia are almost always difficult. It is impossible for any layperson to make a living will so specific that it can fully guide actions to be taken by others in the future. And when individuals are actually dying, even if they are aware and alert, and even if the hospital informs them of their right to decide the course of their treatment, and even if they are given all the facts of their case, it still is difficult for them to know what specific measures will be the most humane in their particular case. Efforts to have all terminally ill patients sign a living will have been resisted by many—especially low-income, younger patients who may be suspicious that advance statements regarding the wish for a speedy death might deprive them of life-support systems and even routine nursing care when they need them (Dubler, 1993). At the same time, many of the elderly "wish to delegate the decision making to professionals," often not realizing that these same professionals are themselves "in some disarray on the issue and are under pressure from lawyers, economists, and philosophers" (Coni, 1991).

The truth is that, such pressures aside, doctors can rarely predict with complete accuracy the progression of any illness or the consequences of any measure to prevent, postpone, or hasten death. Thus, informing a patient of his or her options always involves some guesswork and subjective interpretation as well as science. More wrenching to all concerned, it is almost never clear at what point the expenditure of further effort, money, and emotional energy in the hopes of gaining at least a few more days of meaningful life actually undermines the patient's good death, the family's emotional and economic health, and the larger community's human and financial resources.

At the heart of these problems is the fact that "no one is unambivalent about the process of dying, and respect for choices to die must coexist with robust determination to preserve life" (Dubler, 1993). Unfortunately, in many hospitals the balance seems tilted away from a good death and toward procedures that prolong suffering (Solomon et al., 1993). This may be even more true in the United States, where the cost of medical interventions on the terminally ill is usually borne by private insurance, than in other nations, where health care is publically financed. American doctors, for example, tend to treat terminal cancer patients aggressively with surgery, radiation, and intensive chemotherapy long after most European physicians would have stopped such measures and turned instead to palliative care (Rees, 1988).

Although much progress has been made in recent years, it is clear that much still needs to be done to assure that when death does come, it will be a good death, not only for the sake of the dying person but for the sake of those who live after them. This idea is reflected in the thoughts of one college student following the death of a grandmother:

> We had enabled my grandmother to die at home. This brought all the family members home from all over the U.S. . . . She accepted death—which in turn made us accept death. When she died we all had the feeling of emptiness/loneliness because she would no longer be with us. But on the other hand we were very happy because she no longer had to suffer physical pain. We are a very close family and being with her when she died tied the knots even tighter. [Lagrand, 1981]

Bereavement

In keeping with the denial of death in the modern Western world, **mourning,** as all the ways of expressing grief at the death of a loved one are called, seemed by the mid-twentieth century to have gone out of fashion (Ariès, 1981). In earlier times, the bereaved were encouraged to express their emotions openly and fully. After the funeral itself, mourners followed age-old rituals to help release and control their grief. For example, they wore black, pulled down their window shades, and refused social invitations for a defined mourning period. During this time, friends and family members were expected to visit, bringing food and drink, to help the bereaved talk about their emotions without being overcome by them. When the mourning period was over, people were helped to pick up the pieces of their lives again, neither forgetting nor dwelling on their loss.

However, in recent times, much of this has changed for many people. The bereft are now often encouraged to "bear up"; friends and relatives often do less consoling than advising—to keep busy, to remarry, to look on the bright side; the large funeral has generally given way to a small memorial service; the deceased is less likely to be buried in a commemorative family plot and more likely to be cremated without ceremony. If current trends continue, according to one observer, we may eventually reach the point where death becomes little more than a minor annoyance, to be handled as efficiently and unemotionally as possible (Kastenbaum, 1992).

What are the results of these trends? Certainly they do not abolish the grief; they merely stifle its expression. Many psychologists and psychiatrists have warned that if grief cannot be expressed openly, its indirect manifestations may cripple a person's life (Osterweis et al., 1984). Gorer (1973), for example, describes instances of **mummification,** in which the bereaved leave intact the belongings of the dead. Widowers polish their late wives' knickknacks and clean their clothes; widows burn their husbands' pipe tobacco and air out their suits. Many widowers and widows sanctify their late spouses to the point where they would not consider remarriage (Kalish, 1985). Death of the mourner, either from suicide or a refusal to eat or care for oneself, is not uncommon among the elderly. It may be that, in many such cases, the pain of loss was compounded by the feeling that no one else seemed to care for the deceased, and therefore it must be that no one cares for the mourner either.

The Phases of Mourning

To be able to be sensitive to a bereaved person's needs, it is useful to know the emotional progression that seems typical of the mourning process. First there is *shock,* during which some people seem very calm and rational and others seem dazed and distant. The second phase is an intense *longing* to be with the deceased: memories, thoughts, dreams, and even hallucinations of the dead person flood the mind. The third major phase is *depression and despair,* often characterized by irrational anger and confused thinking. This is the period when friends and family members need to be especially understanding, since the mourner's behavior may at times be self-defeating if not self-destructive. Finally, the death is put into perspective, and *recovery,* the last phase of mourning, occurs.

How long it takes to achieve recovery depends in part on how well the particular culture provides for the needs of the mourner. Among the traditional practices that aid recovery are meaningful rituals that keep the bereaved from feeling isolated; the encouragement and opportunity to grieve openly; memorial customs that ease the transition back to normal life; emotional support and companionship in the months and years (not just days) after the death; and practical help to gradually overcome the many problems that result from the death of an important person in one's life. Even when all these avenues of comfort are available, however, the bereavement process is likely to last for many months, even years.

Indeed, the phases of mourning, like the stages of dying, do not follow a schedule. While a degree of numbness almost always occurs at first, longing, sorrow, and acceptance seem to come in waves. So a bereaved person might seem to accept the death and then might suddenly be overwhelmed with sadness when the realization surfaces again that an attachment that has helped to sustain life has been broken (Jacobs et al., 1987–1988). Such responses are particularly likely to occur on holidays, or birthdays, or the anniversary of the death and are accompanied by a new period of mourning. These **anniversary reactions** should be expected and accepted: the mourner who lights a candle or visits a grave on an anniversary is better off psychologically than the mourner who is surprised, and depressed or troubled, by a new surge of sadness.

Figure 4 *The quiet dignity of a cemetery helps many individuals experience all the emotions of bereavement—not only sadness but anger and acceptance as well.*

The crucial problem for many mourners in contemporary Western cultures is that outsiders sometimes do not understand and sympathize with their grief. For example, it might seem that an elderly person should accept the death of a very elderly mother or father, or that a young parent should not be unduly distressed over the death of an unborn baby. However, every death—especially a death that changes the generational line—is potentially grievous. The older person who now becomes part of the oldest generation of the family, or the parent whose hopes for the next generation are unfulfilled, can be, temporarily at least, devastated by his or her loss.

Because the elderly are likely to experience the death of a number of close friends and relatives in a fairly short span of time, they are particularly vulnerable to **bereavement overload,** as each new death starts the mourning process up again before the earlier ones have been completed. When this happens, other people need to be particularly sympathetic. Further, elderly widows and widowers often have a more difficult time adjusting than their younger counterparts do, in part because age has already diminished the size of their social circle, as well as their ability to fashion a new life for themselves (Sable, 1991).

In truth, reactions to death and the process of bereavement are as varied as the many circumstances, personalities, histories, and cultures of human life. Generally, death is somewhat easier to cope with if it is expected. Sometimes the diagnosis of terminal illness allows for a period of **anticipatory grief,** when both the dying person and the mourners can cry together and can share their affection for each other (Rando, 1986). Having time for anticipation does not necessarily ease the pain of loss, since attachment is often strengthened during the period of anticipatory grief. However, the emotions expressed at this time can make the leave-taking less conflicted than when such exchanges never occur. When individuals achieve the cognitive maturity to realize that death is final and universal, this awareness of mortality often leads them to anticipate eventual grief and make a special effort to express affection and appreciation of their elderly relatives, even when there is no evidence of impending death.

The sudden death of someone who is not "supposed to" die is the most difficult to bear. The clearest example is the death of a child, especially one who has lived long enough to have a distinct personality and position in the family. If the death is a violent and sudden one, as most young people's deaths are, the loss is particularly devastating (Shanfield et al., 1986–1987). Parents and siblings are often racked by powerful and personal emotions of guilt, denial, and anger, as well as sorrow. Similar emotions occur when someone is struck down in their prime, by accident, suicide, or homicide. The real victim, in such cases, is the family and close friends, who often find their entire outlook on life unalterably changed, as emotions of guilt and bitterness become twisted into the sadness of the loss (Sanders, 1989).

Recovery

What can others do, then, to help the bereaved person? The first step is simply to be aware that powerful and complicated emotions are likely: a friend should listen, sympathize, and not ignore the pain. The second step is to understand that bereavement is often a lengthy process, demanding sympathy, honesty, and social support for months or even years. As time passes,

Figure 5 *This widower looks at the photo of his wife of many years. Such reminders and mementos, while evoking sadness, often help the mourner come to terms with the loss of a loved one.*

the bereaved person should become involved in other activities, but should not be expected to forget the person to whom they were attached: sorrow and memory usually continue. Interestingly, sadness does not necessarily correlate with depression (Jacobs et al., 1987–1988). In fact, several studies have found that those who take steps to remember a dead person—to save mementos or photographs, to talk about experiences shared, to visit the gravesite—cope better with death than those who do not (Kastenbaum, 1986; Murphy, 1986–1987). If the emotions of grief have been given expression, the time will come when the person "feels a sense of weary relief in having worked through the bitter emotions of grief, and is ready to approach . . . the new situation more calmly" (Bowlby, 1974).

After working through the emotions of grief, the bereaved may develop a deeper appreciation of themselves, as well as of the value of human relationships. In fact, a theme frequently sounded by those who work with the bereaved is that there are lessons in the processes of dying and mourning that we all could learn. The most central of these is the value of intimate, caring relationships. As one counselor who works with the bereaved expresses it:

> I often have heard phrases such as 'I wish I had told him I loved him' or 'I wish we could have resolved our differences earlier.' There may be things we need to say, appreciations that need to be expressed, distances to bridge . . . Loving and being loved is not just something that happens to us. It is a creative art that must be worked in a variety of ways. [Sanders, 1989]

It is fitting to end this book with just such a reminder of the creative work of loving. As first described in Chapter 1, the study of the process of human development is a science—a topic to be researched, understood, and explained in order to enhance human lives. But the process of actually living one's own life is an art as well as a science, with strands of love and sorrow and recovery that are woven into each person's unique tapestry. Death, when accepted, grief, when allowed expression, and bereavement, when it leads to recovery, give added meaning to birth, growth, development, and all human relationships.

conservation of liquids The idea that the volume of a liquid remains constant, even if the containers into which it is poured are quite different in size and shape. A child who has entered the stage of concrete operational thought will understand that when 6 ounces of juice in a short, squat glass are poured into a tall, narrow glass, the total amount of juice remains the same. (54)

conservation of matter The idea that the volume or weight of an object remains the same even if the form is changed. For example, when two balls of clay have the same volume, rolling one ball into a long rope will not increase the amount of clay. (232)

conservation of number The idea that the number of a set does not change even if the objects in it are repositioned. For example, if two sets have the same number of coins, spacing out one set so that it is distributed over a larger area will not increase the number of coins in that set. (233)

continuity A term used to label development that is seen as a gradual and steady progression. (17)

continuity theory The theory that each person copes with late adulthood in much the same way that he or she coped with earlier periods of life. (643)

control group In research, a group of subjects who are similar to the experimental group on all relevant dimensions (e.g., sex, age, educational background) but who do not experience special experimental conditions or procedures. (23)

control processes That part of the information-processing system which regulates the analysis and flow of information within the system, such as using memory and retrieval strategies, selective attention, and rules or strategies for problem-solving. Control processes become increasingly efficient with development but usually show some specific individual declines in late adulthood. (56, 616)

conventional moral reasoning Kohlberg's term for the middle stages of moral reasoning, in which social standards are the primary moral values. (399)

corpus callosum A network of nerves connecting the two hemispheres (the left side and right side) of the brain. (214)

correlation A statistical term that indicates that two variables are somehow related. Whenever one variable changes in the same direction as another (for example, both decrease), the correlation is *positive*. Whenever one variable increases as another decreases, the correlation is *negative*. (25)

critical period The period during prenatal development, usually said to occur during the first eight weeks, when the basic organs and body structures are forming and are therefore particularly vulnerable to teratogenic exposure. (100)

cross-modal perception The ability to use perceptual information from one sensory system to imagine something in another sensory system. For example, when one sees food and imagines how it tastes. (158)

cross-sectional research Research involving the comparison of groups of people who are different in age but similar in other important ways (e.g., sex, socioeconomic status, level of education). Differences among the groups—as, for instance, between a group of 20-year-olds and a group of 40-year-olds— are presumably the result of development, rather than some other factor. (29)

crystallized intelligence Cattell's term for those types of intellectual ability that reflect accumulated learning. Vocabulary and general information are examples. Some developmental

psychologists think crystallized intelligence increases with age, while fluid intelligence declines. (544)

decenter A child's ability to move away from intuitive, perceptual focusing on a single aspect of an event or problem and to think more objectively, understanding such logical principles as *reversibility* and *conservation*. According to Piaget, children are usually able to decenter at around age 7 or 8. (304)

deferred imitation The ability to re-create an action, or mimic a person, that one has witnessed at some time in the past. According to Piaget, infants are usually first able to do this between 18 and 24 months of age. (150)

dementia Irreversible loss of intellectual functioning caused by organic brain damage or disease. Dementia becomes more common with age, but even in the very old, dementia is abnormal and pathological. Sometimes dementia is misdiagnosed, since reversible conditions such as depression and drug overdose can cause the symptoms of dementia. (625)

democratic-indulgent A style of parenting that is warm, responsive, and permissive. (265)

demographic pyramid The shape that results when populations are graphed by numbers of individuals in each age group. In the past, the largest population group was the youngest and the smallest group was the oldest, giving the graph the shape of a pyramid. Currently, however, the pyramid is becoming more square, with equal numbers of older and younger persons in the population. (589)

demography The study of populations and social statistics associated with these populations. (589)

dendrites Communication networks in the cortex of the brain which are available for the processing and integration of many different kinds of information. (126)

developmental theory A systematic statement of hypotheses and general principles that attempts to explain human development and provides a framework for future research and interpretation. (35)

dialectical thought Thought that is characterized by understanding the pros and cons, advantages and disadvantages, and possibilities and limitations inherent in every idea and course of action. In daily life, dialectical thinking involves the constant integration of one's beliefs and experiences with all the contradictions and inconsistencies one encounters. (468)

disability A measure of health that refers to the inability to perform activities that most others can. (524)

discontinuity A term used to label development that is seen to occur in stages, or which is characterized by abrupt or uneven changes. Many developmental psychologists emphasize the discontinuity of development. (Also called the *stage view of development*.) (17)

disengagement theory A theory of psychosocial development in late adulthood that holds that elderly people voluntarily withdraw from involvement in society and that society responds by withdrawing as well. (642) (See *activity theory*.)

disequilibrium Piaget's term for the cognitive imbalance and confusion that result from difficulties with integrating new information into existing schemas. (52)

dizygotic twins Simultaneously born offspring who develop from two separate zygotes, each the product of a different sperm and ovum. These twins are no more similar genetically than any other two children born to the same parents. (71)

DNA (deoxyribonucleic acid)   Carrier of genetic information in cells. (69)

dominant-recessive pattern   A pattern of genetic inheritance in which certain genes (referred to as dominant) act in a controlling manner in certain gene interactions, hiding the influence of other (recessive) genes involved in those interactions. (72)

Down syndrome   A genetic abnormality caused by an extra chromosome in the twenty-first chromosome pair. Individuals with this syndrome have such characteristics as round faces and short limbs and are underdeveloped physically and intellectually, although the specific number of symptoms exhibited, as well as their intensity, varies from case to case. (Also called *trisomy-21*.) (81)

drug abuse   The use of a drug to the extent that it impairs one's physical, cognitive, or social well-being. (452)

dyscalcula   A specific learning disability involving unusual difficulty in arithmetic. (293)

dyslexia   A specific learning disability involving unusual difficulty in reading. (293)

eclectic perspective   A view incorporating what seems to be the best, or most useful, from various theories, rather than working from a single perspective. (64)

ecological approach   A way of looking at human development that emphasizes the impact of society, culture, physical setting, and other people on the development of each individual. (Also called *systems approach*.) (6)

ego   As conceptualized by Freud, the rational, reality-oriented part of the personality. (39)

egocentrism   Thinking that is limited to one's own point of view. In the egocentrism of early childhood, children often do not take into account that other people have thoughts and feelings different from their own. (233) (See also *adolescent egocentrism*.)

ego involvement learning   An educational approach in which academic grades are based solely on individual test performance, and students are ranked against each other. (395)

elaborated code   A form of speech used by children in school and in other formal situations, characterized by extensive vocabulary, complex syntax, lengthy sentences, and conformity to other middle-class norms for correct language. (317) (See also *restricted code*.)

Elderhostel   A program in which older people live on college campuses and take special classes, usually during college vacation periods. (650)

elder maltreatment   Elder abuse and neglect, ranging from direct physical attack to ongoing emotional neglect, and involving such underlying factors as the social isolation and powerlessness of the victim, mental impairment or drug addiction of the perpetrator, and inadequate education and poverty within the household. (671)

Electra complex   The female version of the Oedipus complex. According to psychoanalytic theory, at about age 4, girls have sexual feelings for their father and accompanying hostility toward their mother. (274)

embryo   The human organism from about two to eight weeks after conception, when basic body structures and organs are forming. (95)

endangerment   Any act that puts a child at risk for serious harm. (194)

endometriosis   A condition in which fragments of the uterine lining become implanted and grow on the surface of the ovaries or the Fallopian tubes, blocking the reproductive tract and leaving many women with fertility problems. (450)

environment   All the external forces that can interact with the individual's genetic inheritance at any point in life—everything from the impact of the immediate cell environment on the genes themselves to the effects on the individual of nutrition, climate, medical care, socioeconomic status, family dynamics, and the broader economic, political, and cultural contexts. (75)

equilibrium   Piaget's term for the state of mental balance achieved through the assimilation and accommodation of conflicting experiences and perceptions. (51)

error catastrophe   A key idea in a theory of aging that holds that, while the body can isolate and repair a certain number of errors in cell duplication, at some point, accumulating errors can no longer be controlled and fatally impair the body's ability to function. (601)

estrogen   A hormone produced primarily by the ovaries that regulates sexual development in puberty. Although boys' adrenal glands produce some estrogen, it is chiefly a female hormone. During menopause, estrogen levels drop, producing a number of physiological changes. (371)

ethnic group   A collection of people who share certain attributes, such as national origin, religion, culture, and language, and, as a result, tend to have similar values and experiences. (8)

exchange theory   The theory that marriage is an arrangement in which each person contributes something useful to the other, something the other would find difficult to attain alone. (496)

executive stage   In Schaie's stages of adult cognitive development, a concern for, and involvement with, some aspects of the larger society, such as one's company or town government, that lead the individual to take on broad obligations, especially those related to coordinating the needs of various groups and individuals. (466)

exosystem   In the ecological approach to studying development, this term refers to the neighborhood and community structures, for example, local government agencies and newspapers, that affect the functioning of the smaller systems. (6)

experiment   The research method in which the scientist tests a hypothesis by bringing people into a controlled setting, and then manipulating a variable and observing the results. (25)

experimental group   In research, a group of subjects who experience special experimental conditions or procedures. (23)

expertise   The acquisition of knowledge in a specific area. As individuals grow older, they concentrate their learning in certain areas that are of the most importance to them, becoming experts in these areas while remainig relative novices in others. (554)

extrinsic reinforcer   A reinforcing stimulus that comes from the environment. For example, allowing a child to stay up late as a reward for good behavior. (45) (See also *reinforcer*.)

extroversion   A personality dimension characterized by a tendency to be outgoing, active, and assertive. (576)

family structures Households composed of people connected to each other in various legal and biosocial ways. (344)

fast mapping A process through which young children rapidly acquire new words, assimilating them—on the basis of a partial understanding of their meaning derived from the context in which they were encountered—into word categories that are already established in the child's vocabulary. (243)

fear of strangers The distress experienced by some infants when confronted with a new person, especially an adult who looks unusual or who acts in an unusual way. This emotion is first noticeable at about six months, and is full-blown at a year. (Also called *stranger anxiety*.) (173)

fetal alcohol effects (FAE) A congenital condition with similar but less pronounced symptoms than those of fetal alcohol syndrome (FAS). (101)

fetal alcohol syndrome (FAS) A congenital condition characterized by a small head, abnormal eyes, malproportioned face, and retardation in physical and mental growth, that sometimes appears in children whose mothers used alcohol frequently or heavily during pregnancy. (101)

fetus The name given to human prenatal life between the ninth week of pregnancy and birth: the term denotes that the basic body parts of an embryo have been formed but that the developing organism is dependent on the mother's body. (96)

filial obligation The sense, experienced by most adult children, of a duty and need to protect and care for their aging parents. (652)

fine motor skills Skills involving small body movements, especially with the hands and fingers. Drawing, writing, and tying a shoelace demand fine motor skills. (131, 218)

5-to-7 shift According to Piaget, a transitional period in cognitive development between preoperational thought and concrete operational thought, occurring between ages 5 and 7. During this period, children sometimes intuit the correct answers to tests of concrete operational logic but cannot explain the underlying principles. (304)

flextime A work policy that permits employees some choice in establishing their work hours. (504)

fluid intelligence Cattell's term for those types of basic intelligence that make learning of all sorts quick and thorough. Underlying abilities such as short-term memory, abstract thought, and speed of thinking are all usually considered part of fluid intelligence. (543) (See *crystallized intelligence*.)

foreclosure Erikson's term for premature identity formation, in which the young person accepts parental values and goals without exploring alternative roles. (412)

formal operational thought Piaget's term for the last period of cognitive development, characterized by hypothetical, logical, and abstract thought. This stage is not reached until adolescence, if at all. (51, 388)

fragile-X syndrome A disorder caused by chromosomal abnormality in the twenty-third pair, the sex chromosomes, in which the "fragile-X" chromosome transmits certain of its genetic information improperly. Although this syndrome is highly variable in its effects, it causes mental deficiency in about 30 percent of the women who carry it and in an even larger percentage of the men who carry it. (83)

frail elderly Older people who are physically infirm, very ill, or cognitively impaired. (665)

free radicals Atoms that, as a result of metabolic processes, have an unpaired electron. Free radicals are believed to damage cells, affect organs, accelerate diseases, and decrease the ability of DNA to maintain and repair the body. (601)

game of thinking Flavell's term for the adolescent's ability to suspend knowledge of reality and think creatively about hypothetical possibilities. (389)

gamete A human reproductive cell. Female gametes are called ova, or eggs; male gametes are called spermatozoa, or sperm. (68)

gender constancy The realization in children at age 4 or 5 that they are permanently male or female. According to cognitive-development theory, this realization motivates them to adopt appropriate gender-role behavior. (277)

gender differences Differences between males and females that arise from the special customs, values, and expectations that a particular culture attaches to one sex or the other. (223)

gender schemas The ways children organize their knowledge about people in terms of gender-based categories and evaluations. (277)

gene The basic unit of heredity, carried by the chromosomes. Genes provide guidelines for the growth and development of every organism. (69)

generational equity Equal contributions from, and fair benefits for, each generation. (648)

generational stake The need of each generation to view the parent-adolescent relationship differently, particularly with regard to problems between them; for example, parents might view a conflict over appropriate dress as temporary, based on peer influences, whereas adolescents might view the same conflict as an impingement on their freedom to make their own decisions and resist their parents' outmoded values. (418)

generation gap The differences between the younger and older generations. Numerous studies have shown few differences in opinion between adolescents and their parents on crucial issues, indicating the strong impact of parental values on adolescents. (415) (See also *generational stake*.)

generativity versus stagnation Erikson's seventh stage of development, in which adults seek to be productive through vocation, avocation, or child-rearing. Without such productive work, adults stop developing and growing. (484)

genetic clock According to one theory of aging, a regulatory mechanism in the DNA of cells regulates the aging process. (602)

genetic counseling A program of consultation and testing through which couples learn about their genetic inheritance in order to make informed decisions about childbearing. (84)

genital stage Freud's term for the last stage of psychosexual development, in which the primary source of sexual satisfaction is an erotic relationship with another adult. (38)

genotype A person's entire genetic heritage, including those characteristics carried by the recessive genes but not expressed in the phenotype. (72)

germinal period The first three weeks after conception, during which rapid cell division occurs. (Also called the *period of the ovum*.) (94)

gerontology The study of old age. This is one of the fastest-growing special fields in the social sciences. (588)

GH The growth hormone which rises steadily in both sexes during puberty. (371)

glass ceiling An invisible barrier experienced by many women in male-dominated occupations—and by many minority workers in majority-dominated occupations—that halts promotion and undercuts their power at a certain managerial level. (505)

glaucoma An eye disease, increasingly common after age 40, that begins without apparent symptoms and often causes eventual blindness. Early detection and treatment can prevent vision impairment from glaucoma. (522)

goal-directed behavior Behavior characterized by purposeful actions, such as crawling towards an object and ignoring distractions along the way. According to Piaget, this behavior usually begins between 8 and 12 months of age, during the fourth stage of sensorimotor intelligence. (147)

gross motor skills Those physical skills that use large body movements. Running, jumping, and climbing involve gross motor skills. (130, 217)

growth spurt A period of relatively rapid physical growth that occurs during puberty. (372)

habituation A process whereby a particular stimulus becomes so familiar that physiological responses initially associated with exposure to it are no longer present. For instance, a newborn might initially stare wide-eyed at a mobile, but gradually look at it less often as habituation occurs. (127)

Hayflick limit The number of times a human cell is capable of dividing into two new cells. Leonard Hayflick determined that the limit for most human cells is approximately fifty divisions, suggesting that the life span is limited by our genetic program, which does not allow cells to reproduce themselves indefinitely. (603)

healthspan The period of vital and vigorous years. (604)

heterogamy Marriage between individuals who tend to be dissimilar with respect to such variables as attitudes, interests, goals, SES, religion, ethnic background, and local origin. (496) (See *homogamy*.)

holistic Referring to a view that sees human development as unified and whole; this perspective emphasizes the interaction among the many diverse aspects of development. (59)

holophrase A single word that is intended to express a complete thought. Young children (usually about 1 year of age) use this early form of communication. (164)

homeostasis The adjustment of the body's systems to keep physiological functions in a state of equilibrium. As the body ages, it takes longer for these homeostatic adjustments to occur, making it harder for older bodies to adapt to stresses. (446)

homogamy Marriage between individuals who tend to be similar with respect to such variables as attitudes, interests, goals, SES, religion, ethnic background, and local origin. (496)

homogeneous grouping The educational practice of separating individuals into groups according to their perceived ability—the slow learners in one class, the fast in another, and so forth. (295)

hormone replacement therapy (HRT) Treatment for women who are experiencing notable difficulties from menopausal symptoms or who have undergone an abrupt drop in hormonal level because their ovaries have been surgically removed. (533)

hospice Originally a religious way station where poor travelers could obtain lodging, the hospice is now a place where the dying can die as painlessly as possible and with dignity, surrounded by friends and family. (684)

hostile aggression An attack against someone rather than a fight about some thing. (269) (See also *instrumental aggression*.)

Human Genome Project A worldwide effort to map all 3 billion codes of the 100,000 human genes. (88)

human immunodeficiency virus (HIV) The agent that causes AIDS, carried in the blood and certain other bodily fluids of infected persons and transmitted chiefly through sexual contact. (403)

humanistic theory A theory that regards every individual as unique and worthy of respect and sees human development as being guided by a variety of basic needs; including the need for achieving one's full potential. (59)

id As conceptualized by Freud, that part of the personality containing primitive, unconscious sexual and aggressive impulses striving for immediate gratification. (38)

identification A defense mechanism through which a person feels like, or adopts the perspective of, someone more powerful than himself or herself. Children identify with their parents for many reasons; one of them, according to psychoanalytic theory, is to cope with the powerful emotions of the Oedipus (or Electra) complex. (274)

identity As a term used by Piaget, the principle of logic which states that a given quantity of matter remains the same no matter what changes occur in its shape or appearance. Before they enter the concrete operational period, children do not recognize this principle. (305)

identity As a term used by Erikson, a person's definition of himself or herself as a separate individual. According to Erikson, the search for identity is a basic human need, as important as food and security. (412)

identity achievement Erikson's term for a person's achievement of a sense of who he or she is as a unique individual. The main task of adolescence, according to Erikson, is the establishment of the young person's identity, including sexual, moral, political, and vocational identity. (412)

identity diffusion Erikson's term for the experience of a young person who is uncertain what path to take toward identity formation, and therefore becomes apathetic and disoriented. (413)

imaginary audience A term referring to the constant scrutiny that many adolescents typically imagine themselves to be under which often leads them to fantasize about people's reactions to their appearance and behavior. (392)

immersion A language-learning approach in which the student's instruction in all or most subjects occurs entirely in the second language. (319)

implantation After conception, the burrowing of the organism into the lining of the uterus where it can be nourished and protected during growth. (94)

inadequate families An assessment label used in child-maltreatment intervention: refers to families that are so impaired by deep emotional problems or serious cognitive deficiencies that they may never be able to meet the needs of their children. (203)

industry versus inferiority The fourth of Erikson's eight "crises" of development, in which school-age children attempt to master many skills and develop a sense of themselves as either industrious or incompetent. (332)

infertility The inability to conceive a child after one year of trying. (449)

information-processing theory A theory of human learning that uses the functioning of the computer as an analogy for the functioning of the human mind—how it analyzes, stores, and retrieves information and how these processes change as one matures. (55, 308)

initiative versus guilt The third of Erikson's eight "crises" of psychosocial development. During this stage, the preschool child begins, or initiates, new activities—and feels guilt when efforts result in failure or criticism. (256)

injury control The implementation of educational measures (such as television announcements and poster campaigns) and legal measures (such as requiring safety caps on medicine bottles and automobile seats for infants and children) to reduce the risk of childhood accidents and injuries. (220)

insecure attachment A caregiver-child bond marked by the child's overdependence on, or lack of interest in, the caregiver. Insecurely attached children are not readily comforted by their caregiver and are less likely to explore their environment than are children who are securely attached. (185)

instrumental activities of daily life (IADLs) Actions that are important to independent living and that require some intellectual competence and forethought. (665)

instrumental aggression Fighting over an object, territory, or privilege. Examples include quarreling over a toy, a seat at the front of the classroom, or a chance to wash the blackboard. Instrumental aggression peaks during the preschool years and then declines sharply. (269) (See also *hostile aggression*.)

integrity versus despair The last of Erikson's eight stages of development. During late adulthood, according to Erikson, people either feel that their lives have had meaning, and look back on their past experiences with a sense of integrity and wholeness, or they despair at their past and therefore dread the future. (674)

intergenerational transmission Refers to the phenomenon of mistreated children growing up to become abusive or neglectful parents themselves, a phenomenon that is less common than is generally supposed. (201)

interindividual variation Differences between individuals that are the result of the uniqueness of each person's genetic make-up and particular environment. (549)

interiority According to Neugarten, the increased introspection and reflection that many people develop as they grow older. (634)

intermodal perception The ability to associate perceptual information from one sensory system with information from another. For example, when we sit next to a fireplace, we realize that the heat, smokey odor, and flickering light all come from the same source. (157)

intimacy versus isolation The sixth of Erikson's eight stages of development. Adults seek to find someone with whom to share their lives, in an enduring and self-sacrificing commitment. Without such commitment, they risk profound aloneness, isolated from their fellow humans. (484)

intrinsic reinforcer A reinforcing stimulus that comes from within the individual, such as feelings of satisfaction and achievement. (45) (See also *reinforcer.*)

invincibility fable The idea, fostered by adolescent egocentrism, that one is immune to normal troubles and dangers. (391)

in vitro fertilization A technique in which ova (egg cells) are surgically removed from a woman and fertilized with sperm in the laboratory. After the original fertilized cells (the zygotes) have divided several times, they are inserted into a woman's uterus (usually but not necessarily the ova provider's) for implantation or are frozen for later use. This method of reproduction is used to bypass problems that cause infertility, such as blocked Fallopian tubes. (450)

kinkeepers The people who celebrate family achievements, gather the family together, and keep in touch with family members who no longer live nearby. (568)

knowledge base That part of the information-processing system that stores long-term information and has a virtually limitless capacity. (Also called *long-term memory*.) (55, 615)

kwashiorkor A disease resulting from protein-calorie deficiency in children. The symptoms include thinning hair, paleness, and bloating of the stomach, face, and legs. (136)

Lamaze method A technique of childbirth that involves breathing and relaxation exercises during labor. (114)

latency Freud's term for the period between the phallic stage and the genital stage. During latency, which lasts from about age 7 to age 11, the child's sexual and emotional drives are relatively quiet and they begin to consider their social world. (38, 332)

learned helplessness The assumption—based on past failures—that one is unable to do anything to improve one's performance or situation, an assumption that undermines self-confidence and impairs performance. (337)

learning disability A particular difficulty in mastering basic academic skills, without apparent deficit in intelligence or impairment of sensory functions. (292) (See also *dyslexia* and *dyscalcula*.)

learning theory A major theory of psychology which maintains that most human behaviors are learned, or conditioned, and which formulates laws of behavior that are applicable to animals and to people of all ages. (Also called *behaviorism*.) (43)

life review The examination of one's own past life that many elderly people engage in. According to Butler, the life review is therapeutic, for it helps the older person to come to grips with aging and death. (635)

longitudinal research A study of the same people over a long period of time. Longitudinal research is designed to measure both changes and continuity in behavior and personality over time. (30)

low-birth-weight infant A newborn who weighs less than 5½ pounds (2,500 grams) at birth. (109) (See also *preterm infant*.)

macrosystem In the ecological or systems approach to development, the larger patterns of culture, politics, economy, and society that affect the smaller systems and the individual. (6)

marasmus A disease that afflicts infants suffering from severe malnutrition. Growth stops, body tissues waste away, and eventually death occurs. (136)

marital equity Refers to the marriage partners' perception of the relative equality of their respective contributions to the marriage. (496)

markers In genetic testing, particular physiological characteristics or gene clusters that suggest but do not prove that the individual is a carrier of a harmful gene. (88)

mastery motivation An innate drive in young children to develop all their skills and competencies, whether or not adults provide incentives for them to do so. (257)

mastery play Any form of play that leads to a mastering of new skills. During the play years, mastery play tends to develop physical skills (such as skipping or using scissors). Later, mastery play includes intellectual activities such as play with words and ideas. (219)

maximum life span The oldest age to which members of a species have been known to live. For humans, that age is 115 years. (602)

memory self-efficacy Refers to the individual's sense of confidence in his or her own memory and related cognitive skills. (618)

menarche A female's first menstrual period. This occurs toward the end of puberty. (376)

menopause The time in middle age, usually around age 50, when a woman's menstrual periods cease completely and the production of estrogen drops considerably. Strictly speaking, menopause is dated one year after a woman's last menstrual period. (533)

mental combinations The mental playing-out of various courses of action before actually exercising one of them. According to Piaget, this ability usually becomes apparent between 18 and 24 months of age, during the sixth stage of sensorimotor intelligence. (149)

mental representation The ability to create mental images of objects, events, or people that have been seen or experienced at an earlier time but are not actually in view. According to Piaget, this ability develops between 18 and 24 months of age during the sixth stage of sensorimotor intelligence. (149)

mentor In career development, a mentor is a more experienced coworker or supervisor who provides advice, instruction, and support. In many professions, the mentor system operates informally, with great impact. Finding a good mentor may make the difference between success or failure in a new career. (504)

mesosystem In the ecological or systems approach to development, the interlocking relationships, such as the parent-teacher communications, or the employment practices impinging on family life, that link one microsystem to another. (6)

metacognition The ability to evaluate a cognitive task to determine how to accomplish it with which cognitive strategies (such as selective attention or mnemonics) and to monitor one's performance on the task. (312)

microsystem In the ecologic or systems approach to development, the immediate systems, such as the family and the classroom, that affect an individual's daily life. (6)

middle age The years from age 40 to age 60. (559)

midlife The point, at about age 40, when the adult has about as many years of life ahead as have already past. Midlife ushers in middle age, which lasts until about age 60. (559)

midlife crisis A time in middle age when adults question their goals and achievements, perhaps becoming depressed or engaging in atypical behavior. For instance, the seemingly happy husband might suddenly demand a divorce, or the seemingly contented mother might want to leave her children and travel to a distant place. Not everyone has a midlife crisis: it seems more typical of middle-class American men than of other people. (560)

mnemonics Memory aids, including storage and retrieval strategies. (310) (See also *rehearsal* and *organization*.)

modeling The patterning of one's behavior after that of someone else. New responses can be learned, and old ones modified, through modeling. (46)

monozygotic twins Two offspring who began development as a single zygote (formed from one sperm and one ovum) that subsequently divided into two zygotes. They have the same genetic make-up, are of the same sex, and look alike. (71)

moratorium Erikson's term for the informal pause in identity formation that allows young people to explore alternatives without making final choices. For many young people, college or military service or a service internship provides such a moratorium. (413)

morbidity A measure of health that refers to the rate of diseases of all kinds in a given population. (524)

mortality A measure of health that refers to the number of deaths each year per thousand members of a given population. (524)

motility The ability of sperm to swim quickly and far enough to reach an ovum for fertilization. Deficiencies in sperm motility diminish male fertility. (449)

mourning All the ways of expressing grief at the death of a loved one. (688)

multidimensional A description of cognitive abilities emphasizing that intelligence is composed of several distinct dimensions, all of which must be studied independently. (548)

multidirectional A way of describing variations in specific cognitive abilities over time. (549)

multifactorial characteristics Those abilities or qualities that are determined by the interaction among several genetic and environmental influences. Characteristics such as intelligence, personality, and talent are multifactorial. (72)

multi-infarct dementia (MID) The form of dementia characterized by sporadic, and progressive, memory loss. The cause is repeated infarcts, or temporary obstructions of blood vessels, preventing insufficient blood from reaching the brain. Each infarct destroys some brain tissue. The underlying cause is an impaired circulatory system. (629)

mummification A reaction to the death of a loved one in which an individual acts as if the dead person were still alive, by preserving the deceased's belongings, setting the deceased's dinner place, and the like. (688)

myelin A fatty insulating substance that coats the nerve cells (neurons), facilitating quicker, more efficient transmission of neural impulses. The myelination process continues until adolescence. (126)

naturalistic observation   The research method in which the scientist tests a hypothesis by observing people in their usual surroundings (home, school, work place). Specific methods of data collection and special training for the observers are generally used to make this method more objective than our usual daily observations of each other. (21)

naturally occurring retirement communities (NORCs)   Neighborhoods or apartment complexes where more than half the residents happen to be elderly. (659)

nature   All the innate traits, capacities, and limitations, that affect development. (15)

negative identity   Erikson's term for a chosen identity that is the opposite of the identity one is expected to adopt by one's parents or society. (412)

negative reinforcer   The removal of an unpleasant stimulus in response to a particular behavior, such removal serving to increase the likelihood that the behavior will occur again. (45)

neglect   A form of child maltreatment in which parents or caregivers fail to meet a child's basic needs. (192) (See also *child maltreatment.*)

neural tube   The fold of cells that appears in the embryonic disc about three weeks after conception and later develops into the central nervous system (brain and spinal cord). (95)

neural tube defects   Defects in which the neural tube does not grow properly: either the lower spine does not close, causing spina bifida, or the upper part of the central nervous system does not develop, causing anencephaly. (104)

neurons   Nerve cells. (125)

neuroticism   A personality dimension characterized by a tendency to be anxious, moody, and self-punishing. (576)

neurotransmitters   Chemicals in the brain that communicate nerve impulses from one nerve cell to another. (593)

norms   Statistical averages based on the results of research derived from a large, representative sample of a given population. Norms are not to be taken as implying "the best." For instance, the norm for an infant's first step is 12 months of age, but the infant who doesn't walk until 14 months is not necessarily less smart or less healthy than the infant who walks at 12 months. (134)

nurture   All the environmental influences that affect development. (15)

obesity   Body weight that is more than 20 percent greater than that of the average person of the same height, age, and sex. Obesity in middle childhood can seriously affect physical as well as emotional health. (286)

object permanence   The understanding that objects and people continue to exist even when they cannot be seen. This concept develops gradually between 6 and 18 months of age. (147)

Oedipus complex   In psychoanalytic theory, both the sexual desire that boys in the phallic stage have for their mother and the associated feelings of hostility they have toward their father. This complex is named after Oedipus, a character in ancient Greek mythology who unwittingly killed his father and married his mother. (274)

Older Americans Act   Legislation passed by the American Congress in 1965 that provides every older person, regardless of income, a wealth of benefits—from subsidized meals at over 15,000 locations to community services offered by over 20,000 agencies. One result, as intended, has been better health, less dependence, and improved morale for many seniors. (666)

old-old   Older adults who suffer from severe physical, mental, or social deficits and thus require supportive services such as nursing homes and hospital stays. (587)

openness   A personality dimension characterized by a tendency to be imaginative, curious, and open to new experiences. (576)

operant conditioning   A learning process, conceptualized by B. F. Skinner, through which a person or animal is more likely to perform or refrain from performing a certain behavior because of past reinforcement or punishment. (Also called *instrumental conditioning.*) (44)

oral stage   Freud's term for the first stage of psychosexual development, when the infant gains both nourishment and pleasure through sucking and biting. (38, 176)

organization   Piaget's term for the process of synthesizing and analyzing perceptions and thoughts in cohesive ways. At every stage of cognitive development, according to Piaget, people actively organize their existing ideas and adapt to new experiences. (53)

organization   In information-processing, a memory technique involving the regrouping of information to make it memorable. (309)

organ reserve   The extra capacity of the heart, lungs, and other organs that makes it possible for the body to withstand moments of intense or prolonged stress. With age, organ reserve is gradually depleted, but the rate of depletion depends on how good the individual's health habits are. (446)

osteoporosis   A loss of calcium within the bone that makes the bone more porous and fragile. It occurs somewhat in everyone with aging, but serious osteoporosis is more common in elderly women than men. Osteoporosis is the main reason the elderly suffer broken hip bones much more often than the young. (533)

ova (singular **ovum**)   The reproductive cells of the human female, which are present, from birth, in the ovaries. (68)

overextension   The use of a given word to describe several objects that share a particular characteristic. For example, toddlers often use "doggie" to label all four-legged animals. (164)

overregularization   The tendency of young children to apply grammatical rules and forms without recognizing exceptions and irregularities. Overregularization might, for example, lead a child to use the suffix "ed" to form the past tense of all verbs and say "bringed" instead of "brought." (246)

parental monitoring   Parental watchfulness over where their child is and what he or she is doing. Authoritarian monitoring, such as curfews and other restrictions, is more likely to occur in families who live in areas where young people are in greater danger because of drugs and violence. (420)

parent-infant bond   The strong feelings of attachment between parents and newborns in the early moments of their relationship. Although this bond has received much popular attention, developmental scientists do not regard it as essential to overall development. (117)

Parkinson's disease   A chronic progressive disease that is characterized by muscle tremors and rigidity, and sometimes dementia, caused by a reduction of dopamine production in the brain. (629)

passive euthanasia The practice whereby a person is allowed to die by withholding some procedure or drug that would have allowed life to continue a bit longer. Passive euthanasia is practiced in many hospitals and hospices, when the extension of life seems only to prolong misery. (686)

peer group A group of individuals of roughly the same age and social status who play, work, and learn together. (337)

pelvic inflammatory disease (PID) A common result of recurring pelvic infections in women. Pelvic inflammatory disease often leads to blocked Fallopian tubes, which, in turn, can lead to sterility. (450)

penis envy The psychoanalytic idea that girls, beginning at about age 4, realize that boys have a penis and become jealous because they themselves do not. (274)

perception The brain's processing or interpretation of sensations that brings them into conscious awareness and makes them comprehensible. (127)

period of acquisition Schaie's characterization of cognitive development in childhood and adolescence. During this period, information is absorbed and problem-solving techniques are learned with little regard for their actual importance or usefulness in the young person's life. (465)

period of the embryo From approximately the fourth through the eighth week after conception, during which time the rudimentary forms of all anatomical structures develop. (94)

period of the fetus From the ninth week after conception until birth. In a full-term pregnancy, this period lasts seven months. (94)

permissive parenting A style of child-rearing in which parents allow their children to do virtually anything they want to do. Permissive parents rarely punish, guide, or control their children; they are nurturant and communicate well with their children. (264)

personal fable Elkind's term for the egocentric idea, held by many adolescents, that they are special and destined for great accomplishments. (392)

person-environment fit The compatibility between the individual and his or her environment as a setting for personal growth. (393)

phallic stage The third stage of psychosexual development, according to Freud, in which the penis, or phallus, is the focus of psychological concern as well as of physiological pleasure. This stage occurs during the preschool years. (38, 274)

phenomenological Refers to the approach to others, stressed by Carl Rogers, in which one maintains an openness to viewing the world from the other person's perspective. (60)

phenotype An individual's observable characteristics, which are the result of the interaction of the genes with each other and with the environment. (72) (See also *genotype*.)

phobia An irrational fear that is out of proportion to the real threat the person experiences, cannot be reasoned away, and interferes with a person's normal functioning. Many phobias have specific names, such as claustrophobia (fear of enclosed places), aquaphobia (fear of water), and agoraphobia (fear of open spaces). (272)

placenta An organ made up of blood vessels leading to both the mother's and the fetus' bloodstream and having membranes to prevent mixture of the two bloodstreams. These membranes serve as screens through which oxygen and nourishment pass to the fetus and wastes pass from the fetus to the mother to be excreted through her system. (95)

planned retirement communities Housing units designed exclusively for older adults. (658)

plasticity In developmental psychology, a term used to indicate that a particular characteristic is shaped by many environmental influences. Many human characteristics, once thought to be firmly fixed before adulthood, are now known to have much more plasticity than was once believed. (550)

play face A facial expression, such as a smile or laugh, that accompanies playful activity. The play face helps distinguish rough-and-tumble play from real hostility. (222)

polygenic inheritance The interaction of many genes to produce a particular characteristic. For example, skin color, body shape, and memory are all polygenic. (72)

positive reinforcer A reward or something pleasant that is given in response to a particular behavior and which increases the likelihood that that behavior will occur again. (44)

postconventional moral reasoning Kohlberg's term for the highest stages of moral reasoning in which the person formulates and follows universal ethical principles, realizing that the rules of society may need to be overridden if they become destructive. (399)

postformal thought A type of adult thinking that is suited to solving real-world problems. Postformal thought is less abstract and absolute than formal thought, more adaptive to life's inconsistencies, and more dialectical—capable of combining contradictory elements into a comprehensive whole. (467) (See *dialectical thought*.)

practical intelligence The intellectual skills used in everyday problem solving. (552)

pragmatics In the study of language, a term for the practical aspects of communication, for example, the skill a person shows in adjusting vocabulary and grammar to fit the social context. (247)

preconventional moral reasoning Kohlberg's term for the first stages of moral reasoning, in which the person's own welfare is paramount and the customs or mores of society are relatively unimportant. (399)

preoperational thought Piaget's term for the second period of cognitive development. Children in this stage of thought, which usually occurs between the ages of 2 and 7, are unable to grasp logical concepts such as conservation, reversibility, or classification. (231)

preterm infant An infant born more than three weeks before the due date. (109)

primary sex characteristics Those sex organs that are directly involved in reproduction. Changes in the primary sex characteristics occur during puberty; in girls, the uterus begins to grow and the vaginal lining thickens, and in boys, the testes begin to grow followed by the penis and the scrotal sac. (375)

private speech The mental use of language to formulate ideas to oneself. Private speech enhances memory and other cognitive abilities. (243)

problem finding The capacity to formulate new questions from ambiguous or ill-defined problems or situations—that is, to "go beyond the information given" to raise more searching issues. (468)

processing capacity The ability to hold information in working memory, the part of the information-processing system where reasoning and thinking occur. (310). (See also *sensory register, working memory*, and *knowledge base*.)

progeria   A rare genetic disease which causes young children to age prematurely and to die by their teens. (602)

programmed senescence   Refers to the theory that the human body is genetically programmed to age. Many researchers believe that the timetable for aging, like the timetable for biological maturation, is contained within the DNA. (601)

Project Headstart   A special preschool educational program designed to provide culturally deprived or disadvantaged 4-year-olds with a variety of intellectual and social experiences that might better prepare them for school. (251)

prosocial behavior   Any behavior that is performed to benefit other people without expected reward for oneself. Cooperation, helping, sharing, and generosity are all prosocial behaviors. (340)

provocation ecologies   Classroom environments that provoke or exacerbate hyperactive behavior in some children by imposing either an unusually rigid classroom structure or none at all. (300)

proximo-distal development   Growth proceeding from the center (spine) toward the extremities (literally, from near to far). Human growth, from the embryonic period through childhood, follows this pattern. (95)

psychoanalytic theory   A theory of psychology, originated by Sigmund Freud, that stresses the influence of unconscious motivation and drives on all human behavior. (37)

psychosexual stages   The idea, held by psychoanalytic theorists, that development occurs in a series of stages (oral, anal, phallic, and genital), each of which is characterized by the focusing of sexual interest and gratification on one part of the body. (38)

psychosocial domain   The domain of human development involving emotions, personality characteristics, interpersonal relationships, and the social contexts in which they occur. (5)

psychosocial theory   A psychoanalytic theory of development emphasizing social and cultural effects on the individual. (41)

puberty   The period of early adolescence characterized by rapid physical growth and the attainment of the physiological capability of sexual reproduction. Puberty usually begins between ages 8 and 14, although there is much variation caused by genes and nutrition. (370)

punishment   An unpleasant event that occurs in response to a particular behavior, making it less likely that the behavior will be repeated. (45)

rarefaction ecologies   Classroom environments that ameliorate or diminish hyperactive behavior in some children by reacting flexibly to disruptive behavior, but also providing sufficient classroom structure. (300)

reaction time   The time it takes a person to react to a particular stimulus. (291)

reciprocal determinism   A social learning theory that regards behavior as the result of the interaction between one's expectations, self-perceptions, and goals, and one's social environment, which influence and affect each other. (47)

reciprocity   The logical principle that a change in one dimension of an object is compensated for by a change in another dimension. For example, a ball of clay, rolled out, will be both longer and thinner. According to Piaget, children begin to understand these relationships during the period of concrete operational thought. (305)

reflexes   Involuntary physical responses, such as an eye blink, to a given stimulus. (131) (See also *breathing reflex, sucking reflex,* and *rooting reflex.*)

rehearsal   A memory technique involving repetition of the material to be remembered. (309)

reinforcement   In operant conditioning, the process whereby a particular behavior is strengthened through a pleasurable or useful consequence making it more likely that the behavior will be repeated. (44)

reinforcer   Anything (for example, food, money, a smile) that increases the likelihood that a given response will occur again. For example, giving a child a warm hug for being polite will increase the chances that that behavior will be repeated. (44) (See also *positive reinforcer, negative reinforcer, extrinsic reinforcer,* and *intrinsic reinforcer.*)

reintegrative stage   Schaie's last stage of cognitive development, during which the individual focuses on the larger purposes of life and existence. (466)

rejecting-neglecting   A style of parenting that is cold and unengagedly permissive. (265)

replicate   To repeat or duplicate. Scientists describe their experiments in detail sufficient to allow others to replicate their test procedures. (20)

representative sample   A group of subjects in a research project who have the relevant characteristics (e.g., sex, race, socioeconomic level) of the general population or of a particular segment of the population that the researcher wants to learn about. (22)

repression   A defense mechanism in which anxiety-provoking thoughts and fantasies are excluded from consciousness. (39)

respiratory distress syndrome   A syndrome in which some preterm infants have trouble getting sufficient oxygen because their immature reflexes do not regulate breathing properly. (109)

response   A behavior (either instinctual or learned) following a specific cue. (43) (See *stimulus.*)

response generator   A network of mental processes, involving the sensory register, working memory, and knowledge base, that analyze sensory information and organize reactions to environmental stimuli. (56)

responsible stage   In Schaie's stages of adult cognitive development, a period during which the adult cares for the well-being of not only the self, but of others, too, such as a family and friends. (465)

restorable families   An assessment label used in child-maltreatment intervention: refers to families in which the caregivers seem to have the potential to provide adequate care, and perhaps have done so in the past, but they have many problems, caused by their immediate situation, by their past history, and by their temperament, that seriously impair their parenting abilities. (202)

restricted code   A form of speech characterized by limited use of vocabulary and syntax. Meaning is communicated by gestures, intonation, and shared understandings. (317)

retrieval strategies Procedures to recollect previously learned information, such as thinking of associated information, trying to create a mental image of the thing to be remembered, or using clues from others. (310)

reversibility The idea that something that has been changed can be returned to its original state simply by reversing the process of change. For example, a ball of clay that has been rolled out into a long, thin rope can be rerolled into a ball. According to Piaget, preschoolers cannot regularly apply the rule of reversibility. (231, 305)

risk analysis In teratology, the attempt to evaluate the combination of factors, such as exposure to teratogens, timing, and nutrition, that have the potential to cause prenatal damage. (99) (See also *teratogens*.)

rooting reflex A normal neonatal reflex that helps babies find a nipple by causing them to turn their heads toward the stimulus and start to suck whenever something brushes against their cheek. (131)

rough-and-tumble play Play such as wrestling, chasing, and hitting that mimics aggression, but that actually occurs purely in fun, with no intent to harm. (222) (See also *play face*.)

sample size In research, the size of a group of individuals that are studied in order to draw conclusions about a larger group or segment of the population. Sample size can greatly affect the validity of research results. (22)

sandwich generation The generation "in between," having both grown children and elderly parents. Many middle-aged people feel pressured by the needs and demands of their adult children, on the one side, and of their elderly (and perhaps ailing or widowed) parents on the other. (568)

schema Piaget's term for a general way of thinking about, or interacting with, ideas and objects in the environment. (52)

scientific method A procedural model used to formulate questions, collect data, test hypotheses, and draw conclusions. Use of the scientific method helps researchers overcome biases, test assumptions, and in short, be "scientific." (20)

scientific reasoning The ability to understand and use the principles of science. According to Piaget, scientific reasoning is characteristic of the last stage of cognitive development, formal operational thought. (388)

secondary sexual characteristics Sexual features other than the reproductive organs, such as a man's beard or a woman's breasts, that develop during puberty. (377)

secure attachment A healthy caregiver-child bond in which the child feels comfort and confidence when the caregiver is present, experiences moderate distress at the caregiver's absence, and quickly reestablishes contact when the caregiver returns. In secure attachment, the infant uses the caregiver as a secure base from which to venture forth to explore the environment. (185)

selective attention The ability to concentrate on relevant information and ignore distractions. (309)

self-actualization The ultimate goal of human development, according to humanistic theories. A self-actualized person has fulfilled his or her potential to the maximum, making *actual*, or real, the unique and creative self that each person can become. (59)

self-awareness A person's sense of himself or herself as a separate person, with particular characteristics. The development of this sense of self begins at birth, but only between 1 and 2 years of age do children begin to truly differentiate themselves from others. (174)

self-efficacy A person's sense of his or her own capabilities and aspirations, which, according to social learning theory, motivate one to learn from and aspire to certain social influences and models. (47)

senescence The state of physical decline, in which the body gradually becomes less strong and efficient with age. (443, 588)

sensation The response of a given sensory system to a particular stimulus. (127)

sensorimotor intelligence Piaget's term for the first stage of cognitive development (from birth to about 2 years old). Children in this stage primarily use the senses and motor skills (i.e., grasping, sucking, etc.) to explore and manipulate the environment. (51, 144)

sensorimotor play Play that captures the pleasures of using the senses, including the primary senses (touching, tasting, hearing, etc.) and one's motor abilities. For example, children who mash their food, or whirl their bodies around for the pure fun of it are engaging in sensorimotor play. (219)

sensory register A memory system that functions for only a fraction of a second during sensory processing, retaining a fleeting impression of the stimulus that has just impinged on a particular sense organ (e.g., the eyes). If a person looks at an object, for example, and then closes his or her eyes, the visual image of the object is briefly maintained. Significant information is transferred to working memory. (55, 612)

separation anxiety An infant's fear of being left or abandoned by the mother or other caregiver. This emotion emerges at about 8 or 9 months, peaks at about 14 months, then gradually subsides. (173)

separation-individuation Mahler's term to describe the period during which the child gradually develops a sense of self, apart from the mother. This period extends from about 5 months to 3 years, and is marked by the child's increasingly secure attempts to achieve psychological separation from the mother. (178)

serial monogamy A series of intimate, committed relationships, with only one person at a time, inside or outside of the marriage contract. (491)

seriation The concept that items can be arranged in a logical series, as by sorting a group of sticks from longest to shortest, or arranging a group of crayons from lightest to darkest. This concept is mastered during the period of concrete operational thought, according to Piaget. (306)

sex differences Differences between males and females that arise from differences between male and female chromosomes and hormones. (223)

sexually transmitted disease (STD) Diseases spread by sexual contact. Such diseases include syphilis, gonorrhea, herpes, chlamydia, and AIDS. (403)

sibling abuse Serious and intentional harm done to a child by a brother or sister. (198)

significance A statistical term that reflects whether a measured difference (for example between an experimental and control group) is a relevant scientific finding, or perhaps merely the result of chance. Usually, if the likelihood that a particular result occurred by chance is less than one chance in twenty, the result is termed significant. (23)

sleeper effects   Results that become apparent sometime after the precipitating event. (251)

small-for-gestational-age (SGA)   A term applied to newborns who weigh substantially less than they should given how much time has passed since conception. (109)

social clock   Neugarten's term for the idea that the stages of life, and the behaviors "appropriate" to them, are set by social standards rather than by biological maturation. For instance, "middle age" begins when the culture believes it does, rather than at a particular age in all societies. (17, 486)

social cognition   A person's understanding of people and the dynamics of human interaction, including gender, maturity, and achievement. (333)

social comparison   The practice—particularly common among school-age children—of comparing one's own and one's family's social status and material well-being with that of peers and neighbors. As children grow older, this broadens to include not only one's immediate experience but also the larger community, as depicted on television or as viewed by the child in traveling outside the neighborhood. (358)

social convoy   Each person's family members, friends, and acquaintances who move through life with him or her are called the social convoy. While peripheral members of the convoy can drop out or join without much disruption, the arrival or departure of central members, as in the birth of an offspring or the loss of a spouse, can have great impact on the individual. People whose social convoy is large and close are better able to endure the various physical and psychological assaults that life brings. (657)

social inoculation   A procedure that uses role-playing and discussion to gradually expose individuals to various kinds of pressures and problems they might face in the future. This technique has been shown to be quite effective with adolescents in sex education. (407)

social learning theory   The theory that learning occurs through imitation of, and identification with, other people. (46)

social referencing   The capacity to look to trusted adults for emotional cues in uncertain situations; for example, an infant might look to the mother when they encounter a stranger, and the mother's reaction then influences the child's reaction. Infants begin to engage in social referencing by 10 months of age. (174)

social smile   An infant's smile in response to someone else. In full-term infants, this kind of smile first appears at about 6 weeks after birth. (172)

society of children   A term for the subculture of games, vocabulary, dress codes, and rules of behavior that regulates children's play and distinguishes it from the general culture. (338)

socioeconomic status (SES)   A measure that takes into account an individual's education, income, occupation, and residence. Socioeconomic status is one of the major contextual factors influencing a person's development. (9)

sonogram   A method of determining the size and position of the fetus by means of sound waves. (89)

spermarche   The first ejaculation of seminal fluid containing sperm. (376)

spermatozoa (singular, **spermatozoon**)   The male reproductive cells, which begin to be produced by the testicles at puberty. (Usually abbreviated to *sperm*.) (68)

stimulus   An external condition or event that elicits a bodily response or prompts a particular action. For example, the sight or aroma of an appetizing meal is a stimulus to which the response is usually salivation. (43)

storage strategies   Procedures for retaining new information, such as rehearsal (repeating the information to be remembered) and organization (regrouping the information to make it more memorable). (309)

Strange Situation   An experiment devised by Mary Ainsworth to assess the nature of an infant's attachment by analyzing his or her reactions to the comings and goings of the mother and a friendly stranger. (185)

stress   The adverse physical and emotional reaction to demands put on the individual by unsettling conditions or experiences, also known as stressors. Adverse reactions to stress have been linked to increased incidence of disease and health problems. (529)

stressors   Unsettling conditions or experiences that cause stress. (529)

sucking reflex   A normal neonatal reflex that causes newborns to suck anything that touches their lips. (131)

superego   Freud's term for that part of the personality that contains the conscience, including the internalization of moral standards set by one's parents. (39)

supportable families   An assessment label used in child-maltreatment intervention: refers to families that will probably never be able to function adequately and independently until the children are grown but that, with ongoing support, could meet their children's basic needs for physical, educational, and emotional care. (203)

survey   A research method consisting of personal interviews or formal questionnaires that ask people for information about themselves or for their opinions. (28)

synchrony   Carefully coordinated interaction between infant and parent (or any other two people) in which each is exquisitely, often unknowingly, attuned to the other's verbal and nonverbal cues. (183)

syndrome   A cluster of distinct personal characteristics that tend to occur together, although the number of characteristics exhibited, and their intensity, vary from individual to individual. (81)

task-involvement learning   An educational approach in which grades are based on acquiring certain competencies and knowledge that everyone, with enough time and effort, is expected to attain. (395)

T-cells   Cells created in the thymus that produce substances that attack infected cells in the body. (598)

temperament   Inherent, relatively consistent dispositions in a person that underlie and affect his or her response to things and people, and are reflected in, for example, one's activity level, intensity of reaction, emotions, and sociability. (179)

teratogens   External agents, such as viruses, drugs, chemicals, and radiation, which can cross the barrier of the placenta and harm the embryo or fetus. (99)

teratology   The scientific study of birth defects caused by genetic or prenatal problems, or by birth complications. (98)

testosterone   A hormone that is produced primarily by the testes and regulates sexual development in puberty. Although girls' adrenal glands produce some testosterone, it is chiefly a male hormone. (371)

thanatology A field of research that studies death. (681)

theory of mind A personal understanding of one's own and others' mental processes, that is, of the complex interaction of emotions, perceptions, thoughts, and actions, that explain individual behavior. Differing theories of mind explain why two people might interpret a third person's intentions quite differently. (237)

threshold effect A term applied to the teratogenic potential of a substance (usually a drug) that is virtually harmless until a pregnant woman's exposure to it reaches a certain frequency or dosage level. (103)

toddler A child, usually between the ages of 1 and 2, who has just begun to master the art of walking. (132)

traditional parenting A style of parenting in which the parents take somewhat traditional male and female roles, the mother being primarily nurturant and permissive, while the father is more authoritarian. (265)

trimester One of the three-month periods in the nine months of pregnancy. (97)

trust versus mistrust Erikson's term for the infant's basic experience of the world either as a secure place where basic needs are met or as a threatening, unreliable one. Early caregiving experiences usually mold the child's viewpoint. This is the first of Erikson's eight stages of development. (177)

twenty-third pair The pair of human chromosomes that determines the individual's sex. (70)

unconditional positive regard Love and respect for an individual in any and all circumstances. (60)

vasomotor instability The temporary disruption of the homeostatic mechanisms of the vascular system, which usually constrict or dilate the blood vessels to maintain body temperature. Vasomotor instability causes moments of feeling suddenly hot or cold, a typical experience during the climacteric at menopause. (533)

violent death Death from accident, homicide, or suicide. It afflicts mostly young men and is often brought about by stereotypically "manly" attitudes and behavior. (458)

vitality A measure of health that refers to how healthy and energetic, physically, intellectually, and socially, an individual actually feels. (524)

vulnerable to crisis An assessment label used in child-maltreatment intervention: refers to families who are experiencing unusual problems and needing temporary help to resolve them. (202)

wear-and-tear theory A theory of aging that states that the human body wears out merely by being lived-in and by being exposed to environmental stressors. The wear-and-tear theory sees the human body as a machine that wears out over time. (599)

working memory That part of the information-processing system that handles current, conscious mental activity. Working memory is constantly receiving new information, so thoughts and memories are either discarded or transferred to the more permanent knowledge base. (Also called *short-term memory*.) (55, 613)

X-linked genes Genes that are carried on the X chromosome exclusively. X-linked genes account for the fact that certain recessive genetic diseases or conditions are more likely to occur in males, who have only one X chromosome, than in females, who have two. (73)

young-old Healthy, vigorous, financially secure older adults who are well-integrated into the lives of their families and their communities. (587)

zone of proximal development Vygotsky's term for the difference between a child's actual level of development (occurring independently) and his or her potential level of development (occurring with the guidance of an adult or more capable peer). (241)

zygote The one-celled organism formed from the union of a sperm and an ovum. (68)

Bibliography

AARP. (1990). *Understanding senior housing for the 1990s: An American Association of Retired Persons survey of consumer preferences, concerns and needs.* Washington, DC: American Association of Retired Persons.

Abbey, Antonia, Andrews, Grank M. and Halman, L. Jill. (1992). Infertity and subjective well-being: The mediating roles of self-esteem, internal control, and interpersonal conflict. *Journal of Marriage and the Family, 54,* 408–417.

Abel, E., and Sokol, R. (1987). Incidence of fetal alchohol syndrome and economic impact of FAS-related anomalies. *Drug and Alcohol Dependency, 19,* 51–70.

Aboud, F. (1985). Children's application of attribution principles to social comparisons. *Child Development, 56,* 682–688.

Abramovitch, R., Corter, C., and Lando, B. (1979). Sibling interaction in the home. *Child Development, 50,* 997–1003.

Abramovitch, R., Pepler, D., and Corter, C. (1982). Patterns of sibling interaction among preschool children. In M. Lamb and B. Sutton-Smith (Eds.), *Sibling relationships.* Hillsdale, NJ: Erlbaum.

Achenbach, Thomas M. (1982). *Developmental psychopathology* (2nd ed.). New York: Wiley.

Achenbach, Thomas M., and Edelbrock, Craig S. (1981). Behavioral problems and competencies reported by parents of normal and disturbed children aged four through sixteen. *Monographs of the Society for Research in Child Development, 46* (Serial No. 188).

Achenberg, W. Andrew. (1985). Religion in the lives of the elderly. In Gari Lesnoff-Caravalglia (Ed.), *Values, ethics, and aging.* New York: Human Sciences Press.

Adams, C.G., and Turner, B.F. (1985). Reported change in sexuality from young adulthood to old days. *The Journal of Sex Research, 21,* 126–141.

Adams, Cynthia, and Labouvie-Vief, Gisela. (1986). *Modes of knowing and language processing.* Symposium on developmental dimensions of adult adaptation: Perspectives on mind, self, and emotion. Presented at 1986 meeting of the Gerontological Association of America, Chicago, November 20.

Adams, Edgar H., Gfroerer, Joseph C., and Bourse, Beatrice A. (1989). Epidemiology of substance abuse, including alcohol and cigarette smoking. In Donald Hutchings (Ed.), *Prenatal abuse of licit and illicit drugs.* New York: New York Academy of Sciences.

Adams, G.R., and Jones, R.M. (1981). Imaginary audience behavior: A validation study. *Journal of Early Adolescence, 1,* 1–10.

Adams, Marilyn Jager. (1990). *Beginning to read: Thinking and learning about print.* Cambridge, MA: MIT Press.

Adams, Paul L., Milner, Judith R. and Schrept, N.A. (1984). *Fatherless children.* New York: Wiley-Interscience.

Adams, Rebecca G. (1987). Patterns of network change: A longitudinal study of friendship of elderly women. *Journal of Gerontology, 27,* 222–227.

Ades, A.E., Newell, M.L., and Peckham, C.S. (1991). Children born to women with HIV-1 infection: Natural history and risk of transmission. *The Lancet, 337,* 253–260.

Ahmedzai, Sam, and Wilkes, Eric. (1988). Dying with dignity: A British view. In Basil A. Stoll (Ed.), *Cost versus benefit in cancer care.* Baltimore, MD: Johns Hopkins University Press.

Ainsworth, Mary D. Salter. (1973). The development of infant-mother attachment. In Bettye M. Caldwell and Henry N. Ricciuti (Eds.), *Review of child development research* (Vol. III). Chicago: University of Chicago Press.

Ainsworth, Mary D. Salter. (1985). Attachments across the lifespan. *Bulletin of the New York Academy of Medicine, 61,* 792–812.

Ainsworth, Mary D. Salter, and Bell, Silvia M. (1970). Attachment, exploration, and separation: Illustrated by the behavior of one-year-olds in a strange situation. *Child Development, 41,* 49–67.

Alberts-Corush, J., Firestone, P., and Goodman, J.T. (1986). Attention and impulsivity characteristics of the biological and adoptive parents of hyperactive and normal control children. *American Journal of Orthopsychiatry, 56,* 413–423.

Allan, Graham. (1989). *Friendship: Developing a sociological perspective.* Boulder, CO: Westview.

Allen, J.R., Barsotti, D.A., and Carsten, L.A. (1980). Residual effect of polychlorinated biphenyls on adult nonhuman primates and their offspring. *Journal of Toxicology and Environmental Health, 6,* 55–66.

Allen, Katherine R., and Pickett, Robert S. (1987). Forgotten streams in the family life course: Utilization of qualitative retrospective interviews in the analysis of lifelong single women's family careers. *Journal of Marriage and the Family, 49,* 517–526.

Allison, Clara. (1985). Development direction of action programs: Repetitive action to correction loops. In Jane E. Clark and James H. Humphrey (Eds.), *Motor development: Current selected research*. Princeton, NJ: Princeton Book Company.

Allison, Paul D., and **Furstenberg, Frank F.** (1989). How marital dissolution affects children: Variations by age and sex. *Developmental Psychology, 25,* 540–549.

Altman, Lawrence K. (1991, August 6). Men, women, and heart disease: More than a question of sexism. *New York Times,* C1, 8.

Alwin, Duane F., Converse, Philip E., and **Martin, Steven S.** (1985). Living arrangements and social integration. *Journal of Marriage and the Family, 47,* 319–334.

Amaro, Hortensia, Fried, Lise E., Cabral, Howard, and **Zuckerman, Barry.** (1990). Violence during pregnancy and substance use. *American Journal of Public Health, 80,* 575–579.

Amato, Paul R., and **Keith, Bruce.** (1991). Parental divorce and adult well-being: A meta-analysis. *Journal of Marriage and the Family, 53,* 43–58.

American Psychological Association. (1990). Ethical principles of psychologists. *American Psychologist, 45,* 390–395.

American Society on Aging. (1992). *Serving elders of color: Challenges to providers and the Aging Network.* San Francisco: American Society of Aging.

Ammerman, Robert T., and **Hersen, Michel** (Eds.). (1989). *Treatment of family violence.* New York: Wiley.

Anastasi, Anne. (1988). *Psychological testing* (6th ed.). New York: Macmillan.

Anderson, Erin and Geden. (1991). Nurses knowledge of breastfeeding. *Journal of Obstetric, Gynecological and Neonatal Nursing, 20,* 58–64.

Anderson, Robert L., and **Golbus, Mitchel S.** (1989). Chemical teratogens. In Mark I. Evans, Alan O. Dixler, John C. Fletcher, and Joseph D. Schulman (Eds.), *Fetal diagnosis and therapy*. Philadelphia: Lippincott.

Andrews, Gary Robert, Esterman, A.J., Braunack-Mayer, A.J., and **Rungie, C.M.** (1986). *Aging in the Western Pacific.* Manila: World Health Organization.

Angier, Natalie. (1991, August 6). Erroneous triple helping of DNA is implicated in disease. *New York Times,* C3.

Anglin, Jeremy M. (1977). *Word, object, and conceptual development.* New York: Norton.

Anthony, E.J. (1987). Risk, vulnerability, and resiliance: An overview. In E.J. Anthony and B.J. Cohler (Eds.), *The invulnerable child.* New York: Guilford.

Antonucci, Toni C. (1985). Personal characteristics, social support, and social behavior. In Robert H. Binstock and Ethel Shanas (Eds.), *Handbook of aging and the social sciences.* New York: Van Nostrand.

Antonucci, Toni C. (1990). Attachment, social support, and coping with negative life events. In E.M. Cummings, A.L. Greene, and K.H. Karraker (Eds.), *Life-span developmental psychology: Vol. 11. Stress and coping across the life-span.* Hillsdale, NJ: Erlbaum.

Apgar, Virginia. (1953). A proposal for a new method of evaluation in the newborn infant. *Current Research in Anesthesia and Analgesia, 32,* 260.

Apple, Rima D. (1988). *Mothers and medicine: A social history of infant feeding, 1890–1950.* Madison, WI: University of Wisconson Press.

Applebaum, Mark I., and **McCall, Robert B.** (1983). Design and analysis in developmental psychology. In Paul H. Mussen (Ed.), *Handbook of child psychology: Vol. I. History, theory, and methods.* New York: Wiley.

Aquilino, William S. (1991). Family structure and home-leaving: A further specification of the relationship. *Journal of Marriage and the Family, 53,* 999–1010.

Arbuthnot, Jack, Gordon, Donald A., and **Jurkovic, Gregory J.** (1987). Personality. In Herbert C. Quay (Ed.), *Handbook of juvenile delinquency.* New York: Wiley.

Archer, Sally L., and **Waterman, Alan S.** (1990). Varieties of identity diffusions and foreclosures: An exploration of the subcategories of the identity statuses. *Journal of Adolescent Research, 5,* 96–111.

Arenberg, David. (1982). Changes in age with problem-solving. In Fergus I.M. Craik and Sandra Trehub (Eds.), *Aging and cognitive processes.* New York: Plenum.

Arend, Richard, Gove, Frederick L., and **Sroufe, L. Alan.** (1979). Continuity of individual adaptation from infancy to kindergarten: A predictive study of ego-resiliency and curiosity in preschoolers. *Child Development, 50,* 950–959.

Aries, E.J. and **Johnson, F.L.** (1983). Close friendship in adulthood: Conversational content between same-sex freinds. *Sex roles, 9,* 1183–1196.

Ariès, Philippe. (1981). *The hour of our death.* New York: Knopf.

Arlin, Greg. (1976). The elderly widow and her family, neighbors, and friends. *Journal of Marriage and the Family, 38,* 757–768.

Arlin, Patricia K. (1984). Adolescent and adult thought: A structural interpretation. In Michael L. Commons, Francis A. Richards, and Cheryl Armon (Eds.), *Beyond formal operations: Late adolescent and adult cognitive development.* New York: Praeger.

Arlin, Patricia K. (1989). Problem solving and problem finding in young artists and young scientists. In Michael L. Commons, Jan D. Sinnott, Francis A. Richards, and Cheryl Armon (Eds.), *Adult development: Vol. 1. Comparisons and applications of developmental models.* New York: Praeger.

Arnold, Elaine. (1982). The use of corporal punishment in child-rearing in the West Indies. *Child Abuse and Neglect, 6,* 141–145.

Arnold, M. Diane. (1989). The politics of assuring quality of care for elders. *Generations, 13* (1), 34–37.

Asher, Steven R. (1983). Social competence and peer status: Recent advances and future directions. *Child Development, 54,* 1427–1434.

Asher, Steven R., and **Renshaw, Peter D.** (1981). Children without friends: Social knowledge and social skill training. In Steven R. Asher and John M. Gottman (Eds.), *The development of children's friendships.* Cambridge, England: Cambridge University Press.

Ashton-Warner, Sylvia. (1963). *Teacher.* New York: Simon and Schuster.

Aslin, Richard N. (1987). Visual and auditory development in infancy. In Joy Doniger Osofsky (Ed.), *Handbook of infant development* (2nd ed.). New York: Wiley.

Aslin, Richard. (1988). Visual perception in early infancy. In Albert Yonas (Ed.), *Perceptual development in infancy.* Hillsdale, NJ: Erlbaum.

Astington, J.W., Harris, P.L., and Olson, D.R. (Eds.). (1988). *Developing theories of mind.* New York: Cambridge University Press.

Atchley, R.C. (1989). A continuity theory of normal aging. *The Gerontologist, 29,* 183–190.

Atkinson, Janette, and Braddick, Oliver. (1988). Infant precursors of later visual disorders: Correlation or causality? In Albert Yonas (Ed.), *Perceptual development in infancy.* Hillsdale, NJ: Erlbaum.

Ausman, L.M., and Russell, R.M. (1990). Nutrition and aging. In E.L. Schneider and J.W. Rowe (Eds.), *Handbook of the biology of aging* (3rd ed.). New York: Academic Press.

Axia, Giovanna, and Baroni, Rosa. (1985). Linguistic politeness at different age levels. *Child Development, 56,* 918–927.

Axline, Virginia. (1964). *Dibs in search of self.* New York: Ballantine.

Bachrach, Christine A. (1984). Contraceptive practice among American women, 1973–1982. *Family Planning Perspectives, 16,* 253–259.

Bahrick, H.P. (1984). Semantic memory content in permastore: Fifty years of memory for Spanish learned in school. *Journal of Experimental Psychology: General, 113,* 1–35.

Bahrick, L.E. (1983). Infants' perception of substance and temporal synchrony in multimodal events. *Infant Behavior and Development, 6,* 429–451.

Bailey, Lynn B. (1986). Nutritional anemias: Iron, folacin, vitamin B-12. In Linda H. Chen (Ed.), *Nutritional aspects of aging* (Vol. 2). Boca Raton, FL: CRC Press.

Baillargeon, Renee, Graber, Marcia, Decops, Julia, and Black, James. (1990). Why do young infants fail to search for hidden objects? *Cognition, 36,* 255–284.

Bakeman, Roger, and Brown, J.V. (1980). Early interaction: Consequences for social and mental development at three years. *Child Development, 51,* 437–447.

Bakeman, Roger, Adamson, Lauren B., Konner, Melvin, and Barr, Ronald G. (1990). Kung! infancy: The social context of object exploration. *Child Development, 61,* 794–809.

Bakker, D.J., and Vinke, J. (1985). Effect of hemispheric-specific stimulation on brain activity and reading in dyslexics. *Journal of Clinical Neuropsychology, 7,* 505–525.

Ball, Jean A. (1987). *Reactions to motherhood.* New York: Cambridge University Press.

Baltes, Margret M., and Reisenzein, Rainer. (1986). The social world in long-term care institutions: Psychosocial control toward dependency? In Margret M. Baltes and Paul B. Baltes (Eds.), *The psychology of control and aging.* Hillsdale, NJ: Erlbaum.

Baltes, Paul B. (1987). Theoretical propositions of life-span developmental psychology: On the dynamics between growth and decline. *Developmental Psychology, 23,* 611–626.

Baltes, Paul B., and Baltes, Margret M. (1990). Psychological perspectives on successful aging: The model of selective optimization with compensation. In Paul B. Baltes and Margret M. Baltes (Eds.), *Successful aging: Perspectives from the behavioral sciences.* Cambridge, England: Cambridge University Press.

Baltes, Paul B., and Lindenberger. (1988). On the range of cognitive plasticity in old age as a function of experience: 15 years of Intervention research. *Behavior Therapy, 19,* 283–300.

Baltes, Paul B., and Schaie, K. Warner. (1974). Aging and IQ: The myth of the twilight years. *Psychology Today, 7* (10), 35–40.

Baltes, Paul B., and Schaie, K. Warner. (1976). On the plasticity of intelligence in adulthood and old age: Where Horn and Donaldson fail. *American Psychologist, 31,* 720–725.

Baltes, Paul B., and Willis, Sherry L. (1982). Enhancement (plasticity) of intellectual functioning in old age: Penn State's Adult Development and Enrichment Project (ADEPT). In Fergus I.M. Craik and Sandra E. Trehub (Eds.), *Aging and cognitive processes.* New York: Plenum.

Baltes, Paul B., Dittman-Kohli, F., and Dixon, Roger A. (1984). New perspectives on the development of intelligence in adulthood: Toward a dual-process conception and a model of selective optimization with compensation. In Paul B. Baltes and Orville G. Brim, Jr. (Eds.), *Life-span development and behavior* (Vol. 6). New York: Academic Press.

Baltes, Paul B., Smith, Jacqui, and Staudinger, Ursula. (1992). Wisdom and successful aging. In T. Sonderegger (Ed.), *Psychology and aging: Nebraska symposium on motivation* (Vol. 39). Lincoln, NE: University of Nebraska Press.

Bamford, F.N., Bannister, R. Pr., Benjamin, C.M., Hillier, V.F., Ward, B.S., and Moore, W.M.O. (1990). Sleep in the first year of life. *Developmental and Child Neurology, 32,* 718–734.

Band, Eve Brotman. (1988). Coping among school-aged children: The influence of development and environment. In Jaan Valsiner (Ed.), *Child development within culturally structured environments: Vol. 2. Social co-construction and environmental guidance in development.* Norwood, NJ: Ablex.

Band, Eve Brotman, and Weisz, John R. (1988). How to feel better when it feels bad: Children's perspectives on coping with everyday stress. *Developmental Psychology, 24,* 247–253.

Bandura, Albert. (1977). *Social learning theory.* Englewood Cliffs, NJ: Prentice-Hall.

Bandura, Albert. (1981). Self-referent thought: A developmental analysis of self-efficacy. In John H. Flavell and Lee Ross (Eds.), *Social cognitive development: Frontiers and possible futures.* Cambridge, England: Cambridge University Press.

Bandura, Albert. (1986). *Social foundations of thought and action: A social cognitive theory.* Englewood Cliffs, NJ: Prentice-Hall.

Bandura, Albert. (1989). Social cognitive theory. In R. Vasta (Ed.), *Annals of Child Development* (Vol. 6). Greenwich, CT: JAI Press.

Bane, Share DeCroix. (1991). Rural minority populations. *Generations, 27* (3), 63–65.

Baranowski, Tom, Bryan, George T., Rassin, David K., Harrison, Joel A., and Henske, Janice C. (1990). Ethnicity, infant-feeding, and childhood adiposity. *Developmental and Behavioral Pediatrics, 11,* 234–239.

Bardin, C. Wayne. (1986). The pituitary-testicular axis. In Samuel S.C. Yen and Robert B. Jaffe (Eds.), *Reproductive endocrinology: Physiology, pathophysiology, and clinical management* (2nd ed.). Philadelphia: Saunders.

Bardo, Michael T., and Mueller, Charles W. (1991). Sensation seeking and drug abuse prevention from a biological perspective. In Lewis Donohew, Howard E. Sypher, and William J.

Bukoski (Eds.), *Persuasive communication and drug abuse prevention.* Hillsdale, NJ: Erlbaum.

Barnes, Deborah M. (1987a). Defect in Alzheimer's is on chromosome 21. *Science, 235,* 846–847.

Barnes, Deborah M. (1987b). Brain damage by AIDS under active study. *Science, 235,* 1574–1577.

Barnett, Mark A. (1986). Sex bias in the helping behavior presented in children's picture books. *Journal of Genetic Psychology, 147,* 343–351.

Barnett, Rosaline C., and **Baruch, Grace K.** (1987). Determinants of fathers' participation in family work. *Journal of Marriage and the Family, 49,* 29–40.

Barnett, Rosaline C., Marshall, Nancy, L., and **Singer, Judith D.** (1992a). Job experiences over time, multiple roles, and women's mental health: A longitudinal study. *Journal of Personality and Social Psychology, 62,* 634–644.

Barnett, Rosaline C., Marshall, Nancy, L., and **Pleck, Joseph H.** (1992b). Men's multiple roles and their relationship to men's psychological distress. *Journal of Marriage and the Family, 54,* 358–367.

Barnett, W.S., and **Escobar, C.M.** (1987). The economics of early educational intervention: A review. *Review of Educational Research, 57,* 387–414.

Barresi, Charles M., and **Menon, Geeta.** (1990). Diversity in Black family caregiving. In Zev Harel, Edward A. McKinney, and Mischel Williams (Eds.), *Black aged.* Newbury Park, CA: Sage.

Barrett, Martyn D. (1986). Early semantic representations and early word-usage. In Stan A. Kuczaj and Martyn D. Barrett (Eds.), *The development of word meaning: Progress in cognitive developmental research.* New York: Springer-Verlag.

Baruch, Grace K. (1984). The psychological well-being of women in the middle years. In Grace K. Baruch and Jeanne Brooks-Gunn (Eds.), *Women in midlife.* New York: Plenum.

Baruch, Grace K., and **Barnett, Rosaline C.** (1986). Fathers' participation in family work and children's sex-role attitudes. *Child Development, 57,* 1210–1223.

Baruch, Grace K., Barnett, Rosaline C., and **Rivers, C.** (1983). *Lifeprints: New patterns of work and love for today's women.* New York: McGraw-Hill.

Baruch, Grace K., Barnett, Rosaline C., and **Rivers, C.** (1984). *Lifeprints: New patterns of love and work for today's women.* New York: New American Library.

Basseches, Michael. (1984). *Dialectical thinking and adult development.* Norwood, NJ: Ablex.

Basseches, Michael. (1989). Dialectical thinking as an organized whole: Comments on Irwin and Kramer. In Michael L. Commons, Jan D. Sinnott, Francis A. Richards, and Cheryl Armon (Eds.), *Adult development: Vol. 1. Comparisons and applications of developmental models.* New York: Praeger.

Bassuk, E.L., and **Rosenberg, L.** (1990). Psychosocial characteristics of homeless children and children with homes. *Pediatrics, 85,* 257–261.

Bates, Elizabeth, O'Connell, Barbara, and **Shore, Cecilia.** (1987). Language and communication in infancy. In Joy Doniger Osofsky (Ed.), *Handbook of infant development* (2nd ed.). New York: Wiley.

Bateson, Mary Catherine. (1990). *Composing a life.* New York: Plume.

Baugh, J. (1983). *Black street speech: Its history, structure, and survival.* Austin: University of Texas Press.

Baumrind, Diana. (1967). Child-care practices anteceding three patterns of preschool behavior. *Genetic Psychology Monographs, 75,* 43–88.

Baumrind, Diana. (1971). Current patterns of parental authority. *Developmental Psychology, 4* (Monograph 1), 1–103.

Baumrind, Diana. (1982). Are androgynous individuals more effective persons and parents? *Child Development, 53,* 44–75.

Baumrind, Diana. (1987). A developmental perspective on adolescent risk-taking behavior. In C.E. Irwin (Ed.), *Adolescent social behavior and health.* San Francisco: Jossey-Bass.

Baumrind, Diana. (1989). Rearing competent children. In William Damon (Ed.) *New directions for child development: Adolescent health and human behavior.* San Francisco: Jossey-Bass.

Baumrind, Diana. (1991). The influence of parenting style on adolescent competence and substance use. *Journal of Early Adolescence, 11,* 56–95.

Baumrind, Diana. (1991). Parenting styles and adolescent development. In Jeanne Brooks-Gunn, Richard Lerner, and Anne C. Petersen (Eds.), *The encyclopedia of adolescence.* New York: Garland.

Bayley, Nancy. (1935). The development of motor abilities during the first three years. *Monographs of the Society for Research in Child Development, 1.*

Bayley, Nancy. (1955). On the growth of intelligence. *American Psychologist, 10,* 805–818.

Bayley, Nancy. (1966). Learning in adulthood: The role of intelligence. In Herbert J. Klausmeier and Chester W. Harris (Eds.), *Analysis of concept learning.* New York: Academic Press.

Bayley, Nancy, and **Oden, Melita.** (1955). The maintenance of intellectual ability in gifted adults. *Journal of Gerontology, 10,* Section B (1), 91–107.

Beal, Carole R., and **Flavell, John H.** (1983). Young speakers' evaluation of their listeners' comprehension in a referential communication task. *Child Development, 54,* 148–153.

Beard, Belle Boone. (1991). *Centenarians: The new generation.* Westport, CT: Greenwood.

Beauvoir, Simone de. (1964). *Force of circumstances.* Richard Howard (Trans.). New York: G. P. Putnam's Sons.

Becker, Joseph. (1989). Preschoolers' use of number words to denote one-to-one correspondence. *Child Development, 60,* 1147–1157.

Beckwirth, Leila, and **Rodning, Carol.** (1991). Intellectual functioning in children born preterm: Recent research. In Lynn Okagaki and Robert J. Sternberg (Eds.), *Directors of development: Influences on the development of children's thinking.* Hillsdale, NJ: Erlbaum.

Bell, A.P., Weinberg, M.S., and **Mammersmith, S.** (1981). *Sexual preference: Its development in men and women.* Bloomington: University of Indiana Press.

Bell, Richard Q., and **Harper, Lawrence V.** (1977). *Child effects on adults.* Hillsdale, NJ: Erlbaum.

Bell, T.A., and **Hein, K.** (1984). The adolescent and sexually transmitted disease. In K.K. Holmes (Ed.), *Sexually transmitted disease.* New York: McGraw Hill.

Bellinger, David D., and **Needleman, Herbert L.** (1985). Prenatal and early postnatal exposure to lead: Developmental effects, correlations, and implications. *International Journal of Mental Health, 14,* 78–111.

Belmont, John M. (1989). Cognitive strategies and strategic learning: The socio-instructional approach. *American Psychologist, 44,* 142–148.

Belsky, Jay. (1986). Infant day care: A cause for concern? *Zero to Three, 6,* 1–7.

Belsky, Jay. (1990). Infant day care, child development, and family policy. *Society, 27* (5), 10–12.

Belsky, Jay, Gilstrap, Bonnie, and **Rovine, Michael.** (1984). The Pennsylvania Infant and Family Development Project I: Stability and change in mother-infant and father-infant interaction in a family setting at one, three, and nine months. *Child Development, 55,* 692–705.

Belsky, Jay, and **Rovine, Michael.** (1987). Temperament and attachment security in the Strange Situation. *Child Development, 58,* 787–795.

Belsky, Jay, Steinberg, Laurence, and **Draper, Patricia.** (1991). Childhood experience, interpersonal development, and reproductive strategy: An evolutionary theory of socialization. *Child Development, 62,* 647–670.

Belsky, Jay, and **Vondra, Joan.** (1989). Lessons from child abuse: The determinents of parenting. In Dante Cicchetti and Vicki Carlson (Eds.), *Child maltreatment: Theory and research on the causes and consequences of child abuse and neglect.* Cambridge, England: Cambridge University Press.

Bem, Sandra L. (1974). The measurement of psychological androgyny. *Journal of Consulting and Clinical Psychology, 42,* 155–162.

Bem, Sandra L. (1981). Gender schema theory: A cognitive account of sex typing. *Psychological Review, 88,* 354–364.

Bem, Sandra L. (1985). Androgyny and gender schema theory: A conceptual and empirical integration in T.B. Sondegegger (Ed.), *Nebraska symposium on motivation 1984: Psychology and gender* (Vol. 32). Lincoln, NE: University of Nebraska Press.

Bem, Sandra L. (1989). Genital knowledge and gender constancy in preschool children. *Child Development, 60,* 649–662.

Benack, Suzanne, and **Basseches, Michael A.** (1989). Dialectical thinking and relativistic epistemology: Their relation in adult development. In Michael L. Commons, Jan D. Sinnott, Francis A. Richards, and Cheryl Armon (Eds.), *Adult development: Vol. 1. Comparisons and applications of developmental models.* New York: Praeger.

Benbow, C.P., and **Stanley, J.C.** (1983). Sex differences in mathematical reasoning ability: More facts. *Science, 222,* 1029–1031.

Benedek, Elissa. (1989). Baseball, apple pie, and violence: Is it American? In Leah J. Dickerson and Carol Nadelson (Eds.), *Family violence: Emerging issues of national crisis.* Washington, DC: American Psychiatric Press.

Benenson, J.F., and **Dweck, C.S.** (1986). The development of trait explanations and self-evaluations in the academic and social domains. *Child Development, 57,* 1179–1187.

Benet, Sula. (1974). *Abkhasians: The long-lived people of the Caucasus.* New York: Holt, Rinehart and Winston.

Bengston, Vern L. (1975). Generation and family effects in value socialization. *American Sociological Review, 40,* 358–371.

Bengston, Vern L. (1986). Sociological perspectives on aging, families, and the future. In M. Bergener (Ed.), *Perspectives on*

aging: The 1986 Sandoz lectures in gerontology New York: London Press.

Bengston, Vern L., and **Robertson, Joan F.** (Eds.). (1985). *Grandparenthood.* Beverly Hills, CA: Sage.

Bengston, Vern L., Reedy, Margaret N., and **Gordon, Chad.** (1985). Aging and self-conceptions: Personality processes and social contexts. In James E. Birren and K. Warner Schaie (Eds.), *Handbook of the psychology of aging* (2nd ed.). New York: Van Nostrand.

Bengston, Vern L., Rosenthal, Carolyn, and **Burton, Linda.** (1990). Families and aging: diversity and heterogeneity. In Robert H. Binstock and Linda K. George (Eds.), *Handbook of aging and the social sciences* (3rd ed.). San Diego, CA: Academic Press.

Benin, Mary Holland, and **Nienstedt, Barbara Cable.** (1985). Happiness in single and dual-earner families: The effects of marital happiness, job satisfaction, and life cycle. *Journal of Marriage and the Family, 47,* 975–984.

Beres, Cathryn A., and **Baron, Alan.** (1981). Improved digit symbol substitution by older women as a result of extended practice. *Journal of Gerontology, 36,* 591–597.

Berg, Cynthia A., and **Sternberg, Robert J.** (1985). A triarchic theory of intellectual development during adulthood. *Developmental Review, 5,* 334–370.

Berg, Robert L., and **Cassells, Joseph E.** (1990). *The second fifty years: Promoting health and preventing disability.* Washington, DC: National Academy Press.

Berger, Joseph. (1990, September 28). What students think about condom plan. *New York Times,* B1, 4.

Berger, Raymond M. (1982). *Gay and grey: The older homosexual man.* Urbana: University of Illinois Press.

Bergler, Edmund. (1985). *The revolt of the middle-aged man.* New York: International Universities Press.

Bergstrom, Steffan, and **Liljestrand, Jerker.** (1988). Application to developing countries. In B.S. Lindblad (Ed.), *Perinatal nutrition.* San Diego, CA: Academic Press.

Berndt, Thomas J. (1981). Relations between social cognition, nonsocial cognition, and social behavior. In John H. Flavell and Lee Ross (Eds.), *Social cognitive development: Frontiers and possible futures.* Cambridge, England: Cambridge University Press.

Berndt, Thomas. (1989). Friendships in childhood and adolescence. In William Damon (Ed.), *Child development today and tomorrow.* San Francisco: Jossey-Bass.

Berndt, Thomas J., and **Heller, K.A.** (1985). Measuring children's personality attributions: Responses to open-ended questions versus trait ratings and predictions of future behavior. In Stephen R. Yussen (Ed.), *The growth of reflection in children.* New York: Academic Press.

Bernstein, Basil. (1971, 1973). *Class, codes, and control* (Vols. 1, 2). London: Routledge and Kegan Paul.

Berry, Ruth E., and **Williams, Flora L.** (1987). Assessing the relationship between quality of life and marital and income satisfaction: A path analytic approach. *Journal of Marriage and the Family, 49,* 107–116.

Bertenthal, Bennett I., and **Campos, Joseph J.** (1990). A systems approach to the organizing effect of self-produced locomotion during infancy. In Carolyn Rovee-Collier and Lewis P. Lipsitt (Eds.), *Advances in infancy research* (Vol. 6). Norwood, NJ: Ablex.

Berzonsky, Michael D. (1989). Identity style: Conceptualization and measurement. *Journal of Adolescent Research, 4,* 268–282.

Besharov, Douglas J. (1992). A balanced approach to reporting child abuse. *Child, Youth, and Family Service Quarterly, 15* (1), 5–7.

Betancourt, Raoul Louis. (1991). *Retirement and men's physical and social health.* New York: Garland.

Bettes, Barbara A. (1988). Maternal depression and motherese: Temporal and intonational features. *Child Development, 59,* 1089–1096.

Beunen, Gaston P., Malina, Robert M., Van't Hof, Martin A., Simons, Jan, Ostyn, Michel, Renson, Roland, and **Van Gerven, Dirk.** (1988). *Adolescent growth and motor performance: A longitudinal study of Belgian boys.* Champaign, IL: Human Kinetics Books.

Bialystok, E. (1988). Levels of bilingualism and levels of linguistic awareness. *Developmental Psychology, 24,* 560–567.

Biegel, D.E., Sales, E., and **Schultz, R.** (1991). *Family caregiving in chronic illness.* London: Sage.

Bierman, Karen Lynn, and **Furman, Wyndol.** (1984). The effects of social skills training and peer involvement on the social adjustment of preadolescents. *Child Development, 55,* 151–162.

Bigelow, B.J. (1977). Children's friendship expectations: A cognitive developmental study. *Child Development, 48,* 246–253.

Bigelow, B.J., and **La Gaipa, J.J.** (1975). Children's written descriptions of friendship: A multidimensional analysis. *Developmental Psychology, 11,* 857–858.

Biggs, John B., and **Collins, K.F.** (1982). *Evaluating the quality of learning: The SOLO taxonomy (Structure of the Observed Learning Outcome).* New York: Academic Press.

Bijou, S.W. (1989). Behavior analysis. In R. Vasta (Ed.), *Annals of child development* (Vol. 6). Greenwich, CT: JAI Press.

Billingham, Robert E., and **Sack, Alan R.** (1986). Courtship and violence: The interactive status of the relationship. *Journal of Adolescent Research, 1,* 315–326.

Binder, Arnold, Geis, Gilbert, and **Bruce, Dickson.** (1988). *Juvenile delinquency: Historical, cultural and legal perspectives.* New York: Macmillan.

Bing, Elizabeth D. (1983). *Dear Elizabeth Bing: We've had our baby.* New York: Pocket Books.

Bingham, C. Raymond, Miller, Brent C., and **Adams, Gerald R.** (1990). Correlates of age at first sexual intercourse in a national sample of young women. *Journal of Adolescent Research, 5,* 7–17.

Birch, Leann L. (1990). Development of food acceptance patterns. *Developmental Psychology, 26,* 515–519.

Birren, James E., and **Fisher, Laurel M.** (1992). Aging and slowing of behavior: Consequences for cognition and survival. In T. Sonderegger (Ed.), *Psychology and aging: Nebraska symposium on motivation* (Vol. 39). Lincoln, NE: University of Nebraska Press.

Birren, James E., Woods, Anita M., and **Williams, M. Virtrue.** (1980). Behavioral slowing with age: Causes, organization, and consequences. In Leonard W. Poon (Ed.), *Aging in the 80's: Psychological issues.* Washington, DC: American Psychological Association.

Bittles, Alan H., Mason, William M., Greene, Jennifer, and **Rao, N. Appagi.** (1991). Reproductive behavior and health in consanguineous marriages. *Science, 252,* 789–794.

Bjorklund, David. (1990). (Ed.) *Children's strategies: Contemporary views of cognitive development.* Hillsdale, NJ: Erlbaum.

Black, Rebecca, and **Mayer, Joseph.** (1980). Parents with special problems: Alcoholism and opiate addiction. In C. Henry Kempe and Ray E. Helfer (Eds.), *The battered child* (3rd ed.). Chicago: University of Chicago Press.

Blake, Judith. (1989). *Family size and achievement.* Berkeley, CA: University of California Press.

Blank, Robert H. (1988). The challenge of emergent public policy issues in genetic counseling. In Susie Ball (Ed.), *Strategies in genetic counseling: The challenge of the future.* New York: Human Sciences Press.

Blazer, Dan G., Bachar, James R., and **Manton, Kenneth G.** (1986). Suicide in later life: Review and commentary. *Journal of the American Geriatrics Society, 34,* 519–525.

Blevins-Knabe, Belinda. (1987). Development of the ability to insert into a series. *Journal of Genetic Psychology, 148,* 427–441.

Blewitt, Pamela. (1982). Word meaning acquisition in young children. A review of theory and research. In H.W. Reese and L.P. Lipsitt (Eds.), *Advances in child development and behavior.* New York: Academic Press.

Blieszner, Rosemary, and **Hamon, Raeann R.** (1992). Filial responsibility: Attitude, motivators, and behaviors. In Jeffrey W. Dwyer and Raymond R. Coward (Eds.), *Gender, families and elder care.* Newbury Park, CA: Sage.

Bloch, Marianne N. (1989). Young boys' and girls' play at home and in the community: A cultural ecological framework. In Marianne N. Bloch and Anthony D. Pellegrini (Eds.), *The ecological context of children's play.* Norwood, NJ: Ablex.

Bloch, Marianne N., and **Pellegrini, Anthony D.** (1989). Ways of looking at children, context, and play. In Marianne N. Bloch and Anthony D. Pellegrini (Eds.), *The ecological context of children's play.* Norwood, NJ: Ablex.

Bloom, Lois, Merkin, Susan, and **Wootten, Janet.** (1982). Wh-questions: Linguistic factors that contribute to the sequence of acquisition. *Child Development, 53,* 1084–1092.

Blumstein, Philip, and **Schwartz, Pepper.** (1991). Intimate relationships and the creation of sexuality. In David P. McWhirter, Stephanie A. Dangers, and June Machover Reinisch (Eds.), *Homosexuality/heterosexuality: Concepts of sexual orientation.* New York: Oxford University Press.

Blythe, Ronald. (1979). *The view in winter: Reflections on old age.* New York: Penguin.

Boehm, Corinne D. (1990). Prenatal diagnosis and carrier detection by DNA analysis. In Susie Ball (Ed.), *Strategies in genetic counseling: The challenge of the future.* New York: Human Sciences Press.

Bogin, Barry, and **MacVean, Robert B.** (1983). The relationship of socioeconomic status and sex to body size, skeletal maturation, and cognitive status of Guatemala City schoolchildren. *Child Development, 54,* 115–128.

Bolton, Frank G., Morris, Larry A., and **MacEacheron, Ann E.** (1989). *Males at risk: The other side of child sexual abuse.* Newbury Park, CA: Sage.

Booth, Alan, and **Johnson, E.** (1988). Premarital cohabitation and marital success. *Journal of Family Issues, 9,* 387–394.

Boring, E.G. (1950). *A history of experimental psychology* (2nd ed.). New York: Appleton-Century-Crofts.

Bornstein, Marc H. (1985). Habituation of attention as a measure of visual information processing in human infants: Summary, systematization, and synthesis. In Gilbert Gottlieb and Norman A. Krasnegor (Eds.), *Measurement of audition and vision in the first year of postnatal life: A methodological overview*. Norwood, NJ: Ablex.

Bornstein, Marc H., Tal, Joseph, and **Tamis-Lemonda, Catherine S.** (1991). Parenting in cross-cultural perspective: The United States, France, and Japan. In Marc H. Bornstein (Ed.), *Cultural approaches to parenting*. Hillsdale, NJ: Erlbaum.

Bornstein, Marc H., Tal, Joseph, Rahn, Charles, Galperin, Celia Z., Pecheaux, Marie-Germaine, Lamour, Martine, Toda, Sueko, Azuma, Hiroshi, Ogino, Misako, and **Tamis-LeMonda, Catherine S.** (1992). Functional analysis of the content of maternal speech to infants of 5 and 13 months in four cultures: Argentina, France, Japan, and the United States. *Developmental Psychology, 28,* 593–603.

Botwinick, Jack. (1973). *Aging and behavior.* New York: Springer.

Botwinick, Jack, and **Storandt, Martha.** (1980). Recall and recognition of old information in relation to age and sex. *Journal of Gerontology, 35,* 70–76.

Botwinick, Jack, West, Robin, and **Storandt, Martha.** (1978). Predicting death from behavioral test performance. *Journal of Gerontology, 33,* 755–762.

Bouchard, Thomas J., Lykken, David T., McGue, Matthew, Segal, Nancy L., and **Tellegen, Auke.** (1990). Sources of human psychological differences: The Minnesota study of twins reared apart. *Science, 250,* 223–228.

Boulton, Michael, and **Smith, Peter K.** (1989). Issues in the study of children's rough-and-tumble play. In Marianne N. Bloch and Anthony D. Pellegrini (Eds.), *The ecological context of children's play*. Norwood, NJ: Ablex.

Bower, Bruce. (1987a). The character of cancer. *Science News, 131,* 120–121.

Bower, Bruce. (1987b). IQ's generation gap. *Science News, 132,* 108–109.

Bower, T.G.R. (1989). *The rational infant: Learning in infancy.* New York: Freeman.

Bowerman, Melissa. (1982). Reorganizational processes in lexical and syntactic development. In Eric Wanner and Lila R. Gleitman (Eds.), *Language acquisition: The state of the art*. Cambridge, England: Cambridge University Press.

Bowlby, John. (1974). Psychiatric implications in bereavement. In A.A. Kutscher (Ed.), *Death and bereavement*. Chicago: Charles C. Thomas.

Bowman, James E., and **Murray, Robert F.** (1980). *Genetic variation and disorders in peoples of African origin*. Baltimore, MD: Johns Hopkins University Press.

Boyer, Debra, and **Fine, David.** (1992). Sexual abuse as a factor in adolescent pregnancy and child maltreatment. *Family Planning Perspectives, 24,* 4–11, 19.

Braddick, Oliver, and **Atkinson, Janette.** (1988). Sensory selectivity, attentional control, and cross-channel integration in early visual development. In Albert Yonas (Ed.), *Perceptual development in infancy*. Hillsdale, NJ: Erlbaum.

Bradley, Robert H., and **Caldwell, Bettye M.** (1984). The HOME inventory and family demographics. *Developmental Psychology, 20,* 315–320.

Braine, Martin D.S., and **Rumain, Barbara.** (1983). Logical rea-soning. In Paul H. Mussen (Ed.), *Handbook of child psychology: Vol 3. Cognitive development*. New York: Wiley.

Brandes, Stanley. (1985). *Forty: The age and the symbol.* Knoxville, TN: University of Tennessee Press.

Bray, D.W., and **Howard, A.** (1983). The AT&T longitudinal studies of managers. In K. Warner Schaie (Ed.), *Longitudinal studies of adult psychological development*. New York: Guilford.

Brayfield, April A. (1992). Employment resources and housework in Canada. *Journal of Marriage and the Family, 54,* 19–30.

Breckenridge, James N., Dallagher, Dolores, Thompson, Larry W., and **Peterson, James.** (1986). Characteristic depressive symptoms of bereaved elders. *Journal of Gerontology, 41,* 163–168.

Breitner, John C.S. (1988). Alzheimer's disease: Possible evidence for genetic causes. In Miriam K. Aronson and Robert N. Butler (Eds.), *Understanding Alzheimer's disease*. New York: Charles Scribner's Sons.

Bremner, J. Gavin. (1988). *Infancy.* Oxford, England: Blackwell.

Bretherton, Inge, and **Beeghly, M.** (1982). Talking about internal states: The acquisition of an explicit theory of mind. *Developmental Psychology, 18,* 906–921.

Bretherton, Inge, and **Waters, Everett.** (1985). Growing points of attachment theory and research. *Monographs of the Society for Research in Child Development, 50* (1–2, Serial No. 209).

Bretherton, Inge, Fritz, Janet, Zahn-Waxler, Carolyn, and **Ridgeway, Doreen.** (1986). Learning to talk about emotions: A functionalist perspective. *Child Development, 57,* 529–548.

Bridge, Lisa J., O'Connell, James P., and **Belsky, Jay.** (1988). Similarities and differences in infant-mother and infant-father interaction in the Strange Situation: A component process analysis. *Developmental Psychology, 24,* 92–100.

Bril, B. (1986). Motor development and cultural attitudes. In H.T.A. Whiting and M.G. Wade (Eds.), *Themes in motor development*. Dordrecht, Netherlands: Martinus Nijhoff Publishers.

Broman, Clifford L. (1991). Gender, work-family roles, and psychological well-being of Blacks. *Journal of Marriage and the Family, 53,* 509–520.

Broman, Clifford L., Hamilton, V.L., and **Hoffman, W.S.** (1990). Unemployment and its effects on families: Evidence from a plant closing study. *American Journal of Community Psychology, 18,* 643–659.

Bronfenbrenner, Urie. (1979). *The ecology of human development: Experiments by nature and design*. Cambridge, MA: Harvard University Press.

Bronfenbrenner, Urie. (1985). Freedom and discipline across the decades. In G. Becker, H. Becker, and L. Huber (Eds.), *Ordnung and Unordnung*. Weinheim, Germany: Beltz Berlag.

Bronfenbrenner, Urie. (1986). Ecology of the family as a context for human development research perspectives. *Developmental Psychology, 22,* 723–742.

Bronson, Gordon W. (1990). Changes in infants' visual scanning across the 2- to 14-week age period. *Journal of Experimental Child Psychology, 49,* 101–125.

Bronson, Wanda C. (1985). Growth in the organization of behavior over the second year of life. *Developmental Psychology, 21,* 108–117.

Bronstein, Phyllis. (1984). Differences in mothers' and fathers' behaviors toward children: A cross-cultural comparison. *Developmental Psychology, 20,* 995–1003.

Brooks, George A., and Fahey, Thomas D. (1984). *Exercise physiology: Human bioenergetics and its application.* New York: Wiley.

Brooks-Gunn, Jeanne, and Kirsch, Barbara. (1984). Life events and the boundaries of midlife for women. In Grace K. Baruch and Jeanne Brooks-Gunn (Eds.), *Women in midlife.* New York: Plenum.

Brooks-Gunn, Jeanne, Attie, Ilana, Burrow, Carolyn, Rosso, James T., and Warren, Michelle P. (1989). The impact of puberty on body and eating concerns in athletic and nonathletic contexts. *Journal of Early Adolescence, 9,* 269–290.

Brooks-Gunn, Jeanne, Warren, Michelle P., Samelson, Marion, and Fox, Richard. (1986). Physical similarity of and disclosure of menarchal status to friends: Effects of grade and pubertal status. *Journal of Early Adolescence, 6,* 3–14.

Brown, B. Bradford, Lohr, Mary Jane, and McClenahan, Eben L. (1986). Early adolescents' perception of peer pressure. *Journal of Early Adolescence, 6,* 139–154.

Brown, Barry S., and Mills, Arnold R. (1987). *Youth at high risk for substance abuse.* Rockville, MD: National Institute on Drug Abuse.

Brown, J.K., and Kerns, V. (Eds.). (1985). *In her prime: A new view of middle-aged women.* South Hadley, MA: Bergin and Garvey.

Brown, W.T., Jenkins, E.C., Gross, A.C., Chan, C.B., Krawczun, M.S., Duncan, C.J., Sklower, S.L., and Fisch, G.S. (1987). Further evidence for genetic heterogeneity in the Fragile X syndrome. *Human Genetics, 75,* 311–321.

Brown, W. Ted, Zebrower, Michael, and Kieras, Fred J. (1990). Proferia: A genetic disease model of premature aging. In David E. Harrison (Ed.), *Genetic effects on aging II.* Caldwell, NJ: Telford.

Brownell, Kelly D., Marlatt, G. Alan, Lichtenstein, Edward, and Wilson, G. Terrence. (1986). Understanding and preventing relapse. *American Psychologist, 41,* 765–782.

Brownson, Ross C., Alavanja, Michael C.R., Hock, Edward T., and Loy, Timothy S. (1991). Passive smoking and lung cancer in nonsmoking women. *American Journal of Public Health, 82,* 1525–1530.

Bruce, Patricia R., and Herman, James P. (1986). Adult age differences in spatial memory. *Journal of Gerontology, 41,* 774–777.

Bruce, Patricia R., Coyne, Andrew C., and Botwinick, Jack. (1982). Adult age differences in metamemory. *Journal of Gerontology, 37,* 354–357.

Bruner, Jerome Seymour. (1983). *Child's talk: Learning to use language.* New York: Norton.

Bruner, Jerome Seymour. (1986). *Actual minds, possible worlds.* Cambridge, MA: Harvard University Press.

Brunswick, Ann F., Messerie, Peta A., and Titus, Stephen P. (1992). Predictive factors in adult substance abuse: A prospective study of African-American adolescents. In Meyer Glantz and Roy Pickens (Eds.), *Vulnerability to drug abuse.* Washington, DC: American Psychological Association.

Bryant, Brenda K. (1985). The neighborhood walk: Sources of support in middle childhood. *Monographs of the Society for Research in Child Development, 50* (3, Serial No. 210).

Bryant, Peter E. (1985). The distinction between knowing when to do a sum and knowing how to do it. *Educational Psychology, 5,* 207–215.

Buhrmester, Duane, and Furman, Wyndol. (1987). The development of companionship and intimacy. *Child Development, 58,* 1101–1113.

Bumpass, Larry L., Sweet, James A., and Cherlin, Andrew. (1991). The role of cohabitation in declining rates of marriage. *Journal of Marriage and the Family, 53,* 913–927.

Burchinal, Margaret, Lee, Marvin, and Ramey, Craig. (1989). Type of day care and preschool intellectual development in disadvantaged children. *Child Development, 60,* 128–137.

Burelson, Brant R. (1982). The development of comforting communication skills in childhood and adolescence. *Child Development,* 1578–1588.

Burger, Sarah G., Miller, Brenoa H.S., and Mauney, Brenda Fay. (1986). *A guide to management and supervision in nursing homes.* Springfield, IL: Thomas.

Burns, Alisa. (1992). Mother-headed families: An international perspective and the case of Australia. *Society for Research in Child Development: Social Policy Report, 6,* 1–22.

Burton, Linda M., Dilworth-Anderson, Peggye, and Bengston, Vern L. (1991). Creating culturally relevant ways of thinking about diversity and aging. *Generations, 15* (4), 67–72.

Buss, Arnold H., and Plomin, Robert. (1984). *Temperament: Early developing personality traits.* Hillsdale, NJ: Erlbaum.

Buss, David M., Larsen, Randy J., Westen, Drew, and Semmelrother, Jennifer. (1992). Sex differences in jealousy: Evolution, physiology, and psychology. *Psychological Science, 3,* 251–255.

Busse, Ewald W. (1985). Normal aging: The Duke longitudinal studies. In M. Bergener, Marco Ermini, and H.B. Stahelin (Eds.), *Thresholds in aging.* London: Academic Press.

Butler, John A., Starfield, Barbara, and Stemark, Suzanne. (1984). Child health policy. In Harold W. Stevenson and Alberta E. Siegel (Eds.), *Child development research and social policy.* Chicago: University of Chicago Press.

Butler, Robert N. (1963). The life review: An interpretation of reminiscence in the aged. *Psychiatry, 26,* 65–76.

Butler, Robert N., and Golding, Jean. (1986). *From birth to five: A study of the health and behaviour of Britain's 5-year-olds.* Oxford: Pergamon.

Butler, Robert N., and Lewis, Myrna I. (1982). *Aging and mental health: Positive psychosocial and biomedical approaches* (3rd ed.). St. Louis, MO: Mosby.

Cadoret, Remi J. (1991). Genetic and environmental factors in initiation of drug use and the transition to abuse. In Meyer Glantz and Roy Pickens (Eds.), *Vulnerability to drug abuse.* Washington, DC: American Psychological Association.

Cahalan, Don. (1991). *An ounce of prevention: Strategies for solving tobacco, alcohol, and drug problems.* San Francisco: Jossey-Bass.

Cairns, Robert B. (1983). The emergence of developmental psychology. In Paul H. Mussen (Ed.), *Handbook of child psychology: Vol. 1. History, theory, and methods.* New York: Wiley.

Callahan, Daniel. (1990). Afterward. In Paul Homer and Martha Holstein (Eds.), *A good old age?* New York: Simon and Schuster.

Cameron, Judy L. (1990). Factors controlling the onset of puberty in primates. In John Bancroft and June Machover Reinisch (Eds.), *Adolescence and puberty.* New York: Oxford University Press.

Camp, Cameron J., Doherty, Kathleen, Moody-Thomas, Sarah, and **Denney, Nancy W.** (1989). Practical problem solving in adults: A comparison of problem types and scoring methods. In Jan D. Sinnott (Ed.), *Everyday problem solving*. New York: Praeger.

Campbell, Angus. (1981). *The sense of well-being in America: Recent patterns and trends*. New York: McGraw Hill.

Campos, Joseph J., Barrett, Karen C., Lamb, Michael L., Goldsmith, H. Hill, and **Stenberg, Craig.** (1983). Socioemotional development. In Paul H. Mussen (Ed.), *Handbook of child psychology: Vol. 2. Infancy and developmental psychobiology*. New York: Wiley.

Canada, Andrew T., and **Calabrese, Edward J.** (1991). Free radicals, aging, and toxicology. In Ralph L. Cooper, Jerome M. Goldman, and Thomas J. Harbin (Eds.), *Aging and environmental toxicology*. Baltimore, MD: Johns Hopkins Press.

Carey, James R., Liedo, Pablo, Orozco, Dina, and **Vaupel, James W.** (1992). Slowing of mortality rates at older ages in large medfly cohorts. *Science, 258,* 457–461.

Carey, William B., and **McDevitt, Sean C.** (1978). Stability and change in individual temperament diagnoses from infancy to early childhood. *Journal of the American Academy of Child Psychiatry, 17,* 331–337.

Carew, Jean V. (1980). Experience and the development of intelligence in young children at home and in day care. *Monographs of the Society for Research in Child Development, 45* (Serial No. 187).

Carmen, Elaine. (1989). Family violence and the victim-to-patient process. In Leah J. Dickstein and Carol C. Nadelson (Eds.), *Family violence: Emerging issues of national crisis*. Washington, DC: American Psychiatric Press.

Carnegie Council on Adolescent Development. (1989). *Turning points: Preparing American youth for the 21st century*. New York: Carnegie Corporation.

Caron, Albert J., and **Caron, Rose F.** (1981). Processing of relational information as an index of infant risk. In S.L. Friedman and M. Sigman (Eds.), *Preterm birth and psychological development*. New York: Academic Press.

Caron, Albert J., and **Caron, Rose F.** (1982). Cognitive development in infancy. In Tiffany M. Field, Aletha Huston, Herbert C. Quay, Lillian Troll, and Gordon E. Finley (Eds.), *Review of human development*. New York: Wiley.

Carstensen, Laura L. (1987). Age-related changes in social activity. In Laura L. Carstensen and Barbara A. Edelstein (Eds.), *Handbook of clinical gerontology*. New York: Pergamon.

Case, Robbie. (1985). *Intellectual development: Birth to adulthood*. Orlando, FL: Academic Press.

Casey, R., and **Rozin, Paul.** (1989). Changing children's food preferences: Parent opinions. *Appetite, 12,* 171–182.

Caspi, Avshalom, Elder, Glen H., and **Bem, Daryl J.** (1988). Moving away from the world: Life-course patterns of shy children. *Developmental Psychology, 24,* 824–831.

Caspi, Avshalom, Elder, Glen H., and **Herbener, Ellen S.** (1990). Childhood personality and the prediction of life-course patterns. In Lee N. Robins and Michael Rutter (Eds.), *Straight and devious pathways from childhood to adulthood*. Cambridge, England: Cambridge University Press.

Caspi, Avshalom, Herbener, Ellen S., and **Ozer, Daniel J.** (1992). Shared experiences and the similarities of personalities: A longitudinal study of married couples. *Journal of Personality and Social Psychology, 62,* 281–291.

Cassill, Kay. (1982). *Twins reared apart*. New York: Atheneum.

Cavanaugh, John C., and **Green, Elizabeth E.** (1990). I believe, therefore I can: Self-efficacy beliefs in memory aging. In Eugene A. Lovelace (Ed.), *Aging and cognition: Mental processes, self-awareness, and interventions*. North-Holland: Elsevier.

Cavenaugh, John L., Kramer, Dierdre A., Sinnott, Jan C., Camp, Cameron J., and **Markley, Robert P.** (1985). On missing links and such: Interfaces between cognitive research and everyday problem-solving. *Human Development, 28,* 146–168.

Ceci, Stephen J. (1990). *On intelligence . . . more or less: A bioecological treatise on intellectual development*. Englewood Cliffs, NJ: Prentice-Hall.

Ceci, Stephen J. (1991). How much does schooling influence general intelligence and its cognitive components? *Developmental Psychology, 27,* 703–722.

Ceci, Stephen J., and **Cornelius, Steven W.** (1990). Commentary. *Human Development, 33,* 198–201.

Cefalo, Robert C., and **Moos, Merry-K.** (1988). *Preconceptual health promotion*. Rockville, MD: Aspen.

Centers for Disease Control. (1989, May 7). AIDS weekly surveillance report. Atlanta, GA: Center for Disease Control.

Centers for Disease Control. (1992). Selected behaviors that increase the risk for HIV infection among high school students—U.S. 1990. *MMWR, 41,* 231–240.

Centers for Disease Control. (1992). *Setting the national agenda for injury control in the 1990s*. Washington, DC: United States Department of Health and Human Services, Public Health Service.

Cerella, John. (1990). Aging and information-processing rate. In James E. Birren and K. Warner Schaie (Eds.), *Handbook of the psychology of aging* (3rd ed.). San Diego, CA: Academic Press.

Chalfant, J.C. (1989). Learning disabilities: Policy issues and promising approaches. *American Psychologist, 44,* 392–398.

Chandler, Lynette A. (1990). Neuromotor assessment. In Elizabeth D. Gibbs and Douglas M. Teti (Eds.), *Interdisciplinary assessment of infants*. Baltimore, MD: Brookes.

Chandler, Michael. (1987). The Othello effect: Essay on the emergence and eclipse of skeptical doubt. *Human Development, 30,* 137–159.

Chandler, Michael, Fritz, Anna S., and **Hala, Suzanne.** (1989). Small-scale deceit: Deception as a marker of two-, three-, and four-year-olds' early theories of mind. *Child Development, 60,* 1263–1277.

Chap, Janet Blum. (1985–1986). Moral judgment in middle and late adulthood: The effects of age-appropriate moral dilemmas and spontaneous role-taking. *International Journal of Aging and Human Development, 22,* 161–172.

Charness, Neil. (1986). Expertise in chess, music, and physics: A cognitive perspective. In L.K. Obler and D.A. Fein (Eds.), *The neuropsychology of talent and special abilities*. New York: Guilford.

Charness, Neil. (1989). Age and expertise: Responding to Talland's challenge. In Leonard W. Poon, David C. Rubin, and Barbara A. Wilson (Eds.), *Everyday cognition in adulthood and later life*. Cambridge, England: Cambridge University Press.

Charness, Neil, and **Bosman, Elizabeth A.** (1990). Expertise and aging: Life in the lab. In Thomas M. Hess (Ed.), *Aging and cognition: Knowledge, organization and utilization.* North-Holland: Elsevier.

Chasnoff, Ira J. (1986). Perinatal addiction: Consequences of intrauterine exposure to opiate and nonopiate drugs. In Ira J. Chasnoff (Ed.), *Drug use in pregnancy: Mother and child.* Lancaster, England: MTP Press.

Chasnoff, Ira J. (1989). Drug use and women: Establishing a standard of care. In Donald Hutchings (Ed.), *Prenatal abuse of licit and illicit drugs.* New York: New York Academy of Sciences.

Chasnoff, Ira J., Chisu, G.M., and **Kaplan, W.E.** (1988). Maternal cocaine use and genitourinary tract malformations. *Teratology, 37,* 201–204.

Chen, Linda H. (1986). Biomedical influences on nutrition of the elderly. In Linda H. Chen (Ed.), *Nutritional aspects of aging* (Vol. 1). Boca Raton, FL: CRC Press.

Chen, S.-J., and **Miyake, K.** (1986). Japanese studies of infant development. In H. Stevenson, H. Azuma, and K. Hakuta (Eds.), *Child development and education in Japan.* New York: Freeman.

Cherlin, Andrew, and **Furstenberg, Frank F., Jr.** (1986). *The new American grandparent: A place in the family, a life apart.* New York: Basic Books.

Chess, Stella, and **Thomas, Alexander.** (1982). Infant bonding: Mystique and reality. *American Journal of Orthopsychiatry, 52,* 213–222.

Chess, Stella, and **Thomas, Alexander.** (1990). Continuities and discontinuities in development. In Lee N. Robins and Michael Rutter (Ed.), *Straight and devious pathways from childhood to adulthood.* New York: Cambridge University Press.

Chi, Michelene T.H. (1985). Developmental perspectives on content specific knowledge and memory performance. In F. Weinart and Marion Perlmutter (Eds.), *Memory development: Universal changes and individual differences.* Hillsdale, NJ: Erlbaum.

Chickering, Arthur W. (1981). Conclusion. In Arthur W. Chickering (Ed.), *The modern American college: Responding to the new realities of diverse students and a changing society.* San Francisco: Jossey-Bass.

Children's Defense Fund. (1990). *Children 1990: A report card, briefing book, and action primer.* Washington, DC: Children's Defense Fund.

Chilman, Catherine S. (1983). *Adolescent sexuality in a changing American society* (2nd ed.). New York: Wiley.

Chin, J., Sato, D.A., and **Mann, J.M.** (1990). Projections of HIV infections and AIDS cases to the year 2000. *Bulletin of the World Health Organization, 68,* 1–32.

Chipuer, H.M., Plomin, Robert, Pedersen, Nancy L., McClearn, Gerald E., and **Messelroade, John R.** (1993). Genetic influence on family environment: The role of personality. *Developmental Psychology, 29,* 110–118.

Chiriboga, David A. (1982). Adaptation to marital separation in later and earlier life. *Journal of Gerontology, 37,* 109–114.

Chisu, G.M., and **Kaplan, W.E.** (1988). Maternal cocaine use and genitourinary tract malformations. *Teratology, 37,* 201–204.

Chomsky, Carol. (1969). *The acquisition of syntax in children from five to ten.* Cambridge, MA: MIT Press.

Chomsky, Noam. (1968). *Language and mind.* New York: Harcourt, Brace, World.

Chomsky, Noam. (1980). *Rules and representations.* New York: Columbia University Press.

Christoffel, Katherine K., and **Forsyth, Brian W.C.** (1989). Mirror image of environmental deprivation: Severe childhood obesity of psychosocial origin. *Child Abuse and Neglect, 13,* 249–256.

Christophersen, Edward R. (1989). Injury control. *American Psychologist, 44,* 237–241.

Chung, Chin S., Villafuerte, Arnold, Wood, William, and **Lew, Ruth.** (1992). Trends in prevalence of behavioral risk factors: Recent Hawaiian experience. *American Journal of Public Health, 82,* 1544–1546.

Cicchetti, Dante, and **Beeghly, Marjorie.** (1990). *Children with Down Syndrome: A developmental perspective.* Cambridge, England: Cambridge University Press.

Cicchetti, Dante, and **Carlson, Vicki** (Eds.). (1989). *Child maltreatment: Theory and research on the causes and consequences of child abuse and neglect.* Cambridge, England: Cambridge University Press.

Cicirelli, G. Victor. (1985). The role of siblings as family caregivers. In W.J. Sauer and R.T. Coward (Eds.), *Social support networks and the care of the elderly.* New York: Springer.

Clark, Jane E., and **Phillips, Sally J.** (1985). A developmental sequence of the standing long jump. In Jane E. Clark and James H. Humphrey (Eds.), *Motor development: Current selected research.* Princeton, NJ: Princeton Book Company.

Clark, Robert D. (1983). *Family life and school achievement: Why poor black children succeed or fail.* Chicago: University of Chicago Press.

Clarke-Stewart, K. Alison. (1978). And daddy makes three: The father's impact on mother and young child. *Child Development, 49,* 466–478.

Clarke-Stewart, K. Alison. (1984). Day care: A new context for research and development. In Marion Perlmutter (Ed.), *Parent-child interactions and parent-child relations in child development: The Minnesota symposia on child psychology* (Vol. 17). Hillsdale, NJ: Erlbaum.

Clarke-Stewart, K. Alison. (1989). Infant day care: Maligned or malignant? *American Psychologist, 44,* 266–273.

Clarkson, Marsha G., and **Berg, W. Keith.** (1983). Cardiac orienting and vowel discrimination in newborns: Crucial stimulus parameters. *Child Development, 54,* 162–171.

Clarkson, Marsha G., Clifton, Rachel K., and **Morrongiello, Barbara A.** (1985). The effects of sound duration on newborns' head orientation. *Journal of Experimental Child Psychology, 39,* 20–36.

Clay, Marie. (1972). *Reading: The patterning of complex behavior.* Aukland, New Zealand: Heinemann.

Clayton, Richard R. (1992). Transitions in drug use: Risk and protective factors. In Meyer Glantz and Roy Pickens (Eds.), *Vulnerability to drug abuse.* Washington, DC: American Psychological Association.

Clayton, Vivian P., and **Birren, James E.** (1980). The development of wisdom across the lifespan: A reexamination of an ancient topic. In Paul B. Baltes and Orville G. Brim (Eds.), *Life-span development and behavior* (Vol. III). New York: Academic Press.

Clemens, Andra W. and **Axelson, Leland J.** (1985). The not-so-empty nest: The return of the fledgling adult. *Family Relations, 34,* 259–264.

Clifford, Edward. (1971). Body satisfaction in adolescence. *Perceptual and Motor Skills, 33,* 119–125.

Clinchy, Blythe, and **Zimmerman, Claire.** (1982). Epistemology and agency in the development of undergraduate women. In Pamela J. Perun (Ed.), *The undergraduate woman: Issues in educational equity.* Lexington, MA: Lexington Books.

Coe, Christopher, Kayashi, Kevin T., and **Levine, Seymour.** (1988). Hormones and behavior at puberty: Activation or concatenation? In Megan R. Gunnar and W. Andrew Collins (Eds.), *Development during the transition to adolescence.* Hillsdale, NJ: Erlbaum.

Cohen, David. (1987). *The development of play.* New York: New York University Press.

Cohn, Jeffrey F., and **Tronick, Edward Z.** (1983). Three-month-old infants' reaction to stimulated maternal depression. *Child Development, 54,* 185–193.

Cohn, Jeffrey F., and **Tronick, Edward Z.** (1987). Mother-infant face to face interaction: The sequence of dyadic states at 3, 6, and 9 months. *Developmental Psychology, 23,* 68–77.

Cohn, Jeffrey P. (1987). The molecular biology of aging. *Bioscience, 37,* 99–102.

Cohn, Lawrence D.S., and **Adler, Nancy E.** (1992). Female and male perception of ideal body shapes. *Psychology of Women Quarterly, 16,* 69–79.

Coie, John D., and **Dodge, Kenneth A.** (1983). Continuities and changes in children's social status: A five-year longitudinal study. *Merrill-Palmer Quarterly, 29,* 261–282.

Coie, John D., and **Krehbiel, Gina.** (1984). Effects of academic tutoring on the social status of low-achieving, socially rejected children. *Child Development, 55,* 1465–1478.

Coie, John D., and **Kupersmidt, J.B.** (1983). A behavioral analysis of emerging social status in boys' groups. *Child Development, 54,* 1400–1416.

Coie, John D., Dodge, Kenneth A., and **Coppotelli, H.** (1982). Dimensions and types of social status: A cross-age perspective. *Developmental Psychology, 18,* 557–570.

Coie, John D., Dodge, Kenneth A., Terry, Robert, and **Wright, Virginia.** (1991). The role of aggression in peer relations: An analysis of aggression episodes in boys' play groups. *Child Development, 62,* 812–826.

Colby, Anne, Kohlberg, Lawrence, Gibbs, John, and **Lieberman, Marcus.** (1983). A longitudinal study of moral development. *Monographs of the Society for Research in Child Development, 48* (1–2, Serial No. 200).

Coleman, John C. (1980). Friendship and the peer group in adolescence. In Joseph Adelson (Ed.), *Handbook of adolescent psychology.* New York: Wiley.

Coleman, Marilyn, and **Ganong, Lawrence H.** (1990). Remarriage and stepfamily research in the 1980s: Increased interest in an old family form. *Journal of Marriage and the Family, 52,* 925–940.

Coles, Robert. (1990). *The spiritual life of children.* Boston: Houghton Mifflin.

Collins, W.A. (Ed.). (1984). *Development during middle childhood: The years from 6 to 12.* Washington, DC: National Academy Press.

Comfort, Alex. (1980). Sexuality in later life. In J.E. Birren and R.B. Sloane (Eds.), *Handbook of mental health and aging.* New York: Van Nostrand Reinhold.

Comings, David E. (1990). *Tourette syndrome and human behavior.* Durante, CA: Hope Press.

Commons, Michael L., and **Richards, Francis A.** (1984). A general model of stage theory. In Michael L. Commons, Francis A. Richards, and Cheryl Armon (Eds.), *Beyond formal operations.* New York: Praeger.

Compas, Bruce E., Banez, Gerard A., Malcarne, Vanessa, and **Worsham, Nancy.** (1991). Perceived control and coping with stress: A developmental perspective. *Journal of Social Issues, 47,* 23–34.

Coni, Nicholas K. (1991). Ethical dilemmas faced in dealing with the aged sick. In Frederick C. Ludwig (Ed.), *Life span extension.* New York: Springer.

Conners, C.K. (1980). *Food additives and hyperactive children.* New York: Plenum.

Connor, J.M., and **Ferguson-Smith, M.A.** (1991). *Essential medical genetics.* Oxford, England: Blackwell Scientific Publications.

Consortium for Longitudinal Studies. (1983). *As the twig is bent: Lasting effects of preschool programs.* Hillsdale, NJ: Erlbaum.

Constanzo, P.R., and **Woody, E.Z.** (1985). Domain-specific parenting styles and their impact on the child's development of particular deviance: The example of obesity proneness. *Journal of Social and Clinical Psychology, 3,* 425–430.

Cook, Ellen P. (1985). *Psychological androgyny.* Oxford, England: Pergamon.

Cook, Michael, and **Birch, R.** (1984). Infant perception of the shapes of tilted plane forms. *Infant Behavior and Development, 7,* 389–402.

Cooney, George H., Bell, A., McBride, W., and **Carter, C.** (1989). Low-level exposures to lead: The Sydney Lead Study. *Developmental Medicine and Child Neurology, 31,* 640–649.

Cooper, Ralph L., Goldman, Jerome M., and **Harbin, Thomas J.** (1991). *Aging and environmental toxicology.* Baltimore, MD: Johns Hopkins Press.

Copeland, L., Wolraich, M., Lindgren, S., Milich, R., and **Woolson, R.** (1987). Pediatricians' reported practices in the assessment and treatment of attention deficit disorders. *Developmental and Behavioral Pediatrics, 8,* 191–197.

Cornelius, Steven W. (1990). Aging and everyday cognitive abilities. In Thomas M. Hess (Ed.), *Aging and cognition: Knowledge, organization and utilization.* North-Holland: Elsevier.

Costa, Paul T., and **McCrae, Robert R.** (1988). Personality in adulthood: A six-year longitudinal study of self-reports and spouse ratings of the NEO Personality Inventory. *Journal of Personality and Social Psychology, 54,* 853–863.

Costa, Paul T., and **McCrae, Robert R.** (1989). Personality continuity and the changes of adult life. In Martha Storandt and Gary R. Vandenbos (Eds.), *The adult years: Continuity and change.* Washington, DC: American Psychological Association.

Costa, Paul T., Zonderman, A.B., McCrae, R.R., Coroni-Huntley, J., Locke, B.Z., and **Barbano, H.E.** (1987). Longitudinal analyses of psychological well-being in a national sample: Stability of mean levels. *Journal of Gerontology, 42,* 50–55.

Coste, Joel, Job-Spira, Nadine, and **Fernandez, Herve.** (1991). Increased risk of ectopic pregnancy with maternal cigarette smoking. *American Journal of Public Health, 81,* 199–201.

Cotman, Carl W., and **Holets, Vicky R.** (1985). Structural changes at synapses with age: Plasticity and regeneration. In Caleb E. Finch and Edward L. Schneider (Eds.), *Handbook of the biology of aging* (2nd ed.). New York: Van Nostrand.

Cowan, Carolyn Pape, and **Cowan, Philip A.** (1992). *When partners become parents.* New York: Basic Books.

Cowan, Philip A. (1978). *Piaget, with feeling: Cognitive, social, and emotional dimensions.* New York: Holt, Rinehart and Winston.

Coward, Raymond T., Horne, Claydell, and **Dwyer, Jeffrey W.** (1992). Demographic perspectives on gender and family caregiving. In Jeffrey W. Dwyer and Raymond T. Coward (Eds.), *Gender, families and elder care.* Newbury Park, CA: Sage.

Cox, Maureen V. (1986). *The child's point of view: The development of cognition and language.* New York: St. Martin's Press.

Craik, Fergus I.M. (1977). Age differences in human memory. In James E. Birren and K. Warner Schaie (Eds.), *Handbook of the psychology of aging.* New York: Van Nostrand Reinhold.

Craik, Fergus I.M., and **Byrd, Mark.** (1982). Aging and cognitive deficits: The role of attentional resources. In Fergus I.M. Craik and Sandra Trehub (Eds.), *Aging and cognitive processes.* New York: Plenum.

Crain, W. (1992). *Theories of development: Concepts and applications* (3rd ed.). Englewood Cliffs, NJ: Prentice Hall.

Crimmins, E.M., and **Ingegneri, D.G.** (1990). Interaction and living arrangements of older parents and their children: Past trends, present determinants, future implications. *Research of Aging, 2,* 3–35.

Crittenden, Patricia M. (1992). The social ecology of treatment: Case study of a service system for maltreated children. *American Journal of Orthopsychiatry, 62,* 22–34.

Crittenden, Patricia M., and **Ainsworth, Mary D.S.** (1989). Child maltreatment and attachment theory. In Dante Cicchetti and Vicki Carlson (Eds.), *Child maltreatment: Theory and research on the causes and consequences of child abuse and neglect.* Cambridge, England: Cambridge University Press.

Crnic, Keith A., and **Booth, Carolyn L.** (1991). Mothers' and fathers' perceptions of daily hassles of parenting across early childhood. *Journal of Marriage and the Family, 53,* 1042–1050.

Crnic, Keith A., Ragozin, Arlene S., Greenberg, Mark T., Robinson, Nancy M., and **Basham, Robert B.** (1983). Social interaction and developmental competence of preterm and full term infants during the first year of life. *Child Development, 54,* 1199–1210.

Crohan, Susan E., and **Antonucci, Toni C.** (1989). Friends as a source of social support in old age. In Rebecca G. Adams and Rosemary Bleiszner (Eds.), *Older adult friendship.* Newbury Park, CA: Sage.

Crook, Thomas. (1987). Dementia. In Laura L. Carstensen and Barry A. Edelstein (Eds.), *Handbook of clinical gerontology.* New York: Pergamon.

Cross, W.W., Jr. (1991). *Shades of black: Diversity in African-American identity.* Philadelphia: Temple University Press.

Crowe, Mary. (1992). Some common and uncommon health and medical problems. In The Boston Women's Health Collective (Eds.), *The new our bodies, ourselves.* New York: Simon and Schuster.

Cruickshank, J.K., and **Beevers, D.G.** (1989). *Ethnic factors in health and disease.* London: Wright.

Crum, Julie F., and **Eckert, Helen M.** (1985). Play patterns of primary school children. In Jane E. Clark and James H. Humphrey (Eds.), *Motor development: Current selected research.* Princeton, NJ: Princeton Book Company.

Crystal, Howard A. (1988). The diagnosis of Alzheimer's disease and other dementing disorders. In Miriam K. Aronson and Robert N. Butler (Eds.), *Understanding Alzheimer's disease.* New York: Charles Scribner's Sons.

Culliton, Barbara. (1987). Osteoporosis reexamined: Complexity of bone biology is a challenge. *Science, 235,* 833–834.

Cumming, Elaine, and **Henry, William H.** (1961). *Growing old: The process of disengagement.* New York: Basic Books.

Cummings, E.M., Iannotti, R.J., and **Zahn-Waxler, C.** (1985). Influence of conflict between adults on the emotions and aggression of young children. *Developmental Psychology, 21,* 495–507.

Cummins, Jim. (1991). Interdependence of first- and second-language proficiency. In Ellen Bialystok (Ed.), *Language processing in bilingual children.* Cambridge, England: Cambridge University Press.

Cunningham, Walter R. (1987). Intellectual abilities and age. In K. Warner Schaie (Ed.), *Annual review of gerontology and geriatrics* (Vol. 7). New York: Springer.

Cunningham, Walter R. (1989). Intellectual abilities, speed of response, and aging. In Vern L. Bengston and K. Warner Schaie (Eds.), *The course of later life.* New York: Springer.

Cunningham, Walter R. (1980). Speed, age and qualitative differences in cognitive functioning. In Leonard W. Poon (Ed.), *Aging in the 1980s.* Washington, DC: American Psychological Association.

Cunningham, Walter R., and **Tomer, Adrian.** (1990). Intellectual abilities and age: Concepts, theories and analyses. In Eugene A. Lovelace (Ed.), *Aging and cognition: Mental processes, self-awareness and interventions.* North-Holland: Elsevier.

Curran, David K. (1987). *Adolescent suicidal behavior.* Washington, DC: Hemisphere Publishing.

Cutler, Richard G. (1984). Antioxidants and longevity. In Donald Armstrong, R.S. Sohol, Richard G. Cutler, and Trevor F. Slater (Eds.), *Free radicals in molecular biology, aging, and disease.* New York: Raven Press.

Damon, William. (1984). Self understanding and moral development from childhood to adolescence. In William M. Kurtines and Jacob L. Gewirtz (Eds.), *Morality, moral behavior, and moral development.* New York: Wiley.

Daniels, Denise H., Dunn, Judy, Furstenberg, Frank, and **Plomin, Robert.** (1985). Environmental differences within the family and adjustment differences within pairs of adolescent siblings. *Child Development, 56,* 764–774.

Daro, Deborah. (1988). *Confronting child abuse.* New York: The Free Press.

Dasen, P., Inhelder, B., Lavallee, M., and **Retschitzki, J.** (1978). *Naissance de l'intelligence chez l'enfant Baoule de Côte d'Ivoire.* Berne, Switzerland: Hans Huber.

Dasen, P.R. (Ed.). (1977). *Piagetian psychology: Cross-cultural contributions.* New York: Gardner.

Datan, Nancy. (1986). Oedipal conflict, Platonic love: Centrifugal forces in intergenerational relations. In Nancy Datan, Anita L. Greene, and Hayne W. Reese (Eds.), *Life-span developmental psychology: Intergenerational relations.* Hillsdale, NJ: Erlbaum.

Davajan, Val, and **Israel, Robert.** (1991). Diagnosis and medical treatment of infertility. In Annette L. Stanton and Christine Dunkel-Schetter (Eds.), *Infertility.* New York: Plenum.

Davidson, Lucy. (1986, March 7). Is teenage suicide contagious? *Atlanta Constitution,* B1, B7–B9.

Davies, A. Michael. (1991). Function in old age: Measurement, comparability, and service planning. *Proceedings of the 1988 International Symposium on Aging,* Series 5, No. 6. (DHHS Publication No. 91–1482). Hyattsville, MD: United States Department of Health and Human Services.

Davies, Bronwyn. (1982). *Life in the classroom and playground.* London: Routledge and Kegan Paul.

Davies, D. Roy, and **Sparrow, Paul R.** (1985). Age and work behavior. In Neil Charness (Ed.), *Aging and human performance.* New York: Wiley.

Davies, Louise. (1990). Nutrition education of the elderly. In Derek M. Prinsley and Harold H. Sandstread (Eds.), *Nutrition and aging.* New York: Liss.

Davies, Peter. (1988). Alzheimer's disease and related disorders: An overview. In Miriam K. Aronson and Robert N. Butler (Eds.), *Understanding Alzheimer's disease.* New York: Charles Scribner's Sons.

Davis, Debra Lee. (1991, March 1). Fathers and fetuses. *New York Times,* A19.

Davis, G. Cullom. (1985). Accounts of lives and times. In Gari Lesnoff-Caravalglia (Ed.), *Values, ethics, and aging.* New York: Human Sciences Press.

Davis, Janet M., and **Rovee-Collier, Carolyn.** (1983). Alleviated forgetting of a learned contingency in 8-week-old infants. *Developmental Psychology, 19,* 353–365.

Dawis, Rene V. (1984). Job satisfaction: Worker aspirations, attitudes and behavior. In Norman C. Gysbers (Ed.), *Designing careers.* San Francisco: Jossey-Bass.

Dawood, M. Yusoff. (1985). Overall approach to the management of dysmenorrhea. In M. Yusoff Dawood, John L. McGuire, and Laurence M. Demers (Eds.), *Premenstrual syndrome and dysmenorrhea.* Baltimore, MD: Urban and Schwartzenberg.

Dawson, Deborah A. (1991). Family structure and children's health and well-being: Data from the 1988 national health interview study on child health. *Journal of Marriage and the Family, 53,* 573–584.

DeCasper, Anthony J., and **Fifer, William P.** (1980). Of human bonding: Newborns prefer their mothers' voices. *Science, 208,* 1174–1175.

DeFriese, Gordon H., and **Woomert, Alison.** (1992). Informal and formal health care. In Marcia G. Ory, Ronald P. Ables, and Paula Darby Lipman (Eds.), *Aging, health, and behavior.* Newbury Park, CA: Sage.

Deimling, Gary T., and **Bass, David M.** (1986). Symptoms of mental impairment among elderly adults and their effects on family caregivers. *Journal of Gerontology, 41,* 778–784.

DeMaris, Alfred, and **Rao, K. Vaninadha.** (1992). Premarital cohabitation and subsequent marital stability in the United States: A reassessment. *Journal of Marriage and the Family, 54,* 178–190.

Dement, William, Richardson, Gary, Prinz, Patricia, Carskadon, Mary, and **Kripke, Daniel.** (1985). Changes in sleep and wakefulness with age. In Caleb E. Finch and Edward L. Schneider (Eds.), *Handbook of the biology of aging* (2nd ed.). New York: Van Nostrand.

Demo, David H. (1992). Parent-child relations: Assessing recent changes. *Journal of Marriage and the Family, 54,* 104–117.

Demopoulus, Harry B. (1982). Oxygen free radicals in the central nervous system. In A.P. Autor (Ed.), *Pathology of oxygen.* New York: Academic Press.

Denney, Nancy Wadsworth. (1982). Aging and cognitive changes. In Benjamin B. Wolman and G. Sticker (Eds.), *Handbook of developmental psychology.* Englewood Cliffs, NJ: Prentice Hall.

Denney, Nancy Wadsworth. (1989). Everyday problem solving: Methodological issues, research findings, and a model. In Leonard W. Poon, David C. Rubin, and Barbara A. Wilson (Eds.), *Everyday cognition in adulthood and late life.* Cambridge, England: Cambridge University Press.

Denney, Nancy Wadsworth. (1990). Adult age differences in traditional and practical problem solving. In Eugene A. Lovelace (Ed.), *Aging and cognition: Mental processes, self-awareness and interventions.* North-Holland: Elsevier.

Denney, Nancy Wadsworth, and **Palmer, Ann M.** (1981). Adult age differences on traditional and practical problem-solving measures. *Journal of Gerontology, 36,* 323–328.

Denney, Nancy Wadsworth, and **Thisson, David M.** (1983–1984). Determinants of cognitive ability in the elderly. *International Journal of Aging and Human Development, 16,* 29–41.

Dennis, Wayne. (1966). Creative productivity between the ages of 20 and 80 years. *Journal of Gerontology, 21,* 1–8.

Denny, B. Michael, and **Thomas, Susan.** (1986). The relationship of proportional reasoning ability to self-concept: A cognitive developmental approach. *Journal of Early Adolescence, 6,* 45–54.

DeParle, Jason. (1991, March 12). A state's fight to save babies enters round 2. *New York Times,* A1, A20.

Department of Commerce. (1990). *Statistical abstract of the United States.* Washington, DC: U.S. Bureau of the Census.

de Ribaupierre, Anik, Rieben, Laurence, and **Lautrey, Jacques.** (1985). Horizontal decalages and individual differences in the development of concrete operations. In Valerie L. Shulman, Lillian C.R. Restaino-Bauman, and Loretta Butler (Eds.), *The future of Piagetian theory: The neo-Piagetians.* New York: Plenum.

Deutsch, Helene. (1944–1945). *The psychology of women: A psychoanalytic interpretation* (Vol. 2). New York: Grune and Stratton.

Deutscher, Irwin. (1988). Misers and wastrels: Perceptions of the depression and yuppie generations. In Suzanne K. Steinmetz (Ed.), *Family and support systems across the life span.* New York: Plenum.

de Villiers, Jill G., and **de Villiers, Peter A.** (1978). *Language acquisition.* Cambridge, MA: Harvard University Press.

de Villiers, Jill G., and **de Villiers, Peter A.** (1986). *The acquisition of English.* Hillsdale, NJ: Erlbaum.

Diamond, Adele. (1985). Development of the ability to use recall to guide action, as indicated by infants' performance on AB. *Child Development, 56,* 868–883.

Diamond, Jared. (1986, November). I want a girl just like the girl. . . *Discover, 7* (11), 65–68.

Diamond, Marion Cleeves. (1988). *Enriching heredity.* New

York: The Free Press.

Diaz, Rafael M. (1985). Bilingual cognitive development: Addressing three gaps in current research. *Child Development, 56,* 1376–1388.

Diaz, Rafael M. (1987). The private speech of young children at risk: A test of three deficit hypotheses. *Early Childhood Research Quarterly, 2,* 181–197.

Diaz, Rafael M., and **Klinger, Cynthia.** (1991). Toward an explanatory model of the interaction between bilingualism and cognitive development. In Ellen Bialystok (Ed.), *Language processing in bilingual children.* Cambridge, England: Cambridge University Press.

Dickinson, David K. (1984). First impressions: Children's knowledge of words gained from a single exposure. *Applied Psycholinguistics, 5,* 359–374.

Dick-Read, Grantly. (1972). *Childbirth without fear: The original approach to natural childbirth* (rev. ed.). Helen Wessel and Harlan F. Ellis (Eds.). New York: Harper & Row.

DiClemente, Ralph J. (1990). The emergence of adolescents as a risk group for human immunodeficiency virus infection. *Journal of Adolescent Research, 5,* 7–17.

Dietz, William H., Jr., and **Gortmaker, Steven L.** (1985). Do we fatten our children at the television set? Obesity and television viewing in children and adolescents. *Pediatrics, 75,* 807–812.

Digman, J.M. (1990). Personality structure: Emergence of the five-factor model. *Annual Review of Psychology, 41,* 417–440.

Dion, Kenneth L., and **Dion, Karen K.** (1988). Romantic love: Individual and cultural perspectives. In Robert J. Sternberg and Michael L. Barnes (Eds.), *The psychology of love.* New Haven, CT: Yale University Press.

DiPietro, Janet Ann. (1981). Rough and tumble play: A function of gender. *Developmental Psychology, 17,* 50–58.

Dittmann-Kohli, Freya and **Baltes, Paul B.** (1990). Toward a neofunctionalist conception of adult intellectual development: Wisdom as a prototypical case of intellectual growth. In Charles N. Alexander and Ellen J. Langer (Eds.), *Higher stages of human development.* New York: Oxford University Press.

Dixon, Roger A. (1992). Contextual approaches to adult intellectual development. In Robert J. Sternberg and Cynthia A. Berg (Eds.), *Intellectual development.* New York: Cambridge University Press.

Dixon, Roger A., and **Baltes, Paul B.** (1986). Toward life-span research on the functions and pragmatics of intelligence. In Robert J. Sternberg and Richard K. Wagner (Eds.), *Practical intelligence.* Cambridge, England: Cambridge University Press.

Dixon, Roger A., Kramer, Dierdre A., and **Baltes, Paul B.** (1985). Intelligence: A life-span developmental perspective. In Benjamin B. Wolman (Ed.), *Handbook of intelligence: Theories, measurements, and applications.* New York: Wiley.

Dobbing, John (Ed.). (1987). *Early nutrition and later achievement.* London: Academic Press.

Dobkin, Leah. (1992). If you build it, they may not come. *Generations, 16* (2), 31–32.

Dockrell, J., Campbell, R., and **Neilson, I.** (1980). Conservation accidents revisited. *International Journal of Behavioral Development, 3,* 423–439.

Dodge, Kenneth. (1986). A social information processing model of social competence in children. In M. Perlmutter (Ed.), *Cognitive perspectives on children's social and behavioral develop-* *ment: Minnesota symposia on child psychology* (Vol. 18). Hillsdale, NJ: Erlbaum.

Dodge, Kenneth A., Coie, John D., Pettit, Gregory S., and **Price, Joseph M.** (1990). Peer status and aggression in boys' groups: Developmental and contextual analysis. *Child Development 61,* 1289–1309.

Dodge, Kenneth A., and **Somberg, Daniel R.** (1987). Hostile attributional biases among aggressive boys are exacerbated under conditions of threats to self. *Child Development, 58,* 213–224.

Dodge, Kenneth A., Murphy, Roberta R., and **Buchsbaum, Kathy.** (1984). The assessment of intention-cue detection skills in children: Implications for developmental psychopathology. *Child Development, 55,* 163–173.

Dodge, Kenneth A., Pettit, G.S., McClaskey, C.L., and **Brown, M.M.** (1986). Social competence in children. *Monographs of the Society for Research in Child Development, 51* (2, Serial No. 213).

Donaldson, Margaret, Grieve, Robert, and **Pratt, Chris.** (1983). General introduction. In Margaret Donaldson, Robert Grieve, and Chris Pratt (Eds.), *Early childhood development and education: Readings in psychology.* New York: Guilford.

Doris, John (Ed.). (1991). *The suggestibility of children's recollections.* Washington, DC: American Psychological Corporation.

Dorris, Michael. (1989). *The broken cord: A family's ongoing struggle with fetal alcohol syndrome.* New York: Harper & Row.

Downs, A. Chris. (1990). The social biological constraints of social competency. In Thomas P. Gullotta, Gerald R. Adams, and Raymond R. Montemayor (Eds.), *Developing social competency in adolescence.* Newbury Park, CA: Sage.

Drigotas, Stephen M., and **Rusbult, Caryl E.** (1992). Should I stay or should I go? A dependence model of relationships. *Journal of Personality and Social Psychology, 62,* 62–87.

Drotan, Dennis, Eckerle, Debby, Satola, Jackie, Pallotta, John, and **Wyatt, Betsy.** (1990). Maternal interactional behavior with nonorganic failure-to-thrive infants: A case comparison study. *Child Abuse and Neglect, 14,* 41–51.

Dryfoos, Joy G. (1990). *Adolescents at risk: Prevalence and prevention.* New York: Oxford University Press.

Duany, Luis, and **Pittman, Karen.** (1990). *Latino youth at the crossroads.* Washington, DC: Children's Defense Fund.

Dubas, Judith Semon, Graber, Julia A., and **Petersen, Anne C.** (1991). A longitudinal investigation of adolescents' changing perceptions of pubertal timing. *Developmental Psychology, 27,* 580–586.

Dubler, Nancy Neveloff. (1993). Commentary: Balancing life and death—proceed with caution. *American Journal of Public Health, 83,* 23–25.

Dubow, Eric R., and **Luster, Tom.** (1990). Adjustment of children born to teenage mothers: The contribution of risk and protective factors. *Journal of Marriage and the Family, 52,* 393–404.

Dugger, Celia W. (1991, March 9). Neighbors ask, how could parents let that baby starve? *New York Times,* 25–26.

Dunham, Roger G., and **Alpert, Gregory P.** (1987). Keeping juvenile delinquents in school: A prediction model. *Adolescence, 22,* 45–57.

Dunkel-Schetter, Christine and **Lobel, Marci.** (1991). In Annette L. Stanton and Christine Dunkel-Schetter (Eds.), *Infertility.* New York: Plenum.

Dunn, Judy. (1983). Sibling relationships in early childhood. *Child Development, 54,* 787–811.

Dunn, Judy. (1985). *Sisters and brothers.* Cambridge, MA: Harvard University Press.

Dunn, Judy. (1988). *The beginnings of social understanding.* Cambridge, MA: Harvard University Press.

Dunn, Judy. (1992). Siblings and development. *Current Directions in Psychological Science, 1,* 6–9.

Dunn, Judy, and **Munn, Penny.** (1985). Becoming a family member: Family conflict and the development of social understanding in the second year. *Child Development, 56,* 480–492.

Dunn, Judy, and **Plomin, Robert.** (1990). *Separate lives: Why siblings are so different.* New York: Basic Books.

Dunn, Judy, Brown, Jane, Slomkowski, Cheryl, Tesla, Caroline, and **Youngblade, Lisa.** (1991). Young children's understanding of other people's feelings and beliefs: Individual differences and their antecedents. *Child Development, 62,* 1352–1366.

Du Randt, Ross. (1985). Ball-catching proficiency among 4-, 6-, and 8-year-old girls. In Jane E. Clark and James H. Humphrey (Eds.), *Motor development: Current selected research.* Princeton, NJ: Princeton Book Company.

Dustman, R.E., Ruhling, R.O., Russell, E.M., Shearer, D.E., Bonekat, H.W., Shigeoka, J.W., Wood, J.S., and **Bradford, D.C.** (1984). Aerobic exercise training and improved neuropsychological function of older individuals. *Neurobiology of Aging, 5,* 35–42.

Dweck, Carol S., and **Elliott, Elaine S.** (1983). Achievement motivation. In Paul H. Mussen (Ed.), *Handbook of child psychology: Vol. 4. Socialization and personality development.* New York: Wiley.

Dweck, Carol S., Davidson, W., Nelson, S., and **Enna, B.** (1978). Sex differences in learned helplessness, II: The contingencies of evaluative feedback in the classroom, and III: An experimental analysis. *Developmental Psychology, 14,* 268–276.

Dwyer, Jeffrey W., and **Coward, Raymond T.** (1992). Gender, family, and long-term care of the elderly. In Jeffrey W. Dwyer and Raymond T. Coward (Eds.), *Gender, families and elder care.* Newbury Park, CA: Sage.

Easley, Jack, and **Taylor, Harold.** (1990). Conceptual splatter and dialogues in selected Japanese and U.S. first grade mathematics classes. In Leslie P. Steffe and Terry Wood (Eds.), *Transforming children's mathematics education: International perspectives.* Hillsdale, NJ: Erlbaum.

East, Whitfield B., and **Hensley, Larry D.** (1985). The effects of selected sociocultural factors upon the overhand-throwing performance of prepubescent children. In Jane E. Clark and James H. Humphrey (Eds.), *Motor development: Current selected research.* Princeton, NJ: Princeton Book Company.

Easterbrooks, M. Ann. (1989). Quality of attachment to mother and to father: Effects of perinatal risk status. *Child Development, 60,* 825–830.

Easterbrooks, M. Ann, and **Goldberg, W.A.** (1984). Toddler development in the family: Impact of father involvement and parenting characteristics. *Child Development, 55,* 740–752.

Eaton, Warren O., and **Yu, Alice Piklai.** (1989). Are sex differences in child motor activity level a function of sex differences in maturational status? *Child Development, 60,* 1005–1011.

Eaves, L.J., Eysenck, H.J., and **Martin, N.G.** (1989). *Genes, culture, and personality.* London: Academic Press.

Eccles, Jacquelynne S., and **Jacobs, J.E.** (1986). Social forces shape math attitudes and performance. *Signs, 11,* 367–389.

Eccles, Jacquelynne S., and **Midgley, Carol.** (1989). Stage/environment fit: Developmentally appropriate classrooms for early adolescents. In R.E. Ames and C. Ames (Eds.), *Research on motivation education* (Vol. 3). New York: Academic Press.

Eckenrode, John, and **Gore, Susan** (Eds.). (1990). *Stress between work and family.* New York: Plenum.

Edinger, Jack D., Hoelscher, Timothy J., Marx, Gail R., Lipper, Steven, and **Ionescu-Pioggia, Martin.** (1992). A cognitive behavioral therapy for sleep-maintenance insomnia in older adults. *Psychology and Aging, 7,* 282–289.

Edwards, Carolyn Pope. (1987). Culture and the construction of moral values: A comparative ethnography of moral encounters in two cultural settings. In Jerome Kagan and Sharon Lamb (Eds.), *The emergence of morality in young children.* Chicago: University of Chicago Press.

Edwards, D.D. (1987). Alcohol-breast cancer link. *Science News, 131,* 292.

Edwards, John N. (1969). Familiar behavior as social exchange. *Journal of Marriage and the Family, 31,* 518–526.

Egley, Lance C. (1991). What changes the societal prevalence of domestic violence? *Journal of Marriage and the Family, 53,* 885–897.

Eichorn, Dorothy H. (1979). Physical development: Current foci of research. In Joy Doniger Osofsky (Ed.), *Handbook of infant development.* New York: Wiley.

Eichorn, Dorothy H., Hunt, Jane V., and **Honzik, Marjorie P.** (1981). Experience, personality, and IQ: Adolescence to middle age. In Dorothy Eichorn, John A. Clausen, Marjorie P. Honzik, and Paul H. Mussen (Eds.), *Present and past in middle life.* New York: Academic Press.

Eiger, Marvin S. (1987). The feeding of infants and children. In Robert A. Hoekelman, Saul Blatman, Stanford B. Friedman, Nicholas M. Nelson, and Henry M. Seidel (Eds.), *Primary pediatric care.* St. Louis, MO: Mosby.

Eimas, Peter D., Sigueland, Einar R., Jusczyk, Peter, and **Vigorito, James.** (1971). Speech perception in infants. *Science, 171,* 303–306.

Eisdorfer, Carl. (1977). Intelligence and cognition in the aged. In Ewald W. Busse and Eric Pfeiffer (Eds.), *Behavior and adaptation in late life* (2nd ed.). Boston: Little, Brown.

Eisdorfer, Carl. (1985). The conceptualization of stress and a model for further study. In Michael R. Zales (Ed.), *Stress in health and disease.* New York: Brunner/Mazel.

Eisenberg, Nancy. (1982). *The development of prosocial behavior.* New York: Academic Press.

Eisenberg, Nancy. (1986). *Altruistic emotion, cognition, and behavior.* Hillsdale, NJ: Erlbaum.

Eisenberg, Nancy. (1990). Prosocial development in early and mid-adolescence. In Raymond Montemayor, Gerald R. Adams, and Thomas P. Gullotta (Eds.), *From childhood to adolescence: A transitional period?* Newbury Park, CA: Sage.

Eisenberg, Nancy, Lunch, Teresa, Shell, Rita, and **Roth, Karlsson.** (1985). Children's justifications for their adult and peer-direction compliant (prosocial and nonprosocial) behaviors. *Developmental Psychology, 21,* 325–331.

Eisenberg, Nancy, Shell, Rita, Pasternack, J., Lennon, R.,

Beller, R., and Mathy, R.M. (1987). Prosocial development in middle childhood: A longitudinal study. *Developmental Psychology, 23,* 712–718.

Eisenberg-Berg, Nancy, Boothby, Rita, and Matson, Tom. (1979). Correlates of preschool girls' feminine and masculine toy preferences. *Developmental Psychology, 48,* 1411–1416.

Eisenson, Jon. (1986). *Language and speech disorders in children.* New York: Pergamon.

Elder Abuse Project. (1991, October/November). Aging today. *American Society on Aging,* 14–15.

Elder, Glen H., Jr., Nguyen, Tri Van, and Caspi, Avshalom. (1985). Linking family hardship to children's lives. *Child Development, 56,* 361–375.

Elevenstar, D. (1980, January 8). Happy couple a tribute to old-fashioned virtues. *The Los Angeles Times,* 2.

Elias, Merrill F., Elias, Jeffrey W., and Elias, Penelope K. (1990). In James E. Birren and K. Warner Schaie (Eds.), *Handbook of the psychology of aging* (3rd ed.). San Diego, CA: Academic Press.

Elkind, David. (1974). *Children and adolescents: Interpretive essays on Jean Piaget.* New York: Oxford University Press.

Elkind, David. (1978). *The child's reality: Three developmental themes.* Hillsdale, NJ: Erlbaum.

Elkind, David. (1985). Egocentrism redux. *Developmental Review, 5,* 218–226.

Elkind, David, and Bowen, R. (1979). Imaginary audience behavior in children and adolescents. *Developmental Psychology, 15,* 38–44.

Ellis, Nancy Borel. (1991). An extension of the Steinberg accelerating hypothesis. *Journal of Early Adolescence, 11,* 221–235.

Elstein, A.S., Shulman, L.S., and Sprafka, S.A. (1978). *Medical problem-solving: An analysis of clinical expertise.* Cambridge, MA: Harvard University Press.

Emde, Robert N., and Harmon, R.J. (1972). Endogenous and exogenous smiling systems in early infancy. *Journal of the American Academy of Child Psychiatry, 11,* 77–100.

Emery, Alan E.H. (1983). *Elements of medical genetics* (6th ed.). Edinburgh: Churchill Livingstone.

Emery, Robert E. (1988). *Marriage, divorce, and children's adjustment.* Newbury Park, CA: Sage.

Endo, R., Sue, S., and Wagner, N.N. (Eds.). (1980). *Asian-Americans: Social and psychological perspectives.* Palo Alto, CA: Science and Behavior Books.

Engstrom, Paul F. (1986). Cancer control objectives for the year 2000. In Lee E. Mortenson, Paul F. Engstrom, and Paul N. Anderson (Eds.), *Advances in cancer control.* New York: Liss.

Enkin, Murray, Keirse, Marc J.N.C., and Chalmers, Iain. (1989). *Effective care in pregnancy and childbirth.* Oxford, England: Oxford University Press.

Epstein, L.H. (1985). Family-based treatment for pre-adolescent obesity. In M. Wolraich and D.K. Routh (Eds.), *Advances in developmental and behavioral pediatrics* (Vol. 6). Greenwich, CT: JAI Press.

Erber, Joan T. (1982). Memory and age. In Tiffany M. Field, Aletha Huston, Herbert C. Quay, Lillian Troll, and Gordon E. Finley (Eds.), *Review of human development.* New York: Wiley.

Erdrich, Louise. (1989). Foreward. In Michael Dorris (Ed.), *The broken cord: A family's ongoing struggle with fetal alcohol syndrome.* New York: Harper & Row.

Erikson, Erik H. (1963). *Childhood and society* (2nd ed.). New York: Norton.

Erikson, Erik H. (1968). *Identity, youth, and crisis.* New York: Norton.

Erikson, Erik H. (1975). *Life history and the historical moment.* New York: Norton.

Erikson, Erik H., Erikson, Joan M., and Kivnick, Helen Q. (1986). *Vital involvement in old age.* New York: Norton.

Ernhart, Claire B., Landa, Beth, and Wolf, Abraham. (1985). Subclinical lead level and developmental deficit: Re-analysis of data. *Journal of Learning Disabilities, 18,* 474–479.

Ernhart, Claire B., Sokol, Robert J., Ager, Joel W., Morrow-Tlucak, Mary, and Martier, Susan. (1989). Alcohol-related birth defects: Assessing the risk. In Donald Hutchings (Ed.), *Prenatal abuse of licit and illicit drugs.* New York: New York Academy of Sciences.

Essex, Marilyn J., and Nam, Sunghee. (1987). Marital status and loneliness among older women. *Journal of Marriage and the Family, 49,* 93–106.

Eveleth, Phillis B., and Tanner, James M. (1976). *Worldwide variation in human growth.* Cambridge, England: Cambridge University Press.

Ewing, Charles Patrick. (1990). *Kids who kill.* Lexington, MA: Lexington Books.

Fagot, Beverly. (1978). The influence of sex of child on parental reactions to toddler children. *Child Development, 49,* 459–465.

Fagot, Beverly. (1985). Changes in thinking about early sex role development. *Developmental Review, 5,* 83–98.

Falbo, Toni. (1984). Only children: A review. In Toni Falbo (Ed.), *The single-child family.* New York: Guilford.

Farrar, Michael Jeffrey. (1992). Negative evidence and grammatical morpheme acquisition. *Developmental Psychology, 28,* 90–98.

Farrell, Michael P., and Rosenberg, Stanley D. (1981). *Men at midlife.* Boston: Auburn House.

Farrington, David P. (1987). Epidemiology. In Herbert C. Quay (Ed.), *Handbook of juvenile delinquency.* New York: Wiley.

Fasick, Frank A. (1984). Parents, peers, youth culture and autonomy in adolescence. *Adolescence, 19,* 143–157.

Faust, Margaret S. (1983). Alternative constructions of adolescent growth. In Jeanne Brooks-Gunn and Anne C. Petersen (Eds.), *Girls at puberty: Biological and psychological aspects.* New York: Plenum.

Feather, Norman T. (1980). Values in adolescence. In Joseph Adelson (Ed.), *Handbook of adolescent psychology.* New York: Wiley.

Featherstone, Helen. (1980). *A difference in the family.* New York: Basic Books.

Fein, Edith. (1981). Issues in foster family care: Where do we stand? *American Journal of Orthopsychiatry, 61,* 578–583.

Feinman, S. (1985). Emotional expression, social referencing, and preparedness for learning in infancy—Mother knows best, but sometimes I know better. In G. Ziven (Ed.), *The development of expressive behavior.* Orlando, FL: Academic Press.

Feiring, Candice, and Lewis, Michael. (1984). Changing characteristics of the U.S. family: Implications for family networks, relationships, and child development. In Michael Lewis (Ed.), *Beyond the dyad*. New York: Plenum.

Feiring, Candice, and **Lewis, Michael.** (1989). The social network of girls and boys from early through middle childhood. In Deborah Belle (Ed.), *Children's social networks and social supports*. New York: Wiley.

Feldman, Harold. (1981). A comparison of intentional parents and intentionally childless couples. *Journal of Marriage and the Family, 43,* 593–600.

Feldman, Nina S., and **Ruble, Diane N.** (1988). The effect of personal relevance on psychological inference: A developmental analysis. *Child Development, 59,* 1339–1352.

Feldman, S. Shirley, Biringen, Zeynap C., and **Nash, Sharon Churnin.** (1981). Fluctuations of sex-related self-attributions as a function of stage of family life cycle. *Developmental Psychology, 17,* 24–35.

Felmlee, D., Sprecher, S., and **Bassin, E.** (1990). The dissolution of intimate relationships: A hazard mode. *Social Psychology Quarterly, 53,* 13–30.

Felner, R.D., and **Terre, L.** (1987). Child custody dispositions and children's adaptation following divorce. In L.A. Weithorn (Ed.), *Psychology and child custody determinations*. Lincoln, NE: University of Nebraska Press.

Ferber, Marianne A., and **O'Farrell, Brigid.** (1991). *Work and family: Policies for a changing work force*. Washington, DC: National Academy Press.

Ferguson, Charles A. (1977). Baby talk as a simplified register. In Catherine E. Snow and Charles A. Ferguson (Eds.), *Talking to children: Language input and requisition*. Cambridge, England: Cambridge University Press.

Fernald, Anne. (1985). Four-month-old infants prefer to listen to motherese. *Infant Behavior and Development, 8,* 181–195.

Fernald, Anne, and **Massie, Claudia.** (1991). Prosady and focus in speech to infants and adults. *Developmental Psychology, 27,* 209–221.

Fiati, Thomas A. (1991). Cross-cultural variation in the structure of children's thought. In Robbie Case (Ed.), *The mind's staircase: Exploring the conceptual underpinning of children's thought and knowledge*. Hillsdale, NJ: Erlbaum.

Field, Dorothy, Schaie, K. Warner, and **Leino, E. Victor.** (1988). Continuity in intellectual functioning: The role of self-supported health. *Psychology and Aging, 3,* 385–392.

Field, Tiffany M. (1980). Interactions of high risk infants: Quantitative and qualitative differences. In D.B. Sawin, R.C. Hawkins, L.P. Walker, and J.H. Penticuff (Eds.), *Exceptional infant: Vol. 4. Psychosocial risks in infant environmental transactions*. New York: Brunner/Mazel.

Field, Tiffany M. (1982). Individual differences in the expressivity of neonates and young infants. In R. Feldman (Ed.), *Development of nonverbal behavior in children*. New York: Springer-Verlag.

Field, Tiffany M. (1987). Affective and interactive disturbances in infants. In Joy Doniger Osofsky (Ed.), *Handbook of infant development* (2nd ed.). New York: Wiley.

Field, Tiffany M. (1991). Quality infant day-care and grade school behavior and performance. *Child Development, 62,* 863–870.

Field, Tiffany M., and **Reite, Martin.** (1984). Children's re-sponses to separation from mother during the birth of another child. *Child Development, 55,* 1308–1316.

Field, Tiffany M., and **Schanberg, Saul A.** (1990). Massage alters growth and catecholamine production in preterm newborns. In Nina Gunzenhauser (Ed.), *Advances in touch: New implications in human development*. Skillman, NJ: Johnson and Johnson.

Field, Tiffany M., Gewirtz, Jacob L., Cohen, Debra, Garcia, Robert, Greenberg, Reena, and **Kerry, Collins.** (1984). Leave-takings and reunions of infants, toddlers, preschoolers, and their parents. *Child Development, 55,* 628–634.

Field, Tiffany M., Woodson, R., Greenberg, R., and **Chen, D.** (1982). Discrimination and imitation of facial expression by neonates. *Science, 218,* 179–181.

Fincham, Frank D., and **Cain, Kathleen M.** (1986). Learned helplessness in humans: A developmental analysis. *Developmental Review, 6,* 301–333.

Fincham, Frank D., Hokoda, Audrey, and **Sanders, Reliford, Jr.** (1989). Learned helplessness, test anxiety, and academic achievement: A longitudinal analysis. *Child Development, 60,* 138–145.

Fine, Michelle. (1991). *Framing dropouts: Notes on the politics of an urban school system*. Albany, NY: SUNY Press.

Fingerhut, Lois A., and **Makuc, Diane M.** (1992). Mortality among minority populations in the United States. *American Journal of Public Health, 82,* 1168–1170.

Finkelhor, David. (1979). What's wrong with sex between adults and children? Ethics and the problems of sexual abuse. *American Journal of Orthopsychiatry, 49,* 692–697.

Finkelhor, David. (1992). New myths about the child welfare system. *Child, Youth, and Family Service Quarterly, 15* (1), 3–5.

Firth, Shirley. (1989). The good death: Approaches to death, dying, and bereavement among British Hindus. In Arthur Berger, Paul Badham, Austin H. Kutscher, Joyce Berger, Ven. Michael Petty, and John Beloff (Eds.), *Perspectives on death and dying: Cross-cultural and multi-disciplinary views*. Philadelphia: Charles Press.

Fischer, Judith L., Sollie, Donna L., and **Morrow, K. Brent.** (1986). Social networks in male and female adolescents. *Journal of Adolescent Research, 1,* 1–14.

Fischer, Kurt W. (1980). A theory of cognitive development: The control of hierarchies of skill. *Psychological Review, 87,* 477–531.

Fischman, Joshua. (1987). Type A on trial. *Psychology Today, 21* (2), 42–50.

Fitzpatrick, Mary Ann. (1984). A typological approach to marital interaction: Recent theory and research. In Leonard Berkowitz (Ed.), *Advances in experimental social psychology* (Vol. 18). New York: Academic Press.

Flanagan, Constance A. (1990). Change in family work status: Effects on parent-adolescent decision making. *Child Development, 61,* 163–177.

Flavell, John H. (1963). *The developmental psychology of Jean Piaget*. Princeton, NJ: Van Nostrand.

Flavell, John H. (1970). Cognitive changes in adulthood. In L.R. Goulet and Paul B. Baltes (Eds.), *Life-span developmental psychology: Research and theory*. New York: Academic Press.

Flavell, John H. (1982). Structures, stages, and sequences in cognitive development. In W. Andrew Collins (Ed.), *The concept of development: Minnesota symposia on child psychology* (Vol. 15). Hillsdale, NJ: Erlbaum.

Flavell, John H. (1985). *Cognitive development* (2nd ed.). Englewood Cliffs, NJ: Prentice Hall.

Flavell, John H., Speer, James Ramsey, Green, Frances L., and **August, Diane L.** (1981). The development of comprehension monitoring and knowledge about communication. *Monographs of the Society for Research in Child Development, 46* (5, Serial No. 192).

Flesh, Rudolph. (1955). *Why Johnny can't read.* New York: Harper and Row.

Flesh, Rudolph. (1985). *Why Johnny can't read.* (2nd ed.) New York: Harper and Row.

Fodor, J. (1983). *The moduality of mind.* Cambridge, MA: MIT Press.

Foege, William H. (1985). Preface. National Research Council (Ed.), *Injury in America: A continuing public health problem.* Washington, DC: National Academy Press.

Folberg, Jay (Ed.). (1991). *Joint custody and shared parenting* (2nd ed.). New York: Guilford.

Folkins, C.H., and **Sime, W.E.** (1981). Physical fitness training and mental health. *American Psychologist, 36,* 373–389.

Fonda, Jane. (1984). *Women coming of age.* New York: Simon and Schuster.

Fowler, James W. (1981). *Stages of faith: The psychology of human development and the quest for meaning.* New York: Harper & Row.

Fowler, James W. (1986). Faith and the structuring of meaning. In Craig Dykstra and Sharon Parks (Eds.), *Faith development and Fowler.* Birmingham, AL: Religious Education Press.

Fox, Margery, Gibbs, Margaret, and **Auerbach, Doris.** (1985). Age and gender dimensions of friendship. *Psychology of Women Quarterly, 9,* 489–502.

Fox, N.A., and **Davidson, R.J.** (1984). Hemispheric substrates of affect: A developmental model. In N.A. Fox and R.J. Davidson (Eds.), *The psychobiology of affective development.* Hillsdale, NJ: Erlbaum.

Fozard, James L. (1990). Vision and hearing in aging. In James E. Birren and K. Warner Schaie (Eds.), *Handbook of the psychology of aging* (3rd ed.). San Diego, CA: Academic Press.

Frances, Carol. (1980). *College enrollment trends: Testing the conventional wisdom against the facts.* Washington, DC: American Council on Education.

Francis, P.L., and **McCroy, G.** (1983, April). *Bimodal recognition of human stimulus configurations.* Paper presented at the meeting of the Society for Research in Child Development. Detroit, MI.

Frankenburg, W.K., Frandel, A., Sciarillo, W., and **Burgess, D.** (1981). The newly abbreviated and revised Denver Developmental Screening Test. *Journal of Pediatrics, 99,* 995–999.

Freedman, Samuel G. (1990). *Small victories.* New York: Harper and Row.

French, Doran C. (1984). Children's knowledge of the social functions of younger, older, and same-age peers. *Child Development, 55,* 1429–1433.

Freud, Sigmund. (1935). *A general introduction to psychoanalysis.* Joan Riviare (Trans.). New York: Modern Library.

Freud, Sigmund. (1938). *The basic writings of Sigmund Freud.*

A.A. Brill (Ed. and Trans.). New York: Modern Library.

Freud, Sigmund. (1963). *Three case histories.* New York: Collier. (Original work published 1918).

Freud, Sigmund. (1964). *An outline of psychoanalysis: Vol. 23. The standard edition of the complete psychological works of Sigmund Freud.* James Strachey (Ed. and Trans.). London: Hogarth Press. (Original work published 1940).

Freud, Sigmund. (1965). *New introductory lectures on psychoanalysis.* James Strachey (Ed. and Trans.). New York: Norton. (Original work published 1933).

Freud, W. Ernest. (1989). Prenatal attachment and bonding. In Stanley I. Greenspan and George H. Pollock (Eds.), *The course of life: Volume I. Infancy.* Madison, WI: International Universities Press.

Frey, K.S., and **Ruble, D.N.** (1987). What children say about classroom performance: Sex and grade differences in perceived competence. *Child Development, 58,* 1066–1078.

Frick, Paul J., and **Lehey, Benjamin B.** (1991). The nature and characteristics of attention-deficit hyperactivity disorder. *School Psychology Review, 20,* 163–173.

Fried, Peter A. (1989). Postnatal consequences of maternal marijuana use in humans. In Donald Hutchings (Ed.), *Prenatal abuse of licit and illicit drugs.* New York: New York Academy of Sciences.

Fried, Peter A., and **Watkinson, Barbara.** (1990). 36- and 48-month neurobehavioral follow-up of children prenatally exposed to marijuana, cigarettes, and alcohol. *Developmental and Behavioral Pediatrics, 11,* 49–58.

Friedman, Meyer, and **Rosenman, R.H.** (1974). *Type A behavior and your heart.* New York: Knopf.

Friedrich-Cofer, Lynette, and **Huston, Aletha C.** (1986). Television violence and aggression: The debate continues. *Psychological Bulletin, 100,* 364–371.

Fries, James F. (1989). Reduction of the national morbidity. In Stephen J. Lewis (Ed.), *Aging and health: Linking research and public policy.* Chelsea, MI: Lewis Publishers.

Fries, James F. (1990). The compression of morbidity: Progress and control. In M. Bergener, M. Ermini, and H.B. Stahelin (Eds.), *Challenges in aging.* New York: Academic Press.

Fries, James F., and **Crapo, Lawrence M.** (1981). *Vitality and aging.* San Francisco: Freeman.

Frisch, Rose E. (1983). Fatness, puberty, and fertility: The effects of nutrition and physical training on menarche and ovulation. In Jeanne Brooks-Gunn and Anne C. Petersen (Eds.), *Girls at puberty: Biological and psychosocial aspects.* New York: Plenum.

Fritz, Janet, and **Wetherbee, Sally.** (1982). Preschoolers' beliefs regarding the obese individual. *Canadian Home Economics Journal, 33,* 193–196.

Frye, Douglas, Braisby, Nicholas, Lowe, John, Marouda, Cline, and **Nicholls, Jon.** (1989). Young children's understanding of counting and cardinality. *Child Development, 60,* 1158–1171.

Fullard, W., McDevitt, S.S., and **Carey, W.B.** (1984). Assessing temperament in one- to three-year-old children. *Journal of Pediatric Psychology, 9,* 205–217.

Furman, Wyndol. (1987). Acquaintanceship in middle childhood. *Developmental Psychology, 23,* 563–570.

Furstenberg, Frank F., and **Cherlin, Andrew J.** (1991). *Divided* *families: What happens to children when parents part.* Cambridge, MA: Harvard University Press.

Furstenberg, Frank F., Jr., and **Nord, Christine Winquist.** (1985). Parenting apart: Patterns of childbearing after marital disruption. *Journal of Marriage and the Family, 47,* 893–912.

Furstenberg, Frank F., and **Spanier, Graham.** (1984). *Recycling the family: Remarriage after divorce.* Beverly Hills, CA: Sage.

Furstenberg, Frank F., Brooks-Gunn, Jeanne, and **Morgan, S.** (1987). *Adolescent mothers in later life.* New York: Cambridge University Press.

Fuson, Karen C. (1988). *Children's counting and concepts of number.* New York: Springer-Verlag.

Gaddis, Alan, and **Brooks-Gunn, Jeanne.** (1985). The male experience of pubertal change. *Journal of Youth and Adolescence, 14,* 61.

Gaensbauer, Theodore J. (1980). Anaclitic depression in a three-and-a-half month old child. *American Journal of Psychiatry, 137,* 841–842.

Galinsky, Ellen. (1981). *Between generations: The six stages of parenthood.* New York: Berkley.

Galler, Janina. (1989). A follow-up study of the influence of early malnutrition on development: Behavior at home and at school. *Journal of the American Academy of Child and Adolescent Psychiatry, 28,* 254–261.

Galotti, Kathleen M., Kozberg, Steven R., and **Farmer, Maria C.** (1991). Gender and developmental differences in adolescents' conceptions of moral reasoning. *Journal of Youth and Adolescence, 20,* 13–30.

Galvin, Ruth Mehrtens. (1992). The nature of shyness. *Harvard Magazine, 94* (4), 40–45.

Gandour, M.J. (1989). Activity level as a dimension of temperament in toddlers: Its relevance for the organismic specificity hypothesis. *Child Development, 60,* 1092–1098.

Garbarino, James. (1988). Preventing childhood injury: Developmental and mental health issues. *American Journal of Orthopsychiatry, 58,* 25–45.

Garbarino, James. (1989). An ecological perspective on the role of play in child development. In Marianne N. Bloch and Anthony D. Pellegrini (Eds.), *The ecological context of children's play.* Norwood, NJ: Ablex.

Garbarino, James, Kostelny, Kathleen, and **Dubrow, Nancy.** (1991). *No place to be a child: Growing up in a war zone.* New York: Lexington Books.

Gardner, Howard. (1980). *Artful scribbles: The significance of children's drawings.* New York: Basic Books.

Gardner, Howard. (1983). *Frames of mind: The theory of multiple intelligences.* New York: Basic Books.

Garmezy, Norman. (1985). Stress-resistant children: The search for protective factors. In J. E. Stevenson (Ed.), *Recent research in developmental psychopathology.* Oxford, England: Pergamon.

Garrett, C.J. (1985). Effects of residential treatment on adjudicated delinquents. *Journal of Research on Crime and Delinquency, 22,* 287–308.

Garvey, Catherine. (1976). Some properties of social play. In Jerome S. Bruner, Alison Jolly, and Kathy Sylva (Eds.), *Play.* New York: Basic Books.

Garvey, Catherine. (1977). *Play.* Cambridge, MA: Harvard University Press.

Garvey, Catherine. (1984). *Children's talk.* Cambridge, MA: Harvard University Press.

Garvey, Catherine, and **Kramer, Thayer L.** (1989). The language of social pretend play. *Developmental Review, 9,* 364–382.

Gatz, Margaret, Bengston, Vern L., and **Blum, Mindy J.** (1990). Caregiving families. In James E. Birren and K. Warner Schaie (Eds.), *Handbook of the psychology of aging* (3rd ed.). San Diego, CA: Academic Press.

Gauvain, Mary. (1990). Review of Kathleen Berger, *The developing person through childhood and adolescence* (3rd ed.). New York: Worth.

Gazzaniga, Michael S. (1983). Right hemisphere language following brain bisection: A 20-year perspective. *American Psychologist, 43,* 184–188.

Geiger, Roger L. (1986). *Private sectors in higher education: Structure, function, and change in eight countries.* Ann Arbor: University of Michigan Press.

Gelles, Richard J. (1987). *Family violence* (2nd ed.). Newbury Park, CA: Sage.

Gelles, Richard J. (1988). *Intimate violence.* New York: Simon and Schuster.

Gelman, Rochel, and **Baillargeon, Renee.** (1983). A review of some Piagetian concepts. In Paul H. Mussen (Ed.), *Handbook of child psychology: Vol. 3. Cognitive development.* New York: Wiley.

Gelman, Rochel, and **Gallistel, C.R.** (1978). *The child's understanding of number.* Cambridge, MA: Harvard University Press.

Gelman, Rochel, Maccoby, Eleanor, and **Le Vine, Robert.** (1982). Complexity in development and developmental studies. In W. Andrew Collins (Ed.), *The concept of development: Minnesota symposia on child psychology* (Vol. 15). Hillsdale, NJ: Erlbaum.

Genesse, F. (1983). Bilingual education of majority language children: The immersion experiments in review. *Applied Linguistics, 4,* 1–46.

Genishi, Celie, and **Dyson, Anne Haas.** (1984). *Language assessment in the early years.* Norwood, NJ: Ablex.

George, Victor, and **Wilding, Paul.** (1972). *Motherless families.* London: Routledge and Kegan Paul.

Gergen, Mary M. (1990). Finished at 40. *Psychology of Women Quarterly, 14,* 471–493.

Gesell, Arnold. (1926). *The mental growth of the pre-school child: A psychological outline of normal development from birth to the sixth year including a system of developmental diagnosis.* New York: Macmillan.

Gesell, Arnold, and **Amatruda, Catherine S.** (1947). *Developmental diagnosis: Normal and abnormal child development, clinical methods and pediatric applications* (2nd ed.). New York: Hoeber.

Gesell, Arnold, and **Ilg, Frances L.** (1946). *The child from five to ten.* New York: Harper & Row.

Gesell, Arnold, Ames, Louise Bates, and **Ilg, Frances L.** (1977). *The child from five to ten* (rev. ed.). New York: Harper & Row.

Getzels, J.W., and **Csikszentmihalyi, M.** (1976). *The creative vision: A longitudinal study of problem finding in art.* New York: Wiley.

Giambra, Leonard M., Camp, Cameron J., and **Grodsky, Alicia.** (1992). Curiosity and stimulation-seeking across the adult life span: Cross-sectional and 6- to 8-year longitudinal findings. *Psychology and Aging, 7,* 150–157.

Gianino, A., and **Tronick, Edward.** (1988). The Mutual Regulation Model: The infant's self and interactive regulation and coping and defensive capacities. In T. Field, P. McCabe, and N. Schneiderman (Eds.), *Stress and coping* (Vol. 2). Hillsdale, NJ: Erlbaum.

Gibson, Eleanor. (1988). Levels of description and constraints on perceptual development. In Albert Yonas (Ed.), *Perceptual development in infancy.* Hillsdale, NJ: Erlbaum.

Gibson, Eleanor, and **Walker, Arlene S.** (1984). Development of knowledge of visual-tactile affordances of substance. *Child Development, 55,* 453–460.

Gilbert, Enid F., Arya, Sunita, Loxova, Renata, and **Opitz, John M.** (1987). Pathology of chromosome abnormalities in the fetus: Pathological markers. In Enid F. Gilbert and John M. Opitz (Eds.), *Genetic aspects of developmental pathology.* New York: Liss.

Giles-Sims, Jean, and **Crosbie-Burnett, Margaret.** (1989). Adolescent power in stepparent families: A test of normative resource theory. *Journal of Marriage and the Family, 51,* 1065–1078.

Gilligan, Carol. (1981). Moral development. In Arthur W. Chickering (Ed.), *The modern American college: Responding to the new realities of diverse students and a changing society.* San Francisco: Jossey-Bass.

Gilligan, Carol. (1982). *In a different voice: Psychological theory and women's development.* Cambridge, MA: Harvard University Press.

Gilligan, Carol. (1990). *Making connections: The relational worlds of adolescent girls at Emma Willard School.* Cambridge, MA: Harvard University Press.

Gilligan, Carol, and **Attanucci, J.** (1988). Two moral orientations: Gender differences and similarities. *Merrill-Palmer Quarterly, 34,* 223–237.

Gilligan, Carol, and **Belensky, M.F.** (1980). A naturalistic study of abortion decisions. In R. Sleman and R. Yando (Eds.), *New directions for child development: Clinical developmental psychology.* San Francisco: Jossey-Bass.

Gilligan, Carol, and **Murphy, John M.** (1979). Development from adolescence to adulthood: The philosopher and the dilemma of the fact. In William Damon (Ed.), *New Directions for Child Development* (Vol. 5). San Francisco: Jossey-Bass.

Gilligan, Carol, Murphy, John M., and **Tappan, Mark B.** (1990). Moral development beyond adolescence. In Charles N. Alexander and Ellen J. Langer (Eds.), *Higher stages of human development.* New York: Oxford University Press.

Gittelman, R., Mannuzza, S., Shenker, R., and **Bonagura, N.** (1985). Hyperactive boys almost grown up: Psychiatric status. *Archives of General Psychiatry, 42,* 937–947.

Glass, Jennifer. (1992). Housewives and employed wives: Demographic and attitudinal change. *Journal of Marriage and the Family, 54,* 559–569.

Gleason, Jean Berko. (1967). Do children imitate? *Proceedings of the International Conference on Oral Education of the Deaf, 2,* 1441–1448.

Glenn, Norval D. (1991). The recent trend in marital success in the United States. *Journal of Marriage and the Family, 53,* 261–270.

Glenn, Norval D., and **Weaver, Charles N.** (1988). The changing relationship of marital status to reported happiness. *Journal of Marriage and the Family, 50,* 317–324.

Glick, Paul C., and **Lin, Sung-Ling.** (1986). Recent changes in divorce and remarriage. *Journal of Marriage and the Family, 48,* 737–748.

Glidden, Laraine Mastes. (1991). Adopted children with developmental disabilities: Post-placement family functioning. *Children and Youth Services Review, 13,* 363–377.

Gnepp, Jackie, and **Chilamkurti, Chinni.** (1988). Children's use of personality attributions to predict other people's emotional and behavioral reactions. *Child Development, 59,* 743–754.

Goedert, James J., Mendez, Hermann, Drummond, James E., Robert-Guroff, Marjorie, Minkoff, Howard L., Holman, Susan, Stevens, Roy, Rubinstein, Arye, Blattner, William A., Willoughby, Anne, and **Landesman, Sheldon H.** (1989). Mother-to-infant transmission of human immunodeficiency virus type I: Association with prematurity or low anti-gp120. *The Lancet, 335,* 1351–1354.

Goetz, T.E., and **Dweck, Carol.** (1980). Learned helplessness in social situations. *Journal of Personality and Social Psychology, 39,* 246–255.

Goggin, Judith M. (1992). Elderhostel: The next generation. *Aging Today, 13* (2), 8.

Gold, Herbert. (1987). Social ecology. In Herbert C. Quay (Ed.), *Handbook of juvenile delinquency.* New York: Wiley.

Goldberg, W.A., and **Easterbrooks, M.A.** (1984). Role of marital quality in toddler development. *Developmental Psychology, 20,* 504–514.

Goldberg, Wendy A. (1990). Marital quality, parental personality, and spousal agreement about perceptions and expectations for children. *Merrill Palmer Quarterly, 36,* 531–556.

Goldberg-Reitman, Jill. (1992). Young girls' conception of their mother's role: A neo-structural analysis. In Robbie Case (Ed.), *The mind's staircase: Exploring the conceptual underpinning of children's thought and knowledge.* Hillsdale, NJ: Erlbaum.

Goldhaber, M.K., Polen, M.R., and **Hiatt, Robert A.** (1988). The risk of miscarriage and birth defect among women who use visual display terminals during pregnancy. *American Journal of Industrial Medicine, 13,* 685–706.

Goldman, Connie. (1991). Late bloomers: Growing older or still growing? *Generations, 15,* 41–44.

Goldsmith, H. Hill, Buss, Arnold H., Plomin, Robert, Rothbart, Mary Klevjord, Thomas, Alexander, Chess, Stella, Hinde, Robert A., and **McCall, Robert B.** (1987). Roundtable: What is temperament? Four approaches. *Child Development, 58,* 505–529.

Goldstein, Beth L. (1990). Refugee students' perception of curriculum differentiation. In Rebe Page and Linda Valli (Eds.), *Curriculum differentiation: Interpretive studies in U.S. secondary schools.* Albany, NY: SUNY Press.

Goldstein, Harold. (1984). Changing structure of work: Occupational trends and implications. In Norman C. Gysbers (Ed.), *Designing careers.* San Francisco: Jossey-Bass.

Golinkoff, Roberta Michnick, Hirsh-Pasak, Kathy, Bailey, Leslie M., and **Wenger, Neill R.** (1992). Young children and adult use lexical principles to learn new nouns. *Developmental Psychology, 28,* 99–108.

Gonsiorek, John C., and **Weinrich, James D.** (1991). The definition and scope of sexual orientation. In John C. Gonsiorek and

James D. Weinrich (Eds.), *Homosexuality: Research implications for public policy.* Newbury Park, CA: Sage.

Goode, W.J. (1956). *After divorce.* Glencoe, IL: The Free Press.

Goodman, N.C. (1987). Girls with learning disabilities and their sisters: How are they faring in adulthood? *Journal of Clinical Child Psychology, 16,* 290–300.

Goodnow, Jacqueline J., and **Collins, W. Andrew.** (1990). *Development according to parents: The nature, sources, and consequences of parents' ideas.* Hillsdale, NJ: Erlbaum.

Goodwin, J. (1982). *Sexual abuse: Incest victims and their families.* Boston: John Wright.

Goodwin, Megan P., and **Roscoe, Bruce.** (1990). Sibling violence and agonistic interactions between middle adolescents. *Adolescence, 25,* 451–467.

Gordon, Debra Ellen. (1990). Formal operational thinking: The role of cognitive-developmental processes in adolescent decision-making about pregnancy and contraception. *American Journal of Orthopsychiatry, 60,* 346–356.

Gorer, Geoffrey. (1973). Death, grief, and mourning in Britain. In James E. Anthony and Cyrille Koupernik (Eds.), *The child in his family: The impact of disease and death.* New York: Wiley.

Gottesman, Irving I. (1991). *Schizophrenia genesis.* New York: Freeman.

Gottlieb, Gilbert, and **Krasnegor, Norman.** (1985). *Measurement of audition and vision in the first year of postnatal life: A methodological overview.* Cambridge, England: Cambridge University Press.

Gottlieb, Jay, and **Leyser, Yona.** (1981). Friendship between mentally retarded and nonretarded children. In Steven R. Asher and John M. Gottman (Eds.), *The development of children's friendships.* Cambridge, England: Cambridge University Press.

Gottman, John M. (1983). How children become friends. *Monographs of the Society for Research in Child Development, 48* (3, Serial No. 201).

Gould, Roger L. (1978). *Transformations: Growth and change in adult life.* New York: Simon and Schuster.

Graff, H. (1987). *The labyrinths of literacy: Reflections on literacy past and present.* London: Falmer Press.

Grant, James P. (1982). *The state of the world's children: 1982–1983.* New York: UNICEF and Oxford University Press.

Grant, James P. (1986). *The state of the world's children.* Oxford, England: Oxford University Press.

Gratch, Gerald, and **Schatz, Joseph.** (1987). Cognitive development: The relevance of Piaget's infancy books. In Joy Doniger Osofsky (Ed.), *Handbook of infant development* (2nd ed.). New York: Wiley.

Gray, William M., and **Hudson, Lynne M.** (1984). Formal operations and the imaginary audience. *Developmental Psychology, 20,* 619–627.

Green, A.L., and **Boxer, Andres M.** (1986). Daughters and sons as young adults. In Nancy Datan, Anita Greene, and Hayne W. Reese (Eds.), *Life-span developmental psychology: Intergenerational relations.* Hillsdale, NJ: Erlbaum.

Greenberger, Ellen, and **Goldberg, Wendy A.** (1989). Work, parenting, and the socialization of children. *Developmental Psychology, 25,* 22–35.

Greer, Germaine. (1986, May). Letting go. *Vogue, 176,* 141–143.

Greer, Jane. (1992). *Adult sibling rivalry.* New York: Crown.

Grinker, Joel A. (1981). Behavioral and metabolic factors in childhood obesity. In Michael Lewis and Leonard A. Rosenblum (Eds.), *The uncommon child.* New York: Plenum Press.

Grossman, Frances K., Pollack, William S., and **Golding, Ellen.** (1988). Fathers and children: Predicting the quality and quantity of fathering. *Developmental Psychology, 24,* 82–91.

Grotevant, Harold D., and **Cooper, Catherine R.** (1985). Patterns of interaction in family relationships and the development of identity exploration in adolescence. *Child Development, 56,* 415–428.

Guelzow, Maureen G., Bird, Gloria W., and **Kobal, Elizabeth, H.** (1991). Analysis of the stress process for dual-career men and women. *Journal of Marriage and the Family, 53,* 151–164.

Gump, Paul V. (1989). Ecological psychology and issues of play. In Marianne N. Bloch and Anthony D. Pellegrini (Eds.), *The ecological context of children's play.* Norwood, NJ: Ablex.

Gunzenhauser, Nina (Ed.). (1990). *Advances in touch: New implications in human development.* Skillman, NJ: Johnson and Johnson.

Gurin, G., Veroff, J., and **Feld, S.** (1960). *Americans view their mental health.* New York: Basic Books.

Guthrie, Sharon R. (1991). Prevalence of eating disorders among intercollegiate athletes: Contributing factors and preventative measures. In David R. Black (Ed.), *Eating disorders among athletes.* Reston, VA: American Alliance for Health, Physical Education, Recreation and Dance.

Gutmann, David. (1975). Parenthood: Key to the comparative psychology of the life cycle. In Nancy Datan and L. Ginsberg (Eds.), *Life span developmental psychology.* New York: Academic Press.

Gutmann, David. (1987). *Reclaimed powers: Toward a new psychology of men and women in later life.* New York: Basic Books.

Haan, Norma. (1981). Adolescents and young adults as producers of their development. In Richard M. Lerner and Nancy A. Busch-Rossnagel (Eds.), *Individuals as producers of their development: A life-span approach.* New York: Academic Press.

Haan, Norma. (1985a). Common personality dimensions or common organizations across the life span. In Joep M.A. Munnichs, Paul H. Mussen, Erhard Olbrich, and Peter G. Coleman (Eds.), *Life span and change in a gerontological perspective.* Orlando, FL: Academic Press.

Haan, Norma. (1985b). Processes of moral development: Cognitive or social disequilibrium. *Developmental Psychology, 21,* 996–1006.

Haan, Norma, Millsap, R., and **Hartka, E.** (1986). As time goes by: Change and stability in personality over fifty years. *Psychology and Aging, 1,* 220–232.

Hackman, J. Richard. (1986). The psychology of self-management in organizations. In Michael S. Pallak and Robert O. Perloff (Eds.) *Psychology and work.* Washington, DC: American Psychological Association.

Hagestad, G.O. (1986). The aging society as a context for family life. *Daedalus, 115,* 119–139.

Hagestad, G.O. (1988). Demographic change and the life course: Some emerging trends in the family realm. *Family Relations, 37,* 405–410.

Hahn, Martin E., and **Benno, Robert H.** (1990). Integrative approaches to the study of behavior. In Martin E. Hahn, John K. Hewitt, Norman D. Henderson, and Robert H. Benno (Eds.), *Developmental behavior genetics: Neural, biometrical, and evolutionary approaches.* Oxford, England: Oxford University Press.

Hakuta, K. (1986). *Mirror of language.* New York: Basic Books.

Hale, Janice E. (1982). *Black children: Their roots, culture, and learning styles.* Provo, UT: Brigham Young University Press.

Hale, Sanora, Myerson, Joel, and **Wagstaff, David.** (1987). General slowing of non-verbal information processing: Evidence for a power law. *Journal of Gerontology, 42,* 131–136.

Hall, G. Stanley. (1904). *Adolescence: Its psychology and its relations to physiology, anthropology, sociology, sex, crime, religion and education.* New York: Appleton.

Halliday, M.A.K. (1979). One child's protolanguage. In Margaret Bullowa (Ed.), *Before speech: The beginning of interpersonal communication.* Cambridge, England: Cambridge University Press.

Hamon, Raeann R., and **Blieszner, Rosemary.** (1990). Filial responsibility expectations among adult child-older parent pairs. *Journal of Gerontology: Psychological Sciences, 45,* 110–112.

Hans, Sydney L. (1989). Developmental consequences of prenatal exposure to methadone. In Donald Hutchings (Ed.), *Prenatal abuse of licit and illicit drugs.* New York: New York Academy of Sciences.

Hanson, David J., Conaway, Loren, P. and **Christopher, Jeanette Smitt.** (1989). Victims of child physical abuse. In Robert T. Ammerman and Micheal Hersen (Eds.), *Treatment of family violence.* New York: Wiley.

Hanson, James W., Streissguth, Ann P., and **Smith, David W.** (1978). The effects of moderate alcohol consumption during pregnancy on fetal growth and morphogenesis. *Journal of Pediatrics, 92,* 457–460.

Hanson, Sandra L., Myers, David E., and **Ginsberg, Alan L.** (1987). The role of responsibility and knowledge in reducing teenage out-of-wedlock childbearing. *Journal of Marriage and the Family, 49,* 241–256.

Hanson, Susan. (1990). The college preparatory curriculum across schools: Access to similar opportunities? In Reba Page and Linda Valli (Eds.), *Curriculum differentiation: Interpretive studies in U.S. secondary schools.* Albany, NY: SUNY Press.

Hardy, Janet B., Duggan, Anne K., Masnyk, Katya, and **Pearson, Carol.** (1989). Fathers of children born to young urban mothers. *Family Planning Perspectives, 21,* 159–163.

Hardy, John A., and **Higgins, Gerald A.** (1992). Alzheimer's disease: The amyloid cascade hypothesis. *Science, 256,* 184–185.

Hardy, Melissa. (1985). Occupational structure and retirement. In Zena Smith Blau (Ed.), *Current perspectives on aging and the life cycle: Work retirement and social policy.* Greenwich, CT: JAI.

Haring-Hidore, Marilyn, Stock, William A., Okun, Morris A., and **Witter, Robert A.** (1985). Marital status and subjective well-being: A research synthesis. *Journal of Marriage and the Family, 47,* 947–953.

Harley, B., Allen, P., Cummins, Jim, and **Swain, M.** (1987). *Final report. The development of bilingual proficiency study.* Toronto: Ontario Institute for Studies in Education.

Harman, Denham. (1984). Free radicals and the origination, evolution, and present status of the free radical theory of aging. In Donald Armstrong, R.S. Sohol, Richard G. Cutler, and Trevor P. Slater (Eds.), *Free radicals in molecular biology, aging, and disease.* New York: Raven Press.

Harman, S.M. (1978). Clinical aspects of the male reproductive system. In E.L. Schneider (Ed.), *Aging: Vol. 4. The aging reproductive system.* New York: Raven Press.

Harper, Lawrence V., and **Sanders, Karen M.** (1975). Preschool children's use of space: Sex differences in outdoor play. *Developmental Psychology, 11,* 119.

Harper, Rita G., and **Yoon, Ing (Jing) Ja.** (1987). *Handbook of neonatology* (2nd ed.). Chicago: Year Book Medical Publishers.

Harrington, Michael. (1962). *The other America: Poverty in the United States.* New York: Macmillan.

Harris, P.L. (1987). The development of search. In Philip Salapatek and Leslie Cohen (Eds.), *Handbook of infant perception: Vol. 2. From perception to cognition.* Orlando, FL: Academic Press.

Harris, P.L., Olthof, T., and **Meerum Terwogt, M.** (1981). Children's knowledge of emotion. *Journal of Child Psychology and Psychiatry, 22,* 247–261.

Harris, Paul L., Brown, Emma, Marriott, Crispin, Whittal, Semantha and **Harmer, Sarah.** (1991). Monsters, ghosts, and witches: Testing the limits of the fantasy-reality disctinction in young children. *British Journal of Developmental Psychology, 9,* 105–123.

Harris, Raymond. (1986). *Clinical geriatric cardiology.* Philadelphia: Lippincott.

Harrison, Algea O., Wilson, Melvin N., Pine, Charles J., Chan, Samuel Q., and **Bureil, Raymond.** (1990). Family ecologies of minority children. *Child Development, 61,* 347–362.

Harrison, David E. (1990). *Genetic effects on aging II.* Caldwell, NJ: Telford.

Harrison, James B. (1984). Warning: The male sex role may be dangerous to your health. In Janice M. Swanson and Katherine A. Forrest (Eds.), *Men's reproductive health.* New York: Springer-Verlag.

Hart, Craig G., Ladd, Gary W., and **Burelson, Brant R.** (1990). Children's expectations of the outcomes of social strategies: Relations with sociometric status and maternal disciplinary styles. *Child Development, 61,* 127–137.

Hart, Stuart N., and **Brassard, Marla R.** (1991). Psychological maltreatment: Progress achieved. *Development and Psychopathology, 3,* 61–70.

Harter, Susan. (1982). Children's understanding of multiple emotions: A cognitive developmental approach. In W.F. Overton (Ed.), *The relationship between social and cognitive development.* Hillsdale, NJ: Erlbaum.

Harter, Susan. (1983). Developmental perspectives on the self-system. In Paul H. Mussen (Ed.), *Handbook of child psychology: Vol. 4. Socialization, personality and social development.* New York: Wiley.

Harter, Susan. (1990). Processes underlying adolescent self-concept formation. In Raymond Montemayor, Gerald R. Adams, and Thomas P. Gullotta (Eds.), *From childhood to adolescence: A transitional period?* Newbury Park, CA: Sage.

Harter, Susan, and **Pike, Robin.** (1984). The pictorial scale of perceived competence and social acceptance for young children. *Child Development, 55,* 1969–1982.

Harter, Susan, and **Ward, C.** (1978). A factor-analysis of Coopersmith's self-esteem inventory. Unpublished manuscript, University of Denver. (Cited in Harter, 1983).

Harter, Susan, and **Whitesell, N.R.** (1989). Developmental changes in children's understanding of single, multiple, and blended emotion concepts. In C. Saarni and P.L. Harris (Eds.), *Children's understanding of emotion.* Cambridge, England: Cambridge University Press.

Hartshorne, Hugh, May, Mark A., and **Maller, J.B.** (1929). *Studies in service and self-control.* New York: Macmillan.

Hartsough, Carolyn S., and **Lambert, Nadine M.** (1985). Medical factors in hyperactive and normal children: Prenatal, developmental, and health history findings. *American Journal of Orthopsychiatry, 55,* 190–201.

Hartup, Willard W. (1974). Aggression in childhood: Developmental perspectives. *American Psychologist, 29,* 336–341.

Hartup, Willard W. (1983). Peer relations. In Paul H. Mussen (Ed.), *Handbook of child psychology: Vol. 4. Socialization, personality and social development.* New York: Wiley.

Hartup, Willard W., Laursen, B., Stewart, M.I., and **Eastenson, A.** (1988). Conflict and the friendship relations of young children. *Child Development, 59,* 1590–1600.

Haskett, Mary E., and **Kistner, Janet A.** (1991). Social interactions and peer perceptions of young physically abused children. *Child Development, 62,* 979–990.

Haskins, Ron. (1989). Beyond metaphor: The efficacy of early childhood education. *American Psychologist, 44,* 274–282.

Hass, Aaron. (1979). *Teenage sexuality: A survey of teenage sexual behavior.* New York: Macmillan.

Hatch, Laurie Russell, and **Bulcroft, Chris.** (1992). Contact with friends in later life: Disentangling the effects of gender and marital stability. *Journal of Marriage and the Family, 54,* 222–232.

Hatfield, Elaine. (1988). Theories of romantic love. In Robert J. Sternberg and Michael L. Barnes (Eds.), *The psychology of love.* New Haven, CT: Yale.

Hausman, Perrie B., and **Weksler, Marc E.** (1985). Changes in the immune response with age. In Caleb E. Finch and Edward L. Schneider (Eds.), *Handbook of the biology of aging* (2nd ed.). New York: Van Nostrand.

Havik, Richard J. (1991). Physical, social, and mental vitality. *Proceedings of the 1988 International Symposium on Aging,* Series 5, No. 6. (DHHS Publication No. 91–1482). Hyattsville, MD: United States Department of Health and Human Services.

Haviland, J.M., and **Lelwica, M.** (1987). The induced affect response: 10-week-old infants' responses to three emotion expressions. *Developmental Psychology, 23,* 97–104.

Havlik, Richard J. (1991). Physical, social and mental vitality. *Proceedings of the 1988 International symposium on aging.* Series 5, No. 6. (DHHS Publication No. 91-1482). Hyattsville, MD:United States Department of Health and Human Services.

Hawkins, Alan J., and **Eggebeen, David J.** (1991). Are fathers fungible? *Journal of Marriage and the Family.* 958–972.

Hay, D.F., and **Ross, H.S.** (1982). The social nature of early conflict. *Child Development, 53,* 105–113.

Hayachi, Y., and **Endo, S.** (1982). All-night sleep polygraphic recordings of healthy aged persons: REM and slow wave sleep. *Sleep, 5,* 277–283.

Hayden-Thompson, Laura, Rubin, Kenneth H., and **Hymel, Shelley.** (1987). Sex preferences in sociometric choices. *Developmental Psychology, 23,* 558–562.

Hayes, Cheryl (Ed.). (1987). *Risking the future.* Washington, DC: National Academy Press.

Hayflick, Leonard. (1979). Cell aging. In Arthur Cherkin (Ed.), *Physiology and cell biology of aging.* New York: Raven Press.

Hayflick, Leonard, and **Moorhead, Paul S.** (1961). The serial cultivation of human diploid cell strains. *Experimental Cell Research, 25,* 585.

Hayne, Harleen, Rovee-Collier, Carolyn, and **Perris, Eve E.** (1987). Categorization and memory retrieval by three-month-olds. *Child Development, 58,* 750–767.

Heap, Kari Killen. (1991). A predictive and follow-up study of abusive and neglectful families by case analysis. *Child Abuse and Neglect, 15,* 261–273.

Heath, Shirley Brice. (1989). Oral and literate traditions among Black Americans living in poverty. *American Psychologist, 44,* 367–373.

Heaton, Tim, and **Albrecht, Stan L.** (1991). Stable unhappy marriages. *Journal of Marriage and the Family, 53,* 747–758.

Heckler, Margaret H. (1985). *Black and minority health.* U.S. Department of Health and Human Services. Washington, DC: U.S. Government.

Hein, Karen. (1993). "Getting real" about HIV in adolescents. *American Journal of Public Health, 83,* 492–493.

Helson, Ravenna. (1992). Women's difficult times and the rewriting of the life story. *Psychology of Women Quarterly, 16,* 331–347.

Helson, Ravenna, and **Moane, Geraldine.** (1987). Personality change in women from college to midlife. *Journal of Personality and Social Psychology, 52,* 1176–1186.

Hemmings, Annette, and **Metz, Mary Haywood.** (1990). Real teaching: How high school teachers negotiate societal, local community, and student pressures when they define their work. In Reba Page and Linda Valli (Eds.), *Curriculum differentiation: Interpretive studies in U.S. secondary schools.* Albany, NY: SUNY Press.

Henker, B., and **Whalen, C.K.** (1989). Hyperactivity and attention deficits. *American Psychologist, 44,* 216–223.

Herman, Judith. (1981). *Father-daughter incest.* Cambridge, MA: Harvard University Press.

Herron, Robert E., and **Sutton-Smith, Brian.** (1971). *Child's play.* New York: Wiley.

Herzog, Christopher, Dixon, Roger A., and **Hultsch, David F.** (1990). Metamemory in adulthood: Differentiating knowledge, belief, and behavior. In Thomas M. Hess (Ed.), *Aging and cognition: Knowledge organization and utilization.* North-Holland: Elsevier.

Herzog, Christopher, Raskind, Cheryl L., and **Cannon, Constance J.** (1986). Age-related slowing in semantic information-processing speed: An individual difference analysis. *Journal of Gerontology, 41,* 500–512.

Herzog, Regula A. (1991). Measurement of vitality in the American's Changing Lives study. *Proceedings of the 1988 International Symposium on Aging.* Series 5, No. 6. (DHHS Publication No. 91–1482). Hyattsville, MD: United States Department of Health and Human Services.

Herzog, Regula A., and **House, James S.** (1991). Productive activities and aging well. *Generations, 15* (1), 49–54.

Herzog, Regula A., House, James S., and **Morgan, James N.**

(1991). Relation of work and retirement to health and well-being in older age. *Psychology and Aging, 6,* 202–211.

Hetherington, E. Mavis. (1989). Coping with family transitions: Winners, losers, and survivors. *Child Development, 60,* 1–14.

Hetherington, E. Mavis, and Camara, Kathleen A. (1984). Families in transition: The process of dissolution and reconstitution. In Ross D. Parke (Ed.), *Review of child development research* (Vol. 7). Chicago: University of Chicago Press.

Hetherington, E. Mavis, and Clingempeel, W. Glenn. (1992). Coping with marital transitions. *Monographs of the Society for Research in Child Development, 57* (2–3, Serial No. 227).

Hetherington, E. Mavis, and McIntyre, C.W. (1975). Developmental psychology. In M.R. Rosenzweig and L.W. Porter (Eds.), *Annual Review of Psychology.* Palo Alto, CA: Annual Reviews.

Hetherington, E. Mavis, Hagan, Margaret Stanley, and Anderson, Edward R. (1989). Marital transitions: A child's perspective. *American Psychologist, 44,* 303–312.

Hewitt, Paul. (1986). *A broken promise.* Washington, DC: Americans for Generational Equity.

Heyman, Gail D., Dweck, Carol S., and Cain, Kathleen M. (1992). Young children's vulnerability to self-blame and helplessness: Relationship to beliefs about goodness. *Child Development, 63,* 401–415.

Hiebeck, Tracy H., and Markman, Ellen M. (1987). Word learning in children: an examination of fast mapping. *Child Development, 58,* 1021–1034.

Higgins, E. Tory. (1981). Role taking and social judgment: Alternative developmental perspectives and processes. In John H. Flavell and Lee Ross (Eds.), *Social cognitive development: Frontiers and possible futures.* Cambridge, England: Cambridge University Press.

Hill, John, and Holmbeck, G.N. (1987). Familial adaptation to biological change during adolescence. In Richard M. Lerner and Terryl T. Foch (Eds.), *Biological-psychosocial interactions in early adolescence.* Hillsdale, NJ: Erlbaum.

Hilts, Philip J. (1991, October 8). Lower lead limits are made official. *New York Times,* C3.

Hingson, R.J., Alpert, N., Day, E., Dooling, H., Kayne, S., Morelock, E., Oppenheimer, E., and Zuckerman, B. (1982). Effects of maternal drinking and marijuana use on fetal growth and development. *Pediatrics, 70,* 539–546.

Hirschi, Travis. (1969). *Causes of delinquency.* Berkeley, CA: University of California Press.

Hochschild, Arlie. (1989). *The second shift: Working parents and the revolution at home.* New York: Viking.

Hoff-Ginsberg, Erica. (1991). Mother-child conversation in different social classes and communicative settings. *Child Development, 62,* 782–796.

Hoffman, Lois Wladis. (1989). Effects of maternal employment in the two-parent family. *American Psychologist, 44,* 283–292.

Hoffman, Michelle. (1991). How parents make their mark on genes. *Science, 252,* 1250–1251.

Holden, Constance. (1980). Identical twins reared apart. *Science, 207,* 1323–1328.

Holden, Constance. (1987). OTA cites financial disaster of Alzheimer's. *Science, 236,* 253.

Hollander, P. (1982). Legal context of educational testing. In National Research Council, Committee on Ability Testing, *Ability testing: Uses, consequences and controversies.* Washington, DC: National Academy Press.

Holroyd, K.A., and Boyne, J. (1984). The health belief model: A decade later. *Journal of Personality, 55,* 359–375.

Holzman, Mathilda. (1983). *The language of children: Development in home and in school.* Englewood Cliffs, NJ: Prentice-Hall.

Holzman, Philip S., and Matthyusse, Steven. (1990). The genetics of schizophrenia: A review. *Psychological Science, 1,* 279–286.

Homer, Paul, and Holstein, Martha. (1990). *A good old age? The paradox of setting limits.* New York: Simon and Schuster.

Honig, Alice Sterling. (1987). The shy child. *Young Children, 42,* 54–64.

Hopwood, Nancy J., Kelch, Robert P., Hale, Paula M., Mendes, Tarina M., Foster, Carol M., and Beitins, Inese Z. (1990). The onset of human puberty: Biological and environmental factors. In John Bancroft and June Machover Reinisch (Eds.), *Adolescence and puberty.* New York: Oxford University Press.

Horn, John L. (1976). Human abilities: A review of research and theory in the early 1970's. *Annual Review of Psychology, 27,* 437–485.

Horn, John L. (1982). The aging of human abilities. In Benjamin B. Wolman (Ed.), *Handbook of developmental psychology.* Englewood Cliffs, NJ: Prentice-Hall.

Horn, John L. (1985). Remodeling old models of intelligence. In Benjamin B. Wolman (Ed.), *Handbook of intelligence: Theories, measurements, and applications.* New York: Wiley.

Horn, John L., and Donaldson, Gary. (1976). On the myth of intellectual decline in adulthood. *American Psychologist, 31,* 701–719.

Horn, John L., and Donaldson, Gary. (1977). Faith is not enough: A response to the Baltes-Schaie claim that intelligence does not wane. *American Psychologist, 32,* 369–373.

Horn, John L., and Hofer, Scott M. (1992). Major abilities and development in the adult period. In Robert J. Sternberg and Cynthia A. Berg (Eds.), *Intellectual development.* New York: Cambridge University Press.

Horney, Karen. (1967). *Feminine psychology.* Harold Kelman (Ed.). New York: Norton.

Horwitz, A., Macfadyen, D.M., Munro, H., Scrimshaw, N.S., Steen, B., and Williams, T.F. (Eds.). (1989). *Nutrition in the elderly.* Oxford, England: Oxford University Press.

Howard, Anne. (1992). Work and family crossroads spanning the career. In Sheldon Zedeck (Ed.), *Work, families and organizations.* San Francisco: Jossey-Bass.

Howard, Darlene V., Heisy, Jane Gillette, and Shaw, Raymond J. (1986). Aging and the priming of newly learned associations. *Developmental Psychology, 22,* 78–85.

Howard, Marion, and McCabe, Judith Blamey. (1990). Helping teenagers postpone sexual involvement. *Family Planning Perspectives, 22,* 21–26.

Howes, C. (1987). Social competence with peers in young children: Developmental sequences. *Developmental Review, 7,* 252–272.

Hoyer, William J., and Plude, Dana J. (1980). Attentional and perceptual processes in the study of cognitive aging. In Leonard W. Poon (Ed.), *Aging in the 1980's: Psychological is-*

sues. Washington, DC: American Psychological Association.

Hsu, Jeng M., and **Smith, James C.** (1984). B-vitamins and ascorbic acid in the aging process. In J. Marc Ordy, Denham Harman, and Roslyn B. Alfin-Slater (Eds.), *Nutrition in gerontology*. New York: Raven Press.

Hsu, L.K. George. (1990). *Eating disorders*. New York: Guilford.

Hudson, Judith A. (1986). Memories are made of this: General event knowledge and development of autobiographic memory. In Katherine Nelson (Ed.), *Event knowledge: Structure and function in development*. Hillsdale, NJ: Erlbaum.

Hughes, Diane, Galinsky, Ellen, and **Morris, Anne.** (1992). The effects of job characteristics on marital quality: Specifying linking mechanisms.

Hughes, Martin, and **Donaldson, Margaret.** (1979). The use of hiding games for studying coordination of viewpoints. *Educational Review, 31,* 133–140.

Hughes, Martin, and **Grieve, Robert.** (1980). On asking children bizarre questions. *First Language, 1,* 149–160.

Hull, Valerie, Thapa, Shyam, and **Pratomo, Hadi.** (1990). Breast-feeding in the modern health sector in Indonesia: The mother's perspective. *Social Science and Medicine, 30,* 625–633.

Hultsch, David F., and **Dixon, Roger A.** (1990). Learning and memory in aging. In James E. Birren and K. Warner Schaie (Eds.), *Handbook of the psychology of aging*. San Diego, CA: Academic Press.

Humphreys, Anne P., and **Smith, Peter K.** (1987). Rough and tumble, friendship, and dominance in schoolchildren: Evidence for continuity and change with age. *Child Development, 58,* 201–212.

Hunt, M.E., and **Ross, L.** (1990). Naturally-occurring retirement communities: A multiattribute examination of desirability factors. *Gerontologist, 30,* 667–674.

Hunter, Fumiyo Tao. (1985). Adolescents' perception of discussion with parents and friends. *Developmental Psychology, 21,* 433–440.

Hunter, Laura Russell, and **Membard, Polly Hunter.** (1981). *The rest of my life*. Stamford, CT: Growing Pains Press.

Hunter, Mic. (1990). *Abused boys: The neglected victims of sexual abuse*. Lexington, MA: Lexington Books.

Hurrelmann, K., and **Engel, W.** (1989). *The social world of adolescents: International perspectives*. Berlin: Walter de Gruyter.

Huston, Aletha C. (1983). Sex-typing. In Paul H. Mussen (Ed.), *Handbook of child psychology: Vol. 4. Socialization, personality and social development*. New York: Wiley.

Huston, Aletha C. (1985). The development of sex-typing: Themes from recent research. *Developmental Review, 5,* 1–17.

Huston, Aletha C., and **Alvarez, Mildred A.** (1990). The socialization context of gender-role development in early adolescents. In Raymond Montemayor, Gerald R. Adams, and Thomas P. Gullotta (Eds.), *From childhood to adolescence: A transitional period?* Newbury Park, CA: Sage.

Huston, Aletha C., Watkins, Bruca A., and **Kunkel, Dale.** (1989). Public policy and children's television. *American Psychologist, 44,* 424–433.

Huttenlocher, Janellen, Waight, Wendy, Bryk, Anthony, Seltzer, Michael, and **Lyons, Thomas.** (1991). Early vocabulary growth: Relation to language input and gender. *Child Development, 27,* 236–248.

Hyde, Kenneth E. (1990). *Religion in childhood and adolescence: A comprehensive review of the research*. Birmingham, AL: Religious Education Press.

Hynd, George W., Hern, Kelly L. Voeller, Kytja K., and **Marshall, Richard M.** (1991). Neurobiological basis of attention-deficit hyperactivity disorder. *School Psychology Review, 20,* 174–186.

Iber, Frank L. (1990). Alcoholism and associated malnutrition in the elderly. In Derek M. Prinsley and Harold H. Sandstread (Eds.), *Nutrition and aging*. New York: Liss.

Imbert, Michel. (1985). Physiological underpinnings of perceptual development. In Jacques Mehler and Robin Fox (Eds.), *Neonate cognition: Beyond the blooming confusion*. Hillsdale, NJ: Erlbaum.

Inclan, Jaime, and **Hernandez, Miguel.** (1992). Cross-cultural perspectives and codependence: The case of poor Hispanics. *American Journal of Orthopsychiatry, 62,* 245–255.

Ingleby, David. (1987). Psychoanalysis and ideology. In John M. Broughton (Ed.), *Critical theories of psychological development*. New York: Plenum.

Inhelder, Bärbel, and **Piaget, Jean.** (1958). *The growth of logical thinking from childhood to adolescence*. New York: Basic Books.

International Assessment of Educational Progress. (1989). *A world of differences: An international assessment of math and science*.

Isabella, Russell A., and **Belsky, Jay.** (1991). Interactional synchrony and the origins of infant-mother attachment: A replication study. *Child Development, 62,* 373-384.

Israel, A.C., and **Shapiro, L.S.** (1985). Behavior problems of obese children enrolling in a weight reduction program. *Journal of Pediatric Psychology, 10,* 449–460.

Izard, C.E. (1980). *The maximally discriminative facial movement scoring system*. Unpublished manuscript, University of Delaware.

Izard, C.E., and **Malatesta, C.Z.** (1987). Perspectives on emotional development I: Differential emotions theory of early emotional development. In Joy Doniger Osofsky (Ed.), *Handbook of infant development* (2nd ed.). New York: Wiley.

Izard, C.E., Hembree, E.A., and **Huebner, R.R.** (1987). Infants' emotional expressions to acute pain: Developmental change and stability of individual differences. *Developmental Psychology, 23,* 105–113.

Izard, Carroll E., Porges, Stephen W., Simons, Robert F., Maynes, O. Maurice, and **Cohen, Ben.** (1991). Infant cardiac activity: Developmental changes and relations with attachment. *Developmental Psychology, 27,* 432–439.

Jacklin, Carol Nagy, Wilcox, K.T., and **Maccoby, Eleanor E.** (1988). Neonatal sex-steroid hormone and intellectual abilities of six-year-old boys and girls. *Developmental Psychobiology, 21,* 567–574.

Jackson, Sonia. (1987). Great Britain. In Michael E. Lamb (Ed.), *The father's role: Cross cultural perspectives*. Hillsdale, NJ: Erlbaum.

Jacobs, Bruce. (1990). Aging and politics. In Robert H. Binstock and Linda K. George (Eds.), *Handbook of aging and the social sciences* (3rd ed.). San Diego, CA: Academic Press.

Jacobs, Selby C., Kosten, Thomas R., Kasl, Stanislav V., Ostfeld, Adrian M., and **Berkman, Lisa.** (1987–1988). Attachment theory and multiple expressions of grief. *Omega, 18,* 41–52.

Jacobson, Joseph L., and **Jacobson, Sandra W.** (1990). Methodological issues in human behavioral teratology. In Carolyn Rovee-Collier and Lewis P. Lipsitt (Eds.), *Advances in infancy research* (Vol. 6). Norwood, NJ: Ablex.

Jacobson, Joseph L., Boersma, David C., Fields, Robert B., and **Olson, Karen L.** (1983). Paralinguistic features of adult speech to infants and small children. *Child Development, 54,* 436–442.

Jacobson, Joseph L., Jacobson, Sandra W., Fein, Greta G., Schwartz, Pamela M., and **Dowler, Jeffrey K.** (1984). Prenatal exposure to an environmental toxin: A test of multiple effects. *Developmental Psychology, 20,* 523–532.

Jacobson, Sandra W., and **Frye, Karen F.** (1991). Effect of maternal social support on attachment: Experimental evidence. *Child Development, 62,* 572–582.

Jahoda, Marie. (1981). Work, employment, and unemployment. *American Psychologist, 36,* 184–191.

James, Sherman, Keenan, Nora L., and **Browning, Steve.** (1992). Socioeconomic status, health behaviors, and health status among Blacks. In K. Warner Schaie, Dan Blazer, and James S. House (Eds.), *Aging, health behaviors, and health outcomes.* Hillsdale, NJ: Erlbaum.

James, William. (1950). *The principles of psychology* (Vol. 1). New York: Dover. (Original work published 1890).

Jefferys, Margot (Ed.). (1989). *Growing old in the twentieth century.* London: Routledge.

Jelliffe, Derrick B., and **Jelliffe, E.F. Patrice.** (1977). Current concepts in nutrition: "Breast is best": Modern meanings. *New England Journal of Medicine, 297,* 912–915.

Jenkins, Jennifer. (1992). Sibling relationships in disharmonious homes: Potential difficulties and protective effects. In Fritz Boer and Judy Dunn (Eds.), *Children's sibling relationships: Developmental and clinical issues.* Hillsdale, NJ: Erlbaum.

Jessor, Richard, Donovan, John E., and **Costa, Frances M.** (1991). *Beyond adolescence: Problem behavior and young adult development.* Cambridge, England: Cambridge University Press.

John, O.P. (1990). The "Big Five" factor taxonomy: Dimensions of personality in the natural languages and in questionnaires. In L.A. Pervin (Ed.), *Handbook of personality: Theory and research.* New York: Guilford.

Johnson, Clifford M., Mirands, Leticia, Sherman, Arloc, and **Weill, James D.** (1991). *Child poverty in America.* Washington, DC: Children's Defense Fund.

Johnson, Colleen Leahy. (1985). The impact of illness on late-life marriages. *Journal of Marriage and the Family, 47,* 165–172.

Johnson, Craig, and **Conners, Mary E.** (1987). *The etiology and treatment of bulimia nervosa: A biopsychosocial perspective.* New York: Basic Books.

Johnson, Edward S., and **Meade, Ann C.** (1987). Developmental patterns of spatial ability: An early sex difference. *Child Development, 58,* 725–740.

Johnson, Harold R., Gibson, Rose C., and **Luckey, Irene.** (1990). Health and social characteristics. In Zev Brown, Edward A.

McKinney, and Michael Williams (Eds.), *Black aged.* Newbury Park, CA: Sage.

Johnson, Helen L., Glassman, Marc B., Fiks, Kathleen B., and **Rosen, Tove S.** (1990). Resilient children: Individual differences in developmental outcome of children born to drug users. *Journal of Genetic Psychology, 151,* 523–539.

Johnson, Russell R., Greenspan, Stephen, and **Brown, Gwyn M.** (1984). Children's ability to recognize and improve upon socially inept communications. *Journal of Genetic Psychology, 144,* 255–264.

Johnson, Tanya Fusco. (1991). *Elder mistreatment: Deciding who is at risk.* New York: Greenwood.

Johnson, Toni Cavanaugh. (1989). Female child perpetrators: Children who molest other children. *Child Abuse and Neglect, 13,* 571–585.

John-Steiner, Vera. (1986). *Notebooks of the mind: Explorations of thinking.* Albuquerque: University of New Mexico Press.

Johnston, Janet R., Kline, Marsha, and **Tschann, Jeanne.** (1989a). Ongoing post-divorce conflict in families contesting custody: Do joint custody and frequent access help? *American Journal of Orthopsychiatry, 59,* 576–592.

Johnston, Lloyd D., O'Malley, Patrick M., and **Bachman, Jerald G.** (1989b). *Drug use, drinking, and smoking: National survey results from high school, college, and young adult populations, 1975–1988.* Rockville, MD: National Institute for Drug Abuse.

Jondrow, J., Brechling, F., and **Marcu, A.** (1987). Older workers in the market for part-time employment. In S.H. Sandell (Ed.), *The problem isn't age: Work and older Americans.* New York: Praeger.

Jones, Celeste Pappas, and **Adamson, Lauren B.** (1987). Language use in mother-child and mother-child-sibling interactions. *Child Development, 58,* 356–366.

Jones, Elise F., Forrest, Jacqueline Darroch, Goldman, Noreen, Henshaw, Stanley, Lincoln, Richard, Rosoff, Jeannie I., Westoff, Charles F., and **Wulf, Deirdre.** (1986). *Teenage pregnancy in industrialized countries.* New Haven: Yale University Press.

Jones, Harold E., and **Conrad, Herbert S.** (1983). The growth and decline of intelligence: A study of a homogeneous group between the ages of ten and sixty. *Genetic Psychology Monographs, 13,* 223–298.

Jones, Lovell A. (1989). *Minorities and cancer.* New York: Springer-Verlag.

Jones, Mary Cover. (1957). The later careers of boys who were early- or late-maturing. *Child Development, 28,* 113–128.

Jones, Mary Cover. (1965). Psychological correlates of somatic development. *Child Development, 36,* 899–911.

Jones, Mary Cover, and **Bayley, Nancy.** (1950). Physical maturing among boys as related to behavior. *Journal of Educational Psychology, 41,* 129–248.

Jones, N. Burton. (1976). Rough-and-tumble play among nursery school children. In Jerome S. Bruner, Alison Jolly, and Kathy Sylva (Eds.), *Play.* New York: Basic Books.

Jones, Susan S., Smith, Linda B., and **Landau, Barbara.** (1991). Object properties and knowledge in early lexical learning. *Child Development, 62,* 499–516.

Juel-Nielsen, Neils. (1980). *Individual and environment: Monozygotic twins reared apart.* New York: International Universities Press.

Jung, Carl. (1933). *Modern man in search of a soul.* New York: Harvest.

Jurich, Anthony P., Polson, Cheryl J., Jurich, Julie A., and **Bates, Rodney A.** (1985). Family factors in the lives of drug users and abusers. *Adolescence, 20,* 143–159.

Kach, Nick, Mazurek, Kas, Patterson, Robert S., and **DeFaveri, Ivan.** (1991). *Essays on Canadian education.* Calgary, Alberta: Detselig.

Kagan, Jerome. (1984). *The nature of the child.* New York: Basic Books.

Kagan, Jerome. (1989). Temperamental contributions to social behavior. *American Psychologist, 44,* 668–674.

Kagan, Jerome, and **Snidman, Nancy.** (1991). Infant predictors of inhibited and uninhibited profiles. *Psychological Science, 2,* 40–44.

Kahn, Joan R., and **London, Kathryn A.** (1991). Premarital sex and the risk of divorce. *Journal of Marriage and the Family, 53,* 845–855.

Kail, R. (1990). *The development of memory in children* (3rd ed.). New York: Freeman.

Kalish, Richard A. (1985). The social context of death and dying. In Robert H. Binstock and Ethel Shanas (Eds.), *Handbook of aging and the social sciences.* New York: Van Nostrand Reinhold.

Kantrowitz, Barbara, Wingert, Pat, and **Hager, Mary.** (1988, May 16). Premies. *Newsweek.*

Kaplan, B.J., McNichol, J., Conte, R.A., and **Moghadam, H.K.** (1989). Overall nutrient intake of preschool hyperactive and normal boys. *Journal of Abnormal Child Psychology, 17,* 127–132.

Kaplan, Cynthia, Heneghan, Randi J., Trunca, C., and **Rochelson, B.** (1987). Femoral cylinder index in the diagnosis of the Ullrich-Turner syndrome. In Enid F. Gilbert and John M. Opitz (Eds.), *Genetic aspects of developmental pathology.* New York: Liss.

Kaplan, George A. (1992). Health and aging in the Alameda Country Study. In K. Warner Schaie, Dan Blazer, and James S. House (Eds.), *Aging, health behaviors, and health outcomes.* Hillsdale, NJ: Erlbaum.

Kaplan, Howard B., and **Johnson, Robert J.** (1992). Relationship between circumstances surrounding initial illicit drug use and escalation of drug use: Moderating effect of gender and early adolescent experiences. In Meyer Glantz and Roy Pickens (Eds.), *Vulnerability to drug abuse.* Washington, DC: American Psychological Association.

Karp, David A. (1985–1986). Academics beyond midlife: Some observations on changing consciousness in the fifty to sixty year decade. *Aging and Human Development, 22,* 81–103.

Kart, Cary S., and **Metress, Seamus P.** (1984). *Nutrition, the aged, and society.* Englewood Cliffs, NJ: Prentice Hall.

Kastenbaum, Robert J. (1986). *Death, society, and the human experience.* Columbus, OH: Merrill.

Kastenbaum, Robert. (1992). *The psychology of death.* New York: Springer-Verlag.

Katchadourian, Herant A. (1977). *The biology of adolescence.* San Francisco: Freeman.

Katchadourian, Herant A. (1987). *Fifty: Midlife in perspective.* New York: Freeman.

Katz, Joseph and **Sanford, Nevitt.** (1979). Curriculum and personality. In Nevitt Sanford (Ed.), *College and character.* Berkeley, CA: Montaigne.

Katz, S. (1983). Assessing self-maintenance: Activities of daily living, mobility and instrumental activities of daily living. *Journal of the American Geriatrics Society, 31,* 721–727.

Katzell, Raymond A., and **Thompson, Donna E.** (1990). Work motivation: Theory and practice. *American Psychologist, 45,* 144–153.

Katzman, Robert. (1987). Alzheimer's disease: Advances and opportunities. *Journal of the American Geriatrics Society, 35,* 69–73.

Kaufman, Alan S., Reynolds, Cecil R., and **McLean, James E.** (1989). Age and WAIS-R intelligence in a national sample of adults in the 20- to 74-year age range: A cross-sectional analysis with educational level controlled. *Intelligence, 13,* 235–253.

Kaufman, Joan, and **Zigler, Edward.** (1989). The intergenerational transmission of child abuse. In Dante Cicchetti and Vicki Carlson (Eds.), *Child maltreatment: Theory and research on the causes and consequences of child abuse and neglect.* Cambridge, England: Cambridge University Press.

Kaufman, Sharon R. (1986). *The ageless self.* Madison, WI: University of Wisconsin Press.

Kaye, Kenneth. (1982). *The mental and social life of babies: How parents create persons.* Chicago: University of Chicago Press.

Kaye, Leonard, and **Applegate, Jeffrey S.** (1990). *Men as caregivers to the elderly.* Lexington, MA: Lexington Books.

Kazniak, Alfred W. (1990). Psychological assessment of the aging individual. In James E. Birren and K. Warner Schaie (Eds.), *Handbook of the psychology of aging* (3rd ed.). San Diego, CA: Academic Press.

Keele, Reba. (1986). Mentoring or networking? Strong and weak ties in career development. In Linda L. Moore (Ed.), *Not as far as you think.* Lexington, MA: Heath.

Keil, F. C. (1984). Mechanisms of cognitive development and the structure of knowledge. In Robert J. Sternberg (Ed.), *Mechanisms of cognitive development.* New York: Freeman.

Keith, Jennie. (1990). Age in social and cultural context: Anthropological perspectives. In Robert H. Binstock and Linda K. George (Eds.), *Handbook of aging and the social sciences* (3rd ed.). San Diego, CA: Academic Press.

Keith, Pat M. (1986). Isolation of the unmarried in later life. *International Journal of Aging and Human Development, 23,* 81–96.

Keith, Pat M. (1989). *The unmarried in later life.* New York: Praeger.

Keith, Pat M., and **Schafer, Robert B.** (1991). *Relationships and well-being over the life stages.* New York: Praeger.

Kellam, Sheppard G. (1990). Black grandmothers in multigenerational households: Diversity in family structure and parenting involvement in the Woodlawn community. *Child Development, 61,* 434–442.

Kelvin, Peter, and **Jarret, Joanna A.** (1985). *Unemployment: Its social and psychological effects.* Cambridge, England: Cambridge University Press.

Kempe, Ruth S., and **Kempe, C. Henry.** (1978). *Child abuse.* Cambridge, MA: Harvard University Press.

Kempe, Ruth S., and **Kempe, C. Henry.** (1984). *The common secret: Sexual abuse of children and adolescents.* New York: Freeman.

Kendig, Hal L. (1990). Comparative perspectives on housing, aging, and social structure. In Robert H. Binstock and Linda K. George (Eds.), *Handbook of aging and the social sciences* (3rd ed.). San Diego, CA: Academic Press.

Kendig, Hal L., Coles, R., Pittelkow, Y., and **Wilson, S.** (1988). Confidants and family structure in old age. *Journal of Gerontology, 43,* 31–40.

Keniston, Kenneth, and **The Carnegie Council on Children.** (1977). *All our children: The American family under pressure.* New York: Harcourt, Brace, Jovanovich.

Kennell, John H. (1990). Doula-mother and parent-infant contact. In Nina Gunzenhauser (Ed.), *Advances in touch: New implications in human development.* Skillman, NJ: Johnson and Johnson.

Kenney, Asta M., Guardada, Sandra, and **Brown, Lisanne.** (1989). Sex education and AIDS education in the schools: What states and large school districts are doing. *Family Planning Perspectives, 21,* 56–64.

Kerber, Linda K. (1980). Laura Ingalls Wilder. In Barbara Sicherman and Carol Hurd Green (Eds.), *Notable American women: The modern period.* Cambridge, MA: Belknap Press.

Kerr, Robert. (1985). Fitts' law and motor control in children. In Jane E. Clark and James H. Humphrey (Eds.), *Motor development: Current selected research.* Princeton, NJ: Princeton Book Company.

Keshet, Jamie. (1988). The remarried couple: Stresses and successes. In William R. Beer (Ed.), *Relative strangers.* Totowa, NJ: Rowman and Littlefield.

Kessler, Ronald C., Foster, Cindy, Webster, Pamela S., and **House, James S.** (1992). The relationship between age and depressive symptoms in two national surveys. *Psychology and Aging, 7,* 119–126.

King, Cheryl A., Raskin, Allan, Gdowski, Charles L., Butku, Michael, and **Opipari, Lisa.** (1990). Psychosocial factors associated with urban adolescent female suicide attempts. *Journal of the American Academy of Child and Adolescent Psychiatry, 29,* 289–294.

King, P.M., Kitchner, K.S., Davison, M.L., Parker, C.A., and **Wood, P.K.** (1983). The justification of beliefs in young adults: A longitudinal study. *Human Development, 26,* 106–116.

Kirby, Douglas. (1984). *Sexuality education: An evaluation of programs and their effects.* Atlanta, GA: Bureau of Health Education, Centers for Disease Control.

Kirby, Douglas, Barth, Richard P., Leland, Nancy, and **Fetro, Joyce V.** (1991). Reducing the risk: Impact of a new curriculum on sexual risk-taking. *Family Planning Perspectives, 21,* 253–263.

Kirkwood, Thomas B.L. (1985). Comparative and evolutionary aspects of longevity. In Caleb E. Finch and Edward L. Schneider (Eds.), *Handbook of the biology of aging* (2nd ed.). New York: Van Nostrand.

Kirp, David L. (1989). *Learning by heart: AIDS and schoolchildren in America's communities.* NJ: Rutgers University Press.

Kitchener, Karen S., and **King, Patricia M.** (1990). The Reflective Judgment Model: Ten years of research. In Michael L. Commons, Cheryl Armon, Lawrence Kohlberg, Francis A. Richards, Tina A. Grotzer, and Jan D. Sinnott (Eds.), *Adult development: Vol. 2. Models and methods in the study of adolescent and adult thought.* New York: Praeger.

Kitchens, J. (1991). *Understanding and treating codependence.* Englewood Cliffs, NJ: Prentice Hall.

Kitson, Gay C. and **Morgan, Leslie A.** (1990). The multiple consequences of divorce: A decade review. *Journal of Marriage and the Family, 52,* 913–924.

Kitson, Gay C., and **Sussman, Marvin B.** (1982). Marital complaints, demographic characteristics, and symptoms of mental distress in divorce. *Journal of Marriage and the Family, 44,* 87–101.

Klahr, D. (1989). Information-processing approaches. In R. Vasta (Ed.), *Annals of child development* (Vol. 6). Greenwich, CT: JAI Press.

Klatt, Heinz-Jahchim. (1991). In search of a mature concept of death. *Death Studies, 15,* 177–187.

Klaus, Marshall H., and **Kennell, John H.** (1976). *Maternal-infant bonding: The impact of early separation or loss on family development.* St. Louis, MO: Mosby.

Klaus, Marshall H., and **Kennell, John H.** (1982). *Parent-infant bonding.* St. Louis, MO: Mosby.

Klebanoff, Mark A., Shiono, Patricia, and **Rhoads, George G.** (1990). Outcomes of pregnancy in a national sample of resident physicians. *New England Journal of Medicine, 323,* 1040–1045.

Kleemeier, Robert W. (1962). Intellectual changes in the senium. In *Proceedings, American Statistical Association, social statistics section.* Washington, DC: American Statistical Association.

Klein, Melanie. (1957). *Envy and gratitude.* New York: Basic Books.

Klein, Robert P. (1985). Caregiving arrangements by employed women with children under 1 year of age. *Developmental Psychology, 21,* 403–406.

Klein, T.W. (1988). *Program evaluation of the Kaemhameha Elementary Education Program's reading curriculum in Hawaii public schools: The cohort analysis 1978–1986.* Honolulu: Center for Development of Early Education.

Kleinman, J.C., Fingerhut, L.A., and **Prager, K.** (1991). Differences in infant mortality by race, nativity status, and other maternal characteristics. *American Journal of the Diseases of Children, 145,* 194–199.

Klesges, Robert. (1993). Effects of television on metabolic rate: Potential implications for childhood obesity. *Pediatrics, 19* (2).

Kleyman, Paul. (1992). A new beginning in Washington. *Aging Today, 8* (6), 1.

Kliegl, Reinhold, Smith, Jacqui, and **Baltes, Paul B.** (1989). Testing-the-limits and the study of adult age differences in cognitive plasticity of mnemonic skill. *Developmental Psychology, 25,* 247–256.

Kliegl, Reinhold, Smith, Jacqui, and **Baltes, Paul B.** (1990). On the locus and process of magnification of age differences during mnemonic training. *Developmental Psychology, 26,* 894–904.

Kligman, Albert M., Grove, Gary L., and **Balin, Arthur K.** (1985). Aging of the human skin. In Caleb E. Finch and Edward L. Schneider (Eds.), *Handbook of the biology of aging* (2nd ed.).

New York: Van Nostrand.

Kline, D.W., and **Szafran, J.** (1975). Age differences in backward monoptic visual noise masking. *Journal of Gerontology, 30,* 307–311.

Kline, Marsha, Tschann, Jeanne M., Johnston, Janet R., and **Wallerstein, Judith S.** (1989). Children's adjustment in joint and sole physical custody families. *Developmental Psychology, 25,* 430–438.

Klinnert, M.D. (1984). The regulation of infant behavior by maternal facial expression. *Infant Behavior and Development, 7,* 447–465.

Klinnert, M.D., Campos, J.J., Sorce, J.F., Emde, R.N., and **Svejda, M.** (1983). Emotions as behavior regulators: Social referencing in infancy. In R. Plutchik and H. Kellerman (Eds.), *Emotion: Theory, research, and experience: Vol 2. Emotions in early development.* New York: Academic Press.

Knapp, Mary, and **Knapp, Herbert.** (1976). *One potato, two potato: The secret education of American children.* New York: Morton.

Knappert, Jan. (1989). The concept of death and afterlife in Islam. In Arthur Berger, Paul Badham, Austin H. Kutscher, Joyce Berger, Ven. Michael Petty, and John Beloff (Eds.), *Perspectives on death and dying: Cross-cultural and multi-disciplinary views.* Philadelphia: Charles Press.

Knight, Bob G. (1982). There is no continuum of care. *Newsletter of Adult Development and Aging, Division 20, American Psychological Association, 10,* 1, 7, 10–11.

Koch, Patricia Barthalow. (1988). The relationship of first intercourse to later sexual functioning concerns of adolescents. *Journal of Adolescent Research, 3,* 345–362.

Koff, Elissa, Rierden, Jill, and **Stubbs, Margaret.** (1990). Gender, body image, and self-concept during adolescence. *Journal of Early Adolescence, 10,* 56–68.

Kohlberg, Lawrence. (1963). Development of children's orientation towards a moral order (Part I). Sequencing in the development of moral thought. *Vita Humana, 6,* 11–36.

Kohlberg, Lawrence. (1966). A cognitive developmental analysis of children's sex-role concepts and attitudes. In Eleanor Maccoby (Ed.), *The development of sex differences.* Stanford, CA: Stanford University Press.

Kohlberg, Lawrence. (1969). Stage and sequence. The cognitive developmental approach to socialization. In D.A. Goslin (Ed.), *Handbook of socialization theory and research.* Chicago: Rand McNally.

Kohlberg, Lawrence. (1971). Stages of moral development as a basis for moral education. In C.M. Beck, B.S. Crittenden, and E.V. Sullivan (Eds.), *Moral education: Interdisciplinary approaches.* Toronto: University of Toronto Press.

Kohlberg, Lawrence. (1973). Continuities in childhood and adult moral development revisited. In Paul B. Baltes and K. Warner Schaie (Eds.), *Life-span developmental psychology: Personality and socialization.* New York: Academic Press.

Kohlberg, Lawrence, and **Ullian, Dorothy Z.** (1974). Stages in the development of psychosexual concepts and attitudes. In Richard C. Friedman, Ralph M. Richart, and Raymond L. Vande-Wiele (Eds.), *Sex differences in behavior: A conference.* New York: Wiley.

Kohn, Robert R. (1979). Biomedical aspects of aging. In David D. Van Tassel (Ed.), *Aging, death, and the completion of being.* Philadelphia: University of Pennsylvania Press.

Kohn, Willard K., and **Kohn, Jane Burgess.** (1978). *The widower.* Boston: Beacon.

Kolata, Gina. (1985). Down Syndrome—Alzheimer's linked. *Science, 230,* 1152–1153.

Kolata, Gina. (1990, February 6). Rush is on to capitalize on test for gene causing cystic fibrosis. *New York Times,* C3.

Kolata, Gina. (1991, April 16). The aging brain: The mind is resistent, it's the body that fails. *New York Times,* C-1, 10.

Kolodny, Robert C. (1985). The clinical management of sexual problems in substance abusers. In Thomas E. Bratter and Gary G. Forrest (Eds.), *Alcoholism and substance abuse: Strategies for clinical intervention.* New York: The Free Press.

Konker, Claudia S. (1992). Rethinking child sexual abuse: An anthropological perspective. *American Journal of Orthopsychiatry, 62,* 147–153.

Koo, Helen P., Suchindran, C.M., and **Griffith, Janet D.** (1987). The completion of childbearing: Change and variation in timing. *Journal of Marriage and the Family, 49,* 281–294.

Koopman, Peter, Gubbay, John, Vivian, Nigel, Goodfellow, Peter, and **Lovell-Badge, Robin.** (1991). Male development of chromosomally female mice transgenic for Sry. *Nature, 351,* 117–122.

Koplowitz, Herb. (1984). A projection beyond Piaget's formal-operations stage: A general system stage and a unitary stage. In Michael L. Commons, Francis A. Richards, and Cheryl Armon (Eds.), *Beyond formal operations.* New York: Praeger.

Kopp, Clair B. (1982). Antecedents of self-regulation: A developmental perspective. *Developmental Psychology, 18,* 199–214.

Kopp, Clair B., and **Kaler, Sandra R.** (1989). Risk in infancy: Origins and implications. *American Psychologist, 44,* 224–230.

Korbin, Jill. (Ed.). (1981). *Child abuse and neglect: Cross-cultural perspectives.* Berkeley, CA: University of California Press.

Kornhaber, Arthur, and **Woodward, Kenneth L.** (1981). *Grandparents/grandchildren: The vital connection.* Garden City, NJ: Anchor.

Kosik, Kenneth S. (1992). Alzheimer's disease: A cell biological perspective. *Science, 256,* 780–783.

Kosnik, W., Winslow, L., Kline, D., Rasinski, K., and **Sekuler, R.** (1988). Visual changes in daily life. *Journal of Gerontology, 5,* 227–235.

Kotch, Jonathan B., Blakely, Craig H., Brown, Sarah S., and **Wong, Frank Y.** (Eds.). (1992). *A pound of prevention: The case for universal maternity care in the U.S.* Washington, DC: American Public Health Association.

Kotler-Cope, Susan, and **Camp, Cameron J.** (1990). Memory interventions in aging populations. In Eugene A. Lovelace (Ed.), *Aging and cognition: Mental processes, self-awareness, and interventions.* North-Holland: Elsevier.

Kotlowitz, Alex. (1991). *There are no children here.* New York: Doubleday.

Kotre, John. (1984). *Outliving the self: Generativity and the interpretation of lives.* Baltimore, MD: Johns Hopkins University Press.

Kovar, Mary Grace. (1991). Functional ability and the need for care: Issues in measurement research. *Proceedings of the 1988 International Symposium on Aging,* Series 5, No. 6. (DHHS Publication No. 91–1482). Hyattsville, MD: United States Department of Health and Human Services.

Kozol, Jonathan. (1991). *Savage inequalities.* New York: Crown.

Kramer, Dierdre A. (1983). Post-formal operations? A need for further conceptualization. *Human Development, 26,* 91–105.

Kramer, Dierdre A. (1989). Development of an awareness of contradiction across the life span and the question of postformal operations. In Michael L. Commons, Jan D. Sinnott, Francis A. Richards, and Cheryl Armon (Eds.), *Adult development: Vol. 1. Comparisons and applications of developmental models.* New York: Praeger.

Kramer, Dierdre A., and **Melchior, Jacqueline.** (1990). Gender, role conflict, and the development of relativistic and dialectical thinking. *Sex Roles, 23,* 553–575.

Kramer, Dierdre A., and **Woodruff, Diana S.** (1986). Relativistic and dialectical thought in three adult age groups. *Human Development, 29,* 280–290.

Kranichfeld, Marion L. (1987). Rethinking family power. *Journal of Family Issues, 8,* 42–56.

Krause, Neal, and **Wray, Linda A.** (1991). Psychosocial correlates of health and illness among minority elders. *Generations, 15* (4), 25–30.

Krause, Neal, Liang, Jersey, and **Keith, Verna.** (1990). Personality, social support, and psychological distress in later life. *Psychology and Aging, 5,* 315–326.

Krim, Kathy E. (1985). *Mentoring at work: Developmental relationships in organizational life.* Glenview, IL: Scott Foresman.

Kroger, Jane. (1989). *Identity in adolescence: The balance between self and other.* London: Routledge.

Kromelow, Susan, Harding, Carol, and **Touris, Margot.** (1990). The role of the father in the development of stranger sociability during the second year. *American Journal of Orthopsychiatry, 60,* 521–530.

Kropp, Joseph P., and **Haynes, O. Maurice.** (1987). Abusive and nonabusive mothers' ability to identify general and specific emotion signals of infants. *Child Development, 58,* 187–190.

Krupka, Lawrence, and **Vener, Arthur M.** (1979). Hazards of drug use among the elderly. *The Gerontologist, 19,* 90–95.

Kübler-Ross, Elisabeth. (1969). *On death and dying.* New York: Macmillan.

Kübler-Ross, Elisabeth. (1975). *Death: The final stage of growth.* Englewood Cliffs, NJ: Prentice Hall.

Kuczaj, Stan A. (1986). Thoughts on the intentional basis of early object word extension: Evidence from comprehension and production. In Stan A. Kuczaj and Martyn D. Barrett (Eds.), *The development of word meaning: Progress in cognitive developmental research.* New York: Springer-Verlag.

Kuczaj, Stan A., and **Lederberg, A.R.** (1977). Height, age and function: Differing influences on children's comprehension of "older" and "younger." *Journal of Child Language, 4,* 395–416.

Kuhn, Deanna. (1978). Mechanisms of cognitive and social development: One psychology or two? *Human Development, 25,* 233–249.

Kuhn, Deanna. (1988). Cognitive development. In M.H. Bornstein and M.E. Lamb (Eds.), *Developmental psychology: An advanced textbook* (2nd ed.). Hillsdale, NJ: Erlbaum.

Kuhn, Deanna, Nash, Sharon Churnin, and **Brucken, Laura.** (1978). Sex role concepts of two- and three-year-olds. *Child Development, 49,* 445–451.

Kunkel, Suzanne R. (1989). An extra eight hours a day. *Generations, 13* (2), 57–60.

Kurdek, Lawrence A. (1989). Relationship quality for newly married husbands and wives: Marital history, stepchildren, and individual difference predictors. *Journal of Marriage and the Family, 52,* 1053–1064.

Kurdek, Lawrence A. (1991). The relations between reported well-being and divorce history, availability of a proximate adult, and gender. *Journal of Marriage and the Family, 53,* 71–78.

Kurdek, Lawrence A., and **Schmitt, J. Patrick.** (1986). Early development of relationship quality in heterosexual married, heterosexual cohabiting, gay, and lesbian couples. *Developmental Psychology, 22,* 305–309.

Kurnit, D.M., Layton, W.M., and **Matthyusse, Steven.** (1987). Genetics, change and morphogenesis. *American Journal of Human Genetics, 41,* 979–995.

Labouvie-Vief, Gisela. (1985). Intelligence and cognition. In James E. Birren and K. Warner Schaie (Eds.), *Handbook of the psychology of aging* (2nd ed.). New York: Van Nostrand Reinhold.

Labouvie-Vief, Gisela. (1986, November 20). *Mind and self in life-span development.* Symposium on developmental dimensions of adult adaptation: Perspectives on mind, self, and emotion. Presented at the 1986 meeting of the Gerontological Association of America, Chicago, IL.

Labouvie-Vief, Gisela. (1992). A neo-Piagetian perspective on adult cognitive development. In Robert J. Sternberg and Cynthia A. Berg (Eds.), *Intellectual development.* New York: Cambridge University Press.

Lafer, Barbara. (1991). The attrition of hospice volunteers. *Omega, 23,* 161–168.

La Freniere, Peter, Strayer, F.F., and **Gauthier, Roger.** (1984). The emergence of same-sex affiliative preferences among preschool peers: A developmental/ethological perspective. *Child Development, 55,* 1958–1965.

Lagrand, Louis E. (1981). Loss reactions of college students: A descriptive analysis. *Death Education, 5,* 235–248.

Lamb, David R. (1984). *Physiology of exercise: Response and adaptation* (2nd ed.). New York: Macmillan.

Lamb, Michael E. (1981). The development of father-infant relationships. In Michael E. Lamb (Ed.), *Nontraditional families: Parenting and child development.* Hillsdale, NJ: Erlbaum.

Lamb, Michael E. (1987). *The father's role: Cross-cultural perspectives.* Hillsdale, NJ: Erlbaum.

Lamb, Michael E., and **Hwang, C.P.** (1982). Maternal attachment and mother-neonate bonding: A critical review. In Michael E. Lamb and Ann L. Brown (Eds.), *Advances in developmental psychology* (Vol. 2). Hillsdale, NJ: Erlbaum.

Lamb, Michael E., and **Sternberg, Kathleen J.** (1990). Do we really know how day care affects children? *Journal of Applied Developmental Psychology, 11,* 351–379.

Lamb, Michael E., and **Sutton-Smith, B.** (Eds.). (1982). *Sibling relationships.* Hillsdale, NJ: Erlbaum.

Lamb, Michael E., Thompson, R.A., Gardner, W.P., and **Charnov, E.L.** (1985). *Infant-mother attachment.* Hillsdale, NJ: Erlbaum.

Lambert, Nadine M., and **Hartsough, Carolyn S.** (1984). Contribution of predispositional factors to the diagnosis of hyperactivity. *American Journal of Orthopsychiatry, 54,* 97–109.

Lamborn, Susie D., Mounts, Nina S., Steinberg, Laurence, and **Dornbusch, Sanford M.** (1991). Patterns of competence and adjustment among adolescents from authoritarian, authoritative, indulgent, and neglectful families. *Child Development, 62,* 1049–1065.

Lamm, S.S., and **Fisch, M.L.** (1982). *Learning disabilities explained.* Garden City, NY: Doubleday.

Landale, Nancy S., and **Fennelly, Katherine.** (1992). Informal unions among mainland Puerto Ricans: Cohabitation or an alternative to legal marriage. *Journal of Marriage and the Family, 54,* 269–280.

Langer, E.J., and **Rodin, J.** (1976). The effects of choice and enhanced personal responsibility for the aged: A field experiment in an institutional setting. *Journal of Personality and Social Psychology, 34,* 191–198.

Langford, Peter E. and **Claydon, Leslie R.** (1989). A non-Kohlbergian approach to the development of justifications for moral judgements. *Educational Studies, 15,* 261–279.

Langlois, J.H., and **Downs, A.C.** (1980). Mothers, fathers, and peers as socialization agents of sex-typed play behaviors in young children. *Child Development, 51,* 1237–1247.

Langone, John. (1981). Too weary to go on. *Discover, 2* (11), 72–77.

Lansing, L. Stephen. (1983). *The three worlds of Bali.* New York: Praeger.

Lapsley, Daniel. (1990). Continuity and discontinuity in adolescent social cognitive development. In Raymond Montemayor, Gerald R. Adams, and Thomas P. Gullotta (Eds.), *From childhood to adolescence: A transitional period?* Newbury Park, CA: Sage.

La Rue, Asenath, Dessonville, Connie, and **Jarvik, Lissy F.** (1985). Aging and mental disorders. In James E. Birren and K. Warner Schaie (Eds.), *Handbook of the psychology of aging.* New York: Van Nostrand Reinhold.

Lau, Christopher. (1991). The impact of aging on cardiovascular function and reactivity. In Ralph L. Cooper, Jerome M. Goldman, and Thomas J. Harbin (Eds.), *Aging and environmental toxicology.* Baltimore, MD: Johns Hopkins Press.

Lawton, M. Powell. (1985). Housing and living environments of older people. In Robert H. Binstock and Ethel Shanas (Eds.), *Handbook of aging and the social sciences.* New York: Van Nostrand Reinhold.

Lay, Keng-Ling, Waters, Everett, and **Park, Kathryn A.** (1989). Maternal responsiveness and child compliance: The role of mood as a mediator. *Child Development, 60,* 1405–1411.

Lazarus, Richard S., and **DeLongis, Anita.** (1983). Psychological stress and coping in aging. *American Psychologist, 38,* 245–254.

Leach, Penelope. (1989). *Babyhood* (2nd ed.). New York: Knopf.

Leadbeater, B. (1986). The resolution of relativism in adult thinking: Subjective, objective, or conceptual. *Human Development, 29,* 291–300.

Leaf, Alexander. (1982). Long-lived populations: Extreme old age. *Journal of the American Geriatric Society, 30,* 485–487.

Leaper, D.J., Gill, P.W., Staniland, J.R., Horrocks, J.C., and **DeDombal, F.T.** (1973). Clinical diagnostic process: An analysis. *British Medical Journal, 3,* 569–574.

Lee, D.J., and **Markides, K.S.** (1990). Activity and mortality among aged persons over an eight year period. *Journal of Gerontology, 45,* 539–542.

Lee, G.R. (1987). The invisible lives of Canada's grey gays. In V.W. Marshall (Ed.), *Aging in Canada: Social perspectives.* Markham, ON: Fitzhenry and Whiteside.

Lee, Gary R., Seccombe, Karen, and **Shehan, Constance L.** (1991). Marital status and personal happiness: An analysis of trend data. *Journal of Marriage and the Family, 53,* 839–844.

Lee, James Michael. (1980). Christian religious education and moral development. In Brenda Munsey (Ed.), *Moral development, moral education and Kohlberg: Basic issues in philosophy, psychology, religion and education.* Birmingham, AL: Religious Education Press.

Lee, John Alan. (1988). Love-styles. In Robert J. Sternberg and Michael L. Barnes (Eds.), *The psychology of love.* New Haven, CT: Yale University Press.

Lee, Valerie E., Brooks-Gunn, Jeanne, and **Schnur, Elizabeth.** (1988). Does Head Start work? A 1 year follow-up comparison of disadvantaged children attending Head Start, no preschool, and other preschool programs. *Developmental Psychology, 24,* 210–222.

Leifer, A.D., Leiderman, P.H., Barnett, C.R., and **Williams, J.A.** (1972). Effects of mother-infant separation on maternal attachment behavior. *Child Development, 43,* 1203–1218.

Leifer, Myra. (1980). *Psychological effects of motherhood: A study of first pregnancy.* New York: Praeger.

Lemon, B.W., Bengston, V.L., and **Peterson, J.A.** (1972). An exploration of the activity theory of aging: Activity types and life satisfaction among in-movers to a retirement community. *Journal of Gerontology, 27,* 511–523.

Lendler, Marc. (1990). *Just the working life: Opposition and accommodation in daily industrial life.* London: Sharpe.

Lentzner, Harold R., Pamuk, Elsie R., Rhodenhiser, Richard R., and **Powell-Griner, Eve.** (1992). The quality of life in the year before death. *American Journal of Public Health, 82,* 1093–1098.

Leon, Gloria R., Perry, Cheryl L., Mangelsdorf, Carolyn, and **Tell, Grethe J.** (1989). Adolescent nutritional and psychological patterns and risk for the development of an eating disorder. *Journal of Youth and Adolescence, 18,* 273–282.

Leridon, Henri, and **Villeneurve-Gokalp, Catherine.** (1989). The new couples: Number, characteristics, and attitudes. *Population, 44* (1), 203–235.

Lerner, H.E. (1978). Adaptive and pathogenic aspects of sex-role stereotypes: Implications for parenting and psychotherapy. *American Journal of Psychiatry, 135,* 48–52.

Lerner, Jacqueline V., and **Lerner, R.M.** (1983). Temperament and adaptation across life: Theoretical and empirical issues. In P.B. Baltes and O.G. Brim, Jr. (Eds.), *Life-span development and behavior* (Vol. 5). New York: Academic Press.

Lerner, Richard A., Delaney, Mary, Hess, Laura E., Jovanovic, Jasna, and **von Eye, Alexander.** (1990). Adolescent physical attractiveness and academic competence. *Journal of Early Adolescence, 10,* 4–20.

Lester, Barry M., Corwin, Michael J., Sepkoski, Carol, Seifer, Ronald, Peucker, Mark, McLauglin, Sarah, and **Golub, Howard L.** (1991). Neurobehavioral syndromes in Cocaine-exposed newborn infants. *Child Development, 62,* 694–705.

Lester, Barry M., and **Dreher, Melanie.** (1989). Effects of marijuana use during pregnancy on newborn cry. *Child Development, 60,* 765–771.

Lester, Barry M., Hoffman, Joel, and **Brazelton, T. Berry.** (1985). The rhythmic structure of mother-infant interaction in term and preterm infants. *Child Development, 56,* 15–27.

Lester, David. (1989). Self-destructive tendencies and depression as predictors of suicidal ideation in teenagers. *Journal of Adolescence, 12,* 221–223.

Levin, J., and **Levin, W.C.** (1980). *Ageism: Prejudice and discrimination against the elderly.* Belmont, CA: Wadsworth.

Levine, Laura E. (1983). Mine: Self-definition in 2-year-old boys. *Developmental Psychology, 19,* 544–549.

Le Vine, Robert A. (1989). Cultural influences in child development. In William Damon (Ed.), *Child development today and tomorrow.* San Francisco: Jossey-Bass.

Levinson, Daniel J. (1978). *The seasons of a man's life.* New York: Knopf.

Levinson, Daniel J. (1986). A conception of adult development. *American Psychologist, 41,* 3–13.

Levy, G.D., and **Carter, D.B.** (1989). Gender schema, gender constancy, and gender-role knowledge: The roles of cognitive factors in preschoolers' gender-role stereotype attributions. *Developmental Psychology, 25,* 444–449.

Levy, Sandra M. (1991). Behavioral and immunological host factors in cancer risk. In Philip M. McCabe, Neil Schneiderman, Tiffany M. Field, and Jay S. Skylet (Eds.), *Stress, coping, and disease.* Hillsdale, NJ: Erlbaum.

Lewin, Roger. (1987). More clues to the cause of Parkinson's disease. *Science, 237,* 978.

Lewin, Tamar. (1991, July 21). Communities and their residents age gracefully. *New York Times,* A1, A16.

Lewis, Jay. (1990). CDC report alcohol-related deaths top 105,000. *Alcoholism and drug abuse week, 2* (13), 708.

Lewis, Michael, and **Brooks, Jeanne.** (1978). Self-knowledge and emotional development. In Michael Lewis and Leonard A. Rosenblum (Eds.), *The development of affect.* New York: Plenum.

Lewis, Michael, and **Michalson, Linda.** (1983). *Children's emotions and moods.* New York: Plenum.

Lewis, Michael, Sullivan, M.W., Stanger, C., and **Weiss, M.** (1989). Self development and self-conscious emotions. *Child Development, 60,* 146–156.

Lewis, Richard M., and **Cavagnaro, Joy.** (1991). Age-related changes in immune function and toxicity. In Ralph L. Cooper, Jerome M. Goldman, and Thomas J. Harbin (Eds.), *Aging and environmental toxicology.* Baltimore, MD: Johns Hopkins Press.

Lickona, Thomas. (1978). *Moral development and behavior: Theory, research and social issues.* New York: Holt Rinehart Winston.

Lidz, Theodore. (1976). *The person: His and her development throughout the life cycle* (rev. ed.). New York: Basic Books.

Lieberman, Alicia F., Waston, Donna R., and **Pawl, Jeree H.** (1991). Precentive intervention and outcome with anxiously attached dyads. *Child Development, 62,* 199–209.

Lieberman, Morton A. (1965). Psychological correlates of impending death: Some preliminary observations. *Journal of Gerontology, 20,* 181–190.

Lightfoot, Sara Lawrence. (1983). *The good high school.* New York: Basic Books.

Lindahl, Elina, Michelsson, Katarina, Helenius, Maija, and **Parre, Marjatta.** (1988). Neonatal risk factors and later neurodevelopmental disturbances. *Developmental medicine and Child Neurology. 30,* 571–589.

Linde, Eleanor Vander, Morrongiello, Barbara A., and **Rovee-Collier, Carolyn.** (1985). Determinants of retention in 8-week-old infants. *Developmental Psychology, 21,* 601–613.

Lindsey, Duncan. (1991). Factors affecting the foster care placement decision: An analysis of national survey data. *American Journal of Orthopsychiatry, 61,* 272–281.

Lipkowitz, Rochelle. (1988). Services for Alzheimer's patients and their families. In Miriam K. Aronson and Robert N. Butler (Eds.), *Understanding Alzheimer's disease.* New York: Charles Scribner's Sons.

Lipschultz, Larry I., and **Howards, Stuart S.** (Eds.). (1983). *Infertility in the male.* New York: Churchill Livingstone.

Lipsitt, Lewis P. (1990). Learning and memory in infants. *Merrill-Palmer Quarterly, 36,* 53–66.

Liston, Daniel P. and **Zeichner, Kenneth M.** (1991). *Teacher education and the social conditions of schooling.* New York: Routledge.

Livesley, W.J., and **Bromley, D.B.** (1973). *Person perception in childhood and adolescence.* London: Wiley.

Livson, Norman, and **Peskin Harvey.** (1980). Perspectives on adolescence from longitudinal research. In Joseph Adelson (Ed.), *Handbook of adolescent psychology.* New York: Wiley.

Lockery, Shirley. (1991). Caregiving among racial and ethnic minority elders. *Generations, 15* (4), 58–62.

Lockman, Jeffrey J. (1990). Perceptuomotor coordination in infancy. In C.A. Hauert (Ed.), *Developmental psychology: Cognitive, perceptual-motor, and neuropsychological perspectives.* Amsterdam: North-Holland.

Loehlin, John C. (1992). *Genes and environment in personality development.* Newbury Park, CA: Sage.

Loehlin, John C., Willerman, Lee, and **Horn, Joseph M.** (1982). Personality resemblances between unwed mothers and their adopted-away offspring. *Journal of Personality and Social Psychology, 42,* 1089–1099.

Loevinger, J. (1976). *Ego development.* San Francisco: Jossey-Bass.

Lomranz, J., Bergman, S., Eyal, N., and **Shmotkin, D.** (1988). Indoor and outdoor activities of men and women as related to depression and well-being. *International Journal of Aging and Human Development, 26,* 303–314.

Longman, Philip. (1987). *Born to pay: The new politics of aging.* Boston: Houghton Mifflin.

Lopata, Helena Z., and **Barnewolt, Debra.** (1984). The middle years: Changes and variations in social role commitments. In Grace Baruch and Jeanne Brooks-Gunn (Eds.), *Women in midlife.* New York: Plenum.

Lorion, Raymond P., Tolan, Patrick H., and **Wahler, Robert G.** (1987). Prevention. In Herbert C. Quay (Ed.), *Handbook of juvenile delinquency.* New York: Wiley.

Lovelace, Eugene A. (1990a). Basic concepts in cognition and aging. In Eugene A. Lovelace (Ed.), *Aging and cognition: Mental processes, self-awareness, and interventions.* North-Holland: Elsevier.

Lovelace, Eugene A. (1990b). Cognitive aging: A summary overview. In Eugene A. Lovelace (Ed.), *Aging and cognition:*

Mental processes, self-awareness, and interventions. North-Holland: Elsevier.

Lovelace, Eugene A. (1990c). Aging and metacognitions concerning memory function. In Eugene A. Lovelace (Ed.), *Aging and cognition: Mental processes, self-awareness, and interventions.* North-Holland: Elsevier.

Lowman, Rodney M. (1991). *Career assessment.* Washington, DC: American Psychological Association.

Lowrey, George H. (1986). *Growth and development of children* (8th ed.). Chicago: Year Book Medical Publishers.

Lozoff, Betsy. (1989). Nutrition and behavior. *American Psychologist, 44,* 231–236.

Lucas, Tamara, Hense, Rosemary, and **Donato, Ruben.** (1990). Promoting the success of Latino language-minority students: An exploratory study of six high schools. *Harvard Educational Review. 60,* 315–340.

Ludwig, Frederick C. (Ed.). (1991). *Life span extension.* New York: Springer.

Luepnitz, Deborah A. (1986). A comparison of maternal, paternal, and joint-custody: Understanding the varieties of post-divorce family life. *Journal of Divorce, 9,* 1–12.

Lujan, Carol, De Bruyn, Llemyra M., May, Philip A., and **Bird, Michael E.** (1989). Profile of abused and neglected American Indian children in the Southwest. *Child Abuse and Neglect, 13,* 449–461.

Luria, Zella, and **Meade, Robert G.** (1984). Sexuality and the middle-aged woman. In Grace Baruch and Jeanne Brooks-Gunn (Eds.), *Women in midlife.* New York: Plenum.

Luthar, Suniya S., and **Zigler, Edward.** (1991). Vulnerability and competence: A review of research on resilience in childhood. *American Journal of Orthopsychiatry, 61,* 6–22.

Lutkenhaus, Paul. (1984). Pleasure derived from mastery in three-year-olds: Its function for persistence and the influence of maternal behavior. *International Journal of Behavioral Development, 7,* 343–358.

Lynn, R. (1982). IQ in Japan and the United States shows a growing disparity. *Nature, 297,* 222–223.

Lyons-Ruth, Karlen, Connell, David B., Grunebaum, Henry U., and **Botein, Sheila.** (1990). Infants at social risk: Maternal depression and family support services as mediators of infant development and security of attachment. *Child Development, 61,* 85–98.

Lyytinen, Paula. (1991). Developmental trends in children's pretend play. *Child: Care, Health, and Development, 17,* 9–25.

Maccoby, Eleanor Emmons. (1980). *Social development: Psychological growth and the parent-child relationship.* New York: Harcourt Brace Jovanovich.

Maccoby, Eleanor Emmons. (1984). Socialization and developmental change. *Child Development, 55,* 317–328.

Maccoby, Eleanor Emmons. (1988). Gender as a social category. *Developmental Psychology, 24,* 755–765.

Maccoby, Eleanor Emmons. (1989, August). *Gender and relationships: A developmental account.* Distinguished Scientific Achievement Award address to the annual meeting of the American Psychological Association, New Orleans, LA.

Maccoby, Eleanor Emmons, and **Hagen, John W.** (1965). Effect of distraction upon central versus incidental recall: Developmental trends. *Journal of Experimental Child Psychology, 2,* 280–289.

Maccoby, Eleanor Emmons, and **Martin, John A.** (1983). Socialization in the context of the family: Parent-child interaction. In Paul H. Mussen (Ed.), *Handbook of child psychology: Vol. 4. Socialization, personality and social development.* New York: Wiley.

Maccoby, Eleanor Emmons, Depner, Charlene E., and **Mnookin, Robert H.** (1990). Coparenting in the second year after divorce. *Journal of Marriage and the Family, 52,* 141–155.

MacDonald, A.D., McDonald, J. Corbett, Armstrong, B., Cherry, N.M., Nolin, A.D., and **Robert, D.** (1988). Prematurity and work in pregnancy. *British Journal of Industrial Medicine, 45,* 56–62.

MacDonald, Kevin, and **Parke, Ross D.** (1984). Bridging the gap: Parent-child play interaction and peer interactive competence. *Child Development, 55,* 1265–1277.

MacDonald, Kevin, and **Parke, Ross D.** (1986). Parent-child physical play: The effect of sex and age of children and parents. *Sex Roles, 15,* 367–378.

MacEwen, Karyl E., and **Barling, Julian.** (1991). Effects of maternal employment experiences on children's behavior via mood, cognitive difficulties, and parenting behavior. *Journal of Marriage and the Family, 53,* 635–644.

Macey, Terri J., Harmon, Robert J., and **Easterbrooks, M. Ann.** (1987). *Journal of Clinical and Child Psychology, 55,* 846–852.

Mackenzie, Thomas B., Collins, Nancy M., and **Popkin, Michael E.** (1982). A case of fetal abuse? *American Journal of Orthopsychiatry, 52,* 699–703.

MacKinnon, Carol E. (1989). An observational investigation of sibling interactions in married and divorced families. *Developmental Psychology, 25,* 36–44.

Magnusson, David, Stattin, Hakan, and **Allen, Vernon L.** (1985). Biological maturation and social development: A longitudinal study of some adjustment processes from mid-adolescence to adulthood. *Journal of Youth and Adolescence, 14,* 267–283.

Mahler, Margaret. (1968). *On human symbiosis and the vicissitudes of individuation.* New York: International Universities Press.

Mahler, Margaret S., Pine, Fred, and **Bergman, Anni.** (1975). *The psychological birth of the human infant: Symbiosis and individuation.* New York: Basic Books.

Main, Mary, and **George, Carol.** (1985). Responses of abused and disadvantaged toddlers to distress in agemates: A study in the day care setting. *Developmental Psychology, 21,* 407–412.

Main, Mary, and **Solomon, J.** (1986). Discovery of an insecure-disorganized/disoriented attachment pattern. In T.B. Brazelton and M.W. Yogman (Eds.), *Affective development in infancy.* Norwood, NJ: Ablex.

Malina, Robert M. (1990). Physical growth and performance during the transitional years (9–16). In Raymond Montemayor, Gerald R. Adams, and Thomas P. Gullotta (Eds.), *From childhood to adolescence: A transitional period?* Newbury Park, CA: Sage.

Malina, Robert M., Bouchard, C., and **Beunen, G.** (1988). Human growth: Selected aspects of current research on well-nourished children. *Annual Review of Anthropology, 17,* 187–219.

Mangen, David J., Bengston, Vern L., and **Landry, Pierre H.**

(1988). *Measurement of intergenerational relations.* Newbury Park, CA: Sage.

Manton, Kenneth G., Siegler, Ilene C., and Woodbury, Max A. (1986). Patterns of intellectual development in later life. *Journal of Gerontology, 41,* 486–499.

Marcia, James E. (1966). Development and validation of ego identity status. *Journal of Personality and Social Psychology, 3,* 551–558.

Marcia, James E. (1980). Identity in adolescence. In Joseph Adelson (Ed.), *Handbook of adolescent psychology.* New York: Wiley.

Margolin, Leslie, and White, Lynn. (1987). The continuing role of physical attractiveness in marriage. *Journal of Marriage and the Family, 49,* 21–27.

Margolis, Lewis H., and Runyan, Carol W. (1983). Accidental policy: An analysis of the problem of unintended injuries of childhood. *American Journal of Orthopsychiatry, 53,* 629–644.

Markell, Richard A., and Asher, Steven R. (1984). Children's interactions in dyads: Interpersonal influence and sociometric status. *Child Development, 55,* 1412–1424.

Markman, E.M. (1989). *Categorization and naming in children: Problems of induction.* Cambridge, MA: MIT Press.

Markstrom, Carol A., and Mullis, Ronald L. (1986). Ethnic differences in imaginary audience. *Journal of Adolescent Research, 1,* 289–301.

Marsh, H.W., Barnes, J., Cairns, L., and Tidman, M. (1984). Self-description questionnaire: Age and sex effects in the structure and level of self-concept for preadolescent children. *Journal of Educational Psychology, 76,* 940–956.

Martin, C.L., and Halverson, C.F. (1981). A schematic processing model of sex-typing and stereotyping in children. *Child Development, 52,* 1119–1132.

Martin, Teresa Castro, and Bumpass, Larry L. (1989). Recent trends in marital disruption. *Demography, 26,* 37–51.

Maruyama, Fudeko. (1986). Dietary characteristics of the elderly. In Linda H. Chen (Ed.), *Nutritional aspects of aging* (Vol. 2). Boca Raton, FL: CRC Press.

Marx, Jean L. (1987). Oxygen-free radicals linked to many diseases. *Science, 235,* 529–531.

Marx, Jean L. (1991). Zeroing in on individual cancer risk. *Science, 252,* 612–626.

Maslow, Abraham H. (1968). *Toward a psychology of being* (2nd ed.). Princeton, NJ: Van Nostrand.

Maslow, Abraham H. (1970). *Motivation and personality* (2nd ed.). New York: Harper & Row.

Maslow, Abraham H. (1971). *The farther reaches of human nature.* New York: Penguin.

Masten, Ann S. (1992). Homeless children in the United States: Mark of a nation at risk. *Current Directions in Psychological Science, 1,* 41–43.

Masters, William H., and Johnson, Virginia E. (1966). *Human sexual response.* Boston: Little, Brown.

Masters, William H., and Johnson, Virginia E. (1981). Sex and the aging process. *Journal of the American Geriatrics Society, 29,* 385–390.

Matheny, Adam P. (1990). Developmental behavior genetics: Contributions from the Louisville Twin Study. In Martin E. Hahn, John K. Hewitt, Norman D. Henderson, and Robert H. Benno (Eds.), *Developmental behavior genetics: Neural, biometrical, and evolutionary approaches.* Oxford, England: Oxford University Press.

Mazess, R.B., and Forman, S.H. (1979). Longevity and age exaggeration in Vilcabamba, Ecuador. *Journal of Gerontology, 34,* 94–98.

McCabe, Maryann. (1985). Dynamics of child sexual abuse. In Maryann McCabe, Ronald E. Cohen, and Victor Weiss (Eds.), *Child sexual abuse.* New York: Goldner Press.

McCachren, S. Spense, Crawford, Jeffrey, and Cohen, Harvey Jay. (1991). Molecular aspects of aging and carcinogenes. *Aging and environmental toxicology.* Baltimore: Johns Hopkins Press.

McCall, Robert B. (1981). Nature-nurture and the two realms of development: A proposed integration with respect to mental development. *Child Development, 52,* 1–12.

McCarthy, Dorothea. (1954). Language development in children. In Leonard Carmichael (Ed.), *Manual of child psychology* (2nd ed.). New York: Wiley.

McCartney, Kathleen. (1984). Effect of quality of day care environment on children's language development. *Developmental Psychology, 20,* 244–260.

McCauley, Elizabeth, Kay, Thomas, Ito, Joanne, and Treder, Robert. (1987). The Turner Syndrome: Cognitive deficits, affective discrimination, and behavior problems. *Child Development, 58,* 464–473.

McClearn, Gerald, and Foch, Terry T. (1985). Behavioral genetics. In James E. Birren and K. Warner Schaie (Eds.), *Handbook of the psychology of aging.* New York: Van Nostrand Reinhold.

McClearn, Gerald E., Plomin, Robert, Gora-Maslak, Grazyna, and Crabbe, John C. (1991). The gene chase in behavioral science. *Psychological Science, 2,* 222–229.

McClelland, Kent A. (1982). Adolescent subculture in the schools. In Tiffany Field, Aletha Huston, Herbert C. Quay, Lillian Troll, and Gordon E. Finley (Eds.), *Review of human development.* New York: Wiley.

McCrae, Robert R. (1982). Age differences in the use of coping mechanisms. *Journal of Gerontology, 37,* 454–460.

McCrae, Robert R., and Costa, Paul T. (1984). *Emerging lives, enduring dispositions: Personality in adulthood.* Boston: Little, Brown.

McCrae, Robert R., and Costa, Paul T. (1990). *Personality in adulthood.* New York: Guilford.

McDowd, Joan M., and Birren, James E. (1990). Aging and attentional processes. In James E. Birren and K. Warner Schaie (Eds.), *Handbook of the psychology of aging* (3rd ed.). San Diego, CA: Academic Press.

McFadden, Robert D. (1990, June 19). Tragic end to adoption of crack baby. *New York Times,* B1, B4.

McGarrigle, J., and Donaldson, Margaret. (1974). Conservation "accidents." *Cognition, 3,* 341–350.

McGee, Robin A., and Wolfe, David A. (1991). Psychological maltreatment: Toward an operational definition. *Development and psychopathology, 3,* 3–18.

McGue, Matt and Lykken, David T. (1992). Genetic influence on risk of divorce. *Psychological Science, 6,* 368–373.

McHale, Susan M., and Pawletko, Terese M. (1992). Differential treatment of siblings in two family contexts. *Child Development, 63,* 68–91.

McKay, Jennifer (Ed.). (1984). *Adolescent fertility: Report of an international consultation.* London: International Planned Parenthood.

McKeough, Anne. (1992). A neo-structural analysis of children's narrative and its development. In Robbie Case (Ed.), *The mind's staircase: Exploring the conceptual underpinning of children's thought and knowledge.* Hillsdale, NJ: Erlbaum.

McKinlay, Sonja. (1992). Massachusetts study of women and menopause. Harvard. Massachusetts Women's Health Study.

McKusick, Victor A. (1986). *Mendelian inheritance in man* (7th ed.). Baltimore, MD: Johns Hopkins University Press.

McKusick, Victor A. (1990). *Mendalian inheritance in humans.* (9th ed.) Baltimore: Johns Hopkins Press.

McLaughlin, Barry. (1984). *Second language acquisition in childhood: Vol. I. Preschool children* (2nd ed.). Hillsdale, NJ: Erlbaum.

McLaughlin, Barry. (1985). *Second language acquisition in childhood: Vol. II. School-age children* (2nd ed.). Hillsdale, NJ: Erlbaum.

McLeish, John A.B. (1976). *The Ulyssean adult.* Toronto: McGraw-Hill, Ryerson Limited.

McLoyd, Vonnie C. (1989). Socialization and development in a changing economy. *American Psychologist, 44,* 293–302.

Mellinger, Jeanne C., and **Erdwins Carol.** (1985). Personality correlates of age and life roles in adult women. *Psychology of Women Quarterly, 9,* 503–514.

Mellor, Steven. (1990). How do only children differ from other children. *Journal of Genetic Psychology, 151,* 221–230.

Menaghan, Elizabeth G., and **Lieberman, Morton A.** (1986). Changes in depression following divorce: A panel study. *Journal of Marriage and the Family, 48,* 319–328.

Menken, Jane, Trussell, James, and **Larsen, Ulla.** (1986). Age and infertility. *Science, 233,* 1389–1394.

Meredith, Howard V. (1978). Research between 1960 and 1970 on the standing height of young children in different parts of the world. In Hayne W. Reese and Lewis P. Lipsitt (Eds.), *Advances in child development and behavior* (Vol. 12). New York: Academic Press.

Mertz, W. (1989). Minerals. In A. Horwitz, D.M. Macfadyen, H. Munro, N.S. Scrimshaw, B. Steen, and T.F. Williams (Eds.), *Nutrition in the elderly.* Oxford, England: Oxford University Press.

Messer, David J., Rachfor, D., McCarthy, M.E., and **Yarrow, L.J.** (1987). Assessment of mastery behavior at 30 months: Analysis of task-directed activities. *Developmental Psychology, 23,* 771–781.

Michelsson, Katarina, Rinne, Arto, and **Paajanen, Sonja.** (1990). Crying, feeding and sleeping patterns in 1 to 12-month-old infants. *Child: Care, Health, and Development, 116,* 99–111.

Midgley, Carol, Feldlauger, Harriet, and **Eccles, Jacquelynne S.** (1989). Change in teacher efficacy and student self- and task-related beliefs in mathematics during the transition to junior high school. *Journal of Educational Psychology, 81,* 247–258.

Midgley, Carol, Feldlauger, Harriet, and **Eccles, Jacquelynne S.** (1988). The transition to junior high school: Beliefs of pre- and post-transition teachers. *Journal of Youth and Adolescence, 17,* 543–562.

Miedzian, Miriam. (1991). *Boys will be boys: Breaking the link between masculinity and violence.* New York: Doubleday.

Miller, A. (1985). A developmental study of the cognitive basis of performance impairment after failure. *Journal of Personality and Social Psychology, 49,* 529–538.

Miller, Louise B., and **Bizzell, Rondeall P.** (1983). Long-term effects of four preschool programs: Sixth, seventh, and eighth grades. *Child Development, 54,* 727–741.

Miller, Louise B., and **Dyer, Jean L.** (1975). Four preschool programs: Their dimensions and effects. *Monographs of the Society for Research in Child Development, 40* (5–6, Serial No. 162).

Miller, Norman S., and **Gold, Mark S.** (1991). *Alcohol.* New York: Plenum.

Miller, Patricia H. (1983). *Theories of developmental psychology.* San Francisco: Freeman.

Miller, Patricia H., and **Aloise, Patricia A.** (1989). Young children's understanding of the psychological causes of behavior: A review. *Child Development, 60,* 257–285.

Miller, Randi L. (1989). Desegregation experiences of minority students: Adolescent coping strategies in five Connecticut High Schools. *Journal of Adolescent Research, 4,* 173–189.

Milne, Ann M., Myers, David E., Rosenthal, Alvin S., and **Ginsburg, Alan.** (1986). Single parents, working mothers, and the educational achievement of school children. *Sociology of Education, 59,* 125–139.

Milunsky, Aubrey. (1989). *Choices, not chances.* Boston: Little, Brown.

Minkler, Meredith. (1991). Generational equity or interdependence? *Generations, 15* (4), 36, 40–42.

Minkler, Meredith, and **Roe, K.** (1991). *Preliminary findings from the grandmother caregiver study of Oakland, California.* Berkeley, CA: University of California Press.

Minuchin, Patricia, and **Shapiro, Edna K.** (1983). The school as a context for social development. In Paul H. Mussen (Ed.), *Handbook of child psychology: Vol. 4. Socialization, personality and social development.* New York: Wiley.

Mischel, Walter. (1970). Sex typing and socialization. In Paul H. Mussen (Ed.), *Carmichael's manual of child development* (Vol. 2). New York: Wiley.

Mischel, Walter. (1977). On the future of personality measurement. *American Psychologist, 32,* 246–254.

Mischel, Walter. (1979). On the interface of cognition and personality: Beyond the person-situation debate. *American Psychologist, 34,* 740–754.

Mischel, Walter, and **Peake, P.K.** (1983). Analyzing the construction of consistency in personality. In M.M. Page (Ed.), *Personality: Current theory and research.* Lincoln: University of Nebraska Press.

Mitchell, Donald E. (1988). The recovery from early monocular visual deprivation in kittens. In Albert Yonas (Ed.), *Perceptual development in infancy.* Hillsdale, NJ: Erlbaum.

Mitchell, G., and **Shively, C.** (1984). Naturalistic and experimental studies of nonhuman primate and other animal families. In Ross D. Parke (Ed.), *Review of child development research: Vol. 7. The family.* Chicago: University of Chicago Press.

Mitchell, John J. (1986). *The nature of adolescence.* Calgary, Alberta: Detselig.

Mitteness, L. (1987). The management of urinary incontinence by community-living elderly. *Gerontologist, 27,* 185–193.

Moberg, David O. (1965). Religiousity in old age. *The Gerontologist, 5,* 78–87.

Moen, Phyllis. (1991). Transitions in mid-life: Women's work and family roles in the 1970s. *Journal of Marriage and the Family, 53,* 135–150.

Moen, Phyllis, and **Dempster-McClain, Donna I.** (1987). Employed parents: Role strain, work time, and preferences for working less. *Journal of Marriage and the Family, 49,* 579–590.

Moen, Phyllis, Kain, E., and **Elder, Glen H.** (1983). Economic considerations and family life: Contemporary and historical perspectives. In Richard R. Nelson and Felicity Skidmore (Eds.), *American families and the economy.* Ann Arbor, MI: Bks Demand MRI.

Moessinger, Adrian C. (1989). Mothers who smoke and the lungs of their offspring. In Donald Hutchings (Ed.), *Prenatal abuse of licit and illicit drugs.* New York: New York Academy of Sciences.

Moffit, T.E. (1990). Juvenile delinquency and attention deficit disorder: Boys' developmental trajectories from age 3 to age 15. *Child Development, 61,* 893–910.

Moffit, T., Caspi A., and **Belsky, Jay.** (1990). Family context, girls' behavior, and the onset of puberty: A test of a sociobiological model. Paper presented at the biennial meeting of the Society for Research in Adolescence. Atlanta, GA.

Molfese, Dennis L., and **Segalowitz, Sidney J.** (Eds.). (1988). *Brain lateralization in children: Developmental implications.* New York: Guilford.

Molfese, Victoria J. (1989). *Perinatal risk: Developmental assessment and prediction.* New York: Guilford.

Monteiro, C.A., Zuniga, H.P. Pino, Benecio, M.H., and **Victori, C.G.** (1989). Better prospects for child survival. *World Health Forum, 10,* 222–227.

Montemayor, Raymond. (1986). Family variation in parent-adolescent storm and stress. *Journal of Adolescent Research, 1,* 15–31.

Moore, Keith L. (1988). *The developing human: Clinically oriented embryology* (4th ed.). Philadelphia: Saunders.

Moore, Keith L. (1989). *Before we are born: Basic embryology and birth defects* (3rd ed.). Philadelphia: Saunders.

Moore, Susan, and **Rosenthal, Doreen.** (1991). Adolescent invulnerability and perceptions of AIDS risk. *Journal of Adolescent Research, 6,* 164–180.

More, Vin. (1987). *Hospice care systems.* New York: Springer-Verlag.

Morin, C.M., and **Azrin, Nathan H.** (1988). Behavioral and cognitive treatment of geriatric insomnia. *Journal of Consulting and Clinical Psychology, 56,* 748–753.

Morris, Edward K., and **Braukmann, Curtis J.** (Eds.). (1987). *Behavioral approaches to crime and delinquency: A handbook of applications, research, and concepts.* New York: Plenum.

Morrison, Ann M., and **Von Glinow, Mary Ann.** (1990). Women and minorities in management. *American Psychologist, 45,* 200–208.

Morton, Teru. (1987). Childhood aggression in the context of family interaction. In David H. Crowell, Ian M. Evans, and Clifford R. O'Donnell (Eds.), *Childhood aggression and violence: Sources of influences, prevention, and control.* New York: Plenum.

Moscovitch, Morris. (1982). Neuropsychology of perception and memory in the elderly. In Fergus I.M. Craik and Sandra Trehub (Eds.), *Aging and cognitive processes.* New York: Plenum.

Moscovitch, Morris (Ed.). (1984). *Infant memory.* New York: Plenum.

Moss, Madelyn, Colombo, John, Mitchell, D. Wayne, and **Horowitz, Frances Degen.** (1988). Neonatal behavioral organization and visual processing at three months. *Child Development, 59,* 1211–1220.

Moyer, Marth Sebastian. (1992). Sibling relationships among older adults. *Generations, 27* (3), 55–60.

Mueller, Edward, and **Silverman, Nancy.** (1989). Peer relations in maltreated children. In Dante Cicchetti and Vicki Carlson (Eds.), *Child maltreatment: Theory and research on the causes and consequences of child abuse and neglect.* Cambridge, England: Cambridge University Press.

Mulvihill, John J. (1986). Fetal alcohol syndrome. In John L. Sever and Robert L. Brent (Eds.), *Teratogen update: Environmentally induced birth defect risks.* New York: Liss.

Murphy, John M., and **Gilligan, Carol.** (1980). Moral development in late adolescence and adulthood: A critique and reconstruction of Kohlberg's theory. *Human Development, 23,* 77–104.

Murphy, Lois Barclay, and **Moriarty, Alice E.** (1976). *Vulnerability, coping, and growth: From infancy to adolescence.* New Haven: Yale University Press.

Murphy, Patricia Ann. (1986–1987). Parental death in childhood and loneliness in young adults. *Omega, 17,* 219–228.

Mussen, Paul Henry, and **Jones, Mary Cover.** (1957). Self-conceptions, motivations, and interpersonal attitudes of late- and early-maturing boys. *Child Development, 28,* 243–256.

Mutschler, Phyliss H. (1992). Where elders live. *Generations, 16* (2), 7–14.

Muuss, Rolf E. (1988). *Theories of adolescence.* New York: Random House.

Muwahidi, Ahmad Anisuzzaman. (1989). Islamic perspective on death and dying. In Arthur Berger, Paul Badham, Austin H. Kutscher, Joyce Berger, Ven. Michael Petty, and John Beloff (Eds.), *Perspectives on death and dying: Cross-cultural and multi-disciplinary views.* Philadelphia: Charles Press.

Myers, Barbara J. (1984). Mother-infant bonding: The status of this critical period hypothesis. *Developmental Review, 4,* 240–274.

Nathan, Peter E. (1983). Failures in prevention: Why we can't prevent the devastating effects of alcoholism and drug abuse. *American Psychologist, 38,* 459–467.

National Center for Health Statistics. (1985). *Health: United States 1985.* Washington, DC: United States Department of Health and Human Services.

National Center for Health Statistics. (1990). *Health status of the disadvantaged: Chartbook 1990.* United States Department of Health and Human Services. Washington, DC: Public Health Administration.

National Center for Health Statistics. (1991, June). Family structure and children's health: United States, 1988. *Vital and Health Statistics.* US Department of Health and Human Services. Series 10, No. 178.

National Center on Child Abuse and Neglect. (1988). *Study findings: Study of national incidence and prevalence of child abuse and neglect, 1988.* Washington, DC: Author.

National Council of Teachers of Mathematics. (1989). *Curriculum and evaluation standards for school mathematics.* Reston, VA: National Council of Teachers of Mathematics.

National Institute of Drug Abuse. (1988). *National survey on drug abuse: Main findings, 1985.* Rockville, MD: Author.

National Safety Council. (1989). *Accident facts: 1989 edition.* Chicago: Author.

Needleman, Herbert. (1985). The neurobehavioral effects of low-level exposure to lead. *International Journal of Mental Health, 14,* 64–77.

Needleman, Herbert, Schell, Alan, Bellinger, David, Leviton, Alan, and **Allred, Elizabeth N.** (1990). The long-term effects of exposure to low doses of lead in childhood: An 11-year follow-up report. *The New England Journal of Medicine, 322,* 83–89.

Nelkin, Dorothy, and **Tancredi, Laurence.** (1989). *Dangerous diagnostics: The social power of biological information.* New York: Basic Books.

Nelson, Charles A., and **Horowitz, Frances Degen.** (1987). Visual motion perception in infancy: A review and synthesis. In Philip Salapatek and Leslie Cohen (Eds.), *Handbook of infant perception: Vol. 2. From perception to cognition.* Orlando, FL: Academic Press.

Nelson, J. Ron, Smith, Deborah, and **Dodd, John.** (1990). The moral reasoning of juvenile delinquents. *Journal of Abnormal Child Psychology, 18,* 231–239.

Nelson, Katherine. (1986). Preface. In Katherine Nelson (Ed.), *Event knowledge: Structure and function in development.* Hillsdale, NJ: Erlbaum.

Nelson-Le Gall, Sharon A., and **Gumerman, Ruth A.** (1984). Children's perceptions of helpers and helper motivation. *Journal of Applied Developmental Psychology, 5,* 1–12.

Neugarten, Bernice L. (1973). Personality change in late life: A developmental perspective. In C. Eisdorfer and M.P. Lawton (Eds.), *The psychology of adult development and aging.* Washington, D.C.: American Psychological Association.

Neugarten, Bernice L., and **Neugarten, Dail A.** (1986). Changing meanings of age in the aging society. In Alan Pifer and Lynda Bronte (Eds.), *Our aging society: Paradox and promise.* New York: Norton.

Neumann, C.G. (1983). Obesity in childhood. In M.D. Levine, W.B. Carey, A.C. Crocker, and R.T. Gross (Eds.), *Developmental-behavioral pediatrics.* Philadelphia: Saunders.

Newberger, Carolyn Moore, and **White, Kathleen M.** (1989). Cognitive foundations for parental care. In Dante Cicchetti and Vicki Carlson (Eds.), *Child maltreatment: Theory and research on the causes and consequences of child abuse and neglect.* Cambridge, England: Cambridge University Press.

Newcomb, Michael D., and **Bentler, Peter M.** (1990). Antecedents and consequences of cocaine use: An eight-year study from early adolescence to young adulthood. In Lee N. Robbins and Michael Rutter (Eds.), *Straight and devious pathways from childhood to adulthood.* Cambridge, England: Cambridge University Press.

Newman, K. (1988). *Falling from grace: The experience of downward mobility in the American middle class.* New York: The Free Press.

Newton, Robert A. (1984). The medical work up: Male problems. In Miriam D. Mazor and Harriet F. Simons (Eds.), *Infertility: Medical, emotional, and social considerations.* New York: Human Sciences Press.

New York Times. (1980, September 19). *Mistaken identity leads to surprising discovery.* p. 17.

Nicholls, John G. (1978). The development of the concepts of effort and ability, perception of academic attainment, and the understanding that difficult tasks require more ability. *Child Development, 49,* 800–814.

Nicholls, John G. (1989). *The competitive ethos and democratic education.* Cambridge, MA: Harvard University Press.

Nisan, Mordecai. (1987). Moral norms and social conventions: A cross-cultural comparison. *Developmental Psychology, 23,* 719–725.

Noelker, L.S. (1990). Family caregivers: A valuable but vulnerable resource. In Z. Harel, P. Ehrlich, and R. Hubbard (Eds.), *The vulnerable aged: People, services, and policies.* New York: Springer.

Noller, Patricia, and **Callan, Victor J.** (1988). Understanding parent-adolescent interactions: Perceptions of family members and outsiders. *Developmental Psychology, 24,* 707–714.

Norbeck, J.S., and **Tilden, V.P.** (1983). Life stress, social pregnancy: A prospective multivariate study. *Journal of Health and Social Behavior, 24,* 30–46.

Nordin, B.E.C., and **Need, A.G.** (1990). Prediction and prevention of osteoporosis. In M. Bergener, M. Ermini, and H.B. Stahelin (Eds.), *Challenges of aging.* New York: Academic Press.

Nordio, S., Sormi, M., and **deWonderweid, V.** (1986). Neonatal intensive care: Policy, plans, services, and evaluation. In J.M.L. Phaff (Ed.), *Perinatal health services in Europe: Searching for better childbirth.* London: Croom Helm.

Notman, Malkah. (1980). Adult life cycles: Changing roles and changing hormones. In Jacquelynne E. Parsons (Ed.), *The psychology of sex differences and sex roles.* New York: McGraw-Hill.

Nottelmann, Edith D., and **Walsh, C. Jean.** (1986). The long and the short of physical stature in early adolescence. *Journal of Early Adolescence, 6,* 15–27.

Nottelmann, Edith D., Inoff-Germain, Gale, Susman, Elizabeth J., and **Chrousos, George P.** (1990). Hormones and behavior at puberty. In John Bancroft and June Machover Reinisch (Eds.), *Adolescence in puberty.* New York: Oxford University Press.

Nugent, J. Kevin. (1991). Cultural and psychological influences on the father's role in infant development. *Journal of Marriage and the Family, 53,* 475–485.

Nugent, J. Kevin, Lester, B.M., and **Brazelton, T.B.** (1989). *The cultural context of infancy* (Vol. 1). Norwood, NJ: Ablex.

Nussbaum, N.L., Grant, M.L., Roman, M.J., Poole, J.H., and **Bigler, E.D.** (1990). Attention deficit disorder and the mediating effect of age on academic and behavioral variables. *Developmental and Behavioral Pediatrics, 11,* 22–26.

Nydegger, Corinne N. (1986). Asymmetrical kin and the problematic son-in-law. In Nancy Datan, Anita L. Greene, and Hayne W. Reese (Eds.), *Life-span developmental psychology: Intergenerational relations.* Hillsdale, NJ: Erlbaum.

Oakes, Jeanne. (1985). *Keeping track: How schools structure inequality.* New Haven: Yale University Press.

Oakes, Jeanne. (1986). *Educational indicators: A guide for policymakers.* Santa Monica, CA: The RAND Corporation.

Oakes, Jeanne, and **Lipton, Martin.** (1990). *Making the best of* schools: A handbook for parents, teachers, and policymakers. New Haven: Yale University Press.

Oakley, Ann. (1980). *Women confined: Toward a sociology of childbirth.* Oxford, England: Martin Robertson.

Oberle, I., Rousseau, F., Heitz, D., Kretz, C., Devys, D., Hanauer, A., Boule, J., Bertheas, M.F., and **Mandel, J.L.** (1991). Instability of a 550-base pair DNA segment and abnormal methylation in Fragile X syndrome. *Science, 252,* 1097–1102.

Oberman, Albert. (1980). The role of exercise in preventing coronary heart disease. In Elliot Rapaport (Ed.), *Current controversies in cardiovascular disease.* Philadelphia: Saunders.

O'Brien, Marion, Huston, Aletha C., and **Risley, Todd R.** (1983). Sex-typed play of toddlers in a day care center. *Journal of Applied Developmental Psychology, 4,* 1–9.

Obrist, W.D. (1980). Cerebral blood flow and EEG changes associated with aging and dementia. In E.W. Busse and D.G. Blazer (Eds.), *Handbook of geriatric psychiatry.* New York: Van Nostrand Reinhold.

Ochs, Elinor. (1988). *Culture and language development.* Cambridge, England: Cambridge University Press.

O'Connor, Terence. (1989). Cultural voices and strategies for multi-cultural education. *Journal of Education, 171,* 57–74.

O'Donnell, Lydia N. (1985). *The unheralded majority: Contemporary women as mothers.* Lexington, MA: Heath.

Offer, Daniel, and **Offer, Judith.** (1975). *From teenage to young manhood.* New York: Basic Books.

Offermann, Lynn R., and **Gowing, Marilyn K.** (1990). Organizations of the future: Changes and challenges. *American Psychologist, 45,* 95–108.

Olds, D.L., and **Henderson, C.R., Jr.** (1989). The prevention of maltreatment. In D. Cicchetti and V. Carlson (Eds.), *Child maltreatment.* Cambridge, England: Cambridge University Press.

O'Leary, Daniel S. (1990). Neuropsychological development in the child and the adolescent: Functional maturation of the central nervous system. In C.A. Hauert (Ed.), *Developmental psychology: Cognitive, perceptual-motor, and neuropsychological perspectives.* Amsterdam: North-Holland.

Oliver, J.M., Cole, Nancy Hodge, and **Hollingsworth, Holly.** (1991). Learning disabilites as functions of familial learning problems and developmental problems. *Exceptional Children, 57,* 427–440.

Oller, D. Kimbrough, and **Eilers, Rebecca.** (1988). The role of audition in infant babbling. *Child Development, 59,* 441–449.

Olsen, L. (1988). *Crossing the schoolhouse border: Immigrant students and the California public schools.* San Fransico: California Tomorrow.

Olsho, Lynn Werner. (1984). Infant frequency discrimination. *Infant Behavior and Development, 7,* 27–35.

Olsho, Lynne Werner, Harkins, Stephen W., and **Lenhardt, Martin L.** (1985). Aging and the auditory system. In James E. Birren and K. Warner Schaie (Eds.), *Handbook of the psychology of aging.* New York: Van Nostrand Reinhold.

Olsho, Lynn Werner, Koch, E.G., Carter, E.A., Halpin, C.F., and **Spetner, N.B.** (1988). Pure tone sensitivity in human infants. *Journal of the Acoustical Society of America, 84,* 1316–1324.

O'Malley, J.M. (1982). Instructional services for limited English proficiency students. *NABE Journal, 7,* 21–36.

Opie, Iona, and **Opie, Peter.** (1959). *The lore and language of*

schoolchildren. Oxford: Clarendon Press.

Opoku, Kofi Asare. (1989). African perspectives on death and dying. In Arthur Berger, Paul Badham, Austin H. Kutscher, Joyce Berger, Ven. Michael Petty, and John Beloff (Eds.), *Perspectives on death and dying: Cross-cultural and multidisciplinary views.* Philadelphia: Charles Press.

O'Rand, Angela M. (1990). Stratification and the life course. In Robert H. Binstock and Linda K. George (Eds.), *Handbook of aging and the social sciences* (3rd ed.). San Diego, CA: Academic Press.

Ory, Marcia G., and **Warner, Huber R.** (1990). *Gender, health, and longevity.* New York: Springer.

Osgood, Nancy J. (1992). *Suicide in later life.* Lexington MA: Lexington Books.

Osherson, Daniel N., and **Markman, Ellen.** (1974–1975). Language and the ability to evaluate contradictions and tautologies. *Cognition, 3,* 213–226.

Osman, B.B. (1979). *Learning disabilities: A family affair.* New York: Random House.

Osterweis, Marian, Soloman, Fredric, and **Green, Morris** (Eds.). (1984). *Bereavement: Reactions, consequences, and care.* Washington, DC: National Academy Press.

Ouslander, J.G. (1989). Urinary incontinence: Out of the closet. *Journal of the American Medical Association, 261,* 2695–2696.

Pagal, Mark D., Smilksteign, Gabriel, Regan, Hari, and **Montano, Dan.** (1990). Psychosocial influences on newborn outcomes: A controlled prospective study. *Social Science and Medicine, 30,* 597–604.

Page, Reba. (1990). A "relevant" lesson: Defining the lower-track student. In Reba Page and Linda Valli (Eds.), *Curriculum differentiation: Interpretive studies in U.S. secondary schools.* Albany, NY: SUNY Press.

Page, Reba, and **Valli, Linda** (Eds.). (1990). *Curriculum differentiation: Interpretive studies in U.S. secondary schools.* Albany, NY: Suny Press.

Palca, Joseph. (1991). Get-the-lead-out guru challenged. *Science, 253,* 842–844.

Paley, V.G. (1984). *Boys and girls: Superheros in the doll corner.* Chicago: University of Chicago Press.

Palmer, Carolyn F. (1989). The discriminating nature of infants' exploratory actions. *Developmental Psychology, 25,* 885–893.

Palmore, Erdman B. (1990). *Ageism: Negative and positive.* New York: Springer.

Palmore, Erdman B., and **Maeda, Daisaku.** (1985). *The honorable elders revisited.* Durham, NC: Duke University Press.

Papernow, Patricia. (1988). Stepparent role development: From outsider to intimate. In William R. Beer (Ed.), *Relative strangers.* Totowa, NJ: Rowman and Littlefield.

Parke, Ross D. (1981). *Fathers.* Cambridge, MA: Harvard University Press.

Parke, Ross D., and **Slaby, Ronald G.** (1983). The development of aggression. In Paul H. Mussen (Ed.), *Handbook of child psychology: Vol. 4. Socialization, personality and social development.* New York: Wiley.

Parke, Ross D., and **Tinsley, Barbara R.** (1981). The father's role in infancy: Determinants of involvement in caregiving and play. In Michael E. Lamb (Ed.), *The role of the father in child development* (2nd ed.). New York: Wiley.

Parker, Jeffrey G., and **Asher, Steven R.** (1987). Peer relations and later personal adjustment: Are low-accepted children at risk? *Psychological Bulletin, 102,* 357–389.

Parmelee, Arthur H., Jr., and **Sigman, Marian D.** (1983). Perinatal brain development and behavior. In Paul H. Mussen (Ed.), *Handbook of child psychology: Vol. 2. Infancy and developmental psychobiology.* New York: Wiley.

Parnes, Herbert S., and **Less, Lawrence.** (1985). Variation in selection forms of leisure activity among elderly males. In Zena Smith Blau (Ed.), *Current perspectives on aging and the life cycle: Work retirement and social policy.* Greenwich, CT: JAI.

Pascarella, Ernest T., and **Terenzini, Patrick T.** (1991). *How college affects students: Findings and insights from twenty years of research.* San Francisco: Jossey-Bass.

Pasley, Kay, and **Ihinger-Tallman, Marilyn.** (1987). *Remarriage and Stepparenting.* New York: Guilford.

Patel, Pragna, and **Lupski, James R.** (1991). DNA duplication associated with Charst-Marie-Tooth Disease Type 1A. *Cell, 66,* 219–232.

Patterson, Gerald R. (1980). Mothers: The unacknowledged victims. *Monographs of the Society for Research in Child Development, 45* (5, Serial No. 186).

Patterson, Gerald R. (1982). *Coercive family processes.* Eugene, OR: Castalia Press.

Patterson, Gerald R., Littman, R.A., and **Bricker, W.** (1967). Assertive behavior in children: A step toward a theory of aggression. *Monographs of the Society for Research in Child Development, 32* (Serial No. 113).

Paunonen, Sampo V., Jackson, Douglas N., Trzebinski, Jerzy, and **Forsterling, Friedrich.** (1992). Personality structure across cultures: A multimodal evaluation. *Journal of Personality and Social Science, 62,* 447–456.

Pearl, David. (1987). Familial, peer, and television influences on aggressive and violent behavior. In David H. Crowell, Ian M. Evans, and Clifford R. O'Donnell (Eds.), *Childhood aggression and violence: Sources of influence, prevention, and control.* New York: Plenum.

Pearlin, Leonard I. (1982). Discontinuities in the study of aging. In Tamara K. Hareven and Kathleen J. Adams (Eds.), *Aging and life course transitions: An interdisciplinary perspective.* New York: Guilford.

Pearson, Jane L., Hunter, Andrea G., Ensminger, Margaret E., and **Kellam, Sheppard G.** (1990). Black grandmothers in multigenerational households: Diversity in family structure and parenting involvement in the Woodlawn community. *Child Development, 61,* 434–442.

Pederson, Frank A. (1981). Father influences viewed in a family context. In Michael E. Lamb (Ed.), *The role of the father in child development* (2nd ed.). New York: Wiley.

Pederson, Nancy L., Plomin, Robert, McClearn, Gerald E., and **Friberg, L.** (1988). Neuroticism, extraversion, and related traits in adult twins reared apart and reared together. *Journal of Personality and Social Psychology, 55,* 950–957.

Pederson, Nancy L., Plomin, Robert, Nesselroade, John R., and **McClearn, Gerald E.** (1992). A quantitative genetic analysis of cognitive abilities during the second half of the life span. *Psychological Science, 6,* 346–353.

Pellegrini, Anthony D. (1987). Rough and tumble play: Developmental and educational significance. *Educational Psychologist, 23*–44.

Pena, Sally, Grench, Judy, and **Doerann, Judy.** (1990). Heroic fantasie: A cross-generational comparison of two children's television heros. *Early Childhood Research Quarterly, 5,* 393–406.

Pepitone, E.A. (1980). *Children in cooperation and competition: Toward a developmental social psychology.* Lexington, MA: Lexington Books.

Peplau, Letitia, and **Cochran, Susan D.** (1990). A relationship perspective on homosexuality. In David P. McWhirter, Stephanie A. Dangers, and June Machover Reinisch (Eds.), *Homosexuality/heterosexuality: Concepts of sexual orientation.* New York: Oxford University Press.

Peplau, Letitia, and **Gordon, S.L.** (1985). Women and men in love: Sex differences in close heterosexual relationships. In Virginia O'Leary, Rhosa K. Unger, and Barbara S. Wallston (Eds.), *Women, gender, and social psychology.* Hillsdale, NJ: Erlbaum.

Perlmutter, Marion. (1986). A life-span view of memory. In Paul B. Baltes, David L. Featherman, and Richard M. Lerner (Eds.), *Life-span development and behavior.* Hillsdale, NJ: Erlbaum.

Perlmutter, Marion, Adams, Cynthia, Berry, Jane, Kaplan, Michael, Person, Denise, and **Verdonik, Frederick.** (1987). Aging and memory. In K. Warner Schaie (Ed.), *Annual review of gerontology and geriatrics* (Vol. 7). New York: Springer.

Perlmutter, Marion, Kaplan, Michael, and **Nyquist, Linda.** (1990). Development of adaptive competence in adulthood. *Human Development, 33,* 185–197.

Perner, Josef, Leekam, S.R., and **Wimmer, Heinz.** (1987). Three-year-olds' difficulty with false belief: The case for conceptual deficit. *British Journal of Developmental Psychology, 5,* 125–137.

Perris, Eve Emmanuel, Myers, Nancy Angrist, and **Clifton, Rachel Kern.** (1990). Long-term memory for a single infancy experience. *Child Development, 61,* 1796–1807.

Perry, William G., Jr. (1981). Cognitive and ethical growth: The making of meaning. In Arthur W. Chickering (Ed.), *The modern American college: Responding to the new realities of diverse students and a changing society.* San Francisco: Jossey-Bass.

Pertschuk, M., Collins, M., Kreisberg, J., and **Rager, S.** (1986). Psychiatric symptoms associated with eating disorders in a college population. *International Journal of Eating Disorders, 5,* 563–568.

Pervin, Lawrence A. (1990). *Handbook of personality: Theory and research.* New York: Guilford.

Pesce, Rosario, and **Harding, Carol Gibb.** (1986). Imaginary audience behavior and its relationship to operational thought and social experience. *Journal of Early Adolescence, 6,* 83–94.

Peskin, Joan. (1992). Ruse and representations: On children's ability to conceal information. *Developmental Psychology, 28,* 84–89.

Peters, S.D., Wyatt, G.E., and **Finkelhor, David.** (1986). Prevalence. In David Finkelhor (Ed.), *A sourcebook on child sexual abuse.* Beverly Hills, CA: Sage.

Peters-Martin, Patricia, and **Wachs, Theodore D.** (1984). A longitudinal study of temperament and its correlates in the first 12 months. *Infant Behavior and Development, 7,* 285–298.

Peterson, James L., and **Zill, Nicholas.** (1986). Marital disruption, parent-child relationships, and behavior problems in children. *Journal of Marriage and the Family, 48*, 295–307.

Petitto, Anne, and **Marentette, Paula F.** (1991). Babbling in the manual mode: Evidence for the ontogeny of language. *Science, 251,* 1493–1496.

Petzel, Sue V., and **Riddle, Mary.** (1981). Adolescent suicide: Psychosocial and cognitive aspects. In Sherman Feinstein, John Looney, Allan Schwartzberg, and Arthur Sorosky (Eds.), *Adolescent psychiatry: Developmental and clinical studies.* Chicago and London: University of Chicago Press.

Pezdek, Kathy, and **Miceli, Laura.** (1982). Life-span differences in memory integration as a function of processing time. *Developmental Psychology, 18,* 485–490.

Pfeiffer, Eric. (1977). Sexual behavior in old age. In Ewald W. Busse and Eric Pfeiffer (Eds.), *Behavior and adaptation in late life* (2nd ed.). Boston: Little, Brown.

Pfeiffer, Eric, and **Davis, Glenn C.** (1972). Determinants of sexual behavior. *Journal of American Geriatrics Society, 20,* 151–158.

Phinney, Jean S., Lochner, Bruce T., and **Murphy, Rodolfo.** (1990). Ethnic identity development and psychological adjustment in adolescence. In Arlene Rubin Stiffman and Larry E. Davis (Eds.), *Ethnic issues in adolescent mental health.* Newbury Park, CA: Sage.

Phinney, Jean S., and **Rotheram, Mary Jane.** (Eds.), *Children's ethnic socialization: Pluralism and development.* Beverly Hills, CA: Sage.

Piaget, Jean. (1951). *Play, dreams, and imitation in childhood.* New York: Norton.

Piaget, Jean. (1952a). *The origins of intelligence in children.* Margaret Cook (Trans.). New York: International Universities Press.

Piaget, Jean. (1952b). *The child's conception of number.* London: Routledge and Kegan Paul.

Piaget, Jean. (1954). *The construction of reality in the child.* Margaret Cook (Trans.). New York: Basic Books.

Piaget, Jean. (1959). *The language and thought of the child* (3rd ed.). Marjorie Gabain and Ruth Gabain (Trans.). London: Routledge and Kegan Paul.

Piaget, Jean. (1970a). *The child's conception of time.* A.J. Pomerans (Trans.). New York: Basic Books.

Piaget, Jean. (1970b). *The child's conception of movement and speed.* G.E.T. Holloway and M.J. Mackenzie (Trans.). New York: Basic Books.

Piaget, Jean. (1972). Intellectual evolution from adolescence to adulthood. *Human Development, 15,* 1–12.

Piaget, Jean. (1976). *The grasp of consciousness: Action and concept in the young child.* Susan Wedgewood (Trans.). Cambridge, MA: Harvard University Press.

Piaget, Jean. (1980). Intellectual evolution from adolescence to adulthood. In Rolf E. Muuss (Ed.), *Adolescent behavior and society: A book of readings* (3rd ed.). New York: Random House.

Piaget, Jean, and **Inhelder, Bärbel.** (1963). *The child's conception of space.* F.J. Langdon and J.L. Lunzer (Trans.). London: Routledge and Kegan Paul.

Piaget, Jean, and **Inhelder, Bärbel.** (1974). *The child's construction of quantities: Conservation and atomism.* London: Routledge and Kegan Paul.

Pianta, Robert, Egeland, Byron, and **Ericson, Martha Farrell.** (1989). The antecedents of maltreatment: Results of the mother-child interaction project. In Dante Cicchetti and Vicki Carlson (Eds.), *Child maltreatment: Theory and research on the causes and consequences of child abuse and neglect.* Cambridge, England: Cambridge University Press.

Pifer, Alan, and **Bronte, Lynda** (Eds.). (1986). *Our aging society: Paradox and promise.* New York: Norton.

Pillemer, Karl A., and **Finkelhor, David.** (1988). The prevalence of elder abuse: A random sample survey. *The Gerontologist, 29,* 51–57.

Pinderhughes, Ellen E. (1991). The delivery of child welfare services to African-American clients. *American Journal of Orthopsychiatry, 61,* 599–605.

Pines, Ayala M., and **Aronson, Elliot.** (1981). *Burnout: From tedium to personal growth.* New York: The Free Press.

Pinholt, E.M., Kroenke, K., Hanley, J.F., Kussman, M.J., Twyman, P.L., and **Carpenter, J.L.** (1987). Functional assessment of the elderly: A comparison of standard instruments with clinical judgment. *Archive of Internal Medicine, 147,* 484–488.

Pintrich, P.R., and **Blumenfeld, P.C.** (1985). Classroom experience and children's self-perceptions of ability, effort, and conduct. *Journal of Educational Psychology, 77,* 646–657.

Piotrkowski, Chaya S. (1979). *Work and the family system.* New York: The Free Press.

Piper, Alison I., and **Langer, Ellen J.** (1986). Aging and mindful control. In Margret M. Baltes and Paul B. Baltes (Eds.), *The psychology of control and aging.* Hillsdale, NJ: Erlbaum.

Pipp, S., Fischer, K.W., and **Jennings, S.** (1987). Acquisition of self- and mother knowledge in infancy. *Developmental Psychology, 23,* 86–96.

Pitskhelauri, G.Z. (1982). *The long-living of Soviet Georgia.* Gari Lesnoff-Caravaglia (Trans.). New York: Human Sciences Press.

Pittman, Robert B. (1991). Social factors, enrollment in vocational/technical course, and high school dropout rates. *Journal of Educational Research, 84,* 288–295.

Pleck, J.H. (1985). *Working wives/working husbands.* Beverly Hills, CA: Sage.

Plomin, Robert. (1990a). *Nature and nurture: An introduction to human behavioral genetics.* Pacific Grove, CA: Brooks/Cole.

Plomin, Robert. (1990b). The role of inheritance in behavior. *Science, 248,* 183–188.

Plomin, Robert, Corley, Robin, DeFries, J.C., and **Fulker, D.W.** (1990). Individual differences in television viewing in early childhood: Nature as well as nurture. *Psychological Science, 1,* 371–377.

Plomin, Robert, DeFries, J.C., and **McClearn, Gerald E.** (1990). *Behavioral genetics: A primer.* New York: Freeman.

Plomin, Robert, Lichtenstein, Paul, Pederson, Nancy L., McClearn, Gerald, and **Nesselroade, John R.** (1990). Genetic influence on life events during the last half of the life span. *Psychology and Aging, 5,* 25–30.

Plomin, Robert, McClearn, Gerald E., Pederson, N.L., Nesselroade, J.R., and **Bergeman, C.S.** (1989). Genetic influences on adults' ratings of their current family environment. *Journal of Marriage and the Family, 51,* 791–803.

Poffenberger, Thomas. (1981). Child rearing and social structure in rural India: Toward a cross-cultural definition of child abuse and neglect. In Jill E. Korbin (Ed.), *Child abuse and neglect: Cross-cultural perspectives.* Berkeley: University of California Press.

Polit, Denise. (1984). The only child in single-parent families. In Toni Falbo (Ed.), *The single-child family.* New York: Guilford.

Polit, Denise F. (1989). Effects of a comprehensive program for teenage parents: Five years after project redirection. *Family Planning Perspectives, 21,* 164–169.

Pollack, William S., and **Grossman, Frances K.** (1985). Parent-child interaction. In L. L'Abate (Ed.), *The handbook of family psychology and therapy* (Vol. I). Homewood, IL: Dorsey Press.

Pomerleau, Andree, Malcuit, Gerard, and **Sabatier, Colette.** (1991). Child-rearing practices and parental beliefs in three cultural groups of Montreal: Quebeçois, Vietnamese, Haitian. In Marc H. Bornstein (Ed.), *Cultural approaches to parenting.* Hillsdale, NJ: Erlbaum.

Poon, Leonard W. (1985). Differences in human memory with aging: Nature, causes, and clinical implications. In James E. Birren and K. Warner Schaie (Eds.), *Handbook of the psychology of aging.* New York: Van Nostrand Reinhold.

Poon, Leonard W. (1992). *The Georgia Centenarian Study,* Amityville, NY: Baywood.

Poon, Leonard W., Rubin, David C., and **Wilson, Barbara A.** (Eds.). (1989). *Everyday cognition in adulthood and late life.* Cambridge, England; Cambridge University Press.

Pope, H.G., Hudson, J.I., Yurgelun-Todd, D., and **Hudson, M.S.** (1984). Prevalence of anorexia nervosa and bulimia in three student populations. *International Journal of Eating Disorders, 3,* 45–51.

Poussaint, Alvin F. (1990). Introduction. In Bill Cosby, *Fatherhood.* New York: Berkley Books.

Powers, Stephen, and **Wagner, Michael J.** (1984). Attributions for school achievement of middle school students. *Journal of Early Adolescence, 4,* 215–222.

Preston, George A.N. (1986). Dementia in elderly adults: Prevalence and institutionalization. *Journal of Gerontology, 41,* 261–267.

Price, Richard H. (1992). Psychosocial impact of job loss on individuals and families. *Current Directions in Psychological Science, 1,* 9–11.

Price, Sharon J., and **McHenry, Patrick C.** (1988). *Divorce.* Newbury Park, CA: Sage.

Prince, R.L., Smith, M., Dick, I.M., Price, R.I., Webb, P.G., Henderson, K., and **Harris, M.P.** (1991). Prevention of postmenopausal osteoporosis. *New England Journal of Medicine, 325,* 1189–1195.

Public Health Service. (1990). Health interview survey. National Center for Health Statistics. Washington, DC: United States.

Purvis, George A., and **Bartholmey, Sandra J.** (1988). Infant feeding practices: Commercially prepared baby foods. In Reginald C. Tsang and Buford L. Nicholas (Eds.), *Nutrition during infancy.* Philadelphia: Hanley and Belfus.

Putallaz, Martha, and **Wasserman, Aviva.** (1990). Children's entry behavior. In Steven R. Asher and John David Coie (Eds.), *Peer rejection in childhood.* New York: Cambridge University Press.

Quay, Herbert C. (1987). Institutional treatment. In Herbert C.

Quay (Ed.), *Handbook of juvenile delinquency.* New York: Wiley.

Quinn, Joan L. (1987). Attitude of professionals toward the aged. In George L. Maddox (Ed.), *The encyclopedia of aging.* New York: Springer-Verlag.

Quinn, Joseph F., and **Burkhauser, Richard V.** (1990). Work and retirement. In Robert H. Binstock and Linda K. George (Eds.), *Handbook of aging and the social sciences* (3rd ed.). San Diego, CA: Academic Press.

Quirk, Daniel A. (1991). The aging network: An agenda for the nineties and beyond. *Generations, 15,* (3), 23–26.

Rabiner, David, and **Coie, John.** (1989). Effect of expectancy inductions on rejected children's acceptance by unfamiliar peers. *Developmental Psychology, 25,* 450–457.

Rafferty, Yvonne, and **Shinn, Marybeth.** (1991). The impact of homelessness on children. *American Psychologist, 46,* 1170–1179.

Rallison, Marvin L. (1986). *Growth disorders in infants, children, and adolescents.* New York: Wiley.

Ralston, Davis A., and **Flanagan, Michael E.** (1985). The effect of flex-time on absenteeism and turnover for male and female employees. *Journal of Vocational Behavior, 26,* 206–217.

Rando, Therese A. (1986). *Loss and anticipatory grief.* Lexington, MA: Lexington Books.

Rao, K. Vaninadha. (1990). Marriage risks, cohabitation, and premarital births in Canada. *European Journal of Population, 6,* 27–49.

Rathunde, Kevin, and **Csikszentmihalyi, Mihlaly.** (1991). Adolescent happiness and family interaction. In Karl Pillemer and Kathleen McCartney (Eds.), *Parent-child relations throughout life.* Hillsdale, NJ: Erlbaum.

Rauste-von Wright, Maijaliisa. (1989). Body image satisfaction in adolescent girls and boys: A longitudinal study. *Journal of Youth and Adolescence, 18,* 71–83.

Ravitch, Diane. (1983). *The troubled crusade: American education 1945–1980.* New York: Basic Books.

Rawlins, William K. (1992). *Friendship matters.* Hawthorne, NY: Aldine de Gruyter.

Read, M.H., and **Graney, A.S.** (1982). Food supplement use by the elderly. *Journal of American Dietetic Association, 80,* 250.

Rees, Gareth J.G. (1988). What is best for the patient? A European view. In Basil A. Stoll (Ed.), *Cost versus benefit in cancer care.* Baltimore, MD: Johns Hopkins University Press.

Reese, Hayne W., and **Rodeheaver, Dean.** (1985). Problem solving and complex decision making. In James E. Birren and K. Warner Schaie (Eds.), *Handbook of the psychology of aging* (2nd ed.). New York: Van Nostrand Reinhold.

Register, Cheri. (1991). *Are those kids yours?* New York: The Free Press.

Reich, Peter A. (1986). *Language development.* Englewood Cliffs, NJ: Prentice-Hall.

Reid, B.V. (1984). An anthropological reinterpretation of Kohlberg's stages of moral development. *Human Development, 27,* 56–74.

Reid, Barbara Van Steenburgh. (1989). Socialization for moral reasoning: Maternal strategies of Samoans and Europeans in New Zealand. In Jaan Valsiner (Ed.), *Child development in cultural context.* Toronto: Hogrefe and Huber.

Reiff, T.R. (1989). Body composition with special reference to water. In A. Horwitz, D.M. Macfadyen, H. Munro, N.S. Scrimshaw, B. Steen, and T.F. Williams (Eds.), *Nutrition in the elderly.* Oxford, England: Oxford University Press.

Reilly, R.R., Brown, B., Blood, M.R., and Malatesta, C.Z. (1981). The effects of realistic previews: A study and discussion of the literature. *Personnel Psychology, 34,* 832–834.

Reinke, Barbara J., Ellicott, Abbie M., Harris, Rochelle L., and Hancock, Emily. (1985). Timing of psychosocial changes in women's lives. *Human Development, 28,* 259–280.

Reisberg, Barry. (1981). *Brain failure: An introduction to current concepts of senility.* New York: The Free Press.

Reisberg, Barry, Ferris, Steven, de Leon, Mony J., and Crook, Thomas. (1985). Age-associated cognitive decline and Alzheimer's disease: Implications for assessment and treatment. In M. Bergener, Marco Ermini, and H.B. Stahelin (Eds.), *Thresholds in aging.* London: Academic Press.

Rest, James R. (1983). Morality. In Paul H. Mussen (Ed.), *Handbook of child psychology: Vol. 3. Cognitive development.* New York: Wiley.

Rest, James R., and Thoma, Stephen J. (1985). Relation of moral judgment development to formal education. *Developmental Psychology, 21,* 709–714.

Rholes, William S., Blackwell, Janette, Jordan, Carol, and Walters, Connie. (1980). A developmental study of learned helplessness. *Developmental Psychology, 16,* 616–624.

Rhyne, Darla. (1981). Basis of marital satisfaction among men and women. *Journal of Marriage and the Family, 43,* 941–955.

Ricciuti, Henry N. (1991). Malnutrition and cognitive development: Research policy linkages and current research directions. In Lynn Okagaki and Robert J. Sternberg (Eds.) *Directors of development.* Hillsdale, NJ: Erlbaum

Rice, G. Elizabeth, and Meyer, Bonnie J.F. (1986). Prose recall: Effects of aging, verbal ability, and reading behavior. *Journal of Gerontology, 41,* 469–480.

Rice, Mabel L. (1982). Child language: What children know and how. In Tiffany Field, Aletha Huston, Herbert C. Quay, Lillian Troll, and Gordon E. Finley (Eds.), *Review of human development.* New York: Wiley.

Rice, Mabel L. (1984). Cognitive aspects of communicative development. In Richard L. Schiefelbusch and Joanne Pickar (Eds.), *The acquisition of communicative competence.* Baltimore, MD: University Park Press.

Rice, Mabel L. (1989). Children's language acquisition. *American Psychologist, 44,* 149–156.

Rice, Mabel, and Schiefelbusch, R. (Eds.). (1989). *The teachability of language.* Baltimore, MD: Brookes.

Rice, Mabel L., and Woodsmall, L. (1988). Lessons from television: Children's word learning when viewing. *Child Development, 59,* 420–429.

Richman, Amy L., Miller, Patrice M., and Le Vine, Robert A. (1992). Cultural and educational variations in maternal responsiveness. *Developmental Psychology, 28,* 614–621.

Richman, Judith A., and Flaherty, Joseph A. (1987). Adult psychosocial assets and depressive mood over time: Effects of internalized childhood attachments. *Journal of Nervous and Mental Disease, 175,* 703–712.

Riegel, Klaus F. (1975). Toward a dialectical theory of development. *Human Development, 18,* 50–64.

Riegel, Klaus F., and Riegel, Ruth M. (1972). Development, drop, and death. *Developmental Psychology, 6,* 306–319.

Riegel, Klaus F., Riegel, Ruth M., and Meyer, Günther. (1967). A study of the dropout rates in longitudinal research on aging and the prediction of death. *Journal of Personality and Social Psychology, 5,* 342–348.

Rierden, Jill, Koff, Elissa, and Stubbs, Margaret. (1987). Depressive symptomology and body image in adolescent girls. *Journal of Early Adolescence, 7,* 205–216.

Rierden, Jill, Koff, Elissa, and Stubbs, Margaret. (1988). Gender, depression, and body image in early adolescents. *Journal of Early Adolescence, 8,* 109–117.

Rikaus, Lora. (1986). Toxicological factors affecting nutritional status: Drugs. In Linda H. Chen (Ed.), *Nutritional aspects of aging* (Vol. 2). Boca Raton, FL: CRC Press.

Riordan, Jan. (1983). *A practical guide to breastfeeding.* St. Louis, MO: Mosby.

Risman, B.J. (1987). Intimate relationships from a microstructural perspective: Men who mother. *Gender and Society, 1,* 6–32.

Rispens, Jan, Van Ypern, Tom A., and Van Duijn, Gijs A. (1991). The irrelevance of IQ to the definition of learning disabilities: Some empirical evidence. *Journal of Learning Disabilities, 24,* 434–438.

Ritchie, Jane, and Ritchie, James. (1981). Child rearing and child abuse: The Polynesian context. In Jill E. Korbin (Ed.), *Child abuse and neglect: Cross-cultural perspectives.* Berkeley: University of California Press.

Roberto, Karen A., and Scott, Jean Pearson. (1986). Equity considerations in the friendships of older adults. *Journal of Gerontology, 41,* 241–247.

Roberts, Laura R., and Petersen, Anne C. (1992). The relationship between academic achievement and social self-image during early adolescence. *Journal of Early Adolescence, 12,* 197–219.

Roberts, Leslie. (1991a). Does egg beckon sperm when the time is right? *Science, 252,* 214.

Roberts, Leslie. (1991b). Report card on the genome project. *Science, 253,* 376.

Robertson, C.M.T., Etches, P.C., and Kyle, J.M. (1990). Eight year school performance and growth of preterm, small for gestational age infants: A comparative study with subjects matched for birth weight or for gestational age. *Journal of Pediatrics. 116,* 19–26.

Robertson, Elizabeth B., Elder, Glen H., Kinner, Martie L. and Conger, Rand D. (1991). The costs and benefits of social supports in families. *Journal of Marriage and the Family, 53,* 403–416.

Robins, Lee N., Helzer, John E., Weissman, Myrna M., Orvaschel, Helen, Gruenberg, Ernest, Burke, Jack D., and Regier, Darrel A. (1984). Life-time prevalence of specific psychiatric disorders in three sites. *Archives of General Psychiatry, 41,* 949–958.

Robins, Lee, and Rutter, Michael. (1990). *Straight and devious pathways from childhood to adulthood.* Cambridge, England: Cambridge University Press.

Robinson, Clyde C., and Morris, James T. (1986). The gender-stereotyped nature of Christmas toys received by 36-, 48-, and 60-month old children: A comparission between nonrequested vs. requested toys. *Sex Roles, 15,* 21–32.

Robinson, Ira, Ziss, Ken, Ganza, Bill, Katz, Stuart, and **Robinson, Edward.** (1991). Twenty years of the sexual revolution, 1965–1985: An update. *Journal of Marriage and the Family, 53,* 216–220.

Rochat, Phillip. (1989). Object manipulation and exploration in 2- to 5-month-old infants. *Developmental Psychology, 25,* 871–884.

Rodeheaver, Dean, and **Thomas, Jeanne L.** (1986). Family and community networks in Appalachia. In Nancy Datan, Anita L. Greene, and Hayne W. Reese (Eds.), *Life-span developmental psychology: Intergenerational relations.* Hillsdale, NJ: Erlbaum.

Rodin, J. and **Langer, E.** (1977). Long-term effects of a control-relevant intervention with the institutionalized aged. *Journal of Personality and Social Psychology, 35,* 897–902.

Rodin, M. McAvay, G., and **Timko, C.** (1988). A longitudinal study of depressed mood and sleep disturbances in elderly adults. *Journal of Gerontology: Psychological Sciences, 43,* P45–P53.

Rogan, Walter J. (1986). PCB's and Cola-colored babies: Japan 1968 and Taiwan 1979. In John J. Sever and Robert L. Brent (Eds.), *Teratogen update: Environmentally induced birth defect risks.* New York: Liss.

Rogers, Sally J., and **Pennington, Bruce F.** (1991). A theoretical approach to the deficits in infantile autism. *Development and Psychopathology, 3,* 137–162.

Rogers, Sinclair. (1976). The language of children and adolescents and the language of schooling. In Sinclair Rogers (Ed.), *They don't speak our language.* London: Edward Arnold.

Rogoff, Barbara. (1986). Adult assistance of children's learning. In T.E. Raphael (Ed.), *The contexts of school-based literacy.* New York: Random House.

Rogoff, Barbara. (1990). *Apprenticeship in thinking.* New York: Oxford University Press.

Rogoff, Barbara, and **Morelli, Gilda.** (1989). Perspectives on children's development from cultural psychology. *American Psychologist, 44,* 343–348.

Rogosch, Fred A., and **Newcomb, Andrew F.** (1989). Children's perceptions of peer reputations and their social reputations among peers. *Child Development, 60,* 597–610.

Rohlen, Thomas P. (1983). *Japan's high schools.* Berkeley: University of California Press.

Rohner, Ronald P. (1984). Toward a conception of culture for cross-cultural psychology. *Journal of Cross-cultural Psychology, 15,* 111–138.

Rohner, Ronald P., Kean, Kevin J., and **Cournoyer, David E.** (1991). Effects of corporal punishment, perceived caretaker warmth, and cultural beliefs on the psychological adjustment of children in St. Kitts, West Indies. *Journal of Marriage and the Family, 53,* 681–693.

Roll, J. (1989). *Lone parent families in the European community.* London: Family Policy Studies Center.

Romaine, Suzanne. (1984). *The language of children and adolescents: The acquisition of communication competence.* Oxford: Blackwell.

Roopnarine, Jaipual L. (1984). Sex-typed socialization in mixed-age preschool classrooms. *Child Development, 55,* 1078–1084.

Rose, Susan A., and **Ruff, Holly A.** (1987). Cross-modal abilities in infants. In Joy Doniger Osofsky (Ed.), *Handbook of infant development* (2nd ed.). New York: Wiley.

Rosel, Natalie. (1986). Growing old together: Neighborhood, communality among the elderly. In Thomas R. Cole and Sally A. Gadow (Eds.), *What does it mean to grow old?* Durham, NC: Duke University Press.

Rosenberg, Allison Anne, and **Kagan, Jerome.** (1987). Iris pigmentation and behavioral inhibition. *Developmental Psychobiology, 20,* 377–392.

Rosenberg, Elinor B. (1992). *The adoption life cycle.* Lexington, MA: Lexington Books.

Rosenberg, Harry M., Chevarley, Frances, Powell-Griner, Eve, Kochankek, Kenneth, and **Feinleib, Manning.** (1991). Causes of death among the elderly: Information from the death certificate. *Proceedings of the 1988 International Symposium on Aging.* Series 5, No. 6. (DHHS Publication No. 91–1482). Hyattsville, MD: United States Department of Health and Human Services.

Rosenberg, Mindy S., and **Rossman, Robbie.** (1989). The child witness to marital violence. In Robert T. Ammerman and Michel Hersen (Eds.), *Treatment of family violence.* New York: Wiley.

Rosenfeld, Albert. (1985). *Prolongevity II: An updated report on the scientific prospects for adding good years to life.* New York: Knopf.

Rosenfeld, Albert, and **Stark, E.** (1987, May). The prime of our lives. *Psychology Today,* 62–72.

Rosenman, Ray H., and **Chesney, Margaret A.** (1983). Type A behavior patterns and coronary heart disease. In Richard N. Podell and Michael M. Stewart (Eds.), *Primary prevention of coronary heart disease.* Menlo Park, CA: Addison Wesley.

Rosenstein, Diana, and **Oster, Harriet.** (1988). Differential facial responses to four basic tastes. *Child Development, 59,* 1555–1568.

Rosow, Irving. (1985). Status and role change through the life cycle. In Robert H. Binstock and Ethel Shanas (Eds.), *Handbook of aging and the social sciences* (2nd ed.). New York: Van Nostrand.

Ross, Dorothea M., and **Ross, Sheila A.** (1982). *Hyperactivity: Current issues, research, and theory* (2nd ed.). New York: Wiley.

Ross, Jennie Keith. (1977). *Old people, new lives: Community creation in a retirement residence.* Chicago: University of Chicago Press.

Ross, Lee. (1981). The "intuitive scientist" formulation and its developmental implications. In John H. Flavell and Lee Ross (Eds.), *Social cognitive development: Frontiers and possible futures.* Cambridge, England: Cambridge University Press.

Rosser, Pearl L., and **Randolph, Suzanne M.** (1989). Black American infants: The Howard University normative study. In J. Kevin Nuegent, Barry M. Lester, and T. Berry Brazelton (Eds.), *The cultural context of infancy: Vol I. Biology, culture, and infant development.* Norwood, NJ: Ablex.

Rossi, Alice S. (1980). Life-span theories in women's lives. *Signs, 6,* 4–32.

Rotberg, Iris C. (1982). Some legal and research considerations in establishing federal policy in bilingual education. *Harvard Educational Review, 52,* 149–168.

Rotenberg, Ken J., and **Mann, Luanne.** (1986). The development of the norm of reciprocity of self-disclosure and its function in children's attraction to peers. *Child Development, 57,* 1349–1357.

Rotenberg, Ken J., and **Sliz, Dave.** (1988). Children's restrictive disclosure to friends. *Merrill-Palmer Quarterly, 34,* 203–215.

Roth, Martin, Wischik, Claude M., Evans, Nicholas, and **Mountjoy, Christopher.** (1985). Convergence and cohesion of recent neurobiological findings in relation to Alzheimer's disease and their bearing on its aetiological basis. In M. Bergener, Marco Ermini, and H.B. Stahelin (Eds.), *Thresholds in aging.* London: Academic Press.

Roth, William F. (1991). *Work and rewards: Redefining our work-life reality.* New York: Praeger.

Rourke, Byran P. (1989). *Nonverbal learning disabilities: The syndrome and the mode.* New York: Guilford Press.

Rovee-Collier, Carolyn. (1987). Learning and memory in infancy. In Joy Doniger Osofsky (Ed.), *Handbook of infant development* (2nd ed.). New York: Wiley.

Rowe, John W., and **Kahn, Robert L.** (1987). Human aging: Usual and successful. *Science, 237,* 143–149.

Rowe, John W., and **Minaker, Kenneth L.** (1985). Geriatric medicine. In Caleb E. Finch and Edward L. Schneider (Eds.), *Handbook of the biology of aging* (2nd ed.). New York: Van Nostrand.

Rozin, Paul. (1990). Development in the food domain. *Developmental Psychology, 26,* 555–562.

Rubin, Kenneth H., and **Krasnor, L.R.** (1986). Social-cognitive and social behavioral perspectives on problem solving. In M. Perlmutter (Ed.), *Cognitive perspectives on children's social and behavioral development: Minnesota symposia on child psychology* (Vol. 18). Hillsdale, NJ: Erlbaum.

Rubin, Zick. (1980). *Children's friendships.* Cambridge, MA: Harvard University Press.

Ruble, D. (1983). The development of social comparison processes and their role in achievement-related self-socialization. In E.T. Higgins, D.N. Ruble, and W.W. Hartup (Eds.), *Social cognition and social development.* Cambridge, England: Cambridge University Press.

Ruble, D., Boggiano, A., Feldman, N., and **Loebl, J.** (1980). A developmental analysis of the role of social comparison in self-evaluation. *Developmental Psychology, 16,* 105–115.

Ruff, Holly A. (1982). The development of object perception in infancy. In Tiffany M. Field, Aletha Huston, Herbert C. Quay, Lillian Troll, and Gordon E. Finley (Eds.), *Review of human development.* New York: Wiley.

Ruff, Holly A. (1984). An ecological approach to infant memory. In Morris Moscovitch (Ed.), *Infant memory.* New York: Plenum.

Ruffman, Ted K., and **Olson, David R.** (1989). Children's ascriptions of knowledge to others. *Developmental Psychology, 25,* 601–606.

Rush, D., and **Callaghan, K.R.** (1989). Exposure to passive cigarette smoking and child development. In Donald Hutchings (Ed.), *Prenatal abuse of licit and illicit drugs.* New York: New York Academy of Sciences.

Russell, Diana E.H. (1984). Sexual exploitation: Rape, child sexual abuse, and workplace harassment. *Sage Library of Social Research, 155.* Beverly Hills, CA: Sage Publications.

Rutherford, Andrew. (1986). *Growing out of crime.* Middlesex, England: Penguin.

Rutter, D.R., and **Durkin, K.** (1987). Turn-taking in mother-infant interaction: An examination of vocalization and gaze. *Developmental Psychology, 23,* 54–61.

Rutter, Michael. (1979). Protective factors in children's responses to stress and disadvantage. In Martha Whalen Kent and Jon E. Rolf (Eds.), *Primary prevention of psychopathology: Vol. III. Social competence in children.* Hanover, NH: University Press of New England.

Rutter, Michael. (1980). *Changing youth in a changing society: Patterns of development and disorder.* Cambridge, MA: Harvard University Press.

Rutter, Michael. (1982). Epidemiological-longitudinal approaches to the study of development. In W. Andrew Collins (Ed.), *The concept of development: Minnesota symposia on child psychology* (Vol. 15). Hillsdale, NJ: Erlbaum.

Rutter, Michael. (1982). Socio-emotional consequences of day care for preschool children. In E.F. Zigler and E.W. Gordon (Eds.), *Day care: Scientific and social policy issues.* Boston: Auburn House.

Rutter, Michael. (1987). Psychosocial resilience and protective mechanisms. *American Journal of Orthopsychiatry, 57,* 316–331.

Rutter, Michael. (1989). Intergenerational continuities and discontinuities. In Dante Cicchetti and Vicki Carlson (Eds.), *Child maltreatment: Theory and research on the causes and consequences of child abuse and neglect.* Cambridge, England: Cambridge University Press.

Rutter, Michael. (1991). Nature, nurture, and psychopathology: A new look at an old topic. *Development and Psychopathology, 3,* 125–136.

Rutter, Michael, and **Garmezy, Norman.** (1983). Developmental psychopathology. In Paul H. Mussen (Ed.), *Handbook of child psychology: Vol. 4. Socialization, personality and social development.* New York: Wiley.

Rutter, Michael, and **Giller, Henri.** (1984). *Juvenile delinquency: Trends and perspectives.* New York: Guilford.

Rybash, John M., Hoyer, William J., and **Roodin, Paul A.** (1986). *Adult cognition and aging: Developmental changes in processing, knowing, and thinking.* New York: Pergamon.

Saarni, C. (1989). Children's understanding of strategic control of emotional expression in social transactions. In C. Saarni and P.L. Harris (Eds.), *Children's understanding of emotion.* Cambridge, England: Cambridge University Press.

Sable, Pat. (1991). Attachment, loss of spouse, and grief in elderly adults. *Omega, 23,* 129–142.

Sagi, A., and **Lewkowicz, K.S.** (1987). A cross-cultural evaluation of attachment research. In L.W.C. Tavecchio and M.H. van Ijzendoorn (Eds.), *Attachment in social networks.* Amsterdam: Elsevier Science.

Sagi, Abraham, van Ijzendoorn, Marinus H., and **Koren-Karie, Nina.** (1991). Primary appraisal of the Strange Situation: A cross-cultural analysis of preseparation episodes. *Developmental Psychology, 27,* 587–596.

Sainsbury, Peter. (1986). The epidemiology of suicide. In Alec Roy (Ed.), *Suicide.* Baltimore, MD: Williams and Wilkins.

St. George-Hyslop, Peter H., Tanzi, Rudolph E., Polinsky, Ronald J., and **others.** (1987). Absence of duplication of chromosome 21 genes in familiar and sporadic Alzheimer's disease. *Science, 238,* 664–666.

Salt, P., Galler, J.R., and **Ramsey, F.C.** (1988). The influence of early malnutrition on subsequent behavioral development. *Developmental and Behavioral Pediatrics, 9,* 15.

Salthouse, Timothy A. (1984). Effects of age and skill in typing. *Journal of Experimental Psychology: General, 113,* 345–371.

Salthouse, Timothy A. (1985). Speed of behavior and its implications for cognition. In James E. Birren and K. Warner Schaie (Eds.), *Handbook of the psychology of aging* (2nd ed.). New York: Van Nostrand Reinhold.

Salthouse, Timothy A. (1986). Effects of age and skill in typing. *Journal of Experimental Psychology: General, 113,* 345–371.

Salthouse, Timothy A. (1987a). Age, experience, and compensation. In C. Schooler and K. Warner Schaie (Eds.), *Cognitive functioning and social structure throughout the life course.* Norwood, NJ: Ablex.

Salthouse, Timothy A. (1987b). The role of experience in cognitive aging. In K. Warner Schaie (Ed.), *Annual review of gerontology and geriatrics* (Vol. 7). New York: Springer.

Salthouse, Timothy A. (1990). Working memory as a processing resource in cognitive aging. *Developmental Review, 10,* 101–124.

Salthouse, Timothy A. (1991). *Theoretical perspectives on cognitive aging.* Hillsdale, NJ: Erlbaum.

Salthouse, Timothy A. (1992). The information-processing perspective on cognitive aging. In Robert J. Sternberg and Cynthia A. Berg (Eds.), *Intellectual development.* New York: Cambridge University Press.

Sanders, Catherine M. (1989). *Grief: The mourning after.* New York: Wiley.

Santrock, John W., Warshak, Richard A., and **Elliott, Gary L.** (1982). Social development and parent-child interaction in father-custody and stepmother families. In Michael E. Lamb (Ed.), *Non-traditional families: Parenting and child development.* Hillsdale, NJ: Erlbaum.

Sarlo, Gregory, Jason, Leonard A., and **Lonak, Cheryl.** (1988). Parents strategies for limiting children's television viewing. *Psychological Reports, 63,* 435–438.

Saudino, Kimberly J., and **Eaton, Warren O.** (1989, July). Heredity and infant activity level: An objective twin study. Paper presented to the International Society for the Study of Behavioral Development, Jybaskyla, Finland.

Saudino-Troike, Muriel, McClure, Erica, and **Fritz, Mary.** (1984). Communicative tactics in children's second language acquisition. In Fred R. Eckman, Lawrence H. Bell, and Diane Nelson (Eds.), *Universals of second language acquisition.* Rowley, MA: Newbury House.

Sauter, Steven L., Murphy, Lawrence R., and **Hurrell, Joseph J., Jr.** (1990). Prevention of work-related psychological disorders. *American Psychologist, 45,* 1146–1158.

Savin-Williams, Ritch C., and **Demo, David H.** (1984). Developmental change and stability in adolescent self-concept. *Developmental Psychology, 20,* 1100–1110.

Savin-Williams, Ritch C., and **Small, S.A.** (1986). The timing of puberty and its relationship to adolescent and parent perceptions of family interactions. *Developmental Psychology, 22,* 342–347.

Savitz, David A., Whelan, Elizabeth A., and **Kleckner, Robert C.** (1989). Self-reported exposure to pesticides and radiation related to pregnancy outcome: Results from National Natality and Fetal Mortality Surveys. *Public Health Reports, 104,* 473–477.

Sayre, Robert F. (1979). The parents' last lessons. In David D. Van Tassel (Ed.), *Aging, death, and the completion of being.* Philadelphia: University of Pennsylvania Press.

Scarr, Sandra. (1985). Constructing psychology: Making facts and fables for our times. *American Psychologist, 40,* 499–512.

Scarr, Sandra, and **McCartney, Kathleen.** (1983). How people make their own environments. A theory of genotype/environmental effects. *Child Development, 54,* 424–435.

Scarr, Sandra, and **Weinberg, Richard A.** (1983). The Minnesota adoption studies: Genetic differences and malleability. *Child Development, 54,* 253–259.

Schaal, B. (1986). Presumed olfactory exchanges between mother and neonate in humans. In J. Le Camus and J. Cosnier (Eds.), *Ethology and psychology.* Toulouse, France: Private, I.E.C.

Schachter, Stanley. (1982). Recidivism and self-cure of smoking and obesity. *American Psychologist, 37,* 436–444.

Schacter, Daniel L., and **Moscovitch, Morris.** (1984). Infants, amnesiacs, and dissociable memory systems. In Morris Moscovitch (Ed.), *Infant memory.* New York: Plenum.

Schaffer, H. Rudolf. (1984). *The child's entry into a social world.* New York: Academic Press.

Schaie, K. Warner. (1977–1978). Toward a stage theory of adult cognitive development. *Journal of Aging and Human Development, 8,* 129–138.

Schaie, K. Warner. (1983). The Seattle longitudinal study. A twenty-one year investigation of psychometric intelligence. In K. Warner Schaie (Ed.), *Longitudinal studies of adult psychological development.* New York: Guilford.

Schaie, K. Warner. (1989a). Individual differences in rate of cognitive change in adulthood. In Vern L. Bengston and K. Warner Schaie (Eds.), *The course of later life.* New York: Springer.

Schaie, K. Warner. (1989b). Perceptual speed in adulthood: Cross-sectional and longitudinal studies. *Psychology and Aging, 4,* 443–453.

Schaie, K. Warner. (1990a). Intellectual development in adulthood. In James E. Birren and K. Warner Schaie (Eds.), *Handbook of the psychology of aging.* San Diego, CA: Academic Press.

Schaie, K. Warner. (1990b). The optimization of cognitive functioning in old age: Predictions based on cohort-sequential and longitudinal data. In Paul B. Baltes and Margret M. Baltes (Eds.), *Successful aging.* Cambridge, England: Cambridge University Press.

Schaie, K. Warner. (1990c). Individual differences in rate of cognitive change in adulthood. In Vern L. Bengston and K. Warner Schaie (Eds.), *The course of later life.* New York: Springer.

Schaie, K. Warner, and **Baltes, Paul B.** (1977). Some faith helps to see the forest: A final comment on the Horn and Donaldson myth of the Baltes-Schaie position on adult intelligence. *American Psychologist, 32,* 1118–1120.

Schaie, K. Warner, and **Willis, Sherry L.** (1986). Can decline in adult intellectual functioning be reversed? *Developmental Psy-*

chology, 22, 223–232.

Schanfield, Stephen. (1986–1987). Parents' responses to the death of adult children from accidents and cancer: A comparison. Omega, 17, 289–297.

Schein, Edgar H. (1990). Organizational culture. American Psychologist, 45, 109–119.

Scheper-Hughes, Nancy. (1983). Deposed kings: The demise of the rural Irish gerontology. In Jay Sokolovsky (Ed.), Growing old in different societies: Cross-cultural perspectives. Belmone, CA: Wadsworth.

Scheper-Hughes, Nancy, and Stein, H. (1987). Child abuse and the unconscious in American popular culture. In N. Scheper-Hughes (Ed.), Child survival. Dordrecht, Netherlands: Reidel.

Schick, Frank L. (Ed.). (1986). Statistical handbook on aging Americans. Phoenix, AZ: Oryx Press.

Schiefelbusch, Richard L. (1984). Assisting children to become communicatively competent. In Richard L. Schiefelbusch and Joanne Pickar (Eds.), The acquisition of communicative competence. Baltimore, MD: University Park Press.

Schieffelin, Bambi B., and Eisenberg, Ann R. (1984). Cultural variation in children's conversations. In Richard L. Schiefelbusch and Joanne Pickar (Eds.), The acquisition of communicative competence. Baltimore, MD: University Park Press.

Schiff, Donald W. (1992). Health consequenes of inadequate access to maternity and infant health care. In Jonathan B. Kotch, Craig H. Blakely, Sarah S. Brown, and Frank Y. Wong (Eds.). A pound of prevention: The case for universal maternity care in the U.S. Washington, DC: American Public Health Association.

Schilling, R.F. (1987). Limitations of social support. Social Services Review, 61, 19–31.

Schlegal, Alice, and Barry, Herbert. (1991). Adolescence: An anthropological inquiry. New York: The Free Press.

Schlesinger, Benjamin. (1982). Sexual abuse of children. Toronto: University of Toronto Press.

Schlundt, David G., and Johnson, William G. (1990). Eating disorders: Assessment and treatment. Boston: Allyn and Bacon.

Schneider, Anne L. (1990). Detterence and juvenile crime. New York: Springer-Verlag.

Schneider, Edward L., and Reed, John D. (1985). Modulations of the aging process. In Caleb E. Finch and Edward L. Schneider (Eds.), Handbook of the biology of aging (2nd ed.). New York: Van Nostrand.

Schneider-Rosen, Karen, and Cicchetti, Dante. (1991). Early self-knowledge and emotional development: Visual self-recognition and affect reactions to mirror self-images in maltreated and non-maltreated toddlers. Developmental Psychology, 27, 471–478.

Schnorr, Teresa M., Grajewski, Barbara A., Hornung, Richard W., Thun, Michael J., Egeland, Grace M., Murray, William E., Conover, David L., and Halperin, William E. (1991). Video display terminals and the risk of spontaneous abortion. New England Journal of Medicine, 324, 727–734.

Schoendorf, Kenneth C., Hogue, C.J.R., Kleinman, J.C., and Rowley, D. (1992). Mortality of infants of Black as compared to White college educated parents. New England Journal of Medicine, 326, 1522–1526.

Schoof-Tams, Karin, Schlaegel, Jürgen, and Walezak, Leonhard. (1976). Differentiation of sexual morality between 11 and 16 years. Archives of Sexual Behavior, 5, 353–370.

Schor, Juliet B. (1991). The overworked American: The unexpected decline of leisure. New York: Basic Books.

Schumm, Walter R., and Bugaighis, Margaret A. (1986). Marital quality over the marital career. Journal of Marriage and the Family, 48, 165–168.

Schwartz, Richard H., Luxenberg, Michael G., and Hoffman, Norman G. (1991). "Crack" use by American middle-class adolescent polydrug abusers. Journal of Pediatrics, 118, 150–155.

Schweinhart, Laurence J., and Weikart, David (Eds.). (1993). Significant benefits: High/Scope Perry preschool study through age 27. Ypsilanti, MI: High/Scope Press.

Schwenger, Cope W. (1989). Institutionalization of elderly Canadians: Future allocations to non-health sectors. In Stephen J. Lewis (Ed.), Aging and health: Linking research and public policy. Chelsea, MI: Lewis Publishers.

Scott, John Paul. (1990). Forward. In Martin E. Hahn, John K. Hewitt, Norman D. Henderson, and Robert H. Benno (Eds.), Developmental behavior genetics: Neural, biometrical, and evolutionary approaches. Oxford, England: Oxford University Press.

Scott-Maxwell, Florida. (1968). The measure of my days. New York: Knopf.

Sears, Robert R., Rau, Lucy, and Alpert, Richard. (1965). Identification and child rearing. Stanford, CA: Stanford University Press.

Segerberg, Osborn. (1982). Living to be 100: 1,200 who did and how they did it. New York: Scribners.

Seifer, R., and Sameroff, Arnold J. (1987). Multiple determinants of risk and invulnerability. In E.J. Anthony and B.J. Cohler (Eds.), The invulnerable child. New York: Guilford.

Selkoe, Dennis J. (1990). Deciphering Alzheimer's disease: The amyloid precursor protein yields new clues. Science, 248, 1058–1060.

Seltzer, Judith A. (1991). Relationships between fathers and children who live apart: The father's role after separation. Journal of Marriage and the Family, 53, 79–102.

Seltzer, Judith A., and Bianchi, S.M. (1988). Children's contact with absent parents. Journal of Marriage and the Family, 50, 663–677.

Sena, Rhonda, and Smith, Linda B. (1990). New evidence on the development of the word Big. Child Development, 61, 1034–1052.

Service, V. (1984). Maternal styles and communicative development. In A. Lock and E. Risher (Eds.), Language development. London: Crown Helm.

Seyle, Hans. (1982). History and present status of the stress concept. In L. Goldberger and S. Breznitz (Eds.), Handbook of stress: Theoretical and clinical aspects. New York: The Free Press.

Seyle, Hans. (1985). History and present status of the stress concept. In A. Monat and Richard Lazarus (Eds.), Stress and coping. New York: Columbia University Press.

Shannon, Lyle W. (1988). Criminal career continuity: Its social context. New York: Human Sciences Press.

Shantz, C.U. (1987). Conflicts between children. Child Development, 58, 283–305.

Shatz, M., and Gelman, R. (1973). The development of communication skills: Modifications in the speech of young children as a function of the listener. Monographs of the Society for Re-

search in Child Development, 38 (5, Serial No. 152).

Shaw, Lois Banfill (Ed.). (1986). *Midlife women at work: A fifteen year perspective.* Lexington, MA: Lexington Books.

Shay, Kathleen A., and **Roth, David L.** (1992). Association between aerobic fitness and visual-spatial performance in healthy older adults. *Psychology and Aging, 7,* 15–24.

Shaywitz, S.E., and **Shaywitz, B.A.** (1983). Biologic influences on attentional disorders. In M.D. Levine, W.B. Carey, A.C. Crocker, and R.T. Gross (Eds.), *Developmental-behavioral pediatrics.* Philadelphia: Saunders.

Shea, John D.C. (1981). Changes in interpersonal distances and categories of play behavior in the early weeks of preschool. *Developmental Psychology, 17,* 417–425.

Shedler, Jonathan, and **Block, Jack.** (1990). Adolescent drug use and psychological health: A longitudinal inquiry. *American Psychologist, 45,* 612–630.

Sheehy, Gail. (1976). *Passages: Predictable crisis of adult life.* New York: Dutton.

Sheehy, Gail. (1992). *The silent passage.* New York: Random House.

Shevron, Ronald H., and **Lumsden, D. Barry.** (1985). *Introduction to educational gerontology* (2nd ed.). New York: Hemisphere.

Shiffrin, R.M., and **Atkinson, R.C.** (1969). Storage and retrieval processes in long-term memory. *Psychological Review, 76,* 179–193.

Shipp, E.E. (1985, November 4). Teen-agers taking risks: When pregnancy is the result. *New York Times,* A16.

Shirley, Mary M. (1933). The first two years: A study of twenty-five babies. *Institute of Child Welfare Monograph No. 8.* Minneapolis: University of Minnesota Press.

Shneidman, Edwin S. (1978). Suicide. In Gardner Lindzey, Calvin S. Hall, and Richard F. Thompson, *Psychology* (2nd ed.). New York: Worth.

Shock, Nathan W. (1985). Longitudinal studies of aging in humans. In Caleb E. Finch and Edward L. Schneider (Eds.), *Handbook of the biology of aging* (2nd ed.). New York: Van Nostrand.

Shy, Kirkwood K., Luth, David A., Bennett, Forrest C., Whitfield, Michael, Larson, Eric B., van Belle, Gerald, Hughes, James P., Wilson, Judith A., and **Stenchever, Morton A.** (1990). Effects of electronic fetal-heart-rate monitoring, as compared with periodic auscultation, on the neurologic development of premature infants. *The New England Journal of Medicine, 322,* 588–594.

Siegfried, Donna. (1990, April 2). Conversation with technical safety specialist of the National Safety Council.

Siegler, Irene C. (1975). The terminal drop hypothesis: Fact or artifact? *Experimental Aging Research, 1,* 169–185.

Siegler, Irene, and **Costa, Paul.** (1985). Health behavior relationships. In J.E. Birren and K.W. Schaie (Eds.), *Handbook of the psychology of aging.* New York: Van Nostrand.

Siegler, Robert. (1983a). Information processing approaches to development. In Paul H. Mussen (Ed.), *Handbook of child psychology: Vol. 1. History, theory, and methods.* W. Kessen (Vol. Ed.). New York: Wiley.

Siegler, Robert. (1983b). Five generalizations about cognitive development. *American Psychologist, 38,* 263–277.

Siegler, Robert. (1986). *Children's thinking.* Englewood Cliffs,

NJ: Prentice-Hall.

Sigel, Irving E., Dreyer, Albert S., and **McGillicuddy-DeLisi, Ann V.** (1984). Psychological perspectives on the life course. In Ross D. Parke (Ed.), *Review of child development research: Vol. 7. The family.* Chicago: University of Chicago Press.

Sigler, Robert T. (1989). *Domestic violence: An assessment of community attitudes.* Lexington, MA: Lexington Books.

Silbereisen, Rainer K., Petersen, Anne C., Albrecht, Helfried T., and **Kracke, Barbel.** (1989). Maturational timing and the development of problem behavior: Longitudinal studies in adolescence. *Journal of Early Adolescence, 9,* 247–268.

Silbergeld, Ellen K., Mattison, Donald R., and **Bertin, Joan E.** (1989). Occupational exposures and female reproduction. In Mark I. Evans, Alan O. Dixler, John C. Fletcher, and Joseph D. Shulman (Eds.), *Fetal diagnosis and therapy: Science, ethics, and the law.* Philadelphia: Lippincott.

Sill, J.S. (1980). Disengagement reconsidered: Awareness of finitude. *Gerontologist, 20,* 457–462.

Silva, Phil A., Hughes, Pauline, Williams, Sheila, and **Faed, James M.** (1988). Blood lead, intelligence, reading attainment and behavior in eleven-year-old children in Dunedin, New Zealand. *Journal of Child Psychology and Psychiatry, 29,* 43–52.

Silver, A.A., and **Hagin, R.A.** (1990). *Disorders of learning in childhood.* New York: Wiley.

Simmons, Roberta G., and **Blyth, Dale A.** (1987). *Moving into adolescence: The impact of pubertal change and school context.* New York: Aldine de Gruyter.

Simmons, Roberta G., Blyth, Dale A., and **McKinney, Karen L.** (1983). The social and psychological effects of puberty on white females. In Jeanne Brooks-Gunn and Anne C. Petersen (Eds.), *Girls at puberty: Biological and psychosocial aspects.* New York: Plenum.

Simmons, Roberta G., Burgeson, Richard, and **Reef, Mary Jo.** (1988). Cumulative change at entry to adolescence. In Megan R. Gunnar and W. Andrew Collins (Eds.), *Development during the transition to adolescence: Minnesota symposia on child psychology* (Vol. 21). Hillsdale, NJ: Erlbaum.

Simmons, Roberta G., Rosenberg, Florence, and **Rosenberg, Morris.** (1973). Disturbance in the self-image at adolescence. *American Sociological Review, 38,* 553–568.

Simons, Ronald L., Whitbeck, Les B., Conger, Rand D., and **Chyi-In, Wu.** (1991). Intergenerational transmission of harsh parenting. *Developmental Psychology, 27,* 159–171.

Sinclair, David. (1978). *Human growth after birth* (3rd ed.). London: Oxford University Press.

Sinclair, David. (1989). *Human growth after birth.* New York: Oxford.

Sinnot, Jan D. (Ed.). (1989). *Everyday problem solving.* New York: Praeger.

Sinnot, Jan D. (1989). Life-span relativistic postformal thought: Methodology and data from everyday problem-solving studies. In Michael L. Commons, Jan D. Sinnott, Francis A. Richards, and Cheryl Armon (Eds.), *Adult development: Vol. 1. Comparisons and applications of developmental models.* New York: Praeger.

Sizer, Theodore R. (1985). *Horace's compromise: The dilemma of the American high school.* Boston: Houghton Mifflin.

Skeels, H.M. (1966). Adult status of children with contrasting early life experiences. *Monographs of the Society for Research in Child Development, 31* (3).

Skinner, B.F. (1953). *Science and human behavior.* New York: Macmillan.

Skinner, B.F. (1957). *Verbal behavior.* New York: Appleton-Century-Crofts.

Skinner, B.F. (1972). *Beyond freedom and dignity.* New York: Knopf.

Skinner, John H. (1992). Aging in place: The experience of African American and other minority elders. *Generations, 16* (2), 49–52.

Skolnick, Andrew. (1990). Cocaine use in pregnancy: Physicians urged to look for problem where they least expect it. *Journal of the American Medical Association, 264,* 306–307.

Slaughter, Diana T., and Dombrowski, Joseph. (1989). Cultural continuities and discontinuities: Impact on social and pretend play. In Marianne N. Bloch and Anthony D. Pellegrini (Eds.), *The ecological context of children's play.* Norwood, NJ: Ablex.

Slavin, Robert E. (1987). Ability grouping and student achievement in elementary schools: A best evidence synthesis. *Review of Educational Research, 57,* 293–336.

Sloane, Ethel. (1985). *Biology and women* (2nd ed.). New York: Wiley.

Sloane, J.H., Kellerman, A.L., Reay, D.T., Ferris, J.A., Koepsell, T., and Rivara, F.P. (1988). Handgun regulation, crime, assault and homicide: A tale of two cities. *New England Journal of Medicine, 319,* 1256–1262.

Sloane, John Henry, Rivara, Frederick P., Reay, Donald T., Ferris, James A., Path, M.R,C., and Kellerman, Arthur. (1990). Firearm regulations and rates of suicide: A comparison of two metropolitan areas. *New England Journal of Medicine, 322,* 369-373.

Small, Stephen A., Eastman, Gay, and Cornelius, Steven. (1988). Adolescent automomy and parental stress. *Journal of Youth and Adolescence, 17,* 377–391.

Smetana, Judith G., Yau, Jenny, Restrepo, Angela, and Braeges, Judith L. (1991). Adolescent-parent conflict in married and divorced families. *Developmental Psychology, 27,* 1000–1010.

Smith, Jacqui, and Baltes, Paul B. (1990). Wisdom-related knowledge: Age/cohort differences in response to life-planning problems. *Developmental Psychology, 26,* 494–505.

Smith, Ken R., and Zick, Cathleen D. (1986). The incidence of poverty among the recently widowed: Mediating factors in the life course. *Journal of Marriage and the Family, 48,* 619–630.

Smith, Linda. (1989). A model of perceptual classification in children and adults. *Psychological Review, 96,* 125–144.

Smith, M. Brewster. (1983). Hope and despair: Keys to the socio-psychodynamics of youth. *American Journal of Orthopsychiatry, 53,* 388–399.

Smith, Thomas Ewin. (1990). Parental separation and the academic self-concepts of adolescents: An effort to solve the puzzle of separation effects. *Journal of Marriage and the Family, 52,* 107–118.

Smith, Wrynn. (1987). *Cancer: A profile of health and disease in America.* New York: Facts on File.

Smyser, A.A. (1982). Hospices: Their humanistic and economic value. *American Psychologist, 37,* 1260–1262.

Snarey, John R., Reimber, Joseph, and Kohlberg, Lawrence. (1985). Development of social-moral reasoning among Kibbutz adolescents: A longitudinal cross-cultural study. *Developmental Psychology, 21,* 3–17.

Snider, Vicki E., and Tarver, Sara G. (1989). The relationship between achievement and IQ in students with learning disabilities. *Psychology in the Schools, 26,* 346–353.

Snow, Catherine E. (1984). Parent-child interaction and the development of communicative ability. In Richard L. Schiefelbusch and Joanne Pickar (Eds.), *The acquisition of communicative competence.* Baltimore, MD: University Park Press.

Snow, Catherine E. (1987). Language and the beginning of moral understanding. In Jerome Kagan and Sharon Lamb (Eds.), *The emergence of morality in young children.* Chicago: University of Chicago Press.

Snyder, D.L. (1989). *Dietary restriction and aging.* New York: Liss.

Snyder, Dona J. (1985). Psychosocial effects of long-term antepartal hospitalization. In Manohar Rathi (Ed.), *Clinical aspects of perinatal medicine.* New York: Macmillan.

Snyder, James, and Patterson, Gerald R. (1987). Family interaction and delinquent behavior. In Herbert C. Quay (Ed.), *Handbook of juvenile delinquency.* New York: Wiley.

Snyder, James, Dishion, T.J., and Patterson, Gerald R. (1986). Determinants and consequences of associating with deviant peers during preadolescence and adolescence. *Journal of Early Adolescence, 6,* 29–43.

Society for Research in Child Development. (1990, Winter). SRCD ethical standards for research with children. *SRCD Newsletter,* 5–7.

Soloman, Mildred Z., O'Donnell, Lydia, Jennings, Bruce, Guifoy, Vivian, Wolff, Susan M., Nolan, Kathleen, Jackson, Rebecca, Koch-Weser, Dieter, and Donnelley, Strachan. (1993). Decisions near the end of life: Professional views on life-sustaining treatments. *American Journal of Public Health, 83,* 14–23.

Sonenstein, Freya, Pleck, Joseph H., and Ku, Leighton C. (1989). Sexual activity, condom use, and AIDS awareness among adolescent males. *Family Planning Perspectives, 21,* 152–158.

Sonnenschein, Susan. (1984). How feedback from a listener affects children's referential communication skills. *Developmental Psychology, 20,* 287–292.

Sonnenschein, Susan. (1986). Development of referential communication skills: How familiarity with a listener affects a speaker's production of redundant messages. *Developmental Psychology, 22,* 549–552.

South, Scott J. (1991). Sociodemographic differentials in mate selection preferences. *Journal of Marriage and the Family, 53,* 928–940.

Southard, B. (1985). Interlimb movement control and coordination in children. In Jane E. Clark and James H. Humphrey (Eds.), *Motor development: Current selected research.* Princeton, NJ: Princeton Book Company.

Spanier, Graham, and Thompson, Linda. (1984). *Parting: The aftermath of separation and divorce.* Beverly Hills, CA: Sage.

Spearman, Charles. (1927). *The abilities of man.* New York: Macmillan.

Spelke, Elizabeth. (1979). Perceiving bimodally specified

events in infancy. *Developmental Psychology, 15,* 626–636.

Spelke, Elizabeth. (1987). The development of intermodal perception. In Philip Salapatek and Leslie Cohen (Eds.), *Handbook of infant perception: Vol. 2. From perception to cognition.* Orlando, FL: Academic Press.

Spence, Janet T., and Helmreich, Robert L. (1978). *Masculinity and femininity: Their psychological dimensions, correlates, and antecedents.* Austin: University of Texas Press.

Spencer, Margaret Beale, and Markstrom-Adams, Carol. (1990). Identity processes among racial and ethnic minority children in America. *Child Development, 61,* 290–310.

Spitze, Glenna. (1988). Women's employment and family relations. *Journal of Marriage and the Family, 50,* 595–618.

Spock, Benjamin. (1945). *The common sense book of baby and child care.* New York: Duell, Sloan and Pearce.

Sprague, R.L., and Ullman, R.K. (1981). Psychoactive drugs and child management. In J.M. Kaufman and D.P. Hallahan (Eds.), *Handbook of special education.* New York: Prentice-Hall.

Spreen, Otfried. (1988). *Learning disabled children growing up: A follow-up into adulthood.* New York: Oxford University Press.

Springer, Sally P., and Deutsch, Georg. (1989). *Left brain, right brain.* New York: Freeman.

Sroufe, L. Alan. (1979). Socioemotional development. In Joy Doniger Osofsky (Ed.), *Handbook of infant development.* New York: Wiley.

Sroufe, L. Alan, and Ward, Mary Jo. (1980). Seductive behavior of mothers of toddlers. Occurrence, correlates, and family origins. *Child Development, 51,* 1222–1229.

Sroufe, L. Alan, Fox, Nancy E., and Pancake, Van R. (1983). Attachment and dependency in developmental perspective. *Child Development, 54,* 1615–1627.

Sroufe, L. Alan, Jacobvitz, Deborah, Mengelsdorf, Sarah, DeAngelo, Edward, and Ward, Mary Jo. (1985). Generational boundary dissolution between mothers and their preschool children: A relationship systems approach. *Child Development, 56,* 317–325.

Sroule, L., and Fischer, A.K. (1980). The midtown Manhattan longitudinal study vs. the mental paradise lost doctrine. *Archives of General Psychiatry, 37,* 209–221.

Sroule, L., Langner, T.S., Michael, S.T., Opler, M.K., and Rennie, T. (1962). *Mental health in the metropolis: The midtown study.* New York: McGraw-Hill.

Staines, Graham L., Pottick, Kathleen J., and Fudge, Deborah A. (1986). Wives' employment and husbands' attitude toward work and life. *Journal of Applied Psychology, 71,* 118–128.

Stampfer, Meir, et al. (1991). Post-menopausal estrogen therapy and cardiovascular diseases: Ten-year follow-up from the Nurses Health Study. *New England Journal of Medicine, 325,* 756–762.

Stanton, Annette L. (1991). Cognitive appraisal, coping processes, and adjustment to infertility. In Annette L. Stanton and Christine Dunkel-Schetter (Eds.), *Infertility.* New York: Plenum.

Stanton, Annette L., and Dunkel-Schetter, Christine (Eds.). (1991). *Infertility.* New York: Plenum.

Stanton, M. Duncan. (1985). The family and drug abuse: Concepts and rationale. In Thomas E. Bratter and Gary G. Forrest (Eds.), *Alcoholism and substance abuse: Strategies for clinical*

intervention. New York: The Free Press.

Starr, Bernard D., and Weiner, Marcella Baker. (1981). *Sex and sexuality in the mature years.* New York: Stein and Day.

Steele, Brandt. (1980). Psychodynamic factors in child abuse. In C. Henry Kempe and Ray E. Helfer (Eds.), *The battered child* (3rd ed.). Chicago: University of Chicago Press.

Steffe, Leslie P. and Wood, Terry (Eds.). (1990). *Transforming children's mathematics education: International Perspectives.* Hillsdale, NJ: Erlbaum.

Stein, Marvin and Schleifer, Steven J. (1985). Frontiers of stress research: Stress and immunity. In Michael R. Zales (Eds.). *Stress in health and disease.* New York: Brunner/Mazel.

Steinberg, Lawrence. (1986). Stability (and instability) of Type A behavior from childhood to young adulthood. *Developmental Psychology, 22,* 393–402.

Steinberg, Lawrence. (1988). Reciprocal relation between parent-child distance and pubertal maturation. *Developmental Psychology, 24,* 122–128.

Steinberg, Lawrence. (1990). Interdependency in the family: Autonomy, conflict and harmony in the parent-adolescent relationship. In Shirley S. Feldman and G.R. Elliot (Eds.), *At the threshold: The developing adolescent.* Cambridge, MA: Harvard University Press.

Steinberg, Lawrence, Elmen, J.D. and Mounts, N.S. (1989). Authoritative parenting, psychosocial maturity and academic success among adolescents. *Child Development, 60,* 1424–1436.

Steinberg, Lawrence, Mounts, Nina S., Lamborn, Susan D., and Dornbusch, Sanford M. (1991). Authoritative parenting and adolescent adjustment across various ecological niches. *Journal of Research on Adolescence, 1,* 19–36.

Steinmetz, Suzanne. (1988). *Duty bound: Elderly abuse and family care.* Beverly Hills, CA: Sage.

Stenberg, Craig, and Campos, Joseph J. (1983). The development of the expression of anger in human infants. In Michael Lewis and Carolyn Saarni (Eds.), *The socialization of affect.* New York: Plenum.

Stephen, J. Claiborne, Cavanaugh, Mark L., Gradie, Margaret I., Mador, Martin L., and Kidd, Kenneth K. (1990). Mapping the human genome: Current status. *Science, 250,* 237–250.

Stephens, Joyce. (1976). *Loners, losers, and lovers: Elderly tenants in a slum hotel.* Seattle: University of Washington Press.

Stern, Daniel. (1977). *The first relationship: Mother and infant.* Cambridge, MA: Harvard University Press.

Stern, Daniel N. (1985). *The interpersonal world of the infant.* New York: Basic Books.

Stern, J.A., Oster, P.J., and Newport, K. (1980). Reaction time measures, hemispheric specialization, and age. In Leonard W. Poon (Ed.), *Aging in the 80's: Psychological issues.* Washington, DC: American Psychological Association.

Sternberg, Kathleen J., and Lamb, Michael E. (1991). Can we ignore context in the definition of child maltreatment? *Development and Psychopathology, 3,* 87–92.

Sternberg, Robert J. (1985). *Beyond IQ: A triarchic theory of human intelligence.* Cambridge, England: Cambridge University Press.

Sternberg, Robert J. (1988). Intellectual development: Psychometric and information-processing approaches. In M.H. Bornstein and M.E. Lamb (Eds.), *Developmental psychology: An advanced textbook* (2nd ed.). Hillsdale, NJ: Erlbaum.

Sternberg, Robert J. (1990). *Wisdom: Its nature and development*. New York: Cambridge University Press.

Sternberg, Robert J., and Barnes, Michael L. (Eds.). (1988). *The psychology of love*. New Haven, CT: Yale University Press.

Sternberg, Robert J., and Berg, Cynthia. (1987). What are theories of adult intellectual development theories of? In C. Schooler and K. Warner Schaie (Eds.), *Cognitive functioning and social structure over the life course*. Norwood, NJ: Ablex.

Sternberg, Robert J., and Wagner, Richard K. (Eds.). (1986). *Practical intelligence*. Cambridge, England: Cambridge University Press.

Stets, Jan E. (1991). Verbal and physical aggression in marriage. *Journal of Marriage and the Family, 52*, 501–514.

Stevenson, Harold W., and Lee, Shin-ying. (1990). Contexts of achievement: A study of American, Chinese, and Japanese children. *Monographs of the Society for Research in Child Development, 55* (1–2, Serial No. 221).

Stevenson, Harold W., and Stigler, Robert W. (1992). *The learning gap: Why our schools are failing and what we can learn from Japanese and Chinese education*. New York: Summit Books.

Stewart, Robert B. (1990). *The second child: Family transitions and adjustment*. Newbury Park, CA: Sage.

Stipek, Deborah J. (1984). Young children's performance expectations: Logical analysis or wishful thinking? In J. Nicholls (Ed.), *The development of achievement motivation*. Greenwich, CT: JAI.

Stipek, Deborah J., and Hoffman, J. (1980). Development of children's performance-related judgments. *Child Development, 51*, 912–914.

Stipek, Deborah J., and Mac Iver, D. (1989). Developmental change in children's assessment of intellectual competence. *Child Development, 60*, 521–538.

Stipek, Deborah J., Recchia, Susan, and McClinic, Susan. (1992). Self-evaluation in young children. *Monographs of the Society for Research in Child Development, 57*, Serial No. 226, 1–79.

Stipek, Deborah J., Roberts, Theresa A., and Sanborn, Mary E. (1984). Preschool-age children's performance expectations for themselves and another child as a function of the incentive value of success and the salience of past performance. *Child Development, 55*, 1983–1989.

Stoll, Basil A. (Ed.). (1988). *Cost versus benefit in cancer care*. Baltimore, MD: Johns Hopkins University Press.

Stoller, Eleanor Palo. (1992). Gender differences in the experiences of caregiving spouses. In Jeffrey W. Dwyer and Raymond T. Coward (Eds.), *Gender, families and elder care*. Newbury Park, CA: Sage.

Stones, M.J., and Konza, A. (1989). Age, exercise and coding performance. *Psychology and Aging, 4*, 190–194.

Straus, Murray A., and Gelles, Richard J. (1986). Societal change and change in family violence from 1975 to 1985 as revealed by two national surveys. *Journal of Marriage and the Family, 48*, 465–479.

Straus, Murray A., and Sweet, Stephen. (1991). Verbal/symbolic aggression in couples: Incidence rates and relationships to personal characteristics. *Journal of Marriage and the Family, 54*, 346–357.

Strauss, C.C., Smith, K., Frame, C., and Forehand, R. (1985). Personal and interpersonal characteristics associated with childhood obesity. *Journal of Pediatric Psychology, 10*, 337–343.

Strein, William. (1986). Sex and age difference in preschool children's behavior: Partial support for the Knight/Karan hypothesis. *Psychological Reports, 58*, 915–921.

Streissguth, Ann Pytkowicz, Barr, Helen M., Sampson, Paul D., Darby, Betty L., and Martin, Donald C. (1989). IQ at age 4 in relation to maternal alcohol use and smoking during pregnancy. *Developmental Psychology, 25*, 3–11.

Streitmatter, Janice L. (1988). Ethnicity as a mediating variable of early adolescent identity development. *Journal of Adolescence, 11*, 335–346.

Streitmatter, Janice L. (1989). Identity status development and cognitive prejudice in early adolescents. *Journal of Early Adolescence, 9*, 142–152.

Streri, Arlette. (1985). *Tactile discrimination of form in 2- to 3-month-old infants: Is cross-modal transfer to vision possible?* Paper presented to the International Society for the Study of Behavioral Development, Tours, France.

Striegel-Moore, Ruth H., Silberstein, Lisa, and Rodin, Judith. (1986). Understanding of risk factors for bulimia. *American Psychologist, 41*, 246–263.

Stroebe, Margaret S., and Stroebe, Wolfgang. (1983). Who suffers more? Sex differences in health risks of the widowed. *Psychology Bulletin, 93*, 279–301.

Strube, M.J., Berry, J.M., Goza, B.K., and Fennimore, D. (1985). Type A behavior, age, and psychological well-being. *Journal of Personality and Social Psychology, 49*, 203–218.

Stueve, Ann, and O'Donnell, Lydia. (1984). The daughter of aging parents. In Grace K. Baruch and Jeanne Brooks-Gunn (Eds.), *Women in midlife*. New York: Plenum.

Suitor, J. Jill. (1992). Marital quality and satisfaction with the division of household labor across the family life cycle. *Journal of Marriage and the Family, 53*, 221–230.

Sullivan, Margaret Wolan. (1982). Reactivation: Priming forgotten memories in human infants. *Child Development, 53*, 516–523.

Sullivan, Susan A., and Birch, Leann L. (1990). Pass the sugar, pass the salt: Experience dictates preference. *Developmental Psychology, 26*, 546–551.

Sunderland, Alan, Watts, Kathryn, Baddeley, Alan D., and Harris, John E. (1986). Subjective memory assessment and test performance in elderly adults. *Journal of Gerontology, 41*, 376–384.

Super, Charles M., and Harkness, Sara. (1982). The development of affect in infancy and early childhood. In Daniel A. Wagner and Harold W. Stevenson (Eds.), *Cultural perspectives on child development*. San Francisco: Freeman.

Surbey, M. (1990). Family composition, stress, and human menarche. In F. Bercovitch and T. Zeigler (Eds.), *The socioendocrinology of primate reproduction*. New York: Liss.

Sutherland, David H., Olshen, Richard A., Biden, Edmund N., and Wyatt, Marilyn P. (1988). *The development of mature walking*. Philadelphia: Lippincott.

Sutton-Smith, Brian. (1986). *Toys as culture*. New York: Gardner Press.

Swadener, Elizabeth Blue, and **Johnson, James E.** (1989). Play in diverse social contexts: Parent and teacher roles. In Marianne N. Bloch and Anthony D. Pellegrini (Eds.), *The ecological context of children's play.* Norwood, NJ: Ablex.

Swan, Gary E., Dame, Alison, and **Carmelli, Dorit.** (1991). Involuntary retirement, Type A behavior, and current functioning in elderly men: 27-year follow-up of the Western Collaborative Group Study. *Psychology and Aging, 6,* 384–391.

Swann, William B., Stein-Seroussi, Alan, and **Giesler, R. Brian.** (1992). Why people self-verify. *Journal of Personality and Social Psychology, 62,* 392–401.

Taitz, L.S., and **Wardley, B.L.** (1989). *Handbook of child nutrition.* New York: Oxford.

Tannen, Deborah. (1990). *You just don't understand.* New York: Morrow.

Tanner, James M. (1970). Physical growth. In Paul H. Mussen (Ed.), *Carmichael's manual of child psychology: Vol. 1.* (3rd ed.). New York: Wiley.

Tanner, James M. (1971). Sequence, tempo, and individual variation in the growth and development of boys and girls aged twelve to sixteen. *Daedalus, 100,* 907–930.

Tanner, James M. (1978). *Fetus into man: Physical growth from conception to maturity.* Cambridge, MA: Harvard University Press.

Tanzer, Deborah, and **Block, Jean Libman.** (1976). *Why natural childbirth? A psychologist's report on the benefits to mothers, fathers and babies.* New York: Shocken.

Taylor, H. Gerry. (1988). Neuropsychological testing: Relevance of assessing children's learning disabilities. *Journal of Consulting and Clinical Psychology, 56,* 795–800.

Taylor, Robert Joseph. (1986). Family support among black Americans. *Journal of Marriage and the Family, 48,* 67–78.

Taylor, Shelly E. (1989). *Positive illusions: Creative self-deception and the healthy mind.* New York: Basic Books.

Teale, W.H., and **Sulzby, E.** (1986). *Emergent literacy: Writing and reading.* Norwood, NJ: Ablex.

Teller, Davida Y., and **Bornstein, Marc H.** (1987). Infant color vision and color perception. In Philip Salapatek and Leslie Cohen (Eds.), *Handbook of infant perception: Vol. 2. From perception to cognition.* Orlando, FL: Academic Press.

Teri, Linda, and **Reifler, Burton V.** (1987). Depression and dementia. In Laura L. Carstensen and Barry A. Edelstein (Eds.), *Handbook of clinical gerontology.* New York: Pergamon.

Termine, N.T., and **Izard, C.E.** (1988). Infants' responses to their mothers' expressions of joy and sadness. *Developmental Psychology, 24,* 223–229.

Tharp, Roland G. (1989). Psychocultural variables and constants: Effect on teaching and learning in the schools. *American Psychologist, 44,* 349–359.

Tharp, Roland G., and **Fallimore, Ronald.** (1988). *Rousing minds to life: Teaching, learning, and schooling in social context.* Cambridge, England: Cambridge University Press.

Thelan, Esther. (1987). The role of motor development in developmental psychology: A view of the past and an agenda for the future. In Nancy Eisenberg (Ed.), *Contemporary topics in developmental psychology.* New York: Wiley.

Thelan, Esther, and **Ulrich, Beverly D.** (1991). Hidden skills. *Monographs of the Society for Research in Child Development, 56,* Serial No. 223.

Thiederman, Sondra. (1991). *Bridging cultural barriers for corporate success.* Lexington, MA: Lexington Books.

Thoman, E.B. (1975). Sleep and wake behaviors in neonates: Consistencies and consequences. *Merrill Palmer Quarterly, 21,* 295–314.

Thomas, Alexander. (1981). Current trends in developmental theory. *American Journal of Orthopsychiatry, 51,* 580–609.

Thomas, Alexander, and **Chess, Stella.** (1977). *Temperament and development.* New York: Brunner/Mazel.

Thomas, Alexander, Chess, Stella, and **Birch, Herbert G.** (1963). *Behavioral individuality in early childhood.* New York: New York University Press.

Thomas, Alexander, Chess, Stella, and **Birch, Herbert G.** (1968). *Temperament and behavior disorders in children.* New York: New York University Press.

Thomas, Alexander, Chess, Stella, and **Mendez, O.** (1974). Cross-cultural study of behavior in children with special vulnerabilities to stress. In D. Ricks, Alexander Thomas, and M. Roff (Eds.), *Life history research in psychopathology* (Vol. 3). Minneapolis: University of Minnesota Press.

Thomas, Jeanne L. (1986). Age and sex differences in perceptions of grandparents. *Journal of Gerontology, 41,* 417–423.

Thompkins, Linda, and **Walker, Alexis J.** (1989). Gender in families: Women and men in marriage, work, and parenthood. *Journal of Marriage and the Family, 51,* 845–871.

Thompson, Elizabeth, and **Colella, Ugo.** (1992). *Journal of Marriage and the Family, 54,* 259–267.

Thompson, Elizabeth, McLanahan, Sara S., and **Curtin, Roberta Braun.** (1992). Family structure, gender and parental socialization. *Journal of Marriage and the Family, 2,* 368–378.

Thompson, Larry W., Gong, Vincent, Haskins, Edmund, and **Gallagher, Dolores.** (1987). Assessment of depression and dementia during the late years. In K. Warner Schaie (Ed.), *Annual review of gerontology and geriatrics* (Vol. 7). New York: Springer.

Thompson, Lee Anne, Detterman, Douglas K., and **Plomin, Robert.** (1991). Associations between cognitive abilities and scholastic achievement: Genetic overlap but environmental differences. *Psychological Science, 2,* 158–165.

Thompson, Linda, and **Walker, Alexis J.** (1989). Gender in families: Women and men in marriage, work, and parenthood. *Journal of Marriage and the Family, 5,* 845–871.

Thompson, Ross A. (1990). Emotion and self-regulation. In R.A. Thompson (Ed.), *Socioemotional development: Nebraska symposium on motivation* (Vol. 36). Lincoln, NE: University of Nebraska Press.

Thompson, Ross A. (1990). Vulnerability in research: A developmental perspective on research risk. *Child Development, 61,* 1–16.

Thompson, Ross A. (1991). Attachment theory and research. In Melvin Lewis (Ed.), *Child and adolescent psychiatry: A comprehensive textbook.* Baltimore, MD: Williams and Wilkins.

Thompson, Ross A. (1991). Infant day care: Concerns, controversies, choices. In Jacqueline V. Lerner and Nancy Galambos (Eds.), *Employed mothers and their children.* New York: Garland.

Thompson, Ross A. (1992). Maturing the study of aging: Discussant's commentary. In T. Sondregger (Ed.), *Psychology and aging: Nebraska symposium on motivation* (Vol. 39). Lincoln, NE: University of Nebraska Press.

Thompson, Ross A., and **Jacobs, Janis E.** (1991). Defining psychological maltreatment: Research and policy perspectives. *Development and Psychopathology, 3,* 93–102.

Thompson, Ross A., Lamb, M.E., and **Estes, D.** (1982). Stability of infant-mother attachment and its relationship to changing life circumstances in an unselected middle-class sample. *Child Development, 53,* 144–148.

Thompson, Ross A., and **Limber, S.P.** (1990). "Social anxiety" in infancy: Stranger and separation anxiety. In H. Leitenberg (Ed.), *Handbook of social anxiety.* New York: Plenum.

Thompson, Ross A., Tinsley, Barbara R., Scalora, Mario J., and **Parke, Ross D.** (1989). Grandparents' visitation rights. *American Psychologist, 44,* 1217–1222.

Thornburg, Herschel D., and **Aras, Ziya.** (1986). Physical characteristics of developing adolescents. *Journal of Adolescent Research, 1,* 47–78.

Tice, Raymond R., and **Setlow, Richard B.** (1985). DNA repair and replication in aging organisms and cells. In Caleb E. Finch and Edward L. Schneider (Eds.), *Handbook of the biology of aging* (2nd ed.). New York: Van Nostrand.

Tillich, Paul. (1958). *Dynamics of faith.* New York: Harper and Row.

Tisi, Gennaro M. (1988). Pulmonary problems: Smoking, obstructive lung disease, and other lung disorders. In Dorothy Reycroft Hollingsworth and Robert Resnik (Eds.), *Medical counseling before pregnancy.* New York: Churchill Livingstone.

Todd, Judith, Friedman, Ariella, and **Kariuki, Priscilla Wanjiru.** (1990). Women growing stronger with age. *Psychology of Women Quarterly, 14,* 567–577.

Torres-Gil, Fernanda M. (1992). *The new aging.* New York: Auburn.

Toth, Sheree, Manly, Jody Todd, and **Cicchetti, Dante.** (1992). Child maltreatment and vulnerability to depression. *Development and Psychopathology, 4,* 97–112.

Tough, Allen. (1982). *Intentional changes: A fresh approach to helping people change.* Chicago: Follet.

Trasler, Gordon. (1987). Biogenetic factors. In Herbert C. Quay (Ed.), *Handbook of juvenile delinquency.* New York: Wiley.

Treboux, Dominique, and **Busch-Rossnagel, Nancy.** (1990). Social network influences on adolescent sexual attitudes and behaviors. *Journal of Adolescent Research, 5,* 175–189.

Tremblay, Helene. (1988). *Families of the world: East Asia, Southeast Asia, and the Pacific.* New York: Farrar, Straus, and Giroux.

Trent, Katherine, and **South, Scott.** (1989). Structural determinants of the divorce rate: A cross-cultural analysis. *Journal of Marriage and the Family, 51,* 391–404.

Troll, Lillian E. (1980). Grandparenting. In Leonard W. Poon (Ed.), *Aging in the 80's: Psychological issues.* Washington, DC: American Psychological Association.

Troll, Lillian E. (1983). Grandparents: The family watchdogs. In T. Brubake (Ed.), *Family relationships in later life.* Beverly Hills, CA: Sage.

Troll, Lillian E. (1986). Parents and children in later life. *Generations, 10* (4), 23–25.

Tronick, Edward Z. (1989). Emotions and emotional communication in infants. *American Psychologist, 44,* 112–119.

Tronick, Edward Z., and **Cohn, Jeffrey F.** (1989). Infant-mother face-to-face interaction: Age and gender differences in coordination and the occurrence of miscoordination. *Child Development, 60,* 85–92.

Tronick, Edward Z., Als, H., Adamson, L., Wise, S., and **Brazelton, T.B.** (1978). The infant's response to entrapment between contradictory measures in face-to-face interaction. *Journal of the American Academy of Child Psychiatry, 17,* 1–13.

Trussell, James. (1988). Teenage pregnancy in the United States. *Family Planning Perspectives, 20,* 262–272.

Tschann, Jeanne M., Johnston, Janet R., and **Wallerstein, Judith S.** (1989). Resources, stressors, and attachment as predictors of adult adjustment after divorce: A longitudinal study. *Journal of Marriage and the Family, 51,* 1033–1047.

Turiel, Elliot. (1983). *The development of social knowledge: Morality and convention.* Cambridge, England: Cambridge University Press.

Turiel, Elliot, Smetana, Judith G., and **Killen, Melanie.** (1991). Social context in social cognitive development. In William M. Kurtines and Jacob L. Gewirtz (Eds.), *Handbook of moral behavior and development: Vol. 2. Research.* Hillsdale, NJ: Erlbaum.

Turner, B.F., and **Adams, C.G.** (1988). Reported change in preferred sexual activity over the adult years. *Journal of Sex Research, 25,* 289–303.

Tzeng, Meei-Shenn. (1992). The effects of socioeconomic heterogamy and changes on marital dissolution for first marriages. *Journal of Marriage and the Family, 54,* 609–619.

Uchino, Bert N., Kiecolt-Glaser, Janice K., and **Cacioppo, John T.** (1992). Age-related changes in cardiovascular response as a function of chronic stressor and social support. *Journal of Personality and Social Psychology, 63,* 839–846.

Udry, J. Richard. (1981). Marital alternatives and marital disruption. *Journal of Marriage and the Family, 43,* 889–897.

Udry, J. Richard. (1990). Hormonal and social determinants of adolescent sexual initiation. In John Bancroft and June Machover Reinisch (Eds.), *Adolescence and puberty.* Oxford, England: Oxford University Press.

Uhlenberg, Peter. (1980). Death and the family. *Journal of Family History, 5,* 313–320.

Uhlenberg, Peter, and **Myers, M.A.** (1981). Divorce and the elderly. *The Gerontologist, 21,* 276–282.

Umberson, Debra. (1992). Relationship between adult children and their parents: Psychological consequences for both generations. *Journal of Marriage and the Family, 54,* 664–674.

UNESCO. (1985). *Demographic yearbook.* New York: United Nations.

UNICEF. (1990). *Children and development in the 1990's: A UNICEF sourcebook.* New York: United Nations.

United Nations. (1990). *Human Development Report, 1990.* New York: United Nations Development Program.

United Nations. (1991). *Human Development Report, 1991.* New

York: Oxford University Press.

United States Bureau of the Census. (1976). *Historical statistics of the United States: Colonial times to 1970.* Washington, DC: United States Department of Commerce.

United States Bureau of the Census. (1986). *Statistical abstract of the United States, 1986.* Washington, DC: United States Department of Commerce.

United States Bureau of the Census. (1988). *Statistical abstract of the United States, 1988.* Washington, DC: United States Department of Commerce.

United States Bureau of the Census. (1991). *Statistical abstract of the United States, 1991* (111th ed.). Washington, DC: United States Department of Commerce.

United States Bureau of the Census. (1992). *Statistical abstract of the United States, 1992* (112th ed.). Washington, DC: United States Department of Commerce.

United States Department of Commerce. (1991). *Money income of households, families, and persons in the United States, 1990.* Current Population Reports, Series P-60, No. 174. Washington, DC: Author.

United States Department of Education. (1987). *Japanese education today.* Washington, DC: United States Government.

United States Department of Education. (1989). *High school and beyond: 1987 transcript study.* Washington, DC: National Center for Educational Statistics.

United States Department of Education. (1991). *The condition of education, 1991: Vol 1. Elementary and secondary education.* Washington, DC: National Center for Educational Statistics.

United States Department of Health and Human Services. (1990). *Long-term care for the functionally dependent elderly.* Series 13: Data from the National Health Survey, No. 104. Hyattsville, MD: Author.

United States Department of Justice. (1989). *Criminal victimization in the United States, 1987.* Washington, DC: Bureau of Justice Statistics.

United States Department of Justice. (1990). *Crime in the United States.* Washington, DC: Federal Bureau of Investigation.

Uttal, David H., and **Perlmutter, Marion.** (1989). Toward a broader conceptualization of development: The role of gains and losses across the life span. *Developmental Review, 9,* 101–132.

Vachon, M.L.S., Lyall, W.A.L., Rogers, J., Freedman-Letofsky, K., and **Freeman, S.J.A.** (1980). A controlled study of self-help intervention for widows. *American Journal of Psychiatry, 137,* 1380–1384.

Vaillant, George E. (1977). *Adaptation to life.* Boston: Little, Brown.

Vandell, Deborah Lowe. (1987). Baby sister/baby brother. Reactions to the birth of a sibling and patterns of early sibling relations. *Journal of Children in Contemporary Society, 19* (3/4), 13–37.

Vandenberg, Steven G. (1987). Sex differences in mental retardation and their implications for sex differences in ability. In June Machover Reinisch, Leonard A. Rosenblum, and Stephanie A. Sanders (Eds.), *Masculinity/femininity: Basic perspectives.* New York: Oxford University Press.

Vandenberg, Steven G., Singer, Sandra Manes, and **Paula, David L.** (1986). *The heredity of behavior disorders in adults and children.* New York: Plenum.

Vanderkolk, Barbar Schwartz, and **Young, Ardis Armstrong.** (1991). *The work and family revolution.* New York: Facts on File.

Van Ijzendoorn, M.H., and **Kroonenberg, P.M.** (1988). Cross-cultural patterns of attachment: A meta-analysis of the Strange Situation. *Child Development, 59,* 147–156.

Van Keep, Pieter A., and **Gregory, Ann.** (1977). Sexual relations in the ageing female. In John Money and Herman Musaph (Eds.), *Handbook of sexology.* Great Britain: Elsevier/North-Holland Biomedical Press.

van Lier, L. (1988). *The classroom and the language learner.* London: Longman.

Van Nostrand, Joan F. (1991). Long-term care in the United States: Issues in measuring nursing home outcomes. *Proceedings of the 1988 International Symposium on Aging.* Series 5, No. 6. (DHHS Publication No. 91–1482). Hyattsville, MD: United States Department of Health and Human Services.

Varley, C.K. (1984). Attention deficit disorder (the hyperactivity syndrome): A review of selected issues. *Developmental and Behavioral Pediatrics, 5,* 254–258.

Vaughn, Brian E. (1987). Maternal characteristics measured prenatally are predictive of ratings of temperamental "difficulty" on the Carey Infant Temperament Questionnaire. *Developmental Psychology, 23,* 152–161.

Vega, William A., Kolody, Bohdan, and **Valle, Juan Ramon.** (1986). The relationship of marital status, confidant support, and depression among Mexican immigrant women. *Journal of Marriage and the Family, 48,* 597–605.

Verbrugge, Lois M. (1979). Marital status and health. *Journal of Marriage and the Family, 41,* 267–285.

Verbrugge, Lois M. (1983). Multiple roles and physical health of women and men. *Journal of Health and Social Behavior, 24,* 16–30.

Verbrugge, Lois M. (1989). The dynamics of population aging and health. In Stephen J. Lewis (Ed.), *Aging and Health: Linking research and public policy.* Chelsea, MI: Lewis Publishers.

Verbrugge, Lois M. (1990). The twain meet: Empirical explanations of sex differences in health and mortality. In Marcia G. Ory and Huber R. Warner (Eds.), *Gender, health, and longevity.* New York: Springer.

Verillo, Ronald T., and **Verillo, Violet.** (1985). Sensory and perceptual performance. In Neil Charness (Ed.), *Aging and human performance.* New York: Wiley.

Veroff, Joseph, Douvan, Elizabeth, and **Kulka, Richard A.** (1981). *The inner American: A self-portrait from 1957 to 1976.* New York: Basic Books.

Veroff, Joseph, and **Veroff, Joanne B.** (1980). *Social incentives: A life-span developmental approach.* New York: Academic Press.

Vestal, Robert E., and **Dawson, Gary W.** (1985). Pharmacology and aging. In Caleb E. Finch and Edward L. Schneider (Eds.), *Handbook of the biology of aging* (2nd ed.). New York: Van Nostrand.

Vickery, Florence E. (1978). *Old age and growing.* Springfield, IL: Thomas.

Vohr, Betty R., Coll, Cynthia Garcia, and **Oh, William.** (1989). Language and neurodevelopmental outcome of low-birth-weight infants at three years. *Developmental Medicine and Child Neurology, 31,* 582–590.

Volpe, E. Peter. (1987). *Test-tube conception: A blend of love and science.* Macon, GA: Mercer University Press.

Vondra, Joan I., Barnett, Douglas, and **Cicchetti, Dante.** (1990). Self-concept, motivation, and competence among children from maltreating and comparison families. *Child Abuse and Neglect, 14,* 525–540.

von Hofsten, Claes. (1983). Catching skills in infancy. *Journal of Experimental Psychology: Human Perception and Performance, 9,* 75–85.

von Tetzchner, Stephen, Siegel, Linda S., and **Smith, Lars** (Eds.). (1989). *The social and cognitive aspects of normal and atypical language.* New York: Springer.

Voyat, Gilbert. (1982). *Piaget systematized.* Hillsdale, NJ: Erlbaum.

Vygotsky, Lev S. (1978). *Mind in society: The development of higher psychological processes.* Cambridge, MA: Harvard University Press.

Vygotsky, Lev S. (1987). *Thinking and speech.* N. Minick (Trans.). New York: Plenum.

Wachs, T.D., and **Gruen, G.E.** (1982). *Early experience and human development.* New York: Wiley.

Waggoner, J.E., and **Palermo, D.S.** (1989). Betty is a bouncing bubble: Children's comprehension of emotion-descriptive metaphors. *Developmental Psychology, 25,* 152–163.

Wagner, Richard K., and **Sternberg, Robert J.** (1986). Tacit knowledge and intelligence in the everyday world. In Robert J. Sternberg and Richard K. Wagner (Eds.), *Practical intelligence.* Cambridge, England: Cambridge University Press.

Wahlquist, M.L., and **Flint-Richter, D.M.** (1989). Vitamins. In A. Horwitz, D.M. Macfadyen, H. Munro, N.S. Scrimshaw, B. Steen, and T.F. Williams (Eds.), *Nutrition in the elderly.* Oxford, England: Oxford University Press.

Wald, M.S., Carlsmith, J.M., and **Leiderman, P.H.** (1988). *Protecting abused and neglected children.* Stanford, CA: Stanford University Press.

Walford, Roy L. (1983). *Maximum life span.* New York: Norton.

Walker, Alan. (1989). The social division of early retirement. In Margot Jefferys (Ed.), *Growing old in the twentieth century.* London: Routledge.

Walker, Alexis, Shin, Haw-Yong, and **Bird, David N.** (1990). Perceptions of relationship change and caregiver satisfaction. *Family Relations, 39,* 147–152.

Walker, Arlene S. (1982). Intermodal perception of expressive behaviors by human infants. *Journal of Experimental Child Psychology, 33,* 514–535.

Walker, Lawrence J. (1984). Sex differences in the development of moral reasoning: A critical review. *Child Development, 55,* 677–691.

Walker, Lawrence J. (1988). The development of moral reasoning. *Annals of Child Development, 55,* 677–691.

Walker, Lawrence J., de Vries, Brian, and **Trevethan, Shelley D.** (1987). Moral stages and moral orientations in real-life and hypothetical dilemmas. *Child Development, 58,* 842–858.

Wallace, James R., Cunningham, Thomas F., and **Del Monte, Vickie.** (1984). Change and stability in self-esteem between late childhood and early adolescence. *Journal of Early Adolescence, 4,* 253–257.

Wallerstein, Judith S., and **Blakeslee, S.** (1989). *Second chances: Men, women, and children a decade after divorce.* New York: Ticknor & Fields.

Wallwork, Ernest. (1980). Morality, religion and Kohlberg's theory. In Brenda Munsey (Ed.), *Moral development, moral education and Kohlberg: Basic issues in philosophy, psychology, religion and education.* Birmingham, AL: Religious Education Press.

Wang, Margaret C., Reynolds, W.C., and **Walberg, Herbert J.** (Eds.). (1988). *The handbook of special education: Research and practices.* Oxford, England: Pergamon.

Ward, M.C. (1982). *Them children: A study in language learning.* New York: Irvington Press. (Original work published 1971).

Ward, Nicholas, Sneddon, Joan, Densem, James, Frost, Christopher, and **Stone, Rossana** (The MRC Vitamin study research group). (1991). Prevention of neural tube defects: Results of the Medical Research Council vitamin study. *The Lancet, 138,* 131–136.

Ward, Russell, Logan, John, and **Spitze, Glenna.** (1992). The influence of parent and child needs on coresidence in middle and later life. *Journal of Marriage and the Family, 54,* 209–221.

Warr, Peter. (1992). Age and occupational well-being. *Psychology and Aging, 7,* 37–45.

Waterman, Alan S. (1985). Identity in the context of adolescent psychology. In Alan S. Waterman (Ed.), *Identity in adolescence: Processes and contents: Vol. 30. New directions in child development.* San Francisco: Jossey-Bass.

Waterson, E.J., and **Murray-Lyon, Iain M.** (1990). Preventing alcohol related birth damage: A review. *Social Science and Medicine, 30,* 349–364.

Watson, John B. (1927, March). What to do when your child is afraid (interview with Beatrice Black). *Children,* 25–27.

Watson, John B. (1928). *Psychological care of the infant and child.* New York: Norton.

Watson, John B. (1967). *Behaviorism* (rev. ed.). Chicago: University of Chicago Press. (Original work published 1930).

Weber, Hans U., and **Miquel, Jamie.** (1986). Nutritional modulation of the aging process. Part II: Antioxidant supplementation and longevity. In Linda H. Chen (Ed.), *Nutritional aspects of aging* (Vol. 1). Boca Raton, FL: CRC Press.

Webster, Harold, Freedman, Mervin B., and **Heist, Paul.** (1979). Personality change in students. In Nevitt Sanford and Joseph Axelrod (Eds.), *College and character.* Berkeley, CA: Montaigne.

Weddle, Karen D., McHenry, Patric C., and **Leigh, Geoffrey K.** (1988). Adolescent sexual behavior: Trends and issues in research. *Journal of Adolescent Research, 3,* 245–257.

Weinberg, Richard. (1989). Intelligence and IQ: Landmark issues and great debates. *American Psychologist, 44,* 98–104.

Weinraub, M., Clemens, L.P., Sockloff, A., Ethridge, T., Gracely, E., and **Myers, B.** (1984). The development of sex role stereotypes in the third year: Relationships to gender labeling, gender identity, sex-typed toy preferences, and family characteristics. *Child Development, 55,* 1493–1503.

Weiss, Gabrielle, and **Hechtman, Lily Trokenberg.** (1986). *Hy-*

peractive children grow up: Empirical findings and theoretical considerations. New York: Guilford.

Weiss, Rick. (1989). Predisposition and prejudice. *Science News, 135,* 40–42.

Weitzman, Lenore J. (1985). *The divorce revolution: The unexpected social and economic consequences for women and children in America.* New York: The Free Press.

Welford, Alan T. (1980). On the nature of higher-order skills. *Journal of Occupational Psychology, 53,* 107–110.

Welford, Alan T. (1985). Changes of performance with age: An overview. In Neil Charness (Ed.), *Aging and human performance.* New York: Wiley.

Wells, J.C. (1982). *Accents of English* (Vols. 1–3). New York: Cambridge University Press.

Wender, Paul H. (1987). *The hyperactive child, adolescent and adult: Attention deficit disorder through the lifespan.* New York: Oxford.

Werner, Emmy E., and **Smith, Ruth S.** (1982). *Vulnerable but invincible: A study of resilient children.* New York: McGraw-Hill.

Werner, Emmy E., and **Smith, Ruth S.** (1992). *Overcoming the odds: High risk children from birth to adulthood.* Ithaca, NY: Cornell University Press.

Werner, J.S., and **Perlmutter, Marion.** (1979). Development of visual memory in infants. In Haynes W. Reese and Lewis P. Lipsitt (Eds.), *Advances in child development and behavior* (Vol. 14). New York: Academic Press.

Whalen, C.K., Henker, B., Collins, B.E., Finck, D., and **Dotemoto, S.** (1979). A social ecology of hyperactive boys: Medication effects in systematically structured classroom environments. *Journal of Applied Behavioral Analysis, 12,* 65–81.

Wheeler, L., Reis, H., and **Nezlek, J.** (1983). Loneliness, social interaction, and sex roles. *Journal of Personality and Social Psychology, 45,* 943–953.

While, Alison K. (1989). Early infant feeding practice: Socioeconomic factors and health visiting support. *Child: Care, Health, and Development, 15,* 129–136.

Whitbourne, Susan Krauss. (1985a). *The aging body.* New York: Springer-Verlag.

Whitbourne, Susan Krauss. (1985b). The psychological construction of the life span. In James E. Birren and K. Warner Schaie (Eds.), *Handbook of the psychosocial of aging* (2nd ed.). New York: Van Nostrand Reinhold.

Whitbourne, Susan Krauss, Zuschlag, Michael K., Elliot, Lisa B., and **Waterman, Alan S.** (1992). Psychosocial development in adulthood: A 22-year sequential study. *Journal of Personality and Social Psychology, 63,* 260–271.

White, Charles B., and **Janson, Philip.** (1986). Helplessness in institutional settings: Adaptation or iatropic disease. In Margaret M. Baltes and Paul B. Baltes (Eds.), *The psychology of control and aging.* Hillsdale, NJ: Erlbaum.

White, Lynn K. (1990). Determinants of divorce: A review of research in the eighties. *Journal of Marriage and the Family, 52,* 904–912.

White, Lynn K., and **Booth, Alan.** (1985). The quality and stability of remarriages: The role of stepchildren. *American Sociological Review, 50,* 689–698.

White, Nancy, and **Cunningham, Walter R.** (1988). Is terminal drop pervasive or specific? *Journal of Gerontology, 43,* 141–144.

White, Robert W. (1979). Competence as an aspect of personal growth. In Martha Whalen Kent and Jon E. Rolf (Eds.), *Primary prevention of psychopathology: Vol. III. Social competence in children.* Hanover, NH: University Press of New England.

White, Sheldon H. (1965). Evidence for a hierarchical arrangement of learning processes. In Lewis P. Lipsitt and Charles C. Spikes (Eds.), *Advances in child development and behavior* (Vol. 2). New York: Academic Press.

Whiting, Beatrice Blyth, and **Edward, Carolyn Pope.** (1988). *Children of different worlds: The formation of social behavior.* Cambridge, MA: Harvard University Press.

Whiting, Beatrice Blyth, and **Whiting, John W.M.** (1975). *Children of six cultures.* Cambridge, MA: Harvard University Press.

Whitlock, F.A. (1986). Suicide and physical illness. In Alec Roy (Ed.), *Suicide.* Baltimore, MD: Williams and Wilkins.

Widholm, Olaf. (1985). Epidemiology of premenstrual tension syndrome and primary dysmenorrhea. In M. Yusoff Dawood, John L. McGuire, and Laurence M. Demers (Eds.), *Premenstrual syndrome and dysmenorrhea.* Baltimore, MD: Urban and Schwartzenberg.

Widom, Cathy Spatz. (1991). The role of placement experience in mediating the criminal consequences of early childhood victimization. *American Journal of Orthopsychiatry, 61,* 195–209.

Wiggins, Jerry S., and **Holzmuller, Ana.** (1978). Psychological androgyny and interpersonal behavior. *Journal of Consulting and Clinical Psychology, 46,* 40–52.

Wilbur, Ken. (1986). The spectrum of development. In Ken Wilbur, J. Engler, and D.P. Brown (Eds.), *Transformations of consciousness.* Boston: New Science Library.

Wilk, Carole. (1986). *Career women and childbearing.* New York: Van Nostrand Reinhold.

Wilkinson, Richard G. (1992). National mortality rates: The impact of inequality. *American Journal of Public Health, 82,* 1082–1084.

Williams, Sharon, Denney, Nancy Wadsworth, and **Schadler, Margaret.** (1983). Elderly adults' perception of their own cognitive development during the adult years. *International Journal of Aging and Human Development, 16,* 47–158.

Williams, Terry, and **Kornblum, William.** (1985). *Growing up poor.* Lexington, MA: Lexington Books.

Williamson, David F., Serdula, Mary K., Anda, Robert F., Levy, Alan, and **Byers, Tim.** (1992). Weight loss attempts in adults: Goals, duration, and rate of weight loss. *American Journal of Public Health, 82,* 1251–1257.

Willis, Sherry L. (1990a). Current issues in cognitive training research. In Eugene A. Lovelace (Ed.), *Aging and cognition: Mental processes, self-awareness, and interventions.* North-Holland: Elsevier.

Willis, Sherry L. (1990b). Introduction to the special section on cognitive training in later adulthood. *Developmental Psychology, 26,* 875–878.

Willis, Sherry L., and **Baltes, Paul B.** (1980). Intelligence in adulthood and aging: Contemporary issues. In Leonard W. Poon (Ed.), *Aging in the 80's: Psychological issues.* Washington, DC: American Psychological Association.

Willis, Sherry L., and **Nesselroade, Carolyn S.** (1990). Long-term effects of fluid ability training in old-old age. *Developmental Psychology, 26,* 905–910.

Willis, Sherry L., and **Schaie, K. Warner.** (1986). Practical intelligence in later adulthood. In Robert J. Sternberg and Richard K. Wagner (Eds.), *Practical intelligence.* Cambridge, England: Cambridge University Press.

Willis, Sherry L., and **Schaie, K. Warner.** (1986). Training the elderly on the ability factors of spatial orientation and inductive reasoning. *Psychology and Aging, 1, 239–247.*

Wilson, B.L., and **Corcoran, T.B.** (1988). *Successful secondary schools.* New York: Falmer Press.

Wilson, Geraldine S. (1989). Clinical studies of infants and children exposed prenatally to heroin. In Donald Hutchings (Ed.), *Prenatal abuse of licit and illicit drugs.* New York: New York Academy of Sciences.

Wilson, James Q. (1983). Raising kids. *The Atlantic Monthly, 252* (4), 45–56.

Wilson, James Q., and **Herrnstein, Richard J.** (1985). *Crime and human nature.* New York: Simon and Schuster.

Wilson, Jerome. (1989). Cancer incidence and mortality differences of Black and White Americans. In Lovell A. Jones (Ed.), *Minorities and cancer.* New York: Springer-Verlag.

Wilson, Melvin N. (1989). Child development in the context of the Black extended family. *American Psychologist, 44,* 380–385.

Wilson, M.R. (1989). Glaucoma in Blacks: Where do we go from here? *Journal of the American Medical Association, 261,* 281–282.

Wilson, Ronald S. (1979). Analysis of longitudinal twin data: Basic model and applications to physical growth measures. *Acta Geneticae Medicae et Gemellologiae, 28,* 93–105.

Wilson, William J. (1987). *The truly disadvantaged.* Chicago: University of Chicago Press.

Wimmer, Heinz, Hogrefe, G. Jurgen, and **Perner, Josef.** (1988). Children's understanding of informational access as source of knowledge. *Child Development, 59,* 386–396.

Winger, Gail, Hofmann, Frederick G., and **Woods, James H.** (1992). *A handbook on drug and alcohol abuse.* New York: Oxford University Press.

Winick, Myron (Ed.). (1975). *Childhood obesity.* New York: Wiley.

Winn, Steve, Tronick, Edward Z., and **Morelli, Gilda A.** (1989). The infant and the group: A look at Efe caregiving practices in Zaire. In J. Kevin Nugent, Barry M. Lester, and T. Berry Brazelton (Eds.), *The cultural context of infancy: Biology, culture and infant development.* Norwood, NJ: Ablex.

Wolfe, D.A. (1987). *Child abuse: Implications for child development and psychopathology.* Newbury Park, CA: Sage.

Wong Fillmore, Lily. (1976). *The second time around: Cognitive and social strategies in second language acquisition.* Doctoral Dissertation, Stanford University. (Cited in McLaughlin, 1984).

Wong Fillmore, Lily. (1987, April 25). *Becoming bilingual: Social processes in second language learning.* Paper presented at the Society for Research in Child Development, Baltimore, MD.

Wong Fillmore, Lily. (1991a). Second-language learning in children: A model of language learning in social context. In Ellen Bialystok (Ed.), *Language processing in bilingual children.* Cambridge, England: Cambridge University Press.

Wong Fillmore, Lily. (1991b, April 20). Asian-Americans and bilingualism. Paper at Society for Research in Child Development Biennial meeting, Seattle, WA.

Woodhead, Martin. (1991). Psychology and the cultural construction of "children's needs." In Martin Woodhead, Paul Light, and Ronnie Carr (Eds.), *Child development in social context: Vol. 3. Growing up in a changing society.* London: Routledge.

Woodruff, Diana. (1983). The role of memory in personality continuity: A 25-year follow-up. *Experimental Aging Research, 9,* 31–34.

Woody, George E., Urschell, Harold C., and **Alterman, Arthur.** (1992). The many paths to drug dependence. In Meyer Glantz and Roy Pickens (Eds.), *Vulnerability to drug abuse.* Washington, DC: American Psychological Association.

Worobey, John, and **Brazelton, T. Berry.** (1990). Newborn assessment and support for parenting. In Elizabeth D. Gibbs and Douglas M. Teti (Eds.), *Interdisciplinary assessment of infants.* Baltimore, MD: Brookes.

Wright, Fay D. (1986). *Left to care alone.* Hampshire, England: Gower.

Wright, Paul H. (1982). Men's friendships, women's friendships, and the alleged inferiority of the latter. *Sex Roles, 8,* 1–20.

Wright, Paul H. (1989). Gender differences in adults' same- and cross-gender friendships. In Rebecca G. Adams and Rosemary Bleiszner (Eds.), *Older adult friendship.* Newbury Park, CA: Sage.

Wrightsman, Lawrence S. (1988). *Personality development in adulthood.* Newbury Park, CA: Sage.

Wyatt, Gail Elizabeth. (1990). Changing influences on adolescent sexuality over the past forty years. In John Bancroft and June Machover Reinisch (Eds.), *Adolescence and puberty.* Oxford, England: Oxford University Press.

Yasilove, Daniel. (1978). The effect of riddle-structure on children's comprehension and appreciation of riddles. Doctoral Dissertation, New York University. *Dissertation Abstracts International, 36,* 6.

Yerkes, R.M. (1923). Testing and the human mind. *Atlantic Monthly, 131,* 358–370.

Yglesias, Helen. (1980). Moses, Anna Mary Robertson (Grandma). In Barbara Sicherman and Carol Hurd Green (Eds.), *Notable American women: The modern period.* Cambridge, MA: Belknap Press.

Yost, J. Kelley, and **Mines, Robert A.** (1985). Stress and alcoholism. In Thomas E. Bratter and Gary G. Forrest (Eds.), *Alcoholism and substance abuse: Strategies for clinical intervention.* New York: The Free Press.

Youniss, James. (1980). *Parents and peers in social development: A Sullivan-Piaget perspective.* Chicago: University of Chicago Press.

Youniss, James. (1989). Parent-adolescent relationships. In William Damon (Ed.), *Child development today and tomorrow.* San Francisco: Jossey-Bass.

Zadig, J.M., and **Meltzer, L.J.** (1983). Special education. In M.D. Levine, W.B. Carey, A.C. Crocker, and R.T. Gross (Eds.), *Developmental-behavioral pediatrics.* Philadelphia: Saunders.

Zaks, Peggy M., and **Labouvie-Vief, Gisela.** (1980). Spatial perspective taking and referential communication skills in the elderly: A training study. *Journal of Gerontology, 35,* 217–224.

Zales, Michael R. (1985). *Stress in health and disease.* New

York: Brunner/Mazel.

Zametkin, A.J., Nordahl, T.E., Gross, M., King, A.C., Semple, W.E., Rumsey, J., Hamburger, S., and **Cohen, R.M.** (1990). Cerebral glucose metabolism in adults with hyperactivity of childhood onset. *New England Journal of Medicine, 323,* 1361–1366.

Zaslow, Martha J., Pederson, Frank A., Cain, Richard L., Suwalksy, Joan T.D., and **Kramer, Eva L.** (1985). Depressed mood in new fathers: Associations with parent-infant interaction. *Genetic, social, and general psychology monographs, 111,* 133–150.

Zayas, L. (1988). Puerto Rican familism: Consideration for family therapy. *Family Relations, 37,* 260–268.

Zedeck, Sheldon (Ed.). (1992). *Work, families, and organizations.* San Francisco: Jossey-Bass.

Zelazo, P.R. (1979). Infant reactivity to perceptual-cognitive events: Application for infant assessment. In Richard B. Kearsley and Irving E. Sigel (Eds.), *Infants at risk: Assessment of cognitive functioning.* Hillsdale, NJ: Erlbaum.

Zelinski, Elizabeth M., Light, Leah L., and **Gilewski, Michael J.** (1984). Adult age differences in memory for prose: The question of sensitivity to passage structure. *Developmental Psychology, 20,* 1181–1192.

Zietlow, Paul H., and **VanLear, C. Arthur.** (1991). Marriage duration and relational control: A study of developmental patterns. *Journal of Marriage and the Family, 53,* 773–786.

Zigler, Edward, and **Berman, Winnie.** (1983). Discerning the future of early childhood intervention. *American Psychologist, 38,* 894–906.

Zigler, Edward, and **Hall, Nancy W.** (1989). Physical child abuse in America: Past, present, and future. In Dante Cicchetti and Vicki Carlson (Eds.), *Child maltreatment: Theory and research on the causes and consequences of child abuse and neglect.* Cambridge, England: Cambridge University Press.

Zill, N. (1983). *Happy, healthy, and insecure.* New York: Doubleday.

Zill, Nicholas. (1988). Behavior, achievement, and health problems among children in stepfamilies: Findings from a national survey of child health. In E. Mavis Hetherington and Josephine D. Aresteh (Eds.), *Impact on divorce, single parenting, and stepparenting on children.* Hillsdale, NJ: Erlbaum.

Ziven, Gail (Ed.). (1979). *The development of self-regulation through private speech.* New York: Wiley-Interscience.

Zopf, Paul E. (1986). *America's older population.* Houston: Cap and Gown Press.

Zukow, Patricia Goldring (Ed.). (1989). *Sibling interaction across cultures: Theoretical and methodological issues.* New York: Springer-Verlag.

Photo Acknowledgments

Chapter 5

Opener Laura Dwight; **page 127** Jason Lauré/Woodfin Camp; **page 130** Laura Dwight; **page 131** Ken Karp; **page 133** Elizabeth Crews; **page 134** Anthony Jalandoni/Monkmeyer Press; **page 135** Elizabeth Crews; **page 136** Laura Dwight; **page 138** *(top)* J. P. Laffonte/United Nations; *(bottom)* AP/Wide World Photos; **page 140** Michael Tchereukoff/The Image Bank.

Chapter 6

Opener Elizabeth Crews; **page 145** Joe Epstein/Design Conceptions; **page 146** Laura Dwight; **page 148** Yoav Levy/Phototake; **page 149** Laura Dwight; **page 150** Elizabeth Crews; **page 151** Carol Palmer/The Picture Cube; **page 153** Davis/United Nations; **page 157** Laura Dwight; **page 158** Elizabeth Crews; **page 160** Tom Pollak/Monkmeyer Press; **page 164** Laura Dwight; **page 165** Elliott Varner Smith; **page 166** Elizabeth Crews; **page 168** Elizabeth Crews.

Chapter 7

Opener Maratea/International Stock Photo; **page 172** Alan Carey/The Image Works; **page 173** Ken Karp; **page 174** Erika Stone; **page 175** Sybil Shackman/Monkmeyer Press; **page 176** Tom McCarthy/The Picture Cube; **page 177** Bill Ross/Woodfin Camp; **page 178** Anthony Jalandoni/The Picture Cube; **page 179** Elizabeth Crews; **page 180** Rip Griffith/Photo Researchers; **page 183** Anthony Edgeworth/The Stock Market; **page 184** *(top)* Laura Dwight; *(bottom)* Bruce Plotkin/The Image Works; **page 188** Erika Stone; **page 191** AP/Wide World Photos; **page 196** Wolfgang Kaehler; **page 197** Everett Collection; **page 200** George Ancona/International Stock Photo; **page 202** AP/Wide World Photos.

Chapter 8

Opener Philip Jon Bailey/Stock, Boston; **page 213** Tony Freeman/PhotoEdit; **page 214** Gale Zucker/Stock, Boston; **page 217** *(top)* Elizabeth Crews; *(bottom)* Lester Sloan/Woodfin Camp; **page 218** *(top)* Adam Woolfitt/Woodfin Camp; *(bottom)* Shirley Zeiberg; **page 219** Bob Krist/Black Star; **page 221** *(left)* Gabor Kemjen/Stock, Boston; *(right)* Renate Hiller/Monkmeyer Press; *(bottom)* Carol Palmer/The Picture Cube; **page 222** Myrleen Ferguson/PhotoEdit; **page 224** *(left)* Bob Daemmrich/Stock, Boston; *(right)* Jerry Howard/Stock, Boston; **page 226** Donald Dietz/Stock, Boston.

Chapter 9

Opener Erika Stone; **page 230** Sybil Shackman/Monkmeyer Press; **page 233** Hazel Hankin; **page 238** Elizabeth Crews/The Image Works; **page 241** Elizabeth Crews/The Image Works; **page 248** Mike Greenlar/The Image Works; **page 251** Susan Lapides/Design Conceptions.

Chapter 10

Opener Lynn Johnson/Black Star; **page 257** Erika Stone; **page 259** Alan Carey/The Image Works; **page 260** *(top)* Tom McHugh/Photo Researchers; *(bottom)* MacDonald Photography/The Picture Cube; **page 261** Randy Matusow/Monkmeyer Press; **page 262** Erika Stone; **page 264** Laura Dwight; **page 265** Michael Heron/Woodfin Camp; **page 267** Erika Stone; **page 269** Mimi Forsyth/Monkmeyer Press; **page 271** Movie Still Archives; **page 276** *(top)* Joel Gordon; *(bottom)* Frank Siteman/The Picture Cube; **page 277** Mike Mazzaschi/Stock, Boston; **page 278** Joseph Schuyler/Stock, Boston.

Chapter 11

Opener Palmer & Brilliant/The Picture Cube; **page 286** Elizabeth Crews; **page 288** Shirley Zeiberg; **page 291** *(top)* Ross Thompson; *(bottom)* Michael Heron/Woodfin Camp; **page 292** Jean-Claude Lejeune/Stock, Boston; **page 293** Will McIntyre/Photo Researchers; **page 296** Alice Kandell/Photo Researchers; **page 298** Elizabeth Crews.

Chapter 12

Opener Nancy J. Pierce/Black Star; **page 305** Bob Daemmrich/The Image Works; **page 306** George Ancona/International Stock Photo; **page 308** *(top)* Robert Kalman/The Image Works; *(bottom)* Bohdan Hrynewych/Stock, Boston; **page 309** Elizabeth Crews; **page 310** Mark M. Walker/The Picture Cube; **page 312** John Eastcott (Yva Momatiuk)/The Image Works; **page 316** Charles Harbutt/Actuality; **page 319** Paul Conklin/Monkmeyer Press; **page 322** *(left)* John Elk III/Stock, Boston; *(right)* Michael S. Yamashita/Woodfin Camp; **page 325** Joanne Gebhardt; **page 327** Karen Kasmauski/Woodfin Camp.

Chapter 13

Opener Steve and Mary Skjold/The Image Works; **page 332** *(left)* George Ancona/International Stock Photo; *(right)* Victor Englebert/Photo Researchers; **page 334** Shirley Zeiberg; **page 337** David Lissy/The Picture Cube; **page 338** Jean-Claude Lejeune/Stock, Boston; **page 340** Bob Daemmrich/Stock, Boston; **page 341** Nancy Sheehan/The Picture Cube; **page 343** Bob Daemmrich/Stock, Boston; **page 344** Lawrence Migdale/Stock, Boston; **page 348** Erika Stone; **page 353** Lew Merrim/Monkmeyer Press; **page 354** Joel Gordon; **page 357** George Ancona/International Stock Photo; **page 358** Andy Levin/Photo Researchers; **page 362** Peter Chapman/Stock, Boston.

Chapter 14

Opener Spencer Grant/Stock, Boston; **page 370** Kit Hedman/Jeroboam; **page 372** Alan Carey/The Image Works; **page 373** Audrey Gottlieb/Monkmeyer Press; **page 374** Shirley Zeiberg; **page 375** Billy E. Barnes/Stock, Boston; **page 376** Bob Daemmrich/Stock, Boston; **page 377** Rick Kopstein/Monkmeyer Press; **page 379** *(top)* Joseph Neumayer/Design Conceptions; *(bottom)* Joseph Rodriquez/Black Star; **page 380** Bob Daemmrich/The Image Works; **page 381** Joel Gordon; **page 382** Elizabeth Crews.

Chapter 15

Opener Randall Hymann/Stock, Boston; **page 390** Elizabeth Crews; **page 393** Elizabeth Crews; **page 399** Lester Sloan/Woodfin Camp; **page 401** Sybil Shackman/Monkmeyer Press; **page 403** Gale Zucker/Stock, Boston; **page 404** Joel Gordon; **page 407** Elizabeth Crews.

Chapter 16

Opener Lawrence Migdale/Stock, Boston; **page 412** Sybil Shackman/Monkmeyer Press; **page 413** *(left)* Terry E. Eiler/Stock, Boston; *(right)* Robert V. Eckert, Jr./Stock, Boston; **page 417** Mike Yamashita/Woodfin Camp; **page 418** Bob Daemmrich/Stock, Boston; **page 420** Billy E. Barnes/Stock, Boston; **page 421** *(top)* Sybil Shackman/Monkmeyer Press; *(bottom)* Audrey Gottlieb/Monkmeyer Press; **page 423** Laura Dwight; **page 427** Mark M. Walker/The Picture Cube; **page 429** Rhoda Sidney/Stock, Boston; **page 436** Gwyn M. Kibbe/Stock, Boston.

Chapter 17

Opener Brown/The Picture Cube; **page 446** *(top)* John Coletti/Stock, Boston; *(bottom)* J. Pickerell/The Image Works; **page 447** Reuters/Bettmann; **page 451** Hank Morgan/Photo Researchers; **page 455** Evan P. Schneider/Monkmeyer Press; **page 456** Tony Freeman/PhotoEdit; **page 460** Robert Frerck/Woodfin Camp.

Chapter 18

Opener Alan Becker/The Image Bank; **page 465** L. Rorke/The Image Works; **page 466** Sybil Shackman; **page 468** Ted Speigel/Black Star; **page 469** Sybil Shackman/Monkmeyer Press; **page 471** Paul Conklin/Monkmeyer Press; **page 473** *(left)* Margaret Bourke-White/*Life Magazine* ©1946 Time, Inc.; *(right)* Neal Boenzi/NYT Pictures; **page 475** Margot Granitsas/The Image Works; **page 477** Rafael Macia/Photo Researchers; **page 478** *(top)* Terry Wild Studio; *(bottom)* AP/Wide World Photos.

Chapter 19

Opener Jeffry W. Myers/FPG International; **page 485** Guy Gillette/Photo Researchers; **page 486** Owen Franken/Stock, Boston; **page 487** Henley & Savage/Stock, Boston; **page 489** *(top)* M. Eastcott/The Image Works; *(bottom)* Al Lock/International Stock Photo; **page 491** Daemmrich/The Image Works; **page 493** *(top)* Zao Grimberg/The Image Bank; *(bottom)* Will and Deni McIntyre/Photo Researchers; **page 496** Spencer Grant/The Picture Cube; **page 500** Lawrence Migdale/Photo Researchers; **page 502** Mark Richards/PhotoEdit; **page 504** *(left)* Spencer Grant/The Picture Cube; *(right)* Mark Antman/The Image Works; **page 505** David Burnett/Contact Press Images; **page 510** Maratea/International Stock Photo.

Chapter 20

Opener David Madison; **page 520** Joel Gordon; **page 527** Michael R. Abramson/Woodfin Camp; **page 529** John Chiasson/Gamma Liaison; **page 530** John Elk III/Stock, Boston; **page 533** Blair Seitz/Photo Researchers; **page 535** *(left)* Erika Stone; *(right)* Frank Siteman.

Chapter 21

Opener Wayne Hoy/The Picture Cube; **page 540** *(top)* Bob Daemmrich/The Image Works; *(bottom)* Will and Deni McIntyre/Science Source, Photo Researchers; **page 542** Bachmann/The Image Works; **page 543** Julie Houck/Stock, Boston; **page 544** Michael Heron/Woodfin Camp; **page 545** Inga Spence/The Picture Cube; **page 549** *(left)* Lionel Delevingne/Stock, Boston; *(right)* Joel Gordon; **page 552** Mug Shots/The Stock Market; **page 553** Bob Daemmrich/Stock, Boston; **page 555** Edward Letiau/Photo Researchers; **page 556** J. Y. Rabeuf/The Image Works.

Chapter 22

Opener J. Pickerell/The Image Works; **page 563** *(left)* Everett Collection; *(right)* Charlesworth/UNICEF; **page 566** Phil Huber/Black Star; **page 569** *(left)* Cary Wolinsky/Stock, Boston; *(right)* Phil Huber/Black Star; **page 570** Michael Philip Manheim/International Stock Photo; **page 573** Margaret Miller/Photo Researchers; **page 575** Skjold/The Image Works; **page 576** Jodi Cobb/Woodfin Camp; **page 577** Cindy Loo/The Picture Cube; **page 579** David Butow/Black Star.

Chapter 23

Opener Mark Antman/The Image Works; **page 587** Bob Daemmrich/The Image Works; **page 591** Elizabeth Crews; **page 593** Mark Tuschman; **page 594** Chris Sorensen; **page 599** Ira Berger; **page 600** *(top)* Claus Meyer/Black Star; *(bottom)* Kathryn Dudek (Photo News)/International Stock Photo; **page 605** *(all)* John Launois/Black Star; **page 606** Sal di Marco/Black Star.

Chapter 24

Opener Scott Thode/International Stock Photo; **page 613** Bill Bachmann/Stock, Boston; **page 614** Richard Hutchings/PhotoEdit; **page 616** Ira Kirschenbaum/Stock, Boston; **page 617** Abigail Heyman/Archive Pictures; **page 620** Rick Smolan/Stock, Boston; **page 621** Elizabeth Crews; **page 625** AP/Wide World Photos; **page 627** Ira Wyman/Sygma; **page 631** Ann Marie Rousseau/The Image Works; **page 632** Ira Berger/Woodfin Camp; **page 634** *(left)* Robert Brenner/PhotoEdit; *(right)* Ann Purcell; **page 635** Lawrence Migdale/Stock, Boston.

Chapter 25

Opener Spencer Grant/The Picture Cube; **page 643** Elizabeth Crews; **page 645** *(top)* Will and Deni McIntyre/Photo Researchers; *(bottom)* Sobel-Klonsyk/The Image Bank; **page 646** *(left)* Steve Hansen/Stock, Boston; *(center)* Edward L. Miller/Stock, Boston; *(right)* Frank Fournier/Contact Press Images; **page 650** *(left)* Bob Daemmrich/Stock, Boston; *(center)* Rhoda Sidney/Gamma Liaison; *(right)* Howard Chapnick/Black Star; **page 652** Paul Conklin/Monkmeyer Press; **page 653** *(left)* Glyn Cloyd; *(right)* Tom McCarthy/The Picture Cube; **page 654** Sybil Shackman/The Picture Cube; **page 655** Alex Goff/Monkmeyer Press; **page 657** Owen Franken/Stock, Boston; **page 659** Ellis Herwig/The Picture Cube; **page 661** Ginger Chih/Peter Arnold, Inc.; **page 664** Spencer Grant/Photo Researchers; **page 669** *(left)* Susan Lapides/Design Conceptions; *(right)* Phil Huber/Black Star; **page 672** *(left)* Joel Gordon; *(right)* Elizabeth Crews; **page 674** Robert Deutsch/*USA Today*.

Epilogue

Opener Gregory Edwards/International Stock Photo; **page 680** Kal Muller/Woodfin Camp; **page 683** Kay Chernosh/The Image Bank; **page 684** George W. Gardner/Stock, Boston; **page 685** Scott Thode/International Stock Photo; **page 689** Phyllis Picardi/International Stock Photo; **page 691** Rae Russel/International Stock Photo.

Name Index

Abel, E., 101
Abramovitch, R., 261
Achenbach, T., 213, 269, 296, 360
Achenberg, W., 637
Ackerman, 297
Adams, C., 105, 448, 468
Adams, C. G., 535, 536
Adams, E., 353
Adams, G., 392
Adams, P., 353
Adams, R., 642
Adamson, L., 167
Ades, A., 99
Adler, N., 458
Ahmedzai, S., 684
Ainsworth, M., 185, 190
Alberts-Corush, J., 297
Albrecht, S., 499
Allan, G., 487, 489, 490
Allen, K., 662
Allison, C., 218,
Allison, P., 350, 355
Aloise, P., 238, 257, 334
Alpert, G., 418
Altman, L., 526
Alvarez, M., 395
Alwin, D., 488
Amato, P., 345, 355
Ammerman, R., 192
Anastasi, A., 19
Anderson, R., 252
Andrews, G., 645, 665
Angier, N., 82
Anglin, J., 243
Anisfeld, W., 117
Anolik, S., 392
Anthony, E., 360
Antonucci, T., 487, 643, 657, 658
Apgar, V., 108
Apple, R., 137
Applebaum, M., 31
Applegate, J., 667, 669, 670
Aquilino, W., 513, 568
Aras, Z., 373, 374, 376, 380
Arbuthnot, J., 431
Archer, S., 415
Arenberg, D., 617
Arend, R., 187
Ariès, P., 488, 680
Arlin, G., 555
Arlin, P., 468
Arnold, E., 194
Aronson, E., 574

Asher, S., 343, 344
Aslin, R., 128
Astington, J., 238
Atchley, R., 643
Atkinson, J., 128
Atkinson, R., 55
Attanucci, J., 401
Ausman, L., 528
Axelson, 355
Axia, G., 316
Axline, V., 60
Azrin, N., 595

Bachrach, C., 485
Bahrick, H., 616
Bahrick, L., 158
Bailey, L., 606
Baillargeon, R., 151, 235
Bakeman, R., 172
Baker, 297
Bakker, D., 215
Ball, J., 114, 118
Baltes, M., 49, 546, 624, 673
Baltes, P., 54, 57, 540, 546, 548, 550, 552, 619, 624, 636–637
Bamford, F., 126
Band, E., 335
Bandura, A., 46, 47, 276, 333
Bane, S., 667
Bardin, C., 449
Bardo, M., 452
Barkley, 299
Barling, J., 508, 509
Barnes, D., 630
Barnes, J., 336
Barnes, M., 492
Barnett, R., 510, 563, 571
Barnett, W., 252, 276
Barnewolt, D., 564
Baron, A., 623
Baroni, R., 316
Barresi, C., 566, 655, 655, 656
Barrett, M., 164
Barry, H., 419, 423, 437
Bartholmey, S., 136
Baruch, G., 510, 563, 564, 571
Bass, D., 628
Basseches, M., 467 468, 469, 477
Bassuk, E., 359
Bates, E., 163, 248
Bateson, 573
Bauer, C., 21

Baugh, J., 318
Baumrind, D., 264, 265, 266, 267, 278, 419
Bayley, N., 18, 382, 540–541
Beard, B., 607
Beauvoir, S. de, 520
Becker, J., 236
Beckwith, L., 111, 113
Beeghly, M., 81, 238, 257
Beevers, D., 524
Belensky, M., 405
Bell, A., 423
Bell, R., 266
Bell, T., 403, 423
Bellinger, D., 216
Belsky, J., 184, 186, 187, 188, 199, 200, 381
Bem, S., 273, 277, 278, 279
Benack, S., 467
Benbow, C., 16
Benedek, E., 197
Benenson, J., 336
Benet, S., 604
Bengston, V., 42, 418, 578, 654, 655, 656, 660, 667
Benin, 570
Beres, C., 623
Berg, C., 548, 552
Berg, R., 592
Berg, W., 129, 166
Berger, J., 405, 662
Bergler, E., 561
Bergstrom, S., 109, 110
Berman, W., 251
Berndt, T., 334, 341, 421
Berry, R., 570
Berzonsky, M., 414
Besharov, D., 202
Betancourt, R., 647
Bettes, B., 166
Beunen, G., 372
Bhatia, 297
Bialystok, E., 319
Bianchi, S., 354
Bibi, S., 605
Biegel, D., 670
Bierman, K., 344
Bigelow, B., 341
Biggs, J., 305
Bijou, S., 46
Billingham, R., 434
Binder, A., 430
Bing, E., 114
Bingham, C., 381
Birch, H., 179

Subject Index